This modern text is designed to prepare you for your future professional career. While theories, ideas, techniques, and data are dynamic, the information contained in this volume will provide you a quick and useful reference as well as a guide for future learning for many years to come. Your familiarity with the contents of this book will make it an important volume in your professional library.

EX LIBRIS

STRATEGIC MANAGEMENT
Concepts and Cases

STRATEGIC MANAGEMENT
Concepts and Cases

Arthur A. Thompson, Jr.
and
A. J. Strickland III
both of
The University of Alabama

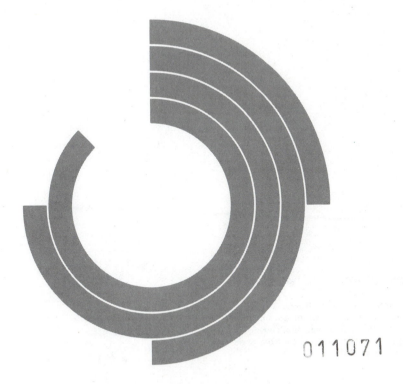

011071

1987 Fourth Edition

BUSINESS PUBLICATIONS, INC.
Plano, Texas 75075

To Hasseline and Kitty

ISBN 0-256-03717-5

Library of Congress Catalog Card No. 86–72250

Printed in the United States of America

2 3 4 5 6 7 8 9 0   K   4 3 2 1 0 9 8 7

Preface

This fourth edition of *Strategic Management: Concepts and Cases* is over 60 percent "new" and plows a lot of fresh ground. We have reorganized the seven chapters covering the concepts and tools of strategic analysis into nine chapters; condensed our treatments of the subject matter into fewer pages; added discussion of some important new topics and techniques; created a three-chapter module on business-level strategy and a two-chapter section on strategic analysis in diversified companies; inserted Analytical Checklists at the end of most chapters to signal to students the key steps in conducting thorough strategic analysis; and developed 12 new Illustration Capsules. Throughout, the content reflects new contributions to the strategic management literature, a stronger conceptual framework, and clear focus on "principles," analytical approaches, and real world practice.

Of the 36 cases we have selected for this edition, 26 are new and one of the 10 holdovers has been updated and revised. The cases are grouped into four sections. Four cases introduce students to the issues and tasks of strategic management, 14 cases zero in on industry and competitive analysis and business-level strategy, 6 cases concern strategic analysis in diversified companies, and 12 cases deal with managing strategy implementation. Quite frankly, we're enthusiastic about the case lineup for this edition; the companies are unusually interesting and the case situations are targeted closely to current strategic management problems and practices.

In addition, we have expanded the available teaching package in a most exciting way. Instructors wishing to introduce students to meaningful *computer-assisted* strategic analysis techniques now have the option of adopting a specially packaged version of the fourth edition containing *Strat-Analyst™*—a set of two case analysis disks for use with Lotus® 1–2–3® on IBM-compatible personal computers with two disk drives. The *Strat-Analyst* option makes it simple and quick for students to do financial ratio analysis, construct graphs from data in a case, build "what if" scenarios, make five-year financial projections, and conduct industry and competitive analysis. *Strat-Analyst* is user-friendly and requires no knowledge of microcomputers, programming, or Lotus 1–2–3 beyond that of knowing how to boot up a disk on a personal computer. The novice can learn to use *Strat-Analyst* successfully in less than an hour, and step-by-step instructions are built into every *Strat-Analyst* option. The case analysis results that students can get with *Strat-Analyst* have been incorporated into the teaching notes in the *Instructor's Manual*. Our students have given *Strat-Analyst* high marks—an outcome which leads us to believe that computer-assisted strategic analysis is destined to become a standard feature in today's courses in strategic management.

Complementing the textbook and the *Strat-Analyst* option are a new edition of *Readings in Strategic Management* (with 65 percent new readings) and a substantially enhanced *Instructor's Manual*. The four-part package creates the most complete, best integrated set of teaching materials that we have ever offered. It gives instructors wide latitude in course design, convenient access to the latest developments in instructional technology, and expanded opportunity to vary the nature of student assignments. The added choices, student supplements, and features of this new edition put the instructor in an even stronger position to put together a course that is fully capable of winning student approval.

What's New in the Text Chapters?

The rapid-fire development of the strategic management literature dictates that major edition-to-edition refinements be made in the treatment given to concepts and analytical techniques. In our updating and adjusting, however, we have kept the focus of this edition strongly centered on the strategy-related tasks of managers and on the methods of strategic analysis. Senior managers (major department heads on up) are cast firmly in the twin roles of chief strategy maker and chief strategy implementer, charged with presiding over insightful strategic analysis, formulating and reviewing strategic action plans, and leading the process of strategy implementation and execution in their respective areas of responsibility. Every key aspect of strategic management is thoroughly examined: defining the business, setting strategic objectives, conducting industry and competitive analysis, evaluating diversified business portfolios, checking out the various generic corporate and business strategy options, seeking ways to achieve a sustainable competitive advantage, building a capable organization, shaping the corporate culture, creating strategy-related administrative fits, and exerting strategic leadership.

We've made several changes worth calling to your attention:

- An all-new chapter on building and defending competitive advantage has been integrated into the presentation. To make room for this material and other new topics *without* expanding the number of pages devoted to text coverage, the writing style has been tightened, wordiness eliminated, and discussions streamlined. Even with the inclusion of new topics, the nine chapters of this edition consume less space than the seven chapters of the last edition.
- What was three-chapter coverage of strategy alternatives and the tools of strategic analysis in the previous edition has been refashioned into a five-chapter presentation: a three-chapter, stand-alone sequence on business-level strategy and a two-chapter, stand-alone sequence on corporate-level strategy. Business strategy is treated first, then corporate strategy, because the concepts and techniques of corporate strategy rely so heavily on a good grasp of business strategy concepts. However, because of their stand-alone nature, instructors who prefer to do so can cover the material on corporate strategy (Chapters 6 and 7) ahead of the business strategy chapter grouping (Chapters 3, 4, and 5).
- The new three-chapter discussion of business-level strategy follows the trail blazed by Professor Michael Porter in his two pioneering books, *Competitive Strategy* (1980) and *Competitive Advantage* (1985). The first chapter in the sequence covers the fundamentals of industry and competitive analysis, the second concerns generic business strategies and industry environments, and the third deals exclusively with how to build and defend competitive advantages at the line-of-business level. The coverage of business strategy has important sections on strategic group map-

ping, driving forces, diagnosing key success factors, Porter's "five forces model" of competition, strategic cost analysis and activity-cost chains, competitor analysis, company situation analysis, profiling a firm's competitive market position and relative competitive strength, ways to tailor business strategies to fit a variety of industry environments, matching strategy to competitive advantage opportunities, and the development of offensive and defensive strategies.

- The role of experience curve economics in business-level strategy formulation is given increased emphasis; the concept of the experience curve is developed fully in a much revised Illustration Capsule.
- An easy-to-follow generic approach to conducting industry and competitive analysis is presented at the end of Chapter 3. It draws together the tools for profiling the strategic features of industry structure and overall industry attractiveness, the competitive forces at work in an industry, and a company's situation in this environment. In addition, it lays out the format for a strategic action plan based on the preceding industry and competitive diagnosis. (This approach has been incorporated in *Strat-Analyst* to give students a time-saving and convenient way to do first-rate situation analysis and then use the results directly in formulating a strategic plan.)
- One of the two new chapters on strategic analysis in diversified companies explains the various corporate strategy alternatives, with emphasis on building a diversified business portfolio and postdiversification portfolio management. The other chapter concentrates on the analytical tools for appraising diversified corporate portfolios; it contains an enhanced treatment of strategic fit and a major new section on creating *corporate-level* competitive advantage.
- Chapter 1 has been greatly condensed to focus only on the process of strategic management—what it is, why it matters, and who is responsible for it.
- In Chapter 2 the spotlight is on the direction-setting entrepreneurial tasks—defining the business, establishing strategic objectives, and formulating a strategic plan. The levels of strategy, a model of the primary determinants of strategy, and how managers tackle the strategy formation process are all laid out in some detail.
- The discussion of strategy implementation is organized around the five internal administrative aspects most crucial to putting the chosen strategy into place: building a capable organization, allocating resources and creating action programs, galvanizing organizational commitment to the chosen strategy, implementing strategy-supportive policies and administrative systems, and exercising strategic leadership. Chapter 8 deals with the first two and Chapter 9 deals with the last three.
- The strategy-related pros and cons of alternative forms of organization are more prominently highlighted in our presentation of how to link strategy and structure. The importance of building a strategy-supportive corporate culture continues to get center stage treatment as a key to successful strategy execution.
- Analytical checklist sections appear at the end of Chapters 3 through 9 to draw student attention again to key concepts and techniques and to serve as a handy reminder to students of what ground to cover in doing a thorough job on assigned cases.
- Shorter, crisper Illustration Capsules have been developed to highlight real world application of core concepts. Twelve of the 21 capsules are new to this edition,

and we have continued to lace every chapter with concrete examples of how strategic management concepts are used by companies and managers.

As before, we have devoted a special chapter to introducing students to case method pedagogy and pointers on how to analyze a case. In our experience, many students are unsure about what they need to do in preparing a case and they are certainly inexperienced in analyzing a company from a strategic point of view. Chapter 10 orients them to what to expect and focuses their attention on the traditional analytical sequence of (1) identify, (2) evaluate, and (3) recommend. This chapter includes a table on how to calculate and interpret key financial ratios; it, along with the step-by-step "what to do" checklists at the end of the text chapters, should get students off on the right foot for both class discussion of cases and written case assignments.

All in all, we are confident that you will find the text portion of this edition better organized, more tightly written, comfortably mainstream, and as close to the cutting edge of both theory and practice as basic textbook discussions can be.

The Collection of Cases

This edition includes over 70 percent new cases and a richer diversity of companies and situations. There are five cases involving non–U.S. based—or international—firms, two cases concerning not-for-profit organizations, five cases involving firms listed in *The 100 Best Companies to Work For in America,* four cases about young start-up companies, six cases involving the ins and outs of corporate diversification, nine cases dealing with the strategic problems of family-owned or relatively small entrepreneurial businesses, two cases about companies whose founder-CEOs now rank among the 400 richest people in the United States, and paired cases showing the contrasting strategies of firms in the same industry. Sprinkled into the mix are cases involving service industries, cases about high-tech companies, cases concerning acknowledged industry leaders, cases involving up-and-coming companies, cases on companies with high-interest products, cases situated in all phases of the industry chain (natural resources, energy, manufacturing, wholesaling, and retailing), cases about companies in trouble, long cases, short cases, "two-day" cases, and cases that rate as tried-and-true favorites. Five of the cases have serial parts (which are reprinted in the *Instructor's Manual*), further expanding the menu and the tempo.

Several criteria have driven our choice of cases for this edition. We have tried to adhere to our traditional practice of choosing cases which senior-level students can suitably handle, which will stimulate student interest, and which involve situations that will produce a lively, exciting classroom discussion. We have looked long and hard for new cases that are current and timely, and have then blended them in with cases whose situations are timeless, classic, and always relevant. And we have been mindful of the need for every case to contain key teaching points and offer real opportunity for students to become skilled in using the tools of strategic analysis. Each of the cases has been conscientiously researched, carefully written, and class-tested. We believe you will find this case collection durable, representative of strategic problems and analytical applications, flexible as to sequencing, and eminently teachable.

The New *Strat-Analyst*™ Option

Scarcely anything is producing more dramatic change in business schools today than the growing use of personal computers for instructional purposes. It is fast becoming standard for upper-level undergraduates to use PCs for one assignment or another on at least a weekly basis. With more business application software becoming available (some of it strategy-related) and with more employers on the lookout for students who have working knowledge of personal computers, the time seems right to start utilizing the power of personal computer technology in the strategic analysis arena.

We have created the *Strat-Analyst* supplement as a way of educating students to the analytical potential of personal computers in the strategic management course. The use of *Strat-Analyst,* however, is strictly *optional* with adopters—the text can be ordered *with* or *without* the *Strat-Analyst* disks. *Strat-Analyst* is designed to work on all IBM-compatible PCs with standard 256k memories, but it must be used in conjunction with Lotus 1–2–3 (this presents no real barrier to students because virtually any university's PC lab will have multiple copies of the Lotus 1–2–3 software package readily available for student use).

Strat-Analyst is multipurpose so as to give instructors the ability to make several different types of computer-assisted strategic analysis assignments. There are two main sections in *Strat-Analyst.* The first section contains files of the financial exhibits for 16 cases and has case-specific templates (a different one for each case) that allow students to *quickly* do any of the following:

- Calculate financial and operating ratios, common-size income statements, and annual compound rates of change in any of several performance variables.
- Construct line graphs, bar graphs, pie charts, and scatter diagrams using any of the case data on file.
- Do "what if" scenarios and five-year financial performance projections.
- Obtain hard copy printouts of all of the analytical work they do.

While students often do some financial analysis of case data using hand calculators, they are often discouraged from doing regular, systematic financial analysis because of the time-consuming nature of punching so many calculator buttons and writing down the results. *Strat-Analyst* makes such calculations so easy to get that instructors can insist on and expect thorough financial assessments. And students can spend their time analyzing the results of the number-crunching rather than on doing a time-consuming series of repetitive calculations on several years of data. *Strat-Analyst's* graphing capabilities are particularly valuable to students in preparing written assignments and visual aids for oral presentations. The "what if" features make it easier to quantify the effects of particular strategic actions and to examine the outcomes of alternative scenarios.

The second section of *Strat-Analyst* features an easy-to-use, step-by-step generic procedure for conducting industry and competitive analysis (ICA) on any assigned case. The menu of ICA options here includes

- Industry situation analysis.
- Competitive situation analysis.

- Company situation analysis.
- Development of a strategic action plan.

Students can choose to go through one, two, three, or all of the ICA options and, when finished, get a neatly organized, final-copy printout of their analysis in a report format (which can then be conveniently graded by the instructor).

We believe that *Strat-Analyst* offers students three important benefits:

1. It gives students a major assist in doing higher-caliber strategic analysis.
2. It will significantly cut the time that it takes students to do a thorough job of case preparation.
3. It will build student comfort levels and skills in the use of PCs for managerial analysis purposes.

The instructor profits too—from improved student performance, from the added dimension *Strat-Analyst* gives the course, and from increased flexibility of course design and variety in instructional techniques. Testing of *Strat-Analyst* in our own classes indicates that it is a win-win approach for both students and instructors.

If You Also Want to Use Readings

For instructors who like to incorporate samples of the strategic management literature into their course syllabus, the second edition of *Readings in Strategic Management* is now available. It contains 31 selections, varying in length from a few pages to 20 pages. All are current (only one was published prior to 1980); all are quite readable; and all are suitable for seniors and MBA students. Most of the selections (22) are articles reprinted from leading journals; they add in-depth treatment to important topic areas covered in the text. Nine of the articles are drawn from practitioner sources and were chosen to stress how particular tools and concepts relate directly to actual companies and managerial practices. In tandem, these readings provide an effective, efficient vehicle for reinforcing and expanding the text-case approach.

Acknowledgments

We have benefited from the help of many people during the evolution of this book. Students, adopters, and reviewers have generously supplied an untold number of insightful comments and helpful suggestions. Our intellectual debt to those academics, writers, and practicing managers who have blazed new trails in the strategy field will be obvious to any reader familiar with the literature of strategic management. We are particularly indebted to the case researchers whose casewriting efforts appear herein and to the companies and organizations whose experiences and situations comprise the case studies.

To each of the case contributors goes a very special thank you. The importance of good, timely cases cannot be overestimated in contributing to a substantive study of strategic management issues and practices. From a research standpoint, cases in strategic management are invaluable in exposing the generic kinds of strategic issues that companies face, in forming hypotheses about strategic behavior, and in drawing experienced-based generalizations about the practice of strategic management. Pedagogically, strategy cases give students essential practice in diagnosing and evaluating strategic situations, in learning to use the tools and concepts of strategy analysis, in sorting through the pros and cons of various strategic options, and in tailoring strategic action plans to fit the prevailing circumstances. Without an ample supply of fresh, well-researched, and well-written cases, the discipline of business policy would fall into disrepair, losing much of its energy and excitement. We trust, therefore, that sentiment and support for first-class case research will thrive and that case researchers will be recognized and justly rewarded for their scholarly contributions.

The following reviewers have been of considerable help in directing our efforts at various stages in the evolution of the manuscript through four editions: W. Harvey Hegarty, Indiana University; Roger Evered, Penn State University; Charles B. Saunders, the University of Kansas; Rhae M. Swisher, Troy State University; Claude I. Shell, Eastern Michigan University; R. Thomas Lenz, Indiana University–Purdue University at Indianapolis; James B. Thurman, Virginia Polytechnic Institute and State University; Michael C. White, Texas Tech University; Dennis Callahan, University of Rhode Island; R. Duane Ireland, Baylor University; William E. Burr II, University of Oregon; C. W. Millard, Iowa State University; Richard Mann, University of Southern California; Kurt Christensen, Purdue University; Neil W. Jacobs, Northern Arizona University; Louis W. Fry, University of Washington; D. Robley Wood, Virginia Commonwealth University; George J. Gore, University of Cincinnati; William R. Soukup, San Diego State University; William Acar, Kent State University; George B. Davis, Cleveland State University; and John F. Preble, University of Delaware.

Naturally, as custom properly dictates, we are responsible for whatever errors of fact, deficiencies in coverage or in exposition, and oversights that remain. As always we value your recommendations and thoughts about the book. Your comments regarding coverage and content will be most welcome, as will your calling our attention to specific errors. Please write us at P.O. Box J, Department of Management and Marketing, The University of Alabama, Tuscaloosa, AL 35487-9725.

A.A.T.
A.J.S.

Contents

6   Generic Types of Corporate Strategies,   159

7   Techniques for Analyzing Corporate Diversification Strategies,   182

PART 3
CASES IN STRATEGIC MANAGEMENT

Part 1

The Process of
Strategic Management

1 Strategic Management: What It Is, Whose Responsibility It Is, and Why It Matters

As long as companies have conducted business, some have been outstanding successes while others have been dismal failures. Some companies act with purpose and direction, others drift. Some companies are adept at seizing new opportunities, others watch passively or let them slip through the cracks. Some companies perform well because of good internal management, others barely survive because of inefficiency and misdirected operations.

The management practices of successful and unsuccessful enterprises have been scrutinized in an effort to learn the really important managerial do's and don'ts that separate the winners from the losers. Although what research and experience have taught us so far falls short of a genuine theory of "how to manage," we have nonetheless zeroed in on some notable managerial differences between high-performing and low-performing enterprises:[1]

1. In high-performing organizations, there is a clear sense of direction. Senior managers have a strong vision of where the company needs to be headed and why. They are not afraid to blaze new trails or initiate major changes in the organization's business makeup. By contrast, the managers of low-performing organizations are characteristically so absorbed in the latest crisis and

---

[1] For a sampling of some of the findings and conclusions, see Joel Ross and Michael Kami, *Corporate Management in Crisis: Why the Mighty Fall* (Englewood Cliffs, N.J.: Prentice-Hall, 1973); Alfred D. Chandler, *The Visible Hand* (Cambridge, Mass.: Harvard Univ. Press, 1977); William K. Hall, "Survival Strategies in a Hostile Environment," *Harvard Business Review* 58, no. 5 (September–October 1980), pp. 75–85; Thomas J. Peters and Robert H. Waterman, Jr., *In Search of Excellence: Lessons from America's Best-Run Companies* (New York: Harper & Row, 1982); and Michael E. Porter, *Competitive Advantage* (New York: Free Press, 1985).

tending to administrative detail that they neglect the task of thinking deeply about where the organization will be in five years if it sticks to doing just what it is already doing. Big direction-setting decisions stay on the back burner. They are more comfortable being late-movers instead of first-movers. Major strategic issues are often studied but less often acted on decisively.

2. In high-performing companies, there is an abundance of skilled entrepreneurship, with unmatched knowledge about customer needs and behavior, market trends, and emerging opportunities. Managers doggedly pursue ways to do things better or differently, often getting their best ideas from listening to customers. The innovative approach they practice is persistence—try, fail, learn, try again, keep at it, and eventually succeed. They aggressively search out new opportunities and move boldly to pursue those they find most attractive. Poorly run enterprises are neither customer-driven nor opportunity-driven. Their managers are normally less perceptive about customer needs and attitudes; their instinct is to react to market trends rather than initiate them. They are reluctant to try out new ideas for fear of making a mistake. Actions and decisions don't stray far from the "tried and true" ways. Real entrepreneurial drive is missing.

3. In high-performing companies, managers are committed to having a first-rate strategic action plan—one aimed at achieving superior financial performance and a strong, defendable competitive position. They see competitive advantage (if possible, competitive dominance) as the key to superior profitability and long-term performance. Weak-performing organizations are nearly always on the short end of the strategy stick. Their managers, preoccupied with internal brush fires and paperwork deadlines, do a comparatively poor job of maneuvering their organizations into favorable competitive positions; they don't develop effective ways to compete more successfully. Often they underestimate the strength of competitors and overestimate the ability of their own organizations to offset the competitive advantages of the market leaders.

4. High-performing organizations are strongly results-oriented and performance-conscious. Doing a good job of managing means achieving the targeted results on time. Outstanding individual performance is valued and well rewarded. The managers of poorly performing organizations excuse weak performance on the basis of such uncontrollable factors as a depressed economy, slack demand, strong competitive pressures, rising costs, and unforeseen problems.[2] Rewards are loosely tied to standards of superior performance. Making modest progress is rated as "doing a great job."

5. In the best-performing companies, managers are deeply involved in implementing the chosen strategy and making it work as planned. They understand the internal requirements for successful strategy implementation and they insist that careful attention be paid to the tiny details required for first-rate execution of the chosen strategy. They engage in "managing by wandering around,"

---

[2] Sometimes, of course, organizations perform badly in the short run because of adverse external circumstances beyond management's ability to control. But such adversity never really has long-run validity as a reason for poor performance. Over time, it is management's responsibility to adjust the organizational game plan to these adverse conditions and, moreover, to devise a game plan that will succeed in spite of them.

staying in touch with down-the-line personnel, and maintaining a personal feel for how things are going. They personally lead the process of strategy implementation and execution. In contrast, the managers of poorly performing organizations are into the machinations of corporate bureaucracy; the bulk of their time is taken up with studies, reports, meetings, policymaking, memos, and administrative procedure. They do not see systematic implementation of strategic plans as their prime administrative responsibility. They spend most of the workday in their offices, remaining largely invisible to their organizations, using immediate subordinates as a conduit to the rest of the organization, and keeping tight control over most decisions.

These contrasts in mindsets and approaches are striking and managerially instructive about do's and don'ts. The managers of successful organizations are action-oriented "strategic thinkers" who make a habit of training their eyes externally on customer needs, new opportunities, and competitive positioning, as well as internally on operations. They have a talent for entrepreneurship combined with a flair for day-to-day management and internal leadership. They are aware of their responsibility to shape their organization's long-term direction, lead the organization down a clear-cut path, formulate a coherent strategic action plan that will produce competitive advantage and long-term financial success, and orchestrate successful implementation of the chosen strategy. They watch like hawks to see that their organization has a good strategy and executes it to perfection. They are good strategists and entrepreneurs as well as good inside leaders.

In unsuccessful organizations managers fail to appreciate the importance of charting a clear organizational course and being good entrepreneurs. They lack an instinct for strategic thinking and ignore the lesson implicit in the familiar expression, "If you don't know where you are going, any road will take you there." Their downfall seems to be getting so wrapped up in administrative activities and solving internal "problems" that they neglect the tasks of consciously shaping the organization's business makeup, directing where the business is headed, and managing the process of getting there.

WHAT IS STRATEGIC MANAGEMENT?

The success-causing power of clear direction, good strategy, and effective implementation of organizational action plans is now generally recognized. *Strategic management is the process whereby managers establish an organization's long-term direction, set specific performance objectives, develop strategies to achieve these objectives in the light of all the relevant internal and external circumstances, and undertake to execute the chosen action plans.*

The strategic management function is perhaps the most fundamental and most important aspect of management and managing. It takes superior entrepreneurship (a well-conceived strategic plan that positions the organization in the right way at the right time) *and* competent strategy implementation and execution to produce superior organizational performance over the long-run. A great strategic plan that is subsequently marred by poor execution reduces performance. Likewise, a subpar strategic plan that is flawlessly executed seldom produces gold star results either.

The optimal condition is superior entrepreneurship and strategy formation on the one hand, combined with first-rate implementation and strategy execution on the other. The chances are excellent that when an organization has a well-conceived, well-executed strategy it will be a high performer—a winner. Superior performance is the most trustworthy sign of good management.

The Components of Strategic Management

Strategic management has five critical components:

1. *Defining the organization's business and developing a strategic mission* as a basis for establishing what the organization does and doesn't do and where it is headed.
2. *Establishing strategic objectives and performance targets.*
3. *Formulating a strategy* to achieve the strategic objectives and targeted results.
4. *Implementing and executing the chosen strategic plan.*
5. *Evaluating strategic performance and making corrective adjustments* in strategy and/or how it is being implemented in light of actual experience, changing conditions, and new ideas and opportunities.

Defining the Business   A basic direction-setting question facing the senior managers of any enterprise is "What is our business and what will it be?" Addressing this question thoughtfully compels executives to think through the scope and mix of organizational activities, to reflect on what kind of organization they are presently trying to create, to consider what markets they believe the organization should be in, and to be specific about which needs of which buyers to serve. The answers that managers settle upon say a lot about the organization's character, identity, and direction. Defining the business as it is now and will be later is a necessary first step in establishing a meaningful direction and developmental path for the organization. Management's view of what the organization seeks to do and to become over the long-term is the organization's *strategic mission.* It broadly charts the future course of the organization. Since decisions about long-term direction fall squarely upon the shoulders of senior officers, the strategic mission nearly always reflects the personal vision and thinking of top-level managers, especially that of the chief executive officer. Some examples of corporate mission statements are presented in Illustration Capsule 1.

Establishing Strategic Objectives   Specific performance targets are needed in all areas affecting the survival and success of an enterprise, and they are needed at all levels of management, from the corporate level on down deep into the organization's structure. The act of establishing formal objectives not only converts the direction an organization is headed into specific performance targets to be achieved but also guards against drift, aimless activity, confusion over what to accomplish, and loss of purpose. Both short-run and long-run objectives are needed. The strategic objectives for the organization as a whole should at a minimum specify the following: the market position and competitive standing the organization aims to achieve, annual profitability targets, key financial and operating results to be achieved through the organization's chosen activities, and any other yardsticks by which strategic success

ILLUSTRATION CAPSULE 1

Examples of How Companies Define Their Business

Presented below are verbatim quotations that illustrate how several firms have defined their business and strategic mission:

Hershey Foods Corporation

Hershey Foods Corporation's basic business mission is to become a major, diversified food company. The company uses four approaches in pursuit of this mission: (1) to capitalize on the considerable growth potential of the company's existing brands and products in current markets; (2) to introduce new products; (3) to expand the distribution of Hershey's long-established, well-known brands and new products into new markets—domestic and foreign; and (4) to make acquisitions and other types of alliances. These approaches are pursued within the context of maintaining the financial strength of the company.

A basic principle which Hershey will continue to embrace is to attract and hold consumers with products and services of consistently superior quality and value.

General Motors

The fundamental purpose of General Motors is to provide products and services of such quality that our customers will receive superior value, our employees and business partners will share in our success, and our stockholders will receive a sustained, superior return on their investment.

Levi Strauss & Co.

Levi Strauss & Co. is the world's largest producer of branded apparel, marketing a broad range of clothing, most of it leisure oriented, to customers of both sexes and all ages throughout the world. The company strives to be among the leading brands—in volume and image—in all markets it serves. The company's products are sold in approximately 40,000 U.S. retail outlets and through sales facilities located in many foreign countries. Principal operating groups are The Jeans Company, which markets jeans and related merchandise in the United States; Battery Street Enterprises, with nonjeans product lines that range from hand-tailored Oxford Clothes to BendOver ® women's slacks; and Levi Strauss International, which sells jeanswear and leisure apparel outside the United states.

Polaroid

Polaroid manufactures and sells photographic products based on inventions of the company in the field of one-step instant photography and light-polarizing products, utilizing the company's inventions in the field of polarized light. The company considers itself to be engaged in one line of business.

General Portland Cement Co., Inc.

It's long been a business philosophy of General Portland that "we manufacture and sell cement, but we market concrete." Our job, as we see it, is to manufacture

ILLUSTRATION CAPSULE 1 *(concluded)*

top-quality cement and to work with our customers to develop new applications for concrete while expanding current uses.

TECO Energy (Parent Corporation of Tampa Electric, TECO Transport, and TECO Coal)

Corporate Purpose: Produce optimum, long-range returns to our investors by nurturing a family of well-managed, customer-oriented operating companies.

Tampa Electric Mission: Provide reliable electric service in ways that earn public support.

TECO Transport Mission: Be the pre-eminent provider of bulk-cargo water transport and transfer services to shippers of the world.

TECO Coal Mission: Supply quality coal at competitive prices to Tampa Electric and other customers.

MCI Communications, Inc.

MCI's mission is leadership in the global telecommunications services industry. Profitable growth is fundamental to that mission, so that we may serve the interests of our stockholders and our customers.

To maintain profitable growth, MCI will: Provide a full range of high-value services for customers who must communicate or move information electronically throughout the United States and the world; manage our business so as to be the low-cost provider of services; make quality synonymous with MCI to our growing customer base; set the pace in identifying and implementing cost-effective technologies and services as we expand our state-of-the-art communications network; continue to be an entrepreneurial company, built of people who can make things happen in a competitive marketplace.

will be measured. Because performance objectives are needed up and down the organization, the objective-setting task of strategic management involves all managers; each must identify what their area's contribution to strategic success will be and then establish concrete, measurable performance targets. Standard Oil of Indiana's performance objectives are presented in Illustration Capsule 2.

Formulating Strategy   This component of strategic management brings into play the critical issue of just *how* the targeted results are to be accomplished. Objectives are the "ends" and *strategy* is the "means" of achieving them. The task of formulating strategy entails taking into account all of the relevant aspects of the organization's internal and external situation and coming up with a detailed action plan for achieving the targeted short-run and long-run results. *Strategy is a blueprint of all the important entrepreneurial, competitive, and functional area actions that are to be taken in pursuing organizational objectives and positioning the organization for sustained success.*

ILLUSTRATION CAPSULE 2

The Strategic Performance Objectives at Standard Oil of Indiana (Amoco)

In a recent corporate annual report, Standard Oil Company of Indiana, which markets its products under the Amoco brand, indicated that its primary objectives were:

- To preserve shareholders' capital.
- To increase earnings on an average of 10 percent a year.
- To earn a return of 13 to 15 percent each year on shareholders' equity (the company's net worth).
- To pay out 35 to 45 percent of earnings in the form of dividends to shareholders.
- To maintain a prudent financial structure, retaining the company's triple-A rating for the purpose of borrowing large sums of money.
- To compare favorably with competitors.

General Electric, a pioneer of strategic management techniques, once defined strategy as "a statement of how what resources are going to be used to take advantage of which opportunities to minimize which threats to produce a desired result." This definition points toward the issues that strategy must address:

1. *How to respond to changing conditions*—specifically, what to do about shifting customer needs and emerging industry trends, which new opportunities to pursue, how to defend against competitive pressures and other externally imposed threats, and how to strengthen the mix of the firm's activities by doing more of some things and less of others.

2. *How to allocate resources* over the organization's various business units, divisions, and functional departments—making decisions that steer capital investment and human resources in behind the chosen strategic plan is always critical; some kind of strategy-supportive guidelines for resource allocation have to exist.

3. *How to compete* in each one of the industries in which the organization participates—decisions about how to develop customer appeal, to position the firm against rivals, to emphasize some products and de-emphasize others, and to meet specific competitive threats are always integral to competitive survival and the achievement of a defendable competitive advantage.

4. Within each line of business of the organization, *what actions and approaches to take in each of the major functional areas and operating departments* to create a unified and more powerful strategic effort throughout the business unit. Obviously, the different functional and operating level strategies ought to be coordinated rather than be allowed to go off on independent courses; they need to support the creation of a sustainable competitive advantage.

The issues of strategy thus go up and down the managerial hierarchy; strategy is not just something that only top management wrestles with. While there is indeed a strategy for the organization as a whole that is top management's responsibility, there are strategies for each line of business the organization is in; there are strategies at the functional area level (manufacturing, marketing, finance, human resources, and so on) within each business; and there are strategies at the operating level (for each department and field unit) to carry out the details of functional area strategy. Optimally, the strategies at each level are formulated and implemented by those managers closest to the scene of the action and then sufficiently coordinated to produce a unified action plan for the whole organization.

Strategy formation is largely an exercise in entrepreneurship. The content of a strategic action plan reflects entrepreneurial judgments about the long-term direction of the organization, any need for major new initiatives (increased competitive aggressiveness, a new diversification move, divestiture of unattractive activities), and actions aimed at keeping the organization in position to enjoy sustained success. Specific entrepreneurial aspects of the strategy formation process include:

- Searching actively for innovative ways the organization can improve on what it is already doing.
- Ferreting out new opportunities for the organization to pursue.
- Developing ways to increase the firm's competitive strength and put it in a stronger position to cope with competitive forces.
- Devising ways to build and maintain a competitive advantage.
- Deciding how to meet threatening external developments.
- Encouraging individuals throughout the organization to put forth innovative proposals and championing those that have promise.
- Directing resources away from areas of low or diminishing results toward areas of high or increasing results.
- Deciding when and how to diversify.
- Choosing which businesses (or products) to abandon, which of the continuing ones to emphasize, and which new ones to enter or add.

The critical entrepreneurial skill is making strategic choices that keep the organization in position to enjoy sustained success.

Analysis and judgment are always factors. The right choice and strategy for one organization need not be right for another organization—even one in the same business. Why? Because situations differ from organization to organization, as well as from time to time. Strongly positioned firms can do things that weakly positioned ones can't do, and weak firms need to do things that strong ones don't. A good strategy is one that is right for the organization, considering all of the relevant specifics of its situation. The entrepreneurial task of formulating strategy thus always requires heavy doses of _situational analysis_ and judgment, with the aim being to achieve "goodness of fit" between strategy and all the relevant aspects of the organization's internal situation and external environment. Indeed, one of the special values and contributions of managers is an ability to develop customized solutions that fit the unique features of an organization's situation.

As an example of what strategy is and how it works, read Illustration Capsule 3 on Beatrice Companies, Inc.

Strategy Implementation and Execution
Putting the strategy into place and getting individuals and organizational subunits to go all out in executing their

Strategy at Beatrice Companies: From a Local Dairy to a Diversified Corporate Giant

Originally a butter and egg company serving a portion of Nebraska, the corporate management of Beatrice Companies, Inc. launched an effort in the 1950s to reduce the company's dependence on local conditions. It started by acquiring small dairies in other midwestern locations. Only firms headed by independent-minded entrepreneurs were brought into the fold, and the former owners were allowed wide latitude to continue running their operations as they saw fit. Although Beatrice found that the dairy business had the disadvantage of low profit margins, it had the advantage of generating big cash flows (mainly because of low capital requirements and rapid inventory turnover). This allowed Beatrice to finance its acquisitions mostly with cash rather than with debt or new stock. Over the years, Beatrice's management broadened the company's geographic scope, acquiring dairies from coast to coast and growing into a $200 million dairy company.

Then the strategic focus at Beatrice shifted to diversification, and cash flows were used to purchase higher-margin food companies. La Choy Food Products, a well-known producer of Chinese foods, was the first acquisition outside the dairy industry and, when it worked out well, Beatrice began to push into other food lines at an accelerating rate. Along the way Beatrice decided to acquire some nonfood firms, and by the 1970s it owned several different kinds of manufacturing operations, a warehousing division, and an insurance company. The major acquisitions were Samsonite (luggage), Dannon (yogurt), Clark (candy bars), Eckrich (meats), Gebhardt's (chili and tamales), and La Choy (Chinese foods).

Beatrice's diversification strategy followed some strict guidelines. Commodity-oriented firms were excluded because of unpredictable price swings. Companies in head-on competition with such powerhouses as Kellogg's and Campbell Soup were avoided. In the nonfood areas, Beatrice shied away from labor-intensive companies because of the risks of sharply rising labor costs. Industries such as steel and chemicals were avoided because of their heavy capital demands.

The basic acquisition strategy was to go after companies with at least five years of sales and profit increases, and to eliminate from consideration any firm so large that failure could seriously damage Beatrice's overall profitability. While Beatrice sought companies with a growth rate higher than its own, management's financial strategy called for a purchase price keyed to a price-earnings multiple about one-third below Beatrice's own current price-earnings ratio. Beatrice was generally successful in buying firms it wanted at a "discount" because the Beatrice stock it was offering in return had performed so well over the years.

Once acquired, the new businesses were managed under a decentralized structure; the general managers of each unit were given broad-ranging authority and were turned loose to formulate and implement their own strategies, thereby permitting each business to be operated in tune with the specifics of its own market and competitive environment.

By 1977 Beatrice's strategy of acquisition and diversification propelled the company into the position of being the largest food processing enterprise in the United States.

SOURCE: Linda Grant Martin. "How Beatrice Foods Sneaked Up on $5 Billion." *Fortune.* April 1976. pp. 118–29.

part of the strategic plan successfully is essentially an *administrative* task. The managerial challenge to "make it happen" involves:

- Building an organization capable of carrying out the strategic plan.
- Developing strategy-supportive budgets and programs.
- Instilling a strong organizationwide commitment both to organizational objectives and the chosen strategy.
- Linking the motivation and reward structure directly to achieving the targeted results.
- Creating an organization "culture" that is in tune with strategy in every success-causing respect.
- Installing policies and procedures that facilitate strategy implementation.
- Developing an information and reporting system to track and control the progress of strategy implementation.
- Exerting the internal leadership needed to drive implementation forward and to keep improving how the strategy is being executed.

Developing an *action agenda* for implementing and executing strategy involves managers at all levels, from headquarters on down to each operating department, deciding on answers to the question, "What is required for us to implement our part of the overall strategic plan and how can we best get it done?" Doing this task well means scrutinizing virtually every operating activity to see what actions can be taken to improve strategy execution and to instill strategy-supportive practices and behavior.

The administrative tasks of implementing and executing strategy involve a process of moving incrementally and deliberately to create a variety of "fits" that bring an organization's conduct of its internal operations into good alignment with strategy. The value of consciously fitting the "way we do things around here" to the requirements of first-rate strategy execution is that it produces a strategy-supportive organizational culture and work climate. Implementation is soon defeated if the ingrained attitudes and habits of managers and employees are hostile or at cross-purposes with the needs of strategy and if their customary ways of doing things block strategy implementation instead of facilitating it. A number of fits are thus needed:

- Between strategy and the internal organizational structure.
- Between strategy and organizational skills/technical know-how/operating capabilities.
- Between strategy and the allocation of budgets and staff size.
- Between strategy and the organization's system of rewards and incentives.
- Between strategy and internal policies, practices, and procedures.
- Between strategy and the internal organizational atmosphere (as determined by the values and beliefs shared by managers and employees, the philosophies and decision-making styles of senior managers, and other factors that make up the organization's personality and culture).

The stronger these fits, the more strategy-supportive an organization's way of doing things.

Broadly viewed, the management task of strategy implementation is one of scrutinizing the whole internal organization to diagnose what strategy-supportive approaches are needed and what actions to take to accomplish them. Then the different pieces of the implementation plan need to be arranged into a pattern of action that will produce orderly change (from the old strategy to the new strategy) rather than creating disruption and dissatisfaction with the way things are being handled. Both the sequence of actions and the speed of the implementation process are important aspects of uniting the entire organization behind strategy accomplishment. The leadership challenge is to so stimulate the enthusiasm, pride, and commitment of managers and employees that an organizationwide crusade emerges to carry out the chosen strategy and to achieve the targeted results.

Evaluating Strategic Performance and Making Corrective Adjustments

Neither strategy formulation nor strategy implementation is a once-and-for-all-time task. In both cases, circumstances arise which make corrective adjustments desirable. Strategy may need to be modified because it is not working well or because changing conditions make fine-tuning, or even major overhaul, necessary. Even a good strategy can be improved, and it requires no great argument to see that changes in industry and competitive conditions, the emergence of new opportunities or threats, new executive leadership, a reordering of objectives, and the like can all make a change in strategy desirable. Likewise, with strategy implementation there will be times when one or another aspect of implementation does not go as well as planned, making adjustments necessary. And changing internal conditions, as well as experiences with current strategy execution, can drive different or improved implementation approaches. Testing out new ideas and learning what works and what doesn't through trial and error is common.

Thus, it is always incumbent upon management to monitor both how well the chosen strategy is working and how well implementation is proceeding, making corrective adjustments whenever better ways of doing things can be supported. The function of strategic management is ongoing, not something to be done once and then neglected.

The Process of Strategic Management

Because each component of strategic management entails judging whether to continue with things as they are or to make changes, *the task of managing strategy is a dynamic process*—all strategic decisions are subject to future modification. Changes in the organization's situation and ups and downs in financial performance are constant drivers of strategic adjustments.

A model of the strategic management process is shown in Figure 1–1. The first three components, in combination, give direction to the enterprise, establish the directional map for strategic action, and, in effect, define what we shall call an organization's *strategic plan.* The fourth component is easily the most complicated and challenging one because it involves not only deciding on but also undertaking the administrative actions needed to convert the strategic plan into results; indeed, orchestrating the execution of strategy is probably 5 to 10 times more time-consuming than is formulating the strategic plan. The fifth component, evaluating strategic performance and making corrective adjustments, is both the end and the beginning of the strategic management cycle. The march of external and internal events guarantees that the

Figure 1–1   The Strategic Management Process

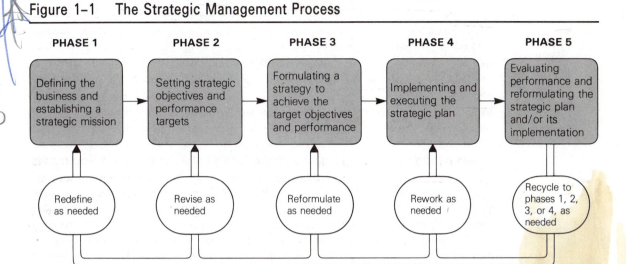

time will come for making revisions in the four previous components. Most of the time, revisions will be of the fine-tuning variety, but occasions for major overhaul in one or more components arise—sometimes because of significant external developments and sometimes because of sharply sliding financial performance.

Characteristics of the Process   While defining the business, establishing strategic objectives, formulating a strategy, implementing and executing the strategic plan, and evaluating performance accurately portray the conceptual elements in managing an enterprise's strategy, the process is not quite so cleanly divided and neatly performed in actual practice. First, managers do not necessarily, or even usually, go through the sequence in rigorous lockstep fashion. Often there is interplay back and forth between the elements; for example, consideration of what strategic actions to take can provoke discussions of whether and how the strategy can be implemented with real effectiveness. Moreover, the boundaries between the components are sometimes hard to distinguish in practice: establishing a strategic mission shades into setting objectives for the organization to achieve (both involve direction-setting); objective-setting shades into considering whether and how strategies can be formulated to achieve them; and deciding on a strategy is nearly always entangled in discussions about the direction the organization needs to take and the position it should try to assume.

Second, the tasks involved in strategic management are never isolated from everything else that falls within a manager's purview. Strategy has to be formulated and implemented in the midst of a managerial schedule that is fragmented with appointments, meetings, paperwork deadlines, unexpected problems, and momentary crises. It is incorrect to construe the job of managing strategy as the exclusive task of managers, even though it may well be the most important function they perform where organizational success or failure is concerned.

Third, the demands that strategy management puts on the manager's time are irregular. Strategic issues, new opportunities, and bright ideas about strategy or its implementation do not appear according to some ordered timetable; they have to be dealt with whenever they arise. Strategic issues soak up big chunks of management time during some weeks and take a backseat in other weeks.

Finally, formulating and implementing strategy must be regarded as something that is *ongoing* and that *evolves*.[3] What qualifies as a surefire high-performance strategy today is sooner or later rendered stale by events unfolding both inside and outside the enterprise. The task of "strategizing" can never therefore be a one-time exercise. While the "whats" of an organization's strategic mission and long-term strategic objectives, once established, usually present fairly stable targets to shoot for, the "hows" of strategy evolve regularly in response to changes in an organization's internal situation and external environment. As a consequence, fine-tuning-type changes in strategic plans, and an occasional major change in strategic thrust, are normal and expected (big strategy changes, however, cannot be made often). The need to keep strategy in tune with an organization's changing situation makes the strategic management process dynamic and means that the prevailing strategy is rarely the result of a single comprehensive analysis. Strategic decisions are made over a period of time, not all at once; moreover, previous decisions are modified and decisions to initiate new strategic moves are forthcoming from time to time. Much of the time strategy evolves in a fairly orderly manner, but sometimes the strategy is crisis-driven, forcing a number of big strategic decisions to be made rapidly.

Similarly, strategy implementation is the product of incremental improvements, internal fine-tuning, the pooling effect of many administrative decisions, and gradual adjustments in the actions and behavior of both managerial subordinates and employees. Implementation is not something that can be made to happen overnight. The transition from the old strategy to executing the new strategy takes time; normally, the larger the degree of strategic change, the more time it takes for the new methods of implementation to take hold.

WHO ARE THE STRATEGY MANAGERS?

It goes without saying that an organization's chief executive officer and chief operating officer are *strategy managers*, with ultimate authority and responsibility for formulating and implementing the strategic plans of the organization as a whole. Most, if not all, of an organization's vice presidents have important strategy-formulating and strategy-implementing responsibilities as well. But managerial positions with strategic management responsibility are by no means restricted to a few senior executives; in organizations of much size and complexity, *there are strategy managers up and down the management hierarchy. The strategic management function directly involves all managers with line authority at the corporate, line-of-business, functional area, and major operating department levels.*

[3] Robert N. Anthony, *Planning and Control Systems: A Framework for Analysis* (Boston: Division of Research, Graduate School of Business Administration, Harvard University, 1965), pp. 38–39; and James B. Quinn, *Strategies for Change: Logical Incrementalism* (Homewood, Ill.: Richard D. Irwin, 1980), chap. 2, especially pp. 58–59.

For the process of managing strategy to work very well, managers must place their imprint on those aspects of the plan to be carried out in their area of responsibility. As one corporate executive succinctly put it, "Those who implement the plan must make the plan." Corporate experiences with strategic planning over the last two decades clearly demonstrate that strategic planning should not be a high-level staff function performed by professionals who then hand over CEO-approved plans to others to carry out in their respective areas of responsibility; rather, the *strategy-making/strategy-executing tasks need to fall directly into the laps of those managers who run those parts of the organization where the strategic results must be achieved.* Putting responsibility and authority for strategy-making in the hands of those who ultimately must put the strategy into place and make it work fixes accountability for strategic success or failure directly on those who are in charge of the results-producing organizational units. As a consequence, the strategy managers in business enterprises include:

- The chief executive officer and other senior corporate-level executives who have primary responsibility and personal authority for big strategic decisions affecting the total enterprise.
- The general managers of subsidiary line-of-business units who have profit-and-loss responsibility for the unit and consequently a leadership role in formulating and implementing the business-level strategy of the unit.
- The functional area managers within a given business unit who have direct authority over a major piece of the business (manufacturing, marketing and sales, finance, R&D, personnel) and therefore must support overall business strategy with strategic actions in their own areas.
- The managers of major operating departments and geographic field units who have frontline responsibility for the details of strategic efforts in their areas and for carrying out their pieces of the overall strategic plan.

A diversified corporation has strategy managers at all four of these levels. A single-business enterprise usually has only three levels: the corporate-level and business-level strategy managers merge into a single group with responsibility for directing the strategic efforts of the total enterprise in that one business. The smallest enterprises, of course, usually have only a single strategy manager (as in the case of the owner-manager of a sole proprietorship or the managing partner in a partnership-type firm) because just one person performs the entire management function.

There are many rather than few strategy managers in not-for-profit organizations as well. For example, a multicampus state university has four identifiable levels of strategic management: (1) The president of the whole university system is a strategy manager with broad direction-setting responsibility and strategic decision-making authority over all the campuses. (2) The chancellor for each campus is a strategy manager with strategy-making/strategy-implementing authority over all academic, student, athletic, and alumni matters, and budgetary, programmatic, and coordinative responsibilities for the whole campus. (3) The deans of the various colleges are strategic managers with direction-setting leadership responsibility for the academic programs, budgets, faculty, and students in the college. (4) The heads of the various academic departments are strategy managers with first-line strategic and supervisory responsibility for the departmental budget, the department's undergraduate and graduate program offerings, the faculty, and students majoring in the department. In federal and state government, the heads of local, district, and regional offices function as strategy managers because they are responsible for custom-tailoring the actions of their agencies to meet the specific needs of the geographical area their units serve and because they are in charge of seeing that their agency's strategic mission, programs, and services are carried out in that area. In municipal government, the heads of the police department, the fire department, the water and sewer department, the parks and recreation department, the health department, and so on are strategy managers in the sense that they are in charge of the entire operations (services and programs offered, day-to-day decisions, facilities, personnel, policies and practices, budget allocations) under their direction.

Managerial jobs with strategy-making/strategy-implementing roles are thus quite numerous and common. The need to understand the ins and outs of strategic management and to be skilled in strategic thinking, strategic analysis, and methods of strategy execution is a basic aspect of managing and is not something that only top managers need to know and to worry about.

Since the scope of a strategy manager's role in the strategy-making/strategy-implementing process plainly varies according to the manager's position in the organizational hierarchy, "the organization" under a strategy manager's direction should henceforth be understood to mean whatever kind of organizational unit the strategy manager is in charge of—whether it is an entire company or not-for-profit organization, a business unit within a diversified company, a major geographic division, an important functional area unit within a business, or an operating department or field unit reporting to a specific functional area head. This will permit us to avoid using the awkward phrase "the organization or organizational subunit" to indicate the alternative scope of the strategy manager's area of responsibility and place in the managerial hierarchy.

WHY STRATEGIC MANAGEMENT MATTERS

The approach we will take throughout this book is that doing a good job of managing necessarily means doing a good job of managing strategy. Looking at the job of managing through strategic eyes and learning how to use the tools of strategic analysis as they affect both strategy formulation and implementation open such a new perspective that the fundamentals of strategic management actually drive the whole approach to managing organizations. The signs are everywhere. Issues pertaining to new strategic moves and to better internal strategy execution enjoy high priority on managerial action agendas. Formal strategic analysis and annual strategy reviews are standard activities in most professionally managed companies. A substantial literature has blossomed forth on the concept of strategy, the elements of strategic thinking," the methods of strategic analysis, the tasks and processes associated with strategy formation and implementation, and all the ramifications of aligning internal operations to match the requirements of strategy. In short, what strategic management is and what it involves is something every manager and would-be manager needs to know about.

The Benefits of Good Strategic Management   Every organization has both a strategy and an internal action agenda for executing it, however conscious or well considered or imperfect they may be. Sometimes strategic plans are openly stated

by management, and sometimes they remain implicit in management decisions and the organization's patterns of operation. Sometimes courses of action are chosen after exhaustive analysis, and sometimes strategic decisions emerge haphazardly from chance occurrences and historical accidents occasioned by the experiences and personalities of previous leaders, the position of the company in the industry, and the economic circumstances surrounding its development. Or, in perhaps the most frequent case, an enterprise's menu of strategic actions and approaches is the product of many internal analyses and reviews, years of market feedback regarding what worked and what didn't, prior strategic moves and decisions, assessments about what the future will bring, and a solid dose of experience and judgment.

It is fair to inquire, though, whether a conscious, analysis-based approach to strategic management is better than one that is the outcome of intuition, "gut feel," and/ or "muddling through." Do firms whose managers work hard at strategic thinking do any better than firms whose managers don't strategize much or don't place much stock in formal strategic planning? The answer is not an absolute, unequivocal yes, because there are organizations that have performed well for reasons other than their managers having done a superior job of strategizing. For instance, in some enterprises fortuitous possession of key raw materials, superior finances and/or labor skills, key patents and proprietary technical know-how, outstanding location, or even just the luck and coincidence of having been in the right place at the right time have produced successful performance—doing or not doing a good job of strategic management seems to have been secondary. Nonetheless, there is credible research showing that thorough strategy analysis and effective strategic management practices have a positive impact on organization performance.[4] The competitive significance of leading-edge strategy management has been underscored by the chief executive officer of one successful company:

> In the main, our competitors are acquainted with the same fundamental concepts and techniques and approaches that we follow, and they are as free to pursue them as we are. More often than not, the difference between their level of success and ours lies in the relative thoroughness and self-discipline with which we and they develop and execute our strategies for the future.

The advantages of first-rate strategic thinking and a deep commitment to the strategic management process include (1) the guidance it provides to the entire management hierarchy in making clear just "what it is we are trying to do and to achieve"; (2) the contribution it makes to recognizing and responding to the winds of change, new opportunities, and threatening developments; (3) the rationale it provides for management in evaluating competing requests for investment capital and new staff; (4) the coordination it adds to all the strategy-related decision making done by manag-

---

[4] For a representative sample of studies in addition to those cited in note 1, see Stanley Thune and Robert House, "Where Long-Range Planning Pays Off," *Business Horizons* 13, no. 4 (August 1970), pp. 81–87; Joseph O. Eastlack and Phillip R. McDonald, "CEO's Role in Corporate Growth," *Harvard Business Review* 48, no. 3 (May–June 1970), pp. 150–63; David M. Herold, "Long-Range Planning and Organizational Performance: A Cross-Validation Study," *Academy of Management Journal* 15, no. 1 (March 1972), pp. 91–102; Dan Schendel, G. R. Patton, and James Riggs, "Corporate Turnaround Strategies," *Journal of General Management* 3, no. 3 (Spring 1976), pp. 3–11; S. Schoeffler, Robert Buzzell, and Donald Heany, "Impact of Strategic Planning on Profit Performance," *Harvard Business Review* 52, no. 2 (March–April 1974), pp. 137–45; Donald W. Beard and Gregory G. Dess, "Corporate-Level Strategy, Business-Level Strategy, and Firm Performance," *Academy of Management Journal* 24, no. 4 (December 1981), pp. 663–88; and Michael E. Porter, *Competitive Strategy* (New York: Free Press, 1980). In addition, dozens of case studies of companies document how and why there is a positive payoff to solid strategic thinking and strategic analysis.

ers across the organization; and (5) the *proactive* instead of *reactive* posture that it gives to the organization.[5] The fifth advantage of trying to influence rather than merely respond to competitive forces and to the larger circumstances of customer-market-technological-environmental change is of acute importance. As discussed earlier, high-performing enterprises deliberately try to impact their target markets with a powerful, opportunistic strategy; they like to *initiate* and *lead,* not just *react* and *defend.* In their view, the real purpose and value of strategy is to come up with an action plan that will successfully attract buyers, produce a sustainable competitive advantage, boost the firm's market stature, put added competitive pressure on rivals, shape the nature of the competitive battle, influence the direction of industry change in their favor, and push performance to superior levels. The ideal outcome is one where the firm's strategy propels it to a leadership position above and apart from rival firms in the industry, such that earnings prosper and its products/services become the standard for industry comparison.

DEFINITION OF TERMS

There is perhaps no more helpful way to conclude this introductory overview of strategic management than by emphasizing the meaning of those key terms and concepts that will be used again and again in the chapters to come:

Strategic mission—consists of a long-term vision of what an organization seeks to do and what kind of organization it intends to become. It provides an answer to the question, "What is our business and what will it be?" It indicates what the organization does and where it is headed.

Strategic objectives—indicate both the specific performance an organization seeks to produce through its activities and the competitive position the enterprise wishes to occupy in the markets for its products.

Long-range strategic objectives—specify the desired performance and market position on an ongoing basis.

Short-range strategic objectives—specify the near-term organizational performance targets and market standing an organization desires to attain in progressing toward its long-range objectives.

Strategy—refers to management's action plan for achieving the chosen objectives. It specifies *how* the organization will be operated and run, and *what* entrepreneurial, competitive, and functional area approaches and actions will be taken to put the organization into the desired position.

Strategic plan—a comprehensive statement of an organization's strategic mission, objectives, and strategy; a detailed road map of the direction and course the organization presently intends to follow in conducting its activities.

Strategy formulation—the process whereby management develops an organization's strategic mission, derives specific strategic objectives, and chooses a strategy;

---

[5] Kenneth R. Andrews, *The Concept of Corporate Strategy,* rev. ed. (Homewood, Ill.: Richard D. Irwin, 1980), pp. 15–16, 46, 123–29; and Seymour Tilles, "How to Evaluate Corporate Strategy," *Harvard Business Review* 41, no. 4 (July–August 1963), p. 116.

it includes all the direction-setting components of managing the total organization.

Strategy implementation—embraces the full range of managerial activities associated with putting the chosen strategy into place, supervising its pursuit, and achieving the targeted results.

When the course winds down and you get to the end of this book, we think you will understand and appreciate why we maintain that two things lie at the root of what separates the best-managed organizations from the rest:

1. Superior entrepreneurship (a well-conceived strategic plan that positions the organization in the right way at the right time).
2. Competent implementation and execution of the chosen strategy.

Good management really means good strategic management. A well-formulated, well-executed strategy is the most surefire route to achieving an attractive competitive advantage and enhanced organizational performance over the long term.

SUGGESTED READINGS

Andrews, Kenneth R. *The Concept of Corporate Strategy.* Rev. ed. Homewood Ill.: Richard D. Irwin, 1980, chap. 1.

Drucker, Peter F. *Management: Tasks, Responsibilities, Practices.* New York: Harper & Row, 1974, chaps. 2, 4, 30, 31, and 50.

Gluck, Frederick W. "A Fresh Look at Strategic Management." *Journal of Business Strategy* 6, no. 2 (Fall 1985), pp. 4–21.

Hofer, Charles W. *Strategy Formulation: Analytical Concepts.* St. Paul, Minn.: West Publishing, 1986, chap. 1.

Katz, Robert L. "Skills of an Effective Administrator." *Harvard Business Review* 33, no. 1 (January–February 1955), pp. 33–42.

Kelley, C. Aaron. "The Three Planning Questions: A Fable." *Business Horizons* 26, no. 2 (March–April 1983), pp. 46–48.

Kotter, John P. *The General Managers.* New York: Free Press, 1982.

Livingston, J. Sterling. "Myth of the Well-Educated Manager," *Harvard Business Review* 49, no. 1 (January—February 1971), pp. 79–87.

Mintzberg, Henry. "The Manager's Job: Folklore and Fact." *Harvard Business Review* 53, no. 4 (July–August 1975), pp. 49–61.

Ohmae, Kenichi. *The Mind of the Strategist.* New York: Penguin Books, 1983, pp. 1–35.

Peters, Thomas J., and Robert H. Waterman. *In Search of Excellence: Lessons from America's Best-Run Companies.* New York: Harper & Row, 1982.

Peters, Thomas J., and Nancy Austin. *A Passion for Excellence: The Leadership Difference* New York: Random House, 1985, chaps. 16–21.

Quinn, James B. *Strategies for Change: Logical Incrementalism.* Homewood, Ill.: Richard D. Irwin, 1980, chaps. 2 and 3.

Ross, Joel, and Michael Kami. *Corporate Management in Crisis: Why the Mighty Fall.* Englewood Cliffs, N.J.: Prentice-Hall, 1973.

Yip, George S. "Who Needs Strategic Planning?" *Journal of Business Strategy* 6, no. 2 (Fall 1985), pp. 22–29.

2 The Essential Entrepreneurial Tasks: Defining the Business, Setting Strategic Objectives, and Formulating Strategy

Without a strategy the organization is like a ship without a rudder, going around in circles. It's like a tramp; it has no place to go.
—*Joel Ross and Michael Kami*

You've got to come up with a plan. You can't wish things will get better.
—*John F. Welch*

The secret of success is to be ready for opportunity when it comes.
—*Disraeli*

While it is easy to understand that a strategic plan is a directional map for where an organization is headed and how it intends to achieve its objectives, it is much harder to understand what goes into a strategic plan and how the strategy-making task is performed. This chapter explores each direction-setting step: defining the business, establishing strategic objectives, and formulating a comprehensive strategy. It also explores the hierarchical levels of strategy within an organization, the kinds of factors that shape strategy, and how managers approach the task of developing strategic plans.

THE THREE ENTREPRENEURIAL COMPONENTS OF DIRECTION-SETTING

The entrepreneurial responsibilities of a manager entail putting one's imprint on all the direction-setting decisions for his or her areas of authority. Three elements comprise the entrepreneurial task:

1. Defining the organization's business and strategic mission.
2. Establishing strategic objectives and performance targets.
3. Formulating a strategy to achieve targeted objectives.

The work product of these three elements is a strategic plan (see Figure 2–1). For an example of a real-world strategic

Figure 2-1   The Entrepreneurial Components of a Strategic Plan

DEFINING THE ORGANIZATION'S BUSINESS AND STRATEGIC MISSION	+	ESTABLISHING STRATEGIC OBJECTIVES	+	FORMULATING A STRATEGY	=	AN ORGANIZATION'S STRATEGIC PLAN
Developing a clear concept and vision of "who we are and where we are headed"; providing answers to the questions "What customer groups and customer needs will we serve?" and "What is our business and what will it be?"		Translating the chosen strategic mission into specific measurable performance targets and results; agreeing on what is to be *accomplished* through the organization's activities		Selecting an action-oriented game plan that indicates *how* chosen objectives will be pursued and *what* entrepreneurial, competitive, and functional area approaches management will adopt to get the organization in the position it wants to be in		A detailed blueprint indicating the direction and strategy that the organization presently intends to follow in conducting its activities

plan, read Illustration Capsule 4 describing Niagara Mohawk Power's corporate plan.

Defining the Business: The First Element in Setting Direction

Organizational direction-setting should always begin with a clear concept and vision of what business the organization is in and what path its development should take. The following questions pose the issues squarely:

- Should the enterprise concentrate on a single business or should it be diversified?
- If managers opt for diversification, should the enterprise's several lines of business be related or unrelated?
- What products, technologies, and industries does the enterprise need to have a stake in and why?
- What needs of which customer groups should the organization try to satisfy?

Normally, how an organization answers "Who are we and where are we headed?" is a function of past experiences, the specifics of its present situation, the outlook if it continues to do just what it is doing now, opportunities and threats on the horizon, and what senior managers conclude about the organization's best long-term course.

The question, "What is our business and what will it be?" can be answered in at least eight different ways:

1. *In terms of the products or services being provided.* Thus, a pecan grower may define its business simply as one of producing pecans; a microwave manufacturer may see itself as being in the convenience cooking business; and a local fire department may view its business as the fire-fighting and fire-prevention business.

2. *In terms of the principal ingredient in a line of products.* Paper companies, for example, can use the same machines to turn out a variety of paper products— newsprint, stationery, notebook paper, and slick printing papers; yet they see themselves as being in the paper business rather than in the newsprint business or the stationery business or the notebook paper business because they can vary production and sales mixes across end-use segments as market conditions warrant.

3. *In terms of the technology that spawns the product.* General Electric's thousands of products have sprung from the technology of electricity, and 3M's lineup of some 50,000 products has emerged from the company's distinctive expertise in finding new applications for chemical coating and bonding technology.

4. *In terms of the customer groups being served.* General Motors has long seen itself as being a full-line car manufacturer, with models to fit every purse and lifestyle. Personal computers sold to corporations and business professionals define a business/ market segment that is quite distinct from home computers sold to individuals through mass-merchandise retail chain stores. Likewise, the business of a neighborhood convenience food store entails a narrower product line for a narrower customer group than does the business of a large supermarket.

5. *In terms of the customer needs and wants being met.* The business of small appliance manufacturers hinges on offering a variety of effort-saving and time-saving

ILLUSTRATION CAPSULE 4

Niagara Mohawk Power's Corporate Strategic Plan for 1985 (sample excerpts)

Corporate Mission

Niagara Mohawk is an energy company with diversified interests and resources committed to providing for the current and future needs of its customers through economical products and services of superior quality.

The Company is dedicated to maintaining an efficient, progressive, cost-conscious organization that provides a fair and equitable return to its owners.

Management is committed to retaining and motivating talented, productive, effective employees by providing reasonable compensation, incentives and a good working environment.

The Company pursues opportunities to improve the economic climate and well-being of citizens, industry and business within the markets it serves. Appropriate actions are taken to meet socioeconomic responsibilities. Such actions include seeking those necessary improvements in the regulatory and legislative environment that best serve the interests of the Company's customers, employees and owners.

Management maintains high ethical standards and strives for open communications with all its constituencies.

The Company takes an active role in the development of technologies and opportunities advantageous to its customers and owners. It is dedicated to maintaining and developing dependable energy resources and delivery systems that are safe and environmentally sound.

Management will actively pursue strategies in support of objectives to accomplish this mission.

Objective 1: *Generate a level of earnings and cash flows which will sustain a competitive dividend policy and achieve a strong "A" credit rating and a common stock price greater than book value.*

Strategies

1.1   Manage and operate the Company in the most efficient manner possible to enhance financial performance and to assist in controlling the rate of increase in electric and gas prices.

1.2   Avoid capital expenditures for new facilities when reliable and cost effective alternatives exist.

1.3   Maintain financial flexibility through prudent financial management techniques, primarily using conventional financing methods.

- Achieve and maintain a minimum SEC interest coverage ratio of 3.25.
- Maintain a common stock capitalization ratio between 40 and 45 percent.
- Maintain dividends at a level competitive with other investments.

Objective 2: *Reinforce the commitment of our entire organization to serving the energy related needs of each customer in a safe, sensitive and responsible manner.*

ILLUSTRATION CAPSULE 4 *(continued)*

Strategies

2.1   Strive for customer satisfaction through superior quality of service and reliability of supply.

2.2   Reinforce an awareness in all employees of the importance of a caring and concerned attitude and a willingness to respond to customer needs.

2.3   Identify customers' energy related needs and monitor their perception of our performance in meeting those needs.

2.4   Review and update policies, procedures and practices in order to enhance our ability to better serve customers.

2.5   Strengthen our commitment to the training and development of all employees and provide adequate resources so that customers' energy related needs can be responsibly addressed.

2.6   Enhance customers' awareness of our commitment to serve their energy related needs and of the value of our products, services and energy expertise.

Objective 3: *Maintain and further develop a strong, productive, informed organization to effectively manage our human, capital and other resources.*

Strategies

3.1   Promote organizational effectiveness by openly communicating, as appropriate, in a timely fashion, Company plans, policies, practices and procedures to all employees.

- Provide channels of communication that permit employees to request and receive responses to their ideas and concerns.
- Increase the visibility and availability of all management to the employee force.

3.2   Cultivate a working environment that fosters positive motivation for improved performance.

- Recognize an employee's exemplary contribution to the community.
- Recognize job performance or innovation which results in significant benefit to the Company and develop incentive and award programs.

3.3   Assess human resource systems and their contribution toward achieving the Corporate Mission.

- Identify short and long-range human resource needs.
- Provide programs that develop and retain existing employees and attract qualified personnel.
- Develop and maintain management support systems and data bases to identify and utilize the talents of the existing work force.

3.4   Develop the qualities of leadership necessary for effective management by strengthening the management development program.

- Train and develop first and second level supervision to improve productivity.
- Address career path planning, interdepartmental experience, human relations and communications skills.

ILLUSTRATION CAPSULE 4 *(concluded)*

3.5   Promote the positive aspects of Company-Union relations.

3.6   Improve productivity by eliminating practices that are counterproductive, by developing uniform productivity standards and by integrating the application of technology to improve efficiency.

3.8   Identify, evaluate, revise and/or develop, as appropriate, policies, procedures and standards related to performance in areas that affect the Company's efficiency of operations.

Objective 4: *Pursue selective marketing and growth opportunities, including those that are conservation related, that identify and satisfy customer needs, optimize the utilization of existing and committed facilities and meet competitive forces.*

Strategies

4.1   Develop and nurture consistent marketing policies and integrate market research and marketing goals and programs into overall Company operations.

- Increase direct contact with customers to better understand customers' needs and to cultivate a closer relationship between the Company and its customers.
- Link conservation and marketing in all energy utilization programs to satisfy customer demands for energy efficiency and economy.
- Strengthen the Company's credibility with customers as the primary source of end-use application and energy efficiency expertise.

4.2   Strengthen the Company's service area economic development plans to include:

- Innovative rate structures and incentives to attract new customers, to compete with alternate fuels and enhance the economic competitiveness of existing customers.
- Development of required expertise, resources, including economic development funds, support systems and regional community data bases.
- Promotional campaign tied to the strengths of the service area.
- Coordination of plans with state, private and local programs.
- Utilization of land holdings and physical properties to provide sites for commercial, industrial and other appropriate uses.
- Utilization of process steam for cogeneration and other opportunities.

4.3   Promote increased market penetration of high efficiency appliances and equipment.

4.4   Contract for reliable power purchases and sales with domestic and foreign sources to reduce electric energy costs and improve the competitive position of electricity.

SOURCE: *Niagara Mohawk Corporation.*

conveniences to household members. The educational program offerings of a two-year community college are intended to meet a different set of student needs than are the programs of a major, multicampus state university.

6. *In terms of the scope of activities within an industry.*   At one end of the spectrum, organizations can be highly *specialized,* with a mission of performing a limited service or function to fill a particular industry niche; for example, an oil service firm that exclusively supplies parts and equipment to well drillers and well operators. At the other end of the spectrum, firms may seek to be *fully integrated,* participating in every aspect of the industry's production chain. Such is the case of the leading international oil companies, all of which: lease drilling sites, drill their own wells, pump crude oil out of the wells, transport their own crude oil in their own ships and through their own pipelines to their own refineries, and sell gasoline and other refined products at wholesale and retail through their own networks of branded distributors and service station outlets. In between these two extremes of industry scope, firms can stake out *partially integrated* positions, participating only in selected stages of the industry.

7. *In terms of creating a diversified enterprise that engages in a group of related businesses.*   The "related" aspect can be based on a core skill, a core technology, complementary relationships among products, common channels of distribution, common customer groups, or overlapping customer functions and applications. Procter & Gamble's (P & G) lineup of products, for instance, includes Jif peanut butter, Duncan Hines cake mixes, Folger's coffee, Tide laundry detergent, Crest toothpaste, Head and Shoulders shampoo, Crisco vegetable oil and shortening, Charmin toilet tissue, and Ivory soap—all different businesses with different competitors, different manufacturing techniques, and so on. But what ties them together into a package of related diversification is that they are all marketed through a common distribution system to be sold in retail food outlets to customers everywhere. Similar consumer marketing and merchandising skills are used for all of P & G's products.

8. *In terms of creating a multi-industry portfolio of unrelated businesses.*   Here the answer to "What is our business?" can be based on any of several considerations: opportunism, a preference for not putting all of the firm's eggs in one basket, attempts to stabilize earnings over the cycle of economic ups and downs, the fun of making a profit by shifting and shuffling the assets of several companies, a belief in growth via diversification, or even "getting into any business where we can make good money." In companies built around unrelated diversifications, there is a conceptual theme that links different businesses in terms of customer needs, customer groups, and technology.[1]

Management's concept of what the organization seeks to do and the customer groups and customer needs it intends to serve *defines the business* and establishes the organization's *strategic mission.* The mission statement specifies what activities the organization as a whole intends to pursue now and in the future; it says something about what kind of organization it is now and is to become and, by omission, what

---

[1] For a discussion of how broadly diversified companies tackle the question of "What is our business?" see Richard F. Vancil and Peter Lorange, "Strategic Planning in Diversified Companies," *Harvard Business Review* 53, no. 1 (January–February 1975), pp. 81–90.

it is not to do and not to become.[2] It depicts an organization's character, identity, and scope of activities.

"What Is Our Business?"   Peter Drucker, a widely respected authority on managing, asserts that management failure to examine the question, "What is our business?" in a timely, probing fashion is the most important single cause of organization frustration and subpar performance. He argues that when the concept of an organization's business is not thought through and spelled out clearly, the enterprise lacks a solid foundation for establishing realistic objectives, strategies, plans, and work assignments.[3] Drucker maintains that any business definition needs to be grounded in how the enterprise intends to "create a customer"; he states:

> A business is not defined by the company's name, statutes, or articles of incorporation. It is defined by the want the customer satisfies when he buys a product or a service. To satisfy the customer is the mission and purpose of every business. The question "What is our business?" can, therefore, be answered only by looking at the business from the outside, from the point of view of customer and market. What the customer sees, thinks, believes, and wants, at any given time, must be accepted by management as an objective fact.
>
> . . . to the customer, no product or service, and certainly no company, is of much importance. . . . The customer only wants to know what the product or service will do for him tomorrow. All he is interested in are his own values, his own wants, his own reality. For this reason alone, any serious attempt to state "what our business is" must start with the customer, his realities, his situation, his behavior, his expectations, and his values.[4]

The Three Dimensions of Defining "What Is Our Business?"   Derek Abell has expanded on the importance of a customer-focused concept and suggests defining a business in terms of three dimensions: (1) customer groups, or *who* is being satisfied; (2) customer needs, or *what* is being satisfied; and (3) technologies, or *how* customer needs are satisfied.[5] Abell points out that a product, in effect, is a physical manifestation of the application of a particular technology to the satisfaction of a particular function or need for a particular customer group. The decision of what business to be in, therefore, is necessarily a joint choice of technologies, needs satisfied/values received, and customers to serve; the choice is not simply which products to offer or which industries to be in. The products offered and the markets served are *results* of choices about whom to satisfy, what to satisfy, and how to produce the satisfaction; the specific combination of these three choices really comprises the answer to "What is our business?"[6]

---

[2] C. Roland Christensen, Kenneth R. Andrews, and Joseph L. Bower, *Business Policy: Text and Cases,* 4th ed. (Homewood, Ill.: Richard D. Irwin, 1978), p. 125; for a more extended discussion see Kenneth R. Andrews, *The Concept of Corporate Strategy,* Rev. ed. (Homewood, Ill.: Richard D. Irwin, 1980), chaps. 1 and 2.

[3] Peter F. Drucker, *Management: Tasks, Responsibilities, Practices* (New York: Harper & Row, 1974), pp. 77–79.

[4] Ibid., pp. 79–80.

[5] Derek F. Abell, *Defining the Business: The Starting Point of Strategic Planning* (Englewood Cliffs, N.J.: Prentice-Hall, 1980), p. 169.

[6] Note how thoroughly the approach to defining the business is grounded in *external* considerations as opposed to *internal* considerations. While there is some temptation to view a company's mission and ultimate purpose as one of "making a profit," this typifies all profit-seeking enterprises and thus fails to distinguish one enterprise from another

"What Will Our Business Be?"   Sooner or later, today's answer to "What is our business?" becomes obsolete. Therefore, managers need to keep looking beyond the present definition of the business, always probing for answers to the additional question, "and what *will* it be?"[7] This latter part of the question forces managers to think ahead and act to position the firm in response to the impact of change. The future is always uncertain (sometimes it is totally unpredictable), and keeping a watchful eye out for the time to institute conscious redirection of the organization reduces the chances of complacency and unpleasant surprises. Good entrepreneurship always requires attention to such questions as: What customer wants and needs are presently going unsatisfied? How will the requirements of present customers change? What new end-use applications are likely to emerge? What new technologies will be used to meet which needs of which customer groups? What will competitors do and what difference will this make? Which new product ideas and new technological potentials can be converted into new businesses? What customer needs and customer groups should the organization be getting in position to serve? Should diversification be pursued and, if so, what kind and how much diversification makes sense? What business should the organization continue in and what should it plan to abandon? What new business positions need to be taken now that can yield big payoffs down the road? *In the best-run organizations, the senior management task of consciously taking actions to shape the organization's future seems to be grounded firmly in thinking deeply about where the organization is now and where it needs to be headed, what it should and should not be doing and for whom, and when it is time to shift to a new direction and to redefine the business.*

The Importance of a Clear Mission and Future Direction   In practice, many statements of "who we are, what we do, and where we are headed" have both broad and narrow connotations (see, for example, the business definitions for the companies in Illustration Capsule 2). They can be broad in the sense of embracing several distinct types of products, industries, customer groups, technologies, and needs to be served, yet narrow in the sense of limiting the scope of the organization's activities to an understandable, meaningful arena. Consider the following definitions of scope:

Broad Definition	*Narrow Definition*
Home entertainment	Stereo equipment
Furniture	Upholstered chair manufacturing
Travel and tourism	Luxury hotel
Air transportation	Commuter airline
Publishing	College textbooks

Distinctions between broad and narrow are relative. Home entertainment is probably too broad a definition for a firm that makes only stereo equipment, but it is quite

---

(the mission of a bank is plainly different from that of a manufacturer of shoes). Profit objectives are properly viewed as a *result* of doing something. It is the answer to the question, "Make a profit doing what and for whom?" that is the real definition of an organization's business.

[7] Drucker, *Management*, pp. 88–89.

appropriate for a firm that manufactures TV sets, stereo equipment, radios, and VCRs. What is important about the broad or narrow definition is that it should be functionally useful: Overly narrow business definitions carry the risk that management's peripheral vision will be unduly restricted and important strategic threats or opportunities in nearby markets may be overlooked. On the other hand, broadly defining an organization's strategic mission in language with high "fog intensity" can obscure the essential character and present or future operating scope of the enterprise. An umbrellalike definition that "Our business is to serve the food needs of the nation" offers no sense of direction or organizational identity; it can mean the organization's business is anything from growing wheat or operating a vegetable cannery to running a supermarket chain, manufacturing farm machinery, or running a Kentucky Fried Chicken franchise. Both the U.S. Postal Service and Federal Express are in the "mail business," but this definition hides their very different business concepts and target clientele. The broader the language used to define the organization's business, the less focus it directs to specific customer groups, customer needs, technologies, and types of products.

The managerial value of a clear mission statement is in crystallizing the firm's long-term direction and in steering entrepreneurial decisions into a coherent pattern. An unambiguous answer to "What is our business and what will it be?" can help managers avoid the trap of trying to march in too many directions at once, and its counterpart, the trap of being unclear about when or where to march at all.[8] When managers don't have a clear vision of what the organization is trying to do and to become, their decisions and actions are as likely to blockade the path ahead as to clear it.

Establishing Strategic Objectives: The Second Element in Setting Direction

Strategic objectives set forth the competitive market position that an enterprise seeks to have and the specific performance targets that management seeks to achieve in pursuing the strategic mission.[9] Some strategic objectives relate *externally* to the attractiveness and mix of industries the firm is in, the competitive position it aspires to in each industry, the reputation it wants to have with customers and the public, the standing it wants in the financial investment community, and its capabilities

[8] H. Igor Ansoff, *Corporate Strategy* (New York: McGraw-Hill, 1965), pp. 105–8.

[9] The literature of management is filled with references to *goals* and *objectives*. These terms are used in a variety of ways, many of them conflicting. Some writers use the term goals to refer to the long-run results an organization seeks to achieve and use the term objectives to refer to immediate, short-run performance targets. Other writers reverse the usage, referring to objectives as the desired long-run results and goals as the desired short-run results. Still other writers use the terms interchangeably, as synonyms. And still others use the term *goals* to refer to general organizationwide performance targets and the term *objectives* to mean the specific targets set by subordinate managers in response to the broader, more inclusive goals of the whole organization. *In our view, semantical distinctions in the usage of the terms goals and objectives are secondary; the important thing is to recognize that the results an enterprise seeks to attain vary both in scope and in time perspective.* In nearly every instance, those organizations which are results oriented tend to establish a hierarchy of both long-range and short-range performance targets. Practically speaking, it makes no difference what labels one attaches to these targets. *Thus we have deliberately chosen to use the single term* objectives *to refer to the performance targets and results an organization seeks to attain.* We will use the adjectives *long-range (or long-run)* and *short-range (or short-run)* to identify the relevant time frame, and we will endeavor to describe objectives in such a way as to indicate their intended scope and level in the organization.

vis-à-vis competitors; other strategic objectives relate *internally* to the desired organizational performance and financial results. The most common strategic objectives concern market share, growth in revenues and earnings, return on investment, competitive strength, technological capability, recognition as an industry leader, reputation with customers, overall size and degree of diversification, earnings stability over the cycle of ups and downs in the economy, financial strength, being well represented in industries with attractive prospects, and the like.

Strategic objectives are needed in all areas on which the survival and success of the organization depend, and they are needed at all levels of management from the corporate level on down deep into the organization structure.[10] Moreover, it is normally desirable to develop both long-range and short-range objectives. *Long-range objectives* keep management alert to what has to be done now to attain the desired results later. *Short-range objectives* indicate the speed and momentum which management seeks to maintain; they call the attention of managers and organizational subunits to the level of performance expected in the near term.

Why Have Strategic Objectives?

This second direction-setting element is a big one. Unless and until the direction an organization is headed is converted into specific performance targets, into achieving a specific market standing and competitive position, and into specific commitments to action, there is great risk that the strategic mission will remain a statement of good intentions and unrealized achievement. Setting strategic objectives reduces this risk. *The hard knocks of experience tell a powerful story about the use of objectives: Managements that establish objectives for themselves and for their organizations are more likely to achieve them than managements that operate without performance targets.* Spelling out the targeted strategic position and results in concrete, measurable terms helps prevent organization drift, establishes organizational priorities, and provides benchmarks for judging how well the organization is doing.

What Performance Targets Are Realistic?

Strategic objectives and performance targets cannot be set on the basis of whatever management decides would be "nice." If objectives are to be something other than "pie-in-the-sky wishful thinking," and if, at the same time, they are to serve as a tool for stretching the enterprise to achieve its full potential, then *they must meet the criterion of being challenging but achievable.* Satisfying this criterion means setting objectives in the light of several important "inside-outside" considerations:

- What performance levels will economic, industry, and competitive conditions realistically allow?
- What financial performance does the organization need to achieve (from an income statement and balance sheet perspective) in order to (1) "look good" to investors and the financial community and (2) have the financial resources requisite for executing the chosen strategic plan?

---

[10] Drucker, *Management,* p. 100; see also, Charles H. Granger, "The Hierarchy of Objectives," *Harvard Business Review* 42, no. 3 (May–June 1963), pp. 63–74.

- What market share and competitive standing can the enterprise realistically aspire to ?
- What performance is the organization capable of when pushed?

Therefore, setting challenging but achievable objectives requires managers to judge what performance is possible in light of external conditions as opposed to what performance the internal organization is really capable of achieving. In addition, there can be two-way direction-setting interaction between objectives and strategy: whereas strategy is the means for accomplishing strategic objectives, the choice of a strategy implies that the organization's financial performance objectives will be set high enough to fund successful strategy execution.

Direction-Setting and the Hierarchy of Strategic Objectives   For direction-setting to penetrate either deeply or meaningfully into the organizational hierarchy, strategic objectives must be established not only at the corporate level for the organization as a whole but also for each of the specific lines of business and products in which the organization has an interest and, further, for each functional area and department within the organization structure. When every involved manager, from the chief executive officer on down to the first-line supervisor, formulates objectives at his or her level of job responsibility and is rewarded on the basis of whether the agreed-upon objectives are achieved, then chances are that all managers will know precisely what they need to accomplish; they will also have a clear understanding of their unit's expected contribution to overall organizational performance.

An example will clarify how strategic objectives at one level drive the objectives and strategic plans of the next level in the organizational hierarchy. Suppose the senior executives of a diversified corporation establish a corporate profit objective of $5 million for next year. Suppose further that, after discussion between corporate management and the general managers of the firm's five different businesses, each business is given the challenging but achievable profit objective of $1 million (the plan being that if the five business divisions can contribute $1 million each in profit, the corporation as a whole can reach its $5 million profit objective). Observe so far, with respect to profit only, that corporate executives have set a priority of $5 million in total profit for the year, and that the general managers of each business division have been assigned responsibility for $1 million in profit by year-end. A concrete result has thus been agreed upon and translated into measurable action commitments to achieve something at two levels in the managerial hierarchy. Next, the general manager of business unit X may, after some analytical calculations and discussion with functional area subordinates, conclude that reaching the $1 million profit objective will require selling 100,000 units at an average price of $50 and producing them at an average cost of $40 (the $10 profit margin multiplied by 100,000 units yields a $1 million profit). Consequently, the general manager and the manufacturing manager may settle upon manufacturing objectives of producing 100,000 units at a unit cost of $40; and the general manager and the marketing manager may agree upon a sales objective of 100,000 units and an average target selling price of $50. In turn, the marketing manager may break the sales objective of 100,000 units down into unit sales targets for each salesperson, sales territory, customer type, and/ or item in the product line. In similar fashion, objectives can be agreed upon for every other strategically relevant area of concern and priority.

The key idea in this example is that the process of establishing objectives for each manager and organizational subunit leads to a clearer definition of what results are expected and who is responsible for achieving them. If done right, *setting objectives energizes the organization,* heads it down the chosen path at a measurable pace, and creates a *results-oriented* organizational climate. At the same time, a hierarchy of strategic objectives that transcends and links organizational levels brings the answer to "Where are we now and where are we headed?" home to every manager and organizational unit. The effect is to add both concreteness and standards for performance to the statement of strategic mission and business definition. By specifying in measurable terms what contribution and results are expected from each manager and unit within the organization, *everyone in the managerial hierarchy comes to understand the direction of the total enterprise and their role in it*—a major leap forward in getting the whole organization moving along the chosen course. In summary, managing with clearly defined strategic objectives in mind is likely to produce better organizational performance than managing without objectives.

Illustration Capsule 5 explains some of the finer points in stating objectives clearly and precisely enough to make them managerially useful.

Formulating Strategy: The Third Element in Setting Direction

In almost every instance, managers have choices about which path to take in achieving strategic objectives. As the old adage goes, "There's more than one way to skin a cat." An organization's strategy thus represents the pattern of choices management has made among the alternative means. *Strategy* is the trajectory or flight path toward the bull's-eye (the target objectives) and *is made up of the entrepreneurial, competitive, and functional area approaches management intends to employ in positioning the enterprise and in managing its overall portfolio of activities.* Because each organization's situation is unique, strategy tends to be custom tailored by management to fit all of the relevant internal and external circumstances that make up its situation. And because an organization's circumstances change, its strategy is always evolving as managers either fine-tune or overhaul the ways they try to achieve strategic objectives.

ILLUSTRATION CAPSULE 5

Stating Objectives: "Good' versus "Bad" Examples

For the direction-setting purpose of objectives to be fulfilled, objectives need to meet five specifications:

1. An objective should relate to a single, specific topic. (It should not be stated in the form of a vague abstraction or a pious platitude—"We want to be a leader in our industry" or "Our objective is to be more aggressive marketers.")
2. An objective should relate to a result not to an activity to be performed. (The objective is the result of the activity, not the performing of the activity.)

ILLUSTRATION CAPSULE 5 *(continued)*

3. An objective should be measurable (stated in quantitative terms whenever feasible).
4. An objective should contain a time deadline for its achievement.
5. An objective should be challenging but achievable.

Consider the following examples:

- *Poor:* Our objective is to maximize profits.
  Remarks: How much is "maximum"? The statement is not subject to measurement. What criterion or yardstick will management use to determine if and when actual profits are equal to maximum profits? No deadline is specified.
  Better: Our total profit target in 1988 is $1 million.

- *Poor:* Our objective is to increase sales revenue and unit volume.
  Remarks: How much? Also, because the statement relates to two topics, it may be inconsistent. Increasing unit volume may require a price cut, and if demand is price inelastic, sales revenue would fall as unit volume rises. No time frame for achievement is indicated.
  Better: Our objective this calendar year is to increase sales revenues from $30 million to $35 million; we expect this to be accomplished by selling 1 million units at an average price of $35.

- *Poor:* Our objective in 1989 is to boost advertising expenditures by 15 percent.
  Remarks: Advertising is an activity, not a result. The advertising objective should be stated in terms of what result the extra advertising is intended to produce.
  Better: Our objective is to boost our market share from 8 percent to 10 percent in 1989 with the help of a 15 percent increase in advertising expenditures.

- *Poor:* Our objective is to be a pioneer in research and development and become the technological leader in the industry.
  Remarks: Very sweeping and perhaps overly ambitious; implies trying to march in too many directions at once if the industry is one with a wide range of technological frontiers. More a platitude than an action commitment to a specific result.
  Better: During the 1980s our objective is to continue as a leader in introducing new technologies and new devices that will allow buyers of electrically powered equipment to conserve on electric energy usage.

- *Poor:* Our objective is to be the most profitable company in our industry.
  Remarks: Not specific enough; by what measures of profit—total dollars or earnings per share or unit profit margin or return on equity investment or all of these? Also, because the objective concerns how well other companies will perform, the objective, while challenging, may not be achievable.
  Better: We will strive to remain atop the industry in terms of rate of return on equity investment by earning a 25 percent after-tax return on equity investment in 1989.

The Levels of Strategy

Just as there is a direction-setting logic for establishing a hierarchy of objectives that span the enterprise from top to bottom, there is an accompanying rationale for developing a strategic game plan at each level of management to achieve the objectives set at that level. Thus, corporate-level objectives underlie the formation of *corporate-level strategy;* line-of-business objectives underlie the formation of *line-of-business strategy* (or just *business strategy*); functional area objectives (in manufacturing, marketing, finance, and so on) underlie the formation of *functional area support strategy;* and departmental and field unit objectives underlie the formation of *operating-level strategy.* The networkings are illustrated in Figure 2–2.

Corporate-Level Strategy   *Corporate-level strategy* is senior management's game plan for directing and running the organization as a whole; it cuts across all of an organization's activities—its different businesses, divisions, product lines, and technologies. The task of developing a corporate strategy has three elements:

1. *Developing plans for managing the scope and mix of the firms' various activities in order to improve corporate performance.* Managing the business portfolio requires decisions and actions regarding when and how the enterprise should get into new businesses, which existing businesses the company should get out of (and whether it should do so quickly or gradually), which opportunities of which existing businesses to go forward with, and what corporate management itself should do to improve the performance of the overall corporate portfolio. The portfolio management plan may, in addition, involve designating a common strategic theme to be pursued by all of the company's lines of business, and it may involve selecting a general strategic posture (aggressive expansion, maintain position, retrench and overhaul, or fix up in preparation to sell out) for each business in the portfolio.

2. *Providing for coordination among different businesses in the portfolio.* Coordination of interrelated activities allows a diversified firm to enhance the competitive strength of its business units and makes overall corporate strategy more than just a collection of the action plans of independent subunits. Several issues have to be addressed: Is there cost-reduction potential in sharing technological know-how, R&D efforts, sales forces, distribution facilities, and so on across any business units? Do other cross-fertilization opportunities exist? Are the benefits worth capturing? What coordination is needed? Will such actions bolster the competitive positions and competitive strengths of the company's various business divisions?

3. *Establishing investment priorities and allocating corporate resources across the company's different activities.* Decisions about how much of the corporate investment budget each organizational unit will get and actions to control the *pattern* of corporate resource allocation commit the firm to pursue some opportunities aggressively and to hold back on others; in addition, these decisions and actions serve to channel resources out of areas where earnings potentials are lower into areas where they are higher.

The portfolio management actions of corporate officers in entering or exiting certain businesses and in pursuing some opportunities more boldly than others are strategically important because they determine the organization's business positions. Which customer needs a firm is meeting and is moving to meet, which customer groups it

Figure 2–2　The Organizational Hierarchy of Objectives and Strategies

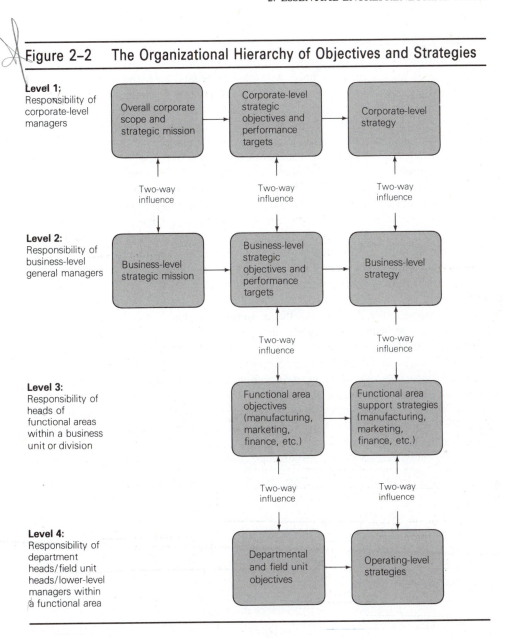

Level 1:
Responsibility of corporate-level managers

Overall corporate scope and strategic mission

Corporate-level strategic objectives and performance targets

Corporate-level strategy

Two-way influence　　Two-way influence　　Two-way influence

Level 2:
Responsibility of business-level general managers

Business-level strategic mission

Business-level strategic objectives and performance targets

Business-level strategy

Two-way influence　　Two-way influence

Level 3:
Responsibility of heads of functional areas within a business unit or division

Functional area objectives (manufacturing, marketing, finance, etc.)

Functional area support strategies (manufacturing, marketing, finance, etc.)

Two-way influence　　Two-way influence

Level 4:
Responsibility of department heads/field unit heads/lower-level managers within a functional area

Departmental and field unit objectives

Operating-level strategies

serves and is moving to serve, which technologies it employs and is becoming capable of employing, and which skills it has and is building are typically a combination of (1) *offensive* moves to pursue selected opportunities and build new or stronger business positions and (2) *defensive* moves to protect existing positions against emerging threats. Such moves strongly affect future levels of corporate performance.

The second element of corporate strategy, coordinating strategic plans *across* business units, is an important corporate headquarters task because it is through coordination of the interrelated activities of the corporation's different business units that a *corporate-level competitive advantage* can be created.[11] Horizontal coordination of divisional strategies enhances cross-fertilization of skills, proprietary know-how, and technology; it pushes business units with closely related activities to either engage in interdivisional cost-sharing or combine operations into a single unit that is more cost-effective, and it can strengthen differentiation of the firm's products and overall reputation. All of these actions can add up to a bigger net competitive advantage for divisional business units and increased corporate profitability.

The third element of corporate-level strategy—controlling the pattern of corporate resource allocation—is crucial because the number of "worthy projects" and "can't miss" opportunities put forward for funding may entail capital requirements that exceed the available dollars. Ultimately, the pot of corporate moneys and resources limits what strategies can be supported. With limited resources, it makes sense to (1) channel investment capital to support those strategic moves with the highest expected profitability and (2) deploy the available internal resources in close alignment with the success requirements of each line of business the corporation is in.

In diversified firms, developing a corporate strategy is chiefly an exercise in deciding how to build and manage the corporate portfolio of businesses. The strategic challenge is to get sustained high performance out of a multi-industry mix of business activities, some or many of which have nothing in common. When single-business enterprises start to contemplate diversification, they face similar strategic issues. In either single-business or multibusiness enterprises, corporate managers have to think strategically about what new businesses (if any) to enter; how much and what kind of diversification to pursue; which current activities to emphasize or downplay; whether to sell off or close down any existing activities; what strategic approach to follow in each of the company's businesses; and how to allocate financial capital and other organizational resources across the enterprise.

The specific strategy-related responsibilities of corporate-level managers include:

- Managing the scope and mix of businesses the corporation is in (and restructuring the makeup of the business portfolio whenever circumstances warrant).
- Establishing corporate-level strategic objectives and financial performance targets.
- Deciding what, if any, general strategic theme or unifying concept will be used to give the enterprise a distinctive character and/or keynote its business mission.
- Deciding what role each business unit will play in the overall corporate portfolio and approving a general strategic direction for each line of business.
- Striving to produce a corporate-based competitive advantage through coordination of the strategies and related activities of divisional business units.
- Maintaining a capacity to intervene should a business unit's strategic performance go awry.
- Reviewing and approving the major strategic recommendations/actions of subordinate managers.
- Controlling the pattern of corporate resource allocation.

---

[11] The desirability of explicit horizontal strategy coordination in diversified firms is incisively exposed in Michael E. Porter, *Competitive Advantage* (New York: Free Press, 1985), chaps. 9 and 10. Porter's work blazes a new trail in corporate strategy analysis and in building corporate-level competitive advantage.

The different parts of corporate strategy are shown in Figure 2–3. The spokes around the corporate strategy wheel indicate what to consider in piecing together the whole of an enterprise's corporate-level strategy. Keep in mind, however, that just observing what the firm does or reviewing what is written down in the formal strategic plan is no guarantee that all of corporate strategy is seen. Illustration Capsule 3 in Chapter 1 provides an example of corporate strategy.

Line-of-Business Strategy

Line-of-business (or business) strategy is the managerial action plan for directing and running a particular business unit. Business strategy deals explicitly with: (1) how the enterprise intends to compete in that specific business; (2) what the role or thrust of each key functional area will be in building a competitive advantage (thereby contributing to the success of the business in the marketplace); (3) developing responses to changing industry and competitive conditions; and (4) controlling the pattern of resource allocation *within* the business unit. Figure 2–4 illustrates the various business strategy elements.

The primary element of line-of-business strategy is always how to make the company entrepreneurially and competitively effective in the marketplace. Questions to consider include: what sort of competitive edge to strive for; which customer groups to go after; how to "position" the business in the marketplace vis-à-vis rivals; what product/

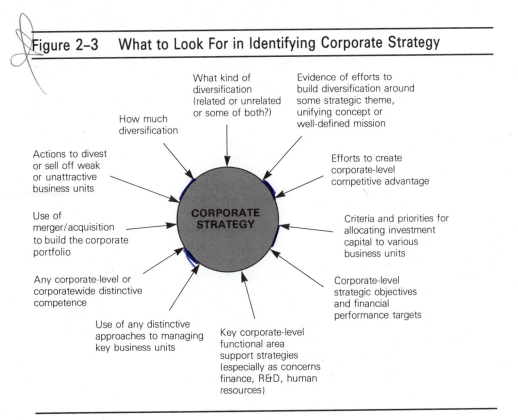

Figure 2–3   What to Look For in Identifying Corporate Strategy

How much diversification

What kind of diversification (related or unrelated or some of both?)

Evidence of efforts to build diversification around some strategic theme, unifying concept or well-defined mission

Actions to divest or sell off weak or unattractive business units

Efforts to create corporate-level competitive advantage

Use of merger/acquisition to build the corporate portfolio

Criteria and priorities for allocating investment capital to various business units

Any corporate-level or corporatewide distinctive competence

Corporate-level strategic objectives and financial performance targets

Use of any distinctive approaches to managing key business units

Key corporate-level functional area support strategies (especially as concerns finance, R&D, human resources)

CORPORATE STRATEGY

Figure 2–4   What to Look For in Identifying Business-Level Strategy

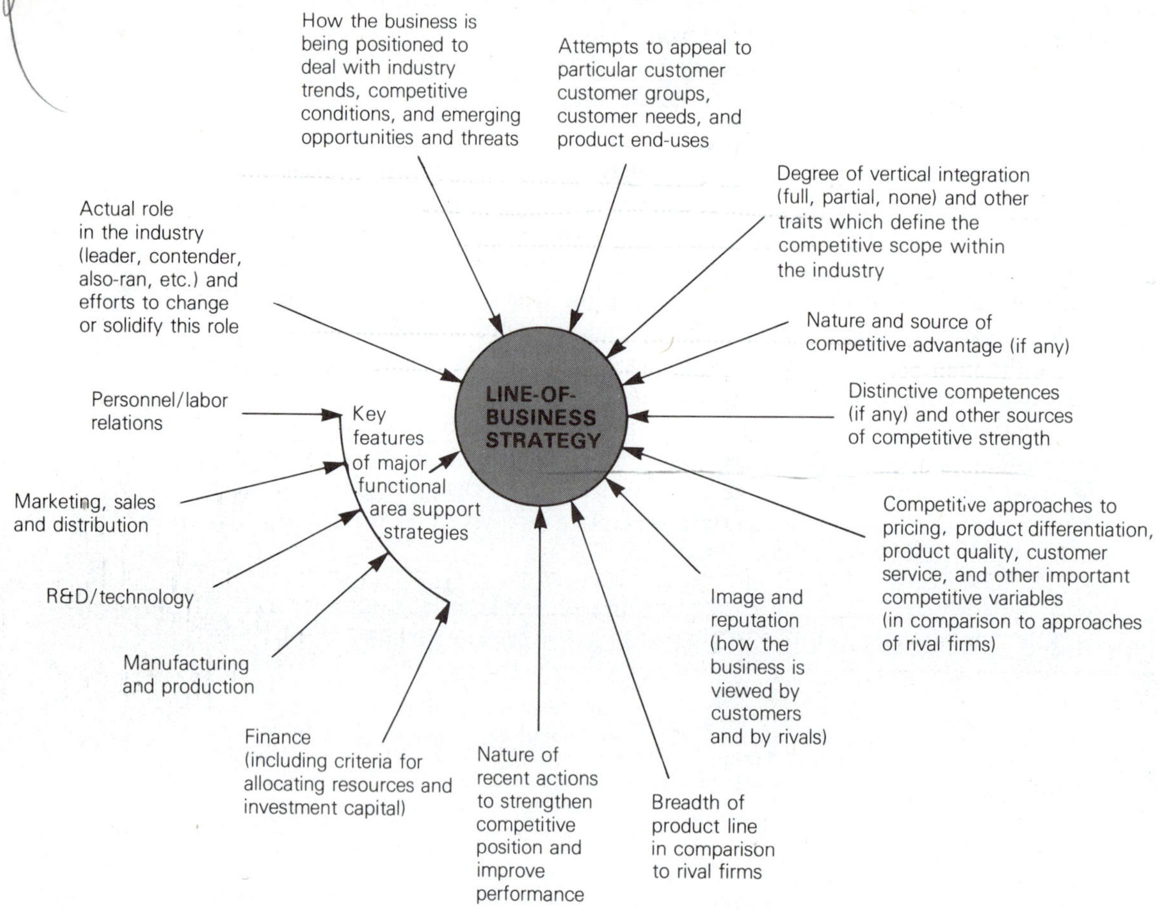

How the business is being positioned to deal with industry trends, competitive conditions, and emerging opportunities and threats

Attempts to appeal to particular customer customer groups, customer needs, and product end-uses

Degree of vertical integration (full, partial, none) and other traits which define the competitive scope within the industry

Actual role in the industry (leader, contender, also-ran, etc.) and efforts to change or solidify this role

Nature and source of competitive advantage (if any)

Personnel/labor relations

LINE-OF-BUSINESS STRATEGY

Key features of major functional area support strategies

Distinctive competences (if any) and other sources of competitive strength

Marketing, sales and distribution

Competitive approaches to pricing, product differentiation, product quality, customer service, and other important competitive variables (in comparison to approaches of rival firms)

R&D/technology

Image and reputation (how the business is viewed by customers and by rivals)

Manufacturing and production

Finance (including criteria for allocating resources and investment capital)

Nature of recent actions to strengthen competitive position and improve performance

Breadth of product line in comparison to rival firms

service attributes to emphasize in appealing to customers for their patronage; how to defend against the competitive moves of rivals; and what actions to take in light of industry trends, societal and political changes, and economic conditions. Internally, business strategy must deal with how the different functional pieces of the business (manufacturing, marketing, finance, R&D, and so on) will be aligned and made responsive to those market factors on which the desired competitive advantage depends. Often the internal key to good business strategy concerns the development and use of a strategy-supportive distinctive competence. The term *distinctive competence* refers to a skill or activity that a firm does especially well in comparison to rival firms.[12] Superior capability in some competitively important aspect of creating, producing,

---

[12] The term *distinctive competence* was originally set forth in Philip Selznick, *Leadership in Administration* (Evanston, Ill.: Row, Peterson & Company, 1957), p. 42.

or marketing the company's product or service can be the vehicle for establishing a competitive advantage and then leveraging this advantage into better-than-otherwise business performance.

Selecting a business strategy that is closely matched to the firm's skills and resource base is essential. It is foolhardy to decide on a strategy that is not suited to what the firm is good at doing (its skills and competences) and to what it is capable of doing with the available resources. Unless business strategy considerations drive the pattern of internal resource allocation, there is a strong chance that strategically important subactivities within the business will not be funded in ways that correspond directly to what is needed in order to achieve and maintain an attractive competitive advantage.

For a single-business enterprise, corporate strategy and business strategy become one and the same, except when a single-business firm begins to contemplate diversification. The distinction between corporate and business strategy is mainly relevant for firms that are sufficiently diversified to have divisional units competing in two or more different industries.

A good example of line-of-business strategy is Kellogg's approach to the ready-to-eat cereals business:

> From the beginning of the company in 1906, when Will Keith Kellogg accidentally discovered a way to make ready-to-eat cereal, Kellogg has aimed its strategy at being the dominant leader in the ready-to-eat cereal business. Kellogg's strategy for competing is based on product differentiation and market segmentation. The company's product line features a diverse number of brands, differentiated according to grain, shape, form, flavor, color, and taste—a something-for-everyone approach.
>
> Competing on the basis of low price is deemphasized in favor of a differentiation strategy keyed to extensive product variety, regular product innovation, substantial TV advertising, periodic promotional offers and prizes, and capturing more space on the grocery shelf than rivals. Much of Kellogg's sales efforts are targeted at the under-25 age group (the biggest cereal eaters with an average annual consumption of 11 pounds per capita), and 33 percent of its cereal sales are in presweetened brands promoted almost totally through TV advertising to children.
>
> Kellogg has tried to sidestep industry maturity and product saturation with introductions of fresh, "new" types of cereals (presweetened cereals in the 1940s, "nutritional" cereals in the 1950s, "natural" and health-conscious cereals in the 1960s and early 1970s, and adult cereals in the late 1970s) and also by advertising a variety of times and places for eating cereals other than at the morning breakfast table. Product-line freshness is additionally enhanced by introduction of brands which differ only slightly from existing brands (flakes versus shredded, plain versus sugar-frosted, puffed versus cocoa flavored).
>
> In 1979, Kellogg introduced five new cereal brands, more than it had ever launched in a single year, as part of a stepped-up and redirected effort to attract consumers in the 25–50 age group (where consumption levels were only half those of the younger age groups). Kellogg also introduced its cereals in four additional countries in South America and the Middle East using campaigns that featured free samples, demonstration booths in food stores, and heavy local advertising to promote the use of ready-to-eat cereals as a substitute for traditional breakfast foods (corn meal and bulgur). Both of these moves were aimed at changing the eating habits of adults who had shied away from cereals or who had spurned breakfast altogether.
>
> In further support of its attempt to appeal to more customer groups, Kellogg continued to increase its research budget (already the industry's most extensive) in an effort to

develop more nutritional, health-conscious cereals and breakfast foods for the older consumer segment. In 1979 Kellogg had three strategic objectives: (1) increasing Kellogg's 42 percent market share, (2) increasing sales by 5 percent annually (compared to an industry growth of 2 percent), and (3) boosting annual cereal consumption from 8.6 pounds per capita to 12 pounds by 1985.

The strategy formulation role of the manager in charge of a business usually includes:

- Making sure that the proposed strategic plan for the business adequately supports achievement of corporate strategic objectives and is consistent with corporate strategy themes.
- Serving as chief strategist and leading the process of assessing the business's strategic situation, evaluating alternative strategies, and making strategy decisions.
- Seeing that the various functional area support strategies are coordinated in ways that promote achieving and maintaining an attractive competitive advantage.
- Controlling the pattern of resource allocation within the business in ways that support the chosen strategy.
- Keeping higher-level management informed of market changes, deviations from plan, and potential business strategy revisions.

Diagnosing a company's strategic posture on each spoke of the "business strategy wheel" in Figure 2–4 usually yields a good overall picture of its business strategy.

Functional Area Support Strategy   *Functional area support strategies* are the action plans for managing the principal subordinate activities *within* a business. There is a functional area support strategy for each part of the business: production, marketing, finance, human resources, R&D, and so on. Functional area support strategies are major corollaries of line-of-business strategy. Their role is to flesh out the business game plan, giving it more substance, completeness, and concrete meaning as applied to a specific part of the business. They are important because they explicitly indicate the contribution of each major subactivity in the business to the overall business strategy. When all of the principal activities within a single business, particularly the activities crucial to successful strategy execution, are integrated and exhibit a consistent fit, the whole strategy obtains added power.

Whereas developing line-of-business strategy is the responsibility of the general manager of the business unit, the task of working out the details of functional area support strategy is typically delegated by the business-level manager to the functional area heads. And just as the business-level manager is obliged to establish a set of business-unit objectives and a business strategy that is deemed by corporate management to contribute adequately toward corporate-level performance objectives, functional area managers are typically delegated a lead role in establishing functional area performance objectives and strategies that will help accomplish business-level objectives and strategy. However, just as business-level strategies and objectives are subject to the approval of the corporate manager, functional area strategies and objectives are subject to the approval of the business manager.

Illustration Capsule 6 provides a detailed look at a sample functional area support strategy—the approach IBM employed in pricing and marketing mainframe computers.

ILLUSTRATION CAPSULE 6

IBM's Marketing Approach—A Sample Functional Area Strategy*

IBM's strategic approach to pricing and marketing its products during the 1967–1972 period is considered by industry observers to be a prime reason for the firm's success in capturing about a 65 to 70 percent share of the computer systems market. At the heart of the IBM approach was the "systems selling" concept whereby IBM salespeople were encouraged to sell customers a complete data processing system. The IBM package included a central processing unit, peripheral equipment (tape storage, disk storage, high-speed printers, card readers, keypunch machines), software, maintenance, emergency repairs, applications support, and consulting services to train the customer's personnel. By offering a total systems package, IBM attempted to supply the full range of a customer's data processing needs.

IBM encouraged customers to lease rather than purchase its products. The advantage to the customer of a leasing arrangement was protection against rapid technological obsolescence. As new equipment was introduced and/or as customer requirements changed, the old system could be turned in for a bigger, better (albeit, generally more costly) new system. In introducing new systems, IBM priced the new equipment *lower* than the older system on a performance/price basis; thus for a given set of jobs, the new system represented a savings to the customer over the old system. However, because the customer's usage of the new system expanded to cover more tasks and applications, the upgrading to the new system produced higher rentals for IBM.

Initially, IBM charged rentals for hardware and provided service, software, and consulting free to its customers—a pricing strategy which motivated customers to accept the total IBM package (to the exclusion of rivals who offered only a partial package—just service or just hardware and software). When IBM was charged by the Justice Department in the late 1960s with monopolizing and attempting to monopolize the computer market (one complaint being the "one-price" rental system), IBM's marketing strategy shifted to one of pricing its equipment rental and services separately. IBM began using a standard base contract for all equipment which provided for a monthly rental and required a 30-day notice for cancellation (a feature which facilitated upgrading of customers as new products were introduced). The base rental fee covered the use of equipment for a specified number of hours per week; usage beyond this amount (usually 40 to 50 hours) resulted in "additional use" rental fees of up to 40 percent of the base rental. All rented equipment was serviced by IBM under a separate service contract, with the amount of the service fee being pegged to equipment usage.

However, when IBM's competitors began to introduce attractively priced peripheral equipment (printers, tapes, disks, and memories) that were compatible with IBM central processing units, IBM adopted a fixed-term plan (FTP) leasing approach for its tape, disk, and printer products. Under the FTP, customers were allowed an 8 percent discount on one-year leases, a 16 percent discount on two-year leases, and all extra use charges were eliminated; the penalty for canceling an FTP was two and a half times the monthly rental for one-year contracts and five times the monthly rental for two-year contracts. The FTP not only made

ILLUSTRATION CAPSULE 6 *(continued)*

IBM products more price competitive, but it also shielded IBM's leased products from competition for a longer period. To make up for the lost revenues under the FTP price discounts, IBM raised its prices for products not covered by the FTP and also raised prices for maintenance and services. The net effect was that while most customers ended up paying IBM about the same total amount as before FTP, they paid less for those IBM products which faced active competition.

When the peripheral equipment manufacturers responded to the FTP with price cuts of their own, IBM initiated a second round of price cuts, along with product design changes. IBM's basic marketing strategy continued to be to induce customers to trade up to progressively higher performance computers.

---

* The content of this capsule has been extracted and synthesized from Derek F. Abell, *Defining the Business: The Starting Point of Strategic Planning* (Englewood Cliffs, N.J.: Prentice-Hall, 1980), pp. 32–48.

(Departmental)

Operating-Level Strategy

Operating-level strategies refer to how departmental and supervisory-level managers intend to carry out the fine details of functional area support strategies.[13] Consider the following examples of operating-level strategy:

A cosmetics firm relies on ads placed in women's magazines as an integral part of its marketing effort to promote the attributes of its product line with women. The strategy of the advertising director is to spend 75 percent of the advertising budget on three big campaigns during the month prior to each of the company's three peak sales periods of Christmas, Easter, and Mother's Day, with full-page ads placed in *Cosmopolitan* and *Ladies Home Journal* and quarter-page ads placed in *Seventeen* and *Family Circle.*

A company with a low-price, high-volume business strategy and a need to achieve very low manufacturing costs develops a three-pronged operating strategy aimed at boosting labor productivity: (1) the hiring director develops procedures that ensure careful selection and training of all employees, (2) the purchasing director makes unhesitating purchases of time-saving tools and equipment, and (3) the employee benefits director develops a superior wage–fringe benefit package designed to attract the best-qualified employees.

A distributor of heating and air-conditioning equipment emphasizes quick, reliable delivery of replacement parts as the feature component of its dealer service package. Accordingly, the inventory strategy of the warehouse manager is to maintain such an ample supply of each part that the chance of a stockout on a given item is virtually nil. His warehouse staffing strategy is to maintain a large enough work force to ship each order within 24 hours.

Note that in each example cited the logic of the operating-level strategy flowed directly from a higher-order strategic requirement, and that the operating strategy was handled by the managers in charge of carrying out the day-to-day details of specific functional

---

[13] Richard F. Vancil, "Strategy Formulation in Complex Organizations," *Sloan Management Review* 17, no. 2 (Winter 1976), p. 12.

Table 2–1   The Strategy-Making Hierarchy: Who Has Primary Responsibility for What Kinds of Strategic Actions

Strategy Level	Primary Strategy Development Responsibility	Strategy-Making Functions and Areas of Focus
Corporate strategy	CEO, other key executives (Decisions are typically reviewed/ approved by board of directors.)	• Structuring and managing the portfolio of business units (making acquisitions, initiating divestitures, strengthening existing business positions) • Coordinating business-level strategies; building corporate-level competitive advantage • Controlling the pattern of resource allocation across business units
Line-of-business strategy	General manager/head of business unit (Decisions are typically reviewed/ approved by senior corporate executive, usually CEO.)	• Choosing how to compete and what kind of competitive advantage to build • Developing responses to changing industry and competitive conditions • Coordinating the role/thrust of functional area strategies • Controlling the pattern of resource allocation *within* the business unit
Functional area support strategy	Functional area heads (Decisions are typically reviewed/ approved by business unit head.)	• Fleshing out the business strategy as it applies to specific functional area and developing specific functional area action plans to support successful execution of business strategy
Operating-level strategy	Department heads/field unit heads/ lower-level managers within functional areas (Decisions are often made after consultations with lateral peers in closely related areas and are reviewed/approved by functional area head.)	• Developing action plans to carry out the day-to-day requirements of functional area support strategies

activities. Ideally, corporate strategy, business strategy, functional area support strategy, and operating-level strategy are developed in sufficient detail that each manager in the organization has a confident understanding of how to manage his or her area of responsibility in accordance with the total organizationwide game plan.[14] This is why many layers of strategy are typically needed (especially in large, diversified organizations), with each layer being progressively narrower in focus and more explicit about the actions to be taken and the programs to be initiated. Table 2–1 illustrates the various levels of strategy-making responsibilities within the organizational structure.

Coordination of the Levels of Strategy   Coordination is essential. A strategy is well formulated when its separate pieces and layers are consistent and interlock smoothly like a jigsaw puzzle. The power of business-level strategy is enhanced when functional area and operating-level strategies are matched and fitted to each other

---

[14] Ibid.

to form a unified whole—clearly, manufacturing strategy, marketing strategy, financial strategy, and so on cannot go off on independent courses. Having all the various elements of business strategy "pulling together" neutralizes some of the effects of organizational politics and acts to keep the sometimes myopic views and loyalties of functional departments from blunting the priorities of what is best for the total enterprise.[15] Likewise, in a multibusiness enterprise, welding diverse business-level strategies together in some coherent fashion increases the power of corporate strategy. It is thus useful to view the links between the pieces and levels of strategy as (1) the conceptual glue that binds an organization's activities together and (2) the merging force behind a well-formulated strategy.[16]

Figure 2–5 depicts a hypothetical composite strategy and the levels of directional actions and decisions needed to make it operationally complete. Note the logical flow from corporate strategy to business strategy to functional support strategies to operating-level strategies. It should be evident from an examination of this figure that an organization's strategic plan is the sum total of the directional actions and decisions it must make in trying to accomplish its objectives—in effect, a collection of strategies. These strategies form a hierarchical network encompassing the broad-ranging to the very specific, and they are linked together by analysis and soul-searching, as well as by an interactive, iterative process of negotiation and agreement on objectives, approaches, and constraints.

THE PRIMARY DETERMINANTS OF STRATEGY

Many, many factors have to be considered in formulating strategy. In general, the goal is to achieve a good match between the organization's internal skills, capabilities, and resources on the one hand and all of the relevant external considerations on the other hand. Six broad categories of considerations usually dominate the design of strategy:

1. Market opportunity, industry attractiveness, and competitive forces.
2. What a company's skills, capabilities, and resources allow it to do best.
3. Emerging threats to the company's well-being and performance.
4. The personal values, aspirations, and vision of managers, especially those of the most senior executive.
5. Social, political, regulatory, ethical, and economic aspects of the external environment in which the enterprise operates.
6. The organization's culture, core beliefs, and business philosophy.

Figure 2–6 is a simple model illustrating how these factors come into play.

---

[15] Functional area managers can sometimes be more interested in doing what is best for their own areas, in building personal empires, and in consolidating their power and organizational influence than they are in cooperating with other functional managers to unify behind the overall business strategy. As a consequence it is easy for functional area support strategies to be at cross purposes; this forces the business-level general manager to expend time and energy refereeing functional strategy conflicts and building support for a more unified approach.

[16] Vancil, "Strategy Formulation in Complex Organizations," p. 18.

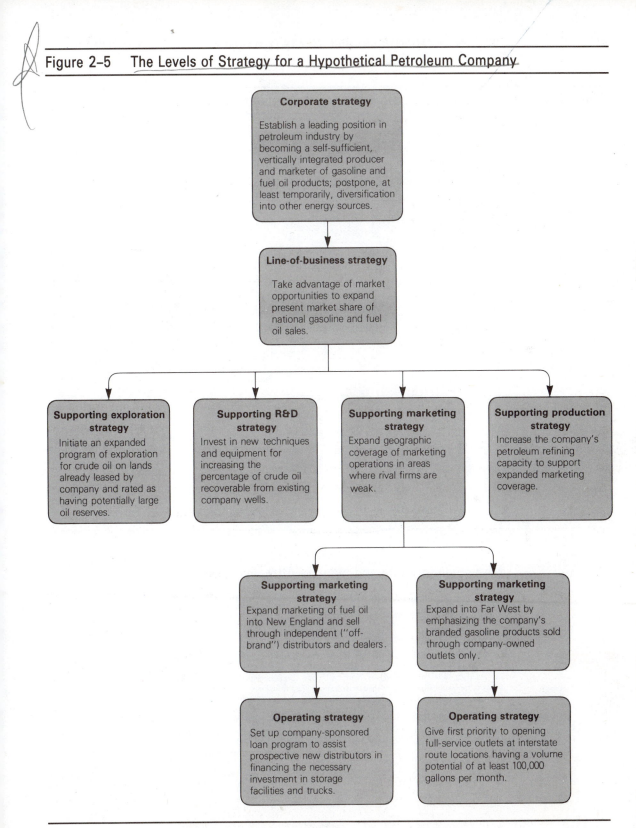

Figure 2–6   A Simple Model of the Primary Determinants of Strategy

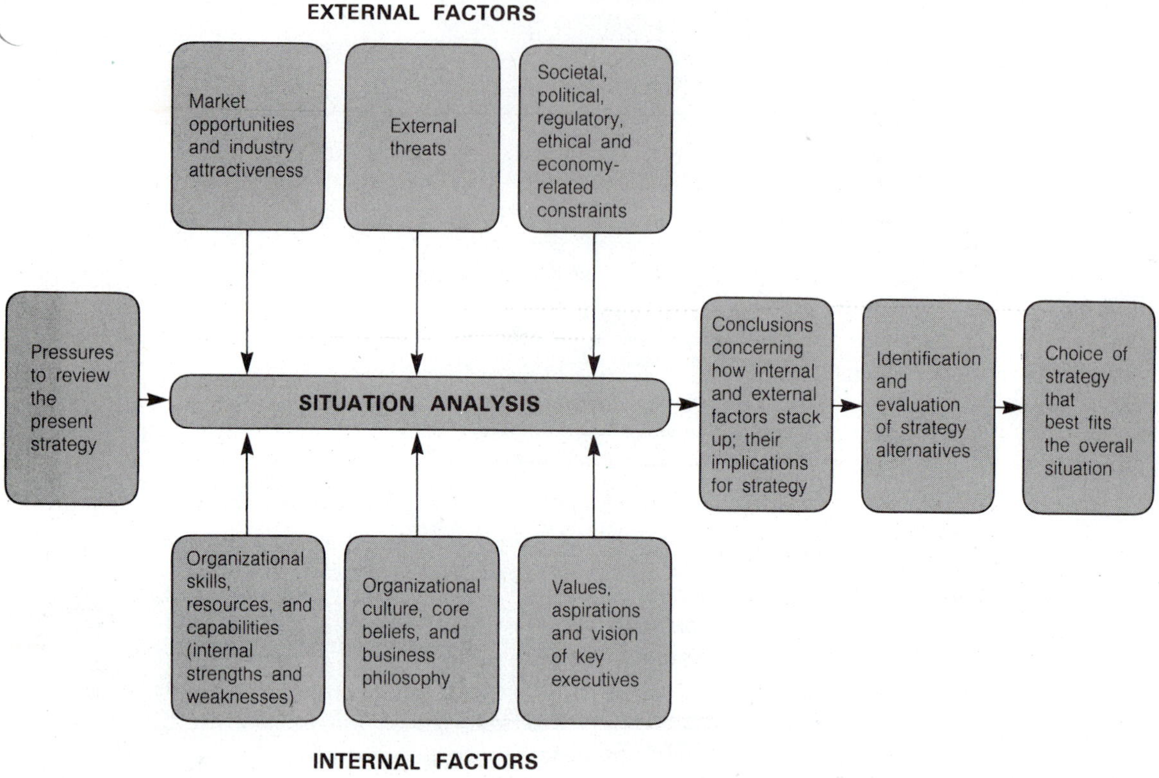

EXTERNAL FACTORS

| Market opportunities and industry attractiveness | External threats | Societal, political, regulatory, ethical and economy-related constraints |

| Pressures to review the present strategy | → | **SITUATION ANALYSIS** | → | Conclusions concerning how internal and external factors stack up; their implications for strategy | Identification and evaluation of strategy alternatives | Choice of strategy that best fits the overall situation |

| Organizational skills, resources, and capabilities (internal strengths and weaknesses) | Organizational culture, core beliefs, and business philosophy | Values, aspirations and vision of key executives |

INTERNAL FACTORS

Market Opportunity and Industry Attractiveness

Market opportunity, the attractiveness of the industry environment, and competitive forces are always factors in formulating strategic plans.[17] Most of the time they are

---

[17] As cogently pointed out by Philip Kotler, there is a difference of opinion in the literature of management regarding whether the strategy formulation process should begin with an identification of attractive opportunities or with defining the business and setting objectives. Those who say the first step should be to identify opportunities argue that: (1) many organizations have gotten their start because they recognized the existence of a major market opportunity (Xerox, Polaroid, Holiday Inns, IBM, and Coca-Cola, among others); (2) many organizations that lack sharply defined objectives and are unable to articulate what they are really trying to do have nonetheless compiled a good record of seizing opportunities; and (3) a number of organizations have changed their focus and their objectives when their opportunities changed (as did the March of Dimes in shifting to a concentration on birth defects when the Salk vaccine virtually eliminated polio). Those who argue that establishing a strategic mission and objectives should logically precede a search for opportunity point out that: (1) a number of organizations search for opportunities that will allow them to achieve sales, profit, and growth objectives; (2) the environment is simply too full of opportunities for companies to look merely for opportunities without a guiding mission and a set of objectives; and (3) organizations can and do, from time to time, change their objectives—an event which, subsequently, leads them to search for new and different opportunities. Both viewpoints have merit in theory and in practice. Quite clearly there is a close link between an organization's search for opportunity and its strategic mission and objectives. As long as this is recognized, there is little need to become embroiled in a "chicken or egg—which comes first" type of controversy. See Philip Kotler, *Marketing Management: Analysis, Planning, and Control,* 3rd ed. (Englewood Cliffs, N.J.: Prentice-Hall, 1976), p. 46.

key strategy-shaping considerations, for unless an enterprise believes it is positioned to pursue an attractive opportunity there is usually the option of choosing some other strategic course. But once an interesting opportunity is spotted, the choice of strategy depends on industry and competitive conditions. The strategy-shaping issues are *how to capture the opportunity, what kind of competitive strategy to use,* and *how to position the enterprise* in light of industry conditions, competition, the strategies of rivals, and the enterprise's own situation. This assessment of the industry and competitive environment entails many facets: analyzing it; predicting it; attempting to change it; deciding how best to adapt to it; and/or electing to get into or get out of some parts of it (in terms of specific customer groups, customer needs, technologies, and products). The choice of strategy is shaped by all relevant industry aspects: key market trends, R&D and technology considerations, the economics of the industry, competitive forces, competitors' strategies, government policies and regulations, buyer demographics and profiles, competition from substitute products, general economic trends and conditions, the factors that govern competitive success—essentially anything and everything that really bears on how to get into a strong competitive position.

Industry versus Company Opportunities   In viewing the role of opportunity in the strategy formation process, it is important to distinguish between *industry opportunities* and *company opportunities.*[18] It is fair to say that there are always attractive industry opportunities in an economy, and new ones emerge as wants, needs, technologies, market demographics, and competitive factors change. But whether these create opportunities for a specific company is another matter. New forms of health care delivery are probably not a relevant opportunity for Exxon, nor is the growing popularity of videocassette recorders a likely opportunity for McDonald's. *The prevailing and emerging industry opportunities that are likely to be most relevant to a particular company are those where the company in question will be able to enjoy some kind of competitive advantage.*

Opportunity, Timing, and First-Mover Advantages   *When* to pursue an opportunity can affect strategy almost as much as what opportunity to pursue. The timing of strategic moves is especially important when *first-mover advantages* or *disadvantages* exist.[19] Being the first competitor to initiate a fresh strategy can have a high payoff when (1) pioneering adds greatly to a firm's image and reputation with buyers; (2) early commitments to supplies of raw materials, new technologies, distribution channels, and so on can produce an absolute cost advantage over rivals; (3) customer loyalty is high, so that long-term benefits accrue to the firm that first convinces the customer to use its product; and (4) moving first can be a preemptive strike, making imitation extremely difficult or unlikely. The stronger any first-mover advantages are, the greater the danger of being late.

However, being late or following a "wait and see" approach is wise if first-mover disadvantages exist. Pioneering is risky when: (1) the costs of opening up a new market are great but customer loyalty is weak, (2) technological change is so rapid

---

[18] Ibid., p. 47.

[19] Michael E. Porter, *Competitive Strategy* (New York: Free Press, 1980), pp. 232–33.

that early investments can be rendered obsolete (thus allowing following firms to have the advantage of the newest products and processes), and (3) the industry is developing so rapidly that skills and know-how built up during the early competitive phase are easily bypassed and overcome by late movers. Good timing, therefore, is an important ingredient in good business strategy formulation.

Organizational Skills, Competences, and Resources

No matter how appealing or abundant an enterprise's opportunities may be, a strategist is forced to validate each opportunity by inquiring into whether the organization has the means to capitalize on it, given the opposing forces of competition and organizational circumstances. Opportunity without the organizational resources and competence to capture it is an illusion. An organization's strengths (demonstrated and potential) may make it particularly suited to seize some opportunities; likewise, its weaknesses may make the pursuit of other opportunities excessively risky or disqualify it entirely. *A good strategy must be doable as well as tuned to attractive opportunity;* hence objective appraisal of what a firm can do and what it shouldn't try to do always needs to guide the choice of strategy.

Experience shows that in seeking an attractive match between a firm's opportunities and its capabilities a firm should try to build on what it does well and should avoid strategies whose key requirements involve what it does poorly, what it has never done at all, and what goes heavily against the ingrained corporate culture. If managers will have to turn an organization upside down and inside out to make a particular strategy doable, then that strategy should usually be ruled out.

Moreover, because of the strategic importance of organizational strengths, weaknesses, and resource capabilities, it makes sense to consider whether the organization has or can build a distinctive competence to help capture the target opportunity. Distinctive competences can take several forms: excelling in the manufacture of a quality product; offering customers superior service after the sale; finding innovative ways to achieve low-cost production efficiency, and then offering customers the attractiveness of a lower price; excelling at developing innovative products that buyers consider a step ahead of rivals' products; designing more clever advertising and sales promotion techniques; having the best technological expertise; being better at working with customer new applications and uses of the product; having the best network of dealers and distributors; and so on. *The importance of distinctive competence to strategy formation rests with (1) the unique capability it gives an organization in capitalizing on a particular opportunity, (2) the competitive edge it may give a firm in the marketplace, and (3) the potential for using a distinctive competence as the cornerstone of strategy.* It is always easier to develop competitive advantage in a market when a firm has a distinctive competence in one of the key requirements for market success, where rival organizations do not have offsetting competences, and where rivals are not able to attain a similar competence except at high cost and/or over an extended period of time.[20]

---

[20] David T. Kollat, Roger D. Blackwell, and James F. Robeson, *Strategic Marketing* (New York: Holt, Rinehart & Winston, 1972), p. 24.

Thomas Peters, coauthor of *In Search of Excellence,* observes:[21]

> Above all, the top performers—school, hospital, sports team, business—are a *package of distinctive skills.* In most cases, one particularly distinctive strength—innovation at 3M, J & J, or Hewlett-Packard; service at IBM, McDonald's, Frito-Lay, or Disney; quality at Perdue Farms, Procter & Gamble, Mars, or Maytag—and the distinctive skill—which in all cases is a product of some variation of "50 million moments of truth a year"—are a virtual unassailable barrier to competitor entry or serious encroachment. . . . Jan Carlzon of SAS puts it this way, "We do not wish to do one thing 1000 percent better, we wish to do 1000 things 1 percent better." Frank G. (Buck) Rodgers, IBM's corporate marketing vice president, made a parallel remark; "Above all we want a reputation for doing the little things well." And a long-term observer of Procter & Gamble noted, "They are so thorough, it's boring."

Experiences such as these teach that attending to the development of a useful distinctive competence is one of the "trade secrets" of first-rate strategic management.

Even if an organization has no distinctive competence (and many do not), it is still incumbent upon a firm to shape its strategy to suit its particular skills and available resources. It never makes sense to develop a strategic plan that cannot be executed with the skills and resources a firm is able to muster.

Emerging Threats to the Company's Well-Being and Performance

Very often, certain factors in a company's external environment pose *threats* to its long-term well-being. These externally imposed threats may stem from the emergence of cheaper technologies, the advent of new substitute products, adverse economic trends, restrictive government action, changing consumer values and lifestyles, projections of natural resource depletion, unfavorable demographic shifts, new sources of strong competition, and the like. Such threats can be a major factor in shaping organizational strategy, and a wise strategist is as much alert to the threats of environmental change as to the opportunities that it may present.

Several examples of strategy-related environmental threats are cited below:

- The potential of nationalization and government takeover threatens the investment strategy of transnational corporations whenever they locate facilities in countries having a record of political instability.
- The business of many American manufacturers has been severely threatened by cheaper foreign imports of comparable or better quality.
- The health and nutrition concerns of consumers have produced sharp declines in the use of foods with high contents of salt, sugar, fat, additives, and preservatives; the long-term sales threats have forced food manufacturers to revolutionize food processing techniques.
- Growing popularity of satellite dishes, cable TV, and videocassette recorders poses a major new competitive threat to NBC, CBS, and ABC. The sizes of the audiences

---

[21] Thomas J. Peters, "Strategy Follows Structure: Developing Distinctive Skills," in *Strategy and Organization: A West Coast Perspective* ed., Glenn Carroll and David Vogel, (Marshfield, Mass.: Pitman Publishing, 1984), p. 104.

watching programs on the three major networks show signs of slippage as more and more households tune in to the cable channels and use VCRs to watch movies. Major advertisers, observing the networks' declining share of home viewers, have shifted some of their advertising budgets to cable TV, thus cutting into the bread-and-butter ad revenues of the major networks.

- Increased costs of regulatory compliance and public concerns about the safety of nuclear-generated electric power have threatened both the business of manufacturing nuclear generating equipment and the financial ability of power companies to install and operate nuclear powered plants. Indeed, during the 1978–1986 period, no new nuclear facilities were ordered and over 50 previously contracted-for units were canceled. A market once thought to be promising dried up quickly.

Most organizations react to environmental threats rather than predicting them. Actually, this is not a strong criticism of managers; many strategically important environmental changes are not readily predicted. Some occur without warning and with few, if any, advance clues; others are "bound to happen" but the uncertainty is when. And still others are simply unknowable. Even when threatening signals are detected early, it is not always easy to assess the extent of their strategic significance. Trying to forecast the strategic significance of future events is scarcely an exact science. Nonetheless, managers have to stay alert to threatening developments and try to develop a strategy that is effective even with adverse environmental change.

The Personal Values, Aspirations, and Vision of Managers

Strategy formulation is rarely so dominated by objective analysis of prevailing circumstances that the subjective imprint of managers is purged. Managers do not dispassionately assess what strategic course to steer. Their decisions are often influenced by their own vision of how to compete and to position the enterprise and by what image and standing they want the company to have. Both casual observation and formal studies indicate that the ambitions, values, business philosophies, attitudes toward risk, and personal vision of managers usually have important influences on strategy.[22] Sometimes the influence of the manager's personal values and experiences is conscious and deliberate; at other times it may be unconscious. As Professor Andrews has noted in explaining the relevance of personal factors to strategy, "Somebody has to have his heart in it."[23]

Two well-known examples of how the strong personal beliefs and values of key managers affect strategy can be cited.[24] The publishers and editors of the *New York Times* have a strong, long-standing commitment to reporting the news intelligently, accurately, and without bias or sensationalism. Their dedication to this style of journalism has caused them to reject changing the nature and character of the *New York*

---

[22] See, for instance, William D. Guth and Renato Tagiuri, "Personal Values and Corporate Strategy," *Harvard Business Review* 43, no. 5 (September–October 1965), pp. 123–32; Kenneth R. Andrews, *The Concept of Corporate Strategy*, rev. ed. (Homewood, Ill.: Richard D. Irwin, 1980), chap. 4; and Vancil, "Strategy Formulation in Complex Organizations," pp. 4–5.

[23] Andrews, *The Concept of Corporate Strategy*, p. 85.

[24] Guth and Tagiuri, "Personal Values and Corporate Strategy," p. 128.

Times, even though their decision to stick with this strategic approach may have restricted circulation and produced a lower return on investment. Hugh Hefner, the founder and publisher of *Playboy,* worked initially for several other magazines, but he found himself wanting to strike out on his own and create a magazine which reflected his own preferences and lifestyle. As he soon discovered, there was indeed a market for *Playboy* and Hefner, guided partly by his own sense of values and lifestyle, pioneered a new concept in magazine publishing.

Attitudes toward risk also have a big influence on strategy. Risk-averters are inclined toward "safe" strategies where external threats appear minimal, profits are adequate but not spectacular, and in-house resources are ample to satisfy anticipated needs. Quite often, risk-averse managers insist on following a financial approach that emphasizes internal financing rather than debt-financing; likewise they may opt to defer major financial commitments as long as possible or until the effects of uncertainty are deemed minimal. They may view pioneering-type innovations as "too chancy" compared to proven, well-established techniques, or they may simply prefer to be followers rather than leaders. In general, the risk-averter places a high premium on "conservative" strategies which minimize the downside risk.

On the other hand, eager risk-takers lean more toward opportunistic strategies where the payoffs are greater, the challenges are more demanding, and the glamour is more appealing, despite the chance of failure. For the risk-taker, innovation is preferred to imitation, and launching a strategy offensive ranks ahead of defensive conservatism. A confident optimism about market prospects overrules pessimism, and attempts to improve the firm's market position are more attractive than maintaining the status quo.

Illustration Capsule 7 on L. L. Bean provides another example of how strongly held values (in this instance regarding customer satisfaction) have a big impact on strategy.

Social, Political, Regulatory, Ethical, and Economic Considerations

Social, political, regulatory, ethical, and economic factors can obviously impinge upon the choice of strategy. Although the interaction between strategy and such factors is a two-way street, here we wish to focus on how the need for overall societal approval of a firm's behavior, together with a firm's perceived social and ethical obligations, constrain strategy formation. That consumerism, truth-in-packaging, equal opportunity employment, occupational health and safety, open housing, product safety, concern for environmental protection, nutritional issues, beliefs about ethics and morals, and other similar societal-based factors have an impact on organization strategies requires no discussion. Adapting strategy to accommodate these factors is commonplace. Toys have been redesigned to improve safety features. The manufacturers of home heating equipment have introduced new energy-saving models in response to consumer concern about high energy costs. Cigarette manufacturers have dramatically reduced the tar and nicotine content of cigarettes and are aggressively marketing new low-tar, low-nicotine brands. Growers of exportable agricultural products and manufacturers of military weapons have adjusted production and sales approaches

ILLUSTRATION CAPSULE 7

The L. L. Bean Tradition of Customer Satisfaction: An Example of How Values and Philosophy Shape Strategy

"THE GOLDEN RULE OF L.L.BEAN"

"Sell good merchandise at a reasonable profit, treat your customers like human beings and they'll always come back for more."

Leon Leonwood Bean started a company 74 years ago based on this simply stated business philosophy. We call it L.L.'s Golden Rule and today we still practice it.

Everything we sell is backed by a 100% unconditional guarantee. We do not want you to have anything from L.L. Bean that is not completely satisfactory. Return anything you buy from us at any time for any reason if it proves otherwise.

L.L. Bean pays all regular postage and handling charges on orders shipped within the United States. This means that the price listed is the only amount that you pay. There are no additional costs.

Send for our FREE fully illustrated 1986 catalogs. They feature a full range of quality products for men and women who enjoy the outdoors. Active and casual apparel and footwear, winter sports equipment, luggage, bedding and furnishings for home or camp. Practical and functional gift ideas. All fully illustrated and honestly described.

Order anytime 24 hours a day, 365 days a year by mail or with our convenient TOLL FREE phone number. Our Customer Service and Telephone Representatives are always here to serve you. We maintain large inventories and ship promptly.

☐ **Please send FREE 1986 L.L. Bean Catalogs!**

Name_____
Address_____
City_____
State_____ Zip_____

L.L. Bean, Inc., 7255 Alder St., Freeport, ME 04033

L.L. Bean®

in international markets to conform to emerging U.S. foreign policy and to the unfolding of international "crises." The efforts of Mothers Against Drunk Driving and other such groups have not gone unnoticed by the makers of alcoholic beverages.

Managerial alertness to the implications of societal forces and political-economic concerns is now an essential part of the strategy formulation process. The desirability (if not the imperative) of relating an organization to the needs and expectations of society is not really a controversial issue today. Making sure that an organization's strategy is responsive to societal concerns means: (1) keeping organizational activities in tune with what is generally perceived as in the public interest; (2) responding positively to emerging societal priorities and expectations; (3) demonstrating a willingness to take needed action ahead of regulatory confrontation; (4) balancing stockholder interests against the larger interest of society as a whole; (5) being a "good citizen" in the community; and (6) making the corporation's social and ethical obligations an explicit and high-priority consideration in the way the enterprise conducts its affairs.

Keeping an organization's strategy socially responsive has both "carrot" and "stick" aspects. There is the positive appeal for an organization to pursue a strategy that will improve its public image and at the same time enhance performance opportunities (and these are always inexorably tied to the general health and well-being of society). And then there is the negative burden of a tarnished reputation and potentially onerous regulation if a firm ignores the changing priorities and expectations of society.

Strategy and Organization Culture

Every organization has policies, values, traditions, behaviors, and ways of doing things which become so ingrained that the organization takes on a distinctive culture. Some companies are noted for being pioneers and exhibiting innovative leadership; others are cautious and conservative, often quite content to assume a follow-the-leader role. Still others are dominated by such traits as a long-standing dedication to superior craftsmanship, a proclivity for financial wheeling and dealing, a desire to grow rapidly by acquiring other companies, a strong social consciousness, or unusual emphasis on customer service and total customer satisfaction.

A couple of examples illustrate the strong link between strategy and culture.[25] IBM's founder, Thomas Watson, once stated, "We must be prepared to change all the things we are in order to remain competitive in the environment, but we must never change our three basic beliefs: (1) respect for the dignity of the individual, (2) offering the best customer service in the world, and (3) excellence." IBM's staunch commitment to these values underlies the company's big competitive edge over rivals in software availability (thus giving IBM users more computing productivity for their money) and customer service, and perhaps it explains why IBM is (at least arguably) the best-managed company in the world.

At AT&T, the value system for nearly a century has emphasized (1) universal service, (2) fairness in handling personnel matters, (3) a belief that work should be

---

[25] For more details, see Richard T. Pascale, "Perspectives on Strategy: The Real Story behind Honda's Success," in Carroll and Vogel, *Strategy and Organization: A West Coast Perspective*, p. 60.

held in balance with commitments to one's family and community, and (4) relationships (from one part of the organization to another). These values have been viewed by AT&T's management to be essential in getting things done in a technologically dynamic, highly structured company. At both IBM and AT&T, the value system is deeply ingrained and widely shared by managers and employees, to such an extent that a definite corporate culture has emerged—the shared values are not empty slogans; they are a way of life within the company.

In companies with strong corporate cultures, the cultural or personality traits are typically reflected in strategy; in some cases these traits even dominate the choice of strategy. This is because culture-related values and policies become imbedded in the thoughts and actions of executives, in the way the enterprise shapes its responses to external events, and in the skills and expertise it builds into the company structure, thereby creating a culture-driven bias about what strategy to select and also, shaping what strategy a firm may be most capable of executing with some proficiency.

MANAGING THE STRATEGY FORMATION PROCESS

Companies and managers go about the strategy-making task differently. In small, owner-managed companies strategic plans tend to be developed informally; the plan itself is not likely to be written but instead may exist mainly in the entrepreneur's own mind and in oral agreements with key subordinates. The largest firms, however, develop their plans via an annual strategic planning cycle (complete with prescribed procedures, forms, and timetables) that includes broad management participation, numerous studies, and multiple meetings to probe and question. The larger and more diverse the enterprise, the more that managers feel it is better to have a structured process that is done annually, involves written plans, and requires management scrutiny and official approval at each level.

Along with variations in the organizational process of formulating strategy come variations in the way the manager, as chief entrepreneur and organizational leader, personally participates in the actual work of strategic analysis and strategic choice. Most managers use one of four approaches to strategy-making:[26]

- *The master strategist approach.* Here the manager personally functions as chief strategist, and chief entrepreneur, exercising *strong* influence over the kinds and amount of analysis conducted, over the strategy alternatives to be explored, and over the details of strategy. This does not mean that the manager personally does all of the work. What it does mean is that the manager is the chief architect of strategy and wields a proactive hand in shaping some or all of the major pieces of strategy. The manager acts as strategy commander, with a big ownership stake in the chosen strategy.
- *The delegate-it-to-others approach.* Here the manager in charge delegates virtually all of the strategic planning to others, perhaps a planning staff or a task force. The manager does little more than suggest minor changes and place a stamp of

---

[26] The following list and discussion is based on David R. Brodwin and L. J. Bourgeois, "Five Steps to Strategic Action," in *Strategy and Organization: A West Coast Perspective,* ed. Carroll and Vogel, especially pp. 168–78.

approval on the plan that emerges, ending up with little personal stake in the formal strategy statement. The great hazard facing the planners and the company whose chief executive turns too much of the strategy formulation task over to others is that the resulting plan will gather dust on the shelf rather than become a blueprint for action. When the ownership of the proposed strategy rests with those who wrote the plan instead of those who must take responsibility for carrying out the recommended strategy, the stage is set for the plan to be largely ignored as nothing more than a ceremonial exercise.

- *The collaborative approach.* This is a middle approach whereby the manager enlists the help of key subordinates in hammering out a consensus strategy which all "the key players" will support and do their best to implement successfully. The greatest strength of this style of managing the formulation process is that those who are charged with strategy formulation are also those who are charged with implementing the chosen strategy. Giving subordinate managers a clear-cut ownership stake in the strategy they subsequently must implement not only enhances commitment to successful execution but also when subordinates have had a hand in proposing their part of the overall strategy they can be held accountable for making it work—the "I told you it was a bad idea" alibi won't fly.

- *The champion approach.* In this style of presiding over strategy formulation, the manager is interested neither in a big personal stake in the details of strategy nor in the time-consuming tedium of leading others through participative brainstorming or a collaborative "group wisdom" exercise. Rather, the idea is to encourage subordinate managers to develop, champion, and implement sound strategies. Here strategy moves upward from the "doers" and the "fast-trackers". The executive serves as a judge, evaluating the strategy proposals that reach his desk. This approach is especially well suited for large diversified corporations where it is impossible for the CEO to be on top of all the strategic and operating problems facing each of many business divisions. Therefore, if the CEO is to exploit the fact that there are many people in the enterprise who can see strategic opportunities that he cannot, then he must give up some control over strategic direction in order to foster strategic opportunities and new strategic initiatives. The CEO may well articulate general strategic themes as organizationwide guidelines for strategic thinking, but the real skill is stimulating and rewarding new strategy proposals put forth by a champion who believes in an opportunity and badly wants the latitude to go after it. With this approach, the total "strategy" is strongly influenced by the sum of the championed initiatives that get approved.

GOOD ENTREPRENEURSHIP EQUALS GOOD
STRATEGIC PLANNING

How well managers have performed the entrepreneurial task of direction-setting and strategy development can be appraised from two angles.[27] One is from the perspective of whether the chosen strategic plan is right for the organization given its particular

---

[27] Vancil, "Strategy Formulation in Complex Organizations," p. 3.

situation. Does it offer a potentially effective match with the organization's internal and external environments? Does it allow the enterprise to exploit attractive opportunities and/or to escape the impact of externally imposed threats? Is it compatible with the organization's internal strengths and resources? Is it timely? All things considered, *is there "goodness of fit" between the chosen strategy and the relevant external/internal considerations?*

The second angle involves whether the strategy has been fleshed out in enough detail to constitute an action plan for the whole organization. A complete strategy is always a combination of many distinct actions and decisions, rather than a single point of attack. Thus the strategic plan must affect every manager, beginning at the corporate level and continuing in increasingly detailed layers down to the operating level. However, as Illustration Capsule 8 points out, there are often different degrees to which those inside and outside the top management ranks know all the strategy details and plans.

Ultimately, of course, the test of good entrepreneurship is whether the chosen strategy produces the desired levels of performance and culminates in the achievement of the target objectives.

ILLUSTRATION CAPSULE 8

Corporate Strategy: Out in the Open or Kept under Wraps?

There are several issues concerning how open the discussion of corporate-level strategy ought to be: To what extent should the details of corporate strategy be expressly articulated to the board of directors, to the various levels of management, to stockholders, and to the outside world? Should a large, multibusiness corporation's board of directors be involved in formulating corporate strategy or is its role the more narrow one of reviewing it and monitoring the process that produces it? What is the best clue of a success-producing corporate strategy—a clearly thought-out strategy that is articulated, questioned, and evaluated before it is approved and used as a basis for decisions *or* an entrepreneurially astute chief executive officer *or* the circumstances of being in the right place at the right time? How can one know what a firm's corporate strategy really is?

There are no nice, neat, pat answers to the questions posed. But partial answers, at least, are emerging. As Professor Edward Wrapp cogently observed in the *Harvard Business Review,* there can be four different perspectives about what a firm's corporate strategy is:[1]

1. *Corporate strategy for the annual report.* Usually the discussions of corporate strategy in annual reports are sterilized by top management and carefully edited by the public relations staff. Nonetheless, pressures for such statements are growing because they give stockholders a sense of direction about where the company is headed and convey an assurance that management has a conscious game plan for directing and running the enterprise.

2. *Corporate strategy for the board of directors, middle managers, and outside securities analysts.* The articulation of corporate strategy for these groups is more comprehensive and detailed than annual report statements. It includes more information about the hows and whys of corporate direction, gives some details

ILLUSTRATION CAPSULE 8 *(continued)*

on growth opportunities, offers information about specific businesses and markets, and contains more documentation of top management's plans for the company. Yet, even these audiences get only part of the strategy; discussions and documentation are kept simple and somewhat superficial—possible pitfalls and drawbacks are seldom explicitly discussed.

3. *Corporate strategy for top management.* In organizations of much size or complexity, all of the key top executives usually participate in comprehensive, in-depth discussions of basic corporate direction, corporate strengths and weaknesses, emerging threats and opportunities, and what moves and countermoves are under contemplation. Typically, special studies and analyses may be prepared as a basis for deciding what course to follow. A full airing of the pros and cons and the various ramifications of each option often precedes strategic decisions. The chief executive/general manager, needing the support of key subordinates, may strive to reach broad consensus on strategy. In the process, key executives come to understand, question, evaluate, and formalize the chosen corporate-level strategy.

4. *The chief executive's own private version of corporate strategy.* The chief executive/general manager commonly mulls a range of moves that are disclosed to almost no one. The chief executive's reasons for keeping some aspects of strategy private may be dictated by a belief that he or she has the best entrepreneurial instincts to sort out the pros and cons and to decide how best to proceed; or it may be because of the risks of premature disclosure of sensitive maneuvers; or it may reflect the CEO's own perception of needs and circumstances that others have not yet recognized and diagnosed; or it may stem from a desire to maneuver informally and flexibly. Given that the chief executive bears ultimate responsibility for corporate strategy and must preside over the strategy formulation process, it should come as no surprise that his or her own personal vision of the game plan (which no doubt undergoes constant change as events unfold and new information is assimilated) is an authentic and highly relevant "source" of what an organization's corporate strategy really is and is going to be. The importance of the top executive's private version of strategy explains why "strategy-watchers" both inside and outside the organization pay so much attention to the CEO's actions and pronouncements for whatever "signals" they may contain.

How much one knows about corporate strategy is thus a variable: it depends on who you are, how much an organization elects to reveal about its strategy, and what can be deduced and inferred from the organization's actions.

As concerns the role of the board of directors in the corporate strategy formulation process, this, too, is a variable. Some organizations involve board members much more heavily in corporate strategy decisions than do others. Texas Instruments, for example, has its board members attend a four-day strategic planning conference each year to discuss business opportunities for the next 10 years; some members stay on for another two days of meetings with 500 managers from all the company's activities. In addition, there is a corporate objectives committee composed of board members, and each director is furnished a wealth of strategy-related information. The outcome is that the TI board is heavily involved in reviewing and monitoring the TI strategy.

ILLUSTRATION CAPSULE 8 *(concluded)*

In other companies, though, corporate executives prefer to keep board members "splashing around in the shallow end of the pool, never letting them venture into deep water." As one former chief executive officer of a multibusiness firm expressed it, "The idea of exposing my strategy for a full discussion by the board never crossed my mind."[2] Another chief executive related, "My board members spent too much time talking about how they did things in their own companies. We listened to their stories, but for the most part they had remote relevance."[3]

One of the originating pioneers of the concept of corporate strategy, Kenneth R. Andrews, argues:

The board must sense at least how well the chief strategic officer of the company (in almost all cases the CEO) has investigated market opportunity, appraised and invested in the distinctive competence and total resources of his company, and combined opportunity and resources, consistent with the economic resources, personal values, and ethical aspirations that define the character of the company. Since no one has a monopoly on insight, not only should top management agree on what it will try to accomplish, but so should the board.[4]

Andrews' point is that board review and discussion of strategy presents individual directors the opportunity (1) to test whether top management has done a creditable job of formulating a durable corporate strategy, however sparsely stated, (2) to get some idea of its validity and feasibility, (3) to relate it to individual project and capital investment decisions, and (4) to ask strategically relevant questions.

While Andrews and others argue that the cause of corporate strategy formulation is enhanced when it is brought out of the closet and becomes a candidly participative process, the contrary view is that so long as the chief executive and other important general managers are creative entrepreneurs and skilled strategic thinkers, they can find ways to make businesses healthy and keep them that way—a consideration that outweighs the issue of whether the strategy is articulated and made explicit or not.

---

[1] As quoted by Kenneth R. Andrews in "Corporate Strategy as a Vital Function of the Board," *Harvard Business Review* 59, no. 6 (November–December 1981), p. 176.
[2] Ibid., p. 180.
[3] Ibid.
[4] Ibid.

SUGGESTED READINGS

Andrews, Kenneth R. *The Concept of Corporate Strategy.* Rev. ed. Homewood, Ill.: Dow Jones-Irwin, 1980, chaps. 2, 3, 4, and 5.

Ansoff, H. Igor. *Corporate Strategy.* New York: McGraw-Hill, 1965, chap. 6.

Drucker, Peter F. *Management: Tasks, Responsibilities, Practices.* New York: Harper & Row, 1974, chaps. 6 and 7.

Foster, Lawrence W. "From Darwin to Now: The Evolution of Organizational Strategies." *Journal of Business Strategy* 5, no. 4 (Spring 1985), pp. 94–98.

Granger, Charles H. "The Hierarchy of Objectives." *Harvard Business Review* 42, no. 3 (May–June, 1964), pp. 63–74.

Hofer, Charles W., and Dan Schendel. *Strategy Formulation: Analytical Concepts.* St. Paul, Minn.: West Publishing, 1978, chap. 2.

McLellan, R., and G. Kelly. "Business Policy Formulation: Understanding the Process." *Journal of General Management* 6, no. 1 (Autumn 1980), pp. 38–47.

Quinn, James Brian. *Strategies for Change: Logical Incrementalism.* Homewood, Ill.: Richard D. Irwin, 1980, chaps. 2 and 4.

Vancil, Richard F. "Strategy Formulation in Complex Organizations." *Sloan Management Review* 17, no. 2 (Winter 1976), pp. 1–18.

Vancil, Richard F., and Peter Lorange. "Strategic Planning in Diversified Companies." *Harvard Business Review* 53, no. 1 (January–February 1975), pp. 81–90.

3 Techniques of Industry and Competitive Analysis

Analysis is the critical starting point of strategic thinking.

—*Kenichi Ohmae*

Awareness of the environment is not a special project to be undertaken only when warning of change becomes deafening. . . .

—*Kenneth R. Andrews*

Competitive strategy must grow out of a sophisticated understanding of the rules of competition that determine an industry's attractiveness.

—*Michael E. Porter*

The bread-and-butter tasks of strategy analysis are performed at the business-unit level. And while many factors always enter into diagnosing what sort of strategy makes the most sense for a particular business, two things emerge time and again as dominant analytical considerations.[1] The first concerns how attractive an industry is in terms of its prospects for long-term profitability and what factors make the industry more or less attractive. There are big differences in the relative attractiveness of industries; some industries are full of opportunity and growth potential while others are stagnant or in decline. Some industries are intensely competitive, with no prospect for winning a meaningful competitive edge; other industries, though quite competitive, still have strategic windows that offer interesting competitive advantage possibilities. Industries differ so much in their attractiveness that even an industry leader may be unable to earn respectable profits when the industry's prospects are grim.

The second big analytical consideration concerns the determinants of relative competitive position within an industry. Competition is a game with winners and losers. It inevitably leads to differences in competitive position and competitive advantage among industry participants. These differences are so important that, even in industries with wide open opportunities, firms will fail if they lack competitive advantage or if they are unable to get out of poor competitive market positions. Disparities in competitive strength and the uneven distribution of competitive advantage explain why some firms are more

---

[1] Michael E. Porter, *Competitive Advantage* (New York: Free Press, 1985), p. 1.

profitable than others and why all industries have leaders and laggards. However, the particulars of how the game of competition is played are not the same from industry to industry. Every industry has its own competitive "rules" and its own weighted ranking of what factors count most/least in determining competitive position and competitive advantage. Identifying all these factors thus becomes fundamental.

This chapter examines the techniques for conducting a full-scale industry and competitive analysis. The results of such an analysis pave the way for deciding what business strategy to pursue.

THE ELEMENTS OF INDUSTRY AND COMPETITIVE ANALYSIS

The entrepreneurial task of assessing whether and how a company's present line-of-business strategy can be improved consists of a three-pronged diagnosis:

1. *Industry situation analysis*—an examination of industry structure, direction, economics, and long-term attractiveness.
2. *Competitive situation analysis*—an analysis of competitive forces and key competitors.
3. *Company situation analysis*—an assessment of the company's own present business situation and competitive position.

Figure 3–1 presents a schematic of the diagnostic framework and the key concerns associated with each analytical element.

INDUSTRY SITUATION ANALYSIS AND INDUSTRY ATTRACTIVENESS

The overriding purpose of "industry situation analysis" is *not* to just "learn all one can" about the industry but rather is to probe the industry's long-term profit potential and discover the factors that make the industry more or less attractive. Industry analysis needs to be focused on four questions:

1. How is the industry structured?
2. What driving forces are causing the industry to change and how important will these changes be?
3. What economic factors and business characteristics have the most influence on the requirements for competitive success in the industry; or, to put it another way, what do firms in this industry have to do well to make money and to succeed?
4. What strategic issues and problems face the industry?

Good, solid answers to these questions enable a strategist to understand what factors are causing changes in an industry, to make predictions about where the industry is headed and why, to judge what the industry's future structure will be like, and

Figure 3–1   The Framework of Industry and Competitive Analysis

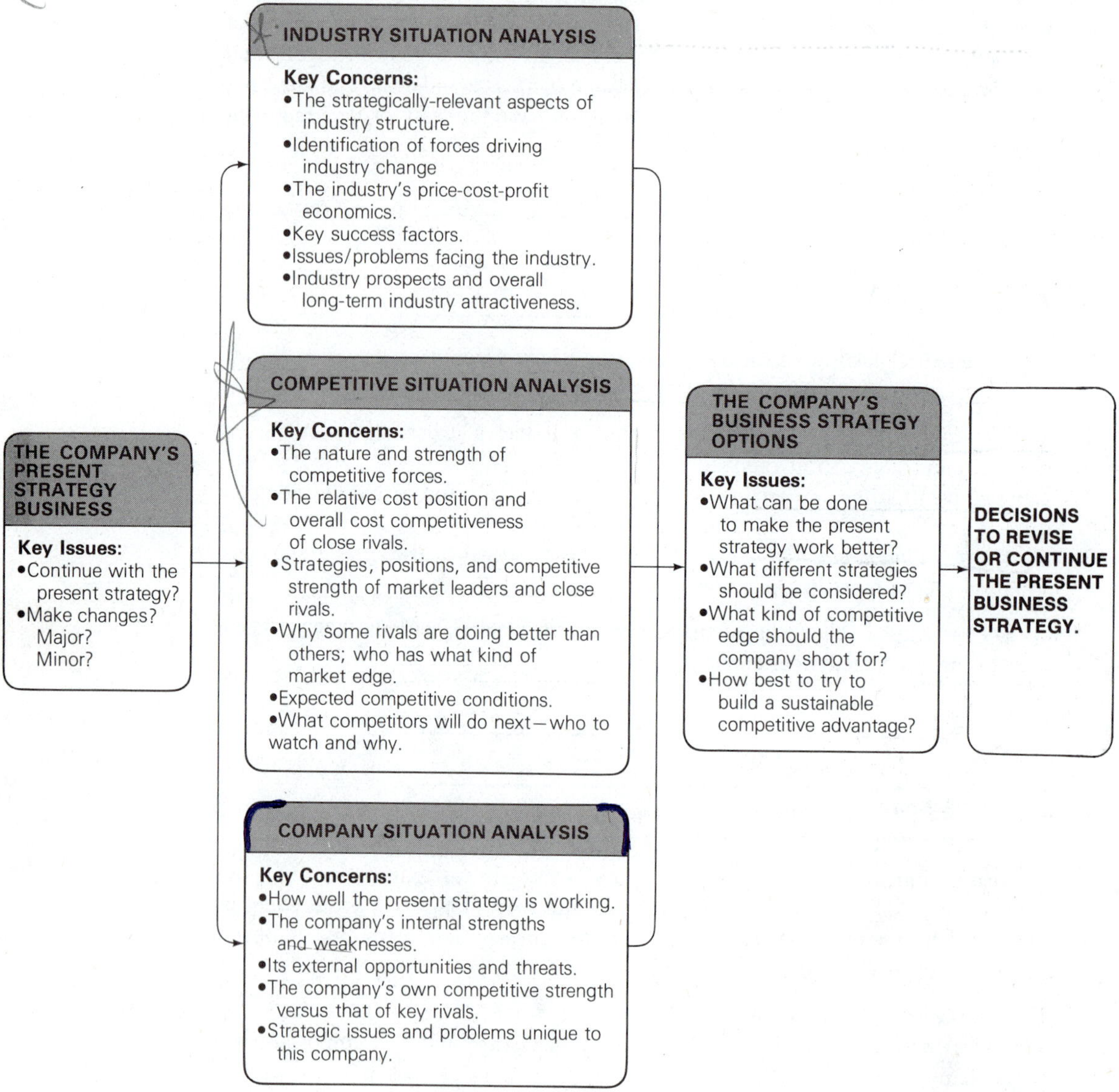

INDUSTRY SITUATION ANALYSIS

Key Concerns:
- The strategically-relevant aspects of industry structure.
- Identification of forces driving industry change
- The industry's price-cost-profit economics.
- Key success factors.
- Issues/problems facing the industry.
- Industry prospects and overall long-term industry attractiveness.

COMPETITIVE SITUATION ANALYSIS

Key Concerns:
- The nature and strength of competitive forces.
- The relative cost position and overall cost competitiveness of close rivals.
- Strategies, positions, and competitive strength of market leaders and close rivals.
- Why some rivals are doing better than others; who has what kind of market edge.
- Expected competitive conditions.
- What competitors will do next—who to watch and why.

THE COMPANY'S PRESENT STRATEGY BUSINESS

Key Issues:
- Continue with the present strategy?
- Make changes? Major? Minor?

THE COMPANY'S BUSINESS STRATEGY OPTIONS

Key Issues:
- What can be done to make the present strategy work better?
- What different strategies should be considered?
- What kind of competitive edge should the company shoot for?
- How best to try to build a sustainable competitive advantage?

DECISIONS TO REVISE OR CONTINUE THE PRESENT BUSINESS STRATEGY.

COMPANY SITUATION ANALYSIS

Key Concerns:
- How well the present strategy is working.
- The company's internal strengths and weaknesses.
- Its external opportunities and threats.
- The company's own competitive strength versus that of key rivals.
- Strategic issues and problems unique to this company.

to conclude whether the industry's attractiveness and profit prospects are bright or dim and why.

Strategic Group Mapping and Industry Structure

The first step in industry analysis is to examine industry structure. As a working definition, we will use the word *industry* to mean a group of firms whose products are so similar that they are drawn into close competition, serving the same needs of the same types of buyers. The raw data for profiling industry structure are fairly standard: the number of sellers and their relative sizes, identification of the market leaders, the structure of the buying side of the market, the channels of distribution from manufacturer to final user, the prevalence of backward and forward integration within the industry, the ease of entry and exit, the size of the industry and its geographical boundaries (local, regional, national, or global), and any other basic characteristics peculiar to the industry in question that shape the industry arena in which firms compete. It is important to understand the generic environment of the industry— that is, whether the industry can be broadly characterized as fragmented (many relatively small competitors), mature, emerging, declining, characterized by global competition, dominated by rapid technological change, or whatever. Some specific industry structure factors to be alert for include the following:

Factor	Reason for Importance
Market size	Small markets don't tend to attract big/new competitors.
Market growth rate	Fast growth breeds new entry; growth slowdowns breed increased rivalry and a shakeout of weaker competitors.
Capacity surpluses or shortages	Surpluses push prices and profit margins down; shortages pull them up.
Relative profitability	High-profit industries attract new entrants; depressed conditions encourage exit.
Entry/exit barriers	High barriers protect positions and profits of existing firms.
Product is a big-ticket item for buyers	More buyers will shop for lowest price.
Rapid technological change	Raises risk factor; investments in technology, facilities, or equipment may become obsolete before they wear out.
Capital requirements	Big requirements make investment decisions critical; timing becomes important; creates a barrier to entry and exit.
The products of sellers are standardized	Buyers have more power because it is easier to switch from seller to seller.
Vertical integration	Raises capital requirements; often creates competitive differences and cost differences among fully versus partially versus nonintegrated firms.
Economies of scale	Affects volume and market share needed to be cost competitive.
Rapid product innovation	Shortens product life cycle; more risk because of opportunities for leapfrogging.

Strategic Group Mapping One of the newest and most revealing techniques for pushing beneath the surface of industry structure is *strategic group mapping*.[2] This analytical tool is useful whenever an industry is populated with several distinct

---

[2] Michael E. Porter, *Competitive Strategy: Techniques for Analyzing Industries and Competitors* (New York: Free Press, 1980), chap. 7.

groups of competitors, each group occupying an identifiable position in the overall market and having an identifiable appeal to buyers. A *strategic group* consists of those rival firms with competitively similar market approaches.[3] Companies in the same strategic group can resemble one another in any of several ways: offering comparable product line breadth; utilizing similar distribution channels; being vertically integrated to much the same degree; offering buyers similar services and technical assistance; appealing to similar customer groups; appealing to buyer needs with the same product features; making extensive use of mass media advertising; depending on identical technological approaches; and/or selling in the same price/quality range.

An industry contains only one strategic group when all sellers approach the market with essentially identical strategies. At the other extreme, there are as many strategic groups as there are competitors when each rival pursues a distinctively different market approach. The major home appliance industry, for example, contains three identifiable strategic groups. One cluster (composed of such firms as GE, Frigidaire, and Whirlpool) produces a full line of home appliances (refrigerators, freezers, clothes washers and dryers, dishwashers, stoves, cooking tops, ovens, garbage disposals, and microwave ovens), employs heavy national advertising, is vertically integrated, and has established a national network of distributors and dealers. Another cluster consists of premium quality, specialist firms (like Amana in refrigerators and freezers, Maytag in washers and dryers, Kitchen Aid in dishwashers, and Jenn-Air in cooking tops) that focus on high-price market segments and have selective distribution. A third cluster, consisting of firms like Roper, Design and Manufacturing, and Hardwick, concentrates on supplying private label retailers and budget-priced, basic models for the low end of the market.

A *strategic group map* is constructed by plotting the market positions of the industry's strategic groups on a two-dimensional map using two strategic variables as axes (see the retail jewelry industry example in Illustration Capsule 9). The map serves as a convenient bridge between looking at the industry as a whole and considering the standing of each firm separately.

The method for constructing a strategic group map and deciding which firms belong in which strategic group can be summarized as follows:

- Identify the broad characteristics that differentiate firms in the industry from one another.
- Plot the firms on a two-variable map using pairs of these differentiating characteristics.
- Assign firms that fall in about the same strategy space to the same strategic group.
- Draw circles around each strategic group, making the circles proportional to the size of the group's respective share of total industry sales revenues.

There are five important guidelines to observe in trying to map the relative competitive positions of firms in the industry's overall "strategy space":[4] First, the two variables selected as axes for the map should *not* be highly correlated; if they are, the circles on the map will fall along a diagonal, rendering one of the variables useless. For

---

[3] Ibid., pp. 129–30.
[4] Ibid., pp. 152–54.

ILLUSTRATION CAPSULE 9

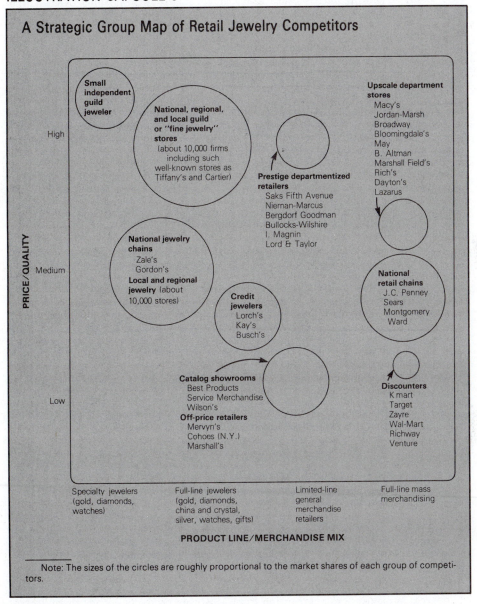

A Strategic Group Map of Retail Jewelry Competitors

PRICE/QUALITY

High

Small independent guild jeweler

National, regional, and local guild or "fine jewelry" stores
(about 10,000 firms including such well-known stores as Tiffany's and Cartier)

Prestige departmentized retailers
Saks Fifth Avenue
Nieman-Marcus
Bergdorf Goodman
Bullocks-Wilshire
I. Magnin
Lord & Taylor

Upscale department stores
Macy's
Jordan-Marsh
Broadway
Bloomingdale's
May
B. Altman
Marshall Field's
Rich's
Dayton's
Lazarus

Medium

National jewelry chains
Zale's
Gordon's
Local and regional jewelry (about 10,000 stores)

Credit jewelers
Lorch's
Kay's
Busch's

National retail chains
J.C. Penney
Sears
Montgomery Ward

Low

Catalog showrooms
Best Products
Service Merchandise
Wilson's
Off-price retailers
Mervyn's
Cohoes (N.Y.)
Marshall's

Discounters
K mart
Target
Zayre
Wal-Mart
Richway
Venture

Specialty jewelers (gold, diamonds, watches)

Full-line jewelers (gold, diamonds, china and crystal, silver, watches, gifts)

Limited-line general merchandise retailers

Full-line mass merchandising

PRODUCT LINE/MERCHANDISE MIX

Note: The sizes of the circles are roughly proportional to the market shares of each group of competitors.

example, if companies with broad product lines use multiple distribution channels while companies with narrow lines use a single distribution channel, then a map based on the number of distribution channels and product line breadth will fail to identify anything more about the relative competitive positioning of rivals than would just one of the variables by itself.

Second, the best strategic variables to choose as axes for the map are those which expose big differences in how rivals have positioned themselves to compete against one another in the marketplace. This, of course, requires identifying the characteristics that differentiate rival firms from one another and then using these differences (a) as variables for the axes on the map and (b) as the basis for deciding which firm belongs in which strategic group.

Third, the variables used as axes need not be either quantitative or continuous; rather, they can be discrete variables or defined in terms of distinct classes and combinations (as turned out to be the case in Illustration Capsule 9). Fourth, drawing the sizes of the circles on the map proportional to the combined sales of the firms in each strategic group allows the map to reflect the relative sizes of each strategic group. Fifth, if there are more than two good strategic variables that can be used as axes for the map, then several maps can be drawn to give different exposures to the competitive positioning relationships present in the industry's structure. Because there need not be one best map for portraying industry structure and strategic positioning, it is advisable to experiment with different pairs of strategic variables.

Strategic group analysis adds to the picture of "what life is like" in the industry:[5]

1. Industry trends often have different implications for different strategic groups. It is worth studying each industry trend to explore (a) whether the trend is closing off the viability of one or more strategic groups and, if so, where competitors in the affected groups may try to shift; (b) whether the trend will raise or lower the entry barriers into a group and the degree to which competitive pressures in the group will be increased or decreased; and (c) how the companies in each group will otherwise be affected by the trend and their probable response to it.
2. The profit potential of firms in different strategic groups often varies because of strengths and weaknesses in each group's market position. Strategic group maps help pinpoint those firms whose position is tenuous or marginal; firms in marginal groups are candidates for exit or for launching attempts to move into another strategic group.
3. Entry barriers vary according to the particular strategic group that an entrant seeks to join (some strategic groups are easier to enter than others).
4. Firms in different strategic groups often enjoy differing degrees of bargaining leverage with suppliers and/or with customers, and they may also face differing degrees of exposure to competition from substitute products outside the industry.
5. Greater numbers of strategic groups generally increase competitive rivalry in an industry because of the possibility for both intragroup and intergroup competition.

---

[5] Ibid., pp. 130, 132–38, and 154–55.

If there are strong indications that certain strategic groups (or specific firms) are trying to change their positions in the strategy space on the map, then attaching arrows to the circles showing the targeted direction enhances the picture of industry structure.

The Concept of Driving Forces

While mapping an industry's structure has analytical benefit, any such picture tells only part of the story about industry conditions. Except in the rarest of cases, every industry is in a state of constant flux—forces of change are constantly at work and new ones are usually gathering steam. One popular hypothesis about how industries change is that they often go through observable evolutionary phases or life-cycle stages. The sequence of stages is usually: *early development, rapid growth and takeoff, competitive shake-out and consolidation, early maturity, saturation,* and *decline and decay.*

Whether industries will actually evolve in orderly sequence according to the life-cycle hypothesis is debatable.[6] Many do, but some do not. There are cases where industries have skipped maturity, passing from rapid growth to decline very quickly. Sometimes growth reoccurs after a period of decay (this occurred in the radio broadcasting, bicycle, and motorcycle industries). Sometimes the paths of different industries collide, causing them to reform and merge as one industry (this is now occurring among banks, savings and loan associations, and brokerage firms, which were in distinctly separate industries but are now reforming into a single financial services industry). And sometimes the growth phase of the cycle can be lengthened by product innovation.[7] Because of these facets, it is difficult to predict when the "usual" cycle pattern will hold, when it will not, and how long the phases will last.

Hence, while it is worthwhile to diagnose where an industry is in the life cycle, it is equally fruitful to identify what forces are at work causing important changes in the industry landscape. *Industries evolve because forces are in motion that create incentives or pressures for change.*[8] The most dominant of these forces are called *driving forces* because they have the strongest influence on what kind of changes will take place in the industry's structure and environment.

The Kinds of Driving Forces and How They Work

There are numerous types of driving forces with power to produce strategically relevant changes in an industry:[9]

 Changes in the long-term industry growth rate   Increases or decreases in industry growth are powerful variables in the investment decisions of existing firms to expand capacity. A strong upsurge in growth frequently attracts new firms to enter the market,

---

[6] For an extended discussion of this point, see Porter, *Competitive Strategy,* pp. 157–62.

[7] For a discussion of how firms can accomplish this, see Theodore Levitt, "Exploit the Product Life Cycle," *Harvard Business Review* 43, no. 6 (November–December 1965), pp. 81–94.

[8] Porter, *Competitive Strategy,* p. 162.

[9] What follows is a brief summary of Porter's discussion in *Competitive Strategy;* see pp. 164–83 for more details.

and a shrinking market often causes some firms to exit the industry. Upward or downward shifts in industry growth are a force for industry change because they affect the balance between industry supply and buyer demand and the intensity of competition.

Changes in who buys the product and how they use it. Increases or decreases in the kinds of customers who purchase the product have potential for changing customer service requirements (credit, technical services, maintenance, and repair); creating a need to alter distribution channels; and precipitating broader/narrower product lines, increased/decreased capital requirements, and different marketing practices. The hand-held calculator industry became a different market requiring different strategies when students and households began to use them as well as engineers and scientists. The computer industry was transformed by the surge of buyers for personal and home computers. Consumer interest in cordless telephones and mobile telephones for use in cars and trucks created a major new buyer segment for telephone equipment manufacturers. Predictions of industry change should, therefore, include an assessment of potential new buyer segments and their characteristics.

Product innovation   Product innovation can broaden demand, promote entry into the industry, enhance product differentiation among rival sellers, and impact manufacturing methods, economies of scale, marketing costs and practices, and distribution. Industries in which product innovation has been a key driving force include copying equipment, cameras and photographic equipment, computers, electronic videogames, toys, prescription drugs, soft drinks (sugar-free and caffeine-free), beer (low-calorie), and cigarettes (low-tar, low-nicotine).

Process innovation   Frequent and important technological advances in manufacturing methods can dramatically alter unit costs, capital requirements, minimum efficient plant sizes, the desirability of vertical integration, and learning curve effects. Process innovation can alter the relative cost positions of rival firms and change the number of firms of cost-efficient size the market can support.

Marketing innovation   From time to time firms opt to market their products in new ways that spark a burst of buyer interest, widen demand, increase product differentiation, and/or lower unit costs, thus setting in motion new forces which alter the industry and the competitive positions of participant firms.

Entry or exit of major firms   When an established firm from another industry enters a new market, it usually brings with it new ideas and perceptions about how its skills and resources can be innovatively applied; the outcome can be a "new ball game" with new rules for competing and new key players. Similarly, the exit of a major firm changes industry structure by reducing the number of market leaders (perhaps increasing the dominance of the leaders who remain) and causing a rush to capture the former customers of the exiting firm.

Diffusion of proprietary knowledge   As a technology becomes more established and knowledge about it spreads through the conduits of rival firms, suppliers, distributors, and customers, the advantage held by firms with proprietary technology erodes. This makes it easier for new competitors to spring up and, also, for suppliers or customers to integrate vertically into the industry. Except where strong patent protection effectively blockades the diffusion of an important technology, it is likely that rapid diffusion of proprietary knowledge will be an important driver of industry change.

Changes in cost and efficiency In industries where new economies of scale are emerging or where strong learning curve effects cause unit costs to decline, large firm size and production experience become distinct advantages, causing all firms to adopt volume-building strategies—a "race for growth" emerges as the driving force. Likewise, sharply rising costs for a key ingredient input (either raw materials or necessary labor skills) can cause a scramble to either *(a)* line up reliable supplies of the input at affordable prices or else *(b)* search out lower-cost substitutes.

Moving from a differentiated to a commodity product emphasis (or vice versa) Sometimes growing numbers of buyers decide that a standard "one-size-fits-all" product with a bargain price meets their requirements just as effectively as do premium-priced brands offering a broad choice of styles and options. Such a swing in buyer demand can be a driver of industry change, shifting patronage away from sellers of more expensive, differentiated products to sellers of cheaper commodity products and creating a strongly price-oriented market focus—a feature that literally can dominate the industry landscape and limit the strategic freedom of industry participants. On the other hand, a shift away from standardized products occurs when sellers are able to win a bigger and more loyal buyer following by bringing out new performance features, making style changes, offering options and accessories, and creating image differences via advertising and packaging; then the driver of change is the struggle among rivals to out-differentiate one another. Industries evolve differently depending on whether the forces in motion are acting to increase or decrease the emphasis on product differentiation.

Regulatory influences and government policy changes Regulatory and governmental influences can significantly affect the character of industry change. Medicare and Medicaid provisions affect hospital and nursing home operations. The decisions of government regulators weigh heavily on the natural gas, telephone, and electric utility industries. Deregulation has been a major driving force in the airline and banking industries. Changes in defense spending affect the defense contracting business. Drunk driving laws and drinking age legislation have recently become driving forces in the alcoholic beverage industry.

The diverse nature of the driving forces, together with the rather obvious unpredictability about when such forces will be triggered in an industry and how strong they will be explain why an industry can suddenly switch gears and head off in a new direction and why it is too simplistic to look at industry change only in terms of the life-cycle perspective.

Diagnosing an Industry's Economic and Business Characteristics

Every industry has an underlying set of price-cost-profit characteristics. The economics of a business tend to be governed by such factors as capital requirements, economies of scale, the make up of the cost structure, how prices are determined, typical operating profit margins, the variability of unit costs at various rates of capacity utilization, the ways that greater efficiency can be realized, the roles of advertising and marketing in generating added volume, and the like. A command of the economics of the business is fundamental to industry and competitive analysis, since revenue-cost-profit relationships effectively establish constraints on how firms must operate their businesses to be successful.

Take the convenience food store business, for example. A breakdown of the margins, expenses, and net profit for a representative convenience food store for a recent year showed:

Sales	$400,000	100.0%
Cost of goods sold	284,800	71.2
Gross profit margin	115,200	28.8
Expenses:		
Wages and benefits	50,000	12.5
Advertising and promotion	2,800	0.7
Rents and property upkeep	13,200	3.3
Utility costs	12,800	3.2
Other expenses	22,800	5.7
Total expenses	101,600	25.4
Profit before taxes	$ 13,600	3.4%

A typical investment in an urban convenience store location was about $200,000, the bulk of which represented the cost of acquiring a choice location with adequate parking on a heavily traveled thoroughfare. Convenience stores tended to have about 600 customers daily; on the average, patrons spent about $2 and took three to five minutes to make their purchase. Convenience store prices were 10 to 15 percent above the levels in most supermarkets, reflecting customer willingness to pay extra for the convenience such stores offered (location, easy access, 24-hour service, popular selections, and quick check-out). Stores generally stocked 3,000 items in their 2,400-square-foot space and could be staffed with a single clerk. With these underlying economic characteristics, it was generally agreed in the industry that success hinged upon:

1. *Choosing good store locations.* Visible, easily accessible sites on well-traveled routes were essential to drawing an ample clientele.
2. *Selecting the "right" products to stock and merchandising them effectively.* Customers expected to find what they were looking for and, in many instances, also made an impulse purchase (factors that made it important to stock popular, high-turnover items and to do a good job of merchandising and positioning them in the store).
3. *Pricing.* Given that most operating expenses were fixed (not sensitive to changes in sales volume), it was important for prices to be set high enough to produce an average 28–30 percent gross margin on the mix of goods sold, yet pricing had to be sensitive to any big erosion of lost sales to supermarkets.
4. *Operating efficiency.* With only a 28–30 percent gross margin, sloppy management practices and inefficiencies in store operations could quickly erode the typically slim 3.0–3.5 percent pre-tax profit margin.

There are often important size and market share requirements attached to the industry's economics. Scale economies can dictate minimum plant sizes and production volumes needed to be cost competitive with established firms. Capital-intensive production technologies can put firms with burdensome investments in new plants under the gun to utilize capacity and spread fixed costs out over more units. And in some industries there are big learning and *experience curve effects* that allow firms to realize major unit cost reductions as production experience accumulates and volume grows. The presence of strong experience curve effects in an industry makes having a big cumulative production volume crucial to being cost competitive. (See Illustration Capsule 10 for a discussion of experience curve economics and its implications for strategy).

ILLUSTRATION CAPSULE 10

Experience Curve Economics: Its Implications for Industry Analysis

The Boston Consulting Group (BCG), one of the premier strategy consulting firms, has made a big impact on industry analysis with a concept called *the experience curve*. The origins of the experience curve reside with studies in the 1930s showing that a doubling of the cumulative production of airframes was accompanied by a 20 percent reduction in unit labor costs. This phenomenon, termed the learning curve, was attributed to (1) the ability of workers to get better at doing a repetitive task the more times they did it and (2) the discovery of more efficient ways to perform the task.

In the late 1960s Bruce Henderson, BCG's founder and president, noticed a recurring theme that kept running through the cost studies being done for client companies: the declining cost principle underlying the learning curve went beyond just labor costs and seemed to apply to the total value-added costs (all costs except purchased materials and components) measured in constant dollars. Further analysis of the empirical evidence BCG had accumulated showed that each time the cumulative number of units manufactured doubled, the deflated value-added cost per unit declined by a fixed percentage. In integrated circuits and cement a doubling of cumulative production volume entailed about a 30 percent unit cost reduction, in air conditioners and power tools the deflated unit cost declines ran about 20 percent, and in primary magnesium and industrial trucks the declines averaged 10 percent. Deflating the actual historical cost data was necessary to correct for the effects of inflation (when the cost data were not expressed in constant dollars, inflationary factors tended to obscure the true size of the cost savings being realized). The decline in unit cost with each doubling of cumulative production experience was attributed to the combined effects of:

- Learning associated with the repetitive performance of labor tasks.
- Cost-effective improvements in product design.
- Incremental gains associated with "debugging" the production technology.
- The making of bit-by-bit improvements in the whole operating process (better use of materials, more efficient inventory handling, more efficient distribution

ILLUSTRATION CAPSULE 10 *(continued)*

methods, and computerization and automation of assorted production, sales, and clerical tasks).
- An increased scale of operation that yielded access to new operating economies.
- Enriched know-how in managing and operating the business.

BCG plotted the declines in unit cost against cumulative production volume on a graph—the resulting graphical relationship was labeled the experience curve.

In the figure below is an 85 percent experience curve. Unit cost drops from $100 at a production volume of 10 to $85 (= $100 × 0.85) when production reaches an accumulated volume of 20 units and further to $72.25 at a volume of 40 units.

An 85 Percent Experience Curve

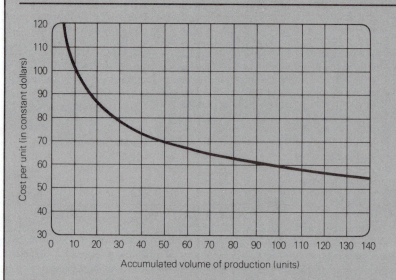

Accumulated volume of production (units)

The significance of the experience curve effect for a given *industry* depends not only on the percentage decline (whether it is 15 percent as in the case of an 85 percent curve or 30 percent as in the case of a 70 percent curve) but also on the rate at which experience accumulates, reflected by the annual rate of market growth. The table below shows the potential for annual cost reductions for different combinations of experience curve effects and market growth:

Experience Curve Effect	Annual Cost Reduction Based on a Rate of Market Growth of				
	2%	*5%*	*10%*	*20%*	*30%*
90%	0.3%	0.7%	1.4%	2.7%	4.1%
80%	0.6	1.6	3.2	6.4	9.6
70%	1.0	2.5	5.0	10.0	15.0
60%	1.4	3.5	7.0	14.0	21.0

ILLUSTRATION CAPSULE 10 *(continued)*

A firm can achieve even bigger annual cost reductions than the industry averages shown above if its market share of industry volume is increasing (this is because the firm's rate of growth in production volume is bigger than the overall industry rate, allowing the firm to accumulate production experience faster than the industry as a whole). As a consequence, the stronger the experience curve effect in an industry, the greater the strategic importance of a firm's market share in determining its ability to remain cost competitive and achieve above-average profitability.

Strategic Implications

Bruce Henderson and BCG argued that the presence of a strong experience curve produced the following cause-effect chain:

High Market Share ⟶ High Accumulated Volume ⟶ Low Unit Cost ⟶ High Profitability

The implications of this chain can be seen by looking at the graph below, which shows the relative position of three competing firms on an industry's experience curve. Firm A, with the largest cumulative volume, has a commanding cost advantage over firms B and C. At the current industry price, firm C is losing money; to become profitable, it has little choice but to move aggressively to increase its market share and thereby move down the experience curve quickly enough to get its costs below the industry price level. Firm B, though able to survive, must live with subpar profitability (in comparison to the leader). Plainly, as long as firm A maintains greater cumulative experience than competitors, it can sustain its cost advantage.

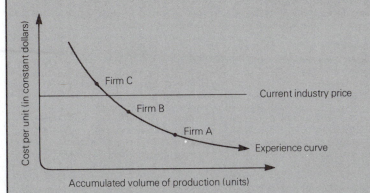

When an industry is characterized by a fairly strong experience curve effect, competitors with less than one quarter of the market share of the largest firm are hard pressed to survive. A shake-out of the low-share firms is virtually inevitable, barring some unusual external constraint or control on competition. As firms exit, the remaining competitors have to grow faster than the industry at large

ILLUSTRATION CAPSULE 10 *(continued)*

just to maintain their relative positions; if runner-up firms want to gain on the leader, then they have to use the exit of weak firms as their opportunity to add volume faster than the leader and move down the experience curve closer to the leader's position. If they fail to capture enough volume to approach the leader's experience curve position, very likely their profits will remain subpar or negative; the best long-run choice then may be to cash out their investment in the industry and reinvest elsewhere.

Estimates of the experience curve effect can be used to forecast costs. Such forecasts become the basis for setting realistic cost reduction goals and for setting prices based on anticipated costs rather than on current or historical costs. Lowering prices at the same rate at which costs decline may well discourage the entry of competing firms into the industry.

Some Added Complexities

There are some subtleties in diagnosing experience curve economics in an industry:

- Occasionally experience effects are lumpy and uneven, causing the curve to decline not at a smooth, uniform rate but rather at rates that change at somewhat unpredictable intervals—the experience curve becomes flatter, then steeper, then flatter again.
- A new entrant firm with improved technology and/or smart followership abilities may be able to ride its own experience curve down more quickly and achieve a cost position significantly closer to the low-cost leaders than would be the case if it was forced to operate on the same experience curve as established competitors.
- There can be different experience curve effects in each part of the industry chain: R&D, design engineering, manufacturing of parts and components, assembly of the final product, marketing, wholesale distribution, and retailing. While the accumulation of experience may result in cost reductions in all stages, seldom will the sizes of the reductions be the same. In like fashion, if a firm produces a whole line of different models, experience will accrue faster for the best-selling models and their costs may fall faster than for slower-selling models.

Applications of Experience Curve Techniques by BCG Clients

One of BCG's first efforts at applying experience curve theory was with the Norton Company of Worcester, Massachusetts. Norton was having trouble profitably penetrating the market for pressure-sensitive tape—a market dominated by 3M. Norton had successfully cut production costs and lowered prices but still was unable to make a dent in increasing its market share. BCG's experience curve analysis showed that Norton, in effect, was chasing 3M down the cost curve, and that so long as 3M followed pricing and growth strategies to maximize market share, it was a fruitless struggle for Norton. Subsequently, Norton concluded it could not compete successfully against 3M by trying to produce a broad range of products sold in a large number of markets; rather, the company decided it was better off concentrating in selected areas. In BCG's view, the Norton situation illustrated an important experience curve commandment: If you

ILLUSTRATION CAPSULE 10 *(concluded)*

cannot get enough market share to be cost competitive, then get out of the business.

Another instance where the same lesson applied was the effort of Allis-Chalmers Company to compete against General Electric and Westinghouse in steam turbine engines. Between 1946 and 1963, Allis-Chalmers' market share was too small for it to be competitive on cost (and therefore on price) with large-volume manufacturers; thus Allis-Chalmers' best decision was to withdraw from the industry.

Black & Decker, Texas Instruments, and Weyerhaeuser have all applied experience curve analysis at one time or another. In 1973 Texas Instruments described its strategy in semiconductors in strong experience curve language: "Follow an aggressive pricing policy, focus on continuing cost reduction and productivity improvement, build on shared experience gained in making related products, and keep capacity growing ahead of demand."

Some Cautions

Three warnings about the experience curve are in order. One, experience curve effects do not exist in all industries; the size of the experience curve effect can range from tiny (or inconsequential) to large, and it is the analyst's task to appraise how important experience is in cost determination. Two, even where a fairly strong experience curve exists, the cost reduction benefits do not occur automatically—a concerted effort has to be made to capitalize on the cost reduction opportunities.

Three, an overly strong emphasis on driving costs down the experience curve can produce some unwanted strategic consequences. Selecting a strategy based on sustained cost reduction associated with growing experience means putting cost-price-efficiency considerations ahead of differentiation-market-effectiveness considerations. For an "efficiency" or low-cost leadership strategy to succeed, significant numbers of customers must want low price, as opposed to differentiating features (quality, service, product innovation, specialized use). Moreover, once a firm decides to pursue a low-cost leadership strategy, it has to guard against losing its ability to respond to product-technology-customer changes. Strategies based on tight adherence to experience curve effects frequently result in narrow skills-building, rigid task performance, and relatively inflexible facilities and technologies. As a consequence, aggressive attempts to ride down the experience curve rapidly can sometimes entail great difficulty in (1) responding to changes in customer needs and product uses, (2) matching or surpassing the product innovations of rival firms, (3) accommodating major changes in process technology and implementing technological breakthroughs, and (4) initiating these changes to drive the market in new directions.

SOURCES: "Selling Business a Theory of Economics," *Business Week,* September 8, 1973, pp. 85–90; Derek F. Abell and John S. Hammond, *Strategic Market Planning* (Englewood Cliffs, N.J.: Prentice-Hall, 1979), pp. 106–21; Arnaldo C. Hay and Nicolas S. Majluf, *Strategic Management: An Integrative Perspective* (Englewood Cliffs, N.J.: Prentice-Hall, 1984), chap. 6; David A. Aaker, *Developing Business Strategies* (New York: John Wiley & Sons, 1984), chap. 10; and Pankaj Ghemawat, "Building Strategy on the Experience Curve." *Harvard Business Review* 63, no. 2 (March–April 1985), pp. 143–49.

Key Success Factors   Without a real understanding of the basic economic features of an industry, strategists may misjudge the key factors required for success. *Key success factors* in an industry consist of the three or four major determinants of financial and competitive success. Key success factors point to the things a firm must concentrate on doing well, the specific kinds of skills and competences that are needed, and which aspects of which internal operating activities are the most crucial and why. Identification of key success factors, then, is a top-priority consideration in industry analysis. At the very least, a firm's business strategy cannot ignore an industry's key success factors; at the most, key success factors can serve as *the cornerstones* on which business strategy is built. Frequently, competitive advantage is built by concentrating on one (or several) key success factors and performing them in a manner that is superior to rivals.

While it would be nice to be able to generalize about key success factors, the truth is that they vary from industry to industry and even from time to time within the same industry (as industry conditions and driving forces change).[10] And even where two industries may have some of the same kinds of key success factors, the subtleties surrounding each factor can differ greatly as well as can their *relative* role and rank in the overall industry scheme. For instance, the key success factors outlined above for the convenience food store industry differ from the key success factors in many other retailing businesses (such as jewelry, tires, gasoline, or appliances). And the kinds of key success factors in retailing businesses are not like those in manufacturing businesses. In beer, the keys are utilization of brewing capacity, a strong dealer distribution network, and advertising effectiveness. In copying equipment, the keys are product innovation and service; in apparel manufacturing, the keys are fashion design and manufacturing efficiency. In industries with high transportation costs, the keys are plant location and the ability to market plant output within economical shipping distances (regional market share proves far more crucial than national share). Because the subtleties of key success factors vary significantly across industries and across time, this aspect of industry analysis is especially crucial when it comes to evaluating how well an organization's skills and resources match up with the requirements for success in the industry.

Identifying Industrywide Strategic Issues

The last component of industry analysis is identification of strategic issues and problems confronting the industry. Every industry has its own set of issues and problems; these nearly always have a bearing on strategy because of the constant concern about the adequacy of a company's present business strategy in responding to these industry-related problems and issues. The list of strategic issues and problems builds from scanning the industry environment and looking for telltale clues of fundamental change. Generally, the most pertinent issues and problems are a function of:

---

[10] For one approach to identifying key success factors, see Kenichi Ohmae, *The Mind of the Strategist* (New York: Penguin Books, 1983), chap. 3 and pp. 84–85.

- The factors that are causing the industry to become more or less attractive.
- Whether the industry is headed for a shake-out of the weaker firms and what will transpire in the wake of industry consolidation.
- How much the industry landscape is likely to be impacted by such factors as the expected changes in costs, supply conditions, competitive pressures, technology, the entry of new firms, or maneuvering between strategic groups.
- Whether general economic influences (demographic shifts, inflation, unemployment, interest rates, economic growth, foreign trade, taxation policies, and so on) are likely to produce any *unusual* changes or have any special impact on industry conditions, particular firms or strategic groups, and the prevailing key success factors.
- Changes in government legislation, spending programs, and regulatory controls.

Sizing up the seriousness of the industry's problems or issues and evaluating their implications is more an art than a science. Different managers may review the same industry situation and reach different conclusions. Nonetheless, judgmental differences based on solid analysis are better than shooting from the hip and guessing what lies on the road ahead. At the very least, assumptions can be made explicit and the hard-to-call areas explored fully for the various probable scenarios. The different outcomes can be tested for their sensitivity to changes in the underlying assumptions.

One way to get a jump on what issues are likely to emerge is to utilize *environmental scanning* techniques as an early warning detector of "new straws in the wind."[11] *Environmental scanning* is a term used to describe a broad-ranging, mind-stretching effort to monitor and interpret social, political, economic, and technological events in an attempt to spot budding trends and conditions that could eventually have an impact on a firm's operations and strategic plans. Companies that undertake formal environmental scanning on a fairly continuous and comprehensive level include General Electric, AT&T, Coca-Cola, Ford, General Motors, Du Pont, and Shell Oil. Using environmental scanning gives a firm more lead time to adjust its plans and prepare for change.

Drawing Conclusions about Industry Attractiveness

While all of the foregoing analysis serves to deepen understanding of the industry environment, its most important purpose is to develop reasoned conclusions about the relative attractiveness of the overall industry environment, both short term and long term. The factors to be especially alert for in determining industry attractiveness are:

- Market size, growth potential, stage in the life cycle.
- Whether the industry will be favorably or unfavorably impacted by the prevailing driving forces.

---

[11] For an excellent short and direct discussion of the linkage between environmental scanning and industry analysis, see Ian H. Wilson, "Environmental Scanning and Strategic Planning," *Business Environment/Public Policy: 1979 Conference Papers,* (St. Louis: American Assembly of Collegiate Schools of Business, 1980), pp. 159–63.

- Industry structure. (Is the field of participants overcrowded? Is a shake-out coming? Is the industry dominated by a few very strong firms?)
- Potential for the entry or exit of major firms (Low barriers to entry reduce attractiveness to existing firms; the exit of a major firm or several weak firms opens more room for remaining firms.)
- Capital requirements. (The larger the capital requirements the less attractive the industry, at least to capital-short firms or risk-averse firms—unless, of course, the payback period is short and profit prospects are high.)
- The stability/dependability of demand (as affected by seasonality, the business cycle, the volatility of consumer preferences, inroads from substitutes, and the like).
- Regulatory, political, societal, and environmental considerations.
- Technology and innovation factors (patents, proprietary know-how, the potential for break-throughs, the pace of innovation).
- Industrywide opportunities and threats.
- How favorable the industry's price-cost-profit economics are.
- Whether competition is more or less intense than is "normal" in competitive markets.
- The severity of the problems or issues confronting the industry; the degrees of risk and uncertainty; the industry's overall prospects for prosperity and profitability.

Aside from these general industry considerations, it is important to realize that an industry which is relatively unattractive overall can still be very attractive to a particular firm, especially one that is already favorably situated in the industry. Appraising industry attractiveness from the standpoint of a particular firm means looking at the following *additional* aspects:

- The firm's position in the industry (being the recognized leader in an otherwise lackluster industry can still produce good profitability).
- The firm's competitive strength and ability to capitalize on the vulnerabilities of weaker rivals.
- Whether continued participation in this industry adds importantly to the firm's ability to be successful in its other business activities.
- Whether the firm is at least partially insulated from, or else able to defend against, the factors that make the industry as a whole unattractive.

COMPETITIVE SITUATION ANALYSIS

Industry analysis sets the stage for digging deeply into the industry's competitive process—the sources of competitive pressures, how strong those pressures are, what competitors are doing, and what future competitive conditions will be like. Here four areas of inquiry are paramount:

1. What competitive forces exist and how strong are they?
2. What are the relative cost positions of rival firms in the industry?

3. What are the competitive positions and relative strengths of key rivals—what are their strategies, how well are they working, why are some rivals doing better than others, and who has what kind of competitive edge?
4. What moves can key rivals be expected to make next?

This phase of business strategy analysis is important because competitive forces shape strategy and because the strategies of rival firms shape competitive forces. A company in a very attractive industry may fail to earn attractive profits if, beleaguered by competitive pressures, it gets maneuvered into a weak competitive position and has little defense from the attacks of aggressive rivals. Some firms are more profitable than others, regardless of the average profitability of the industry. Thus, a company, in seeking a strategy that will put (or keep) it in an attractive market position, needs to look broadly at the whole competitive environment. A leader will seek to build defenses against competition, and a distressed firm may elect to retreat to market niches where competition is comparatively weak.

The Five Forces Model of Competition: A Key Analytical Tool

Even though each industry has its own particular set of competitive characteristics and "rules of the game," there are enough similarities in the nature of competitive forces from market to market to allow for the use of a common analytical framework. Generally speaking, competition in the marketplace is a function of five competitive forces:

1. The jockeying for position among rival firms that flows from their strategic moves and countermoves to gain competitive advantage.
2. The competitive intrusions and threats from the substitute products of companies in other industries.
3. The potential entry of new competitors.
4. The economic power and bargaining leverage of suppliers.
5. The economic power and bargaining leverage of customers.

The *five forces model* depicted in Figure 3–2 is a welcome ally in putting together a picture of the nature and intensity of competition in an industry—indeed, it is the best single analytical tool for understanding the complexities of how competition works. The model was developed by Professor Michael E. Porter of the Harvard Business School (which explains why Figure 3–2 is often referred to as "the Porter model").[12]

The Competitive Force of Rivalry between Firms
The center ring of the competitive arena is nearly always dominated by the competitive maneuvering of rival firms.[13] Indeed the vigor with which sellers jockey for a stronger market position

---

[12] For a more thorough treatment of "the Porter model" by Porter himself, see his *Competitive Strategy,* chap. 1.

[13] Parts of this section are based on the discussion in Arthur A. Thompson, Jr., "Competition as a Strategic Process," *Antitrust Bulletin* 25, no. 4 (Winter 1980), pp. 777–803. See, also, William A. Cohen, "War in the Marketplace," *Business Horizons* 29, no. 2 (March–April 1986), pp. 10–20.

Figure 3-2   The "Five Forces" Model of Competition

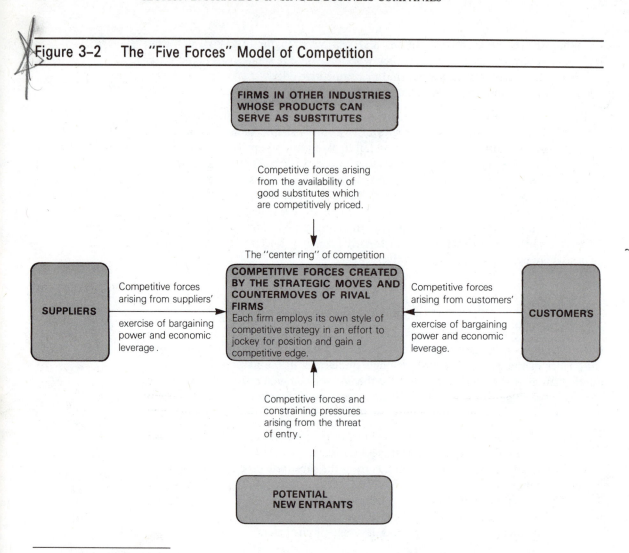

Source: Adapted from Michael E. Porter, "How Competitive Forces Shape Strategy," *Harvard Business Review,* 57, no. 2 (March–April 1979), p. 141.

and a competitive edge over rivals is a solid indicator of the pulse of competition. A firm's *competitive strategy* is the narrower portion of business strategy dealing with its *action plans for achieving market success and, whenever possible, gaining a competitive edge over rival firms.*[14] The motivation of competitors to develop a "win-

---

[14] The distinction between *competitive strategy* and *business strategy* is useful here. As we defined it in Chapter 2, business strategy not only addresses squarely the issue of how to compete but it also embraces all of the functional area support strategies, any other overarching strategic themes for operating the business, and resource allocation within the business. Competitive strategy, however, is narrower in scope and zeroes in on the firm's competitive approach, the competitive edge strived for, and linkages to the industry's key success factors.

ning" competitive strategy results in a competitive interplay with the following characteristics:

1. The competitive strategies which rival firms may devise and the ways they
may seek out new openings to compete are limited only by imagination, by what
will work in the marketplace (i.e., the constraints and reactions of buyers), and by
what is legally permissible (based on antitrust legislation and definitions of "fair competitive practices").

2. Fresh competitive pressures are activated any time one or more competitors
initiates a new "offensive" strategic move to increase sales and profits or launches a
new "defensive" move to protect its established position.

3. How long a firm goes without fine-tuning its strategy or subjecting it to major
overhaul is a function of its market successes (or failures) and the durability of its
competitive approach in withstanding strategic challenges from rival firms. When a
firm realizes that its competitive strategy has been stalemated or defeated by rivals'
strategies, then it is challenged to seek out a better strategy or else be content with
a subpar market position.

4. In considering which of several optional moves to make, there is good reason
for competitors to gravitate toward competitive strategies that are neither easily imi-
tated nor easily thwarted; in this regard, there is advantage in building strategy around
a *distinctive competence* that is hard to copy and also hard to offset. Offering buyers
something that competitors cannot duplicate easily or cheaply gives a firm a market
edge that protects it somewhat from the competitive pressures created by rival firms.

5. As the competitive process unfolds over the long term, active rivalry will result
in firms both *creating* and *responding* to new driving forces, market trends, and
customer preferences. In other words, the competitive strategies of rivals are to a
degree both controlling and controlled by market events and by the sequence of
move and countermoves—*the behavior of rival firms affects the market and the market
affects how rivals behave.*

These characteristics of interfirm rivalry drive how firms "play the game of competition" in the market arena. The real challenge in formulating a winning competitive
strategy, of course, is *how to gain an edge over rivals,* given that the success of any
one firm's strategy hinges in large part on what strategies its rivals employ in conjunction with the resources they are willing and able to invest. The "best" strategy choice
for firm A in its struggle for competitive advantage depends partly (or mostly) on
rivals' competitive strength and choices of strategy; rivals, in turn, may elect to refine
their strategies in light of A's strategic moves.

While many factors influence the strength of rivalry between firms, certain ones
seem to crop up again and again:[15]

1. *Rivalry tends to intensify as the number of competitors increases and as they
become more equal in size and capability.* Up to some point, the greater the number
of competitors the greater the probability for fresh, creative strategic initiatives; in
addition, greater numbers reduce the effects of any one rival's actions on the others,
thereby lessening somewhat the probability of direct retaliation. When rivals are more
equal in size and capability, the chances are better that they will compete on a fairly

---

[15] These indicators of the intensity of interfirm rivalry are based on Porter, "How Competitive Forces Shape Strategy,"
pp. 142–43; and Porter, *Competitive Strategy,* pp. 17–19.

even footing. This feature makes it harder for one or two firms to "win" the competitive battle and then dominate the market on more or less their own terms.

2. *Rivalry is usually stronger when demand for the product is growing slowly.* In a rapidly expanding market, there tends to be enough business to support growth in all competing firms; indeed, it may take all of a firm's financial and managerial resources just to keep abreast of the growth in buyer demand (much less devoting efforts to steal the customers of rivals). But when growth slows, expansion-minded firms and/or firms with excess capacity usually initiate price cuts and thereby ignite a battle for market share that often results in a shake-out of the weak and less efficient firms. The industry "consolidates" to a smaller, but individually stronger, group of sellers. Anytime market share is a key driver of profitability (and maybe even survival) some firms will initiate fresh strategic moves aimed at taking customers away from rivals.

3. *Rivalry is more intense when competitors are tempted by industry conditions to use price cuts or other competitive weapons to boost unit volume.* Whenever fixed costs are high and marginal costs are low, firms are under strong economic pressure to produce at or very near full capacity. Hence, if market demand weakens and capacity utilization declines, rival firms frequently resort to secret price concessions, special discounts, rebates, and other sales-increasing tactics. A similar situation arises when a product is perishable, seasonal, costly, or difficult to store or hold in inventory.

4. *Rivalry is stronger when the products and services of competitors are so weakly differentiated that customers incur low costs in switching from one brand to another.* Product differentiation per se is not a deterrent to competition; indeed, it can enliven rivalry by forcing firms to seek creative new ways of improving their price-quality-service-performance offering. The strategic moves of one firm to differentiate its product may well result in important countermoves from rivals. However, when rivals' products are so strongly differentiated that customers are locked in by the high costs of switching over to a rival brand, competition is weaker because sellers are more insulated from raids on their customers.

5. *Rivalry increases in proportion to the size of the payoff from a successful strategic move.* The greater the potential reward, the more likely some firm will give in to the temptation of a particular strategic move. How big the strategic payoff is varies partly with the speed of retaliation. When competitors can be expected to respond slowly (or maybe even not at all), the initiator of a fresh competitive strategy can reap the benefits in the intervening period and perhaps gain a first-mover advantage which is not easily surmounted. The greater the benefits of moving first, the more likely that some firm will accept the risk of making the first move and the consequences of eventual retaliation.

6. *Rivalry tends to be more vigorous when it costs more to get out of a business than to stay in and compete.* The higher the exit barriers (and thus the more costly it is to abandon a market), the stronger the incentive for firms to remain and compete as best they can, even though they may be earning low profits or even incurring a loss.

7. *Rivalry becomes more volatile and unpredictable the more diverse competitors are in terms of their strategies, personalities, corporate priorities, resources, and countries of origin.* A diverse range of views and approaches enhances the probability that

one or more firms will behave as "mavericks" and employ strategies that produce more competitive interplay than would otherwise occur.

8. *Rivalry is increased when strong companies outside the industry acquire weak firms in the industry and launch aggressive, well-funded moves to transform the newly acquired competitor into a major market contender.* A classic example of this occurred when Philip Morris, a leading cigarette firm with excellent marketing know-how, shook up the whole beer industry's approach to marketing by its acquisition of stodgy Miller Brewing Company in the late 1960s. In short order, Philip Morris revamped the marketing of Miller High Life and pushed it to become the number two best-selling brand; Philip Morris also pioneered low-calorie beer with the introduction of Miller Lite, a move which made light beer the fastest growing segment in the beer industry.

In assessing the nature and strength of the interfirm rivalry between sellers, the important understanding is that fresh strategic moves are likely from time to time and that these moves will stir competitive pressures. Because the jockeying for position among competitors can assume many forms and levels of intensity, it is the strategist's job to identify what the current weapons of competitive rivalry are and to size up how strong the forces of rivalry between competing firms are.

The Competitive Force of Potential Entry   New entrants to a market bring new production capacity, the desire to establish a secure place in the market, and sometimes substantial resources with which to compete.[16] Just how serious the competitive threat of entry is into a particular market depends on two classes of factors: *barriers to entry* and the *expected reaction of firms to new entry.* A barrier to entry exists whenever it is hard for a newcomer to break into the market and/or if the economics of the business puts a potential entrant at a price/cost disadvantage compared to its competitors. There are several major sources of entry barriers:[17]

1. *Economies of scale.*   The presence of important scale economies deters entry because the potential entrant is forced to enter the market on a large-scale basis (a costly and perhaps risky move) or accept a cost disadvantage (and lower profitability). Large-scale entry could result in chronic overcapacity in the industry, and it could threaten the market shares of existing firms that they are pushed into aggressive competitive retaliation (in the form of price cuts, increased advertising and sales promotion, and similar such steps) to maintain their position. Either way, the entrant's outlook is for lower profits. Scale-related barriers may be encountered in advertising, marketing and distribution, financing, after-sale customer service, raw materials purchasing, and R&D, as well as in production.

2. *The existence of learning and experience curve effects.*   When achieving lower unit costs is partly or mostly a function of experience in producing the product and other learning curve benefits, a new entrant is put at a disadvantage in competing with older, established firms with more accumulated know-how (see Illustration Capsule 10 for more details).

3. *Brand preferences and customer loyalty.*   When the products of rival sellers

---

[16] Porter, "How Competitive Forces Shape Strategy," p. 138.

[17] Porter, *Competitive Strategy,* pp. 7–17.

are differentiated, buyers usually have some degree of attachment to existing brands. A potential entrant must therefore be prepared to spend enough money on advertising and sales promotion to overcome customer loyalties and build its own clientele; substantial time, as well as money, can be involved. A new entrant may have to budget more funds for marketing than existing firms, which gives existing firms a cost advantage. In addition, the capital invested in establishing a new brand (unlike the capital invested in facilities and equipment) has no resale or recoverable value, which makes such expenditures a riskier "investment." Product differentiation can be costly to buyers who switch brands, in which case the new entrant must persuade buyers that the changeover or switching costs are worth incurring. This may require lower prices, better quality, better service, or better performance features (which may result in lower expected profit margins for new entrants—a significant barrier for start-up companies dependent on sizable, early profits to support their new investments).

4. *Capital requirements*.   The larger the total dollar investment needed to enter the market successfully, the more limited is the pool of potential entrants. The most obvious capital requirements are associated with manufacturing plant and equipment, working capital to finance inventories and customer credit, introductory advertising and sales promotion to establish a clientele, and covering start-up losses.

5. *Cost disadvantages independent of size*.   Existing firms may enjoy cost advantages not available to potential entrants, regardless of the entrant's size. The most typical sources of cost advantage include access to the best and cheapest raw materials, possession of patents and proprietary technology, the benefits of any learning and experience curve effects, acquisition of fixed assets at preinflation prices, favorable locations, and lower-cost access to financial capital due to a strong income statement and balance sheet.

6. *Access to distribution channels*.   When a product is distributed through established market channels, a potential entrant may face the barrier of gaining adequate distribution access. Some distributors may be reluctant to take on a product that lacks buyer recognition. The more limited the number of wholesale and retail outlets and the more that existing producers have these tied up, the tougher entry will be. To overcome this barrier potential entrants may have to lure distribution access by offering better margins to dealers and distributors or by giving advertising allowances and other promotional incentives. As a result, the potential entrant's profits may be squeezed until its product gains such good market acceptance that distributors and retailers want to carry it because of its popularity.

7. *Government actions and policies*.   Government agencies can limit or even bar entry by instituting controls over licenses and permits. Regulated industries such as trucking, radio and television stations, liquor retailing, and railroads all feature government-controlled entry. Entry can also be restricted, and certainly made more expensive, by stringent government-mandated safety regulations and environmental pollution standards.

Even if a potential entrant is willing to tackle the problems of entry barriers, it may be dissuaded by its expectations about how existing firms will react to new entry.[18] Will incumbent firms "move over" grudgingly and let the new entrant take

---

[18] Porter, "How Competitive Forces Shape Strategy," p. 140.

a viable share of the market, or will they launch a vigorous, "survival-of-the-fittest" defense of their market positions—including prices cuts, increased advertising, new product improvements, and whatever else is calculated to hinder the success of a new entrant as well as other rivals. A firm is likely to have second thoughts about entry:

- When incumbent firms have previously been aggressive in defending their market positions against entry.
- When incumbent firms have substantial financial resources for defense against new entry.
- When incumbent firms are in a position to use leverage with distributors and customers to keep their business.
- When incumbent firms are able and willing to cut prices to preserve their market shares.
- When product demand is expanding slowly, thus limiting the market's ability to absorb and accommodate the new entrant without adversely affecting the profit performance of all the participant firms.
- When it is more costly for existing firms to leave the market than to fight to the death, because the costs of exit are very high, owing to heavy investment in specialized technology and equipment, union agreements that contain high severance costs, or important shared relationships with other products.

One additional point needs to be made about the threat of entry as a competitive force: Entry barriers can rise or fall as economic and market conditions change. For example, the expiration of a key patent can greatly increase the threat of entry. New technological discovery can create a big scale economy where none existed before. New actions by incumbent firms to increase advertising, strengthen distributor-dealer relations, accelerate R&D, or improve product quality can erect higher road-blocks to entry.

The Competitive Force of Substitute Products   Firms in one industry are quite often in close competition with firms in another industry because their respective products are good substitutes. Soft-drink producers are in competition with the sellers of fruit juices, milk, coffee, tea, powdered-mix drinks, and perhaps some alcoholic beverages (wine and beer). The producers of wood stoves are in competition with the producers of kerosene heaters and portable electric heaters. Sugar producers are in competition with firms that produce artificial sweeteners. The producers of plastic containers are in competition with the makers of glass bottles and jars, the manufacturers of paperboard cartons, and the producers of tin and aluminum cans. The producers of rival brands of aspirin are in competition with the makers of other pain relievers and headache remedies.

The competitive force of closely related substitute products impacts sellers in several ways. First, the price and availability of acceptable substitutes for product X places a ceiling on the prices which the producers of product X can charge; at the same time, the ceiling price places a limit on the profit potential for product X.[19] Second,

---

[19] Ibid., p. 142.

unless the sellers of product X can upgrade quality, reduce prices via cost reduction, or otherwise differentiate their product from its substitutes, they risk a low growth rate in sales and profits because of the inroads substitutes may make. The more sensitive the sales of X are to changes in the prices of substitutes, the stronger is the competitive influence of the substitutes.

Third, the competition from substitutes is affected by the ease with which buyers can change over to a substitute. A key consideration is usually the buyer's *switching costs*—the one-time costs facing the buyer in switching from use of X over to a substitute for X.[20] Typical switching costs include employee retraining, the costs to purchase additional equipment that will also be needed, payments for technical help in making the changeover, time and money spent testing the quality and reliability of the substitute, and the psychological costs of severing old supplier relationships and establishing new ones. If buyers' switching costs are high, then the sellers of substitutes must offer a major cost or performance benefit in order to attract users away from X. If switching costs are low, it is easier for sellers of substitutes to overcome the barrier of convincing buyers to change over from X to their product.

As a rule, then, the lower the price of substitutes, the higher their quality and performance, and the lower the user's switching costs, the more intense are the competitive pressures posed by substitute products. One very telling indicator of the strength of competitive pressures emanating from the producers of substitutes is their growth rate in sales; other indicators are their plans for expansion of capacity and the profits they are earning.

The Economic Power of Suppliers
The competitive impact suppliers can have on an industry is chiefly a function of how significant the input they supply is to the buyer.[21] When the input of a particular group of suppliers makes up a sizable proportion of total costs, is crucial to the buyer's production process, or significantly affects the quality of the industry's product, then the *potential* bargaining power and influence of suppliers over firms in the buying industry is enhanced. The extent to which this potential impact is realized depends on a number of factors; in general, a group of supplier firms has more bargaining power:

- When the input is, in one way or another, important to the buyer.
- When the supplier industry is dominated by a few large producers who enjoy reasonably secure market positions and who are not beleaguered by intensely competitive conditions.
- When suppliers' respective products are differentiated to such an extent that it is difficult or costly for buyers to switch from one supplier to another.
- When the buying firms are *not* important customers of the suppliers; in such instances, suppliers are not constrained by the fact that their own well-being is tied to the industry they are supplying. They have no overriding incentive to protect the customer industry via reasonable prices, improved quality, or new products which might well enhance the buying industry's sales and profits.
- When the suppliers of an input do *not* have to compete with the substitute inputs

---

[20] Porter, *Competitive Strategy,* p. 10.
[21] Porter, *Competitive Strategy,* pp. 27–28.

of suppliers in other industries. (For instance, the power of the suppliers of glass bottles to the soft drink bottlers is checked by the ability of the soft drink firms to use aluminum cans and plastic bottles.)

- When one or more suppliers pose a credible threat of forward integration into the business of the buyer industry (attracted, perhaps, by the prospect of higher profits than it can earn in its own market).
- When the buying firms display no inclination toward backward integration into the suppliers' business.

The power of suppliers can be an important economic factor in the marketplace because of the impact they can have on their customers' profits. Powerful suppliers can squeeze the profits of a customer industry via price increases which the latter is unable to pass on fully to the buyers of its own products. An industry's suppliers can also jeopardize industry profits through reductions in the quality of materials they supply. For example, if semiconductor manufacturers supply lower-quality components to the makers of hand-held calculators, they can increase the warranty and defective goods costs of the calculator firms so that the latter's profits and reputation are seriously impaired.

The Economic Power of Customers

Just as powerful suppliers can exert a competitive influence over an industry, so also can powerful customers.[22] The leverage and bargaining power of customers tends to be relatively greater:

- When customers are few in number and when they purchase in large quantities. Large customer groups often have success using their volume-buying leverage to obtain important price concessions and other favorable terms and conditions of sale.
- When customers' purchases represent a sizable percentage of the selling industry's total sales (the actions of the very biggest customers usually carry a lot of clout; and the bigger customers are, the more clout they have in negotiating with sellers).
- When the supplying industry is comprised of large numbers of relatively small sellers (a few big buyers are often able to dominate a group of smaller suppliers).
- When the item being purchased is sufficiently standardized among sellers that customers can not only find alternative sellers but they can also switch suppliers at virtually zero cost.
- When customers pose a credible threat of backward integration, attracted by the prospects of earning greater profits or by the benefits of reliable prices and delivery.
- When sellers pose little threat of forward integration into the product market of their customers.
- When the item being bought is *not* an important input.
- When it is economically feasible for customers to purchase the input from several suppliers rather than one.
- When the product or service being bought does not save the customer money.

A firm can enhance its profitability and market standing by seeking out customers who are in a comparatively weak position to exercise adverse power. Rarely are all

---

[22] Porter, *Competitive Strategy*, pp. 24–27.

buyer groups in a position to exercise equal degrees of bargaining power, and some may be less sensitive to price, quality, or service than others. An example is the automobile tire industry, where the major tire manufacturers on the one hand confront very significant customer power in selling original equipment tires to the automobile manufacturers and on the other hand find themselves in a position to get much better prices selling replacement tires to individual car owners through their own retail dealer networks.

The Strategic Implications of the Five Competitive Forces

The unique analytical contribution of Figure 3–2 (see p. 80) is the systematic way it exposes the makeup of competitive forces. *Analysis of the competitive environment requires that the strength of each one of the five competitive forces be assessed.* The collective impact of these forces determines what competition is like in a given market and, ultimately, the profits that industry participants will be able to earn. As a rule, the collective profitability of participant firms decreases as the competition intensifies. From a business perspective, the sternest and most brutally competitive condition occurs when the five forces combine to create pressures so severe that the industry outlook is for prolonged subpar profitability or even losses for most or all firms. On the other hand, when an industry offers the prospect of superior long-term profit performance, it can be inferred that competitive forces are not unduly strong and that the competitive structure of the industry is "favorable" and "attractive."

In coping with the five competitive forces, it makes sense for a firm to search out a market position and competitive approach that will (1) insulate it as much as possible from the forces of competition, (2) influence the industry's competitive rules in its favor, and (3) give it a strong position from which to "play the game" of competition as it unfolds in the industry. Doing this requires analysis-based judgments about what the competitive pressures are and will be, where they are coming from, and how they can be defended against or otherwise lived with.

Strategic Cost Analysis and Activity-Cost Chains: Tools for Assessing Relative Cost Positions

Along with an assessment of competitive forces must come an assessment of the *relative cost positions* of firms in the industry (if not every firm, then certainly how one's own firm stacks up against key rivals). Competitors do not necessarily, or even usually, incur the same costs in supplying their products to end-users. The disparities in costs among rival producers can stem from:

- Differences in the prices paid for raw materials, component parts, energy, and other items purchased from suppliers.
- Differences in basic technology and the age of plants and equipment. Because rival companies have usually invested in plants and key pieces of equipment at different points in time, they enter into competition with facilities having somewhat different technological efficiencies and different fixed costs. Older facilities built when technology was less developed are typically less efficient, but because they

were constructed in times when it took less money to put them in place, they *may* still be reasonably cost competitive with modern facilities costing more to build. Whether older plants with lower fixed investment costs are, on balance, as cost efficient as newer plants having higher fixed investment costs depends on the trade-off between the lower depreciation and other fixed costs of older plants and the increased operating efficiency of newer plants.

- Differences in internal operating costs due to the economies of scale associated with different size plants, learning and experience curve effects, different wage rates, different productivity levels, different administrative overhead expenses, different tax rates, and the like.
- Differences in rival firms' exposure to rates of inflation and changes in foreign exchange rates (as can occur in global industries where competitors have plants located in different nations).
- Differences in marketing costs, sales and promotion expenditures, and advertising expenses.
- Differences in inbound transportation costs and outbound shipping costs.
- Differences in forward channel distribution costs (the costs and markups of distributors, wholesalers, and retailers in getting the product to end-users).

Plainly enough, for a company to be competitively successful, its costs must be "in line with" those of rival producers, after taking into account, of course, that product differentiation creates justification for some cost differences. The need to be cost competitive is not so stringent as to *require* the costs of every firm in the industry to be *equal;* but, as a rule, the more a firm's costs are above those of the low-cost producers the more vulnerable its market position becomes. With the numerous opportunities for cost disparities among competing companies, it is important for firms to know how their costs compare with rivals' costs and how they can remain cost competitive over the long term. This is where *strategic cost analysis* comes in.

Strategic cost analysis focuses on a firm's relative cost position vis-à-vis its rivals. The primary analytical tool of strategic cost analysis is a completely integrated *activity-cost chain* showing the makeup of costs all the way from purchase of raw materials to the end price paid by customers.[23] The activity-cost chain thus goes beyond a producer's own internal cost structure and includes the buildup of cost (and thus the "value added") at each stage in the whole industry chain of producing the product and distributing it to final users, as shown in Figure 3–3. Construction of an integrated activity-cost chain is especially revealing to a manufacturing firm because its overall ability to furnish end-users with its product at a competitive price can easily depend on cost factors originating either *backward* in the suppliers' portion of the activity-cost chain or *forward* in the distribution channel portion of the chain.

The task of constructing a complete cost chain is not easy. It requires breaking a firm's own historical cost accounting data out into several principal cost categories and also developing cost estimates for the backward and forward channel portions of getting the product to the end-user as well. In addition, it requires estimating

---

[23] The ins and outs of strategic cost analysis are discussed in greater length in Michael E. Porter, *Competitive Advantage,* (New York: Free Press, 1985), chap. 2. What follows is a distilled adaption of the approach pioneered by Porter.

Figure 3-3

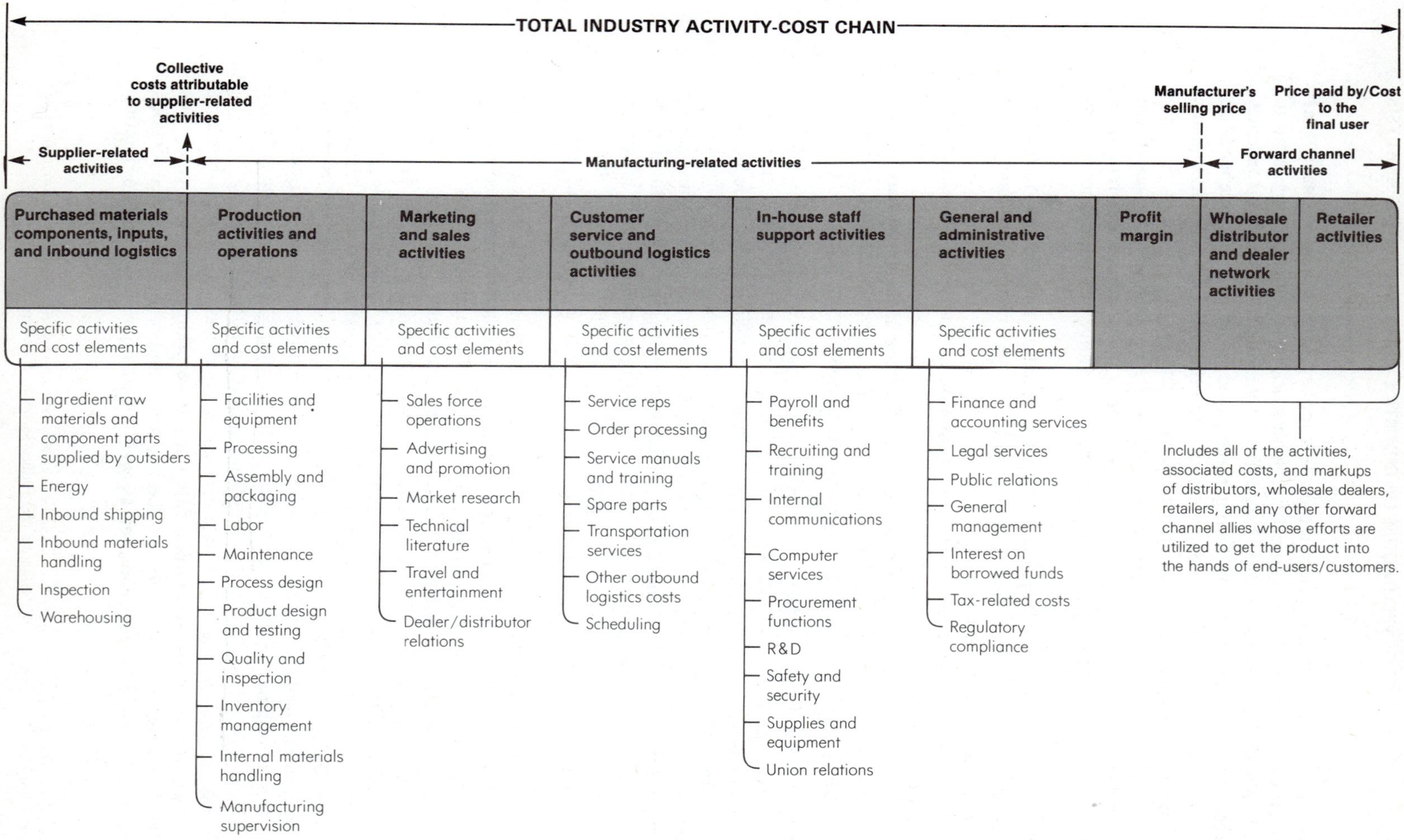

TOTAL INDUSTRY ACTIVITY-COST CHAIN

Supplier-related activities ← Collective costs attributable to supplier-related activities → Manufacturing-related activities

Manufacturer's selling price | Profit margin | Price paid by/Cost to the final user

Forward channel activities

Purchased materials, components, inputs, and inbound logistics	Production activities and operations	Marketing and sales activities	Customer service and outbound logistics activities	In-house staff support activities	General and administrative activities	Profit margin	Wholesale distributor and dealer network activities	Retailer activities

Specific activities and cost elements

Purchased materials, components, inputs, and inbound logistics
- Ingredient raw materials and component parts supplied by outsiders
- Energy
- Inbound shipping
- Inbound materials handling
- Inspection
- Warehousing

Production activities and operations
- Facilities and equipment
- Processing
- Assembly and packaging
- Labor
- Maintenance
- Process design
- Product design and testing
- Quality and inspection
- Inventory management
- Internal materials handling
- Manufacturing supervision

Marketing and sales activities
- Sales force operations
- Advertising and promotion
- Market research
- Technical literature
- Travel and entertainment
- Dealer/distributor relations

Customer service and outbound logistics activities
- Service reps
- Order processing
- Service manuals and training
- Spare parts
- Transportation services
- Other outbound logistics costs
- Scheduling

In-house staff support activities
- Payroll and benefits
- Recruiting and training
- Internal communications
- Computer services
- Procurement functions
- R&D
- Safety and security
- Supplies and equipment
- Union relations

General and administrative activities
- Finance and accounting services
- Legal services
- Public relations
- General management
- Interest on borrowed funds
- Tax-related costs
- Regulatory compliance

Forward channel activities: Includes all of the activities, associated costs, and markups of distributors, wholesale dealers, retailers, and any other forward channel allies whose efforts are utilized to get the product into the hands of end-users/customers.

the same cost elements for rival firms and estimating their cost chains—an advanced art in competitive intelligence in itself. But despite the tedious nature of the task and the imprecision of some of the estimates, the payoff in exposing the cost competitiveness of one's position and the attendant strategic alternatives makes it a valuable analytical tool. Illustration Capsule 11 shows a simplified activity-cost chain comparison of the cost competitiveness of U.S. steel producers and Japanese steel producers over a 20-year period. The shifts in several cost components over the period are dramatic. Some resulted from relative shifts in input prices which built up gradually over time, but technological changes in input requirements and labor productivity were also at work.

While the example in Illustration Capsule 11 shows the relative cost positions of firms in one country versus those in another, the most important application of the activity-cost technique is to expose how a particular firm's cost position compares with those of its rivals. Thus, the relevant level at which to develop cost estimates is usually a single line of business for a given firm and not for an industry or group of firms. Plainly, the makeup of each firm's overall activity-cost chain is unique and can vary from item to item in the product line, from customer group to customer group (if different distribution channels are used), and from plant to plant (if plants employ different technologies or are located in widely different geographic locations—different countries, for example). Once a firm has constructed combined cost chains for itself and its major competitors, it is in position to diagnose the degree to which it is cost competitive.

Looking again at Figure 3–3, observe that there are three main areas in the cost chain where important differences in the *relative* costs of competing firms can occur: (1) in the suppliers' part of the cost chain; (2) in the firm's own respective activity segments; or (3) in the forward channel portion of the chain. When a firm's cost disadvantage lies principally in the backward end of the activity-cost chain, there are five strategic options for moving towards cost parity:

- Negotiate more favorable prices with suppliers.
- Integrate backward to gain more control over material costs.
- Try to use lower-priced substitute inputs.
- Search out sources of savings in inbound shipping and materials logistics costs.
- Try to make up the difference by initiating cost savings elsewhere in the overall cost chain.

When a firm's cost disadvantage occurs in the forward end of the cost chain, there are three corrective options:

- Push for more favorable terms with distributors and other forward channel allies.
- Change to a more economical distribution strategy, including the possibility of forward integration.
- Try to make up the difference by initiating cost savings earlier in the cost chain.

When the source of relative cost disadvantage is internal, five options for restoring cost parity emerge:

- Initiate internal cost-saving measures.
- Invest in cost-saving technological improvements.

Activity-Cost Chains for U.S. Steel Producers versus Japanese Steel Producers, 1956 and 1976

Cost Chain Elements	Per Ton Cost for Cold-Rolled Sheet Steel, 1956		Net Cost Advantage 1956	ACTIVITIES	Net Cost Advantage 1976	Per Ton Cost for Cold-Rolled Sheet Steel, 1976		Cost Chain Elements
	Typical U.S. Producer	Typical Japanese Producer				Typical U.S. Producer	Typical Japanese Producer	
Coking coal	$ 12.02	$ 19.90	$ 7.88 (U.S.)		$10.70 (Japan)	$ 52.15	$ 41.45	Coking coal
Other energy	9.65	12.35	2.70 (U.S.)	Purchased inputs and basic materials	8.76 (Japan)	30.25	21.49	Other energy
Scrap steel	17.80	34.75	16.95 (U.S.)		.95 (U.S.)	20.80	21.75	Scrap steel
Iron ore	16.70	26.17	9.47 (U.S.)		20.30 (Japan)	47.90	27.60	Iron ore
Subtotal	$ 56.17	$ 93.17	$37.00 (U.S.)		$38.81 (Japan)	$151.10	$112.29	Subtotal
Manufacturing labor	$ 54.07	$ 28.80	$25.27 (Japan)		$90.66 (Japan)	$142.93	$ 52.25	Manufacturing labor
Capital charges for facilities and all other operating costs	9.80	31.17	21.37 (U.S.)	Manufacturing operations and administrative support	7.93 (U.S.)	55.95	63.88	Capital charges for facilities and all other operating costs
Profit margin	5.00	4.00	1.00 (Japan)		1.40 (Japan)	4.90	3.50	Profit margin
Subtotal	$ 68.87	$ 63.97	$ 4.90 (Japan)		$84.15 (Japan)	$203.78	$119.63	Subtotal
Transocean shipping Import duties	0	$ 35.69	$35.69 (U.S.)	Distribution and forward channel activities	$36.36 (U.S.)	0	$ 36.36	Transocean shipping Import duties
Price paid by U.S. end-user	$125.04	$192.83	$67.79 (U.S.)		$86.60 (Japan)	$354.88	$268.28	Price paid by U.S. end-user

SOURCES: Compiled by the author from data in U.S. Federal Trade Commission, The United States Steel Industry and Its International Rivals: Trends and Factors Determining International Competitiveness (Washington, D.C.: U.S. Government Printing Office, 1978); and Robert W. Crandall, The U.S. Steel Industry in Recurrent Crisis (Washington, D.C.: Brookings Institution, 1981).

- Innovate around the troublesome cost components as new investments are made in plant and equipment.
- Redesign the product to achieve cost reductions.
- Try to make up the internal cost disadvantage by achieving cost savings in the backward and forward portions of the cost chain.

The construction of activity-cost chains is a valuable component of competitive diagnosis because it reveals a firm's overall cost competitiveness and the relative cost positions of firms in the industry. Examining the makeup of one's own activity-cost chain and comparing it to the chains of important rival firms indicates who has how much of a cost advantage or disadvantage vis-à-vis major competitors and pinpoints which components in the cost chain are the source of the cost advantage or disadvantage. Strategic cost analysis adds much to the picture of the competitive environment, particularly regarding who the low-cost producers are, who is in the best position to compete on the basis of price, and who may be vulnerable to attack because of a poor relative cost position.

Competitor Analysis

Competitor analysis is important for two reasons. First, good strategy cannot be formulated in a competitive vacuum; without perceptive understanding of rivals' strategies, the would-be strategist is "flying blind." It is foolish to expect to outmaneuver market rivals without knowing a good bit about what strategies close rivals are using, why some rivals have been more successful in the marketplace than others, and what moves which rival firms are likely to make next. Second, because rivals' strategies are highly interdependent (the strategic moves of one rival directly impact the others and may prompt counterstrategies), the positions and success of competitors have direct relevance to choosing one's own best strategy.

As a way of profiling the positions and strategies of rivals, consider that there are at least three approaches a firm can pursue with respect to *market share.*

- Grow and build, with a commitment to invest in new capacity as needed (capture a bigger market share by growing faster than the industry as a whole)
- Hold and maintain (protect market share, grow at a rate equal to the industry average)
- Surrender share, with or without a strong fight (maybe in preparation for later withdrawal from the market).

There are at least six different postures a firm can take insofar as its overall *market position* objective is concerned:

- Seek to be a dominant leader (have the biggest market share, have the best-known name and industry reputation, and be the acknowledged front-runner).
- Seek to be one of the industry leaders (in the top five, for example).
- Be a follower, content with a middle-of-the-pack position.
- Be resigned to a position as an also-ran, fringe firm (because doing much better is not realistic, given the firm's skills and resources).
- Make a major move to move up a notch or two in market standing (an overhaul

and reposition approach) because management sees a need and an opportunity to break out of an underdog status or trailing position.
- Play the role of an aggressive newcomer (for firms that have just entered the industry and need to establish an image and reputation).

When it comes to the issue of "how to compete," there are three generic types of *competitive strategies:* [24]

- Striving to be the low-cost producer (a *cost leadership strategy*).
- Seeking to differentiate one's product offering in one way or another from the offerings of rivals (a *differentiation strategy*).
- Concentrating on catering to a narrower group of buyers and a limited part of the market rather than going after the whole market with a "something-for-every-one" approach (a *focus strategy*).

In doing competitor analysis, one needs to watch for:

- How many firms are following each strategic approach, and what degree of success each approach is enjoying.
- The different impacts the driving forces of competition have on each strategic approach and any differences in competitive intensity among strategic groups.
- The skills and organizational requirements needed to execute each basic type of strategy being followed.
- The relative market shares and competitive strength of the group of firms employing each different type of strategy.

Doing a thorough job of diagnosing what competitors are up to and predicting what moves they may make next has five aspects: (1) assessing whether the rival is under pressure to improve performance; (2) listening to what the rival's managers are saying about what they think is going to happen in the industry and what these managers think it will take to be successful, (3) examining the rival's current competitive strategy and how well it is working, (4) studying the backgrounds and experiences of the rival's managers for clues about what moves they may be inclined to make, and (5) appraising the competitive capabilities of close rivals (their strengths and weaknesses, what they can and can't do).[25]

A Rival's Priorities and Performance Objectives   Doing the detective work to discover how a competitor's current performance compares with its target performance objectives has several payoffs. It can reveal whether the rival is satisfied with its current performance and thus its current strategy. It can aid in assessing both the likelihood of a shift in strategy and the vigor with which the rival might respond to new driving forces or strategic moves by other competitors. Some particulars to be alert for include:

---

[24] Porter, *Competitive Strategy*, chap. 2.

[25] The following discussion of these five aspects of competitor analysis is based on Porter, *Competitive Strategy*, chap. 3. See, also, Michael E. Porter and Victor Miller, "How Information Gives You Competitive Advantage," *Harvard Business Review* 63, no. 4 (July–August, 1985), pp. 149–60.

1. Is the rival's financial performance satisfactory or is it in trouble? Is it trying to achieve some important new market objective? Does it aspire to industry leadership in pricing, technological proficiency, market share, product quality, or some other aspect?
2. Is the competitor a subsidiary of a larger corporate parent? If so, is the subsidiary under pressure to contribute more in terms of profitability, growth, and cash flow? Does the parent view this industry as one of its main strategic interests (in which case it will fight hard to protect or improve its position) or is it comparatively unimportant? To what extent does the parent give its subsidiary financial support?
3. Can the rival meet its profit objective and other performance objectives without doing anything different or without launching a major strategic offensive? Can the rival afford to be happy or content with its current performance?

The Rival's Beliefs about the Industry and Competitive Success   Every firm's management operates on assumptions and beliefs about the industry and about how the business ought to be run. How a firm sees itself and its situation is often a good barometer of its strategic thinking. The relevant areas to probe here include: What do the rival's managers believe (based on speeches, advertising claims, representations by its sales force to customers, and so on) about their firm's standing in the marketplace? Is the rival's reputation tightly identified with some competitive aspect (superior service, quality of manufacture, product innovation, breadth of product line, or focus on particular products or market segments) and, if so, will it fight to keep its reputation intact? What are the rival's managers saying about industry trends and future competitive conditions? What views do they have about the strengths and weaknesses of other firms in the industry? Do they use certain consultants, advertising agencies, banks, or other advisers that are known for particular techniques and approaches?

The Rival's Current Strategy   Assessments of a rival firm's competitive strategy should include the following: What generic competitive strategy is the rival pursuing (cost leadership, differentiation, or focus)? What competitive advantage, if any, does the rival have and how strong is it? Is the rival considered to be a leader or a follower in some respect? Does the rival have any distinctive competences? Where is the rival strongest or weakest in products, customer groups, and geographic market penetration? What is the rival doing in terms of R&D, advertising, sales effort, and pricing? Is the rival gaining or losing ground in the marketplace and why? Is it locked into its present competitive approach because of facilities commitments or some other factor? Does it have much strategic flexibility?

The Backgrounds, Experiences, and Styles of the Rival's Senior Managers   Sometimes important clues about the behavior and strategies of a firm can be gleaned from the personal experiences, philosophies, and styles of its senior-level managers; while the information may be hard to acquire, it is worth the effort. The most important areas of inquiry include:

1. What are the work backgrounds of the key managers (accounting, finance, sales, production, R&D), and how likely is it that they lean toward strategies which emphasize their own areas of expertise and experience?

2. Has the firm's current chief executive held the position for a long time (which may suggest continuation of the same basic strategy), or have new senior-level managers come recently from outside the company (which may suggest some changes can be expected)? Is the firm known for selecting managers with a certain track record or managerial philosophy?

3. Is there reason to believe that the actions decided upon by rival managers will be conditioned by some previous major event in their background or experience (a sharp recession, having managed a rapid growth business, a traumatic plant closing, a severe strike, or a near bankruptcy)?

A Rival's Ability to Compete Effectively

One of the things that matters most about a rival is the competitive edge it may have and its capacity for competing effectively in the marketplace. Its strengths and weaknesses regarding product line, marketing and selling, dealer distribution network, R&D, engineering, manufacturing, cost and efficiency, financial condition, and managerial competence determine its ability to respond to competitive moves or to deal with industry driving forces. In assessing a rival's competitive advantages and overall strength, attention has to be paid to what it does best and worst, what flexibility it has to adapt to a change in competitive conditions, and why it is doing better or worse than other rivals. Most important, though, is an appraisal of the degree to which it is likely to be a major factor in the marketplace over the long haul and why its market standing is likely to increase or decrease.

Predicting a Competitor's Next Moves—The Payoff of Competitor Analysis

Gaining useful answers to the kinds of questions and issues posed above is not a simple, short-run task. Compiling a profile of a rival's true competitive strength is a task where the relevant information comes in bits and pieces, and it takes both time and hard work to get a real "feel" for both a competitor's situation and how its management thinks. But if the task is done systematically, the result can be a good ability to predict:

- How a rival will respond to changes in market trends or economic conditions.
- How satisfied a rival is with its present market position and profitability, and thus whether it is likely to initiate a fresh strategic move.
- The most likely moves a rival will make, given its strategic objectives, its management approach, and its competitive strengths and weaknesses.
- How vulnerable a rival is to new strategic moves by other industry participants.
- How much a rival can be pushed before it will be provoked into retaliation.
- The meaning and intent of a rival's new strategic move and how seriously it should be taken.

Such predictive ability is immensely valuable in drawing conclusions about what the future weapons of competition will be, who is vulnerable to attack and who is not, a rival's probable next move, and one's own best time, place, and method for "fighting it out" with competitors.

SELF-ANALYSIS: A FIRM'S OWN SITUATION AND COMPETITIVE STRENGTH

The business-level strategist's task is to construct a strategy that has the best "goodness of fit" between the external industry-competitive environment and the firm's own internal situation. The previous two sections covered how to size up the industry environment and the competitive environment. This section shifts the spotlight to the strategy-shaping aspects of a firm's own competitive capability and overall position. Four self-analysis elements are involved:

1. How well the firm's own present strategy is working and how well it seems to match the anticipated industry and competitive environment.
2. An appraisal of the firm's internal strengths and weaknesses, the availability of external market opportunities, and the strategic threats it faces.
3. An assessment of the firm's competitive position and competitive strength (probing especially into reasons why the firm is gaining ground, losing ground, or holding its own) and how the firm matches up against rivals on each of the industry's key success factors.
4. Any special strategic issues and problems unique to the firm and its business.

How Good the Present Strategy Looks *(a on handout)*

The indicators of how well a firm's present strategy is working include (1) whether the firm's market share is rising or falling, (2) the size of the firm's profit margins in relation to other firms, (3) trends in the firm's net profits and its return on investment, (4) whether the firm's sales are growing faster or slower than the market, and (5) whether the firm's competitive position is improving or slipping. The signs of strategic success or failure are fairly easy to spot. What is usually not so obvious is how well the present strategy is matched to the expected future industry and competitive environment. There are several things to consider:

*   Whether the present strategy is responsive to the industry's driving forces and the strategic issues confronting the industry.
*   How closely the present strategy is geared to the industry's *future* key success factors.
*   How good a defense the present strategy offers against the five competitive forces (the future ones, not the past ones).
*   Whether the firm's functional area support strategies appear adequate for the road ahead.

While these inquiries open the door of self-analysis, a broader and deeper probe into the firm's situation is needed.

The SWOT Analysis

SWOT is an acronym for a firm's internal *Strengths* and *Weaknesses* and its external *Opportunities* and *Threats.* A SWOT analysis consists of a candid appraisal of a

---

Figure 3–4   The SWOT Analysis—a Checklist of What to Look For

Potential Internal Strengths

A distinctive competence?
Adequate financial resources?
Good competitive skills?
Well thought of by buyers?
An acknowledged market leader?
Well-conceived functional area strategies?
Access to economies of scale?
Insulated (at least somewhat) from strong
    competitive pressures?
Proprietary technology?
Cost advantages?
Competitive advantages?
Product innovation abilities?
Proven management?
Ahead on experience curve?
Other?

Potential Internal Weaknesses

No clear strategic direction?
A deteriorating competitive position?
Obsolete facilities?
Subpar profitability because . . . ?
Lack of managerial depth and talent?
Missing any key skills or competences?
Poor track record in implementing strategy?
Plagued with internal operating problems?
Vulnerable to competitive pressures?
Falling behind in R&D?
Too narrow a product line?
Weak market image?
Competitive disadvantages?
Below-average marketing skills?
Unable to finance needed changes in
    strategy?
Higher overall unit costs relative
    to key competitors?
Other?

Potential External Opportunities

Serve additional customer groups?
Enter new markets or segments?
Expand product line to meet broader range of
    customer needs?
Diversify into related products?
Add complementary products?
Vertical integration?
Ability to move to better strategic group?
Complacency among rival firms?
Faster market growth?
Other?

Potential External Threats

Likely entry of new competitors?
Rising sales of substitute products?
Slower market growth?
Adverse government policies?
Growing competitive pressures?
Vulnerability to recession and business cycle?
Growing bargaining power of customers or
    suppliers?
Changing buyer needs and tastes?
Adverse demographic changes?
Other?

---

firm and is a quick, easy-to-use tool for sizing up a firm's overall situation. The diagnostic thrust is not on identifying just any kind of strengths, weaknesses, opportunities, and threats but rather on singling out those that are *strategy related.* Figure 3–4 suggests what to look for in performing the SWOT analysis.

However, the SWOT needs to be more than an exercise in making four lists. Some strategy-related strengths are more important than others because they count for more in the marketplace and in executing an effective strategy. Some strategy-related weaknesses can be fatal, while others might not matter much or can be easily remedied. Some opportunities may be more attractive to pursue than others. And a firm may find itself much more vulnerable to some threats than to others. Hence it is essential to draw conclusions from the SWOT listing about the firm's overall situation and assess the implications these have for selecting a strategy.

Competitive Position Assessment

In addition to the overall diagnosis that SWOT provides, a more focused assessment needs to be made of the firm's relative competitive strength. Particular elements to single out for evaluation are: (1) how strongly the firm holds its present competitive position; (2) whether the firm's position can be expected to improve or deteriorate if the present strategy is continued (allowing for fine-tuning); (3) how the firm ranks *in relation to key rivals* on each important competitive variable and industry key success factor (ratings of stronger, weaker, or equal may be adequate); (4) the net competitive advantage(s) the firm has; and (5) the firm's ability to defend its position in light of industry driving forces, competitive pressures, and the anticipated moves of rivals.

Figure 3–5 contains a checklist of factors that often come into play; a firm's own situation usually suggests other points to consider. Again, more is needed than just a count of the pros and cons. The important thing is to assess how much each plus and minus really matters (given the industry and competitive environment) and to think through the implications for strategy.

The really telling part of strategic self-analysis, however, comes in appraising the firm's competitive strength versus key rivals on each key success factor and important competitive variable. The information for this piece of self-analysis comes from what has been done before: industry analysis reveals the key success factors and competitor analysis provides a basis for judging the strengths and capabilities of key rivals. Step one is to make a list of key success factors and any other relevant measures of competitive strength. Step two is to rate the firm and its key rivals on each factor; rating scales from 1 to 5 or 1 to 10 can be used (or ratings of just stronger, weaker,

Figure 3–5   Identifying the Pluses and Minuses in a Firm's Competitive Market Position

Potential Pluses	*Potential Minuses*
Competitive advantages?	No really good competitive advantage?
Important distinctive competences?	Under attack from key rivals?
Strong in particular market segments?	Losing ground to rival firms because . . . ?
Rising market share?	Below average growth?
A tough, proven competitor?	Lacks some key skills to compete effectively?
A pacesetting or distinctive strategy?	Short on financial resources?
Growing customer base and customer loyalty?	A slipping reputation with customers?
Above-average market visibility?	Trailing in product development?
In a favorably situated strategic group?	In a strategic group that is destined to lose ground?
Concentrating on fastest-growing market segments?	Weak in areas where there is the most market potential?
Strongly differentiated products?	Hard pressed to cope with competitive pressures?
Cost competitive?	Inadequate distribution?
Above-average profit margins?	A higher-cost producer?
Above-average marketing skills?	Too small to be a major factor in the marketplace?
Above-average technological and innovational capability?	No real distinctive competences?
A creative, entrepreneurially alert management?	A relative newcomer with an unproven track record in this business?
Good market savvy?	A history of poorly timed or ill-chosen strategic moves?
Capable of capitalizing on opportunities?	Not in good position to deal with emerging threats?
Other?	Other?

Table 3–1   Sample Assessment of Competitive Strength

Key success factor/Competitive variable	Strength rating			
	Own firm	Rival A	Rival B	Rival C
Adequacy of product line	5	4	5	3
Product, quality and performance	4	3	5	3
Reputation/image with buyers	4	3	5	3
Raw material access and cost	3	3	3	3
Technological skills and know-how	4	3	4	4
Manufacturing capability	4	4	5	3
Marketing and distribution capability	3	3	4	4
Financial strength	4	3	5	4
Adequacy of management	4	3	4	3
Relative cost position	4	3	5	3
Overall rating of competitive strength	39	32	45	33

Rating Scale: 1 = very weak, 5 = extremely strong.

Note: A somewhat more sophisticated rating assessment can be done by assigning weights to each key success factor/competitive variable, in recognition of the fact that they may not be equally important in gauging competitive strength. The procedure involves (1) assigning each key success factor/competitive variable a weight based on its perceived importance (the sum of the weights, of course, should add up to 1.0), (2) deciding how the firm stacks up on each factor (using the 1 to 5 rating scale), and then (3) obtaining a weighted rating by multiplying the weight by the rating score (a weight of .25 times a rating score of 4 gives a weighted rating of 1.0). The sum of the weighted ratings for a firm represents a measure of its overall competitive strength. Comparisons of the weighted scores across firms indicate which firms are stronger and which are weaker.

and about equal may be adequate). Step three is to judge each firm's overall competitive strength. A sample analysis is shown in Table 3–1.

The Firm's Own Strategic Issues and Problems

Because the best strategy for a firm is ultimately a unique action plan reflecting its particular circumstances, it is necessary to factor into the business strategy evaluation process those strategy-related issues and problems which are peculiar to the firm. This is largely a case-by-case exercise in which the firm's present strategy has to be evaluated in light of whatever special constraints are imposed by the firm's own situation. The important thing to realize here is that the strategic issues and problems confronting a given firm need not coincide exactly with the more general set of industrywide issues and problems—and the differences can make a difference in formulating the firm's own strategic plans.

ANALYTICAL CHECKLIST

The first three panels of Figure 3–6 provide a *format* for profiling a firm's situation and highlighting the dominant features of its industry and competitive environment. These parts of Figure 3–6 capture most of what we have covered in this chapter and, if completed conscientiously, reveals the strategy-critical character of a firm's overall business situation (without having to prepare or read a 50-page treatise!). The fourth panel of Figure 3–6 is a generic outline of a business-level strategic action plan; the nature of the recommended strategies and actions should flow readily from the analysis and conclusions of the industry situation analysis, competitive situation analysis, and company situation analysis.

[handwritten marginalia: $ROI = \frac{P}{TA}$ = Profit Margin Multiply total asset turnover]

Checklist for Conducting Industry and Competitive Analysis

Conducting a full-fledged industry and competitive analysis means exploring all of the following:

The Industry Situation

- How is the industry structured? What does the industry's strategy group map look like? Are entry/exit barriers high or low?
- What trends and driving forces are evident? What stage of the life cycle is the industry in now? How far ahead is the next stage?
- What factors stand out in the industry's price-cost-profit economics?
- What are the key success factors in this industry?
- What strategic issues does the industry face?
- All things considered, is this an attractive industry to be in? Why? What are the industry's short-term and long-term profit prospects?

The Competitive Situation

- What competitive forces exist and how strong are they? (Do a five forces analysis and assess the specific nature and strength of each.)
- What are the strategies, marketing positions, and competitive strengths of key rivals? Who is gaining ground, who is losing ground, and for what reasons? Who has what kind of competitive advantage?
- What will future competition be like? Who will likely make what kind of moves next? Which competitors should be watched and worried about most?

Self-Analysis: The Firm's Own Situation

- How well is the present strategy working? How good is the firm's performance compared to others in the industry?
- What conclusions does the SWOT analysis reveal? Any distinctive competences?
- How strong is the firm's competitive position? How does it stack up against specific competitors on specific competitive variables? Any competitive advantage?
- How strong is the firm's relative cost position? (Use activity-cost chain analysis to identify specific sources of cost advantage or disadvantage.)
- What specific strategic issues and problems does the firm need to address?

With solid answers to these questions, the strategist is ready to investigate the firm's strategic options and prepare a strategic action plan like that shown in panel four of Figure 3–6.

Figure 3-6   Industry and Competitive Analysis Summary Profile

INDUSTRY SITUATION ANALYSIS

1. **Description of Industry Structure**

2. **Strategic Characteristics:**
   - Stage in Industry Life Cycle
     Current: _____
     Future: _____
   - Driving Forces

   - Pertinent Price-Cost-Profit Economics

   - Key Success Factors

   - Issues/Problems Facing the Industry

3. **Industry Prospects and Overall Attractiveness:**
   *Factors making the industry attractive

   *Factors making the industry unattractive

   *Conclusions Concerning Industry
     Attractiveness:

	Short-term	Long-term
Very Attractive	_____	_____
Attractive	_____	_____
Neutral/Average	_____	_____
Unattractive	_____	_____
Very Unattractive	_____	_____

COMPETITIVE SITUATION ANALYSIS

1. **Analysis of Competitive Forces:**
   *Rivalry among Competitors in the Industry
     Strength (strong, moderate, weak): _____
     Reasons/Analysis:

   *Threat of Potential Entry
     Strength (strong, moderate, weak): _____
     Reasons/Analysis:

   *Competition from Substitutes
     Strength (strong, moderate, weak): _____
     Reasons/Analysis:

   *Economic Power of Suppliers
     Strength (strong, moderate, weak): _____
     Reasons/Analysis:

   *Economic Power of Customers
     Strength (strong, moderate, weak): _____
     Reasons/Analysis:

2. **Competitor Analysis** (market shares, strategies,
   competitive capabilities, and positions of key rivals):
     Competitor A—

     Competitor B—

     Competitor C—

3. **Expected Competitive Conditions/Predicted
   Moves of Key Competitors:**

4. **Who to Watch and Why:**

COMPANY SITUATION ANALYSIS

1. Strategic Performance Indicators:

Performance Indicator	Period 1	2	3	4
Market Share	___	___	___	___
Sales Growth	___	___	___	___
Net Profit Margin	___	___	___	___
Return on Equity Investment	___	___	___	___

2.

Internal Strengths	Internal Weaknesses

3.

External Opportunities	External Threats:

4. Relative Competitive Strength versus Key Rivals:

Key Success Factor/ Competitive Variable	Weight	Strength Own Firm	Rival A	Rating Rival B	Rival C
Quality/product performance	___	___	___	___	___
Reputation/image	___	___	___	___	___
Raw material access/cost	___	___	___	___	___
Technological skills	___	___	___	___	___
Manufacturing capability	___	___	___	___	___
Marketing/distribution	___	___	___	___	___
Financial strength	___	___	___	___	___
Relative cost position	___	___	___	___	___
Other	___	___	___	___	___
Overall strength rating	═══	═══	═══	═══	═══

Rating Scale (1 = very weak; 5 = extremely strong)

5. Competitive Position Assessment (improving/slipping?):
Pluses/Advantages/Competitive strengths

Minuses/Disadvantages/Competitive weaknesses

6. Major Strategic Issues/Problems Which the Company Must Address:

STRATEGIC PLAN AND ACTION RECOMMENDATIONS

1. Basic Strategic Direction (strategic mission and key strategic objectives)

2. Overall Business Strategy

3. Specific Competitive Approaches and Competitive Moves:

4. Major Functional Support Strategies:

5. Short-Term Action Recommendations (with supporting justifications):

6. Long-Term Action Recommendations (with supporting justifications):

SUGGESTED READINGS

Cohen, William A. "War in the Marketplace." *Business Horizons* 29, no. 2 (March–April 1986), pp. 10–20.

Ghemawat, Pankaj. "Building Strategy on the Experience Curve." *Harvard Business Review* 63, no. 2 (March–April 1985), pp. 143–49.

Henry, Harold W. "Appraising a Company's Strengths and Weaknesses." *Managerial Planning,* July/August 1980, pp. 31–36.

Linneman, Robert E., and Harold E. Klein. "Using Scenarios in Strategic Decision Making." *Business Horizons* 28, no. 1 (January–February 1985), pp. 64–74.

Ohmae, Kenichi. *The Mind of the Strategist.* New York: Penguin Books, 1983, chaps. 3, 6, 7, and 13.

Porter, Michael E. "How Competitive Forces Shape Strategy." *Harvard Business Review* 57, no. 2 (March–April 1979), pp. 137–45.

————. *Competitive Strategy: Techniques for Analyzing Industries and Competitors.* New York: Free Press, 1980.

————. *Competitive Advantage.* New York: Free Press, 1985, chap. 2.

————and Victor Miller. "How Information Gives You Competitive Advantage." *Harvard Business Review* 63, no. 4 (July–August 1985), pp. 149–60.

South, Stephen E. "Competitive Advantage: The Cornerstone of Strategic Thinking." *Journal of Business Strategy* 1, no. 4 (Spring 1981), pp. 15–25.

4 Generic Business Strategies and Industry Environments

Industry environments vary widely in their structural characteristics, growth prospects, stage of evolution, price-cost-profit economics, and combinations of competitive pressures. The circumstances of individual competitors vary widely, too—there are the situations of strong industry leaders, aggressive challengers, content followers, firms in distress and decline, and weak also-rans. And there are several basic competitive approaches, each of which can be tailored to fit a variety of situations.

In the midst of all this diversity there is some degree of order: There are some very common (we shall call them *generic*) strategic approaches and there are generic types of industry environments and company situations. Depending on the industry environment, some strategic options are more appropriate than others. Depending on a firm's competitive position and the strategies of rivals, some competitive approaches have greater appeal than others.

This chapter begins with an examination of the generic strategies and then surveys the strategic alternatives for commonly encountered industry environments and company situations. The emphasis is on matching company strategy to the company's competitive position and industry environment. By the end of this chapter it should be apparent that strategy is what positions a firm to be successful.

> Strategy isn't something you can nail together in slap-dash fashion by sitting around a conference table.
>
> —*Terry Haller*

> The essence of formulating competitive strategy is relating a company to its environment. . . . The best strategy for a given firm is ultimately a unique construction reflecting its particular circumstances.
>
> —*Michael E. Porter*

GENERIC BUSINESS AND COMPETITIVE STRATEGIES

A firm's competitive approach consists of the combination of offensive, defensive, and functional area support actions employed to cope with the five competitive forces in order to achieve target objectives. There are many business strategy approaches, and firms have imaginatively explored them all. Virtually every type of strategy, at one time or another in one industry or another, has produced acceptable results. And because firms tailor their strategies to fit particular circumstances, every firm's strategy has at least several unique components and wrinkles—in this sense there are countless strategy variations and options, ultimately yielding as many business strategies as there are businesses. However, when one delves beneath the differences in detail and looks at the basic character of the different strategies that firms employ, the amount of fundamental strategy variation narrows considerably. From this more generalized perspective, it is possible to single out three generic approaches to competing in the marketplace:

1. Striving to be the overall low-cost producer in the industry.
2. Seeking to differentiate one's product offering in one way or another from rivals' products.
3. A focused approach based on catering (via low cost leadership or differentiation) to a narrow portion of the market rather than going after the whole market.[1]

Table 4–1 profiles the distinctive features of these three generic strategies.

Striving to Be the Low-Cost Producer

The impetus for striving to be the industry's low-cost producer can drive from sizable economies of scale, strong learning and experience curve effects, other cost-cutting and efficiency-enhancing opportunities, and a market comprised of many price-conscious buyers. Trying to be the industry leader in achieving an overall low-cost position typically entails being out in front of rivals in constructing the most efficient-sized plants, in implementing cost-reducing technological advances, in getting the sales and market share needed to capitalize on learning and experience curve effects, in maintaining a tight rein on overhead and other administrative types of fixed costs, and in containing costs in such areas as R&D, advertising, service, and distribution. Low cost *relative to competitors* is the theme of the firm's entire strategy, though low cost is not so zealously pursued that a firm's product offering loses its competitiveness as concerns those product attributes which buyers value highly (such as optional performance features, rapid delivery, spare parts availability, low maintenance, reliability, technical assistance, or whatever). There are attractive advantages to being the low-cost producer in an industry:

- As concerns competitors, the low-cost company is in the best position to compete offensively on the basis of price, to defend against price war conditions, to use the appeal of a lower price as a weapon for both grabbing sales (and market share) away from rivals and attacking whatever success rivals have enjoyed with their competitive strategies, and to earn above-average profits (based on bigger profit margins or greater sales volume) in markets where price competition thrives.

---

[1] Michael E. Porter, *Competitive Strategy: Techniques for Analyzing Industries and Competitors* (New York: Free Press, 1980), chap. 2. The following discussion of these generic strategies relies on Porter's presentation, pp. 35–39 and 44–46.

Table 4–1   Distinctive Features of the Generic Competitive Strategies

Overall low-cost leadership

- Production emphasis—"nobody does it cheaper."
- Marketing emphasis—"budget prices/good values."
- Standardized products (only a few models and limited optional features).
- No frills operating culture ("lean and mean" reputation).
- Stay out front in riding experience curve downward (lower prices ⟶ added volume and market share ⟶ lower costs due to experience effects).
- High productivity per employee.
- Cost-cutting innovations.
- Can set the floor on market price (in best position to use price-cutting as an offensive or defensive weapon).
- Accept low profit margins in return for high volume.

Differentiation

- Production emphasis—"nobody makes it better."
- Marketing emphasis—"ours is better than theirs."
- Many frills (models, options, features, services).
- Create one or more points of difference.
- Frequent innovation.
- Premium pricing to cover added cost of differentiation.
- Intensive advertising and sales efforts.

Focus

- Production emphasis—"made especially for you."
- Marketing emphasis—"ours meets your needs better."
- Specialization (buyer segments, geographic areas, end-use applications).
- Competitive advantage depends on
  —Being the low-cost leader *in the target segment* or
  —Successful differentiation (doing something that is especially appealing to customers comprising the target segment).

- As concerns *customers*, the low-cost company has partial profit margin protection from powerful customers since the latter will rarely be able to bargain prices down past the survival level of the next most efficient firm.
- As concerns *suppliers*, the low-cost producer can, in some cases, be more insulated than competitors from powerful suppliers if its greater efficiency allows more pricing room to cope with increases in the costs of purchased materials.
- As concerns *potential entrants*, the low-cost producer is in a favorable competitive position because having the lowest costs not only acts as a barrier for a new entrant to hurdle but it also provides the leeway to use price-cutting as a defense against market inroads made by a new competitor.
- As concerns *substitutes*, a low-cost producer is, compared to its rivals, in a favorable position to use price cuts to defend against competition from attractively priced substitutes.

Consequently, a low-cost position provides a measure of protection against all five types of competitive forces. Whenever price competition is a major market force, less efficient rivals are squeezed the most. Being the low-cost producer allows a firm to use its cost advantage to earn higher profit margins and/or charge a lower price. Firms in a low-cost position compared to rivals have a significant edge in appealing to those buyers who base their purchase decisions on low price; plainly, *a low-cost producer has the ability to exert a heavy hand in determining the industry's price floor.*

The strategy of trying to be the low-cost producer is a particularly powerful strategy when: (1) demand is price elastic; (2) all firms in the industry produce essentially standardized, commodity-type products (newsprint, sheet steel, fertilizer, plastic pipe, lumber, and bulk chemicals) so that the marketplace is dominated by price competition and "the name of the game" is cost efficiency; (3) there are not many ways of achieving product differentiation that have much value to buyers; (4) most buyers utilize the product in the same ways; and (5) buyers incur few (if any) switching costs in changing from one seller to another and thus are strongly inclined to shop for the best price.

However, trying to be the low-cost leader is not without risk and disadvantage. Technological changes can result in cost or process breakthroughs that nullify past investments and efficiency gains. Rival firms may find it comparatively easy and/or inexpensive to imitate the leader's low-cost methods, thus making any advantage short lived. A tunnel-vision approach to cost reduction can cause a firm to overlook such things as a growing preference of buyers for added quality or service features, subtle shifts in buyer uses of the product, and declining buyer sensitivity to price—thus the firm could be left behind if the strategy of competitors swings more to nonprice variables and use of differentiation. Finally, heavy investments in cost minimization can lock a firm into both its present technology and present strategy, leaving it vulnerable to new state-of-the-art technologies and to a widening of customer interest in something other than a cheaper price. In short, being the low-cost leader imposes a significant burden in terms of staying on top of cost-saving technological improvements, scrapping existing equipment (even if it is not worn out) as soon as something more efficient is available, and risking technological and strategic inflexibility if buyers begin to be attracted by rivals' introduction of new product attributes. Moreover, strategic success in trying to be the low-cost producer usually requires a firm to be *the* overall cost leader, not just one of the several firms vying for this position.[2] When there is more than one aspiring low-cost producer, rivalry among them is typically fierce; unless one firm can get a clear enough cost lead to "persuade" the others to abandon their low-cost strategy, the profit prospects can be grim.

Examples of firms that are well known for low-cost leadership strategies are Lincoln Electric in arc welding equipment and supplies, Briggs & Stratton in small horsepower gasoline engines, BIC Pen in ballpoint pens, Black & Decker in tools, People Express in commercial airline travel, Beaird-Poulan in chain saws, Ford in heavy-duty trucks, Whirlpool in major home appliances, and R. J. Reynolds in cigarettes.

Pursuing a Strategy of Differentiation

The approaches to differentiating one's product from rival firms take many forms: a different taste (Dr Pepper and Listerine); special features (Jenn-Air's indoor cooking tops with a vented built-in grill for barbecueing); superior service (IBM in computers and Federal Express in overnight package delivery); spare parts availability (Caterpillar

---

[2] Michael E. Porter, *Competitive Advantage* (New York: Free Press, 1985), p. 13.

Tractor guarantees that it will deliver spare parts for its construction equipment to any customer anywhere in the world within 48 hours, or the part is furnished free); overall value to the customer (Sears and McDonald's); engineering design and performance (Mercedes-Benz in automobiles); unusual quality and distinctiveness (Rolex in watches and Chivas Regal in Scotch whiskey); product reliability (Johnson & Johnson in baby products); quality manufacture (Karastan in carpets and Curtis Mathes in television sets); technological leadership (Hyster in lift trucks and 3M Corporation in bonding and coating products); convenient payment (American Express); a full range of services (Merrill Lynch); a complete line of products (General Motors in automobiles and Campbell Soup in soups); and top-of-the-line image and reputation (Brooks Brothers and Ralph Lauren in menswear, Chanel in perfumes and fragrances, and Cross in writing instruments).

Differentiation provides some insulation against the strategies of rivals because customers establish a preference or loyalty for the brand or model they like best and are often willing to pay a little (perhaps a lot!) more for it. In addition, successful differentiation (1) erects entry barriers in the form of customer loyalty and uniqueness for newcomers to hurdle, (2) mitigates the bargaining power of large buyers since the products of alternative sellers are less attractive to them, and (3) puts a firm in a better position to ward off threats from substitutes to the extent that it has built a loyal clientele. To the extent that differentiation allows a seller to charge a higher price and earn bigger profit margins, then the seller is in a stronger economic position to negotiate with powerful suppliers. Thus, as with cost leadership, successful differentiation creates lines of defense for dealing with the five competitive forces. Employing a differentiation strategy also has risks.

- The cost of adding enough product attributes to achieve differentiation can result in such a high selling price that buyers opt for lower-priced brands. Buyers are usually willing to pay only so much extra for differentiation; when this extra differential is exceeded, low-cost/low-price firms gain an edge over firms pursuing high-cost differentiation. In such circumstances, despite the unique product features offered by the high-priced firms, a cost-leadership strategy can defeat a differentiation strategy.

- Over a period of time, buyers may decide that they do not need or want extra features, concluding that a basic or standard model serves just as well. Then the market emphasis shifts away from differentiation toward a commodity product situation where the name of the game is low-cost, efficient production of a more or less standardized product.

- Rival firms may imitate the product attributes of the leaders to an extent such that buyers see little meaningful difference from seller to seller. The differentiation attempts of rivals thus cancel each other out and buyers shop chiefly on the basis of price.

The most appealing types of differentiation strategies are those that are least subject to quick or inexpensive imitation. Here is where a distinctive competence comes into play. When a firm has skills and competences that competitors cannot match easily, it can use these skills as a basis for successful differentiation. Differentiation is most likely to produce an attractive and lasting competitive edge when it is based on:

- Technical superiority.
- Quality.
- Giving customers more support services.
- The appeal of more value for the money.

As a rule, differentiation strategies work best in situations where (1) there are many ways to differentiate the product or service and these differences are perceived by some buyers to have value, (2) buyer needs and uses of the item are diverse, and (3) not many rival firms are following a differentiation strategy. Often, the most attractive avenue for product differentiation is the one least traveled by rival firms—as the saying goes, "never follow the crowd." And experience indicates that it is hard to excel in several approaches to differentiation simultaneously. Attempting to differentiate in many ways at once can deteriorate into trying to be too many things to too many people, thus blurring the image the firm presents to its target markets. In formulating a differentiation strategy it is usually wise to stress one key value and to develop a distinctive competence in delivering it. It can also be a good tactic to select a basis for differentiation that *(a)* makes it easy for first-time buyers to try the product and *(b)* makes it hard for regular users to abandon the product (because the costs of switching to other brands or substitutes are high).

Focus and Specialization Strategies

A focus or specialization strategy aims at building a competitive edge and carving out a market position by catering to the somewhat special needs of a particular group of customers, by concentrating on a limited geographic market, or by concentrating on certain uses for the product. *The distinguishing feature of a focus strategy is that the firm specializes in serving only a portion of the total market.* The underlying premise is that a firm can serve its narrow target market more effectively or more efficiently than rivals that position themselves broadly.

The competitive advantage of a focus strategy is earned either by differentiation (better meeting the needs of the target market segment), achieving lower costs in serving the target market segment, or both. A firm using a focus strategy can gain a cost advantage because more than one cost curve can prevail in an industry. The cost curve for a specialist firm concentrating on custom orders and short production runs can differ substantially from the cost curve for a firm pursuing a high-volume, low-cost strategy (as shown in Figure 4–1). In such cases small firms are positioned to be cost-effective focusers in the small-volume, custom-order buyer segments, leaving the mass market to large-volume producers.

Because of its specialized approach and unmatched skills in serving a limited market target, a focused firm develops a defense against the five competitive forces. Rivals do not have the same ability to serve the focused firm's target clientele. Entry into the focused firm's market niche is made harder by the competitive edge generated by the focused firm's distinctive competence. The focused firm's distinctive competence also acts as a hurdle that producers of substitutes must overcome. Focusers are partially shielded from the bargaining leverage of powerful customers by the latter's unwillingness to shift their business to firms with lesser capabilities to serve their needs.

A competitive strategy based on focus or specialization has merit (1) when there

Figure 4–1   When a Focus Strategy Can Allow a Small Firm to Be Cost Competitive with a Large, Mass Production Rival

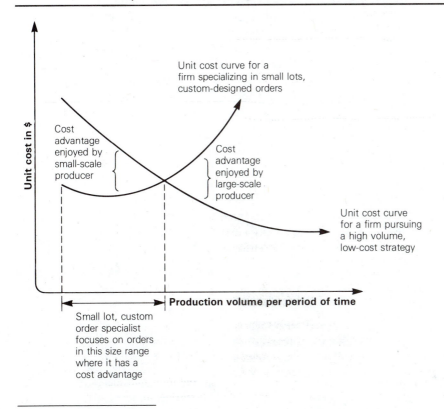

Source: Michael E. Porter, *Competitive Strategy: Techniques for Analyzing Industries and Competitors* (New York: Free Press, 1980), p. 245.

are distinctly different groups of buyers who either have different needs or utilize the product in different ways; (2) when no other rival is attempting to specialize in the same target segment; (3) when a firm's resources do not permit it to go after a wide segment of the total market; or (4) when industry segments differ widely in size, growth rate, profitability, and intensity of the five competitive forces, thereby making some segments much more attractive than others.

Examples of firms employing a focus strategy include Tandem Computers (a specialist in "nonstop" computers for customers who need a "fail-safe" system that can support thousands of on-line terminals and preserve data integrity and reliability); Rolls-Royce (in super luxury automobiles); Thermidor (a maker of top-of-the-line refrigerators, freezers, trash compactors, and cooking appliances); Fort Howard Paper (specializing in paper products for industrial and commercial enterprises only); the numerous commuter airlines (which specialize in low-traffic, short-haul flights linking major airports with smaller population centers 50 to 250 miles away); and Ficks and Reed, a maker of premium quality rattan furniture.

The risks of using a focus strategy include (1) the possibility that broad-range competitors will find effective ways to match the focused firm in serving the narrow target market; (2) shifts in buyer preferences and needs away from the focuser's special product attributes toward more generally available features desired by the target segment (a condition which makes the market as a whole narrower and allows broad-range rivals a stronger competitive footing in the target markets of the focused firms); and (3) the chance that competitors will find smaller segments within the target segment and "outfocus" the focuser. Illustration Capsule 12 describes the successful use of a focus strategy.

ILLUSTRATION CAPSULE 12

Cheerleader Supply Company: A Successful User of a Focus Strategy

Cheerleader Supply Company, a Dallas-based company with sales over $20 million, trains and outfits the lion's share of the 600,000-odd cheerleaders in the United States. Lawrence Herkimer, the company's founder, chairman, and principal owner, claims to be the only person to have a cheerleading move named after him—the "Herkie jump." Herkimer, now a portly 60 years old, occasionally demonstrates the Herkie jump at his numerous cheerleader clinics, always to the delight of enthusiastic audiences.

Herkimer first got into cheerleading at Southern Methodist University. Herkimer was a gymnast in high school but tried out for the cheerleading squad at SMU because SMU didn't have a gymnastics team. With his jumping ability he was soon a crowd favorite, and by the time he graduated in 1948, national sportswriters had dubbed him "Mr. Cheerleader." After graduate school in physical education, Herkimer took a job teaching gymnastics at SMU; before long, schools began calling him to train their cheerleading squads on weekends. The weekend sessions soon evolved into cheerleading clinics and his reputation spread. One weekend at Ohio State netted him $21,000 when Ohio State, anxious to have Herkimer, agreed to pay him a fee of $5 per attendee (his usual fee was $1); 4,200 teenagers showed up for the clinic. That prompted Herkimer to go into the cheerleading business full-time.

At first, Cheerleader Supply was a vehicle to promote the clinics and help Herkimer sell his books—*Championship Cheers and Chants* and *Pep Rally Skits and Stunts*. When schools started asking him to help line up uniforms, Herkimer saw an opportunity:

> *Cheerleaders have very special requirements in clothes, not only in design but in delivery. You pick the squad in April, and the uniforms have to be there in August. And every school wants something special—braid trim on the sweater, two-color lining on the skirt. For four months of the year, you're turning out special orders in small batches, and for eight months you're doing nothing.*

ILLUSTRATION CAPSULE 12 *(continued)*

Herkimer spent $100,000 in the early 1960s to buy a knitting mill and workshop in a rural town south of Dallas. Owning the plant offered the advantages of quality control and elimination of the high premium charged by subcontract apparel manufacturers for small custom orders. Low-wage labor was also plentiful because local farm women, who were needed at home in the spring and fall, were willing to work double overtime shifts in the summer. Other products were added to the line as Herkimer ferreted out old buildings (at bargain prices) in which to set up production: a nearby milk-carton factory was converted into a plant to make plastic megaphones and drinking cups; an old warehouse was used to make plastic buttons and badges.

The company's strategy has evolved to where little is overlooked in training and outfitting cheerleaders:

1. Herkimer and 300 college-age assistants run clinics across the United States all summer long.
2. Cheerleader Supply knits sweaters, makes skirts and slacks, hand-hooks chenille emblems, distributes dyed-to-match saddle shoes, and carries matching knee socks—to provide complete cheerleading outfits.
3. The company holds a design patent on pompons which are made at a company-owned plant outside Houston.
4. Cheerleader Supply sells a line of spirit-building items (miniature megaphones stamped with school mascots, custom-made buttons and ribbons with any desired inscriptions), which in turn can be sold by school clubs or its cheerleaders to raise money (to help finance trips to the next cheerleading clinic).

In the 1980s, Cheerleader Supply succeeded in making sales to about two thirds of the estimated 70,000 high school cheerleading squads and to over half of the 2,500 college squads.

SOURCE: "Go! Fight! Win" *Forbes*, September 27, 1982, pp. 136–40.

STRATEGIES FOR GENERIC TYPES OF INDUSTRY ENVIRONMENTS AND COMPETITIVE SITUATIONS

How firms custom tailor the three generic strategic approaches is conditioned partly by the industry environment in which they compete and partly by each firm's situation in that environment. To demonstrate some of the considerations that shape how a firm can try to compete, we will highlight some ways of tailoring business strategy in nine classic types of generic industry environments and competitive situations:

1. Competitive strategies for leaders and dominant firms.
2. Competitive strategies for runner-up firms.
3. Competitive strategies for also-ran and declining firms.
4. Turnaround strategies for distressed businesses and crisis situations.

5. Competing in a young, emerging industry.
6. Competing during the transition to industry maturity.
7. Competing in mature or declining industries.
8. Competing in fragmented industries.
9. Competing in global markets.

Competitive Strategies for Leaders and Dominant Firms

The competitive positions of industry leaders and dominant firms normally range from stronger-than-average to powerful. Leaders are typically well known; strongly entrenched leaders have proven strategies keyed either to low-cost leadership or to differentiation. Some of the best-known industry leaders are Anheuser-Busch (beer), IBM (computers), McDonald's (fast foods), Gillette (razor blades), GM (automobiles), Campbell Soup (canned soup), Gerber (baby food), Xerox (photocopying machines), AT&T (long-distance telephone service), and Levi Strauss (jeanswear).

The main competitive strategy issue for an industry leader is how best to sustain what has been achieved and how to become or remain *the* leader (as opposed to *a* leader). However, the pursuit of industry leadership and large market share per se is seldom competitively important; what matters more is the competitive advantage enjoyed by the leader. At least three different competitive postures are open to industry leaders and dominant firms:[3]

1. *Stay-on-the-Offensive Strategy*.   This strategy is based on the principle that the best defense is a good offense. The keys to success in offensive strategies are constant innovation and the launching of initiatives that keep rivals guessing, off-balance, and scrambling to respond. The innovative goal is to be *the* source of innovative products, special performance features, quality enhancements, improved customer services, ways to cut production costs, use of different distribution channels, and/or whatever matters to leadership status. Innovations may also include initiatives to expand overall industry demand—discovering new uses for the product, attracting new users of the product, and promoting more frequent usage of the product. A clever offensive leader stays alert for ways to make it easier and less costly for potential customers to switch their purchases over from runner-up firms. Aggressive leaders try to be "first-movers," the aim being to translate "being first" into a sustainable competitive advantage as well as into solidifying their reputation as *the* leader.

2. *Hold and Maintain Strategy*.   The essence of "hold and maintain" is a good defense, which makes it harder for new firms to enter and for challengers to gain ground, lowers the probability of attack, lessens the intensity of attack, or diverts attack to less threatening arenas. The goal of a strong defense is to make the leader's competitive advantage more sustainable by erecting "fortifications" to protect its present market standing. Specific defensive actions can include:

- Attempting to raise entry barriers via increased spending for advertising, customer service, and production capacity.

---

[3] Kotler, *Marketing Management,* 5th ed. (Englewood Cliffs, N.J.: Prentice-Hall, 1984), chap. 23; Porter, *Competitive Advantage,* chap. 14; and Ian C. MacMillan, "Seizing Competitive Initiative," *Journal of Business Strategy* 2, no. 4 (Spring 1982), pp. 43–57.

- Introducing more of the company's own brands to match the product attributes that challenger brands have or could employ.
- Figuring out ways to increase the costs for customers who switch to rival products.
- Broadening the product line to close off possible vacant niches for competitors to slip into.
- Keeping prices reasonable and quality attractive.
- Preserving or even raising the level of customer service.
- Investing enough to remain cost competitive, to stay technologically progressive, and to maintain the firm's existing share of new market growth (thus staving off any market share slippage and decline).
- Patenting the feasible alternative technologies (as Xerox did early in the development of the copier industry).
- Signing exclusive contracts with the best suppliers.

The primary appeals of "hold and maintain" are to lessen the chances of antitrust charges (if the leader's market share is dominant enough to approach monopoly proportions) and to "milk" the firm's present position for profits and cash flow (if the industry's prospects for growth are low or if further gains in market share do not appear profitable enough to pursue).

3. *Competitive Harassment Strategy*. With this strategy the leader sends clear messages to rivals that any moves to cut into the leader's business will be "bloody" and will provoke heavy-handed retaliation. The strategic themes include being quick to meet all competitive price cuts (with even larger cuts if necessary); being ready to counter with large-scale promotional campaigns if lesser-sized firms boost their advertising budgets in a market-share-increasing attempt of their own; offering better deals to the major customers of next-in-line or "maverick" firms; and using "hardball" measures to signal aggressive-minded small firms regarding who should lead and who should follow (possible signaling options include pressuring distributors not to carry rivals' products, having salespersons "bad-mouth" the products of aggressive small firms, or trying to hire away the better executives of firms that "get out of line"). The objective of a harassment/confrontation type of competitive strategy is to enforce an unwritten but well understood tradition among lesser-sized firms of "playing follow the leader." Assuming the role of industry policeman gives the leader added strategic flexibility, as well as "raising the ante" for would-be challengers who might take the offensive.

Competitive Strategies for Runner-Up Firms (under dog)

Runner-up firms occupy weaker market positions than do industry leaders. Some runner-up firms are market challengers willing to fight one another and the leader(s) for a bigger market share and a stronger market position. Other runner-up firms play the role of followers—unwilling to rock the boat and content with their current positions. If a firm is content to be a follower, perhaps because profits are still adequate, then it has no urgent strategic issue to confront beyond that of "What kinds of strategic changes do the leaders seem to have in mind, and what do we need to do to follow along?" However, an ambitious underdog firm may try to capitalize on whatever opportunities come its way to improve its market position. A firm with a subpar market share may have little choice but to aggressively increase its market penetration to at least a "middle-of-the-pack" position.

Normally, if a challenger firm is to make a credible attempt to improve its market standing, it will need a strategy aimed at building a competitive advantage of its own. Rarely can a runner-up firm improve its competitive position just by imitating what leading firms in the industry are doing; indeed, a cardinal rule in offensive strategy is not to attack a leader head-on with an imitative strategy, regardless of the resources and staying power an underdog may have.[4] Moreover, if an underdog has a 5 percent market share and needs a 20 percent share to earn attractive profits, then it needs a more creative approach to competing than just "try harder."

In cases where large size produces a significantly stronger market position and perhaps is accompanied by lower unit costs, small-share firms have only two strategic options: fight to increase share or withdraw from the business (gradually or quickly). The most used competitive strategies for building market share are based on (1) striving to become the low-cost producer and, in turn, using the attractiveness of a lower price to win increased customer favor, and (2) differentiation strategies based on quality, technological superiority, better customer service, or innovation. Striving for low-cost leadership is usually open to an underdog only when one of the market leaders is not already solidly positioned as the industry's low-cost producer.

In cases where scale economies or experience curve effects are small and a large market share produces no appreciable competitive cost advantage, the practical competitive strategy options for runner-up companies usually boil down to six approaches:[5]

1. *Vacant Niche Strategy.* The principle underlying this competitive approach is to concentrate on those customers or end-use applications that major firms have bypassed or neglected. An ideal vacant niche is of sufficient size and scope to be profitable, has some growth potential, and is well suited to a firm's own capabilities and skills, as well as being outside the realm of interest of leading firms. Two examples of successful use of a vacant niche type of focus strategy are the regional commuter airlines which serve small- and medium-sized population centers having too few passengers to attract the interest of the major airlines, and the small, "no-name" tire manufacturers that have managed to find enough holes in the market to survive alongside Goodyear, Firestone, B. F. Goodrich, Uniroyal, and Michelin.

2. *Specialist Strategy.* A specialist firm trains its competitive efforts on a few carefully chosen segments and does not try to compete with a full product line appealing to all different needs and functions. Stress is placed only on those differentiating variables where the company has or can develop special expertise and where such expertise will be highly valued by customers. Smaller companies that have successfully used a specialist type of focus strategy include Formby's (which specializes in making stains and finishes for wood furniture, especially refinishing); Liquid Paper Co. (which made a reputation for itself producing correction fluid for use by typists); Canada Dry (known for its ginger ale, tonic water, and carbonated soda water); and American Tobacco (which specializes in chewing tobacco and snuff).

---

[4] Porter, *Competitive Advantage,* p. 514.

[5] For more details, see Kotler, *Marketing Management,* pp. 397–412; R. G. Hamermesh, M. J. Anderson, Jr., and J. E. Harris, "Strategies for Low Market Share Businesses," *Harvard Business Review* 56, no. 3 (May–June 1978), pp. 95–102; and Porter, *Competitive Advantage,* chap. 15.

3. *"Ours-Is-Better-Than-Theirs" Strategy.* The approach here is to use a combination focus-differentiation strategy keyed to product quality. Sales and marketing efforts are focused on quality-conscious and performance-oriented buyers. Fine craftsmanship, prestige quality, frequent product innovations, and/or working closely with customers to develop a better product usually undergird this "superior product" type of approach. Some examples: Beefeater's approach in gin, Tiffany's stance in diamonds and jewelry, Chicago Cutlery in premium quality kitchen knives, Baccarat in fine crystal, Mazola in cooking oil and margarine, Bally in shoes, Pennzoil in motor oil, and Neiman-Marcus's approach to department store retailing.

4. *Content Follower Strategy.* Follower firms deliberately refrain from being the first to make a new competitive move, and they avoid aggressive attempts to steal customers away from the leaders. Followers use focus and differentiation approaches that will not provoke competitive retaliation and that keep them out of the leaders' paths. They react and respond, rather than initiate and attack. They prefer defense to offense. And they don't get out of line with the leaders on price. Burroughs (in computers) and Union Camp (in paper products) have been successful market followers by consciously concentrating on selected product uses and applications for specific customer groups, effectively focused R&D, profit emphasis rather than market share emphasis, and cautious, but efficient, management.

5. *Guppy Strategy.* A "swallow up the small fish" approach has appeal when a financially strong underdog is able to grow at the expense of still weaker rivals either by directly taking sales away from them or by acquiring them outright to form an enterprise that has more competitive strength. Such beer manufacturers as Heileman, Stroh's, and Pabst owe their market standing share growth to having acquired smaller brewers. Likewise, a number of the "second tier" public accounting firms have achieved rapid growth by acquiring or merging with smaller regional and local CPA firms.

6. *Distinctive Image Strategy.* Some underdogs structure their competitive approach around being unique and distinctive in ways that are highly visible to customers. This can take a variety of forms: lower prices achieved through cost reductions, prestige quality at a good price, superior customer services, unique product attributes, innovative distribution channels, leadership in new product introduction, or unusually creative advertising. Examples include Dr Pepper's strategy of calling attention to its distinctive taste, Apple Computer's approach to making it easier and interesting for people to use a personal computer, and Hyatt's use of architecture and luxurious hotel accommodations to appeal to upscale travelers and conventions.

Table 4–2 highlights risks and pitfalls associated with certain market challenger strategies.

Without a doubt, in industries where size is a key success factor, firms with low market shares have some obstacles to overcome: (1) less access to economies of scale in manufacturing, distribution, or sales promotion; (2) difficulty in gaining customer recognition; (3) inability to afford mass media advertising on a grand scale; and (4) difficulty in funding capital requirements.[6] But *it is erroneous to view runner-up firms as necessarily being less profitable or unable to hold their own against the bigger firms.* Many smaller firms earn healthy profits and enjoy good reputations with customers.

---

[6] Hamermesh, Anderson, and Harris, "Strategies for Low Market Share Businesses," p. 102.

Table 4–2   Risks and Pitfalls of Market Challenger Strategies

Higher Risk Strategy Alternatives

- Price-cutting (without having a cost advantage)
- Cheapening the quality (to save on cost and fund price cuts)
- Product innovation (R&D can be expensive and many new product ideas fail in the marketplace)
- Going after the high end of the market (without having the reputation to attract buyers who want name-brand prestige goods)

Lower Risk Strategy Alternatives

- Improving the levels of customer services
- Opening up new channels of distribution
- Looking for ways to reduce costs

Pitfalls

- Adding lots of models and optional features (product line proliferation is costly and often leads to lower profit margins)
- Spending heavily on promotional and advertising (may provoke a promotional war; the sales gains may not offset the added costs)
- Imitating what the leaders do ("me-too" strategies seldom close the gap on the leaders)
- Depending on cosmetic product improvements to serve as a substitute for real innovation and extra customer value

Oftentimes, the handicap of smaller size can be surmounted and a profitable competitive position established by: (1) focusing on carefully chosen market segments where particular strengths can be developed and not attacking dominant firms head-on with price cuts and increased promotional expenditure; (2) developing a distinctive competence in new product development or technical capabilities, but only for the target market segments; and (3) using innovative ("dare to be different" or "beat-the-odds") entrepreneurial approaches to outmanage stodgy, slow-to-change market leaders. Runner-up companies have a golden opportunity to make major market share gains if they make a leapfrogging technological breakthrough, if the leaders stumble or become complacent, or if they have the patience to nibble away at the leaders and expand their customer base over a long period of time.

Competitive Strategies for Also-Ran and Declining Firms

A firm in an also-ran or declining competitive position has four basic options:[7] If enough resources are available, it can pursue a modest *grow-and-build* strategy based on either low-cost production or "new" differentiation themes, pouring enough money and talent into the effort to make the enterprise a respectable market contender. It

---

[7] Charles W. Hofer and Dan Shendel, *Strategy Formulation: Analytical Concepts* (St. Paul, Minn.: West Publishing, 1978), pp. 164–65.

can adopt a *hold-and-maintain* mode, continuing the present strategy and scrounging up enough resources to keep sales, market share, profitability, and competitive position at survival levels. It can opt for an *abandonment* strategy and get out of the business, either by selling out to another firm or by closing down operations if a buyer cannot be found. Or, it can pursue a *harvest strategy* whereby reinvestment in the business is held to a bare-bones minimum and the dominant short-run objective is to harvest short-term profits and/or maximize short-term cash flow; the long-term objective of harvesting is orderly market exit. The first three options are self-explanatory; the fourth needs clarification.

A *harvest strategy* steers a middle course between maintenance and abandonment. Harvesting entails resource commitments in between what is required for hold-and-maintain and a decision to get out as soon as possible. Harvesting is a phasing down or endgame approach in which strategy is aimed at an orderly market pullback and surrender of market share, but the process includes reaping a "harvest" of cash to deploy in other business endeavors. Professor Kotler has suggested seven indicators of when a business should be harvested:[8]

1. When the business is in a saturated or declining market and the industry's long-term prospects are unattractive.
2. When the business has gained only a small market share, and building it up would be too costly or not profitable enough; or when it has a respectable market share that is becoming increasingly costly to maintain or defend.
3. When profit prospects are subpar because of the firm's competitive weakness or because of a forecast of poor long-term market conditions.
4. When reduced levels of competitive effort will not immediately trigger sharp declines in sales and market position.
5. When the enterprise can redeploy the freed-up resources in higher opportunity areas.
6. When the business is *not* a major component of a diversified corporation's portfolio of existing business interests.
7. When the business does not contribute other desired features (sales stability, prestige, a well-rounded product line) to a company's overall business portfolio.

The more of these seven conditions that are present, the more ideal the business is for harvesting.

The actions to harvest are fairly standard. The operating budget is reduced to a bare bones level, and stringent cost control is pursued. Capital investment in new equipment is given little, if any, financial priority, depending on the current condition of fixed assets and on whether the harvest is to be fast or slow. Price may be raised, promotional expenses cut, quality reduced in subtle ways, nonessential customer services curtailed, equipment maintenance decreased, and the like. The harvest objective is to maximize short-term cash flow and shift the money over to diversification efforts or to expansion in other existing businesses. It is understood that sales will fall, but if costs can be cut in proportion, then profits will erode slowly rather than rapidly.

Harvesting strategies make the most sense in diversified companies with business

---

[8] Phillip Kotler, "Harvesting Strategies for Weak Products," *Business Horizons* 21, no. 5 (August 1978), pp. 17–18.

units that are in the declining stages of the life cycle or that are "dogs." In such cases, the cash flows from harvesting unattractive business units can be reallocated to business units with greater profit potential and better long-term industry attractiveness.

Turnaround Strategies for Distressed Businesses

#3

Turnaround strategies come into play when a business worth rescuing has fallen into disrepair and perhaps into a crisis situation. The goal is to arrest and reverse the sources of competitive and financial weakness as quickly as possible. The first task of rescue is diagnosis: What lies at the root of poor performance? Is it bad competitive strategy or poor implementation and execution of an otherwise workable strategy? Or are the causes of distress beyond management control? Can the business be saved? Discerning what is wrong and how serious the firm's strategic problems are is a prerequisite to formulating a turnaround strategy.

Some of the most common causes of business trouble are ignoring the profit-depressing effects of an overly aggressive effort to "buy" market share with deep price cuts, being burdened with heavy fixed costs because of an inability to utilize plant capacity, betting on R&D efforts to boost competitive position and profitability and failing to come up with effective innovations, betting on technological long shots, being too optimistic about the ability to penetrate new markets, making frequent changes in strategy (because the previous strategy didn't work out); and being overpowered by the competitive advantages enjoyed by close rivals. There are five generic approaches to achieving a business turnaround:[9]

- Revamping the existing strategy.
- Revenue-increasing strategies.
- Cost-reduction strategies.
- Asset reduction/retrenchment strategies.
- A combination of these.

When the cause of weak performance is diagnosed as "bad" strategy, the task of strategy overhaul can proceed along any of several paths: (1) shifting to a new competitive approach and thus trying to rebuild the firm's market position; (2) overhauling internal operations and functional area strategies to produce better support of the same basic overall business strategy; (3) merging with another firm in the industry and converting to its basic strategy; and (4) retrenching into a reduced core of products and customers more closely matched to the firm's strengths. Which of these paths proves most appealing depends on conditions prevailing in the industry, on the firm's particular strengths and weaknesses compared to rival firms, and on the severity of the crisis. Consequently, "situation analysis" of the industry, major competitors, the firm's own competitive position, and its skills and resources are prerequisites to action.

---

[9] For excellent discussions of the ins and outs of rescuing distressed firms, see Charles W. Hofer, "Turnaround Strategies," *Journal of Business Strategy* 1, no. 1 (Summer 1980), pp. 19–31; Donald F. Heany, "Businesses in Profit Trouble," *Journal of Business Strategy* 5, no. 4 (Spring 1985), pp. 14–25.

Usually, reformulating the strategy of an ailing business needs to be predicated on a firm's strengths and what it is best at doing.

Revenue-increasing turnaround efforts aim at generating increases in sales volume. There are a number of revenue-building options: price cuts, increased promotion, a bigger sales force, added customer services, and quickly achieved product improvements. If demand happens to be price inelastic, revenues can be boosted by instituting a price increase instead of a price cut. Attempts to increase sales revenues are necessary when there is little or no room in the operating budget to cut back on expenses and still break even, and when the key to restoring profitability is increased utilization of existing capacity.

Cost-reducing turnaround strategies work best when an ailing firm's cost structure is flexible enough to permit radical surgery, when operating inefficiencies are identifiable and readily correctable, and when the firm is relatively close to its break-even point. Accompanying a general belt-tightening can be an increased emphasis on budgeting and cost control, elimination of jobs and hirings, modernization of existing plant and equipment to gain greater productivity, or postponement of capital expenditures.

Asset reduction/retrenchment strategies become essential to rescue a firm when cash flow is a critical consideration and when the most practical way to generate cash is (1) through the sale of some assets (plant and equipment, land, patents, inventories, or profitable subsidiaries) and (2) through retrenchment (pruning of marginal products from the product line, closing or sale of older plants, a reduced work force, withdrawal from outlying markets, cutbacks in customer service, and so forth). Sometimes the purpose of unloading some of a firm's assets is not just to stem cash drains and get rid of losing operations, but to raise funds which can be used to strengthen remaining activities.

Combination turnaround strategies are usually essential in grim situations where fast action on a broad front is required. Likewise, combination actions frequently come into play when the rescue effort entails bringing in new managers and giving them a relatively free hand to make whatever changes they see fit in restoring the business to a good condition. The tougher the problems, the more likely that the solutions will involve a multipronged approach rather than just one category of turnaround actions.

Turnaround efforts tend to be high-risk undertakings and often fail. An oft-cited study of 64 companies found no successful turnarounds among the most troubled companies in eight basic industries.[10] Many waited until it was too late to begin a turnaround, and others found themselves short of both cash and entrepreneurial talent needed to compete in a mature industry characterized by a fierce battle for market share; better positioned rivals simply proved too strong to defeat in head-to-head combat for the market share needed to survive. This study found that as market maturity approaches and competitive hostility intensifies, a firm's range of strategic options narrows. For a crisis-ridden firm to be successful in a turnaround effort, its management has to be alert to the signs of an impending competitive shake-out and launch an early effort to reposition the firm and restore its competitive status.

---

[10] William K. Hall, "Survival Strategies in a Hostile Environment," *Harvard Business Review* 58, no. 5 (September–October 1980), pp. 75–85.

Strategies for Competing in Young, Emerging Industries

Two crucial strategic issues confront firms trying to participate in a young, emerging industry with high-growth potential: (1) how to acquire the resources needed to support a *grow-and-build strategy* aimed at growing faster than the market as a whole and achieving/maintaining a position among the industry leaders; and (2) what market segments and competitive advantage to go after in preparation for the time when growth slows and the weakest firms fall prey to competitive shake-out and industry consolidation.[11] Ironclad prescriptions cannot be given for resolution of these two issues since emerging industries are not all alike. The form of the grow-and-build strategy has to be matched to the firm's situation and the character of the emerging industry itself—it can emphasize differentiation or low cost. The market environments of emerging industries have several strategy-shaping features:[12]

- There are no "rules of the game"; the issue of how the market will function is open-ended.
- Much of the technological know-how tends to be proprietary, having been developed in-house by pioneering firms.
- There is uncertainty about which production technology will prove to be the most efficient and which product attributes will be preferred by buyers. The result is erratic product quality, absence of industrywide product and technological standardization, and a situation where each firm is (at least until a broader consensus develops) committed to pioneering its own approach to technology, product design, marketing, and distribution.
- Firms lack solid information about competitors, buyer needs and preferences, when demand will take off, how fast the market will grow, and how big the market will get; industry participants are forced to grope for the "right" strategy and the right timing.
- As volume increases, experience curve effects permit significant cost reductions.
- Low entry barriers exist (even for newly formed companies) unless initial investment costs in new technology create a high financial barrier.
- Since all buyers will be first-time users, the marketing task is one of inducing initial purchase and eliminating customer confusion over the multiplicity of product attributes, technologies, and claims of rival firms. Many potential buyers may perceive that second- or third-generation technologies will make current products obsolete; hence, they may delay purchase until the product "matures" and a consensus emerges regarding design and technology.
- Difficulties in securing ample supplies of raw materials and components may be encountered (until suppliers gear up to meet the industry's needs).
- Because of the above conditions, firms in an emerging industry need enough financial strength to "get over the hump" of industry start-up problems and to gain the cash flow benefits of strong sales growth and a declining experience curve.
- Raising the capital needed to finance rapid growth can be a strain.

---

[11] Hofer and Schendel, *Strategy Formulation,* pp. 164–65.

[12] Porter, *Competitive Strategy,* pp. 216–22.

Dealing with these conditions is a challenging business strategy problem. The experiences of firms in emerging industries have produced the following growth-stage strategy guidelines:[13]

1. Manage with a willingness to take risks. A venturesome firm that makes a good strategic choice can shape the rules, gain first-mover advantages, and propel itself into a leadership position.
2. Work hard at improving product quality and developing attractive performance features.
3. Try to capture any advantages associated with adding models, better product styling, early commitments to technologies and suppliers of raw materials, experience curve effects, and new distribution channels.
4. Search out new customer groups, new geographical areas to enter, and new user applications. Make it easier and cheaper for first-time buyers to try the new product.
5. Gradually shift the advertising focus from building product awareness to increasing frequency of use and creating brand loyalty.
6. Move quickly when technological uncertainty diminishes and a "dominant" technology emerges; then try to pioneer the "dominant design" approach (but be cautious when technology is moving so rapidly that early investments are likely to be rendered obsolete).
7. Use price cuts to attract the next layer of price-sensitive buyers into the market.
8. Try to prepare for the entry of powerful competitors by forecasting *(a)* who the probable entrants will be (based on present and future entry barriers) and *(b)* the strategies they are likely to employ.

However, the value of winning the early race for growth and market share leadership has to be balanced against the longer-range need to build a durable competitive edge and a defendable market position.[14] Large, established firms may enter, attracted by the growth potential. Sooner or later, the battle for market share will trigger a competitive shake-out and the industry will consolidate to a smaller number of competitors. A young, single-business enterprise in a fast-developing industry can help its cause by electing knowledgeable members to its board of directors, bringing in entrepreneurial managers with experience in guiding young businesses through the developmental and takeoff stages, or gaining added expertise and a stronger resource base via merger with other firms in the industry.

Strategies for Competing during the Transition to Industry Maturity

Rapid industry growth cannot go on forever. The transition to a slower-growth, maturing industry environment does not occur after any fixed period of time, and

---

[13] Kotler, *Marketing Management*, p. 296; Porter, *Competitive Strategy*, chap. 10; and Steven P. Schnaars, "When Entering Growth Markets, Are Pioneers Better than Poachers?" *Business Horizons* 29, no. 2 (March–April 1986), pp. 27–36.

[14] Hofer and Schendel, *Strategy Formulation*, pp. 164–65.

it can be forestalled by innovations or other driving forces that renew rapid growth. Nonetheless, when maturity occurs, the transition usually produces fundamental changes in the industry's competitive environment:[15]

1. *Slowing growth in buyer demand generates more head-to-head competition for market share.* Since firms are unable to maintain their historical growth rates by merely holding the same market share, rivalry turns toward trying to take customers away from other firms. Outbreaks of price-cutting, increased advertising, and other aggressive tactics are common.

2. *Buyers become more sophisticated, often driving a harder bargain on repeat purchases.* Since the product is no longer new but an established item with which buyers are familiar the attention of buyers is on which of several brands to buy the next time around.

3. *Competition often produces a greater emphasis on cost and service.* As sellers all begin to offer the product attributes buyers prefer, buyer choice among competing brands depends more and more on which seller offers the best combination of price and service.

4. *Firms have a "topping out" problem in adding production capacity.* Slower growth in industry demand means slower rates of capacity additions—or industry overcapacity occurs. Each firm has to monitor rivals' capacity additions carefully and time its own capacity additions so that excess capacity is minimized. Rapid demand growth no longer quickly covers up the mistake of adding too much capacity too soon.

5. *Product innovation and new end-use applications are harder to come by.* Whereas R&D usually produces a stream of new product attributes and applications during the takeoff and rapid growth stages, the ability to generate marketable innovations tends to drop off. Firms run out of big new ideas.

6. *International competition increases.* Technological maturity, product standardization, and increased emphasis on low-cost production act to produce a more globally competitive industry. Growth-minded domestic firms seek out new foreign markets and, also become interested in locating plant facilities in countries where production costs are lower. Domestic and foreign firms are drawn into head-to-head competition, creating political issues over trade barriers and protectionism.

7. *Industry profitability falls, sometimes temporarily and sometimes permanently.* Slower growth, increased competition, more sophisticated buyers, and the erosion of competitive advantages frequently shrink industry profits. The profits of weaker, inefficient firms are usually more adversely affected than are those of strong competitors.

8. *The resulting competitive shake-out induces mergers and acquisitions among former competitors, drives some firms out of the industry, and produces industry consolidation.* In a rapid-growth environment, even inefficient firms and firms with weak competitive strategies can survive. (However, strategic sloppiness is generally exposed by the stiffer competition accompanying industry maturity).

These characteristics usually force firms to reexamine their business strategies. A refashioned competitive approach can sometimes be a matter of survival. There are several strategic moves that characterize maturing industries.[16]

---

[15] Porter, *Competitive Strategy,* pp. 238–40.

[16] The following discussion draws from Porter, *Competitive Strategy,* pp. 241–46.

Pruning the Product Line   Although numerous product models, sizes and options may be competitively useful in a rapidly growing market, product line proliferation can be costly in a mature industry environment characterized by price competition and battles for market share. Squeezed profit margins prompt cost studies that become the basis for pruning unprofitable items from the product line and concentrating on items where margins are highest and/or where the firm has a comparative advantage. Average costing for groups of products and arbitrary allocations of overhead expenses become inadequate for evaluating the product line and for deciding which new items to add. Unwittingly subsidizing the losses incurred on one item with above-average profits earned on another item hides those products whose demand does not support their true costs and invites price-cutting or new product introductions by rivals. In intensely competitive markets, an enhanced "profit consciousness" is needed to be successful.

More Emphasis on Process Innovation   The intensifying price competition that accompanies market maturity puts greater relative importance on process-oriented technological innovation. Innovations that permit lower-cost product design, lower-cost manufacturing methods, and lower cost distribution have high competitive value in markets where buyers are increasingly price conscious. Japanese firms have successfully emphasized technological process strategies aimed at becoming the low-cost producer of a quality product.

A Stronger Focus on Cost Reduction   Stiffening price competition gives firms the incentive to reduce unit costs. The efforts can cover a broad front: pushing suppliers for better prices, switching to lower-priced components, adopting more economical product designs, emphasizing manufacturing and distribution efficiency, retrenching sales efforts (to concentrate on the best type of buyers), and trimming administrative overhead.

Increasing Sales to Present Customers   In a mature market, growing by taking customers away from rivals may not hold as much appeal as a strategy of expanding sales to existing customers. Increasing the purchases of existing customers can take the form of broadening the lines offered to include complementary products and ancillary services, finding more ways for customers to use the product, performing more functions for the buyers (assembling components prior to shipment), and so on.

Purchasing Rival Firms at Bargain Prices   Sometimes the facilities and assets of distressed rivals can be acquired cheaply. Such acquisitions can improve margins and help create a low-cost position if these facilities are not inefficient or likely to be rendered obsolete by technological change. Heileman Brewing Company rose from relative obscurity to become the fourth largest beer company by acquiring small regional brewers and used equipment at bargain prices.

Expanding Internationally   As its domestic market matures, a firm may seek to enter foreign markets where attractive growth potential still exists and where competitive pressures are not so strong. Foreign expansion can also be attractive if manufacturing facilities that have become obsolete domestically are still suitable for competing in less developed foreign markets (a condition that lowers entry costs). This can occur when (1) foreign buyers have less sophisticated needs and simpler, old-fashioned end-use applications; (2) foreign competitors are smaller, are less formidable, and do not employ the latest production technology; (3) squeezing exportable production volume from fully depreciated plants and equipment offers the prospects of bigger profit margins; and (4) a domestic firm's skills and reputation are readily transferable to foreign markets.

Strategic Pitfalls   Perhaps the biggest pitfall during the transition to industry maturity is not making a clear strategic choice and, instead, steering a middle course between low-cost, differentiation, and focus. Middle strategies leave the firm without a solid competitive advantage and blur its image with buyers. Other pitfalls include sacrificing long-term position for short-term profit, waiting too long to respond to price-cutting, not reducing excess capacity as growth slows, and overinvesting in efforts to boost sales growth.

Strategies for Firms in Mature or Declining Industries

Many firms operate in industries where demand is growing slower than the economy or is even declining. Although harvesting, selling out, and closing down are candidate strategies for weaker competitors with dim survival prospects, strong competitors may well find it possible to work within a stagnant market environment and achieve good performance.[17] Stagnant demand by itself is not enough to make an industry unattractive. Selling out may or may not be practical and closing down operations is always a last resort.

Firms competing in slow-growth or declining industries must accept the unpleasant realities of continuing stagnancy and resign themselves to performance goals consistent with the market opportunities that are available. Cash flow and return on investment criteria are more appropriate than growth-oriented performance measures, but sales and market share growth are by no means ruled out. Strong competitors may be able to take sales away from rivals, and either the acquisition of or exit of weaker firms creates opportunities for the market shares of the remaining companies to rise.

In general, three themes characterize the strategies of firms that have succeeded in stagnant industries:[18]

1. *Pursue a focus strategy by identifying, creating, and exploiting the growth segments within the industry.* Slow-growth or declining markets, like other markets, are composed of numerous segments and subsegments. Frequently, one or more of these segments is growing rapidly, despite a lack of growth in the industry as a whole. An astute competitor who is first to concentrate efforts in the most attractive segments can overcome stagnating sales and profits and possibly achieve a competitive advantage in serving the target segments.

---

[17] R. G. Hamermesh and S. B. Silk, "How to Compete in Stagnant Industries," *Harvard Business Review* 57, no. 5 (September–October 1979), p. 161.

[18] Ibid., p. 162.

2. *Emphasize quality improvement and product innovation.* Either enhanced quality or innovation can rejuvenate demand by creating important new growth segments or attracting buyers to trade up. Successful product innovation provides an avenue for competing besides that of meeting or beating the prices of rival sellers. Differentiation based on successful innovation has the additional advantage of being difficult and expensive for rival firms to imitate.

3. *Work diligently and persistently to improve production and distribution efficiency.* When increases in sales cannot be counted upon to generate increases in earnings, an alternative is to improve profit margins and return on investment by reducing operating costs. The paths for achieving a lower cost position include: *(a)* improving the manufacturing process via automation and increased specialization, *(b)* consolidating underutilized production facilities, *(c)* adding more distribution channels to ensure the unit volume needed for low-cost production, and *(d)* closing down low-volume, high-cost distribution outlets.

Plainly enough, these three strategic themes are not mutually exclusive.[19] Attempts to introduce innovative versions of a product can *create* a fast-growing market segment. Similarly, increased efficiency paves the way for price reductions that can produce price-conscious growth segments. Note, also, that all three themes are variations of the three generic competitive strategies—creatively applied to fit opportunities and conditions in an otherwise unattractive industry environment.

The most attractive declining industries are those where the decline is reasonably slow and smooth and where some profitable niches remain. The pitfalls of choosing to continue to compete in a stagnating market are: (1) getting trapped in a profitless war of attrition, (2) trying to harvest from a weak initial position, and (3) excess optimism about the industry's future.

Strategies for Competing in Fragmented Industries

Many firms compete in an industry made up of numerous small and medium-sized companies, many of which are privately held and none of which has a king-sized share of total industry sales.[20] The key competitive feature of a fragmented industry is the absence of highly visible, well-known market leaders with the power to "dominate" the industry and set the tone of competition. Examples of fragmented industries include book publishing, landscaping and plant nurseries, kitchen cabinets, oil tanker shipping, auto repair, restaurants, public accounting, women's dresses, poultry processing, metal foundries, meat packing, paperboard boxes, log homes, hotels and motels, and furniture.

Industries are structured with a host of fairly small competitors for many reasons, some historical and some economic:

- Low entry barriers.
- An absence of scale economies.
- Diverse market needs from geographic area to geographic area, such that the

---

[19] Ibid., p. 165.

[20] This section is summarized from Porter, *Competitive Strategy,* chap. 9.

demand for any particular product version is small, and adequate volume is not present to support producing, distributing, or marketing on a scale that yields advantages to a large firm.

- The need of buyers for relatively small quantities of customized products (as in the business forms industry, advertising, and interior design) that are just as well provided by small firms as by larger firms.
- Strong image-based product differentiation from seller to seller creates so many market niches that many competitors secure a loyal clientele.
- High transportation costs (which limit the area a plant can economically service, as in concrete blocks, mobile homes, milk, and gravel).
- Local regulatory requirements that make each geographic area somewhat unique.
- Newness of the industry (no firms have yet developed the skills and resources to command a significant market share).

Some fragmented industries consolidate naturally as they mature—the stiffer competition that comes with a slow-growth industry environment produces a shake-out of weak, inefficient firms and a greater concentration of fairly large, visible sellers. Other fragmented industries remain atomistically competitive because it is inherent in the nature of their business. And still others remain "stuck" in a fragmented state because existing firms lack the resources or ingenuity to employ a strategy that might promote industry consolidation.

Firms in fragmented industries are usually in a weak bargaining position with buyers and suppliers. Entry into the industry is usually easy. Competition from substitutes may or may not be a major factor. In such an environment, about the best a firm can hope for is to rank among the most successful firms and to garner a modest market share. Competitive strategies based on low-cost, differentiation, or focus approaches are all viable except when the industry's product is highly standardized; then competitors are relegated to a strategy based on low cost or focused specialization. Specific competitive strategy options in fragmented industries include:

1. *Constructing and operating "formula" facilities*   This is an attractive approach to achieving low cost when the firm must operate facilities at multiple locations. It involves designing a standard facility, constructing it in an optimum location at minimum cost, and then polishing to a science how to operate it in super-efficient manner. McDonald's and 7-Eleven have pursued this strategy to perfection, earning excellent profits in their respective industries.

2. *A bare-bones/no frills posture*   When price competition is intense and profit margins are constantly under pressure, a lean operation (based on low overhead, use of low-wage labor, tight budget control, and rigid adherence to a no-frills expenditure policy) can place a firm in the best position to play the price-cutting game and still earn profits above the industry average.

3. *Increasing customer value through integration*   Backward or forward integration may present opportunities to lower costs or enhance the value given to customers (for example, cutting an item to size, assembling components before shipment to customers, or providing technical advice to customers).

4. *Specializing by product type*   When a fragmented industry produces a broad product line with many models and styles, a focus strategy based on specialization in a limited portion of the line can be very effective. In furniture, there are firms

that specialize in only one furniture type, such as brass beds, rattan and wicker furniture, lawn furniture, or early American furniture. In auto repair, there are specialist firms for transmission repair, body work, and mufflers, brakes, and shocks.

5. *Specializing by customer type*   A firm can try to cope with the intense competition of a fragmented industry by catering to customers who have the least bargaining leverage (because they are small in size or because they purchase only a small volume each year), by specializing in serving customers who are the least price sensitive, by going after those buyers who are interested in additional services or product attributes or other "extras," by serving customers who place custom orders, or by targeting buyers who have special needs or tastes.

6. *Focusing on a limited geographic area*   Even though a firm in a fragmented industry is unable to win a big industrywide market share, it may be able to realize significant internal operating economies by blanketing a local or regional geographic area. Concentrating facilities and marketing activities on a limited territory can produce greater sales force efficiency, speed delivery and customer services, and permit saturation advertising, while avoiding the diseconomies of trying to duplicate the strategy on a national scale. Convenience food stores, dry cleaning establishments, savings and loan associations, and department store retailers have been successful in operating multiple locations within a limited geographic area.

In fragmented industries, firms have a wide degree of strategic freedom—many different strategic approaches can exist side by side.

Strategies for Competing in Global Industries

A global industry is one for which the marketplace is worldwide and major firms are driven to employ some type of worldwide competitive strategy.[21] Global competition exists in oil, steel, automobiles, television receivers, motorcycles, sewing machines, heavy construction, aircraft, telecommunications equipment, and apparel. Although the types of structural variables and competitive forces operating in global industries parallel those in less expansive markets, there are some unique features of a globally competitive market environment:

- Varying prices and costs from country to country (due to flexible currency exchange rates, sharp variations in prevailing wage rates from country to country, different inflation rates and other economic conditions, and variations in input supply capability).
- Differences in buyer habits and needs from country to country.
- Differences among foreign governments in trade rules and regulations.
- Differences in competitors and competition from country to country.

There are three basic strategic options for gaining global market coverage: (1) license foreign firms to produce and distribute one's products, (2) maintain a national (one-country) production base and export goods to foreign countries, and (3) establish

---

[21] This section is adapted from Porter, *Competitive Strategy*, chap. 13. See, also, Michael E. Porter, "Changing Patterns of International Competition," *California Management Review* 28, no. 2 (Winter 1986), pp. 9–40.

foreign-based plants and distribution networks to compete directly in the markets of foreign countries.

Competing in globally competitive market environments is complicated by the degree to which technology can flow freely from country to country, by protective national governments (who try to insulate domestic industry from foreign competitors), by the differing emphasis companies put on expanding in international markets, and by the size of any scale economies that accrue to firms which capture a significant share of the global market. These situational factors give rise to four generic approaches to competing on a global scale:

1. *Broad line global competition*—where strategy is directed at competing worldwide with a full product line and plant locations in many countries.
2. *A global focus strategy*—where competitive energies are aimed at serving the same identifiable market segment in each of many target countries.

ILLUSTRATION CAPSULE 13

Ten Common Strategic Mistakes

Experience has shown that some strategic actions fail more often than they succeed. Ten samples of strategic moves that usually produce poor results are presented below:

1. Imitating the moves of leading or successful competitors when the market has no more room for copycat products and look-alike competitors.
2. Spending more money on marketing and sales promotion to try to get around problems with product quality and product performance.
3. Establishing many weak market positions instead of a few strong ones.
4. Trying to achieve greater productivity and lower unit costs by making heavy investments in new facilities and equipment (the risk here is that an unforeseen downturn in industry demand will give rise to excess capacity and put the firm in a bind to meet high fixed overhead costs and debt repayment obligations).
5. Allocating R&D efforts to weak products instead of to strong products.
6. Attacking the market leaders head-on without having either a good competitive advantage or adequate financial strength.
7. Making such aggressive attempts to take market share that rivals are provoked into strong retaliation and a costly "arms-race" struggle ensues (such battles seldom produce a substantial change in market shares; the usual outcome is higher costs and profitless sales growth).
8. Harvesting a weak business in a declining industry.
9. Trying to repeat the same strategy in a new business (what worked elsewhere may not work again, even in similar industry environments, because of subtle differences in industry key success factors and competitive forces).
10. Giving higher priority to cost reduction than to opportunities for building a stronger position in selected market segments.

These mistakes are usually born out of acts of desperation, poor analysis of industry and competitive conditions, and/or misjudgments of one sort or another.

3. *A nation-by-nation focus strategy*—where the firm sees important market and buyer differences from country to country and concludes that a single worldwide competitive approach is not as strong as a multiple country-by-country approach. The end result is a competitive approach that is flexible enough to be tailored to meet the specific needs of buyers in a particular country.

4. *A protected niche strategy*—where a firm seeks out situations having local government restrictions that preclude global or national approaches and, instead, require a localized geographic strategy that fits local government requirements. The aim is to achieve a local competitive advantage by being more responsive to local market variables and the customized requirements of particular localities within a country.

As a conclusion to our review of generic business strategies, read Illustration Capsule 13 describing 10 of the most common business strategy mistakes.

ANALYTICAL CHECKLIST

The task of strategy analysis always goes beyond the first step of identifying alternatives; the real challenge is deciding which strategy option best fits the firm's overall industry environment and competitive position. Table 4–3 provides a summary check-

Table 4–3   Matching Strategy to the Situation: A Checklist of Optional Strategies and Generic Situations

Market Share and Investment Options	Generic Competitive Strategy Options	Generic Industry Environments	Generic Company Positions/Situations

• Grow and build
  Capture a bigger market share by growing faster than industry as a whole
	• Overall low-cost leadership
	• Differentiation
	• Focus
	  Based on low-cost
	  Based on differentiation
		• New emerging industry
		• Rapid growth
		• Transition to maturity/competitive shake-out and industry consolidation
			• Dominant leader
			• Leader
			• Strong runner-up/aggressive challenger

• Hold and maintain
  Protect market share; grow at least as fast as whole industry
  Invest enough resources to maintain competitive strength and market position
		• Mature/slow growth
		• Aging/declining
		• Fragmented
		• Globally competitive
			• Weak runner-up
			• Weak/in trouble/distressed
			• Aggressive newcomer
			• Candidate for exit/failing
			• No-name, also-ran

• Withdraw and abandon
  Give up market share gradually
  Harvest; prepare for orderly market withdrawal
  Manage to maximize cash flow			

• Liquidate
  Sell out
  Close down			

list of the optional strategies and generic situations. The first analytical step in matching strategy to the situation is to diagnose the industry environment and the firm's competitive standing in the industry. Answers to the following questions need to be developed:

1. What stage of the life cycle is the industry in (emerging, growth, transition to maturity, mature, aging)? What strategic options and strategic postures are usually best suited for this stage?
2. What position does the firm have in the industry (strong versus weak versus crisis-ridden; leader versus runner-up versus also-ran)? How does the firm's standing influence its strategic options, given the stage of the industry's development—which options have to be ruled out?

Once these questions have been answered, step two is choosing which of the three generic competitive approaches to build the firm's strategy around:

- Strive to be the low-cost producer and become the overall cost leader.
- Pursue some sort of differentation theme (which one?).
- Specialize or focus on selected market segments (as opposed to trying to compete across-the-board).

To this must be added the firm's market share and investment options (see column 1 of Table 4–3).

Step three is to tailor the chosen generic approaches (see column 1 and 2 of Table 4–3) to fit *both* the industry environment and the firm's standing vis-à-vis competitors. Here, it is important to be sure that (1) the customized aspects of the proposed strategy are well matched to the firm's skills and capabilities and (2) the strategy addresses all of the strategic issues confronting the firm.

Step four is to formulate functional area support strategies to undergird the overall business and competitive strategy. Step five is to recommend a set of specific strategic actions that the company needs to take in the short-term (now) and in the long-term (a bit later).

SUGGESTED READINGS

Carroll, Glenn R.   "The Specialist Strategy." in *Strategy and Organization: A West Coast Perspective,* ed. Glenn Carroll and David Vogel. Marshfield, Mass.: Pitman Publishing, 1984, pp. 117–28.

Feldman, Lawrence P., and Albert L. Page.   "Harvesting: The Misunderstood Market Exit Strategy." *Journal of Business Strategy* 5, no. 4 (Spring 1985), pp. 79–85.

Finkin, Eugene F.   "Company Turnaround." *Journal of Business Strategy* 5, no. 4 (Spring 1985), pp. 14–25.

Hall, William K.   "Survival Strategies in a Hostile Environment." *Harvard Business Review* 58, no. 5 (September–October 1980), pp. 75–85.

Harrigan, Kathryn R.   *Strategic Flexibility.* Lexington, Mass.: Lexington Books, 1985, chaps. 6 and 8.

Heany, Donald F.   "Businesses in Profit Trouble." *Journal of Business Strategy* 5, no. 4 (Spring 1985), pp. 4–13.

Hofer, Charles W.   "Turnaround Strategies." *Journal of Business Strategy* 1, no. 1 (Summer 1980), pp. 19–31.

Hout, Thomas; Michael E. Porter; and Eileen Rudden.   "How Global Companies Win Out." *Harvard Business Review* 60, no. 5 (September–October 1982), pp. 98–108.

Ohmae, Kenichi.   *The Mind of the Strategist.* New York: Penguin Books, 1983, chaps. 8, 9, and 11.

Porter, Michael E.   *Competitive Strategy: Techniques for Analyzing Industries and Competitors.* New York: Free Press, 1980, chaps. 9–13.

————.   "Changing Patterns of International Competition." *California Management Review* 28, no. 2 (Winter 1986), pp. 9–40.

Schnaars, Steven P.   "When Entering Growth Markets, Are Pioneers Better than Poachers?" *Business Horizons* 29, no. 2 (March–April 1986), pp. 27–36.

Stevenson, H. H. and J. C. Jarrillo-Mossi.   "Preserving Entrepreneurship as Companies Grow." *Journal of Business Strategy* 7, no. 1 (Summer 1986), pp. 10–24.

Thompson, Arthur A., Jr.   "Strategies for Staying Cost Competitive." *Harvard Business Review* 62, no. 1 (January–February 1984), pp. 110–117.

Wright, Peter.   "The Strategic Options of Least-Cost, Differentiation, and Niche." *Business Horizons* 29, no. 2 (March–April 1986), pp. 21–26.

5 Building and Defending Competitive Advantages

Any business strategy, to be capable of sustained success, must be predicated on building and maintaining a competitive advantage. Competitive advantage grows out of positioning a firm in its competitive and industry environment so that it has an edge in coping with competitive forces. Many different positioning advantages exist: offering the highest quality product, providing the best customer service, being the biggest firm in the market, having the lowest prices, dominating a particular geographic region, having the best product to meet the needs of a narrowly targeted group of buyers, guaranteeing the highest degree of performance and reliability, and offering the most value for the money (a combination of good quality, good service, and acceptable price)—to mention some of the most frequently used competitive edge possibilities. But whichever positioning option is pursued, the essential competitive advantage requirement is that a viable number of buyers end up preferring the firm's product offering because of its perceived "superior value." Superior value is nearly always created in either of two ways: (1) by offering buyers a "standard" product at a lower price or (2) by using some differentiating technique to provide a "better" product that more than offsets the higher price it usually carries.

This chapter spotlights the ways a competitive advantage can be achieved or defended.[1] Attention is trained on how competitive advantages are built and sustained with:

---

[1] Michael E. Porter of the Harvard Business School has done more than anyone else to expose the *hows* of achieving and defending competitive advantage. His 1980 book, *Competitive Strategy,* quickly won status as a classic and in five years has totally reshaped the approach to analyzing business and competitive strategy; no discussion of the tools and techniques of industry and competitive analysis is adequate without relying heavily on Porter's work. His latest book, *Competitive Advantage* (published by The

- Strategies aimed at being the industry's low-cost producer.
- Differentiation strategies.
- Focus strategies.
- Offensive strategies.
- Defensive strategies.

BUILDING COMPETITIVE ADVANTAGE VIA
LOW-COST LEADERSHIP

A firm's cost position is the result of the behavior of costs in each one of the activities comprising its total activity-cost chain.[2] Nine *major types of cost drivers* can come into play in determining costs in each activity segment of the chain:[3]

1. *Economies or diseconomies of scale*.   Economies or diseconomies of scale can exist in virtually any segment of the activity-cost chain. For example, manufacturing economies can sometimes be achieved by simplifying the product line and scheduling longer production runs for fewer models. A geographically organized sales force can realize economies as regional sales volume grows because a salesperson can write larger orders at each sales call and/or because of reduced travel time between calls. On the other hand, a sales force organized by product line can encounter travel-related diseconomies if salespersons have to spend disproportionately more travel time calling on distantly spaced customers. In global industries, modifying products by country instead of selling a standard product worldwide can boost unit costs because of lost time in model changeover, shorter production runs, and inability to reach the most economic scale of production for each model. Boosting local or regional market share can lower sales and marketing costs per unit, whereas opting for a bigger national market share by entering new regions can create scale diseconomies unless and until the market penetration in the newly entered regions reaches efficient proportions.

2. *Learning and experience curve effects*.   Experience-based cost savings can come from improved layout, gains in labor efficiency, debugging of technology, product design modifications that enhance manufacturing efficiency, redesign of machinery and equipment to gain increased operating speed, getting samples of rival's products and having design engineers study how they are made, and tips from suppliers, consultants, and ex-employees of rival firms. Learning tends to vary with the amount of management attention devoted to capturing the benefits of experience of both the

---

Free Press in 1985), is undoubtedly destined to serve as the definitive original treatment of how to capture a competitive advantage and, as such, is required reading for anyone who expects command of the subject. Because of its pathbreaking nature, this chapter necessarily draws heavily upon Porter's *Competitive Advantage* in an attempt to present the best, most up-to-date summary survey of how competitive advantages can be achieved and maintained. The material in this chapter only skims the surface and can, at most, serve as an introduction to the subject. Porter's *Competitive Advantage*, and the other references cited as sources for this chapter, offer more sweeping and much more intensive treatments of what is a complex and critical consideration in strategy formulation.

[2] The construction of activity-cost chains was briefly discussed in chapter 3. For greater detail and discussion of this analytical approach by its original author, see Michael E. Porter, *Competitive Advantage* (New York: Free Press, 1985), chap. 2. The strategic importance of looking at the whole industry chain has also been recognized and discussed by Ian MacMillan; see his article "Preemptive Strategies," *Journal of Business Strategy* 4, no. 2 (Fall 1983), pp. 18–26.

[3] This listing and explanation is condensed from Porter, *Competitive Advantage*, pp. 70–83.

firm and others. Learning benefits can be kept proprietary by building or modifying production equipment in-house, retaining key employees, limiting the dissemination of information through employee publications, and enforcing strict nondisclosure provisions in employment contracts.

3. *The percentage of capacity utilization.* High fixed costs as a percentage of total costs create a stiff unit cost penalty for underutilization of existing capacity. Increasing the percentage of capacity utilization spreads indirect and overhead costs over a larger unit volume and enhances the efficiency of fixed asset utilization. The more capital intensive the business, the more important this cost driver becomes. Finding ways to minimize the ups and downs in seasonal capacity utilization can be an important source of cost advantage.[4]

4. *Linkages with other activities in the chain.* When the cost of one activity is affected by the way other activities are performed, there is opportunity to lower the costs of the linked activities via superior coordination and/or joint optimization. Linkages with suppliers tend to center on suppliers' product design characteristics, quality assurance procedures, delivery and service policies, and the manner by which the supplier's product is furnished (for example, delivery of nails in prepackaged 1-pound, 5-pound, and 10-pound assortments instead of 100-pound bulk cartons can reduce a hardware dealer's labor costs in filling individual customer orders). The easiest supplier linkages to exploit are those where both a supplier's and a firm's costs fall because of coordination and/or joint optimization. Linkages with forward channels tend to center on location of warehouses, materials handling, outbound shipping, and packaging.

5. *Sharing opportunities with other business units within the enterprise.* When an activity can be shared with a sister unit, there can be significant cost savings. Cost sharing is potentially a way to achieve scale economies, ride the learning curve down at a faster clip, and/or achieve fuller capacity utilization. Sometimes the experience gained in one division can be used to help reduce costs in another; sharing know-how is significant when the activities are similar and the knowledge can be readily transferred from one unit to another.

6. *The extent of vertical integration.* Partially or fully integrating into the activities of either suppliers or forward channel allies can allow an enterprise to detour suppliers or buyers with considerable bargaining power. Vertical integration can also result in cost savings when it is feasible to coordinate or closely mesh adjacent activities in the overall cost chain.

7. *Timing considerations associated with first-mover advantages and disadvantages.* The first major brand in the market may achieve lower costs of establishing and maintaining a brand name. Late movers can, in a fast-paced technology development situation, benefit from purchasing the latest equipment or avoiding the high product/market development costs of early-moving pioneers.

8. *Strategic choices and operating decisions.* A number of strategic decisions and operating decisions can affect costs:

---

[4] A firm can improve its capacity utilization by *(a)* serving a mix of accounts having peak volumes spread throughout the year, *(b)* finding off-season uses for its products, *(c)* serving private label customers that can intermittently use the excess capacity, *(d)* selecting buyers with stable demands or demands that are counter to the normal peak-valley cycle, *(e)* letting competitors serve the buyer segments whose demands fluctuate the most, and *(f)* sharing capacity with sister units having a different pattern of needs.

- Increasing/decreasing the number of products offered.
- Adding/cutting the services provided to buyers.
- Incorporating more/less performance and quality features into the product.
- Paying higher/lower wages and fringes to employees relative to rivals and firms in other industries.
- Increasing/decreasing the number of different forward channels utilized in distributing the firm's product.
- Raising/lowering the levels of R&D support as compared to rivals.
- Having more/less emphasis on achieving higher levels of productivity, as compared to rivals.
- Raising/lowering the specifications set for purchased materials.

A firm intent on being the low-cost producer needs to scrutinize each portion of the activity-cost chain to identify the costs associated with its strategic and operating choices. An examination of competitors' choices can suggest ways they can be modified or improved to obtain a stronger relative cost position.

9. _Locational variables._ Locations differ in their prevailing wage levels, tax rates, energy costs, inbound and outbound shipping and freight costs, and so on. Opportunities may exist for reducing costs by relocating plants, field offices, warehouses, and headquarters operations. Moreover, the distance between sister facilities affects intra-firm shipping, inventory, outbound freight on goods shipped to customers, and coordination.

Cost drivers can either reinforce or counteract one another. The cost savings of vertical integration, for example, may be strongly reinforced if it also opens up opportunities for sharing activities with sister units. Counteraction can occur when constructing capital-intensive, automated plants to achieve scale economies also has the effect of driving up the cost of capacity underutilization.

Ways to Achieve a Cost Advantage

A cost advantage is achieved when a firm's cumulative costs across the overall activity-cost chain are lower than competitors' cumulative costs.[5] How valuable a cost advantage is from a competitive strategy perspective depends on its sustainability. Sustainability, in turn, hinges on whether a firm's sources of cost advantage are difficult to copy or match in some other way. A cost advantage generates superior profitability when buyers consider the firm's product to be comparable to the products of competitors (and underpricing competitors is not necessary to win sales).

In a generic sense there are two ways to pursue a cost advantage: (1) do a better job of controlling the cost drivers vis-à-vis competitors; and (2) revamp the makeup of the activity-cost chain by doing things differently and saving enough in the process that customers can be supplied more cheaply. The two approaches are not mutually exclusive; low-cost producers usually achieve their cost advantage from any and all sources they can identify. More often than not, low-cost producers have a strong cost-conscious operating culture undergirded by symbolic traditions of spartan facili-

---

[5] This section is adapted from the presentation by Porter, _Competitive Advantage_, pp. 97–115.

ties, frugal screening of all budget requests, and limited perks and frills for employees at all levels.

The primary ways to achieve a cost advantage via revamping the makeup of the activity-cost chain include:

- Stripping away all the extras and offering only a basic, no-frills product or service.
- Using a different production process.
- Automating a particularly high-cost activity.
- Finding ways to use cheaper raw materials.
- Using new kinds of advertising media and promotional approaches relative to the industry norm.

ILLUSTRATION CAPSULE 14

Winning a Cost Advantage: Iowa Beef Packers and Federal Express Corp.

Iowa Beef Packers (IBP) and Federal Express Corp. have been able to win strong competitive positions by restructuring the traditional activity-cost chains in their industries. In beef packing the traditional cost chain involved raising cattle on scattered farms and ranches, shipping them live to labor-intensive, unionized slaughtering plants, and then transporting whole sides of beef to grocery retailers whose butcher departments cut them into smaller pieces and packaged them for sale to grocery shoppers. Iowa Beef Packers revamped the traditional chain with a radically different strategy: large automated plants employing nonunion workers were built near economically transportable supplies of cattle; then the meat was partially butchered at the processing plant into smaller high-yield cuts (sometimes sealed in plastic casing ready for purchase), boxed, and shipped to retailers. IBP's inbound cattle transportation expenses, traditionally a major cost item, were cut significantly by avoiding the weight losses that occurred when live animals were shipped long distances; major outbound shipping cost savings were achieved by not having to ship whole sides of beef with their high waste factor. Iowa Beef's strategy was so successful that it was, in 1985, the largest U.S. meat-packer, surpassing the former industry leaders, Swift, Wilson, and Armour.

Federal Express Corp. innovatively redefined the activity-cost chain for rapid delivery of small parcels. Traditional firms like Emery Air Freight Corporation and Airborne Express, Inc. operated by collecting freight packages of varying sizes, shipping them to their destinations via air freight and commercial airlines, and then delivering them to the addressee. Federal Express opted to focus only on the market for overnight delivery of small packages. These were collected at local drop points during the late afternoon hours, flown on company-owned planes during early evening hours to a central hub in Memphis where all parcels were sorted, then reloaded on company planes and flown during the late night/early morning hours to their destinations where they were delivered the next morning by company personnel using company trucks.

SOURCE: Michael E. Porter, *Competitive Advantage* (New York: Free Press, 1985), p. 109.

- Selling directly through one's own sales force instead of indirectly through dealers and distributors.
- Relocating facilities closer to suppliers and/or customers.
- Achieving a more economical degree of forward or backward vertical integration relative to competitors.
- Going against the "something for everyone" approach of others and focusing on a limited product/service to meet a special, but important, need of the target buyer segment.

Illustration Capsule 14 describes how two companies won strong competitive positions by restructuring the traditional activity-cost chain.

Pitfalls in Pursuing a Cost Advantage

Gaining a sustainable cost advantage is no easy chore; there are a number of common pitfalls:[6]

- Focusing too heavily or even exclusively on manufacturing costs (in many businesses, a significant portion of the activity-cost chain consists of sales and marketing, customer services, the development of new products and production process improvements, and internal staff support).
- Ignoring the payoff of first-rate, diligent efforts to reduce the cost of purchased materials and equipment (many senior executives view purchasing as a secondary staff function).
- Overlooking activities that represent a small fraction of total costs.
- Not understanding what factors really affect costs per unit (for example, a large regional market share may be more important to unit cost than having a large national share arising from scattered sales across many regions).
- Striving exclusively for incremental cost improvements in the existing activity-cost chain and not broadening the search to include ways to revamp the chain.
- Unwitting pursuit of conflicting functional strategies, as when a firm tries to gain market share to reap the benefits of scale economies and long production runs while at the same time dissipating the potential benefits of larger volume by adding more models and optional features.
- Pursuing cost reductions so zealously that differentiation of the firm's product is undermined by cutting out performance features, overstandardizing models, and eliminating helpful customer services.

BUILDING COMPETITIVE ADVANTAGE
VIA DIFFERENTIATION

Successful differentiation requires being unique at something buyers consider valuable.[7] When differentiation offers value to the customer, it yields competitive advantage.

---

[6] Ibid., pp. 115–18.

[7] Porter, *Competitive Advantage*, pp. 119–20. This section is based on Chapter 4 of *Competitive Advantage;* for an alternative treatment, see David A. Aaker, *Developing Business Strategies* (New York: John Wiley & Sons, 1984), pp. 251–57.

Differentiation is unsuccessful when the forms of uniqueness pursued by a firm are not valued highly by enough buyers to cause them to choose the firm's product over rivals' products. Successful differentiation allows a firm to: (1) command a premium price; and/or (2) sell more units of its product at a given price; and/or (3) realize greater degrees of buyer loyalty. Differentiation can produce superior profitability if the price premium achieved exceeds any added costs associated with accomplishing differentiation. Differentiation strategies may be aimed at broad customer groups or narrowly focused on a limited buyer segment having particular needs.

Ways to Differentiate

Successful differentiation strategies can grow out of activities performed anywhere in the overall activity-cost chain; they do not arise solely from marketing and advertising departments. The places in the chain where differentiation can be achieved include:[8]

1. *The procurement of raw materials* that affect the performance or quality of the end product. (McDonald's is more selective and particular than its competitors in selecting the potatoes it uses in its french fries.)
2. *Product-oriented R&D efforts* that lead to improved designs, performance features, expanded end-uses and applications, product variety, shorter lead times in developing new models, and being the first to come out with new products.
3. *Production process oriented R&D efforts* that lead to improved quality, reliability, and product appearance.
4. *The manufacturing process* insofar as it emphasizes zero defects, carefully engineered performance designs, long-term durability, improved economy to end-users, maintenance-free use, flexible end-use application, and consistent product quality.
5. *The outbound logistics system* to the extent that it improves delivery time and accurate order fulfillment.
6. *Marketing, sales, and customer service activities* that result in helpful technical assistance to buyers, faster maintenance and repair services, more and better product information provided to customers, more and better training materials for end-users, better credit terms, better warranty coverages, quicker order processing, more frequent sales calls, and greater customer convenience.

Differentiation is thus much broader than just "quality and service" aspects. Quality is primarily a function of the product's physical properties, whereas differentiation possibilities that create value to buyers can be found throughout the whole activity-cost chain.

Creating a Differentiation-Based Advantage

Anything a firm can do to lower the buyer's total costs of using a product or to raise the performance the buyer gets represents a potential basis for differentiation. [9] Specific ways to reduce a buyer's total costs include:

[8] Porter, *Competitive Advantage,* pp. 120–24.
[9] Ibid., pp. 135–38.

- Reduced waste and scrap in raw materials use.
- Lower labor costs (fewer hours, less training, lower skill requirements).
- Less down-time or idle time (because of short lead times in supplying spare parts).
- Faster processing times.
- Lower delivery, installation, or financing cost.
- Reduced inventory costs (because of reliable delivery capability from suppliers).
- Less maintenance and/or ease of maintenance.
- Reduced need for other inputs (energy, safety equipment, security personnel, inspection personnel).
- Higher trade-in value for used models.
- Compatibility to interface with other ancillary equipment.
- Multipurpose flexibility to handle a variety of needs and potential applications (reduces buyer's need for other equipment).
- Free advice and technical assistance on end-use applications (lowers need for technical personnel, enhances efficiency of use).
- The desire to avoid risk in the purchase decision should the product fail later at a big cost to the user.

Specific approaches to enhancing the performance of the product from the buyer's perspective include:

- Greater convenience and ease of use.
- More features that meet the full range of a buyer's requirements, as compared to competitors' products.
- Capacity to add on or change later.
- Optional extras to meet occasional needs.
- Flexible applications that give buyers more options to tailor their own products to the needs of customers.
- Ability to fill noneconomic needs such as status, image, prestige, appearance, comfort.
- Capability for meeting the customer's need to accommodate future growth and expansion requirements.

Real Value, Perceived Value, and Signals of Value

Buyers will seldom pay for value they do not perceive, no matter how real the unique extras may be.[10] Thus the price premium that a differentiation strategy commands is a reflection of the value actually delivered to the buyer and the value perceived by the buyer (even if not actually delivered). The difference between actual value and perceived value often emerges because buyers have a difficult time assessing in advance what their experience with the product will actually be. Sometimes, buyers cannot completely or accurately gauge value even *after* the product has been used; this is especially true in trying to compare the outcome with what might have been experienced with rival brands.

---

[10] This discussion draws from Porter, *Competitive Advantage,* pp. 138–42. Porter's insights here are particularly important to formulating differentiation strategies because they highlight the strategic relevance of *intangibles* and *signals.*

When buyers have incomplete knowledge about value, there is competitive opportunity for a seller to adopt a new differentiating feature, educate buyers to value it, and gain the first-mover advantage of reputation for being a leader. In addition, incomplete knowledge on the part of buyers often prompts buyers to judge or infer what the real value may be on the basis of such *signals* as: seller's word-of-mouth reputation; how attractively the product is packaged; how extensively the brand is advertised and thus how "well known" it is; the content of the ads and the image they project; the manner in which information is presented in brochures and sales presentations; the attractiveness and aura of quality associated with the seller's facilities; the list of customers a seller has; the market share the firm has; the time the firm has been in business; the price being charged (where price connotes "quality"); and the professionalism, appearance, and personality of the seller's employees. These signals of value may be as important as actual value when (1) the nature of differentiation is subjective or hard to quantify, (2) buyers are making their first-time purchases, (3) repurchase is infrequent, and (4) buyers are unsophisticated. A seller whose differentiation strategy delivers only modest extra value but who signals the existence of extra value very effectively may be able to command a higher price than a firm that actually delivers higher value but signals it poorly.

Keeping the Cost of Differentiation in Line

Attempts to achieve differentiation usually raise costs. The trick to profitable differentiation is either to raise unit costs by less than the price premium that the differentiation approach commands (this widens the profit margin per unit sold) or to more than offset the cost increase with enough added volume to cause total profits to be greater (larger volume can make up for smaller margins provided differentiation adds enough extra sales). In pursuing differentiation, a firm must be careful not to get its overall costs so far out of line with competitors that the resulting price premium is eaten up by the added costs of differentiating. From a cost perspective, the most attractive differentiating activities are those which enable a firm to achieve differentiation more cheaply than competitors or to charge a price that price more than offsets the added costs of achieving uniqueness. There may also be good reason to pursue all sources of differentiation that are not costly.

The Pitfalls of Pursuing a Differentiation-Based Competitive Advantage

There are, of course, no guarantees that differentiation will produce a meaningful competitive advantage. If buyers see little value in uniqueness and a "standard" item sufficiently meets customer needs, then a low-cost strategy can easily defeat a differentiation strategy. In addition, differentiation can be defeated when competitors are able to quickly copy most kinds of differentiation attempts. Rapid imitation, of course, means that real differentiation is never achieved and that competing brands remain pretty much alike despite the efforts of sellers to create uniqueness. Thus, to be successful at differentiation a firm must search out durable sources of uniqueness that are protected by barriers to quick or cheap imitation. Aside from these considerations, the most common pitfalls to pursuing differentiation include:[11]

- Trying to differentiate on the basis of something that does not lower buyer cost or enhance the buyer's well-being, as perceived by the buyer.
- Overdifferentiating so that price is too high as compared to competitors or that product quality or service levels go well past the needs of buyers.
- Trying to charge too high a price (the bigger the premium the more buyers can be attracted to competitors by means of a lower price).
- Ignoring the need to signal value and depending only on the "real" bases of differentiation.
- Not knowing the cost of differentiation and plodding ahead on the blind assumption that differentiation makes good economic and competitive sense.
- Not understanding or identifying what the buyer will consider as value.

BUILDING COMPETITIVE ADVANTAGE VIA FOCUSING

Buyer segments within an industry are far from homogeneous.[12] The strengths of the five competitive forces vary from segment to segment, and different segments can have significantly different activity-cost chains. As a consequence, segments differ in competitive attractiveness and in what it takes to achieve competitive advantage in each segment. It is these differences that give rise to the appeal of a focus strategy. The two crucial issues concerning adoption of a focus strategy revolve around (1) choosing which industry segments to compete in and (2) how to build competitive advantage in the target segments.

Deciding which segments to compete in hinges on the attractiveness of the various segments. Segment attractiveness is typically a function of segment size and growth rate, the intensity of the five competitive forces in the segment, segment profitability, the strategic importance of the segment to other major competitors, and the match between a firm's capabilities and the segment's needs. These are self-explanatory except for the differences between analyzing the five forces at the segment level as compared to the industry level.[13] In five forces analysis at the segment level, potential entrants include firms serving other segments, as well as firms not presently in the industry. Substitutes for the product varieties already included in the segment can be product varieties in the rest of the industry, as well as products produced in other industries. Rivalry in the segment involves both firms focusing exclusively on the segment and firms that serve this and other segments. Buyer and supplier power, while mostly segment-specific, can be influenced by buyer purchases in other segments and supplier sales to other segments. As a rule, then, five forces analysis of a segment tends to be heavily influenced by the amount of competitive spillover from other segments.

---

[11] Ibid., pp. 160–62.

[12] This section is based on Porter, *Competitive Advantage*, chap. 7; for a different but related approach to focusing and segmentation, see Kenichi Ohmae, *The Mind of the Strategist* (New York: Penguin Books, 1983), chap. 9. See also, Aaker, *Developing Business Strategies*, pp. 261–64.

[13] Porter, *Competitive Advantage*, pp. 256–57.

The segments most attractive for focusing have one or more of the following characteristics:

- The segment is of sufficient size and purchasing power to be profitable.
- The segment has good growth potential.
- The segment is not crucial to the success of major competitors.
- The focusing firm has the skills and resources to serve the segment effectively.
- The focuser can defend itself against challengers via the customer goodwill it has built up and its superior ability to serve buyers in the segment.

Choosing the Segment to Focus On

Segments are often related in ways that affect the choice of segments in which to compete.[14] The most important of these is the opportunity to share activities in the overall activity-cost chain across segments. There are times when (1) the same sales force can effectively sell to different buyer groups, (2) the same manufacturing plants can produce enough product varieties to supply two or more segments, (3) R&D can be done simultaneously for several product groups within the industry family, or (4) outbound shipping and distribution activities for two or more buyer groups can be closely coordinated, all with resultant cost savings in serving multiple segments. Such sharing interrelationships become strategically important whenever the benefits of sharing exceed the cost of sharing. This can occur when sharing promotes significant scale economies, more rapid learning, improved capacity utilization, increased differentiation, or lower differentiation costs. However, the benefits associated with segment interrelationships can be offset when:

- The costs of coordinating shared activities are high (because of greater operating complexity).
- The activity-cost chain designed to serve one segment is not optimally suitable for serving another segment, thereby compromising a firm's ability to serve both segments well.
- Sharing activities across segments limits the flexibility of modifying strategies in the target segments.

The net competitive advantage of focusing on one versus several target segments is a function of the balance between the benefits and costs of sharing activities. In general, the stronger the interrelationships among several segments, the more attractive is a multisegment focus strategy.

Creating a Focus-Based Competitive Advantage

A focuser, to achieve competitive advantage, has to succeed at low-cost leadership or differentiation *in its chosen segment or segments.* If a focuser opts to pursue low-cost leadership, then the same kinds of cost-reducing approaches as explained above

---

[14] Philip Kotler, *Marketing Management: Analysis, Planning and Control,* 5th ed. (Englewood Cliffs, N.J.: Prentice-Hall, 1984), p. 411.

for industrywide cost leadership have to be used in managing the activity-cost chain for the segment. If a focusing firm opts for differentiation, then it must look at buyer needs and develop ways to lower their costs or enhance the performance they get from the product. The specific kinds of differentiating approaches are the same for focusers as for broad competitors. What sets the creation of competitive advantage by focusing apart is that focus strategies are grounded in differences among segments. A focuser excels in serving the target segment. A focuser can gain a segment-based competitive advantage whenever differences across segments make it more costly for broadly targeted competitors to meet the specific needs of buyers in the focuser's target segments at the same time they are trying to serve other specific needs of buyers in other segments. This is the condition that makes focusing really attractive. When the differences among the segments are slight, a focuser has little defense against more broadly targeted competitors because they can serve the needs of the buyers' segment about as well as the focuser can.

Sustaining a Focus Strategy

For a focus strategy to be successful over time, three conditions must be present:[15]

- A focuser must be able to defend its position against inroads from more broadly targeted competitors. This is easier when segment differences are big and harder when they are small.
- A focuser needs to erect barriers to imitation from other focusers. Another competitor, either new to the industry or one dissatisfied with its current strategy, may try to replicate the focus strategy. The more attractive the segment and the more successful a focuser's strategy, the greater the threat of imitation (unless the focuser has built a good defense against imitation).
- A focuser must not be threatened by conditions that will cause the segment to dissolve into the broader market or to shrink to an unattractive size. Competitors serving broader parts of the industry may well use product innovation, advertising, promotional efforts, and other marketing tactics to induce buyers to leave the focuser's segment and come into theirs.

Pitfalls in Pursuing a Focus Strategy

Focusing on a segment or group of segments is not by itself a basis for competitive advantage.[16] For focusing to have a chance for real success, the target segment must involve buyers with different needs or require a seller to employ an activity-cost chain that is different from the chain needed to serve other segments. When more broadly targeted competitors do not face much compromise in serving multiple segments, a focus strategy involves an uphill struggle.

A second focus strategy pitfall is viewing the choice of segments served as a permanent decision. The strategically relevant segments evolve over time due to shifts in

---

[15] Porter, *Competitive Advantage*, pp 267–69.

[16] These and other pitfalls were identified by Porter; see *Competitive Advantage*, pp. 270–72.

buyer behavior, demographic changes in the demand side of the marketplace, the emergence of new buyer groups, and developments in new technology. The nature of the target segment must be continually monitored.

Two other pitfalls are (1) choosing a segment that cannot be successfully defended against challengers attracted by the segment's size and profitability and (2) going with a single-segment focus strategy and then having the target segment dry up.

OFFENSIVE STRATEGIES

To the extent that a firm can capture and maintain the initiative, competitors are forced to respond to the initiator's moves defensively and to do so under conditions not of their own choosing.[17] The strategic management challenge in capturing and retaining an offensive initiative involves:[18]

- Anticipating what it will take to be an industry leader during the next few rounds of strategic moves.
- Planning a *series* of moves aimed at throwing competitors off balance, keeping them on the defensive, and giving them little time to launch initiatives of their own.
- Gaining a shrewd understanding of offensive strategy tactics and what organizational capabilities are needed to carry them out.

As it turns out, military warfare principles are particularly instructive in designing offensive attacks on competitors' market positions. Three military maxims speak to how to attack an enemy:

- *Principle of mass*—Superior combat power must be concentrated at the critical time and place for a decisive purpose.
- *Principle of the offensive*—The commander who exercises the initiative, capitalizes on emergent opportunities, and exploits enemy weakness is in the best position to dominate the enemy and to maintain control of the campaign.
- *Principle of surprise*—Surprise results from striking an enemy at a time and place and in a manner for which he is not prepared.

And four additional offensive guidelines have been proposed by business strategists:[19]

- A challenger firm should concentrate its strength against its competitors' relative weaknesses.
- A major attack should never be launched against a competent, well-entrenched, competitor without first neutralizing the competitor's ability to counterattack effectively.

---

[17] Ian C. MacMillan, "How Business Strategies Can Use Guerrilla Warfare Tactics," *Journal of Business Strategy* 1, no. 2 (Fall 1980), p. 65.

[18] Ian C. MacMillan, "Seizing Competitive Initiative," *Journal of Business Strategy* 2, no. 4 (Spring 1982), pp. 45–49.

[19] Bruce D. Henderson, "On Corporate Strategy," reprinted in R. B. Lamb, *Competitive Strategic Management* (Englewood Cliffs, N.J.: Prentice-Hall, 1984), pp. 9, 10, 14; and Ian C. MacMillan, "Preemptive Strategies," *Journal of Business Strategy* 4, no. 2 (Fall 1983), p. 16.

- Any strategy of value requires that a firm follow a different course from its competitors *or* initiate action which will not be effective for an imitator *or* follow a course which will have quite different, and more favorable, consequences for it than for rivals.
- Capturing and retaining the initiative requires capitalizing on opportunities to preempt competitors and gain a prime market position. Preemption occurs when one firm moves first (to tie up the best suppliers, to build new capacity, and so on), creating a condition where others find it extremely difficult to follow because of the "first occupancy" benefits gained by the aggressor.

These military principles and experience-based business strategy admonitions have led to the identification of six attack strategies.[20]

Frontal Attacks on Competitors' Strengths

An offensive-minded firm is said to employ a frontal attack when it attacks an opponent head-on, pitting its own strengths against those of rivals. The outcome depends on who has the greater competitive strength and commitment. For a pure frontal attack to succeed, the initiator needs a strength advantage over the intended victim(s). The military "principle of force" holds that whoever has the greatest resources will win out, except if the defender has greater firing efficiency or a terrain advantage. Military wisdom maintains that for an aggressor's frontal attack to succeed against a well-entrenched opponent, the attacker needs at least a 3 to 1 advantage in combat firepower. When aggressor companies have fewer resources and weaker competitive strengths than entrenched defender firms, a frontal attack makes no sense and is generally doomed from the start.

All-out attacks on a competitor's strengths can involve initiatives on any of several fronts: price-cutting, boosts in advertising and promotion, improved quality and performance, added customer services, the construction of major new plant capacity, and/or bigger R&D outlays. Modified frontal attacks are more selective in the choice of offensive tactics and are often restricted to a single, but very important, new initiative. One of the most usual modified frontal ploys is for the aggressor to match the leader's product offering on other counts and beat it on price.[21] This can produce market share gains if the leader has strong reasons for not resorting to price cuts of its own and if the challenger convinces buyers that its product is as good as the leader's. However, whether such a strategy produces improved profits depends on the challenger's price-cost-volume relationships—will the price cuts result in lower margins and, if so, will the gains in volume offset the bottom-line impact of thinner margins per unit sold?

Another type of price-aggressive attack is based on first achieving overall low-cost leadership and then attacking competitors with a lower price.[22] Cost-related

---

[20] Philip Kotler and Ravi Singh, "Marketing Warfare in the 1980s," *Journal of Business Strategy* 1, no. 3 (Winter 1981), pp. 30–41; Kotler, *Marketing Management,* pp. 401–6; MacMillan, "Preemptive Strategies," pp. 16–26; and William A. Cohen, "War in the Marketplace," *Business Horizons* 29, no. 2 (March–April 1986), pp. 10–20.

[21] Kotler, *Marketing Management,* p. 402.

[22] Ibid. p. 403.

price-cutting is perhaps the strongest basis for launching and sustaining a price-aggressive frontal attack. Without a cost advantage, price-cutting works only if the aggressor has more financial resources than its rivals and can outlast them in a war of attrition.

Attacks on Competitors' Weaknesses

This offensive approach draws upon the military principle of mass and involves concentrating one's competitive strengths and resources against the weaknesses of rivals. The common weaknesses and openings that challengers are inclined to attack are:

- Geographic regions where the rival has a low market share and/or is exerting less competitive effort.
- Buyer segments which the rival is neglecting and/or is less equipped to serve.
- Situations where rivals have neglected improving quality and product performance, thus creating opportunities to switch quality and performance-conscious buyers over to the challenger's better-quality offering.
- Instances where rivals have done a poor job of providing adequate customer service, making it relatively easy for a service-oriented challenger to win away the defenders' disenchanted customers.
- Where the defenders have underadvertised and otherwise failed to market the product to its fullest potential, thereby allowing a challenger with strong marketing skills to move in and win substantial sales and market share.
- Where the market leaders have gaps in their product line and opportunities exist to develop these gaps into strong, new market segments.
- Where the market leaders have failed to spot certain buyer needs and an opportunity exists for an aggressor to jump in and serve them.

As a general rule, attacks on competitors' weaknesses have a better chance of succeeding than do frontal attacks on strengths. They may or may not involve the element of surprise.[23]

Simultaneous Attack on Many Fronts

There are times when aggressors launch a grand competitive offensive involving several major initiatives in an effort to throw a rival off-balance, divert its attention in many directions, and force it into channeling resources to simultaneously protect its front, sides, and rear. Hunt-Wesson Foods tried such an offensive several years ago in an attempt to wrest market share away from Heinz in the ketchup market. Simultaneously, Hunt's introduced two new ketchup flavors (pizza and hickory) to disrupt consumers' taste preferences, try to create new product segments, and capture more retail shelf space in groceries. It lowered its price to 70 percent of Heinz's price; it offered sizable trade allowances to retailers; and it raised its advertising budget to over twice the level of Heinz's.[24] The offensive failed because not enough Heinz users tried the

---

[23] For a discussion of the use of surprise to gain an offensive competitive edge, see William E. Rothschild, "Surprise and the Competitive Advantage," *Journal of Business Strategy* 4, no. 3 (Winter 1984), pp. 10–18.

[24] Kotler, *Marketing Management,* p. 404.

Hunt's brands, and many of those who switched over to Hunt's soon switched back to Heinz. Grand offensives have their best chance of success when a challenger, because of superior resources, can overpower its rivals by outspending them across-the-board, thereby "buying its way" into a position of market leadership and competitive advantage.

Bypass Offensives

Bypass offensives eschew any direct assault on a rival in favor of such moves as being the first to expand into new geographic markets, trying to create new segments via the introduction of products with different attributes and performance features, and leapfrogging into new technologies to supplant existing products and/or production processes. Technological leapfrogging is used often in high-tech industries; challengers concentrate on developing the next generation of technology and, when confident of its superiority, bring out a new wave of products that shift the competitive focus to its own new technological arena where it holds an advantage.

When bypass offensives can be disguised or otherwise made to appear as if they pose no *direct* threat to any particular rival, then they may not elicit any immediate competitive response. Aggressors who succeed in avoiding or delaying competitive retaliation may gain a significant first-mover advantage.

Guerrilla Offensives

Guerrilla offensives are particularly well suited to small challengers who have neither the resources nor the market visibility to mount a broad-based attack on the industry leaders. A guerrilla offensive involves attacking in those locations and at those times where an underdog can compete under conditions that suit it rather than its competitors. There are several options for designing a guerrilla offensive:[25]

1. Focus the offensive on a narrow, well-defined segment that is weakly defended by competitors.
2. Attack those fronts where rivals are overextended and have spread their resources thinly (possibilities include serving less populated geographic areas, enhancing delivery schedules at times when competitors' deliveries are running behind, adding to quality when rivals have quality control problems, and boosting technical services when buyers are confused by competitors' proliferation of models and optional features).
3. Make small, scattered raids on the leaders with such harassing tactics as selective lowballing on price, intense bursts of promotional activity, and legal actions charging antitrust violations, patent infringement, and unfair advertising.

---

[25] For more details, see MacMillan, "How Business Strategists Can Use Guerrilla Warfare Tactics," pp. 63–65; and Kathryn R. Harrigan, *Strategic Flexibility* (Lexington, Mass.: Lexington Books, 1985), pp. 30–45.

Preemptive Strategies

Preemptive strategies involve moving first to secure an advantageous position that rivals are foreclosed or discouraged from duplicating. There are several ways to win a prime strategic position with preemptive moves:[26]

- Expanding production capacity well ahead of market demand in hopes of discouraging rivals from following with expansions of their own. When rivals are "bluffed" out of adding capacity by a fear of creating long-term excess supply conditions and having to struggle with the bad profit economics of underutilized plants, the preemptor stands to win a bigger market share as market demand grows and its own plant capacity becomes filled.
- Tying up the best (or the most) raw material sources and/or the most reliable, high-quality suppliers via long-term contracts or backward vertical integration. This move can effectively relegate rivals to struggling for second-best supply positions.
- Securing the best geographic locations. Big first-mover advantages are often locked in by quickly moving to obtain the most favorable sites along a heavily traveled thoroughfare, at a new interchange or intersection, in a new shopping mall, in a scenic location, close to cheap transportation or raw material supplies or market outlets, and so on.
- Obtaining key accounts and the business of prestigious customers.
- Establishing a "psychological" image and position in the minds of consumers that is unique and hard to copy and that establishes a compelling appeal and rallying cry—examples include Avis's well-known "we try harder" theme; Frito-Lay's guarantee to retailers of "99.5 percent service;" Holiday Inns' assurance of "no surprises" and Prudential's "piece of the rock" image of safety and permanence.
- Securing exclusive or dominant access to the best distributors in an area.

Preemption has been used successfully on a number of occasions. General Mills' Red Lobster restaurant chain was notably successful in securing access to excellent seafood suppliers and in getting prime locations for its restaurant sites. DeBeers became the dominant world distributor of diamonds by tying up the production of nearly all of the important diamond mines. Du Pont's aggressive capacity expansions in titanium dioxide, while not blocking all competitors from expanding, did discourage enough competitors to give it a leadership position in the titanium dioxide industry. Coca-Cola has won a strong position in the fountain segment of the soft-drink industry by winning the McDonald's business. Price Waterhouse's image as the most prestigious public accounting firm has always been linked to its list of blue-chip corporate clients.

To be successful, it is not necessary for a preemptive move to totally blockade rivals from following or copying. It is enough to create a competitive advantage if preemption results in occupying a "prime" position. A prime position is one that is easier to defend and one that makes a material difference in how the game of competition unfolds in the industry.

---

[26] The use of preemptive moves is treated comprehensively in MacMillan, "Preemptive Strategies," pp. 16–26. What follows in this section is based on MacMillan's article.

Choosing Whom to Attack

Aggressor firms need to analyze which of their rivals to attack as well as how to attack them. There are basically three types of firms at which an offensive can be aimed:[27]

1. *Attack the market leader(s).* This entails high risk but can carry a potentially big payoff. It makes the best sense when the leader in terms of size and market share is not a "true leader" in terms of serving the market well. The signs of leader vulnerability include unhappy buyers, low profitability, strong emotional commitment to a technology it has pioneered, a history of regulatory problems, and being "stuck in the middle" (lacking real strength based on low-cost leadership or differentiation). Attacks on leaders can also succeed when the challenger is able to revamp its activity-cost chain or otherwise innovate activities in order to get a grip on a fresh cost-based or differentiation-based competitive advantage.[28] Attacks on leaders need not have the objective of making the aggressor the new leader; however, a challenger may "win" by simply wresting enough sales away from the leader to make the aggressor a far stronger runner-up.
2. *Attack runner-up firms.* Launching offensives against weaker runner-up firms whose positions are vulnerable often has strong appeal and carries relatively low risk. In such cases, frontal attacks may work, even if the challenger has smaller resources to work with, because the targeted rival's vulnerabilities are so readily exploitable.
3. *Attack small local and regional firms that are not doing the job and whose customers are dissatisfied.*

As was argued earlier in this chapter, the most successful strategies tend to be grounded in competitive advantage. This goes for offensive strategies, too. The offensive options for obtaining a competitive advantage can be linked to low-cost leadership, differentiation, or focusing. The primary competitive offensive weapons include:[29]

- Coming up with a lower-cost product design.
- Developing product features that deliver superior performance to buyers or that lower buyers' user costs.
- Employing more efficient inbound and/or outbound logistical systems.
- Giving more responsive after-sale support to buyers.
- Escalating the marketing effort in an undermarketed industry.
- Utilizing a more technically proficient sales force.
- Making changes in production operations that lower costs or enhance differentiation.
- Pioneering a new distribution channel.
- Bypassing existing channels and selling direct to the end-user.

---

[27] Kotler, *Marketing Management,* p. 400.

[28] Porter, *Competitive Advantage,* p. 518.

[29] Ibid., pp. 520–22.

USING DEFENSIVE STRATEGIES TO PROTECT COMPETITIVE ADVANTAGES

In a competitive market, all firms are subject to attacks from rivals. Offensive attacks can come both from new entrants into the industry and from established firms seeking to improve their market positions. The purpose of defensive strategy is to lower the risk of being attacked, to lessen the intensity of any attack that occurs, and to influence challengers to opt for less threatening offensive strategies.[30] While defensive strategy usually doesn't enhance a firm's competitive advantage, it should definitely be capable of strengthening a firm's competitive position and thus sustaining whatever competitive advantage the firm has.

The Kinds of Defensive Tactics

There are substantial numbers of defensive tactics to choose from in formulating a comprehensive defensive strategy. One category of defensive tactics involves trying to block off the avenues that challengers can take in mounting an offensive; the options here include:[31]

- Broadening the product line to close off vacant niches and gaps to would-be challengers.
- Introducing models or brands that match the characteristics that challengers' models already have or might have.
- Keeping prices low on those models that most closely match competitors' offerings.
- Signing exclusive agreements with dealers and distributors to keep competitors from using the same ones.
- Granting dealers and distributors sizable volume discounts in order to discourage them from experimenting with other suppliers.
- Offering free or low-cost training to buyers' personnel in the use of the firm's product.
- Making it harder for competitors to get buyers to try their brands by: (1) giving special price discounts to buyers who are considering trial use of rival brands, (2) resorting to high levels of couponing and sample giveaways to buyers most likely to experiment, and (3) leaking information about impending new products or price changes that cause buyers to postpone switching decisions.
- Raising the amount of financing provided to dealers and/or to buyers.
- Reducing delivery times for spare parts.
- Increasing warranty coverages.
- Patenting the feasible alternative technologies.
- Maintaining a participation in alternative technologies.
- Trying to discredit alternative technologies.

---

[30] Ibid., p. 482.

[31] Porter, *Competitive Advantage,* pp. 489–94.

- Protecting proprietary know-how in products, production technologies, and other parts of the activity-cost chain.
- Signing exclusive contracts with the best suppliers to block access of aggressive rivals.
- Purchasing natural resource reserves well in excess of present needs so as to preempt them from competitors.
- Avoiding suppliers that also serve competitors.
- Challenging rivals' products or practices in regulatory proceedings.

A second category of defensive tactics consists of ways to signal challengers that there is a real threat of strong retaliation if the challenger attacks. Such tactics are intended to dissuade challengers from attacking at all (by raising their expectations that the resulting battle will be bloody and more costly to the challenger than it is worth) or, at the least, to blunt and divert the attack to arenas that are less threatening to the defender. A number of defensive moves can be used to signal challengers of a defender's intent to retaliate:[32]

- Publicly announcing management's commitment to maintain the firm's present market share.
- Publicly announcing plans to construct enough production capacity to meet rising demand, and sometimes building just ahead of demand.
- Leaking advance information about a new product generation, a breakthrough in production technology, or the planned introduction of important new brands or models, thereby raising the risk perceived by challengers that such a move will actually be forthcoming and, hopefully, inducing them to delay moves of their own until they see if the signals are credible.
- Publicly committing the firm to a policy of matching the prices or other terms offered by competitors.
- Maintaining a war chest of cash reserves.
- Making an occasional strong counterresponse to the moves of weak competitors to enhance the firm's image as a tough defender.

A third category of defensive maneuvers involves trying to lower the inducement for challengers to launch an offensive. Typically, profit is the inducement for attack—in particular, the defender's current profits and the challenger's assumption about future industry conditions and profitability. A defender can deflect attacks, especially from new entrants, by not being too greedy and deliberately forgoing some short-run profits. When a firm's or an industry's profitability is very high, challengers are more willing to try to hurdle high defensive barriers and to combat strong retaliation.

Benefit-Cost Trade-Offs   The benefits of a successful defense can be hard to measure because when a defense works best, nothing happens in the way of serious challenges. On the other hand, a number of defensive options involve substantial costs to a firm. Defensive tactics become more attractive:[33]

---

[32] Porter, *Competitive Advantage*, pp. 495–97. The listing here is selective; Porter offers a greater number of options.
[33] Ibid., pp. 500–502.

1. When the firm's position with buyers is strengthened through enhanced differentiation or increased sales or increased buyer loyalty.
2. When the cost of the defensive tactic imposes an even greater cost on a challenger.
3. When the defensive tactic has a lasting effect in raising barriers or in creating a credible long-term threat of retaliation.
4. When the tactic will be noticed and taken seriously by challengers (because the defender has the resources to carry out its retaliatory threats and a resolve to do so).

Illustration Capsule 15 relates a fascinating example of the offensive and defensive maneuvers IBM once employed in mainframe computers.

ILLUSTRATION CAPSULE 15

Competitive Strategy at IBM: The System/360 Product Line

IBM'S System/360 computer models included a wide range of central processing unit (CPU) sizes, together with numerous options for tying in input-output equipment (printers, readers) and memory storage. IBM priced its memory and input-output equipment separately from its central processing computer units so as to allow customers maximum flexibility in choosing the best equipment combinations. The design characteristics of the System/360 models, however, allowed rival computer manufacturers to produce almost identical copies of the IBM input-output units and memories; they could then sell these at lower prices directly to users having IBM central processing units. Generally, IBM's central processing units were protected from the competition of rival computer firms because IBM customers were very reluctant to discard their investment in specialized programming and because of the difficulty in manufacturing a CPU having programming logic compatible with IBM processors. There was no such compatibility problem with input-output equipment or with memory units. Potter Instrument Company in 1967 initiated competition with IBM by introducing a replacement for IBM tape drives; a short time later, other peripheral equipment manufacturers came out with replacements for IBM disc drives and then for main memory units.

Because sales of input-output equipment and memory units accounted for over half of IBM's computer revenue, IBM was concerned in early 1970 about the threat posed by the competitive products of the peripheral equipment manufacturers and the great success they were having in getting IBM users to switch to lower-priced non-IBM equipment. At the time, IBM was preparing to introduce its new System/370 line, and while the company felt it could safely ignore the threat to the System/360 memories, it wanted to avoid losing the new System/370 memories to rival firms. IBM assembled a task force to assess how well rival firms would fare in selling IBM-compatible memory units against IBM at various IBM prices; the study was done for a hypothetical new company and also for an established company having the capacity to produce IBM-compatible memory units. Insofar as the hypothetical new company was concerned, the analysis showed that IBM's primary protection from competition was the time required for a new company to become established in the marketplace. The

ILLUSTRATION CAPSULE 15 *(continued)*

IBM task force estimated that if IBM established a lease price of $16,000 to $18,000 per month per megabyte of memory (with initial shipments to begin in 1972), then a new company could not break even competing with IBM until around 1974, and, further, if the IBM lease price was $12,000 and above, the task force projected good profitability for a new company beyond 1976 but at prices of $10,000 and below no break-even point was envisioned until the far future.

For an established company, the task force projected that a firm could enter memory competition and reach the break-even point by 1973 at an IBM lease price of $18,000 per month per megabyte, and by 1975 with a price of $10,000 to $12,000, with high profitability in later years for all lease rentals of $12,000 and above. The task force concluded that if IBM went ahead with its planned $12,000-per-megabyte monthly fee that a new company could be only marginally profitable but that an established peripheral equipment company would be very likely to enter the field because they could make a 20 percent return on investment for a $10 million investment and would enjoy a healthy 23 percent profit margin.

However, additional studies indicated that of the $61 million-per-month rental value which IBM expected to have from its memory units by 1976, 26 percent would be protected through minimum memory sizes tied directly to the CPU, 36 percent through customers who would resist mixing IBM equipment with that of other manufacturers, and 15 percent because of locations in outlying geographical areas where the smaller firms were not expected to compete. This left only 23 percent of IBM's memory business as a possible competitive target, regardless of the exact price set by IBM. Thus, based on the expected customer resistance to using non-IBM equipment and upon the estimated lag time between IBM's introduction to System/370 memory units and the availability of competitive memory units, IBM decided to go ahead with its planned price of $12,000 per month per megabyte for memory units on its 155 and 165 System/370 models. The 370/155 and 165 memory units utilized magnetic cores—the standard computer memory technology. But when IBM came out with its next System/370 model, the 145, a new all-semiconductor memory was used; this semiconductor memory was much faster than magnetic cores, and because it was a new technology, it was not considered subject to immediate competitive attack. As a result, IBM priced its new semiconductor memory units 60 percent higher than its magnetic core memory units. Within less than a year, though, IBM became concerned about the ability of rival firms to introduce not only magnetic core replacements for the earlier System/370 models but also replacement equipment for the new semiconductor unit.

Meanwhile, IBM studies indicated lower prices for central processing units prompted users to install the largest possible system and thus generate the maximum demand for memory and input-output equipment (subject to replacement by competitors), while higher prices on central processing units increased CPU profits but reduced the demand and profit earned on peripheral equipment sales and leases. IBM's solution to this profit trade-off was to package a large amount of memory with a central processing unit and charge a lower CPU price. This had the advantage of raising overall profits, while protecting at least the packaged portion of memory from competition.

ILLUSTRATION CAPSULE 15 *(continued)*

Even so, within a few months, IBM saw that its previous forecast had underestimated the ability of rival firms to keep pace, and still another task force was set up to study alternatives for reducing the competitive threat. Basically, the plans the task force considered were various combinations of minimum memories, lower memory unit prices, and increased CPU prices. The task force also looked at reducing the number of memory options obtainable with a central processing unit and then refusing to sell CPUs without at least the minimum memory. Nonetheless, the final decision was to raise the central processing unit prices by a maximum of 8 percent, cut the purchase price of memory units on 155 and 165 models, and make no change in the rental price of memory units.

This action shortly proved to be ineffective, and IBM came up with a strategy of introducing upgraded 155 and 165 models as new machines having higher CPU prices and lower memory prices. In August 1972 IBM announced new versions of its 155 and 165 models, to be known as the 158 and 168 models (a revision known inside IBM as the SMASH program). The basic CPU price was raised 36 percent on the 165 model and 54 percent on the model 155. The memory price was cut 57 percent and a larger minimum memory size was tied to the basic central processing unit on both models, neither of which could be acquired without the memory units. The effect of the changes was to make the total price of the 158 and 168 models higher in small configurations and lower in large configurations than the original 155 and 165 models. The semiconductor memory was not made available to users of the original 155 and 165 models, thereby prohibiting users from buying the cheaper central process unit and putting on the cheaper memory as well. The SMASH program effectively foreclosed rival firms from the memory market for several months.

In trying to unravel IBM's actions it is important to understand that there are high barriers to entry in the full-line computer systems market but low barriers to entry in the peripheral equipment market. The barriers that do exist in the peripheral equipment market are related primarily to brand loyalty to IBM (including a fear of problems of mixing the equipment of different manufacturers) and the difficulty of producing IBM-compatible products which will match IBM interface specifications. The latter problem causes a lag between the time IBM introduces a product and the time it can be copied. This time lag reduces the rental life of the product of rival firms and gives IBM some time after a new product introduction without competition. Additional barriers to entry in the peripheral market include raising enough working capital to finance a rental business and some small manufacturing economies of scale. However, the disadvantages of small size are not so large as to preclude a satisfactory profit by undercutting IBM's existing price—unless and until IBM also cuts prices.

A second aspect of the computer equipment market is the disruption caused by equipment installation and removal, even if compatibility is not a problem. Normally, lower-priced equipment is introduced as a "new" product having essentially identical performance specifications as existing products. The customer can get the price cut only by physically removing the old model and installing the new one. The freight charges and disruption involved, as well as lack of information or lethargy on the part of some computer users, allowed IBM to

ILLUSTRATION CAPSULE 15 *(concluded)*

come out with a competitive low-priced product while still receiving the higher rent from many users for some time after the price cut.

A third feature which IBM used to good advantage related to the time lag between IBM's introduction of a new product and a rival's introduction of its equivalent. As part of its introductory scheme, IBM induced users to agree to a fixed-term lease period, with heavy penalties for early termination. This effectively locked out competitors until users completed their lease agreements.

ANALYTICAL CHECKLIST

The strategist's task is to judge "how all the factors add up" and "which strategy and competitive approach make the most sense, all things considered." In singling out stronger candidate strategies from the weaker ones and weighing the pros and cons of the most attractive strategic options, the answers to the following questions often indicate the way to go:

- Given the firm's competitive position in the industry and the strategies of rivals, should the firm employ a focus, differentiation, or overall low-cost leadership approach?
- What type of competitive advantage is most attractive in terms of achievability and sustainability? What can the firm do *specially* to achieve this advantage? Does it have the skills/resources to be successful?
- Once built, how can the competitive advantage be protected? What defensive strategies need to be employed? Will rivals counterattack? What will it take to blunt their efforts?
- Are any rivals particularly vulnerable? Should the firm mount an offensive to capitalize on these vulnerabilities? What offensive moves need to be employed?
- What additional strategic moves are needed to deal with driving forces in the industry, specific environmental threats, the industry's key success factors or other issues/problems unique to the firm?

As the choice of strategic initiatives is developed, there are some specific pitfalls to watch out for:

- The combination of strategic actions being contemplated should not represent so many dulled edges and compromises that the firm ends up *stuck in the middle,* with no sharply defined strategic theme and a blurred, inconsistent image with buyers. The strategy should send consistent signals to buyers about the content of its product/service offering, always nurturing and reinforcing the image/reputation the firm is trying to present. Meeting the test of consistency is also important internally; if some of the strategic moves are in conflict and blur what really is trying to be achieved, then managers are likely to see the strategy as flawed and doomed to failure from the start (thereby undercutting effective implementation).

- The strategy ought to be capable of succeeding in a variety of market and economic conditions, not just in an environment that is favorable and benign. Unless some flexibility and room for contingencies is built in, the strategy will lack durability.
- The chosen strategy needs to be compatible with the organization's culture and temperament, as well as consistent with the philosophies and values of top management. Without both, the strategy will almost surely be unacceptable and unattractive to those who have the final authority and to those who must implement it.

SUGGESTED READINGS

Cohen, William A. "War in the Marketplace." *Business Horizons* 29, no. 2 (March–April 1986), pp. 10–20.

Coyne, Kevin P. "Sustainable Competitive Advantage—What It Is, What It Isn't." *Business Horizons* 29, no. 1 (January–February 1986), pp. 54–61.

Harrigan, Kathryn R. "Formulating Vertical Integration Strategies." *Academy of Management Review* 9, no. 4 (October 1984), pp. 638–52.

————. *Strategic Flexibility.* Lexington, Mass.: Lexington Books, 1985, chap. 2.

Henderson, Bruce D. "On Corporate Strategy." Reprinted in R. B. Lamb, ed., *Competitive Strategic Management* (Englewood Cliffs, N.J.: Prentice-Hall, 1984), pp. 1–34.

Hout, Thomas; Michael E. Porter; and Eileen Rudden. "How Global Companies Win Out." *Harvard Business Review* 60, no. 5 (September–October 1982), pp. 98–108.

Kotler, Philip, and Ravi Singh. "Marketing Warfare in the 1980s." *Journal of Business Strategy* 1, no. 3 (Winter 1981), pp. 30–41.

MacMillan, Ian C. "How Business Strategists Can Use Guerrilla Warfare Tactics." *Journal of Business Strategy* 1, no. 2 (Fall 1980), pp. 63–65.

————. "Seizing Competitive Initiative." *Journal of Business Strategy* 2, no. 4 (Spring 1982), pp. 43–57.

————. "Preemptive Strategies." *Journal of Business Strategy* 4, no. 2 (Fall 1983), pp. 16–26.

Ohmae, Kenichi. *The Mind of the Strategist.* New York: Penguin Books, 1983, chaps. 4 and 5.

Porter, Michael E. *Competitive Advantage.* New York: Free Press, 1985, chaps. 3, 4, 5, 7, 14, and 15.

Rothschild, William E. "Surprise and the Competitive Advantage." *Journal of Business Strategy* 4, no. 3 (Winter 1984), pp. 10–18.

Thompson, Arthur A. "Strategies for Staying Cost Competitive." *Harvard Business Review* 62, no. 1 (January–February 1984), pp. 110–17.

6 Generic Types of Corporate Strategies

In this chapter and the next, the spotlight is focused on corporate-level strategy. The issues of corporate strategy are broader than those of line-of-business (or business) strategy. Business strategy is the game plan for competing in a single line of business (in the context of the industry's environment and competitive forces), whereas corporate strategy goes beyond that level to address diversification—the present and future scope for the whole company and plans for getting peak performance from different business divisions. Line-of-business strategy is developed principally by the managers of business units, whereas corporate strategy is nearly always formulated by senior corporate officers. Business strategy and corporate strategy are the same only in enterprises content with single-business concentration.

The managerial function of corporate strategy is to establish a coherent corporate direction and an action plan for the entire enterprise. The core of corporate strategy rests with developing answers to three questions:

1. How should the corporation's diversified business portfolio be managed to improve long-term performance—what scope and mix of business units makes the most sense, which businesses should be divested, what new businesses should be added, and what courses to chart for continuing operations?
2. To what extent should the strategies of the firm's individual business units be coordinated?
3. How should the available corporate resources be allocated across all of the company's various activities in order to get maximum performance from the whole portfolio—which business units deserve what kind of resource and investment priority?

> To acquire or not to acquire: that is the question.
>
> —Robert J. Terry

> Doing too many things isn't always a good idea—no matter how much better you think you can do them than someone else.
>
> —Dan Ciampi

159

In this chapter we will survey the generic corporate strategy alternatives. In Chapter 7 we will examine the techniques for analyzing a multibusiness corporate portfolio and for building competitive advantage at the corporate level.

HOW COMPLEX ORGANIZATIONS DEVELOP—GENERAL PATTERNS OF CORPORATE STRATEGY EVOLUTION

Within the corporate sector where enterprises are complex enough to consist of several distinct business units, company growth seems to follow a fairly standard strategic path. The majority of companies begin as small single-business enterprises serving a local or at most a regional market. During a company's early years the product line tends to be limited and the capital base thin; the company's competitive position tends to be tenuous to weak. The initial strategic theme is nearly always "grow and build," with chief strategic thrusts aimed at increasing sales volume, improving market share, and cultivating customer loyalty. Much attention is devoted to building a stronger competitive position in relation to rival firms. Price, quality, service, and promotion are fine-tuned to respond more precisely to a detailed market need. The product line is broadened to meet variations in customer wants and end-use applications.

Opportunities for geographical market expansion customarily are pursued next. Usually the sequence of geographic expansion proceeds from local to regional to national to international markets, though the degree of penetration may be uneven from area to area because of varying profit potentials. Geographic expansion may, of course, stop short of global or even national proportions because of intense competition, lack of resources, or the unattractiveness of further market coverage.

When the opportunities for geographic expansion start to diminish, the third stage of corporate strategy may be directed toward opportunities for vertical integration— either backward to sources of supply, or forward to the ultimate consumer. For some companies, this is an attractive strategic move, due to the strength vertical integration adds to the firm's core business.

When a firm has reached the practical limits of geographical market expansion for its original product line and has also come to terms with the possibilities of forward and backward integration, there are several strategic options. The firm can either attempt a more intensive implementation of the current line-of-business strategy, or it can begin to focus on diversification opportunities and expanding the kind of businesses the company is in. The strategy of building a diversified business portfolio raises the issue of what new businesses to pursue. Obviously, there are many ways to answer the question, "What kind and how much diversification?" An almost infinite number of diversified business portfolios can be created. And after a diversified portfolio has been put together, the time will come when management has to consider, "What businesses do we need to get out of?"—planned abandonment, divestiture, or liquidation of those business units that no longer are attractive become realistic options. Somewhere along the way and for any number of reasons, the firm's portfolio of businesses may fall into disarray and start to perform poorly. Then the task of corporate strategy becomes one of concocting a game plan to restructure and rebuild the portfolio to fit new conditions and new corporate priorities.

GENERIC CORPORATE STRATEGY APPROACHES

The foregoing sketch of the evolutionary thrusts in formulating corporate strategy highlights the basic approaches to tailoring a corporatewide strategic plan. Seven generic corporate strategy approaches stand out:

1. Concentration on a single business, with little or no diversification.
2. A strategy of partial or full vertical integration.
3. A strategy of related diversification.
4. A strategy of unrelated diversification.
5. Abandonment, divestiture, and liquidation strategies.
6. Corporate turnaround, retrenchment, and portfolio restructuring strategies.
7. Combination strategies (mixing approaches 2 through 6 in varying ways).

Let's explore each of these generic corporate strategy approaches in some detail.

The Single-Business Corporate Strategy

The number of firms that have become household words concentrating in one line of business is impressive. The power of single-business concentration is evidenced by the market prominence of such familiar companies as McDonald's, Holiday Inns, Coca-Cola, BIC Pen, Apple Computer, Timex, Campbell Soup, Anheuser-Busch, Xerox, Gerber, and Polaroid, all of which gained their reputations in a single business. In the nonprofit sector, single activity emphasis has proved successful for the Red Cross, the Salvation Army, the Christian Children's Fund, the Girl Scouts, Phi Beta Kappa, and the American Civil Liberties Union.

Concentrating on a single line of business (whether it is total or with a small dose of diversification) offers some impressive competitive strengths and advantages. To begin with, single-business concentration breeds directional clarity and unity of purpose up and down the whole organization—there is no confusion about "who we are and what we do." A number of key strategic tasks become more manageable: the efforts of the *total* organization can be directed down the *same* business path rather than becoming fragmented into the pursuit of several different business directions simultaneously; the job of setting precise performance objectives for the company and for each department is less complex; and all entrepreneurial eyes can be trained squarely on keeping the firm's business strategy and competitive approach responsive to the winds of industry change and fine-tuned to specific customer needs. There is less chance that senior management's attention and limited organizational resources will be stretched thinly over too many diverse activities. All of the firm's managers, and especially those at the top executive level, can maintain hands-on contact with the core business and can be expected to have in-depth knowledge about operations. Most senior officers will probably have come up through the ranks and possess firsthand experience in field operations—something that is hard to expect of corporate managers in broadly diversified enterprises.

The competitive strength and earning power often associated with single-business concentration cannot be lightly dismissed. There are important sources of competitive advantage stemming from the single-business corporate strategy approach; concentrating on a single business offers opportunity for a firm to:

1. Build a distinctive competence by utilizing the full force of organizational resources and managerial know-how in order to become proficient at doing one thing very well and very efficiently.
2. Use the firm's accumulated experience and distinctive expertise to pioneer fresh approaches in production technology and/or in meeting customer needs and/or in product innovation and/or in any other part of the overall activity/cost chain.
3. Translate the firm's distinctive competence and ability to innovate into a reputation for leadership and excellence.

Many single-business enterprises have parlayed such opportunities into a sustainable competitive advantage and achieved a prominent leadership position in their industry.

Concentrating on a single line of business does pose the risk of putting all of a firm's eggs in one industry basket. If the industry stagnates, declines, or otherwise becomes unattractive, then the single-business enterprise's future outlook dims, the company's growth rate becomes tougher to sustain, and superior profit performance is much harder to achieve. In fact, there are times when changing customer needs, technological innovation, or new substitute products can undermine or virtually wipe out a single-business firm. One has only to recall what plastic bottles and paper cartons did to the market for glass milk bottles, what hand-held calculators did to the makers of slide rules, and what electric typewriters did to the manual typewriter business.

Vertical Integration Strategies

Vertical integration strategies *extend a firm's competitive scope within the same overall industry.* They involve expanding the firm's range of activities backward into sources of supply and/or forward toward end-users of the final product. Thus, if a manufacturer elects to build a new plant to make certain component parts rather than purchase them from outside suppliers, it remains in essentially the same industry as before— all that has changed is that it has business units in two stages of production in the industry's total activity chain. Similarly, if a personal computer manufacturer elects to integrate forward by opening up 100 retail stores to market its brands directly to users, it remains in the personal computer business even though its *competitive scope* within the industry extends further forward in the industry chain.

Plainly, the generic corporate approaches to vertical integration can involve integrating backward or integrating forward or doing both. Corporate strategy can aim at becoming *fully integrated,* participating in all stages of the process of getting products into the hands of final users, or the strategic objective may be limited to becoming *partially integrated.* A firm can accomplish vertical integration via its own internal start-up entry into more stages in the industry's activity chain, or it can choose to acquire an enterprise already positioned in the stage into which it wishes to integrate.

The best reason for pursuing vertical integration is to strengthen a firm's market position and/or to secure a competitive advantage.[1] Integrating backward into the business of one's suppliers can convert a cost center into a profit producer—an attractive option when suppliers have sizable profit margins. Moreover, integrating backward spares a firm the uncertainty of being dependent on suppliers of crucial raw materials or support services, as well as lessening the firm's vulnerability to powerful suppliers intent on jacking up the prices of important component materials at every opportunity.

The strategic impetus for forward integration has much the same roots. Undependable sales and distribution channels can give rise to costly inventory pileups and frequent underutilization of capacity, thereby undermining the economies of steady, near-capacity production operation. When the loss of these economies proves substantial, it is often advantageous for a firm to integrate forward in order to gain dependable channels through which to push its products to end-users.

For a raw materials producer, integrating forward into manufacturing may help achieve greater product differentiation and allow escape from the price-oriented competition of a commodity business. Often, early in the industry production chain, intermediate goods are "commodities" in the sense that they have essentially identical technical specifications irrespective of producer (as is the case with crude oil, poultry, sheet steel, cement, and textile fibers). Competition in the markets for commodity or commodity-like products is usually fiercely price competitive, with the shifting balance between supply and demand giving rise to volatile profits. However, the further the progression toward the ultimate consumer, the greater are the opportunities for a firm to break out of a commodity-like competitive environment and differentiate its end product via design, service, quality features, packaging, promotion, and so on. Often, product differentiation causes the importance of price to shrink in comparison to other competitive variables and allows for improved profit margins.

For a manufacturer, integrating forward may take the form of building a chain of closely supervised dealer franchises or it may mean establishing company-owned and company-operated retail outlets. Alternatively, it could simply entail staffing regional and district sales offices instead of selling through manufacturer's agents or independent distributors.

Whatever its specific format, forward integration is usually motivated by a desire to realize the profit potential of (1) a smoother, more economical production flow, (2) product differentiation, (3) having one's own capability for accessing end-user markets, and/or (4) a distribution cost advantage.

There are, however, some strategic disadvantages of vertical integration. The larger capital requirements that sometimes accompany a strategy of full vertical integration may place a heavy strain on an organization's financial resources. Second, integration introduces additional risks since the effect is to extend the enterprise's scope of activity across the industry chain. Third, vertical integration can so increase a firm's vested interests in technology, production facilities, and ways of doing things that it becomes reluctant to abandon heavy fixed investments even though they are becoming obsolete.

---

[1] Kathryn R. Harrigan, "A Framework for Looking at Vertical Integration," *Journal of Business Strategy* 3, no. 3 (Winter 1983), pp. 30–37; for specific advantages and disadvantages of vertical integration, see Kathryn R. Harrigan, *Strategic Flexibility* (Lexington, Mass.: Lexington Books, 1985), p. 162.

Because of this inflexibility, fully integrated firms are more vulnerable to new technologies and new products than are partially integrated or nonintegrated firms.

Fourth, vertical integration can pose problems of balancing capacity at each stage in the activity chain. The most efficient scale of operation at each step in the activity chain can be at substantial variance. Exact self-sufficiency at each interface is the exception, not the rule. Where internal capacity is not sufficient to supply the next stage, the difference will have to be bought externally. Where initial capacity is excessive, customers will need to be found for the surplus. And if by-products are generated, they will require arrangements for disposal.

All things considered, a strategy of vertical integration can have both important strengths and weaknesses. Which direction the scales tip on vertical integration depends on (1) how compatible it is with the organization's long-term strategic interests and performance objectives, (2) how much it strengthens an organization's position in the overall industry, and (3) the extent to which it creates competitive advantage. Unless these considerations yield solid benefits, vertical integration is not likely to be an attractive corporate strategy option.[2]

Related Diversification Strategies

There are two generic approaches to corporate diversification: *related* and *unrelated*. In related diversification a firm's several lines of business, although distinct, still possess some kind of "fit." The nature of the fit in related diversification can be based on any of several factors: shared technology, common labor skills and requirements, common distribution channels, common suppliers and raw material sources, similar operating methods, similar kinds of managerial know-how, marketing-distribution channel complementarity, or customer overlap—virtually any aspect where significant links or sharing opportunities exist in the respective activity-cost chains. In contrast, with unrelated diversification there is no common linkage or element of fit among a firm's several lines of business; in this sense unrelated diversification is *pure* diversification.

Related Diversification   Related diversification is a very attractive way to expand a firm's field of business interests. It allows a firm to maintain a degree of unity in its business activities and gain any benefits of fit and cost sharing, while at the same time spreading the risks of enterprise over a broader base. But more importantly, perhaps, when a firm has been able to build a distinctive competence in its original business, related diversification offers a way to exploit what it does best and to transfer a distinctive-competence-based competitive advantage from one business to another. Diversifying in ways that extend a firm's expertise to related businesses is a principal way to build corporate-level competitive advantage in a diversified firm; this advantage allows the diversifier to earn a profit greater than the total that would be earned if each business operated as an independent company. Specific approaches to related diversification include:

---

[2] For an extensive, well-researched, and fresh look at the whole family of corporate approaches to vertical integration, see Kathryn R. Harrigan, "Formulating Vertical Integration Strategies," *Academy of Management Review* 9, no. 4 (October 1984), pp. 638–52.

- Expanding via acquisition or internal start-up into products where sales force, advertising, and distribution activities can be shared (a bread bakery buying a firm making crackers and salty snack foods).
- Exploiting closely related technologies (a maker of agricultural seeds and fertilizers diversifying into chemicals for insect and plant disease control).
- Seeking to increase capacity utilization (an aluminum window manufacturer with idle equipment and unused plant space deciding to add aluminum lawn furniture to its product lineup).
- Increasing the utilization of existing natural resource and raw material holdings (a paper products firm electing to harvest more of its timberland and building a new plant to produce plywood).
- Acquiring a firm where the buyer has a distinctive ability to improve the operations of the seller (a successful mass marketer of women's cosmetics buying a distributor of women's jewelry and accessories).
- Building upon the organization's brand name and goodwill (a successful milk producer diversifying into ice cream parlors and frozen yogurt shops).
- Acquiring new businesses that will uniquely help the firm's position in its existing businesses (a canned fruit juice firm diversifying into canned vegetables and frozen pies to give it more clout with food brokers and an expanded distribution system).

Actual examples of related diversification abound. The BIC Corporation, which pioneered inexpensive throwaway ballpoint pens, used the distinctive low-cost production and mass merchandising competences it built up in writing instruments as the basis for diversifying into disposable cigarette lighters, disposable shaving razors, and pantyhose, all three of which were businesses that relied heavily on low-cost production know-how and skilled consumer marketing for competitive success. Tandy Corporation practiced related diversification when its chain of Radio Shack outlets (which originally handled mostly radio and stereo equipment) added telephones, intercoms, calculators, clocks, electronic and scientific toys, microcomputers, and peripheral computer equipment. The Tandy strategy was to use the marketing access provided by its thousands of Radio Shack locations to become one of the world's leading retailers of electronic technology to individual consumers. Philip Morris Incorporated, a leading cigarette manufacturer, employed a marketing-related diversification strategy when it purchased Miller Brewing and General Foods and transferred many of its cigarette marketing skills to the marketing of beer and consumer foods. Lockheed pursued a diversification strategy based on customer needs in creating business units to supply the U.S. Department of Defense with missiles, rocket engines, aircraft, electronic equipment, ships, and contract R&D for weapons. Sears understood that the diverse nature of TV sets, auto repair centers, men's suits, draperies, refrigerators, paint, and homeowner's insurance posed no difficulty to its corporate strategy because the same customers buy them, in very much the same way and with the same value expectations, thereby providing the essential link for its version of customer-based related diversification. Technology-based related diversification has proved successful in process industries (steel, aluminum, paper, and glass), where a single processing technique spawns a multitude of related products.

The Nature and Value of Strategic Fit   The thing that makes related diversification so attractive, in comparison with unrelated diversification, is the opportunity

to capitalize on *strategic fit*. Strategic fit exists when the activity-cost chains of different businesses are sufficiently related that opportunities exist to reduce costs, to enhance differentiation, or to manage more effectively by coordinating those particular activities in the industry chains that are closely related.[3] *A diversified firm which exploits these activity-cost chain interrelationships and captures the benefits of strategic fit can achieve a consolidated performance that is more than the sum of what the businesses can earn pursuing independent strategies.* The presence of strategic fit within a diversified firm's business portfolio, together with corporate management's skill in capturing the benefits of the interrelationships, makes related diversification capable of being a 2 + 2 = 5 phenomenon.

There are three broad categories of strategic fit. *Market-related fits* arise when the activity-cost chains of different businesses overlap so that the products are used by the same customers, sold by essentially the same marketing and sales methods in the same geographic market, or distributed through common dealers and retailers. A variety of opportunities for cost sharing and coordination spring from market-related strategic fit: use of a common sales force to call on customers, advertising the related products in the same ads and brochures, use of the same brand names, coordinated delivery and shipping, combined after-the-sale service and repair organizations, coordinated order processing and billing, use of common promotional tie-ins (cents-off couponing, free samples and trial offers, seasonal specials, and the like), and combined dealer networks. In general, market-related strategic fits enhance a firm's overall ability to economize on its marketing, selling, and distribution costs and/or on product offerings.

Operating fits arise from interrelationships in the procurement of purchased inputs, in production technology, in manufacture and assembly, and in such administrative support areas as hiring and training, finance (efficiency in raising investment capital and in utilizing work capital), government relations, accounting and information systems, security, and facility maintenance. Operating fits nearly always present opportunities for cost-saving; some derive from the potential to tap into more scale economies and some derive from ways to boost operating efficiency through sharing of related activities. The bigger the proportion of cost that an activity represents, the more significant the shared cost savings become and the bigger the relative cost advantage that can accrue to capturing operating fits.

Management fit emerges when different business units present managers with comparable or similar types of entrepreneurial, technical, administrative, or operating problems, thereby allowing the accumulated managerial know-how associated with one line of business to spill over and be useful in managing another line of business. Transfers of managerial know-how can occur anywhere in the activity-cost chain. United Airlines transferred its reservation systems know-how in air travel over to hotels when its corporate parent acquired Westin Hotels; Emerson Electric transferred its skills as a low-cost producer to its newly acquired Beaird-Poulan chain saw business division. In Beaird-Poulan's case, the transfer of management know-how drove its

---

[3] Michael E. Porter, *Competitive Advantage* (New York: Free Press, 1985), pp. 318–19. Porter has added substantially to the concept of strategic fit. The remainder of this section incorporates Porter's contributions into the presentation; for more details see Chapter 9 of *Competitive Advantage,* especially pp. 337–53. The various ways to share resources across business units have also been discussed in Kenichi Ohmae, *The Mind of the Strategist* (New York: Penguin Books, 1983), pp. 121–24; the discussion here incorporates his ideas as well as Porter's.

new strategy, changed the way its chain saws were designed and manufactured, and paved the way for new pricing and distribution emphasis. Management fit can also be based on (1) use of the same type of generic business strategy and competitive approach, (2) similar configuration of the activity-cost chains, and (3) the application of proprietary technology in related products or production processes.

Table 6–1 provides a selective summary of the generic types of sharing opportunities associated with strategic fit, the likely kinds of competitive advantages that can result from each sharing opportunity, and the "hidden factors" that can result in the promise of fit never being realized.

Unrelated Diversification Strategies

While many diversified companies have opted for related diversification to try to benefit from strategic fit opportunities, some firms have been more attracted to unrelated diversification. A simple criterion of venturing into "any industry in which we think we can make a profit" captures the essence of the corporate strategy of some broad diversified firms. Textron, for example, built its business portfolio out of such diverse businesses as Bell helicopters, Gorham silver, Homelite chain saws,

Table 6–1 Specific Types of Strategic Fit, the Competitive Advantage Potentials, and the Impediments to Achieving the Benefits of Fit

Types of Strategic Fit and Opportunities for Sharing	Potential Competitive Advantages	Impediments to Achieving the Benefits of Fit
Market-related strategic fits Shared sales force activities and/or shared sales offices	• Lower selling costs • Better market coverage • Stronger technical advice to buyers • Enhanced buyer convenience (can single source) • Improved access to buyers (have more products to sell)	• Buyers have different purchasing habits toward the products • Different salespersons are more effective in representing the product • Some products get more attention than others • Buyers prefer to multiple source rather than single source their purchases
Shared after-the-sale service and repair work	• Lower servicing costs • Better utilization of service personnel (less idle time) • Faster servicing of customer calls	• Different equipment and/or different labor skills are needed to handle repairs • Buyers may do some in-house repairs
Shared brand name	• Stronger brand image and company reputation • Increased buyer confidence in the brand	• Hurts reputation if quality of one product is lower
Shared advertising and promotional activities	• Lower costs • Greater clout in purchasing ads	• Appropriate forms of messages are different • Appropriate timing of promotions is different

Source: Compiled and adapted from Michael E. Porter, *Competitive Advantage* (New York: Free Press, 1985), pp. 337–51.

Table 6–1 *(concluded)*

Types of Strategic Fit and Opportunities for Sharing	Potential Competitive Advantage	Impediments to Achieving the Benefits of Fit
Common distribution channels	• Lower distribution costs • Enhanced bargaining power with distributors and retailers to gain shelf space, shelf positioning, stronger push and more dealer attention, and better profit margins	• Dealers resist being dominated by a single supplier and turn to multiple sources and lines • Heavy use of the shared channel erodes willingness of other channels to carry or push the firm's products
Shared order processing	• Lower order processing costs • One-stop shopping for buyer enhances service and thus differentiation	• Differences in ordering cycles disrupt order processing economies
Operating fits Joint procurement of purchased inputs	• Lower input costs • Improved input quality • Improved service from suppliers	• Input needs are different in terms of quality or other specifications • Inputs are needed at different plant locations and centralized purchasing is not responsive to separate needs of each plant
Shared manufacturing and assembly facilities	• Lower manufacturing/assembly costs • Better capacity utilization because peak demand for one product correlates with valley demand for other • Bigger scale of operation improves access to better technology and results in better quality	• Higher changeover costs in shifting from one product to another • High-cost special tooling or equipment is required to accommodate quality differences or design differences
Shared inbound and/or outbound shipping and materials handling	• Lower freight and handling costs • Better delivery reliability • More frequent deliveries such that inventory costs are reduced	• Input sources and/or plant locations are in different geographic areas • Needs for frequency and reliability of inbound/outbound delivery differ among the business units
Shared product and/or process technologies and/or technology development	• Lower product and/or process design costs because of shorter design times and transfers of knowledge from area to area • More innovative ability, owing to scale of effort and attraction of better R&D personnel	• Technologies are same but the applications in different business units are different enough to prevent much sharing of real value
Shared administrative support activities	• Lower administrative and operating overhead costs	• Support activities are not a large proportion of cost and sharing has little cost impact (and virtually no differentiation impact)
Management fits Shared management know-how, operating skills, and proprietary information	• Efficient transfer of a distinctive competence—can create cost savings or enhance differentiation • More effective management as concerns strategy formulation, strategy implementation, and understanding of key success factors	• Actual transfer of know-how is costly and/or stretches the key skill personnel too thinly • Increased risks that proprietary information will leak out

Shaeffer pens, Fafnir bearings, Speidel watchbands, Polaris snowmobiles, Sprague gas meters and fittings, Bostitch staplers, air cushion vehicles, iron castings, milling machines, rolling mills, industrial fasteners, insurance, and missile and spacecraft propulsion systems. International Telephone and Telegraph (ITT), another pioneer of unrelated diversification, has had in its portfolio at one time or another such broad-ranging businesses as telephone equipment, Sheraton hotels, Wonder Bread, Smithfield Hams, Bobbs-Merrill Publishing, Hartford Insurance, Aetna Finance, Avis Rent-a-Car, Jabsco Pump, Gotham Lighting, Speedwriting Inc., Transportation Displays, Rayonier chemical cellulose, Bramwell Business School, South Bend Window Cleaning, and Scott lawn care products.

Possible ways to pursue unrelated diversification strategies include:

1. A cash-rich, opportunity-poor company seeking to acquire a number of opportunity-rich, cash-poor enterprises.
2. A firm subject to strong seasonal and cyclical sales patterns diversifying into areas with a counterseasonal or countercyclical sales pattern.
3. A debt-heavy firm seeking to acquire a debt-free firm in order to balance the capital structure of the former and increase its borrowing capacity.
4. Building a diversified portfolio of three or four unrelated groups of businesses, striving for some degree of relatedness within each group.
5. Acquiring companies in any line of business, so long as the projected profit opportunities equal or exceed minimum criteria.

While there are circumstances where unrelated diversification is attractive, such a strategy has three big drawbacks. The Achilles' heel of unrelated diversification is the big demand it places on corporate-level management. The greater the number of diverse businesses that corporate managers must oversee and the more diverse these are, the harder it is for them to (1) stay on top of what is really going on in the divisions, (2) have in-depth familiarity with the strategic issues facing each business unit, and (3) probe deeply into the strategic actions and plans of business-level managers. As one president of a diversified firm expressed it:

> We've got to make sure that our core businesses are properly managed for solid, long-term earnings. We can't just sit back and watch the numbers. We've got to know what the real issues are out there in the profit centers. Otherwise, we're not even in a position to check out our managers on the big decisions. And considering the pressures they're under, that's pretty dangerous for all concerned.[4]

With broad diversification, one has to hope that corporate managers will have the talent (1) to hire "good management" to run each of many entirely different businesses; (2) to discern when the major strategic proposals of division managers are "sound" versus when they represent "good snow jobs"; and (3) to be shrewd in acquiring/divesting businesses of widely varying character. Because every business sooner or later gets into trouble, one test of the risk of diversifying into new unrelated areas is to ask, "If the new business got into trouble, would we know how to bail it out?" If the answer is no, the risk of trouble is high and the profit prospects are chancy.[5]

---

[4] Carter F. Bales, "Strategic Control: The President's Paradox," *Business Horizons* 20, no. 4 (August 1977), p. 17.

[5] Of course, management may be willing to assume the risk that trouble will not strike before it has had time to learn the business well enough to bail it out of most any difficulty. See Peter Drucker, *Management: Tasks, Responsibilities, Practices* (New York: Harper & Row, 1974), p. 709.

As the former chairman of a *Fortune 500* company put it, "Never acquire a business you don't know how to run."

Second, without some kind of strategic fit, consolidated performance of an unrelated multibusiness portfolio will tend to be no better than the sum of what the individual business units could achieve if they were independent firms, and it may be worse to the extent that centralized management policies hamstring the line of business units. Except, perhaps, for the added financial backing that a strong corporate parent can provide, a strategy of unrelated diversification adds little to the competitive strength of individual business units. The value added by corporate managers in a widely diversified firm is primarily, therefore, a function of how good they are at portfolio management—deciding what new businesses to add to the portfolio, which ones to get rid of, and how best to deploy the available financial resources in building a higher-performing portfolio.

Third, although in theory unrelated diversification might seem to offer the potential of greater sales-profit stability over the course of the business cycle, in practice the attempts at countercyclical diversification appear to have fallen short of the mark. The consolidated profits of broadly diversified firms have not been found to be any more stable or less subject to reversal in periods of recession and economic stress than have the profits of firms in general.[6]

Despite its drawbacks, unrelated diversification cannot be ruled out as a desirable corporate strategy alternative. It plainly makes sense for a firm to consider some kind of diversification when its existing business has been expanded to its practical limits and/or when it is severely threatened by outside forces (it may or may not make sense to diversify before this occurs, however). And occasions will arise when the opportunity of acquiring a particular unrelated business is simply too good to pass up. A reasonable way to tackle the issue of how much diversification is by compromising the answers to two questions: "What is the least diversification we need to attain our objectives and remain a healthy, viable entity, capable of competing successfully?" and "What is the most diversification we can manage given the complexity it adds?"[7] In all likelihood, the optimal answer lies in between these two extremes.

Strategies for Entering New Businesses

Entry into new businesses can take any of three forms: acquisition, internal start-up, and joint ventures. *Acquisition of an existing business* is probably the most popular approach to corporate diversification.[8] Acquiring an established organization has the advantage of much quicker entry into the target market (while at the same time offering a way to hurdle such barriers to entry as patents, technological inexperience, access to reliable sources of supplies, size needed to match rival firms in efficiency and unit costs, cost of introductory promotions to gain market visibility and brand recognition, and adequate distribution access). Internally developing the knowledge,

---

[6] Drucker, *Management,* p. 767. Research studies in the interval since 1974, when Drucker made his observation, uphold his conclusion—on the whole, broadly diversified firms do not outperform less diversified firms over the course of the business cycle.

[7] Drucker, *Management,* pp. 692–93.

[8] In recent years, takeovers have become an increasingly used approach to acquisition. The term *takeover* refers to the attempt (often sprung as a surprise) of one firm to acquire ownership or control over another firm against the wishes of the latter's management (and perhaps some of its stockholders).

resources, scale of operation, and market reputation necessary to become an effective competitor can take years and entails all the problems of start-up. Finding the right kind of company to acquire can sometimes present a challenge, though.[9] A firm considering acquisition may face the dilemma of buying a successful company at a high price or a struggling company at a low price. If the buying firm has very little knowledge about the industry it is seeking to enter but has ample capital, then it may be better off acquiring a capable firm—regardless of the higher price. On the other hand, it can be advantageous to acquire a struggling firm at a bargain price when the new parent company sees promising ways for transforming the weak firm into a strong one and has the money and know-how to transform it into a much stronger competitor.

Achieving diversification through *internal development* involves creating a new business entity in the desired industry and, starting from scratch, establishing new production capacity, developing sources of supply, building channels of distribution, developing a customer base, and so on. Generally, internal entry is more attractive when (1) there is ample time to launch the business from the ground up, (2) incumbent firms are likely to be slow or ineffective in responding to new entry, (3) the entrant has lower entry costs than other potential entrants, (4) the entrant has a distinctive ability to compete effectively in the business, (5) the additional capacity will not adversely impact the supply-demand balance in the industry, and (6) the targeted industry is young, fragmented (populated with many relatively small firms), and has potential for rapid growth over the long run.[10]

Joint ventures are a useful way to gain access to a new business in at least three types of situations.[11] First, a joint venture is a good device for doing something that is uneconomical or risky for an organization to do alone. Second, joint ventures make sense when pooling the resources and competences of two or more independent organizations produces an organization with more of the skills needed to be a strong competitor. In such cases, each partner brings to the deal special talents or resources which the other doesn't have and which are important enough that they can spell the difference between success and near-success. Third, joint ventures with foreign partners are sometimes a good way to surmount import quotas, tariffs, nationalistic political interests, and cultural roadblocks. Economic, competitive, and political realities of nationalism often require a foreign company to team up with a domestic partner in order to gain access to the national market in which the domestic partner is located. The drawback to joint ventures is that they create complicated questions about the division of efforts among the partners and who has effective control.[12]

Abandonment, Divestiture, and Liquidation Strategies

Even a shrewd corporate diversification strategy can result in the acquisition of business units that, down the road, just do not work out. Misfits or partial fits cannot be

---

[9] Michael E. Porter, *Competitive Strategy: Techniques for Analyzing Industries and Competitors* (New York: Free Press), 1980, pp. 354–55.

[10] Porter, *Competitive Strategy,* pp. 344–45.

[11] Drucker, *Management,* pp. 720–24. Information regarding the joint venture activities of firms can be found in the periodical, *Mergers and Acquisitions: The Journal of Corporate Venture.*

[12] Porter, *Competitive Strategy,* p. 340.

completely avoided because it is impossible to predict precisely how getting into a new line of business will actually work out. In addition, long-term industry attractiveness changes with the times, and what once was a good diversification move into an attractive industry may later turn sour. Subpar performance by some business units is bound to occur, thereby raising questions of whether to continue. Other business units may simply not mesh as well with the rest of the firm as predicted.

Sometimes, a diversification move that seems sensible from the standpoint of common markets, technologies, or channels turns out to lack the compatibility of values essential to a *temperamental fit.*[13] Several pharmaceutical companies had just this experience. When they diversified into cosmetics and perfume, they discovered their personnel had little respect for the "frivolous" nature of such products as compared to the far nobler task of developing miracle drugs to cure the ill. The absence of "temperamental unity" between the chemical and compounding expertise of the pharmaceutical companies and the fashion-marketing orientation of the cosmetics business was the undoing of what otherwise was diversification into a business with related technology and logical product fit.

When a line of business loses its appeal, the best solution is often *abandonment.* Normally unattractive businesses should be divested as fast as is practical. To drag things out merely drains away valuable organization resources. The more business units in a firm's portfolio, the more it will need a systematic "planned abandonment" strategy for divesting itself of poor performers, "dogs," and misfits. A useful guide for determining if and when to divest a particular line of business is to ask the question, "If we were not in this business today, would we want to get into it now?"[14] When the answer is no or probably not, then divestiture needs to become a priority consideration.

Divestiture can take either of two forms. In some cases, it works fine to divest a business by spinning it off as a financially and managerially independent company, with the parent company retaining partial ownership or not. In other cases, divestiture is best accomplished by selling the unit outright, in which case a buyer needs to be found. As a rule, divestiture should not be approached from the angle of "Who can we pawn this business off on and what is the most we can get for it?"[15] Instead, it is better to proceed by analyzing "For what sort of organization would this business be a good fit and under what conditions would it be viewed as a good deal?" In identifying organizations for whom the business is a good fit, one also finds the buyers who will pay the highest price.

Of all the strategic alternatives, *liquidation* is the most unpleasant and painful, especially for a single-business enterprise where it means terminating the organization's existence. For a multi-industry, multibusiness firm to liquidate one of its lines of business is less traumatic; the hardship of suffering (through layoffs, plant closings, and so on), while not to be minimized, still leaves an ongoing organization, perhaps one that eventually will turn out to be healthier after its pruning than before. In hopeless situations, an early liquidation effort usually serves owner-stockholder inter-

---

[13] Drucker, *Management,* p. 709.

[14] Drucker, *Management,* p. 94.

[15] Ibid., p. 719.

ests better than an inevitable bankruptcy. Prolonging the pursuit of a lost cause simply exhausts an organization's resources and leaves less to liquidate; it can also mar reputations and ruin management careers. Unfortunately, it is seldom simple for management to decide when a cause is lost and when a turnaround is achievable. This is particularly true when emotions and pride get in the way of sound managerial judgment—as they often do.

Corporate Turnaround, Retrenchment, and Portfolio Restructuring Strategies

Corporate turnaround, retrenchment, and portfolio restructuring strategies come into play when senior management undertakes restoration of an ailing corporate business portfolio to good health. The first task here is always diagnosis of the underlying reasons for poor corporate performance. Formulation of curative strategies then follows. Poor performance can be caused by large losses in one or more business units which pull overall performance down, having a disproportionate number of businesses in unattractive industries, a bad economy which has adversely impacted many of the firm's business units, or having weak management at either the corporate or business levels.

How to attempt a *turnaround* necessarily depends on the roots of poor profitability and the urgency of any crisis. Depending on the causes, there are six action approaches that can be used singly or in combination to achieve a turnaround in a diversified enterprise: (1) focus mainly on restoring profitability in the money-losing units; (2) implement harvest/divest strategies in the poorly performing units and allocate money and resources to expansion of better-performing units; (3) institute across-the-board economies in all business units; (4) revamp the composition of the business portfolio by selling off weak businesses and replacing them with new acquisitions in more attractive industries; (5) replace key management personnel at the corporate and/or business levels; and (6) launch profit improvement programs in all business units.

Retrenchment differs from turnaround in that retrenchment is a temporary retreat and trimming back in the face of adverse conditions; the strategic posture of retrenchment is one of "battening down the hatches and weathering out the storm." Retrenchment is a common short-run defensive strategy for responding to conditions of general economic recession, tight money, periods of economic uncertainty, a storm of public criticism, and/or harsh regulation. Corporate retrenchment also makes sense as a response to internal financial crisis brought on by excessively rapid expansion, strain in financing a major capital investment project, or an unexpected business reversal (loss of a major customer, failure to win an anticipated contract, a natural disaster, and so on). Retrenchment strategies are usually dropped as soon as conditions turn favorable enough to resume expansion and otherwise launch new initiatives.

Retrenchment can be approached in either of two ways: one, pursuing stringent across-the-board internal economies aimed at wringing out waste and improving efficiency; and two, singling out the weakest performing businesses in the corporate portfolio for pruning and revamping. In the first instance, a firm that finds itself in a defensive or overextended position elects to remain in most or all of its current businesses and tries to ride out the bad times with various internal economy measures. Ordinarily this type of corporate retrenchment strategy is highlighted by directives to reduce operating expenses, improve efficiency, and boost profit margins. It can involve curtailing the hiring of new personnel, trimming the size of corporate staff, postponing capital expenditure projects, stretching out the use of equipment and delaying replacement purchases in order to economize on cash requirements, retiring obsolete equipment, dropping marginally profitable products, closing older and less efficient plants, reorganizing internal work flows, reducing inventories, and the like.

The second variation of corporate retrenchment singles out the weak-performing parts of the corporate business portfolio for major strategy revisions, internal overhaul, and whatever else may be necessary to restore them to good health. Performing radical surgery on those units that are least profitable is nearly always a by-product of poor overall corporate performance and/or persistently poor performance in the targeted business units. Many diversified firms have been forced into drastic surgery on one or more business units because of an inability to make them profitable after several frustrating years of trying, or because ongoing operating problems proved intractable, or because funds were lacking to support the investment needs of all the businesses in their corporate portfolios.

Portfolio restructuring strategies involve radical surgery on the mix and percentage makeup of the types of businesses in the portfolio. Restructuring can be prompted by any of several conditions: (1) when a strategy review reveals that the long-term performance prospects for the corporation as a whole have become unattractive (because the portfolio contains too many slow-growth, declining, or competitively weak business units); (2) when one or more of the firm's key business units fall prey to hard times; (3) when a new chief executive officer (CEO) takes over the reins and decides that it is time to redirect where the company is headed; (4) when "wave of the future" technologies or products emerge and make a series of foothold acquisitions an attractive way to get a position in a potentially big new industry; or (5) when a "unique opportunity" presents itself to make an acquisition so big that several existing business units have to be sold off to raise money to finance the new acquisition.

Portfolio restructuring frequently involves both divestitures and new acquisitions. The candidate business units for divestiture include not only those that may be competitively weak or are up-and-down performers or are in unattractive industries, but also those that no longer "fit" (even though they may be profitable and in attractive enough industries). Indeed, many broadly diversified corporations, disenchanted with their past experiences and future prospects with unrelated diversification, have recently gone through the process of revamping their business portfolios. Units found not to be compatible with newly established related diversification themes have been divested, the remaining units realigned to capture more strategic fit benefits, and new units acquired to create a stronger mix of related businesses.

Combination Strategies

The six corporate strategy alternatives discussed above are not mutually exclusive. They can be used in combination, either in whole or in part, and they can be chained together in whatever sequences may be appropriate for adjusting to changing internal and external circumstances. For instance, one well-known company over a two-year period added 25 new lines of business to its corporate portfolio (16 through acquisition and 9 through internal start-up), divested 4, and closed down the operations of 4 others. Moreover, there are endless variations of each of the six alternatives, allowing ample room for enterprises to create their own individualized corporate strategy.

Although each firm's corporate strategy tends to be idiosyncratic and otherwise tailor-made to its own particular situation, there are several distinctive types of enterprises that emerge. The most common business portfolios created by corporate strategies are:

- A single-business enterprise operating in only one stage of an industry's activity-cost chain.
- A partially integrated, single-business enterprise operating in *some* of the stages of an industry's activity-cost chain.
- A fully integrated, single-business enterprise operating in *all* stages of an industry's activity-cost chain.
- A "dominant-business" enterprise with sales concentrated in one major core business but with a modestly diversified portfolio of either related or unrelated businesses (amounting to one third or less of total corporatewide sales).
- A narrowly diversified enterprise whose business portfolio includes a "balanced" mixture of a *few* (3 to 10) *related* business units.
- A broadly diversified enterprise whose business portfolio includes a balanced mixture of *many* (mostly *related*) business units.
- A narrowly diversified enterprise whose business portfolio includes a balanced mixture of a *few* (3 to 10) *unrelated* business units.
- A broadly diversified enterprise whose business portfolio includes a balanced mixture of *many* (mostly *unrelated*) business units.
- A multibusiness enterprise which has deliberately diversified into several different and unrelated areas but which has a portfolio of related businesses within each area—thus giving it *several unrelated groups of related businesses.*

Illustration Capsule 16 describes corporate strategy at Hammermill Paper Company.

ILLUSTRATION CAPSULE 16

Corporate Strategy at Hammermill Paper Company

Hammermill Paper Company's operations are all related to the manufacture or distribution of pulp, paper, paper products and lumber. Principal end-use markets are business communications, copiers, graphic arts, industrial manufacturing, furniture manufacturing, and construction.

At the end of 1984, Hammermill had 33 separate manufacturing or processing locations along with 96 distribution facilities, totally within the United States. The company had 13,000 employees. The company was made up of five business

ILLUSTRATION CAPSULE 16 *(continued)*

groups. Each of these occupied a prominent position in its major markets, and each represented a different combination of economic and operating characteristics. The business groups were:

	Percent of 1984 Sales	Percent of 1984 Operating Profit	Percent of 1984 Assets
Fine and printing papers	24%	56%	53%
Industrial and packaging papers	13	12	16
Converted paper products	7	5	5
Wholesale distribution	47	18	17
Forest products	9	9	9

Hammermill's senior management has publicly stated that its corporate strategy for achieving profit growth and better market position is based on five strategic approaches and principles: In the words of Hammermill, these are as follows:[1]

1. *Building leading positions in targeted market segments.* The great size and diversity of the market for paper and paper-based materials divides it into many and varied segments. Accordingly, we select markets in which our unique strengths in manufacturing, technology and distribution give us a competitive advantage. By building leadership positions in new and existing markets, Hammermill can operate with far greater initiative and flexibility.

2. *Achieving cost-competitiveness in our operations.* Being among the lowest-cost producers in each of its markets is a great advantage to any company. At Hammermill, we continue to invest heavily to optimize the productivity of our resources through modernization, streamlining, development, and even pruning when called for. Being highly cost effective yields better profit margins, improves staying power through economic cycles, reduces earnings volatility and makes possible continual new investment.

3. *Balancing five distinct but related businesses.* While most segments of our industry tends to be cyclical, their ups and downs usually don't closely coincide in timing or degree. Such individual business cycles can be effectively counterbalanced by allocating Hammermill's assets to an appropriate mixture of different segments which have enough in common so that management can exercise effective direction of the entire enterprise. The principal rewards of this kind of controlled diversification are reduced risk and greatly improved stability and predictability of company performance.

4. *Expanding productive capacity by increments.* Major increases in construction costs and their large minimum economic size make building totally new pulp and paper mills very costly and complex. While such "greenfield" expansion may occasionally be desirable, the best approach for Hammermill in recent years has been steady growth by adding smaller increments of capacity. By expanding existing plants or by raising their productivity, we benefit

---
[1] *1984 Annual Report.*

ILLUSTRATION CAPSULE 16 *(concluded)*

> from lower operating and capital costs per unit of added output, reduced economic exposure, shorter construction times and smaller amounts of new supply for the market to digest.
>
> 5. *Maintaining a strong, flexible financial position.* To grow and progress in a basic manufacturing industry such as ours, continuous large investment in expansion, productivity, new technology and market development is absolutely vital. Assurance of long-term availability of capital to Hammermill has long been based on detailed preplanning of funding needs, maintaining suitable financial ratios, intelligent use of debt and employment of various forms of equity and innovative financial methods.

Fitting Strategy to a Firm's Situation

Some corporate strategy alternatives offer a stronger fit with a corporation's situation than do others. As one way of analyzing situational fit, consider Figure 6–1 where the variable of competitive position is plotted against various rates of market growth to create four distinct strategic situations that might be occupied by a single-business or diminant-business firm.[16] Firms that fall into quadrant I (rapid market growth and strong competitive position) have several logical corporate strategy options as indicated, the strongest of which in the near term may well be single-business concentration. Given the industry's high growth rate (and implicit long-term attractiveness), it makes sense for quadrant I firms to push hard to maintain or increase their market shares, to further develop their distinctive competences, and to make whatever capital investments are necessary to continue in a strong industry position. At some juncture, a quadrant I company may find it desirable to consider vertical integration as a strategy for undergirding its competitive strength. Later, when market growth starts to slow, prudence dictates looking into related diversification as a means of spreading business risks and capitalizing on the expertise the company has built up.

Firms falling into quadrant II should, first of all, consider what options they have for reformulating their present competitive strategy (given the high rate of market growth) and address the questions of (1) why their current approach to the market has resulted in a weak competitive position and (2) what it will take to become an effective competitor. With the market expanding rapidly, there should be ample opportunity for even a weak firm to improve its performance and to make headway in becoming a stronger competitor. If the firm is young and struggling to develop, then it usually has a better chance for survival in a growing market where plenty of new business is up for grabs than it does in a stable or declining industry. However, if a quadrant II firm lacks the resources and skills to hold its own, then either merger with another company in the industry that has the missing pieces or merger with an outsider having the cash and resources to support the organization's development

---

[16] Roland Christensen, Norman A. Berg, and Malcolm S. Salter, *Policy Formulation and Administration,* 7th ed. (Homewood, Ill.: Richard D. Irwin, 1976), pp. 16–18.

Figure 6–1   Matching Corporate Strategy Alternatives to Fit a Firm's Situation

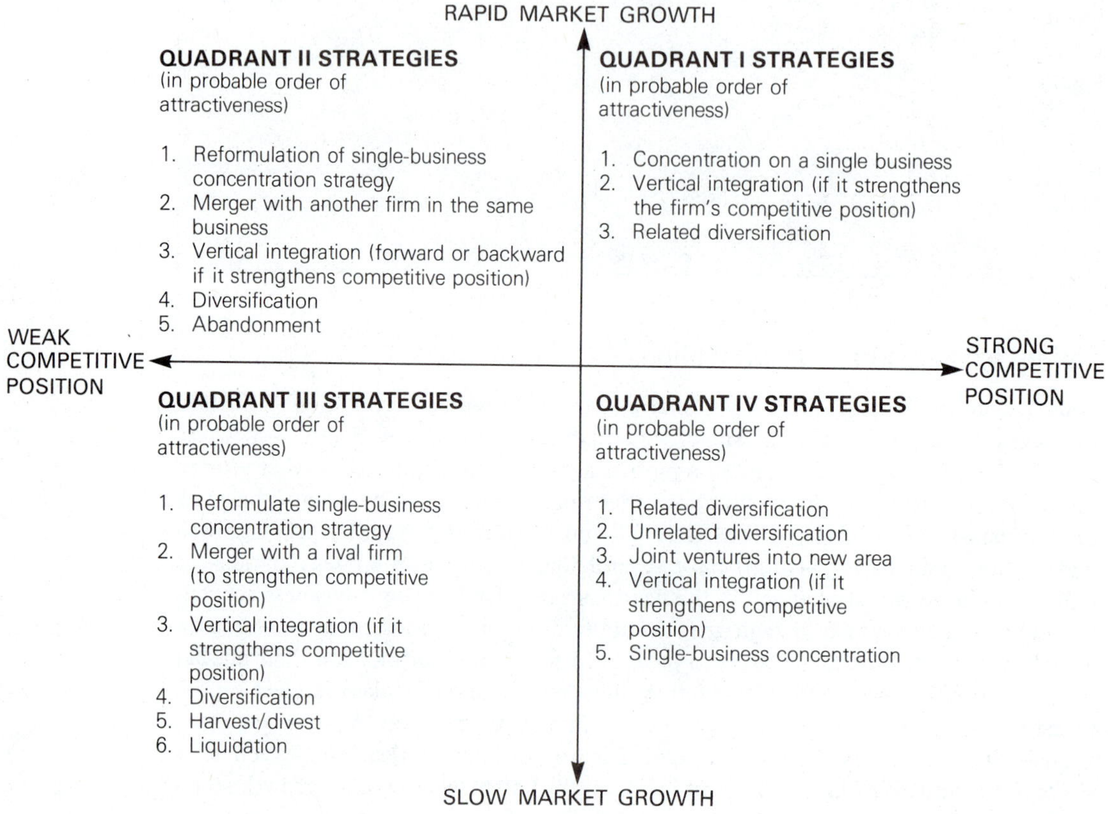

RAPID MARKET GROWTH

QUADRANT II STRATEGIES
(in probable order of
attractiveness)

1. Reformulation of single-business
    concentration strategy
2. Merger with another firm in the same
    business
3. Vertical integration (forward or backward
    if it strengthens competitive position)
4. Diversification
5. Abandonment

QUADRANT I STRATEGIES
(in probable order of
attractiveness)

1. Concentration on a single business
2. Vertical integration (if it strengthens
    the firm's competitive position)
3. Related diversification

WEAK
COMPETITIVE
POSITION

STRONG
COMPETITIVE
POSITION

QUADRANT III STRATEGIES
(in probable order of
attractiveness)

1. Reformulate single-business
    concentration strategy
2. Merger with a rival firm
    (to strengthen competitive
    position)
3. Vertical integration (if it
    strengthens competitive
    position)
4. Diversification
5. Harvest/divest
6. Liquidation

QUADRANT IV STRATEGIES
(in probable order of
attractiveness)

1. Related diversification
2. Unrelated diversification
3. Joint ventures into new area
4. Vertical integration (if it
    strengthens competitive
    position)
5. Single-business concentration

SLOW MARKET GROWTH

may be the best corporate strategy alternative. Vertical integration, either forward or backward or both, becomes a necessary consideration for weakly positioned firms whenever it can materially strengthen the firm's competitive position. A third option is diversification into related or unrelated areas (if adequate financing can be found). If all else fails, then abandonment (divestiture in the case of a multibusiness firm or liquidation in the case of a single-business firm) has to become an active corporate strategy option. While getting out may seem extreme because of the high growth potential, it is wise to remember that a company that is unable to make a profit in a booming market probably does not have the ability to make a profit at all and has little prospect of survival—particularly if recession hits or competition stiffens.

Quadrant III companies with their weak competitive position in a more or less stagnant market should look at: (1) reformulating the present competitive strategy (to turn the firm's situation around and create a more attractive competitive position);

(2) integrating forward or backward, provided good profit improvement and competitive positioning opportunities exist; (3) diversifying into related or unrelated areas; (4) merger with another firm; (5) employing a harvest, then divest strategy; and (6) liquidating its position in the business—by either selling out to another firm or closing down operations.

Quadrant IV organizations, considering the industry's unattractive growth prospects, are likely to be drawn toward using the excess cash flow from their existing business to begin a program of diversification. A related diversification approach keyed to the distinctive competence that gave it its dominant position is an obvious option, but unrelated diversification is an option when related business opportunities do not appear to be especially attractive. Joint ventures with other organizations into new fields of endeavor are another logical possibility, and vertical integration

Figure 6–2   Checklist of Major Corporate Strategy Alternatives

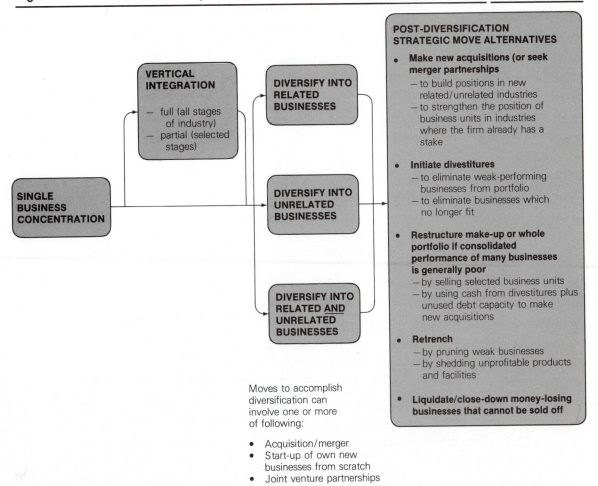

could be attractive if solid profit improvement opportunities exist. Whichever move it selects, the firm will likely wish to put a damper on much new investment in its present facilities (unless important growth *segments* within the industry merit grow-and-build approaches) in order to free up the maximum amount of cash to deploy in new endeavors.

Comparing firms on the basis of competitive position and market growth rate (or any other two variables) is useful for the insight it provides into the importance of situational fit and why companies in the same industry may have good reason to pursue different corporate strategies. The makeup of a firm's current business portfolio, how well the portfolio is performing, the firm's financial strength, capital investment requirements, ability to respond to emerging market opportunities, distinctive competences, and so on all combine to define its situation and what corporate strategy options it should realistically consider.

ANALYTICAL CHECKLIST

Figure 6–2 presents a summary schematic of the generic corporate strategy alternatives. The corporate strategist's task is to tailor these generic options in ways which will boost long-term corporate performance. Step one is to diagnose the current state of the corporate business portfolio and assess the firm's overall situation. Step two is to identify which corporate strategy options should realistically be considered. Step three is to decide which strategic options best match the firm's situation and offer the most attractive long-term performance prospects.

SUGGESTED READINGS

Ansoff, H. Igor. *Corporate Strategy.* New York: McGraw-Hill, 1965, chap. 7.

Ansoff, H. Igor, and John M. Stewart. "Strategies for a Technology-Based Business." *Harvard Business Review* 45, no. 6 (November–December 1967), pp. 71–83.

Bright, William M. "Alternative Strategies for Diversification." *Research Management* 12, no. 4 (July 1969), pp. 247–53.

Buzzell, Robert D. "Is Vertical Integration Profitable?" *Harvard Business Review* 61, no. 1 (January–February 1983), pp. 92–102.

Drucker, Peter. *Management: Tasks, Responsibilities, Practices.* New York: Harper & Row, 1974, chaps. 55, 56, 57, 58, 60, and 61.

Guth, William D. "Corporate Growth Strategies." *Journal of Business Strategy* 1, no. 2 (Fall 1980), pp. 56–62.

Hall, William K. "Survival Strategies in a Hostile Environment." *Harvard Business Review* 58, no. 5 (September–October 1980), pp. 75–85.

Hanan, Mack. "Corporate Growth through Internal Spinouts." *Harvard Business Review* 47, no. 6 (November–December 1969), pp. 55–66.

Harrigan, Kathryn R. "A Framework for Looking at Vertical Integration." *Journal of Business Strategy* 3, no. 3 (Winter 1983), pp. 30–37.

―――. "Formulating Vertical Integration Strategies." *Academy of Management Review* 9, no. 4 (October 1984), pp. 638–52.

_____. *Strategic Flexibility.* Lexington, Mass.: Lexington Books, 1985, chap. 4 and Table A–8 (p. 162).

Hofer, Charles W. "Turnaround Strategies." *Journal of Business Strategy* 1, no. 1 (Summer 1980), pp. 19–31.

Lauenstein, Milton, and Wickham Skinner. "Formulating a Strategy of Superior Resources." *Journal of Business Strategy* 1, no. 1 (Summer 1980), pp. 4–10.

Ohmae, Kenichi. *The Mind of the Strategist.* New York: Penguin Books, 1983, chaps. 10 and 12.

Vancil, Richard F., and Peter Lorange. "Strategic Planning in Diversified Companies." *Harvard Business Review* 53, no. 1 (January–February 1975), pp. 81–90.

Woodward, Herbert N. "Management Strategies for Small Companies." *Harvard Business Review* 54, no. 1 (January–February 1976), pp. 113–21.

7 Techniques for Analyzing Corporate Diversification Strategies

Corporate-level managers add to the value of an enterprise by acting effectively on the answers to three strategy-related questions:

- How strong is the firm's present lineup of business activities?
- If the firm continues to stay in only its present business activities, then what will the enterprise's position be in another 5 to 10 years?
- If continuing to rely upon the present business lineup looks unattractive for the long term, then what can and should be done to boost future performance?

The task of developing and implementing action plans to improve the firm's overall business position, thereby enhancing long-term performance, is the heart of what corporate-level strategic management is all about.

Approaches to strategy evaluation at the corporate level vary with a firm's business makeup. In enterprises which have a broadly diverse revenue base, the main analytic considerations are (1) appraising the health of the firm's current business portfolio, (2) diagnosing the relative long-term attractiveness of each business in the portfolio, and (3) choosing when and how to upgrade the performance of the total business portfolio (through stronger coordination and management of existing businesses, the addition of new business units to the firm's makeup, and/or divestiture of weak performers and misfits). In diversified firms, corporate managers do little more than review and approve line-of-business strategies; on occasion they may suggest broad business strategy direction, but the specifics of business-level and functional area strategies are typically delegated to subordinate managers with profit-and-loss responsibility for particular business units and product lines. Creating a "fit" between corporate and business strategies is, however, something corporate managers and business-unit managers often negotiate; internal consensus must also be reached regarding whether and how related activities of the various business units will be coordinated. Corporate management must be convinced that the chosen business-level strategy has an attractive corporate payoff and be willing to provide whatever corporate-level resources are needed for successful strategy implementation. On the other hand, business strategy must be responsive to corporate priorities and match up with both corporate resources and long-term direction. Thus, there is two-way traffic between the analysis of corporate and business strategy.

In contrast, in single-business or dominant-business enterprises, evaluating the strategy of the core business is the center of corporate headquarter's attention, after which diversification and other portfolio questions relating to corporate strategy are addressed. Such firms generally do not divorce corporate strategy analysis and business strategy analysis because (1) activities outside the core business contribute minimally to sales and profits and (2) the issue of "which way do we go from here" hinges on the health and attractiveness of the main business. Thus, in dominant-business companies, corporate strategy takes its cues from business strategy instead of the reverse.

Whatever approach to corporate strategy formation best fits a company, sound strategy analysis starts with a probing of the organization's present strategy and business makeup. Recall from Figure 2–3 (on p. 37) that the spokes on the corporate strategy wheel are:

- Whether a firm is pursuing a strategy of related diversification, a strategy of unrelated diversification, or a mixed strategy involving both related and unrelated business units.
- The extent to which a firm's business unit portfolio is heavily dominated by one or two core businesses or, instead, is composed of a more balanced and evenly distributed mix of business units (as measured by the proportion of total sales and total corporate profits contributed by each business unit).
- The nature of any recent management moves to expand, revamp, or restructure the makeup of the set of businesses a firm is in.
- Recent divestiture actions.
- The use of various merger and acquisition methods to put the corporate portfolio together.
- The overall direction in which the company seems to be moving.
- The internal efforts of corporate management to realize the benefits of strategic fit relationships and to create a corporate-level competitive advantage (as distinct from a competitive advantage that springs from and is limited to the operations of a single business unit).
- The pattern of investment expenditures and cash flows across the firm's various lines of business.
- Key corporate-level functional area support strategies, especially as concerns finance, efforts in product innovation and new technology development, and human resource policies.
- Whether the firm has any predilection for employing the same generic competitive strategies in most of the firm's business units and/or whether there are any other important approaches to managing the company's business units.

- What, if any, corporate-level or corporatewide distinctive competence the firm has and how it fits into the corporate strategy.

Identification of the corporate strategy lays the foundation for conducting a thorough strategy analysis and subsequently, for reformulating the strategy as it "should be."

MATRIX TECHNIQUES FOR EVALUATING DIVERSIFIED PORTFOLIOS

The most popular analytical technique for probing the overall makeup of a diversified group of business units involves constructing a *business portfolio matrix*, a two-dimensional graphic portrait of the comparative positions of different businesses. Matrixes can be constructed using any pair of strategically relevant variables, but in practice the revealing variables have proved to be industry growth rate, market share, long-term industry attractiveness, competitive strength, and stage of product/market evolution. Use of two-dimensional business portfolio matrixes as a tool of corporate strategy evaluation is based on the relative simplicity of constructing them and on the clarity of the overall picture that they produce. Three types of business portfolio matrixes have been used the most frequently: the Boston Consulting Group's growth-share matrix, the GE 9-cell matrix, and the Hofer–Arthur D. Little product/market evolution matrix.

The Four-Cell BCG Growth-Share Matrix

The first business portfolio matrix to receive widespread usage was a four-square grid pioneered by the Boston Consulting Group (BCG), one of the leading management consulting firms.[1] An illustrative BCG-type matrix is depicted in Figure 7–1. The matrix is formed using *industry growth rate* and *relative market share* as the axes. Each business unit in the corporate portfolio appears as a "bubble" on the four-cell matrix, with the size of each bubble or circle scaled according to the percent of revenues it represents in the overall corporate portfolio.

BCG methodology arbitrarily places the dividing line between "high" and "low" industry growth rates at around twice the real GNP growth rate plus inflation, but the boundary percentage can be raised or lowered when it makes sense to do so. The essential criterion is to place the line so that business units in the "high growth" cells can fairly be said to be in industries growing faster than the economy as a whole and those in the "low growth" cells are growing slower than the economywide rate and are in industries that merit labels like mature, aging, stagnant, or declining.

---

[1] For a readily available, more extensive treatment, see Barry Hedley, "A Fundamental Approach to Strategy Development," *Long Range Planning,* December 1976, pp. 2–11. The original presentation is Bruce D. Henderson, "The Experience Curve—Reviewed, IV. The Growth Share Matrix of the Product Portfolio," (Boston: The Boston Consulting Group, 1973), Perspectives no. 135. For two more recent discussions of the strategic importance of the experience curve, see Pankaj Ghemawat, "Building Strategy on the Experience Curve," *Harvard Business Review* 64, no. 2 (March–April 1985), pp. 143–49; and Bruce D. Henderson, "The Application and Misapplication of the Experience Curve," *Journal of Business Strategy* 4, no. 3 (Winter 1984), pp. 3–9. For an excellent treatment of the use of the BCG growth-share matrix in strategic portfolio analysis, see Arnoldo C. Hax and Nicholas S. Majluf, *Strategic Management: An Integrative Perspective* (Englewood Cliffs, N.J.: Prentice-Hall, 1984), chap. 7.

Figure 7–1   The BCG Growth-Share Business Portfolio Matrix

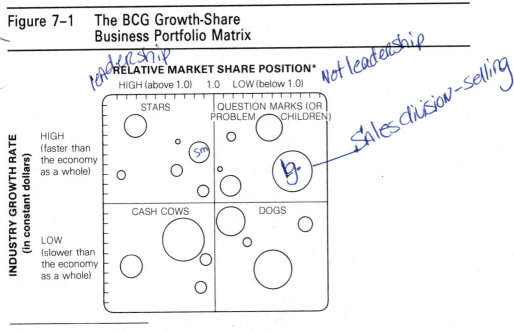

leadership   *Not leadership*   *Sales division–selling*

Relative market share is defined by the ratio of one's own market share to the market share held by the largest *rival* firm. When the vertical dividing line is set at 1.0, the only way a firm can achieve a "star" or "cash cow" position in the growth-share matrix is to have the largest market share in the industry. Since this is a very stringent criterion, it may be "fairer" to locate the vertical dividing line in the matrix at about .75 or .8.

Relative market share is defined as the ratio of a business's market share to the market share held by the largest rival firm in the industry, with market share being measured in terms of unit volume, not dollars. For instance, if business A has a 15 percent share of the industry's total volume and the share held by the largest rival is 30 percent, then A's relative market share is 0.5. If business B has a market-leading share of 40 percent and its largest rival has a 30 percent share, then B's relative market share is 1.33. Given this definition, only business units that are market share leaders in their respective units will have relative market share values greater than 1.0; business units in the portfolio that trail rival firms in market share will have ratios below 1.0.

The most stringent BCG standard calls for the border between "high" and "low" relative market share on the grid to be set at 1.0, as shown in Figure 7–1. With 1.0 as the boundary, those circles in the two left-side cells of the matrix identify how many and which businesses in the firm's portfolio are leaders in their industry; those falling in the two right-side cells trail the leaders, with the degree to which they trail being indicated by the size of the relative market share ratio. A ratio of .10 indicates that the business has a market share only one tenth of the market share of the largest firm in the market, whereas a ratio of .80 indicates a market share that is four-fifths, or 80 percent as big as the leading firm's share. A less stringent criterion is to fix the high-low boundary so that businesses to the left enjoy positions as market leaders (though not necessarily *the* leader), and those to the right are in below-average or underdog market-share positions. Locating the dividing line between "high" and "low" at about .75 or .8 is a reasonable compromise.

The merit of using *relative* market share instead of the actual market share percentage to construct the growth-share matrix is that the former is a better indicator of comparative market strength and competitive position—a 10 percent market share is much stronger if the leader's share is 12 percent than if it is 50 percent; the use of relative market share captures this feature. An equally important consideration in using relative market share is that it is also likely to be a reflection of relative cost based on experience in producing the product and on economies of large-scale production. The potential of large businesses to operate at lower unit costs than smaller firms because of technological and efficiency gains related to larger size is a well-understood possibility. But personnel from BCG accumulated evidence that the phenomenon of lower unit costs went beyond the effects of economies of scale; they found that as the cumulative volume of production increased, the resulting knowledge and experience gained often led to the discovery of additional efficiencies and ways to reduce costs even further. The relationship between cumulative production experience and lower unit costs was labeled by BCG as *the experience curve effect* (for more details, see Illustration Capsule 10 in Chapter 3). When an important experience curve effect is present in the activity-cost chain of a particular business or industry, it places a strategic premium on market share: the firm that gains the largest market share rides down the experience curve fastest and improves its relative cost position the most.

With these features of the BCG growth-share matrix in mind, we are ready to explore the portfolio implications for businesses falling into each cell of the matrix in Figure 7–1.

Question Marks and Problem Children

Question Marks and Problem Children   Business units falling in the upper-right quadrant of the growth-share matrix have been tagged by BCG as "question marks" or "problem children." Rapid market growth makes such business units attractive from an industry standpoint, but their low relative market share positions (and thus reduced access to experience curve effects) raise questions whether the profit potential associated with market growth can realistically be captured—hence, the "question mark" or "problem child" designation. Question mark businesses, moreover, are typically, "cash hogs"—so labeled because their cash needs are high (because of the investment requirements of rapid growth and product development) and their internal cash generation is low (because of low market share, less access to experience curve effects and scale economies, and consequently thinner profit margins). The corporate parent of a cash hog business has to decide whether it is worthwhile to invest corporate capital to support the needs of a question mark division.

BCG has argued that the two best strategic options for a question mark business are (1) an aggressive grow-and-build strategy to capitalize on the high growth opportunity, or (2) divestiture (in the event that the costs of strengthening its market share standing via a grow-and-build strategy outweigh the potential payoff and financial risk). Pursuit of a grow-and-build strategy is imperative anytime an attractive question mark business is characterized by strong experience curve effects because of the lower-cost position enjoyed by firms with the cumulative production experience that attends bigger market shares. The stronger the experience curve effect, the more powerful the competitive position enjoyed by the competitor that is the low-cost producer. Consequently, according to the BCG thesis, unless a question mark/problem child business is managed via a grow-and-build type strategy, it will not be in a position to remain cost competitive vis-à-vis large-volume firms—in which case divestiture becomes the only other viable long-term alternative. The corporate strategy prescriptions for managing question mark/problem child business units thus become straightforward: divest those that are weaker and less attractive and groom the attractive ones to become tomorrow's "stars."

Stars   Businesses with high relative market share positions in high growth markets rank as "stars" in the BCG grid because they offer both excellent profit and excellent growth opportunities. As such, they are the business units that an enterprise comes to depend on for boosting overall performance of the total portfolio.

Given their dominant market-share position and rapid growth environment, stars typically require large cash investments to support expansion of production facilities and working capital needs, but they also tend to generate their own large internal cash flows due to the low-cost advantage that results from economies of scale and cumulative production experience. Star-type businesses vary as to whether they can support their investment needs totally from within or whether they require infusions of investment funds from corporate headquarters to support continued rapid growth and high performance. According to BCG, some stars (usually those that are well established and beginning to mature) are virtually self-sustaining in terms of cash flow and make little claim on the corporate parent's treasury. Young stars, however, often require substantial investment capital *beyond what they can generate on their own* and may thus be cash hogs.

Cash Cows   Businesses with a high relative market share in a low-growth market have been designated as "cash cows" by BCG because their entrenched position tends to yield substantial *cash surpluses* over and above what is needed for reinvestment and growth in the business. Many of today's cash cows are yesterday's stars. Cash cows, though less attractive from a growth standpoint, are nonetheless a valuable corporate portfolio holding because they can be "milked" for the cash to pay corporate dividends and corporate overhead; they provide cash for financing new acquisitions; and they provide funds for investing in young stars and in those problem children that are being groomed as the next round of stars (cash cows provide the dollars to "feed" the cash hogs). Strong cash cows are not "harvested" but are maintained in a healthy status to sustain long-term cash flow. The idea is to preserve market position while efficiently generating dollars to reallocate to business investments elsewhere. Weak cash cows, however, may be designated as prime candidates for harvesting and eventual divestiture if their industry becomes unattractive.

Dogs   Businesses with low growth and low relative market share carry the label of "dogs" in the BCG matrix because of their weak competitive position (owing, perhaps, to high costs, low-quality products, less effective marketing, and the like) and the low profit potential that often accompanies slow growth or impending market decline. Another characteristic of dogs is their inability to generate attractive cash flows on a long-term basis; sometimes they do not even produce enough cash to adequately fund a rear-guard hold-and-maintain strategy—especially if competition is brutal and profit margins are chronically thin. Consequently, except in unusual cases, the BCG corporate strategy prescription is that dogs be harvested, divested, or liquidated, depending on which alternative yields the most attractive amount of cash for redeploying to other businesses or to new acquisitions.

Implications for Corporate Strategy   The chief contribution of the BCG growth-share matrix is the attention it draws to the cash flow and investment characteristics of various types of businesses and how corporate financial resources can be shifted from business unit to business unit in an effort to optimize the long-term strategic position and performance of the whole corporate portfolio. According to BCG analysis, the foundation of a sound, long-term corporate strategy is to utilize the excess cash generated by cash cow business units to finance market-share increases for cash hog businesses—the young stars still unable to finance their own growth internally and those problem children that have been singled out as having the best potential to grow into stars. If successful, the cash hogs eventually become self-supporting stars and then, when the markets of the star businesses begin to mature and their growth slows down, they will become the cash cows of the future. The "success sequence" is thus problem child/question mark to young star (but perhaps still a cash hog) to self-supporting star to cash cow.

The weaker, less attractive question mark businesses not deemed worthy of the financial investment necessary to fund a long-term grow-and-build strategy are often portfolio liabilities. These question marks become prime divestiture candidates unless they can be kept profitable and viable with their own internally generated funds (all problem child businesses are not untenable cash hogs; some may be able to generate the cash to finance a "hold-and-maintain" strategy and thus contribute enough to corporate earnings and return on investment to justify retention in the portfolio). Even so, such question marks still have a low-priority claim on corporate financial resources; as market growth slows and maturity-saturation sets in, they will move vertically downward in the matrix, becoming less and less a source of corporate growth.

Dogs should be retained only as long as they can contribute positive cash flow and do not tie up assets and resources that could be more profitably redeployed. The BCG recommendation for managing a weakening or already weak dog is to employ a harvesting strategy. If and when a harvesting strategy is no longer attractive, then a weak dog buiness becomes a candidate for elimination from the portfolio.

There are two "disaster sequences" in the BCG scheme of things: (1) when a star's position in the matrix erodes over time to that of a problem child and then falls to become a dog, and (2) when a cash cow loses market leadership to the point where it becomes a dog on the decline. Other strategic mistakes include overinvesting in a safe cash cow; underinvesting in a question mark so that instead of moving into the star category it tumbles into a dog; and shotgunning resources thinly over many question marks rather than concentrating them on the best question marks to boost their chances of becoming stars.

Strengths and Weaknesses in the Growth-Share Matrix Approach   The
BCG business portfolio matrix makes a definite contribution to the strategist's toolbox
when it comes to diagnosing the portfolio makeup and reaching broad prescriptions
regarding the strategy and direction for each business unit in the portfolio. Viewing
a diversified corporation as a collection of cash flows and cash requirements (present
and future) is a major step forward in understanding the financial aspects of corporate
strategy. The BCG matrix highlights the financial "interaction" within a corporate
portfolio, shows the kinds of financial considerations that must be dealt with, and
explains why the priorities for corporate resource allocation can legitimately be different from business to business. It also provides good rationalizations for both grow-
and-build strategies and divestiture. Yet, several legitimate shortcomings exist:

1. A four-cell matrix based on high-low classifications hides the fact that many
businesses (the majority?) are in markets with an "average" growth rate and have
relative market shares that may be best characterized as neither high nor low but
rather in between or intermediate. A three-cell classification of high, medium, and
low may be more accurate.

2. While viewing all businesses as being stars, cash cows, dogs, or question marks
does indeed add a useful element of flavor and communicative appeal, it is a misleading
simplification to neatly categorize the members of a corporate portfolio in terms of
just four types of businesses. Some market leaders may be getting stronger while
other are getting weaker—a few one-time stars or cash cows have encountered hard
times, and some have ended up in bankruptcy as dogs. Some market-share leaders
have never really been stars in terms of profitability. All businesses with low relative
market shares are not dogs or question marks—in many cases, trailing firms have
proven track records in terms of growth, profitability, and competitive ability, even
gaining on the so-called leaders. Hence, a key characteristic to assess is the *trend*
in a firm's relative market share—is it gaining ground or losing ground and why?
This weakness is partially corrected by indicating each business's present and future
position in the matrix (see Figure 7–2).

3. The BCG matrix is not a reliable indicator of relative investment opportunities
across business units.[2] For example, investing in a star is not necessarily more attractive
than investing in a lucrative cash cow. The matrix results are silent as to when a
question mark business is a potential winner versus being a likely loser. It says nothing
about whether shrewd investments can turn a strong dog into a star or a cash cow.

4. Being a market leader in a slow-growth industry is not a surefire guarantee of
cash cow status because *(a)* the investment requirements of a hold-and-maintain
strategy, given the impact of inflation on the costs of replacing worn-out facilities
and equipment, can soak up much or all of the available internal cash flow; and
(b) as markets mature, competitive forces often stiffen and the ensuing vigorous battle
for volume and market share can shrink profit margins and surplus cash flows.

5. The connection between relative market share and profitability is not as tight
as the experience curve effect implies. The importance of cumulative production experi-

---

[2] Derek F. Abell and John S. Hammond, *Strategic Market Planning* (Englewood Cliffs, N.J.: Prentice-Hall, 1979),
p. 212.

Figure 7–2   Present versus Future Positions in the Portfolio Matrix

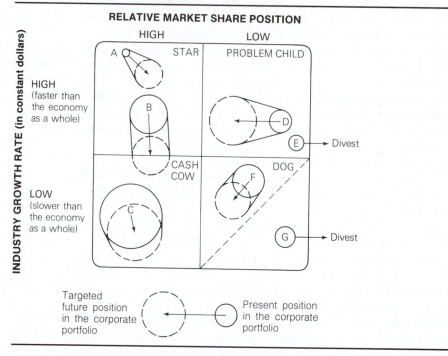

ence in lowering unit costs varies from industry to industry. In some cases, a larger market share can be translated into a unit-cost advantage; in others it cannot. Hence, it is wise to be cautious in basing strategy prescriptions on the assumption that experience curve effects are strong enough and cost differences among competitors big enough to totally drive competitive advantage.

6. A thorough assessment of the relative long-term attractiveness of business units in the business portfolio requires an examination of more than just market growth and relative market share variables.

The Nine-Cell GE Matrix

An alternative matrix approach that avoids some of the shortcomings of the BCG growth-share matrix has been pioneered by General Electric, with help from the consulting firm of McKinsey & Company. The GE effort is a nine-cell portfolio matrix based on the two dimensions of long-term product-market attractiveness and business strength/competitive position.[3] In this matrix, depicted in Figure 7–3, the

---

[3] For an expanded treatment, see Michael G. Allen, "Diagramming G.E.'s Planning for What's WATT," in *Corporate Planning: Techniques and Applications,* ed. Robert J. Allio and Malcolm W. Pennington (New York: AMACOM, 1979); and Hax and Majluf, *Strategic Management,* chap. 8.

area of the circle is proportional to the size of the industry, and the pie slices within the circle reflect the business's market share. The vertical axis represents each industry's *long-term attractiveness* (defined as a composite weighting of market growth rate, market size, historical and projected industry profitability, market structure and competitive intensity, scale economies, seasonality and cyclical influences, technological and capital requirements, emerging threats and opportunities, and social, environmental, and regulatory influences). The procedure involves assigning each industry attractiveness factor a weight according to its perceived importance, rating the business on each factor (using a 1 to 5 rating scale), and then obtaining a weighted composite rating as shown below:

Industry Attractiveness Factor	Weight	Rating	Value
Market size	.15	5	0.75
Projected rate of market growth	.20	1	0.20
Historical and projected profitability	.10	1	0.10
Intensity of competition	.20	5	1.00
Emerging opportunities and threats	.15	1	0.15
Seasonality and cyclical influences	.05	2	0.10
Technological and capital requirements	.10	3	0.30
Environmental impact	.05	4	0.20
Social, political, regulatory factors	Must be acceptable	—	—
	1.00		2.90

To arrive at a measure of business strength/competitive position, each business is rated (using the same approach shown above) on such aspects of business strength/competitive position as relative market share, success in increasing market share and profitability, ability to match rival firms in cost and product quality, knowledge of customers and markets, how well the firm's skills and competences in the business match the various requirements for competitive success in the industry (distribution network, promotion and marketing, access to scale economies, technological proficiency, support services, manufacturing efficiency), adequacy of production capacity, and caliber of management. The two composite values for long-term product-market attractiveness and business strength/competitive position are then used to plot each business's position in the matrix.

Corporate Strategy Implications

The nine cells of the GE matrix are grouped into three categories or zones. One zone (vertical lines) consists of the three cells at the upper left where long-term industry attractiveness and business strength/competitive position are favorable. The general strategic prescription here is *grow-and-build,* and businesses in these zones are accorded a high priority in allocating investment funds. The second zone (unshaded) consists of three diagonal cells stretching from the lower left to the upper right; businesses falling into these cells usually carry a medium investment allocation priority in the portfolio (*hold-and-maintain* is the strategy type). The third zone (horizontal lines) is composed of the three cells in the lower right corner of the matrix; the strategy prescription for these businesses

---

Figure 7–3   General Electric's Nine-Cell Business Portfolio Matrix

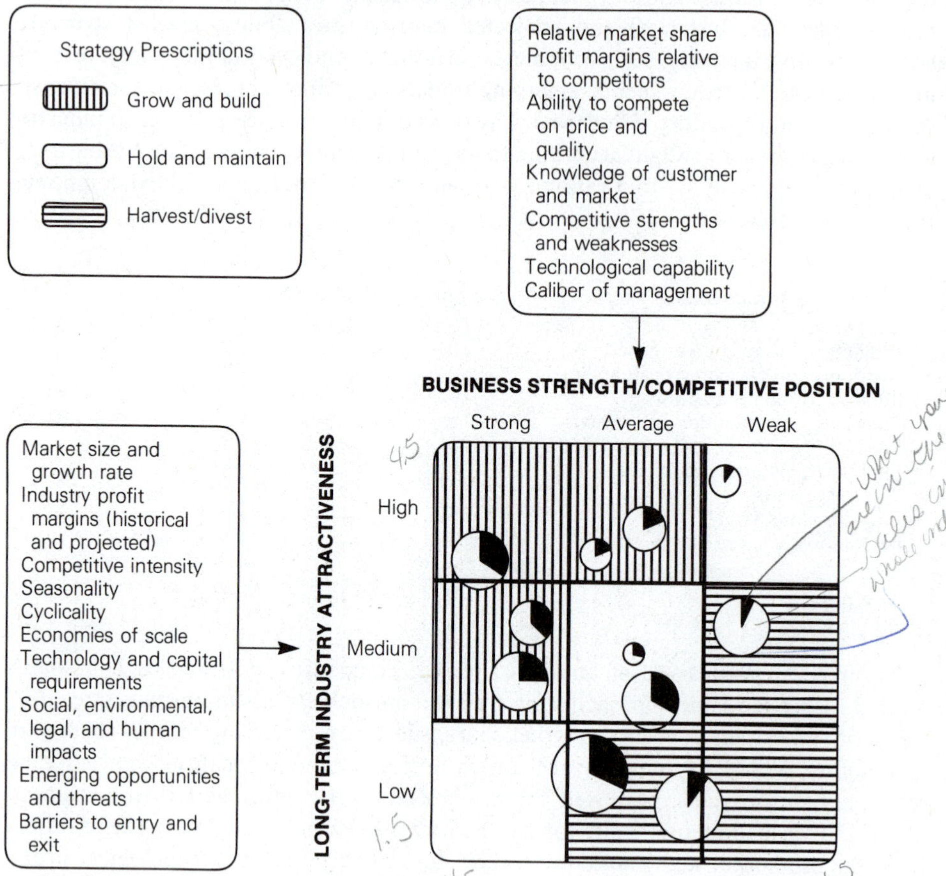

Strategy Prescriptions

[IIIIIIII] Grow and build

[ ] Hold and maintain

[≡≡≡] Harvest/divest

Relative market share
Profit margins relative
  to competitors
Ability to compete
  on price and
  quality
Knowledge of customer
  and market
Competitive strengths
  and weaknesses
Technological capability
Caliber of management

BUSINESS STRENGTH/COMPETITIVE POSITION

Strong   Average   Week

Market size and
  growth rate
Industry profit
  margins (historical
  and projected)
Competitive intensity
Seasonality
Cyclicality
Economies of scale
Technology and capital
  requirements
Social, environmental,
  legal, and human
  impacts
Emerging opportunities
  and threats
Barriers to entry and
  exit

LONG-TERM INDUSTRY ATTRACTIVENESS

High

Medium

Low

---

is typically *harvest or divest* (in exceptional cases it can be *rebuild and reposition* using some type of turnaround approach).[4]

The strength of the nine-cell GE approach is threefold: (1) it allows for intermediate rankings between high and low and between strong and weak; (2) it incorporates explicit consideration of a much wider variety of strategically relevant variables; and most important, (3) the powerful logic of GE's approach is its emphasis on channeling corporate resources to those businesses that combine medium-to-high product-market attractiveness with average-to-strong business strength or competitive position (the

---

[4] At GE each business actually ended up in one of five categories: (1) *high-growth potential* products deserving top investment priority, (2) *stable base* products deserving steady reinvestment to maintain position, (3) *support* products deserving periodic investment funding, (4) *selective pruning or rejuvenation* products deserving reduced investment funding, and (5) *venture* products deserving heavy R&D investment.

thesis is that the greatest probability of competitive advantage and superior performance lies in these combinations).

However, the nine-cell GE matrix, like the four-cell growth-share matrix, provides no real clues or hints about the specifics of business strategy. The GE matrix analysis yields only *general* prescriptions: grow and build, hold and maintain, or harvest-divest. Such prescriptions may occasionally suffice insofar as corporate-level strategy formulation is concerned, but the issue of specific competitive approaches remains wide open. Another weakness has been pointed out by Hofer and Schendel: the GE approach does not depict as well as it might the positions of businesses that are about to emerge as winners because the product/market is entering the takeoff stage.[5]

The Life-Cycle Matrix

To better identify a *developing-winner* type of business, Hofer developed a 15-cell matrix in which businesses are plotted in terms of stage of industry evolution and competitive position, as shown in Figure 7–4.[6] Again, the circles represent the sizes of the industries involved and pie wedges denote the business's market share. Looking at the plot in Figure 7–4, business A would appear to be a *developing winner;* business C might be classified as a *potential loser;* business E might be labeled an *established winner;* business F could be a cash cow; and business G a loser or a dog. The power of the life-cycle matrix is the story it tells about the distribution of the firm's businesses across the stages of industry evolution.

Actually, there is no need to force a choice as to which type of portfolio matrix to use; any or all can be constructed to gain insights from different perspectives, and each matrix type has its pros and cons. The important thing is analytical accuracy and completeness in describing the firm's current portfolio position—all for the larger purpose of discerning how to manage the portfolio as a whole and get the best performance from the allocation of corporate resources.

EVALUATING CORPORATE STRATEGY: BEYOND THE
BUSINESS PORTFOLIO MATRIX

Constructing business portfolio matrixes is a useful first step in appraising a diversified firm's current strategic situation because of the insight and clarity they provide about the overall character of a firm's business makeup. But business portfolio matrix analysis by no means constitutes the whole corporate strategy evaluation process. At most, a business portfolio matrix offers a snapshot comparison of different business units and some general prescriptions for the direction of business strategy. This is too skimpy a framework on which to base long-term direction-setting, make strategic

---

[5] Charles W. Hofer and Dan Schendel, *Strategy Formulation: Analytical Concepts* (St. Paul, Minn.: West Publishing, 1978), p. 33.

[6] Ibid., p. 34. This approach to business portfolio analysis was reportedly first used in actual practice by consultants at Arthur D. Little, Inc. For a full-scale review of this portfolio matrix approach, see Hax and Majluf, *Strategic Management,* chap. 9.

Figure 7–4   The Life-Cycle Portfolio Matrix

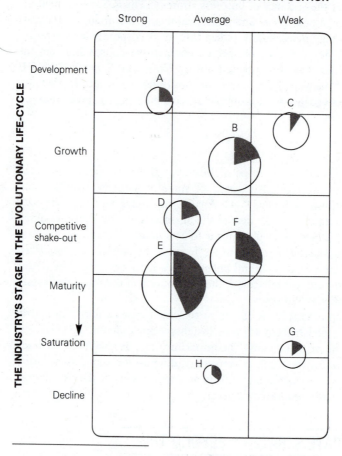

Source: Adapted from C. W. Hofer, "Conceptual Constructs for Formulating Corporate and Business Strategies" (Boston: Harvard Case Services, #9–378–754, 1977), p. 3.

decisions, and allocate corporate resources. Substantially more probing into the status and prospects of each business unit in the portfolio is needed to guide corporate strategy decisions. The kinds of additional probing that round out the task of evaluating corporate strategy have been identified by Hofer and Schendel:[7]

1. Constructing a summary profile of the industry environment and competitive environment of each business unit (as presented in Figure 3–6).
2. Appraising each business unit's strength and competitive position in its industry.

---

[7] Hofer and Schendel, *Strategy Formulation*, pp. 72–86.

Understanding how each business unit ranks against its rivals and on the key factors for competitive success affords corporate managers a basis for judging the business unit's chances for real success in its industry.

3. Identifying and comparing the specific external opportunities, threats, and strategic issues peculiar to each business unit. This adds to corporate management's understanding of each business unit's situation.

4. Determining the total amount of corporate financial support needed to fund each unit's business strategy and what corporate skills and resources could be deployed to boost the competitive strength of the various business units.

5. Comparing the relative attractiveness of different businesses in the corporate portfolio. This includes not only industry attractiveness/business strength comparisons but also a look at how the different business units compare on various historical and projected performance measures—sales growth, profit margins, return on investment, and the like.

6. Checking the overall portfolio to ascertain whether the mix of businesses is adequately "balanced"—not too many losers or question marks, not so many mature businesses that corporate growth will be slow, enough cash producers to support the stars and developing winners, too few dependable profit performers, and so on.

The methods for accomplishing items 1, 2, and 3 above were discussed at length in Chapter 3 and need not be iterated here. However, Illustration Capsule 17 presents an example of how a business unit can be profiled and its strategic plan summarized for review by corporate management and for comparison with other business units. A discussion of items 4, 5, and 6 follows.

Determining Resource and Skills Requirements

This evaluation step entails considering whether and how corporate resources and skills can be used to enhance the competitive standing of particular business units.[8] This is especially important when the firm has business units judged to be in a less than desirable competitive position and/or where improvement in some key success area is indicated. It is also important when corporate strategy is predicated on strategic fit and the game plan calls for transferring corporate skills and strengths to business units in an effort to give them a competitive edge and make their market position stronger.[9] One key to realizing the potential of strategic fit is matching corporate skills and resources with the key success factors in the industries in the firm's portfolio—the closer the match and the more potent the corporate skills and resources the more powerful is the strategy of a related-business portfolio approach. Another key is achieving corporate-level coordination of those portions of the activity-cost chains of business units where cost sharing and/or differentiation enhancement are attractive possibilities.

---

[8] Ibid., p. 80.

[9] Michael E. Porter, *Competitive Advantage* (New York: Free Press, 1985), chap. 9.

ILLUSTRATION CAPSULE 17

Profiling a Business Unit: An Actual Case—Allied Corporation's Sulfur Products Business

SITUATION ANALYSIS

- **Statement of Scope**

  Sulfuric acid manufactured or purchased for resale is sold to domestic petroleum, fibers, steel, paint, paper, chemical, and agricultural industries. Related activities also include specialty reprocessing of sulfur-containing products.

  About 30 percent of Allied's sulfur products produced in this business unit are captively consumed in upgraded products (used by other Allied businesses), with the remaining 70 percent moving to the merchant market. Specifically excluded from the scope of this unit are sulfuric manufacturing facilities where product is totally consumed in captive on-site upgrading for fibers, agriculture and hydrofluric acid (HF) products.

- **Industry Description**

  Sulfuric acid, the largest volume commodity chemical in the United States, is produced both by burning sulfur and as a recovered by-product. Total sulfuric acid production in the United States is valued at about $2.0 billion, typically representing 40 million net tons of product annually. Most sulfuric acid is consumed captively in production of other industrial chemicals, primarily fertilizers. Only about 30 percent of U.S. production moves to the merchant market. The U.S. industry comprises 140 producing locations with capacity of about 55 million net tons, and about 5,000 customers. Markets are primarily regional in nature.

  There are 70 companies producing sulfuric acid in the United States at 140 producing locations. Major merchant market producers include:

	Capacity (MM tons)
Stauffer	3.8
Du Pont	2.5
Allied:	
Sulfur products	0.8
Other (by-product acid)	0.4
Total Allied	1.2
Tennessee Chemical	1.4
American Cyanamid	1.1
Canadian Industries, Ltd.	0.6
Essex Chemical	0.6

- **Industry Maturity**

Current:	Aging
Future:	Aging
Cyclicality:	Linked to GNP; strong agricultural influences because of big fertilizer end-use.
Timing:	Coincident
Amplitude:	Medium

- **Market**

  Total consumption of sulfuric acid in the United States grew at an average annual rate of 3.0 percent from 1972 to 1981. Consumption declined significantly in 1982 and 1983 due to the general economic slowdown. This has been particularly true in the hard-hit fertilizer sector, which (excluding ammonium sulfate) accounts for some 60 percent of sulfuric acid consumption. Overall, U.S. consumption of sulfuric acid is projected to grow at an average annual rate of 2.5 percent from a 1984 base for the next several years, reflecting in part a recovery from the economic downturn. Growth in fertilizer use will exceed this rate, while other uses will be static or exhibit slower growth.

  Nonfertilizer segment growth:

			Sulfuric Acid	
			Allied Growth Rate	
End-Uses	U.S. (MM)	Allied (MM)	Past Five Years	Next Five Years
Chemicals	3.2	.5	−6.0	2.0
Petroleum	2.5	.2	−9.6	—
Other	7.6	.4	−4.4	2.0
Total	13.3	1.1	−5.8	1.7

- **Major Threats/Concerns**

  East Coast competition will result in lower market share and margins as new producers establish position and excess capacity continues.

  Major customer plant closings could be announced.

  Acceleration of resolution of acid rain issue could impact on sulfuric acid.

  Additional imported acid on East Coast (Canada, Europe).

- **Expected Competitive Conditions**

  Expect continued price and margin pressures in East Coast market due to:
  CIL operation of Sayreville, N.J. Plant (600M tons) at one train rate to provide backup for smelter acid resale position.

  Essex operation of Baltimore, Md. plant (350M tons) continues tenable near term.

  American Cyanamid will operate Warners, N.J. for energy value.

  Du Pont will consolidate capacity on East Coast.

  Increased competition for Allied resale arrangements.

PLAN ANALYSIS

- **Key Assumptions**

  Economic recovery continues; fertilizer demand improves.

ILLUSTRATION CAPSULE 17 *(concluded)*

Captive demand remains stable at 1982 levels.

Decomposition volume remains constant on East Coast; customer mix changes.

Continuation of long-term contractual arrangements.

Continued supply/demand imbalance on East Coast limits margin improvement near term.

Du Pont shutdown at Rapunto, N.J. facility; Allied to supply.

Additional production rationalization occurs within three to five years.

By-product acid resale arrangements continue, but greater competitive pressure for participation.

Acid rain issue resolution will not impact in plan period.

- **Business-Unit Description**
Allied's plants are managed to support captive requirements of about 300 million tons/year ($23 million) for upgraded chemical group products, profitable service related reprocessing of sulfur containing materials, and stand-alone profitable locations which have defendable competitive positions.

Manufacturing plants include:

	Millions of Net Tons		
	Capacity	*Current Volume Estimate*	*Utilization*
Bakersville	90	77	86%
Sacramento	150	100	67
Philadelphia	370	377	91
Baltimore	152	113	74
Total	762	667	82%

Additionally, approximately 400M tons/year of by-product acid are either resold or captively consumed.

8 customers = 50 percent of Allied's total trade tons
24 customers = 80 percent of Allied's total trade tons

- **Competitive Position/Strength vis-à-vis Rivals**

	Competitor				
	A	*B*	*C*	*D*	*E*
Protected market position	+	=	+	+	+
Total cost	=	+	=	=	=
Profitability	=	=	+	=	=
Net cash throw-off	=	=	+	=	=
Location & size of facility	=	+	=	+	=
Summary: Equal/favorable			+ Favorable = Comparable − Unfavorable		

- **Current/Future Strategic Situation**

	Embryo	Growth	Mature	Aging
Leading				
Strong				
Favorable				X
Tenable				
Weak				

- **Past Strategies**
Maintenance
Market rationalization
Product rationalization

- **Strategic Thrust and Positioning**
Hold niche/defend position.
Stand alone manufacturing locations (product/market segments) will be managed to maximize return and cash flow. Resale arrangements will be continued wherever profitable. Bakersville and Sacramento will focus on maintaining existing niche, while Baltimore and Philadelphia locations will orient to defending position based upon geographical advantage.

- **Acquisition Activities**
None

- **Strategic Manufacturing Focus**
Objective is to be a dependable supplier with a competitive cost structure, including a secure sulfur raw material supply, while controlling investment in inventories and facilities.

- **Strategic Technological Development Focus**
R&D spending is focused on process improvement (spent decomposition efficiencies) and energy savings projects.

- **Major Action Programs**
Maintain long-term contractual positions to defend positions.
Continue cost reduction program at Philadelphia.
Continue to explore potential change in Philadelphia customer/product mix to isolate from Northeast merchant market.
Improve efficiencies on inventory and distribution management.

SOURCE: Allied Corporation. Certain figures and locations have been disguised, as have other sensitive parts of the profile; some editing has also been done by the authors.

Comparing the Attractiveness of Different Business Units

After the businesses in the firm's portfolio have each been assessed on their own merits, the next step is to rank their relative attractiveness in terms of *(a)* their historical and projected performance (sales growth, profitability, and return on investment), *(b)* their priority for receiving corporate investment funds based on comparative industry attractiveness/business strength, and *(c)* which, if any, business units should become candidates for divestiture. The groundwork for this is contained in the assessments of each business. But other factors may also enter in. In addition to weighing the intangibles of how each business adds to or subtracts from the total portfolio outlook, two more considerations often creep into play. One is whether any material difference exists between the assessments of short-run and long-run potential and how this affects the business-unit comparisons across the portfolio. The second is the importance management attaches to building a portfolio that has good strategic fit and how this will alter judgments about which businesses should form the core of the corporation's future and which ought to be divested.

Overall "Balance" in the Portfolio

The final evaluation phase involves judging the mix of businesses in the portfolio.[10] The kinds of key questions to be answered include: Does the portfolio contain enough businesses in very attractive industries? Does it contain too many losers or question marks? Is the proportion of mature or declining businesses so great that corporate growth will be sluggish? Does the firm have enough "cash cows" to finance the stars and emerging winners? Are there enough businesses that generate dependable profits and/or cash flow? Is the portfolio overly vulnerable to inflation or recessionary influences? Does the firm have too many businesses that it really doesn't need to be in or otherwise needs to divest? Does the firm have its share of businesses with strong competitive positions, or is it burdened with too many businesses in average-to-weak competitive positions? Does the makeup of the business portfolio put the corporation in good position for the future?

CHECKING FOR PERFORMANCE GAPS

The whole of corporate-level strategy analysis points toward determining whether the aggregate performance of the businesses in the portfolio can be expected to achieve corporate objectives and, if not, what kinds of corporate strategy changes can be devised to close the performance gap. If a performance gap is found to exist, then there are at least five basic types of action top management can take to reduce or close the gap between the target and projected levels of corporate performance:[11]

    1. *Alter the strategic plans for some (or all) of the businesses in the portfolio.* This option essentially involves renewed corporate efforts to get better performance out

[10] Barry Hedley, "Strategy and the Business Portfolio," *Long Range Planning* 10, no. 1 (February 1977), p. 13; and Hofer and Schendel, *Strategy Formulation,* pp. 82–86.

[11] Hofer and Schendel, *Strategy Formulation,* pp. 93–100.

of its present business units. However, squeezing out better short-term performance, if pursued too zealously, can impair long-term performance of the adversely affected business units (and in any case there are limits to how much extra performance can be squeezed out to close the gap).

2. *Add new business units to the corporate portfolio.*   Making new acquisitions and/or implementing internal start-up of new businesses to boost overall performance, however, raises some new strategy issues. Expanding the corporate portfolio to close a performance gap means taking a close look at *(a)* what kind and size of new business should be added and what, if any, types of strategic fit they should have; *(b)* how the new units would be absorbed into or grafted onto the present corporate structure; *(c)* what specific features should be looked for in an acquisition candidate; and *(d)* whether portfolio expansion can be financed without shortchanging the present business units.

3. *Delete weak-performing or money-losing businesses from the corporate portfolio.*   The most likely candidates for divestiture are those businesses that are in a weak competitive position or in a relatively unattractive industry or in an industry which does not "fit."

4. *Join forces with other groups to try to alter conditions responsible for subpar performance potentials.*   In some situations, concerted actions with rival firms, trade associations, suppliers, unions, customers, or other interested groups may help ameliorate adverse performance prospects. Forming or supporting a political action group may be an effective way to lobby for solutions to import-export problems, tax disincentives, and onerous regulatory requirements.

5. *Reduce corporate performance objectives.*   On occasion, adverse economic circumstances or declining fortunes in one or more big business units can render corporate objectives unreachable. Closing the gap between actual and desired performance may then require downward revision of corporate objectives to bring them more in line with reality. As a practical matter, though, this tends to be a "last-resort" option, being used only after other options have come up short.

BUILDING CORPORATE-LEVEL COMPETITIVE ADVANTAGE IN DIVERSIFIED COMPANIES

One of the most important strategic tasks of corporate-level general managers is how to coordinate the strategies of the various business units—and to do so in ways that produce a corporate-driven contribution to the competitive advantage of business units.[12] It is the effective performance of this task that makes the corporate-level managers of diversified companies *more than portfolio managers* and the firm itself *more than a holding company.* Indeed, effective performance of this task is perhaps the chief way that corporate executives *add value* to a diversified enterprise.[13] Some

---

[12] Porter, *Competitive Advantage,* p. 364. This point is also emphasized in Kenichi Ohmae, *The Mind of the Strategist* (New York: Penguin Books, 1983), pp. 137–40.

[13] The term *add value* is used here to mean that performance of the corporate-level management functions is done in a manner that causes the profit performance of a diversified firm to be more than the total of what its business units would earn operating as independent companies. To put it another way, unless a diversified firm turns in a better performance than its business units could earn in the aggregate on their own, corporate management adds no pecuniary value to the enterprise.

other ways that corporate managers can add value to a diversified firm, besides building corporate-level competitive advantage, include:

- Excelling in portfolio management (selecting new businesses to get into that prove to be outstanding performers, selling business units off at their peak and getting premium prices, and so on), so that the enterprise consistently outperforms other firms in generating dividends and capital gains for stockholders.
- Doing such a good job of helping to manage the various business units (by providing expert problem-solving skills, innovative ideas, and improved decision-making acumen to the business-level managers) that the business units perform at a higher level than they would otherwise be able to do.
- Providing such inspirational leadership that subordinate managers and employees are motivated to perform "over their heads" on a sustained basis, thereby adding an "extra" measure of performance.

All of these ways amount to "better management"—which is to say that if corporate executives are to add value to a diversified firm in some way other than building a corporate-level competitive advantage, they must be "managerially superior" and produce results that business-level managers cannot. That this occurs very regularly would be hard to prove (but easy to claim!).

Building competitive advantage at the corporate level is grounded in coordinating and managing the interrelationships in the activity-cost chains of a firm's business units (the concept of activity-cost chains was first discussed in Chapter 3; the remainder of this section draws heavily on the presentation of "Strategic Cost Analysis" and Figure 3–4 in Chapter 3, and also on the material in Table 6–1 in Chapter 6). Step one is to analyze the activity-cost chains of each business unit to identify opportunities for cost sharing and/or differentiation enhancement.[14] In searching for business unit interrelationships to capitalize on, care has to be taken to distinguish between those opportunities where real sharing benefits can actually be achieved and those where the degree of relatedness is insignificant or disappears when put under the microscope and specifics are closely scrutinized. Moreover, there are many sources of business unit linkages: (1) supplier and/or component parts interrelationships, (2) technology and production process overlaps, (3) distribution channel interrelationships, (4) customer overlaps, (5) common managerial know-how requirements, and (6) competitor interrelationships (different business units may have common competitors and, often, two or more business units of one diversified firm may be in competition with two or more business units of another diversified firm—a condition that makes them *multipoint competitors*).

Once the interrelationships among business units in the corporate portfolio are identified, step two is to identify important interrelationships between a firm's present business units and other industries not represented in its portfolio.[15] Looking for sharing potentials in industries outside the portfolio can turn up interesting acquisition candidates and is a fruitful way of developing stronger strategic fits. Studying the portfolios of other firms with related portfolios can yield clues about which industries may offer attractive sharing possibilities.

[14] Porter, *Competitive Advantage,* p. 368; see also Ohmae, *The Mind of the Strategist,* pp. 137–38.
[15] Porter, *Competitive Advantage,* pp. 370–71.

Step three is to assess the potential of the interrelationships identified in steps one and two for building an attractive corporate-based competitive advantage.[16] The size of any net gain in competitive advantage here is a function of the sharing benefits, the costs of capturing the sharing benefits, and the difficulty of matching up and coordinating the business unit interrelationships. Analysis usually reveals that while there are many actual and potential business unit interrelationships and linkages, only a few of these have enough strategic importance to generate competitive advantage.

Step four is to develop a corporate action plan to coordinate those targeted business unit interrelationships where an attractive net competitive potential exists.[17] Corporate coordination of these interrelationships can be pursued in several different ways:[18]

1. Implement sharing of the related activities in the cost chain. Examples include centralizing the procurement of raw materials, combining R&D and design activities in one unit, integrating manufacturing facilities wholly or partially, combining dealer networks and sales force organizations, and combining order processing and shipping (for more possibilities refer to Table 6–1 in Chapter 6).
2. Coordinating the strategies of the related business units in order to unify and strengthen the firm's overall approach to customers, suppliers, and/or distribution channels, and also to present a stronger offensive or defensive front against the actions of competitors.
3. Formulating a corporate-level game plan for attacking and/or defending against multipoint competitors, the thrust of which is to strengthen the firm's overall position and to put multipoint rivals under added competitive pressure.
4. Setting up interbusiness task forces, standing committees, or project teams to transfer generic know-how, proprietary technology, and skills from one business unit to another and/or to implement sharing.
5. Diversifying into new businesses that enhance or extend strategic fit relationships in the activity-cost chains of existing businesses.
6. Divesting units that do not have strategic fit relationships or that make sharing and coordination more difficult.
7. Establishing incentives for business unit managers to work together in realizing strategic fit potentials.

Illustration Capsule 18 describes how one company pursued and achieved an attractive type of strategic fit.

GUIDELINES FOR MANAGING THE CORPORATE
STRATEGY FORMATION PROCESS

Although formal analysis and entrepreneurial brainstorming are important contributors to corporate strategy selection, there is more to where corporate strategy comes

---

[16] Ibid., pp. 371–72.
[17] Ibid., p. 372.
[18] Ibid., pp. 372–75; and Ohmae, *The Mind of the Strategist,* pp. 142–62.

ILLUSTRATION CAPSULE 18

Harry and David: Pursuing Strategic Fit

Harry and David is a mail-order company specializing in fresh fruit and bakery goods. Headquartered at a 23-acre site south of Medford, Oregon, Harry and David grows much of its own fruit, bakes its own cakes and pastries, processes a variety of preserves, and weaves over 120,000 gift baskets for its products. The company is internationally known for its Fruit-of-the-Month Club and for its Royal Riviera pears. The pears are Harry and David's most popular product and are grown at the company-owned Bear Creek Orchards near Medford. The company's hallmark is an old-fashioned concern for quality and personal attention. The fruit shipped by Harry and David is of exceptionally fine quality and meets exacting standards. Attention to detail extends to hand-tying the bows on each gift basket, and every box of fruit and gift basket contains a card identifying the packer to signal the pride and care taken with each order.

Sales at Harry and David's are highly seasonal. Over two-thirds of the company's orders are received during the October–December period, following the mailing of the company's Christmas catalog. To help relieve the strong seasonal nature of its business, Harry and David elected to diversify by purchasing Jackson and Perkins, a New York–based firm specializing in selling roses by mail order. Jackson and Perkins had gained national prominence selling roses at the 1939 New York World's Fair; sales had thrived since that time and orders were shipped nationwide.

Shortly after Jackson and Perkins was acquired by Harry and David, it was relocated to the West Coast. Arrangements were made to grow Jackson and Perkins' roses in production fields in California and truck them to Medford for packing and shipping. The packing and shipping operations of the two businesses meshed nicely. Both are seasonal; pears are packed and shipped from October through December, and roses from mid-December through May. Both businesses are thus able to share the same facilities and labor for packing and shipping, to utilize common order processing personnel and procedures, and to benefit from economies in preparing and mailing their catalogs. The strategic fit potential between the two businesses was the main factor shaping Harry and David's decision to acquire Jackson and Perkins.

from and how it evolves. The process used to arrive at major strategic decisions is typically fragmented, incremental, and the product of a shared consensus for action among key members of corporate-level management.[19] Rarely is there an all-inclusive grand formulation of the total corporate strategy. Instead, corporate strategy in major enterprises emerges incrementally from the unfolding of many different internal and external events, the result of probing the future, experimenting, gathering more information, sensing problems, building awareness of the various options, developing ad

---

[19] James Brian Quinn, *Strategies for Change: Logical Incrementalism* (Homewood, Ill.: Richard D. Irwin, 1980), p. 15.

hoc responses to unexpected "crises," communicating partial consensus as it emerges, and acquiring a "feel" for all the strategically relevant factors, their importance, and their interrelationships.[20]

One should not think, therefore, of corporate strategy analysis as a time executives set aside to undertake a single comprehensive review. Such big reviews may be scheduled, but the evidence is that major strategic decisions emerge gradually rather than from periodic, full-scale analysis followed by a prompt decision. Typically, top executives approach major strategic decisions a step at a time, often starting from broad, intuitive concepts and then embellishing, fine-tuning, and modifying their original thinking as more information is gathered, as formal analysis confirms or modifies emerging judgments about the situation, and as confidence and consensus build for what strategic moves need to be made. Often, attention and resources are concentrated on a few critical strategic thrusts that illuminate and integrate corporate direction, objectives, and strategies.

ANALYTICAL CHECKLIST

Diagnostic work on a diversified firm's business portfolio should be routinely conducted, not just at regular intervals but also when new developments cause the outlook for one or more business units to change significantly. Full-fledged portfolio analysis is an eight-step process. Step one is to construct business portfolio matrixes as needed to see what the overall composition of the present portfolio looks like. Step two is to profile the industry and competitive environment of each business unit and to draw conclusions about how attractive each industry represented in the portfolio is. Step three is to probe the competitive strength of the individual businesses and how well situated each one is in its respective industry. Step four is to probe further into each business's situation, identifying the strategic issues that must be addressed and weighing the implications of specific threats and opportunities. Step five is to determine the corporate financial support needed to fund each unit's business strategy and what corporate skills can be used to boost their competitive strength. Step six is to compare the different business units in terms of relative industry attractiveness/business strength and relative profitability, ending up with a ranking of their relative investment priority and conclusions about where the firm should be putting its money. Step seven is to check whether the portfolio has a balanced mix of business units. Step eight is to ascertain whether the projected performance of the portfolio will meet corporate objectives, and if a performance gap is evident then what actions to take to close the gap. Out of this should come:

- General strategy recommendations for managing each business unit (grow and build, hold and maintain, overhaul and reposition, harvest, or divest).
- Conclusions concerning whether to add new units to the portfolio and, if so, whether they should be related or unrelated to those already in the portfolio.
- Decisions regarding the need to promote more strategic fit and whether and how to try to build what kind of corporate-level competitive advantage.

---

[20] Ibid., pp. 58, 196.

SUGGESTED READINGS

Bettis, Richard A., and William K. Hall. "Strategic Portfolio Management in the Multibusiness Firm." *California Management Review* 24, no. 1 (Fall 1981), pp. 23–38.

————. "The Business Portfolio Approach—Where It Falls Down in Practice." *Long Range Planning* 16, no. 2 (April 1983), pp. 95–104

Christensen, H. Kurt; Arnold C. Cooper; and Cornelis A. Dekluyver. "The Dog Business: A Reexamination," *Business Horizons* 25, no. 6 (November–December 1982), pp. 12–18.

Hamermesh, Richard G. *Making Strategy Work.* New York: John Wiley & Sons, 1986, chaps. 1, 4, and 7.

Haspeslagh, Phillippe. "Portfolio Planning: Uses and Limits." *Harvard Business Review* 60, no. 1 (January–February 1982), pp. 58–73.

Hax, Arnoldo, and Nicolas S. Majluf. *Strategic Management: An Integrative Perspective* (Englewood Cliffs, N.J.: Prentice-Hall, 1984), chaps. 7–9.

Hedley, Barry. "A Fundamental Approach to Strategy Development." *Long Range Planning* 9, no. 6 (December 1976), pp. 2–11.

————. "Strategy and the Business Portfolio." *Long Range Planning* 10, no. 1 (February 1977), pp. 9–15.

Henderson, Bruce D. "The Application and Misapplication of the Experience Curve." *Journal of Business Strategy* 4, no. 3 (Winter 1984), pp. 3–9.

Hofer, Charles W., and Dan Schendel. *Strategy Formulation: Analytical Concepts.* St. Paul, Minn.: West Publishing, 1978, chaps. 2 and 4.

Hussey, D. E. "Portfolio Analysis: Practical Experience with the Directional Policy Matrix." *Long Range Planning* 11, no. 4 (August 1978), pp. 2–8.

Lorange, Peter. *Corporate Planning: An Executive Viewpoint.* Englewood Cliffs. N.J.: Prentice-Hall, 1980, chaps. 1–3.

Porter, Michael E. *Competitive Advantage.* New York: Free Press, 1985, chaps. 9–11.

Quinn, James B. *Strategies for Change: Logical Incrementalism.* Homewood, Ill.: Richard D. Irwin, 1980.

Salter, Malcolm, and Wolf Weinhold. *Diversification through Acquisition.* New York: Macmillan, 1979.

8 Implementing Strategy: Organization Structure, Distinctive Competences, and Resource Allocation

Once the course of strategy has been charted, the manager's priorities swing to converting the chosen strategic plan into actions and good results. Putting the strategy into effect and getting the organization moving in the direction of strategy accomplishment calls for a fundamentally different set of managerial tasks and skills. Whereas formulation has an entrepreneurial focus, strategy implementation has primarily an administrative focus. Whereas strategy formulation entails heavy doses of vision, analysis, and entrepreneurial judgment, successful strategy implementation depends on the skills of working through others, organizing, motivating, culture-building, and creating stronger fits between strategy and how the organization operates. Ingrained behavior does not change just because a new strategy has been announced.

In comparison, implementing strategy poses the tougher management challenge. Practitioners emphatically state that it is a whole lot easier to develop a sound strategic plan than it is to "make it happen." To see why, let's look at what strategy implementation involves.

> Just being able to conceive bold new strategies is not enough. The general manager must also be able to translate his or her strategic vision into concrete steps that "get things done."
> —*Richard G. Hamermesh*

> . . . organizations are creatures of habit just like people. They are cultures, heavily influenced by the past.
> —*Robert H. Waterman, Jr.*

A GENERAL FRAMEWORK FOR STRATEGY IMPLEMENTATION

What makes the job of the strategy manager so complicated when it comes to implementation is the number of tasks involved and the variety of ways to approach each task. Strategy implementation has to be tailored to the organization's overall condition and setting, to the nature of the strategy and the amount of strategic change involved (shifting to a bold new strategy poses different implementation problems than fine-tuning a strategy already in place), and to the manager's own skills, style, and methods. Figure 8–1 illustrates the wide-ranging administrative concerns that shape a manager's action agenda for implementing strategy. Four broad areas stand out:

1. Performing the recurring administrative tasks associated with strategy implementation.
2. Creating "fits" between strategy and the various internal "ways of doing things" in order to align the whole organization behind strategy accomplishment.
3. Figuring out an agenda and a set of action priorities that matches up well with the organization's overall situation and the context of the setting in which implementation must take place.

Figure 8–1   Implementing Strategy: A Diagnostic Framework

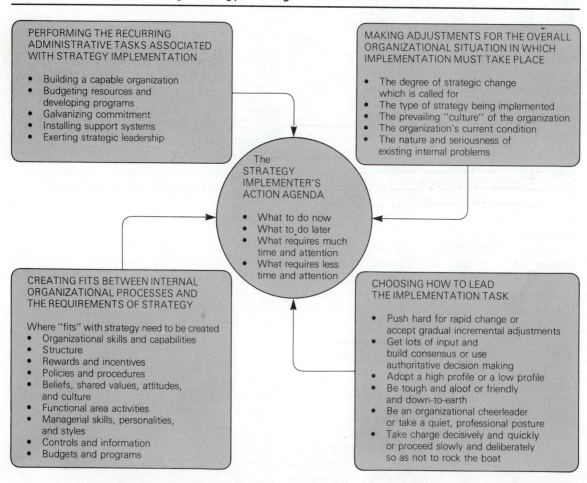

PERFORMING THE RECURRING ADMINISTRATIVE TASKS ASSOCIATED WITH STRATEGY IMPLEMENTATION

- Building a capable organization
- Budgeting resources and developing programs
- Galvanizing commitment
- Installing support systems
- Exerting strategic leadership

MAKING ADJUSTMENTS FOR THE OVERALL ORGANIZATIONAL SITUATION IN WHICH IMPLEMENTATION MUST TAKE PLACE

- The degree of strategic change which is called for
- The type of strategy being implemented
- The prevailing "culture" of the organization
- The organization's current condition
- The nature and seriousness of existing internal problems

The STRATEGY IMPLEMENTER'S ACTION AGENDA

- What to do now
- What to do later
- What requires much time and attention
- What requires less time and attention

CREATING FITS BETWEEN INTERNAL ORGANIZATIONAL PROCESSES AND THE REQUIREMENTS OF STRATEGY

Where "fits" with strategy need to be created
- Organizational skills and capabilities
- Structure
- Rewards and incentives
- Policies and procedures
- Beliefs, shared values, attitudes, and culture
- Functional area activities
- Managerial skills, personalities, and styles
- Controls and information
- Budgets and programs

CHOOSING HOW TO LEAD THE IMPLEMENTATION TASK

- Push hard for rapid change or accept gradual incremental adjustments
- Get lots of input and build consensus or use authoritative decision making
- Adopt a high profile or a low profile
- Be tough and aloof or friendly and down-to-earth
- Be an organizational cheerleader or take a quiet, professional posture
- Take charge decisively and quickly or proceed slowly and deliberately so as not to rock the boat

4. What managerial approach and leadership style to adopt in inducing the needed organizational changes.

In general, every unit of an organization, from headquarters on down to each operating department, has to ask, "What is required for us to implement our part of the overall strategic plan and how can we best get it done?" A thorough answer to this question entails scrutinizing the whole internal organization to diagnose what strategy-supportive changes are needed and how to accomplish them.

The administrative components of strategy implementation and the recurring administrative issues relating to each are highlighted in Figure 8–2. The strategy implementer's challenge in performing these tasks is to bring the organization's conduct of its internal operations into good alignment with strategy and to unite the total organization behind strategy accomplishment. The implementer's job is one of building such determined enthusiasm and commitment up and down the ranks that a virtual organizationwide crusade emerges to carry out the chosen strategy. The stronger the strategy-supportive culture that can be created, the greater the chances of successful strategy implementation. Strategy-supportive matches are needed with organizational skills and capabilities, functional area activities, organization structure, reward systems and incentives, policies and procedures, information systems and control mechanisms, budgets and programs, and shared values and cultural norms. Making these fits strong prevents internal activities from being at cross purposes with strategy and brings the organization's actual work into closer harmony with the strategic plan.

The Manager's Role in the Implementation Process

The chief executive officer and the heads of major organizational subunits are obviously the persons most responsible for leading and keynoting the tone, pace, and style of strategy implementation. There are many ways to proceed. A strategy implementer can opt for an active, visible role or a low-key, behind-the-scenes role. He or she can elect to make decisions authoritatively or on the basis of consensus, to delegate much or little, to be deeply involved in the details of implementation or to remain aloof from the day-to-day problems. It is up to the strategy implementer to decide whether to proceed swiftly (launching implementation initiatives on many fronts) or to move deliberately, content with gradual progress over a long time frame. Moreover, work on all the central administrative tasks (Figure 8–2) has to be launched and supervised, and decisions must be made regarding which of the several administrative fits to work on first and what steps to take to create the fits.

How a manager goes about the implementation task is, in addition, a function of his or her experience and accumulated knowledge about the business; whether the manager is new to the job or a secure incumbent; the manager's network of personal relationships with others in the organization; the manager's own diagnostic, administrative, interpersonal, and problem-solving skills; the authority which the manager has been given; and the manager's own leadership preferences for how to proceed. The remaining determinant of the manager's approach to strategy implementation is the context of the organization's situation—the seriousness of the firm's strategic difficulties; the nature and extent of the strategic change involved; the type of strategy being implemented; the strength of the ingrained behavior patterns; the available financial and organizational resources; the configuration of personal and organization

Figure 8–2 The Administrative Aspects of Strategy Implementation

Building an Organization Capable of Carrying Out the Strategic Plan	+	Allocating and Focusing Resources on Strategic Objectives	+	Galvanizing Organizationwide Commitment to the Chosen Strategic Plan	+	Installing Internal Administrative Support Systems	+	Exerting Strategic Leadership
Key recurring tasks: 1. Developing a strategy-supportive organization structure. 2. Building and nurturing the skills and distinctive competence on which strategy is grounded. 3. Selecting people for key positions.		*Key recurring tasks:* 1. Seeing that each organizational unit has the budget and programs to carry out its part of the strategic plan. 2. Getting individuals and organization units to gear their efforts closely to achieving the target strategic objectives.		*Key recurring tasks:* 1. Motivating organizational units and individuals to accomplish strategy. 2. Creating a strategy-supportive work environment and corporate culture. 3. Promoting a results orientation and a spirit of high performance. 4. Keeping the reward structure tightly linked to strategic performance and the achievement of target objectives.		*Key recurring tasks:* 1. Establishing strategy-facilitating policies and procedures. 2. Generating the right strategic information on a timely basis. 3. Instituing internal "controls" to keep the organization on its strategic course. 4. Creating fits between strategy and the various internal ways of doing things.		*Key recurring tasks:* 1. Leading the process of shaping values, molding culture, and energizing strategy accomplishment. 2. Keeping the organization innovative, responsive, and opportunistic. 3. Dealing with the politics of strategy, coping with power struggles, and building consensus. 4. Initiating corrective actions to improve strategy execution.

relationships that have permeated the firm's history; the pressures for short-term performance; and other such factors that make up the firm's "personality" and overall internal condition.

To some extent, therefore, each strategy implementation situation is unique enough to require the strategy manager to tailor his or her action agenda to fit the specific organizational environment at hand. This forces the manager to be conscious of all that strategy implementation involves and to diagnose carefully the action priorities and in what sequence things need to be done. The manager's role is thus all-important. His or her agenda for action and conclusions about how hard and how fast to push for change are decisive in shaping the character of implementation and moving the process along.

In the remainder of this chapter and in Chapter 9, we shall survey the ins and outs of the manager's role as chief implementer and administrator of strategy. For convenience, the discussion will be organized around the administrative components of the strategy implementation process and the recurring administrative issues associated with each—as displayed in Figure 8–2. This chapter will explore the management tasks of organization building, budgetary allocation, and skills development. Chapter 9 deals with galvanizing organizationwide commitment to the chosen strategy, installing administrative support systems to fit strategy, and exerting strategic leadership.

BUILDING A CAPABLE ORGANIZATION

Successful strategy execution depends greatly on good internal organization and competent personnel. Building a capable organization is thus always a top strategy implementation priority. Three organizational issues stand out as dominant:

1. Developing an internal organization structure that is responsive to the needs of strategy.
2. Developing the skills and distinctive competences in which the strategy is grounded and seeing that the organization has the managerial talents, technical know-how, and competitive capabilities it needs.
3. Selecting people for key positions.

Matching Organization Structure to Strategy

There are few hard and fast rules for designing a strategy-supportive organization structure. Every firm's internal organization is partly idiosyncratic, the result of many organizational decisions and historical circumstances. Moreover, every strategy is grounded in its own set of key success factors and critical tasks. The only ironclad imperative is to design the internal organization structure around the key success factors and critical tasks inherent in the firm's strategy. The following five-sequence procedure serves as a useful guide for fitting structure to strategy:[1]

---

[1] LaRue T. Hosmer, *Strategic Management: Text and Cases on Business Policy* (Englewood Cliffs, N.J.: Prentice-Hall, 1982), chap. 10; and J. Thomas Cannon, *Business Strategy and Policy* (New York: Harcourt Brace Jovanovich, 1968), p. 316.

1. Pinpoint the key functions and tasks requisite for successful strategy execution.
2. Reflect on how the strategy-critical functions and organizational units relate to those that are routine and to those that provide staff support.
3. Make strategy-critical business units and functions the main organizational building blocks.
4. Determine the degrees of authority needed to manage each organizational unit, bearing in mind both the benefits and costs of decentralized decision making.
5. Provide for coordination among the various organizational units.

Pinpointing the Strategy-Critical Activities　　In any organization, some activities and skills are always more critical to strategic success than others. From a strategy perspective, much of an organization's total work effort is routine and falls under the rubric of administrative good housekeeping and necessary detail (handling payrolls, managing cash flows, controlling inventories, processing grievances, taking care of warehousing and shipping, processing customer orders, and complying with regulations). Other activities are primarily support functions (data processing, accounting, training, public relations, market research, and purchasing). Yet there are usually certain crucial tasks and functions which have to be exceedingly well done for the strategy to be successful. For instance, tight cost control is essential for a firm trying to be the low-cost producer in a commodity business where margins are low and price-cutting is a widely used competitive weapon. For a luxury goods manufacturer, the critical skills may be quality craftsmanship, distinctive design, and sophisticated promotional appeal. The strategy-critical activities vary according to the particulars of a firm's strategy and competitive requirements.

To help identify what an organization's strategy-critical activities are, two questions can usefully be posed: "What functions have to be performed extra well and on time for the strategy to succeed?" and "In what areas would malperformance seriously endanger strategic success?"[2] The answers to these two questions should point squarely at what activities and skills are crucial and where to concentrate organization-building efforts.

Understanding the Relationships among Activities　　Activities can be related by the flow of material through the production process, the type of customer served, the distribution channels used, the technical skills and know-how needed to perform them, a strong need to centralize authority over them, the sequence in which tasks must be performed, and geographic location, to mention some of the most obvious ways. Such relationships are important because one (or more) of the interrelationships usually become the basis for grouping activities into organizational units. If the needs of strategy are to drive organization design, then the relationships to look for are those that link one piece of the strategy to another.

Grouping Activities into Organization Units　　The chief guideline here is to make strategy-critical activities the main building blocks in the organization struc-

[2] Peter F. Drucker, *Management: Tasks, Responsibilities, Practices* (New York: Harper & Row, 1974), pp. 530, 535.

ture. If activities crucial to strategic success are to get the attention and visibility they merit, then they have to be a prominent part of the organizational scheme. When key functions and critical tasks take a backseat to less important activities, the politics of organizational budget making usually leads to them being given fewer resources and accorded less significance than they actually have. On the other hand, when they form the core of the whole organization structure, their role and power in the overall scheme of things is highlighted and institutionalized. Senior managers can seldom give a stronger signal as to what is strategically important than by making key functions and critical skills the most prominent organizational building blocks and, further, assigning them a high position in the organizational pecking order.

Determining the Degree of Authority and Independence to Give Each Unit   How much authority and decision-making latitude to give each organization unit, especially line-of-business units, is important. In the case of line-of-business units, one polar alternative is to centralize authority for the big strategy and policy decisions at the corporate level and delegate only operating decisions to business-level managers. At the other extreme, line-of-business units can be delegated enough autonomy to function independently, with little direct authority being exerted by corporate headquarters staff.

Several guidelines for parceling out authority across the various units can be offered. Activities and organizational units with a key role in strategy execution should not be made subordinate to routine and nonkey activities. Revenue-producing and results-producing activities should not be made subordinate to internal support or staff functions. With few exceptions, decisions should be delegated to those managers closest to the scene of the action. Corporate-level authority over operating decisions at the business-unit level and below should be held to a minimum. The crucial administrative skill is selecting *strong* managers to head up each unit and delegating them enough authority to formulate and execute an appropriate strategy for their unit. If the results such managers produce prove unsatisfactory, then those with a poor track record of "right" and "wrong" decisions should be weeded out.

Providing for Coordination among the Units   Providing for coordination of the activities of organizational units is accomplished mainly through positioning them in the hierarchy of authority. Managers higher up in the pecking order generally have authority over more organizational units and thus the clout to coordinate, integrate, and otherwise arrange for the cooperation of the units under their supervision. The chief executive officer, the chief operating officer, and business-level managers are, of course, central points of coordination because they have broad authority. Besides positioning organizational units along the vertical scale of managerial authority, coordination of strategic efforts can also be achieved through informal meetings, project teams, special task forces, standing committees, formal strategy reviews, and annual strategic planning and budgeting cycles. Additionally, the formulation of the strategic plan itself serves a coordinating role; the whole process of negotiating and deciding on the objectives and strategies of each organizational unit and making sure that related activities mesh together suitably help coordinate operations across organizational units.

The Structure-Follows-Strategy Thesis   The practice of *consciously* matching organization design and structure to the particular needs and requirements of strategy is a fairly recent management development, and it springs from research evidence about the actual experiences of firms. The landmark study is Alfred Chandler's *Strategy and Structure*.[3] Chandler found that changes in an organization's strategy bring about new administrative problems which, in turn, require a new or refashioned structure if the new strategy is to be successfully implemented. His study of 70 large corporations revealed that structure tends to follow the growth strategy of the firm—but often not until inefficiency and internal operating problems provoke a structural adjustment. The experience of these firms followed a consistent sequential pattern: new strategy creation, emergence of new administrative problems, a decline in profitability and performance, a shift to a more appropriate organizational structure, and then recovery to more profitable levels and improved strategy execution. Chandler found this sequence to be often repeated as firms grew and modified their corporate strategies. The lesson of Chandler's research is that the choice of organization structure *does make a difference* in how an organization performs. Not all forms of organization structure are equally supportive in implementing a given strategy.

The *structure-follows-strategy* thesis is undergirded with powerful logic: How the work of an organization is structured is just a means to an end—not an end in itself. Structure is no more than a managerial device for facilitating the implementation and execution of the organization's strategy and, ultimately, for achieving the intended performance and results. Toward this end, the structural design of an organization acts both as a "harness" that helps people pull together in their performance of diverse tasks and as a means of tying the organizational building blocks together in ways that promote strategy accomplishment and improved performance. Without *deliberately* organizing responsibilities and activities to produce linkages between structure and strategy, the outcomes are likely to be disorder, friction, and malperformance.[4]

How Structure Evolves as Strategy Evolves: The Stages Model

In a number of respects, the strategist's approach to organization-building is governed by the size and growth stage of the enterprise, as well as by the key success factors inherent in the organization's business. For instance, the type of organization structure that suits a small specialty steel firm relying on a concentration strategy in a regional market is not likely to be suitable for a large, vertically integrated steel producer doing business in geographically diverse areas. The organization form that works best in a corporation pursuing unrelated diversification is, understandably, likely to

---

[3] Alfred D. Chandler, *Strategy and Structure* (Cambridge, Mass.: MIT Press, 1962). Although the stress here is on matching structure to strategy, it is worth noting that structure can and does influence the choice of strategy. A "good" strategy must be doable. When an organization's present structure is so far out of line with the requirements of a particular strategy that the organization would have to be turned upside down and inside out to implement it, then the strategy may, as a practical matter, not be doable and ought not to be given further consideration. In such cases, structure shapes the choice of strategy. The point here, however, is that once strategy is chosen, structure must be made to fit the strategy if, in fact, an approximate fit does not already exist. Any influence of structure on strategy should, logically, come before the point of strategy selection rather than after it.

[4] Drucker, *Management*, p. 523.

be different yet again. Recognition of this characteristic has prompted several attempts to formulate a model linking changes in organizational structure to stages in an organization's strategic development.[5]

The underpinning of the stages concept is that enterprises can be arrayed along a continuum running from very simple to very complex organizational forms and that there is a tendency for an organization to move along this continuum toward more complex forms as it grows in size, market coverage, and product-line scope, and as the strategic aspects of its customer-technology-business portfolio become more intricate. Four distinct stages of strategy-related organization structure have been singled out.

Stage I   Stage I organizations are small, single-business enterprises managed by one person. The owner-entrepreneur has close daily contact with employees and each phase of operations. Most employees report directly to the owner, who makes all the pertinent decisions regarding mission, objectives, strategy, and daily operations.

Stage II   Stage II organizations differ from Stage I enterprises in one essential respect: an increased scale and scope of operations force a transition from one-person management to group management. However, a Stage II enterprise, although run by a team of managers with functionally specialized responsibilities, remains fundamentally a single-business operation. Some Stage II organizations prefer to divide strategic responsibilities along classic functional lines—marketing, production, finance, human resources, engineering, public relations, procurement, planning, and so on. In vertically integrated Stage II companies, the main organizational units often relate to the distinct production stages in the industry chain; for example, the organizational building blocks of a large oil company usually consist of exploration, drilling, pipelines, refining, wholesale distribution, and retail sales. In practice, there is wide variation in the ways Stage II firms define the functional area building blocks.

Stage III   Stage III consists of organizations whose operations, though concentrated in a single field or product line, are scattered over a wide geographical area and large enough to justify having geographically decentralized operating units. These units all report to corporate headquarters and conform to corporate policies, but they are given the flexibility to tailor their unit's strategic plan to meet the specific needs of each respective geographic area. Ordinarily, each of the geographic operating units of a Stage III organization is structured along functional lines.

The key difference between Stage II and Stage III, however, is that while the functional units of a Stage II organization stand or fall together (in that they are built around one business and one end market), the geographic operating units of a Stage III firm can stand alone (or nearly so) in the sense that the operations in each geographic unit are not dependent on those in other areas. Typical firms in this category are breweries, cement companies, and steel mills having production

---

[5] See, for example, Malcolm S. Salter, "Stages of Corporate Development," *Journal of Business Policy* 1, no. 1 (Spring 1970), pp. 23–27; Donald H. Thain, "Stages of Corporate Development," *Business Quarterly,* Winter 1969, pp. 32–45; Bruce R. Scott, "The Industrial State: Old Myths and New Realities," *Harvard Business Review* 51, no. 2 (March–April 1973), pp. 133–48; and Alfred D. Chandler, *Strategy and Structure,* chap. 1.

capacity and sales organizations in several geographically separate market areas. Corey and Star cite Pfizer International as a good example of a company whose strategic requirements made geographic decentralization propitious:

> With sales of $223 million in 1964, Pfizer International operated plants in 27 countries and marketed in more than 100 countries. Its product lines included pharmaceuticals (antibiotics and other ethical prescription drugs), agriculture and veterinary products (such as animal feed supplements and vaccines and pesticides), chemicals (fine chemicals, bulk pharmaceuticals, petrochemicals, and plastics), and consumer products (cosmetics and toiletries).
>
> Ten geographic area managers reported directly to the president of Pfizer International and exercised line supervision over country managers. According to a company position description, it was "the responsibility of each area manager to plan, develop, and carry out Pfizer International's business in the assigned foreign area in keeping with company policies and goals."
>
> Country managers had profit responsibility. In most cases a single country manager managed all Pfizer activities in his country. In some of the larger, well-developed countries of Europe there were separate country managers for pharmaceutical and agricultural products and for consumer lines.
>
> Except for the fact that New York headquarters exercised control over the to-the-market prices of certain products, especially prices of widely used pharmaceuticals, area and country managers had considerable autonomy in planning and managing the Pfizer International business in their respective geographic areas. This was appropriate because each area, and some countries within areas, provided unique market and regulatory environments. In the case of pharmaceuticals and agriculture and veterinary products (Pfizer International's most important lines), national laws affected formulations, dosages, labeling, distribution, and often price. Trade restrictions affected the flow of bulk pharmaceuticals and chemicals and packaged products, and might in effect require the establishment of manufacturing plants to supply local markets. Competition, too, varied significantly from area to area.[6]

Stage IV   Stage IV includes large, diversified firms decentralized by line of business. Typically, each separate business unit is headed by a general manager who has profit-and-loss responsibility and whose authority extends across all of the unit's functional areas except, perhaps, accounting and capital investment (both of which are traditionally subject to corporate approval). Both business strategy decisions and operating decisions are concentrated at the line-of-business level rather than at the corporate level. The organizational structure within the line-of-business unit may be along the lines of Stage II or III types of organizations. Characteristic Stage IV companies include GE, ITT, Procter & Gamble, Philip Morris, Du Pont, United Technologies, RJR Nabisco, and Litton Industries.

Movement Through the Stages   The stages model provides useful insights into why organization structure tends to change. As firms progress from small, entrepreneurial enterprises following a basic concentration strategy to more complex strategic phases of volume expansion, vertical integration, geographic expansion, and

---

[6] Raymond Corey and Steven H. Star, *Organization Strategy: A Marketing Approach* (Boston: Division of Research, Harvard University Graduate School of Business Administration, 1971), pp. 23–24.

line-of-business diversification, their organizational structures tend to evolve from unifunctional to functionally centralized to multidivisional decentralized organizational forms. Firms that remain single-line businesses almost always have some form of a centralized functional structure. Enterprises predominantly in one industry but slightly diversified typically have a hybrid structure; the dominant business is managed via functional organization and the diversified activities are handled through a decentralized divisionalized form. The more diversified an organization becomes, regardless of whether the diversification is along related or unrelated lines, the more it moves toward some form of decentralized business units. In short, as a firm's strategy course shifts from a small, single-product business to a large, dominant-product business and then on to broad diversification, its organizational structure evolves from one-man management to large group functional management to decentralized, line-of-business management. About 90 percent of the Fortune 500 firms (nearly all of which are diversified to one degree or another) have a divisionalized organizational structure with the primary basis for decentralization being line-of-business considerations.

One final lesson that the stages model teaches is that a reassessment of organization structure and authority is always useful whenever strategy is changed.[7] A new strategy is likely to entail new or subtly different skills and key activities. If these changes go unrecognized, especially the subtle ones, the resulting mismatch between strategy and organization can pose implementation problems and curtail performance.

The Strategy-Related Pros and Cons of Alternative Organization Forms

There are essentially five strategy-related approaches to organization: (1) functional specialization, (2) geographic organization, (3) decentralized business divisions, (4) strategic business units, and (5) matrix structures featuring dual lines of authority and strategic priority. Each form relates structure to strategy in a different way and, consequently, has its own set of strategy-related pros and cons.

The Functional Organization Structure   A functional organization structure tends to be effective in single-business units where key activities revolve around well-defined skills and areas of specialization. In such cases, in-depth specialization and focused concentration on performing functional area tasks and activities can enhance both operating efficiency and the development of a distinctive competence. Generally speaking, organizing by functional specialties promotes full utilization of the most up-to-date technical skills and helps a business capitalize on the efficiency gains resulting from use of those technical skills; it also helps a business capitalize on the efficiency gains resulting from the use of specialized manpower, facilities, and equipment. These are strategically important considerations for single-business organizations, dominant-product enterprises, and vertically integrated firms, and account for why they usually have some kind of centralized, functionally specialized structure.

---

[7] For an excellent documentation of how a number of well-known corporations revised their organization structures to meet the needs of strategy changes and specific product/market developments, see Corey and Star, *Organization Strategy,* chap. 3.

However, just what form the functional specialization will take varies according to customer-product-technology considerations. For instance, a technical instruments manufacturer may be organized around research and development, engineering, production, technical services, quality control, marketing, personnel, and finance and accounting. A municipal government may, on the other hand, be departmentalized according to purposeful function: fire, public safety, health services, water and sewer, streets, parks and recreation, and education. A university may divide up its organizational units into academic affairs, student services, alumni relations, athletics, buildings and grounds, institutional services, and budget control. Two types of functional organizational approaches are diagrammed in Figure 8–3.

The Achilles' heel of a functional structure is getting and keeping tight strategic coordination across the separated functional units. Functional specialists, partly because of how they were trained and the technical "mystique" of their jobs, tend to develop their own mindset and ways of doing things. The more that functional specialists differ in their perspectives and approaches to task accomplishment, the more difficult it becomes to achieve both strategic and operating coordination between them. They neither "talk the same language" nor have sympathetic appreciation for one another's strategic role, problems, and changed circumstances. Each functional group is more interested in its own "empire" and promoting its own strategic interest and importance (despite the lip service given to cooperation and "what's best for the company"). Tunnel vision and empire building in functional departments impose a time-consuming administrative burden on a business-level manager in terms of resolving cross-functional differences, enforcing joint cooperation, and opening lines of communication. In addition, a purely functional organization tends to be myopic when it comes to promoting entrepreneurial creativity, adapting quickly to major customer-market-technological changes, and pursuing opportunities that go beyond the conventional boundaries of the industry.

b) *Geographic Forms of Organization*

Organizing according to geographic areas or territories is a rather common structural form for large-scale enterprises whose strategies need to be tailored to fit the particular needs and features of different geographical areas. As indicated in Figure 8–4, geographic organization has its advantages and disadvantages, but the chief reason for its popularity is that, for one reason or another, it promotes improved performance.

In the private sector, a territorial structure is typically utilized by chain store retailers, power companies, cement firms, and dairy products enterprises. In the public sector, such organizations as the Internal Revenue Service, the Social Security Administration, the federal courts, the U.S. Postal Service, the state troopers, and the Red Cross have adopted territorial structures in order to be directly accessible to geographically dispersed clienteles.

c) *Decentralized Business Units*

Grouping activities along business and product lines has been a clear-cut trend among diversified enterprises for the past half-century, beginning with the pioneering efforts of Du Pont and General Motors in the 1920s. Separate business/product divisions emerged because diversification made a functionally specialized manager's job incredibly complex. Imagine the problems a manufacturing executive and staff would have if put in charge of, say, 50 different

Figure 8–3   Functional Organizational Structures

A. The building blocks of a ''typical'' functional organization structure

B. The building blocks of a process-oriented functional structure

Strategic Advantages	*Strategic Disadvantages*
• Permits centralized control of strategic results.	• Poses problems of functional coordination.
• Very well-suited for structuring a single business.	• Can lead to interfunctional rivalry, conflict, and empire building.
• Structure is linked tightly to strategy by designating key activities as functional units.	• May promote overspecialization and narrow management viewpoints.
• Promotes in-depth functional expertise.	• Hinders development of managers with cross-functional experience because the ladder of advancement is up the ranks within the same functional area.
• Well suited to developing a functional-based distinctive competence.	• Forces profit responsibility to the top.
• Conducive to exploiting learning/experience curve effects associated with functional specialization.	• Functional specialists often attach more importance to what's best for the functional area than to what's best for the whole business.
• Enhances operating efficiency where tasks are routine and repetitive.	• May lead to uneconomically small units or underutilization of specialized facilities and manpower.
	• Functional myopia often works against creative entrepreneurship, adapting to change, and attempts to restructure the activity-cost chain.

Figure 8–4   A Geographic Organizational Structure

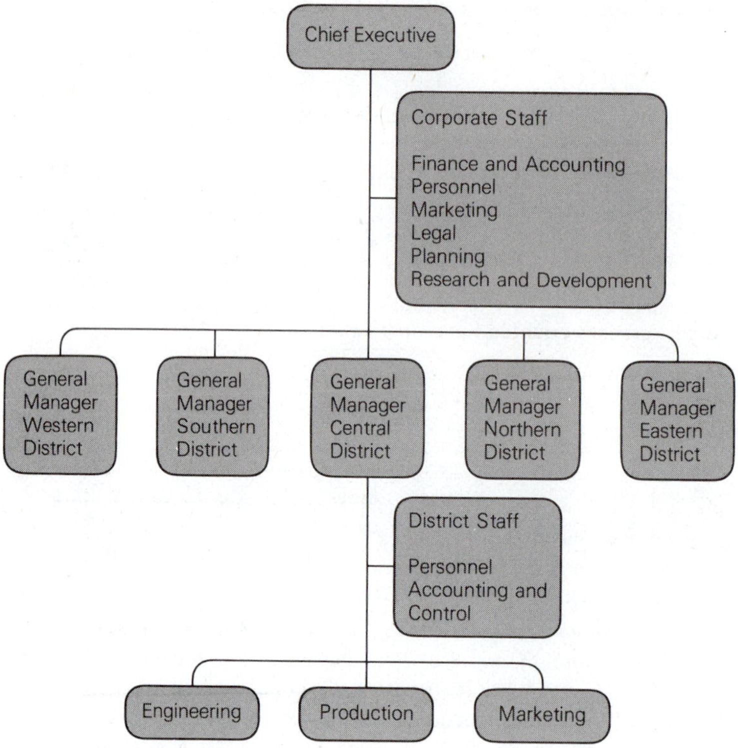

Strategic Advantages

- Allows tailoring of strategy to needs of each geographic market.
- Delegates profit/loss responsibility to lowest strategic level.
- Improves functional coordination within the target market.
- Takes advantage of economies of local operations.
- Area units make an excellent training ground for higher-level general managers.

Strategic Disadvantages

- Poses a problem of how much geographic uniformity headquarters should impose versus how much geographic diversity should be allowed.
- Greater difficulty in maintaining consistent company image/ reputation from area to area when area managers exercise much strategic freedom.
- Adds another layer of management to run the geographic units.
- Can result in duplication of staff services at headquarters and district levels, creating a relative cost disadvantage.

plants using 20 different technologies to produce 30 different products in 8 different businesses or industries. In a multibusiness enterprise, the needs of strategy virtually dictate that the organizational sequence be corporate *to* line of business *to* functional area within a business, rather than corporate *to* functional area (aggregated for all businesses). The latter produces a nightmare in making sense out of business strategy and achieving functional area coordination for a given business.

Strategy implementation is facilitated by grouping key activities belonging to the same business under one organizational roof, thereby creating line-of-business units (which then can be subdivided into whatever functional subunits suit the key activities/ critical tasks makeup of the business). The outcome is not only a structure which fits strategy but also a structure which makes the jobs of managers more doable. The creation of separate business units is then accomplished by decentralizing authority over the unit to the business-level manager. The approach, very simply, is to put entrepreneurial general managers in charge of the business unit, giving them enough authority to formulate and implement the business strategy that they deem appropriate, motivating them with incentives, and then holding them accountable for the results they produce. However, when a strong strategic fit exists across related business units, it can be tough to get autonomy-conscious business-unit managers to cooperate in coordinating and sharing related activities. They are prone to argue long and hard about "turf" and about being held accountable for activities not totally under their control.

A typical line-of-business organizational structure is shown in Figure 8–5, along with the strategy-related pros and cons of this type of organizational form.

Strategic Business Units   In the really large, diversified companies, the number of decentralized business units can be so great that the span of control is too much for a single chief executive. Then it may be useful to group those that are related and to delegate authority over them to a senior executive who reports directly to the chief executive officer. While this imposes a layer of management between business-level managers and the chief executive, it may nonetheless improve strategic planning and top-management coordination of diverse business interests. This explains both the popularity of the group vice president concept among broadly diversified firms and the recent trend toward the formation of *strategic business units*.

A strategic business unit (SBU) is a grouping of business units based on some important strategic elements common to each; the possible elements of relatedness include an overlapping set of competitors, a closely related strategic mission, a common need to compete globally, an ability to accomplish integrated strategic planning, common key success factors, and technologically related growth opportunities. At GE, a pioneer in the concept of SBUs, 190 units were grouped into 43 SBUs and then aggregated further into 6 "sectors."[8] At Union Carbide Corporation, 15 groups and divisions were subdivided into 150 "strategic planning units" and then regrouped and combined into 9 new "aggregate planning units." At General Foods, SBUs were

[8] William K. Hall, "SBUs: Hot, New Topic in the Management of Diversification," *Business Horizons* 21, no. 1 (February 1978), p. 19. For an excellent discussion of the problems of implementing the SBU concept at 13 companies, see Richard A. Bettis and William K. Hall, "The Business Portfolio Approach—Where It Falls Down in Practice," *Long Range Planning* 16, no. 2 (April 1983), pp. 95–104.

Figure 8–5   A Decentralized Line-of-Business Type of Organization Structure

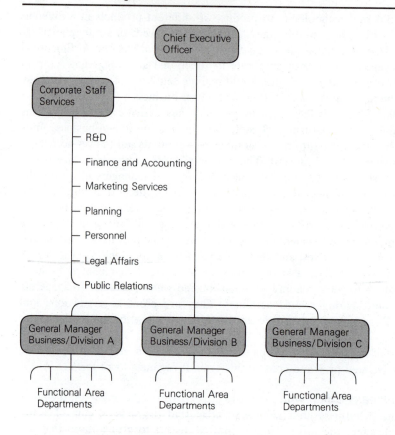

Strategic Advantages

- Offers a logical and workable means of decentralizing responsibility and delegating authority in diversified organizations.

- Puts responsibility for business strategy in closer proximity to each business's unique environment.

- Allows each business unit to organize around its own set of key activities and functional area requirements.

- Frees CEO to handle corporate strategy issues.

- Puts clear profit/loss accountability on shoulders of business unit managers.

Strategic Disadvantages

- May lead to costly duplication of staff functions at corporate and business unit levels, thus raising administrative overhead costs.

- Poses a problem of what decisions to centralize and what decisions to decentralize (business managers need enough authority to get the job done, but not so much that corporate management loses control of key business level decisions).

- May lead to excessive division rivalry for corporate resources and attention.

- Business/division autonomy works against achieving coordination of related activities in different business units, thus blocking to some extent the capture of strategic fit benefits.

- Corporate management becomes heavily dependent on business unit managers.

- Corporate managers can lose touch with business unit situations, end up surprised when problems arise, and not know much about how to fix such problems.

originally defined on a product-line basis but were later redefined according to menu segments (breakfast foods, beverages, main meal products, desserts, and pet foods).

The managerial value of the SBU concept is that it provides diversified companies with a way to rationalize the organization of many different businesses and a way to give cohesive direction to separate but related areas within the total enterprise. SBUs are particularly helpful in reducing the complexity of dovetailing corporate strategy and business strategy and in "cross-pollinating" the growth opportunities in different industries, perhaps to create altogether new industries. SBUs also make headquarters' reviews of the strategies of lower-level units less imposing (there is no practical way for a CEO to conduct in-depth reviews of a hundred or more different businesses). Figure 8–6 illustrates the SBU form of organization, along with its strategy-related pros and cons.

Matrix Forms of Organization

A matrix organization is a structure with two (or more) channels of command, two lines of budget authority, and two sources of performance and reward. The key feature of the matrix is that product (or business) and functional lines of authority are overlaid (to form a matrix or grid), and managerial authority over the activities in each unit/cell of the matrix is shared between the product manager and functional manager (as shown in Figure 8–7). In a matrix structure, subordinates have a continuing dual assignment: to the business/product line/project and to their home base function.[9] The outcome is a compromise between functional specialization (engineering, R&D, manufacturing, marketing, finance) and product line or market segment or line-of-business specialization (where all of the specialized talent needed for the product line/market segment/line of business are assigned to the same divisional unit).

A matrix-type organization is a genuinely different structural form and represents a "new way of life." One reason is that the unity-of-command principle is broken; two reporting channels, two bosses, and shared authority create a new kind of organizational climate. In essence, the matrix is a conflict resolution system through which strategic and operating priorities are negotiated, power is shared, and resources are allocated internally on a "strongest case for what is best overall for the unit" type basis.[10]

The impetus for matrix organizations stems from the growing use of strategies that add new sources of diversity (products, customer groups, technology, lines of business) to a firm's range of activities. This diversity produces product managers, functional managers, geographic area managers, new venture managers, and business-level managers—all of whom have important strategic responsibilities. When at least two of several variables (product, customer, technology, geography, functional area, and market segment) have roughly equal strategic priorities, then a matrix organization can be an effective structural form. A matrix arrangement promotes internal checks and balances among competing viewpoints and perspectives, with separate managers for different dimensions of strategic initiative. A matrix approach thus allows each

[9] A more thorough treatment of matrix organizational forms can be found in Jay R. Galbraith, "Matrix Organizational Designs," *Business Horizons* 15, no. 1 (February 1971), pp. 29–40.

[10] An excellent critique of matrix organizations is presented in Stanley M. Davis and Paul R. Lawrence, "Problems of Matrix Organizations," *Harvard Business Review* 56, no. 3 (May–June 1978), pp. 131–42.

Figure 8-6 An SBU Type of Organization Structure

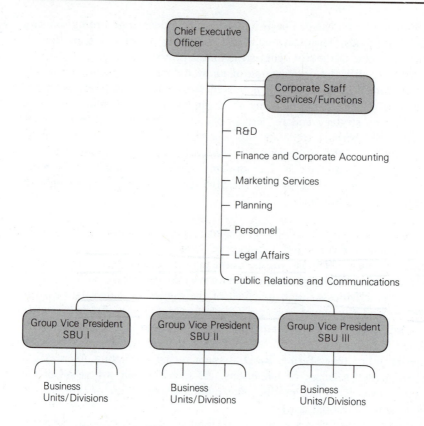

Strategic Advantages

- Provides a strategically relevant way to organize large numbers of different business units.
- Improves coordination between the role and authority of the businesses with similar strategies, markets, and growth opportunities.
- Allows strategic planning to be done at the most relevant level within the total enterprise.
- Makes the task of strategic review by top executives more objective and more effective.
- Helps allocate corporate resources to areas with greatest growth opportunities.
- Promotes more cohesiveness among the new initiatives of separate but related businesses.
- Facilitates the coordination of related activities *within* an SBU, thus helping to capture the benefits of strategic fits in the SBU.

Strategic Disadvantages

- It is easy for the definition and grouping of businesses into SBUs to be so arbitrary that the SBU serves no purpose other than administrative convenience. If the criteria for defining SBUs are rationalizations and have little to do with the nitty-gritty of strategy coordination, then the groupings lose real strategic significance.
- The SBUs can still be myopic in charting their future direction.
- Adds another layer to top management.
- The roles and authority of the CEO, the group vice president, and the business-unit manager have to be carefully worked out or the group vice president gets trapped in the middle with ill-defined authority.
- Unless the SBU head is strong willed, very little strategy coordination is likely to occur across business units in the SBU.
- Performance recognition gets blurred; credit for successful business units tends to go to corporate CEO, then to business unit head, last to group vice president.

Figure 8-7   A Matrix Organization Structure*

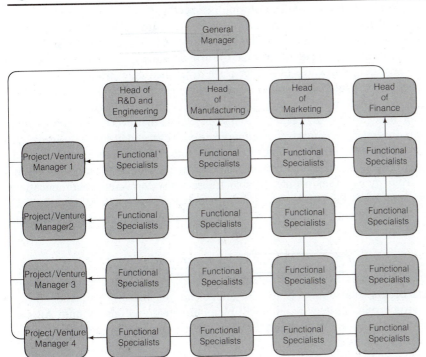

Strategic Advantages

- Permits more attention to each dimension of strategic priority.
- Creates checks and balances among competing viewpoints.
- Facilitates simultaneous pursuit of different types of strategic initiative.
- Promotes making trade-off decisions on the basis of "what's best for the organization as a whole."
- Encourages cooperation, consensus-building, conflict resolution, and coordination of related activities.

Strategic Disadvantages

- Very complex to manage.
- Hard to maintain "balance" between the two lines of authority.
- So much shared authority can result in a transactions logjam and disproportionate amounts of time being spent on communications.
- It is hard to move quickly and decisively without getting clearance from many other people.
- Promotes an organizational bureaucracy and hamstrings creative entrepreneurship.

* Arrows indicate reporting channels.

of several strategic considerations to be managed directly and to be formally represented in the organization structure. In this sense, it helps middle managers make trade-off decisions from an organizationwide perspective.[11]

Companies using matrix structures include GE, Texas Instruments, Citibank, Shell Oil, TRW, Bechtel, Boeing, and Dow Chemical. However, most applications of matrix organization are limited to a portion of what the firm does (certain important functions) rather than spanning the whole of a large-scale diversified enterprise.

A number of companies shun matrix organization because of its chief weaknesses.[12] It is a complex structure to manage; people often end up confused over whom to report to for what. Moreover, because the matrix signals that everything is important and, further, that everybody needs to communicate with everybody else, a "transactions logjam" can emerge. Action turns into paralysis since, with shared authority, it is hard to move decisively without first considering many points of view and getting clearance from many other people. Sizable transactions costs and communications inefficiency can arise, as well as delays in responding. Even so, there are situations where the benefits of conflict resolution and consensus building outweigh these weaknesses.

Combination and Supplemental Methods of Organization

A single type of structural design is not always sufficient to meet the requirements of strategy. When this occurs, one option is to mix and blend the basic organization forms, matching structure to strategy requirement by requirement and unit by unit. Another is to supplement a basic organization design with special-situation devices. Three of the most frequently used ones are:

1. The *project manager* or *project staff approach*, where a separate, largely self-sufficient subunit is created to oversee the completion of a special activity (setting up a new technological process, bringing out a new product, starting up a new venture, consummating a merger with another company, seeing through the completion of a government contract, supervising the construction of a new plant). Project management is a relatively popular means of handling one-of-a-kind situations that have a finite life expectancy when the normal organization is ill equipped to achieve the same results in addition to regular duties.

2. The *task force approach*, where a number of top-level executives and/or specialists are brought together to work on unusual assignments of a problem-solving or innovative nature. Special task forces provide increased opportunity for creativity, open communication across lines of authority, tight integration of specialized talents, expeditious conflict resolution, and common identification for coping with the problem at hand. One study showed that task forces were most effective when they had less than 10 members, membership was voluntary, the seniority of the members was proportional to the importance of the problem, the task force moved swiftly to deal with its assignment, the task force was pulled together only on an as-needed basis, no staff was assigned, and documentation was scant.[13] In these companies, the prevailing

---

[11] Ibid., p. 132.

[12] Thomas J. Peters and Robert H. Waterman, Jr., *In Search of Excellence* (New York: Harper & Row, 1982), pp. 306–7.

[13] Peters and Waterman, *In Search of Excellence*, pp. 127–32.

philosophy about task forces is to use them to solve real problems, produce some solution efficiently, and then disband them. At the other extreme, Peters and Waterman report one instance where a company had formed 325 task forces, none of which had completed its charge in three years and none of which had been disbanded.

3. The *venture team approach,* whereby a group of individuals is formed for the purpose of bringing a specific product to market or a specific new business into being. Dow Chemical, General Mills, Westinghouse, GE, and Monsanto have used the venture team approach to infuse more entrepreneurial thinking. The difficulties with venture teams include deciding to whom the venture manager should report; whether funding for ventures should come from corporate, business, or departmental budgets; how to keep the venture clear of bureaucratic and vested interests; and how to coordinate large numbers of different ventures.

Perspectives on Matching Strategy and Structure

The foregoing discussion brings out two points: (1) there is no such thing as a perfect or ideal organization design, and (2) there are no universally applicable rules for matching strategy and structure. All of the basic organizational forms have their strategy-related strengths and weaknesses. Moreover, use of one of the basic organizational forms does not preclude simultaneous use of others. Many organizations are large enough and diverse enough to have subunits organized by functional specialty, geographical area, market segment, line of business, SBU, and matrix principles—there is no need to adhere slavishly to one basic organization type. In a very real sense, *the best organizational arrangement is the one that best fits the firm's situation at the moment.* Experience shows that firms have a habit of regularly outgrowing their prevailing organizational arrangement—either an internal shake-up is deemed periodically desirable or changes in the size and scope of customer-product-technology relationships make the firm's structure strategically obsolete. An organization's structure thus is dynamic; changes are not only inevitable but typical.

There is room to quibble over whether organization design should commence with a strategy-structure framework or with a pragmatic consideration of the realities of the situation at hand—the corporate culture, the constraints imposed by the personalities involved, and the way things have been done before. By and large, agonizing over where to begin is unnecessary; both considerations have to be taken into account. However, strategy-structure factors usually have to take precedence if structure is to be firmly built around the organization's strategy-critical tasks, key success factors, and high-priority business units. Adapting structure to the peculiar circumstances of the organization's internal situation and personalities is usually done to modify the strategy-structure match in "minor" ways.

Drucker has summed up the intricacies of organization design thusly:

> The simplest organization structure that will do the job is the best one. What makes an organization structure "good" are the problems it does not create. The simpler the structure, the less that can go wrong.
>
> Some design principles are more difficult and problematic than others. But none is without difficulties and problems. None is primarily people-focused rather than task-focused; none is more "creative," "free," or "more democratic." Design principles are

tools; and tools are neither good nor bad in themselves. They can be used properly or improperly; and that is all. To obtain both the greatest possible simplicity and the greatest "fit," organization design has to start out with a clear focus on *key activities* needed to produce *key results*. They have to be structured and positioned in the simplest possible design. Above all, the architect of organization needs to keep in mind the purpose of the structure he is designing.[14]

Peters and Waterman, in their study of excellently managed companies, confirm what Drucker says; their organization prescription is "simple form, lean staff."[15] Illustration Capsule 19 explains some of the organizational principles and approaches being used at these companies.

ILLUSTRATION CAPSULE 19

Organization Lessons from the "Excellently Managed" Companies

Peters and Waterman's study of America's best-managed corporations provides some important lessons in building a strategically capable organization:

1. The organizational underpinning of most of the excellently managed companies is a fairly stable, unchanging form—usually a decentralized business/product division—that provides the structural building block which everyone in the enterprise understands and that serves as the base for approaching day-to-day issues and complexities.

2. Beyond the crystal-clear primacy of this basic and simple organizational building block, the rest of the organization structure is deliberately kept fluid and flexible to permit response to changing environmental conditions. Much use is made of task forces, project teams, and the creation of new, small divisions to address emerging issues and opportunities.

3. New divisions are created to pursue budding business opportunities, as opposed to letting them remain a part of the originating division. Often, there are established guidelines when a new product or product line automatically becomes an independent division.

4. People and even products and product lines are frequently shifted from one division to another—so as to improve efficiency, promote shared costs, enhance competitive strength, and/or adapt to changing market conditions.

5. Many excellently managed companies have comparatively few people at the corporate level, and many of these are out in the field frequently rather than in the home office all the time. Emerson Electric with 54,000 employees had a headquarters staff of fewer than 100 people. Dana Corporation employed 35,000 people and had a corporate staff numbering about 100. Schlumberger Ltd., a $56 billion diversified oil service company, ran its worldwide organization with a corporate staff of 90 people. At Intel (sales of over $1 billion), all staff assignments were temporary ones given to line officers. Rolm managed a $200 million business with about 15 people in corporate headquarters. In addition, corporate planners were few and far between. Hewlett-Packard Company, Johnson & Johnson, and 3M had no planners

---

[14] Drucker, *Management*, pp. 601–2.
[15] Peters and Waterman, *In Search of Excellence*, chap. 11.

ILLUSTRATION CAPSULE 19 *(concluded)*

at the corporate level; Fluor Corporation ran a $6 billion operation with three corporate planners. At IBM, management rotated staff assignments every three years. Few IBM staff jobs were manned by "career staffers"; most were manned temporarily by managers with line jobs in the divisions who will rotate back to line jobs.

6. Functional organization forms are efficient and get the basic activities performed well; yet they are not particularly creative or entrepreneurial, they do not adapt quickly, and they are apt to ignore important changes.

7. The key to maintaining an entrepreneurial, adaptive organization is *small size*—and the way to keep units small is to spin off new or expanded activities into independent units. Division sizes often run no bigger than $50 to $100 million in sales, with a maximum of 1,000 or so employees. At Emerson Electric, plants rarely employed more than 600 workers so that management could maintain personal contact with employees. (Emerson, by the way, has a good track record on efficiency; its strategy of being the low-cost producer has worked beautifully in chain saws and several other products.) At Blue Bell, a leading apparel firm, manufacturing units usually employ under 300 people. The lesson seems to be that small units are both more cost-effective and more innovative.

8. To prevent "calcification" and stodginess, it helps to rely on such "habit-breaking" techniques as *(a)* reorganizing regularly; *(b)* putting top talent on project teams and giving them a "charter" to move quickly to solve a key problem or execute a central strategic thrust (i.e., the creation of the General Motors Project Center to lead the downsizing effort); *(c)* shifting products or product lines among divisions to take advantage of special management talents or the need for market realignments; *(d)* breaking up big, bureaucratic divisions into several new, smaller divisions; and *(e)* being flexible enough to try experimental organization approaches and support the pursuit of new opportunities.

9. It is useful to adopt a simultaneous "loose-tight" structure that on the one hand fosters autonomy, entrepreneurship, and innovation from rank-and-file managers yet, on the other hand, allows for strong central direction from the top. Such things as regular reorganization, flexible form (the use of teams and task forces), lots of decentralized autonomy for lower-level general managers, and extensive experimentation all focus on the excitement of trying things out in a slightly "loose" fashion. Yet, regular communication, quick feedback, concise paperwork, strong adherence to a few core values, and self-discipline can impose "tight" central control so that nothing gets far out of line.

Application of these "principles" in the best-managed companies tends to produce an environment that fosters entrepreneurial pursuit of new opportunities and adaptation to change. A fluid, flexible structure is the norm—the basic form is stable, but there is frequent reorganization "around the edges." The aim is to keep structure matched to the changing needs of an evolving strategy and to avoid letting the current organization structure become so ingrained and political that it becomes a major obstacle to be hurdled.

SOURCE: Thomas J. Peters and Robert H. Waterman, Jr., *In Search of Excellence* (New York: Harper & Row, 1982), especially chaps. 11 and 12.

Building a Distinctive Competence

A good match between structure and strategy is plainly one key facet of a strategically capable organization. But an equally dominant organization-building concern is that of staffing the chosen structure with the requisite managerial talent and technical skills—and, most particularly, staffing in a manner calculated to give the firm a distinctive competence in performing one or more critical tasks. The strategic importance of deliberately trying to develop a distinctive competence within an organization stems from the extra contribution which special expertise and a competitive edge make both to performance and to strategic success. To the extent that an organization can build an astutely conceived distinctive competence in its chosen business domains, it creates a golden opportunity for achieving a competitive advantage and posting a superior record of performance.

However, distinctive competences do not just naturally appear. They have to be consciously developed and nurtured. Consequently, for a distinctive competence to emerge from organization-building actions, strategy implementers have to push aggressively to secure an inventory of technical skills and capabilities in those few subunits where superior performance of strategically critical tasks can make a real difference to greater strategic success. Usually, this means (1) giving above-average operating budget support to strategy-critical tasks and activities, (2) seeing that these tasks and activities are staffed with high-caliber managerial and technical talent, and (3) insisting on high performance standards from these subunits, backed up with a policy of rewarding superior performance. In effect, strategy implementers must take premeditated actions to see that the organization is staffed with enough of the right kinds of people and that these people have the budgetary and administrative support needed to generate a distinctive competence.

Once developed, the strengths and capabilities that attach to distinctive competences become cornerstones for successful strategy implementation as well as for the actual strategy itself. Moreover, really distinctive internal skills and capabilities are not easily duplicated by other firms; this means that any differential competitive advantage so gained can give a lasting boost to performance over the long term. Conscious management attention to the task of building strategically relevant internal skills and strengths into the overall organizational scheme is therefore one of the central tasks of organization building.

Selecting People for Key Positions

Assembling a capable management team is an obvious part of the strategy implementation task. The recurring administrative issues here center around what kind of core management team is needed to carry out the strategy and finding the people to fill each slot. Sometimes the existing management team is suitable and sometimes the core executive group needs to be strengthened and/or expanded, either by promoting qualified people from within or by bringing in skilled managerial talent from the outside to help infuse fresh ideas and fresh approaches into the organization's management. In turnaround situations, in rapid-growth situations, and in those cases where the right kinds of managerial experience and skills are not present in-house, recruiting outsiders to fill key management slots is a fairly standard part of the organization-building process.

The important dimension of assembling a core executive group is discerning what mix of backgrounds, experiences, know-how, values, beliefs, styles of managing, and personalities will reinforce and contribute to successful strategy execution. As with any kind of team-building exercise, it is important to put together a compatible group of managers who possess a full set of skills to get things done—the personal "chemistry" needs to be right and the talent base needs to match the managerial requirements of the chosen strategy. Picking good lieutenants and adequately staffing key activities are always essential strategy implementing functions.

ALLOCATING AND FOCUSING RESOURCES ON STRATEGIC OBJECTIVES

Keeping an organization on the strategy implementation path thrusts a manager squarely into directing the resource allocation process. Not only must a strategy implementer oversee "who gets how much," but this must also be followed up with an equal concern for "getting the biggest bang for the buck." Two issues stand out:

1. What budgets and programs are needed by each organizational unit to carry out its part of the strategic plan.
2. How to focus the energies of people on achieving organizationwide objectives as opposed to just carrying out their assigned duties.

How well a strategy implementer handles these two issues determines whether the organization will be results-oriented and directed toward strategy accomplishment or whether it gets bogged down and wanders off the path of "making it happen."

Allocating Resources: Budgets and Programs

Little discussion is needed to establish the role of budgets and programs in the strategy implementation process. Obviously, organizational units must have the resources needed to carry out their part of the strategic plan. This includes having enough of the right kinds of people and having enough operating funds for them to carry out their work. Moreover, each subunit must program its activities to meet its objectives, establish schedules and deadlines for accomplishment, and parcel out assignments which specify exactly who is responsible for what by when. Budgets and programs go hand in hand. Programs lay out detailed, step-by-step action plans, and budgets specify the costs of the planned activities.

The resource allocation issues that confront strategy managers range across the whole landscape. A sampling of some of the more important ones include:

- How many extra dollars to allocate to a business unit trying to rebuild and reposition itself after having just gone through a period of market decline and competitive weakness.

- How much to budget for advertising and promoting a major new item in the firm's product line.
- What extra resources it will take to assimilate a newly acquired subsidiary and to establish effective reporting systems and financial controls.
- What extra R&D efforts will have to be made to defend against a new outbreak of rapid technological developments by competitors.
- What additional resources it will take to bring a new plant on-stream at the scheduled time.
- What budgetary changes in which areas it will take to achieve low-cost producer status.
- What the resource allocation implications are of shifting from a "grow-and-build" strategy to a "maintain-and-hold" strategy.
- What it will cost to build a distinctive competence in providing technical support services to customers.
- How much new funding of which departments it will take to support a 5 percent increase in market share.

How well a manager resolves strategy-related resource allocation decisions of this magnitude can, quite clearly, either promote or impede the process of strategy implementation and execution. Too little funding deprives subunits of the capability to carry out their pieces of the strategic plan. Too much funding is a waste of organizational resources and reduces financial performance. Both outcomes argue for strong management involvement in the budgeting process and in reviewing the programs and proposals of strategy-critical subunits within the organization.

A ready willingness to shift resources in support of strategic change is especially critical. For example, at Harris Corporation, where one element of strategy is to diffuse research ideas into areas that are commercially viable, top management regularly shifts groups of engineers out of government projects and moves them (as a group) into new commercial venture divisions. Boeing has a similar approach to reallocating ideas and talent; according to one Boeing officer, "We can do it (create a big new unit) in two weeks. We couldn't do it in two years at International Harvester."[16] A fluid, flexible approach to reorganization and reallocation of people and budgets is characteristic of implementing strategic change successfully.

Fine-tuning existing strategy usually involves less reallocation and more of an extrapolation approach. Big movements of people and money from one area to another are seldom necessary. Fine-tuning can usually be accomplished by incrementally increasing or decreasing the budgets and staffing of existing organization units. The chief exception occurs where a prime ingredient of corporate/business strategy is to generate fresh, new products and business opportunities from within; then, as attractive ventures "bubble up" from below, decisions have to be made regarding funding and staffing. Companies like 3M, GE, Boeing, IBM, and Digital Equipment all shift resources and people from area to area on an "as-needed" basis to support budding ideas and ventures. They empower "product champions" and small bands of would-be entrepreneurs by giving them financial and technical support and by setting up organizational units and programs to facilitate moving things along.

---

[16] Peters and Waterman, *In Search of Excellence*, p. 125.

Focusing Work Efforts on Strategic Objectives

As previously indicated, successful strategy implementation and execution is assisted when critical tasks and key activities are linked directly and clearly to accomplishing the strategic plan. Matching structure to strategy provides a valuable linkage. Defining jobs and assignments in terms of the strategic results to be accomplished (as well as in terms of the duties and functions to be performed) adds an equally important linkage.

The value of defining jobs and assignments in terms of what is to be accomplished is that it makes the work environment results oriented and performance oriented. From a strategy perspective, what is to be accomplished is (1) carrying out the strategy and (2) achieving the target levels of organization performance. When an organization's attention and energies are kept firmly trained on executing strategy and achieving the agreed-upon objectives, the chances for accomplishing the strategic plan are decidedly greater.

The question, then, is how to keep the organization trained on achieving the right strategic results as opposed to routinely carrying out duties and functions in hopes that the by-product will be strategic success. Making the right things happen rather than hoping they will happen is, of course, what *managing with objectives* is all about. For the tool of managing with objectives to be of real assistance in implementing and executing the strategic plan, two things must happen. One, the strategy manager must insist that jobs and assignments be defined *primarily* in terms of the results to be accomplished and *secondarily* in terms of descriptions of the duties and functions to be performed. The danger of the latter is that it is very easy for people and organization subunits to become so engrossed in doing their duties and performing their functions that they lose sight of what it is the functions and duties are intended to accomplish in the first place. By defining jobs and activities in terms of what strategic results and objectives are to be achieved, the spotlight is kept on accomplishment of the strategic plan. Two, the strategy manager must not waver far from the standard that "doing a good job" *equals* "achieving the agreed-upon strategic objectives and performance." Any other standard simply serves to undermine strategy implementation and to channel energies and efforts into other directions.

Using strategic objectives as the ultimate results for work and job assignments, therefore, begins with the question, "What are our objectives, and what results do we want to show for our efforts?" If the levels of strategy have been fleshed out thoroughly from the corporate level on down to the operating level, the answers to this question are explicit in the strategic plan itself or, at least, are reasonably unambiguous in the minds of the managers of each organizational unit. Otherwise, the answers are suggested by the role and contribution expected of the organization unit in achieving financial performance targets and in carrying out day-to-day operations. Keep in mind that specific objectives and performance targets are needed not only for the organization as a whole but also for each organizational subunit. While there is ample room for the agreed-upon objectives and results to reflect both top-down and bottom-up considerations, the key is to promote understanding and emphasis on what each organizational unit's part is in achieving the target levels of strategic performance. This makes clearer the kind of work and effort that can be strategically productive. It relates departments and functional areas to the strategic needs of the organization as a whole. But most important, it lets people know what is expected of them—from a results perspective instead of from an activity and effort perspective. The pressure to perform should be nothing short of brutal. A "no excuses" environment has to prevail.[17]

Next, it must be asked, "What specific activities, work assignments, and jobs are needed to produce the target levels of performance?" The answers here should suggest the skills, technical expertise, staffing, and funding needed to reach the established objectives.

Finally, managers have to address the question, "How can jobs and work efforts in my unit be designed around the unit's strategy-related objectives?" Placing the emphasis of job design and work assignments on "what to accomplish" instead of "what to do" is an important difference. As any student knows, just because an instructor conducts his or her classes regularly, it cannot be safely assumed that students are learning what they are being taught—teaching and learning are different things. The first is an activity and the second is a result.

In any job, doing an activity is not equivalent to achieving the intended objective. Working hard, staying busy, and diligently attending to one's duties do not guarantee results. Hence, the creativity of managers in drawing attention to the right things to shoot for (accomplishing our part of the strategic plan) and creating a results-oriented work environment (where work efforts are aimed squarely at reaching the unit's target performance objectives) is more than incidental. Indeed, figuring out how to make the achievement of strategy-related objectives a "way of life" up and down the whole organization is central to the task of strategy implementation. *The more that organizational energies and efforts flow in the direction of strategy execution, the more that strategy implementation stays on track.*

ANALYTICAL CHECKLIST

Linking daily activities and work efforts directly and clearly to accomplishing the organization's strategic plan is critical to successful strategy implementation. The two strategy-implementing tasks of a manager which aim at creating this linkage are (1) building a capable organization and (2) allocating resources and focusing work efforts on strategic objectives. The first task centers around the strategy-critical components of matching the structure to fit the requirements of strategy and staffing each organizational unit with the skills, expertise, and competences it needs to carry out its assigned role in the strategic plan. The second task involves providing organizational units with the budgetary resources and programs requisite for accomplishing their piece of the overall strategy and then keeping organizationwide attention focused on "what to achieve" (the target strategic objectives) and not letting work efforts aim simply at "what to do."

Figures 8–1 and 8–2 serve as good reminders of what the primary strategy implementation considerations are. In addressing how to match internal structure to strat-

---

[17] Tom Peters and Nancy Austin, *A Passion for Excellence* (New York: Random House, 1985), p. XIX.

egy, consult Figure 8–3 through 8–7 for the basic structural options and for the pros and cons of each option.

SUGGESTED READINGS

Bettis, Richard A., and William K. Hall. "The Business Portfolio Approach—Where It Falls Down in Practice." *Long Range Planning* 16, no. 2 (April 1983), pp. 95–104.

Chandler, Alfred D. *Strategy and Structure.* Cambridge, Mass.: MIT Press, 1962.

Corey, Raymond E., and Steven H. Star. *Organization Strategy: A Marketing Approach.* Boston: Division of Research, Harvard University Graduate School of Business Administration, 1971, chaps. 2, 3, 4, and 5.

Davis, Stanley M., and Paul R. Lawrence. "Problems of Matrix Organizations." *Harvard Business Review* 56, no. 3 (May–June 1978), pp. 131–42.

Drucker, Peter. *Management: Tasks, Responsibilities, Practices.* New York: Harper & Row, 1974, chaps. 41–48.

Hall, William K. "SBUs: Hot, New Topic in the Management of Diversification." *Business Horizons* 21, no. 1 (February 1978), pp. 17–25.

Leontiades, Milton. "Choosing the Right Manager to Fit the Strategy." *Journal of Business Strategy* 3, no. 2 (Fall 1981), pp. 58–69.

Lorsch, Jay W., and Arthur H. Walker. "Organizational Choice: Product vs. Function." *Harvard Business Review* 46, no. 6 (November–December 1968), pp. 129–38.

Mintzberg, Henry. "Organization Design: Fashion or Fit." *Harvard Business Review* 59, no. 1 (January–February 1981), pp. 103–16.

Paulson, Robert D. "Making It Happen: The Real Strategic Challenge." *The McKinsey Quarterly,* Winter 1982, pp. 58–66.

Peters, Thomas J. "Beyond the Matrix Organization." *Business Horizons* 22, no. 5 (October 1979), pp. 15–27.

Peters, Thomas J., and Robert H. Waterman, Jr. *In Search of Excellence.* New York: Harper & Row, 1982.

Rumelt, Richard. *Strategy, Structure, and Economic Performance.* Cambridge, Mass.: Harvard University Press, 1974.

Salter, Malcolm S. "Stages of Corporate Development." *Journal of Business Policy* 1, no. 1 (1970), pp. 23–37.

Waterman, Robert H.; Thomas J. Peters; and Julien R. Phillips. "Structure Is Not Organization." *Business Horizons* 23, no. 3 (June 1980), pp. 14–26.

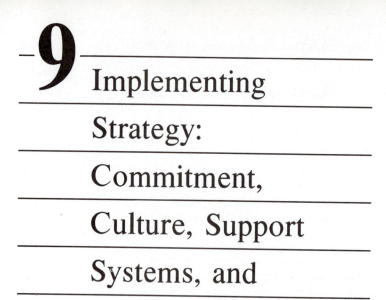

9 Implementing Strategy: Commitment, Culture, Support Systems, and Leadership

Weak leadership can wreck the soundest strategy; forceful execution of even a poor plan can often bring victory.
—*Sun Zi*

What gets measured gets done.
—*Mason Haire*

. . . an organization should approach all tasks with the idea that they can be accomplished in a superior fashion.
—*Thomas Watson, Jr.*

In the previous chapter we examined two of the strategy manager's implementation tasks: building a capable organization and steering resources into strategy-critical programs and activities. In this chapter we explore the three remaining central tasks: galvanizing organizationwide commitment to strategic accomplishment, installing internal administrative support systems, and exerting strategic leadership. The first two tasks embraced structure, staffing, and resource allocation issues; the last three involve the day-to-day aspects of strategy execution, including motivation and reward, building a strategy-supportive corporate culture, instituting strategy-related policies and procedures, implementing strategic controls, gathering information about strategic progress, and exercising whatever leadership is needed to keep strategy implementation on course.

GALVANIZING ORGANIZATIONWIDE COMMITMENT TO THE STRATEGIC PLAN

The task of generating, maintaining, and otherwise orchestrating organizationwide commitment to strategy implementation and execution has four components:

1. Motivating organizational units and individuals to execute the strategic plan and achieve the targeted results.
2. Building a strategy-supportive corporate culture.

3. Creating a strong results orientation and a spirit of high performance.
4. Linking the reward structure to actual strategic performance.

Motivating People to Achieve the Target Results

It is important for organizational subunits and individuals to be committed to implementing and accomplishing strategy. Solidifying organizationwide commitment to putting the strategic plan in place is typically achieved via motivation, incentives, and the rewarding of good performance. The range of options for getting people and organizational subunits to push hard for successful strategy implementation involves creatively using the standard reward-punishment mechanisms—salary raises, bonuses, stock options, fringe benefits, promotions (or fear of demotions), assurance of not being "sidelined" and ignored, praise, recognition, constructive criticism, tension, peer pressure, more (or less) responsibility, increased (or decreased) job control and decision-making autonomy, the promise of attractive locational assignments, and the bonds of group acceptance. The aim here must be to inspire employees to do their best and to be winners, giving them in the process a sense of ownership in the strategy and a commitment to make it work.

Some actual examples of strategy-supportive motivational approaches indicate the range of options:[1]

- At Mars Inc. (best known for its candy bars), every employee, including the president, gets a weekly 10 percent bonus by coming to work on time each day that week.
- In a number of Japanese companies, employees meet regularly to hear inspirational speeches, sing company songs, and chant the corporate litany. In the United States, Tupperware sales managers conduct weekly Monday night rallies to honor, applaud and fire up its salespeople who conduct Tupperware parties. Amway and Mary Kay Cosmetics hold similar inspirational get-togethers for their sales force organizations.
- A San Diego area company assembles its 2,000 employees at its six plants the first thing every workday to listen to a management talk about the state of the company. Then they engage in brisk calisthenics. This company's management believes "that by doing one thing together each day, it reinforces the unity of the company. It's also fun. It gets the blood up." Managers take turns making the presentations. Many of the speeches "are very personal and emotional, not approved beforehand or screened by anybody."
- Texas Instruments and Dana Corp. insist that teams and divisions set their own goals and have regular peer reviews.
- Procter & Gamble's brand managers are asked to compete fiercely against each other; the official policy is "a free-for-all among brands with no holds barred." P&G's system of purposeful internal competition breeds people who love to compete and excel. Those who "win" become corporate "heroes," and around them emerges a folklore of "war stories" of valiant brand managers who waged uphill

---

[1] The list that follows is abstracted from Thomas J. Peters and Robert H. Waterman, Jr., *In Search of Excellence* (New York: Harper & Row, 1982), pp. xx, 213–14, 276, 285.

struggles against great odds and made a market success out of their assigned brands.

Whereas the above motivational approaches accentuate the positive, others blend positive and negative features. Consider the way Harold Geneen, former president and chief executive officer of ITT, allegedly combined the use of money, tension, and fear:

> Geneen provides his managers with enough incentives to make them tolerate the system. Salaries all the way through ITT are higher than average—Geneen reckons 10 percent higher—so that few people can leave without taking a drop. As one employee put it: "We're all paid just a bit more than we think we're worth." At the very top, where the demands are greatest, the salaries and stock options are sufficient to compensate for the rigors. As some said, "He's got them by their limousines."
>
> Having bound his men to him with chains of gold, Geneen can induce the tension that drives the machine. "The key to the system," one of his men explains, "is the profit forecast. Once the forecast has been gone over, revised, and agreed on, the managing director has a personal commitment to Geneen to carry it out. That's how he produces the tension on which the success depends." The tension goes through the company, inducing ambition, perhaps exhilaration, but always with some sense of fear: what happens if the target is missed?[2]

If (and when) a strategy implementer's use of rewards and punishments induces too much tension, anxiety, and job insecurity, the results can be counterproductive. Yet, it is doubtful whether it is ever useful to completely eliminate tension, pressure for performance, and anxiety from the strategy implementation process; there is, for example, no evidence that "the quiet life" is highly correlated with superior strategy implementation. On the contrary, high-performing organizations need a cadre of ambitious people who relish the opportunity to climb the ladder of success, who love a challenge, who thrive in a performance-oriented environment, and who thus find some degree of competition and pressure useful in order to satisfy their own drives for personal recognition, career advancement, and self-satisfaction.

The conventional view is that a manager's push for strategy implementation should incorporate more positive than negative motivational elements, because when cooperation is positively enlisted rather than negatively strong-armed, people tend to respond with more enthusiasm and more effort. Nevertheless, how much of which incentives to use depends on how hard the task of strategy implementation will be in light of all the obstacles to be overcome. A manager has to do more than just talk to everyone about how important strategy implementation is to the organization's future well-being. Talk, no matter how inspiring, seldom commands people's best efforts for long. Ensuring sustained, energetic commitment to strategy virtually always requires resourceful use of incentives. The more that a manager understands what motivates subordinates and the more that motivational incentives are relied on to implement and execute strategy, the greater will be the commitment to carrying out the strategic plan.

---

[2] Anthony Sampson, *The Sovereign State of ITT* (New York: Stein and Day, Publishers, 1973), p. 132.

Building a Strategy-Supportive Corporate Culture

Every organization is a unique culture. It has its own special history of how the organization has been managed, its own set ways of approaching problems and conducting activities, its own mix of managerial personalities and styles, its own established patterns of "how we do things around here," its own legendary set of war stories and heroes, its own experiences of how changes have been instituted—in other words, its own climate, folklore, and organization personality. This says something important about the leadership task of orchestrating strategy implementation: *Anything so fundamental as implementing and executing the chosen strategic plan involves moving the whole organizational culture into alignment with strategy.* The optimal condition is an organizational culture so in tune with strategy that execution of the game plan can be truly powerful. As one observer noted:

> It has not been just strategy that led to big Japanese wins in the American auto market. It is a culture that enspirits workers to excel at fits and finishes, to produce moldings that match and doors that don't sag. It is a culture in which Toyota can use that most sophisticated of management tools, the suggestion box, and in two years increase the number of worker suggestions from under 10,000 to over 1 million with resultant savings of $250 million.[3]

The taproot of corporate culture is the philosophy, attitudes, beliefs, and shared values on and around which the organization operates. Such things in a company's activities can be hard to pin down, even harder to characterize accurately—in a sense they are intangible and "soft." They are manifest in people's attitudes and feelings, the war stories they tell, and the "chemistry" and "vibrations" which emanate from the work environment.

The best way to understand corporate culture is by example. Illustration Capsule 20 on the culture at Tandem Computers provides one good example.

ILLUSTRATION CAPSULE 20

The Corporate Culture at Tandem Computers

Tandem Computers is a leading producer of modular, expandable, multiple-processor computing systems designed so that failure of no one module can substantially affect system operations—Tandem calls it "the fail-safe nonstop computing system." Tandem's success is tied to offering customers the assurance that they will always have computer power available—if one processing unit breaks down, the backup unit carries on. Tandem's nonstop computer system can support thousands of terminals in on-line, nonstop conditions, thus preserving data integrity, reliability, and system flexibility. According to Tandem, "no one else has this capability." Key applications are in businesses in which computer "down time" can have serious consequences: electric power monitoring, emer-

---

[3] Robert H. Waterman, Jr., "The Seven Elements of Strategic Fit," *Journal of Business Strategy* 2, no. 3 (Winter 1982), p. 70.

ILLUSTRATION CAPSULE 20 *(continued)*

gency vehicle dispatching, back office transaction processing for financial institutions, on-line order entry, credit verification, and inventory control.

Tandem's main operations are in California's famous Silicon Valley where many other electronics firms are located. The Silicon Valley is noted for the fierceness with which area companies compete for talent; demand for talented employees is so high that assembly people, operators, and engineers can literally walk across the street and get a job with another company the next day. The Valley's high-technology companies are constantly "pirating" employees from each other's staffs. Moreover, many of the most creative people are unique personality types, sometimes labeled as "semifreakies" and "pseudohippies," and are products of the California culture of the 1960s and early 1970s, with a preference for openness, spontaneity, nonjudgmental acceptance, brotherhood, freedom, and expressiveness.

The Tandem Gospel

As conceived largely by cofounder-president James G. Treybig, pronounced Try-big, Tandem Computers' approach to dealing with its high-technology employees in the Silicon Valley culture represents "the convergence of capitalism and humanism, and incorporates a blend of ideology and incentives." The ideology centers around Treybig's five cardinal principles for running a company:

1. All people are good.
2. People, workers, management, and company are all the same thing.
3. Every single person in a company must understand the essence of the business.
4. Every employee must benefit from the company's success.
5. You must create an environment where all the above can happen.

These principles are pushed in a continual stream of orientation lectures, breakfast meetings, newsletters, a company magazine, and periodic communications with employees—the content of which is predicated on and inspired by a company manual entitled *Understanding Our Philosophy.* All employees are given a copy of the manual and are put through a two-day indoctrination course.

As an example of how conventional platitudes are instilled with new meaning, Treybig took the oft-said phrase "All employees should be treated with respect" and translated it at Tandem into "You never have the right at Tandem to screw a person or to mistreat him. It's not allowed. . . . No manager mistreats a human without a fear of his job." This statement is given teeth by giving any aggrieved employee ready access to anyone in the company—"guilty" managers have been fired.

In indoctrinating employees to the Tandem philosophy, pains are taken to explain the essence of the company's business, to give them a companywide perspective, and to go through the company's five-year plan. *Understanding Our Philosophy,* a road map–size chart which took Treybig two weeks to draw up, shows how a performance breakdown in one area spills over into lower performance in other parts of the company. While the main purpose of the big picture

ILLUSTRATION CAPSULE 20 *(continued)*

approach is to explain what various groups in the company are doing and how it all fits together and thus to point people in the direction of strategy accomplishment, it also helps to boost employee enthusiasm and loyalty. As one of the company founders put it, "People really get a great kick out of being part of the team and trusted with the corporate jewels."

Another key part of Tandem's philosophy is that companies can be overmanaged. According to Treybig; "most people need less management than you think." At Tandem, top management control is not accomplished with numerous reviews, meetings, and reports but rather with giving employees a full understanding and appreciation of the company's business concepts and managerial philosophy. Supervision is loose and flexible. There is no formal organization chart and there are few formal rules. Employees are encouraged to exercise freedom and creativity. They speak in glowing terms about how the company has helped them grow. The importance of people and personal growth is emphasized in Tandem's corporate philosophy which states: "Tandem's greatest resource—its people, creative action, and fun." T-shirts and bulletin boards proclaim:

"Get the job done no matter what it takes."

"Tandemize it—means make it work."

"It takes two to Tandem."

"It's so nice, it's so nice, we do it twice."

Company literature speaks of efforts to foster not just the welfare of employees but also their spouses and "spouse equivalents." Most employees respond positively to all this, describing Tandem's management as "people oriented."

Tandem's Incentive Package

Undergirding the ideology and philosophy is a package of reinforcing incentives and practices. *Every* employee participates in the company's stock option plans. As of mid-1982, an employee who had been with the company since its stock began to be traded publicly in 1977 had received stock options worth almost $100,000. At the company's 1981 Halloween costume party (which was so well attended that the crowd filled most of a large warehouse), the company announced the granting of a 100-share stock option to each of 3,000-plus employees. Even with Tandem's rapid growth three out of five new managers have risen from within the company's ranks.

An abundance of attention is paid to employee working conditions and amenities. Working hours are kept flexible and no one punches a time clock, the philosophy being, "We don't want to pay people for attendance but for output." The company has built a swimming pool, jogging trails, spaces for yoga classes and dance exercise, and a basketball court. There are periodic company-supplied weekend barbecues for employees working overtime. Employees get six-week sabbatical leaves every four years. On Friday afternoons at 4:30, the company conducts its weekly beer bust (attended by about 60 percent of the employees). Treybig is seen regularly at the beer busts, once coming in a cowboy hat

ILLUSTRATION CAPSULE 20 (continued)

and boots. Associates note that Treybig deliberately does and says things for their shock value. The result, says one vice president, is that "a lot of people when they meet Jim for the first time think he's a bullshitter, just shuckin' and jivin'." Yet, beneath the rhetoric and philosophy are some hardnosed policies.

Enhanced Loyalty and Commitment

Managers are pushed to hire new employees who are smarter and more qualified than they are. Normally, only experienced and proven applicants are seriously considered (to help Tandem gain access to new ideas and the best talent available). Interviews are very thorough, sometimes running 20 hours. Managers, not the personnel department, do the hiring, and prospective co-workers play a big role in the selection process. One employee observed, "A manager will never hire somebody his people don't think is good. Basically, he says will you work with this person, and you say yes or no." Employees are paid a $500 bonus for referring prospective candidates who subsequently are employed over 90 days. The hiring system exposes new employees to the Tandem culture before their first day on the job and endeavors to convey the feeling that they have been chosen by an exacting process. Tandem believes that such an initiation builds dedication because, by being ordeals, people tend to place a higher value on what has cost them a lot.

The results have been impressive. Tandem's productivity figures are among the highest in the industry. The work culture is one of commitment, hard work, loyalty, self-esteem, creativity, learning, personal growth, light supervision, and self-discipline. Tandem's turnover rate is about one third the average for the U.S. computer industry. Many employees are convinced that their jobs are filling their innermost goals of self-realization. Several employee comments about the company's approach and its effects are telling:

> I feel like putting a lot of time in. There is a real kind of loyalty here. We are all working in this together—working a process together. I'm not a workaholic—it's just the place. I love the place.

> I don't think someone who thought Tandem was just a job would work out because Tandem expects commitment.

> I feel like I'm accomplishing something with myself.

> I speak to my manager about once a month—that's how often my manager manages me.

> Its progressive. It's ahead of the times. I don't know what's right or wrong. I know that it's very unique. It sure feels right to me: it fits in with the way I like to see people treated.

WHY DOES TANDEM'S CORPORATE CULTURE WORK?

Part of what makes the corporate culture at Tandem Computers successful, however, is its close fit with the situation. Tandem has one basic product and

---

ILLUSTRATION CAPSULE 20 *(concluded)*

one clearly defined market. Most of its parts and components are supplied by subcontractors. Everything is cleaned by a contract janitorial service. What manufacturing Tandem does itself is skilled assembly and massive testing—activities that are conducted in quiet, airy rooms more like labs than factories. Most employees are well trained, highly skilled, self-disciplined, and intelligent enough to work well without close supervision. Much of Tandem's work activity is creative and highly technical, and workers need freedom and solitude to perform well. Good performance is handsomely rewarded (although some of the stock options are carefully calibrated to make leaving the company before four years very expensive). Rapid growth and financial success have funded the payment of generous benefits, created numerous promotion opportunities, and otherwise helped to make Tandem's unique blend of ideology and incentive work well up to this point. In addition, Tandem's management is strong, and the company dominates its market niche via careful product engineering, attention to manufacturing and skill in marketing—aspects that are also critical in the computer business.

Irrespective of whether the Tandem approach could be successful in other companies (and it may not continue to work as well at Tandem if growth slows and the company's fortunes slacken), the Tandem experience does spotlight the value of deliberately creating a corporate culture that is in close alignment with strategy.

SOURCE: Based on information reported in Myron Magnet, "Managing by Mystique at Tandem Computers," *Fortune,* June 28, 1982, pp. 84–91; and Terence E. Deal and Allen A. Kennedy, *Corporate Cultures* (Reading, Mass.: Addison-Wesley Publishing, 1982), pp. 8–13.

Peters and Waterman, in their already classic report on America's best-managed companies, provide some additional insights on what culture is, where to look for it, and why it is relevant:[4]

- At Frito-Lay, stories abound about potato chip route salesman slogging through sleet, mud, hail, snow, and rain to uphold the 99.5 percent service level to customers in which the entire organization takes such great pride. At IBM, the key themes are respect for the individual and services to the customer. At Procter & Gamble (P & G), the overarching value is product quality. At McDonald's the dominant factors are quality, service, cleanliness, and value, and the emphasis is on attention to detail and perfecting every fundamental of the business. At Delta Airlines, the culture is driven by "Delta's family feeling" that builds a team spirit and nurtures each employee's cooperative attitude toward others, cheerful outlook toward life, and pride in a job well done. At Johnson & Johnson, the credo is that customers come first, employees second, the community third, and shareholders fourth and last. At Du Pont, there is a fixation on safety—a report of every

---

[4] Peters and Waterman, *In Search of Excellence,* pp. xxi, 75–77, 280–85; see also, Thomas J. Peters and Nancy Austin, *A Passion for Excellence,* (New York: Random House, 1985), pp. 282–83, 334.

accident must be on the chairman's desk within 24 hours (Du Pont's safety record is 17 times better than the chemical industry average and 68 times better than the all-manufacturing average).

- Companies with strong cultures are unashamed collectors and tellers of stories, anecdotes, and legends in support of basic beliefs. L. L. Bean tells customer service stories. 3M tells innovation stories. P & G, Johnson & Johnson, Perdue Farms, and Maytag tell quality stories. From an organizational standpoint, such tales are very important because people in the organization take pride in identifying strongly with the stories, and they start to share in the traditions and values which the stories relate.

- The most typical values and beliefs which shape culture include: (1) a belief in being the best (or as at GE "better than the best"); (2) a belief in superior quality and service; (3) a belief in the importance of people as individuals and a faith in their ability to make a strong, positive contribution; (4) a belief in the importance of the details of execution, the nuts and bolts of doing the job well; (5) a belief that customers should reign supreme; (6) a belief in inspiring the best of people whatever their ability; (7) a belief in the importance of informality to enhance communication; and (8) a recognition that growth and profits are essential to a company's well-being. While the themes are common, however, every company implements them differently (to fit their particular situations), and every company's values are the articulated handiwork of one or two legendary figures in leadership positions. Accordingly, each company has its own distinct culture which, they believe, no one can copy successfully.

- In companies with strong cultures, managers and workers either "buy in" to the culture and accept its norms or else they opt out and leave the company.

- The stronger the corporate culture and the more it is directed toward customers and markets, the less a company uses policy manuals, organization charts, and detailed rules and procedures to enforce discipline and norms. The reason is that the guiding values inherent in the culture convey in crystal clear fashion what everybody is supposed to do in most situations. Often, poorly performing companies have strong cultures, too. The difference is that their cultures are dysfunctional, being focused on internal politics or operating by the numbers as opposed to emphasizing customers and the people who make and sell the product.

- Companies with strong cultures are clear on what they stand for, and they take the process of shaping values and reinforcing cultural norms. Significantly, the values these companies espouse undergird the strategies they employ.

While one can become impressed quickly with the contribution culture can have on strategic performance, the most interesting question is how the values get laid down and instilled in an organization's norms and activities. The answer has everything to do with the abilities and actions of the strategy manager. As organizational leader, the strategy manager keynotes both the ideas and the actions to give the ideas real content and meaning. The value-shaping task of the manager is concerned, on the one hand, with specifying lofty, inspirational visions that will generate organization-wide enthusiasm—not just among a few top-level subordinates and, on the other hand, with instilling these values mainly through actions and deeds rather than emotional rhetoric.[5] Words alone don't work. Instead, value building and culture shaping hinge on scores of actions at the most mundane levels of detail. No opportunity is too small or too insignificant. Implanting the desired values derives from obvious, sincere, sustained commitment by the chief executive coupled with extraordinary persistence in reinforcing those values. Neither charisma nor personal magnetism are necessary. However, being highly visible around the organization on a regular basis is essential; the job cannot be done from one's office.

Creating a Fit between Strategy and Culture   As chief entrepreneur, it is the strategy manager's responsibility to choose a strategy that can be executed given whatever constraints may be imposed by the "sacred" parts of the prevailing corporate culture. As chief administrator of the strategic plan, it is the manager's leadership task, once strategy is chosen, to bring the corporate culture into alignment with strategy and keep it there.

The variables of corporate culture are a useful perspective from which to check out the climate for strategic success. Given the chosen strategic plan, are the various parts of the corporate culture aligned to support the strategy and make execution doable? Which ones will have to be changed to create a better fit? Can these changes be made with a reasonable prospect of success? If the answer is no, then reformulation of the strategic plan is indicated. If the answer is yes, then management has to (1) address the problem of needed changes and (2) consider how long it will take for the changes, once initiated, to bear fruit (an overnight transformation is not possible!).

Normally, managerial *actions taken to modify corporate culture need to be symbolic and substantive.* The strategy manager's leadership role is essential here. In addition to being out front, personally keynoting the push for new attitudes and communicating widely and often the reasons for new approaches, the manager has to convince the organization that more than cosmetics is involved. Talk has to be backed up by substance and real movement. The actions taken have to be credible and highly visible, and must serve as unmistakable signals to the whole organization of the seriousness of management's commitment to a new climate and culture. Some quick successes in reorienting the way some things are done help to highlight the value of the new order, thus making enthusiasm for the changes contagious. However, figuring out how to get some instant results is usually not as important as having the will and patience to mold the parts of the organization into a solid, competent team which is psychologically committed to superior strategy execution.

Creating an organizational culture which is fully harmonized with the strategic plan offers a strong challenge to the strategy implementer's administrative leadership abilities. The first step is to be consciously alert to the importance of shaping the organization's habits, mindsets, and personality variables to fit the needs of strategy. The second step is to use the available opportunities to make incremental changes that improve the alignment of culture and strategy. Such opportunities crop up regularly: new and vacant positions can be filled with people who are willing and able to refashion the old ways of doing things; the appearance of a new problem can

---

[5] Peters and Waterman, *In Search of Excellence,* pp. 287–88. The leadership role of the general manager is discussed in considerably more detail in Peters and Austin, *A Passion for Excellence,* chaps. 16–19.

pave the way for making a desirable policy change; those proposals of subordinates which have positive impacts on culture can be strongly supported; individuals and subunits that "get with the program" can be visibly rewarded and singled out for praise; and the annual budgetary process can be used as a vehicle to steer resources from one area to another.

Step three is to insist that subordinate managers do things in ways that instill and reinforce the desired culture and organizational values. Step four is to proactively build and nurture the organization's emotional commitment to strategy so as to produce a temperamental fit between culture and strategic mission.

Creating a Results Orientation and a High Performance Spirit

An ability to instill high levels of commitment to strategic success and to create an atmosphere where there is constructive pressure to perform is one of the most valuable strategy-implementing skills. When an organization performs consistently at or near peak capability, the outcome is not only improved strategic success but also an organizational climate where the emphasis is on excellence and achievement—a spirit of high performance pervades. Such a spirit of performance should not be confused with whether employees are "happy" or "satisfied" or whether they "get along well together." For an organization to be instilled with and sustain a spirit of performance, it must maintain a focus on achievement and excellence. It must strive at developing a consistent ability to produce results over prolonged periods of time. It must succeed in utilizing the full range of rewards and punishment to establish and enforce high standards of performance.

Usually a number of performance measures are needed at each level; rarely will a single measure suffice. At the corporate and line-of-business levels, the typical performance measures include profitability (measured in terms of total profit, return on equity investment, return on total assets, return on sales, operating profit, and so on), market share, growth rates in sales and profits, and evidence that competitive position and future prospects have improved. In the manufacturing area, the strategy-relevant performance measures may focus on unit manufacturing costs, productivity increases, meeting production and shipping schedules, quality control, the number and extent of work stoppages due to labor disagreements and equipment breakdowns, and so on. In the marketing area, the measures may include unit selling costs, the increases in dollar sales and unit volume, the degree of sales penetration of each target customer group, increases in market share, the success of newly introduced products, the severity of customer complaints, advertising effectiveness, and the number of new accounts acquired. While most performance measures are quantitative in nature, there are always several which have elements of subjectivity—improvements in labor-management relations, whether employee morale is up or down, whether customers are more or less satisfied with quality of the firm's products, what impact advertising is having, and how far the firm is ahead or behind rivals on quality, service, technological capability, and other key success factors.

The successful approaches to creating a spirit of high performance involve an intense focus on people, reinforced at every conceivable occasion in every conceivable way and mirrored to people down the line in every activity. The goal is to get everybody in the organization involved and emotionally committed. The idea is to try to generate contagious enthusiasm at all levels and among all employees, utilizing a tough-minded respect for the individual employee, a willingness to train each employee thoroughly, a belief in setting reasonable and clear performance expectations, and a painstaking effort to grant employees enough autonomy to stand out, excel, and contribute. An important aspect of creating a results-oriented organizational culture is making champions out of the people who turn in winning performances; examples of how this is done are cited below:[6]

- At Boeing, IBM, GE, and 3M, top executives deliberately make "champions" out of individuals who believe so strongly in their ideas that they take it upon themselves to hurdle the bureaucracy, maneuver their projects through the system, and turn them into improved services, new products, or even new businesses. In these companies, "product champions" are given high visibility, room to push their ideas, and strong executive support. Champions whose ideas prove out are usually handsomely rewarded; those whose ideas don't pan out still have secure jobs and are given chances to try again.
- The manager of a New York area sales office rented the Meadowlands Stadium (home field of the New York Giants) for an evening. After work, the salesmen were all assembled at the stadium and then asked to run one at a time through the player's tunnel onto the field. As each one emerged, the electronic scoreboard flashed his name to those gathered specially in the stands—executives from corporate headquarters, employees from the office, family, and friends. Their role was to cheer loudly in honor of the individual's sales accomplishments. The company involved was IBM. The occasion for this action was to reaffirm IBM's commitment to satisfy an individual's need to be part of something great and to reiterate IBM's concern for championing individual accomplishment.
- Some companies upgrade the importance and status of individual employees by referring to them as cast members (Disney), crew members (McDonald's), or associates (Wal-Mart and J. C. Penney). Companies like IBM, Tupperware, and McDonald's actively seek out reasons and opportunities to give pins, buttons, badges, and medals to good showings by average performers—the idea being to show appreciation and help give a boost to the "middle 60 percent" of the work force.
- McDonald's has a contest to determine the best hamburger cooker in its entire chain. It begins with a competition to determine the best hamburger cooker in each store. Store winners go on to compete in regional championships, and regional winners go on to the "All-American" contest. The winners get trophies and an All-American patch to wear on their shirts.
- Milliken & Co. holds corporate sharing rallies once every three months at which teams come from all over the company to swap success stories and ideas. A hundred or more teams make 5-minute presentations over a two-day period. Each rally has a major theme—quality, cost reduction, and so on. No criticisms and

---

[6] Peters and Waterman, *In Search of Excellence,* pp. xviii, 240, 269; and Peters and Austin, *A Passion for Excellence,* pp. 304–07.

negatives are allowed, and there is no such thing as a big idea or a small one. Quantitative measures of success are used to gauge improvement. All those present vote on the best presentation and several ascending grades of awards are handed out. Everyone, however, receives a framed certificate for participating.

What makes a spirit of high performance come alive is more than a belief or statement or philosophy or program. It is a complex network of practices, words, symbols, styles, values, and policies pulling together to form a system that produces an ability to achieve extraordinary results with ordinary people. The drivers of the system are a belief in the worth of the individual, attention to detail, and an effort to do the "itty-bitty, teeny-tiny things" right.

While emphasizing a spirit of high performance nearly always accentuates the positive, there are negative aspects, too. Managers whose units consistently rank poor on performance have to be removed. Aside from the organizational benefits, weak-performing managers should be reassigned for their own good; people who find themselves in a job they cannot handle are usually frustrated, anxiety ridden, harassed, and unhappy.[7] Moreover, subordinates have a right to be managed with competence, dedication, and achievement; unless their boss performs well, they themselves cannot perform well.

Linking Rewards to Performance

If strategy accomplishment is to be a top-priority activity, then the reward structure must be linked *explicitly* and *tightly* to actual strategic performance. *Decisions on salary increases, promotions, who gets which key assignments, and the ways and means of awarding praise and recognition are the strategy implementer's foremost attention-getting, commitment-generating devices.* How a manager parcels out the rewards signals who is perceived as doing a good job and what sort of behavior and performance management wants. Such matters seldom escape the closest scrutiny of every member of the organization. If anything, an organization will overreact to the system of incentives and how rewards are handed out.

Creating a tight fit between strategy and the reward structure is generally best accomplished by agreeing upon strategic objectives, fixing responsibility and deadlines for achieving them, and then treating their achievement as a *contract*. Next, the contracted-for strategic performance has to be the *real* basis for designing incentives, evaluating individual efforts, and handing out rewards. To prevent undermining and undoing the whole managing-with-objectives-approach to strategy implementation, a manager must insist that actual performance be judiciously compared against the contracted-for target objectives. The reasons for any deviations have to be explored fully to determine whether the causes are attributable to poor management or to circumstances beyond management control. All managers need to understand clearly how their rewards have been calculated. In short, managers at all levels have to be held accountable for carrying out their assigned part of the strategic plan, and they have to know their rewards are based on the caliber of their strategic accomplishments

---

[7] Peter F. Drucker, *Management: Tasks, Responsibilities, Practices* (New York: Harper & Row, 1974), p. 457.

(allowing for both the favorable and unfavorable impacts of uncontrollable, unforesee-able, and unknowable circumstances).

INSTALLING INTERNAL ADMINISTRATIVE SUPPORT
SYSTEMS: CREATING MORE FITS

The fourth central task of strategy implementation concerns installing internal adminis-trative support systems which fit the needs of strategy. The recurring administrative issues here are:

1. What kinds of strategy-facilitating policies and procedures to establish.
2. How to get the right strategy-critical information on a timely basis.
3. What "controls" are needed to keep the organization on its strategic course.

The Role of Strategy-Related Policies and Procedures

Changes in strategy generally call for some changes in how internal activities are conducted and administered. The process of changing from the old ways to the new ways has to be initiated and managed. Asking people to alter actions and practices always upsets the internal order of things somewhat. It is normal for pockets of resistance to emerge and, certainly, questions will be raised about the "hows" as well as the whys of change. The role of new and revised policies is to promulgate "standard operating procedures" that will (1) facilitate strategy implementation and (2) counteract any tendencies for parts of the organization to resist or reject the chosen strategy. Policies help enforce strategy implementation in five respects:

1. Policy acts as a lever for institutionalizing strategy-supportive practices and operat-ing procedures on an organizationwide basis, thus pushing day-to-day activities in the direction of efficient strategy execution.
2. Policy places limits on independent action and sets boundaries on the kinds and directions of action that can be taken. By making a statement about how things are now to be done, policy communicates what is expected, guides strategy related activities in particular directions, and places bounds on unwanted variations.
3. Policy acts to align actions and behavior with strategy throughout the organization, thereby minimizing zigzag decisions and conflicting practices and establishing some degree of regularity, stability, and dependability in how the organization is attempting to make the strategy work.
4. Policy helps to shape the character of the internal work climate and to translate the corporate philosophy into how things are done, how people are treated, and what the corporate beliefs and attitudes mean in terms of everyday activities.
5. Policy operationalizes the corporate philosophy, thus playing a key role in estab-lishing a fit between corporate culture and strategy.

From a strategy implementation perspective, managers need to be inventive in establishing policies that can supply vital support to an organization's strategic plan. IBM's policy of trying to offer the best service of any company in the world undergirds its whole competitive strategy and corporate philosophy. At McDonald's, to channel "crew members" into stronger quality and service behavior patterns, the policy manual spells out such detailed procedures as: "Cooks must turn, never flip, hamburgers. If they haven't been purchased, Big Macs must be discarded in 10 minutes after being cooked and french fries in 7 minutes. Cashiers must make eye contact with and smile at every customer." At Delta Airlines, it is corporate policy to check out all stewardess applicants thoroughly regarding their aptitudes for friendliness, cooperativeness, and teamwork. Caterpillar Tractor has a policy of giving its customers 48-hour guaranteed parts delivery anywhere in the world, and if it fails to fulfill the promise the part is supplied free of charge. Hewlett-Packard has a policy requiring R&D people to make regular visits to customer premises to learn of their problems, to talk about new product applications, and, in general, to keep R&D activities customer oriented.

There is, therefore, a definite role for policies and procedures in the strategy implementation process. Wisely constructed policies and procedures help enforce strategy implementation by channeling actions, behavior, decisions, and practices in directions which promote strategy accomplishment. Checking out the alignment between existing policies and strategy is thus a recurring administrative part of the strategy implementation process. Failure to examine existing policies and procedures from a strategy perspective runs the risk that some existing policies will act as burdensome obstacles or hurdles to overcome and that people who have vested interests to protect will thwart or even defeat the strategic plan (either because they disagree with the strategy or because their thinking is colored by an administrative and bureaucratic mindset rather than a strategic results and performance mindset). On the other hand, consciously instituting policies and procedures that promote strategy-supportive behavior build organization commitment to the strategic plan and create a tighter fit between corporate culture and strategy.

None of this is meant to imply, however, that a fat omnibus manual of policies is called for. Too much policy can be as stifling as wrong policy or as chaotic as no policy. Sometimes, the best policy for implementing strategy is a willingness to let subordinates "do it any way they want if it makes sense and works." A little "structured chaos" can be a good thing where individual creativity is more essential to strategy than standardization and strict conformity. When Rene McPherson became CEO at Dana Corp., he dramatically threw out 22½ inches of policy manuals and replaced them with a one-page statement of philosophy focusing on "productive people."[8] Creating a strong supportive fit between strategy and policy can mean more policies, fewer policies, or different policies. It can mean policies that require things to be done a certain way or policies that give the person performing a job the autonomy to do it the way he or she thinks best.

Gathering Strategy-Critical Information—The MBWA Approach

To stay on top of how well the strategy implementation process is going, a manager needs to develop a broad network of contacts and sources of information, both

---

[8] Peters and Waterman, *In Search of Excellence*, p. 65.

formal and informal. The regular channels include talking with key subordinates, reading written reports, gleaning statistics from the latest operating results, getting feedback from customers, watching the competitive reactions of rival firms, tapping into the flow of gossip through the grapevine, listening to what is on the minds of rank-and-file employees, and firsthand observation. However, some pieces of information tend to be more trustworthy than others. The content of formal written reports may represent "the truth but not the whole truth." "Bad news" may be covered up, minimized, or not reported at all. Sometimes subordinates delay reporting failures and problems in hopes that more time will give them room to turn things around. As information flows up an organization, there is a tendency for it to get "censored" and "sterilized" to the point that it may fail to reveal strategy-critical information. Hence, there is reason for strategy managers to guard against major surprises by making sure that they have accurate information and a "feel" for the existing situation. The chief way this is done is by regular visits "to the field" and talking with many different people at many different levels. The technique of managing by wandering around (MBWA) is practiced in a variety of styles:[9]

- At Hewlett-Packard (HP), there are weekly beer busts in each division, attended by both executives and employees, to create a regular opportunity to keep in touch. Tidbits of information flow freely between down-the-line employees and executives—facilitated in part because "the HP Way" is for people at all ranks to be addressed by their first names. Bill Hewlett, one of HP's cofounders, had a companywide reputation for getting out of his office and "wandering around" the plant greeting people, listening to what was on their minds, and asking questions. He found this so valuable that he made MBWA a standard practice for all HP managers. Furthermore, ad hoc meetings of people from different departments spontaneously arise; they gather in rooms with blackboards and work out solutions informally.

- McDonald's founder, Ray Kroc, regularly visited store units and did his own personal inspection on Q.S.C. & V. (Quality, Service, Cleanliness, and Value)—the themes he preached regularly. There are stories of him pulling into a unit's parking lot, seeing litter lying on the pavement, getting out of his limousine to pick it up himself, and then lecturing the store staff at length on the subject of cleanliness.

- The CEO of a firm making titanium products, spends much of his time riding around the factory in a golf cart, waving and joking with workers, listening to them, and calling all 2,000 employees by their first names. In addition, he spends a lot of time with union officials, inviting them to meetings and keeping them well informed about what is going on.

- Sam Walton, Wal-Mart's founder, insists "The key is to get out into the store and listen to what the associates have to say. Our best ideas come from the clerks and stockboys." Walton himself visits every one of Wal-Mart's 700-plus stores every year (a policy he has followed since 1962 when there were just 18 stores. On one occasion he flew the company plane to a Texas town, got out, and instructed the copilot to meet him 100 miles down the road. Then he flagged

---

[9] Ibid., pp. xx, 15, 120–23, 191, 242–43, 246–47, 287–90; For an extensive report on the benefits of MBWA, see Peters and Austin, *A Passion for Excellence*, chap. 2, 3, and 19.

a Wal-Mart truck and rode the rest of the way to "chat with the driver—it seemed like so much fun." Walton makes a practice of greeting store managers and their spouses by name at annual meetings and has been known to go to the company's distribution centers at 2 A.M. (carrying boxes of doughnuts to share with all those on duty) to have a chance to find out what was on their minds.

- When Ed Carlson became CEO at United Airlines, he traveled about 200,000 miles a year talking with United's employees. He observed, "I wanted these people to identify me and to feel sufficiently comfortable to make suggestions or even argue with me if that's what they felt like doing. . . . Whenever I picked up some information, I would call the senior officer of the division and say that I had just gotten back from visiting Oakland, Reno, and Las Vegas, and here is what I found." Carlson insisted that his top 15 executives travel 200,000 miles yearly, too; all 15 spent 65 percent or more of their time in the field.

- At Marriott Corp. Bill Marriott not only personally inspects all Marriott hotels at least once a year but he also invites all Marriott guests to send him their evaluations of Marriott's facilities and services. He personally reads every customer complaint and has been known to telephone hotel managers about them.

Managers at many companies attach great importance to informal communications. They report that it is essential to have a "feel" for situations and to gain quick, easy access to information. When executives stay in their offices, they tend to become isolated and often surround themselves with people who are not likely to offer criticisms and different perspectives; as a result, prompt, flexible, timely solutions to problems go by the wayside.

Instituting Formal Reporting of Strategic Information

Naturally, more than informal communications and personal contacts with field operations are called for. A formal effort to gather and report strategy-critical information is necessary. The work of individuals and subunits has to be monitored beyond just the "controls" of budgets, the reward structure, established policies and procedures, cultural norms, and networks of personal contacts.

In designing formal reports to monitor strategic progress, five guidelines can be recommended:[10]

1. Information and reporting systems should involve no more data and reporting than is really needed to give a reliable picture of what is going on. The information gathered should emphasize strategically meaningful variables and symptoms of potentially significant developments. Temptations to supplement "what managers need to know" with other "interesting" but marginally useful information should be avoided.

2. Reports and statistical data-gathering have to be timely—not come too late to take corrective action nor generated so often as to cost more than it's worth.

[10] Drucker, *Management,* pp. 498–504; Harold Koontz, "Management Control: A Suggested Formulation of Principles," *California Management Review* 2, no. 2 (Winter 1959), pp. 50–55; and William H. Sihler, "Toward Better Management Control Systems," *California Management Review* 14, no. 2 (Winter 1971), pp. 33–39.

3. The flow of information and statistics should be kept simple. Complicated reports are likely to confound and obscure because of the attention that has to be paid to mechanics, procedures, and interpretive guidelines instead of measuring and reporting the really critical variables.

4. Information and reporting systems should aim at "no surprises" and generating "early-warnings signs" rather than just producing information. It is debatable whether reports should receive wide distribution ("for your information"), but they should, without fail, be put directly into the hands of managers who are in a position to act when trouble signs appear.

5. Statistical reports should make it easy to flag big or unusual variances from plan and the "exceptions," thus directing management attention to significant departures from targeted performance.

Statistical information gives the strategy manager a feel for the numbers; reports and meetings provide a feel for new developments and the problems that exist; and personal contacts and conversations add a feel for the people dimension. All are good barometers of the overall tempo of performance and which things are on and off track. Identifying deviations from plan and problem areas to be addressed are prerequisites for initiating actions to either improve implementation or fine-tune strategy.

BONDING THE ADMINISTRATIVE FITS: THE ROLE OF SHARED VALUES AND BELIEFS

As emphasized earlier, strategy implementation is made more certain of success when an organization's various internal administrative activities and practices are aligned with the requirements of strategy. "Fits" with strategy need to be created in many areas, including structure, staffing (both managerial and technical), organizational skills and distinctive competences, resource allocation, rewards and incentives, policies and procedures, functional area activities, shared values and culture, and managerial skills and styles. The better the "goodness of fit" among these variables, the more powerful strategy execution is likely to be.

McKinsey & Co., a leading consulting firm with wide-ranging experiences in strategic analysis, has developed a framework for examining the fits in seven broad areas: (1) strategy; (2) structure; (3) shared values, attitudes, and philosophy; (4) approach to staffing the organization and its overall "people orientation"; (5) administrative systems, practices, and procedures used to run the organization on a day-to-day basis, including the reward structure, formal and informal policies, budgeting and programs, training, cost accounting, and financial controls; (6) the organization's skills, capabilities and distinctive competences; and (7) style of top management (how they allocate their time and attention, symbolic actions, their leadership skills, the way the top management team comes across to the rest of the organization).[11] McKin-

---

[11] For a more extended discussion, see Robert H. Waterman, Jr., Thomas J. Peters, and Julien R. Phillips, "Structure Is Not Organization," *Business Horizons* 23, no. 3 (June 1980), pp. 14–26; and Robert H. Waterman, Jr., "The Seven Elements of Strategic Fit," *Journal of Business Strategy* 2, no. 3 (Winter 1982), pp. 68–72.

sey has diagrammed these seven elements into what it calls the McKinsey 7-S Framework (the seven Ss are strategy, structure, shared values, staff, systems, skills, and style—so labeled to promote recall), shown in Figure 9–1. Shared values are the central core of the framework because they are the heart-and-soul themes around which an organization rallies; they define its main beliefs and aspirations, its guiding concepts of "who we are, what we do, where we are headed, and what principles we will stand for in getting there." They drive the corporate culture.

The virtue of the McKinsey 7-S Framework is that it draws attention to some important organizational interconnections and why these interconnections are relevant in trying to effect change. In orchestrating a major shift in strategy and gathering full momentum for implementation, the pace of real change will be governed by all seven Ss. The 7-S framework is a simple way to illustrate that the job of implementing strategy is one of bringing all seven Ss into harmony. When the seven Ss are in good alignment, an organization is poised and energized to execute strategy to the best of its ability.

Figure 9–1   Bonding the Administrative Fits: The McKinsey 7-S Framework

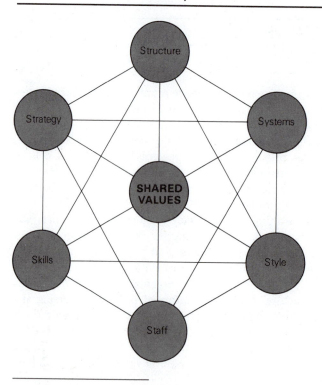

Source: Thomas J. Peters and Robert H. Waterman, Jr., *In Search of Excellence* (New York: Harper & Row, 1982), p. 10.

EXERTING STRATEGIC LEADERSHIP

The litany of good strategic management is simple enough: Formulate a sound strategic plan, implement it, execute it to the fullest, win! Clearly, this is "easier said than done." Exerting "take charge" leadership, being a "spark plug," ramrodding things through, being one of the "movers and shakers" in the organization, and getting things done by coaching others to do it are not easy skills. Moreover, a strategy manager has many different leadership roles to play: chief entrepreneur, chief administrator, crisis solver, taskmaster, figurehead, spokesman, resource allocator, negotiator, motivator, adviser, inspirationist, consensus builder, policymaker, and so on. Sometimes it is useful to be authoritarian and hardnosed; at other times being a perceptive listener and a compromising decision maker works best; and still other times a strongly participative, collegial approach is called for. Many occasions call for a highly visible role and extensive time commitments, while others entail a brief ceremonial performance with the details being mostly delegated to subordinates.

In general, the problem of strategic leadership is one of diagnosing the situation at hand and choosing from any of several ways to handle it. Four leadership issues dominate the manager's action agenda:

#7

1. What actions to take in promoting a climate and culture in which the organization is "energized" to accomplish strategy and perform at a high level.
2. How to keep the organization responsive to changing conditions, alert for new opportunities, and bubbling with innovative ideas.
3. How to deal with the politics of strategy formulation and implementation, cope with "power struggles," and build consensus.
4. When and how to push corrective actions to improve strategy execution and overall strategic performance.

Fostering a Strategy-Supportive Climate and Culture

Strategy implementers have to be "out front" in promoting a strategy-supportive organizational climate. When major strategic changes are being implemented, scarcely anything else is likely to constitute a better use of the manager's time than personally leading the way on creating a more strategy-supportive work environment. When only strategic fine-tuning is being implemented, less generally needs to be done in bringing values and culture into better alignment with strategy, but there is still a lead role for the manager to play in pushing ahead. As organizational commander-in-chief, the manager always stands in the center ring of attention, keynoting the belief that the chosen strategy is right and that implementing it to the best of the organization's ability is "top priority."

Both words and deeds play a part. Words are needed to inspire accomplishment of the strategy, to infuse spirit and drive, to define strategy-supportive cultural norms and values, to articulate the reasons for strategic organizational change, to legitimize new viewpoints and priorities, to urge and reinforce commitment to the course being charted, and to arouse confidence in the new strategy being implemented. Deeds are essential to add credibility to the words, to create strategy-supportive symbols, to set examples, to give meaning and content to the language, and to teach the organization what sort of behavior is needed and expected.

Highly visible symbols and imagery are needed to complement substantive actions. As an example of the value of symbolic actions, consider the explanation one GM manager gave for the striking difference in performance between two large plants:[12]

> At the poorly performing plant, the plant manager probably ventured out on the floor once a week, always in a suit. His comments were distant and perfunctory. At South Gate, the better plant, the plant manager was on the floor all the time. He wore a baseball cap and a UAW jacket. By the way, whose plant do you think was spotless? Whose looked like a junkyard?

At GE, a company consistently rated by other CEOs as one of the best-managed industrial corporations in the United States, the recently appointed new chairman and chief executive officer, John Welch, has tried to install a new cultural norm by challenging GE's 250-plus business-level managers to "be better than the best." He has translated this theme into a single, overarching performance standard: they must establish their business as no. 1 or no. 2 in their industries or else achieve a competitive advantage by virtue of decided technological superiority. All business unit managers are asked to visit the corporate R&D labs for brainstorming sessions for developing "clear technological edge businesses." His plan calls for divesting businesses that are unable to meet these standards, his belief being that future economic and competitive conditions will leave "no room for the mediocre suppliers of products and services."

As a rule, the greater the degree of strategic change being implemented and/or the greater the shift in cultural norms needed to accommodate a new strategy, the more visible the strategy implementer's words and deeds need to be. The lesson from well-managed companies is that what the manager says and does has a significant bearing on down-the-line strategy implementation and execution.[13] According to one view, "It is not so much the articulation . . . about what an [organization] should be doing that creates new practice. It's the imagery that creates the understanding, the compelling moral necessity that the new way is right."[14] Moreover, the actions and images, both substantive and symbolic, have to be hammered out regularly, not just restricted to ceremonial speeches and special occasions. This is where a high profile and "managing by wandering around" comes heavily into play. As a Hewlett-Packard official expresses it in the company publication *The HP Way:*

> Once a division or department has developed a plan of its own—a set of working objectives—it's important for managers and supervisors to keep it in operating condition. This is where observation, measurement, feedback, and guidance come in. It's our "management by wandering around." That's how you find out whether you're on track and heading at the right speed and in the right direction. If you don't constantly monitor how people are operating, not only will they tend to wander off track but also they will begin to believe you weren't serious about the plan in the first place. It has the

---

[12] As quoted in Peters and Waterman, *In Search of Excellence,* p. 262.

[13] Peters and Waterman, *In Search of Excellence,* chap. 9.

[14] Warren Bennis, *The Unconscious Conspiracy: Why Leaders Can't Lead* (New York: AMACOM, 1976), p. 93.

extra benefit of getting you off your chair and moving around your area. By wandering around, I literally mean moving around and talking to people. It's all done on a very informal and spontaneous basis, but it's important in the course of time to cover the whole territory. You start out by being accessible and approachable, but the main thing is to realize you're there to listen. The second is that it is vital to keep people informed about what's going on in the company, especially those things that are important to them. The third reason for doing this is because it is just plain fun.

Such contacts give the manager a feel for how things are progressing, and they provide opportunity to speak with encouragement, to uplift spirits, to shift attention from the old to the new priorities, to create some excitement, and to project an atmosphere of informality and fun—all of which drive implementation along in a positive fashion and intensify the organizational energy behind strategy execution. John Welch of GE sums up the hands-on role and motivational approach well: "I'm here every day, or out into a factory, smelling it, feeling it, touching it, challenging the people."[15]

Keeping the Internal Organization Responsive and Innovative

While formulating and implementing strategy is very much a manager's responsibility, the task of generating fresh ideas, identifying new opportunities, and being responsive to changing conditions cannot be accomplished by a single person. It is an organization-wide task, particularly in large corporations. One of the toughest parts of exerting strategic leadership is generating a dependable supply of fresh ideas from the rank and file, managers and employees alike, and promoting an entrepreneurial, opportunistic spirit that permits continuous adaptation to changing conditions. A flexible, responsive, innovative internal environment is critical in fast-moving high technology industries, in businesses where products have short life cycles and growth depends on new product innovation, in managing widely diversified business portfolios (where opportunities are varied and scattered), in industries where successful product differentiation is a key success factor, and in businesses where the strategy of being the low-cost producer hinges on productivity improvement and continuous cost reduction. One cannot mandate such an environment by simply exhorting people to be "creative."

One useful leadership approach is to take special pains to foster, nourish, and support people who are willing to champion new ideas, better services, and new products and product applications, and who are eager for a chance to try to turn their ideas into new divisions, new businesses, and even new industries. When Texas Instruments recently reviewed its last 50 or so successful and unsuccessful new product introductions, one factor marked every failure: "Without exception we found we hadn't had a volunteer champion. There was someone we had cajoled into taking on the task. When we take a look at a product and decide whether to push it or not these days, we've got a new set of criteria.

Number one is the presence of a zealous, volunteer champion. After that comes market potential and project economics in a distant second and third."[16] The rule

---

[15] As quoted in Ann M. Morrison, "Trying to Bring GE to Life," *Fortune,* January 25, 1982, p. 52.

[16] As quoted in Peters and Waterman, *In Search of Excellence,* pp. 203–4.

seem to be that the idea of something new or something better either finds a champion or it dies. And the champion is usually persistent, competitive, tenacious, committed, and more than a bit fanatic about the idea and seeing it through to success. An example of a typical champion is presented in Illustration Capsule 21.

ILLUSTRATION CAPSULE 21

How the Product Champion Thinks and Works: The Case of Howard Head

Product champions seem to be different types of people. Oftentimes they appear to be obsessed with their ideas, slightly fanatic, bullheaded, willing to battle the status quo and struggle against heavy odds. Nearly always they have the know-how, energy, daring, and staying power to see their ideas through to implementation. A well-known case of a champion at work and what the process is like comes from *Sports Illustrated*'s story of Howard Head's invention of the metal snow ski:[1]

In 1946 Head went off to Stowe, Vermont, for his first attempt at skiing. "I was humiliated and disgusted by how badly I skied," he recalls, "and, characteristically, I was inclined to blame it on the equipment, those long, clumsy, hickory skis. On my way home I heard myself boasting to an Army officer beside me that I could make a better ski out of aircraft materials than could be made from wood."

Back at Martin [Head's workplace], the cryptic doodles that began appearing on Head's drawing board inspired him to scavenge some aluminum from the plant scrap pile. In his off-hours he set up shop on the second floor of a converted stable in an alley near his one-room basement flat. His idea was to make a "metal sandwich" ski consisting of two layers of aluminum with plywood sidewalls and a center filling of honeycombed plastic.

Needing pressure and heat to fuse the materials together, Head concocted a process that would have made Rube Goldberg proud. To achieve the necessary pressure of 15 pounds per square inch, he put the ski mold into a huge rubber bag and then pumped the air out through a tube attached to an old refrigerator compressor that was hooked up backward to produce suction. For heat, he welded together an iron, coffinlike tank, filled it with motor oil drained from automobile crankcases and, using two Sears Roebuck camp burners, cooked up a smelly 350-degree brew. Then he dumped the rubber bag with the ski mold inside into the tank of boiling oil and sat back like Julia Child waiting for her potato puffs to brown.

Six weeks later, out of the stench and smoke, Head produced his first six pairs of skis and raced off to Stowe to have them tested by pros. To gauge the ski's chamber, an instructor stuck the end of one into the snow and flexed it. It broke. So, eventually, did all six pairs. "Each time one of them broke," says Head, "something inside me snapped with it."

[1] The following excerpts are reprinted courtesy of *Sports Illustrated* from the September 29, 1980, issue (pp. 68–70). © 1980 Time. "Howard Head says, 'I'm giving up the thing world'" by Ray Kennedy.

ILLUSTRATION CAPSULE 21 *(concluded)*

Instead of hanging up his rubber bag, Head quit Martin the day after New Year's 1948, took $6,000 in poker winnings he had stashed under his bed, and went to work in earnest. Each week he would send a new and improved pair of skis to Neil Robinson, a ski instructor in Bromley, Vermont, for testing, and each design would take 40 versions before the ski was any good. I might have given it up," says Head, "but fortunately, you get trapped into thinking the next design will be it."

Head wrestled with his obsession through three agonizing winters. The refinements were several: steel edges for necessary bite, a plywood core for added strength, and a plastic running surface for smoother, ice-free runs. One crisp day in 1950, Head stood in the bowl of Tuckerman's Ravine in New Hampshire and watched ski instructor Clif Taylor come skimming over the lip of the headwall, do a fishtail on the fall line, and sweep into a long, graceful curve, swooshing to a stop in front of the beaming inventor.

"They're great, Mr. Head, just great," Taylor exclaimed. At that moment, Head says, "I knew deep inside I had it."

In order to promote an organizational climate where champion innovators can blossom and thrive, strategy managers need to do several things. One, individuals and groups have to be encouraged to bring their ideas forward. Two, the maverick style of the champion has to be tolerated and given room to operate. People's imaginations need to be encouraged to "fly in all directions." Autonomy to experiment and informal brainstorming sessions need to become ingrained behavior. Above all, people with creative ideas must not be looked upon as disruptive or troublesome. Three, managers have to induce and promote lots of "tries" and be willing to tolerate mistakes and failures. Most ideas will not pan out, yet it is likely that a good try results in learning even when it fails. Four, strategy managers should demonstrate a willingness to use all kinds of ad hoc organizational forms to support ideas and experimentation— venture teams, task forces, internal competition among different groups working on the same project (IBM calls the showdown between the competing approaches a "performance shootout"), informal "bootlegged" projects composed of volunteers, and so on. Five, strategy managers have to see that the rewards for a successful champion are large and visible and that people who champion an unsuccessful idea are encouraged to try again rather than being punished or sidetracked. In effect, the leadership task here is one of putting internal support systems for entrepreneurial innovation into place.

Dealing with Company Politics

It would be naive to presume that a manager can effectively formulate and implement strategy without being perceptive about company politics and being adept at political maneuvering.[17] Politics virtually always comes into play in formulating the strategic plan. Inevitably, key individuals and groups will form coalitions around the issues of which direction the organization should be headed, with each group pressing the benefits and potential of its own ideas and vested interests. Political considerations enter into which strategic objectives will take precedence and which lines of business in the corporate portfolio will have top priority in resource allocation. Internal politics is a factor in building a consensus for which business strategy alternative to employ and in settling on the role and contribution of each functional area in supporting line-of-business strategy.

Likewise, politics play a part in implementing strategy. Typically, internal political considerations enter into decisions affecting organization structure (whose areas of responsibility need to be reorganized, who reports to whom, who has how much authority over subunits), the choice of individuals to fill key positions and head up strategy-critical activities, and which organizational units get the biggest budget increases. As a case in point, Quinn cites a situation where three strong managers who fought each other constantly formed a potent coalition to resist a reorganization scheme to coordinate the very things that caused their friction.[18]

In short, political considerations and the forming of alliances are an integral part of building organizationwide support for the strategic plan and in gaining consensus on the various mechanics of how to implement strategy. Indeed, having astute political skills is a definite, and maybe even a necessary, asset for a manager to have in orchestrating the whole strategic process.

There is a clear-cut imperative for a strategy manager to understand how an organization's power structure works, who it is that wields influence in the executive ranks, which groups and individuals are "activists" and which are "defenders of the status quo," who can be helpful in a "showdown" on key decisions, and which direction the political winds are blowing on a given issue. On those occasions where major decisions have to be made, strategy managers need to be especially sensitive to the politics of managing coalitions and reaching some consensus on which way to go. As the chairman of a major British corporation expressed it:[19]

> I've never taken a major decision without consulting my colleagues. It would be unimaginable to me, unimaginable. First, they help me make a better decision in most cases. Second, if they know about it and agree with it, they'll back it. Otherwise, they might challenge it, not openly, but subconsciously.

The politics of strategy centers chiefly around stimulating options, nurturing support for strong proposals and killing the weak ones, guiding the formation of coalitions on particular issues, and achieving consensus and commitment. A landmark study of strategy management in nine large corporations showed that the political tactics of successful executives included:[20]

---

[17] For further discussion of this point, see Abraham Zaleznik, "Power and Politics in Organizational Life," *Harvard Business Review* 48, no. 3 (May–June 1970), pp. 47–60; R. M. Cyert, H. A. Simon, and D. B. Trow, "Observation of a Business Decision," *Journal of Business*, October 1956, pp. 237–48; and James Brian Quinn, *Strategies for Change: Logical Incrementalism* (Homewood, Ill.: Richard D. Irwin, 1980).

[18] Quinn, *Strategies for Change*, p. 68.

[19] This statement was made by Sir Alastair Pilkington, Chairman, Pilkington Brothers, Ltd.; the quote appears in Quinn, *Strategies for Change*, p. 65.

[20] Quinn, *Strategies for Change*, pp. 128–45.

- Letting weakly supported ideas and proposals die through inaction.
- Establishing additional hurdles or tests for strongly supported ideas which the manager views as unacceptable but which are best not opposed openly.
- Keeping a low political profile on unacceptable proposals by getting subordinate managers to say no.
- Letting most negative decisions come from a group consensus that the manager merely confirms, thereby reserving one's own personal vetoes for big issues and crucial moments.
- Leading the strategy but not dictating it—giving few orders, announcing few decisions, depending heavily on informal questioning, and seeking to probe and clarify until a consensus emerges.
- Staying alert to the symbolic impact of one's actions and statements, lest a false signal stimulate proposals and movements in unwanted directions.
- Ensuring that all major power bases within the organization have representation in or access to top management.
- Injecting new faces and new views into considerations of major changes, so as to preclude those who are primarily involved from coming to see the world the same way and then acting as systematic screens against other views.
- Minimizing one's own political exposure on issues which are highly controversial and in circumstances where opposition from major power centers can trigger a "shootout."

The politics of strategy implementation is especially critical in attempting to introduce a new strategy against the support enjoyed by the old strategy. Except for crisis situations where the old strategy is plainly revealed as out-of-date, it is usually bad politics to push the new strategy via attacks on the old strategy.[21] Bad-mouthing old strategy can easily be interpreted as an attack on those who formulated it and those who supported it in the enterprise's climb to its present success. Besides, the former strategy and the judgments behind it may have been well suited to the organization's earlier circumstances, and the people who made these judgments may still be in positions where support for the new strategy is important.

In addition, a wise manager will recognize that there are a variety of legitimate views as to what can and should be done in the present circumstances; the new strategy and/or the plans for implementing it may thus not have been the first choices of others and lingering doubts may remain. Consequently, in trying to surmount resistance, nothing is gained by "knocking" the views of those who argued for alternative approaches. Such attacks are likely to produce alienation instead of cooperation.

In short, to bring the full force of an organization behind a strategic plan calls for the strategy manager to assess and deal with the most important centers of potential support and opposition to new strategic thrusts.[22] One needs to secure the support of key people, co-opt or neutralize serious opposition and resistance when and where necessary, and learn where the zones of indifference are.

---

[21] Ibid., pp. 118–19.
[22] Ibid., p. 205.

Leading the Process of Making Corrective Adjustments

No strategic plan and no scheme for strategy implementation can foresee all the events and problems that will arise. Making adjustments and "mid-course" corrections are therefore a normal and necessary part of strategic management.

Consider, first, the case of reacting and responding to new conditions involving either the strategy or its implementation. The process of what to do starts with an evaluation of whether immediate action needs to be taken or whether time permits a more deliberate response. In a crisis, the approach typically is to wield a heavy hand in pushing key subordinates to gather as much information as time permits and to formulate recommendations for consideration, personally presiding over extended discussions of the pros and cons of proposed responses, and trying to build a quick consensus among members of the executive "inner circle." If no consensus emerges or if several key subordinates remain divided in their views, the burden falls on the strategy manager to choose the response and urge "best efforts" support of it.

In cases where time permits a full-fledged evaluation, strategy managers seem to prefer a process of incrementally solidifying commitment to a response.[23] The approach seems to be one of consciously:

1. Staying flexible and keeping a number of options open.
2. Asking a lot of questions.
3. Gaining in-depth information from specialists.
4. Encouraging subordinates to participate in developing alternatives and proposing solutions.
5. Getting the reactions of many different people to proposed solutions, as a test of their potential and political acceptability.
6. Seeking to build commitment to a response by gradually moving toward a consensus solution.

The governing principle seems to be to make a final decision as late as possible so as to (1) bring as much information to bear as is needed, (2) let the situation clarify enough to know what to do, and (3) allow the various political constituencies and power bases within the organization to move toward a consensus solution. Executives are often wary of committing themselves to a major change too soon because it discourages others from asking questions that need to be raised.

Corrective adjustments to strategy need not be just reactive, however. Proactive adjustments constitute a second approach to improving strategy or its implementation. The distinctive feature of a proactive posture is that adjusting actions arise out of management's own drives and initiatives for better performance as opposed to forced reactions. Successful strategy managers have been observed to employ a variety of proactive tactics.[24]

1. Commissioning studies to explore areas where they have a "gut feeling" or clue that something needs to be done.
2. Shopping ideas among trusted colleagues and putting forth trial balloons.

---

[23] Ibid., pp. 20–22.

[24] Ibid., chap. 4.

3. Teaming people with different skills, interests, and experiences, and letting them push and tug on interesting ideas to expand the variety of approaches considered.
4. Contacting a variety of people inside and outside the organization to sample viewpoints, probe, and listen, thereby trying to get early warning signals of impending problems/issues and deliberately short-circuiting all the careful screens of information flowing up from below.
5. Stimulating proposals for improvement from lower levels, encouraging the development of competing ideas and approaches, and letting the momentum for change come from below, with final choices being postponed until it is apparent which option best matches the organization's situation.
6. Seeking options and solutions that go beyond mere extrapolations from the status quo.
7. Accepting and committing to partial steps forward as a way of building up comfort levels before going on ahead.
8. Managing the politics of change so as to promote managerial consensus-building and to solidify management's commitment to whatever course of action is chosen.

Both the reactive and proactive approaches exhibit commonality in the process of deciding what adjusting actions to take. The leadership sequence seems to be one of sensing needs, gathering information, amplifying understanding and awareness, developing options, exploring the pros and cons, testing proposals, generating partial solutions, empowering champions, building a managerial consensus, and formally adopting an agreed-upon course of action.[25] The ultimate managerial prescription may have been given by Rene McPherson, former CEO at Dana Corporation. In speaking to a class of students at Stanford, he said, "You just keep pushing. You just keep pushing. I made every mistake that could be made. But I just kept pushing."[26]

This points to a key feature of strategic management. The job of formulating and implementing strategy is not one of steering a clear-cut, linear course of carrying out the original strategy intact according to some preconceived and highly detailed implementation plan. Rather, it is one of creatively (1) adapting and reshaping strategy to unfolding events and (2) employing analytical-behavioral-political techniques to bring internal activities and attitudes into alignment with strategy. The process is iterative, with much looping and recycling to fine-tune and adjust in a continuously evolving process whereby the conceptually separate acts of strategy formulation and strategy implementation blur and join together.

ANALYTICAL CHECKLIST

The action menu for implementing strategy is expansive. Virtually every aspect of administrative work comes into play; the checklist of what is involved includes

- Building a capable organization—choosing an appropriate structure, establishing a distinctive competence, and selecting people for key positions.

---

[25] Quinn, *Strategies for Change,* p. 146.
[26] As quoted in Peters and Waterman, *In Search of Excellence,* p. 319.

- Formulating strategy-supportive budget allocations and programs.
- Galvanizing commitment to strategy execution via creative use of reward systems and recognition of high performers.
- Devising policies, information and reporting networks, and internal support systems to facilitate strategy execution.
- Trying to build a strategy-supportive culture and work climate.
- Aligning and coordinating internal organization processes to fit the requirements of strategy.
- Taking into account the overall organizational situation in which implementation must take place—the degree of strategic change called for, the type of strategy being implemented, and the nature and seriousness of existing internal problems.
- Deciding on a leadership approach—whether to push hard for rapid change or accept gradual adjustments, whether to be authoritative or seek consensus and broad participation, and whether to adopt a high profile or a low profile.

Use Figures 8–1 and 8–2 to check whether you have touched all the main bases.

Because the organizational circumstances of strategy implementation are so idiosyncratic, a manager's action agenda for implementing a given strategy is always a function of the specifics of the situation at hand. This makes the challenge to "make it happen" big, varied, and interesting, with lots of room for managerial creativity.

SUGGESTED READING

Adizes, Ichak. "Mismanagement Styles." *California Management Review* 19, no. 2 (Winter 1976), pp. 5–20.

Bennis, Warren and Burt Nanus. *Leaders: The Strategies for Taking Charge.* New York: Harper & Row, Publishers, 1985.

Deal, Terence E., and Allen A. Kennedy. *Corporate Cultures.* Reading, Mass.: Addison-Wesley Publishing , 1982, especially chaps. 1 and 2.

Drucker, Peter F. *Management: Tasks, Responsibilities, Practices.* New York: Harper & Row, 1974, chaps. 16–19 and 33–39.

Gabarro, J. J. "When a New Manager Takes Charge." *Harvard Business Review* 64, no. 3 (May–June 1985), pp. 110–23.

Hall, Jay. "To Achieve or Not: The Manager's Choice." *California Management Review* 18, no. 4 (Summer 1976), pp. 5–18.

Herzberg, Frederick. "One More Time: How Do You Motivate Employees." *Harvard Business Review* 51, no. 3 (May–June 1973), pp. 162–80.

Hosmer, LaRue T. "The Importance of Strategic Leadership." *Journal of Business Strategy* 3, no. 2 (Fall 1982), pp. 47–57.

Machiavelli, Niccolo. *The Prince.* New York: Washington Square Press, 1963.

McClelland, David C., and David H. Burnham. "Power Is the Great Motivator." *Harvard Business Review* 54, no. 2 (March–April 1976), pp. 100–110.

Oliver, Alex R., and Joseph R. Garber. "Implementing Strategic Planning: Ten Sure-Fire Ways to Do It Wrong." *Business Horizons* 16, no. 2 (March–April 1983), pp. 49–51.

Pascale, Richard. "The Paradox of 'Corporate Culture': Reconciling Ourselves to Socialization." *California Management Review* 27, no. 2 (Winter 1985), pp. 26–41.

Peters, Thomas J., and Robert H. Waterman. *In Search of Excellence.* New York: Harper & Row, 1982, chaps. 4, 5, and 9.

Peters, Thomas J., and Nancy Austin. *A Passion for Excellence.* New York: Random House, 1985, especially chaps. 11, 12, 15–19.

Quinn, James Brian. *Strategies for Change: Logical Incrementalism.* Homewood, Ill.: Richard D. Irwin, 1980, chap. 4.

————. "Managing Innovation: Controlled Chaos." *Harvard Business Review* 64, no. 3 (May–June 1985), pp. 73–84.

Schwartz, Howard, and Stanley H. Davis. "Matching Corporate Culture and Business Strategy." *Organizational Dynamics,* Summer 1981, pp. 30–48.

Tannenbaum, Robert, and Warren H. Schmidt. "How to Choose a Leadership Pattern." *Harvard Business Review* 51, no. 3 (May–June 1973), pp. 162–80.

Zalenik, Abraham. "Power and Politics in Organizational Life." *Harvard Business Review* 48, no. 3 (May–June 1970), pp. 47–60.

Part 2

From Concepts to Cases: Practicing Strategic Analysis

10 Analyzing a Case

In most courses in strategic management, students practice at being strategy managers via case analysis. A case sets forth, in a factual manner, the events and organizational circumstances surrounding a particular managerial situation. It puts the readers at the scene of the action and familiarizes them with the situation as it prevailed. A case on strategic management can concern a whole industry, a single organization, or some part of an organization; the organization involved can be either profit-seeking or not-for-profit. The essence of the student's role in case analysis is to *diagnose* and *size up* the situation described in the case and recommend what, if any, actions need to be taken.

Why Use Cases to Practice Strategic Management?

A student of business with tact
Absorbed many answers he lacked.
But acquiring a job,
He said with a sob,
"How *does* one fit answer to fact?"

The foregoing limerick was offered some years ago by Charles I. Gragg in a classic article, "Because Wisdom Can't Be Told," to characterize the plight of business students who had no exposure to cases.[1] Gragg observed that the mere act of listening to lectures and sound advice about managing does little for anyone's management skills and that the accumulated managerial experience and wisdom cannot effectively be passed

---

[1] Charles I. Gragg, "Because Wisdom Can't Be Told," in *The Case Method at the Harvard Business School,* ed. M. P. McNair (New York: McGraw-Hill, 1954), p. 11.

on by lectures and readings alone. Gragg suggested that if anything has been learned about the practice of management, it is that a storehouse of ready-made textbook answers does not exist. Each managerial situation has unique aspects, requiring its own diagnosis, judgment, and tailor-made actions. Cases provide would-be managers with a valuable way to practice wrestling with the actual problems of actual companies.

The case approach to strategic analysis is, indeed, learning by doing. The case method of instruction builds on the benefits of acquiring managerial "experience" and skills by analyzing company after company and situation after situation. Another big justification for case analysis is that few college students have much direct personal contact with different kinds of companies and real-life strategic situations. Cases offer a viable substitute by bringing a variety of industries, organizations, and strategic problems into the classroom, permitting students to assume the manager's role, and providing a test of how to apply the tools and techniques of strategic management.

Objectives of Case Analysis

Using cases to learn about strategic management produces four student-related results:[2]

1. Helping you to apply textbook knowledge about strategic management and to become more skilled in the art and science of situation analysis.
2. Getting you out of the habit of being a receiver of facts, concepts, and techniques and into the habit of diagnosing problems, analyzing and evaluating alternatives, and formulating workable plans of action.
3. Training you to work out answers and solutions for yourself, as opposed to relying on the authoritative crutch of the professor or "back-of-the-book" answers.
4. Providing you with exposure to a range of firms and strategy-related situations (which might take a lifetime to experience personally), thus creating a background of "experience" for beginning your own business career.

If you understand that these are the objectives of case analysis, then you are less likely to be consumed with curiosity about "the answer to the case." Being accustomed to textbook statements of fact and supposedly definitive lecture notes, students find that case discussions often do not produce concrete answers. Usually, a good argument can be made for more than one course of action. If the class discussion concludes without clear indications of what to do, some students become frustrated because they are not told "what the answer is" or "what the company actually did."

However, business situations where answers are not clear cut are common. In reality, several feasible courses of action may exist. Moreover, in the business world when one elects a particular course of action, there is no peeking at the back of a book to see if you have chosen the best thing to do and no provably correct answers exist. The only really valid test of management action is results. If the results turn out to be "good," the decision may be presumed "right"; if not, then it was "wrong" in the sense that it "didn't work out." Hence, the important thing for a student to

---

[2] Ibid., pp. 12–14; and D. R. Schoen and Philip A. Sprague, "What Is the Case Method?" in McNair, *The Case Method at the Harvard Business School*, pp. 78–79.

understand in case analysis is that it is the managerial exercise of identifying, diagnosing, and recommending that builds your skills; discovering "the right answer" or finding out what actually happened is no more than frosting on the cake.

To put it another way, *the purpose of case analysis is not to run to the library to look up what the company actually did but rather to become skilled in evaluating the options for solving the actual problems of actual companies using only the information the company's managers had when they had to make their decisions.* The aim of case analysis is for you to bear the strains of thinking actively, of making managerial assessments which may be vigorously challenged, of offering your analysis, and of proposing action plans—this is how you are provided with meaningful practice at being a manager.

The Student's Role in Case Analysis

If this is your first experience with the case method, you may have to reorient your study habits. Unlike lecture courses, where there is no imperative of specific preparation before each class and where assigned readings and reviews of lecture notes may be done at irregular intervals, *a case assignment requires conscientious preparation before class.* You will not get much out of hearing the class discuss a case with which you are totally unfamiliar, and you certainly won't be able to contribute anything to the discussion yourself. The case method of teaching/learning represents a radical departure from the lecture/discussion/problem classroom technique. Members of the class do most of the talking. The instructor's role is to solicit student participation and guide the discussion. Typically, members of the class will evaluate and test their opinions as much in discussions with each other as with the instructor. But regardless of whether the discussion emphasis is instructor-student or student-student, *members of the class carry the burden for analyzing the situation and for being prepared to present and defend their diagnosis and recommendations.* Be prepared for a discussion involving *your* size-up of the situation, what actions *you* would take, and why would *you* take them.[3]

Begin preparing for class by reading the case once for familiarity. An initial reading should give you the general flavor of the situation and make possible preliminary identification of issues. On the second reading, attempt to gain full command of the facts. Strive for a sharp, clear-cut "size-up" of the issues posed in the case situation.

To help diagnose the situation, put yourself in the position of some manager portrayed in the case and pick out the key issues where decisions have to be made. Do not be dismayed if you find it impractical to isolate the problems and issues into distinct categories; in addition, expect the cases in this book to contain several problems and issues, not just one. Guard against making an oversimplified statement of the problem unless the strategic issue is very clear cut. Work at getting a good grip on the condition of the company, the industry situation, and the economics of the business. Get a handle on what it takes to be successful in the industry and assess the nature and strength of competition; this is essential if you are to come up with solutions

---

[3] Schoen and Sprague, "What Is the Case Method?" p. 80.

which will be both workable and acceptable in light of the prevailing external constraints and internal organizational realities.

Conducting a Strategic Analysis of a Company

Developing an ability to evaluate companies and size up their situations is the core of what strategic analysis is all about. The cases in this book are all strategy related and each requires some form of strategic analysis. To help you analyze them, consult the fairly comprehensive analytical checklists presented at the ends of Chapters 3 through 9. Not all of the checklist items have to be dealt with in each case; use the checklists to jog your thinking about what needs to be considered in the case at hand and quickly skip over the items that don't come into play. Use Table 10–1 to stimulate and guide whatever financial calculations are called for.

In preparing the case, do not rely solely on your opinion; support it with evidence! Crunch the numbers! *If your instructor has provided you with specific study questions for the case, by all means prepare notes on how you would answer them. Include in your notes all the reasons and evidence you can muster to support your diagnosis and evaluation.*

When information in the case is conflicting or various opinions are contradictory, decide which is more valid and why. Forcing you to make judgments about the validity of the data and information presented in the case is to help you develop your powers of judgment and inference. It is realistic because a great many managerial situations entail conflicting points of view.

Once you have thoroughly diagnosed the company's situation and weighed the pros and cons of various alternative courses of action, the final step of case analysis is to decide what you think the company needs to do to improve its performance. Draw up your set of recommendations on "what to do" and be prepared to present your "action agenda." This is really the most crucial part of the process of case analysis; diagnosis divorced from corrective action is sterile. But bear in mind that proposing realistic, workable solutions and offering a hasty, ill-conceived "possibility" are not the same. *Don't recommend anything you would not be prepared to do yourself if you were in the decision maker's shoes.* Be sure you can give reasons why your recommendations are preferable to other options which exist. Be wary of rushing to include as part of your recommendation "the need to get more information." From time to time, of course, a search for additional information may be entirely appropriate, but you must also recognize that the organization's managers may not have had any more information available than that presented in the case. Before recommending that action be postponed until additional facts are uncovered, be sure that you think it will be worthwhile to get them and that the organization can afford to wait. In general, though, try to recommend a course of action based on the evidence you have at hand.

Remember that rarely is there a "right" decision or just one "optimal" plan of action or an "approved" solution. Your goal should be to develop what you think is a pragmatic, defensible course of action which is based on a serious analysis of the situation and which appears to you to be "right" in view of your assessment and weighing of the facts. Admittedly, someone else may evaluate the same facts in

Table 10–1   A Summary of Key Financial Ratios, How They Are Calculated, and What They Show

Ratio	How Calculated	What It Shows
Profitability ratios:		
1. Gross profit margin	$$\frac{\text{Sales} - \text{Cost of goods sold}}{\text{Sales revenues}}$$	An indication of the total margin available to cover internal operating expenses and yield a profit.
2. Operating profit margin	$$\frac{\text{Profits before taxes and interest}}{\text{Sales revenues}}$$	An indication of the firm's profitability from current operations without regard to the interest charges accruing from the capital structure.
3. Net profit margin (or net return on sales)	$$\frac{\text{Profits after taxes}}{\text{Sales revenues}}$$	Shows aftertax profits per dollar of sales. Subpar-profit margins indicate that the firm's sales prices are relatively low or that its costs are relatively high, or both.
4. Return on total assets	$$\frac{\text{Profits after taxes}}{\text{Total assets}}$$ or $$\frac{\text{Profits after taxes} + \text{Interest}}{\text{Total assets}}$$	A measure of the return on total investment in the enterprise. It is sometimes desirable to add interest to the numerator of the ratio since total assets are financed by creditors as well as by stockholders; hence, it is accurate to measure the productivity of assets by the returns provided to both classes of investors.
5. Return on stockholders' equity (or return on net worth)	$$\frac{\text{Profits after taxes}}{\text{Total stockholders' equity}}$$	A measure of the rate of return on stockholders' investment in the enterprise.
6. Return on common equity	$$\frac{\text{Profits after taxes} - \text{Preferred stock dividends}}{\text{Total stockholders equity} - \text{Par value of preferred stock}}$$	A measure of the rate of return on the investment that the owners of common stock have made in the enterprise.
7. Earnings per share	$$\frac{\text{Profits after taxes} - \text{Preferred stock dividends}}{\text{Number of shares of common stock outstanding}}$$	Shows the earnings available to the owners of common stock.
Liquidity ratios:		
1. Current ratio	$$\frac{\text{Current assets}}{\text{Current liabilities}}$$	Indicates the extent to which the claims of short-term creditors are covered by assets that are expected to be converted to cash in a period roughly corresponding to the maturity of the liabilities.
2. Quick ratio (or acid-test ratio)	$$\frac{\text{Current assets} - \text{Inventory}}{\text{Current liabilities}}$$	A measure of the firm's ability to pay off short-term obligations without relying on the sale of its inventories.
3. Inventory to net working capital	$$\frac{\text{Inventory}}{\text{Current assets} - \text{Current liabilities}}$$	A measure of the extent to which the firm's working capital is tied up in inventory.
Leverage ratios:		
1. Debt to assets ratio	$$\frac{\text{Total debt}}{\text{Total assets}}$$	Measures the extent to which borrowed funds have been used to finance the firm's operations.

Table 10–1 *(concluded)*

Ratio	How Calculated	What It Shows
2. Debt to equity ratio	$\dfrac{\text{Total debt}}{\text{Total stockholders' equity}}$	Provides another measure of the funds provided by creditors versus the funds provided by owners.
3. Long-term debt to equity ratio	$\dfrac{\text{Long-term debt}}{\text{Total stockholders' equity}}$	A widely used measure of the balance between debt and equity in the firm's long-term capital structure.
4. Times-interest-earned (or coverage) ratio	$\dfrac{\text{Profits before interest and taxes}}{\text{Total interest charges}}$	Measures the extent to which earnings can decline without the firm becoming unable to meet its annual interest costs.
5. Fixed-charge coverage	$\dfrac{\text{Profit before taxes and interest} + \text{Lease obligations}}{\text{Total interest charges} + \text{Lease obligations}}$	A more inclusive indication of the firm's ability to meet all of its fixed charge obligations.

Activity ratios:

Ratio	How Calculated	What It Shows
1. Inventory turnover	$\dfrac{\text{Sales revenues}}{\text{Inventory of finished goods}}$	When compared to industry averages, it provides an indication of whether a company has excessive or perhaps inadequate finished goods inventory.
2. Fixed assets turnover	$\dfrac{\text{Sales revenues}}{\text{Fixed assets}}$	A measure of the sales productivity and utilization of plant and equipment.
3. Total assets turnover	$\dfrac{\text{Sales revenues}}{\text{Total assets}}$	A measure of the utilization of all the firm's assets; a ratio below the industry average indicates the company is not generating a sufficient volume of business given the size of its asset investment.
4. Accounts receivable turnover	$\dfrac{\text{Annual credit sales}}{\text{Accounts receivable}}$	A measure of the average length of time it takes the firm to collect the sales made on credit.
5. Average collection period	$\dfrac{\text{Accounts receivable}}{\text{Total sales} \div 365}$ or $\dfrac{\text{Accounts receivable}}{\text{Average daily sales}}$	Indicates the average length of time the firm must wait after making a sale before its receives payment.

Other ratios:

Ratio	How Calculated	What It Shows
1. Dividend yield on common stock	$\dfrac{\text{Annual dividends per share}}{\text{Current market price per share}}$	A measure of the return to owners received in the form of dividends.
2. Price-earnings ratio	$\dfrac{\text{Current market price per share}}{\text{After-tax earnings per share}}$	Faster growing or less risky firms *tend* to have higher price-earnings ratios than do slower growing or more risky firms.
3. Dividend payout ratio	$\dfrac{\text{Annual dividends per share}}{\text{After-tax earnings per share}}$	Indicates the percentage of profits paid out as dividends.
4. Cash flow per share	$\dfrac{\text{After-tax profits} + \text{Depreciation}}{\text{Number of common shares outstanding}}$	A measure of the discretionary funds over and above expenses available for use by the firm.

Note: Industry-average ratios against which a particular company's ratios may be judged are available in *Modern Industry* and *Dun's Reviews* published by Dun & Bradstreet (14 ratios for 125 lines of business activity), Robert Morris Associates' *Annual Statement Studies* (11 ratios for 156 lines of business), and the FTC–SEC's *Quarterly Financial Report* for manufacturing corporations.

another way and thus have a different "right" solution; but since several good plans of action can normally be conceived, you should not be afraid to stick by your own analysis and judgment.

The Classroom Experience

During class discussion of a case, you will see very quickly that you have not thought of everything in the case that your fellow students have thought of. While you will see things others did not, they will see things you did not. Do not be dismayed or alarmed by this. It is normal. As the old adage goes, "Two heads are better than one." So it is to be expected that the class as a whole will do a more penetrating and searching job of case analysis than will any one person working alone. This is the power of group effort, and one of its virtues is that it will give you more insight into the management options and how to wrestle with differences of opinion. Keep the following points in mind:

1. The case method enlists a maximum of individual participation in class discussion. It is not enough to be present as a silent observer; if every student took this approach, then there would be no discussion. (Thus, do not be surprised if a portion of your grade is based on your participation in case discussions.)

2. Although you should do your own independent work and independent thinking, don't hesitate to discuss the case with other students. Managers often discuss their problems with other key people.

3. During case discussions, expect and tolerate challenges to the views expressed. Be willing to submit your conclusions for scrutiny and rebuttal. State your views without fear of disapproval and overcome the hesitation of speaking out.

4. In orally presenting and defending your ideas, strive to be convincing and persuasive. Always give supporting evidence and reasons.

5. Expect the instructor to assume the role of extensive questioner and listener. Expect to be "cross-examined" for evidence and reasons by your instructor or by others in the class. Expect students to dominate the discussion and do most of the talking.

6. Although discussion of a case is a group process, this does not imply conformity to group opinion. Learning respect for the views and approaches of others is an integral part of case analysis exercises. But be willing to "swim against the tide" of majority opinion. In the practice of management, there is always room for originality, unorthodoxy, and unique personality.

7. In participating in the discussion, make a conscious effort to contribute, rather than just talk. There is a big difference between saying something that builds the discussion and offering a long-winded, off-the-cuff remark that leaves the class wondering what the point was.

8. In making your points, assume that everyone has read the case and knows what "the case says"; avoid reciting and rehashing information in the case— instead, use the data and information to support your position.

9. Avoid the use of "I think . . . ," "I believe . . . ," and "I feel . . . "; instead, say "My analysis shows . . . " and "The company should do . . . because . . . ."

10. Don't be surprised if you change your mind about some things as the discussion unfolds. Be alert for how these changes affect your analysis and recommendations (in case you get called on). You will learn a lot from each case discussion; use what you learn to be better prepared for the next case discussion.

Preparing a Written Case Analysis

Preparing a written case analysis is much like preparing a case for class discussion, except that your analysis must be more complete and reduced to writing. Unfortunately, though, *there is no ironclad procedure for doing a written case analysis.* All that we can offer are some general guidelines and words of wisdom—this is because company situations and management problems are so diverse that no one mode of analysis can really suffice.

Your instructor may assign you a specific topic around which to prepare your written report. Or, alternatively, you may be asked to do a "comprehensive written case analysis" where the expectation is that you will: (1) *identify* all the pertinent issues that management needs to address; (2) perform whatever *analysis* and *evaluation* is appropriate; and (3) propose an *action plan* and set of *recommendations* addressing the issues you have identified. In going through the exercise of *identify, evaluate,* and *recommend,* you should keep the following pointers in mind.[4]

Identification   It is essential that your paper reflect a sharply focused diagnosis of strategic issues and key problems and, further, that you "size up" the company's present situation. Make sure you can identify the firm's strategy (use Figures 2–3 and 2–4 in Chapter 2 as your diagnostic aids) and that you have pinpointed whatever strategy implementation issues exist (consult Figures 8–1 and 8–2 for diagnostic help). You should consider beginning your paper by "sizing up" the company's situation, its strategy, and the significant problems and issues which confront management. State problems/issues as clearly and precisely as you can. Unless it is necessary to do so for emphasis, avoid recounting facts and history about the company (assume your professor has read the case and is familiar with the organization).

Analysis and Evaluation   This is usually the hardest part of the report. Analysis is hard work! Study the tables, exhibits, and financial statements in the case carefully. Check out the firm's financial ratios, its profit margins and rates of return, and its capital structure, and decide how strong the firm is financially. Table 10–1 contains a summary of various financial ratios and how they are calculated. Similarly, look at marketing, production, managerial competences, and other factors underlying the organization's strategic successes and failures. Decide whether it has a distinctive competence and, if so, whether it is capitalizing on it.

Check to see if the firm's strategy is working and determine the reasons why or why not. Use the Analytical Checklists at the end of Chapters 3–9 as guides for

---

[4] For some additional ideas and viewpoints, you may wish to consult Thomas J. Raymond, "Written Analysis of Cases," in *The Case Method at the Harvard Business School,* ed. McNair pp. 139–63. In Raymond's article is an actual case, a sample analysis of the case, and a sample of a student's written report on the case.

conducting your strategy analysis. Probe the nature and strength of the competitive forces confronting the company. Decide whether and why the firm's competitive position is getting stronger or weaker. Use the tools and concepts presented in the text to perform whatever analysis and evaluation is appropriate.

In writing your analysis and evaluation, bear in mind four things:

1. You are obliged to offer supporting evidence for your views and judgments. Do not rely on unsupported opinions, overgeneralizations, and platitudes as a substitute for tight logical argument backed up with facts and figures.
2. If your analysis involves some important quantitative calculations, then use tables and charts to present the calculations clearly and efficiently. Don't just tack the exhibits on at the end of your report and let the reader figure out what they mean and why they were included. Instead, in the body of your report cite some of the key numbers, highlight the conclusions to be drawn from the exhibits, and refer the reader to your charts and exhibits for more details.
3. Demonstrate that you have command of the tools and concepts presented in the text. Use them in your analysis.
4. Your interpretation of the evidence should be reasonable and objective. Be wary of preparing a one-sided argument which omits all aspects not favorable to your conclusions. Likewise, try not to exaggerate or overdramatize. Endeavor to inject balance into your analysis and to avoid emotional rhetoric. Strike phrases like "I think," "I feel," and "I believe" when you edit your first draft.

Recommendations   The final section of the written case analysis should consist of a set of definite recommendations and a plan of action. Your set of recommendations should address all of the problems/issues you identified and analyzed. If the recommendations come as a surprise or do not follow logically from the analysis, the effect is to weaken greatly your suggestions of what to do. Obviously, your recommendations for action should offer a reasonable prospect of success. High risk, bet-the-company recommendations should be made with caution. State how your recommendations will "solve" the problems you identified. Be sure that the company is financially able to carry out what you recommend; also check to see if your recommendations are workable in terms of acceptance by the persons involved, the organization's competence to implement them, and prevailing market and environmental constraints. Try not to hedge or weasel on the actions you believe should be taken.

By all means state your recommendations in sufficient detail to be meaningful— get down to some definite "nitty-gritty" specifics. Avoid such unhelpful statements as "the organization should do more planning" or "the company should be more aggressive in marketing its product." For instance, do not stop with saying, "the firm should improve its market position," but continue on with exactly how you think this should be done. Offer a definite agenda for action, stipulating a timetable and sequence for initiating actions, indicating priorities, and suggesting who should be responsible for doing what.

In proposing an action plan, remember there is a great deal of difference between being responsible, on the one hand, for a decision which may be costly if it proves in error and, on the other hand, casually suggesting courses of action which might be taken when you do not have to bear the responsibility for any of the consequences.

A good rule to follow in making your recommendations is to *avoid recommending anything you would not yourself be willing to do if you were in management's shoes.* The importance of learning to develop good judgment in a managerial situation is indicated by the fact that, while the same information and operating data may be available to every manager or executive in an organization, the quality of the judgments about what the information means and what actions need to be taken do vary from person to person.[5]

Your report should be well organized and well written. Great ideas amount to little unless others can be convinced of their merit—this takes tight logic, the presentation of convincing evidence, and a persuasively written argument.

---

[5] Gragg, "Because Wisdom Can't Be Told," p. 10.

Part 3

Cases in Strategic Management

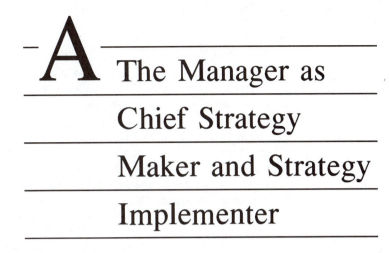

A The Manager as Chief Strategy Maker and Strategy Implementer

CASE 1 ROBERT E. (TED) TURNER III*

Robert E. (Ted) Turner III was born in 1938 in Cincinnati, where his father, Ed, was in the outdoor advertising business. In the early 1940s, Ed Turner purchased a billboard firm in Savannah, Georgia, and moved his family there, where Ted got his first taste of the sea and sailing. Ted Turner's father was a stern, tough, self-made man who came from a poor, farm background in Mississippi. As a youngster, Ted was told to read a book every two days.[1] He was disciplined with a wire coat hanger. At 11, Ted was sent to McCallie Military School in Chattanooga, Tennessee; even though he professed dislike of the school, he completed six years at McCallie and graduated in the top 15 percent of his class as a company commander. (Later, he sent his own son, Robert Edward Turner IV, to McCallie.) At 17, he won the Tennessee State Debate Championship by redefining the basic question and taking an approach no one was prepared to debate.

During the summers of his high school years, he worked in the family business digging postholes and doing other manual labor tasks; one summer Ted worked a 40-hour week, was paid $50, and then was charged $25 a week to live at home.

In this, the heyday of the large corporation that follows the morally and socially neutral judgments of committees of lawyers and accountants, Ted Turner is a character—in the best sense of that much misused word. He is in the great tradition of the individual entrepreneur who had a dream and backed it with his money and his sweat.
—George N. Allen
Washington Journalism Review

---

* Prepared by Professor Arthur A. Thompson, Jr., the University of Alabama, with the research assistance of Miriam Aiken.

[1] Curry Kirkpatrick, "Going Real Strawwng," *Sports Illustrated,* October 14, 1977.

As Ted viewed it, "My father put the screws to me early. If he hadn't, I never would have survived. My father made me a man."

Upon graduation from McCallie, it was agreed by Ted and his father that he would enroll at Brown University in Providence, Rhode Island. When Ted informed his businessman father that he was planning to major in classics, his father wrote him a letter (which Ted had published in the school newspaper) describing Plato and Aristotle as "old bastards" and ending with the observation that "you are rapidly becoming a jackass, and the sooner you get out of that filthy atmosphere, the better. . . . You are in the hands of the Philistines, and dammit, I sent you there. I am sorry, Devotedly, Dad." Later, Ted switched his major to economics.

Turner's college years at Brown were eventful. He shot a rifle from his dorm window and was thrown out of his fraternity for burning down its homecoming display. During his sophomore year when his father refused to let him take a summer job at a Connecticut yacht club, he broke his agreement to refrain from drinking until he was 21 (for which he was to get a $5,000 reward), got drunk, and then got caught in a dorm room at Wheaton, a girl's college in nearby Norton, Massachusetts; Brown University officials expelled him. He joined the Coast Guard for a short stint and then was readmitted to Brown. He became vice president of the debating union and commodore of the yacht club. But in his senior year he was expelled again when a Wheaton girl was caught in his dorm room.

Without a degree, he returned in 1960 to Georgia, where he went to work for his father and learned the business from the bottom up. His assigned tasks included posting the books and cutting weeds around billboards. A short time later, his father sent him to Macon to run the firm's branch office. In 1962 the elder Turner arranged to more than triple the size of his company and, with borrowed funds, he purchased billboard operations in Atlanta; Richmond, Virginia; and Roanoke, Virginia. Within a year Turner's father had a breakdown and committed suicide.

THE FIRST CHALLENGE

Ted, at age 24, found himself in charge of a struggling business that was short of cash and $6 million in debt. The company's bankers advised Ted that they didn't believe the business could survive under his unseasoned management and expressed reluctance at financing further operations. Turner was given an opportunity to sell out but refused and ended up persuading the lenders to stick with him a while longer. He then sold off some assets to improve the company's cash position, arranged for some innovative financing, reworked contracts with customers, hired a sales force, and proceeded to turn things around. Within two years the company was making its loan payments on time, and by 1969 the debt was paid off.

THE SECOND CHALLENGE

With the company now secure, Turner began to prospect for new growth opportunities. He felt that the billboard business had only limited growth potential and was not challenging enough (it took only about half of his time to run things), so he elected to diversify into something more exciting. The first acquisitions were two radio stations in Chattanooga, a move which prompted Ted Turner to rename his company Turner Communications Corporation. Turner wanted to buy a radio outlet in Atlanta, but nothing attractive was available at the right price. In 1970 he settled for acquiring financially strapped WTCG-TV, Channel 17, a two-year-old, independent UHF station that was losing $50,000 per month trying to compete with Atlanta's three network affiliates, WSB-TV, WAGA-TV, and WXIA-TV. To finance the acquisition of Channel 17, Turner Communications Corporation went public, and its stock was traded in local over-the-counter markets; Ted Turner retained about 47 percent of the stock.

Turner's biggest problem in turning Channel 17's operations around was how to get Atlanta TV viewers to watch Channel 17 programs instead of the programs carried on the three major network stations. Writer Roger Vaughn, who knew Turner in college, has written two books about him, and has sailed with him, described Turner's efforts:

> When Turner bought Channel 17, there was another independent in the Atlanta market. It belonged to United States Communications and was one of five stations in the country owned by that company, a subsidiary of the American Viscose conglomerate. It was a fact that the Atlanta market could not support two independents. "Ted knew this," one of the early Channel 17 employees says, "but I doubt if he realized how serious the situation was." Only one of the stations was going to survive, and it didn't look like it would be Channel 17, which was running a solid fifth out of five Atlanta stations.
>
> The instability of the situation was reflected in the fact that in the first 22 months of Turner's ownership, the personnel of the station turned over twice. By the spring of 1971, every spare dollar Turner could find had been poured into the station. As Will Sanders recalls, the whole show was about to sink. Then overnight, without warning, the U.S. Communications station folded. It was a high stroke of luck for Turner, a lifeline for a drowning man.
>
> In one day, Channel 17 went from fifth of five stations to fourth of four. As the only independent in Atlanta, the way ahead was clear for development, but the problems were still immense. UHF reception was terrible, for one thing. . . .
>
> "I can remember going into an advertiser's office and asking him to buy time on Channel 17," Turner says. "The answer would be 'We don't buy UHF.' And I would tell them, 'Why not? It's coming, like FM radio. We're not asking you to pay for the future. We're just asking you to buy our audience at the same cost per thousand. Our audience isn't very big, but our viewers are way above the average viewers' mentality.'
>
> "And they would say, 'How do you know that? How come!' and I would tell them, 'Because you have got to be smart to figure out how to tune in a UHF antenna in the first place. Dumb guys can't do it. Can you get Channel 17? No? Well, neither can I. We aren't smart enough. But my viewers are.'
>
> "Then I would ask them if their commercials were in color. And they would say, 'Of course.' And I would tell them their commercials would stand out better on my station. Why? Because most of the programs were in black and white and when the commercial came on, it would have more shock value, it would catch the viewers' attention. They fell over. They hadn't thought of that.
>
> "And finally I told them my audience was richer. Every set with UHF capability was color, which costs more. Don't you think that was a pretty good sales pitch?"

With the competition gone, Turner put more money into strengthening his signal. Then he got his second break. The Atlanta ABC affiliate was forced by the network to pick up the 6 P.M. news, which they had not been running. It is a television fact of life that roughly 25 percent of an audience will actively avoid the news. So Turner scheduled "Star Trek" at 6 P.M. and not only increased his rating at that hour but got a few more people acquainted with Channel 17's presence. In Turner's mind, a philosophy was beginning to take shape. As he told *Television/Radio Age* in 1974, "All three stations had big group-ownership money behind them. They all programmed pretty much alike. I felt the people of Atlanta were entitled to something different than a whole lot of police and crime shows with murders and rapes going on all over the place. I believe that people are tired of violence and psychological problems and all the negative things they see on TV every night."

Turner concentrated his energies on buying films, the titles of which he selected himself, and on composing a lineup of old shows that sounded like the sitcom hall of fame: "I Love Lucy," "Gilligan's Island," "Leave It to Beaver," "Petticoat Junction," "Father Knows Best," "Gomer Pyle," and "Andy Griffith." "We're essentially an escapist station," Turner announced to those who hadn't noticed. "As far as our news is concerned, we run the FCC minimum of forty minutes a day."

Having moved into the entertainment void left by ABC's commitment to news, Turner attacked the NBC affiliate (WSB-TV), Atlanta's number-one station. WSB had chosen not to air five network shows, which meant that those shows could be picked up by an independent in the area. Turner grabbed all five, and soon billboards (Turner's, of course) around Atlanta were announcing, "The NBC network moves to Channel 17," and listing the five shows.

"We didn't think we could take over as the number-one station in the market," Turner said at the time. "But we felt we could shake 'em up a bit, get 'em to think about us, let 'em know we were in the race." They were shook and started thinking. The move was splashed all over the newspapers, and if success could be measured in phone calls from NBC lawyers, it was a hit.

While WSB-TV was still fuming over their public embarrassment, Turner grabbed their rights to telecast Atlanta Braves games. At the time, the Braves were paying WSB to run 25 games a year. Turner made the Braves an offer they couldn't refuse, paying them $2.5 million for the TV rights to games for five years.

"The Braves games were the top-rated locally produced program in the Atlanta market," Gerry Hogan says. Hogan is general sales manager of Channel 17. He is a dapper, precise fellow with styled red hair and the office manner of a Park Avenue physician discussing a social disease of moderate seriousness. He left Chicago advertising in 1971 to take a chance with Turner.

"Signing the Braves did a lot for our image," Hogan says, "It changed our image from that of a kiddie station. It forced people to tune us in. We became a factor. Atlanta went from a three-station market plus WTCG to a four-station market. We were in it after the Braves signed with us.[2]

Atlanta-area residents were attracted by the new style of programming and began to tune in to Channel 17's programs more regularly. Viewers and advertising revenues increased steadily, and by 1972 Channel 17 had positive operating profits:

---

[2] Roger Vaughn, "Ted Turner's True Talent," *Esquire,* October 10, 1978, pp. 35–36. Quoted with permission.

Year	Channel 17's Operating Profits
1970	$ (550,707)
1971	(531,584)
1972	181,406
1973	1,043,316
1974	732,340
1975	1,707,987
1976	3,687,447
1977	3,714,648

While Channel 17 was still in the red, Turner acquired (at a bankruptcy sale) a second UHF station, in Charlotte, North Carolina. It was purchased with Turner's personal funds because the directors of Turner Communications were not willing to risk corporate funds on the deal, given Channel 17's still unprofitable status and the high risk of trying to turn the Charlotte operation around. To help get the Charlotte station on track, Turner appeared on a series of televised "beg-a-thons" asking Charlotte viewers for financial support; more than 36,000 contributions were received, ranging from 25 cents to $80. Turner collected $25,000 and used the proceeds to help finance the same movie-sports-rerun programming emphasis that he had pioneered in Atlanta. By 1975 the Charlotte station was breaking even, and Turner sold a controlling interest in the station to Turner Communications; later the station became an NBC affiliate.

THE EMERGENCE OF TURNER BROADCASTING SYSTEM

In 1975 the billboard advertising operations were spun off from Turner Communications and made a separate company, Turner Advertising, with Ted Turner as majority stockholder. Turner Advertising succeeded in becoming the largest billboard firm in the Atlanta and Chattanooga markets; the remaining branches were sold. Meanwhile, Turner Communications began repurchasing its stock on the open market, increasing Ted Turner's ownership percentage to about 85 percent of the shares outstanding.

Turner's 1972 bid to televise the Atlanta Braves baseball games on Channel 17 not only was the first step in the company's major sports involvement, but it also established a business relationship with the Braves owners, Chicago-based Atlanta LaSalle Corporation. In 1975 Atlanta LaSalle's management approached Ted Turner about buying the Braves club. Turner moved quickly, and in January 1976 Turner Communications acquired the Braves through a newly formed, wholly owned subsidiary, Atlanta National League Baseball Club (ANLBC); the purchase price was $9.65 million, to be paid over 12 years at 6 percent interest.

In 1977 the Company acquired, through Atlanta Hawks, Inc., a 95 percent limited partnership interest in Hawks, Ltd., owner of the Atlanta Hawks professional basketball team, which competed in the National Basketball Association. In 1978 Turner Communications acquired a limited partnership interest in Soccer, Ltd., the owner of the Atlanta Chiefs professional soccer team. Also in 1978 the company sold its radio stations in Chattanooga for $1,050,000 cash, realizing a pre-tax gain of $395,000.

Three important developments occurred in 1979. The company launched plans for the first 24-hour news programming network for cable television operators (to be called CNN); by the end of 1979 the Company had invested $6.7 million in the CNN venture, acquired and begun renovations of a headquarters facility, hired key personnel, and obtained purchase commitments to provide the programming. The second development was to change the name of Turner Communications Corporation to Turner Broadcasting System, Inc. and the letters of WTUG (Channel 17) to WTBS. The third involved an agreement to sell the Charlotte TV station for $20 million cash to help finance CNN's start-up.

DEVELOPMENTS DURING 1980–1985

Much managerial time and considerable company resources were invested in making a success out of CNN. The challenge of this project was so big that Turner and TBS were unable to make any major new strategic moves between 1980 and 1985. But by early 1985 CNN was well on its way to earning its first profit and the cash drain of CNN had eased considerably.

In April 1985, Turner announced that he intended to purchase CBS, an organization 17 times the size of TBS. When his initial attempts to gain control of CBS by friendly means failed, Turner made a public tender offer to CBS shareholders. Turner planned to acquire 73 percent of the network's 30 million outstanding shares of stock. CBS's net worth was about $7.6 billion, or $254 per share; the face value of Turner's offer (composed of TBS stock, interest bearing "junk bonds," and zero coupon bonds) was $175 a share, with estimates of the market value of the offer ranging between $130 and $155 a share.

CBS fought Turner's takeover attempt vigorously with a series of moves involving increased debt and the repurchase of 6.4 million shares (21 percent of the outstanding shares) at a cost of $960 million. To make the company unattractive for future takeover attempts, CBS engineered a provision to place a ceiling on the amount of debt that CBS could carry. Turner's court suit to halt the repurchase plan was denied; his lack of cash to compete with CBS's repurchase offer and lack of ability to wage a proxy battle ended the takeover attempt. Turner's abortive efforts to win control of CBS cost TBS $18.2 million in fees and expenses.

One week after his failed bid for CBS, Turner reached an agreement with MGM/ United Artists Entertainment Company to purchase the movie company for $1.5 billion, about $29 a share. MGM's stock was trading at $24 at the time and had traded in the $13–$15 range in 1984. The 2,200-film library of MGM would be used to upgrade the programming of WTBS, and Turner expressed an interest in moviemaking. The acquisition was financed by the issue of $1.4 billion of high-yield, high-risk "junk bonds" that were viewed with skepticism by many institutions.

As of 1986 the business of Turner Broadcasting System (TBS) consisted of (1) the operations of WTBS-TV; (2) two 24-hour cable news services, the Cable News Network (CNN) and CNN Headlines News, which were available to subscribing cable television systems; (3) 100 percent ownership of the Atlanta Braves professional major league baseball team; (4) an equity interest in a limited partnership operating the Atlanta Hawks professional NBA basketball team; (5) a 75 percent interest in

Omni Ventures, which operated a 14-story complex in downtown Atlanta containing the 470 room Omni International Hotel and 775,000 square feet of office and retail shopping space; and (6) 100 percent ownership of MGM's motion picture and TV series production and distribution facilities and movie libraries. In 1985 TBS entered into a 15-year lease with Omni Ventures for 270,000 square feet of space in the Omni complex to house its corporate offices and the operations of CNN and CNN Headlines News.

The company's 10-year revenue growth record was strong but profits were sporadic:

Year	Revenues ($000)	Net Income ($000)
1976	$ 25,345	$ 648
1977	28,799	(1,232)
1978	33,843	1,203
1979	37,721	(1,496)
1980	54,610	(3,775)
1981	95,047	(13,423)
1982	165,641	(3,350)
1983	224,532	7,012
1984	281,732	10,062
1985	351,891	1,157

Exhibits 1, 2, and 3 present more extensive financial data for TBS.

SUPERSTATION WTBS-TV

Turner Broadcasting System's principal revenue and profit source was WTBS-TV. Although WTBS-TV operated as an independent UHF station broadcasting free to the Atlanta market on Channel 17, its signal reached a far greater number of homes via cable-TV systems in 48 states and was transmitted via telecommunications satellite.

From the time Turner purchased WTBS-TV in 1970 to the fall of 1976, only 462,000 cable TV customers were added to the station's viewing audience. But two key events drastically changed the market potential for WTBS's signal. In 1975 the Federal Communications Commission determined that cable growth in many areas had been held back by FCC regulations forbidding cable operators from bringing in a more desirable distant signal over that of a local independent; the FCC lifted its restrictions on "leapfrogging." Then, in December 1975, RCA launched its first communications satellite into orbit some 22,000 miles above the equator; a television signal could be beamed to the orbiting satellite and retransmitted to a receiving earth station antenna anywhere in the United States. Turner took full note of both changes. He quickly joined the cable-operators' association and got to know the operators personally. And upon seeing Home Box Office (a rival subscriber offering movies for home viewing on pay TV) unveil the first satellite broadcast to cable operators, Turner moved quickly. Satellite transmission of the WTBS signal began in December 1976, after being delayed six months by FCC proceedings.

To reflect the size of the station's geographic coverage and its availability to more and more households, the company began in 1979 to refer to WTBS as Superstation.

Exhibit 1 Financial Information for TBS by Business Segment, 1978–1985

		(in thousands)		
	1978	1980	1983	1984	1985
Total revenues					
Broadcasting	$23,772	$36,556	$139,562	$177,432	$205,784
Cable productions	—	7,551	67,489	88,339	126,562
Professional sports (Atlanta Braves)	9,140	10,276	22,456	24,285	23,377
Hotel and office operations (Omni Ventures)	—	—	—	—	8,163
Other	2,947	4,744	9,384	9,676	4,587
Totals	35,859	59,127	238,891	299,732	368,473
Intersegment revenues					
Broadcasting	(338)	(1,061)	(3,345)	(4,168)	(9,494)
Cable productions	—	(350)	(2,320)	(2,790)	(3,615)
Professional sports	(959)	(1,065)	(1,055)	(1,604)	(1,613)
Hotel and office operations	—	—	—	—	(106)
Other	(719)	(2,041)	(7,639)	(9,438)	(1,754)
Totals	(2,016)	(4,517)	(14,359)	(18,000)	(16,582)
Revenues from unaffiliated customers					
Broadcasting	23,434	35,495	136,217	173,264	196,290
Cable productions	—	7,201	65,169	85,549	122,947
Professional sports	8,181	9,211	21,401	22,681	21,764
Hotel and office operations	—	—	—	—	8,057
Other	2,228	2,703	1,745	238	2,833
Totals	$33,843	$54,610	$224,532	$281,732	$351,891
Operating profit (loss)					
Broadcasting	$ 6,089	$10,166	$ 43,335	$ 65,803	$ 55,684
Cable productions	—	(16,024)	(14,162)	(15,285)	18,843
Professional sports	(1,688)	(4,461)	(1,829)	(2,983)	(6,480)
Equity in losses of Atlanta Hawks partnership	(1,225)	(2,905)	(3,350)	(2,490)	(2,707)
Hotel and office operations	—	—	—	—	(138)
Other	418	15,689	—	—	—
Operating profit before interest and general corporate expenses	3,594	2,465	23,994	45,045	65,202
Interest expense	(1,323)	(4,437)	(14,383)	(26,037)	(37,567)
General corporate expenses	(743)	(1,603)	(2,599)	(8,946)	(7,472)
Income (loss) before income taxes	$ 1,528	$ (3,575)	$ 7,012	$ (10,062)	$ 20,163
Identifiable assets at end of year					
Broadcasting	$19,942	$22,196	$ 84,646	$ 97,838	$135,706
Cable productions	—	12,257	58,023	56,771	57,638
Professional sports	6,974	5,894	4,538	14,571	17,808
Investment in limited partnership for Atlanta Hawks	2,578	2,027	1,633	1,433	1,181
Hotel and office operations	—	—	—	—	52,534
Other assets of industry segments	169	22	—	—	—
Corporate assets	735	11,622	56,998	106,317	91,691
Totals	$30,398	$54,018	$205,838	$276,930	$356,558
Capital expenditures					
Broadcasting	$ 2,532	$ 3,828	$ 1,062	$ 4,239	$ 2,123
Cable productions	—	9,731	4,509	4,610	6,168
Professional sports	77	180	237	239	272
Hotel and office operations	—	—	—	—	1,276
Corporate	—	—	2,981	2,332	1,021
Totals	$ 2,609	$13,739	$ 8,798	$ 11,420	$ 10,860

Notes:
1. The broadcasting segment consisted primarily of the operations of WTBS, but also included the operations of program syndication activities.
2. The cable productions segment consisted primarily of the operations of CNN and CNN Headline News; the costs of owning, leasing, and operating the company's satellite access facilities were also included in this segment.
3. The professional sports segment included only the operations of the Atlanta Braves baseball operations.
   Sources: 1985 10-K Report and 1980 Annual Report.

Exhibit 2   Consolidated Statements of Income, Turner Broadcasting System, Inc., 1983, 1984, 1985   In Thousands, except per Share Data

	1983	1984	1985
Revenues			
Broadcasting	$136,217	$173,264	$196,290
Cable productions	65,169	85,549	122,947
Professional sports	21,401	22,681	21,764
Motel and office operations	—	—	8,057
Other	1,745	238	2,833
Total revenues	$224,532	$281,732	$351,891
Cost and expenses			
Cost of operations, exclusive of depreciation and amortization shown below	$105,685	$117,618	$158,161
Selling, general and administrative	80,722	95,748	106,064
Amortization of player, film, and other contract rights	9,674	20,805	16,331
Depreciation and amortization of property, plant, and equipment	4,706	8,972	10,898
Interest expense and amortization of debt discount, restructuring fees, and imputed interest	14,383	26,037	37,567
Total of costs and expenses	$214,170	$269,180	$329,021
Income from internal operations	$ 10,362	$ 12,552	$ 22,870
Equity in losses of limited partnership	(3,350)	(2,490)	(2,707)
Income before provision of income taxes and extraordinary items	7,012	10,062	20,163
Provision for income taxes	(3,655)	(4,987)	(2,862)
Income before extraordinary items	3,357	5,075	17,301
Extraordinary items			
Expensing of costs for proposed exchange offer, net of income tax benefits of $2,325	—	—	(16,326)
Realization of operating loss carryforwards	3,655	4,987	182
Net income	$ 7,012	$ 10,062	$ 1,157
Earnings per share of common stock			
Before extraordinary items	$ .16	$ .25	$ .79
Extraordinary items	.18	.24	(.74)
Net income per common share	$ .34	$ .49	$ .05
Weighted average number of common shares outstanding	20,393	20,436	21,783

Source: 1985 10-K Report.

Exhibit 3   Consolidated Balance Sheets, Turner Broadcasting System, Inc., 1984 and 1985
In Thousands, except Share Data

	December 31, 1984	December 31, 1985
Assets		
Current assets:		
Cash, including short-term investment of $135 and $30,017	$ 51,371	$ 21,082
Accounts receivable, less allowance for doubtful accounts of $3,799 and $2,898	41,548	52,454
Current portion of film contract rights and deferred program costs	14,334	24,974
Prepaid expenses and other current assets	5,591	10,602
Total current assets	112,844	109,122
Property, plant and equipment, less accumulated depreciation	73,559	119,432
Film contract rights and deferred program production costs, less current portion	39,256	57,873
Deferred charges related to the acquisition of MGM	—	25,651
Intangible assets, less accumulated amortization of $8,454 and $4,062	21,938	17,546
Deferred debt restructuring and debt issue costs	13,551	9,060
Other assets, including player contract rights and investment in limited partnership	15,782	17,874
Total assets	$276,930	$356,558
Liabilities and Stockholders' Equity		
Current liabilities:		
Accounts payable and accrued expenses	$ 29,432	$ 38,534
Current portion of long-term debt	2,409	12,458
Current portion of obligations for film contract rights, net of imputed interest of $2,350 and $2,121	10,753	11,533
Deferred income	5,957	9,397
Total current liabilities	48,551	71,922
Long-term debt, less current portion	175,015	226,084
Obligations for film contract rights, net of imputed interest of $1,484 and $1,205, less current portion	9,082	11,989
Obligations under employment contract, net of imputed interest of $3,677 and $2,400	7,060	10,819
Other liabilities	8,760	6,063
Total liabilities	248,468	326,877
Stockholders' equity		
Common stock, par value $125, authorized 32,000,000 shares, issued 22,708,000 shares	2,838	2,838
Capital in excess of par value	29,698	29,750
Accumulated deficit	(2,672)	(1,515)
	29,864	31,073
Less:		
918,000 and 928,000 shares of common stock in treasury	(943)	(933)
Notes receivable from sales of common stock from treasury	(459)	(459)
Total treasury stock	(1,402)	(1,392)
Total stockholders' equity	28,462	29,681
Total liabilities and stockholders' equity	$276,930	$356,558

Source: 1985 10-K Report.

Meanwhile, the number of full-time, cable TV subscribers receiving the WTBS signal soared:

Year	Subscribers
1977	1,350,000
1983	28,492,000
1984	33,111,000
1985	36,100,000

At year-end 1985, WTBS could be seen in 87 percent of U.S. homes with cable service and in 42 percent of U.S. homes with television. Much of the growth in WTBS's viewing audience was due to Turner's own entrepreneurial vision of the potential of cable and the personal sales job he did promoting WTBS to cable operators. As Turner expressed it, "We're what the cable industry needed—something to jazz it up." An article by Barbara Ruger in a 1978 issue of *Cable Vision* described Turner and his efforts:

> Since recognizing it was cable television distribution that could put his fledgling UHF television station on the map, Turner has given the cable industry a massive injection of pizzazz. . . . He has pleaded with the industry to "put me in everywhere.". . .
>
> From the outset, Turner has allied himself with the cable industry. His first exposure to cable came in 1970, when he attended a cable meeting in Myrtle Beach. "That's when I realized you cable guys didn't have big fangs hanging out of your mouths," Turner commented after meeting his first cable operator on the plane to South Carolina. "I was your friend from that day on," Turner reminds operators. . . .
>
> As for competition from other independents, he says assuredly, "We can beat them hands down."
>
> "If we aren't number one of all the people up there, I'm not going to be happy," declares the infamous Turner. "I want all the cable operators to be filthy rich—and I'd like our stockholders to get a little piece of that action too.
>
> "You take my advice—and I'll make you twice as rich a year from now as you are today . . . and of course, I'll be twice as rich too!"[3]

A rival executive observed, "You have to hand it to Turner. He surrounded himself with people who knew the cable industry, and he made friends. He had the timing, the ambition, the foresight, and the will to put his money where his mouth was."[4]

Programming   To fill the time slots for its 24-hour, 7-day-a-week broadcast schedule (8,760 hours per year) WTBS relied on sports events (especially games of its sports affiliates), television feature film suppliers, program syndicators, and a limited amount of internal programming. Movies contributed the most-viewed segment of WTBS programming; more than 40 movies were featured weekly from a library of 4,500 feature films (not including the recently acquired MGM library of 2,200 films). Responding to critics who complained about using so many reruns and old movies instead of new programming, Turner quipped, "At least our shows were successful once."

---

[3] Barbara Ruger, "WTCG: Leader of the Pack," *Cable Vision,* September 11, 1978.

[4] Quoted in Vaughn, "Ted Turner's True Talent," p. 46.

WTBS obtained a significant portion of its sports programming from its sports affiliates. Beginning in 1981, the hours of scheduled sports programming were increased; the most significant change was upping the number of televised Braves baseball games from 100 to 150. TBS paid the National Basketball Association $20 million for rights to televise up to 75 NBA games for each of the 1984–85 and 1985–86 basketball seasons. The number of Atlanta Hawks basketball games to be broadcast was decreased from the 40 televised games in previous years to two games in 1984–85 and to three games in 1985–86. TBS also televised nearly 40 college football games and one postseason bowl during the 1985 season, paying approximately $11 million in rights fees.

In July 1985, TBS entered an agreement with the All-Union Association Soyuzsport and the U.S.S.R. State Committee for Television and Radio to organize a major international sports competition, known as the "Goodwill Games," to be held during 1986 in Moscow and during 1990 in the United States. TBS agreed to pay $7.5 million in participation fees to Soyuzsport for each set of games (which were to feature 18 of the most popular Olympic sports), $5.4 million to The Athletic Congress of the U.S.A., Inc. for assembling the 1986 team, transportation fees for the U.S. team to and from Moscow, and all the costs of the 1990 Goodwill Games. These games added a planned 129 hours to WTBS's sports broadcasting.

Turner proposed to finance the sports venture by selling advertising packages, ranging from $1.5 million to $3.5 million, to advertisers such as General Motors, Anheuser-Busch, PepsiCo, Inc., and the Stroh Brewery Company. Turner's aim was to sell 33 of the packages; however, by early 1986, only two companies had made definite commitments for advertising.

Beginning in July 1981, programming at WTBS was shifted to begin five minutes past the hour and at five minutes past the half hour. The rationale was explained by a WTBS executive:

> Ever since TV programming began, it has been scheduled on the hour and half hour. Since all stations program in this format, millions of viewers have to suffer through commercial clutter on all channels at the same time. Our trademark has been and continues to be innovation, and we're going to give viewers a chance to see something other than ads on those half-hour breaks. We're going to run programs when all other stations are running commercials. When dials are being flipped, we're going to provide an alternative for viewers. Once we have these viewers, we're going to keep them.

According to a TBS vice president, "the development of our own uniquely original programming, both on CNN and WTBS, has brought us into a potential new source of income, the syndication of Turner-created programs." To follow up on this opportunity, a new unit called Turner Program Sales was established in late 1980 to syndicate TBS programming. Approximately 23 percent of the programming broadcast on WTBS in 1985 was produced specifically for the station, either internally or by others under contract. The production facilities of WTBS included two fully equipped studios and two mobile remote units.

Advertising   Advertising revenues of WTBS-TV were largely a function of audience size. Because of its sizable, rapidly growing viewing audience, WTBS was able to compete for national spot advertising and network advertising which otherwise would not be available to an independent station. In January 1979 WTBS instituted substantially higher "Superstation rates" for ads as a result of its greatly increased audience size. Even so, WTBS ad rates were not up to what might be justified by its 1 percent share of the national viewing audience. TBS management offered three reasons why this was so: (1) the Superstation concept was still new to the advertising community and did not conveniently fit into the long-established budgeting practices of major firms for network and national spot ads; (2) some national advertisers did not consider WTBS coverage and audience size large enough to shift some of their allocation of TV advertising away from the major networks; and (3) there was a significant time lag between documenting audience size and being able to establish rates on that basis. Still, scores of national advertisers ran ads on the Superstation; total advertising revenues for WTBS were $173 million in 1985, up from $156 million in 1984. Advertising time for WTBS as well as for CNN and CNN Headline News was marketed by TBS's own advertising sales force of about 100 persons.

In addition to advertising revenues, WTBS derived up to 10 percent of its total revenues from commissions on sales of mail-order products sold to viewers who, upon seeing a product touted on a spot ad over WTBS, would phone their order in on a toll-free 800 number or send a letter to an Atlanta post office box, both reserved by WTBS for all its mail-order house advertisers.

Competition   In the Atlanta market, WTBS competed with affiliates of the three major television networks, two independent TV stations, and two affiliates of the Public Broadcasting System. The PBS affiliates offered programming for educational or intellectual appeal; the two independents generally geared their programs to appeal to a variety of special audiences.

Competition for cable TV viewers came from several other large, independent stations which, like WTBS, were trying to "go national" and offer an alternative to traditional network programming. Two of the biggest independents were WPIX-TV in New York and WGN-TV in Chicago. In 1981 the parent firm of WGN-TV in Chicago bought into the Chicago Cubs National League baseball team. Major competition also came from ESPN, a 24-hour sports network, and from pay TV operators, such as Home Box Office, Showtime, Cinemax, and the Movie Channel, which offered cable subscribers regular showing of movies, some of which were relatively new first- and second-run films. In addition, there were over 30 other cable channels, including the Disney Channel, the Nashville Network, USA, Playboy, CNN, and CBN. As of 1985, most cable TV subscribers could choose between 5 and 25 channels in addition to the 3 major networks (ABC, NBC, and CBS), a PBS channel, and local independent TV stations (at least one independent TV station served virtually every metropolitan area). In mid-1985 the top choices of cable TV watchers were:

ESPN	36.5 million subscribers
WTBS	34.8
CNN	34.0
USA	31.0
CBN	29.7

THE ATLANTA BRAVES BASEBALL CLUB

Turner's purchase of the Atlanta Braves had several entrepreneurial pluses. Sports programming was a key feature of Channel 17, and Braves games had high audience ratings. By owning the Braves, Turner avoided contract disputes and renegotiations over broadcast rights and TV schedules, and the certainty of baseball programming enhanced Channel 17's appeal—especially to cable operators. Moreover, there was "fit" in another respect: Channel 17 could be used locally to promote attendance at Braves games; higher attendance meant more gate receipts, an ability to sign better players, and a better win-loss record. The improved record would attract more viewers to Channel 17. And with more viewers Channel 17 could command higher advertising rates. These considerations, in conjunction with the acquisition terms (a purchase price of $9.65 million, payable $1 million in cash and the balance in quarterly installments over 12 years at 6 percent interest), were attractive to Turner in spite of the fact that (1) there was little likelihood that the Braves club would ever make much profit and (2) at the time of purchase the Braves were doing poorly (some sportswriters labeled them a disaster).

Turner wasted little time in involving himself in the Braves activities and, for the first time, became widely known and highly visible in Atlanta—he did not move in Atlanta's social circles. Bruce Galphin, in a feature article in a 1977 issue of *Atlanta* magazine, described some of what transpired:

> The Braves ended their first Turner season 32 games off the pennant pace, but attendance rose some 300,000 (to a still miserably unprofitable 830,000). Andy Messersmith was the new $1.5 million star on the field, but Ted Turner made the headlines. Before the season was out, everybody knew his name (and quite a few took it in vain).
>
> He turned somersaults for the fans. He vaulted his box-seat rail to congratulate home run–hitting Braves. (Cincinnati Reds' President Bob Howsam threatened to have him arrested if Turner pulled that trick on his turf.) He put Channel 17 promotion on the back of Messersmith's uniform. He played poker with the players. Such varied maverick behavior drew rebukes from National League President Chub Feeney.
>
> The Atlanta sports press was critical of the Braves in general and especially such deals as trading five players for Texas Ranger Jeff Burroughs. Turner retaliated by cutting off the press box's traditional free beer and sandwiches.
>
> Bowie Kuhn fined the Braves $10,000 for making overtures to outfielder Gary Matthews, then a San Francisco Giant, though soon to be a free agent. Blame that one not on Turner but on a now departed employee. But Turner did fly Matthews to Atlanta during the season for a cocktail bash and welcomed him with a Turner billboard at the airport.
>
> That turned into one of Kuhn's charges in suspending Turner. Another was a drunken boasting match at the World Series with Bob Lurie, part owner of the Giants, about who would bid the most for Matthews. (Turner did: $1.75 million for a five-year contract. Kuhn at least left him that.)
>
> "It's only my first year in baseball, OK?" says Turner. "I don't know that much about it, all right. I mean it's all complicated. When you get into a new kind of thing, there's a power structure that you're not really sure of, and there are unwritten rules as well as written rules. There's no book on how to be an owner."
>
> Turner is proud, too, of bringing home-run king Hank Aaron back to the Braves

to take charge of the minor league teams and new-talent search. "His main thing is to go around and to fire up the young players and teach them how to hit the baseball."

He enjoys the company of his players. If he's forbidden to play poker with them, then he takes them hunting and generally treats them "like people." There are other owners who don't like this.

"They'd rather treat them like—well, like an owner-race horse relationship. My ballplayers aren't horses. They're my friends. I want them to be happy here."

In 1976, Ted Turner was suspended from all baseball activities for a year by Commissioner Bowie Kuhn for "conduct unbecoming to baseball." The Braves finished last in the Western Division of the National League the first four seasons under Turner's ownership. Early in the fifth season Turner remarked to a reporter, "I promised Atlanta that the Braves would be winners in five years; I still have one year to do it. Maybe there'll be a miracle. Besides, the Russians never make their five-year programs. They start new ones."[5] (The fifth year the Braves moved up to 4th place in their division, with a win-loss record of 81–80.)

The Atlanta Braves baseball team and associated activities made up the entire professional sports segment of Turner Broadcasting's business (Exhibit 1) and accounted for 9 percent of TBS's revenue in 1983, 8 percent in 1984, and 6 percent in 1985. Operating losses were incurred every year of Turner's ownership, and a continuation of the trend of increasing operating losses was expected. Ticket prices for Braves games were unchanged for the 1978, 1979, and 1980 seasons but were increased for the 1981 season. However, the increased ticket prices were not expected to boost gate receipts substantially; management believed that it would be necessary for the team to contend for its divisional championship in order to achieve a significant revenue increase. During 1985, average home game attendance decreased by 22 percent.

During the 1978–85 period, the operating expenses of the Braves increased rapidly as a result of escalating player salaries, travel costs, and preseason training costs. Record losses for the segment in 1985 resulted from even higher salary costs.

The National League's baseball schedule called for 162 regular-season games—81 home games and 81 road, or away, games. The Braves home games were played in the Atlanta–Fulton County Stadium, seating capacity 52,194. In 1984 and 1985, 150 of the Braves games were telecast by WTBS. Exhibit 4 presents selected statistics on the Braves' performance during Turner's ownership.

THE ATLANTA HAWKS BASKETBALL TEAM

In 1976 Tom Cousins, an Atlanta real-estate developer and principal owner of the Atlanta Hawks, approached Turner about buying the team. The Hawks team was in about the same condition as the Braves; the team had a poor win-loss record, attendance was falling, and financial losses were sizable. The owners wanted out, even if it meant that the franchise would be moved out of Atlanta. When Turner's

---

[5] As quoted in Kim Chapin, "The Man Who Makes Waves," *United Mainliner*, May 1980, p. 86.

Exhibit 4   Selected Statistics of Atlanta Braves Baseball Team under Turner Ownership, 1976–1985

| | Win-Loss Record/Division Standing | | | | Season Attendance | | |
Year	Games Won	Games Lost	Games behind Division Leader	Final Rank in Division (six teams)	Atlanta Braves	All Major League Teams	Braves Attendance Ranking
1976	70	92	32	6th	818,179	31,300,000	26th (out of 26 teams)
1977	61	101	37	6th	872,464	38,700,000	26th
1978	69	93	26	6th	904,494	40,800,000	26th
1979	66	94	23½	6th	769,465	43,600,000	24th
1980	81	80	11½	4th	1,048,412	43,000,000	20th
1981†	50	56	8½	4th	535,418	26,450,000†	25th
1982	89	73	0	1st*	1,801,985	44,587,000	10th
1983	88	74	3	2nd	2,119,935	45,557,000	9th
1984	80	82	12	2nd (tie)	1,724,892	44,735,000	14th
1985	66	96	NA	5th	1,350,127	46,864,000	19th

* Lost National League playoffs to St. Louis, three games to zero in a best-of-five series.
† Shortened season due to players' strike.

board of directors balked at the company acquiring the Hawks, Turner acquired a 95 percent limited partnership interest himself. Turner's investment was financed entirely by the company, however, through a $1 million secured note receivable from Atlanta Hawks, Ltd., and a $400,000 advance to Turner. In addition, for a 2 percent partnership interest, Turner Advertising advanced $742,000 to the Hawks on an unsecured basis. In 1977 the directors of TBS agreed to let Turner transfer his 95 percent interest in the Hawks to the company, at cost plus accrued interest. In 1979 the new general managing partner of AHL was granted a 1 percent ownership interest; in 1980 TBS acquired the 2 percent limited partnership interest of Cousins for $41,000, bringing TBS's share in AHL to 96 percent.

The Atlanta Hawks competed in the Central Division of the 23-team National Basketball Association (NBA). The NBA was recognized as the top professional basketball league in the world, and its champion each year was accorded the "world championship" in professional basketball. Like baseball team owners, basketball team owners received a pro rata distribution of television revenues from telecasts by the national networks, but unlike baseball team owners, they received none of the gate receipts from away games (the home team retained the net gate receipts). Teams were subject to rules and regulations promulgated by the NBA's Commissioner of Basketball. Employment relationships with players were governed by a contract between the NBA and the National Basketball Players Association.

During Turner's first year as owner of the Hawks, Curry Kirkpatrick wrote:

> Turner's ignorance about both baseball and basketball is a matter of public record as well as the basis of many jokes he tells on himself. After two years as owner of the Braves, he thinks he finally knows what a balk is. But much of pro basketball has him stumped.

Exhibit 5   Selected Statistics of Atlanta Hawks Basketball Team, 1975–1986

	Win-Loss Record/Division Standing				Season Attendance		
Season	Games Won	Games Lost	Games Behind Division Leader	Final Rank in Division*	Atlanta Hawks	All NBA Teams	Hawks' Attendance Ranking
1975–76	29	53	20	5th	n.a.	n.a.	n.a.
1976–77	31	51	18	6th	214,775	9,898,521	22nd (out of 22 teams)
1977–78	41	41	11	4th	304,482	9,874,155	19th
1978–79	46	36	2	3rd	329,064	9,761,377	20th
1979–80	50	32	0	1st†	449,843	9,937,975	11th
1980–81	31	51	29	4th	362,702	9,449,340	16th
1981–82	42	40	13	2nd	308,899	9,964,919	20th
1982–83	43	39	8	2nd	292,673	9,637,614	20th
1983–84	40	42	10	3rd	292,690	10,014,543	20th
1984–85	34	48	25	5th	299,514	10,506,355	22nd
1985–86	50	32	7	2nd	377,678	11,214,888	19th

n.a. = Not available.

* There were six teams competing in the Hawks' division each year, except for 1975–1976 when there were five teams.

† Hawks lost in first round of NBA playoffs.

He is forever calling NBA coaches managers and officials umpires. Although Turner knows his Hawks are "not too shabby" but rather "strawwwnnng" (two of the more annoying expressions in the terrific Turner lexicon someone once called "Southern bebop"), he does not seem to know their names or what positions they play. For instance, former Hawk Ron Behagen was always "Ber-hagen" to Turner. When the hulking 6'7" forward, John Brown—whose name Turner appears to have less difficulty pronouncing—fouled out of a game, the owner jumped and yelped, "Golly! Now we've got only three guards left." Later in the same game, after the Hawks were warned for using the illegal zone defense, Turner was bewildered.

"What the hell was that?" he said.

"A zone warning," he was told.

"Awww for Chrissakes, forget it," he concluded, angrily giving up.[6]

But what Turner lacked in knowledge, he substituted with energy, enthusiasm, and a flair for promotion. In the 1979–80 season, the Hawks won the NBA Central Division Championship and compiled the best record of any Hawks team since Atlanta obtained the franchise; the team set a new attendance record, drawing total of 449,843 persons—an average of 10,792 fans per home game. The 1980–81 season was a disappointment, however, and attendance slipped. The Hawks' performance in 1982–83, 1983–84, and 1984–85 was mediocre as well, and attendance remained low—see Exhibit 5. The Hawks games were played at the Omni in downtown Atlanta (seating

---

[6] Kirkpatrick, "Going Real Strawwng," p. 76.

Exhibit 6   Selected Financial Data for Atlanta Hawks Operations   In Thousands of Dollars

			Years Ended December 31,			
	1978	1980	1982	1983	1984	1985
Revenues:						
Game ticket sales, net of league share	$1,675	$3,144	$2,020	$2,266	$2,448	$2,580
Broadcast rights						
National	688	886	1,077	1,206	1,184	1,503
Local	219	708	746	1,094	684	323
Gain on traded players	—	77	—	401	—	—
Other	267	494	355	400	424	716
	2,849	5,309	4,198	5,367	4,740	5,122
Expenses:						
Team and games, exclusive of rent shown below	2,431	4,747	3,625	4,991	4,517	4,941
Promotional, general and administrative	796	2,063	1,319	1,527	1,441	1,671
Rent	221	523	313	328	288	325
Amortization of deferred cost of employment contracts and original player costs	1,489	1,469	879	986	697	578
Interest	632	865	695	850	588	635
	5,569	9,667	6,831	8,682	7,531	8,150
Net loss	(2,720)	(4,358)	(2,633)	(3,315)	(2,791)	(3,028)
Partnership deficit:						
Beginning of year	(2,375)	(6,518)	(11,444)	(14,077)	(17,392)	(20,183)
End of year	$(3,421)*	$(10,876)	$(14,077)	$(17,392)	$(20,183)	$(23,211)

* After additional partners' contributions of $1,674.
Source: 1985 10-K Report and 1980 and 1984 Annual Reports.

capacity 16,181); the lease agreement required payments to the Omni of 15 percent of gate receipts from each home game. The Atlanta Hawks routinely purchased TV advertising from WTBS.

Additional financial data on the Atlanta Hawks operations is shown in Exhibit 6; Ted Turner, using personal funds, and TBS routinely advanced the Hawks partnership the necessary funds to cover the losses and negative cash flows incurred. During 1985, CBS and the NBA entered into an agreement to televise NBA games through 1990; the Hawks pro rata share of the TV rights fees from CBS was $1.7 million in 1987, $1.8 million in 1988, $1.95 million in 1989, and $2.06 million in 1990.

THE ATLANTA CHIEFS PROFESSIONAL SOCCER TEAM

In October 1978 Turner Broadcasting formed a limited partnership, Atlanta Professional Soccer, Ltd. (APSL), to acquire the assets of the Colorado Caribous professional soccer team. The team was moved to Atlanta and its name changed to the Atlanta Chiefs. In 1979 the Chiefs won 12 games, lost 18, and finished last in its four-team division; in 1980 the Chiefs won only 7 games, lost 25 games, and again finished last in its division.

The partners of APSL included Turner Broadcasting (the sole limited partner with a 1 percent equity interest) and Atlanta Professional Soccer, Inc. (the general partner with 99 percent equity interest). TBS paid $1,554,000 cash for its partnership interest. The partnership agreement provided that the operating losses of APSL were to be allocated 99 percent to the limited partner and 1 percent to the general partner. As the sole limited partner, TBS provided all necessary operating funds to the Chief's operations. The Chiefs lost money in 1978 ($115,000), 1979 ($1,224,000), and 1980 ($2,128,000). During the early 1980s, Ted Turner concluded that the popularity of soccer was not growing fast enough to warrant continued financing of this investment; the venture was abandoned.

CABLE NEWS NETWORK

One of the most expensive ventures of Turner Broadcasting was the Cable News Network. After a 19-month development period, CNN began operations on June 1, 1980, as a comprehensive, continuous, 24-hour-a-day programming service, consisting of world, national, and sports news; analysis; commentary; and special features. CNN sold this service by subscription to cable television systems nationwide and distributed it by telecommunication satellite using the transmission services of a satellite common carrier. Like WTBS, CNN also derived revenues from advertising.

At the June 1, 1980, sign-on date, CNN's signal was available to 1.7 million households; seven months later, CNN was providing programming to 663 cable systems having a total of 4.3 million households—a growth rate of 10,000 subscribers per day. At the end of 1985, CNN could be seen on cable in more than 33 million television households; CNN was also broadcast outside the United States—in the Caribbean, Australia, Japan, Germany, Iceland, Italy, Korea, Central America, and the Philippines.

The first national telephone survey for CNN, conducted by a nationally known research firm in the early 1980s, showed that 77 percent of the respondents rated CNN's performance as above average or better relative to all services carried on their cable system; 31 percent ranked CNN as the best or one of the best channels offered. Management said that "a significant number" of viewers who regularly viewed CNN considered it their primary source of national news.

CNN Programming and Personnel   The original CNN staff consisted of more than 400 journalists, reporters, executives, and technical personnel. The first president hired by Ted Turner to run CNN was Reese Schonfield, a 25-year veteran of television news. Schonfield had been founder and managing director of the Independent Television News Association, which supplied a daily 90-minute news package to major independent television stations; prior to running ITNA, Schonfield was with the United Press International Television News service for 17 years.

CNN operations were headquartered at Turner Broadcasting System facilities in Atlanta. Other domestic news bureaus were located in Washington, New York City, Chicago, Dallas, Los Angeles, and San Francisco. CNN foreign bureaus were located in Rome and London, with traveling correspondents based in the Middle East and Bangkok. CNN's own news coverage capability was amplified by the services of United Press International Television News and the wires of United Press International, the Associated Press, and Reuters. CNN management felt that its resource base gave it an unprecedented capability to go "live" anywhere in the world to cover major news breaking at any hour of the day or night. The aim at CNN was to report the news as it broke, not at midday, 6 P.M., or 11 P.M. as the network stations did.

In 1984 CNN programming offered the following features:

- Two-hour, prime-time newscast, "Primenews/120," each weeknight.
- Up-to-the-minute news reports each hour.
- Special early evening and late-night sports reports, including taped highlights from around the country and around the world.
- "Moneyline," business and financial news each weeknight.
- "Pinnacle," profiles of top corporate executives.
- "Your Money," personal money management and investments.
- "Freeman Reports," a one-hour, live national news interview and telephone show hosted each weeknight by Sandi Freeman.
- "Showbiz Today," entertainment around the world.
- "Inside Business," a weekly half-hour program in which business, financial, and government leaders discuss key economic issues of the day.
- "Press Box," a look at the events of the week by the CNN Washington Bureau and guest correspondents.
- Hour-long weekend "Newsmaker" interviews from the Washington bureau.
- Expanded weekend sports coverage.
- Special features: daily medical/health news, daily agricultural reports and interviews, talk shows, commentary, celebrity news, reviews of theater/film/records/TV, veterinarian reports, exercise, cooking, plant care, home furnishings, weather, fashions, and lifestyles.

CNN management saw an all-news channel as having several advantages in covering a breaking news story. First, interrupting normal programming for coverage of breaking news would enhance program content for most of the audience; for the network, the result would be an annoyed audience and a loss of revenue from commercials not aired. Second, CNN could stay with a developing news story without any time restraints. Third, when a network went live on a long-lasting event, it could not easily switch back to entertainment during the dull segments and then break off an entertainment program when the live action picked up; an all-news operation, however, could switch in and out of its normal programming, returning to the live event the moment it became more interesting. Fourth, CNN had the capability to go live whenever and wherever a good news story developed. Turner declared, "The majority of people now depend on TV for their basic news, and I don't think they're getting a straight story, only a few headlines about what bad has happened. That's pretty scary."[7]

The main weakness in CNN's "narrowcasting" approach was that its all-news format was not very appealing to viewers who watched TV for long stretches of time. Many of CNN's news events and stories were reported as many as 25 to 50 times each day. During normal viewing hours, CNN rewrote the script for the news every half hour to update and freshen its stories, but much of the film footage was still identical. Between 2 A.M. and 6 A.M., nearly everything shown was a repeat of material telecast earlier.

Advertising and Subscription Revenues   CNN sold 10 minutes of national advertising each hour, with an additional two minutes an hour to be sold by the local operators. Advertising revenues totaled about $56 million during 1985 up from $46 million in 1984. Over 100 national advertisers had chosen to use CNN, including American Express, Bristol-Myers, General Motors, Campbell Soup, Eastern Airlines, Exxon, General Mills, General Foods, Goodyear, Holiday Inns, K mart, Kraft Foods, Merrill Lynch, Nestle, Procter & Gamble, Quaker Oats, RCA, Schlitz, Sears, Toyota, and Xerox. Bristol-Myers' strategy in electing to advertise on CNN was to get TV exposure for some of its lesser-known brands (Ammens powder and Congespirin cold remedy) whose sales were not large enough to justify paying the much higher ad rates charged by the three major networks. Joining the major advertisers on CNN were numerous mail-order houses, all using the same 800 toll-free number and Atlanta post office box; the mail-order products included records, jewelry, books and magazines, household items (the Amazing Vita-Mix blender), and health and nutrition products. CNN received a commission on these sales of mail-order products bought by CNN viewers.

As had become a tradition in Turner ventures, during the start-up period at CNN, Turner himself appeared live and on tape on both CNN and WTBS to try to raise money for CNN. His ads promoting CNN urged people to send in their orders for bumper stickers, at $5 for a set of five, proclaiming "I Love CNN." Turner also donated a disk antenna to make CNN available to congressmen at their Capitol offices.

---

[7] As quoted in Allen, "Ted Turner's Dream," p. 32.

CNN Headline News   TBS launched CNN Headline News at the beginning of 1982. The goal of Headline News was to give viewers a concise, fast-paced update on current news headlines, business, weather, and sports every half hour. Headline News utilized the news-gathering resources of CNN. Carried by 2,074 cable systems in 1985, Headline News was seen in 18 million households. Total advertising revenues in 1985 for Headline News were $13.7 million, up from $6.4 million during the previous year.

CNN and CNN Headline News Finances   Operating costs of the cable production segment (CNN and CNN Headlines News) rose $12 million in 1984 due to expansion of the company's domestic and foreign news-gathering operations, and extensive coverage of the 1984 election campaigns; in 1985, increased expenses were incurred from coverage of the Beirut hostage crisis and the production of special features and stories. The segment realized its first operating profit in 1985, primarily because cable productions revenues grew by 44 percent, without a significant overall increase in expenses. The operations of CNN (broadcasts started in 1980) and CNN Headline News (first broadcast in 1982) had combined losses of $16 million in 1980, $11 million in 1981, $16 million in 1982, $14 million in 1983, $13 million in 1984, and a combined profit of $20.7 million in 1985.

TED TURNER'S STYLE OF ENTREPRENEURSHIP AND MANAGEMENT

Turner's approach to business and to dealing with people was both colorful and controversial. He was frequently interviewed by the media and seldom hesitated to say exactly what he thought. This, of course, delighted reporters, and when they printed his quotes a swirl of discussion often ensued. During the 1981 baseball strike, it was rumored and reported in the *Atlanta Constitution* that Turner, at one of the owner's meetings to discuss the strike situation, remarked that all the players should be drowned and the teams restaffed from scratch.

Over the years, writers and journalists had used many labels to describe the personality and characteristics of Ted Turner: Captain Courageous, Captain Outrageous, Terrible Ted, the Mouth of the South, honest, petulant, childlike, loud, raucous, profane, impulsive, sentimental, egotistical, rebellious, ruthless, cold, money-grubbing, engrossing, multifaceted, flirtatious, hyperactive, sincere, outspoken, antiestablishment, likable, enjoyable, and chauvinistic; he had been called a humanist, a romantic, and the world's best-known sailor and had been accused of having basic racist tendencies, an elitist view of society, and a fascist ideology. Among his incongruous interests and activities, he had attended a state dinner at the White House, ridden in an ostrich race at Atlanta Stadium, read the Bible twice from cover to cover, permitted the screening of pornographic movies for his baseball players and their wives on a bus ride from Plains, Georgia, to Atlanta, nudged a baseball around the base paths with his nose, arrived drunk at a news conference following his victory in the world-famous America's Cup race, been named Yachtsman of the Year four times, appeared in ads for Cutty Sark Scotch, acquired a taste for Beechnut chewing tobacco, and quoted classical literature. In 1976 Turner was suspended from baseball, and in 1980 he was presented the Private Enterprise Exemplar Medal by the Freedom Foundation at Valley Forge.

Turner was highly motivated, energetic, and willing to do what it took to achieve his goals. He told one interviewer, "I have such a distaste for people who can't roll up their sleeves and get the job done. . . . My father always said to never set goals you can reach in your lifetime. After you accomplished them, there would be nothing left."[8] He valued and appreciated money—"Life is a game, but the way you keep score is money."[9] And he sought out success—"I've always been encouraged since I was a little kid to be a top competitor, and to be a worker, not a shirker."[10] Turner was known for being candid and honest with everyone. Honor, truth, and sincerity were his bywords.

Close associates described Turner as having a strong sense of what to do and when to do it. As one of his vice presidents expressed it, "He's a good concept man. He's got a good eye for where profitable growth lies, where growth potential is. He has ability to put things together that make sense."[11]

Complementing Turner's sense of direction and sense of timing was a knack for picking capable managers to work under him. He delegated authority readily. Administrative matters and day-to-day operating details were left to his vice presidents and lower-echelon managers. He did not, as a general rule, supervise them closely, preferring instead to let them do their jobs with a minimum of interference as long as things seemed to be progressing satisfactorily. The executives under Turner were regarded as devoted to him and seemed motivated by his leadership. A friend and sailing partner observed, "He is always winning, never losing, and he gives that same feeling to people sailing or working with him."

Turner's approach was to throw 100 percent of his energies into a project until he felt he could go on to something else. He got bored sitting still doing the same things over and over and handling routine matters. As one writer described it:

> When he approaches a project, he demonstrates great powers of positive thinking and an even greater innocence. ("It can't be done? Let's find out.") If things aren't going particularly well, Turner is capable of short temper tantrums and brief flurries of petulance. When a project bores him, Turner is quick to turn his back on it and move to something fresh, leaving to his corporate subalterns the job of seeing the project through—as well as the task of pouring oil on the inevitable troubled waters he has left in his wake.[12]

By Turner's own admission, the thing that turned him on was trying to win, the playing of the game, the competition, the matching of wits. He liked to turn losers into winners, in sports and in business. The general manager of WTBS-TV described his perception of Turner:

> He has a tremendous desire to win. He doesn't like to lose. If he does, he is one of the few people I know who benefits from the loss. He asks himself, "Why did I lose?" I don't know why he has to win so. It's a compulsion with him.

[8] As quoted in Kirkpatrick, "Going Real Strawwng," p. 78.

[9] Ibid, p. 75.

[10] As quoted in Bruce Galphin, "Other Things to Do," *Atlanta,* Spring 1977, p. 40.

[11] As quoted in Wayne Minshew and DeWitt Rogers, "A Winner," *Atlanta Constitution,* January 8, 1977.

[12] As quoted in Chapin, "The Man Who Makes Waves," p. 85.

One of my responsibilities is, if I know he is doing something wrong, to try and stop him. But did you ever try and stop a speeding train?

If he wants something, he is going to get it. The problem is, he will pay more than it's worth. And the other guy knows it.[13]

However, Turner did not look at himself as a "win at all costs" practitioner:

I don't think winning is everything. It's a big mistake when you say that. I think *trying* to win is what counts. Be kind and fair, and make the world a better place to live, that's what important. . . .

I think the saddest people I've ever met were people with a lot of wealth. If you polled 90 percent of the people and asked them what they want most, most would want to be millionaires. I'll tell you, you've got to be one to know how unimportant it is.

I'm blessed with some talents. I've made a lot of money, more than I ever thought I would. . . . But if I continue to be successful, I would like to serve my fellow man in some way other than doing a flip at third base. . . .

People want leadership, somebody to rally around, and I want to be a leader.[14]

FUTURE OUTLOOK

In 1981, replying to questions from the casewriter, Ted Turner was confident and optimistic about the prospects for TBS:

The future outlook is excellent. We have not peaked and I feel competition is always good; you continue to do better with competition.

CNN's future is solid and it is proving to be a viable venture, even though as of this month (September 1981) it has not yet turned the corner into the black.

Moreover, we are currently doing well in competing both against the major networks and the other emerging alternatives.

Five years from now, I expect TBS to be five times stronger.

However, two March 1986 articles in *The Wall Street Journal* (see Exhibits 7 and 8) indicated that the challenges facing Ted Turner and his company were even bigger in 1986 than they had been when he "bet the company" to pull off the CNN venture. In addition, there was speculation in the business press that Denver-based Tele-Communications, Inc., one of the largest cable operators, was laying plans to team up with Turner and TBS to form a cable-exclusive network modeled after CBS, NBC, and ABC. TCI's president had recently become a member of the TBS board of directors and TCI had bought 3 percent of TBS's stock. TBS had many of the building blocks for a fourth network—sports and news operations, a sales and marketing force, and (via the recent acquisition of MGM/UA Entertainment Corp.) production studios and a movie library. Turner was said to be considering buying rights to some 1987 National Football League games. According to analysts, a limited start-up of a fourth network would require a programming budget of $350 million—NBC, ABC, and CBS were said to have annual programming budgets of about $1 billion.

---

[13] As quoted in Minshew and Rogers, "A Winner."
[14] Ibid.

After eight gruelling months of fund raising and negotiation, Turner Broadcasting System Inc. expects to close its $1.5 billion purchase of MGM/UA Entertainment Co. Tuesday. But for all its effort, it appears that Turner may end up with far less than it started out bargaining for.

But because of high financing costs, Ted Turner—who owns 81 percent of the Atlanta broadcasting company—not only must quickly sell nearly all that he is buying or risk drowning in a sea of red ink; now he may be forced to accept prices lower than he expected because some prized assets of the Culver City, California, concern have been tarnished while the transaction dragged to its conclusion.

Turner Broadcasting has been sending out conflicting signals on its strategy, leading to questions as to whether it has one. And MGM, already damaged by months of uncertainty, faces the prospect of a public auction far more threatening than its famous sale of studio props—including Judy Garland's ruby slippers from *The Wizard of Oz*—more than a decade ago.

To date, the broadcaster's drive on Hollywood appears to have been shaped more by what investment bankers could sell Wall Street than by any grand corporate vision. When Turner first made his bid last August, he talked not only of his designs on MGM's 2,200-film library but his interest in making movies. By the time Drexel Burnham Lambert Inc. marketed $1.4 billion in high-yield, high-risk "junk bonds" to finance the acquisition this week, everything but the library was marked for possible resale.

This is not, however, to say things couldn't change. "The worst thing that could happen is if one of the movies we have in the pipeline becomes a hit," says one Turner insider. "That would be the tease for Ted to think, 'Hey, this is easy. Let's run a movie studio.' "

But there is widespread skepticism about the wisdom of buying MGM just to get a piece of the company. "It's one of the nuttiest deals of all time," says an analyst for one institution that passed up the junk bonds.

Has Turner Broadcasting finally stretched itself to the financial breaking point? No, maintains its vice president and chief financial officer, William C. Bevins, Jr. "We've always been this leveraged," he says, adding that the company will get a programming source it had long coveted.

The acquisition surely makes Turner Broadcasting one of the more debt-ridden companies of its time. The combined companies would have had an operating loss of $284.4 million for the nine months ended last September 30 because their interest costs would have so far outstripped their revenue. And the combined companies, which had $567.3 million in revenues for that period, will have to make $600 million in principal debt payments six months after closing or face ever-escalating interest rates on the notes.

There is thus enormous pressure on Turner to move quickly in selling assets. Turner will immediately sell United Artists to Kirk Kerkorian, who owns 50.1 percent of MGM/UA shares, for about $470 million. But other asset sales may present big problems. The company doesn't want to settle for fire-sale prices, which it has admitted in a Securities and Exchange Commission filing is a danger. It doesn't want to cannibalize its more attractive continuing operations either. But it has reluctantly shopped around a stake in the newly profitable Cable News Network. Bevins says the network is no longer on the block, but one of the company's investment bankers says its sale must remain an option.

And MGM's production facilities have foundered as the transaction has dragged toward completion. That means that while Turner will begin sitting down next week with a host of possible buyers for the movie and television

---

Turner Before and After

Turner Broadcasting System Inc. as of September 30, 1985

Before		After†	
Operations		Operations	
Television broadcasting, cable TV production and professional sports		Television broadcasting, cable TV production and professional sports, motion picture and television series production and distribution, movie libraries, and film processing laboratory	
Revenue*	$259,440,000	Revenue*	$ 567,341,000
Loss*	5,001,000	Loss*	248,400,000
Total assets	354,006,000	Total assets	2,572,350,000
Working capital	45,492,000	Working capital	450,300,000
Long-term debt	223,954,000	Long-term debt	1,747,168,000

* For nine months ended September 30, 1985.
† Doesn't reflect Turner plan to seek buyers for all or part of MGM's assets, except its movie libraries, or adjustments required to reflect the fair value of the net assets acquired.

Source: Company SEC filings.

Exhibit 7 *(concluded)*

studios, film-processing lab, distribution business, and more, the price he can fetch may be well below what it was last August. "The good news is that there is interest," says a source at Drexel Burnham, which is advising on the sales. "The bad news is that we don't know how high they'll go."

Alan Ladd, Jr., the studio's president and top creative officer, maintains that MGM so far hasn't been permanently hurt by the prospect of a break-up that might sever MGM's library and valuable home video arms from its movie and television operations. "We've never stopped working," says the laconic Ladd, a 48-year-old veteran movie executive who joined the studio early last year. He adds: "Turner has always said, 'Spend what you have to spend and keep going.' "

Nonetheless, MGM executives say movie and television production is being badly hurt as Hollywood agents and producers keep prime projects away from the studio because of doubts about Turner. "For us, this has been a year of begging," says David Gerber, MGM's president of television production. "Network executives read all the news stories and said, 'David, if we do a pilot with you, how do we know Ted Turner can afford it? How do we know the studio is still going to be there?' "

Salvaging the studio's credibility has been an uphill struggle. At one point, says Gerber, Turner personally pleaded MGM's case in a meeting with B. Donald Grant, president of CBS Inc.'s entertainment division. The step was particularly awkward in view of Turner's bitterly resisted takeover bid for CBS last year. At present, MGM says it has sold two pilot programs to ABC and one to NBC, but none to CBS, for next fall.

Gerber also has faced sometimes brutal resistance in recruiting the best Hollywood stars for MGM programs. The longtime television producer tells of one talent agent who was reluctant to commit a star's services to MGM— and offered to bet Gerber $1,000 that the executive would lose his own job by June. "I made the bet to get the client," says Gerber.

That same resistance has taken its toll on MGM's movie division—a perennial laggard that has commanded the lowest market share of any Hollywood studio in 6 of the last 10 years. Despite the enormous success of *Rocky IV*, bottom-ranked MGM accounted for only about $135 million, or 9 percent, of $1.5 billion in total U.S. theatrical film rentals last year.

Bevins admits the studios' value "certainly diminished while we were in the process of the deal." But he figures it bottomed out in December and has since been coming back. He thinks he can dispose assets enough to trim debt by $600 million at year's end.

He also admits the company had to reverse course on its initial plans to become a film producer, after it saw the studio's recent dismal track record. Such movies as *Marie* and *Fever Pitch* grossed less than $1 million, according to Bevins, while costing more than $15 million each.

But he maintains that gaining the film library is still worth all the trial and error, time and money. With about half of the schedule for Turner's WTBS Superstation devoted to movies and with film licensing costs skyrocketing, Turner locked in much of its programming costs and upgraded the quality of its fare.

Some familiar with the operation agree. "From an advertising standpoint, it's certainly going to be beneficial to him," says Bob Geary, an executive at Cargill Wilson & Acree Inc., an Atlanta advertising agency. "You aren't going to see Roy Rogers so much; you're going to see some pretty first-rate movies."

But many question whether the benefits of the library outweigh the costs, even if Turner can sell the production facilities on favorable terms. Long-term rights to many of its top pictures—*The Wizard of Oz*, for instance—have already been sold to the networks or pay TV. Without a studio, Turner can't replenish the library with new movies, the major source of videocassette rentals. And local TV stations may not care to buy packages of films that have already been beamed into their market by the superstation.

For what Turner is getting, says Jeffrey Logsdon, an analyst at Los Angeles-based Crowell, Weedon & Co., "He paid more than top dollar."

Part of the problem, many observers feel, is that Turner went after MGM while on the rebound from his failed CBS Inc. bid. Though he had talked periodically for some time with Kerkorian, his offer came only about a week after the CBS offer ended and his motivation may have involved more ego balm than financial sense.

Now the question is whether that shoot-from-the-hip nature will allow Turner to walk away from the studio. Realistically, he doesn't have the capital to invest in production and he needs the asset sales to pay debt. But, says Freddie Fields, executive producer of a forthcoming MGM film, *Poltergeist II*, there may be "too much show business in him to walk away."

Indeed, when asked whether Turner might change his present thinking and stick with the film business, Bevins says: "There's always that possibility where Ted's concerned. Ted owns the company."

But Turner's free-wheeling entrepreneurial style is decreasingly suited to the scale of the company he has assembled. And his need for control restricts his financial maneuverability.

Talks with Viacom International Inc. regarding a 50 percent interest in the MGM studio broke off in December over issues of control. Talks with RCA Corp.'s National Broadcasting Co. unit for a 50 percent interest in the Cable News Network broke off in November when Turner wouldn't cede editorial control.

Control will continue to be an issue as Turner steps up the pace of divestiture talks—possibly limiting interested buyers. "Not everybody wants to get in bed with him," says Steven Rosenberg of Paul Kagan Associates, a California media consulting concern.

Source: John Helyer, Linda Williams, and Michael Cieply, *The Wall Street Journal*, March 21, 1986. Reprinted by permission of *The Wall Street Journal*. © Dow Jones & Company, Inc., 1986. All rights reserved.

Exhibit 8   Ted Turner's U.S.–Soviet Games Face Olympic Hurdles at Home   *The Wall Street Journal,* March 26, 1986

Ted Turner doesn't want much, just some tasty television programming, a bigger slice of the broadcast pie, and world peace.

So after choking on CBS Inc. and swallowing MGM/UA Entertainment Co. and $1.2 billion of debt whole, the maverick broadcaster has whipped up a souffle called the Goodwill Games, an international competition featuring 18 of the most popular Olympic sports. The first of what Turner hopes will become a quadrennial event will take place July 5–20 in Moscow and will be televised in the United States by—who else?—Superstation WTBS, the cornerstone of Turner's Turner Broadcasting System Inc. (A superstation is a regional station broadcast by satellite to cable television systems nationwide.)

Turner believes the games will promote world peace and prove that private enterprise can join together what politicians tore asunder in the 1980 and 1984 Olympic Games, namely competition between the United States and the USSR. Although invited, the rest of the world is just window dressing.

A FLASHY EVENT

In the process Turner hopes to enhance WTBS's national image and, eventually, its profits. Be it for profits or peace, the Goodwill Games aren't a run-of-the-mill sports event. Indeed, they seem to have taken on some of their flamboyant creator's personality: bold and original, flashy and attention-getting, but to some, half-baked. And they reek of controversy.

They have touched off a turf battle among amateur sports ruling bodies and raised anew concerns about overcommercialization of athletics. Moreover, they add 129 hours to television's already-over-stuffed sports schedule, further straining a dismal advertising market.

Nothing about these games has come easily, starting with months of "gut-wrenching" negotiations with the Soviets, says Robert Wussler, executive vice president of Turner Broadcasting and president of WTBS. And lately, nagging problems have kept Wussler on a monthly shuttle between Atlanta and Moscow. One recent worry: Russian bureaucrats have been moving at a glacier-like pace in securing commitments to compete from other nations. "It's like a doctor visiting his patient," the former CBS network president says wearily.

Meanwhile, Goodwill Games critics have lined up to take potshots at this meshing of sports, television, and private enterprise. The U.S. Olympic Committee, the most vocal, has questioned whether the broadcaster would promote sports with limited viewer appeal, such as events for women and the disabled (the traditional line-up of women's sports will be included, but handicapped events will not).

Turner Broadcasting first ran afoul of the USOC when it appointed the Athletics Congress, the Indianapolis-based governing body for U.S. track and field events, to organize the U.S. Goodwill contingent, instead of the USOC, which some USOC members consider the only proper organizer for international competition in Olympic events. "I didn't know anybody at the USOC," Wussler explains. "And past experience said it would take six months for the USOC to make a decision" about accepting the job, he adds. TAC signed on after one meeting in the Indianapolis airport between Wussler and Ollan Cassell, the group's combative executive director and a long-time acquaintance.

The Olympic Committee has since said it didn't want to organize the Goodwill Games. But insiders admit that some committee members are angry and worried that Turner Broadcasting's choice of the Athletics Congress will weaken the committee's traditional iron grip on U.S. sports.

Turner Broadcasting has given the Athletics Congress $5.4 million to parcel out to participating teams to help them prepare for Moscow. While that is peanuts compared with what the committee hands out for the Olympics, it still could weaken the dominance of the USOC.

Robert Helmick, USOC president, describes talks with Turner Broadcasting as "mostly congenial," but Wussler says the USOC threatened to sue Turner Broadcasting to halt the games. Not true, Helmick replies. "I was threatened by an attorney for Turner that they would sue if we didn't do all they want," he says. In any case, the USOC now says that while it doesn't oppose the games, it doesn't "endorse" them either.

Meanwhile, the Goodwill Games have heightened competition between Turner Broadcasting and the Entertainment and Sports Programming Network, a sports cable channel. ESPN has a contract to broadcast the U.S. Olympic Festival, an annual event designed to develop talent for the Olympics. The problem is that the festival begins just five days after Turner's Goodwill Games wind up, and ESPN officials are worried that top athletes and advertisers will abandon the festival for a chance to face down the Soviets in the Goodwill Games.

Bringing the best American athletes to Moscow this summer is critical to Turner's success. After all, if an inferior team gets creamed early by the Russians, American viewers may switch to something starring Sylvester Stallone.

But even if the top athletes sign up for the Goodwill Games, the support of advertisers is still uncertain. Despite personal appeals by Turner to General Motors Corp., Anheuser-Busch Cos., Wendy's International Inc., PepsiCo Inc. and Stroh Brewery Co.—plus an increase in Goodwill salespeople to 27 from 4—only PepsiCo and Stroh's have bought one of the games' sponsorship-advertising packages. Although several others are pending, Turner had hoped to sell 33 of them. "We're at a Mexican standoff with advertisers," he concedes.

Exhibit 8 *(concluded)*

BILLBOARDS AND FREE TRIPS

The advertising packages range from $1.5 million to about $3.5 million paid by Stroh's, and on up to the $10 million paid by PepsiCo. For that, advertisers get from 27 to 248 half-minute spots during the 16-day broadcast, plus billboards in Moscow, the use of the Goodwill Games logo, and an all-expense-paid trip to the games for 4 to 16 persons. But because promotional events and advertising are handled by different people in most corporations, the combined packaging has hurt sales. "No one knows who to go to in the corporation to get a decision," says Michael Trager, chairman of Greenwich, Connecticut-based Sports Marketing & Television International.

In addition, the Goodwill Games "haven't evoked an emotional appeal" like the Olympics did, says Lesa Ukman, president of International Events Group, which tracks corporate sponsorships. And an executive of a major U.S. brewery notes, "Having a billboard in Moscow doesn't do much for us."

Advertisers also doubt whether a cable station, with its limited audience, can pull in the requisite ratings. To compensate, WTBS is syndicating the games to independent stations worldwide. Turner promises that 7 percent of the viewing audience will watch the games during prime time, making the rates a bargain. But some television sources say he'll never reach that.

He insists he won't cut rates, although many potential advertisers say the prices are too steep for an unproven event in mid-summer, when viewing is down. "It's an enormous load packed into a short period of time," says Mark Reece, corporate media director for Adolph Coors Co.

Turner is betting that he will profit when the games return to the United States in 1990, even though he will have to foot the entire bill for the games (this year he's sharing it with the Soviets). But these are perilous waters, even for an expert yachtsman. "Turner's got guts," says Howard David, senior vice president of Mizlou TV, a major syndicator of television shows. "But I'm glad it's TBS doing it and not us."

CASE 2 PEOPLE EXPRESS AIRLINES, INC. (A)*

It was late Friday afternoon on a windy, drizzly April day in the old North terminal of the Newark International Airport. Donald Burr, chairman and chief executive officer of People Express Airlines, leaned back in his chair, looked out the window of his spartanly furnished office, and reflected on how far his company had come in the last three years and how far it still had to go to live up to his vision. By all accounts, People Express was the fastest-growing airline in the history of aviation; yet, it was not clear how sustainable the company's growth was nor what its ultimate competitive inroads on the industry would be.

Since its first commercial flights on April 30, 1981, People Express had expanded from a company with 250 employees, three Boeing 737s, and routes serving four cities with 24 flights a day to a company which in April 1984 had over 4,000 full- and part-time employees, 49 planes (26 Boeing 727s, 22 Boeing 737s, and 1 Boeing 747), and over 320 flights daily to 20 destinations, including London. In the process People Express had become the busiest airline operating out of the Newark, New Jersey, airport and revenues were up from $38.4 million for the nine months ended December 1981 to $286.6 million for full-year 1983. The 1981 loss of $9.2 million (which included start-up costs) had become a $10.4 million profit in 1983. And all this had been achieved despite a severe national economic recession, an outbreak of price wars among the airlines, a national air traffic controllers strike which created havoc with flight schedules, and such general hard times in the airlines industry that most companies lost money and several flirted with bankruptcy. The ingredients of People's startling success in the midst of a bleak industry environment were no mystery—rock-bottom fares, low-cost operations, astute selection of routes, and savvy marketing. No one could seriously challenge Burr's observation, "We've designed a product which is so popular we can't satisfy the demand for it."

Burr had ambitious growth plans to be implemented over the next two years. Arrangements were in place to expand the flights serving its 20 destinations, to add more routes, and to boost the company's fleet of aircraft from 49 to 77 planes by June 1985. Just an hour ago, Burr had gotten copies of some preliminary operating results for the first three months of 1984, as well as an audited income statement for 1983 (see Exhibits 1 and 2); he had been told informally that the company had operated in a break-even position during the first three months of 1984. He was also furnished statistics comparing People Express with several other airlines (see Exhibit 3). Before calling it a day, Burr decided to review the new figures and to mull over what his priorities and agenda ought to be during the next few months.

---

* Prepared by Professor Arthur A. Thompson, Jr., with the assistance of graduate researcher Elsa Wischkaemper, both of The University of Alabama.
Copyright © 1984 by Arthur A. Thompson, Jr.

Exhibit 1   Recent Performance of People Express Airlines, Inc.

Selected Monthly Operating Statistics, 1983 versus 1984

	1983			
	January	*February*	*March*	*First Quarter*
Passengers	356,994	317,783	396,364	1,071,141
Revenue passenger miles (000)[1]	206,657	197,124	252,738	656,519
Available seat miles (000)[2]	289,749	257,547	313,640	860,936
Load factor[3]	71.3%	76.5%	80.6%	76.3%

	1984			
	January	*February*	*March*	*First Quarter*
Passengers	551,891	567,914	686,556	1,806,361
Revenue passenger miles (000)[1]	410,696	439,311	557,593	1,407,600
Available seat miles (000)[2]	632,081	655,793	730,451	2,018,325
Load factor[3]	65.0%	67.0%	76.3%	69.7%

Selected Quarterly Operating Statistics, 1983

	Three Months Ended			
	March 31, 1983	*June 30, 1983*	*September 30, 1983*	*December 31, 1983*
Operating revenues ($000)	$ 51,770	$ 64,304	$ 81,764	$ 88,751
Passengers carried	1,071,141	1,235,988	1,644,564	1,746,592
Revenue passenger miles (000)[1]	656,519	786,277	1,033,086	1,192,484
Available seat miles (ASM) (000)[2]	860,936	1,001,650	1,308,923	1,745,878
Load factor[3]	76.3%	78.5%	78.9%	68.3%
Break-even load factor[4]	73.1%	73.3%	76.2%	67.3%
Yield per revenue passenger mile[5]	$ 0.0789	0.0818	$ 0.0791	$ 0.0744
Total costs per ASM	$ 0.0577	0.0600	$ 0.0603	$ 0.0501
Average fuel cost per gallon	$ 0.921	$ 0.879	$ 0.856	$ 0.850
Average passenger haul (miles)[6]	613	636	628	683
Aircraft in service at end of period	21	23	29	40
Full-time employees at end of period . . .	1,219	1,690	2,184	2,596

Selected Quarterly Results, 1982 and 1983
(in thousands of dollars, except per share data)

	Three Months Ended							
	March 31, 1982	*June 30, 1982*	*September 30, 1982*	*December 31, 1982*	*March 31, 1983*	*June 30, 1983*	*September 30, 1983*	*December 31, 1983*
Operating revenues	$25,776	$36,524	$36,463	$40,096	$51,770	$64,304	$81,764	$88,751
Operating expenses	25,608	30,924	32,357	39,510	47,074	57,711	76,662	85,515
Net income (loss)	(1,957)	2,978	1,657	(1,676)	2,109	4,208	2,791	1,326
Net income (loss) per common share	(.20)	.30	.14	(.11)	.13	.24	.15	.07

[1] "Revenue passenger miles" are determined by multiplying the number of passengers carried by the distance flown.
[2] "Available seat miles" are determined by multiplying the number of seats available for passengers by the distance flown.
[3] "Load factor" is determined by dividing the revenue passenger miles by the available seat miles.
[4] "Break-even load factor" is the load factor that will result in operating revenues being equal to total costs (including net interest expense).
[5] "Yield per revenue passenger mile" is determined by dividing operating revenues by the revenue passenger miles.
[6] "Average passenger haul" is determined by dividing the revenue passenger miles by the number of passengers carried.
Source: Company reports.

Exhibit 2   Income Statements, People Express Airlines, Inc., 1980–1983   In Thousands of Dollars except per Share Data

	From April 7 1980 to March 31, 1981	Nine Months Ended December 31, 1981	Years Ended December 31	
			1982	*1983*
Operating revenues:				
Passenger	—	$37,046	$133,822	$276,505
Baggage and other revenue, net	—	1,337	5,037	10,084
Total operating revenues	—	38,383	138,859	286,589
Operating expenses:				
Flying operations	—	3,464	9,812	20,115
Fuel and oil	—	16,410	48,009	85,188
Maintenance	21	2,131	8,549	26,113
Passenger service	—	1,785	6,283	13,653
Aircraft and traffic servicing	—	7,833	23,618	53,215
Promotion and sales	146	8,076	17,589	37,680
General and administrative	1,685	3,508	6,119	16,114
Depreciation and amortization	6	1,898	7,423	11,786
Amortization—restricted stock purchase plan	—	479	997	3,098
Total operating expenses	1,858	45,584	128,399	266,962
Income (loss) from operations	(1,858)	(7,201)	10,460	19,627
Interest				
Interest expense	14	3,913	11,263	10,296
Interest income	(1,420)	(1,909)	(1,805)	(1,623)
Interest expense (income), net	(1,406)	2,004	9,458	8,673
Income (loss) before income taxes and extraordinary item	(452)	(9,205)	1,002	10,954
Provision for income taxes	—	—	461	4,500
Income (loss) before extraordinary item	(452)	(9,205)	541	6,454
Extraordinary item—utilization of net operating loss carryforward	—	—	461	3,980
Net income (loss)	$ (452)	$ (9,205)	$ 1,002	$ 10,434
Net income (loss) per common share:				
Income (loss) before extraordinary item	$ (.10)	$ (.96)	$ 0.04	$ 0.35
Extraordinary item	—	—	0.04	0.22
Net income (loss) per common share	$ (.10)	$ (.96)	$ 0.08	$ 0.57
Weighted average number of common shares outstanding	4,598	9,610	12,118	18,300

Source: 1983 10-K Report.

Exhibit 3   Operating Comparisons of Five U.S. Airlines

Operating Expenses per Available Seat Mile

	1982	1st 6 mo. of 1983
Delta	7.97¢	8.11¢
Eastern	8.21	8.42
Piedmont	9.26	8.91
US Air	11.07	10.64
People Express	5.00	5.60

Revenue per Passenger Mile, or "Yield"

	1982	1st 6 mo. of 1983
Delta	13.67¢	12.03¢
Eastern	13.01	12.39
Piedmont	15.87	15.29
US Air	19.51	17.69
People Express	8.90	8.00

Load Factor

	1982	1st 6 mo. of 1983
Delta	52.7%	58.3
Eastern	56.7	60.9
Piedmont	55.6	53.5
US Air	57.2	60.5
People Express	60.9	77.5

Source: Lucien Rhodes, "That Daring Young Man and His Flying Machine," *Inc.*, January 1984, p. 46.

DONALD C. BURR

After getting his MBA at age 25 from the Harvard Business School in 1965, Don Burr went to work for National Aviation Corporation, a closed-end investment company specializing in airline and aerospace securities and venture capital. Six years later at age 31, on the basis of his prowess in the economics of commercial airline operations and in financial strategies for starting and running a new airline company, he was elected president of National Aviation. In June 1973, he was recruited by Houston-based Texas International Airlines, a regional carrier with a history of financial troubles and management problems, to help engineer a rescue and major turnaround. As one of TI's senior executives, Burr was instrumental in designing a set of low-price fares to use as a promotional tactic for increasing TI's passenger traffic; the centerpiece of his marketing strategy was the creation of a character named "Mr. Peanut" to carry the message of Texas International's new low-cost "peanuts fares" between selected cities. Even though the pros and cons of the peanuts fares were debated heatedly inside the company, Burr's ideas were implemented in 1976 and the campaign worked. Later that same year Burr was promoted to chief operating officer and in 1979 was made president and a member of the board of directors. Six months later, Burr had a falling out with Frank Lorenzo, TI's chairman and chief executive officer, partly over a new "Peanuts Payola" marketing plan; Burr resigned, as did two of his close associates, Gerald Gitner, TI's senior vice president of marketing and planning, and Melrose Dawsey, Burr's executive assistant.

When Burr left Texas International, he expected to get a number of interesting offers from other airlines. He was 38, had already been president of two companies, was well known in the industry, and had good connections on Wall Street. What happened surprised him:

> I was thinking that I'll get some calls for sure. There must be a lot of people out there who want somebody like me to run their airlines. But did I get any substantive calls? My mother called and that's pretty much it. That's when I realized that the world really didn't care whether I got up in the morning; it didn't give a damn. But is that bad, is that immoral? No, that's life. That's the way it is. No one would have me, so I had to start my own.[1]

Burr, Gitner, and Dawsey rented an office in Houston. In between telephone calls to industry contacts and reading trade journals trying to unearth a challenging opportunity, they brainstormed about starting a new airline—where the money would come from, how it would be organized, how employees would be motivated and managed, what kind of planes would be best, what geographic areas could be served most successfully, and what the company's strategy should be. Talk gradually turned into commitment and planning. Burr sold his stock in Texas International, his house in Houston, three condominiums he had invested in, and drew out his savings, coming up with $350,000 to put into the venture. Gitner invested $175,000 and Dawsey contributed $20,000. In April 1980, they incorporated People Express Airlines, a new commercial airline whose name was intended to signal a strong people orientation—as concerned both employees and customers.

Burr's effervescent personality and leadership qualities inspired those around him. According to a writer for *Inc.* magazine:

> When friends or business associates talk about Donald Burr today, they invariably say, "He could've been a preacher." They don't say "minister," or "reverend," or "clergy." They say "preacher" because it conveys exactly the right sense of sweating-in-a-hot-tent, evangelical fervor that makes the pulse race. Burr works hard when he talks. He paces; he sits; he stands; he throws out his arms; he condemns and praises, implores and jokes. He moves effortlessly from the blunt, almost slang, of a working-class neighborhood to the polished diction of the corporate boardroom. And all the while, there never seems to be any doubt that he can do exactly what he says he will.[2]

INITIAL START-UP APRIL 1980—APRIL 1981

The 12 months following incorporation were characterized by a nonstop, pellmell agenda: raising capital, purchasing aircraft, selecting an airport to serve as an operations center, filing documents to obtain regulatory approval, selecting routes, working out flight schedules, setting up an ad campaign, getting a reservation system in place, and recruiting and training personnel. Several of Burr's former associates at Texas

---

[1] As quoted in Lucien Rhodes, "That Daring Young Man and His Flying Machine," *Inc.*, January 1984, p. 45.
[2] Ibid., p. 45.

International joined the People Express team. Harold Pareti, 32, formerly legal counsel at TI, became managing officer for flight operations and legal and government affairs. Lori Dubose, 28, TI's director of personnel resources, became managing officer in charge of recruiting, training, and in-flight service. Robert McAdoo, 35, TI's vice president of information systems, became chief financial officer. Donald Hoydu, 39, TI's director of facilities, became a managing officer in charge of the company's facilities and purchasing. By December 1980, there were 15 former TI executives and managers on the People Express payroll and Don Burr at 39 was the oldest person in the group.

In July 1980, People Express filed a 200-page application with the Civil Aeronautics Board for permission to operate a new interstate airline, one of the first such requests since passage of the 1978 Airline Deregulation Act. In its filing People Express proposed to raise about $5 million in capital and to lease several planes to fly in and out of the Newark International Airport until it became financially able to buy its own planes and expand its routes.

However, Burr all along intended to establish a much bigger presence in the industry if he could raise the money. His preferred plan was to assemble a fleet of jet aircraft and deploy them over a "hub-and-spoke" system of routes. All flights would entail nonstop round-trips from a single airport terminal (the hub) to a single destination (the spoke), with there being as many spokes as the company could afford planes to support. Planes would be operated with fast turnaround times at each stop, thus enabling them to make more flights per day. Passengers would be induced to fly People Express by offering fares well below those of competitors.

In August 1980, Burr was invited to lunch by William Hambrecht of Hambrecht & Quist, a San Francisco investment firm which had a national reputation for its success in taking small companies public. Burr described his plan to Hambrecht and Hambrecht agreed to head an effort to take People Express public immediately, even though no airline had ever gone public to raise start-up money. Hambrecht believed that Burr's strategy of low fares, no-frills service, fast turnaround times on the ground, and lean operating costs had a good chance to succeed in a climate of deregulation because established airlines, reluctant to upend the way they had always operated, would be hard-pressed to respond effectively given their higher-cost approaches to doing business.

Later in August, Burr took his first tour of the Newark International Airport. Newark had been designated as the hub in the application People Express had made to the CAB, but it had been on the basis of Burr having only read that space was available—no details had been worked out. The North Terminal at Newark had been vacant since 1973, when the airlines operating out of Newark International Airport had moved to two newly built terminals. The stark facilities were like a ghost town, with abandoned junk scattered around and bad disrepair in plain view. Nonetheless, Burr decided on the spot to go ahead with arrangements to rent the space because the Newark airport was closer to downtown Manhattan and Wall Street than was NYC's John F. Kennedy Airport (even if it was located in the less-fashionable Newark area) and because it was viewed by airline travelers as an acceptable alternative to flying into or out of JFK International Airport or LaGuardia International Airport, both of which served New York City and were among the

---

Exhibit 4   Number of Arriving and Departing Passengers at the Top 30 U.S. Airports, 1982

1.	Chicago O'Hare	37,743,598	16.	Pittsburgh	9,986,374
2.	Atlanta	34,702,494	17.	Seattle	9,278,737
3.	Los Angeles	32,383,105	18.	Philadelphia	9,232,609
4.	New York (JFK)	26,452,508	19.	Las Vegas	8,167,044
5.	Dallas/Ft. Worth	24,726,741	20.	Detroit	8,953,966
6.	Denver	24,553,249	21.	Minneapolis/St. Paul	8,679,359
7.	San Francisco	21,028,788	22.	Tampa	7,747,192
8.	Miami	19,387,619	23.	Phoenix	7,492,142
9.	New York (LaGuardia)	18,516,891	24.	Orlando	6,925,198
10.	Boston	15,867,722	25.	New Orleans	5,895,661
11.	Honolulu	15,610,755	26.	Ft. Lauderdale	5,845,575
12.	Washington (National)	13,036,226	27.	Charlotte	5,719,734
13.	Houston	12,501,370	28.	Salt Lake City	5,693,682
14.	St. Louis	12,007,363	29.	San Diego	5,630,343
15.	Newark	11,731,062	30.	Memphis	5,212,721

Source: Air Transport Association of America.

---

10 busiest airports in the United States (see Exhibit 4). He negotiated a leasing fee which was less than half what other airlines were paying for space in the new terminals at Newark.

In October 1980, the CAB granted a certificate to People Express to operate as an interstate airline. Meanwhile, Hambrecht & Quist had proceeded with preparations for a public issue of People Express common stock and, in November, People Express netted approximately $24 million in equity capital from the sale of 3 million shares at $8.50 per share. The funds became available at a perfect time—Burr had just read in a trade journal that a West German airline, Lufthansa, wanted to sell a fleet of 22 used Boeing 737s. Burr sent Harold Pareti to Frankfurt to try to negotiate a deal. Pareti committed People Express to take delivery of 17 of the Boeing 737s at various dates through 1982 at a total price of around $70 million, or $4.1 million per plane (a new deluxe Boeing 737 could then cost as much as $13 million). Lufthansa agreed to remove the Boeing 737s' first-class and galley sections to allow the number of coach-class seats to be increased from 90 to 118, to refurbish the interiors, and to repaint the exteriors to People Express's specifications. According to the agreement, People Express would forfeit a $6 million deposit if for any reason it failed to accept delivery of any of the 17 planes. Commenting later on developments to this point, Burr said, "When we got the Hambrecht financing and the 17 planes, I knew the sky was the limit."[3] Five months later, 200 people had been hired and trained and planes were flying.

Milestones in the rapid progression of People Express are summarized in Exhibit 5.

---

[3] Ibid., p. 46.

Exhibit 5   Key Dates and Events in People Express's Corporate History

---

April 7, 1980.   The corporation is organized and founded by a group of entrepreneurial individuals intent on creating a new approach to commercial air travel.

October 24, 1980.   The Civil Aeronautics Board grants the company a certificate to offer interstate service between Newark, New Jersey, and 27 major cities in the East. The company then proceeds to raise $100 million in financing for the purchase of 17 Boeing 737 aircraft through the sale of common stock and a long-term debt arrangement with a consortium of major Northeast banks. The financing is backed by government loans guaranteed by the Federal Aviation Administration.

April 30, 1981.   Initial service is inaugurated between Newark and Buffalo, Columbus, (Ohio), and Norfolk, with three Boeing 737 aircraft.

April 30, 1982.   The first year of operation ends with strong growth—a fleet of 17 Boeing 737 aircraft serving 12 cities in the East, including four Florida markets. During its first year, People Express carries 1.7 million passengers and has an average load factor of 60.1 percent.

August 19, 1982.   People Express raises $28 million for future expansion through a second stock offering. The distinguished firm of Morgan Stanley & Company joins Hambrecht & Quist in underwriting this issue, and a Morgan Stanley executive is appointed to serve on the company's board of directors.

November 15, 1982.   People Express opens service to 3 new cities with the purchase of 3 additional Boeing 737 aircraft, bringing the total number of cities served in the East to 16 and the Boeing 737 fleet total to 20.

March, 1983.   People Express obtains a revolving line of credit for $22.5 million from the Bank of America and other New Jersey banks. People Express announces one of the airline industry's highest load factors for the first quarter, 76.3 percent.

April, 1983.   The second anniversary of People Express is marked by continued growth and aircraft acquisition including the purchase of a fleet of Boeing 727 jets, the lease of a 747 jet, and expansion of the Boeing 737 fleet to 22 jets.

April 26, 1983.   People Express sells an additional 1 million shares of stock at public offering and raises $33 million.

May 26, 1983.   People Express inaugurates flights to London's Gatwick Airport using a widebody Boeing 747 with seats for 490 persons. The fare is $149 one-way.

October, 1983.   The company enters into a bank credit agreement providing for eight-year term loans of up to $150 million to finance the acquisition costs of part of its Boeing 727 fleet.

December, 1983.   People Express issues $86.2 million of convertible debentures in a public offering; the proceeds are to be used primarily to acquire aircraft and related equipment.

December 31, 1983.   People Express realizes revenue increases of 100 percent over 1982, net income is more than 10 times the 1982 figure, and earnings per share jump by 7 times the 1982 figure.

March, 1984.   The company reaches agreement with the Port Authority of New York and New Jersey to construct a $150 million addition to Terminal C at the Newark International Airport for use by People Express.

April, 1984.   People Express issues $60 million in 14¾ percent secured Equipment Certificates to the public as part of its program to finance its aircraft fleet.

BUSINESS STRATEGY

By early 1981, People Express's strategy was well-crystallized. The company opted to provide low-price, no-frills, high-frequency passenger service to a select number of cities and to do so at costs substantially below those customary in the airline industry. To operate profitably with low-price fares, People Express developed streamlined, budget-conscious operating systems and put together a set of flight schedules and route patterns which would allow it to keep its planes in the air 10 to 11 hours per day, compared to an industry average of just over 7 hours per day.

To hold down labor costs and at the same time boost employee productivity and performance, Burr instituted some novel approaches to organization, staffing, and motivation, including a flat organizational structure, multiple-task assignments for all job categories, and stock options and bonus payments for all employees. Burr felt compelled to "do things differently" at People Express because, over the years, he had become convinced that traditional corporate authority pyramids smothered individual initiative with layers of supervisory control, frustrating people who really wanted to work. Too many companies, he felt, had designed self-serving personnel policies which conditioned employees to approach their work with indifference, disaffection, and even hostility. He was determined that the work environment at People Express would inspire and empower employees to utilize their creative energies.

Pricing Strategy   People Express believed that a substantial passenger traffic market existed for same-day, low-cost, round-trip service on short-distance routes and for low-cost service on medium- and long-distance routes, provided fare prices were not only much lower than other airlines but also competitive with automobile, bus, or rail transportation. The company's fares were competitive with all modes of transportation. The idea was to stimulate demand by inducing passengers who would otherwise travel by automobile, bus, or rail, or who might not travel at all, to take advantage of the speed and convenience of air travel, thereby increasing the total market for the company's services. Donald Burr viewed air travel as

> a commodity business, like chicken parts or steel. . . . We believe that if you respect people and give them a good deal, they'll use the hell out of it.[4]

A two-tier pricing structure was designed for each of the company's domestic routes. On short-haul routes, peak fares were pegged in the range of 45 to 60 percent of the prevailing standard coach fares of rival airlines prior to the announcement of People Express's service. Off-peak prices varied between 25 and 35 percent of rivals' prevailing coach fares. On medium-haul routes, peak and off-peak fares were set substantially below the standard coach fares in effect prior to announcement of service by People Express. For example, on its Newark to Indianapolis route, People established a one-way ticket price of $79 in peak hours and $59 off-peak, compared to the fares of $150 between New York and Indianapolis being charged by TWA and US Air. People's Newark to Norfolk fare was set at $35 on peak and $23 off-peak, in comparison to Piedmont's $82 fare. To compete with the well-known Eastern Air Lines shuttle service between New York and Boston, which offered 15 flights each weekday for $57 during peak hours and $42 at off-peak times, People Express intended to quickly have 20 flights a day for $38 on peak and $25 off-peak. To bring People Express's low-cost fares to the attention of the public, the company launched a "Fly Smart" advertising campaign that drummed the theme "flying costs less than driving."

A number of "unnecessary free services" were unbundled from the standard fare—

---

4 Ibid, pp. 44 and 48.

passengers paid extra to have baggage checked and for snacks and drinks on board; there were no free magazines; and passengers either were ticketed on board the plane or through travel agents, thus reducing the need for so many agents at ticket counters and for gate attendants. The estimated savings of these actions came to about $18 per passenger. A fee of $3 was established for the first two pieces of luggage checked by passengers; the fee for additional or oversize bags was $9. Beverages and snacks on board the aircraft were priced as follows:

Item	Price
Coffee, juice, pastry, soft drink (full can)	$0.50
Small snack, regular and light beer	$1.00
Cocktails, wine, large snack	$2.00

All products were to be top-quality brands. People's Express's "unbundling" of food and beverages from ticket prices was based on analysis which showed that airlines spent close to $1 billion annually on food costs, amounts that averaged $3 to $5 per passenger (several of the major airlines, namely United, American, TWA, and Pan Am, spent $4 to $7 per passenger). Unbundling lowered both fares and operating costs; as the company later stated in its promotional literature:

> Our customers are smart and they realize that there is no such thing as "free drinks," "free meals," and "free baggage handling." Those costs are usually disguised in the ticket price and the passenger pays for them whether he uses them or not.

Cost Strategy   People Express intended to develop an efficient management organization, simplified operations, and such productive utilization of both aircraft and employees that it would have the lowest costs per available seat per mile flown of any airline in the industry. The target was to achieve a cost per available seat mile in the 5¢ to 6¢ range (against revenues which averaged 8¢ to 9¢ per passenger mile). Burr and his associates calculated that, with revenues averaging 8¢ per passenger mile and operating costs averaging 5¢ per available seat mile, People Express would have to fill only 60 percent of all available seats to break even. Given that most other airlines then had costs of 8¢ to 12¢ per available seat mile and were charging fares which yielded revenues of 10¢ to 15¢ per passenger mile, Burr believed People Express would be in a strong competitive position.

To further its strategic objective of becoming the lowest-cost airline, People Express carried through with its plan for a hub-and-spoke route pattern; all flights were scheduled to make nonstop round trips between Newark International Airport and a selected destination. Passengers connected to all People Express destinations at the Newark terminal. Gerald Gitner, who had a reputation as a wizard of route selection and marketing, supervised the analysis of which routes to fly. Ground times were minimized so planes could make more flights per day (in early 1984, for example, the company's planes were in the air about 10 hours per day—over 2 hours above the industry average). According to one of the company's managers:

> You don't keep costs down by counting pencils and paper clips. You have to squeeze massive productivity out of people and planes.

To reduce personnel and facility requirements, the company set up a reservation system that accepted reservations only for its own flights; it was not a party to interline arrangements with any other airlines for ticketing or for baggage. The company had no ticket counters; all tickets were purchased either on board or through travel agents. To reduce the need for people and for equipment to handle checked baggage, passengers were encouraged to carry their luggage on board themselves and to store it under their seats or in the overhead compartments.

All passengers flew coach class (except that first-class service was available on the Boeing 747 flights later established between Newark and London). The interiors of all People Express's planes were redesigned to increase seating capacity—the Boeing 737s bought from Lufthansa, for example, had 90 seats and a galley for hot meals; the galley and first-class sections were taken out and 28 seats per plane were added. The redesign achieved a higher level of available seat miles per flight and per gallon of fuel consumed.

The company arranged with independent contractors for the performance of substantially all aircraft maintenance and for much of the ground-handling services required at airports. Some of the contractors People Express chose were other airlines with whom it competed. Such arrangements were not unusual in the airline industry, and the company believed that they were more economical than performing such operations directly with company personnel. However, the company did employ a staff of maintenance managers to supervise the activities of the independent contractors and outside ground-handling personnel.

Personnel Strategy   Burr and his inner circle of recruits from Texas International thought longer and harder about how to design the "people structure" at People Express than about anything else. Burr was convinced from his prior experience that "people are the enterprise" and that without the wholehearted, personal commitment of everyone involved the rest of the strategy could fall flat. A decision was made to be very selective in recruiting and to search out only highly motivated employees who would fit the cofounders' concept of "the People Express type." Moreover, every employee was designated as a "manager" and only three job classifications were established: flight managers (who performed as pilots and served as instructors, dispatchers, and schedulers), maintenance managers (who supervised maintenance operations and performed other staff functions), and customer service managers (who did just about everything else—including handing out boarding passes as passengers checked in, ticketing passengers, serving snacks and drinks, handling luggage, and taking on various staff functions on a rotational basis).

The staffing emphasis was on cross-utilization and multiple-job assignments—no employee performed just a single function all of the time. People Express's pilots were scheduled to fly about 70 hours per month (compared to an industry average of about 45 hours), which left ample time for them to take on other duties. No one, not even Burr, was assigned a secretary. Cross-utilization was considered a vital way to hone the company's competitive edge and as a source of productivity-building job enrichment. Burr and his cofounders believed cross-utilization would reduce personnel requirements by at least 10 percent.

Part-time employees were hired to handle telephone reservations; they were given the title of reservations sales representatives. All full-time employees were asked to

Exhibit 6   Sample "Help Wanted" Newspaper Ad Placed by People Express Airlines

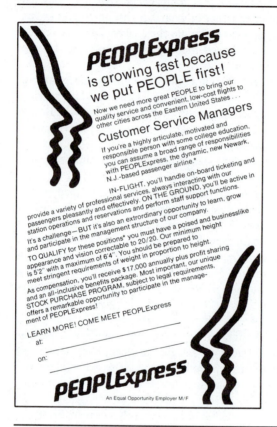

volunteer to help take reservations; signs taped on corridor walls at headquarters announced: "Reservations needs help at peaks on Thursday. Sign up, schedules permitting."

Job openings were advertised in local newspapers; the ads were upbeat and stimulated numerous applications (see Exhibit 6). Every job applicant was thoroughly screened. Recruiters spent about five hours evaluating each individual whose credentials and personality appeared suitable. Those who survived the weeding out at this stage were invited to attend training classes (not equivalent to a job offer). Customer service managers-in-training had to go through a five-week program, during which they learned to display enthusiasm, confidence, and competence and to otherwise shine with a clean-cut, pleasant, collegiate exuberance. Those customer service trainees who best displayed the traits of "the People Express type" were offered a job with a base pay of $17,500 plus fringe benefits (including 100 percent medical and dental coverage) and profit-sharing.

As a condition of employment, all full-time employees had to purchase at least 100 shares of the company's common stock (at prices as much as 60 percent below the current market price); those who didn't have the cash to pay for the stock were given an interest-free loan. Additional incentive stock option opportunities were made available to all employees throughout the year at prices not less than the fair market value on the date the option was granted. A profit-sharing plan for full-time employees was instituted, whereby the company contributed amounts based on pre-tax return on revenue (not to exceed one third of the company's income before income taxes for four consecutive quarters). The employee compensation package was intended to secure a high level of motivation and commitment as well as to minimize the threat of unionization.

Salaries for top executives were set at modest levels—Burr and Gitner received $48,000 per year in 1981. Pilots were recruited at $30,000 a year to start (the average salary for pilots at other airlines was about $60,000 a year); however, the starting pay of customer service managers of $17,500 a year was well above the entry-level pay at rival airlines. Burr explained:

> This is a very democratic company. We've leveled the compensation scales and we intend to keep it that way. We want people motivated by feelings of ownership and peer pressure.[5]

To push even further toward a working environment which was conducive to personal responsibility, accountability, and commitment, Burr and his cofounders established a horizontal organization structure with only the three levels: (1) the managing officers (company founders), (2) general managers, and (3) flight managers, maintenance managers, and customer service managers. Because all individuals were cross-utilized in more than one area of operations on a rotational basis, employees became familiar with several phases of company operations, with more appreciation of the significance of their own individual roles. The cofounders believed that the combination of People Express's unique organizational structure, its cross-utilization of employees, employee ownership requirements, and compensation packages would result not only in operating economies but also in excellent, courteous passenger service. Burr observed, "To be a winner, you have to have the ultimate frill—nice people."

THE U.S. SCHEDULED AIRLINE INDUSTRY

In 1984, the U.S. scheduled airline industry began its 26th year of jet service. Safety, speed, reliability, and convenience were major factors in boosting the number of passengers enplaned from 49 million in 1958 to an estimated 300 million in 1983. Industry revenues were approaching $40 billion annually (Exhibit 7) and there were about 14,000 daily flights. The industry consisted of 12 "major" airlines, 15 "national" airlines, 17 "large regional" airlines, and 49 "medium regional" airlines; about 17 had commenced service since 1981. Exhibit 8 shows data on the 30 largest commercial airlines as of 1982. In 1983, about 2,800 passenger aircraft were in service, about 95 percent of which were jet aircraft. Since 1979, when 317 million passengers were enplaned, passenger air traffic had fallen off (see Exhibit 7).

---

[5] As quoted in Peter Nulty, "A Champ of Cheap Airlines," *Fortune,* March 22, 1982, p. 134.

Exhibit 7   Selected Financial and Operating Statistics of the U.S. Scheduled Airline Industry, 1972–1982

	1972	*1973*	*1974*	*1975*
Traffic—scheduled service:				
Revenue passengers enplaned (000)	191,349	202,208	207,458	205,062
Revenue passenger miles (000)	152,406,276	161,957,307	162,918,594	162,810,057
Available seat miles (000)	287,411,214	310,597,107	297,006,062	303,006,243
Revenue passenger load factor (%)	53.0%	52.1%	54.9%	53.7%
Average passenger trip length (miles)	797	801	785	794
Aircraft departures	5,046,438	5,134,577	4,726,101	4,704,052
Passenger Revenue ($000)	$ 9,271,353	$ 10,274,310	$ 11,879,177	$ 12,353,501
Freight revenue ($000)	906,494	1,038,459	1,216,332	1,295,100
Charter revenue ($000)	448,537	421,007	444,815	489,856
Total operating revenues ($000)	11,163,271	12,418,777	14,699,125	15,355,921
Total operating expenses ($000)	10,578,800	11,833,511	13,973,385	15,228,042
Operating Profit ($000)	584,471	585,266	725,740	127,879
Net income ($000)	214,850	226,693	321,641	(84,204)
Revenue per passenger mile (¢)	6.1¢	6.3¢	7.3¢	7.6¢
Operating profit margin (%)	5.2%	4.7%	4.8%	0.8%
Aircraft in service	2,361	2,361	2,244	2,267
Employees	301,127	311,499	307,318	289,926

Source: Air Transport Association of America.

Five years after passage of the Airline Deregulation Act of 1978, it was evident that the industry was still very much in a state of transition and restructuring. The deregulation act had provided greater freedom for airline carriers to schedule flights into airports they had not served heretofore, to abandon unprofitable flight and routes, and to reprice their fares. No longer was there strict regulatory authority for setting airline fares and for restricting price competition.

Airline carriers responded to the freedom which deregulation afforded by instituting a host of new discount fare packages, rearranging flight schedules, and establishing all kinds of incentive schemes for generating increased passenger traffic (frequent-flyer plans, weekend vacation packages, and off-price tie-ins with rental car agencies and hotel/motel chains). Competition intensified to a significant degree. Price wars were common on heavily traveled routes, yet price increases were common on less traveled routes served by only one or two airlines. The stability of fares and pricing rationality (which under close government regulation had usually been a function of mileage or distance) disappeared. Changes in fare prices and in routes were fast-paced, as airlines scrambled for market position and profitable traffic volumes and load factors. Frequent-flyer plans (whereby travelers could earn added discounts and free tickets as they accumulated mileage flown on a given airline) were instituted by many of the major airlines in an attempt to increase customer loyalty and to combat the propensity of travelers to fly whichever airline offered the lowest fare to their destination.

1976	1977	1978	1979	1980	1981	1982
223,318	240,326	274,719	316,863	296,903	285,976	293,244
178,988,026	193,218,819	226,781,368	262,023,375	255,192,114	248,887,801	259,037,643
322,821,649	345,565,901	368,750,530	416,126,429	432,535,103	424,897,230	438,956,310
55.4%	55.9%	61.5%	63.0%	59.0%	58.6%	59.0%
802	804	826	827	860	870	883
4,832,664	4,936,519	5,013,169	5,399,652	5,352,927	5,211,867	4,930,842
$ 14,265,947	$ 16,273,355	$ 18,806,247	$ 22,791,390	$ 28,048,689	$ 30,722,629	$ 30,549,719
1,482,502	1,687,302	1,939,062	2,155,228	2,370,468	2,512,796	2,351,099
572,580	644,381	578,285	520,916	1,160,524	1,175,154	1,085,537
17,501,215	19,924,800	22,883,955	27,226,665	33,727,806	36,662,555	36,407,635
16,779,282	19,016,760	21,519,092	27,027,610	33,949,421	37,117,325	37,141,070
721,933	908,040	1,364,863	199,055	(221,615)	(454,770)	(733,435)
563,354	752,536	1,196,537	346,845	17,414	(300,826)	(915,814)
8.0¢	8.4¢	8.3¢	8.7¢	11.0¢	12.3¢	11.8¢
4.1%	4.6%	6.0%	0.7%	(0.7)%	(1.2)%	(2.0)%
2,264	2,229	2,266	2,542	2,712	2,808	2,830
303,006	308,068	329,303	340,696	360,517	349,864	330,495

A number of significant events transpired in the wake of deregulation:

- Because the major airlines were no longer required to serve obscure destinations and unprofitable routes, new market opportunities opened up for smaller regional carriers with small planes to serve the less frequently traveled routes which were rapidly being abandoned by the majors.
- Airlines could, under streamlined regulatory procedures, now register and obtain approval for a new fare within 24 hours.
- The major carriers focused more emphasis on expanding their service between major population centers, opting to add more long-haul flights and to attain transcontinental coverage. This was mainly because larger planes, especially the wide-bodied jets, were economical to use on long hauls but not on short hauls.
- The hub-and-spoke route pattern, pioneered by Delta Airlines, was quickly adopted by all of the major carriers and many of the national and large regional carriers because of both marketing and operating advantages. (All airlines did not use the same airports as hubs—Delta's was Atlanta; American's was Dallas; and US Air's was Pittsburgh. Eastern had two major hubs—Miami and Atlanta; United had hubs at Denver and Chicago; and Republic utilized three hubs—Detroit, Memphis, and Minneapolis–St. Paul). Airlines whose hubs were in a particular city usually had dominant market shares in that city because of the large number of flights offered and excellent interconnections to other destinations.

Exhibit 8   The 30 Largest U.S. Commercial Airlines, 1982

	Number of Passengers Enplaned (in thousands)		Revenue Passenger Miles (in thousands)		Total Operating Revenues (in thousands of dollars)
1.	Eastern	35,138	United	38,483,142	United	$4,613,850
2.	Delta	33,678	American	30,900,013	American	3,977,774
3.	United	32,777	Pan American	27,165,791	Eastern	3,769,237
4.	American	27,670	Eastern	26,063,139	Delta	3,741,376
5.	Republic	18,022	Trans World	25,530,720	Pan American	3,471,376
6.	Trans World	17,699	Delta	24,406,576	Trans World	3,236,178
7.	USAir	14,639	Northwest	15,675,196	Northwest	1,888,247
8.	Continental	13,071	Continental	11,157,392	Republic	1,530,668
9.	Pan American	12,255	Republic	9,172,724	Continental	1,415,207
10.	Northwest	11,356	Western	8,884,697	USAir	1,273,012
11.	Western	10,002	USAir	6,078,094	Western	1,065,270
12.	Southwest	9,075	Piedmont	3,888,982	Flying Tiger	877,744
13.	Piedmont	8,511	Frontier	3,545,592	Piedmont	655,340
14.	PSA	7,083	Capitol	3,483,608	Frontier	537,736
15.	Frontier	5,850	Braniff	3,145,903	Ozark	407,155
16.	Ozark	4,286	Southwest	3,022,140	PSA	378,132
17.	Braniff	3,911	PSA	2,638,070	Braniff	360,228
18.	AirCal	3,409	World	2,627,168	Southwest	331,188
19.	Hawaiian	3,165	Ozark	2,155,730	Air Florida	280,800
20.	People Express	2,857	Air Florida	2,103,042	World	269,881
21.	Aloha	2,431	People Express	1,553,805	Capitol	267,194
22.	Air Florida	2,384	AirCal	1,298,261	Transamerica	239,507
23.	New York Air	1,738	Alaska	1,263,582	Alaska	235,372
24.	Capitol	1,627	Midway	646,394	AirCal	214,737
25.	Alaska	1,547	New York Air	606,656	Wien Air Alaska	178,420
26.	Midway	1,260	Wien Air Alaska	565,824	People Express	138,859
27.	World	1,246	Hawaiian	407,528	Hawaiian	99,891
28.	Wien Air Alaska	906	Aloha	324,092	New York Air	95,416
29.	Muse	864	Muse	271,314	Midway	94,690
30.	Air Wisconsin	724	Transamerica	265,701	Aloha	81,342

Source: Air Transport Association of America.

- As price wars erupted, airlines spent more on newspaper and radio advertising to publicize their discount fares and to announce their promotional programs (industrywide advertising, for example, rose from $148 million in 1979 to $187 million in 1980—a 26 percent increase.
- A number of regional carriers entered the market, competing on the basis of low fares, cheaper labor costs, low overhead, and fuel-efficient aircraft. The most prominent of these were People Express, Midway, New York Air (a subsidiary of Texas International), Air Florida, Pioneer, and Southwest Airlines (a subsidiary of Texas International and the role model for the "new breed of discounters"). Many of these new carriers were started by "entrepreneurial alumni" of existing airlines.
- When one airline (either a low-price regional or a major carrier) established a discount fare on a given route, competitors on that route usually saw no other recourse but to do the same and match the discounter's fare. However, in matching the price-cutter's discount fares, competitors often placed restrictive conditions on the matched low-price fare—such as requiring the ticket to be purchased one to four weeks in advance, requiring the interval between the traveler's departing and return flights to include a Saturday, limiting the time of travel to off-peak periods, and limiting the number of seats on a given flight for discount fares.

These developments had made all airlines very cost-conscious and had caused many to pursue cost-cutting programs, including renegotiation of labor contracts with employee unions (especially as concerned salary reductions and elimination of restrictive work practices). Most of the commercial airlines were unionized. The vast majority of commercial airline pilots belonged to a powerful pilot's union (the Air Line Pilots Association) which had been successful in bargaining for lucrative salaries, fringe benefits, and working conditions for pilots; unions representing other airline employees historically had also exercised significant leverage with management, winning good contracts for their members in the process. The new cut-rate airlines were not unionized.

Employment in the industry had exhibited the following patterns:

	1972	1981	1982
Pilots and copilots	26,880	30,230	28,144
Other flight personnel	6,820	6,726	6,900
Flight attendants	39,408	54,726	50,860
Communications personnel	2,080	1,150	838
Mechanics	45,570	45,325	43,393
Aircraft and traffic servicing personnel	88,098	94,897	87,813
Office employees	58,974	68,600	66,997
All other	33,297	40,096	35,564
Total majors and nationals	—	341,750	320,509
Total large and medium regionals	—	8,114	9,986
Total employment	301,127	349,864	330,495

Exhibit 9 shows cost breakdowns for the major and national airlines as a group. Exhibit 10 contains various operating and financial statistics for the industry, with breakouts for the major, nationals, and regionals. Exhibits 11 and 12 present additional industry and company statistics.

Exhibit 9 Selected Operating Costs of U.S. Commercial Airline Industry—Majors and Nationals Only—1972, 1981, and 1982

	1972	1981	1982
Labor:			
Total cost ($millions)	$ 4,627	$ 12,384	$ 12,511
Average number of employees	295,684	340,091	319,225
Average compensation ($)	$ 15,650	$ 36,414	$ 39,193
Percent of total operating expenses	46.8%	34.8%	35.3%
Passenger meals:			
Total cost ($millions)	$ 390	$ 993	$ 1,015
Cost per revenue passenger mile	0.238¢	0.395¢	0.390¢
Percent of total operating expenses	3.9%	2.8%	2.9%
Interest:			
Interest on debt ($millions)	$ 344	$ 1,292	$ 1,431
Average debt outstanding ($millions)	$ 5,950	$ 12,325	$ 13,584
Average book interest rate (%)	5.8%	10.5%	10.5%
Percent of total operating expenses	3.5%	3.6%	4.0%

	1972	1981	1982
Fuel:			
Total cost ($millions)	$ 1,189	$10,461	$9,674
Gallons used (millions)	10,195	10,041	9,834
Avg. cost per gal. (¢)	11.7¢	104.2¢	98.4¢
Percent of total operating expenses	12.0%	30.4%	28.1%
Landing fees:			
Total cost (millions)	$ 257	$ 585	$ 593
Aircraft capacity tons landed (millions)	98	106	106
Cost per ton landed ($)	$ 2.63	$ 5.50	$ 5.60
Percent of total operating expenses	2.6%	1.6%	1.7%
Maintenance materials, and other costs:			
Total cost ($millions)	$ 2,482	$ 6,870	$7,083
Percent of total operating expenses	25.1%	19.3%	20.0%

	1972	1981	1982
Traffic commissions:			
Total cost ($millions)	$ 342	$ 2,063	$ 2,214
Cost per revenue passenger mile	0.209¢	0.821¢	0.850¢
Percent of total operating expenses	3.5%	5.8%	6.2%
Advertising and promotion:			
Total cost ($millions)	$ 254	$ 623	731
Percent of total operating expenses	2.6%	1.8%	2.1%
Total operating expenses ($millions)	$9,885	$35,583	$35,468

Note: Total operating expense includes interest on debt less depreciation and amortization.
Source: Air Transport Association of America.

AIRLINE REGULATION

All regional, national, and major commercial airlines in the United States were subject to the Federal Aviation Act of 1958, under which the Civil Aeronautics Board (CAB) and the administrator of the FAA exercised regulatory authority. The CAB had jurisdiction over issuance of certificates authorizing carriers to provide airline transportation to the public, supervised the fares airlines charged, and approved the routes which carriers flew; routes authorized by the CAB could not be abandoned without notice to the CAB and the communities affected. The CAB was empowered to prohibit unfair methods of competition, to mandate conditions of air travel service, and to approve or disapprove mergers and contracts between air carriers. The FAA had jurisdiction over air safety, flight equipment, flight personnel and their training, certain ground facilities, maintenance programs, communications, and various other aspects of flight operations.

In accordance with the phased-in provisions of the Airline Deregulation Act of 1978, the CAB's control over domestic routes terminated at the end of 1981 and its control over the reasonableness of interstate fares terminated on January 1, 1983; however, the CAB retained authority over foreign routes and fares until 1985. Prior to the deregulation act, it was well-established CAB policy to set commercial airline fares based on the average costs of the industry and to discourage new competitors from entering the industry unless they could present a convincing case on how the public interest would be better served. As a consequence of strict fare regulation, rival airlines competed mainly on service variables; rising costs associated with generous union contracts and service-oriented competition were passed on to travelers by CAB-approved fare increases. Deregulatory conditions, however, had prompted rapid erosion of the CAB's protective pricing practices. The CAB was scheduled to terminate its existence on January 1, 1985, at which time its authority over mergers, acquisitions, and interlocking relationships concerning interstate and overseas air transportation was to be transferred to the Department of Justice. The CAB's authority over foreign air transportation was to be transferred to the Department of Transportation.

Since 1968, the FAA had restricted the number of hourly arrivals and departures at airports where there was high air traffic congestion. At airports where the FAA's "high-density rule" was a limiting factor (Chicago O'Hare, Atlanta, Los Angeles, Dallas/Ft. Worth, and Washington National were prominent examples), airlines were sometimes unable to obtain arrival and departure slots at favorable times and the FAA could reallocate slots of one company to another.

In August 1981, the nation's air traffic controllers went on strike, prompting the FAA to impose an emergency set of procedures for operating the entire U.S. air traffic control system. During the initial phase of the strike, 22 high-traffic airports were singled out for reductions in flights below the normal high-density limits. As the FAA rebuilt its air traffic controller work force (the strikers, because of their government employee status and their role in safe operation of air traffic systems, were fired and not rehired), arrival and departure slots at many of the controlled airports were gradually restored to their former limits and made available to airlines petitioning for them.

Exhibit 10 Selected Operating and Financial Statistics by Type of Carrier, 1981 and 1982

	Total U.S. Scheduled Airlines		Majors		Nationals		Regionals	
	1981	1982	1981	1982	1981	1982	1981	1982
Passenger traffic—scheduled service:								
Revenue passengers enplaned (000)	285,976	293,244	224,802	226,583	51,757	55,292	9,417	11,369
Revenue passenger miles (000)	248,887,801	259,037,643	219,607,064	224,658,799	26,863,623	29,840,484	2,417,114	4,538,360
Available seat miles (000)	424,897,230	438,956,310	377,092,683	380,846,596	43,219,023	49,646,379	4,585,524	8,463,335
Revenue passenger load factor (%)	58.6%	59.0%	58.2%	59.0%	62.2%	60.1%	52.7%	53.6%
Average length of haul (miles)	870	883	977	992	519	540	257	399
Operating revenues—total ($000):	$ 36,662,555	$ 36,407,635	$ 30,457,115	$ 29,976,760	$ 5,211,600	$ 5,260,845	$ 993,840	$1,170,030
Passenger	30,722,629	30,549,719	26,687,200	26,181,013	3,434,757	3,664,642	600,672	704,064
Freight	2,512,796	2,351,099	1,690,594	1,543,363	687,923	695,703	134,279	112,033
U.S. mail	653,996	688,675	549,035	562,010	94,229	111,954	10,732	14,711
Express	84,054	86,604	62,736	72,797	20,776	12,816	542	991
Charter	1,175,154	1,085,537	159,399	214,712	813,177	595,074	202,578	275,751
Public service revenue	113,085	56,048	39,467	20,885	52,353	24,448	21,265	10,715
Other	1,400,842	1,589,953	1,268,685	1,381,980	108,385	156,208	23,772	51,765
Operating expenses—total ($000):	$ 37,117,325	$ 37,141,070	$ 31,053,685	$ 30,693,370	$ 5,031,716	$ 5,281,952	$1,031,924	$1,165,748
Flying operations	15,495,515	14,664,093	12,837,118	12,034,178	2,206,765	2,113,057	451,632	516,858
Maintenance	3,559,636	3,373,473	2,920,849	2,748,957	478,275	468,429	160,512	156,087
General services & administration:								
Passenger service	3,185,661	3,314,544	2,880,699	2,967,560	296,913	335,843	8,049	11,141
Aircraft & traffic servicing	5,520,267	5,629,780	4,634,215	4,646,942	858,364	943,820	27,688	39,018
Promotion and sales	4,731,061	5,202,157	4,206,649	4,537,667	502,453	634,277	21,959	30,213
Administrative	1,728,535	1,881,300	1,096,779	1,202,338	353,014	377,507	278,743	301,455
Transport related	685,670	726,399	629,281	625,208	43,582	65,889	12,807	35,302
Total	15,851,195	16,754,182	13,447,623	13,979,715	2,054,326	2,357,338	349,246	417,129
Depreciation & amortization:	2,210,979	2,349,322	1,848,095	1,930,520	292,350	343,128	70,534	75,674
Operating income or (loss) ($000):	$ (454,770)	$ (733,435)	$ (596,570)	$ (716,610)	$ 179,884	$ (21,107)	$ (38,084)	$ 4,282

Other income statement items ($000):

Interest expense	$ 1,234,898	$ 1,384,084	$ 888,060	$ 974,482	$ 266,971	$ 327,343	$ 79,867	$ 82,259
Income taxes	(140,546)	(102,191)	(237,352)	(122,248)	84,094	15,354	12,712	4,703
Net profit or (loss)	(300,826)	(915,814)	(329,904)	(752,431)	129,997	(121,445)	(100,919)	(41,938)
Assets:								
Current assets	$ 7,389,295	$ 7,411,828	$ 6,165,503	$ 6,304,553	$ 1,009,499	$ 910,502	$ 214,293	$ 196,773
Investments and special funds	1,126,506	1,150,458	707,973	792,150	405,787	316,701	12,746	41,607
Flight equipment	22,739,812	23,463,804	18,475,515	19,211,715	3,490,465	3,613,589	773,832	638,500
Ground property & equipment	5,183,433	5,377,772	4,587,244	4,773,969	530,053	551,155	66,136	52,648
Reserve for depreciation (owned)	(11,090,728)	(11,312,036)	(9,983,752)	(10,227,078)	(937,140)	(911,209)	(169,836)	(173,749)
Leased property capitalized	6,329,378	6,230,986	5,252,018	5,292,023	991,215	911,945	86,145	27,018
Reserved for depreciation (leased)	(2,375,593)	(2,586,920)	(2,076,779)	(2,290,653)	(291,818)	(291,561)	(6,996)	(4,706)
Other property	1,341,590	1,037,226	989,125	879,203	319,331	145,048	33,234	12,975
Deferred charges	365,123	404,331	193,077	256,587	131,528	122,071	40,518	25,674
Total assets	$ 31,008,816	$ 31,177,449	$ 24,309,924	$ 24,992,468	$ 5,648,820	$ 5,368,241	$1,050,072	$ 816,740
Liabilities:								
Current liabilities	$ 9,694,515	$ 9,154,214	$ 7,937,141	$ 7,771,179	$ 1,529,016	$ 1,168,835	$ 228,357	$ 214,200
Long-term debt	7,416,422	8,831,816	5,225,377	6,672,122	1,641,782	1,803,160	549,263	356,534
Other noncurrent liabilities	4,604,919	4,591,542	3,759,419	3,745,501	756,887	788,618	88,613	57,423
Deferred credit	1,553,479	1,521,462	1,332,804	1,323,048	198,399	171,667	22,276	26,747
Stockholders' equity—net of treasury stock	7,739,482	7,078,415	6,055,183	5,480,618	1,522,736	1,435,961	161,563	161,836
Preferred stock	233,508	210,701	193,039	181,109	27,104	16,532	13,365	13,060
Common stock	412,635	386,335	260,361	229,148	139,053	147,538	13,221	9,649
Other paid-in capital	3,840,943	4,046,233	2,889,708	3,074,202	710,500	813,584	240,735	158,447
Retained earnings	3,264,528	2,448,829	2,713,602	1,997,685	647,571	462,658	(96,645)	(11,514)
Less: treasury stock	12,132	13,685	1,527	1,527	1,492	4,351	9,113	7,806
Total liabilities and equity	$ 31,008,816	$ 31,177,449	$ 24,309,924	$ 24,992,468	$ 5,648,820	$ 5,368,241	$1,050,072	$ 816,740

Source: Air Transport Association of America.

Exhibit 11   Financial and Operating Comparisons of Selected U.S. Commercial Airlines, 1982

Company	Number of Employees	Passengers	Annual Number of Flight Departures	Revenue Passenger Miles (in thousands)	Total Operating Revenues (in thousands of dollars)	Operating Profit (Loss) (in thousands of dollars)	Net Profit (Loss) (in thousands of dollars)
AirCal	2,036	3,409,000	58,338	1,298,261	$ 214,737	$ (20,654)	$ (23,992)
Air Florida	1,923	2,384,000	51,455	2,103,042	280,800	(33,940)	(78,507)
Alaska	1,962	1,547,000	34,120	1,263,582	235,372	23,270	10,569
Aloha	877	2,431,000	32,059	324,092	81,342	295	(325)
American	34,095	27,670,000	317,611	30,900,013	3,977,774	(18,247)	(14,476)
Capitol	1,661	1,627,000	7,801	3,483,608	267,194	(12,965)	(21,203)
Continental*	14,506	13,071,000	216,126	11,157,392	1,415,207	(62,078)	(64,710)
Delta	36,158	33,678,000	493,246	24,406,576	3,631,792	(85,948)	(17,058)
Eastern	40,011	35,138,000	500,800	26,063,139	3,769,237	(18,781)	(74,927)
Frontier	5,445	5,850,000	141,420	3,545,592	537,736	6,812	15,922
Hawaiian	966	3,165,000	39,699	407,528	99,891	(6,612)	(16,761)
Midway	712	1,259,921	27,869	646,394	94,690	4,464	346
Muse Air	440	864,000	14,118	271,314	33,056	(4,738)	11,468
Northwest	12,828	11,356,000	152,351	15,675,196	1,888,247	(7,998)	5,019
Ozark	3,941	4,286,000	104,293	2,155,730	407,155	18,099	7,542
Pan Am	30,318	12,255,000	137,734	27,165,791	3,471,376	(372,736)	(485,331)
Piedmont	6,554	8,511,000	187,966	3,888,982	655,341	21,952	30,463
Pacific Southwest	3,540	7,083,000	87,400	2,638,070	378,132	(17,432)	18,552
Republic	14,262	18,022,000	460,215	9,172,724	1,530,668	37,253	(39,861)
Trans World	29,910	17,699,000	194,914	25,530,720	3,236,178	(104,174)	(30,829)
United	41,283	32,777,000	399,874	38,483,142	4,613,850	(68,549)	(10,751)
US Air	10,690	14,639,000	291,524	6,078,094	1,273,012	79,336	59,104
Western	10,257	10,002,000	139,120	8,884,697	1,065,270	(30,798)	(44,016)
Wien Air Alaska	1,365	906,000	91,591	565,824	178,420	6,113	2,140

* Figures include data for Texas International, which merged with Continental on November 1, 1982.
Source: Air Transport Association of America.

Exhibit 12   Selected Airline Traffic Statistics, by Company, 1983

	1983 Revenue Passenger Miles (in billions)	Percent Change from 1982	1983 Available Seat Miles (in billions)	Percent Change from 1982	Load Factors	
					1982	1983
Major carriers:						
American	34.1	+10.3%	52.4	+7.5%	63.3	65.0
Continental	9.3	−16.8	15.4	−20.1	57.9	60.3
Delta	26.8	+9.6	49.5	+6.9	52.7	54.0
Eastern	28.3	+8.4	47.9	+4.1	56.7	59.0
Northwest	17.7	+13.0	29.5	+12.4	59.7	60.0
Pan American	28.9	+6.2	46.3	+2.8	57.1	62.4
Republic	9.6	+5.0	17.7	+7.3	55.7	54.4
Trans World	27.3	+6.8	42.5	+5.1	63.2	64.1
United	43.0	+11.8	67.6	+10.2	62.7	63.6
USAir	7.2	+19.2	12.2	+14.7	57.0	59.2
Western	9.4	+5.9	16.6	+10.1	58.8	56.5
Other carriers:						
AirCal	1.4	+5.8	2.4	−6.4	51.4	58.2
Air Florida	1.8	−14.5	2.9	−18.2	59.5	62.2
Alaska	1.5	+22.5	2.7	+23.7	58.0	57.4
Frontier	3.9	+10.1	6.6	+12.1	61.0	59.9
Jet America	.6	+78.3	.9	+46.5	58.5	71.2
Midway	.6	+0.3	1.3	+12.9	54.4	48.4
Muse Air	.7	+139.8	1.3	+97.0	41.8	50.9
New York Air	.7	+8.2	1.1	+3.3	54.6	57.3
Ozark	2.6	+21.6	⁻4.7	+18.3	54.5	56.1
People Express	3.7	+136.0	4.9	+92.5	60.9	74.6
Piedmont	5.1	+31.9	9.5	+36.3	55.6	53.8
PSA	3.1	+16.6	5.6	+15.9	54.9	55.2
Southwest	3.9	+28.8	6.3	+28.9	61.6	61.6

Source: *Aviation Week & Space Technology*, January 30, 1984.

PEOPLE EXPRESS IN 1981

People Express began its first flights on April 30, 1981, with three Boeing 737s flying to three destinations. By June, the company had five 737s in operation flying to Buffalo, Norfolk, Boston, Columbus, and Jacksonville. To attract passengers, the airline ran newspaper ads headlining "Flying That Costs Less than Driving" and highlighting its rock-bottom fares. Then in early August, when members of the Professional Air Traffic Controllers Organization went on strike, People Express flirted with disaster. The FAA's safety cutbacks in flights at 22 airports, including Newark International, hit the company hard. People Express, with seven planes and 35 departures a day from Newark, was ordered by the FAA to cut out 12 flights. Widespread publicity over the strike and its disruption of scheduled flights prompted a sharp dropoff in passenger travel. From August to October, People Express lost $6 million from cancelled trips and low load factors. Cash flows were insufficient to make the payments to Lufthansa on the delivery of the additional Boeing 737s.

In a move born of desperation to avoid going out of business, Burr and his colleagues abandoned the original hub-and-spoke operation and initiated flights from Buffalo, Columbus, and Baltimore to Sarasota and West Palm Beach, Florida—all uncongested and unrestricted airports. South Florida routes were chosen without careful analysis on the chance that, with Florida's leisure-time attractions, they might prove price sensitive; the thinking was that if fares were cheap enough people might take spur-of-the-moment trips, saying, "Why shouldn't I go to Florida?" or "Why shouldn't I go twice instead of once, like I usually do?" Crews were shifted, new support services were arranged, and ads announcing the new flights were run in local newspapers. Burr said, "We had to create a whole new airline and we had to do it overnight. We had to bet the company a second time."[6] The $59 one-way fares were attractive; early flights were 60 percent full, and traffic built up to an 85 percent load factor on several routes. Revenues improved and cash flows were enough to finance the payments to Lufthansa. As the crisis of the air traffic controllers strike eased and the FAA eased up on the flight restrictions, People Express gradually returned to its original hub-and-spoke scheduling patterns.

The company finished the year on an upbeat note, making a $500,000 profit in December (the eighth month of flying) on revenues of $9 million. That same month, Burr felt it was time to take the philosophy and values that existed in the collective minds of the cofounders and formalize them in writing. In an all-day meeting, the company's senior managers debated just what People Express was trying to accomplish and what the company stood for; six "precepts" emerged:

- Dedication to service, growth, and development of people.
- Becoming the best provider of air transportation in the industry.
- Exhibiting the highest quality of management.
- Serving as an industry role model.
- Simplicity.
- Maximization of profit.

Burr saw these precepts as defining and revealing the soul of People Express.

People Express was not alone in trying to break into the airline business with a discount fare strategy. By year-end 1981, there were eight cut-rate carriers offering no-frills, point-to-point service (see table, page 331).

The established major and national airlines responded to the entry of the discounters by matching their fares and by heavily advertising their service advantages; there were also a few reported instances where established carriers had turned a deaf ear

---

[6] Rhodes, "That Daring Young Man," p. 50.

Company	Home Base	Start-Up Date	Cities Served	Fleet	Capitalization
Midway	Chicago's Midway Airport	1979	Chicago, Kansas City, Detroit, Cleveland, Washington, St. Louis, New York, Omaha, Philadelphia	Nine DC-9-10s	$27.5 million
New York Air	New York's LaGuardia Airport	1980	New York, Washington, Boston, Cleveland, Louisville	Seven DC-9-30s	$33.2 million
People Express	Newark International Airport	1981	New York, Buffalo, Columbus, Norfolk, Jacksonville, Boston	Five 737-100s	$61.3 million
Muse Air	Dallas' Love Field	1981	Houston, Dallas	Two DC-9 Super 80s	$110 million
Sun Pacific	Ontario (Calif.)	1981	Los Angeles, San Francisco, Las Vegas, Ontario, Bakersfield, Fresno	Four DC-9-15s	$16 million
Sun Air	Dallas/Fort Worth Airport	1981	Dallas, Abilene, San Angelo, Beaumont, Houston	Four DC-9-15s	$12 million
Pacific Express	Chico (Calif.)	1981	San Francisco, Los Angeles, Medford (Ore.), Eugene, Boise	Seven BAC 111s	$30 million
Air Chicago	Chicago's Midway Airport	1981	Minneapolis, Atlanta, Pittsburgh, New York, Chicago	Eight DC-9-10s	$50.3 million

Source: *Business Week,* June 15, 1981, p. 80.

to ground service contracts with discounters and had been uncooperative in transferring luggage and in booking connecting reservations. Piedmont, which competed against People Express on the Newark to Norfolk route, matched People's fare and ran ads saying "On Piedmont the extras aren't extra" and referred to People Express's charges for soft drinks and checking baggage. The strategies of established carriers to defend against the discounters frequently paralleled the vows of the chairman of USAir:

> "We're going to stay in our markets, keep our frequencies, in some cases increase them, match the fares, and give better service.

However, major carriers were not always willing to fight hard for traffic on some short-haul routes. American Airlines in mid-1981 dropped its flights from New York to Boston, New York to Washington, and New York to Cleveland. American's president said, "If we find upstarts hurting us in dense markets where we don't have to be, we'll just drop those routes." Pan American's president said, "We are not a major factor in high-density, short-haul markets. We give them (the discounters) the local markets. . . . What we're looking for is the guy who's going beyond."

There were occasions when People Express's low fares did not produce enough passengers. When TWA and USAir dropped their $150 New York to Indianapolis fares to match People's $79 on-peak and $59 off-peak fares between Newark and Indianapolis, People Express failed to obtain enough passengers to make the route profitable. The company soon dropped its flights to Indianapolis. Burr said, "We got blasted out of there." TWA and USAir then raised their fares to $162.

Several events, however, seemed to confirm the success of People Express's strategy of attracting more fliers with its discounted approach to pricing. After People Express started its flights into Norfolk, a Norfolk newspaper reported that Greyhound sharply cut its bus service to the city and surrounding areas, citing a decrease in ticket sales; meanwhile, traffic at Norfolk's airport rose 18 percent. Industry statistics showed a climb in discount fare traffic from 57 percent of total passenger miles in 1980 to 71 percent in 1981.

PEOPLE EXPRESS IN 1982

In 1982, People Express got off to a rocky start. In January, a slow month for air travel, operations slipped back into the red. Then in early March, Gerald Gitner, People's president and a cofounder, resigned suddenly to become senior vice president for marketing and operations at Pan American World Airlines; at the time, Gitner was the company's second largest stockholder with 330,000 shares. The resignation came as a shock to employees; Gitner had been a favorite company personality, highly visible in headquarters, with an infectious spirit of fun and adventure. Don Burr noted, "Our folks were saying, 'We thought you guys started something new and better. Why should we stay committed if the president is going to leave?'" To bolster morale, Burr spent the day after Gitner announced his departure in company meetings explaining that Gitner's favorite challenge was planning, most of which had already been accomplished at People Express. (Later, however, Burr confided that Gitner left not only because he saw the Pan Am job as a bigger challenge but also because he had not been comfortable with the basic direction of the company— its low fares, its simplified operating systems, and its personnel policies and employee motivation approaches.)

Nonetheless, 1982 proved to be a successful year, despite losses in both the first and fourth quarters. By year-end, People Express was flying routes to 16 airports, had 67 daily departures from its Newark hub, and had expanded its fleet to 20 Boeing 737s. Service was expanded to six additional cities and the company had successfully withstood competitive pressures on routes to Florida, a depressed economy, severe winter weather that resulted in the cancellation of a number of flights and additional aircraft maintenance expenses, and the costs of personnel hiring, training, and advertising associated with start-up operations in six new locations.

Price competition on People Express's routes continued to be vigorous. When People Express announced fares on new routes, competitors flying that route promptly instituted matching discount fares (usually subject to multiple restrictions) and advertised them heavily. For its part in the war over airline fares, People Express ran a series of ads that poked fun at other airlines and their approach to restricted discounting; in one TV commercial a reservation clerk at fictitious BSA Airlines told a customer:

> You want the BSA Airlines super low-price special. OK? You simply fly one way, and pay the price you pay the other way if you fly two ways. OK? Simply put, each way costs half of either way, both ways, some days. OK?

A second profit-sharing plan was instituted in 1982, under which the company made quarterly profit-sharing payments to its full-time employees; the payments to employees were equal to a percentage of the quarterly base salary and ranged from 15 to 51 percent depending on position. Total payments under this plan could not exceed the company's quarterly net income.

Industry figures showed a further increase in discount fare traffic in 1982—to 78 percent of total passenger miles traveled (up from 57 percent in 1980 and 71 percent in 1981).

PEOPLE EXPRESS IN 1983

During 1983, People Express's traffic volume improved each quarter:

1983 Quarters	Passenger Traffic (in millions)	Load Factor (percent)
First	1.0	76.3
Second	1.2	78.5
Third	1.6	78.9
Fourth	1.75	68.3

In several months of 1983, People Express had the highest load factor in the entire commercial airline industry. People Express initiated Newark–London service in May 1983, using a Boeing 747 (seating capacity of 490 persons) leased from Braniff for an initial fee of $50,000 per month (later increased to $250,000 per month); during the remainder of 1983, the company carried over 109,000 passengers on its Newark–London route and had a 83.7 percent load factor. People Express charged a one-way fare of $149 between Newark and London; within 24 hours of the time People Express announced its London schedule and fares, every flight in both directions was booked solid for the next two months. Waiting to board People Express's London flight became something of a legend; one media reporter described the scene vividly:

> Waiting for the London flight has since become a spectacle in its own right, a rite of passage, a mark of the veteran traveler. The daily drama enacted before the check-in counters on the main concourse of the North Terminal is perhaps the single most convincing demonstration of the magic of People Express's strategy. A thick crowd of well over 200 people churns around in a sea of knapsacks and baggage. Some sleep on bedrolls in the middle of the aisles. A family with three young children is playing cards on a blanket. Another group is sitting cross-legged on the floor eating pizza. When the 6:30 P.M. standby call is announced, all the standbys rise as one and turn reverentially toward the check-in counters as if the Second Coming has just been revealed. The looks of anguished expectancy, the whoops of joy, and the expletives of bad luck alone are worth a trip to Newark.[7]

However, this scene was not much different from what prevailed on other People Express flights. A *Fortune* reporter had earlier written:

---

[7] Rhodes, "That Daring Young Man," p. 52.

On the planes, briefcases mix with backpacks, blue jeans and sailors' bell-bottoms with pinstripes. The cabins are clean, the seats close together, and the attendants refreshingly chipper. It's like a McDonald's of the air.[8]

In mid-1983, People Express upped the number of flights at Newark from 67 to 105 and in November increased the daily departures to 141, including 6 flights to Houston. Also in November, the company instituted fare increases of about 5 percent on most domestic routes; management believed that this increase, together with a decrease in its costs per available seat mile associated with introducing additional Boeing 727s (which were more cost efficient per seat mile than Boeing 737s), would significantly reduce the company's break-even load factor.

During 1983, the company doubled its fleet from 20 to 40 aircraft and expanded the employment of full-time personnel by 1,300 persons. At year-end 1983, People Express had 2,596 full-time employees (consisting of 7 managing officers, 9 general managers, 1,915 customer service managers, 627 flight managers, and 38 maintenance managers) and 1,641 part-time employees (most of whom functioned as reservations sales representatives). Advertising costs rose substantially over prior periods:

1981 (nine months)	$ 4,304,000
1982	6,946,000
1983	10,835,000

All of the increase in general and administrative expenses for 1983 over 1982 (see Exhibit 2) was primarily attributable to amounts paid to employees under the company's profit-sharing plans.

Donald Burr, as chairman, president, and chief executive officer, in 1983 received a salary of $60,210 and was paid an additional $35,302 in profit-sharing compensation; each of the other six managing officers in 1983 had a salary of $58,911 and received profit-sharing compensation of $30,659.

All full-time employees who had one year or more of service with People Express received profit-sharing compensation in 1983 based upon a specified percentage of their salaries; total profit-sharing compensation exceeded $4.8 million (up from $989,000 in 1982) and averaged over $3,700 per eligible employee. By year-end 1983, under provisions of the company's incentive stock option and stock purchase plans, employees had purchased an aggregate of 3,552,440 shares of common stock, approximately 94 percent of which were owned by employees other than managing officers and general managers. All told, company employees owned an average of about 2,500 shares of stock each, and some employees owned considerably more. Approximately 1,500 employees had options, exercisable over the next four years, to purchase an additional 860,000 shares of common stock at an average purchase price of $14.28.

The company's common stock was traded in the over-the-counter market and had been listed on the NASDAQ national market since November 1982. The stock price had performed well over the past two years:

---

[8] Nulty, "A Champ of Cheap Airlines," p. 130.

Years/Quarters	High	Low
1982:		
First	$ 6½	$ 4¼
Second	7¼	6¼
Third	9	6
Fourth	12¾	7½
1983:		
First	15¾	9¼
Second	24	14
Third	24½	17½
Fourth	23½	17⅞
1984:		
First	22⅝	13

During April 1984, the stock traded in the $11 to $15⅜ range. People Express had not paid any dividends on its common stock and intended, for the foreseeable future, to retain all earnings for use in its business.

Exhibits 13 and 14 present the firm's financial position as of year-end 1983.

THE FUTURE

Donald Burr's plans for People Express were bold and ambitious. Arrangements were already completed to expand the company's aircraft fleet to 77 planes by mid-1985 using a combination of debt and lease financing:

Aircraft Fleet (as of)	Boeing 737–100	Boeing 737–200	Boeing 727–200*	Boeing 747–100†	Boeing 747–200†	Total
March 31, 1984	17	5	26	—	1	49
June 30, 1984	17	5	34	1	3	60
September 30, 1984	17	5	40	1	3	66
December 31, 1984	17	5	44	1	3	70
March 31, 1985	17	5	47	2	3	74
June 30, 1985	17	5	50	2	3	77

* As of April 1984, four of the Boeing 727s were leased to Southwest Airlines Company and negotiations were underway to lease out two additional 727s. A total of 44 of the 50 727s had been acquired at an aggregate purchase price of approximately $252 million (including refurbishment costs of about $650,000 per plane).

† The company had options to purchase the two additional 747–200s for $2.7 million each and an option to purchase the second 747–100 for $18.2 million cash. Lease payments were $250,000 per month on one of the 747s (plus a lump-sum payment of $25 million in October 1988) and $950,000 per month on the other four.

In March 1984, People Express reached an agreement with the Port Authority of New York and New Jersey to relocate the company's flight operations into a to-be-constructed wing of Terminal C at Newark Airport by the end of 1985. Design and construction of the new facilities was anticipated to cost $150 million, with funding advanced by the port authority; the costs were to be repaid by the company over 25 years under a lease arrangement. The company anticipated that its annual lease expense for use of Terminal C would be approximately $19 million, compared with its current annual rental expense of approximately $3 million. The new wing of Terminal C would increase the number of departure gates available to People Express from 22 to 44, thereby enabling significant expansion of flights into and out of People Express's Newark hub. The company intended to continue to lease

Exhibit 13   Balance Sheets, People Express Airlines, 1982 and 1983 In Thousands
of Dollars

	December 31	
	1982	1983
Assets		
Current assets:		
Cash and temporary investments, at cost, which approximates market	$ 12,041	$ 85,780
Accounts receivable, less allowance for doubtful accounts of $350,000 at December 31, 1983, and $160,000 at December 31, 1982	2,888	11,661
Expendable parts	605	1,873
Prepaid expenses and other current assets	2,003	4,469
Total current assets	17,537	103,783
Property and equipment, at cost:		
Flight equipment	108,244	262,702
Facilities and ground equipment	6,503	16,539
Leasehold improvements	1,677	9,403
	116,424	288,644
Less accumulated depreciation and amortization	9,326	21,112
	107,098	267,532
Advance payments on equipment purchase contracts	—	14,405
Net property and equipment	107,098	281,937
Cash designated for expansion	—	20,000
Other assets and deferred charges	2,770	10,013
Total assets	$127,405	$415,733
Liabilities and Stockholders' Equity		
Current liabilities:		
Current portion of long-term debt	$ 6,650	$ 8,313
Current portion of capitalized lease obligations	439	1,339
Accounts payable	6,684	40,962
Accrued liabilities	3,774	12,067
Air traffic liability	979	4,539
Total current liabilities	18,526	67,220
Long-term debt, excluding current portion		
10.56% convertible exchangeable subordinated debentures	—	86,250
Other	48,215	122,448
Capitalized lease obligations, excluding current portion	11,619	37,893
Commitments and contingencies		
Stockholders' equity:		
Common stock $.01 par value:		
Voting, authorized 50,000,000 shares; issued 19,956,240 at December 31, 1983 and 15,702,200 at December 31, 1982	157	200
Nonvoting, authorized and issued 200,000 shares	2	—
Additional paid-in capital	68,758	131,556
Retained earnings (accumulated deficit)	(8,654)	1,780
Less cost of 1,600 shares of common stock held in treasury	(3)	
Less deferred compensation—restricted stock purchase plan, net	(8,143)	(21,730)
Less notes receivable—restricted stock purchase plan	(3,072)	(9,884)
Net stockholders' equity	49,045	101,922
Total liabilities and stockholders' equity	$127,405	$415,733

Source: 1983 10-K Report.

Exhibit 14 Statement of Changes in Financial Position, People Express Airlines, 1981–1983 In Thousands of Dollars

	From April 7, 1980, to March 31, 1981	Nine Months Ended Dec, 31, 1981	Years Ended Dec. 31	
			1982	1983
Source of funds:				
Operations:				
Income (loss) before extraordinary item	$ (452)	$ (9,205)	$ 541	$ 6,454
Items which do not use working capital—				
depreciation and amortization	6	2,437	8,420	14,884
Funds provided by (used in) operations before extraordinary item	(446)	(6,768)	8,961	21,338
Extraordinary item	—	—	461	3,980
Funds provided by (used in) operations	(446)	(6.768)	9,422	25,318
Issuance of common stock	24,239	183	30,047	37,919
Increase in long-term debt:				
Convertible exchangeable subordinated debentures	—	—	—	86,250
Other	4,277	55,915	—	80,883
Increase in capitalized lease obligations	—	—	12,300	27,614
Decrease in other assets and deferred charges	—	543	—	—
Payments received on notes receivable— restricted stock purchase plan	—	626	1,273	1,426
Decrease in working capital	—	626	1,273	1,426
Total source of funds	$28,070	$ 66,490	$ 59,743	$259,410
Application of funds:				
Additions to property and equipment	$ 5,511	$ 62,290	$ 48,623	$172,220
Advance payments on equipment purchase contracts	—	—	—	14,405
Cash designated for expansion	—	—	—	20,000
Increase in other assets	856	—	2,458	7,243
Repayment and current portion of long-term debt and capitalized lease obligations	—	4,200	8,457	7,990
Treasury shares purchased	—	—	205	—
Increase in working capital	21,703	—	—	37,552
Total application of funds	$ 28,070	$ 66,490	$ 59,743	$259,410
Changes in components of working capital:				
Increase (decrease) in current assets:				
Cash and temporary investments	$ 22,152	$ (7,892)	$ (2,219)	$ 73,739
Accounts receivable, net	73	1,180	1,635	8,773
Expendable parts	—	55	550	1,268
Prepaid expenses and other current assets	430	195	1,378	2,466
Total net change in current assets	22,655	(6,462)	1,344	86,246
Increase in current liabilities:				
Current portion of long-term debt	—	4,000	2,650	1,663
Current portion of capitalized lease obligations	—	—	439	900
Accounts payable	138	4,430	2,116	34,278
Accrued liabilities	814	1,099	1,861	8,293
Air traffic liability	—	—	979	3,560
Total increase in current liabilities	952	9,529	8,045	48,694
Increase (decrease) in working capital	$ 21,703	$(15,991)	$ (6,701)	$ 37,552

Source: 1983 10-K Report.

its present North Terminal facilities for administrative and equipment servicing purposes. Two buildings with about 237,000 square feet of space, located adjacent to Newark Airport, were leased for training purposes and for operation of the company's reservation systems.

To finance its expansion program, the company was committed not only to meet its monthly lease payments on airport facilities and aircraft but also to make long-term debt principal payments of $8.3 million in 1984, $25.4 million in 1985, and $17.0 million in each of the years 1986, 1987, and 1988. The company's flight equipment was pledged as collateral for its long-term debt. As of year-end 1983, the company's minimum net lease payments under noncancellable lease agreements were:

	Capital Leases	Operating Leases
1984	$ 6,600	$ 9,800
1985	6,600	13,800
1986	6,600	8,900
1987	6,600	5,000
1988	6,600	4,900
Thereafter	53,400	17,000
Total minimum lease payments	86,400	$59,400
Less amount representing interest	47,168	
Present value of net minimum lease payments	$39,232	

These amounts did not include the anticipated lease costs for the new Terminal C facilities to be constructed, nor the lease costs for the five Boeing 747s which had been negotiated in early 1984.

Just off the press was People Express's new flight schedule to be effective April 29, 1984. It contained the following flights and fares out of the Newark hub:

	Number of Daily Flights	On-Peak Fare	Off-Peak Fare
From Newark to:			
Atlantic City, N.J.	4	$ 40	$ 27
Baltimore	6	40	27
Boston	20	40	27
Buffalo	11	40	27
Burlington, Vt.	8	40	27
Columbus, Ohio	8	65	45
Hartford, Conn.	6	40	27
Houston	6	99	79
Jacksonville	6	79	59
London	1	159*	159*
Melbourne, Fla.	6	99	79
Norfolk	6	40	27
Pittsburgh	12	49	35
Portland, Me.	6	40	27
Tampa/St. Petersburg	8	99	79
Sarasota, Fla.	8	99	79
Syracuse	8	40	27
Washington	11	40	27
West Palm Beach	13	99	79

* Premium service was available at a fare of $439.

In addition, Burr was discussing using one of the 747s to be delivered soon to commence flights from Newark to Los Angeles; the proposed one-way fare was $119. Exhibit 15 shows the company's route system as of April 1984. Top management was shooting for a long-term growth in flights that averaged out to adding one and a half to two planes per month. The company's chief financial officer was on record as predicting that People Express would have revenues of a billion dollars "in a couple of years." And Burr's top management team was in place (Exhibit 16).

One area of particular concern to Burr was getting managers deeply involved in the company's decision-making and policy-setting processes. He believed that, so

Exhibit 15   People Express's Route System, as of April 1984

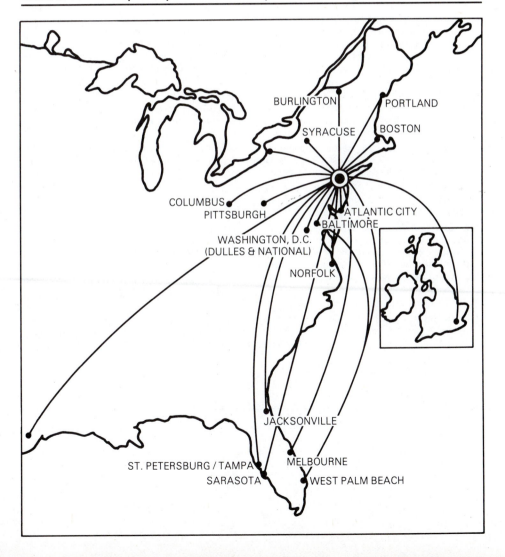

Exhibit 16   Board Members and Managing Officers of People Express Airlines, 1984

Mr. Michael C. Brooks, 39, was elected a director of People Express on August 19, 1982. Mr. Brooks was a managing director of Morgan Stanley & Co., Inc., an investment banking firm, where he has been employed since 1973.

Mr. Donald C. Burr, 42, was one of the founders of People Express and had served as its chairman and chief executive officer and as a director since its incorporation in April 1980. In February 1982, Mr. Burr was elected president of the company. From June 1973 to January 1980, Mr. Burr was employed as a senior executive of Texas International Airlines, Inc., most recently as president, chief operating officer, and director.

Mr. William R. Hambrecht, 48, was elected a director of the company on September 24, 1980. Mr. Hambrecht was president of Hambrecht & Quist, Inc., an investment banking firm. Mr. Hambrecht was also a director of ADAC Laboratories, Inc., Auto-Trol Technology Corporation, Computer & Communications Technology Corporation, Evans & Sutherland Computer Corporation, Granger Associates, Margaux Controls, NBI, Inc., Silicon General, Inc., VLSI Technology, Inc., and Xidex Corporation.

Mr. David F. Thomas, 34, was elected to the company's board of directors on October 6, 1980. Since December 1981, Mr. Thomas had been a vice president of Citicorp Venture Capital, Ltd., where he had been employed as a senior investment manager since March 1980. Mr. Thomas joined Citibank, N.A., in July 1976 and, from June 1978 to March 1980, he served in the bank's transportation finance department, serving most recently as an assistant vice president.

Ms. Melrose K. Dawsey, 35, a founder of the company, had served as a managing officer of the company since its incorporation. From March 1968 to January 1980, Ms. Dawsey was employed by Texas International Airlines, Inc., and served most recently as executive assistant to the president of Texas International Airlines, Inc.

Ms. Lori L. Dubose, 31, had served the company as a managing officer since August 1980. From August 1977 to August 1980, Ms. Dubose was employed by Texas International Airlines, Inc., most recently as its director of personnel resources.

Mr. Donald E. Hoydu, 42, joined the company as a managing officer in August 1980. From August 1972 to August 1980, Mr. Hoydu was employed by Texas International Airlines, Inc., serving most recently as its director of facilities.

Mr. Robert J. McAdoo, 38, joined the company in June 1980 and was a managing officer and the chief financial officer of the company. From August 1974 through June 1980, Mr. McAdoo was employed by Texas International Airlines, Inc., most recently serving as its vice president of information systems.

Mr. David M. McElroy, 38, joined the company as a managing officer in August 1980. From September 1978 to August 1980, Mr. McElroy served as director of technical services for Itel Air Corporation.

Mr. Harold J. Pareti, 35, joined the company in July 1980 as secretary and as a managing officer. From January 1977 to July 1980, Mr. Pareti was employed by Texas International Airlines, Inc., serving most recently as staff vice president of governmental affairs and assistant secretary.

Source: 1983 10-K Report.

far, the company's organizational structure and personnel approach had been only 60 percent successful:

> It's horribly difficult to give everyone a sense of commitment and participation. It's an inch-by-inch, every day, grinding process. There's no magic, no wands.[9]

An earlier internal study had concluded that several areas needed improvement, including giving employees meaningful staff work with built-in feedback, clarifying authority and accountability, providing ample individual recognition, and addressing whether the small number of designated leaders at People Express was adequate for the company's size and rapid growth. Burr believed that cross-utilization and organizing all of the managers into teams would eventually produce the results and working environment he wanted. While cross-utilization required more time and money in training and created problems in maintaining operating continuity as managers switched from area to area (sometimes to tasks in which they were not fully expert), Burr felt the long-term benefits were substantial because employees would not "burn out" from being penned into a particular function.

Teams were Burr's answer to how best to translate People Express's six precepts into action. All managers were on two- or three-person teams which oversaw various tasks and areas of responsibility, in the process eliminating the need for additional layers of supervisory control. Teams participated in large decisions and policy making by electing members to advisory and coordinating councils which met periodically with Burr, the managing officers, and the general managers. Team managers served as liaisons between teams working in any given area and the general manager and managing officers.

While the success of the people structure was short of optimal, it was still adequate to forestall unionization. The Air Line Pilots Association had failed twice in attempts to organize People Express's flight managers. Top management's view of unions was expressed by one managing director:

> Unions have a place in American business, but that place exists only where their role is important to protect the employees against actions of an employer who doesn't have the employees' interest in mind. To the extent you structure an organization that literally spends the majority, if not the total, amount of its time dedicated to working with its people, you don't need a union.

Burr was also concerned about reports that people who flew on People Express were sometimes destructive and careless with the furniture and furnishings in the waiting areas at departure gates; considerable litter and trash had been noted around People Express's gate areas on numerous occasions.[10] While Burr was disturbed by such reports, he felt they were not typical. He believed that the vast number of People Express's employees were loyal to the company's values and committed to making it successful—if for no other reason than it was in their own financial interest. Despite the shortcomings and problems which remained, Don Burr was proud of

---

[9] Rhodes, "That Daring Young Man," p. 52.

[10] Interviews by the case-writer with people who had flown People Express revealed experiences where there had been so much carry-on baggage underneath seats and in the overhead storage compartments that compliance with federal safety regulations concerning carry-on luggage was in doubt. Some interviewees expressed satisfaction with their trips on People Express while others were less than enthusiastic—indicating that the only real appeal was the low fares.

the progress People Express had made in providing each individual employee with a sizable ownership interest, the freedom to fashion a personal contribution, and an opportunity for personal growth:

> We're not sitting around here counting roses. This is capitalism. People are getting rich here. There are millionaires walking around here and tons of 24- and 25-year-olds worth $75,000, $100,000, $200,000. Tons of 'em. The only way I know to wealth in the long term is to own a piece of something and build it.[11]

An *Inc.* magazine writer's report on one such People Express employee seemed to confirm Don Burr's philosophy and convictions:

> Candee Brock is being cross-utilized today.
>
> Wearing the brown and tan uniform of People Express Airlines, Inc., she is checking bags for passengers leaving the North Terminal of Newark International Airport. Between tickets she talks about a day that changed her life.
>
> March 25, 1981, was an unusually pleasant day in Buffalo, after a harsh, lingering winter. Candee thought she had things pretty well figured out. She had just quit her job as a dental hygienist and was enrolled to study business management at State University College at Buffalo. She was at home reading the *Buffalo Courier-Express* and saw an ad announcing great opportunities as a customer-service manager for People Express. "It seemed like it was written just for me," she says. [See Exhibit 6.]
>
> Candee drove to the Sheraton Inn Buffalo East, where the interviews were being held, took a look at the mob of some 12,000 applicants, and drove back home. "They'll never notice me in all those people," she recalls thinking. She considered doing some studying or maybe some errands around the neighborhood, but the ad wouldn't leave her alone. She drove back to the interviews.
>
> On April 2, Candee arrived in Newark, N.J., and checked into the Holiday Inn North, where she would live for a month while she was in training. "When I first got to the People Express office," she says, "I found an empty terminal with garbage cans lying around. There were no planes; you had to imagine them flying in. I said to myself, 'We're going to land people here?' But a month later, I was at the check-in counter. The garbage was gone, the planes were here, and there was wallpaper on the walls, even if it was still wet."
>
> When she is not checking baggage, Candee is team manager for 54 people in the accounts-payable and accounts-receivable section of the accounting department. She works 10 to 12 hours a day, five or six days a week, and says she would work more. She makes $24,000 a year and owns 8,400 shares of People Express stock, trading over-the-counter at $18.50 a share at press time. Candee is 25.
>
> "I've grown a lot in two years," she says. "My job has given me more confidence in every area of my life. Now I'm involved in the day-to-day operations of a very successful airline."[12]

---

[11] Rhodes, "That Daring Young Man," p. 50.

[12] Rhodes, "That Daring Young Man," p. 42.

CASE 3 KOLAPORE, INC.*

In January 1986, Mr. Adriaan Demmers, president and sole employee of Kolapore, Inc., a firm based in Guelph, Ontario, specializing in the importation, processing, and sale of high-quality souvenir spoons, was becoming increasingly frustrated with the pace at which his business was developing. Over a two-year period, Demmers had taken his idea of importing souvenir spoons from Holland to Canada to annual sales of nearly $30,000. He believed the potential existed for well over $100,000 in Canadian sales plus exports to the United States. This success to date had been a strain, however, on Demmers' limited financial resources, and not provided any compensation for the long hours invested. Demmers was beginning to question if he was ever going to have the major breakthrough which he had always believed was "just around the corner."

Recently, Demmers had accepted a full-time position with another firm in an unrelated business. While Demmers realized that he could continue to operate Kolapore, Inc. on a part-time basis, he wondered if he should "face reality" and simply fold the business up, or try to sell it. Alternately, Demmers could not occasionally help wondering if he should be devoting himself full-time to Kolapore.

BACKGROUND

In February/March 1984, Demmers conducted a feasibility study of starting a business to market souvenir spoons. His idea was to offer a high-quality product depicting landmarks, historic buildings, and other unique symbols of the area the spoons were to be sold in.

There were numerous spoons on the market but most tended to be for Canada or Ontario rather than local sites of interest, and were generally poorly made and not visually appealing. There were few quality spoons and the ones that did exist were priced in the $15–$40 range.

Sources of spoons were examined in Canada, the United States, and the Netherlands (Holland). Given Demmers' Dutch heritage, the fact that there existed a well-recognized group of silversmiths in Schoonhoven, plus a particular company which already had over 40 Canadian-specific dies, the limited search process for a country from which to source the spoons was quickly settled.

Demmers felt the key factors for success were a good-quality product using designs of local landmarks, and an eye-catching display. He felt displays should be located in a prominent position in retail stores because souvenir spoons are often bought on impulse.

As part of his feasibility study, Demmers conducted a Market Analysis (including

* Prepared by Professor Paul W. Beamish, School of Business and Economics, Wilfrid Laurier University, as a basis for classroom discussion. © Paul W. Beamish, 1986. Reprinted with permission.

customer and retailer surveys), a Competitive Analysis (both manufacturers and distributors), and developed an Import Plan, Marketing Plan, and Financial Projections (including projected break-even and cash flows). Excerpts from this study follow.

Market Analysis

The market for souvenir spoons consists of several overlapping groups—primarily tourists and the gift market. There are also groups interested in spoons for more specialized purposes (e.g., church groups, service clubs, associations and others). These are very specialized and for special occasions.

A random telephone survey conducted in March 1984 of 50 people in Guelph revealed that 78 percent owned souvenir spoons. Forty six percent of those people had purchased the spoons themselves, while 54 percent had received them as gifts. In total, almost 25 percent of the people in the sample collected souvenir spoons or had a rack to hang them on. Retailers indicated that sales occurred primarily during the summer months and at Christmas time. Twelve retail outlets were visited to obtain information regarding quality, sales, and prices. Backgrounds of a selection of these retailers are summarized in Exhibit 1.

There was a high awareness of souvenir spoons in the market, but the product quality was generally at the low end of the market. For example, rough edges on the bowls were common, and the crests on the spoons were often crooked. In fact, one manufacturer's spoon had a picture of Kitchener City Hall which was out of focus and off-center. (Terms concerning souvenir spoons are explained in Exhibit 2.)

A limited variety of spoons was often available and few of the spoons were of local points of interest even though these were the spoons that were most in demand. One retailer noted that of a total of 140 spoons sold in 1983, 106 were one variety, a spoon with a relief design in plastic of a Conestoga wagon. This was the only unique spoon Demmers found in the area "other than the cheap picture spoons."

There was no advertising for souvenir spoons due to the nature of the product and the lack of identification with a particular brand.

Souvenir spoons appeared to be a low priority in many producing companies, with little marketing effort made to push the products. Even the packaging was poor quality; boxes were often not supplied for gift wrapping.

The sale of spoons was viewed as seasonal by some retailers. Point of purchase displays were removed once the summer rush was over in many instances.

Spoons were not prominently displayed in most stores, yet they are largely an impulse item. In several stores they were kept in drawers and only taken out when requested.

Competitive Analysis

Souvenir spoons essentially serve two customer functions: as gifts or commemoratives. They can be used as gifts for family and friends on special occasions such as Christmas. They can also serve as a commemorative token, of having visited somewhere or for a special anniversary (e.g., the Province of Ontario's 200th anniversary). They can

Exhibit 1   Survey of Spoons Carried by Local Retailers in Guelph and Kitchener–Waterloo Region

- **A Taste of Europe**—Delicatessen and Gift Store.
  Guelph Eaton Centre.
  — A selection of spoons from Holland with Dutch designs.
  — Also one with the Canadian coat of arms which looked good.
  — Rhodium-plated spoons—$5.98 per spoon.
  — Well displayed at front of store.

- **Eatons**—Guelph Eaton Centre.
  — Breadner spoons with maple leaf or Canadian flag and "Guelph" stamped in the bowl.
  — Rhodium-plated—$4.98.
  — No display and hard to find.

- **Pequenot Jewellers**—Wyndham Street, Guelph.
  — Carry Candis spoons, which look cheap and do not sell very well.
  — $4.98.
  — Poorly displayed.

- **Smith & Son, Jewellers**—Wyndham Street, Guelph.
  — Do not carry souvenir spoons because they are not in line with the store's image. They often get requests for them.

- **Franks Jewellers**—King Street, Waterloo.
  — Carry Breadner spoons with the Waterloo coat of arms.
  — Also carry spoons with trilliums and Canadian flag.
  — Rhodium-plated spoons—$4.50 per spoon.
  — Not on display, but kept in drawer.
  — Sell less than 12 per year.

- **Copper Creek**—Waterloo Square Mall, Waterloo.
  — Candis spoons—$5.00 each.

- **Birks**—King Centre, Kitchener.
  — Carry Oneida and Breadner spoons.
  — Rhodium-plated spoons for $5.98.
  — Oneida spoons were $8.95 and looked like a silver alloy.
  — Sterling silver Breadner spoons for $31.95.
  — Displayed in a spoon rack, looked good.
  — Birks regency spoons with crest of each province, $12.50.

- **Eaton's**—Market Square, Kitchener.
  — Breadner spoons, two types for Canada only,
  — Rhodium-plated—$4.98 each.

- **Young's Jewellers**—King Street, Kitchener.
  — Rhodium-plated Breadner spoons, $4.50 each.

- **Walters Jewellers.**
  — Against chain policy to carry souvenir spoons because of poor quality and low turnover.

- **People's Jewellers.**
  — Do not carry souvenir spoons.

- **Engels Gift Shop**—King Street, Kitchener.
  — Carry Breadner, Oneida, Gazelle, and Metropolitan,
  — Altogether about 20 varieties,
  — Well displayed near entrance of store, prices range from $2.25 for Metropolitan spoons to $7.98 for Oneida spoons,
  — Saleslady said they sell hundreds every year, mostly in the summer.

Exhibit 2   Terms Concerning Souvenir Spoons

Crest—Emblem, either metal, plastic, or enamel, that is affixed to a standard spoon.
Picture Spoon—Spoon with a picture under plastic which is heat moulded to the spoon.
Relief Design—Spoon with an engraving or picture which is moulded into the metal of the spoon.
Enamel—Opaque substance similar to glass in composition.
Plated—Thin layer of metal put on by electrolysis.
Rhodium-Plated—Shiny "jeweller's metal" which does not tarnish (no silver content).
Silver-Plated—Silver covering on another metal (e.g., steel).
Sterling Silver—Alloy of 92.5 percent silver and 8.5 percent copper, nickel, and zinc.
Silver Alpacca—Alloy of 82 percent copper and 18 percent nickel.

---

be either functional (used for coffee or tea spoons) or may be used for decorative purposes (hung in a spoon rack or put in a cabinet).

Competition comes from all other gift items and all other souvenir items in approximately the same price range.

Demmers identified 11 companies that distributed souvenir spoons in the southwestern Ontario area and gathered what data he could, much of it anecdotal, on each. This process had provided encouragement for Demmers to proceed. The backgrounds of these competitors are summarized in Exhibit 3.

Southwestern Ontario contained a number of large urban areas, including Toronto (over 2 million people), Hamilton/Burlington, Kitchener/Waterloo, and London, with over 300,000 people in each, plus many smaller cities such as Guelph. Guelph was located roughly in the center of the triangle formed by Toronto, Waterloo, and Burlington and was within an hour's drive of each.

Importing

To import goods into Canada on a regular basis in amounts over $800, an importer number is required. This was available from Revenue Canada, Customs and Excise. Requirements for customs were an advise notice from the shipper and a customs invoice. These were available in office supply stores. A customs tariff number and commodity code were also required to complete the customs B3 form.

Souvenir spoons of either sterling silver or silver plate were listed in the customs tariff under number 42902-1. The Netherlands has Most Favoured Nation status, so the duty is 20.3 percent. On top of the cost of the merchandise (excluding transportation and insurance but including duty), there is a further 10 percent excise tax and 10 percent federal sales tax.

A customs broker can be hired to look after the clearing of goods through customs. Rates were approximately $41 plus $3.60 for every thousand dollars of value, duty included.

Insurance on a shipment of less than $10,000 costs a fixed fee of about $150 with insurance brokers. This can be reduced if insurance is taken on a yearly basis, based on the expected value of imports over the year. Freight forwarders charge approximately $2 per kilo regardless of the total weight of the shipment.

Exhibit 3 Souvenir Spoon Suppliers

Breadner Manufacturing Ltd.

Breadner appears to have national market distribution and includes two major retailers, Birks and Eatons. According to some of the store managers interviewed, their sales of souvenir spoons in each location were low. Several retailers also expressed dissatisfaction with the Breadner line because of the slow turnover. Typically, there was a basic design for the spoon, which did not change except for a different crest glued on for the different locale.

Breadner has been in the jewelry business since 1900 and has a plant in Hull, Quebec. They manufacture to order various types of pins, medals, and advertising specialties but advised Demmers that in general they use their entire output of souvenir spoons for their own sales.

They have many varieties of spoons in their catalog and an established distribution system across the country. Demmers recognized the possibility that they could upgrade their selection in a short time span to compete directly with his intended selection of spoons.

Typical retail prices for Breadner spoons were $4.50 and up, the cost to the retailer being $2.25 and up. Breadner's high-end sterling silver spoons were available at Birks for $31.95, with the cost to Birks estimated at about $15.00 per spoon. Both rhodium-plated and silver-plated spoons were available but rhodium-plated were the most common. Silver-plated spoons were not carried.

Candis Enterprises Ltd.

Candis was located in Willowdale, Ontario. This company had good distribution in gift shops (e.g., the 650 outlet United Cigar Store Chain) and in some jewelry stores. They had a line of rhodium-plated spoons marketed under the Mar-Vel name and silver-plated spoons under the Candis name.

Their strategy appears to be one of putting out a large variety of spoons for each place that they sell in. However, the quality seemed to be toward the low end: many of the spoons had rough edges on the bowls and there was no detail in the dies.

Wholesale cost ranged from $2.00 per spoon for a rodium-plated picture spoon to $3.25 for a silver-plated spoon with a five-color ceramic crest.

Metropolitan Supplies Ltd.

Metropolitan Supplies was located in Toronto and distributed its goods across Canada primarily to gift shops and souvenir shops in tourist areas. This company deals with all sorts of souvenirs and novelty items. They have a large selection of spoons, each of which can be crested to suit the buyer. The quality of the spoons was at the low end. Prices ranged from $0.55 per spoon (wholesale) for iron and nickel-plated spoons to $2.00 per spoon for silver-plated spoons.

Gazelle Importers and Distributors

Gazelle Importers and Distributors was located in Grimsby, Ontario. They previously imported spoons from Holland, but later manufactured in Ontario. They are sold under the Gazelle name. They retail for $5.95 and, therefore, presumably cost the retailer about $3.00. Spoons had designs for Ontario and Canada but nothing local. Quality seemed about the same as Breadner's less expensive line.

Exhibit 3 *(concluded)*

Oneida Canada Ltd.

Oneida is located in Niagara Falls, Ontario, and is a division of Oneida Ltd. in the United States. The Niagara Falls plant manufactures stainless steel and silver-plate flatware. Their product was distributed in several jewelry stores including Birks and gift stores. The quality is better than any other spoons except for Breadner's sterling spoons. Prices are also somewhat higher with a retail price of $7.98, giving a probable cost to the retailer of about $4.00 per spoon. There is little variety: All spoons come in one design with a different engraving in the top of the spoon.

Commemorative Spoons

This firm is located in Ottawa and sells spoons in the $6.95–$8.95 range. They have three basic designs (supplied by Oneida). They have large accounts with Simpsons and Cara and frequently deal with clubs for whom they make up special spoons for fundraising.

Hunnisett and Edmunds

This is a distribution company which specializes in selling to card shops and variety stores. They use a somewhat unique packaging system—selling via fly-top displays of 12 spoons.

Parsons-Steiner

This firm is located in Toronto. The quality of the product was low. Retail prices ranged from $1.99 to $5.98. Spoons tended to be picture spoons and the least expensive ones appeared to be made of cast iron with a decal attached.

Boma

This company is located in Vancouver, B.C. The quality was very good. Spoons were made out of pewter with designs of such things as totem poles. Retail prices ranged from $10 to $20.

Aalco Souvenirs

Located in Vancouver, this company carries over 300 "three dimensional" models of spoons. They are made in Canada and are nickel-plated with a white gold flash. Aalco's products are distributed across Canada. They also carry other souvenir items such as bells, bottle openers, keychains, lapel pins, and charms. Prices for spoons range from $2.50 to $3.00 each.

Souvenir Canada

Located in Downsview, Ontario, and operating throughout Canada and the United States, this company carries spoons with plastic decals, keychains, bottle openers, bells, lapel pins, mugs, plates, glasses, clothing, and special promotional items. They have been in business for about 10 years and use standardized spoons with crests attached. Retail price per spoon is $3.00.

The importing can be easily handled without help on small shipments such as spoons. The product can be sent by airmail and insured with the post office. It can also be sent to a small city like Guelph rather than Toronto, and this avoids the busy Toronto customs office and possible delays of several days. The customs office in Guelph can easily clear the goods the same day they arrive.

Product   Kolapore's souvenir spoons are to be a high-quality product with detailed dies made to give them a relief design far superior to any competitive spoons (except for those retailing in the $30 range). The spoons are to be silver plated or made of alpacca, making them similar to jewelry.

Designs would be of specific points of interest. In the Kitchener-Waterloo area, for example, possible subjects would include Seagram Museum, Schneider House, Doon Pioneer village, University Crests, and City Crests. Kitchener-Waterloo would be printed under the picture, also in relief in the metal, along with the title of the particular picture.

Price Points

- $2.25   Metropolitan Supplies—nickel-plated.
- $4.50–6.00   Breadner Manufacturing—rhodium-plated and silver-plated.
                  Candis.
                  Gaxelle.
- $7.00–8.00   Oneida or Commemorative—simple designs with engraved insignia. Appear to be made of a silver alloy.
- $10.00–14.00   Proposed price range for retail:
                  —Quality comparable to $30.00 spoons but silver content is lower.
                  —Detailed designs of local landmarks.
                  —Variety of 6–10 spoons in each market.
- $30.00 and up   Breadner—Sterling silver.
                  —Fine workmanship.
                  —Very limited variety of designs.

Retail Outlets   Because of the impulse nature of souvenir spoons, locations with high traffic are essential. Jewelry stores and gift stores in malls and tourist areas are probably most suitable in this respect.

Due to the price range proposed and the quality of the merchandise, the quality and image of the store has to be appropriate. This would eliminate discount jewelry stores and cheap souvenir shops for the aforementioned reasons. Second, it would not please higher end retailers if the same spoons were sold for less in the same area and would likely restrict distribution in the appropriate channels.

Jewelry stores are perceived by many people as selling expensive, luxury items that are not part of one's everyday needs. For this reason it would be helpful for these stores to have a window display.

Promotion   Each retail location would carry a minimum product line of six varieties of spoons: one with a Canadian theme, one with a provincial theme, and at least four spoons with designs of local landmarks or points of interest.

The packaging will be suitable for gift wrapping, so will likely consist of a small box with a clear plastic cover.

Marketing Plan

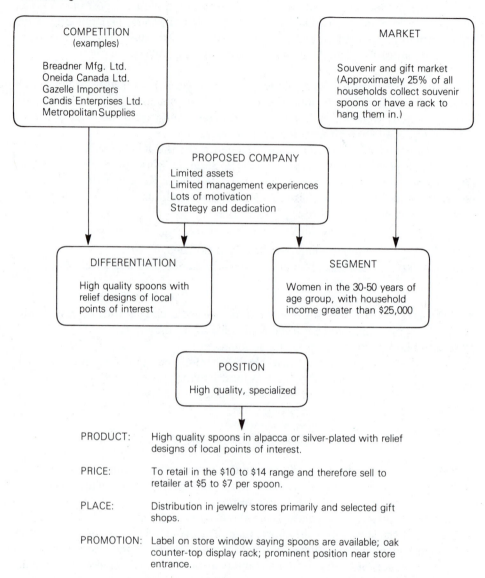

Each retail location will have an oak countertop display rack. There will be a relatively high cost to the displays initially, but they will attract attention and convey the quality of the spoons. Different sizes can be made depending on the number of spoons for a particular market.

Because souvenir spoons are primarily an impulse item, location in the store is important and should be near the entrance or have a window display. This is something which can only be controlled by persuading the retailer that this would increase the turnover and consequently his profits.

Finance

Contribution margin per spoon has been calculated using the most conservative numbers and at a wholesale price of $3.50. Retailers would typically mark prices up by 100 percent (see Exhibit 4). The contribution margins worked out to $2.05 on alpacca spoons and $1.50 on silver-plated spoons.

The break-even, assuming costs of $25,250 per year and a contribution margin of $2.05, would be sales volume of 12,317 spoons with sales value of $43,110 (see Exhibit 5). Assuming the spoons would be introduced in the Toronto market and distribution obtained in 100 retail locations, this means sales of 124 spoons per store.

Upon graduating from a university business school in April 1984, Demmers planned to devote his efforts to Kolapore. Demmers felt that while there could be a short-term financial drain, his cash balance would be positive at the end of the second month of operation (see Exhibit 6).

Exhibit 4   Kolapore, Inc., Forecast Variable Costs and Margins of Spoons

	Alpacca	Silver Plate
Factory cost in $Canadian	$0.95*	$1.33†
Duty @ 20.3%	.19	.27
Cost, duty included	1.14	1.60
Federal sales tax @ 9%	.10	.14
Federal excise tax @ 10%	.11	.16
Freight and insurance	.10	.10
Total variable cost	$1.45	$2.00
Contribution margin	$2.05 to $3.55	$1.50 to $3.00
Cost to retailer	$3.50 to $5.00	$3.50 to $5.00
Retailer markup	$3.50 to $5.00	$3.50 to $5.00
Retail price	$7.00 to $10.00	$7.00 to $10.00

* Based on quote by Dutch manufacturer (Zilverfabriek) of 2.20 guilders (1 Dutch guilder = $.43 Canadian).
† Based on quote by Dutch manufacturer (Zilverfabriek) of 3.10 guilders (1 Dutch guilder = $.43 Canadian).

Exhibit 5   Kolapore, Inc., Forecast Breakeven

Distribution costs (transportation)	$ 4,000
Rent expense (work from home)	nil
Salary	15,000
Office supply costs (including telephone)	1,000
Inventory costs	1,000
Merchandising expenses (displays and boxes)	3,000
Investment in dies (10 @ $125 each)	1,250
Total fixed costs	$25,250

Breakeven volumes at selected contribution margins:
$25,250/$1.50 = 16,833 spoons
$25,250/$2.05 = 12,317 spoons
$25,250/$3.00 = 8,416 spoons

Exhibit 6   Forecast Cash Flow, May–August 1984

	May	June	July	August
Cash, beginning of period	$3,000	$ (750)	$1,000	$ 7,500
Disbursements:				
Moulds	1,250	—	—	—
Purchases	—	7,250	—	7,250
Promotion expenses	2,000	1,000	—	—
Car expenses	500	500	500	500
Total disbursements	3,750	8,750	500	7,750
Net cash, after disbursements	(750)	(9,500)	500	(250)
Receipts:				
Accounts receivable				
(Terms, net 30 days)	nil	10,500	7,000	10,500
Cash balance	(750)*	1,000	7,500	10,250

* To be borrowed.

SUBSEQUENT EVENTS

Soon after graduating in April, it became clear to Demmers that Kolapore was not going to realize forecast sales of $28,000 by September 1984. Due to delays in getting shipments from Holland and difficulty in obtaining distribution in Canada, sales were only $1,830 over the summer. A number of assumptions in the original feasibility study (as described earlier) had proved incorrect:

1. The number of dies ultimately required (each of which cost $125) was not going to be 10 but closer to 50.
2. The federal sales tax rate had increased to 10 percent from 9 percent.
3. Duty was payable on the dies themselves as well as the spoons, at the rate of 20.3 percent excise tax plus federal sales tax.
4. Delivery time for new dies was closer to six months than the forecast 10–12 weeks (the artist had been ill for several months). Several orders were canceled during this period as a result.
5. Packaging costs per spoon were closer to 32 cents/unit than the estimated 10 cents.
6. Distribution had been difficult because the large chain stores which dominated the market all had established suppliers.
7. The target market was not nearly as upscale as originally envisioned. Although Kolapore's spoons were readily identifiable as being of superior quality, most customers would only pay a maximum of $7–$8 retail for any spoon. Demmers had estimated the total Canadian souvenir spoon market at about $1.5 million annually. Within that, a very small portion was for sterling silver (where Demmers could not compete), about $450,000 was at the price point where Demmers was selling (some of his competitors were promoting similar or poorer quality spoons at the same price), with the balance of the market reserved for lower priced/ lower quality spoons.

The goal of 100 stores by September 1984 was still a long way off.

Demmers had also discovered that the chain stores plan all their buying from 6 to 12 months in advance. Because many of the spoons he had designed did not arrive until September 1984, this meant that he had missed much of the tourist season (and nearly all of the Christmas market).

On the positive side, the Dutch guilder had depreciated relative to the Canadian dollar. In September 1984 it cost Canadian $0.39 for 1 guilder rather than $0.43 as forecast. In addition, delivery times for spoons from existing dies required three–four weeks rather than the expected four–six weeks, and the cost of display cases was only about $16 each. These were made of plastic rather than the originally envisioned oak.

Although Kolapore was showing a negative cash balance at the end of August 1984 (see Exhibit 7), sales began to improve in September (see Exhibit 8), growing to nearly $16,000 by the end of the first full year of operation (see Exhibits 9 and 10 for financial statements). A financial loss of $1,800 was incurred for the first year of operation, and this took no account of the countless hours Demmers had invested. Since the business was not yet self-supporting, in September 1984 Demmers had begun to look for other sources of income.

Between September 1984 and January 1986, Demmers worked for five months in a fiberglass factory, acquired a house in Guelph in which he was able to live and to rent out rooms, sold Bruce Trail calendars on a commission basis, worked at organizing and selling several ski tours (which did not take place), and opened

Exhibit 7　Kolapore, Inc., Actual Cash Flow, 1984 (4 months)

	May	June	July	August
Cash (beginning)	$2,600	$1,000	$ 950	$ 530
Disbursements:				
Purchases	1,000	550	870	1,460
Expenses	1,000	80	300	300
Total disbursements	2,000	630	1,170	1,760
Net cash	600	370	(220)	(1,230)
Receipts:				
Accounts receivable	400	580	750	100
Cash balance	$1,000	$ 950	$ 530	$(1,130)

Exhibit 8　Kolapore, Inc., Actual Sales, 1984–1985

May 1984	$ 400
June 1984	580
July 1984	750
August 1984	100
September 1984	2,600
October 1984	2,540
November 1984	1,500
December 1984	1,400
January–March 1985	4,923
Total (11 months)	$14,793

Exhibit 9   Balance Sheet (unaudited), Kolapore, Inc., March 31, 1985

Assets

Current
Cash	$ 1,708
Accounts receivable	1,763
Inventory	2,873
	6,344
Incorporation Expense	466
Total assets	$ 6,810

Liabilities and Shareholders' Equity

Current
Accounts payable and accruals	$ 268
Due to shareholder	8,342
	8,610
Retained earnings (deficit)	(1,800)
Total liabilities and shareholders' equity	$ 6,810

Exhibit 10   Statement of Income (unaudited), Kolapore, Inc., Year Ended March 31, 1985

Sales	$15,793
Cost of sales:	
Inventory at beginning of year	—
Purchases	8,453
Duty and freight	2,288
Dies	3,034
	13,775
Inventory at end of year	2,873
	10,902
Gross profit	4,891
Expenses:	
Office	657
Samples	582
Auto expenses	1,137
Car allowance	3,900
Bank interest and charges	139
Advertising	26
Accounting	250
Total expenses	6,691
Net (loss) for the year	$ (1,800)

Notes:
1. Significant accounting policies:
   - Kolapore, Inc. is a company incorporated under the laws of Ontario on April 6, 1984, and is primarily engaged in the importing and selling of souvenir spoons.
   - The accounting policies are in accordance with generally accepted accounting principles.
   - Inventory is valued at lower of cost or net realizable value.
   - Incorporation expense is not amortized.
2. Due to shareholder is noninterest bearing and payable on demand.

an ice-cream store in a regional resort area (Wasaga Beach). Due to a low volume of traffic, this latter venture in the summer of 1985 resulted in an $8,000 loss. In the fall of 1985, Demmers accepted a position as production manager for a weekly newspaper in Guelph.

By this time, Demmers was selling direct to retailers in 20 towns and cities in Ontario and through five chains, Simpsons, and United Cigar Stores and, to a much smaller extent, Eatons, Birks, and Best Wishes. Other chains such as The Bay, Sears, and Woolco had been approached but so far without success. Demmers was hoping to find the time so that he could approach the buyers at K mart, Zeller's, Consumer's Distributing, Robinson's, Woodwards, and others.

Kolapore spoons were sold in Simpsons stores from Windsor, Ontario, to Halifax, Nova Scotia, and in 18 United Cigar Store locations in southern Ontario. Four months after Demmers' first delivery to the chain outlets in the summer of 1985, about half the stores were sold out of Kolapore spoons. Neither chain would reorder stock part-way through the year.

To sell direct in some of the smaller cities, Demmers' practice had been to drive or walk through the main shopping areas, stopping at jewelry stores or other likely retail outlets. If he was unable to meet with the store owner, he would usually leave a sample and a letter with some information (see Exhibit 11 for a copy of the letter). Demmers' experience had been that unless he personally met with the right person, which sometimes took three or more visits, no sales would occur. When he was able to meet with the owner, his success rate was over 70 percent. To sell direct in larger centers such as Toronto (where he had 40 customers), Demmers had focused his efforts on hotel gift shops. Having established these customers, he could now visit all 40 customers in Toronto personally in two–three days.

By year-end, Demmers had access to a pool of 89 Canadian-specific dies. Demmers' supplier in Holland had 46 dies in stock which another Canadian from western Canada had had designed. Spoons based on these dies were no longer being sold anywhere as far as Demmers could tell.

For the most part Demmers was selling spoons based on his own designs. (For those spoons which Demmers had had designed, he had exclusive rights in Canada.) In less than two years he had 43 more dies made up (see Exhibit 12 for a complete list). In some cases Demmers had asked a particular company/group to pay the cost of the dies; in others, such as for universities, he had built the die cost into his price for the first shipment; while in others he had simply gone ahead on his own with the hope that he could achieve sufficient sales to justify the investment.

There was a wide variability in the sales level associated with each spoon. Sales from his best-seller Toronto Skyline (which depicted major buildings and the CN Tower) were about 1,000 spoons a year. Demmers' second best–selling spoon in Toronto was 300 units of Casa Loma. (For a list of the major tourist sites in Toronto, see Exhibit 13.) This spoon had quickly sold out on-site. (However, the buyer had been unwilling to order more part-way through the year.) Spoons with other Toronto designs were selling less than 50 units a year.

By December 1985, inventories had increased and Kolapore, Inc. was still showing a small loss (see Exhibit 14). Any gains from changes in the rate of import duty on spoons (20.3 percent in 1984 to 18.4 percent in 1986) had been negated by changes in federal sales tax (9 percent in 1984 to 11 percent in 1986) and exchange rates. The fluctuating Dutch guilder was at a two-year high relative to the Canadian dollar.

Exhibit 11   Kolapore, Inc., Letter of Introduction

Kolapore, Inc.
P.O. Box 361
Guelph, Ontario
N1H 6K5

Dear

Kolapore, Inc. would like to offer you the opportunity to have your own design on a spoon, made up in metal relief, for example a logo, coat of arms, crest, building, or whatever you would like.

There is always a large market for souvenir spoons of unique design and high quality. Kolapore Collection Spoons fit this category extremely well and are priced very competitively.

The spoons are available in silver plate at $3.50 per spoon. This price includes a gift box, federal sales tax, and shipping.

The minimum order is 100 spoons to get a new design made up and there is also a one time die charge of $125.00 to help offset the cost of making the new die. Delivery time is approximately three months if a die has to be made up; subsequent orders will take four–six weeks.

The dies for Kolapore Collection Spoons are made by master craftsmen in Schoonhoven, Holland, the silversmith capital of the world. The spoons themselves are made in Canada. As a result the quality of the spoons is exceptional and recognized by the consumer at a glance.

I trust that this is sufficient information. I look forward to hearing from you. If you have any questions or concerns please don't hesitate to contact me. Thank you for your time and consideration.

Sincerely,

Adriaan Demmers
President

From a March 1984 value of Canadian $0.43, the guilder had declined to $0.36 in February 1985 and climbed to $0.50 by December 1985. Partially due to these exchange fluctuations, during the past eight months Demmers had also arranged for the spoons to be silver plated at a cost of $0.40 each in Ontario. This had resulted in a saving of $0.15/spoon (which varied with the exchange rate). More significantly, because many spoons were purchased as souvenirs of Canada, by adding sufficient value by silver plating in Canada, the imported product no longer had to be legally stamped "Made in Holland." In fact, the packaging could now be marked "Made in Canada." Demmers was quite optimistic regarding the implications of this change because a number of potential store buyers had rejected his line because it did not say "Made in Canada." Demmers' supplier was upset, however, with the change.

Meanwhile, the feedback he was receiving from many of his customers was positive—in most cases they were selling more of his spoons than any other brand. Some customers in fact had enquired about other products. Since he had so far not experienced any competitive reactions to his spoons, Demmers was thinking of investigating the possibility of adding ashtrays, letter openers, keychains, lapel pins, and bottle openers to the product line in 1986—if he stayed in business. Each one of these

Exhibit 12   Kolapore Collection Spoons—Designs Available

Canada:
  Deer
  Elk
  Caribou
  Cougar
  Mountain goat
  Moose
  Bighorn sheep
  Grizzly bear
  Salmon
  Coast Indian
  Indian
  Coat of arms
  Mountie
  Maple leaf

Province of Ontario:
  ✓ Trillium
  ✓ Windsor, Ambassador Bridge
  ✓ Sarnia, Bluewater Bridge
  ✓ Chatham, St. Joseph's Church
  ✓ London, Storybook Gardens
  ✓ Woodstock, Old Town Hall
  ✓ Stratford, Swan
  ✓ Kitchener, Schneider Haus
  ✓ Waterloo, The Seagram Museum
  ✓ Waterloo County, Mennonite Horse and Buggy
  ✓ Elora, Mill Street
  ✓ Guelph, Church of Our Lady
  ✓ Guelph, Johnston Hall (U of G)
  ✓ Kitchener-Waterloo, Oktoberfest
  ✓ Hamilton, Dundurn Castle
  ✓ St. Catharines, Old Court House
  ✓ Niagara Falls, Falls, Brock Monument, and Maid of
      the Mist
  ✓ Acton, Leathertown (hide with buildings)
  ✓ Toronto, skyline
  ✓ Toronto, City Hall
  ✓ Toronto, St. Lawrence Hall
  ✓ Toronto, Casa Loma
  ✓ Kingston, City Hall
  ✓ Ottawa, Parliament buildings
  ✓ Collingwood, Town Hall
  ✓ Owen Sound, city crest

Province of Quebec:
  Montreal, skyline
  Montreal, Olympic Stadium

Province of Nova Scotia:
  Bluenose (schooner)

Yukon Territory:
  Coat of arms
  Gold panner

Province of British Columbia:
  Coat of arms
  Prince George
  Victoria, Parliament buildings
  Victoria, lamppost
  Victoria, Empress Hotel
  Nanaimo, Bastion
  Dogwood (flower)
  Totem pole
  Kermode Terrace
  Smithers
  Northlander Rogers Pass, bear
  Northlander Rogers Pass, house
  Kelowna, The Ogopogo
  Okanagan, The Ogopogo
  Vancouver, Grouse Mountain/skyride/chalet
  Vancouver, Grouse Mountain/skyride
  Vancouver, Grouse Mountain/skyride/cabin
  Vancouver, Cleveland Dam
  Vancouver, The Lions
  Vancouver, The Lions Gate Bridge

Province of Alberta:
  Banff, Mount Norquay
  Banff, Mount Rundle
  Banff, Banff Springs Hotel
  Calgary, bronco rider
  Edmonton, Klondike Mike
  Wild rose (flower)
  Oil derrick
  Jasper
  Jasper sky tram

University Crests/Coats of Arms
  ✓ Wilfrid Laurier
  ✓ Waterloo
  ✓ Carleton
  ✓ Trent
  ✓ York
  ✓ Western
  ✓ Windsor
  ✓ McMaster
  ✓ Brock

Community College Crests/Coats of Arms
  ✓ Fanshawe
  ✓ Humber
  ✓ Other: St. Joseph's Hospital, Guelph
            Credit union

Note: Those with a check mark denote those made up on Demmers' initiative.

Exhibit 13   The Major Tourist Sites of Toronto

---

1. Metro Zoo
2. CN Tower
3. Casa Loma
4. Royal Ontario Museum (ROM)
5. Black Creek Pioneer Village
6. Art Gallery of Ontario (AGO)
7. Canada's Wonderland
8. Ontario Place
9. The Ontario Science Centre

Exhibit 14   Statement of Income (unaudited), Kolapore, Inc., Eight Months Ending Nov. 30, 1985*

Sales	$21,000
Cost of sales	
Inventory at beginning of year	2,873
Purchases	12,000
Duty and freight	3,500
Dies	1,950
	20,323
Inventory at end of year	5,000
	15,323
Gross Profit	5,677
Expenses	6,500
Net (loss) for the year to date	$ (823)

* Annual sales expected to be $30,000.

---

products could have a crest attached to it. These crests would be the same as those used on the spoons and would thus utilize the dies to a greater extent. The landed costs per metal crest from the same supplier would be $0.85. Demmers contemplated attaching these crests himself onto products supplied by Canadian manufacturers. However, initial investigations had revealed no obvious economical second product line.

Demmers also planned to phase out alpacca imports—all products would now be silver plated. In fact, Demmers was also wondering if he should acquire the equipment and materials in order to do this silver plating and polishing himself.

With no lack of ideas, many of the original frustrations nonetheless remained. The buyers at major chains such as Eatons and Simpsons had changed once again, and because they did not use an automatic reorder system, new appointments had to be arranged. This was as difficult as ever. Also, Demmers had still not been able to draw anything from the firm for his efforts. These factors, coupled with his lack of cash and the demands of his new full-time position, had left Demmers uncertain as to what he should do next. With the spring buying season approaching, when Demmers would normally visit potential buyers, he realized that his decision regarding the future of Kolapore could not be postponed much longer.

CASE 4 HOUSTON MARINE TRAINING SERVICES, INC.*

In January of 1984, Brant Houston, president of Houston Marine Training Services (HMTS), Inc., was considering alternative solutions to a problem that had plagued his company for the past five years. The problem was that his company had historically experienced a low return on operations outside of the Louisiana area. Increased competition and high overhead had exacerbated the problem. He had to find a way to make operations outside of Louisiana more profitable or discontinue them.

Since 1972, HMTS had served the marine industry by conducting license preparation courses for Coast Guard required licenses. Over 17,000 people in the charter fishing, towing, and offshore oil industries had received Coast Guard licenses after completing an HMTS course. HMTS trained 3,305 students in 1983, 72 percent of whom were trained outside Louisiana.

Geographic expansion started in 1978 in response to existing demand. Sales grew rapidly from $450,000 in 1978 to $780,000 in 1979. By the end of 1983, sales were $1.8 million. Profits, however, peaked in 1978 at $55,000, a level not exceeded until 1983. (See Exhibits 1 and 2 for current financial data.)

During the period from 1979 to 1984, Brant tried numerous measures to increase the profitability of the firm. The first of these measures was an attempt to isolate the revenues and costs of conducting courses outside Louisiana. According to Brant:

> The revenues and costs for each of the two geographic markets were so different that we began asking how much of our money is coming in from these different sources and how much is being used to support them. We didn't know at that point. We just knew that we had a pile of money coming in and a pile going out, and when we subtracted the two we had some left. That's about all we knew. We analyzed the situation and learned what we knew instinctively—that we were making more money inside Louisiana than we were outside Louisiana. But, we had no idea how drastic the difference was.

That was in 1980.

In 1983, the problem persisted; 70 percent of HMTS courses were offered outside Louisiana, and the profitability of these courses had to be increased somehow. Brant considered several options, including partnerships between the company and individuals, joint ventures, strong management incentive programs for local managers, and the hiring of a full-time sales manager. After revealing reservations with regard to these alternatives, Brant reflected on the problem. "Whatever option we choose, it has to work," he said. "If it doesn't, we can hang it up so far as our business outside Louisiana is concerned."

---

* Prepared by Mr. James F. Simpson under the direction of Professor Jeffrey A. Barach, Graduate School of Business Administration, Tulane University, as a basis for class discussion and not to illustrate either effective or ineffective administrative practices. (Revised November, 1984.) Copyright © 1984 by the School of Business, Tulane University. Reprinted with permission.

Exhibit 1   Income Statements, Houston Marine Training Services, 1981–1983

	June 1, 1980– May 31, 1981	June 1, 1981– May 31, 1982	June 1, 1982– May 31, 1983
Total revenues	$1,293,580	$1,536,548	$1,842,128
Direct expenses			
Salaries and benefits	$ 74,465	$ 317,799	$ 389,254
Commissions and contract services	318,454	76,839	271,733
Rentals—classrooms	52,865	116,056	146,680
Advertising	40,506	86,714	97,120
Entertainment	1,137	1,828	3,860
Travel and transportation	85,650	89,787	96,082
Phone	48,834	14,613	50,302
Postage	11,849	6,418	9,184
Supplies		6,947	16,423
Registration		88,775	
Cost of goods sold		98,020	123,516
Training support		34,904	63,904
Marketing and sales		15,305	153,600
Miscellaneous	33,013	14,414	3,988
Intra-company transfers			(49,418)
Total direct expenses	$ 666,773	$ 968,419	$1,376,228
Gross profit	$ 626,807	$ 568,129	$ 465,900
General and administrative expenses			
Equipment expense	$ 47,098	$ 48,167	$ 56,545
Salaries and benefits, officers	10,773	22,524	12,925
Salaries and wages	225,397	330,776	311,511
Professional services	39,865	68,671	34,890
Promotional marketing	22,410	16,019	20,512
Contributions/subscriptions	2,882	4,123	4,212
Taxes, fees, licenses	1,715	3,678	9,157
Telephone	3,542	54,788	23,917
Travel and transportation	1,912	13,368	9,361
Supplies	25,974	35,325	34,852
Postage (office—Kenner)	6,489	13,415	10,509
Janitorial and utilities	8,712	17,505	13,306
Insurance	12,094	8,569	18,565
Entertainment	2,528	3,147	4,987
Depreciation	19,718	56,924	55,715
Miscellaneous operating expenses	6,853	9,053	6,739
Office rent	8,640	26,100	18,804
Applied overhead		(274,887)	(320,072)
Total	$ 446,602	$ 457,265	$ 326,435
Other expenses (income)			
Miscellaneous expenses (income)	$ 1,527	$ 76,241	$ (5,514)
Interest	34,749	1,569	49,677
Bonuses	21,088	3,752	
Accelerated depreciation expense	63,624		
R&D write-off			32,985
Contributions	4,270		
Bad debts	8,704		
Taxes	11,371	(262)	
Profit sharing expenses	31,000	15,000	
Total operating expenses	$ 622,935	$ 553,565	$ 403,583
Net income	$ 3,872	$ 14,564	$ 62,317

Exhibit 2   Balance Sheets, Houston Marine Training Services, 1981–1983

Assets	May 31, 1981	May 31, 1982	May 31, 1983
Current assets:			
Cash	$ 53,051.48	$ 48,655.34	$ 126,731.63
Accounts receivable	30,320.35	52,837.19	84,346.38
Inventory	11,044.15	15,465.31	27,860.16
Prepaid expenses	1,145.00	16,157.64	55.65
Total current assets	95,560.98	133,115.48	238,993.82
Property and equipment:			
Building	368,696.60	396,323.75	412,706.68
Furniture, fixtures, and equipment	36,164.00	51,431.56	75,277.60
Autos	27,569.16	32,235.16	45,293.14
Leasehold improvements (LaRose)	63,656.40	69,652.55	69,652.55
Less: Accumulated depreciation	(54,093.00)	(106,690.00)	(160,157.00)
Net property and equipment	441,993.16	442,953.02	442,772.97
Other assets*	53,242.80	3,283.87	15,629.20
Total assets	$590,796.94	$ 579,352.37	$ 697,395.99
Liabilities and Stockholders' Equity			
Current liabilities:			
Student liabilities	–0–	–0–	$ 41,192.67
Accounts payable	$ 33,547.80	$ 11,110.32	30,585.66
Taxes payable	16,214.68	(818.25)	775.22
Bonus and profit sharing payable	39,088.31	18,752.30	6,000.00
Notes payable (current)	50,000.00	3,645.44	91,114.00
Total current liabilities	138,850.79	32,689.81	169,667.55
Notes payable (net)	274,607.79	354,759.73	273,508.58
Total liabilities	413,458.58	387,449.54	443,176.13
Stockholders' Equity:			
Common stock	100.00	100.00	100.00
Retained earnings	173,420.65	177,238.36	191,802.80
Net income	3,817.71	14,564.47	62,317.06
Total stockholders' equity	177,338.36	191,902.83	254,219.86
Total liabilities and stockholders' equity	$590,796.94	$ 579,352.37	$ 697,395.99

* Other assets [investments, deposits, investments in and amounts due from(to) affiliates].

BACKGROUND

Brant Houston graduated from the U.S. Coast Guard Academy in 1967. For the next three years, he served aboard Coast Guard cutters in Vietnam and the Atlantic. After sea duty, Lieutenant Houston was selected to attend the Coast Guard Marine Safety School. From there he was assigned to the Marine Inspection Office in New Orleans, Louisiana. During the next two years, he worked in the Coast Guard's investigation, vessel inspection, and marine personnel licensing departments.

Brant observed first-hand the rapid expansion of the towing and offshore oil industries on the Gulf Coast. He was aware of the industries' many safety problems. He knew companies had a hard time obtaining trained and licensed personnel to operate vessels in a manner that complied with Coast Guard requirements. He also knew many people wanted these jobs, but they did not know how to qualify themselves.

After identifying these opportunities, Brant resigned from the Coast Guard and founded Houston Marine Training Services, Inc. in suburban New Orleans. His personal skills and reputation gave him a distinctive competence to solve these problems. Establishing his name with potential customers was critical, because customers could not prejudge quality due to the simultaneous creation and delivery of services. Making a go of the business wasn't easy. Often a wrong decision would have meant serious losses and inability to support his wife and children.

For the first year, Brant worked out of a bedroom at home. From 1973 through 1976 he rented a two-room office suite, and in 1977 he rented two additional rooms. Later that same year, HMTS moved into a modern office/classroom facility located along a highway in a commercial strip near the Mississippi River about nine miles from downtown New Orleans. In 1980, Brant purchased an 8,000 square foot building in Kenner, Louisiana, adjacent to the New Orleans International Airport. This location was selected because it was accessible to students and clients; it was convenient to motels and restaurants for out-of-town students; and its administrative and classroom spaces were adequate to serve the company's needs. In addition to the headquarters building, the company had a branch office located in Larose, Louisiana, approximately 60 miles southwest of New Orleans.

INDUSTRY BACKGROUND

HMTS served people in the marine industry who required a Coast Guard license for employment. The company had found that it actually served two separate groups. One category was comprised of people needing a license to gain employment in the oil exploration industry and the towing industry. They enrolled in such courses as Able Seaman, Tankerman, Towing Vessel Operator, and Master/Mate. The other category consisted of individuals who owned their own boat and who wanted to use it to carry "passengers for hire." These people enrolled in the Passenger Vessel Operator (PVO) course.

Federal Regulations required that any individual who carried "passengers for hire" must be properly licensed. The "passenger for hire" definition covered a wide variety of vessel operators and crew boat operators. There were a number of court cases which had stretched the definition of "passengers for hire." Boat owners had been found to have been carrying "passengers for hire" if they accepted food or beer from otherwise nonpaying passengers.

Getting a Coast Guard license was not easy. Both passing a written examination and experience on the water were required. Any person over 18 years of age with at least 365 days on the water using any size motor vessel could qualify for the Motorboat Operator license if he completed the required Coast Guard forms, a medical exam, and passed the license exam. This license authorized the holder to carry a maximum of six passengers for hire on motorboats 65 feet or less in length. To carry more than six passengers, the Ocean Operator license was required. This license also authorized the holder to operate a vessel inspected by the Coast Guard. For this license, two years' experience on the water was required. The experience had to be in the deck department (deckhand, mate, etc.) of a motorboat or small motor vessel on oceans or coastwise waters.

The number of newly licensed personnel was directly related to industry supply and demand. More boats were operated during times of economic prosperity, and licensed personnel were in heavy demand. However, according to Brant, his company's fortunes to some extent worked the opposite of the industry. He explained that when the towing industry was booming, a towing company had more boats, hence more notes to pay. An owner would operate his boat even if he didn't have the proper number of licensed seamen. He could operate his boat illegally because the Coast Guard had insufficient personnel to adequately enforce the licensing laws. It was relatively easy for a seaman to find employment even if he didn't have the proper license.

When the economy was bad, the industry laid people off. The last employee to be laid off was the one with a license. Job security became important and a license, in many cases, was the key to job security. This was also a time when many people upgraded their licenses. These factors partially insulated HMTS during downturns in the economy.

Still, demand varied seasonally and from port to port depending on economic conditions. Despite built-in insulations described in the last paragraph, HMTS had suffered from the recession in the oilfield and towing industries. Decreased sales and increased operating costs created dangerously weak cash positions as the company entered slow seasonal periods.

Brant was encouraged by predictions of turnarounds in the industries he served. One industry newsletter, *Marine Management Newsletter,* reported in July of 1983:

> Many observers of the rig charter market, both foreign and domestic, believe the rig market has, in fact, reached bottom. That should signal the beginning of a turnaround for the offshore service vessel market as well—at least as far as the number of available jobs is concerned.

In another issue of the same newsletter it was reported that:

> Gulf of Mexico Market could show an upturn by late 1983 according to some observers. As a result of the recent central Gulf lease sale, as many as 50 of the 71 idle rigs located in the Gulf could be back at work by the end of 1983. This would raise the rig utilization rate in the Gulf from the present mid 60 percent level to about 90 percent.

If the oilfield and towing industries recovered from the recession as expected, Brant estimated increased demand for qualified marine personnel could result in net operating income of as much as $400,000.

COMPETITION

Although the Coast Guard promoted self-study, it could not offer license prep courses because its responsibility in this area was limited to certifying the competence of marine personnel. Competition did exist among a variety of individuals, state schools, and other commercial schools.

The individuals who taught license prep courses did so on a part-time basis; most were charter boat captains who had a knowledge of the exams. They were interspersed along the Gulf and Atlantic coasts. They advertised in local telephone books, posted notices at marinas, and placed ads in local newspapers. They also found customers through word of mouth or through customer contact established in the normal course of their businesses.

A number of small schools taught license prep courses in Louisiana. Almost all students in these schools were employed in the offshore oil or towing industries. Two state vocational training schools offered license prep courses at no charge to state students and only a token charge for nonresidents. These schools were similar to vocational schools in that their courses covered a longer period of time. Because the courses were substantially longer in duration, these schools did not compete directly with HMTS. Another school offering license prep courses, Page Navigation, was located in downtown New Orleans. This school specialized in classes for higher level licenses, and there was little overlap with HMTS courses.

There were two commercial schools competing directly for HMTS customers. Both schools were owned by former HMTS instructors or sales agents. One, located in New Orleans, competed primarily for mineral and drilling customers. The other school, headquartered in St. Petersburg, Florida, competed for PVO customers in Florida, Alabama, and New Orleans. The success of these schools had caused Brant to re-evaluate his pricing and promotional strategy. Although competition was costly, he maintained that competition had been good for his company in that it had caused exploration of new areas (e.g., computer-assisted instruction) and new strategies to recapture market share.

COMPANY HISTORY

Houston Marine Training Services began as Houston Marine Consultants, Inc. Brant perceived a need for training in 1972, but he believed the greatest need in the oil exploration industry was for a consultant who could advise clients how they could best prepare for Coast Guard inspection of their vessels. He felt that his knowledge of federal regulations and his familiarity with Coast Guard policies with respect to enforcing these regulations qualified him for consulting. He soon found that consulting was less profitable than he anticipated, so he turned to a lucrative market that was not being served—the Coast Guard license prep market.

Growth during the early history of the company was slow. It had all the problems faced by new businesses: undercapitalization, no proven track record, and inexperienced management. Brant freely admitted that he didn't know what direction he was headed and that energy was wasted shifting the company's emphasis from consulting to training.

In 1977, revenues were $221,000. HMTS still had a consulting division, but its contribution to total revenue was minimal. Total revenue in 1978 was $455,000, and Brant estimated that only 5 percent had been generated by consulting activities. License prep courses accounted for 90 percent of the revenue. Courses offered included: Passenger Vessel Operator (Motorboat Operator, Ocean Operator, and Inland Operator), First Class Pilot, Uninspected Towing Vessel Operator, Chief/Assistant Engineer

(Mineral and Oil), Able Seaman, Third Class Radio-Telephone Operator, Tankerman, 300 Ton Master/Mate of Mineral and Oil vessels, Master/Mate—Freight and Towing (1,000 Ton), Loran C, and Celestial Navigation.

A portion of the revenue in 1978 had been provided by a retail operation, the Captain's Locker, Ltd. This was a subsidiary corporation which became a Hallmark Gift store located in a Larose, Louisiana shopping center in 1980. HMTS sold charts, books, course materials, and nautical gifts through the Captain's Locker. In 1981, this venture fell victim to a recession in the oil exploration industry which hit severely the Larose area and the Captain's Locker's shopping mall.

Brant believed that his success in the license prep market was attributed to few competitors, delivery of a quality product, respect for students, and a loyal and experienced corps of instructors. Exhibits 3 and 4 present a description of HMTS's philosophy and instructors.

In 1979, the training division had 18 full-time, salaried instructors. Most instructors taught two classes per month, occasionally traveling to nearby areas where eight or more students enrolled in a course. At the time, Brant estimated that 5 students in an out-of-Louisiana course covered out-of-pocket costs, and 12 covered its full costs. Between 1979 and 1984, the number of courses conducted annually and the number of instructors increased, but in the pursuit of profitability, the company relied less on full-time, salaried instructors and more on contract instructors and training representatives, both of which will be discussed later.

HMTS served two distinct geographic markets—a Louisiana market and a market outside Louisiana. The study confirmed what Brant already knew intuitively—the company was making 60 percent gross profit on sales in Louisiana and 20 percent gross profit on sales outside Louisiana.

"My initial reaction was to terminate operations outside Louisiana," remarked Brant. "I couldn't do that because sales outside Louisiana were contributing to overhead and the contribution was significant. So, I began to look for ways to make this aspect of the business more profitable."

Exhibit 3   The Ten Commandments of Houston Marine

1. The STUDENT is the most important person at Houston Marine.
2. The STUDENT is not an outsider—he is the reason for our existence.
3. The STUDENT is not an interruption of our work—he is the purpose of it.
4. The STUDENT does us a favor when he calls, we are not doing him a favor—nor are we doing a favor when we serve the STUDENT.
5. The STUDENT is not a cold statistic but a human being with feelings and emotions like our own. He does not like to be referred to as a PVO, Master/Mate, UTV, etc.
6. The STUDENT is not someone to argue or match wits with.
7. The STUDENT is a person who brings us his needs. It is our job to assist in the meeting of those needs.
8. The STUDENT is deserving of the most courteous and attentive treatment that can be given.
9. The STUDENT is often dependent on us and we are equally dependent on the STUDENT.
10. The STUDENT is the life blood of Houston Marine.

Exhibit 4   Qualifications and Functions of Selected HMTS Personnel

Name	Year Came to HMTS	Background	Function	Location
Bill Clark	1983	Retired Coast Guard Captain, graduate U.S. Coast Guard Academy	Profit Center Manager; Instructor: (1) Towing (2) Master/ Mate	New Orleans
Babs Cullen	1976	Holds 100-Ton Captain's License	Training Rep: VI, PR	St. Thomas, Virgin Islands
Terry Southerland	1983	Retired U.S. Navy; graduate U.S. Naval Academy	Instructor: Master/ Mate	New Orleans
Heinz Hickethier	1982	Retired U.S. Navy; NROTC Instructor, University of Pennsylvania	Manager, Larose, La., Profit Center; Instructor	Larose, La.
Paul McElroy	1982	Great Lakes Charter Captain; accomplished author	Training Rep, Great Lakes	Hoffman Estates, Ill.
Greg Szczurek	1975	Former Coast Guard Officer	Vice President, Profit Center Manager	New Orleans
George Bishop	1982	Graduate U.S. Naval Academy; 3rd Mate License	Training Rep	Pelham, N.J.
Ken Woods	1978	Retired, U.S. Navy (24 years); graduate U.S. Naval Academy	Profit Center Manager; Instructor: Captain's C.	New Orleans
Tom Webb	1977	Licensed as Master upon Oceans on Steam or Motor Passenger Vessels and Master Freight and Towing Vessels	Profit Center Manager; Instructor	Key Largo, Fla.
Mike Ellison	1983	Graduate U.S. Naval Academy; MBA Naval Post Graduate School, Monterey, California; three years management consulting	Profit Center Manager; Marketing Manager	New Orleans

---

One of the first things he did to improve the profitability of operations outside Louisiana was to create a new and experimental position: area manager. The area manager was a salaried instructor who liked the challenge of organizing his own business territory and performing the administrative functions required to get a student his license.

The first area manager, Tom Webb, was responsible for operations in Florida. His responsibilities included handling local problems with instructors, resolving problems with Coast Guard officials in his territory, teaching courses himself, and promoting Houston Marine Training Services.

The area manager concept was successful in Florida because of the concentrated sales of courses. Other areas of the country had pockets of activity which warranted expansion into these areas but could not support an area manager. Coordination in these areas was done through headquarters. Full-time salaried instructors, mostly residents of the areas where there was a demand for courses, were used to conduct the courses, but the cost of travel and lodging for the instructors made this unprofitable. This led to another experimental concept: the training representative.

The training representative concept was designed and implemented in 1981. Pursuant to an agreement entered into by the company and the training representative, the training rep agreed to promote and organize classes in a designated protected territory. He was responsible for conducting all classes. This included all classroom instruction, locating and paying for the classroom, handling all attendant paperwork, and paying for local promotion when required. Each training rep was responsible for his lodging, travel, and food expenses. These costs were nonreimbursable.

The training rep provided the company with collections and itemized reimbursable expenses (local advertising, classroom rental, etc.) for each class. The net of gross receipts less reimbursable expenses was split between the training rep and the company. For its part, the company provided marketing and administrative support and validated review questions similar to those appearing on actual Coast Guard examinations.

The training representative concept was highly successful in selected geographic areas and significantly improved the overall profitability of operations outside Louisiana. This was done primarily because particular training reps had been able to increase their class sizes. See, for example, Maryland (Conklin) and the Great Lakes area (McElroy) in Exhibits 5 and 6. There were several problems, however:

1. The training representative was limited to a relatively small territory because of the same expense and control problems HMTS had experienced when trying to do business on the road. Because the market was so specialized, there were only a limited number of territories that would support a sufficient number and size of classes to make the proposition attractive to a potential training rep. Many of the courses offered in New Orleans were not marketable because a given territory would not produce enough students at any given time to make a profitable class.
2. The initial recruiting and training costs were high and might be lost if the potential training rep changed his mind during the training process.
3. Once trained, the training rep needed little in terms of ongoing services from HMTS. Should he leave the company, he would be a formidable competitor in an area that he had developed.

Another change which had reduced fixed costs was the addition of contract instructors. They were paid a base for each course, plus a commission for each student. The contract instructor was required to teach the course and collect the tuition from each student. If he failed to get the minimum number of students, HMTS could cancel the class no later than the seventh day before the class was to commence. The use of contract instructors was a recent development, and its profitability was still being evaluated.

The greatest change in operations was in 1980 when the company grouped all products and services offered by Houston Marine into profit centers. Each profit center had a profit center manager who was accountable to Brant. Responsibilities of profit center managers included scheduling of classes, teaching courses, supervising instructors assigned to that profit center, promoting and selling courses. Instructors of all kinds (full-time, part-time, contract, and training reps) reported to their respective profit center manager. Profit centers were organized by product line. In 1983, they

Exhibit 5   Number of Classes Scheduled and Conducted at HMTS, by State and Year

State	1979 Scheduled	1979 Conducted	1980 Scheduled	1980 Conducted	1981 Scheduled	1981 Conducted	1982 Scheduled	1982 Conducted	1983 Scheduled	1983 Conducted
Vt.	0	0	1	1	0	0	0	0	1	1
Me.	9	4	4	1	2	1	0	0	4	3
N.H.	1	1	3	3	2	2	4	4	3	3
Mass.	10	6	7	7	11	11	7	7	7	7
R.I.	10	8	5	5	3	3	4	4	4	4
Conn.	12	7	11	11	4	3	9	8	5	4
N.Y.	15	9	11	7	11	10	8	8	8	8
N.J.	23	15	22	17	20	19	21	18	18	16
Pa.	4	2	4	4	8	8	6	4	4	4
Del.	4	2	2	1	3	3	0	0	2	1
Md.	1	1	3	1	0	0	8	8	8	8
D.C.	0	0	0	0	0	0	1	1	0	0
Va.	3	0	5	2	0	0	1	1	3	2
N.C.	12	7	10	6	3	2	7	5	9	8
S.C.	1	1	2	1	0	0	2	2	4	3
Ga.	0	0	0	0	0	0	0	0	0	0
Fla.	64	48	51	42	39	38	42	33	45	39
V.I.	4	4	7	6	4	2	5	5	6	5
P.R.	1	1	1	1	0	0	0	0	2	2
Ala.	7	6	3	3	1	1	9	9	17	17
Miss.	2	2	3	3	0	0	3	3	5	5
La.	76	76	79	78	78	78	96	96	132	109
Tex.	15	13	13	13	23	23	32	28	41	34
Ind.	0	0	0	0	0	0	1	1	2	2
Ill.	0	0	0	0	1	1	3	3	4	4
Ohio	0	0	0	0	1	1	2	2	4	4
Mich.	0	0	0	0	0	0	0	0	6	6
Wis.	0	0	0	0	1	0	0	0	3	3
Calif.	0	0	1	1	0	0	3	2	0	0
Wash.	0	0	0	0	0	0	2	2	4	3
Oreg.	0	0	1	1	0	0	2	2	1	1
Totals	274	213	249	215	217	206	278	256	352	306

Exhibit 6 Number of Students Enrolled in HMTS Courses, by State

State	1979 PVO*	1979 Other†	1980 PVO	1980 Other	1981 PVO	1981 Other	1982 PVO	1982 Other	1983 PVO	1983 Other
Vt.	0	0	6	0	0	0	0	0	5	0
Me.	39	0	6	0	18	0	0	0	16	0
N.H.	10	0	35	0	13	0	33	0	30	0
Mass.	90	0	115	0	101	0	83	0	131	0
R.I.	93	0	66	0	51	0	61	0	48	0
Conn.	44	0	90	0	28	0	76	0	24	0
N.Y.	76	0	83	0	99	0	59	0	85	0
N.J.	202	0	194	0	172	0	180	0	200	0
Pa.	25	0	45	0	76	0	53	0	49	0
Del.	14	0	8	0	36	0	0	0	8	0
Md.	5	0	29	0	0	0	104	0	128	0
D.C.	0	0	0	0	0	0	13	0	0	0
Va.	0	0	14	0	0	0	12	0	22	0
N.C.	45	0	50	0	3	0	31	0	50	0
S.C.	9	0	6	0	0	0	21	0	13	0
Ga.	0	0	0	0	0	0	0	0	0	15
Fla.	489	0	510	0	441	0	412	0	381	0
V.I.	119	0	158	0	31	0	82	0	22	0
P.R.	8	0	9	0	0	0	0	0	87	11
Ala.	69	0	26	0	9	0	62	0	32	59
Miss.	18	0	31	0	0	0	31	0	37	0
La.	573	315	891	543	860	491	618	592	188	752
Tex.	136	0	154	0	178	0	174	0	249	0
Ind.	0	0	0	0	0	0	29	0	64	0
Ill.	0	0	0	0	3	0	44	0	123	0
Ohio	0	0	0	0	9	0	24	0	139	0
Mich.	0	0	0	0	0	0	0	0	199	0
Wis.	0	0	0	0	0	0	0	0	75	0
Calif.	0	0	6	0	0	0	17	0	0	0
Wash.	0	0	0	0	0	0	0	4	0	52
Oreg.	0	0	6	0	0	0	24	0	0	11
Totals	2,064	315	2,538	543	2,128	491	2,243	596	2,405	900

* PVO included Ocean Operator, Inland Operator, and Motorboat Operator.

† Other included Tankerman, Towing Vessel Operator, Master/Mate, Able Seaman, First Class Pilot, Loran C, and Celestial Navigation.

were changed to geographic organization, as the company became more market oriented.

OPERATIONS

In 1984, HMTS operated in 25 states, Puerto Rico, and the Virgin Islands. Most of its operations were directed at assisting otherwise qualified individuals prepare for Coast Guard examinations. The company offered day courses and night courses in 50 locations to make courses convenient for students. This sometimes resulted in conducting classes with as few as five students (see Exhibits 5 and 6) when a minimum of six students was required to cover variable costs. In 1983, HMTS conducted 302 courses and prepared 3,305 students for Coast Guard examinations.

Students were taught material they needed to know to obtain licenses required for employment in the marine industry. They were also taught how to take the exam and what tricks to watch for in questions. Great care was taken in structuring courses so students covered all relevant material needed to pass the exam.

HMTS acted as a liaison between companies, students, and the Coast Guard in assisting with paperwork, photographs required for documents, application problems, medical examinations (using contract physicians), and testing arrangements. Whenever possible, the company arranged for Coast Guard exams to be administered in its classrooms immediately following the period of instruction. This allowed students to test in a convenient and familiar environment, resulting in improved pass rates.

A recent change in HMTS operations was the addition of multilevel courses. Market research had shown that HMTS customers were of two basic types. One type wanted increased professional knowledge while preparing for the examination. The other type only wanted a license, and he wanted to learn nothing beyond what was absolutely necessary to obtain a license. Two levels of courses were being given in Kenner in 1984: self-paced and professional development. These are described in Exhibit 7.

In 1983, courses were taught by five full-time, salaried instructors; four half-time salaried instructors; seven contract instructors; and six training representatives. Salaries for full-time instructors ranged between $17,000 and $24,000. Because instructors were crucial to the success of the firm, Brant Houston recruited new instructors himself. The process was both long and difficult, sometimes taking a month to hire a new instructor. Once hired, Ken Woods supervised the instructor's two-month training period. Mr. Houston felt that if an instructor stayed for three years, the training effort was worthwhile. Typically, instructors did stay two and a half to three years. Classes in New Orleans were conducted at the company's Kenner location which had three classrooms and computer terminals for the self-paced courses. In Larose, Louisiana, classes were held in classroom/office space leased by HMTS. Self-paced courses were also offered in Larose. Courses conducted outside the New Orleans area were held in rented classrooms, usually motel conference rooms. Net profit for operations varied depending on the location of the course and whether the course was taught by a salaried instructor, contract instructor, or a training representative (see Exhibit 8).

To provide control over operations, all products and services offered by HMTS were grouped into profit centers, with each profit center manager reporting directly

---

Exhibit 7   Descriptions of HMTS's Self-Paced and Professional Development Courses

So you want your license? Well Houston Marine Training Services now offers you a choice in courses. You can take our Professional Development Course or our Self-Paced License Prep Course. The choice is yours!

Self-Paced License Prep

Houston Marine has developed the surest and easiest way to get your Passenger Vessel license in as little as three days! Combining the latest in technology and personalized instruction, we can give you what you want in a license prep course: your license in as little time possible! The course can be scheduled when you want it— call for your appointment today!

How It Works

You learn the course material from a concise study manual based on our lectures. It's written in plain English that is easy to understand. A Houston Marine instructor is on hand to answer your questions and explain any difficult concepts. Once you feel comfortable with the material, you test your knowledge with a computer-assisted review. When you and the instructor are satisfied with your scores on the computer, you take the Coast Guard exam.

No Pressure

This is a *self-paced* course! There's no pressure to keep up with the fastest guy in the class. And if you do your homework, you can have your license in as little as three days! Call today to set up your appointment!

Tuition: Self-Paced, $295

Professional Development

Houston Marine's Professional Development Captain's Course is designed to improve and broaden the student's maritime skills and knowledge. The course is taught by an experienced instructor who covers the material in depth while making difficult concepts and regulations covered on the Coast Guard exam easy to understand. This is for the mariner who wants more than just a license!

Course Date and Times

Location: Houston Marine
            1600 20th St.
            Kenner, LA 70062

Dates: April 25–May 1
          May 15–22
          June 5–12

Time: 8 A.M.–5 P.M.

Class Size Is Limited

Enroll now! A $50 registration fee will reserve a seat for you. When we receive your fee, we will send you the necessary Coast Guard applications and instructions on how to fill them out. We accept certified checks, money orders, cashier's checks, VISA, Mastercard, and American Express. The tuition covers everything you need for the course.

Tuition: Professional Development, $495

Our 11 years of professional maritime training experience makes it easy for us to say: Your success is guaranteed— or your money back!

---

to the director of marketing, Mike Ellison, or the president, Brant Houston. Responsibilities of profit center managers included scheduling of classes, promoting, teaching, and selling.

The profit center manager's primary objective was to maintain a profitable operation and to ensure that the product delivered met the standards set by HMTS and those expected by the customer. He had sales agents, instructors, and headquarters support personnel working to help him achieve these objectives. In addition to managing these resources, the profit center manager was also responsible for formulating and executing the budget for his profit center.

In 1984, the company had 38 employees: two in Florida, one in North Carolina, one in Texas, two in Larose, Louisiana, and the remainder (instructors and administrative employees) at the headquarters location in Kenner, Louisiana. The company was divided into six separate areas with the head of each area reporting directly to Brant. The six areas were: Administration, Finance, Training Support, Electronic Data Processing, Research and Development/Special Products, and Marketing (see Exhibit 9 for organization chart).

Exhibit 8   Revenue-Cost Comparions for Selected HMTS Courses and Enrollments

	Number of Students				
	6	8	10	12	15
I. Company salaried instructor (inside Louisiana)					
Revenue (@ $495 per enrollee)	$2,970	$3,960	$4,950	$5,940	$7,425
Less direct costs:					
Instructor salary	648	648	648	648	648
Travel/transportation	0	0	0	0	0
Lodging/meals	0	0	0	0	0
Classroom rental	1,000*	1,000	1,000	1,000	1,000
Materials	240	320	400	480	600
Direct advertising	128	128	128	128	128
Total direct expenses	1,976	2,096	2,176	2,256	2,376
Gross margin	994	1,864	2,774	3,684	5,049
Less indirect costs:					
Training support	154	154	154	154	154
Marketing	412	412	412	412	412
Administration/accounting	82	82	82	82	82
Total indirect expenses	648	648	648	648	648
Net income per course	$ 346	$1,216	$2,126	$3,036	$4,401
II. Company salaried instructor (outside Louisiana)					
Revenue (@ $495 per enrollee)	$2,970	$3,960	$4,950	$5,940	$7,425
Less direct costs:					
Instructor salary	648	648	648	648	648
Travel/transportation	200	200	200	200	200
Lodging/meals	360	360	360	360	360
Classroom rental	600	600	600	600	600
Materials	240	320	400	480	600
Commissions	180	240	300	360	450
Direct advertising	128	128	128	128	128
Total direct expenses	2,356	2,496	2,636	2,776	2,986
Gross margin	614	1,464	2,314	3,164	4,439
Less indirect costs:					
Training support	154	154	154	154	154
Marketing	412	412	412	412	412
Administration/accounting	82	82	82	82	82
Total indirect expenses	648	648	648	648	648
Net income per course	$ (34)	$ 816	$1,666	$2,516	$3,791
III. Contract Instructor					
Revenue (@ $495 per enrollee)	$2,970	$3,960	$4,950	$5,940	$7,425
Less direct costs:					
Instructor salary†	680	740	800	860	950
Travel/transportation	200	200	200	200	200
Lodging/meals	360	360	360	360	360
Classroom rental	600	600	600	600	600
Materials	240	320	400	480	600
Commissions	0	0	0	0	0
Direct advertising	128	128	128	128	128
Total direct expenses	2,208	2,348	2,488	2,628	2,838
Gross margin	762	1,612	2,402	3,312	4,587
Less indirect expenses:					
Training	154	154	154	154	154
Marketing	412	412	412	412	412
Administration/accounting	82	82	82	82	82
Total indirect expenses	648	648	648	648	648
Net income per course	$ 114	$ 964	$1,814	$2,664	$3,939

Exhibit 8 *(concluded)*

	Number of Students				
	6	8	10	12	15
IV. **Training representative**					
Revenue (@ $495 per enrollee)	$2,970	$3,960	$4,950	$5,940	$7,425
Less direct costs:					
Classroom rental	600	600	600	600	600
Materials	240	320	400	480	600
Direct advertising	128	128	128	128	128
Total direct expenses	968	1,048	1,128	1,208	1,328
Gross margin	2,002	2,912	3,822	4,732	6,097
HMTS gross income (50 percent)	1,001	1,456	1,911	2,366	3,048
Less indirect costs:					
Training support	154	154	154	154	154
Marketing	412	412	412	412	412
Administration/accounting	82	82	82	82	82
Total indirect costs	648	648	648	648	648
Net income per course	$ 353	$ 808	$1,263	$1,718	$2,400

* Allocated cost of headquarters' classroom.
† Instructor salary is $500 + $30 per student.

Administration was headed by Mrs. Jeanne Roy. She served as administrative assistant to the president and as HMTS's personnel officer. In addition, she was also the business office manager and plant/property manager.

The vice president of finance was Robin Houston. Besides performing the duties of that job, she also managed the accounting department.

Ken Woods was manager for the training support and training representative profit centers. As training support manager, he was responsible for maintaining and updating course materials and supervising the distribution center manager. His duties as training representative manager included providing guidance and answering questions they had concerning changes in regulations affecting their courses. Ken was also responsible for ensuring courses conducted by training reps met the standards set by HMTS. This sometimes required that he attend classes given by a training rep who was having problems as evidenced by poor student evaluations. Ken would make suggestions for improvements, and if the course did not improve, he would recommend the termination of the training rep. In addition to training reps, Ken also supervised 12 sales agents.

Data processing had become such an integral part of HMTS that it had been removed from the Accounting Department. It was now an independent department managed by Robert Andre. He worked for Brant, for the marketing department, and for any other department requiring data processing support.

Greg Szczurek was manager of the research and development custom courses and special projects profit centers. He developed course materials (books, videotapes, and study guides) to improve the quality and reduce the costs of HMTS courses. Greg also developed custom courses tailored to the needs of a particular company.

He was a member of and actively involved in a number of professional trade associations.

Custom courses were developed for companies covering the subject matter of any of HMTS's standard courses. These courses offered several advantages for a company. The material was specifically tailored to the company's needs. Training could be held at the company location. Courses could be scheduled to fit the company's work schedule.

Exhibit 9   HMTS's, Inc., Organization Chart

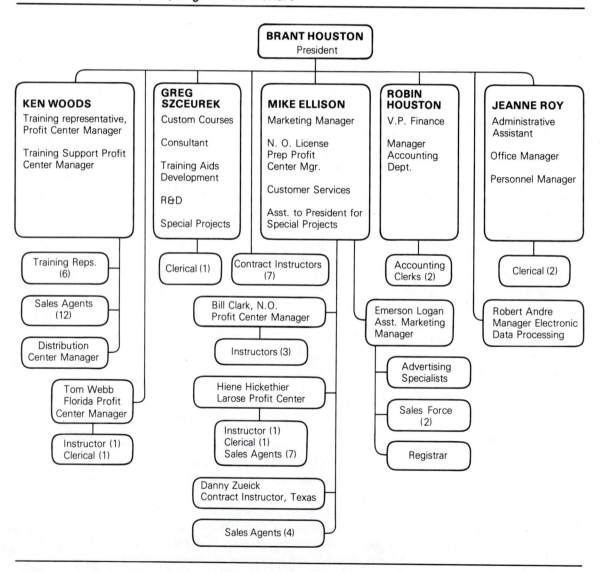

Exhibit 10 Partial List of Books Produced and Sold by HMTS

Unified Rules
- Study guide and reference book.
- Fulfills requirement that vessels over 39 feet carry a copy of Rules aboard.
- Chosen as textbook at U.S. Naval Academy.
- Cost: $10.50 plus shipping.

COLREGS
- Study guide and reference book.
- Easy guide to International Collision Prevention Regulation (COLREGS).
- Chosen as textbook of U.S. Naval Academy.
- Cost: $9.50 plus shipping.

Licensing Procedures Manual
- Contains most Coast Guard licensing policies and procedures.
- Only book available that offers one easy-to-read source.
- Used by personnel managers and Coast Guard personnel.

Greg also produced and sold training aids such as books, videotapes, slides, and outlines (see Exhibit 10 for a description of books published). Most of the sales of training aids had been to the Coast Guard, Navy, and students enrolled in HMTS's courses. Books were sold through *Hooked-Up* (the Houston Marine Newsletter) and by direct mail, but were sold primarily to students by their instructors.

Mike Ellison was marketing manager. The marketing department consisted of an assistant manager, an advertising specialist, a sales force, and a registrar. All courses conducted in New Orleans were promoted and sold through the Marketing Department. In addition, it provided national advertising and marketing support to training reps and other license prep profit center managers. This department also conducted research and feasibility studies for new markets and new courses. Mike was also profit center manager for license prep courses in Louisiana and Texas, and had two other profit center managers and the contract instructor for Texas reporting directly to him. He also supervised four sales agents. In addition, Mike was the profit center manager for customer services, which was responsible for arranging for photographs and physical examinations required for students' licenses. Finally, Mike served as special assistant to the president.

MARKETING

The marketing department assisted each profit center manager in developing his marketing plan and budget. Functions performed by the company's marketing group included:

- Telephone sales—handled incoming calls from prospects and actively solicited new business.
- Maintained sales/prospect files.
- Maintained master company course schedule (tally boards, status boards).
- Used and updated computer information for possible leads.

- Developed advertisements, promotional materials, schedules, and the like at request of profit center managers.
- Placed advertisements.
- Maintained contact with agents and training reps regarding all marketing functions.
- Market research—questionnaire development and implementation.

The marketing department was responsible for coordinating sales force activities, advertising programs, and other promotional activities for each profit center and for the company overall. Additionally, the marketing department conducted surveys to measure the student's perception of courses and the overall services provided by HMTS. It also monitored trade journals to follow industry trends and recommended new courses or modifications to existing courses when it appeared that there was a demand that would justify the addition or change. Finally, in this area, the marketing department researched and presented demographic data to help management keep abreast of its customer bases in the various markets and geographic areas it served.

As a part of the marketing department, there was a local sales force of two people who made telephone calls throughout the country. These individuals also handled all incoming calls from prospective students. After a student was "sold," he or she was referred to a profit center for registration, processing, teaching, and so on. The sales section did not handle incoming calls for custom courses, videotapes, or books.

Outside of Louisiana there was a network of 31 sales agents. These agents were not HMTS employees. Rather, they were part-time salespeople, most of whom were employed in the marine industry, who sold courses on a commission basis per student. The agents promoted and sold courses in their local areas.

The agent had been, and continued to be, the weakest link in the HMTS service chain. Ironically, he was often the only personal contact a prospective student had with the company. Service by the agents was inconsistent according to Jeanne Roy, who had coordinated the activities of sales agents before they were assigned to profit center managers.[1] The biggest problem was motivating them. She said the company had initiated a number of incentives (bonuses, an "early bird" program providing a higher commission for filling classes early, and an agent newsletter), but had failed to find one that worked satisfactorily.

The third method of sales management was with training representatives in locations outside Louisiana. This method had built-in motivation. If the training rep didn't sell, he didn't teach, which meant less income. If he did not watch his expenses, he made less money. An advantage of this method was that the training rep had face-to-face contact with the prospective student. He could hire a sales agent, but he had to pay the commissions.

Mass advertising at HMTS was used most extensively for the PVO classes. Advertisements were placed regularly in the classified or boating sections of boating magazines and local newspapers. Also, regional and national fisherman publications were used, as were national magazines like *Yachting*. Radio had been used on a limited basis, and outdoor billboards were used in the Bayou Lafourche area of Louisiana. Additionally, for all courses, advertising consisted largely of direct mail flyers, course schedules, brochures, and the like. These were sent to former students and practically

---

[1] Sales agents reported to profit center managers in Headquarters, Florida, and Larose, Louisiana.

anyone who had expressed an interest in an HMTS course. Other targeted advertising efforts included postal routes with flyers and brochures in marine stores, personnel offices, yacht and fishing clubs, and other like locations.

Course prices were initially established by executive management, with gradual increases of roughly $25 twice a year. Prices did vary by geographic area, with courses taught in Louisiana priced at $50–$100 lower than other regions, with the exception of Florida. (See Exhibit 7 for PVO course prices in Louisiana.) Tuition in Florida had been lowered in response to strong competition. Training reps set the price of their courses generally at equal or slightly lower costs than the home office. Course prices were largely a function of the length of the course, averaging $350–$450 per week. Customized courses or products were priced to return 30–50 percent gross profit depending on the specifics.

There were companies and schools in the marketplace that provided license preparatory courses or home study materials. For the most part, these schools or companies were lower priced than HMTS. While the services provided were not comparable, they could be used as substitutes for the HMTS products. Home study packages ranged from $14.95 up, and the Captain's Course could be had for as little as $99, or were available free from the Louisiana state schools. Basically, much of the competition, aside from the "free schools," looked to HMTS for a standard and priced their courses accordingly to offer a price advantage. One of the competitive schools stressed that license prep was license prep, and why spend $100–150 more, and why go to school longer, as their program was only five nights, four hours each, for the PVO test. They saved time and still achieved excellent pass rates by stressing test preparation rather than teaching navigation.

According to an in-house marketing report, clients almost never expressed the opinion that HMTS prices were too high. Most recognized the product as worth the price. Also, for many, the company picked up the cost of the course. For a great many who traveled from outside Louisiana to take courses at Kenner, tuition was just a part of the overall cost including hotel, transportation, and meals. To an individual, price mattered, but the goal was to obtain a license as cheaply and as quickly as possible. Thus, high pass rate and scheduling dates could become deciding factors rather than price.

There had been some sense among agents that HMTS's prices were too high. While Mike Ellison recognized that this might have been a fair reflection of resistance in the marketplace, he felt that the agents should have recognized and communicated that the product was worth the price.

Ellison said that there were two basic groups which made up the customer base for HMTS. The target market varied depending on the course content. For PVO classes, customers fell into the following categories:

- Individuals who wanted to charter their boat for hire.
- Individuals who were currently operating illegal charters.
- Recreational boaters who wanted to learn more about their boats for safety and interest.
- Professionals seeking tax deductions and insurance benefits.

Until recently, fishing had been the backbone of the charter industry, but sailing charters, sightseeing, water-skiing, and similar activities were growing as individuals sought ways to increase their incomes or pay for the boat's expenses. Also, using the boat to transport passengers for the drilling industry was a lucrative charter.

For other license prep courses, the market included:

- Individuals employed or seeking employment on towing vessels or supply boats or in the drilling industry.
- Companies owning or managing towing vessels or supply boats.
- Drilling company personnel or management.

Clients with all levels of experience were eligible for different courses. A large part of this market was involved in the offshore drilling industry, but many worked on the Mississippi River transporting such items as coal or grain, as well as in the oil-related fields.

Jobs on boats appealed to young and independent people who preferred being out on the water to a regular job. The river and offshore oil boat operators often alternated seven days on board ship and seven days off. In good times, turnover was high, because the men switched jobs often to suit their own individual schedules, and because they upgraded their licenses and advanced to larger vessels. Still others left the industry or were promoted to jobs on shore. Among deckhands, turnover typically had been 300–500 percent a year. Although not as high, the turnover among licensed officers and operators had often run in excess of 100 percent. Mr. Houston estimated that 20 percent of this turnover was from people who left the industry permanently. Therefore, even if demand remained constant, many new jobs requiring licenses became available every year. The recent recession in the industry had reduced personnel turnover.

Companies were often the target while individuals were the direct consumer. Many times companies paid for or encouraged an individual employee to obtain a particular license. Thus, company management played a large part in the decision-making process by either recommending a particular school or making all the arrangements and requiring that school. When the supply of licensed personnel was less than companies needed to meet their Coast Guard requirements, companies were more likely to send their employees to school.

For training aids, consulting, and special seminars, the target market included the same individuals and companies interested in the license prep courses, as well as Navy, Coast Guard, or Air Force training classes and others involved with or affected by Coast Guard regulations who may be in need of expert advice.

Custom courses were marketed to companies involved in the maritime or drilling industries. Custom courses were less likely to be oriented to license prep and more likely to be focused on safety issues such as stability, hazards on the rig, and firefighting.

The marketing department had been able to develop customer profiles of its students. A majority of HMTS students were between the ages of 20 and 45, males, white, married, high-school educated or less, outdoor oriented, and had a maritime occupation. Incomes varied widely, from $8,000–$10,000 for unlicensed deckhands coming for their first license to $25,000–$35,000 when they got an advanced license.

For the PVO classes, students tended to be fishermen, shrimpers, charter boat captains or those hoping to be charter boat captains, and a small group of professional people—doctors, lawyers, airline pilots—looking for a tax write-off. PVO students tended to be somewhat older than students in Able Seaman, Mate, or Tankerman classes, with a majority 35–50 years old, male, white, and high school educated.

In addition to developing a customer profile, the marketing department had identified reasons individuals engaged HMTS's services. It had found that, among other reasons, customers were motivated to take courses because:

- They were required by the Coast Guard to have a license for the job they had or a job they wanted.
- They wanted a license so that they could legally hire out their vessel for a part-time source of income.
- They wanted a license for prestige, tax deductions, or insurance benefits.
- They were interested in the knowledge and benefits obtained from taking a course, rather than the license itself.

Those who wanted to obtain their Coast Guard license took a course because they knew, or had heard, how difficult it was to qualify without the course. Their objective was usually to get the license in as short a time as possible and return to work. Many had tried on their own and failed, and some had tried the "free" state schools and failed. They saw HMTS as the quickest way to their desired end.

Factors that were considered to affect an individual's decision to study at Houston Marine versus elsewhere were:

- Scheduled dates for classes—class scheduled during time off or availability to start immediately.
- Class location.
- Recommendations from friends, captains, or company personnel officers.
- Previous experiences with HMTS or other schools.
- Good pass rate.
- Their company made the decision.
- Advertising.
- Sales pitch from marketing department or agent.
- Only school the individual knew of was HMTS.
- Price.

BRANT HOUSTON, CHIEF EXECUTIVE OFFICER

When Brant founded HMTS, he was pretty much a one-man show. By 1979, the company had matured and, while he occasionally taught a course, most of his time was spent doing high-level consulting, selling, working with industry groups, and managing the organization. The pace was typical for an entrepreneur—hectic. Exhibit 11 presents a week in Brant Houston's life in 1979.

Commenting on what had happened since then, Brant remarked that the more things changed, the more they remained the same. He did no teaching now, and his direct involvement in consulting had diminished considerably. Industry groups, key customers, and other "outside" matters still took much of his time, but more

---

Exhibit 11   A Week in the Life of HMTS's President, Brant Houston

---

Monday

5:50 A.M.	Leave home for racquetball courts.
6:00 A.M.–7:00 A.M.	Play two games of racquetball.
7:00 A.M.–7:45 A.M.	Sauna, whirlpool, shower, and dress.
8:15 A.M.	Arrive at office.
8:15 A.M.–8:30 A.M.	Coffee, check with key personnel for any crises.
8:30 A.M.–1:30 P.M.	Approve 10 expense reports; take telephone complaint from employee in Florida whose paycheck did not arrive; write letter to government agency to straighten out snafu caused by government personnel changes; discuss personnel and licensing problems in Massachusetts with area manager; read mail, assign various tasks of responding; meet with insurance agent on ramifications of new federal regulations on maternity leave; politely get rid of Chamber of Commerce salesman; brief customer on Coast Guard Industry Day meeting which he could not attend; discuss Coast Guard policies with personnel manager of a customer.
1:30 P.M.–2:00 P.M.	Lunch (can of Sego); discuss progress of computer installation with DP manager and programmer.
2:00 P.M.–5:00 P.M.	Review new policy from Coast Guard HQ on license renewal for special licenses, compare with conflicting regulations, develop strategy to tactfully point out the error to the CG; review sales strategy with marketing manager; revise drafts of sales letter to drilling companies; miscellaneous phone calls; work on rough draft of letter to U.S. Senate Foreign Relations Committee explaining the adverse impact of an international convention scheduled for ratification hearings.
5:00 P.M.–5:30 P.M.	Supervise and generally get in the way of secretary, DP manager, and programmer learning how to type letters into the new computer.
6:00 P.M.	Arrive home.
6:00 P.M.–9:00 P.M.	Eat with family.
9:00 P.M.–10:30 P.M.	Listen to home study tape course on computers; read computer user guide.

Tuesday

6:00 A.M.	Arrive at office.
6:00 A.M.–8:30 A.M.	Continue drafting letter to Congress on international convention.
8:30 A.M.–12:30 P.M.	Review computer insurance proposal; review marketing letters; make last-minute check of air conditioning modification plans for computer room; take 15 minutes for public relations with old customer to show him our facility and discuss his problems; read mail, assign responses; discuss international convention with former delegate for 30 minutes on telephone (promised a copy of 1975 drafts which had been "impossible" to obtain); discuss payroll problems with bookkeeper; miscellaneous phone calls.
12:30 P.M.–1:30 P.M.	Took bookkeeper (wife) to lunch.
1:30 P.M.–5:00 P.M.	Supervised air conditioning work; discussed results of morning exams with CG; discussed relocation plans with an employee; approved payables; wrote two letters; proofread international convention draft letters; developed strategy on mail campaign.

Wednesday

8:30 A.M.	Arrive at office, check with key personnel.
8:45 A.M.–noon	Meet with assistant to finalize agenda for OMSA manning and licensing committee meeting to be held at our facility on Thursday; plan handouts and strategy in general for meeting; review mail; handle miscellaneous calls.
12:00 noon–1:00 P.M.	Have lunch with training director.
1:00 P.M.–5:30 P.M.	Continue preparing for committee meeting.

Exhibit 11 *(concluded)*

Thursday

8:00 A.M.–8:30 A.M.	Work with key personnel to be sure that office work and meeting will go smoothly for the day.
8:30 A.M.–9:00 A.M.	Greet arriving committee members.
9:00 A.M.–noon	Conduct meeting.
12:00 noon–1:30 P.M.	Have lunch with several committee members (who are also customers).
1:30 P.M.–5:30 P.M.	Catch up on morning's work, assign tasks of following up on morning meeting.

Friday

7:00 A.M.–9:00 A.M.	Meeting with training director to review resumes of prospective instructors.
9:00 A.M.–9:15 A.M.	Check with key personnel for any problems.
9:15 A.M.–noon	Prepare for afternoon meeting of Marine Education Association in Thibodaux; agree to work on United Fund campaign in a weak moment; review mail.
12:00 noon–1:00 P.M.	Enroute to Thibodaux; eat hamburger on the way.
1:00 P.M.–4:30 P.M.	Attend meeting.
5:00 P.M.–6:30 P.M.	Attend cocktail party.
6:30 P.M.–8:00 P.M.	Dinner with OMSA Executive Secretary, M&L Committee member, and House of Representatives minority and majority counsels to discuss status of impending legislation (last-minute happening—had planned to be home by 7:00 P.M.).
9:30 P.M.	Arrive home.

---

* Source: Dale A. Aronson and Jeffrey A. Barach, "Houston Marine Consultants, Inc." (New Orleans, La.: School of Business, Tulane University, 1980), pp. 28–30.

---

and more of his time was devoted to working with his management team. The ever-expanding computer system commanded constant attention, as it had in 1979. Running had replaced racquetball because it could be done in less time and at any hour. He still got to take his wife to lunch, though she was now vice president of finance.

His biggest challenge was in developing middle-level managers who could take the load off him in managing the various departments and profit centers. An enormous amount of his time was taken up interacting with these individuals. If a manager had been promoted from within, he usually had been hired because of his technical or teaching experience and skills and had to learn the marketing and business aspects of the job. If a manager had been hired from the outside, he had an equally formidable task of learning the company's organization, products, philosophy, and so on. Brant wanted to delegate more but felt like he was abdicating his responsibility if he did so before the manager was ready to take on more responsibility.

Personally, Brant's family had grown from no children when the business was founded to three. The family needed more and more of his time. Although he still enjoyed his work immensely, he had begun to realize that the day would come when he would want to have the option to retire or at least decrease his day-to-day involvement with the business.

FUTURE

In an in-house document, Brant described Houston Marine as a company on the move. It had thrived for the first year of the national recession in spite of the fact that the oilfield and towing industries were particularly hard hit. The company had upgraded its management, marketing, and operating personnel; improved its marketing tools and techniques; and developed several innovative new products. These changes were part of a strategic plan that established an annual increase in net operating income of 20 percent and predicted gross sales to be $5 million in 1988.

Several factors were to contribute to this growth. Brant was particularly excited about two product innovations. A computer-assisted course had been developed and had been successful in New Orleans and Larose. Plans to expand it to other locations were being considered. This new method of preparing students for examinations was expected to not only reduce operating costs but also to be more attractive to a larger segment of the market, helping to increase the company's market share.

Another development that had been successful was a ballast control simulator program. The course was intended for anyone responsible for maintaining and monitoring stability on mobile offshore drilling units. Tuition ranged from $600 for the two-day course to $1,200 for the full five-day course.

The success of these and other recent developments had fueled Brant's optimism for the future. He anticipated these factors to increase net operating income by more than $200,000 by 1985. If the oilfield and towing industries recovered as predicted from the recession, the increased demand for qualified marine personnel could result in net operating income of $400,000.

Over the next several years, Brant planned to diversify within the training business to offer training prep courses outside the marine industry. He felt that, with slight modifications, his organization was excellently suited to offer GMAT, SAT, LSAT, MCAT, and GRE review courses for the college student market.

Other potential sources for growth were not the products or services offered, but the manner in which they were distributed. Franchising was being considered. Brant believed that operating costs would be decreased and revenues would be increased by going to a self-paced, computer-assisted series of courses offered by local individuals with full control over advertising, sales, and operations under the Houston Marine Training Services name in defined territories. Because of the advent of videotaped instruction materials requiring constant updating, the company would have something substantial to offer franchisees, in addition to the HMTS name, to keep the franchisee paying a percentage to HMTS rather than becoming a competitor.

However profitable franchising might prove to be, Brant did not see it as an immediate solution to the problem associated with geographic expansion. He was considering two or three alternatives to increase the profitability of operations outside Louisiana. One alternative was to increase the number of training reps wherever possible. Over 18 percent of HMTS students in 1983 were trained by the Great Lakes training representative. His compensation for 1983 approached $100,000. HMTS had benefited too. Until 1982, only 12 students had trained in this area. Increasing the number of training reps would mean less supervision required by HMTS, although extra care would be required to safeguard course quality. Brant felt that if he could locate highly motivated, qualified instructors he could negotiate an incentive plan that would increase the company's profits. However, he also knew that this was the kind of individual who was most likely to leave the company, and at the expiration of the noncompeting clause of his employment contract, would become a formidable competitor.

Another alternative was to leave the organizational structure as it was. (See Exhibit 9 for organization chart.) The profit center concept was new; perhaps he should give it time to work. He could use the computer to isolate costs, and he could rid the company of marginal areas. Brant felt that if he could get costs in line, motivate sales agents, and increase the average number of students per class, he might make more money (with less risk of loss of control and creating competition) with his existing mix of full-time, part-time, and contract instructors than by turning more territory over to training reps. He had even entertained the idea of hiring a sales manager. Maybe he could use a sales manager even if he decided to increase the number of training reps. This thought led to another problem: Whom should he hire as sales manager?

Mike Ellison came to mind, but Brant wondered whether he could handle the extra duties. Since coming to HMTS, Mike had sought and had been given increased responsibility. He now had full control of marketing activity and supervisory responsibility for the marketing staff. He was also responsible for exploring and assessing the marketability of new courses for HMTS. In addition, as profit center manager for license prep courses, he had two other profit center managers and one contract instructor reporting to him. They were Bill Clark (New Orleans License Prep), Heinz Hickethier (Larose License Prep), and Danny Duzick of Houston, the contract instructor for Texas.

Brant was not sure what he should do. There was one thing of which he was sure, however; whatever he did had to work.

B
Strategic Analysis in
Single-Business
Companies

CASE 5 THE APARTMENT STORE*

"Our next big step is to arrange the bank financing we will need to start our new venture," Paula Cox said to her two partners on January 5, 1984. "When that matter is settled, we can actually make some physical arrangements and open the business in a matter of weeks." Because Katherine Wallace and Alice Bennett agreed with her, all three founders sat down to go over all the material they had collected.

While working on their MBA degrees at a nearby university, the three women had become interested in opening their own business. Since they wished to utilize their special talents, they decided to begin a venture called, "The Apartment Store." The Apartment Store would be a retail business oriented toward serving the furniture and accessory needs of a rapidly growing market: young people with moderate incomes generally living in rental housing. To serve these needs at a reasonable cost and to retain design flexibility, The Apartment Store was planned as an integrated operation from manufacture to retail.

ORGANIZATION

The founders felt that the success of the venture would largely be a function of the blend of the special talents of the management team. Paula Cox, as president, would have overall coordi-

---

* Prepared by Richard Levin and Bettye Painter of the University of North Carolina at Chapel Hill. Support to write the case was provided by the North Carolina Business Foundation.

nation responsibility, as well as responsibility for handling the financial/accounting duties. Because she had experience as an interior designer, Cox was familiar with the industry. All marketing matters, including the sales effort, would be the direct concern of Katherine Wallace as Vice President—Marketing. Finally, Alice Bennett, as Vice President—Operations, would have direct responsibility for production and distribution.

Despite their well-defined primary responsibilities, all three would act as a team in strategy decisions. Any questions of product design, store locations, and long-range planning would require input from and a decision by the entire group. In this manner, they felt that the strengths of the members could be best utilized to achieve success.

Initially, virtually all work was to be done by the three-person management team, including selling, bookkeeping, production supervision, and so on. When growth of the organization occurred, additional personnel then would be added, primarily in production and sales. The organization chart in Exhibit 1 presents the organization's approach to growth.

MARKETING

Market to Be Served

The Apartment Store, as the name implies, is designed to serve the needs of apartment dwellers and other renters. These needs are furniture and accessories that are moderately priced, easily transportable, designed for flexibility, and value-oriented. The

Exhibit 1 Organization Structure for The Apartment Store

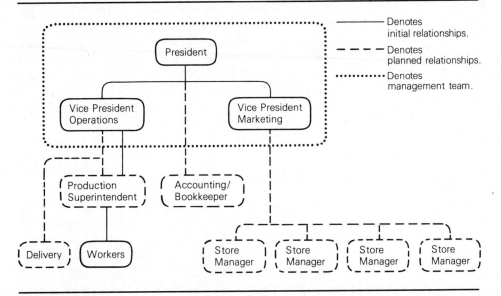

market is characterized by single people and young families (head of household under 34 years old). In general, the customer has a minimum income of $15,000 annually, although this may not be true of students and others with parental support. The market is both price and value-conscious, in addition to demanding innovative styling.

Competition

Competition comes from other retailers and furniture-rental agents. The rental agents tend to have close ties with specific apartment complexes. Considerable business is generated as a result of referrals. For customers, the appeals of renting are (1) minimal investment by apartment dweller, (2) no moving/storage problems, and (3) ability to change furniture as styles change. Major problems that rental dealers face include customer perceptions that rental charges are "high," customer desires for ownership, and the fact that customers wish to avoid the "plastic" atmosphere of rental furniture.

Furniture retailers typically offer a broad range of furniture, most of which has been designed for single-family homes, not apartments. Although the retail trade has developed along price lines to some extent, other types of segmentation are developing. Recent years have seen the development of waterbed stores, unfinished furniture stores, and other specialty approaches. For such stores to be successful, they must locate where there is a sufficiently large market for their product. The founders of The Apartment Store hope to develop an attractive market niche with their strategy.

Product Concept

The Apartment Store would retail two basic product lines: in-house manufactured items and purchased accessories. The latter would be purchased from distributors and include lamps, wall decorations, and bed frames—products that could not be made as cheaply in-house as they could be bought at wholesale. The products manufactured by The Apartment Store are fully described in the writings and drawings in Exhibits 2 and 3. In brief, the product line includes furniture for the living room, dining room, and bedroom. It is characterized by compactness and flexibility. The apartment dweller places a high premium on both because of frequent moves, limited space, and a limited furniture budget. The products will be made of solid wood and available in several finishes or unfinished. The products have been designed to blend well in furniture groups.

Product Pricing

The market for furniture of this general type is value-conscious. If The Apartment Store was strictly a retail operation, it would be difficult to match the value offered by established competition. Because the founders plan to control both manufacturing and retailing, The Apartment Store will be able to offer furniture with a competitive style, quality, and price combination. Exhibit 4 indicates prices by product; in all cases, the price is 10 to 40 percent below that of competitive merchandise. Prices

---

Exhibit 2   Product Descriptions

TRUNDLE BED

This delightful, moderately priced trundle bed is a modern, comfortable couch by day that converts into a comfortable 60″ wide bed by night. The overall dimensions of the couch are 76½″ × 31½″. By sliding out the top drawer, a 76½″ × 61½″ queen-size bed is formed. Two super-firm, 6″ polyfoam mattresses covered in decorator fabrics (or available uncovered for your own fabric) are supplied.

CHAIR BED

By day this is a 30″ × 36″ × 12″-high chair that converts into a full-size bed by night. The chair is made of two 30″ × 36″ × 6″ thick polyfoam mattresses with a detachable 36″ × 6″ × 15″ high bolster. When laid end-to-end, the chair converts into a full-size single bed. Two or more chairs can be used in modular form, placed side-by-side, to create a sofa.

DINING ROOM TABLE

With the two tops stacked, this table measures 34″ × 44″, providing dining space for four. By telescoping out the third pair of legs and turning over the upper top, a 34″ × 88″ table is formed providing dining for eight. For storing or moving, the top lifts off the legs (attached by pins) and the three pairs of legs collapse to form a compact unit making storage easy.

COFFEE/DINING ROOM TABLE

Wherever space is at a premium, this table is perfect. With its legs on end, it is a 52″ × 29″ × 20″ high coffee table. By turning the legs onto its side and placing the top across the two upper legs, the table converts into a 52″ × 29″ × 29″ high dining table.

MODULAR SYSTEM

This storage and shelving system is based on a 25″ × 16″ × 16″ box with almost infinite flexibility. Boxes can be stacked to produce any size book case or storage shelf. Steel pins inserted into mating holes on the top and bottom of the boxes being stacked lock the boxes securely. Drawers can be added to produce drawer cabinets or, by stacking, to produce four, six, and eight-drawer chests. Each drawer comes with two-drawer guide bars that fit into position holes in the box sides. These bars then form the guide bars on which the drawers slide.

Drawers come in three sizes: 24″ × 7½″ high, 24″ × 5″ high, and 15″ × 4″ high. All drawers are 16″ deep. The first two are used with the mod box horizontal. By stacking boxes and using the 7½″ drawer, bedroom chests of different sizes can be created. The 5″ drawers can be used to create different sized general-storage cabinets.

The 15″ × 4″ drawer is used with the mod box vertically to produce general-storage cabinets or with the available desktop to form a 4-, 6-, or 10- (with two mod boxes) drawer desk. The desktop measures 47½″ × 24″ wide and contains two 24″ × 5″ × 16″-deep open-storage bins that can take two 24″ × 5″ drawers. The desktop can be used with the mod boxes fitted with drawers or with shelves or four 25″ legs.

---

for purchased items have margins over cost somewhat below those for in-house manufactured items (see Exhibit 5).

Market Location

Because of the market it will serve, Cox, Wallace, and Bennett wished to locate The Apartment Store in a reasonably young, affluent metropolitan area. They limited their search to several nearby states because of manufacturing considerations, the management team's familiarity with the customs and needs of the area, and family considerations. Analysis of the alternatives centered on several quantitative factors: (1) absolute size of rental living population, (2) level of affluence, (3) mobility, and (4) age of renters. In addition, strength of competition, area growth, local customs, and other qualitative factors were considered.

The three-person management team used data from the 1980 U.S. Census to make the quantitative evaluation. The largest market area was excluded because of the heavy saturation of its retail and apartment rental markets. Manufacturing and market-

Exhibit 3 Coffee/Dining Room Table

52″ × 29″ Detachable Top

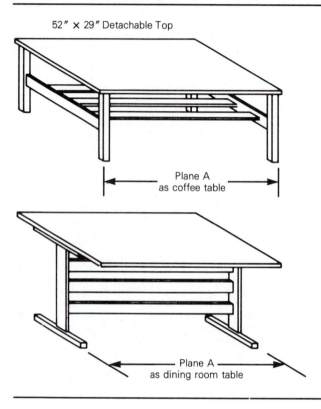

Plane A
as coffee table

Plane A
as dining room table

ing costs would also have been much higher. The city of Alexandria was selected because it was more compact geographically, had a slightly larger mobile population, and was more centrally located to the long-run market area than the other choices. About 17,800 (73 percent) of the 24,400 rental units (with monthly rental in excess of $200) were occupied within two years of the census; in addition, 7,700 or 32 percent of the total units had a 1980 income greater than $15,000.

Retail Strategy

The founders realized that their ultimate success rested on retail success. Although considerable effort was devoted to choosing a market area, the second-level decision was the actual location of the initial store. The management team planned to locate the store adjacent to the plant in Alexandria. They decided against locating The Apartment Store in a shopping mall to avoid casual shoppers and the high overhead of such a location. The site for the free-standing location is advantageous, because it is convenient to major apartment locations and high traffic thoroughfares, has a reasonable rental fee, and is zoned to allow a combination retail/manufacturing facility.

Exhibit 4   Manufactured Products

Product	Labor Cost	Material Cost	Total Cost	Sales Price	Sales Mix*
Table, dining	$23.50	$25.10	$ 48.60	$100	0.12
Table, coffee	43.50	12.30	55.80	110	0.05
Chair, low	3.70	30.10	33.80	100	0.10
Chair, high	3.70	40.10	43.80	120	0.05
Desk, basic	30.60	10.80	41.40	80	0.07
Desk, drawer optional	14.40	10.00	24.40	40	0.05
Sofa, trundle	71.50	44.70	116.20	200	0.03
Sofa, drawer optional	9.00	11.30	20.30	40	0.01
Headboard (single)	10.60	3.30	13.90	30	0.05
Headboard (double)	11.50	4.50	16.00	40	0.10
Module	12.10	5.30	17.40	30	0.15
Drawer (one)	4.70	3.30	8.00	15	0.05
Shelf	1.20	1.60	2.80	5	0.10
Magazine rack	4.50	.60	5.10	15	0.07

Note: In all income and cash flow statements, manufactured products are assumed to constitute 80 percent of total dollar sales volume. For computation purposes, the weighted average figures above are used.

* Sales Mix is an estimate of relative unit sales within this group of manufactured products. Based on it, the following figures were derived:
  Weighted average cost = $29.65
  Weighted average selling price = $59.80.

Source: Costs—engineering estimates. Prices—desired markup and competitive pressures. Sales Mix—management estimate.

Exhibit 5   Purchased Products

Product	Cost	Sales Price	Sales Mix*
Mattress and box spring (double)	$120	$200	0.06
Mattress and box spring (twin)	90	150	0.03
Mattress, air, double	30	60	0.03
Mattress, air, twin	20	40	0.01
Bed frame	8	16	0.12
Bean bag chair	20	25	0.15
Dining chair	12	24	0.10
Bed lamp	6	12	0.10
Table lamp	10	20	0.10
Floor lamp	20	40	0.10
Pole lamp	12	25	0.05
Pictures, framed	10	25	0.15

Note: In all income and cash flow statements, purchased goods are assumed to constitute 20 percent of total dollar sales volume. For computation purposes, the weighted average figures above are used.

* Sales mix is an estimate of relative unit sales within this group of purchased products. Based on it, the following figures were derived:
  Weighted average cost = $20.90.
  Weighted average selling price = $38.95.

Source: Costs—quotations. Prices—estimates based on competitive pricing. Sales Mix—management team estimate.

Since Cox's experience indicated that most furniture is sold to the serious shopper rather than the casual looker, she felt that the free-standing approach was sound.

Wallace plans to use two techniques for attracting customers. First, a substantial advertising budget would be used mostly to run newspaper ads periodically. The remainder of the budget would be used for Yellow Pages, apartment guides, and specialty newspapers (e.g., college papers). In all instances, ad copy would stress the value of the furniture: modest costs, flexibility, compactness, and durability. The second promotion technique would be simply displaying the merchandise. This would, of course, be accomplished primarily at the retail store. Displays would emphasize innovative room settings. Wallace also plans to make supplemental display techniques, used effectively by rental agents, such as providing furnishings for model apartments, part of The Apartment Store display approach. Finally, the owners plan to make shopping convenient for the apartment dweller by accepting cash, checks, and bank credit cards as payment. They also hope to assist in arranging bank credit through their bank. Store hours would be 10 A.M. to 8 P.M., Monday through Saturday, for the convenience of the working customer, and free delivery would be provided within the metropolitan area.

Long-Range Marketing Strategy

Within five years of the initial opening, the management team plans to expand The Apartment Store to five metropolitan areas in a two-state region. Details on this expansion are given in the financial exhibits. This expansion would follow the same approach as was used in the original location in Alexandria. Retail and advertising skills, tested in Alexandria, would become more effective with experience. In general, the limits on growth would be primarily financial and organizational. The latter is crucial, since store managers must be hired and developed as the network of retail outlets expands. Since a poor manager could destroy an excellent marketing effort, future growth is purposely limited to five stores in five years to prevent undertrained management.

PRODUCTION

Physical Requirements

Furniture production requires a substantial investment in equipment, tools, and inventory. These requirements are detailed in a layout (Exhibit 6) and equipment list (Exhibit 7). Since the production requirements are for short runs of differentiated products, a job-shop approach is planned for manufacturing. The system calls for three basic operations: machining, assembly, and finishing. The proposed facility would be adequate for production levels anticipated in the first three years. The purchase of additional equipment (less than $10,000 in cost) would allow the five-year production targets to be met. The proposed facility is designed to meet all applicable OSHA (Occupational Safety and Health Act) and pollution controls regulations.

Exhibit 6 Floor Layout of Initial Factory/Sales Showroom

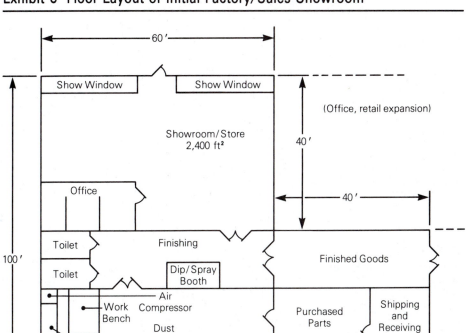

Manufacturing/Operations 6,000 ft²

Staffing

Initially, the operation would be under the direct supervision of Bennett, Vice President—Operations. For most of the first year, her duties would include production guidelines and quality control. During that year, the direct labor force would not exceed three people. In the second year, it would grow to a maximum of five people. With the exception of a lead person, these employees would be semiskilled.

Costing

Bennett has developed product costs based on material and labor estimates made by graduate engineers. In all cases, reasonable allowances were made for additional costs because of inefficiency, scrap, and purchasing variances. All estimates assume sales volume as estimated in the exhibits and the resultant product lot sizes.

Exhibit 7   Plant and Equipment

Item	Price
Dust collector	$ 4,500
Air compressor with tank	1,000
Contour sander	2,000
Band saw	600
Radial arm saw	600
Router	500
Drill	400
Table saw	400
Total	$10,000

Plant Improvements	Cost
Equipment wiring	$ 7,500
Dust collection pipes	3,000
Compressed air pipes	500
Total	$11,000

Miscellaneous	Cost
Material handling carts	$ 1,000
Tools (hammers, buffers, etc.)	1,200
Office equipment	800
Total	3,000
Total cost, plant and equipment	$24,000

Annual straight-line depreciation, based on a seven-year life: $3,400.

Source: Estimates by a woodworking manufacturer. Prices are for top condition used equipment when available.

Long-Range Production Considerations

All production has been planned to be accomplished in the initial building with the addition of some equipment in year three. As volume grows, a production superintendent will be added. Growth in volume will result in reduced cost, principally because of labor and purchasing efficiencies. This improvement is reflected in all *pro-forma* statements (see Exhibits 8–11).

FINANCE

Sales Forecast

The five-year sales forecast (Exhibit 8) is based on three considerations: (1) selling prices, (2) sales levels of competitors and similar businesses, and (3) market size (census data). Sales growth will come partially from individual store growth; it is planned, however, to achieve it primarily by expansion. The forecast includes the slow growth that is characteristic of new furniture retailers at any given location.

Exhibit 8 Five-Year Sales Forecast, The Apartment Store

Year	Month/ Quarter	City 1	City 2	City 3	City 4	City 5	City 6	Total
1	1							$ —
	2	$ 4,000						4,000
	3	5,000						5,000
	4	5,000						5,000
	5	6,000						6,000
	6	6,000						6,000
	7	7,000						7,000
	8	7,000	$ 3,000					10,000
	9	7,000	4,000					11,000
	10	8,000	4,000					12,000
	11	8,000	5,000					13,000
	12	8,000	5,000					13,000
	Year 1 totals	$ 71,000	$ 21,000					$ 92,000
2	1	9,000	6,000					15,000
	2	9,000	6,000					15,000
	3	9,000	6,000					15,000
	4	9,000	6,000	$ 3,000				18,000
	5	9,000	6,000	3,000				18,000
	6	9,000	6,000	4,000				19,000
	7	10,000	7,000	4,000				21,000
	8	10,000	7,000	4,000				21,000
	9	10,000	7,000	4,000				21,000
	10	10,000	8,000	4,000				22,000
	11	10,000	8,000	5,000	$ 3,000			26,000
	12	10,000	8,000	5,000	3,000			26,000
	Year 2 totals	$114,000	$ 78,000	$ 36,000	$ 6,000			$234,000
3	1	30,000	24,000	15,000	12,000			81,000
	2	30,000	24,000	15,000	12,000			81,000
	3	30,000	25,000	18,000	15,000			88,000
	4	30,000	25,000	18,000	15,000	$ 9,000		97,000
	Year 3 totals	$120,000	$ 98,000	$ 66,000	$54,000	$ 9,000		$347,000
4	1	30,000	25,000	21,000	18,000	12,000		116,000
	2	30,000	25,000	21,000	18,000	12,000		116,000
	3	30,000	25,000	24,000	21,000	15,000		125,000
	4	30,000	25,000	24,000	21,000	15,000	$ 9,000	134,000
	Year 4 totals	$120,000	$100,000	$ 90,000	$78,000	$54,000	$ 9,000	$491,000
5	1	30,000	25,000	25,000	24,000	18,000	12,000	144,000
	2	30,000	25,000	25,000	24,000	18,000	12,000	144,000
	3	30,000	25,000	25,000	25,000	21,000	15,000	151,000
	4	30,000	25,000	25,000	25,000	21,000	15,000	151,000
	Year 5 totals	$120,000	$100,000	$100,000	$98,000	$78,000	$54,000	$590,000

Financial Structure

The initial financing is planned to consist of $32,000 in common stock, $12,000 in unsecured convertible debentures, and a $20,000 secured bank loan. Each member of the management team is participating financially by contributing capital and accepting a reduced salary ($8,000 annually) to start.

The common stock will be issued with a par value of $100. Of the authorized 1,000 shares, the management team plans to purchase 40 each and sell 200 shares

Exhibit 9   *Pro-Forma* Cash Flow Statement, The Apartment Store

Year One / Month	1	2	3	4	5
Sales collections (see Notes)	—	$ 3,880	$ 4,850	$ 4,850	$ 5,820
Miscellaneous inflows (see Notes)	$44,000	—	—	20,000	—
Purchased goods	$ 2,000	$ 200	$ 250	$ 250	$ 1,900
Labor	740	980	1,110	1,110	1,110
Materials	3,500	1,370	680	2,700	680
Overhead					
Manufacturing	2,020	2,020	2,020	2,020	2,020
Selling	1,800	2,500	2,000	2,000	2,000
Administrative	1,160	760	760	760	760
Interest	—	—	—	200	200
Miscellaneous outflows (see Notes)	—	10,000	10,000	4,000	—
Total outflow	$11,220	$ 17,830	$ 16,820	$13,040	$ 9,670
Inflow less outflow	$32,780	$(13,950)	$(11,970)	$11,810	$ (3,850)
Cash, end of month	$32,780	$ 18,830	$ 6,860	$18,670	$14,820
Inventory, end of month					
Raw/purchased parts	$ 2,590	$ 2,740	$ 2,050	$ 3,380	$ 2,710
In-process	900	1,200	1,350	1,350	1,350
Finished	900	1,360	1,900	2,580	2,880
Purchased goods	2,000	1,800	1,550	1,300	2,600

Year Two / Month	1	2	3	4	5
Sales collection (see Notes)	$13,580	$ 14,550	$ 15,520	$16,490	$17,460
Purchased goods	$ 2,900	$ 750	$ 800	$ 3,500	$ 900
Labor	2,450	3,170	3,170	3,460	3,600
Materials	6,700	1,670	1,670	7,460	1,270
Overhead					
Manufacturing	2,050	2,050	2,050	2,050	2,050
Selling	3,800	3,800	3,800	5,100	5,100
Administrative	1,200	1,200	1,200	1,300	1,300
Interest	500	200	200	500	200
Miscellaneous outflows (see Notes)	—	—	—	—	—
Total outflow	$19,600	$ 12,840	$ 12,890	$23,370	$14,420
Inflow less outflow	$ (6,020)	$ 1,710	$ 2,630	$ (6,880)	$ 3,040
Cash, end of month	$ 1,830	$ 3,540	$ 6,170	$ (710)	$ 2,330
Inventory, end of month					
Raw/purchased parts	$ 7,100	$ 5,400	$ 3,700	$ 7,500	$ 5,000
In-process	2,200	2,800	2,800	3,100	3,200
Finished	2,000	2,600	2,700	3,200	3,400
Purchased goods	3,600	2,800	2,000	3,800	2,900

Notes: 97 percent of gross sales are collected in the month of the sale; the remainder is lost to service charges. All inventories are at cost. Year 1, Month 1—Inflow is from stock and debenture issues. Year 1, Month 4—Inflow from proceeds of bank loan. Year 1, Months 2–4—Miscellaneous outflow is related to purchase of equipment and plant improvements. The delay reflects expected purchase items.

6	7	8	9	10	11	12	Total
$ 5,820	$ 6,790	$ 9,700	$10,670	$11,640	$12,610	$12,610	$ 89,240
—	—	—	—	—	—	—	64,000
$ 300	$ 350	$ 500	$ 3,600	$ 600	$ 650	$ 650	$153,240
1,110	1,110	2,010	2,300	2,450	2,450	2,450	
680	4,570	1,220	1,290	5,180	1,290	1,290	
2,020	2,020	2,020	2,020	2,020	2,020	2,020	
2,000	2,200	3,500	2,400	2,500	2,400	2,400	
760	760	1,320	1,120	1,120	1,120	1,620	
200	200	200	200	200	200	200	
—	—	—	—	—	—	—	
$ 7,070	$11,210	$10,770	$12,930	$14,070	$10,130	$10,630	$145,390
$ (1,250)	$ (4,420)	$ (1,070)	$ (2,260)	$ (2,430)	$ 2,480	$ 1,980	
$13,570	$ 9,150	$ 8,080	$ 5,820	$ 3,390	$ 5,870	$ 7,850	
$ 2,040	$ 5,240	$ 4,130	$ 2,980	$ 5,570	$ 4,270	$ 2,900	
1,350	1,350	2,100	2,400	2,550	2,550	2,200	
3,180	3,050	2,490	2,580	2,700	2,580	2,400	
2,300	1,950	1,450	3,950	3,350	2,700	2,050	

6	7	8	9	10	11	12	Total
$18,430	$19,400	$20,370	$21,340	$22,310	$23,280	$24,250	$226,980
$ 950	$ 4,700	$ 1,050	$ 1,100	$ 4,000	$ 1,200	$ 1,600	
3,750	3,750	3,750	3,750	4,470	4,470	4,760	
1,320	7,920	1,330	1,320	9,440	2,360	4,000	
2,050	2,050	2,050	2,050	2,050	2,050	2,050	
5,100	5,100	5,100	5,100	6,400	6,400	6,400	
1,300	1,300	1,300	1,300	1,400	1,400	1,400	
200	500	200	200	500	200	200	
—	—	—	—	—	—	8,000	
$14,520	$25,320	$14,770	$14,820	$28,260	$18,080	$28,410	$227,300
$ 3,860	$ (5,920)	$ 5,600	$ 6,520	$ 5,950	$ 5,200	$ (4,160)	
$ 6,240	$ 320	$ 5,920	$12,440	$ 6,490	$11,690	$ 7,530	
$ 2,400	$ 6,300	$ 3,700	$ 1,000	$ 5,800	$ 3,400	$ 2,400	
3,400	3,400	3,400	3,400	4,000	4,000	4,300	
3,600	3,400	2,900	1,800	1,800	1,500	1,500	
2,000	4,700	3,600	2,500	4,200	3,000	2,100	

to outside investors. There will be only one class of common stock, with all having equal voting rights per share.

The convertible debentures are $1,000 face value with an interest rate of 10 percent, payable in the year 2000. The three founders plan to purchase four debentures each. The conversion ratio will be one debenture for 10 shares of common stock, with conversion taking place at the request of the holder. The debentures will be unsecured.

The $20,000 bank loan will be secured by equipment and inventories. The founders anticipate an annual interest rate of 10 percent and that the note will be payable on demand. The pledged security would amount to approximately 175 percent of

Exhibit 10   *Pro-Forma* Income Statements, The Apartment Store, Years 1 and 2

	Year One	Year Two
Gross sales	$ 92,000	$234,000
Less: Discounts and losses*	2,800	7,000
Net sales	89,200	227,000
Cost of goods sold	46,000	117,000
Gross margin	43,200	110,000
Overhead:		
Manufacturing		
Salaries	$ 8,000	$ 8,000
Rent	15,000	15,000
Utilities	1,200	1,500
Depreciation	3,400	3,400
Total manufacturing overhead	$27,600	$27,900
Selling:		
Salaries	$10,000	$25,000
Advertising	7,000	15,000
Delivery	4,000	9,000
Rent	6,000	12,000
Utilities	800	1,800
Total selling overhead	$27,800	$62,800
Administrative:		
Salaries	$ 8,000	$ 8,000
Transportation	1,800	3,600
Telephone	600	1,000
Office	600	1,000
Professional	500	800
Miscellaneous	500	800
Total administrative overhead	$12,000	$15,200
Total overhead	67,400	105,900
Earnings before interest and taxes	(24,200)	4,100
Interest	3,000	3,000
Earnings	$(27,200)	$ 1,100

* Three percent discount allows for losses and service charges for credit sales.

the loan amount. With such a structure, the debt-equity ratio would be 0.625 not including convertibles, 0.50 if they are included.

The Apartment Store will be incorporated in the state where the founders live and will be organized under the provisions of Subchapter S. The Apartment Store meets all Internal Revenue Service requirements for Subchapter S election.

Potential Return

The founders plan to defer debenture interest payments in the first year. This would give The Apartment Store a positive cash balance of $7,850 (Exhibit 9) and a net loss of $27,200 (Exhibit 10). Under Subchapter S, this loss would be passed on directly to the investors. The management team hopes this will be a major selling point for acquiring outside investment. Each investor, if in the 60 percent tax bracket, would realize a tax saving of $5,100 during the first year. In the second year, the return is anticipated to be small. Beginning in the third year, Subchapter S would be revoked, and the operation would begin as a normal corporation. With positive earnings in year three, the investor would receive stock appreciation plus dividends. The tax savings plus appreciation should be sufficient to attract investors. In addition, the downside risk would be minimal. If the entire venture fails in the second year, the outside investors would lose a maximum of $3,500. This includes the $5,100 tax savings, plus balancing a capital loss against a capital gain.

The purpose of the convertible debentures is to increase the tax loss the outside investor can take by reducing the equity position of the management team. In addition, it offers the management team the benefit of capital appreciation. As can be seen in Exhibit 11, the owners of The Apartment Store anticipate dividends of $4,000 in

Exhibit 11 Pro Forma Income Statements, The Apartment Store, Years 3, 4, and 5

	Year Three	Year Four	Year Five
Gross sales	$347,000	$491,000	$590,000
Less: Discounts and losses	10,400	14,700	17,700
Net sales	336,600	476,300	572,300
Cost of goods sold	173,500	245,500	295,000
Gross margin	163,100	230,800	277,300
Overhead:			
Manufacturing	36,200	36,500	37,400
Selling	93,400	111,000	138,600
Administrative	22,500	25,400	28,300
Total overhead	152,100	172,900	204,300
Earnings before interest and taxes	11,000	57,900	73,000
Interest expense	2,000	2,000	2,000
Earnings before taxes	9,000	55,900	71,500
Taxes	2,000	20,500	27,500
Net income	$ 7,000	$ 35,400	$ 44,000
Dividends	$ 4,000	20,000	40,000

year three, $20,000 in year four, and $40,000 in year five. This, combined with a repurchase of the total outside stock for $50,000 in year five, would give the outside investors an annual return over five years of over 30 percent after taxes. Without stock repurchase, the annual after-tax return exceeds 10 percent.

CONCLUSION

As their meeting came to a close, Katherine Wallace turned to her two partners and said, "I think we have completed our plans. When we meet with our bankers this afternoon, we will have to convince them that we have made logical plans, have a marketable idea, and can attract those outside investors." After chatting a little longer, the three founders of The Apartment Store idea gathered their notes and exhibits and prepared to leave for the meeting at the bank.

CASE 6   CERVANTES EQUESTRIAN CENTER*

Have you ever wondered how we landed on the whopper of a name, CERVANTES EQUESTRIAN CENTER, RIDING FOR THE HANDICAPPED?? Well . . . Mr. Cervantes was the author of the book *Don Quixote* from whence the song the "Impossible Dream" came. We felt it appropriate to name our program of riding therapy for the handicapped after the man who inspired us to "dream impossible dreams," and "to reach unreachable stars." Romantic? Idealistic?? You Bet!!! But Cervantes was an impossible dream—and the idea that Ronnie or Jennifer, two of our cerebral palsy students, could ever leave their wheelchairs and ride horses was for them an impossible dream— and yet it is happening!!

So we will continue to dream impossible dreams and reach for unreachable stars. You can be sure that we will continue to inspire our students to dream their impossible dreams and reach out after their unreachable stars. We're betting—and working—and praying—that they will make it.

This is how Linda Smith described the selection of the name "Cervantes" in a newsletter to her students, volunteer staff members, and friends. Linda founded the Cervantes Equestrian Center in the summer of 1979 for the purpose of teaching both handicapped and normal children to ride horses.

Linda Smith grew up in Rockford, Illinois. At an early age she learned to ride horses and began to participate in horse shows, where she later won a number of awards with her horses. She majored in physical education in college and became a certified instructor (1 of only 12 people so certified by NARHA) for teaching horseback riding to the handicapped. After graduation from college, she worked on an assembly line in a manufacturing plant in the Rockford area in order to save some money for her riding school.

Linda became a member of the North American Riding for the Handicapped Association. NARHA was a nonprofit, tax-exempt organization which had been organized in 1969. The stated aims of NARHA were:

- To establish standards and techniques for teaching riding to the handicapped.
- To advise and certify existing programs that wish to be members.
- To approve training programs and provide certification of instructors who plan to teach the handicapped.
- To maintain contact with members of the medical profession in order to ensure the safety and well-being of handicapped riders, and to gain approval and recognition of riding as a valuable therapeutic activity.
- To make periodic inspection of those centers in operation and to visit affiliated programs regularly.
- To provide experienced consultants for lectures and discussions.
- To promote responsible research, and to make the resulting data generally available.

Normal children as well as handicapped were accepted as students by Cervantes because Linda believed that both groups of children could learn from each other.

* Copyright © 1980 by Brigham Young University. Prepared by Professor Melvin J. Stanford.

Moreover, the lessons for the normal children helped bring in enough revenue to get Cervantes started without relying solely on a clientele of handicapped students. There were three other riding schools in the county in which Linda lived. Two of them gave riding lessons, but neither of them had any handicapped students. There were several riding stables and riding schools in a more populous adjoining county. Some of them gave lessons, but so far as Linda knew, none of them was certified to teach handicapped students.

Volunteers consisting of students from a nearby university and neighbors in Linda's community helped her get Cervantes started. She received a very positive response to requests for donated help because of the nature of what was being done for handicapped children. The progress that those children made was rather dramatic in some cases. Linda described her experience with a student, Peter, as follows:

> I remember well the first time I worked with Peter. I heard Peter before I saw him. He came into the arena screaming and crying because he was afraid.
>
> Peter is autistic. He lived isolated in his own little world devoid of emotion, happiness, and human contact. He was afraid of everything and would not speak or communicate in any way with other people except to push them away or to cry.
>
> It took one man and three women to put 10-year-old Peter, kicking, screaming, and pushing us away, up on the back of patient "Little Mike." Little Mike never even batted an ear while all of this was happening. An interesting thing occurred as Peter was walked around on Little Mike's back. Peter realized his world was changed. He was up on the back of some warm and fuzzy creature who was moving. This change and movement caused Peter to focus his mind, to concentrate, and to get in touch with what was happening in the world around him. He stopped crying. He was unable to participate that first evening as member of a team in the relay race, so we had him go solo. Encouraged by the clapping and cheering of his teammates and volunteers, Peter was led to the end of the arena where he was given a piece of red paper and led back down the home stretch of the race, amid clapping and cheers of "Come on Peter!" A faint smile flickered across his face.
>
> I was talking to my volunteers just before Peter's second lesson, telling them not to be upset if Peter struggled as we put him on the pony. Just then the bus pulled up with the students. Peter was the first one off the bus. He came galloping into the arena, grabbed my hand, and pulled me over where Little Mike, his pony, was tied. I was shocked! My mouth hung open and tears filled my eyes as I helped Peter pet Little Mike. Peter wanted to get on. He would start to climb on and then lose his courage. The little boy, who last week had required four people to put him up on the pony's back, this week only required mild encouragement and the helping hand of one person.
>
> National studies have shown that the use of animals can be effective in bringing patients out emotionally so they think better of themselves and interact more effectively with others. The use of horses can also bring students out physically because they want to ride, lead, brush, pet, feed, and play with their horses and ponies. This has certainly been the case with Peter. Peter has made steady improvement from the first day on. He has formed a strong friendship and trust in his pony and his volunteers. He now participates in the games and gets on and off and controls his pony by himself. He loves to feed Little Mike carrots and pet him.
>
> Probably the most exciting event so far occurred about a month ago. We were playing a game of tag on horseback. This exciting game is a favorite of the children and they giggle all the way around the arena. Peter was tagged "it." He laughed and yelled, "Attack!" His volunteer was so shocked at Peter speaking that she stopped the pony and in amazement said, "Peter, what did you say?" Peter was too excited to chase his

classmates. He kicked Little Mike and yelled again, "Attack!!" Peter spoke several words that day; among them were: whoa, carrots, go, thank you, and good-bye.

It fills the hearts of all of us with joy as Peter laughs and interrelates with his volunteers, his pony, and his classmates. He is experiencing happiness and joy—a strong contrast to the lonely, self-isolated Peter of a few months ago.

We at Cervantes feel each student is important. There is great joy as we see each student progressing and reaching goals that will help them enjoy life more. We feel confident that Peter will continue to progress, and we are grateful that for one hour on Saturday we can be part of his life.

Favorable publicity soon began to result from the work done at Cervantes. Several feature articles with photographs were run in some of the larger newspapers in the area. By early summer of 1980, enrollment had built up to nearly 50 students, each taking one riding lesson per week. Linda had a roster of 80 volunteer workers, about 30 of whom were spending 4–5 hours per week with Cervantes. Linda also had 11 horses, 4 of which had been donated to Cervantes. Four of her horses were bearing foals. Cervantes operated in a donated facility that included a stable, outdoor arena, and pasture. During the winter, an indoor arena was used at a cost of $1 per student per hour. The first facility used by Cervantes was also donated rent-free; however, after Linda and her volunteers had cleaned and fixed it up and used it only a short period of time, the owner said he wanted to do something else with it. Linda was thus obliged to find another facility and repeat the cleanup and repair process. Then, in late July of 1980, she was told that her present facility was needed by the owner and that Cervantes would need to vacate it by August 18.

Parents of some of her students offered pasture for Cervantes' horses and for riding lessons if needed temporarily. However, Linda wanted to find a new facility she could stay in. She thought of buying a stable or buying some land and building a stable. With this in mind, she reviewed her financial situation.

When Cervantes was started in August 1979, Linda had $1,500 cash she had saved. She also had five horses and some equipment. In September, Linda applied for a loan from a local bank. She prepared for the banker a list of her assets offered as collateral and a list of what the loan would be used for (see Exhibit 1). She also

---

Exhibit 1   Cervantes Equestrian Center, Loan Application Information

List of Collateral for Bank Loan

1977 AMC Pacer	$ 3,800
1974 Chevrolet ¾-ton pick-up	2,500
1971 Champion six-horse trailer	2,800
Five horses	17,850
Five saddles	500
Miscellaneous	250
Total	

Use of Loan

Insurance	$ 2,000
Six saddles at $200 each	1,200
Three horses at $500 each	1,500
Working captial	2,000
Total	$ 6,700

Exhibit 2 Projected Income and Expenses, Cervantes Equestrian Center, Year 1

	1979				1980							
	September	October	November	December	January	February	March	April	May	June	July	August
Projected expenses												
Taxes	$ 0	$ 0	$ 0	$ 0	$ 0	$ 0	$ 0	$ 0	$ 0	$ 0	$ 0	$ 0
Rent	0	0	0	100	100	100	100	0	0	0	0	0
Repairs	120	5	5	0	5	5	5	5	5	5	5	5
Payroll	100	200	200	200	200	200	250	300	300	400	400	400
Insurance	0	85	85	85	85	85	85	85	85	85	85	85
Legal fees	0	0	0	0	0	0	0	0	0	0	0	0
Bank payment—truck loan	78	78	78	78	78	78	78	78	78	78	78	78
Veterinarian and worming	10	40	10	40	10	40	10	40	10	40	10	40
Blacksmith	36	0	36	0	36	0	36	0	36	0	36	0
Feed	112	137	137	152	162	162	162	162	162	137	137	137
Tack	400	200	200	200	200	0	0	10	10	0	0	10
Advertising	70	70	0	0	70	50	50	50	0	0	0	0
Telephone	6	15	15	15	15	15	15	15	15	15	15	15
Gas	50	50	50	50	50	50	50	50	50	50	50	50
Miscellaneous	25	25	25	25	25	25	25	25	25	25	25	25
Totals	$1,007	$ 905	$ 841	$ 945	$1,006	$ 810	$ 866	$ 820	$ 776	$ 835	$ 841	$ 845
Projected income												
Lessons	$ 120	$ 600	$ 900	$ 720	$1,200	$1,080	$1,320	$2,250	$1,800	$1,920	$2,700	$2,160
Stud service						600	600	600	600	0	0	0
Boarding						150	150	150	150	150	150	150
Training						250	250	250	250	250	250	250
Totals	$ 120	$ 600	$ 900	$ 720	$1,200	$2,080	$2,320	$3,250	$2,800	$2,320	$3,100	$2,610

made a list of projected expenses and income for each month for 12 months (see Exhibit 2). The bank then loaned her $6,700 at 16 percent interest, with monthly payments of $184.49 for five years.

All income was deposited in the bank, and all expenses were paid by check. For several months, Linda summarized her income and expenses. Actual income was $91 in September 1979, $104 in October, and $229 in November. Actual expenses were $607 in September, $1,617 in October, $1,662 in November, and $499 in December. Thereafter, she didn't summarize her income and expenses, but she tried to be very careful with her money. Typically, Linda withdrew only $50 to $100 per week for living expenses. By July 1980, she still had $3,000 of the original bank loan on hand, which she kept in an interest-bearing savings account, making withdrawals only when needed. Linda had estimated that if she took in $360 per week and drew $100 for herself, Cervantes would break even financially. Earlier in the summer of 1980, she had been grossing $1,200 per month, with expenses (other than her draw) running about $600 per month. In July, however, she raised the price of a one-hour lesson for a handicapped student from $5 to $6. As a result, a local handicapped school discontinued 16 of its 18 students that had been coming for a weekly riding lesson. It appeared that this change would reduce Cervantes' gross to $800 for July.

The reason the school gave for discontinuing that many students was that they had to pay for the riding lessons out of a personal money allowance of $25 per month. She wondered how she might get institutions or schools to budget for riding lessons as therapy or recreation. Cervantes' price for a one-hour lesson for a normal child was $7.50. Linda believed that price to be comparable for other stables in the area.

In addition to the 11 horses, valued at $30,000 to $40,000 (depending on the value of the foals, when born), Cervantes had its original equipment, plus three more saddles. Payments on both loans were current, with a principal balance due of $4,356 on the bank loan and $783 on the truck loan.

The local Junior Chamber of Commerce had helped Cervantes with volunteer cleanup projects. Linda wondered whether they could help her find a new facility. Could she make Cervantes profitable as a business without volunteers or donated facilities? If so, were there other locations in the country where a Cervantes Equestrian Center could serve both handicapped and normal children and make enough profit to justify the investment? There were about 100 riding centers for the handicapped in the United States. All of them were nonprofit, and none of them had nonhandicapped students. Linda Smith wanted to control her own operation, and she wondered how she could best develop Cervantes toward success and stability.

CASE 7 CORRECTIONS CORPORATION OF AMERICA (A)*

THE ENTREPRENEURS

Thomas W. Beasley and Doctor R. Crants, Jr., first met at West Point. After graduating in 1966, they served together in Vietnam where Beasley received the silver star and two bronze stars for valor.

The turn of the decade found both men back in school, Beasley at Vanderbilt University's School of Law and Crants enrolled in a joint Law and Business School program at Harvard.

After receiving his law degree in 1973, Beasley returned to his hometown of Dickson Falls, Tennessee, and began his own law practice. One observer said:

> He's really a country boy who likes farming. But he got bored with the practice of law and turned his attention to politics. He'd gotten a taste of that at Vanderbilt and in 1974 he ran Lamar Alexander's losing campaign for the Tennessee governorship. Lamar lost bad, and from 1974 to 1978 the Democrats controlled the House, the Senate, and the State House. Tom became chairman of the Republican Party. Over the next four years he represented the party in all the important debates; he learned how to handle the press; and he developed a certain expertise under fire.

"Doc" Crants came to Tennessee in 1974 at the urging of his old friend Beasley and another West Point classmate then practicing law in Nashville. While Beasley operated in the world of politics, Crants pursued a career in real estate development, banking, and financial consulting. "Somewhere along the line," he says, "I became aware of the value of franchises—nursing homes and radio and television stations, for example. I discovered that the process of applying for licenses was exceedingly cumbersome—dealing with all that bureaucratic red tape—and not many people were willing to put up with it. I *was.* I didn't mind doing the dirty work, and occasionally I found that at the end of the process, I was the only bidder for a valuable property."

In 1978 Beasley ran Lamar Alexander's second, and successful, campaign for the governorship. Afterwards, he was charged with helping find candidates for the governor's cabinet. One job seemed unfillable: that of State Commissioner of Corrections. Beasley said:

> It was the one area where you couldn't find anyone with a good reputation. People would have a good reputation *for awhile* but they always seemed to lose it and get fired. There weren't any exceptions. It's a very difficult job to begin with, of course, but it always gets worse. The prison population grows, and legislatures are unwilling to provide money. So the institutions become more crowded. Indeed, they become inhumane. There are scandals and lawsuits. Many of our state correctional systems have

---

*This case was prepared by Professor Winthrop of the John Fitzgerald Kennedy School of Government, Harvard University. Reprinted with permission of the author.

been declared unconstitutional under the cruel and inhumane treatment of prisoners provision of the Constitution. The commissioner is the one who takes the rap.

While the new governor eventually filled the position, the new commissioner did not last, and during Alexander's first term Beasley kept wondering whether the public sector was really capable of running a decent corrections system. By 1982, with the Republicans in power in Washington, there was much talk in the air of reducing the activities of government in general and providing the private sector with a greater role in solving societal problems. It seemed to Beasley that the corrections area was one where this might be possible. He began taking small groups of Nashville business-men to dinner at the Bellemeade Country Club to see if they could be persuaded to put money in a new venture that would try to run prisons for a profit. One businessman who was interested was his old West Point classmate, "Doc" Crants.

Not long after the two men agreed (late in 1982) to go into business together, they enjoyed two remarkable strokes of good fortune. It turned out that several other Nashville businessmen were considering the same kind of proposition. Jack Massey, the founder of American Hospital Supply of America, and his young colleague, Lucius E. Burch III, had formed a new venture-capital firm, Massey Burch, in June 1981 to provide a formal vehicle for venture-capital investments for a very limited number of large outside clients. Already highly successful in the privatization of hospitals, already committed to the concept of building strong franchises (as in the case of at least one other extraordinarily successful investment, Kentucky Fried Chicken Corporation), Massey Burch was now considering starting a company called Prisons Corporations of America. Hearing of Beasley's and Crants's efforts to launch a similar concern, Burch set up a meeting of the parties, and a deal was quickly struck. For an investment of $500,000 Massey Burch would obtain a 50 percent interest in the Beasley/Crants venture. It would be called Corrections Corporation of America. Beasley would be president and chairman of the Board of Directors; Crants, secretary, treasurer, and vice chairman; and Burch would become a director and senior adviser.

The second lucky stroke came in the form of T. Don Hutto, an experienced correc-tions professional who had just been replaced as head of Virginia's corrections system as a result of the election of a new governor, Democrat Charles Robb. Hutto was the chairman-elect of the American Correctional Association (the ACA), the watchdog trade association that had been struggling since 1977 to formulate humane operating standards for American prisons. The ACA was planning to hold its next convention in Nashville in early 1983. Beasley, Crants, and Hutto met, and Hutto was brought aboard as executive vice president of the new firm.

THE U.S. DETENTION AND CORRECTIONS SYSTEM

The American prison system consists of two broad types of institutions (although, as indicated below, the two sometimes overlap): facilities for detention and for correc-tion.

The most widespread of the former are local jails where individuals are held awaiting trial or, having been convicted, are held awaiting sentencing to a corrections institution.

The most common corrections institutions are penal farms and workhouses, where individuals are sent to serve terms of less than six years and penitentiaries (state and federal) where they serve longer terms for more serious crimes. Because corrections institutions are often overcrowded, some prisoners who would ordinarily be sent to the latter are kept instead in local jails serving out their terms alongside other individuals who have yet to be found guilty of any crime or who have been convicted of relatively minor offenses. Sometimes individuals are "detained" in penal farms and workhouses, so that these serve both as "detention" and "corrections" facilities. In addition, there are a number of specialized institutions where illegal immigrants or juveniles are held for a variety of purposes.

Describing U.S. jails in a 1981 report, the ACA wrote:[1]

Since the first jail built in the Jamestown Colony, Virginia, in 1608, American society has caged human beings like animals with the expectation that they would return to the community and become law-abiding citizens. Traditional jail procedures have changed very little since the beginning of the 17th century, continuing to reflect a punitive "lock 'em up" approach in facilities. Prisoners often languish in idleness and boredom, under primitive conditions. Jails were primarily designed then, and still are, to enable a small number of staff to confine securely a comparatively large number of prisoners.

From the small to the large, today's detention facilities are poorly equipped to handle their diverse populations ranging from homeless drunks and the mentally ill to individuals accused of every conceivable crime. When such human beings are imprisoned with little regard for individual needs and rights their further deterioration is virtually assured. At detention facilities, the intake point in the criminal justice system, petty offenders comingle with hard-core criminals. Contempt for the law as well as knowledge and skills for future criminal careers are readily available to the young and first offenders. Their exposure to and acceptance of such opportunity is reflected by their high rates of failure and recidivism.

Despite decades of failure and criticism, most jails have remained unchanged, continuing to function as human warehouses. The reasons for this phenomenon can be any combination of such factors as limited local financing, public indifference and apathy, emphasis on restraint, and public ambivalence regarding concepts of punishment and treatment. Jails are the least studied and least understood of all penal institutions and are often held in low esteem by the public and its officials. Supporting jail reform has become a politically unpopular cause, and the tendency to minimize the importance of detention facilities and their impact on society is growing. The rare existence of sound operational standards for detention facilities and the failure of the many states to enforce those that do exist further depress the situation.

Justice Department data released in the spring of 1985 indicated:[2]

- In 1974, the United States prison population in federal and state penal institutions totaled approximately 229,000. By 1984, this number had doubled to 464,000. Between 1980 and 1984 the prison population increased by more than 40 percent. These increases were spurred in part by the arrival at the prison-prone ages (20–29 years) of the "baby boom" generation.

---

[1] *Standard for Adult Local Detention Facilities,* 2nd ed. American Correctional Association, 1981.

[2] *Prisoners in 1984,* Bureau of Justice Statistics Bulletin.

- In addition to state and federal prison systems, there are approximately 3,400 local jails within the United States. On any given day, there are approximately 300,000 people residing in these jails. In 1984, a total of 11,500 sentenced prisoners were held in local jails because of state prison overcrowding, an increase of more than 40 percent over the previous year.
- The number of prison admissions from court for every 100 serious crimes reported to the police declined from 6.3 in 1960 to 2.3 in 1970. The ratio began to increase in 1981, reaching 4.0 in 1983. If the 1960 rate of prison admissions relative to crime had prevailed in 1983, the number of offenders sentenced that year would have been about 100,000 higher than the 173,000 who were actually incarcerated.
- The strain placed on prison systems by the rapid influx of prisoners in recent years has been accompanied by a series of court interventions charging that individual prisons or whole state systems are violating the constitutional provision prohibiting "cruel and unusual treatment" of prisoners. In 1984 the entire prison systems in eight states were operating under court order or consent decree. Thirty-three state correctional systems had been declared unconstitutional, either in whole or in part, by the federal courts or were currently defending litigation in that regard.
- Despite substantial increases in expenditures for new prison capacity in recent years, both federal and state systems were operating at over-capacity occupancy rates in 1984: federal institutions at 110–137 percent of capacity and states at 105–116 percent (depending on how capacity is measured). One in 10 prisoners was housed in a facility built before 1875, half of all prisoners in facilities 40 or more years old.

Experts predict that inmate populations will level off from about 1985 to 1990 when they are again expected to increase. These projections are based on expected population age groupings and the fact that young people are the high-risk group and commit most crimes.

The Immigration and Naturalization Service (INS) reports that they arrested 1.2 million illegal aliens in 1983. Because of jail overcrowding and despite the fact that INS operates over 3,000 beds, INS finds itself without places to detain aliens once they are arrested. It is not uncommon for local district offices to stop arresting aliens as early as 9 A.M. each day because there is no further place to detain them.

It is expected that the illegal alien problem will worsen over the next 10 years and that the need for detention of aliens will increase. Even if Congress passes a reform bill, most observers believe that this will increase the numbers in detention. This is based on the premise that declaring amnesty for present aliens within this country will only serve to encourage other aliens to enter illegally in the future.

CCA'S OPERATING STRATEGY

The Company's managers and owners believed that the state of the nation's detention and corrections system provided it with a unique commercial opportunity. (See Exhibit 1.) As Lucius Burch put it, in an early memorandum on CCA:

> It is evident that change in the corrections industry is necessary and imminent. Public entities clearly are not managing the prison systems effectively.

Prodded by the Reagan administration, mayors and county officials are increasingly paying private industry to provide a wide range of public services in a move that has redefined the role of local government.

In the past local officials sought to expand their political bases by expanding services, creating new jobs and constituencies. This approach gathered momentum in the 1960s and 1970s as the federal government sharply increased funds for the cities; they could then increase services without raising taxes.

But federal funds are now running dry, and local officials, facing taxpayer revolts and paying union salaries and benefits they consider high, are turning to private industry to provide public services.

JAILS, HOSPITALS, TRANSIT

Some localities have begun to pay private industry to operate jails, hospitals or mass transit systems, services that local officials often consider both costly and troublesome.

Because this trend is relatively new, there is no conclusive evidence in most areas whether private industry is performing public services better or cheaper than governments do, as those who support the trend say, or whether governments are turning to private contractors in an effort to curtail services, as some critics maintain.

As they move into private services, many local officials are stressing their roles as policy makers rather than providers of service. They have taken a new look at the minimal services they must provide and have restructured their patronage systems.

"Local governments are redefining their role," said Lydia Manchester of the International City Management Association, which represents managers of local governments. "They're making a distinction between making policy and actually delivering the services."

"Local officials are saying, 'We can't do everything for everybody anymore,'" she said. "They are getting elected on the platform of keeping local taxes down and keeping a very close eye on what kinds of services should be provided by local government."

Governor Cuomo of New York said, "It is not government's obligation to provide services but to see that they're provided."

DIVERSE SERVICES OFFERED

Nationally, private industry now provides local governments with a significant fraction of such diverse services as waste collection, street-light operation, vehicle towing, ambulance services, hospital management, legal services and labor relations, according to a survey published last year by the International City Management Association.

The survey, financed by the Department of Housing and Urban Development, was the first comprehensive study of privatization of local services. No comparable data exist for earlier periods because the trend is so new.

"Private contracts act as a good discipline on our own operation," said Mayor George Latimer of St. Paul, where private industry provides sanitation, street paving, some snow plowing, sewers, lighting improvement, and other services. "It gives local government more flexibility. It gives us options. And remember, we write the specifications. We write the contracts."

Privatization of public services affects both large and small cities in all sections of the nation. In New York, Stanley N. Brezenoff, Deputy Mayor for Operations, said, "We weigh two major factors: cost and quality of service." The city pays private industry to provide a wide range of services, from street repair to design services and consulting contracts.

EFFORTS IN NEWARK

The city of Newark pays private industry to provide most sewer cleaning, vehicle maintenance, building trades work, specialty printing, data processing, and street repairing.

In Phoenix, city departments bid against private contractors to provide many city-financed services, including custodial services, trash collection, and major street landscaping.

Los Angeles County maintains 139 contracts with private companies, concentrated in the area of parks and grounds maintenance. La Mirada, California, has contracted for almost all its key services, including police and fire protection, building inspection, public works, and human services.

Stuart M. Butler, director of domestic policy studies of the Heritage Foundation, a research organization, noted the federal role in this trend. "Local governments had to redefine their role and maintain the same levels of service with less federal funds," he said. "They had to either raise taxes, which industry it often lacked the necessary equipment, which it had sold to the private contractor.

"You get locked into a service, and you can't get out," Mr. McEntee said.

John T. Marlin, president of the Council on Municipal Performance who is editor of the book "Contracting Municipal Services," said Mr. McEntee was correct as far as he went. "When New York City closed down its asphalt plant," Mr. Marlin said, "it was at the mercy of all the people who made asphalt."

LOOKING FOR A "GOOD DEAL"

He nevertheless contended, "It's good government to look at all the options," and he said that voters provided the pressure for quality private services. "The voters are saying, 'Show me you've got a good deal,'" Mr. Marlin said.

Mr. Brezenoff cited another case in which New York had become vulnerable to private contractors. "During the fiscal crisis, we had to reduce some of our design capabilities," Mr. Brezenoff said. "In the interim, we will probably be more dependent on private firms for design of projects."

"Periodically there's been a discussion of contracting out sanitation services, but we always decided against it," Mr. Brezenoff added.

In an experiment, Newark paid private industry to provide sanitation for one third of the city. That provided new incentives for the city employees, who retained jurisdiction over the remaining two-thirds, Mayor Kenneth A. Gibson said.

"It's amazing what a little competition will do," Mr. Gibson said, noting that city employees had stepped up their sanitation efforts.

He has now proposed increasing private industry's

Exhibit 1 *(concluded)*

share to two-thirds, however, because, even with the improved work from city employees, he found that the private contractor was more efficient.

TREND HAS DEEP ROOTS

Although local governments have provided most public services directly, they have always paid private industry to perform some services.

In the early 1900s cities and towns around the country turned to private companies to build and run local streetcar systems, collect garbage, or provide fire protection or other basic public services, often because their communities lacked the needed public resources.

There were problems, however. It was the era of big-city political bosses, and corruption was rampant. In New York, for example, municipal contracts became a favorite form of patronage under Tammany Hall. Contractors frequently overcharged municipalities, payoffs by contractors were common, and their services were often poor.

The Progressive movement of the 1920's tried to professionalize the delivery of public services by making them part of the municipal government. But now many experts believe the pendulum is swinging the other way under the prodding of the Reagan philosophy and cuts in funds for the cities.

"We seem to go through these swings," said Dr. A. Lee Fritschler, director of the Center for Public Policy Education at the Brookings Institution, a research organization. "When the marketplace doesn't work well, we let government do it. And when government doesn't work well, we go back to the private sector."

EFFECT ON PATRONAGE

Many public officials acknowledge that privatization has changed the structure of local politics. Major patronage has gone to companies rather than individuals.

Dr. Fritschler says local officials actually have a freer hand in doling out patronage because "there are a lot fewer rules to worry about and less union pressure."

"I'm sure local politicos are saying, 'If we contract this out, I'd like to suggest some people for jobs,'" Dr. Fritschler said. "In a way, it's a lot easier for them."

Mr. McEntee, the union president, said privatization provided a new patronage system for politicians. "Before the unions and the civil service laws," he said, "politicians could hire and promote whoever they wanted. But the private sector can hire and promote as it wishes, and private contractors sometimes end up being the best contributors to either the political party or the politicians."

Many private contractors have historically played an active role in local politics, especially in cities with strong political organizations, like Chicago, New York and Boston. A week after a fund-raising event for the campaign of Jane M. Byrne, then Mayor of Chicago, the city awarded a $2 million contract to a trash-hauling enterprise whose executives had bought $8,300 in tickets.

FINDING THE REAL COST

Bill Donaldson gained considerable experience with privatization as City Manager in Scottsdale, Arizona, Tacoma,

Washington, and Cincinnati. He now is director of the Philadelphia Zoo.

"One of the things I liked about contracting out was that it forced me to look at what it really cost to do a service," Mr. Donaldson said. "In theory, government ought to be more efficient than the private sector, because it doesn't pay taxes or pay for the use of capital. Unfortunately, because there's no competition, most governments don't have the faintest idea of what it costs to do anything."

"Also, if a private contractor falls down on the job, the contract eventually runs out," he added. "But civil service never runs out."

Private Help for Government

National percentage of some public services that cities and counties have turned over to private industry

Public Works and Transportation:	
Commercial solid-waste collection	41%
Residential solid-waste collection	34
Solid waste disposal	26
Street repair	26
Traffic signal installation/maintenance	25
Snow-plowing and sanding	18
Public Utilities:	
Street light operation	18
Utility billing	12
Utility meter reading	0
Safety and Recreation:	
Vehicle towing and storage	73
Ambulance service	23
Emergency medical service	13
Parks maintenance	7
Health Services:	
Operation/management of hospitals	25
Insect/rodent control	13
Support Services:	
Legal services	48
Fleet management and maintenance	
Heavy equipment	31
Emergency vehicles	30
All other vehicles	28
Labor relations	23
Data processing	22
Building/grounds maintenance	18
Payroll	10
Building security	7
Public relations	7
Tax assessing	6
Personnel services	5
Secretarial services	4

Source: International City Management Association.

---

* Source: Martin Tolchin, *New York Times,* May 28, 1985. Reprinted with permission.

While the American public has taken a "hard-line" attitude in regard to the suppression of crime, this attitude has not translated itself into support for tax initiatives to build additional facilities to handle the increased population. There is no political constituency for building and housing criminals. It is a low budget priority and will not receive proper attention absent private intervention.

Further, as public treasuries grow leaner in the years ahead, experts believe that the role of private enterprise in criminal justice will increase.

Prisons in the United States are aging and are in need of repair or replacement. Private entities can relieve municipalities (and ultimately taxpayers) from the burden of additional capital outlays and high operating expenses for these facilities. In fact, a corrections corporation is a tax-paying entity and will provide additional capital through payment of state and federal taxes.

Most importantly, however, a private entity can manage correctional facilities more economically and efficiently than the governmental entities. A private entity can be competitive in its costs relative to governmental operations for several reasons:

- Personnel economies can be achieved through careful attention to the design of the facility. In a twenty-four (24) hour operation, such economies are of major importance.
- Further economies can be achieved through mass purchasing, an advantage not available to small single jail operations.
- Private entities are not required to operate under cumbersome bureaucratic purchasing regulations which, inevitably, increase the cost of supplies and materials. As a result, a private operation can trim an estimated 10–25 percent off the cost of running conventional facilities. The bidding procedures designed to maintain honesty, while resulting in low bids for the government, usually do not result in low prices.

With solid financial backing from Massey Burch, with a small cadre of managers experienced in politics (Beasley), business (Crants), and corrections management (Hutto), CCA determined that it would attempt to contract with local, state, and federal governmental bodies for the detention of persons for whom a minimum to medium level of security was required and who presented, in the management's opinion, "a relatively low risk of violence or other untoward behavior." The company would build, own (or lease), staff, and manage such correctional and detention facilities. It would contract with government bodies to "detain or incarcerate, provide food and other necessities for, and supervise persons in the correctional and detention facilities owned by government bodies."

Although this statement of purpose seemed relatively straightforward, the leaders of the company knew that implementation would be no simple matter. They understood that the process of "selling" their concept to local elective officials (sheriffs, county executives, and county commissions) would be time-consuming and difficult. Many local officials had a stake in the existing system. For them, employment opportunities in county jails represented a source of patronage. At the state and federal level there would be legislative oversight committees to deal with as well as elective and appointive officials in the executive branches. How would these public bodies feel about turning over the administration of corrections facilities to a for-profit body?

What standards would need to be established so that the public sector would feel at home delegating these kinds of responsibilities to private concerns? The ACA had recently set a standard of 70 square feet of cell space for each prisoner. The federal standard was 60 square feet. But it was estimated that only 1 percent of all facilities met these levels. There were numerous instances, in fact, where four prisoners were crowded into cells of less than 60 square feet, where there were no outdoor recreation areas, and where health, sanitation, and hygiene facilities were lamentable (see Appendix 1 for a sampling of the standards that the ACA was attempting, with extremely limited success, to impose on the nation's prison system in 1981). Indeed, it was the public sector's inability or unwillingness to provide these standards that created the opportunity that CCA wished now to exploit. Should CCA strive to build and run facilities that met the ACA standards or some less stringent test that would still substantially improve upon existing practice?

There were a number of other questions on CCA's managers' minds in 1983 as it began formulating its first bids:

- What role, if any, would public sector officials play in monitoring what went on inside a prison once CCA "owned" or managed it?
- How much competition did CCA want? It was important that the public sector have more than one firm bidding for this kind of business. On the other hand, nothing would damage the privatization concept faster than fly-by-night operators who failed to make good on their promises. Was there any way CCA could influence the competitive environment in which it operated? Should it even attempt to do so?
- What liabilities would the company be exposing itself to in the management of detention and corrections facilities? And how could these be contained?
- How would the company meet its staffing requirements—both for its own management and for the staff required within the facilities it operated—given the poor reputation of the public officials now in the business.
- What would the media make of all this? And the liberal academic intelligentsia? And how could *they* be "managed"? Or should the company even try?

THE FIRST CONTRACT

The company submitted its first proposal and bid to manage a detention facility on August 26, 1983, to the Immigration and Naturalization Service for the operation of an approximately 67,600-square-foot, 350-bed detention facility for illegal aliens in Houston, Texas. On October 6, 1983, the company received notification from the INS that its proposal and bid to operate the facility had been accepted and that the INS contract was effective from that date. On October 11, 1983, the company purchased an approximately 5.84-acre site in Houston for construction of the facility for a price of approximately $763,000. On October 21, 1983, the company entered into a construction contract with Trimble & Stephens Co. of Houston, Texas, for the construction of the facility. Construction commenced on October 26, 1983, and was completed on April 20, 1984. The company also incurred architectural and engineering fees in connection with the construction.

The initial term of the INS contract terminated on September 30, 1984, and the INS has renewed the INS contract to September 30, 1985. The INS has the option to renew the INS contract for three consecutive one-year periods with adjustments in the amounts paid by the INS to the company during such renewal periods, which adjustments are designed, in part, to offset inflation. Unless the company operates the facility for at least five years, the company will likely lose a substantial amount of money on the project. The company will receive $25.74 per day per person from the INS through September 1985. The company has received a letter of intent from the INS to renew the INS contract until September 30, 1986.

APPENDIX 1   Recommended Standards of American Correctional Association for Adult Local Detention Facilities (Selected Excerpts)*

I. SUMMARY OF ORIENTATION AND MINIMUM TRAINING HOURS

The following description of general job categories should be used in determining minimum training requirements as outlined in standards 2-5081 thru 2-5085. Contract or part-time employees should receive training similar to full-time employees in their particular category and pertinent to their role in working with inmates.

Title	Position	Prior to Job	First Year On the Job	Each Year Thereafter
(2-5081) Clerical/ support (minimum contact)	Secretaries, clerks, typists, PBX operators, computer and warehouse personnel, accountants, personnel staff	24	16	16
(2-5082) Support (regular or daily contact)	Food service, industry work supervisors, farm work supervisors, maintenance work supervisors	40	40	40
(2-5083) Correctional officers	All staff assigned to full-time custodial and/or security posts	40	120	40
(2-5084) Administrative/ management personnel (additional training)	Facility administrators, business managers, personnel directors, or other supervisors	—	40	24
(2-5085) Emergency unit staff	Members of emergency or confrontation units	40*	—	16†

* May be part of 120 hours of on-the-job training required in first year as correctional officer.
† May be part of 40 hours of required annual training.

---

* American Correctional Association, in cooperation with the Commission on Accreditation for Corrections.

II. PHYSICAL PLANT STANDARDS

Note: As indicated, these standards apply to existing facilities, renovations, additions, when undertaken, and/or for new plant construction. New construction is defined as that for which the final plans were approved after January 1, 1982.

Standard 2–5108 Existing: All activity areas have toilets and wash basins which are accessible to persons using the area. An independent, qualified source has documented that

- Lighting is appropriate to the activity area.
- Circulation is at least 10 cubic feet of fresh or purified air per minute per human occupant.
- Temperatures are appropriate to the summer and winter comfort zones with consideration for the activity performed.

   Discussion.   Activity areas in the facility must have sufficient air, lighting, and sanitary facilities to ensure the health of those using them. These areas include multipurpose rooms, recreation areas or program areas for inmates, or work areas for staff.

Standard 2–5110 Existing, Renovation, Addition, New Plant: Only one inmate occupies each cell and detention room designed for single occupancy.

   Discussion   Single-cell occupancy provides privacy and protection for the inmates, and should be provided based on the designed capacity of the facility.

Standard 2–5111 Existing, Renovation: All single rooms or cells in *detention facilities* have at least 60 square feet of floor space, provided inmates spend no more than 10 hours per day locked in; when confinement exceeds 10 hours per day, there are at least 70 square feet of floor space.

   Discussion   Adequate living space is important to the mental well-being of the inmate. Rooms or cells of sufficient size enable inmates to personalize living space consistent with facility rules and regulations. Inmates who have access to programs and activities throughout the facility require less space in their rooms or cells because they do not spend as much time there.

Standard 2–5112 Existing, Renovation, Addition, New Plant: All rooms or cells in *detention facilities* have, at a minimum

- Access to the following sanitation facilities:
- Toilet above floor level which is available for use without staff assistance 24 hours a day.
- Wash basin and drinking water.
- Shower facilities.
- Hot and cold running water.
- A bed at above floor level, desk or writing surface, hooks or closet space, chair or stool.
- Natural light.

There is documentation by an independent, qualified source that

- Lighting is at least 20 footcandles at desk level and in the personal grooming area; in additions and new plants it is both occupant and centrally controlled.

- Circulation is at least 10 cubic feet of outside or recirculated filtered air per minute per human occupant.
- Temperatures are appropriate to the summer and winter comfort zones.
- Noise levels do not exceed 70 decibels in daytime and 45 decibels at night.

Discussion   Suggested temperatures are 66 to 80 degrees (F) in the summer comfort zone, optimally 71 degrees (F), and 61 to 73 degrees (F) in the winter comfort zone, optimally 70 degrees (F). Sensory deprivation should be reduced by providing variety in terms of space, surface textures, and colors. Natural lighting should be available either by cell or room windows to exterior or from a source within 20 feet of the room or cell. The bed should be elevated from the floor and have a clean, covered mattress with blankets provided as needed. Toilet facilities can be located either in the cell or outside if it is available at all times without requiring staff to unlock a door to provide access.

Standard 2–5114 Existing, Renovation: Where used, multiple occupancy rooms house no less than 4 and no more than 50 inmates each who are screened prior to admission for suitability to group living; the rooms provide

- Continuing observation by staff.
- A minimum floor area of 50 square feet per occupant in the sleeping area and a clear floor to ceiling height of not less than 8 feet.
- Toilet and shower facilities at a minimum of one operable toilet and shower for every eight occupants.
- One operable wash basin with hot and cold running water for every six occupants.
- Natural light.
- Beds above floor level.
- A locker for each occupant.

There is documentation by an independent, qualified source that

- Lighting is at least 20 footcandles at desk level and in the personal grooming area.
- Circulation is at least 10 cubic feet of outside or recirculated filtered air per minute per occupant.
- Temperatures are appropriate to the summer and winter comfort zones.
- Noise levels do not exceed 70 decibels in daytime and 45 decibels at night.

Discussion   When multiple occupancy housing cannot be avoided, as in multiple occupancy cells or dormitories, the number of inmates rooming together should be kept as low as possible. Multiple occupancy rooms in pretrial facilities should not house more than 16 individuals. Where dormitories are used in facilities for sentenced inmates the number of occupants should not exceed 50 per room.

Standard 2–5116 Existing, Renovation, Addition, New Plant: A room used for segregation permits inmates assigned to it to communicate with staff and has a door which permits observation by staff.

Discussion   The segregation units should be designed to permit the staff on duty an unobstructed view of all inmates in the unit. Although inmates may be physically separated from the general population, they should be allowed to talk to other inmates assigned to the same housing unit or to staff members. Total isolation as punishment for a rule violation is not an acceptable practice. When exceptions occur, they should be justified by clear and substantiated evidence and fully documented.

Standard 2–5117 Existing, Renovation, Addition, New Plant: When seriously ill, mentally disordered, injured, or nonambulatory inmates are held in the facility, there is at least one single-occupancy cell or room for them which provides for continuing staff observation.

Discussion   The facility should be equipped to provide temporary medical services. All seriously ill, injured, and nonambulatory inmates should be transported to a hospital as soon as possible after admission.

Standard 2–5118 Existing, Renovation, Addition, New Plant: When both males and females are housed in the same facility they are provided separate sleeping quarters which are separated visually and acoustically.

Standard 2–5119 Existing, Renovation: Designated exits in the facility permit prompt evacuation of inmates and staff members in an emergency.

Discussion   At least two separate means of exit from the facility should be provided to ensure the safety of inmates and staff members. These exits should lead directly from the inmate living area to a hazard-free area, where adequate supervision should be provided.

Standard 2–5120 Addition, New Plant: There are at least two identifiable exits in each inmate housing area/cell block and other high-density area to permit the prompt evacuation of inmates and staff under emergency conditions.

Discussion   Emergency exits must be provided for the safety of inmates and staff. Such exits should lead directly to a hazard-free area, where adequate supervision can be provided.

Standard 2–5121 Existing, Renovation, Addition, New Plant: The facility perimeter is secured in a way which provides that inmates remain within the perimeter and that access by the general public is denied without proper authorization.

Discussion   Most facilities are located in the center of the community usually adjacent to the courthouse, to facilitate movement of inmates to and from court. To prevent introduction of weapons and other contraband into the facility, it is essential that inmates are not given the opportunity for physical contact with any persons outside the facility. Screens or similar devices should be used to protect windows. This does not preclude authorized contact visits for approved inmates.

III. SECURITY AND CONTROL STANDARDS

Standard 2–5185: Written policy and procedure govern the use of firearms and include the following requirements:

- Weapons are subjected to stringent safety regulations and inspections.
- A secure weapons locker is located outside the security perimeter of the facility.
- Except in emergency situations, firearms and weapons such as nightsticks are permitted only in designated areas to which inmates have no access.
- Employees supervising inmates outside the institution perimeter follow procedures for the security of weapons.
- Employees are instructed to use deadly force only after other actions have been tried and found ineffective, unless the employee believes that a person's life is immediately threatened.

- Employees on duty only use firearms or other security equipment which have been issued through the facility and only when directed by or authorized by the facility administrator.

    Discussion   In order to reduce the risk of firearms falling into the hands of inmates, institution personnel who spend most of their time in direct personal contact with inmates must not carry firearms. A system of receipts for the temporary storage or checking of weapons should exist to accommodate law enforcement personnel who must enter the facility. Use of firearms in transporting inmates or in outside work assignments requires officers who are trained in the handling and use of firearms. This should enable the facility to maintain control over the type of firearms or other equipment to be used in the facility and the quality of their care.

Standard 2–5186: Written policy and procedure provide that the facility maintains a written record of routine and emergency distributions of security equipment.

Discussion   A written record detailing who receives security equipment and what equipment they receive is necessary to establish responsibility and accountability for its use.

Standard 2–5187: Written policy and procedure require that personnel discharging firearms, using chemical agents or any other weapon, or using force to control inmates submit written reports to the facility administrator or designee no later than the conclusion of the tour of duty.

Discussion   All instances involving the discharge of firearms and use of chemical agents should be documented to establish the identity of personnel and inmates involved and to describe the nature of the incident.

Standard 2–5189: Written policy and procedure require prompt reporting of all incidents that result in physical harm to or threaten the safety of any person in the facility, or that threaten the security of the facility.

Discussion   A written record of such incidents should be available for administrative review. These reports also can be used to assess training needs and are fundamental to an evaluation of the operation of the facility.

Standard 2–5190: Written policy and procedure govern the control and use of keys.

Discussion   The key control system should provide a current accounting of the location and possessor of each key. All keys should be issued from a central control area, and a log should be used to record the number of each key given out, the location of the lock, the number of keys to that lock, and the names of all employees possessing the key. Keys should be stored in a manner that permits easy determination of either the presence or absence of keys. Keys should be returned to the control center daily. All keys should be numbered, and the facility should maintain at least one duplicate key for each lock. Fire and emergency keys should be color-coded, marked for identification by touch, and readily available. Inmates should not possess keys other than those to living quarters or work assignments, when appropriate, and to personal lockers.

Standard 2–5191: Written policy and procedure govern the control and use of tools, and culinary and medical equipment.

Discussion   Tools and utensils such as hacksaws, welding equipment, butcher knives, and barber shears can cause death or serious injury. They should be locked in control panels and issued in accordance with a prescribed system. Provision should be made for checking tools and utensils in and out, and for the control of their use at all times.

Standard 2–5194: Written policy and procedure regarding escapes are available to all personnel, and are reviewed at least annually and updated if necessary.

> *Discussion   The facility should detail in writing specific procedures that can be used quickly when an escape occurs. The procedures should include:*

- Prompt reporting of the escape to the facility administrator.
- Identification of escapee(s).
- Mobilization of employees.
- Implementation of a predetermined search plan.
- Notification of law enforcement agencies, community groups, and interested media.
- After capture of the escapee, prompt notification of all who were previously alerted to the escape.

> *Because an escape indicates a weakness in the facility's security system, an analysis of the escape should be conducted and defects in the security system should be corrected immediately.*

Standard 2–5195: There are written plans that specify procedures to be followed in situations including, but not limited to, riots, hunger strikes, disturbances, and taking of hostages. These plans are made available to applicable personnel, and reviewed and updated at least annually.

> *Discussion   The plans also should designate who should implement such procedures. They should specify what personnel should be involved, when and which authorities and media should be notified, how the problem should be contained, and what should be done after the incident is quelled. Provision should be made for the emergency housing and supervision of inmates should the facility become uninhabitable. The plan presupposes regular inspection and maintenance of specialized equipment necessary to implement the procedures. All personnel should become familiar with the plans.*

Standard 2–5197: There is a written plan that provides for continuing operations in the event of a work stoppage or other job action. Copies of this plan are available to all supervisory personnel, who are required to familiarize themselves with it.

> *Discussion   A contingency plan for maintaining essential services is crucial. This plan might involve agreements with other law enforcement agencies, such as the state police. Additionally, the facility administrator should attempt to ensure the safety and well-being of employees who do not participate in the job action.*

Standard 2–5198: Written policy and procedure restrict the use of physical force to instances of justifiable self-defense, protection of others, protection of property, and prevention of escapes, and only when it is necessary to control inmates and in accordance with appropriate statutory authority. In no event is physical force justifiable as punishment. A written report is prepared following all uses of force and is submitted to the facility administrator.

> *Discussion   Correctional personnel should be prepared to justify their use of physical force. Immediate medical attention should be provided when warranted or requested by the inmate or staff member involved in an incident where physical force was used.*

IV. MEDICAL AND HEALTH CARE SERVICES STANDARDS

Standard 2–5261: Medical, dental, and mental health matters involving clinical judgments are the sole province of the responsible physician, dentist, and psychiatrist or qualified psychologist respectively; however, security regulations applicable to facility personnel also apply to health personnel.

> *Discussion   The provision of health care is a joint effort of administrators and health care providers and can be achieved only through mutual trust and cooperation. The health authority arranges for the availability of health care services; the official responsible for the facility provides the administrative support for the accessibility of health services to inmates.*

Standard 2–5262: The health authority meets with the facility administrator or designee at least quarterly and submits quarterly reports on the health care delivery system and annual statistical reports.

V. STANDARDS FOR INMATE RIGHTS

Standard 2–5293: Written policy and procedure ensure the right of inmates to have unlimited access to the courts and to address uncensored communications to governmental authorities. Inmates seeking judicial or administrative redress are not subjected to reprisals or penalties as a consequence.

Standard 2–5294: Written policy and procedure ensure and facilitate the right of inmates to have access to attorneys and their authorized representatives.

> *Discussion   Every effort should be made to facilitate privacy in contacts between attorneys and their clients. Unsentenced and sentenced inmates should be able to consult with attorneys, their representatives, or experts retained by them. Provision should be made for contacts during normal facility hours, for uncensored correspondence and telephone communication, and for all after hours visits requested on the basis of special circumstances. Attorney substitutes representing the attorney of record, or other legally authorized attorney substitutes, have access to the facility.*

Standard 2–5295: Inmates have access to legal materials if there is not adequate free legal assistance to help them with criminal, civil, and administrative legal matters.

> *Discussion   The constitutional right of access to the courts requires that, when requested, inmates receive assistance in preparing and filing legal papers. This should include assistance from persons with legal training, law school legal assistance programs, the public defender's office, and law library facilities. If a law library is available, a minimum collection should include: state and federal constitutions, state statutes and decisions, procedural rules and decisions and related commentaries, federal case law materials, court rules and practices treatises, and legal periodicals and indexes.*

Standard 2–5296: Written policy and procedure provide inmates access to paper, typewriters or typing service, and other supplies and services related to legal matters.

> *Discussion   The institution should make reasonable efforts to assist inmates with the preparation and processing of their legal documents. Items such as paper, typewriters or typing services, and carbon paper should be provided all inmates upon request and should be available free of charge to indigent inmates.*

Standard 2–5297: The facility fulfills the right of inmates to basic medical and dental care.

VI. STANDARDS FOR INMATE RULES AND DISCIPLINE

Standard 2–5305: There are written rules of inmate conduct which specify acts prohibited within the facility and penalties that may be imposed for various degrees of violation. These rules are provided to all inmates, and procedures exist for ensuring that all inmates understand the rules.

Standard 2–5306: The written rules of inmate conduct are reviewed annually and updated, if necessary, to ensure that they are consistent with constitutional and legal principles.

Standard 2–5307: All personnel who deal with inmates receive sufficient training so that they are thoroughly familiar with the rules of inmate conduct, the sanctions available, and the rationale for the rules.

Discussion   All facility personnel who deal with inmates in any way should receive continuous inservice training that ensures their understanding of the rules of inmate conduct, the sanctions available, and the rationale for the rules. The clarity and specificity of the rules, together with this training, should preclude discrepancies among staff members in interpretation. (See related standards 2–5082 and 2–5083.)

Standard 2–5308: There are written guidelines for informally resolving minor inmate infractions.

Discussion   Written guidelines should specify misbehavior that may be handled informally. All other rule violations should be handled through formal procedures that include the filing of a disciplinary report.

CASE 8   THE GRAND THEATRE COMPANY*

"There is no better director than me. Some may be as good, but none better."

—Robin Phillips

In December 1982, the Board of Directors of Theatre London in London, Ontario (see Exhibit 1) were considering a proposal to hire Robin Phillips as artistic director, to replace Bernard Hopkins. The hiring decision was complicated by Phillips's ambitious plans for the theatre, which included a change from a subscription theatre to repertory, an increase in budget from $1.9 million to $4.4 million, and even changing the organization's name. The board had to act quickly as plans had to be made, and actors hired, for the next season.

THEATRE IN ONTARIO

Theatre is big business in Ontario. In Toronto alone (including cabaret, dinner theatre, and opera) some 3.5 million people attended 120 productions in 1982, in 28 locations. There are 24 nonprofit professional theatres in Toronto, and 18 in the rest of Ontario.

Virtually all theatre organizations in Ontario and the rest of Canada are nonprofit and are subsidized by local, provincial, and federal grants. Thus theatres compete for funds with charities, educational, and health care organizations. As shown in Exhibit 2, a third of revenue typically comes from government sources and half of this comes from The Canada Council. Another 10 percent comes from individual and corporate donors, and the balance from the box office. Because of the pressing need for box office revenues, most theatre companies sell subscriptions of five or so plays from October to May.

In 1982–83, audience size was 570,000 for the Stratford Festival, the largest art organization in Canada, and 268,000 for The Shaw Festival, the second largest theatre company. According to a Stratford audience study, audiences break down into: (1) committed theatregoers (27 percent) who see a number of plays each year, and who tend to be older and more educated and live in Ontario; (2) casual theatregoers (53 percent) who attend a theatre every year or two to see plays of particular interest; and (3) first-timers (20 percent). The challenge for these theatres is to develop these first-timers to be the audience of the future.

Theatre audiences tend to be well educated, with most having university education, and slightly over 50 percent having attended a graduate or professional school. Those aged 36 through 50 make up 35 percent of the Stratford audience, and the 21-to-35 and 51-to-64 age groups each make up 25 percent. Visitors from the United States

---

* Prepared by Dr. Larry M. Agranove with the assistance of Dr. J. Peter Killing from published sources and interviews with numerous people in theatre, government, and arts organizations. Copyright © 1985, Wilfrid Laurier University. Reprinted with permission.

Exhibit 1   The Grand Theatre Company, Board of Directors, December 1982

J. Noreen De Shane	President, and president of a stationery firm
Peter J. Ashby	Partner, major consulting firm
W. C. P. Baldwin, Jr.	President, linen supply firm
Bob Beccarea	Alderman and civic representative
Art Ender	Life insurance representative
Ed Escaf	Hotel and restaurant owner
Dr. John Girvin	Surgeon
Stephanie Goble	Representative of London Labour Council
Elaine Hagarty	Former alderman, active in arts community
Barbara Ivey	Active board member of various theatre groups
Alan G. Leyland	Entrepreneur
John F. McGarry	Partner, major law firm
C. Agnew Meek	Corporate marketing executive
Robert Mepham	Retired civic leader and businessman
Elizabeth Murray	Board member of theatre groups and Ontario Arts Council
John H. Porter	Vice president and partner, major accounting firm
Peter Schwartz	Partner, major law firm
Dr. Tom F. Siess	University professor
Dr. Shiel Warma	Surgeon

---

account for 35 percent of box office receipts at the Stratford Festival; Toronto accounts for 25 percent, and the remaining 40 percent come from elsewhere in Ontario. Twice as many women attend as men. It is understood that Shaw's market is similar, with slightly fewer coming from the United States.

A recent study[2] showed that while 42 percent of Ontario residents attended live plays and musicals in 1974, this number grew to 55 percent by 1984. Some 24 percent of the Ontario population are "frequent attenders" (at least six times a year). They come from all age groups, but many are "singles," and many are university educated and affluent. In fact, while only 63 percent of Ontarians without a high school education attended live theatre, 94 percent with university degrees have attended live theatre.

There is some price sensitivity: 73 percent said they would attend oftener if tickets were less expensive. However, 77 percent (which included young adults and lower-middle income families) said they would accept a tax increase of up to $25 to support the arts.

THE ORGANIZATION OF A THEATRE COMPANY

The Board of Directors   The board of directors is fiscally and legally responsible for the theatre. They may determine the theatre's artistic objectives, then delegate the fulfilling of these objectives to the artistic director. However, any artistic plan

---

[2] Report to the Honorable Susan Fish, The Minister of Citizenship and Culture, by the Special Committee for the Arts, Spring 1984.

Exhibit 2   The Major Arts Organizations in Canada—Ranked by Size of Total Revenue for 1982–1983

Arts Organizations	Total Revenue 1982–1983	Box Office and Earned	Government Grants	Private Donations	Accumulated Surplus (Deficit) End of 1982–1983
1. Stratford Festival	$12,314,300	$9,678,285	$1,405,939	$1,230,076	$(1,731,492)
2. Toronto Symphony	9,480,503	6,020,112	1,893,100	1,567,291	(149,391)
3. National Ballet	7,271,616	3,233,810	2,943,856	1,093,950	(675,096)
4. Orchestre Symphonique de Montreal	7,071,886	4,048,749	2,164,350	858,787	(857,662)
5. Canadian Opera Company	5,969,077	2,668,698	2,029,100	1,271,279	(290,168)
6. Vancouver Symphony	5,189,041	2,488,690	1,784,315	916,036	(818,951)
7. Shaw Festival	4,801,700	3,848,200	586,000	367,500	(45,167)
8. Royal Winnipeg Ballet	4,021,263	1,884,339	1,611,463	525,461	343,639
9. Centre Stage	3,483,020	1,923,312	1,316,000	243,708	(212,108)
10. Citadel Theatre	3,541,911	2,097,096	1,117,733	327,082	177,821
18. Grand Theatre	1,990,707	1,277,625	390,000	323,082	0*

* Reduced by Wintario Challenge Fund.
Source: Council for Business and the Arts in Canada.

has financial objectives, and the board's responsibility is essentially financial. Artistic directors generally demand, and are generally granted, a great deal of autonomy in such matters as programming and casting; to a large extent the board "bets" on the artistic director's ability to put on a season of theatre, subject to his accountability in meeting budgets and providing an appropriate level of quality.

Board members are typically expected to assist in fund raising, and to set an example by contributing generously themselves.

Board members often have business backgrounds. As a result, they may be—and are certainly often perceived to be—insensitive to the unique needs of an artistic organization. Artistic boards often include lawyers and accountants, who are often recruited to serve a specific function, but who tend to remain on long enough to achieve positions of power.

Busy businesspeople serve on boards for a number of reasons. They may perceive their serving as a civic responsibility. Others may see it as an opportunity to wield power at a board level, something they are not allowed to do in their own organizations. Membership on a board allows people to widen their social and business contacts; this can be important to lawyers and accountants, who are limited in their freedom to advertise. One common motivation for businesspeople to join arts boards is the opportunity to mingle with luminaries in the arts. Here is one view of their performance:

> It has often been charged that many a hard-headed businessman loses his business sense on entering a meeting of an arts board. Lacking a profit motive to guide the affairs of the organization, businessmen who serve on arts boards sometimes feel unsure of themselves and their expertise. Compounding this problem is the inclination on the part of arts organizations to consider themselves a breed apart, outside the realm of normal business practice. But whether a company manufactures widgets or mounts exhibitions, the basic business concerns remain the same: strategic planning, good marketing, adequate financing, and competent management are essential to any enterprise.[3]

Theatre Management   In addition to the artistic director, whose role and relationship with the board were described above, there is usually a general manager who is responsible for the business affairs of the organization. Since artistic directors strive for maximum quality, which is expensive, and since business managers have to find and account for the money to run the theatre, conflicts often occur. Not surprisingly, boards often side with the business manager because of their similarities of culture and values. Typically both artistic director and general manager report directly to the board.

MOUNTING A PRODUCTION

The theatre company selects "products" to suit its objectives and audiences. For example, a theatre might select a playbill of classics or children's plays. A regional theatre might select a Canadian play (to satisfy government grant-giving agencies),

---

[3] "Developing Effective Arts Boards," undated publication of The Council for Business and the Arts in Canada, pp. 28, 29.

a classic (to satisfy the artistic aspirations of the artistic director), a resounding "hit" from Broadway or England (to help sell the series), and one or more plays that have been successful elsewhere.

Each production requires a producer (who may be the artistic director) to act as the "entrepreneur" to put the show together.[4] He acquires the rights to the play, if it is not in the public domain, for a fee of 7 to 10 percent of the box office revenue. He also retains a director, who may be on staff or who may be a free-lance director retained for the run of the play. In the latter case, minimum scale would be $6,174.80 for a run of three weeks of rehearsal and three to four weeks of performance.

Casting is done, beginning with the major parts, on the basis of a uniform contract, which sets out fees (minimum of $416.27 per week for a major company), starting date, billing, working time, and "perks" (e.g., dressing room, accommodation).

Finally, a stage manager is contracted, as are designers for sets, costumes, and lighting. It is essential, of course, that all these people work well together.

The above describes the typical "stock," or subscription, company. However, Stratford and Shaw operate as "repertory" companies, hiring a group of actors for one or more seasons, and allocating roles among the members of the company. Repertory companies typically sell tickets for individual plays, while subscription companies sell their series at the beginning of the season, with few single tickets.

Lead times are considerable; in Stratford, for example, plays that open in May are firmly cast by the previous December, and the entire season is planned by March, when rehearsals begin.

THEATRE LONDON

Background

The Grand Opera House was opened in London on September 9, 1901, by Ambrose J. Small, a Toronto theatrical entrepreneur and frustrated producer. It quickly became the showcase of Small's theatrical chain, opening with such attractions as the Russian Symphony Orchestra, and later offering such performers as Barry Fitzgerald, Bela Lugosi, Clifton Webb, Sidney Poitier, and Hume Cronyn. Small sold his theatre chain in 1919, deposited a million dollars in his bank, and disappeared. There has been no explanation to this day; however, Small's ghost is said to haunt the Grand.

Famous Players bought the theatre in 1924, tore out the second balcony, and converted the theatre to a cinema. They sold to The London Little Theatre for a token amount in 1945, and the building housed an amateur community theatre until the spring of 1971. The theatre employed professional business management and a professional artistic director, but the actors were all amateur. Some of London's leading citizens acted in plays, and some even displayed a high level of competence. The theatre was prominent in the social life of the city and attracted one of the largest subscription sales in North America, both as a percentage of available seats

---

[4] Harry Chartrand, Research Director, "An Economic Impact Assessment of the Canadian Fine Arts," The Canada Council, February 1, 1984, p. 77.

and in absolute terms. It also achieved a reputation for a very high level of quality, given that it was essentially an amateur theatre. Articles about the theatre appeared in such magazines as *Life*. However, there was some concern in the theatre that the level of quality was as high as it was going to get as a company of amateurs, and that the community deserved, and was ready to support, a professional theatre. Another local organization, the London Symphony, had engaged a conductor with an international reputation and was changing from an amateur to a professional orchestra. An active art gallery association was formed to work toward providing London with a major art gallery. Although strong objections were raised against the proposal for a professional theatre, particularly because of the increased financial burden, the risk, and the denial to many of the theatre's supporters of an opportunity to participate in their hobby of acting, London Little Theatre changed to Theatre London in 1971 under Artistic Director Heinar Piller. The progressives were vindicated, as theatregoers in London and area were treated to a decade of artistically and financially successful theatre.

Piller was succeeded, at the end of the 1975 season, by William Hutt, who had achieved great success as an actor at Stratford and was well known to Londoners. He served from 1976 to 1978. Bernard Hopkins arrived in 1979 and was artistic director until May 1983.

The Grand was attractively and authentically renovated at a cost of $5.5 million, reopening in the fall of 1978, after being closed for a full season. (The company had a reduced season during that time in small, rented accommodations.) During the renovation, seating capacity was reduced from 1,100 to 845.

Theatre London ran successful stock seasons from 1979 to 1982. The 1981–82 season was particularly successful, operating at 85 percent of capacity. Eighty percent of its tickets were sold through subscription to some 13,431 subscribers. Financial statements are shown in Exhibits 3 and 4.

THE LONDON ENVIRONMENT

London was founded at the forks of the Thames River in 1793 by Governor Simcoe with the intention of making it the capital of Upper Canada. Instead, it became the cultural and commercial center of southwestern Ontario. Located on three railroad lines and on Highway 401, which serves the Quebec–Windsor corridor, London also has a major airport served by two airlines. London is two hours away from Detroit or Toronto; however, it is in a major snow belt. London is a major retail center, with the second highest per capita retail capacity in North America. However, it serves as a trading area of almost a million people, although its own population is only 259,000—see Exhibit 5. There are four hotels near the core area and motels in outlying areas. Many interesting restaurants had opened with a great deal of excess capacity; a few restaurants closed or changed hands.

There is little heavy industry in London, but there is a major university, a community college, a teacher's college, and two small church-affiliated colleges. Four major hospitals serve a wide area and provide teaching facilities for the university medical school and dental school. In addition to being a retail center, London is the home of major financial institutions and agribusiness firms, as well as a major brewery.

Exhibit 3   Theatre London, Condensed Five-Year Operating Results

Revenue	June 30, 1979	June 30, 1980	June 30, 1981	June 30, 1982	June 30, 1983 (estimate)
Productions					
Ticket sales	$ 551,650	$ 585,938	$ 620,313	$ 664,058	$1,100,000
Sponsored programs	26,000	25,000	26,500	9,000	9,000
Program advertising	17,283	17,270	19,652	24,241	24,000
	594,933	628,208	666,465	697,299	1,133,000
Grants					
Canada Council	145,000	163,000	173,000	185,000	210,000
Ontario Arts Council	145,000	152,000	160,000	170,000	180,000
Wintario	89,254	—	—	—	—
City of London	12,500	—	—	—	—
Cultural Initiative Program	—	—	25,000	—	—
	391,754	315,000	358,000	355,000	390,000
Other					
Operating fund drive	41,222	27,462	182,559	183,188	160,000
Special projects	36,811	36,525	43,881	41,281	65,000
Interest	34,553	50,608	62,128	86,106	80,000
Concessions	33,500	75,073	69,581	62,065	78,000
Theatre school	8,720	17,687	19,481	—	—
Box office commissions	3,319	3,721	651	6,142	3,000
Theatre rental and miscellaneous	3,170	—	—	4,704	2,000
	161,295	211,076	378,281	383,486	388,000
Total revenue	$1,147,982	$1,154,284	$1,402,946	$1,435,785	$1,911,000
Expenses					
Public relations	$ 179,880	$ 128,502	$ 139,907	$ 177,267	$ 270,000
Administration	91,973	115,798	162,723	167,749	330,000
Production overhead	190,911	237,606	282,270	339,474	350,000
Productions	466,906	414,644	416,440	421,151	780,000
Front of house, box office, and concessions	75,563	123,910	107,617	126,673	140,000
Facility operation	131,445	139,215	152,153	142,061	140,000
Theatre school	9,742	20,832	34,804	—	—
Total	1,146,420	1,180,507	1,295,914	1,374,375	2,010,000
Excess of revenue over expense	$ 1,562	$ (26,223)	$ 107,032	$ 61,410	$ (99,000)
Alternate Expense Compilation					
Salaries, fees, and benefits	$ 658,507	$ 754,109	$ 791,954	$ 823,260	$1,100,000†
Supplies and expenses	487,913	426,398	503,960	551,115	910,000
	$1,146,420	$1,180,507	$1,295,914	$1,374,375	$2,010,000

† In addition, development costs for the establishment of a repertory company in the 1983–1984 season could be incurred which could be largely offset by federal and provincial grants.

Exhibit 4 Condensed Balance Sheets, Theatre London, 1979–1982

	June 30, 1979	June 30, 1980	June 30, 1981	June 30, 1982
Assets				
Current assets:				
Cash and term deposits	$351,010	$372,868	$325,631	$316,939
Accounts receivable	3,908	13,957	35,208	10,916
Inventory	7,463	7,146	6,050	
Prepaid expenses	20,257	32,788	46,938	72,471
Total assets	$382,638	$426,759	$413,827	$400,326
Liabilities and Surplus				
Current liabilities:				
Bank loan		$ 25,000		
Accounts payable	$ 26,253	24,041	$ 30,112	$ 67,198
Advance ticket sales	280,431	324,524	319,843	302,983
Advance grants	1,060		15,201	14,805
Payable to Theatre London Foundation		4,523		15,340
	307,744	378,088	365,156	400,326
Surplus	74,894	48,671	48,671*	
Total liabilities and surplus	$382,638	$426,759	$413,827	$400,326

* In addition, there was equity of $453,080 from the Wintario Challenge Fund Program in 1981 and $807,289 in 1982. Under the terms of the program, Wintario will match two dollars for every eligible contributed dollar raised (during the three-year period ending June 30, 1983) in excess of 5.9 percent of the current year's operating expenses. All these matching contributions are placed in a separate investment fund for at least five years, although interest earned on the fund may be used for current operations.

London is also a major cultural center. In addition to Theatre London, London has a professional symphony orchestra and a couple of significant choral groups. The university has an active program of theatre and music, and the community is a center for visual artists. There are various commercial art galleries, an art gallery connected with the university, and a major public art gallery located in the city center. There are several museums, including a unique children's museum and a museum of Indian archaeology. The latter two attract visitors from a wide area.

THE GRAND THEATRE COMPANY

In late 1981, a decade after the company had become professional, concern was again raised in the theatre that the level of quality had stagnated, and the theatre would have to move in new directions. Bernard Hopkins was a superb actor and a competent artistic director. He had directed a few plays, rather than have to pay for a free-lance director, with some success. However, some members of the board believed that he had taken the theatre as far as he was able, and there was no initiative on either side to extend Hopkins' contract beyond its expiration in May 1983.

Exhibit 5   Selected Demographic Statistics for Canadian Metropolitan Areas

	Income Rating		1983 Per Capita Personal Disposable Income	
	Index	Rank	Dollar Amounts	Rank
Toronto	117	6	$12,693	7
Montreal	103	11	11,212	14
Vancouver	118	5	12,793	6
Ottawa-Hull	118	5	12,796	5
Edmonton	126	4	13,668	4
Calgary	132	1	14,324	1
Winnipeg	111	8	11,997	9
Quebec	98	14	10,623	18
Hamilton	112	7	12,114	8
St. Catharines	103	11	11,223	13
Kitchener	101	13	10,974	16
London	106	10	11,462	11
Halifax	101	13	10,923	17
Windsor	107	9	11,602	10
Regina	130	2	14,056	2
Saskatoon	129	3	14,021	3
Oshawa	106	10	11,450	12
Thunder Bay	102	12	11,089	15
Canada	100		10,851	

Note: This list shows all 18 census metropolitan areas in which the principal city had a population of at least 100,000 in the 1981 Census.

London-Centered Seven-County Market Area Data

	Seven Counties	Canada
Population, June 1, 1983 (thousands)	838.5	24,886.6
Ten-Year Growth Rate	5.7%	12.0%
Households (June 1, 1983)	293.7	8,335.0
Wage Earner Average Income (1981)	$14,522	$15,141
Per Capita Disposable Income (1983)	$10,669	$10,851
Per Capita Retail Sales (1983)	$ 4,238	$ 4,153

Source: Canadian Markets, 1984, and 1981 income tax returns.

A planning committee, under one of the board members, addressed the issue of continuing the growth in quality. They conducted a number of retreats and interviewed experts in professional theatre as well as officers of The Canada Council and The Ontario Arts Council. During the course of the investigation, they interviewed Robin Phillips. Phillips had been artistic director at The Stratford Festival and was well known to Barbara Ivey (who served on both the Stratford and Theatre London boards) and to other Theatre London directors. He also had directed, with considerable artistic success, two productions for Theatre London: *The Lady of the Camellias* and *Long Day's Journey into Night*.

Robin Phillips   Robin Phillips is a highly talented artistic director and a person of incredible charm. (In *all* of the interviews conducted by the casewriter, words like *charm, charisma,* and *talent* abounded). Actress Martha Henry said, "Once you've worked with Robin, it's almost impossible to work for anyone else."

He came to Canada from England in 1974 to plan the 1975 Stratford season, although he would not direct any specific plays until 1976. His tenure at Stratford has been described as successful but stormy. When he was contracting to direct a production for The Canadian Opera Company in 1976, he said he would not renew his Stratford contract unless he had more evidence of support for his ambition to make Stratford the focus of Canadian theatre, with film and television productions as well as live theatre. He received a five-year contract to run from November 1, 1976; the contract could be terminated with four months' notice.

There was a series of resignations from, and returns to, Stratford starting in July 1978, until Phillips' departure in 1981. In addition to his Stratford activities, Phillips was involved with theatre in Calgary, New York, Toronto's Harbourfront, and Vancouver. He also filmed *The Wars,* a novel by Timothy Findley. It was generally understood that he was seeking a theatre in Toronto to serve as a base for his stage, film, and television ambitions. However, none was available.

The Phillips Plan   Robin Phillips had a plan for Theatre London and would only come if he had a budget to fulfill his plan and complete artistic autonomy. His plan called for raising Theatre London from 18th place in Canadian theatre to 3rd.

The plan required a budget of $4.7 million, up from $1.9 million. This included $400,000 of capital cost to improve the Grand's facilities. Box office and concessions would provide 73 percent of the budget, 18 percent would come from donations, 5 percent from the Canada Council, and 4 percent from the Ontario Arts Council. Revenue projections were based on playing to 80 percent of capacity; this was considered feasible because Phillips had surpassed that performance at Stratford, and Theatre London had been operating at 85 percent. The theatre requested a permanent tax exemption from the city of London; the deputy mayor described this request as "cavalier."

Three of the stage productions would be adapted for television and filmed by Primedia Productions of Toronto. This would provide some $100,000 of additional revenue for each production, as well as audience exposure.

Robin Phillips strongly favored a repertory company over a subscription policy. He believed, and often stated, that subscriptions denied audiences a choice, and audiences must learn to discriminate. A change had to be made to make the theatre different, special, and exciting. A repertory company would provide a company of salaried actors who could not be lured away during the season, and who would be attracted by steady employment.

Another advantage of the repertory concept is the flexibility afforded patrons, who may choose the dates they see a play and their seat locations.

In a subscription series, patrons are restricted to the same seat location on the same night for each performance. In repertory theatre several productions are typically run simultaneously.

The Playbill   Phillips proposed to offer these plays on the main stage (in addition to a children's program in a small, secondary theatre):

- *Godspell,* by John-Michael Tebelak—A rousing rock musical with audience appeal, especially for younger audiences.
- *The Doctor's Dilemma,* by George Bernard Shaw—An established, classical "hit."
- *Waiting for the Parade,* by John Murrell—A Canadian play, with an all female cast, showing what women did while their men were fighting World War II.
- *Timon of Athens,* by William Shakespeare—A little performed, little known Shakespearean play, ignored by Stratford.
- *The Club,* by Eve Merrian—A musical spoof of men's clubs, with a female cast playing the part of men.
- *Arsenic and Old Lace,* by Joseph Kesselring—A well-known classic comedy of American theatre.
- *The Prisoner of Zenda,* adapted by Warren Graves—A comedy of political intrigue and romance, set in a mythical Eastern European kingdom.
- *Hamlet,* by William Shakespeare—One of his best known plays.
- *Dear Antoine,* by Jean Anouilh—A comedy by a leading contemporary French playwright.

Casting for these plays would not be a problem, as leading actors from Canada, the United States, and England were eager to work with Phillips.

Pricing   Since the plan envisioned a box office yield of $3.2 million, up from the $1.2 million planned for the 1982–83 season, revenue would have to be increased in two ways. The number of productions would be increased, with nine productions in the season instead of the previous six. There would be a record 399 performances, instead of the 230 performances in the 1982–83 season. Thus the plan projected an audience of 217,000, compared with the 137,000 planned for the 1982–83 season. In addition, prices would be increased.

A subscriber in the 1982–83 season could see five plays for $55 on weekends or $45 on weekdays. The pricing schedule proposed for the 1983–84 repertory season was:

Number of Seats	Price	
	Weekdays	Weekends
178	$20	$22.50
245	14.50	15.50
422	10.50	12.50

Promotion   Since the theatre would require an expanded audience from a wider area, the plan envisioned a program of investment spending in major area newspapers: *The Toronto Star* and *Globe and Mail,* the *Kitchener–Waterloo Record,* and the *Detroit Free Press,* as well as the *London Free Press.* The advertising would be directed at a first-time audience.

Group sales would be stressed, particularly to schools. Hotel-restaurant-transportation-theatre ticket packages were planned to attract theatre-goers from neighboring areas.

THE DECISION

The directors were impressed by the charm and the reputation of Robin Phillips. The proposal to hire Phillips—and to accept his plan—was supported by board members who had sound business backgrounds and who had worked in theatre for some years. They had a comfortable, modern theatre, with a recently acquired computer to issue tickets. They had a proven record in selling tickets, as did Robin Phillips.

On the other hand, if Phillips were hired, his artistic strengths might not be matched administratively. There was an administrative director who had been there for only two years, and a chief accountant, but no controller. And Stratford, Canada's leading theatre, was less than an hour's drive down the road.

CASE 9   BIODEL, INC. (A) *

Dr. Oscar Feldman, founder and president of Biodel, Inc., sat back for a moment and reflected. The year 1979 had recently ended. It had been a constructive 12 months for his small biotechnology company, yet Feldman knew that several difficult strategic choices loomed before him in 1980.

Biodel stood at an enviable crossroad. Feldman was confident that Biodel had distinct competencies in its current biotechnologies. These competencies currently provided the company with competitive advantages on which the president had resolved to capitalize. Should the company pursue the significant growth prospects in these current technologies—cell biology, molecular biology, and immunodiagnostics? Or should the company expand its technological focus to include genetic engineering, a field poised at the threshold of exciting advances? If Biodel were to pursue genetic engineering, how should it do so?

Finally, Feldman wondered if Biodel had sufficient personnel and funds to pursue an aggressive strategy.

COMPANY BACKGROUND

Oscar Feldman was originally from Scotland, where his father had been a successful businessman. After a McGill Chemistry PhD and postdoctoral work at Harvard Medical School, Dr. Feldman taught at Stanford University. His work there centered on applying chemistry to biological and medical problems, including cancer research. During his 11 years at Stanford, Dr. Feldman published almost 100 papers, enjoyed widespread popularity, and established a base of contacts in the academic community which he valued highly.

Biodel was founded in 1962 shortly after Dr. Feldman obtained a contract for research which he felt could be executed more effectively in a commercial setting. The contract required the combination of several disciplines, including chemistry, biochemistry, biology, and enzymology, in order to obtain the best results. In an effort to cover initial working capital and facilities requirements for the start-up, Dr. Feldman raised $50,000 from local businessmen. He considered seeking a larger sum but decided that he would rather remain the principal shareholder of a smaller enterprise.

Dr. Feldman's initial business objective for Biodel was simply to establish a position of technological leadership in the biomedical industry. A key to his strategy was the leveraging of his academic contacts. Dr. Feldman relied on his contacts at Stanford,

* Prepared by Jeffrey Crowe under the supervision of Modesto A. Maidique, associate professor of engineering management, Stanford University. The case is based in part on an earlier ICCH (now HCS) case (Biodel, Inc. #9-681-004, Rev. 7/82) prepared by Mason Drew Haupt under the same supervisor. Reprinted from *Stanford Business Cases 1983* with permission of the Publishers, Stanford University Graduate School of Business, © 1983 by the Board of Trustees of the Leland Stanford Junior University.

for example, to bring on scientists to commence work on Biodel's first contract. He also planned to obtain additional government research contracts. Such contracts would provide Biodel with the financial support necessary to build technological leadership through the development of high-quality facilities and staff. Finally, Dr. Feldman began to assemble a small group of leading academics to advise Biodel. He stated at the time: "It is important to associate with none but the very best minds in the field."

During the start-up phase, Dr. Feldman held several views about his company's long-term strategy. Once Biodel had established itself in the contract research marketplace, he expected that the company would expand its focus. Dr. Feldman's exposure to his father's lumber business had convinced him that earning contract revenues and royalties would not be a sufficient long-term business base for Biodel. He envisioned a time when his company would manufacture and market biomedical products developed through its own research. Dr. Feldman was also wary of Biodel depending only on a few government agencies for its revenues. Marketing a product, he believed, would endow his company with a broad base of customers.

Despite slow but steady growth throughout the 1960s, Dr. Feldman's fears about dependence on government contracts were eventually realized. (See Exhibit 1.) In the early 1970s government cutbacks resulted in the loss of Biodel contracts with the Surgeon General, the Quartermaster Corps, and other agencies. At the time, the government had been responsible for 85 percent of Biodel's revenues. Biodel was forced into its first layoff, which troubled Dr. Feldman greatly. He considered the technological expertise of his employees to be one of Biodel's significant assets and regarded layoffs as damaging to the company's long-term potential.

This period of cutbacks and layoffs was a crucial point in the company's history. Biodel faced the threat of bankruptcy. Dr. Feldman later claimed that "It was a good thing I wasn't such a good businessman, otherwise I would have realized that Biodel was insolvent."

Concerns with its long-term survival caused Biodel in the early 1970s to move into the business of scientific research products, an area which Dr. Feldman had not originally anticipated. Biodel's scientific research products, numbering approxi-

---

Exhibit 1　Biodel's Financial History

Fiscal Year	Revenues	Net Income	Net Income as a Percent of Revenues
1962	$ 250,000	$ 5,000	2%
1965	510,000	45,000	9
1968	619,000	31,000	5
1969	647,000	59,000	9
1970	352,000	(32,000)	−8
1971	289,000	(44,000)	−11
1972	394,000	26,000	7
1973	460,000	15,000	3
1974	583,000	49,000	8
1975	748,000	62,000	8
1976	1,011,000	88,000	9

mately 500, were initially items which the company produced to utilize in its own research efforts. Biodel discovered, however, that biochemists and molecular biologists in other organizations also needed such research products, yet often lacked the technical expertise to make them. Biodel found a ready market for various reagents and synthetic nucleic acids which it had been using internally. Relying on word of mouth as its basic marketing tool, Biodel generated enough demand for its research products to reverse the sharp decline in revenues from lost contracts. The company was so successful in commercializing research products throughout the 1970s that research products constituted approximately 60 percent of the company's revenues by 1980.

In January 1980, Biodel conducted all of its research and development at a 14,000-square-foot, leased location in Menlo Park, California. Due to the rapid growth of the late 1970s, quarters in the aging building were becoming cramped and Dr. Feldman knew that he had to start looking for additional space soon.

TECHNOLOGIES AND PRODUCTS

By the end of the 1970s, Biodel had developed special expertise in three areas of biotechnology: molecular biology, cell biology, and immunology. The company conducted research and sold research products to scientists working in each of the three areas.

All of Biodel's researchers were in some way studying cells, which are the basic biological units of life. Each cell possesses the biochemical machinery to grow and reproduce. An important component of this machinery is nucleic acid, a form of which is deoxyribonucleic acid (DNA). DNA is a relatively large molecule which consists of small building blocks called nucleotides. Specific arrangements of nucleotides, called genes, determine the production of specific proteins through a sequence of steps aided by biocatalysts called enzymes. Proteins provide the machinery by which cells utilize nutrients to grow and reproduce.

The techniques of *molecular biology* have played a leading role in determining the molecular structure and function of DNA and relating this structure to the production of proteins. In 1980 Biodel was using the techniques of molecular biology to isolate and prepare biologically active substances, such as nucleic acids and enzymes. The company then marketed the products to other researchers in molecular biology and genetic engineering.

Cell culture technology, a technique of *cell biology,* concerns itself with the growth of mammalian cells. Such cells have stringent nutrition requirements normally supplied by serum, the fluid portion of the blood. In this area, Biodel was primarily involved in manufacturing and marketing cell growth factors, products which could be used, either partially or completely, to replace serum in helping cells to grow. Adequate quantities of uniformly high-quality serum (usually derived from horses, pigs, and calves) were proving difficult for researchers to obtain. Thus, Biodel had enjoyed increasing success in the late 1970s in selling its cell growth factors to scientists who could not locate serum for use in their cell proliferation research. By 1980 Biodel's pioneering efforts had paid off. The company dominated the growth factor market with about a 60 percent share.

Biodel's third area of special expertise was *immunodiagnostics.* Immunodiagnostics is one field within immunology, which is the study of how organisms protect themselves against infection. When foreign substances (antigens) are introduced into an organism, the organism responds by producing antibodies which bond themselves to the antigens. The presence of a specific antigen in a sample may be measured by adding to the sample a known level of antigen which has been radioactively tagged. The radioactive antigen competes with the sample's antigen for the antibodies in the sample. By measuring the residual radioactive antigen not attached to the antibodies, the level of antigen in the sample can be accurately estimated. Biodel had research expertise and a small product line in radioactive immunodiagnostic products.

CURRENT ORGANIZATION

Contract Research

During the 1970s, Biodel reported its revenues in two lines: contract research and research products. (See Exhibit 2.) The contract research activities were projected to generate $1 million in revenues in fiscal 1980. Seventy percent of those revenues related to industrial research, the two prime customers being a large pharmaceutical company and a large chemical company. The government accounted for the remaining 30 percent of the contract research.

The scope of Biodel's contract research included work in the company's three primary areas of expertise (molecular biology, cell biology, and immunology) as well as in fields such as cancer chemotherapy, and enzymology. Within those areas the company offered its customers high-quality technical advice, numerous links to the scientific community, and a highly sophisticated contract research and development service with a record of many successes.

Dr. Feldman marketed Biodel's contract research efforts. He personally secured the contracts through his relationships with scientists in government and industry. Dr. Feldman also supervised the ongoing contract research activities. He managed the activities informally, preferring not to set exceedingly detailed milestones and budgets. He commented: "I consider my researchers to be professionals. I see no need for me to continually monitor them. Scientists are motivated by new technical challenges, not by heavy-handed supervision."

Research Products

Dr. Feldman expected sales of research products to reach $1.5 million in fiscal 1980. Research products consisted of three interrelated product lines corresponding to the company's three areas of scientific expertise: molecular biological products, cell biological products, and immunodiagnostic products. The product lines were generally sold to researchers in universities, private laboratories, and industrial firms. Despite a limited marketing effort, sales had been growing at a 35 percent clip over the last several years.

Exhibit 2   Selected Financial Data for Biodel, Inc., 1977–1980

	For Fiscal Years Ending August 31			
	1977	1978	1979	1980*
Revenues:				
Product sales	$ 598,941	$ 738,732	$1,153,749	$1,450,000
Contract revenue	754,207	836,385	730,942	1,000,000
Royalty and license income	—	—	—	50,000
Total revenue	1,353,148	1,575,117	1,884,691	2,500,000
Cost of revenue:				
Cost of product sales	271,225	324,781	489,091	750,000
Cost of contract revenue	550,652	659,480	667,548	800,000
Total cost of revenue	821,877	984,261	1,156,639	1,550,000
Gross profit	531,271	590,856	728,052	950,000
Operating expenses:				
Research and development	146,228	193,285	274,224	200,000
Selling, general, and administrative	205,592	245,475	436,057	650,000
Total operating expenses	351,820	438,760	710,281	850,000
Net interest income	—	—	2,000	—
Income before income taxes	179,451	152,096	19,771	110,000
Income taxes	81,400	56,200	2,000	10,000
Net income	$ 98,051	$ 95,896	$ 17,771	$ 100,000
Net income per common share	$.08	$.08	$.01	$.07
Common shares outstanding	1,351,875	1,351,875	1,351,875	1,351,875
Working capital	$ 449,209	$ 485,587	$ 476,698	$ 325,000
Total assets	$ 803,238	$ 875,063	$ 965,559	$1,400,000
Long-term debt, including capital lease obligations	$ 127,095	$ 108,414	$ 114,732	$ 30,000
Stockholders' investment	$ 433,233	$ 529,129	$ 546,900	$ 650,000

* Estimated.

In the area of molecular biology, Biodel prepared and stocked the largest commercially available selection of synthetic nucleotides. Researchers used nucleotides as substitutes and primers for nucleic acid enzymes, as reference compounds for sequence analysis in studies of nucleic acids, for the development of new separation techniques, and as tools in recombinant DNA research. Nucleotides accounted for 50 percent of the sales of all research products (Exhibit 3).

Cell growth factors, Biodel's primary product offspring in the cell biology field, generated 40 percent of the research product revenues. Sales of cell growth factors had risen rapidly over the past several years, and Dr. Feldman believed that they represented a fertile area for future growth. There did exist disagreement within the company's management team, however, over the company's current competitive position in cell growth factors. Dr. Feldman considered Biodel to be the technological leader, yet several top employees believed that this assessment might be too optimistic. All did agree, however, that they lacked the necessary market research data to back their conclusions with confidence.

Exhibit 3   Biodel's Research Product Sales

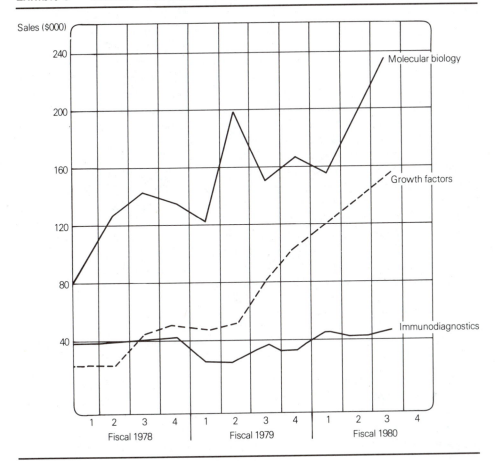

Biodel had been a major factor in the immunodiagnostics market for several years until several large firms aggressively entered the field and slashed the company's market share. The product line had not expanded since that time and constituted 10 percent of the sales of research products in 1980. Further significant growth in radioactive diagnostic products was not considered likely.

Profitability for these research products varied, depending upon the intensity of the product's research and development. Operating profit margins, after charges for product cost, research and development, and marketing, were estimated at 20 percent in the aggregate. Biodel's current accounting system, however, did not provide product-by-product profitability data and aggregate data was clouded by overhead allocations that in the opinion of some managers were "arbitrary."

Personnel

Biodel was organized along lines of scientific expertise (Exhibit 4). The three operating groups—molecular biology, cell biology, and immunodiagnostics—were each under the control of a manager who reported directly to Dr. Feldman. All three managers were experienced scientists who were longtime employees of the company. Each manager supervised R&D and production and held some marketing responsibility. The organization within each operating group was highly fluid. Generally, those scientists who completed research on a particular product would then turn to manufacturing the product in small quantities and would also determine which scientists in other organizations would be likely customers for that product.

From the standpoint of staff, Dr. Feldman had kept Biodel a lean organization. Biodel had 55 employees, most of whom were scientists or technicians. The company employed neither a marketing manager nor a research director. Dr. Feldman filled both roles due to his widespread contacts and scientific expertise. All of Biodel's financial functions were handled by an accountant who was also a longtime employee. Insofar as Dr. Feldman perceived major strategic, financial, or administrative issues, he invariably made the decisions himself. He rarely convened staff meetings and did not require regular reports from his subordinates. Dr. Feldman considered his management style well-fitted to Biodel's organization and atmosphere:

> We are a paternalistic company. I believe in management by walking around and talking to people. That's the best way for me to stay on top of what is happening. I don't want our employees tied up in paper shuffling. And anyway, professional management, goals, budgets, and meetings are not my "schtik."

One employee characterized Biodel's board of directors as "Dr. Feldman and his friends." The board consisted of four members, including Dr. Feldman. A corporate lawyer, age 79, sat on the board. He had been involved with the company since its founding. Dr. Feldman had also wanted scientific expertise on the board and had persuaded a gifted Stanford scientist, now retired, to join him. The fourth member was an associate of Dr. Feldman who was an officer of an investment banking firm. The board was convened infrequently, whenever Dr. Feldman felt a need to discuss the company's affairs.

From the standpoint of the researchers, Biodel was an exciting place to work. Dr. Feldman believed that he placed heavy pressure on his researchers and in return offered them projects at the cutting edge of technology. Although Biodel's equipment was not the most sophisticated and the company's quarters were spartan, the work itself was more challenging and fruitful than that of many commercial labs. In fact, employees likened the company's atmosphere to one of an academic facility. They considered the combination of informality and high challenge to be attractive. Turnover among employees, especially the senior technical people, was extremely low. The technical staff expressed pride in the company's work, and one referred to the firm's reputation as the "Cadillac of the industry." Dr. Feldman, who had distinct automotive preferences, preferred to refer to it as the "Mercedes of the industry."

A second reason for the low turnover was Oscar Feldman himself. Dr. Feldman was generally regarded as the hub of Biodel's universe. The senior employees were

Exhibit 4   Biodel's Organization Chart

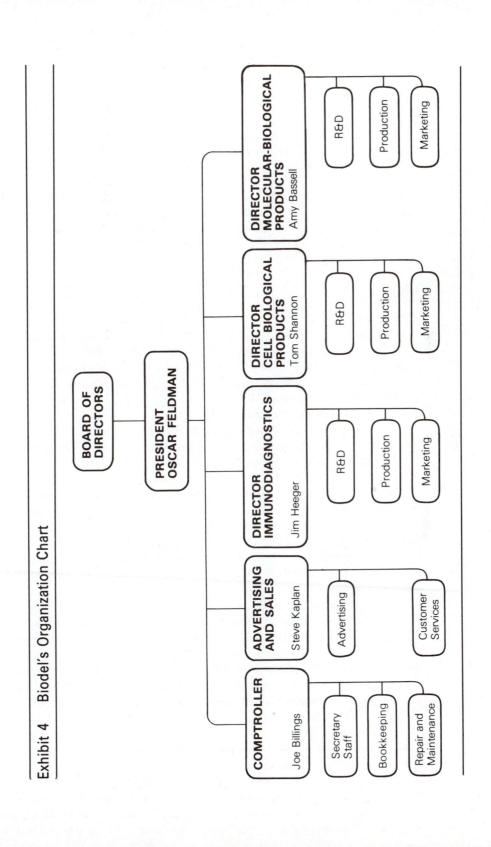

unanimous in their affection for the president. One of the senior scientist explained the phenomenon as follows:

> Simply put, Oscar is an attractive man. His warmth and effusiveness is infectious. He is so naturally witty and charming that you can't help but enjoy working with him. Oscar gets so enthusiastic about the work that it's contagious.

A senior manager added:

> Oscar is unique. Irrespective of the situation, he never fails to appear distinguished. He wears perfectly tailored suits, drives a stately old convertible, and has impeccable manners. He also looks remarkably trim and healthy for his age. There are not too many people still skiing avidly at age 65. True, sometimes he'll forget a fact or two, but he can also be extraordinarily articulate.

Marketing

Throughout the 1970s Biodel's marketing effort was an informal mixture of different activities. Research products were sold by mail, with customers typically having heard of the company through word of mouth. Trade shows, advertising, direct mail, and phone solicitation were also employed from time to time. Order processing and shipping were handled informally, without much emphasis on control. Dr. Feldman cited Biodel's customer service as "almost laughable."

In 1979 Dr. Feldman determined that the company needed to market its research products more aggressively and systematically. He decided that he needed someone who had familiarity both with the sales function and with biotechnology. In May 1979, he hired Steve Kaplan, who had been marketing manager at a large pharmaceutical company.

Tension eventually developed between Dr. Feldman and his new manager. Dr. Feldman wanted Kaplan only to organize a sales effort and gather information on customers and competitors. He still felt that he should direct Biodel's marketing strategy himself. Kaplan, on the other hand, perceived a need for focus in the company's marketing strategy. In addition, he concluded that Biodel was understaffed and proceeded to hire additional salespeople, an administrative assistant, an order clerk, and a secretary.

The results were mixed. Sales of research products increased 65 percent in the first quarter of fiscal 1980, an achievement for which Kaplan took credit. In addition, the customer service function began to respond more systematically to shipment delays and other problems. On the other hand, marketing costs increased 500 percent, resulting in sharply reduced profits despite the jump in sales. Dr. Feldman began to wonder if his marketing group was too large for Biodel, given its size and stage of development. He also began to question Steve Kaplan's tendency to make solo decisions regarding the company's marketing direction.

GROWTH OPPORTUNITIES

While Dr. Feldman was satisfied with the course Biodel had taken over the past 10 years, he knew that important choices remained to be made. Several of his top scientists were excited about two of the company's new product developments in cell biology and immunodiagnostics. At the same time, interest was building rapidly in scientific and financial circles in genetic engineering. The new genetic engineering technology was closely related to Biodel's expertise in molecular biology and could be a natural extension of the company's scientific focus. Each of the growth opportunities looked attractive, and Dr. Feldman wondered how he should decide which path to pursue.

Cell Biology

Based on its experience and expertise in using cell growth factors as components of serum substitutes, Biodel had under development several synthetic sera which were formulated to satisfy the growth requirements of a variety of cell lines in tissue culture. The synthetic serum substitutes would replace natural fetal calf serum, which was currently the most widely used source of growth for cells. Horse serum was second in market importance. The price and quality of fetal calf serum had been unstable over time because the availability of the product depended upon the slaughter of cattle, which tended to be cyclical. Biodel's researchers projected the market for fetal calf serum at about $50 million domestically in 1980 and $80 million worldwide and growing at 15 percent a year. Biodel believed that the market for synthetic sera of uniformly high quality and reliable supply would be even larger. However, these numbers were somewhat speculative, for the firm had not conducted a systematic analysis of the serum market.

Dr. Feldman believed that the company would have a competitive edge in synthetic sera which would be difficult for other firms to overcome. This advantage would allow Biodel to achieve a market share of up to 20 percent of the current market. The sera would be produced by adding to distilled water certain combinations of cell growth factors which would not be easy to break down and analyze. Even if a competitor could break the combinations down, Dr. Feldman believed that developments in this scientific discipline could not be quickly duplicated. It might require several years between the time a firm initially studied an area and the time it commercialized a product. Dr. Feldman was not certain whether other firms were currently pursuing the same course as his company. Finally, Biodel planned to cement its advantage by applying for patent protection, although it was by no means certain that a patent could be obtained.

Tom Shannon, the cell biology manager, felt that Biodel could eventually produce the synthetic sera at costs which would allow it to price the products competitively with fetal calf serum. At this point, Shannon guessed that a $1–2 million investment would be needed in manufacturing facilities. Dr. Feldman thought that the company would also need additional management personnel to oversee the venture. Both he and Tom Shannon were unsure as to just how best to market the product and what product introduction and marketing costs would likely be.

Immunodiagnostics

Within immunodiagnostics lay another opportunity for Biodel to enter markets vastly larger than its current customer base in research organizations. The company had under development a new testing technology based on enzyme membranes rather than radioactivity. Jim Heeger, the immunodiagnostics manager, expected that the new product (called DEMA) would have many applications in clinical, medical, environmental and industrial testing. The product could determine the presence and level of many substances, including hormones, enzymes, drugs, viruses, and bacteria. The tests could include, among others, those for pregnancy, syphilis, hepatitis, cancer, toxins in food, and carcinogens in the environment.

Heeger considered DEMA an alternative to tests based on radioactivity. It appeared to share the high sensitivity of radioactive tests without the drawbacks and hazards associated with radioactivity. In addition, Heeger believed that DEMA tests would be simpler, faster, and less expensive than radioactive tests. Other enzyme-linked immunodiagnostic technologies, such as EMIT and ELISA, were already in existence, but Heeger judged them to be less sensitive and applicable to fewer substances than DEMA. The company had filed for patent protection and had been encouraged to believe by its patent attorneys that a patent for the technology would be forthcoming.

As with synthetic sera, the market for DEMA test appeared to be vast, perhaps in excess of $100 million. One analyst's estimate placed the potential home market at over $1 billion. Again, however, Dr. Feldman and his subordinates were unsure how to bring the product to the marketplace. Investments in the necessary manufacturing and marketing facilities and personnel could easily total in the millions. Further R&D costs would range from $1 to $3 million. On the other hand, several large drug companies had expressed an interest in exploring a joint venture or licensing agreement. Under such conditions license percentages ranged from 4 percent to 7 percent, depending on the fraction of R&D costs funded by the sponsoring firm. Dr. Feldman wanted Biodel to have some manufacturing and marketing capability, but he did not know how much of the marketplace his company could feasibly pursue on its own. One possibility was to have Biodel target the clinical diagnostics market, which was limited and well defined. Medical clinics would be a logical place to introduce the new DEMA technology. On the other hand, drugstore sales of DEMA potentially could generate enormous revenues and would be best pursued in conjunction with a partner that had an established distribution system and brand name. Pharmacies greatly outnumbered clinics, and DEMA would easily have numerous applications in the vast consumer markets.

Genetic Engineering

Dr. Feldman saw genetic engineering as a third opportunity for Biodel's expansion. The company currently had no direct expertise in the field, although it was closely associated with genetic engineering laboratories by virtue of its work as a supplier of molecular biology products. The nucleotides and synthetic genes which Biodel produced and sold were used as support products by genetic engineers. In some cases, Biodel was the sole supplier.

The opportunity for Biodel to move into genetic engineering itself arose through Dr. Feldman's contacts. Dr. Daniel Ballantine, a University of California, Berkeley Nobel Laureate and a pioneer in genetic engineering, was a longtime friend of Dr. Feldman and a consultant to Biodel. He had risen to prominence in the 1970s, and for the last two years he had been suggesting to Dr. Feldman that genetic engineering offered Biodel explosive opportunities for growth. Dr. Feldman began to consider seriously his associate's recommendations when he noticed an intensive interest developing in financial circles in the concept of genetic engineering.

The technology of genetic engineering is not complex in theory. To "engineer" a cell to produce a specific product, DNA containing the desired sequence must be isolated. The desired gene is either obtained from a biological source or is synthesized chemically. The gene is then spliced into a carrier molecule, called a vector, to form a recombinant DNA molecule. Control sequences which program the cell to produce the product coded by the gene are introduced into the vector, which itself could be a virus or a plasmid. The vector carries the new gene into the host cell, thereby programming the host cell to manufacture the desired product. The most widely used host cell has been Escherichia coli. or E. coli. (See the Appendix for more detailed technical explanation of the genetic engineering.) More is known about E. coli than about any other bacteria.

While the theory of genetic engineering may be easy to understand, the techniques have been difficult to perform. Procedures for isolating DNA and for utilizing vectors were not discovered until the early 1970s. By the mid-1970s, however, the academic world realized the future of gene splicing and many major universities launched DNA research programs. A critical breakthrough came in 1973 when Stanley Cohen of Stanford and Herb Boyer of the nearby University of California in San Francisco first chemically translated DNA from one species to another by gene splicing. In contrast, the commercialization of the technology began slowly. In 1971 Cetus was the only genetic research firm. Genentech and Bethesda Research Labs were founded in 1976, followed by Genex in 1977, and Biogen in 1978 (Exhibit 5). Venture capitalists and large pharmaceutical, chemical, and energy companies provided the financing for the start-up phases of the fledgling firms. The large corporate investors had two goals: (1) to establish a technological window in a potentially revolutionary technology and (2) to make a profitable investment.

The early investments were already generating large capital gains by 1979. In 1976 Inco purchased $400,000 of Genentech's stock, only to sell it to Lubrizol four years later for $5.2 million. In early 1980 Genentech estimated that the market value of its privately held stock exceeded $100 million—one half of which was owned by the company's officers, directors, and employees. A frenzy was enveloping the whole field of genetic engineering. Investors seemed willing to stake significant sums of money on almost any company who employed well-known scientists with connections to gene splicing. Financial journals continually touted genetic engineering's revolutionary potential to impact the manufacturing processes of products in the chemical, pharmaceutical, and petrochemical industries. The *New York Times* editorialized, "Recombinant DNA technology seems poised at the threshold of advances as important as antibiotics or electronic semiconductors." (January 19, 1980.)

Despite the euphoria surrounding genetic engineering, no firm had yet sold a genetically engineered product in mass quantities. Investors were lured by the prospects of production of a host of recombinant products, including pharmaceuticals, biologicals, chemicals, and fuels. Several firms had announced product capability—Biogen was making interferon; Genentech, interferon and insulin—but observers believed that years would transpire before any genetically engineered product generated significant revenues. The major pharmaceutical and chemical companies had set up their

---

Exhibit 5   The Four Pacesetting Genetic Engineering Firms

Genentech, Inc.

Headquarters: South San Francisco. Founded in 1976; 110 employees. Has announced more DNA-made products than competitors. Joint ventures with Eli Lilly for human insulin; with A. B. Kabi of Sweden for human growth hormone; with Hoffmann-La Roche for interferon. Half-owned by employees. Lubrizol, a lubricating oil company, holds 20 percent; venture capitalists own the rest.

Cetus Corporation

Headquarters: Berkeley, California. Founded in 1971; 250 employees. Concentrates on industrial and agricultural chemicals, also interferon. Joint ventures with Standard of California for chemicals and fruit sugar; with National Distillers for fuel alcohol. Founders, employees, and private investors own almost 40 percent; Standard California, 24 percent; National Distillers, 16 percent; Standard Indiana, 21 percent.

Genex Corporation

Headquarters: Rockville, Maryland. Founded in 1977; 50 employees. Concentrates on industrial chemicals. Has interferon research contract with Bristol-Myers; another contract with Koppers, a mining and chemicals company. Management owns about 45 percent; Koppers, 30 percent; InnoVen, a venture capital company backed by Monsanto and Emerson Electric, about 25 percent.

Biogen S.A.

Headquarters: Geneva, Switzerland. Founded in 1978; about a dozen employees, plus others under contract. First to make interferon. Schering-Plough, a New Jersey pharmaceutical company that owns 16 percent, plans to begin pilot production of the antiviral drug using Biogen's process. Inco, formerly International Nickel, owns 24 percent. Remainder held by management and various outside investors.

Source: *The New York Times,* June 29, 1980. Section 3, p. 1. Reprinted by permission.

---

own gene splicing departments, but they, as well as the small firms, had yet to understand the intricacies of production on a mass scale.

Amidst the mounting excitement over gene splicing's long-run potential, Dr. Feldman pondered Biodel's role. While the business of selling support products to the genetic engineering firms was expected to grow at a 30 percent–50 percent clip over the next several years, it held neither the glamour nor the potential for explosive expansion associated with genetic engineering. One of Biodel's competitors in the molecular biology products industry was quoted as saying: "Our market won't ever compare to the markets for genetically engineered products. After all, it only takes one dollar of our stuff to make a thousand or a million dollars of their stuff." Cetus was the world's biggest user of enzymes in its genetic engineering research, yet it could have bought one year's supply for $12,000. The market for synthetic nucleotides, enzymes, and the like seemed limited.

What Dr. Ballantine offered Biodel was a route to expand into genetic engineering itself. He proposed a novel approach to the problem of growing cells by using yeast organisms as hosts in place of the E. coli predominantly used by other genetic engineering firms. For the past two years, Dr. Ballantine had been collaborating with three other renowned scientists on the development of yeast as the host cell in the genetic engineering process. The four men believed that yeast cells would ultimately prove more attractive than E. coli for industrial applications of genetic engineering. Yeast cells were easier and less costly to grow and it was believed by Biodel scientists that they could be grown to higher yields and thus with lower costs than E. coli. In addition, yeast cells contained biochemical machinery, absent in E. coli, which allowed for the possibility of programming the yeast cells to produce glycoproteins (proteins which contained carbohydrates).

Interferon and urokinase were two examples of glycoproteins which, although currently produced by conventional extraction processes, could potentially be manufactured by yeast cells through genetic engineering techniques. Interferon was a protein which performed a regulatory function in the body; it appeared to inhibit the multiplication of viruses and cancerous tissue cells. Because of the extraordinary difficulty of producing it in large quantities through conventional techniques, interferon was highly valued in medical circles. In 1980 its price exceeded $1 billion per pound. Urokinase was an enzyme produced in the human body as an agent to dissolve blood clots. Sales of urokinase up to 1980 had been limited due to the complication and high cost of conventional extraction processes. Biodel had already had some experience producing urokinase through a tissue culture process and knew that several drug companies were interested in securing a large, stable supply of the enzyme if it could be genetically engineered. In short, Biodel scientists believed that genetic engineers using yeast might have an advantage over researchers using E. coli in producing both interferon and urokinase.

Dr. Ballantine indicated his willingness to convene his three colleagues with Dr. Feldman in order to discuss a possible association with Biodel. Dr. Ballantine and his friends were all experts in yeast genetics. Full professors at the nation's most distinguished university laboratories, the four had been elected to the National Academy of Sciences and had jointly won all of the coveted biochemistry and molecular genetics prizes in American science. Dr. Feldman was excited at the possibility of attracting them to Biodel. He commented:

> As a group, they have talents unsurpassed in genetic engineering. James Finney, Columbia's leading biochemist, possesses one of the most penetrating intellects I've come across. He is a mature scientist with unimpeachable integrity. He's the type of person you'd want at your side when the going gets tough. Ralph Davidson is noted among the scientists at Cal Tech for his brilliant creativity. Despite his quiet nature, he could make invaluable intellectual contributions to our activities. Dennis Bernstein generates more ideas than 10 scientists combined. His work at University of Wisconsin has earned acclaim throughout scientific circles. And of course, we have my good friend Daniel Ballantine. He is simply the best there is. If the four of them worked with us, it would give our company a tremendous edge. If even one of them joined us, we'd have an advantage over Genentech, Cetus, and the rest. However, if we plan to land any or all of them, we will have to make an extraordinary offer.

Indeed, all four individuals were in high demand. They had offers from large chemical and pharmaceutical companies for positions as senior scientists with salaries ranging from $75,000 to $100,000. Smaller biotechnology firms were luring them with stock option packages which included 1 percent to 4 percent of the companies' outstanding stock. Leading universities were proposing prestigious endowed chairs with unparalleled academic freedom and clout. Even venture capital firms had approached them, exploring the possibilities of a start-up. One venture capitalist had asserted that he could raise $5 million on the strength of Dr. Ballantine's reputation alone.

Biodel, however, was not without its attractions. The company could offer the scientists both the freedom to start up their own gene-splicing R&D operation and the expertise in key related areas. Biodel had placed itself at the leading edge of technology and had earned a position of respect in science. The scientists' ideas could be further developed and enhanced through an association with the company. Despite the intangible benefits, however, Dr. Feldman knew that he would also have to structure a lucrative financial package to lure them away, even on a consulting basis, from their well-established academic environments.

Although there was much uncertainty surrounding genetic engineering—estimates varied widely on market sizes and on the time required for successful refinement of production processes—Dr. Feldman hoped that Biodel would be able to quickly generate revenue if it secured the services of the four scientists. He felt that the company could land a gene-splicing research contract from one of several large corporations for $5 to $10 million over a period of five years. From such an arrangement Biodel could earn as much as a 25 percent margin after deduction for salaries, capital expenditures, and other associated costs. More important, the company would retain licensing rights at agreed-upon rates for potential products. In effect, Biodel would be conducting research at the expense of a commercial sponsor who sought to participate in genetic breakthroughs but who lacked the necessary technical capability.

ACTIONS TO BE TAKEN

Several routes lay open to Biodel at this point. Shannon was pushing to develop synthetic sera. He thought the company would lose any competitive edge it might have in cell biology if it did not bring the sera to market as soon as possible. Heeger, in contrast, pressed for more investment in DEMA. The immunodiagnostics manager argued that DEMA could reach the marketplace in a year if his group could obtain substantial additions in people and facilities. Both managers believed that Biodel could within reason meet whatever goals Dr. Feldman might set simply by pursuing the company's present product opportunities. They saw little reason to look elsewhere. Genetic engineering, on the other hand, represented a potentially lucrative expansion of Biodel's focus and a considerable boost to the company's prestige. Dr. Feldman was fascinated by the idea of having world-famous scientists officially and intimately associated with his firm.

No matter what course Biodel chose, tough financial decisions needed to be made. Development of synthetic sera was projected to cost more than $500,000; development of DEMA was estimated to be several times more expensive. On the advice of a finance professor at the Graduate School of Business at Stanford, Dr. Feldman held informal conversations with local bankers and venture capitalists. He discovered from the bankers that a loan above $500,000 would require his personal guarantee. One bank was willing to supply Biodel with as much as $1 million. In exchange, it wanted two points over the prime rate (currently 17 percent) and covenants restricting further debt, dividend payments, equity issues, and mergers and acquisitions. Venture capitalists generally expressed reluctance to invest in Biodel unless it strengthened its management team. One venture capital firm, however, tentatively offered Dr. Feldman $2 million for 40 percent of the company's equity. On January 1, 1980, Biodel had 1 million shares of common stock outstanding. Upon hearing the proposal, Dr. Feldman exclaimed that his company was worth many times more, prompting the investor to dryly remark that the financial community would not commit large sums of money simply for the potential of developing synthetic sera.

Another issue was the financial package that Biodel might offer to Dr. Ballantine and his cohorts. One alternative was to set up a separate subsidiary of Biodel, with all transactions between the parent and the subsidiary at arm's length. The four scientists would not work directly for the subsidiary, but they would act as an advisory board and recruit other top scientists to work for it. In return, they would receive a consulting fee and restricted stock in the subsidiary, which would vest over a four-year period at 25 percent per year. In this way the four could maintain their affiliation with their respective universities. The finance professor guessed that a per diem of $500 to $1,000 and ownership of 2 percent to 10 percent of the subsidiary for each of the scientists would be a reasonable range within which Dr. Feldman could make an offer.[1]

A second possibility was to hire one or more of the geneticists as employees of the company itself. Dr. Feldman knew that to employ the scientists directly he would have to match any salary and equity combination that another company might offer. This would pose a commitment larger than Dr. Feldman was used to for his own employees. Biodel's three managers currently earned salaries under $35,000, and their ownership of the company's stock jointly totaled less than 2 percent. Dr. Feldman owned over 80 percent of the outstanding stock. Friends, business associates, and relatives of Dr. Feldman owned another 10 percent. On the other hand, by hiring directly, Biodel would get at least one top scientist solely committed to the company's efforts and an immediate boost to its reputation. Dr. Feldman believed that one of the geneticists ought to be employed full-time if Biodel planned to set up and operate a significant genetic engineering operation. He was not certain, however, of how difficult it would be to entice one of the scientists away from his academic research on a full-time basis.

A third alternative was to retain the scientists as technical consultants. Biodel would pay them a per diem fee of $800–$1,200 in exchange for guidance on the company's current projects, proposals for new avenues of research, and recruitment of geneticists. In addition, the company would offer incentive agreements which would allot the scientists stock options on the basis of the company's performance. One possible measure of performance was revenue earned from genetic engineering contracts and products. The Stanford finance professor suggested the following proposal: Biodel would grant the scientists, as a group, options to purchase 50,000 shares at $.10 per share for each incremental $1 million in annual revenues related to genetic engineering. The grants would be made yearly for the next four years, based on Biodel's genetic engineering revenues in the particular year. Dr. Feldman estimated that over a four-year period genetic engineering contract revenue could rise to about

---

[1] Maximum allowed consulting time at major universities was one day per week.

$5 to $10 million. The options would be exercisable starting one year from the date of grant if, and only if, the scientists were still consulting for the company. In this way, the Stanford professor noted, the scientists would have an incentive to remain with Biodel. They would also be motivated to help the company grow enough to go public, a development which would greatly increase the value of their options. A final advantage of this alternative was that Biodel would be able to avoid a drain on its cash flow stemming from large salaries.

Dr. Feldman felt that he had to make a move. Shannon and Heeger were pressing for more money, more people, and more facilities. Dr. Ballantine warned that his colleagues were being pressured to accept individual offers. It was a time for decisions.

CASE 10 THE SOUTHLAND CORPORATION*

In 1978, the world's largest chain of convenience food stores was 7-Eleven markets, a division of the Southland Corporation. The 7-Eleven chain started from very humble beginnings in 1927 to surpass the $3 billion sales figure in 1978. Southland showed all indications of continuing its 15 percent annual growth rate and capitalizing on consumer acceptance of convenience shopping. As the president of a rival chain expressed it, "I think it has to be said that Southland is one of the great retailing stores of our time."

COMPANY HISTORY

In 1924, Jodie Thompson wanted to get married, but his $40-a-week salary from a Dallas ice-making firm was not enough to support a wife and family. From working on the ice docks and overseeing sales that summer, Thompson came upon the solution—chilled watermelons. No one had ever tried to sell chilled watermelons (or any other retail item for that matter) off the ice docks in Texas. Thompson's boss was initially very skeptical, but finally gave approval to try the idea. The venture was a success, and, by the end of the summer, Thompson had made $2,300.

In the summer of 1927, one of the dock managers of the Southland Ice Co. found that he could do a much brisker business by staying open 16 hours a day, seven days a week. He also noted that late-hour ice customers often complained about there being no place to pick up a loaf of bread or a bottle of milk. The dock manager persuaded Mr. Thompson, who by then was secretary-treasurer and a director of Southland Ice Co., to finance an inventory of bread, milk, and eggs and stack them on the dock. The items sold well, and shortly thereafter, when Thompson became president, all the company's ice docks were stocked with grocery items and the enterprising dock manager was assigned the task of finding new store sites. At the advice of a local advertising agency, Thompson named the stores 7-Eleven because they were open from 7 A.M. to 11 P.M.

By the mid-1950s, Southland had expanded to about 300 stores, mostly in Texas and Florida. As the United States became more urbanized, with many people commuting to work from the suburbs, Thompson and his two oldest sons believed that Southland could move into and redefine the niche once dominated by mom-and-pop corner grocery stores; they felt that selling customers convenience in the form of accessible hours, handy locations, big parking lots, and well-selected merchandise would translate into a competitive edge and accelerate a shift of buyer patronage from the rapidly failing corner groceries to Southland's convenience food store concept. Southland's store expansion program began in earnest about 1960.

* Prepared by J. W. Brown, M.B.A., 1979, at the University of Tennessee, under the direction of Prof. John Thiel.

SOUTHLAND'S CURRENT BUSINESS STRUCTURE

In 1978, Southland's business interests were organized into three major groups. The Stores Group was the world's largest operator and franchiser of convenience stores with 6,599 7-Eleven stores in 42 states, the District of Columbia, and 5 provinces of Canada. Its three distribution centers served 3,916 7-Eleven stores with approximately 50 percent of their merchandise needs. Food Centers, located at each distribution center, prepared a variety of sandwiches for distribution to 7-Eleven and other customers. Other retail operations included 109 Gristede's and Charles & Company food stores and sandwich shops in metropolitan New York, 383 R. S. McColl confectionery, tobacco, and news stores, and 7 7-Eleven units in the United Kingdom. Southland also had an equity interest in 5 Super Siete stores in Mexico and 23 Naroppet stores in Sweden. An additional 279 7-Eleven stores were operated by area licensees in the United States, 559 in Japan, 5 in Canada, and 12 in Australia.

The Dairies Group, another part of the Southland Corporation, was a major processor of dairy products which were distributed under 11 well-known regional brand names in 34 states and the District of Columbia.

The Special Operations Group included the Chemical division, Reddy Ice, Hudgins Truck Rental, and Tidel Systems which manufactured money handling devices for retail operations. In addition, Chief Auto Parts, a retail automobile supply chain of 119 stores in Southern California, was added to the Group in late 1978.

Exhibit 1 gives a breakout of the sales revenues and operating profits of these three groups. Exhibit 2 provides a corporatewide financial summary and Exhibit 3 is a condensed statement of consolidated earnings.

CUSTOMER PROFILE OF SOUTHLAND'S
7-ELEVEN STORES

Approximately 5.4 million people patronized 7-Eleven stores daily in 1978. Based on a study it conducted that year, Southland came up with a profile of its customers:

```
69.8 percent male
80.2 percent in 18–49 age group
80.9 percent live/work in area
 4.3 average trips a week
30.1 percent shop weekends
50.2 percent shop 1 P.M. to 10 P.M.
$1.54 average purchase
822 customers daily per store
```

On the average, the typical customer spent less than $2—and three to four minutes—at the store, and often made at least one unplanned impulse purchase. Though these small unplanned purchases did not amount to much extra expense for the individual customer, they resulted in significant extra sales and profits to Southland, given that over five million customers a day were involved.

Exhibit 1 Southland's Revenues and Operating Profits by Major Business Segment   All Dollar Figures Are in Millions

	1974		1975		1976		1977		1978	
Revenues:										
Stores Group	$1,405.4	87%	$1,556.0	87%	$1,857.5	88%	$2,271.9	89%	$2,791.0	90%
Dairies Group	184.0	11	208.3	12	236.1	11	236.5	9	253.4	8
Special Operations Group	22.6	2	25.0	1	26.0	1	33.7	2	40.9	2
Corporate	2.2	—	1.5	—	2.4	—	3.3	—	4.8	—
Total	$1,614.2	100%	$1,790.8	100%	$2,122.0	100%	$2,545.4	100%	$3,090.1	100%
Operating profits:										
Stores Group	$ 68.5	85%	$ 80.8	88%	$ 92.3	86%	$ 115.7	90%	$ 142.7	92%
Dairies Group	8.1	10	10.1	11	8.6	8	6.0	5	6.7	4
Special Operations Group	4.0	5	.9	1	6.4	6	6.7	5	6.0	4
Total	$ 80.6	100%	$ 91.8	100%	$ 107.3	100%	$ 128.4	100%	$ 155.4	100%

Source: Company records.

Exhibit 2 Southland Corporation Financial Summary

	1974	*1975*	*1976*	*1977*	*1978*
Operations (Note 1):					
Total revenues in (000s)	$1,614,188	$1,790,805	$2,122,023	$2,545,415	$3,090,094
Increase over prior year	15.47%	10.94%	18.50%	19.95%	21.40%
Net earnings (in 000s)	$27,167	$32,068	$37,849	$45,317	$57,097
Increase over prior years	25.85%	18.04%	18.03%	19.73%	25.99%
Per revenue dollar	1.68%	1.79%	1.78%	1.78%	1.85%
Return on beginning shareholders' equity	13.16%	13.72%	14.56%	15.62%	17.30%
Assets employed (Note 1):					
Working capital (in 000s)	$72,495	$80,196	$101,536	$136,693	$141,633
Current ratio	1.55	1.58	1.63	1.66	1.54
Property, plant, and equipment including capital leases (net) (in 000s)	$406,486	$447,392	$506,190	$567,442	$677,284
Depreciation and amortization (in 000s)	43,078	47,974	55,029	61,735	67,724
Total assets (in 000s)	639,599	696,107	799,261	942,531	1,134,476
Capitalization (Note 1):					
Long-term debt (in 000s)	$105,609	$119,911	$153,093	$195,520	$261,460
Capital lease obligations (in 000s)	155,918	163,380	178,556	192,547	211,342
Shareholders' equity (in 000s)	233,659	259,940	290,142	329,952	374,467
Total capitalization (in 000s)	495,186	543,231	621,791	718,019	847,269
Shareholders' equity to total capitalization	47.19%	47.85%	46.66%	45.95%	44.20%
Per share data (Notes 1 and 2):					
Primary earnings	$1.42	$1.63	$1.92	$2.26	$2.83
Earnings assuming full dilution	1.35	1.58	1.85	2.19	2.74
Cash dividends	.30	.36	.44	.55	.68
Shareholders' equity	$12.21	$13.23	$14.68	$16.48	$18.55
Other data:					
Cash dividends (in 000s)	$5,834	$7,033	$8,660	$10,961	$13,627
Dividends as a percent of earnings (Note 1)	21.47%	21.93%	22.88%	24.19%	23.87%
Stock dividends	3%	3%	3%	3%	3%
Average shares outstanding (Note 3)	19,137,414	19,642,947	19,761,788	20,015,512	20,181,879
Average diluted shares (Note 3)	20,854,737	20,883,719	20,911,047	21,028,143	21,129,981
Market price range (Note 3)					
High	$18⅞	$26¼	$26⅛	$25⅛	$33¾
Low	11⅜	14	19⅛	19¼	21½
Year-end	14¼	20⅜	25½	24⅝	26¾
Number of shareholders	9,351	9,093	8,881	8,764	8,627
Number of employees	28,200	28,600	31,000	34,000	37,000

Notes:

(1) The years 1974 through 1977 have been restated for the change in the method of accounting for leases to comply with the provisions of *Statement of Financial Accounting Standards No. 13,* which was adopted early in accordance with the requirements of the Securities and Exchange Commission.

(2) Based on average shares outstanding adjusted for stock dividends.

(3) Adjusted for stock dividends.

Source: *1978 Annual Report.*

Exhibit 3 Consolidated Statement of Earnings

	1974	1975	1976	1977	1978
Revenues:					
Net sales	$1,609,257	$1,787,928	$2,115,769	$2,536,109	$3,076,532
Other income	4,931	2,877	6,254	9,306	13,562
	$1,614,188	1,790,805	2,122,023	2,545,415	3,090.94
Cost of sales and expenses:					
Cost of goods sold, including buying and occupancy expenses	$1,184,835	1,323,799	1,577,141	1,903,791	2,311,024
Selling, general, and administrative expenses	348,797	374,234	435,687	510,337	619,519
Interest expense	8,674	7,936	9,707	13,540	15,804
Imputed interest expense on capital lease obligations	12,982	13,969	15,388	18,064	19,325
Contributions to employees savings and profit sharing plan	5,899	6,995	8,346	9,726	11,714
	$1,561,187	1,726,933	2,046,269	2,455,458	2,977,386
Earnings before income taxes	$ 53,001	63,872	75,754	89,957	112,708
Income taxes	25,834	31,804	37,905	44,640	55,611
Net earnings	$ 27,167	$ 32,068	$ 37,849	$ 45,317	$ 57,097
Per share					
Primary earnings	$1.42	$1.63	$1.92	$2.26	$2.83
Earnings assuming full dilution	$1.35	$1.58	$1.85	$2.19	$2.74

All figures are in thousands of dollars except the per share data.
Source: *1978 Annual Report.*

According to a reporter for *The Wall Street Journal:*

Southland's 7-Elevens are successors of the old-fashioned mom-and-pop grocery, but they prosper by catering to the modern urge for instant gratification. Their customers fill their pantries at the supermarket but dash instead to the closest 7-Eleven to fill their latest desire for, say, cigarettes or cold beer. Indeed, well over half the goods a 7-Eleven sells are consumed within 30 minutes.[1]

The same article quoted a 7-Eleven customer who lived in Dallas: "I usually stop by on the way to work to get a roll, in the afternoon to pick up a TV dinner, and sometimes during the day to get a coke. I'm a bachelor and it's quick and convenient." This view reflected management's own perceptions that Southland was really in the convenience business rather than in the retail grocery business.

STORE GROWTH AND LOCATIONS

Southland's management looked upon convenience as "giving customers what they want, when they want it, where they want it." As a consequence, in 1978, 5,407 of Southland's 6,599 7-Elevens were open around the clock and 91 percent were open beyond the traditional 7 A.M. to 11 P.M. hours. Moreover, Southland emphasized easily accessible neighborhood locations and quick, friendly service: its product lines included popular fast foods selections and, at 30 percent of its locations, self-serve gasoline.

In recent years, Southland had opened about 500 new 7-Eleven stores per year. The net gain in stores was smaller, however, because population shifts, changes in traffic patterns, lease expirations, and relocations to newly available and more desirable sites resulted in some existing stores being closed. The number of store openings and closings since 1972 are shown in the table below:

	New Stores Opened	Existing Stores Closed	Total 7-Eleven Stores
1972	424	83	4,455
1973	426	80	4,801
1974	n.a.	n.a.	5,171
1975	566	158	5,579
1976	528	154	5,953
1977	658	254	6,357
1978	550	308	6,599

Southland used a meticulous store site selection system; the primary criteria included such factors as (1) the traffic count in front of the site, (2) the ease with which passing cars could enter and leave the site, (3) the site's visibility from the street or road, (4) the number of people living within a one-mile radius, (5) the site's proximity to apartments, subdivisions, and high-traffic commercial establish-

---

[1] Gerald F. Seib, "Despite High Prices and Sparse Selection, 7-Eleven Stores Thrive," *The Wall Street Journal,* May 1, 1979, p. 1.

ments, (6) the adequacy of parking space, and (7) whether the site was a "natural" stopping-off point in the traffic flow by the site. To make sure its small 2,400-square-foot stores were readily seen from approaching traffic, they were carefully positioned in a heavy traffic area where they could be seen easily and were convenient to passers-by. Traffic patterns and flows were so crucial that stores had failed because a street was made one-way or because the opening of new streets and subdivisions had shifted traffic away from a site. Southland extensively studied potential sites and used a computer to estimate a proposed store's sales for its first five years.

John Thompson, Southland chairman, recently indicated that when a store starts looking like a loser, "We would rather close then and take our licks." The poor performers were identified by computerized analysis; by merely punching the store number into a computer terminal, executives could call up on a terminal display the store's current sales and earnings and tell how close it was to its budget. The company's management kept a close check on each store's operating performance.

In 1977, Southland started opening central-city stores. Located in high-density metropolitan residential areas, Southland saw them as filling a genuine need for walking customers. The company had central-city stores in Philadelphia, Boston, San Francisco, and New York City; more were planned. According to Thompson, the central-city stores "open up a whole new market area we haven't yet been able to serve. We will attempt to build and merchandise stores according to their neighborhoods."

PRODUCT LINES AND MERCHANDISING

Southland continually experimented with the product mix offered in the stores. Some products, like the frozen concoction "Slurpee," became huge successes. Others, like 7-Eleven beer, turned out to be quiet flops.

One Southland executive stated, "There's little risk involved in experimenting. We have a built-in market base of 5 million customers a day. Things that don't work out we can throw out after a week or two. Things that catch on in one store we can try nationwide. Our computers in Dallas can tell us overnight about any new market trends."[2] 7-Eleven stores carried 3,000 different items, about 23 percent of them Southland's own house brands. The larger percentage of brands available in a 7-Eleven store were nationally recognized brands; however, each item was located in a space predetermined by a Southland computer in Dallas. One Southland executive indicated:

> There is no room to stock a lot of different brands of the same product. Our customers don't have time to make choices anyway. We usually put on our shelves only the top one or two sellers of every product line and we put them in the area of the store where we think the customer would like to find them. It's all been researched and market tested. I can walk into most stores blindfolded and find any item you want.[3]

Through 1977, Southland's biggest selling item was tobacco—cigarettes primarily—followed closely by groceries, beer and wine, soft drinks, nonfood items such as maga-

---

[2] "7-Eleven Creates a Mood of Convenience at a Price," *The Washington Star,* November 27, 1978.

[3] Ibid.

Exhibit 4   7-Eleven Store Sales by Principal Product Category

	1974	1975	1976	1977	1978
Groceries	17.1%	15.3%	14.6%	14.0%	13.4%
Gasoline	2.7	3.9	6.8	9.8	13.4
Tobacco products	15.7	15.6	14.7	14.2	12.9
Beer/wine	14.1	14.8	14.4	13.7	12.9
Soft drinks	11.5	11.5	10.7	11.0	10.9
Nonfoods	9.3	9.5	10.2	9.9	9.4
Dairy products	10.5	9.5	9.6	9.3	8.9
Other food items	3.9	4.2	4.7	4.7	5.5
Candy	5.3	5.7	5.4	5.0	4.7
Baked goods	5.9	5.7	5.3	5.0	4.6
Health/beauty aids	4.0	3.9	3.6	3.4	3.4
Total	100.0%	100.0%	100.0%	100.0%	100.0%

* The Company does not record sales by product lines but estimates the percentage of convenience store sales by principal product category based on total store purchases.

Source: *1978 Annual Report.*

zines and Kleenex, and dairy products (see Exhibit 4). However, tobacco products dropped from number one in 1978, the change primarily due to increased gasoline sales. 7-Elevens had at times sold shotgun shells, television tubes, watermelons, and cancer insurance. Among the stores' best selling items were fast-food sandwiches, disposable diapers, and *Playboy* magazines (of which 7-Eleven sold far more than any other retailer). In general, the items carried were products that would be needed on a fill-in basis or else bought on impulse.

By the end of 1978, self-service gasoline accounted for 60 percent of all gasoline sales in the United States and showed every indication of increasing beyond that figure, according to industry sources. In response to this demand, 7-Eleven provided self-service gasoline at 1,857 locations. A substantial increase in volume at existing units, as well as the addition of gasoline at 284 stores during 1978, resulted in a 70 percent gasoline sales increase for the year. The availability of gasoline also led to the generation of additional sales, as more than 30 percent of 7-Eleven's gasoline customers in 1978 purchased other merchandise.

One merchandising trend of particular import was that of adding higher-margin items to each store's product line to try to boost store profitability. Fast-food items like sandwiches, pizza, soup, coffee, fruit punch, and draft soda (like "Slurpee") carried gross margins in the 40 percent range. Nonfood impulse items, which had margins in the 35 percent range, were also being added. Both compared favorably with Southland's recent storewide margins of 25 percent to 27 percent. Southland's fast food division, which in 1978 experienced a 30.5 percent sales gain, produced approximately 30 sandwiches marketed under the 7-Eleven and Landshire labels. These were distributed either fresh or flash-frozen for reheating in microwave or infrared ovens. The division in 1978 sold approximately 80 million sandwiches to 7-Eleven stores, other retailers, and institutional customers; it also furnished 7-Eleven stores with more than 1 million gallons of Slurpee syrup.

Southland's management was optimistic about the potential for increasing its share of the food-away-from-home market. Projections called for this segment to increase its share of the consumer's total food dollar owing to greater numbers of women entering the work force, higher family incomes, smaller families, and more single people—all of which acted to reinforce the lifestyle where a higher percent of disposable personal income would be spent for food prepared outside the home.

PRICING

According to Southland's marketing research director, people just about everywhere are willing to pay a little extra for the convenience a 7-Eleven offers—especially when the consumer is hit by an urge to buy. Most of the items in a 7-Eleven are therefore priced some 10 to 15 percent above the levels in most supermarkets. But, as shown in Exhibit 5, a few items, like milk, are priced more competitively.

Exhibit 5   Sample Comparisons of Prices at 7-Eleven Stores and Safeway Supermarkets in 1978

Item	7-Eleven	Safeway
Cascade (20 oz.)	$ .98	$ .89
Shredded wheat (12 oz.)	.93	.75
Tuna (chunk light, 6 oz.)	1.19	.99
Campbell's chicken noodle soup	.36	.30
Jello instant pudding (4 oz.)	.40	.35
Log Cabin maple syrup (12 oz.)	1.15	.93
Hellman's mayonnaise (16 oz.)	1.23	.99
Franco-American spaghetti (14 oz.)	.39	.34
Domino sugar (5 lbs.)	1.59	1.49
Wesson oil (16 oz.)	1.19	.99
V-8 juice (46 oz.)	1.09	.85
Maxwell House instant coffee (6 oz.)	4.29	3.79
Kellogg's corn flakes (12 oz.)	.85	.69
Hydrox cream-filled cookies	1.19	1.09
6-pack of Budweiser (12 oz.)	2.33	1.99
6-pack of Schlitz Light	2.34	1.99
Gallo burgundy wine	2.23	1.99
6-pack of Pepsi (16 oz.)	2.02	1.89
7Up (32 oz.)	.71	.63
Hostess cup cakes (2)	.35	.33
White bread (22 oz.)	.73	.40
Hostess powdered doughnuts (12)	.99	.99
Dozen eggs (grade A large)	.89	.79
Minute Maid orange juice (quart bottle)	.85	.75
Philadelphia cream cheese (3 oz.)	.43	.34
Salt (26 oz.)	.35	.30
Bayer aspirin (50 tablets)	1.19	.89
Heinz ketchup (14 oz.)	.79	.61
French's mustard (9 oz.)	.55	.43
Carton of Winston cigarettes	4.79	4.49
10 Briggs hot dogs	1.69	1.39
Half-gallon milk	.91	.91
Total (32 items)	$40.97	$35.55

Source: *The Washington Star,* November 26, 1978.

As one 7-Eleven customer put it: "There's a lot I don't like about 7-Eleven stores. They look tacky. They charge too much. They sell stuff that isn't good for you, and they always seem to be getting robbed. But yes, I do shop there. They're so convenient."[4] So far, though, no consumer activist groups had targeted 7-Eleven for either its high prices or its line of merchandise.

Southland seemed to have discovered, and was helping perpetuate, its own market segment—a world of customers caught in a time crisis, willing to pay extra to save themselves a few seconds waiting in line. A Wall Street analyst said:

> It is perplexing to us why Southland's revenue growth has accelerated when rising prices have stretched the consumer's budget to a considerable extent. Perhaps it is time rather than money which is the precious commodity to most Americans at present. The appeal of convenience stores has nothing to do with price. It has to do with people's lifestyles and their constant need for fill-ins. The more tightly the pocketbook is pinched, the less frequently the housewife shops at her supermarket, and the more need she has for last minute fill-ins.[5]

FRANCHISE ACTIVITIES

Of the 6,599 7-Eleven stores operating at the end of 1978, 4,056 were company operated and 2,543 were franchised. The typical franchise agreement allowed for the company to lease the property and equipment to a franchisee in exchange for a fee of $10,000 plus roughly half the store's profits. Southland allowed new franchises a 120-day grace period to pull out of their contracts without losing their initial investments. Most of the franchisees were couples with children and the family typically worked in the store.

SOUTHLAND'S ADVERTISING FOR 7-ELEVEN

In January 1978, Southland introduced its first prime-time network 7-Eleven commercial to the largest audience in television history prior to Super Bowl XII. Product awareness messages featuring Hot-to-Go coffee, Egg Hamlette, Chili Dog, Slurpee, or sunglasses reached 58 million households each broadcast week. In addition to the network television commercials, advertisements were aired on approximately 500 radio stations and published in more than 200 newspapers nationwide.

During 1978, broadcasts remained the company's major advertising vehicle with spot radio getting 30 percent, network television 35 percent, spot television 25 percent, newspapers 4 percent, and outdoor advertising 6 percent. Total television advertising increased 22 percent during the first half of 1978, compared with the same period in 1977.

7-Eleven stores were decidedly male-oriented. However, due to the increased buying power of women in today's society, Southland's advertising had begun to be geared specifically toward women.

---

[4] Southland Is the Best Example I Know of Modern Capitalism," *The Washington Star,* November 26, 1978.

[5] "7-Eleven Creates a Mood of Convenience."

DISTRIBUTION CENTERS

Southland's 7-Eleven stores were served by distribution centers in Florida, Virginia, and Texas that were specifically designed to meet the needs of 7-Eleven for a reliable and efficient source of supply, frequent delivery, and a high in-stock position. The system also enabled the stores to have the flexibility to respond quickly to customer preferences and seasonal changes in demand, as well as to implement promotional programs and introduce new products. The centers serviced 3,916 7-Eleven stores at the end of 1978.

Store stock lists, compiled and updated monthly by computer, were tailored to the merchandise specifications of each store, enabling personnel to easily determine restocking needs. The store orders were then transmitted through a network of computer terminals located at 7-Eleven district offices and connected to the computer center in Dallas, which assimilated the orders and transmitted them to printing terminals at the appropriate distribution center. From these printed lists, the store orders were then "picked" and assembled for delivery. Custom-designed trucks with separate compartments for dry, chilled, and frozen merchandise followed computer-planned routes to achieve maximum savings of energy and time.

Southland's concept of delivering prepriced merchandise in less-than-case-quantities eliminated overstocking, assured fresh merchandise on the store shelves at all times, promoted more productive use of selling space, and improved store profitability. The importance of stores not having to order full cases of merchandise was highlighted by Southland's manager of information services: "Can you imagine how long it would take to sell 48 cans of tomato paste in a 7-Eleven? Now we can give them three cans and keep it fresh." During 1978, the computerized inventory control system enabled the stores to achieve an average inventory turnover of 23 times while maintaining a 99 percent order fill rate.

In many cases, store managers did not even bother to order groceries; that was done by warehouse employees whose only job was visiting each 7-Eleven twice a month to take inventory and order merchandise.[6] The computer then took over, sending hundreds of orders to a warehouse, deciding which orders to ship on what truck, and telling employees how to stack goods inside the truck to fill it to the brim. The trucks were able to begin delivering only hours after the warehouse got the order. Southland's computer also helped analyze the layout of merchandise in the store—by keeping track of what items sold well in which shelf locations.

FINANCING

The long-term policy of Southland was to finance expansion from retained earnings, although other methods of raising funds were used when necessary. In late 1978, the company offered $50 million of unsecured 9⅜ percent Sinking Fund Debentures, due December 15, 2003. These debentures, as well as a 1977 8⅜ percent issue, were

---

[6] Seib, "Despite High Prices."

rated A by both Moody's and Standard & Poor's and were listed on the New York Stock Exchange.

In April 1978, the annual cash dividend rate was increased 20 percent to 72 cents per share. Cash dividends had been paid each year since 1957, and the annual rate had been raised seven times in the last eight years, providing shareholders an average compound growth rate of 20.7 percent. In addition, for the 13th consecutive year, a 3 percent stock dividend was distributed.

In recent years, Southland had been forced to increase its debt burden to finance corporate expansion—especially the growth in the number of 7-Eleven stores. To open a new store, Southland had to invest more than $180,000. This included land costs of about $50,000, a store building costing an average of $70,000, equipment installation of $46,000, and initial inventory costs of $18,000 to $25,000. In the case of franchised stores, Southland advanced most of the up-front investment, with the exception of the $10,000 franchise fee.

The capital costs of financing 400–500 new stores per year had exceeded Southland's retained earnings and internal cash flow capabilities during recent years; the resulting debt increases were in such an amount as to cause a steady decline in Southland's equity capitalization percentage (see Exhibit 2).

Although a 41-year-old Southland official expressed the view that the company would be adding a net of 300–400 stores per year for the rest of his lifetime, it was not clear that Southland could continue to finance such an ambitious store expansion program without adversely affecting earnings. Higher site and construction costs and higher interest rates were becoming significant factors; so was the move to increase store size from 2,400 square feet to the 2,700 to 3,000 square feet range. In 1977, Southland spent an estimated $75.3 million to open 658 stores; in 1978, the figure exceeded $95 million for 550 new stores.

Nor was it clear that such a rate of expansion was consistent with market opportunities. Already there were over 33,000 convenience food stores in the United States—approximately one for every 6,600 persons. Prime sites were becoming hard to find and were increasingly expensive. According to one industry trade publication, several factors were at work:

> Munford executives, like most in the business, have set their sights on prime corner locations with high visibility and heavy traffic counts. Because Munford is selecting former gas station sites for its new units, traffic counts have replaced household density, once the sacred cow of the industry's site selection procedure.
>
> In fact, one Majik Market is making $7,000 per week in food sales—the industry average is $5,257—without a house within a five-mile radius of the store.
>
> Secondary sites, mainly at the mouths of suburban subdivisions and in shopping malls, are a thing of the past. "The suburban, residential convenience store is doomed," explains Tom Ewens, vice president of real estate for Houston-based National Convenience Stores Inc., "because the sales volume that those units produce simply can't keep pace with the costs of land, construction and operation."
>
> But the recently sought-after, first-rate corner spots are getting harder for convenience store chains to find due, in part, to increased competition from other retailers for the same locations. As store sizes creep up to the 3,000-square-foot mark, the lot sizes expand to allow for increased gas and parking facilities, convenience stores are looking

Exhibit 6   Consolidated Balance Sheets, Southland Corp., 1977 and 1978

	December 31, 1977	December 31, 1978
Assets		
Current assets:		
Cash and short-term investments	$ 65,903,801	$ 82,745,504
Accounts and notes receivable	75,171,378	78,968,103
Inventories	126,913,578	161,254,967
Deposits and prepaid expenses	21,436,624	26,777,392
Investment in properties	53,319,492	55,857,419
Total current assets	342,744,873	405,603,385
Investments in affiliates	26,717,136	27,364,352
Property, plant, and equipment	389,251,583	479,554,364
Capital leases	178,190,671	197,730,040
Other assets	5,627,054	24,223,652
Total assets	$942,531,317	$1,134,475,793
Liabilities and Shareholders' Equity		
Current liabilities:		
Accounts payable and accrued expenses	$168,894,391	$ 211,920,848
Income taxes	15,481,417	18,636,987
Long-term debt due within one year	4,142,055	13,254,868
Capital lease obligations due within one year	17,533,856	20,157,217
Total current liabilities	206,051,719	263,969,920
Deferred credits	18,460,424	23,235,908
Long-term debt	195,520,000	261,460,472
Capital lease obligations	192,546,677	211,342,074
Common stock $1 par value, authorized 40 million shares, issued and outstanding 20,200,557 and 19,557,287 shares	195,573	202,006
Additional capital	223,499,143	242,339,822
Retained earnings	106,257,781	131,925,591
Total shareholders' equity	329,952,497	374,467,149
Total liabilities and shareholders' equity	$942,531,317	$ 1,134,475,793

Source: *1978 Annual Report.*

for roughly the same size lot that a fast-food unit, drug store, bank or gas station might want. This means that the sector's traditional strength of flexibility in site selection is being somewhat impaired.

What's happening is that convenience stores are pinning their hopes for higher sales volumes and profits on primary locations, while coping with higher real estate and operations costs than they faced at former sites.

This means that convenience stores' profit and loss statements will likely get tighter and tighter, the line between a winning and losing location more thinly drawn.[7]

Exhibits 6 and 7 contain additional financial data on Southland.

[7] "What's Down the Road for Convenience Stores," *Chain Store Age Executive,* June 1979, pp. 23–24.

Exhibit 7   Consolidated Statements of Changes in Financial Position, Southland Corp., 1977 and 1978

	1977	1978
Sources of working capital:		
From operations:		
Net earnings	$ 45,317,241	$ 57,097,109
Expenses charged to earnings which did not require outlay of working capital:		
Depreciation and amortization	41,991,861	46,839,875
Amortization of capital leases	19,743,097	20,884,330
Deferred income taxes and other credits	3,415,874	6,552,597
Working capital provided from operations	$110,468,073	$131,373,911
Long-term debt	61,534,160	70,658,506
Capital lease obligations	37,409,857	41,907,748
Retirements and sales of property	12,774,857	13,555,200
Retirements and sales of capital leases	6,191,948	1,397,049
Issuance of common stock		
Conversion of notes	2,690,000	—
Acquisitions	2,310,000	—
Key employees incentive plan	462,278	470,992
Employee stock options	97,343	704,463
Total sources of working capital	$233,938,516	$260,067,869
Uses of working capital:		
Property, plant, and equipment	$ 96,324,184	$141,438,084
Capital leases	37,409,857	41,907,748
Reduction of capital lease obligations	23,419,196	23,112,351
Payment of long-term debt	16,862,491	4,718,034
Cash dividends	10,960,976	13,627,443
Net noncurrent assets of businesses purchased for stock and cash	9,111,552	29,180,394
Retirement of long-term debt upon conversion of notes	2,690,000	—
Investments in affiliates	1,061,359	647,216
Other	836,640	366,089
Cash paid in lieu of fractional shares on stock dividends	105,267	130,199
Total uses of working capital	$198,781,522	$255,127,558
Increase in working capital	$ 35,156,994	$ 4,940,311
Changes in working capital:		
Increases in current assets:		
Cash and short-term investments	$ 39,504,544	$ 16,841,703
Accounts and notes receivable	7,788,618	3,796,725
Inventories	21,884,637	34,341,389
Deposits and prepaid expenses	1,482,830	5,340,768
Investment in properties	9,342,429	2,537,927
Total changes in working capital	$ 80,003,058	$ 62,858,512
Increases (decreases) in current liabilities:		
Accounts payable and accrued expenses	38,624,253	43,062,457
Income taxes	4,442,417	3,155,570
Long-term debt due within one year	(611,614)	9,112,813
Capital lease obligations due within one year	2,391,008	2,623,361
Total increases (decreases) in current liabilities	$ 44,846,064	$ 57,918,201
Increase in working capital	$ 35,156,994	$ 4,940,311

Source: *1978 Annual Report.*

RECENT TRENDS IN THE CONVENIENCE FOOD INDUSTRY

In 1957, the industry consisted of 500 stores with an annual volume of $75 million. Ten years later, there were 8,000 convenience stores with combined sales of $1.3 billion. In 1978, the corresponding figures were some 33,000 stores and an annual sales volume of $8.7 billion. Average annual sales growth during the last five years was about 17 percent. Sales volumes in convenience food stores were approaching 5 percent of total U.S. grocery sales, up from 1.7 percent in 1967. Many industry sources predicted favorable sales growth for convenience food stores for the years ahead. Sales revenues were projected to increase at a 15 percent annual rate and volume was expected to reach 8 percent of total grocery sales by 1980.

For the extra convenience and service they offered, convenience food stores took higher mark-ups on the items they sold. Whereas conventional supermarkets had an average gross margin of 22.4 percent in 1978, the gross margins in convenience food stores were typically 28 to 30 percent. Exhibit 8 gives a breakdown of the 1976 gross margin, expenses, and net profits for the representative convenience food store.

Recently, industry observers had become concerned with the increased competition that supermarkets seemed to be initiating. Specifically, the trends of many supermarkets toward longer hours, Sunday openings, and express-lane checkouts had the potential of eroding the market shares of convenience food stores. In response, some convenience chains were keeping prices on selected high volume items as close to those of supermarkets as possible. Munford's Majik Market stores, Southland's biggest competitor, recently adjusted the prices of some 25 of its best-selling items to be competitive with supermarket prices.

In addition to competition from supermarkets, competition from other retail sectors

---

Exhibit 8 Breakdown of 1976 Margins, Expenses, and Net Profit for the Representative Convenience Store*

Sales	100.0%
Cost of goods sold	71.2
Gross margin	28.8
Employee wages	10.6
Employee benefits	1.9
Advertising and promotion	0.7
Property rentals	3.3
Utility expenses	3.2
Other expenses	5.7
Total expenses	25.4
Net profit before taxes	3.4%

* Determined by trade sources from industrywide data.
Source: *Convenience Stores*, September–October 1977, p. 44.

was emerging. Fast-food chains, liquor-delis, gas stations carrying food items, and discount and drug outlets with newly added food items were a new competitive threat. These types of firms were expected to expand their convenience food lines and to begin to carry high-traffic nonfood items. Furthermore, many of the drug stores were staying open longer hours and opting for locations with many of the same features of convenience stores.

7-ELEVEN'S COMPETITORS IN CONVENIENCE FOODS

7-Eleven in 1978 was more than seven times the size of Munford, its nearest competitor. (Munford is the only other convenience chain listed on the New York Stock Exchange.) In recent years, while 7-Eleven had been booming, Munford had been having more than its share of problems. While in the process of closing marginal and unprofitable units, earnings and sales for Munford suffered accordingly. In addition to their stores group, Munford experienced problems with Farmbest Foods, a dairy operation acquired in 1975. The Farmbest operation lost money in 1977 due to unsettled industry conditions in Florida and Alabama.

A new merchandising concept being tried by Munford, in order to catch up with the industry, was to join forces with major oil companies such as Texaco, Gulf, and Amoco by putting Munford's Majik Market convenience stores at existing gasoline station sites. The executives of Munford saw many advantages for this concept and were convinced that consumers were accepting the idea of buying gasoline at convenience stores very well.

Another competitive factor in the convenience store field was Circle K. For a period of four years through 1977, Circle K virtually halted its store expansion program in favor of remodeling and renovating older, existing stores. The Circle K chain, like Munford and others, entered the gasoline business, but with a basic difference from Munford. Circle K's strategy was to retain its recognition and image as convenience first and gasoline second. For this reason, Circle K chose to add gasoline pumps to their existing stores, not vice versa, as Munford did. Circle K planned to add 60 to 70 stores a year through the mid-1980s.

A third competitor of 7-Eleven was the National Convenience Stores chain. In 1976, a young, dynamic man named Pete Van Horn became president of National Convenience. Not being fettered by the bonds of tradition in the industry, Van Horn slashed the number of stores, lowered personnel turnover, increased sales in remaining stores and, in general, put National Convenience on a sound footing. Van Horn was anxious to try out his ideas about store layout, merchandising and expansion; his goal at the end of 1977 was to double earnings in the next four years.[8]

Exhibit 9 presents comparative sales and earnings for ten leading convenience food chains. Exhibit 10 contains per store sales and profit statistics for the 1974–1978 period.

---

[8] "The Convenience Stores," *Financial World,* November 1, 1977.

Exhibit 9   Sales and Earnings of Convenience Chains

Company	Sales ($000)			Earnings ($000)		
	1976	1977	1978	1976	1977	1978
Southland	$2,121,146	$2,544,414	$3,089,000	$40,277	$45,348	$57,000
Munford	334,770	34,0174	378,950e	3,427	(770)	6,090
Circle K	262,362	302,603	363,783	5,122	6,912	8,196
National Convenience Stores	212,606	233,208	263,705	2,652	3,536	5,011
Utotem Group	192,499	206,041	221,423	8,822	8,788	9,658
Convenient Industries of America ...	123,368	146,598	177,732	857	896	1,148
Sunshine-Jr. Stores	68,899	81,225	93,553	1,387	1,432	1,622
Shop & Go	60,780	70,136	82,729	1,650	1,655	2,271
Hop-In Food Stores	14,077	22,739	31,714	280	392	658
Lil' Champ	18,807	21,006	22,727	592	647	778
Grand total	$3,409,314	$3,968,144	$4,725,316	$65,066	$68,836	$92,432

Note: Includes sales and earnings from operations other than convenience stores where applicable.

e Estimated.

Source: *Progressive Grocer*, April 1978.

Exhibit 10   Average Sales and Profit Statistics for Top Ten Publicly Held Convenience Food Store Chains

	1974	1975	1976	1977	1978
Yearly sales per store	$213,890	$232,140	$240,828	$263,895	$274,115
Weekly sales per store	$4,113	$4,452	$4,606	$5,061	$5,257
Profit on pre-tax sales	3.39%	3.32%	3.64%	3.48%	3.65%
Profit on after-tax sales	1.77%	1.71%	1.92%	1.8%	1.98%
Yearly pre-tax profit per store	$7,242	$7,723	$8,762	$9,194	$10,026
Yearly after-tax profit per store	$3,789	$3,978	$4,523	$4,752	$5,431

Source: "Eighth Annual Dollars-per-Day Survey of Small Food Store Industry," as published in *Chain Store Age Executive,* June 1979, p. 26.

SOUTHLAND'S DAIRIES AND SPECIAL
OPERATIONS GROUPS

Initially, the Dairies and Special Operations groups were formed to vertically integrate their activities with 7-Eleven. The Dairies Group processed and distributed milk, ice cream, yogurt, juices, eggnog, dips, and toppings; in 1978, it served 5,295 of Southland's convenience stores and supplied 66 percent of all the dairy products sold in all 7-Eleven stores. The group included 28 processing plants and 86 distribution locations. However, more and more of the Dairies Group sales volume was coming from outside Southland. In 1978, 65 percent of the unit's $400 million sales revenues were to food retailers such as Denny's and Wendy's. The expansion of sales to outside companies was being pursued through the development of new high-margin novelty items such as sundae-style yogurts, cheeses, and frozen dairy items like Big Deal, Gram Daddy, and Big Wheel.

A similar trend was evident in the Special Operations Group. While this division supplied other Southland units with food ingredients, ice, Slurpee concentrate, preservatives, sanitizers, and cleaning agents, in 1978 a total of 72 percent of sales were to outside customers. In 1978, the chemicals unit was expanded by the acquisition of a New Jersey fine chemicals plant; this acquisition allowed Southland to market a broader line of products to customers in the agricultural and pharmaceutical industries. The division's Hudgins Truck Rental unit was expanding its efforts to provide full-maintenance truck leasing to national and regional customers, as well as to Southland operations; in 1978, its outside sales were up 10 percent and accounted for 68 percent of revenues. In 1978, a new unit called Tidel Systems was added to the Special Operations Group; it manufactured an innovative money-handling device designed to reduce losses from robberies and to increase store-site cash handling efficiency. While Southland planned to install the device at its 7-Eleven stores, there was an even greater potential for sales to other retailers and a nationwide sales and maintenance organization was being assembled.

THE ACQUISITION OF CHIEF AUTO PARTS

In December 1978, at a cost of $20 million, Southland acquired the assets of Chief Auto Parts, a chain of 119 retail automobile supply stores in southern California. A typical Chief store was 2,000 square feet in size, open seven days a week, and located in a neighborhood shopping center close to homes or businesses. The stores sold approximately 7,500 replacement parts and accessories and carried both national brands and private-label products. The average purchase was $5 and a large percentage of sales were on weekends when most do-it-yourselfers had time to service their cars. Chief also had a modern warehouse in Los Angeles from which it supplied its stores.

There was some thought that the Chief acquisition signaled a move by Southland to diversify into small store retailing, particularly those kinds of retail businesses which had operating characteristics similar to those of 7-Eleven stores.

FUTURE OUTLOOK

Southland management's view of the future for its 7-Eleven stores was exemplified by John Thompson, chairman:

> We believe that the growth opportunity in the convenience store area is great. I'm very bullish on the future. There are many parts in the United States that are not saturated with convenience stores, and I would say that Texas and Florida are the two most saturated areas. Even in those states we can go 20 to 40 more stores a year, depending on housing. But in the rest of the United States, there is relatively much less saturation, so that as far as we're concerned we think we can build 500-plus stores a year for a long time. Why, the Northeast is a great area. We haven't really saturated that market at all. And the Midwest? Well, we've hardly gotten started there. And California? Well sure we have 900 stores in California, but you can build forever in that state. I guess you could say the future for us looks marvelous.[9]

However, in 1979, several industry observers were taking a more cautious stance and asking if the industry was not on the verge of maturity.

---

[9] "Southland Is the Best Example."

CASE 11 NOTE ON THE AMBULANCE INDUSTRY*

The typical ambulance firm is in the business of providing two categories of medical service. Most observable is the limited on-the-scene emergency aid given to stabilize the effects of accidents or sudden illness, and the subsequent movement of the victim to acute care facilities. While less noticeable, the more profitable facet of the industry involves scheduled transportation of convalescent patients to medical offices, nursing homes, or hospitals. Long dominated by locally owned one-to-five unit firms, the industry has been substantially influenced by competitive struggles rather than an uncompromising concern for the patient's welfare.

THE INDUSTRY'S HISTORICAL POSTURE

Until the early 1970s, ambulance enterprises, unlike other components in the health care industry, appeared to be free of most environmental constraints. Low barriers to entry allowed large numbers of aggressive competitors to battle for the available business and often allowed the least professional to succeed.

Characterizing the industry in 1972, insurance company research reported that less than 3 percent of the nation's ambulance attendants were qualified. Further investigations by the U.S. Public Health Service estimated that 60,000 needless deaths and 100,000 permanent disabilities occurred each year due to poorly trained and ill-equipped emergency personnel. One analyst connected with a 1972 congressional investigation commented:

> Accidents are the leading cause of death among Americans and highway accidents make up by far the largest percentage of these deaths. Fully 15,000 of the 55,000 highway deaths each year could be avoided with proper emergency medical services at the scene of the accident and enroute to the hospital. . . . Experts in emergency medical care estimate that 30 percent of coronary-related deaths each year could be averted with proper emergency medical attention.

Also according to a 1968 University of Michigan research effort:

> 20 percent of accident victims could have been saved by such simple procedures enroute to the hospital as keeping the throat open to permit breathing, or using intravenous fluids. . . . Less than half of the ambulance attendants in the country are trained in even the most rudimentary Red Cross first aid procedures.

---

* The research and written case note information were presented at a Case Research Symposium and were evaluated by the Case Research Association's Editorial Board. This case note was prepared by J. Kim DeDee of the University of Tennessee at Chattanooga as a basis for class discussion. Distributed by the Case Research Association. All rights reserved to the author and the Case Research Association. Reprinted with permission.

Industry Trends Prior to 1970

With varying degrees of intensity, four significant factors had contributed most to the historical nature and structure of the ambulance industry: the personnel, the vehicles and equipment, the regulatory structure, and competitive rivalries.

Personnel   The primary determinant of the industry's quality standards prior to 1970 was the selection, training, and compensation of personnel. Fledgling companies recruited inexperienced employees into a work environment emphasizing contiguous 24-hour shifts with sleep periods often interrupted by high-stress trauma calls. Employees were also responsible for the maintenance and repair of the equipment, vehicles, and housing facilities.

Organizationally, ambulance firms were usually divided into four areas along functional lines. The owner/manager divided his time among general business practices, competitive struggles, and representing the interest of the firm to local governmental offices. The dispatcher managed the normal billing routine, took incoming telephone messages, determined the status of the emergency necessity, and directed the closest unit to the site of the call. The driver was often promoted from within the organization, but in many cases only needed a chauffeur's license and had little, if any, emergency experience. At the lowest level of the organization was the attendant whose principal responsibility focused on the immediate care, comfort, and transportation of the victim. Legal entry-level qualifications normally did not require previous experience but probably included the 26-hour Red Cross standard first-aid course. Ironically, the dimensions of this training program did little to enhance the employee's competency level. Instead of being designed to aid in the safe movement of the patient, the Red Cross program only explained techniques of momentary and initial care. To that end, the course was deficient in such critical areas as emergency childbirth, back and neck injuries, extrication, and transportation.

Vehicles and Equipment   A second major force affecting the industry was the acquisition of the firm's most substantial revenue-generating asset: the vehicle fleet. While numerous criteria would normally be expected to play a role in the vehicle selection decision, aesthetics coupled with myopic consumer demands proved paramount. Job order shops began to lengthen and customize luxury automobiles for ambulance use but, in most cases, critical structural components such as braking, suspension, steering, cooling, and electrical systems remained unaltered. These vehicles were difficult to handle and subject to excessive component failures during adverse driving conditions. Confronted with the high fixed costs of these units, many firms elected to cut costs in equipment and supplies, narrowing their working inventory to a single back board; a few board splints, elastic bandages, and dressings; and an assortment of restraint devices for combative patients.

Regulatory Structure   Contrary to the rest of the health care industry the ambulance segment had not been subject to much federal, state, or local regulation. During the 1960s some states did begin to enact laws setting minimum licensing standards for vehicles and personnel; however, because of wording irregularities, a limited number of inspectors, and the piecemeal approach to most regulations, serious problems of quality control existed in large portions of the industry.

Competition   Competition had an unusual impact on the industry. Consumers requesting emergency services rarely evaluated the final services. Frequently, the non-payment rate on emergency service calls approached 60 percent (the rate for patient transfers was much lower). To counter the risk of revenue losses management exercised a number of options including selective withholding of services, cash discounts for early payment, and collection agencies for overdue accounts.

In addition, pressures were applied by larger firms on local governments to supply partial subsidies covering the costs of indigent use of emergency services. Revenue for the transfer business often originated from federal (medicare), state (medicaid), and private insurance programs. Essentially, these third-party payors offered payments of between 70 and 100 percent for those with insurance coverage.

Competitive rivalry in some geographic locales was often so bitter that it involved call-jumping through the use of transistorized radio monitors, delaying responding to an emergency call until the firm's own unit became available, and sabotage of a rival's vehicles or equipment at the accident scene.

RECENT INDUSTRY DEVELOPMENTS

By 1985 the ambulance service industry had evolved through 15 years of unprecedented and turbulent change. The catalysts for the reversals in the prehospital, or emergency medical services (EMS) industry as it is now known, came from a number of sources. During the 1960s numerous organizations formed focusing special attention on the growing morbidity of highway accidents. President Johnson's Committee on Highway Safety and the National Academy of Sciences provided key impetus in the passage of the Highway Safety Act of 1966. This law essentially allowed states the use of federal monies to establish minimum performance standards for emergency medical processes and to improve their existing ambulance provision systems. Later, in 1967, the Department of Transportation published its "Emergency Medical Services" standards which contained numerous provisions affecting the scope and breadth of emergency medical coverage.

A second major piece of legislation, the Emergency Medical Service Systems Act, was enacted in 1975. It was revised in 1976 to extend through 1980. This legislation provided additional federal money for the design and development of emergency medical systems and to support long-range planning at the state level. The Department of Health, Education and Welfare, the Department of Transportation, and the National Highway Traffic and Safety Administration (DOT-NHTSA) further increased the involvement of the federal government in such areas as standard setting, prehospital critical care system development, and ambulance design criteria.

Realizing these federal funding initiatives were temporary, virtually all states began efforts to establish regional EMS programs. Under these programs clear identification of the individual components of each geographic system became necessary. Also, standardized guidelines and criteria were written as tools of implementation to these regional emergency care processes.

Typically, state EMS systems were divided into four functional elements: (1) system administration—long-range planning, operations, and evaluation of the total prehospital emergency care process; (2) manpower—routine position descriptions and revised training formats; (3) equipment—the vehicles and medical or extraction devices; and (4) communication—the geographic scope of emergency two-way radio traffic and the use of 911 telephone numbers.

The major thrust of the EMS system, however, centered on the increasingly complex network of components necessary to respond to patients in life-threatening situations. The sequence of events associated with a typical emergency medical routine were:

1. *Identification of emergency incident.* The person making the discovery assesses and defines the situation in which immediate aid is required.
2. *Access to EMS system.* A telephone call is placed to the appropriate agency which then dispatches all necessary aid units (police, fire, extrication, or ambulance).
3. *Arrival of first response personnel.* Appropriate personnel arrive at scene and begin initial assessment and treatment of patient(s).
4. *Prehospital stabilization of patient.* Field personnel decide on the use of predetermined procedures for particular life-threatening conditions or make radio contact with a trained physician in a designated hospital. Vital information concerning the patient's condition is provided while the physician directs the application of appropriate medical treatment.
5. *Transport of patient.* Following stabilization, patient's condition is continually monitored while being transported to hospital. Physician may order additional treatment while enroute via radio contact.
6. *Transfer of patient responsibility.* Vital information concerning patient's condition is transmitted as patient undergoes initial hospital examination and/or treatment.

In most cases individual state EMS agencies added further detail to qualifications the DOT-NHTSA specified for ambulance vehicles. Primary design criteria were established covering size, floor plans, ground clearance, emergency equipment, and electrical, cooling, suspension, and braking systems. Normally recommended color schemes included orange accent stripes on a white background with ample room for the blue Star of Life emblem, and the organization's logo and phone number. See Exhibits 1 and 2.

Many city and county agencies refined the governmental momentum through increased operating budgets covering EMS salaries, training, vehicles, equipment, and reimbursements to private firms. This, however, put the local EMS system in the vulnerable position of being heavily supported by tax dollars, while nearly all other health care services were paid for by individuals or third-party payors.

Organized medicine had also stimulated improvements in emergency medical care. The patriarch of health care, the American Medical Association, had moved increasingly toward advancing emergency medical skills, technologies, and research. Other groups such as the American College of Surgeons and the Committee on Injuries of the American Academy of Orthopedic Surgeons, working in concert with concerned local physicians, designed numerous trauma care delivery training programs, instruction films and manuals, and skill-building workshops. By 1983 these organizations

Exhibit 1   Cost Classification of 1985 Emergency Vehicles

Vehicle	Price Range
Type I Converted hearse (used mainly for patient transfers)	$38,000–$42,000
Type II Van ambulance	$25,000–$29,000
Type III Heavy duty cab/chassis Dual rear wheels	$38,000–$40,000
Type IV Chevrolet Suburban 4-wheel drive	$12,000–$17,000

Source: Collins Industries Inc.

further standardized essential position descriptions and equipment criteria (see Exhibit 3).

Currently, the nationally recognized entry-level position for basic life support personnel is the emergency medical technician (EMT). Primary training topics emphasize airway obstruction, pulmonary or cardiac arrest, cardiopulmonary resuscitation, and bleeding control. Closely related subjects include shock treatment, splinting, poisoning, emergency childbirth, and general evaluation of anatomic subsystems.

While several variations exist in the ranks of emergency medical paraprofessionals, the highest level currently attainable is the paramedic. Requirements for certification and licensing specified by state law usually include up to two years of college-level training in advanced airway management, administration of intravenous fluids, cardiac monitoring and defibrillation, and administration of medications for resuscitation.

As increased revenues became more available after the passage of medicare and medicaid acts, the additional demands placed on personnel necessitated commensurate increases in compensation. Currently, in larger cities, salaries for entering employees approach $15,500 annually with top salary levels for EMTs exceeding $25,000 (see Exhibit 4). Probationary paramedics in municipalities can earn $20,700 with advancement potential exceeding $35,700.

A number of indirect factors also contributed to the evolution of EMS care. Physicians modified their practice patterns by eliminating house calls, compelling patients to go directly to local hospitals, often through the use of emergency vehicles. To meet this challenge, many hospitals expanded their trauma center personnel and emergency facilities. As their experience with emergency care grew, hospitals came to view with alarm the lack of sophistication in the transportation arm of emergency care. Many hospital administrators responded with their own hospital-based ambulance systems, while others chose to cooperate more fully in training and developing existing providers.

Exhibit 2   Advanced Life Support (ALS) Internal and External Configurations

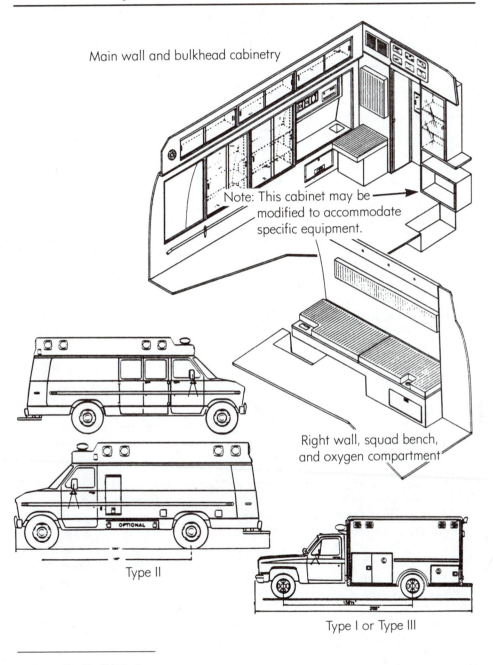

Main wall and bulkhead cabinetry

Note: This cabinet may be modified to accommodate specific equipment.

Right wall, squad bench, and oxygen compartment

Type II

Type I or Type III

Source: Frontline Vehicles Inc.

Exhibit 3   Profile of Equipment and Supplies for Basic and Advanced Life Support Systems

---

Item	Number	Unit Price
Basic life support:		
Ventilation/airway equipment	1	
Suction apparatus		$ 396
Oxygen equipment		288
Airways		Variable*
Immobilization devices/splints		
Traction	2	75
Extremity splints		120
Backboards	2	125
Dressings		Variable*
Pneumatic antishock garment	1	300
Radio		
Two-way permanent	1	1,300
Two-way portable	1	900
Obstetrical kit	2	Variable*
Light equipment		75
Aluminum cot/mattress	1	850
Stretchers	3	200
Audio/lighting equipment	1	800
Miscellaneous		350
Advanced life support system:		
Intravenous equipment		90
Airways/tubing/laryngoscope		130
Cardiac monitor/defibrillator	1	7,875
Drugs		Variable*
Mechanical cardiac compression unit	1	3,917

---

* Variable cost normally charged to the patient.
Source: American College of Surgeons, Dixie U.S.A. Inc., and casewriter's computations.

Interestingly, this myriad of environmental factors proved advantageous to some firms. As the central objective of the industry changed from high-speed transport to more definitive at-the-scene treatment, the image of the paramedic began to parallel those of police and fire department personnel. Also, the increased stature of the industry's professional organizations precipitated additional skill enhancement workshops and seminars as well as more sophisticated research-oriented publication journals. Finally, the growing investment in capital equipment and compensation erected significant barriers to market entry for marginal providers.

The Competitive Arena

The prehospital emergency care industry can normally be divided into four classes of providers, two not-for-profit and two for-profit. The not-for-profit sector consisted of municipal (police and fire department) service units and rural volunteer organiza-

Exhibit 4   Average Annual Pay and Labor Costs, 1985

Provider	Emergency Medical Technician	Paramedic	Administrator	Range of Labor Cost/ Unit Hour	Average Labor Cost/ Unit Hour
Private company	$12,754	$16,721	$29,277	$12.03–35.03	$20.99
Separate municipal	15,248	19,709	24,913	11.01–49.46	31.38
Hospital-based	13,999	19,381	28,091	17.19–35.89	27.40
Fire department	18,818	25,528	35,725	10.30–45.32	25.98
County-operated	14,261	18,664	27,730	11.05–55.89	21.53
Overall average	14,520	18,540	29,516		
Change from 1984	−12.44%	−8.78%	+.08%		

Source: *Journal of Emergency Medical Services,* January 1985.

tions; profit-oriented EMS firms included those operated by hospitals and small private providers. Cost structures differed widely among these industry participants.

Municipal Services   Spurred by various federal programs and growing pressures from constituents, the commitment of local municipalities to upgrade the quality and availability of urban emergency services had shown some growth in recent years. Consequently, the scope of police and fire departments was broadened in some locales to include on-the-scene medical assistance and treatment. While the municipal EMS was increasingly paid for with tax revenues, patient transfer services were normally handled by a private ambulance service.

Volunteer Organizations   The volunteer segment of the industry operating along with rural not-for-profit firefighting associations included those who periodically donated their time and first-aid skills to a particular geographic community. Fees collected supported training and equipment rather than compensation. Industry sources estimated that approximately 25 percent of the total EMS market was served by volunteer providers.

Hospitals   Some hospitals, pressed financially by declining bed use and more competition, instituted ambulance businesses as feeder systems for their more definitive health care facilities. With the hospital name and logo prominently displayed on both the ambulance and the uniforms of EMS personnel, such services often became a powerful marketing tool in the community.

Private Providers   The dominant force in the industry, however, continued to be the small profit-oriented enterprise. This segment was beset with high capital investments in vehicles, heavy insurance costs, and the need to keep personnel on duty for 24-hour time frames. While some firms did pursue the state of the art in equipment and training, many could be characterized as undermanaged and poorly motivated to provide state-of-the-art emergency care.

FUTURE INDUSTRY DIRECTIONS

Analysts believed that a number of important factors would affect the future shape and direction of the emergency medical industry:

1. The increasing costs and sophistication of medical technology would require continued assessment of labor, equipment, and all related performance variables.
2. As demands for quality grew, prior training and experience requirements would place added burdens on the small provider.
3. Private firms would find it increasingly difficult to maintain high operating standards and remain profitable, especially where local governments were interested in starting a municipal EMS.
4. Since municipal EMS programs were expensive, their perceived inefficiencies could come under more careful voter scrutiny in future economic downswings.
5. Pressures would escalate concerning technical malpractice. Providers, technicians, and equipment manufacturers would fall under closer legal observation.
6. Antitrust law complexities would have an increased effect on communities that promote both tax-based and private ambulance services.
7. With more competitive compensation schedules, the ambulance field should be able to attract more career-minded individuals.
8. There would be increased controversy over the amount of on-the-scene care as opposed to more immediate transport of the accident victim.
9. It would become increasingly important for EMS providers to work in closer proximity with health care planning agencies.
10. Comprehensive statewide and interstate EMS systems would be developed further.
11. EMS would become an even more integral process to the total health care delivery system. Competing ambulance firms may be integrated into this unified system, forcing cooperative rather than purely competitive postures.
12. With federal and state budgets in decline, the market could swing back toward heavier reliance on private EMS providers.

REFERENCES

"Ambulance Shortages Puts Firms in Bind." *The Wall Street Journal,* April 17, 1984, p. 37.

Committee on Trauma. "Essential Equipment for Ambulances." *Bulletin, American College of Surgeons,* August 1983, pp. 36–38.

Committee on Trauma. "Qualifications of Trauma-Care Personnel." *Bulletin, American College of Surgeons,* October 1983.

Emergency Medical Services Division: NTS-42 National Highway Traffic Safety Administration. *Emergency Medical Services: Transportation and Communications Field Intervention Medicine.* Washington, D.C.: U.S. Government Printing Office, 1983.

Hering, Alex. Chicago: American College of Surgeons, Interview, June 25, 1985.

"The 1985 Almanac of Emergency Medical Services." *The Journal of Emergency Medical Services* 9, no. 1 (January 1984).

"The 1985 Almanac of Emergency Medical Service." *The Journal of Emergency Medical Services* 10, no. 1 (January 1985).

Page, James O.   *The Paramedics.* Morristown, N.J.: Backdraft Publications, 1976.

Peisner, Michael B., and Eldridge R. Hicks.   *An Evaluation of the Private Ambulance Industry in Michigan.* Ann Arbor: University of Michigan Press, 1973.

Rockwood, Charles A., et al.   "The History of Emergency Medical Services in the United States." *The Journal of Trauma,* April 1976, pp. 299–308.

"State Survey." *Emergency Medical Services* 12 (October 1983), pp. 97–113.

Valisis, John.   Chattanooga Fire Department, Chattanooga, Tennessee, Interview, July 6, 1985.

CASE 12 THE TULIP CITY AMBULANCE COMPANY, INC.*

BACKGROUND OF THE FIRM

On May 10, 1983, the Tulip City Ambulance Company celebrated its 25th anniversary. In an industry characterized by short life cycles and rapid participant turnover, management considered this to be a monumental achievement. Launching the enterprise as a part-time venture on $3,000 of family funds, Marshal (Mart) Berghorst was, for the most part, the driving force behind the company's success.

Following his wife's troubled pregnancy, which required several emergency trips to the hospital, Mart concluded that neither of the two funeral homes nor the existing independent provider offered an acceptable degree of quality in emergency ambulance care. Soliciting some friends who possessed high-speed driving skills and who enjoyed a periodic respite from home each week, the 20-year-old entrepreneur combined a $500 savings with his father's capitalization to place a down payment on a 4-year-old Cadillac hearse. Additional bank financing was obtained to outfit and convert the vehicle into ambulance service, supply working capital, and provide initial rent on an abandoned gas station with a working hoist.

An important reason for the firm's early success came from the "gentlemen's agreement" negotiated with the Poindexter Funeral Home to handle their emergency nighttime calls. This allowed the funeral directors a full night's sleep without any appreciable effect on profits.

In August of 1960, Marshal Berghorst resigned from his daytime job at the local Ford garage and was named president and chief executive officer of the recently incorporated Tulip City Ambulance Company. Berghorst's talents were not limited to mechanical technology alone. When he was not on duty at the company's base of operations or busy with maintenance for the vehicle and equipment, he was out placing the firm's telephone stickers wherever there was a high probability of an emergency occurrence.

To cover mounting fixed costs and to address the expanding nonemergency demands, Mrs. Berghorst began to handle all office and dispatching duties while Mart, in addition to his ambulance duties, concentrated more earnestly on the company's transfer services. By the end of 1962 both funeral homes elected to drop out of the ambulance business by converting their vehicles into hearses and selling their emergency telephone numbers to Tulip City. While this ploy doubled the firm's emergency volume to four daily calls and halved the number of competitors, the fledgling enterprise faced even stiffer competition from the county's only other provider, the DeYoung Ambulance Company.

* Prepared by J. Kim DeDee, The University of Tennessee at Chattanooga and Richard C. Johanson, The University of Arkansas. The research and written information was presented at a Case Research Symposium and were evaluated by the Case Research Association's Editorial Board. All rights reserved to the authors and the Case Research Association. Reprinted with permission. The company's name is disguised; however all key relationships remain intact.

With over 4,000 independent and volunteer organizations in existence, Tyson De-Young had been able to parlay a sizable inheritance and extensive debt financing into the third largest ambulance company in the United States. While most firms served relatively small local areas, DeYoung, by 1965, had operations in Michigan, Illinois, and Indiana, with expansion plans covering Ohio and Kentucky. Stressing emergency transport, DeYoung ambulances were positioned at most regional sporting events, entertainment programs, and the Indianapolis Motor Speedway. This latter tactic exposed the firm's name and logo to almost 350,000 spectators attending the various time trials, parades, and the Memorial Day race. Further recognition was also gained through national radio and regional television coverage of these events.

The DeYoung growth pattern in property and equipment remained consistent through the early 1970s. After committing a series of strategic errors, however, the company's revenue and cash flow plummeted until 1975 when it faced insolvency. Later that year Tyson DeYoung died of alcoholism and his widow sold the one remaining vehicle and the accounts receivable to Tulip City for $5,000. No employees were retained. Tulip City continued to operate the DeYoung service as a wholly-owned subsidiary.

For the rest of the decade, Tulip City held an almost unchallenged monopoly position and under the direction of Marshal Berghorst had accomplished the following results: opened and equipped a second base doubling the firm's operating radius; acquired the assets of two bankrupt competitors; diversified into specialty emergency transport services (hospital to hospital) for premature infants and critically injured adults; vertically integrated into new ambulance construction; and introduced entry-level standards and development courses for all personnel.

THE OPERATING ENVIRONMENT

Located between two interstate highways in Michigan's Lower Peninsula, the Manchester/Springdale area had recently experienced sizable population growth patterns. Part of this 5–6 percent annual increase was due to the favorable economic climate of the region and the strong religious work ethic of its Polish and Dutch inhabitants. Attracted by the community's lower-than-average age and higher-than-average income levels, Sears, J.C. Penney, and other major chains had expanded their retail operations in the Lincoln County area. In addition, a variety of smaller retailers had recently opened stores that appealed to more discriminating buyers. A second force behind this expansion was the continuing industrialization of the tri-county metropolitan area. Since Manchester/Springdale was within close proximity to the huge automotive complexies of eastern Michigan and was the central location for a large university, industry analysts considered it ideal for the location of low-technology manufacturing plants. The general upbeat economic optimism of the community had been further enhanced by the recent announcement by a big three automaker that Manchester was one of two final site choices for its new $500 million final assembly plant.

Prior to 1980, Tulip City Ambulance's biggest threat came from Tyson DeYoung's competitive maneuverings. Beginning in 1980, however, the firm faced a growing number of threatening developments. There were emerging competitive threats from the recently organized "Ambulance for Jesus" movement and the newly started David Vanlaar service. In addition, Tulip City had to contend with an increasingly hostile city government, the likelihood of the downtown hospital entering the business, and the possibility of territorial encroachment by at least one of the area's municipal agencies.

The Competition

Tulip City not only competed directly for consumer acceptance, but also for referrals from medical personnel concerning transfers to and from hospitals, rest homes, and related institutions. In the last five years the company had fared reasonably well in its toughening environment. Total ambulance requests in Manchester/Springdale had risen to one daily call for each 6,600 people. This, however, reflected only partially on Tulip City's effectiveness. While the company held a clearly dominant position, its share of the market had shown an overall steady decline in the last half decade.

The newest competitive threat facing Tulip City originated from a small group of missionaries organized "to provide a fully licensed and highly qualified Christian ambulance service to the people of Manchester and Springdale." Developed solely as a charitable venture, the Ambulance for Jesus firm relied primarily on contributions to cover its variable costs and in 14 months had been able to increase its volume load to five calls a week.

Tulip City's most serious competitive threat came from the now solidly entrenched Van's Ambulance Service. Since its inception in early 1980, the firm's principal objective, according to founder David Vanlaar, "was to obtain market position and respect using luxury emergency vehicles. This company was not created to produce short-term profits but to provide a viable growth-oriented activity for myself and those who follow my business philosophy."

In January of 1976 Vanlaar dropped out of college to enter the U.S. Army. While there, he worked as a heavy equipment operator, lived frugally, and in four years was able to meet the initial payment requirements on one of the few remaining Cadillac ambulances to be produced. The firm had sufficient resources through loan agreements from Manchester's second largest hospital (St. Luke's—400 beds) to penetrate substantially into Tulip City's market position. Rather than rely on personal selling, Vanlaar's primary marketing approach was the ornate vehicle, large Yellow Page advertisements, and sales of a subscription service. This latest technique annually offered families one emergency or one transfer call at less than 35 percent of normal competitive rates. In addition, Vanlaar distributed bright green bumper stickers with the company name, logo, and phone number.

Vanlaar felt that regardless of situational complexities, requests for his ambulance were specific rather than general. Thus to maintain corporate integrity, company policy stated that when the car was tied up on either a transfer or emergency and a second call came in, the initial call would be completed under lights and siren status to avoid referring the later call to a competitor. Despite repeated complaints from medical personnel and patient's families, the policy has not been altered.

Vanlaar's strategy stressed minimizing response time to or from the trauma scene. The speeds attained by the high-performance Vanlaar vehicle, after a number of police warnings and newspaper editorials, resulted in a reckless driving summons

(92 mph in a 25 mph zone) and a court appearance. In an effort to convince the jury and the general public regarding the validity of his methods, Vanlaar retained a Chicago-based law firm known for its truculence.

A motivated prosecution presented a force of expert witnesses including a noted orthopedic surgeon who stated:

> In the past 13 years I have had occasion to be familiar with more than a few emergency cases. In no instance can I recall where speed in transportation of the injured patient materially affected the patient's outcome. . . . Actually, what is necessary is appropriate methodology adequately applied at the scene, which I can state parenthetically, the Van's personnel are either unable or unwilling to provide, and then a reasonable speed, say 10 miles an hour over posted limits with allowed passage through red traffic lights. . . . This is required if our streets are to remain safe for all concerned.

After two days of heated court debate Vanlaar was acquitted of all charges.

As a counter strategy to the growing conflict developing between his firm, the local emergency medical industry, and both municipalities, Vanlaar initiated a series of half-page newspaper ads with a conservative political theme. Each promotion began with "Did you know" and included at least one of the following topics:

1. That firemen, professing to be first-aiders, have stood waiting by dying patients for professional medical help and not attempting any life supporting techniques?
2. Police agencies have ordered ambulance attendants away from persons needing service because the attendants were not of their particular political choice? At least one such patient died.
3. That people in need have waited 45 minutes for ambulance service because they called a police or fire agency first?
4. That the county is going to use hundreds of thousands of dollars to accomplish what is already being done "Tax Free" because of a lack of cooperation with available resources?

The promotional campaign also included quotes relating to "progression without taxation" and "Don't waste time calling a police or fire agency first, call us directly and immediately for your medical emergencies. The Vanlaar Ambulance Company— the state's most progressive service."

The Hospitals

In August of 1983, Bellview General (450 beds), the city's largest and most centrally located hospital, was acquired by a national chain noted for its innovative and aggressive management style. Following a year of extensive reorganization, Jackson Baker was offered and accepted the position of vice president of Hospital Projects and reported directly to the Executive Committee. After preparing in-depth analyses on a number of potential investments, Jackson decided to promote the idea of a hospital-based ambulance service which he felt would better position the trauma center within the organization's overall strategic objectives. Bellview was profitable and in fairly sound financial condition, but recently had experienced a reduced bed-use factor similar to the rest of the industry. To assure future growth patterns for the hospital, the following key points were stressed in his report:

A properly designed and maintained hospital-based ambulance service should:

1. Provide access to additional revenue sources from a relatively small investment base ($125,000).
2. Increase to 41–42 percent the number of patients being admitted through the trauma center.
3. Create a valuable marketing tool and generate goodwill in the community through exposure of the hospital name and logo on vehicles and uniforms.
4. Utilize more effectively the trauma center personnel.
5. Act as an effective feeder system to more definitive care helping alleviate the unused capacity problem.
6. Countervail the market share gained by St. Luke's through their direct financial assistance of Van's Ambulance Service.
7. Allow complete emergency care for the patient from trauma scene to possible extended care admission.

By September the Executive Committee began deliberations on the proposal and instructed Mr. Baker to develop a management team, refine or modify certain objectives, and begin negotiations with principal resource suppliers.

Manchester's Response

Sensing the growing alienation developing within the city emergency medical service (EMS) system, Paul Wynski, recently appointed director of Manchester's Primary Services Department, set out to pursue two principal objectives. First came the desire to put his office at the forefront of the city's growth pattern, and second, he wanted to personally establish some tangible evidence indicating his potential for higher government offices.

As director, Wynski was responsible for the total operations and performance of two separate groups, the City Protection Group (police) and the Fire Protection and Control Group. A simple breakdown of the $22 million budget indicated 76 percent covered salaries for 870 employees, while the remainder went to property, plant, and equipment. Included in this final category was the central administration building, 18 regional fire stations, 21 diesel pumpers, 7 ladder trucks, and a fleet of patrol cars.

To meet his present intentions, Mr. Wynski contemplated a number of alternatives, but settled on a municipal tax-based EMS rescue and transportation system. His initial strategy was to begin strictly as an advanced emergency care treatment and extraction service with later expansion into transport. Paramedic training was estimated to take two years with another six months needed to operationalize the total EMS process. He estimated the billing and collection procedure would allow the system to become self-supporting by year three.

Wynski believed in change and innovation but was practical enough to realize that any major variation in his department would be a formidable task. To help win the approval of the city commission, he sent the memo shown in Exhibit 1.

Director Wynski was pleasantly surprised at the outcome of the meeting. Most commissioners heartily agreed with the general intentions of the proposal and gave tacit approval to the design of his emergency medical paramedic system.

Enthusiastically returning to his office, Wynski promptly scheduled a meeting with his staff intent on furthering development of the EMS model. To increase the profile

Exhibit 1   Memorandum

To: All City Commissioners

From: Paul L. Wynski, Director of Primary Services

Re: Establishment of a class A emergency medical service system
Date: November 16, 1984

As a result of the growing unrest in the current independently operated emergency medical service (EMS) system, I would appreciate your opinions on the following project objectives. I plan to make a more formal presentation of these generalized goals at the commission meeting scheduled December 3, 1984.

Critical Objectives:

1. Establishment of a citywide advanced life support (ALS) emergency rescue and treatment system.
2. Expansion into emergency transport of trauma victims.
3. Development of billing and collection procedures encouraging the service to become self-supporting.

Rationale for the System

1. No paramedics in Manchester.
2. Springdale is currently considering a similar system.
3. Tulip City Ambulance—the city's largest provider—only offers Basic Life Support (BLS).
4. Possibility of Manchester setting a state recognized precedent.
5. Alleviation of expanding turmoil in the current EMS system arising from the Van's Ambulance Company's operating style.

Future tactics include:

1. Additional research focusing on property, plant, equipment, and personnel costs.
2. In-depth observation of municipal services currently operating in adjoining states.
3. Expert judgments detailing legal complexities and antitrust laws.

of his ambulance system concept, the director also called both television stations and the local paper to arrange detailed news releases.

TULIP CITY AMBULANCE OPERATIONS

By 1980, Tulip City and the reorganized DeYoung service (see Exhibit 2) had both achieved solid reputations in the private ambulance sector. Following the acquisition, the parent company and its subsidiary occupied two bases with garages at strategic points in Manchester and Springdale. The bases, both located in low-income areas, were extensively refurbished in 1975 to provide living, office, and meeting space in addition to usual kitchen facilities. The Manchester locations of the two services

Exhibit 2   Organization Chart, Tulip City Ambulance, Inc.

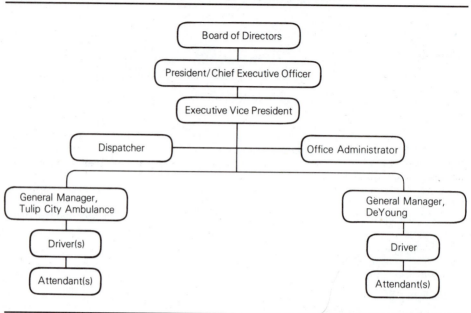

shared the central administration office and a 2,600-square-foot garage that housed a majority of the vehicles and associated maintenance and repair equipment.

In January 1975, as a move to show support for Springdale, Tulip City enlarged its base capacity there and built a similar but smaller garage (1,800 square feet) to cover the primary and backup vehicles and assorted rental wheelchairs, hospital beds, and ancillary devices. All the buildings were either built or reconditioned by Berghorst and construction teams he assembled and were in acceptable operating condition. Between 1975 and 1985, however, despite extensive usage and exposure, no major repairs or upgrading were performed on any of the firm's property or facilities.

Key Personnel

Berghorst served as chief executive officer and board chairman, posts that he had held since 1960. He was considered one of the most knowledgeable experts in ambulance company management and occasionally had acted in this capacity to consult with various EMS agencies and private concerns. Berghorst made all major decisions in the running of the firm, but at some distance. It was generally agreed by the other managers that if Mart liked an idea it was implemented; if he did not, it was dropped. Since 1980, he had become heavily involved with rental property, a used car lot, and foreign travel.

Karl VerBeek was hired into the position of executive vice president and general manager of Tulip City in July of 1974. He had previously been a sales manager with a large international pharmaceutical firm, a position he later gave up as too confining and without challenge to open a small delicatessen specializing in natural foods. Over the years he developed a close, but sometimes strained, friendship with Berghorst on both professional and social levels. His initial responsibilities at Tulip City were to build a more refined technical work force, establish financial stability, and strengthen the firm's tie-ins with the city's political infrastructure. Karl's manner of presenting ideas and his penchant for challenging work brought him immediate success. His 96-hour work weeks were reduced to 70 in 1983. This extra time afforded him the opportunity to continue a graduate degree in business (MBA) and put more sophistication into the daily administration of Tulip City. In anticipation of a larger organization, VerBeek began strengthening the firm's control and planning systems, showing special emphasis on reducing uncollectable accounts and formalizing equipment purchase decisions. With an eye on eventual ownership of the firm, he had maintained his emergency medical qualifications and performed nearly every management task.

From time to time Karl had received executive-level offers from Bellview General and his former employer. Becoming a little irate at the CEO's autocratic style and his occasional override of lower level decisions, VerBeek was beginning to weigh more carefully his personal costs for such a move.

Phillip Lasser joined Tulip City in 1976 as manager/driver of the newly acquired DeYoung service. Coming to the firm from a technical position in Bellview General's Emergency Department, he faced the effort of rebuilding the tarnished image of De-Young as an exacting challenge. Lasser kept his team small but continued to stress the state of the art in emergency ambulance technology.

Mrs. Berghorst, while continuing her role as director, had long since left the office and dispatching duties to devote more time to her family and various social obligations.

The remainder of the work force was balanced between full- and part-time people. Except for the office personnel, all were licensed EMTs, with a few pursuing paramedic level training at the local community college. With access to temporary help from various fire and police department EMTs, the personnel needs for the immediate future were deemed adequate.

The Marketing and Operating Culture

From the beginning Tulip City had been a market-oriented company retaining a wide view of its role in emergency health care. Rather than viewing itself as a provider of luxury convalescent transportation, or as an overextension of trauma center technology, the Tulip City/DeYoung organization saw itself in the business of offering high-quality but cost-effective methods while utilizing efficiently designed and maintained resources. The company further believed there were substantial differences in these three approaches. In the first, emphasis was placed strictly on the vehicle, avoiding almost all personal responsibility. In the second, the growing but limited understanding of the EMT tended to be stressed beyond its intended realm during critical time frames when the patient needed to be moved to facilities with more specialized trauma care capability. In the final method, a balance had to be reached between immediate care and stabilization of the patient and that of appropriately timed and prepared transport.

The Tulip City organization's philosophy began with the training and indoctrination of new members. Only those near completion of the 100-hour EMT course were considered for employment. Their skills and personalities were then evaluated by current team members during a two-week trial period. Once accepted, individuals were expected to cooperate fully with the team effort and to update their abilities through periodic seminars and training programs.

The Tulip City philosophy was further enhanced through the production and use of its ambulance fleet. Since 1970, the company had become almost totally integrated by producing all but one of its own heavy-duty emergency vehicles. Few firms in the industry could duplicate this capability. To minimize production costs and allow for immediate recognition on the road, specialization had played an important role in the construction of the company's two types of vehicles.

After extensive negotiations with a number of local dealers, Berghorst settled on the Ford F-250 Econoline and F-350 chassis (driver compartment and frame/wheels only) for the Type II and Type III units, respectively. Structurally, these trucks were purchased with the "ambulance preparation package" which, in addition to deluxe driving compartments, included extended-duty cooling, air conditioning, braking, suspension, and electrical systems. The first half of 1980 was a critical time in the upgrading of the company ambulance fleet with the purchase of three vans and two F-350 chassis.

Getting these vehicles ready for service was a temporary but central activity for Berghorst and was characterized by expert craftsmanship, coordination of a host of detail work, and a deep sense of personal pride. Upon completion of each project, Berghorst often remarked, "These units are dependable, durable, good looking, and cost about 80 percent of the normal going price." Both styles of Tulip City emergency ambulance were made up of many individual parts such as cabinetry, stainless steel support and hinge devices, leather work, vacuum and pressure lines, and a labyrinth of electronic circuitry.

The production process basically involved six stages. First, various pressure and vacuum lines were positioned alongside the electrical wiring harnesses and cables. Second, the fiberboard flooring was anchored, on which a balance of right and left side cabinets were installed. Next, the linoleum, Formica, and other veneers were cut, fitted, and bonded into position for all countertops, cabinetry, and floor surfaces. Fourth, the ventilation, internal lighting, support mechanisms, and switches were installed, as was the leather seating and padding devices. The fifth stage involved the securing of the scene lights, warning lights, and siren apparatuses. Finally, the car was driven to a custom detail shop where the federally mandated accent strips and company name and logo were hand painted into place. The entire operation took about five weeks per unit to complete.

Toward the end of 1978 an awkward situation started to develop in the geographic area surrounding Manchester and Springdale. A number of peripheral hospitals found they could no longer cope with the increased severity of some trauma victims and the growing number of neonatal (premature) births. At the culmination of much discussion and negotiation, Tulip City and Bellview General jointly agreed to build two vehicles capable of addressing these unique needs. The specifics of the program stated that Berghorst would design and build customized patient treatment chambers retrofitted on a Type III/Modulance chassis for stable emergency transportation between the outlying hospital and Bellview General.

The value of the baby unit was its capacity to carry a neonatologist, registered nurse, inhalation therapist, and ancillary equipment to the smaller outlying hospital and return with the crew and one to four incubators. The patient(s) could then be stabilized by the team before and during transport to Bellview's recently expanded Neonatal Intensive Care Unit (NICU).

Slightly larger in size than the baby bus, but with a similar internal configuration, the trauma unit was intended mainly for emergency transfers of adults between hospitals. Staffed by an emergency room physician and a carefully selected and trained crew, the use of this unit to date had been very disappointing. Revenue, maintenance, and repairs of either vehicle were shared equally by both program partners.

The normal maintenance routine of the fleet included periodic servicing every 5,000 miles of the engine and structural lubrication systems. Every 30,000 miles, the brakes, shock absorbers, batteries, and related components were upgraded or replaced, while at 100,000 miles the drive train (engine, transmission, etc.) and other major components were completely rebuilt. This final measure, which was supervised closely by Berghorst, was estimated to cost at least $5,200 and extend the life of the vehicle another 30,000 miles.

The remainder of the company's fleet consisted of three Ford vans, five Cadillacs, and a recently purchased Chevrolet high top custom-built ambulance. Management rebuilt the Fords according to schedule, using them only as backup vehicles. In contrast, the 1975 Cadillacs were purchased in poor condition and, unlike the rest of the fleet, were not upgraded; they were mainly utilized for long distance transfers. The Chevrolet was purchased rather impetuously by Berghorst during a convention, but when confronted by his executive vice president on the decision, his response was "I got a deal that I couldn't pass up," and the matter was dropped.

Tulip City/DeYoung facilities and equipment were specifically designed to meet the expanding needs of Lincoln County and, in a growing number of cases, an even larger circle of operations. The two bases, the radio network, the skill level of the work force, and the complexity of the vehicle fleet gave the company flexibility to respond quickly to ever-widening consumer use of ambulance and emergency services.

Realizing the consumer's purchase of ambulance service was difficult to segment into any workable classification scheme and that a note of urgency normally circumvented the unsought nature of the product offering, management utilized a variety of promotional techniques. Supplementing the prominent positioning of the company's name and logo on vehicles and uniforms was the widespread use of Yellow Page advertisements. Since the first reaction of a person in need of an ambulance was to use the telephone or Yellow Pages, the company concentrated much of its promotional efforts around the telephone.

In March 1981, Tulip City introduced its first prime time television commercial. Product awareness messages featuring the transfer, EMS, and specialty units reached approximately 300,000 people in the lower portion of the state. In addition to the single-station TV commercials, other advertisements were aired on three local radio stations and published in the area newspaper.

Exhibit 3   Tulip City Ambulance Vehicle Evaluation Schedule as of December 31, 1984

Date in Service	Vehicle	Unit Cost ($000)	Annual Mileage (000)	Evaluation
1/76	Van (3)	$13.9	5.0	Moderate/poor condition Life: 30,000 miles
1/78	Cadillac (5)	$12.5	2.0	Very poor condition Life: 7,500 miles
7/80*	Van	$16.9	20.5	Good condition Life: 8,000 miles
7/80	Van	$16.9	20.0	Good condition Life: 10,000 miles
7/80	Van	$16.9	18.0	Good condition Life: 19,000 miles
7/80	Modulance baby unit	$29.7	12.5	Good condition Life: 44,000 miles
7/80	Modulance trauma unit	$26.3	3.0	Excellent condition Life: 5 years
1/83	Van†	$26.3	14.0	Excellent condition Life: 70,000 miles

* All units purchased since 1980 are expected to be rebuilt or replaced at 100,000 miles.
† Chevrolet.
Source: Company records.

Finance and Accounting

Tulip City retained a local CPA firm to draw up financial statements for management decision making and income tax purposes. Earnings not retained were taxed as personal income at both the federal and state levels. Even with the growing complexity of the business, and the resultant financial documentation, no management/accountant discussions of consequence have taken place since 1979. Exhibits 3 through 9 contain supplemental data and consolidated financial information for the years 1980–84.

From 1980 to 1985 TCA experienced steady increases in total revenue aided in part by consumer acceptance, community growth, and the special utility vehicles. Management was not sure whether TCA's billing rates were set at premium levels. This was due mainly to the uncertainty over the pricing strategies of both competitors in the greater Manchester area. While it was relatively easy to obtain reliable estimates of what Van's was charging at any one point in time, the company deliberately varied its prices up or down often to keep competitors guessing. Moreover, it was increasingly evident that rates patients found acceptable varied depending on the services performed and the image of the firm within the community.

Payroll was distributed biweekly, with nonexempt personnel receiving 76 regular hours and 8 overtime hours for each of the 26 pay periods. To minimize morale and turnover problems, Berghorst advocated steady increases in pay levels (at something less than inflation) for the 12 full-time and various part-time EMTs. After the addition of the new vehicle in 1983, the number of EMTs was increased to 14. Selected compensation costs are shown below:

Position	1980	1981	1982	1983	1984
EMT hourly wage	$ 6.00	$ 6.30	$ 6.60	$ 7.00	$ 7.30
Part-time employee payroll	29,500	30,975	32,520	34,146	35,860
Dispatcher salary	10,200	10,700	11,235	11,800	12,390
Office administrator salary	11,500	12,100	12,705	13,340	14,000
Office part-time	12,000	12,600	13,230	13,840	14,585
CEO salary	35,000	40,000	45,000	50,000	55,000
Executive vice president salary	22,500	23,650	24,883	26,075	27,380
Payroll taxes (percent)	7.13%	7.86%	7.78%	7.78%	8.00%

Exhibit 4 Comparative Ambulance Volume, TCA versus Van's, 1980–1984

Year	Population†	Purpose	Average Number of Daily Calls* TCA	Van's	Total‡	TCA's Collection Rate (percent)
1980	145,500	EMS	12.0	.5	12.5	62%
		Transfer	12.5	1.0	13.5	86
1981	147,525	EMS	11.0	1.0	12.0	62
		Transfer	13.5	1.2	14.7	86
1982	154,900	EMS	10.0	2.0	12.0	62
		Transfer	14.5	2.0	16.5	87
1983	162,650	EMS	10.0	2.5	12.5	63
		Transfer	14.5	2.5	17.5	87
1984	170,780	EMS	9.5	3.5	13.5‡	63
		Transfer	15.0	2.0	18.0‡	87

* EMS and transfers only
† Manchester 85 percent, Springdale 15 percent.
‡ Totals here include calls to "Ambulance for Jesus" group.
Source: Company records and casewriter's computations.

Exhibit 5 Special Vehicle Use, Tulip City Ambulance, 1980–1984

Year	Neonatal Unit Calls	Neonatal Call Price	Collection Rate (percent)	Trauma Unit Calls	Trauma Call Price	Collection Rate (percent)
1980	125	$218.75	85%	5	$249.0	88%
1981	265	227.50	85	12	257.1	87
1982	280	235.30	84	11	255.4	89
1983	300	249.75	83	13	277.8	86
1984	320	270.50	86	13	288.8	84

Note: Both special units were put into service on July 1, 1980.
Source: Company records.

Exhibit 6   Revenue and Critical Expense Summary, Tulip City Ambulance, 1980–1984

	1980	1981	1982	1983	1984
Ambulance/EMS					
Revenue:					
Base rate	$ 60.00	$ 65.00	$ 65.00	$ 65.00	$ 65.00
Mileage rate	.50	.50	.60	.60	.65
Distance	8.00	8.00	8.00	9.00	10.00
Miscellaneous	12.00	11.50	12.50	13.00	13.50
Total	$ 76.00	$ 80.50	$ 82.30	$ 83.40	$ 85.00
Expenses:					
Fuel (9/mpg)	$ .84	$ .84	$ .84	$ .95	$ 1.05
Labor	12.00	12.60	13.20	14.00	14.60
Maintenance	310.00	335.00	350.00	370.00	390.00
Insurance	450.00	450.00	470.00	470.00	470.00
Ambulance/transfer					
Revenue:					
Base rate	$ 60.00	$ 60.00	$ 65.00	$ 65.00	$ 65.00
Mileage rate	.75	.85	.90	1.00	1.00
Distance	17.00	17.00	17.00	18.00	18.50
Total	$ 72.75	$ 74.45	$ 80.30	$ 83.00	$ 83.50
Expenses:					
Fuel (12/mpg)	$ 1.35	$ 1.35	$ 1.35	$ 1.43	$ 1.43
Labor	18.00	18.90	19.80	21.00	21.90
Baby van unit					
Revenue:					
Base rate	$125.00	$130.00	$130.00	$135.00	$140.00
Mileage rate	1.25	1.30	1.30	1.35	1.45
Distance	75.00	75.00	81.00	85.00	90.00
Total	$218.75	$227.50	$235.30	$249.75	$270.50
Expenses:					
Fuel (12/mpg)	$ 6.00	$ 6.00	$ 6.50	$ 6.75	$ 7.15
Labor	24.00	25.20	26.40	28.00	29.20
Maintenance	365.00	785.00	835.00	880.00	925.00
Insurance	350.00	725.00	730.00	740.00	750.00
Trauma unit					
Revenue:					
Base rate	$150.00	$150.00	$150.00	$150.00	$150.00
Mileage rate	1.65	1.70	1.70	1.75	1.85
Distance	60.00	63.00	62.00	73.00	75.00
Total	$249.00	$257.10	$255.40	$277.75	$288.95
Expenses:					
Fuel (11/mpg)	$ 5.20	$ 5.50	$ 5.35	$ 6.30	$ 6.50
Labor	24.00	25.20	26.40	28.00	29.20
Maintenance	75.00	150.00	600.00	175.00	190.00
Insurance	275.00	550.00	560.00	560.00	600.00

Note: All maintenance and insurance amounts are annual expenses per unit, fuel at $.95/gallon, and distance in miles.

Exhibit 7   Comparative Income Statements, Tulip City Ambulance, 1980–1984

	1980	1981	1982	1983	1984
Operating income:					
EMS	$332,880	$323,207	$300,395	$304,410	$294,738
Transfers	331,922	366,852	424,988	439,278	441,924
Special units:					
Baby unit	13,672	30,143	32,942	37,462	43,280
Trauma unit	623	1,543	1,405	1,805	1,877
Total operating revenue	$679,097	$721,745	$759,730	$782,955	$781,818
Operating expenses:					
Wages	$194,236	$203,948	$213,730	$258,370	$269,694
Depreciation	51,350	51,350	36,350	42,850	16,600
Maintenance	4,190	4,935	5,555	6,350	9,200
Fuel	13,788	5,253	15,885	15,678	17,218
Uncollectible accounts:					
EMS	126,494	122,818	114,150	112,632	109,053
Transfer	46,469	51,360	55,248	57,106	57,450
Special units	1,015	2,218	2,404	2,847	3,387
Linen and supplies	1,348	1,482	1,556	1,635	1,715
Total operating expenses	$438,890	$453,364	$444,878	$497,468	$484,317
Gross margin	$240,207	$268,381	$314,852	$285,487	$297,502
Administrative expenses:					
Salaries	$ 91,200	$ 99,050	$107,000	$115,105	$123,355
Payroll taxes	20,350	23,816	24,950	29,056	31,444
Employee benefits	52,716	56,055	59,335	69,093	72,714
Telephone	3,685	3,870	5,070	5,365	5,680
Utilities	5,460	6,000	6,550	6,870	7,220
Insurance	5,525	6,175	6,195	8,225	8,275
Advertising	0	800	900	1,000	1,100
Property taxes	9,300	9,300	12,100	12,100	12,100
Supplies	1,208	1,260	1,330	1,400	1,460
Postage	2,480	2,497	2,800	2,813	2,933
Miscellaneous	1,606	1,680	1,815	1,905	2,000
Professional services	3,000	3,300	3,565	3,750	3,930
Total administrative expenses	$196,530	$213,803	$231,610	$256,682	$272,211
Income from operations	$ 43,677	$ 54,578	$ 83,242	$ 28,805	$ 25,291
Nonoperating income expenses					
Interest expense	34,947	27,842	19,440	16,527	8,452
Income before taxes	8,370	26,736	63,802	12,278	16,839
Taxes	2,183	6,684	21,055	3,069	4,210
Income after taxes	$ 6,548	$ 20,052	$ 42,747	$ 9,208	$ 12,629

Exhibit 8   Comparative Balance Sheets, Tulip City Ambulance, 1980–1984

| | As of December 31 | | | | |
	1980	1981	1982	1983	1984
Assets					
Current assets:					
Cash	$ 2,500	$ 511	$ 2,232	$ 1,364	$ 1,536
Accounts receivable	84,187	90,356	92,777	81,517	82,364
Inventory	337	371	389	409	429
Prepaid insurance	6,175	6,195	8,225	8,275	8,690
Total current assets	93,199	97,433	103,623	91,565	93,019
Fixed assets:					
Land	75,000	75,000	75,000	75,000	75,000
Buildings	128,000	128,000	128,000	128,000	128,000
Less: Accumulated depreciation . .	−73,000	−81,000	−89,000	−97,000	−105,000
Vehicles	208,275	208,275	208,275	234,275	234,275
Less: Accumulated depreciation . .	−97,100	−138,350	−164,600	−197,350	−203,850
Equipment	20,000	20,000	20,000	23,000	23,000
Less: Accumulated depreciation . .	−8,500	−10,500	−12,500	−14,500	−16,500
Furniture and fixtures net	4,000	3,900	3,800	3,700	3,600
Total fixed assets	256,675	205,325	168,975	155,125	138,525
Total assets	$349,874	$ 302,758	$ 272,598	$ 246,690	$ 231,544
Liabilities and Owners' Equity					
Current liabilities:					
Current maturity of notes	$ 51,582	$ 39,272	$ 45,642	$ 21,409	$ 11,532
Accounts payable	310	425	390	450	680
Payroll taxes payable	13,320	14,140	14,968	17,429	18,342
Wages/salaries payable	4,391	4,662	4,935	5,746	6,047
Income taxes payable	546	1,671	5,263	767	1,052
Other	245	380	589	325	430
Total current liabilities	70,394	60,550	71,787	46,126	38,083
Noncurrent liabilities					
Notes payable	131,139	91,867	46,223	43,768	32,236
Total liabilities	201,533	152,417	118,010	89,894	70,319
Owners' Equity:					
Common stock ($10 par)	40,000	40,000	40,000	40,000	40,000
Paid in capital	5,000	5,000	5,000	5,000	5,000
Retained earnings	103,341	105,341	109,588	111,796	116,225
Total equity	148,341	150,341	154,588	156,796	161,225
Total liabilities and owners' equity . .	$349,874	$ 302,758	$ 272,598	$ 246,690	$ 231,544

Exhibit 9   Summary of Notes to TCA's Financial Statements

1. TCA uses the accrual method of accounting for reporting and tax purposes.
2. Accounts receivable are stated at actual amounts minus an estimated sum for uncollectibles based on past trends.
3. All fixed assets are stated at cost. Depreciation for tax and reporting requirements is computed with the straight line method with minimum salvage values. The useful lives of the assets are: buildings, 15 years; furniture and fixtures, 15 years; vehicles, 4 years; and equipment, 10 years. Full depreciation of the fixed assets are: primary base, 1984; secondary base, 1989; vehicles (Chevrolet), 1986. All other assets are fully depreciated.
4. Repairs and maintenance are generally charged to operations as they occur. When an asset is sold or removed from service, its cost and related depreciation are omitted from the accounts with the gain or loss being recognized at the time of removal.
5. The real estate mortgage is 9 percent on both items of property. The debt on the primary base will be released in December of 1985 and the debt on the secondary base in December of 1989.

Whenever feasible TCA financed expansion from retained earnings; debt was used whenever internal cash flows had to be supplemented. Through the first 15 years of the company, the small family of investors continued to reinvest a large portion of earnings in the business. Short-term requirements were met through open lines of credit with the state's two largest banks and were generally secured by corporate accounts receivable. Bank debt was also used to finance the vehicle fleet at prevailing interest rates, with collateral coming from the ambulances and corporate property holdings.

Since 1978 the firm had purchased ambulances in four or five lot sizes causing periodic strains to its interest and debt capacity. Also since 1979, Berghorst had withdrawn cash from TCA to help finance his other business ventures.

VIEW OF THE FUTURE

Karl VerBeek once again had to contemplate the growing myriad of problems facing TCA as of 1985. He knew that TCA had to clarify its direction if it were to remain a leader in the industry. Revenue from EMS operations showed almost constant decline; price battles with Vanlaar were always a threat; and volume related to the transfer business appeared headed for a plateau.

Even the specialty vehicles raised new problems, not the least of which was how these units would be used and what would happen to total revenue if Bellview Hospital went ahead with plans to incorporate its own ambulance service.

The city government's challenge to Tulip City was also increasing; not only were plans well under way to establish municipal-based emergency aid and treatment at the scene but it was generally assumed that once this operation was in place, a transport process for the victims would soon follow.

As the executive vice president glanced at the financial documents he had accumulated on his desk, his attention shifted to the meeting Mart had requested take place that afternoon.

In addition to the ambulance business, Mart Berghorst made frequent trips overseas to buy high-priced European automobiles to be converted to American pollution control standards and sold on his retail lot. Immediately after returning from one such trip a few months earlier, Berghorst had called in his executive vice president for the following conversation:

> I am quite pleased with the way you have managed the operations of Tulip City and DeYoung over the past few years. I don't have your formal education, but I do have a nose for what is right or wrong concerning expenses and profits. This business seems to be doing as well as can be expected. We have talked in the past about setting up a more sophisticated planning process with budgets, objectives, goals, strategies, and a computer. I again gave your idea some thought while I was in Europe but I still feel that this business is changing so rapidly and Vanlaar has thrown so much confusion into the local area with his severe price-cutting and antagonistic operations that we can only plan a few days at a time. Your efforts to obtain cost data on different aspects of this business have been helpful, but that is as detailed as I want to go.
>
> It has been my policy on past occasions to buy vehicles or equipment when I thought the price was right. I've made some mistakes especially with the Cadillacs and the high interest rates we paid on them and the Fords. We've gotten fairly good use out of the truck fleet but the luxury cars were a complete waste of money and I wish I had never bought them.

VerBeek wondered what this latest meeting would be about. Berghorst's primary reason for the meeting soon became evident:

> Personally, Karl, I have struggled to reach a position in this business where I would have more time to spend on my other interests and with my family. I have been tempted to milk this venture dry and then walk away from it. Now, I feel it is only fair to let you know that much to my surprise, David Vanlaar called me about six weeks ago with an initial offer to buy the company. While at first I thought he was joking, he went on to say that St. Luke's would support his intention by providing partial financing for the acquisition.
>
> The CPA and I were to meet with Vanlaar, Dykema (administrator of St. Lukes), and some bank officials to discuss our records, books, and financial operations. No meeting ever took place, however, and I thought the matter was dropped. Then yesterday morning Vanlaar and Dykema called from the bank and gave me an offer, which I feel is much more (but I really don't know) than the firm is worth. Even though I seriously doubt that Vanlaar could handle an operation like this one, I also think I would be foolish not to accept the offer.
>
> As I have mentioned to you before, Karl, I will sell this company to you as well. But you know our relationship with Bellview is becoming strained and it is up for grabs if they will bankroll you like St. Luke's is doing for Vanlaar.

Karl VerBeek left the meeting angry and resentful to call his wife and ponder the future.

CASE 13 COMPETITION IN THE U.S. BREWING INDUSTRY*

In 1983, the U.S. beer brewing manufacturers had to reassess the competitive consequences of a much-revised industry structure. So-called second tier producers had
engaged in a flurry of mergers and acquisitions over the past four years to try to
bolster their ability to compete with the two largest producers, Anheuser-Busch and
Miller Brewing Company. At one point or another, during the 1979–83 period, all
of the second tier brewers except Adolph Coors had been involved in some sort of
merger proposal:

March 1979. Sixth-ranked G. Heileman Brewing Company acquired Carling National
Brewing for $33.7 million. Carling's 3.5 million barrels of capacity gave Heileman
14.5 million barrels of capacity and a 6.4 percent market share. Brands acquired
included Colt 45, Tuborg, Carling Black Label, Heidelberg, and Stag.

April 1979. Fifth-ranked Pabst acquired Blitz-Weinhard Brewing for $8.4 million giving
Pabst an 8.8 percent market share at the end of 1979. Brands acquired included
Blitz-Weinhard, Henry Weinhard Private Reserve, and Olde English 800 Malt Liquor.

May 1981. Seventh-ranked Stroh Brewery acquired ninth-ranked F. M. Schaefer Brewing Company for $32 million, adding 3.6 million barrels of brewing capacity to Stroh's
6.2 million barrels and giving Stroh a combined market share of 5.5 percent (based
on 1980 totals).

July 1981. Sixth-ranked G. Heileman offered to buy fourth-ranked Jos. Schlitz Brewing
Company for $494 million. Schlitz's 1980 sales of 14.7 million barrels (8.3 percent
market share) would have given G. Heileman a third place ranking—approximately
10 million barrels behind Miller Brewing.

August 1981. Schlitz closed its 6.8 million barrel capacity Milwaukee brewery after a
bitter strike. Third-ranked Pabst Brewing Company offered to buy Schlitz for $588
million.

October 1981. Heileman's proposed merger with Schlitz was blocked by the Justice
Department on antitrust grounds.

December 1981. Dissident stockholder Irwin Jacobs initiated a proxy fight for control
of fifth-ranked Pabst.

February 1982. Pabst, struggling to maintain its 5th-place industry ranking, made an
unsuccessful offer to acquire 12th-ranked Pittsburgh Brewing Company for $7.8 million
(had the purchase succeeded, it would have added one million barrels and 0.5 percent
market share to Pabst's totals).

February 1982. C. Schmidt and Sons, the 10th largest brewer, made an offer to acquire
Pabst for $128 million (the offer later proved unsuccessful).

March 1982. The Stroh Brewery made an offer for control of struggling but still third-
ranked Schlitz; the bid was later approved by Schlitz shareholders. As a condition
for not opposing the merger, however, the Justice Department required Stroh to sell
off Schlitz's breweries in Memphis, Tennessee, and in Winston-Salem, North Carolina.

* Prepared as a basis for student analysis and class discussion by Professor Arthur A. Thompson, Jr., with the
assistance of graduate student researchers Tom McLean and Elsa Wischkaemper, all of The University of Alabama.
Copyright © 1984 by Arthur A. Thompson, Jr.

Based on 1981 data, the merger gave Stroh a market share of 12.8 percent (compared to Anheuser Busch's 29.9 percent and Miller's 22.1 percent). The brands acquired included Schlitz, Schlitz Light, Erlanger, Schlitz Malt Liquor, Old Milwaukee, and Old Milwaukee Light.

June 1982. Fourth-ranked G. Heileman offered, in the first of a series of attempts, to buy fifth-ranked Pabst for $196.8 million. The acquisition of Pabst would give G. Heileman 27.5 million barrels or 15.1 percent market share based on 1981 data and would move Heileman up from a regional brewer to a national brewer. Pabst at the same time offered $35.6 million for 49 percent ownership of eighth-ranked Olympia Brewing Co. During the following months, Pabst and Olympia agreed to merge in a cash and stock transactions valued at $70.2 million. Meanwhile a three-way bidding war for control of Pabst unfolded.

December 1982. Fourth-ranked G. Heileman, in battling for control of Pabst, emerged partly victorious, receiving two breweries of Pabst (Georgia and Oregon) and one of Olympia's (Texas) for $183.5 million. The transaction added 8.5 million barrels of capacity and gave G. Heileman a 26 million barrel per year production capacity and an 8 percent market share. In addition, Heileman acquired production and marketing rights to six of Pabst's former brands: Lone Star, Blitz Weinhard, Henry Weinhard Private Reserve, Red White and Blue, Burgermeister, and Buckhorn. Heileman agreed to produce 3.15 million barrels of beer for Pabst. New Pabst emerged with 14.5 million barrels of capacity. Brands that remained with Pabst included Pabst Blue Ribbon, Olympia, Olympia Gold, Hamm's, Hamm's Light, Pabst Extra Light, Jacob Best Premium, Jacob Best Premium Light, and Andeker.

May 1983. Pabst swapped its brewing and malting facilities in St. Paul, Minnesota, to Stroh for Stroh's Tampa, Florida, brewing and can-making operations.

Exhibit 1 Brewing Industry Volume, Brewing Capacity, and Number of Years, 1972–1983

Company	Brewing Volume (in millions of 31-gallon barrels)					
	1972	1976	1980	1981	1982	1983
Anheuser-Busch	26.5	29.1	50.2	54.5	59.1	60.5
Miller Brewing	5.3	18.4	37.3	40.3	39.3	37.5
Stroh	28.7	35.2	24.7	23.5	22.9	24.3
Pabst Brewing	12.6	17.0	15.1	13.5	12.3	12.8
Adolph Coors	9.8	13.5	13.8	13.3	11.9	13.7
Heileman	10.0	9.5	13.3	14.0	14.5	17.5
Total majors	92.9	122.7	154.4	159.1	160.0	166.3
Others	40.7	29.7	22.1	20.2	19.1	13.8
Total	133.5	152.4	176.5	179.3	179.1	180.1
Less exports	(1.6)	(1.9)	(3.1)	(2.6)	(2.4)	(2.6)
Imports	0.9	2.4	4.6	5.2	5.8	6.3
Total U.S. consumption	132.8	152.9	111.0	181.9	182.4	183.8

Sources: Goldman Sachs research department and various company annual reports.

The end result of the merger consolidations was an industry dominated by six firms—see Exhibits 1 and 2.

HISTORY AND BACKGROUND

Beers had been in existence since perhaps 6000 B.C. In ancient Egypt and other Mediterranean countries, beer was considered as nutritious and more hygienic than drinking water. Beer and bread were standard components of the basic adult diet in medieval Germany and England. Knowledge about brewing beer came to America with the Pilgrims, and English-style ales were a favorite of the Colonial era. In the 1840s, an influx of German immigrants with brewmaster skills and production know-how stimulated growth in the number of breweries. By the 1870s, there were several thousand breweries in operation in the United States; total production was about 6.6 million barrels annually, and per capita consumption was 5.3 gallons. By the early part of the 20th century, a series of technical innovations—refrigerated freight cars, new pasteurization processes, and mechanized bottling equipment—resulted in greater production capacity, the ability to distribute beer regionally rather than just locally, and economies of scale. As the strongest and most aggressive brewers began to expand operations to exploit the combination of a growing market for beer and scale economies, the smaller and weakest breweries were gradually squeezed out of the market and a long-term decline in the number of breweries began.

Percent Increase	Compound Growth		Brewing Capacity 1983 (in millions of barrrels)	Number of Breweries 1983
	1978–1983	1973–1983		
2.4%	7.8%	7.3%	66.0	11
(4.6)	3.7	18.4	44.0	6
6.1	(4.0)	(2.6)	29.0	7
4.1	(3.6)	(0.2)	14.0	4
15.1	1.7	2.3	15.0	1
20.7	10.8	5.3	26.0	11
2.9	3.3	4.9	193.0	40
(27.7)	(10.6)	(9.6)	27.9	38
0.6	1.7	2.5	220.9	78
8.6	12.5	19.1		
0.8	2.0	2.8		

Exhibit 2   Market Shares of Leading U.S. Brewers, 1973–1983

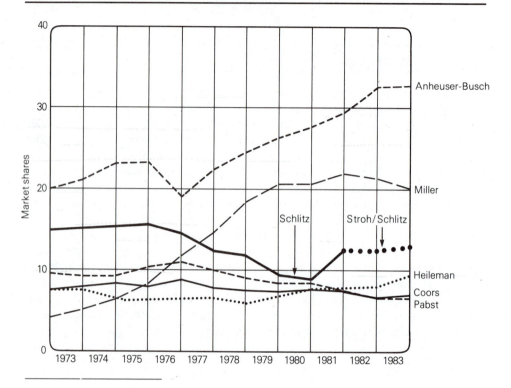

Source: Goldman Sachs research department.

Maintaining a profitable volume of operation had historically been a struggle for small brewers because the product was bulky, costly to distribute, had a fairly short life span before spoilage, was heavily taxed, and entailed high labor costs to produce. After the Prohibition years of 1920–34, brewers began to attack these sources of high cost/low margin operations. Labor productivity was increased via investments in bigger plants, shifts to more capital intensive production methods, and installation of automated equipment. Cost savings were instituted by increasing the speeds of canning and bottling equipment. Some brewers integrated backward into malt production (a key ingredient) and into making their own cans. The introduction of rice and corn as partial substitutes for the more expensive barley in the malt process further reduced costs. Improving transportation networks and declining transportation rates lowered shipping costs and permitted economical distribution over a wider area. The more successful brewers began to construct plants in more than one location to take advantage both of shipping economies and of opportunities to market over a wider geographic area. The guesswork in the brewing process was eliminated during the 1950s as scientific advances in microbiology and equipment technology enabled brewers to control all the variables in the brewing process and thus brew a consistent, uniform beer from batch to batch. Many local and regional breweries lacked the customer base and investment capital to cope with these competitive developments and went out of business.

Meanwhile, as many as 15 of the largest brewers pursued opportunities to move toward national market coverage for their products. The strategies of the up-and-coming national brewers had three main components: (1) to brew "premium" beers with mass appeal taste and a quality image, thus establishing a contrast with the stronger, more distinctly flavorful character of the many locally brewed beers which had native popularity; (2) to get their beers into more supermarkets, bars, and other retail outlets by building a broader geographic network of local distributors; and (3) to pull their beer brands through these channels by increased regional and national advertising. The aim was to achieve volume growth by (1) capitalizing on the expanding population and the trend of more people to drink more beer and (2) by cutting into the market shares of local and regional breweries. The strategy of convincing beer drinkers to switch over from local to nationally advertised brands began to succeed. The use of television advertising during the 1950s and 1960s, growing sponsorship of nationally televised sports events, and the emergence of supermarket chains as major beer sales outlets accelerated the battle for market share among the national, regional, and local brewers. Competition intensified. The national firms pushed their beers as premium quality and they charged premium prices (usually 10 to 20 cents per six-pack more); the locals and regionals touted their traditional flavor and the pride of local manufacture and sold their beers at "popular" prices. It was a battle that the bigger firms continued to win:

Year	Number of Plants	Number of Firms	Combined Market Shares	
			Four Largest Firms	Eight Largest Firms
1947	465	404	21%	30%
1954	310	263	27	41
1963	211	171	34	52
1967	154	125	40	59

Then when cigarette giant Philip Morris acquired seventh-ranked Miller Brewing Company in 1969 and proceeded to introduce a wave of marketing innovations that revolutionized the way beer was marketed, competitive pressures took another quantum leap. Within a 10-year span, Anheuser-Busch (with its Budweiser and Michelob brands) and Miller Brewing (with its Miller High Life and Miller Lite brands) captured combined market shares approaching 55 percent of the U.S. beer market. A scramble by the remaining brewers to remain in the race with the two leaders led to a major industry shake-up and restructuring. Most of the remaining second tier firms found themselves confronted with closing down or accepting a long-term decline in volume and market share or merging with another firm or coming up with fresh ways to maintain their current market positions. Between 1970 and 1983, the number of beer manufacturers declined from just over 110 to less than 45 and the number of brewing plants declined from 137 to 78. Consolidation in the industry's structure was reflected in the 20-year shift in the market share percentages of the top six firms:

1962		1972		1982	
Firm	Market Share	Firm	Market Share	Firm	Market Share
Anheuser-Busch	9.8%	Anheuser-Busch	20.1%	Anheuser-Busch	33.0%
Schlitz	7.5	Schlitz	14.3	Miller	21.9
Pabst	6.4	Pabst	9.6	Stroh	12.8
Carling	5.9	Coors	7.4	Heileman	8.1
Falstaff	5.8	Falstaff	4.7	Pabst	7.0
Ballantine	5.0	Schaefer	4.2	Coors	6.7
All others	59.6	All others	29.7	All others	10.5

THE BEER MANUFACTURING PROCESS

Brewing beer was much like concocting a stew; the recipe could vary and the result was a function of the quantity and quality of the ingredients, the way they were combined, and the processing time. Beer was made from four principal ingredients: a fermentable cereal grain (such as barley, corn, rice, wheat, oats, or rye), a fermenting agent (yeast), a flavoring and preserving agent (hops), and water. The grain contributed color, sweeteners, body, protein, vitamins, minerals, carbohydrates, and most important, the starch that was converted into sugar by means of malting. Barley was considered the best cereal grain for beer making and gave the brew a fuller body and richer flavor. Yeasts were classified as bottom fermenting, top fermenting, or wild; the various yeasts used added to the brew's distinctive taste. Fermentation took place when the yeast agent attacked the natural malt sugar, converting it into approximately equal parts of alcohol and carbon dioxide gas; the alcohol content of most beers was about 4 percent by volume. At the end of the fermentation period, the yeast was removed and a small quantity was kept as the starter for the next batch. Hops were added to the developing beer at the beginning of the brewing stage for flavoring purposes and were added again at the end of the brewing stage to preserve the beer's smell; only the flower from the female hops plant was used—a tiny, yellowish green, soft-leaved cone measuring an inch that came from perennial vinelike plants of the hemp family. Water, fortified with dissolved mineral salts of calcium sulfate and magnesium sulfate, also enhanced the beer's taste and flavor.

There were nine basic steps to the commercial beer making process (Exhibit 3). Depending upon what "recipe" the beer manufacturer opted to use, the brewing process could take anywhere from a couple of weeks to as much as four months per batch. The variability in the quantity and quality of the ingredients chosen and the processing time was what produced differences in taste, body, and "character" from beer to beer. For example, the level of bitterness was a function of malt content and the amount of hops; a lighter color could be achieved by using rice and corn at a ratio of 60 to 40 for the more expensive barley; and the distinctive color and flavor of ales, stouts, and pilsener beers stemmed from the amount of time the malt was roasted. Artificial flavors and colors, carbonic injection, foam stabilizers, and chemical preservatives could also be used to vary the taste and qualities a beer had. The difference in the manufacturing costs between cheap, low-quality beers and the best-tasting, high-quality beers was generally less than $3–$4 per barrel (5 percent

Exhibit 3 The Nine Traditional Brewing Stages

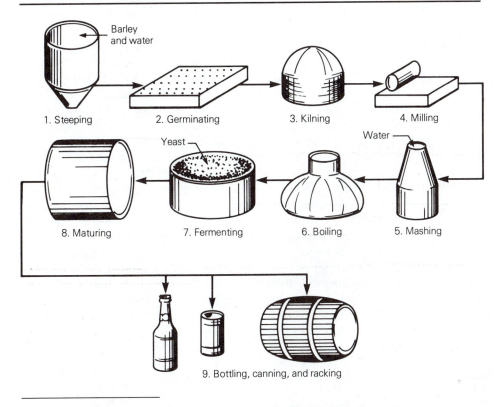

Source: Howard Hillman. *The Gourmet Guide to Beer* (New York: Washington Square Press, 1983), p. 160.

of the manufacturer's selling price) and consisted mainly of differences in ingredient costs and the costs of aging.

As of the 1980s, beer manufacturers had the know-how and brewing skills to make beers with a wide range of taste, smells, colors, body, and caloric content. However, the major U.S. brews looked and tasted pretty much alike, mainly because brewers believed that most American beer drinkers preferred smooth-tasting, relatively bland brews, compared to the heavy-bodied and more flavorful European brews from which American beer descended. To make their beers even smoother and "more drinkable," U.S. brewers had in recent years reduced the hops content of their beers by 15 percent. The whole flavor level had come down, to achieve a milder taste; malt content had also been reduced, to lighten the filling sensation. American beers were described by beer connoisseurs as weak and bland in comparison to European beers, which had strong, often bitter (because of high hops content), distinctive tastes. A 1978 report to the Federal Trade Commission concluded that a person's ability to tell one brand of U.S. beer from another probably declined "drastically as the quantity of beer consumed per sitting increased." The first few sips was said to be where beer drinkers could most readily distinguish the difference in the tastes of various brands.

Brewing Facilities   While the number of brewing plants in the United States had declined over the years, the average size of plants had nonetheless increased dramatically. In 1946, the average U.S. brewery had a capacity of 200,000 barrels annually. The newest and most efficient plants in the 1980s had capacities of 4 to 10 million barrels; the largest brewery in the industry was Coors's 15 million barrel brewery in Golden, Colorado. A modern plant incorporating the largest technology could cost from $50 million to $300 million, depending on its size; capital investment requirements were in the range of $30–$50 per barrel of new capacity. The newest breweries were much more automated than their older counterparts, resulting in important labor cost savings (average hourly wages of production workers were among the highest in the United States). The minimum efficient plant size was said to be about 1.25 million barrels annually, but scale economies existed up to annual capacities of 4–5 million barrels. Depending upon a brewery's size, when it was built, the brewing process it incorporated, the wages paid to production workers, and the use of automation, the brewing costs per barrel could vary considerably. For example, in the early 1970s, one analyst estimated that Falstaff's production costs in its four small, older plants (combined capacity of 4.1 million barrels and 1800 workers) were $4.39 per barrel, an amount four times the $1.08 per barrel costs that Schlitz supposedly incurred at a large newly constructed plant (capacity of 4.4 million barrels and workforce of about 480 people).

TYPES OF BEERS

As of 1983, there was little industry standardization in the way various beers were classified and labeled. Most of the world's major beers were technically either ales (top-fermenting) or lagers (bottom-fermenting). Ales were brewed mainly in Europe. Lagers were predominant in the United States. Over 90 percent of American-style beers were pale lagers—a term commonly used by beer manufacturers and beer connoisseurs to describe a beer with a light body, bland taste, scant flavor, and high carbonation (in comparison to other beer types). During the 1970s, many U.S. manufacturers introduced "light" beers, which had even less body and flavor than "regular" pale lagers; far and away the most attractive characteristic of light beers was that they had about one third fewer calories than regular beers. Another type of beer was commonly referred to as draft beer. From a strictly technical and historical perspective, draft (or draught) beer was a term used to describe a naturally carbonated, unpasteurized, minimally filtered beer drawn by the server directly from a wooden barrel; however, in the United States, the term *draft beer* had over the years come to mean any beer tapped from a keg, regardless of whether it has been pasteurized, filtered, or artificially carbonated—in fact, in the United States the only distinction between draft beer and regular beer was that draft beer was served directly from a keg, whereas regular beer came in cans or bottles (the beer itself was the same). Malt liquor was a classification of beers whose alcoholic content was too high to be legally referred to as "beer"—as defined by state statutes. Near beers were virtually alcohol-free beers (less than 0.5 percent alcohol by weight). Beer could also be "home-brewed"; in the United States it was legal for any adult to brew up to 100 gallons of beer per calendar year for personal or family use without having to obtain a license or pay a tax. There were also a few "hybrid beers" on the market which were a blend of bottom-fermented lagers and top-fermented ales.

From a price standpoint, beers sold in the United States could be grouped into five categories: luxury-priced, super-premium, premium, popular-priced, and budget-priced. However, price was not tightly correlated with quality since how would-be connoisseurs or average beer drinkers rated a beer on "quality" was a matter of personal taste and preference. The luxury-priced classification included most of the foreign import brands; these often retailed for 25 cents to 50 cents more per 12-oz. bottle (or $1.50 to $3.00 more per six-pack) than beers in the super-premium price group. The super-premium beers (the most prominent of which were Anheuser-Busch's Michelob brand and Miller's Lowenbrau brand) typically retailed for about 5 to 10 cents per 12-oz. bottle (or 30 cents to 60 cents per 6-pack) above the premium group. Superpremium beers were a cut above the general run in terms of ingredients, brewing process, aging, and/or taste. Most of the best-selling U.S. beers fell into the premium-priced category (such brands as Budweiser, Miller High Life, Coors, Stroh, and Schlitz). However, because there was no industry or government standard as to what the term *premium beer* stood for, some manufacturers labeled their beers "premium" but priced them below the levels of other premium beers—at so-called popular prices. The popular-priced beer category consisted of those premium beers sold at subpremium prices plus a host of regional and locally brewed beers, most of which retailed for less than the best-selling premium beers; popular-priced beers usually were 20 cents to 50 cents cheaper per six-pack than were premium-priced beers. The budget-priced category consisted mostly of "no name" brands and generic beer—their primary appeal was low price.

The recent U.S. market share breakdowns and 1990 projections by type of beer were as follows:

	1970	1975	1980	1981	1982	1990 Projections
Luxury-priced imports	0.7%	1.1%	2.6%	2.8%	3.1%	8.0%
Super-premium beers	0.9	3.4	6.0	6.1	6.1	11.0
Premium-beers, except light	37.6	47.0	49.6	49.4	46.6	45.0
Light beers	0.0	1.9	13.0	14.7	17.1	20.0
Popular-priced beers	58.3	44.0	25.6	23.8	23.8	15.0
Malt liquor	2.5	2.6	3.2	3.2	3.3	1.0
Total	100.0%	100.0%	100.0%	100.0%	100.0%	100.0%

The brands of the major producers, arranged by category, are shown in Exhibit 4.

DISTRIBUTION CHANNELS

Beer was channeled to consumers through a three-tier system: brewery to wholesaler/distributor to retail outlet. In the case of imports, the network was often brewery

Exhibit 4   Principal Brands of Major U.S. Brewers, as of 1983

Company	Premium Brands	Super-Premium Brands	Light Brands	Popular Brands	Malt Liquor Brands	Imports
Anheuser-Busch	Budweiser Premium Busch Classic Dark	Michelob Michelob Classic Dark	Michelob Light Budweiser Light Natural Light	Busch	Budweiser Malt	
Miller Brewing	Miller High Life	Lowenbrau Special Reserve	Lite	Meister Brau Milwaukee's Best	Magnum Malt Liquor Miller High Life Ale Miller High Life Malt Liquor	Munich Oktoberfest
Stroh Brewery	Stroh Schlitz	Erlanger Stroh Signature	Stroh Light Schlitz Light Old Milwaukee Light Stroh Bohemian Light Schaeffer Light	Old Milwaukee Goebel Schaeffer Schaeffer King's	Schlitz Malt Liquor	—
G. Heileman Brewing	Old Style Rainier National	Special Export Tuborg Gold Henry Weinhard Special Reserve Schmidt Extra Special Tuborg Dark	Heileman's Premium Light Stag Light Lone Star Light Red White & Blue Light Blatz Light Old Style Light Schmidt Light Rainier Light Black Label Light Wiedeman Light Grainbelt Light Falls City Light Heidelberg Light Sterling Light National Light	Sterling Stag Pfeiffer Sterling Special Weidemann Drewery's Grain Belt Schmidt Falls City Extra Special Blatz Dunk's Lone Star Blitz Weinhard Red White & Blue Burgermeister Buckhorn Medalian Special Carling Black Label Heidelberg National Bohemian	Colt 45 Malta Havey, Malt Duck, Mickey's Malt Liquor Fischer's Ale Red Cap Ale Rainer Ale Blatz Light Cream Ale	Beck's
Pabst Brewing	Pabst Blue Ribbon Pabst Special Dark Olympia Hamm's	Andeker Jacob Best Premium	Pabst Light Jacob Best Premium Light Hamm's Light Hamm's Special Light Olympia Light Buckhorn Light	Blitz Burgie Maxx	Olde English "800"	Fuerstenberg
Adolph Coors	Coors	Herman Joseph's 1868	Coors Light			Stella Artois

to importer to wholesaler/distributor to retail outlet. Distributors were appointed by the beer manufacturer; each brewery found it a competitive necessity to have a strong network of wholesale distributors handling their brands in order to gain access to retail outlets and consumers. If, in a beer producer's opinion, a distributor was not doing a good job of representing its products in a given area, then the brewer could arrange for its brands to be handled by another distributor. Every brewer exerted major efforts to see that its brands were handled by strong, aggressive distributorships and spent much time and money building a healthy, profitable relationship with distributors.

In 22 states, laws permitted breweries to assign exclusive territories to wholesale distributors; in the remaining states, looser territorial agreements were arranged. Depending upon population size and density, a distributor's geographic coverage could range from a single county on out to a radius of 300 miles. In 1983, legislation was pending in Congress to exempt exclusive brewer-distributor territorial sales agreements from the federal antitrust laws. Territorial lines were more strict in the agreements Anheuser-Busch and Miller Brewing had with their distributors than was the case with other breweries. Transshipping by one distributor into another distributor's area was looked upon unfavorably by most distributors as causing price cutting and a deterioration of customer service, but it was supported by consumer groups as being conducive to price competition and necessary to reduce distributor complacency.

Merger and consolidation among the U.S. brewers had precipitated a decline in the number of beer wholesaler/distributors and an increase in their size:

	Number of Beer Wholesaler Establishments	Estimated Average Volume (in barrels)	Estimated Average Sales ($ millions)
1963	5,788	16,200	$0.6
1972	5,114	25,800	1.3
1980	4,713	37,700	3.7
1982	4,551	40,200	4.2

Mergers among beer producers reduced the need for as many distributorships. There was no assurance that a distributor handling the brands of a brewery being acquired would continue to handle those brands after the merger. When Stroh acquired Schlitz, management elected not to appoint a number of Schlitz distributors to handle the combined Stroh/Schlitz brands. The trend was toward having only three or four distributors serving an area—one that functioned as the distributor for all the Anheuser-Busch brands (and sometimes several imports and selected brands of a second tier brewer), one that distributed Miller products (and perhaps several brands of one or two other brewers as well as selected import brands), perhaps one that handled the brands of one or more strong second tier or regional brewers along with several imports, and one that handled the remaining brands sold in that area. However, in the 50 or so largest metropolitan areas there were often 5 to 10 distributors, one or more handling the brands of the leading brewers in the area and frequently a distributor which specialized in imported beers.

The prevailing view among distributors was that they could not survive unless they handled a variety of brands; the key to a distributor's success was to represent enough popular-selling brands to be efficient and to produce a big enough gross profit over cost of goods sold. Fewer than 30 percent of the distributors handled only the brands of a single brewer, and the percentage was declining. Increasing numbers (rising to 25 percent in 1983) of beer wholesalers were taking on wine and distilled spirits lines and functioning as alcoholic beverage distributors—integrating complementary lines into their operations was considered an economical move because such retailers as bars, restaurants, supermarkets, and package stores carried all types of alcoholic beverages and were agreeable to dealing with one distributor for all their alcoholic beverage supplies. Distributors benefited from multiple lines because it increased average sales per account; multiple lines did, however, increase the complexities of truck loading and efficient route design. Some distributors were also adding bottled water and snack food items to their lines.

Distributors operated on markups of 20 to 40 percent over the price which they paid brewers; this worked out to a margin of about $1.75 per case (24 12-oz. cans or bottles) for popular-priced beers and about $2.35 per case for super-premium brands. The margins on import brands were bigger—about $3.00 to $4.50 per case in 1983. Margins on keg sales were much smaller (about 20 to 25 percent).

Distributors were usually supplied from the brewery closest to their territory. The area brewery maintained sales information on each affiliated distributor's territory, aided distributors in forecasting brand sales, did market analyses for distributors, and recommended prices and quotas based on past sales. In most cases, beer was shipped FOB the brewery via common carrier.

Distributors were required by their territorial agreements to service all retail accounts irrespective of whether the retailer chose to buy a few cases on an irregular basis or was a high volume retail outlet for the distributor's brands. Each distributor had to have truck fleets of the type and number required to make deliveries on an as-needed basis to supermarkets, convenience food stores, bars, restaurants, fast-food outlets, "mom-and-pop" country stores, and service stations which stocked beer. The primary way beer retailers were serviced was through the use of route sales techniques, whereby truck drivers left the warehouse each day with a fully loaded truck and brand assortment, making scheduled calls on retailers located on an assigned geographic route. The truck driver functioned as salesperson as well as delivery person, filling orders on the spot and generally stocking the cooler or shelves for the retailer in the process. It was important for the driver-salesperson to maintain good relationships with customers, to tailor service to each customer's situation, and to monitor product freshness (removing stale products from shelves when the last sales date had expired). Some distributors, mainly in large population centers, employed a special sales force to presell large chain supermarket accounts and obtain orders for specific quantities in advance; this allowed the distributor to organize more efficient routing of delivery trucks, to know how much of which brands and package types to put on a given load, and to employ more economical on-and-off-loading techniques (using pallets and lift trucks to replace individual handling of cases). Good truck routing and establishing optimal call frequencies for customers made a vast difference in how efficiently a distributor used its truck fleet.

Distributors had several roles to play in promoting and selling a beer producer's brands in the locales they served. One was to sell bars and taverns on stocking the producer's brands and on serving its flagship brands on tap. Most on-premise retailers carried a limited number of brands and were equipped to serve only one to three brands on tap. Distributors competed fiercely with one another to gain access to the on-premise segment. In addition, local distributors helped sponsor area sporting events and community sports teams (softball, bowling, and so on), erected billboards on roads and near roadside taverns, put neon signs in bars, erected point-of-sale displays in supermarkets, designed advertising displays for their trucks, held sampling parties, and participated in price promotions.

Most breweries found it competitively useful (for reasons of excess capacity or overstocked inventory or campaigns to build market share) to run special price discount campaigns from time to time; these were coordinated through local distributors. Such "post-offs" from regular price were conducted over special time periods (such as a Fourth of July holiday weekend), with the intent being to pass the savings through to beer drinkers. Distributors and retailers were not required to participate in the price discounting, though it was customary for distributors and supermarket chains to do so. A number of distributors and retailers were reluctant to engage in price discounting on a regular basis because of drop-offs in sales when they stepped back up to charging regular prices.

Exhibit 5 presents some statistics on the number and size of beer distributors who primarily handled the brands of the major brewers.

Beer Retailers   Distributors sold beer only to retailers who were licensed by state and/or local governments as authorized outlets. Licenses to retailers generally permitted sales either for on-premise consumption (restaurants and bars) or for off-premise consumption (supermarkets, convenience food stores, and package stores).

The retail markup for on-premise consumption was substantial—seldom less than 100 percent and, in the case of draft beer, as much as 700 percent over cost. A bottle of beer might cost a restaurant 40 cents yet it could have a menu price of $1.00 to $1.75. Draft beer was even more profitable. The price of a keg, depending on the brand, had a wholesale cost of about $90–110 from the distributor; a keg provided 350–400 glasses of beer, depending on glass size, retailing at $1.25 to $1.75 per glass, equal to gross revenue of $437 to $700 per keg. (Keg beer, however, was generally little more than a break-even proposition for distributors because of the smaller distributor margin and because kegs were more costly to handle and store.)

Off-premise retailers had variable markup policies on beers, depending on type of store, location, and competitive influences. Premium beers purchased at supermarket chains usually had no more than a 20 percent margin; however, popular-priced brands sold primarily on the basis of price could have as little as a 5 percent markup over distributor cost. Beer sold direct from coolers sometimes was priced slightly above beer sitting on the shelf. The retail markup on superpremium and import brands could be as much as 25–30 percent. Convenience food stores, some package stores, and many low-volume outlets put higher markups on beers than supermarkets. One price survey in Houston showed a six-pack of Coors (12-oz. cans) retailing for $3.29 in package and convenience stores and for $2.79 in major supermarket outlets; Miller Lite 12-packs ran $5.99 in liquor and convenience stores and $5.79 in supermarkets. Retailers could at their own choosing elect to put a given brand of beer "on special," featuring the off-price amount in newspaper ads and at in-store point-of-sale displays.

Exhibit 5   Number and Size of U.S. Beer Distributors, by Primary

Sales Size ($ millions)	Anheuser-Busch No.	Anheuser-Busch %	Miller No.	Miller %	Stroh/ Schlitz/ Schaefer No.	Stroh/ Schlitz/ Schaefer %
$50 or more	4	0.4	1	0.1	—	—
$25 to $50	17	1.6	15	1.7	7	0.8
$10 to $25	86	8.0	103	11.8	34	3.8
$5 to $10	128	11.9	113	12.9	99	11.0
$3 to $5	180	16.8	147	16.8	129	14.4
$2 to $3	230	21.4	230	26.3	234	26.1
$1 to $2	226	21.0	157	17.9	229	25.5
Less than $1	203	18.9	110	12.5	165	18.4
Totals	1,074	100.0	876	100.0	897	100.0

Note: The numbers shown in the exhibit are less than the total number of distributors handling some or all of each brewer's brands; included in the breakdowns above are only the estimated number of distributors whose *majority of sales* are the brands of the indicated brewer.
Source: Beverage marketing Corporation; *Beverage Industry Annual Manual 1984.*

Supermarkets viewed beer as an attractive item to feature in their weekly "on sale" specials because of its ability to generate additional store traffic.

BREWING INDUSTRY COST STRUCTURE

Because of intense rivalry and the need to be competitive on price and cost, brewers stayed on top of all aspects of production and distribution costs, beginning with ingredients and continuing through to the price paid by consumers. To gain some control over ingredient costs, some brewers had integrated backward into grain and malt production, supplying part or all of their needs. An even greater number had integrated into the manufacture of aluminum cans, paper cartons, and labels—packaging costs were the single biggest component of beer manufacture, amounting to about 40 percent of the manufacturer's net selling price. Most brewers were unionized; wage rates were generally above the all-manufacturing average. Labor productivity, however, was primarily a function of the brewing process, the age of the brewery and key pieces of equipment (particularly bottling, can filling, labeling, and packaging), and the degree of capacity utilization. Manufacturing cost of goods sold (ingredients, direct wages and salaries, packaging, and depreciation) ran about 70 percent of the brewer's selling price, although the percentage varied according to whether the beer was super-premium or popular-priced. Most brewers strived to realize at least a 10 percent operating profit margin on their overall sales mix.

Beer was heavily taxed at the federal, state, and local levels. State and local taxes varied appreciably from place to place, but it was not unusual for 20 to 25 percent of the retail price to be taxes of one kind or another.

Affiliation with Major Brewers, 1981

Pabst/ Olympia		Coors		All Others		Total U.S.	
No.	%	No.	%	No.	%	No.	%
—	—	1	0.4	—	—	7	0.2
—	—	2	0.8	1	0.2	42	0.9
25	3.9	18	7.2	9	1.9	286	6.2
59	9.3	20	8.0	24	5.1	473	10.2
97	15.3	38	15.3	43	9.1	689	14.8
160	25.3	78	31.3	89	18.4	1,113	24.0
169	26.7	59	23.7	127	26.8	1,076	23.2
123	19.5	33	13.3	182	38.5	951	20.5
633	100.0	249	100.0	473	100.0	4,637	100.0

Exhibit 6 shows a detailed breakdown of the production-distribution cost chain for two major brewers.

MARKET SIZE AND GROWTH

The market for beer in the United States was the largest of any country in the world. In 1982, retail sales of beer in the United States totaled about $25 billion (including taxes); consumption was an estimated 182.7 million barrels or 5.7 billion gallons (1 barrel = 31 gallons), equal to 22 percent of world consumption of 25 billion gallons. The consumption of beer in the United States had grown at varying rates over the past four decades:

Period	Average Annual Growth Rate
1940–1950	5.1%
1950–1960	0.6
1960–1970	4.1
1970–1980	2.9

Consumption in 1981 was up 2.2 percent over 1980 and in 1982 consumption rose just 0.4 percent. The slowdown was attributed largely to the effects of economic recession and partly to changes in the demographic makeup of the drinking-age population. Industry forecasts called for consumption increases of 2–3 percent in 1983 as the effects of recession waned and for an average annual growth rate of 1.7 percent for the remainder of the decade.

Exhibit 6   Estimated Cost Structure for the Brewing Industry, as of 1982

	Estimated Average Cost Breakdown for Combined Anheuser-Busch Brands		Estimated Average Cost Breakdown for Combined Adolph Coors Brands	
	Per 6-pack of 12-oz. Cans	Per Barrel Equivalent	Per 6-pack of 12-oz. Cans	Per Barrel Equivalent
1. Manufacturing costs:				
Direct production costs:				
Raw material ingredients	$0.1384	$ 7.63	$0.1082	$ 5.96
Direct labor	0.1557	8.58	0.1257	6.93
Salaries for nonunionized personnel	0.0800	4.41	0.0568	3.13
Packaging	0.5055	27.86	0.4663	25.70
Depreciation on plant and equipment	0.0410	2.26	0.0826	4.55
Subtotal	0.9206	50.74	0.8396	46.27
Other expenses:				
Advertising	0.0477	2.63	0.0338	1.86
Other marketing costs and general administrative expenses	0.1096	6.04	0.1989	10.96
Interest	0.0147	0.81	0.0033	0.18
Research and development	0.0277	1.53	0.0195	1.07
Total manufacturing costs	$1.1203	$ 61.75	$1.0951	$ 60.34
2. Manufacturer's operating profit	0.1424	7.85	0.0709	3.91
3. Net selling price	1.2627	69.60	1.1660	64.25
4. Plus federal and state excise taxes paid by brewer	0.1873	10.32	0.1782	9.82
5. Gross manufacturer's selling price to distributor/wholesaler	1.4500	79.92	1.3442	74.07
6. Average margin over manufacturer's cost	0.5500	30.31	0.5158	28.43
7. Average wholesale price charged to retailer (inclusive of taxes in item 4 above but exclusive of other taxes)	$2.00	$110.23	$1.86	$102.50
8. Plus other assorted state and local taxes levied on wholesale and retail sales (this varies from locality to locality)	0.60		0.60	
9. Average 20% retail markup over wholesale cost	0.40		0.38	
10. Average price to consumer at retail	$3.00		$2.84	

Note: The difference in the average cost structures for Anheuser-Busch and Adolph Coors is, to some substantial extent, due to A-B's higher proportion of super-premium beer sales. A-B's super-premium brand, Michelob, was far and away the best-seller in its category (see Exhibit 5) and was somewhat more costly to brew than premium and popular-priced beers. In this sense the cost structure for Coors is perhaps "more representative" than that of A-B. A-B and Coors were chosen for inclusion in this exhibit primarily because of greater data availability to the case researchers.
Source: Compiled by the case researchers from a wide variety of documents and field interviews.

Since the mid-1960s, retail beer sales had risen somewhat more slowly than prices of consumer goods in general. During the 1980–83 period, beer prices increased an average of 7 percent each year.

BEER CONSUMERS

About half of the 165 million adults in the United States in 1982 were thought to drink beer at least occasionally. Total U.S. beer consumption of approximately 183 million barrels in 1982 worked out to an average of 69 gallons per beer drinker (an average of 735 12-oz. cans per year per drinker). About 25 percent of the beer drinking population was thought to consume 70 to 80 percent of the product. Male beer drinkers outnumbered female beer drinkers by a ratio of about 2 to 1; however, this ratio was in decline. Increasing numbers of adult women beer drinkers had been an important factor in the increase in beer consumption since 1970; prior to the 1970s, it was estimated that male beer drinkers outnumbered female beer drinkers by a ratio of at least 5 to 1 and perhaps as much as 10 to 1. Still, in 1983, men accounted for at least 80 percent of beer consumption. Men and women differed in their beer preferences, particularly with regard to low-calorie and imported beers:

	Preferred Types of Beer	
	Male	*Female*
Domestic (regular)	68%	59%
Low-calorie (domestic/imported)	8	27
Imported	8	4
No particular brand	7	5
No reply	9	5
Total	100%	100%

Exhibit 7 profiles the beer consumption patterns of adult males.

The changing male/female ratio was only one of several factors causing revisions in beer consumption patterns. Another factor was the changing age composition of the U.S. population. Over 60 percent of the beer drinkers in 1982 were under 40 years of age, and people in the 18–34 age group were the heaviest beer drinkers; the 18–34 population segment was expected to peak at 29.1 percent of the total population in 1985 and then decline to a level of 22.7 percent by the year 2000. While beer was popular among many young adults, including two-career married couples and those with above-average incomes, it was uncertain whether and how much their consumption patterns would change as they moved into the middle-age population segments. Surveys made in 1983 showed that older adults were less likely to drink beer (only about 25 percent of the adults 50 years of age or older reported drinking beer regularly versus 61 percent among 18- to 24-year-olds).

Another consumption-related factor was the changing attitudes of the population towards health, lifestyles, quality, and status. Exercising and weight consciousness had reached "epidemic" proportions, with fad diets, exercise clinics, jogging, aerobics, bicycling, and leisure sports growing in popularity. Eating habits and the nutritional content of foods were very much on the mind of consumers, particularly as concerned salt, sugar, calories, cholesterol, and artificial additives. There was a pronounced trend toward lighter foods and lighter alcoholic beverages. Lighter wines and lighter beers were seen as trendier, less fattening, more socially desirable, and more in keeping with an active, healthy lifestyle. Most of the rapid growth in the sales of light beers was a reflection of the weight-and-calorie consciousness of many consumers and growing popularity of less filling foods and beverages.

At the same time, broader public awareness of alcohol abuse was said to be a factor in slowing down the consumption of alcoholic beverages in general. Concern

Exhibit 7   Relative Usage Index for Adult Males for Malt Beverage Categories by Demographic Groupings   Per Capita Consumption among All Males = 100 per Category

| | Domestic Beer | | Imported |
	(Light/Low Cal.)	(Regular)	
Total males	100	100	100
Age:			
18–24	95*	143	211
25–34	135	117	119
35–44	104	90	79
45–54	94	92	65
55–64	86	71	42
65+	62	59	34
Education:			
College grad.	135	87	133
Some college	94	105	128
High school grad.	94	110	96
Some high school	88	93	67
Occupation:			
Professional/manager	124	84	109
Clerical/sales	102	111	125
Crafts/foremen	123	111	145
Other	96	118	89
Not employed	68	88	67
Household income:			
$40,000+	136	92	131
$25,000+	122	99	127
$20,000–$24,999	94	101	66
$15,000–$19,999	90	111	70
$10,000–$14,999	83	106	93
Under $10,000	69	84	88
Region:			
Northeast	91	113	167
East Central	94	92	52
West Central	113	96	34
South	95	96	92
Pacific	115	98	131

* Table reads as follows: 18–24-year old males (95 index) consume 5 percent less light beer than the average for all adult males.

Source: Simmons Market Research Bureau, 1981 Study of Media and Markets.

about the drinking excesses of teenagers and college students had prompted states to consider raising the legal drinking age back to 21. A newly formed organization, Mothers Against Drunk Drivers (MADD), had successfully lobbied for tougher penalties for drunk drivers and was supportive of bills to raise the drinking age. Many universities had recently instituted alcohol awareness programs to acquaint students with the harmful effects of heavy alcohol consumption.

Consumers also seemed to be increasingly aware of quality and brand image. Designer clothing was fashionable and upscale adults were trading up in search of quality and the higher status such items afforded. The beer market was affected by the upscale movement. Sales of luxury-priced foreign import beers were growing 5 to 10 times faster than the market for beer as a whole. Guidebooks on beers appeared; *The Great American Beer Book, The Gourmet Beer Book,* and the *Connoisseur's Guide to Beer* lauded the many graces of fine beers and analyzed various brands based on taste, bouquet, ingredients, and color of the bottle. The consumer's economic and social climb upward, reinforced by beer having shed its T-shirt and suspenders image, was said to account for why the super-premium and import segments were the fast-growing portions of the beer market. If import and superpremium sales grew at their expected annual growth rates of 10–12 percent and 6–8 percent, respectively, by 1990 these high-end segments would represent one fifth of the total U.S. market (up from the current shares of 3 percent for imports and 7 percent for superpremiums).

People's consumption varied according to the time of day and location. Six percent of all beer was consumed at lunch, 13.3 percent at dinner, 48.6 percent in the evening, and 28.8 percent at snack times. Almost two thirds of beer consumption occurred either in the drinker's own home (54.5 percent) or in another person's home (11.7 percent); the remaining places of consumption were restaurants (5.2 percent), bars and clubs (12.9 percent), parties (3.5 percent), picnics and camping (2.6 percent), sporting events (2.0 percent), and all other (7.5 percent). Geographically, about 30 percent of the beer consumed in the United States occurred in states in the Midwest; only about 20 percent was consumed in the western states. The southeastern and Sunbelt states were the areas of fastest growth in beer consumption during the early 1980s.

In 1983, beer was sold at between 500,000 and 600,000 retail establishments. Most beer was purchased in supermarkets (60 percent); convenience food stores and other retail outlets accounted for another 20 percent. The remainder was sold through restaurants, bars, and at sporting events. About 12 percent of the beer which consumers bought was "on tap" (draft beer) and was drunk directly on the seller's premises (mostly restaurants and bars). The remaining 88 percent was bought prepackaged in cans and bottles, predominantly for off-premise consumption.

According to one survey, the primary reason people preferred their favorite brand of beers was taste (76 percent). Other reasons cited included low in calories (6 percent), price (5 percent), and conveniently available (5 percent).

SUBSTITUTES

While beer represented about 85 percent of the total alcoholic beverage market (based on gallonage per capita), beer drinkers had numerous other alcoholic and nonalcoholic beverages which they could consume instead of and in addition to beer. Aside from water, the most popular nonalcoholic beverages were, in order, soft drinks, coffee, milk, juices, tea, powdered drinks, and bottled water (see Exhibit 8).

Wine had recently displaced distilled spirits (bourbon, rum, gin, scotch, vodka, and so on) as the most heavily consumed alcoholic beverage next to beer. Wine was equally popular among men and women; about 45 percent of the adults who

Exhibit 8   Trends in the Consumption of Beverages in the United States, Selected Years 1965–1983

	\multicolumn{7}{c}{*Consumption in Gallons Per Capita*}						
	1965	*1970*	*1975*	*1980*	*1981*	*1982*	*1983E*
Soft drinks	20.3	27.0	31.0	38.8	39.5	40.1	42.0
Coffee	37.8	35.7	33.0	26.8	26.7	26.1	25.9
Beer	15.9	18.5	21.6	24.3	24.6	24.4	24.6
Milk	26.0	23.1	22.1	20.7	20.4	20.0	19.8
Juices	3.8	5.2	6.9	6.9	6.7	6.6	6.8
Tea	4.9	5.5	6.2	6.6	6.5	6.3	6.4
Powdered drinks	n.a.	n.a.	4.8	6.0	6.0	6.0	6.5
Wine	1.0	1.3	1.7	2.3	2.3	2.3	2.4
Bottled water	n.a.	n.a.	1.2	1.6	1.9	2.2	2.7
Distilled spirits	1.5	1.8	2.0	2.0	2.0	1.9	1.8
Subtotal	111.2	118.1	130.5	136.0	136.6	135.9	138.9
Imputed water consumption	71.3	64.4	52.0	46.5	45.9	46.6	43.6
Total	182.5	182.5	182.5	182.5	182.5	182.5	182.5

n.a. = Not available; E = Estimate.
Sources: John Maxwell; Lehman Brothers Kuhn Loeb research estimates; *Beverage Industry Annual Manual,* 1984.

drank alcoholic beverages drank wine. The largest percentage of wine drinkers lived in the western United States, and wine was the most popular alcoholic beverage choice of households with annual incomes exceeding $35,000. The highest concentration of wine volume was among people in the 30–39 age group (about 30 percent of total consumption). In the 1980s, wine consumption spread rapidly because of its increasing acceptance and popularity as a social occasion beverage and because more people were drinking wine as a predinner drink instead of a cocktail or highball. One survey found wine was the alcoholic beverage people served most often to guests in their homes. Over 42 percent of the wine was consumed with dinner; the next most popular times for enjoying wine were in the evening (33 percent of volume), and at snack times (18 percent).

About 20–25 percent of the consumers of alcoholic beverages frequently drank distilled spirits or "hard liquor." Over one third of distilled spirits consumption occurred away from home. Men led in distilled spirits consumption with about 60 percent of volume. Consumption of hard liquor was fairly even across all adult age groups (see Exhibit 9). Geographically, consumption of hard liquor was highest in the South, followed by the Northeast, the West, and the Midwest. After-dinner consumption accounted for 45 percent of volume, with 34 percent at snack times, and 15 percent during the dinner hour. Sales of distilled spirits fell over 5 percent in 1982 (to pre-1975 levels); the drop was attributed to a slack economy and to continuation of consumers' switch to beverages with less alcoholic content. The biggest declines were in bourbon, scotch, and gin; vodka and rum sales were flat; and sales of brandy, cordials, and after-dinner liqueurs were up slightly.

Exhibit 9   The Total U.S. Consumption of Alcoholic Beverages Accounted for by Each Age Group, 1982

Age Group	All Beverages	All Wine	Table Wine	Table Wine Color			Distilled Spirits	Malt Beverages
				Red	White	Rose		
Under 20	26.0%	1.0%	1.2%	2.4%	0.6%	1.2%	2.7%	3.1%
20–29	17.2	18.9	20.4	26.6	20.0	15.1	18.2	29.9
30–39	18.9	28.2	30.2	29.8	29.9	31.3	22.3	29.3
40–49	11.9	17.1	19.6	19.3	20.1	18.9	16.8	13.6
50–59	12.6	18.6	18.4	12.4	18.4	24.7	19.1	13.9
60 and over	13.4	16.2	10.2	9.5	11.0	8.9	20.8	10.2

Source: National Family Opinion, Inc.'s Share of Intake Panel (SIP) Study, as reported in *Impact*.

ENTRY INTO THE INDUSTRY

Entry barriers to compete on a scale with the leading breweries were high, owing mainly to the $100–$300 million capital costs of building a modern, large-scale, cost-efficient brewery and $20–$50 million in annual marketing costs associated with gaining adequate market penetration for a new brand on a regional or national basis. All of the leading U.S. brewers in 1983 had origins in the industry going back many decades. The only industry "newcomer" with a major market share was Philip Morris, which in 1969 bought into the industry with a $277 million acquisition of seventh-ranked Miller Brewing Company. Philip Morris, a leading U.S. manufacturer of cigarettes (its top-selling brands were Marlboro, Virginia Slims, Merit, and Benson & Hedges) and also the parent of The Seven-Up Company, proceeded over the next 15 years to invest about $3 billion in new facilities at Miller and to increase its advertising budget to about $130 million annually in supporting its long-range strategy to make Miller a dominant force in the beer industry.

Microbreweries   The newest entrants into the beer industry were tiny, commercial "boutique breweries" or microbreweries with capacities which did not exceed 30,000 barrels per year. These small breweries began to spring up in the 1980s, inspired by the success of the first boutique, Anchor Brewing Company, in San Francisco. Anchor had been a small, ailing brewery and was bought in the late 1960s by Fritz Maytag, the appliance heir, who aspired to produce a top-quality beer. Anchor was the largest of the microbreweries, producing 28,500 barrels in 1983; the company had 17 employees and was well-equipped with stainless-steel fermenting tanks and copper brew kettles. Many beer connoisseurs and gourmet guidebooks ranked Anchor Steam as the "best" beer brewed in the United States, giving it their highest recommendation to "discriminating, taste-conscious beer drinkers." Most microbreweries, however, operated on a shoestring, scrambling to raise the necessary investment capital ($100,000 to $500,000), scrounging secondhand vats, making do with a couple of employees, spending very little on advertising and promotion, and selling less than 10,000 barrels annually.

Buyers of the beers of microbrewers were characterized as "sophisticated" beer drinkers who held American beers in contempt because of their mild, bland taste and who sensed something missing in even the best of the foreign imports—specifically freshness. One microbrewery owner described his customers as "the searchers . . . the folks who search and search but can't seem to find the beer they remember drinking in the little German hofbrau." Other buyers of boutique beers were people who liked to go "super first class" and were willing to pay luxury prices for prestige beers. Still others saw such beers as status products.

Microbrewers had focused almost exclusively on developing local outlets for their beers, depending on the appeal of a tenderly produced, super-quality, distinctive-tasting, local-made product, and word-of-mouth praisings. According to one micro-brewer, "There are three things that sell beer—price, image, and product quality. We operate on the last two." Industry analysts speculated on whether the emergence of the 10 to 20 microbreweries represented the beginning of a significant new market segment or was merely a fad fueled by publicity in the national press and by the curious customers who were adventurous enough to try a different beer, especially if it was made locally and had a prestige mystique.

Foreign Imports   The other major entrants into the U.S. beer market were foreign imports. Sales of imported beers had quadrupled since 1975 and more brands were being introduced in the United States. Strong growth in import sales (about 10–12 percent annually) was expected throughout the 1980s. The growth of imports was driven by several factors: (1) the growing appeal of beer to upscale, white-collar, and professional people; (2) the willingness of more affluent beer drinkers, especially people who had traveled abroad and who liked symbols and status, to experiment with import and super premium beers; (3) the increasing movement of consumers away from hard liquor and distilled spirits; and (4) the existence of enough variety of imports to satisfy discriminating beer connoisseurs. Between 200 and 300 brands of imported beers were being sold in the United States in 1983; only a few, however, enjoyed a significant consumer following and no more than 10 were available nation-ally. The vast majority had spotty distribution and only toehold market shares in those areas where they were sold. Exhibit 10 shows sales of the leading imported beer brands.

While beer importers saw great growth potential for increasing the 3 percent market share which imports had and while the number of foreign brands being imported was growing, most observers foresaw a competitive shakeout. According to a California distributor of import beers, "There are over 200 imported beers in California and that's simply too many" Another importer noted, "There are a lot of dreamers out there. Without a good product, a lot of money, and a lot of patience, none of them has a chance to crack the market."

Marketing costs were a major barrier to the successful entry of imports. Heineken had a U.S. ad budget of $20 million. The U.S. importer of a leading German brand observed, "Today, if you want to operate a viable import, it takes $10 million a year for five years." In 1983, the efforts of imports to make greater market inroads included using radio and TV advertising (including some network TV ads), expanding

Exhibit 10 Leading Brands of Imported Beers in the United States, 1980–1982

Brand	1980		1981		1982	
	Total Volume (millions of gallons)	Percent Share of U.S. Import Segment	Total Volume (millions of gallons)	Percent Share of U.S. Import Segment	Total Volume (millions of gallons)	Percent Share of U.S. Import Segment
Heineken	53.5	37.8%	62.9	38.9%	68.7	38.5%
Molson	31.7	22.4	32.0	19.8	32.0	17.9
Becks	7.3	5.2	10.0	6.2	14.0	7.9
Moosehead	5.6	4.0	7.9	4.9	11.2	6.3
Dos Equis	7.0	4.9	7.0	4.3	10.5	5.9
Labatt	6.9	4.9	9.0	5.6	9.5	5.3
St. Pauli Girl	2.4	1.7	3.0	1.9	4.5	2.5
Guinness Harp	1.7	1.2	3.9	2.4	4.1	2.3
Carling O'Keefe	—	—	4.5	2.8	4.0	2.2
Tecate	—	—	3.8	2.3	2.7	1.5
Others	25.5	17.9	17.8	10.9	17.2	9.7
Total	141.6	100.0	161.8	100.0	178.4	100.0

Sources: John Maxwell; Lehman Brothers Kuhn Loeb research department; and *Beverage Industry 1984 Annual Manual.*

their geographical distribution, trying to increase their penetration of the on-premise segment (bars and restaurants), and relying upon the mystique and personality of their names and ad themes to arouse the curiosity of beer drinkers. Moosehead, a small Canadian brewery, went from a standing start at the bottom of the import heap to the fourth leading import brand in four years on the strength of its colorful name, clever ads featuring the moose as a friendly, noble animal representing the outdoors and Canada, a slogan "The Moose Is Loose" (which became a popular bumper sticker), a very successful Moosehead T-shirt merchandising promotion (1 million were sold), and radio and college newspaper ads headlining "No Moose is an island," "Of Moose and men," "A Moose for all seasons," "The Moose that roared," and "Head and antlers above the rest." Industry analysts attributed the success of the Moosehead brand to original advertising that gave the brand a strong personality and image based on its name and its label symbol. Moosehead sold at retail prices 15 to 20 percent above many other imports partly because it was brewed in small, high-cost breweries and partly because of the higher freight and handling costs associated with marketing small volumes in all 50 states.

CAPACITY EXPANSION AND CONTRACTION

The actions of the major brewers to expand or contract production capacity underscored the changing competitive situation. Anheuser-Busch had plans to boost production capacity to about 75 million barrels by the mid-1980s. A major expansion of A-B's Los Angeles brewery was completed in 1982; a 6-million-barrel New York State brewery, purchased from Schlitz in 1980, came on stream in 1983; and a 5-

million-barrel expansion of A-B's Houston brewery was scheduled for completion in 1985. Miller had in 1983 just completed a 10-million-barrel plant in Ohio. G. Heileman had plans to expand a Wisconsin brewery by 4 million barrels.

Many brewers, however, were wrestling with excess-capacity problems. In 1981, Schlitz closed its large Milwaukee plant, only a year after having sold a 6-million-barrel brewery it had under construction in New York State to Anheuser-Busch. Falstaff in 1981 closed, at least temporarily, its Rhode Island brewery. Pabst Brewing in 1982 closed its Peoria brewery in Illinois despite having to pay unusually large severance payments to workers and decided to keep its Newark, New Jersey, brewery open only after sizable labor union concessions.

Exhibit 11 shows the sales volume and production capacities of the 30 largest U.S. brewers, as of 1982.

Exhibit 11   Sales Volumes and Production Capacities of the 30 Largest U.S. Brewers, 1981–1983

Company	1982 Sales (in 31-gal. barrels)	1981 Sales volume (in 31-gal. barrels)	1982–1983 Production Capacity (in 31-gal. barrels)
1. Anheuser-Busch	59,100,000	54,500,000	66,000,000
2. Miller Brewing	39,300,000	40,300,000	44,000,000
3. The Stroh Brewery	22,900,000	23,500,000	29,000,000
4. G. Heileman Brewing	14,518,000	13,965,000	26,000,000
5. Pabst Brewing	12,306,000	13,465,000	14,000,000
6. Adolph Coors	11,919,000	13,261,000	15,000,000
7. Olympia Brewing	5,172,932	5,708,000	9,000,000
8. Genesee Brewing	3,400,000	3,625,000	4,000,000
9. Falstaff/Pearl/General Brewing	3,187,000	3,596,455	8,800,000
10. Christian Schmidt	3,150,000	3,300,000	4,300,000
11. Pittsburgh Brewing	983,000	922,331	1,250,000
12. Latrobe Brewing	*700,000	—	750,000
13. Hudepohl Brewing	*450,000+	*400,000	1,000,000
14. F. X. Matt Brewing	*400,000+	*400,000	800,000
15. Champale Product	*400,000	—	1,000,000
16. Schoenling Brewing	*300,000	—	400,000
17. Jos. Huber Brewing	275,000	267,000	500,000
18. Eastern Brewing	260,000	—	400,000
19. The Lion, Inc.—Gibbons	230,000	—	300,000
20. D. G. Yuengling & Son	143,000	140,000+	200,000
21. Dixie Brewing	139,000	124,000	300,000
22. Jones Brewing	125,600	125,627	200,000
23. Fred Koch Brewery	70,000	*56,000	80,000
24. Jacob Leinenkugel	66,000	*72,000	95,000
25. Cold Spring Brewing	*40,000	—	350,000
26. Stevens Point Brewing	48,600	*47,500	55,000
27. Walter Brewing	41,000	*50,000	100,000
28. August Schell	40,000+	40,000+	40,000+
29. Spoetzl Brewery	37,100	34,000	60,000
30. Straub Brewery	36,000	*35,000	40,000

* Estimate.
Source: *Modern Brewery Age,* March 21, 1983, p. MS–19.

COMPETITIVE RIVALRY

Competitive maneuvering among the remaining U.S. brewers revolved mainly around pricing, advertising, defining and creating a clientele for their brands, and building a strong distribution network. The pressure on second tier brewers to maintain their ability to compete against the two market leaders was intense. Anheuser-Busch and Miller had capitalized on their greater volume by increasing their total advertising expenditures far above the levels of other brewers while still incurring an advertising cost per barrel close to the industry average (see Exhibit 12). The two leaders also had taken advantage of other economies of scale in the production area to give wage increases to unionized employees that other brewers were hard-pressed to match and still remain cost competitive. The consensus view of industry analysts was that it was absolutely essential for second tier brewers to merge into financially viable entities capable of competing effectively on a national basis.

Exhibit 12   Average Revenues, Advertising Expenditures, and Operating Profit per Barrel Sold of the Six Leading Brewers, 1973–1983

Company	1973	1975	1977	1979	1980	1981	1982	1983
Revenue per barrel:[a]								
Anheuser-Busch	$35.55	$44.19	$46.20	$55.28	$60.39	$69.94	$69.95	$73.96
Miller Brewing	30.90	42.52	46.03	53.47	59.16	61.40	65.30	68.70
Schlitz/Stroh	32.94	39.65	42.36	53.21	59.97	61.65	n.a.	n.a.
Coors	31.83	40.34	41.50	49.47	54.93	59.23	64.36	70.10
Pabst	27.06	33.51	36.42	43.10	47.68	51.24	52.78	53.67
Heileman	5.13	8.41	22.48	42.23	46.89	50.09	52.45	53.83
Industry avg.[b]	29.86	38.10	45.15	52.65	57.38	60.83	63.26	67.89
Advertising expenditures per barrel:								
Anheuser-Busch	0.43	0.55	1.24	1.89	1.87	2.05	2.63	2.72[c]
Miller Brewing	1.45	1.62	1.74	2.10	2.37	2.31	3.04	4.22[c]
Schlitz/Stroh	0.78	0.99	1.85	2.87	2.95	2.37	—	—[c]
Coors	0.06	0.07	0.31	1.16	1.57	1.72	1.86	2.00[c]
Pabst	0.49	0.57	0.68	1.22	1.17	1.28	1.52	2.26[c]
Heileman	—	—	—	1.33	1.03	1.78	1.55	1.77[c]
Industry avg.[b]	0.57	0.74	1.28	1.75	1.63	1.84	2.47	2.89[c]
Operating profit per barrel:								
Anheuser-Busch	3.74	4.58	4.65	4.92	5.73	6.02	7.85	10.50
Miller Brewing	(0.34)	2.24	4.39	5.06	3.88	2.87	4.04	6.06
Schlitz/Stroh	5.14	3.59	2.75	(0.46)	2.01	1.38	n.a.	n.a.
Coors	8.68	9.95	8.50	7.59	6.29	4.83	3.91	10.47
Pabst	3.13	2.28	2.36	1.31	1.42	(0.97)	0.97	1.08
Heileman	1.00	0.87	2.37	4.48	4.78	4.96	5.22	5.94
Industry avg.[b]	4.29	4.32	4.31	4.26	4.56	4.09	5.07	7.96

[a] Excludes federal excise tax.
[b] Weighted by sales volume.
[c] Estimate.
n.a.—Schlitz/Stroh not available.
Source: Goldman Sachs research department.

Pricing   During the 1970s, in an effort to wrest industry leadership away from Anheuser-Busch, Miller Brewing acted as the industry price leader, initiating price increases which other brewers eventually followed. However, some rival brewers, including Anheuser-Busch, would either maintain prices slightly below the new Miller price or else match Miller's price increases after several months' delay, leaving Miller at the high end of the price scale for varying periods of time. The practice was common enough that Miller was hailed as the nominal price leader and Anheuser-Busch as the effective price determiner; it was apparent that smaller brewers were uncomfortable matching Miller's new prices until Anheuser-Busch did so.

In 1980, Miller abandoned its practice of being first to announce price increases, electing instead to follow Anheuser-Busch on pricing. In 1980, concerned about a plateauing of its market share, Miller ran its first price promotion since 1974. Meanwhile, second-tier brewers increasingly turned to price cutting to try to preserve volume and market share. Most of the second-tier firms had excess production capacity and were confronted with whether to use price cuts or other marketing and promotional means to build volume or whether to close plants permanently or temporarily in order to cut costs and protect profit margins.

Average revenue per barrel sold rose significantly during the 1980–83 period (Exhibit 12), beginning with the 5 to 7 percent increases which Anheuser-Busch led the way in implementing between October 1980 and January 1981 when it reassumed the role of industry price leader. The wide differences in average revenue per barrel among the top-six brewers primarily reflected differences in their mix of sales of super-premium, premium, and popular-priced brands, rather than differences in prices among brands competing in the same price segment. Brewers' margins on super-premium brands were about 1.5 times those on premium brands; premium brands had margins about 50 percent bigger than on popular-priced brands. The cost of brewing a super-premium beer was generally less than 5 percent more than the costs of brewing a popular-priced beer, with the cost difference due mainly to ingredient and aging costs. One regional brewer observed, "There is a lot of business out there if you want to cut your margins down to a harrowing edge. Two years ago, we tried that, but never again."

Advertising and Promotional Merchandising   In 1983, domestic brewers spent an estimated $482 million on advertising, mostly buying spot and national TV time (Exhibit 13). Import marketers spent over $50 million in 1982 supporting their brands. Advertising expenditures were expected to rise in 1984 as G. Heileman, Stroh Brewery, Adolph Coors, and Pabst Brewing pushed toward national geographic coverage.

Advertising was a key competitive weapon. According to one industry analyst:

> As far as quality image goes, advertising is the name of the game. Status is the most important element in a brand preference decision. While there are always some people who want the cheapest brand, there are many, many more who are willing to pay a little more for the assurance of quality.[1]

---

[1] Marvin R. Shanken in an interview by Gail Festa reported in *Restaurant Hospitality,* February 1982, p. 78.

Exhibit 13   Top 10 Advertisers in U.S. Brewing Industry $Millions

Brewer	1979	1980	1981	1982	Change 1981–1982 Dollars	Change 1981–1982 Percent
Anheuser-Busch	$105.8	$120.0	$147.2	$193.9	$ 46.7	31.7%
Miller Brewing (P. Morris)	78.6	95.7	107.8	137.9	30.1	27.9
Stroh Brewery*	73.7	68.2	61.8	45.5	−16.3	−26.4
Adolph Coors	17.8	25.5	32.0	32.2	0.2	0.6
G. Heileman†	17.4	15.9	15.2	21.9	6.7	44.1
Olympia Brewing	13.4	16.5	20.2	16.7	−3.5	−17.3
Pabst Brewing	21.2	23.4	24.1	14.3	−9.8	−40.7
Genesee	4.5	6.0	6.4	6.2	−0.2	−3.1
Christian Schmidt	4.1	2.8	2.9	2.0	−0.9	−31.0
Latrobe Brewing	1.7	1.3	1.3	1.5	0.2	15.4
Total top 10	$344.3	$381.6	$423.2	$475.5	$ 52.3	12.4%

* Advertising expenditures reflect purchase of F. & M. Schaefer in 1981 and Jos. Schlitz in 1982.
† G. Heileman's advertising does not include brands transferred from Pabst/Olympia mergers.
Source: *Advertising Age,* January 16, 1984, p. M-10.

Another industry observer expanded on the importance of advertising thusly:

Beer advertising is mainly an exercise in building images.

Its foundation rests upon the brewing industry's thinking that "beer is a badge." That means what you drink says something about you in the presence of peers and woe be to the poor shlump who runs against the grain.

In some parts of the country your barroom reputation is safe only if you order a Bud, while in others—let's say Chicago—you gain stature by slugging back an Old Style.

The imagery must appeal to men. The majority of the nation's beer swillers are males between the ages of 21 and 35, who naturally drink, and therefore, buy the most beer.

But these days beer companies are attempting to appeal to all different men of all different backgrounds with various incomes and lifestyles. Naturally, there is a set beer for every lifestyle, income, and taste.

At the risk of coining some new advertising jargon, they can be called the premium man, super-premium man and popular-price man.

The premium man, for instance, is the hard-working fellow who likes to have a few cold ones after knocking off from work.

Then there is super-premium man. He's upscale.

This fella has a good, high-paying job. That enables him to spend his leisure time, on his boat, in an out-of-the-way cottage or on the soccer field. . . .

The idea here is to get these more affluent types to plunk down an extra $1.50 a 6-pack as a sign of their individuality and stature.

Imports are another matter. You drink them with dinner or when trying to impress someone on your first date and don't want to run the risk of asking for the wine list and not understanding it.

Imports basically attempt to build on snob appeal. The thinking is: No American beer is as good. So you buy an import and then reminisce about your college days tramping through Europe.

Then there is the popular-price man. He's basically strapped for cash but fun-loving.

Traditionally, popular-price beers are seen as a means of filling a beer maker's excess brewing capacity. It has high volume, is sold at a lower price, and doesn't get much ad support.

Finally, there is that not-so-distinct group of light beer drinkers. They are . . . hang on . . . a combination of blue-collar, upscale, young, males who don't want to be thought of as drinking a "diet" beer.

The heavyweight here is Miller Lite. With its long-running ad campaign that uses former athletes and other well-known personalities, it has given that segment of beer drinking legitimacy.

. . . the case remains that advertising—especially TV advertising—is as imperative to a beer's success as its ingredients, taste, packaging, and over-all hangover effect.[2]

Brewers relied heavily on slogans in their ads and promotional efforts. Some of the best known were:

"This Bud's for You" (Budweiser).
"Welcome to Miller Time" (Miller High Life).
"The King of Beers" (Budweiser).
"When You're Out of Schlitz, You're Out of Beer" (Schlitz).
"Let It Be Lowenbrau" (Lowenbrau).
"Bring Out Your Best" (Bud Light).
"The Best of the Rockies Is Yours" (Coors).
"Come to Think of It, I'll Have a Heineken" (Heineken).

Successful themes were used for several years before they were deemed "worn out," whereas unsuccessful themes were dropped quickly. Brewers used professional "Madison Avenue" advertising agencies to develop their themes and media campaigns; it was not uncommon for brewers to switch the account for a brand to a new agency whenever a campaign managed by its current agency was unsuccessful.

The advertising costs to introduce a new brand were substantial. For example, Anheuser-Busch spent $35 million for an ad campaign to introduce Bud Light in 1982. Miller Brewing spent well over $15 million in 1983–84 in a national rollout of its new popular-priced Meister Brau brand; the campaign centered on the theme "Meister Brau tastes as good as Budweiser, at a better price" and utilized TV and some ads in print media. Part of G. Heileman's success in revitalizing sales of some of its regionally popular brands was attributed to its shrewd use of regional advertising.

In addition to media advertising, brewers devoted considerable effort to merchandising and brand promotion. Labels, packaging, logos, and trademarks were carefully designed because of their importance in establishing brand image and brand appeal. Both brewers and their distributors developed campaigns for point-of-sale promotions in retail outlets. Shelf space in retail outlets was generally allocated to various brands based on volume of sales. Most brewers offered a variety of packaging options to consumers, including 6-packs, 12-packs, and cases (24 units) in either aluminum cans or glass bottles. Cans and bottles ranged in size from 7 oz. to 12 oz. to 16 oz. to quarts; and glass bottles were of various shapes and colors (clear, brown, or green); super-premium brands and foreign imports often had more expensive aluminum foil

---

[2] Robert Reed, "Satisfying a Thirst for Images," *Advertising Age,* January 16, 1984, pp. M-9–M-11.

labels and cap wrappers to enhance their packaging appeal. Some brewers, particularly Anheuser-Busch and Miller, sponsored special sports events of local, regional, or national scope (auto racing, snow skiing contests, bicycling races, rodeos, and surfing, sailing, and fishing contests) to get.their names before the public and to establish a strong identification with sports activities. Several brewers, notably Miller, had appointed college representatives to promote their brands at parties and campus events. All brewers had staffs of sales representatives to "work the trade"—building the enthusiasm of distributors and calling on retailers to gain their willing cooperation.

Miller Brewing and Anheuser-Busch were widely considered to be the most successful and capable promoters and marketers of beer, with Miller having the distinction of having revolutionized the way the industry marketed beer. Before 1970, the beer industry was more production-oriented; most brewers used similar mass-marketing methods to try to reach a vaguely defined target—the beer drinker. When Philip Morris, a skillful marketer of cigarettes, acquired Miller Brewing Company and began to utilize the same market segmentation principles and advertising approaches in its beer business that had proved so successful in its cigarette business, the whole complexion of competitive rivalry in beer changed. The lesson Philip Morris taught brewers was that the beer market was not homogeneous but, rather, a diverse collection of definable segments based on lifestyles, incomes, social status, occupation, and other demographics. As Miller moved from seventh to second in market share, Anheuser-Busch's interest in revamping its marketing approaches grew and it began to upgrade its marketing competence. By the late 1970s A-B had learned to be a skillful marketer, too; a Miller executive acknowledged, "They have been good and fast learners." Miller's most dramatic marketing triumph was generally said to be its success in developing a low-calorie beer (Lite), promoting it with a "tastes great and is less filling" ad campaign, transforming a diet product into a product with macho appeal to men and weight-conscious appeal to women, and creating in the process a whole new growth segment called light beer (which by 1983 accounted for over 17 percent of total beer sales).

An analysis of 1980 data of 11 publicly owned brewers conducted by an industry consultant concluded that, to support one major brand and one secondary brand nationally, a brewer needed to be in position to spend $200 million for marketing, administrative, and general expenses (at least 50 percent of which usually went for advertising); to achieve successful 50-state coverage for two major brands and one secondary brand, marketing, administrative, and general expenses were estimated to run $300 million. The same study found that the manufacturing cost of goods sold for the 11 brewers averaged 71.7 percent. Based upon these calculations and the formula

$$\text{Required sales volume (in barrels)} = \frac{\text{Marketing, administrative, and general expenses}}{\dfrac{1 - (\text{Cost of goods sold} + \text{Target operating profit margin})}{\text{Net revenue per barrel}}}$$

the consultant developed the following sales volumes needed to support annual marketing, administrative, and general expenses of $200 million and $300 million:[3]

---

[3] R. S. Weinberg & Associates, as reported in *Beverage World*, October 1982, p. 34.

	Needed Sales Volume (in millions of barrels annually) in 1980 at Net Revenue per Barrel of				
	$60	$55	$50	$45	$40
At $200 million:					
10% operating profit	18.2	19.9	21.9	24.3	27.3
15% operating profit	25.1	27.3	30.1	33.4	37.6
At $300 million:					
10% operating profit	27.3	29.8	32.8	36.4	41.0
15% operating profit	37.6	41.0	45.1	50.1	56.4

A report in *Beer* magazine offered a prescription for what a regional brewery had to do to survive and succeed:

> It should offer a product that is distinctive and noticeably different (or better!) than locally available national brands. It should price its beer competitively, yet avoid waging "guerrilla" pricing wars with the nationals. It should be wary of overexpansion and cultivate a solid local market. To accomplish the latter, an image of strong regional identification is essential, plus a healthy dose of plain old mystique.[4]

Some small brewers were pessimistic about their ability to survive. As one put it, "[Market share, not profitability] is the only thing that seems to matter to the big boys. As long as that attitude prevails, the little brewer is going to be like an ant caught in an elephant dance."[5] Yet, other small, regional brewers were encouraged by the fact that 10 of the brewers ranked from 11th to 30th largest in the industry (see Exhibit 11) had shown volume increases in 1982. According to the head of one regional brewer:

> Distribution of our beers is still a tough fight, but there definitely is a growing interest in regional beers. We can and do produce something different, something better, and people are interested in us.
>
> As long as people continue to think about what they're drinking and more people do, regional brewers will prosper.[6]

Fritz Maytag, owner and brewmaster of the largest of the microbreweries predicted:

> My feeling is that the market eventually will break up into tiny breweries and giants, and the little ones must have a reason for being. They will have to do more than retain brand loyalty in their local markets. They will have to develop a reputation outside their market for quality, and I'm talking about international quality.
>
> Even in their home markets, most small brewers do not come to mind as the best beer. Most aren't as highly regarded as they could be, or even should be.[7]

A profile of each of the six largest brewers follows. Exhibit 14 contains comparative financial data for the six competitors.

---

[4] *Beer,* November 1983, p. 57.

[5] As quoted in *Modern Brewery Age,* March 21, 1983, p. MS-17.

[6] Ibid., p. MS-19.

[7] Ibid., p. MS-18.

Exhibit 14 Comparative Financial Performance of Top Six U.S. Brewers, Selected Years 1970–1983 $ Millions, Except for Percentage Figures

Company	1970	1975	1980	1981	1982	1983
Anheuser-Busch, Inc.:						
Net sales	$ 792.8	$1,645.0	$3,295.4	$ 3,847.2	$ 4,576.6	$ 6,034.2
Operating profit	120.7	175.1	312.9	356.7	492.9	700.8
Operating profit margin	15.2%	10.6%	9.5%	9.3%	10.8%	11.6%
Net aftertax income	62.5	84.7	171.8	217.4	287.3	348.0
Total assets	605.4	1,202.1	2,449.7	2,875.2	3,902.8	3,330.2
Shareholders' equity	385.5	601.9	1,031.4	1,206.8	1,526.6	1,766.5
Return on equity[a]	17.5%	15.6%	17.8%	19.3%	19.9%	18.0%
Philip Morris, Inc./ Miller Brewing:						
Net sales	$1,509.5	$3,642.4	$9,649.5	$10,722.3	$11,586.0	$12,975.9
Operating profit	203.2	492.8	1,273.4	1,446.2	1,715.7	1,958.0
Operating profit margin	13.5%	13.5%	13.2%	13.5%	14.8%	15.1%
Net aftertax income	77.5	211.6	549.1	659.7	781.8	903.5
Total assets	1,239.4	3,134.3	7,301.7	9,115.1	9,622.1	9,667.0
Shareholders' equity	452.8	1,227.8	2,837.0	3,233.7	3,662.9	4,033.7
Return on equity	17.1%	17.2%	19.4%	20.4%	21.3%	22.4%
Miller Brewing Co. only:						
Net sales	$ 198.5	$ 658.3	$2,542.3	$ 2,837.2	$ 2,928.7	$ 2,922.1
Operating profit	11.4	28.6	144.8	115.6	158.8	227.3
Operating profit margin	5.7%	4.3%	5.7%	4.1%	5.4%	7.8%
Stroh Brewery Co.:						
Net sales				$ 467.3[c]	$ 499.1[c]	$ 1,318.0[b]
Operating profit				22.6	11.0	94.6
Operating profit margin				4.8%	2.2%	7.2%
Net aftertax income				7.8	5.6	1.2
Total assets					650.0	721.1
Shareholders' equity						80.7
Return on equity						1.5%
G. Heileman Brewing Co.:						
Net sales	$ 109.4	$ 171.2	$ 722.0	$ 807.0	$ 870.8	$ 1,151.0
Operating profit	11.0	12.7	69.5	76.1	82.9	108.3
Operating profit margin	10.1%	7.4%	9.6%	9.4%	9.5%	9.4%
Net aftertax income	5.3	5.7	34.7	40.2	45.7	57.0
Total assets	48.0	86.6	291.4	321.2	518.7	530.3
Shareholders' equity	22.7	43.0	127.1	158.9	194.1	239.3
Return on equity	23.3%	13.3%	27.3%	25.3%	23.5%	23.8%
Adolph Coors Co.:						
Net sales	$ 246.2[d]	$ 520.0[d]	$ 887.9	$ 929.9	$ 915.3	$ 1,110.4
Operating profit	n.a.	147.4	105.8	79.6	65.1	155.9
Operating profit margin		28.3%	11.9%	8.6%	7.1%	14.0%
Net aftertax income	31.8	59.5	65.0	52.0	40.1	89.3
Total assets			894.4	956.4	1,007.9	1,155.7
Shareholders' equity		375.0	712.1	753.6	783.2	860.2
Return on equity		15.9%	9.1%	6.9%	5.1%	10.4%
Pabst Brewing Co.:						
Net sales	$ 362.7	$ 665.3	$ 719.9	$ 691.9	$ 649.2	$ 687.0
Operating profit	38.3	35.7	21.4	(13.2)	11.9	13.7
Operating profit margin	10.6%	5.4%	3.0%	(1.9%)	1.8%	2.0%
Net aftertax income	23.3	20.7	12.6	(23.5)	2.7	3.6
Total assets	224.2	314.6	430.3	404.0	408.9	243.9
Shareholders' equity	175.3	235.0	281.4	254.8	254.3	37.0
Return on equity	13.3%	8.8%	4.5%	(9.2%)	1.1%	9.7%

[a] As adjusted by the company for the effects of potential conversions of preferred stock into common stock.

[b] Includes data for Schlitz; figures are for 12 months ending March 1983.

[c] Figures do not include operations of Schlitz and represent the 12-month period ending in March. Data for earlier years was not available because the company was privately-held and figures were not released.

[d] Data for 1975 was incomplete and figures for 1970 were unavailable because of the privately-held ownership of the company.

n.a. = Not available.

Sources: Company annual reports and *Moody's Industrial Manual.*

ANHEUSER-BUSCH COMPANIES

Anheuser-Busch was a diversified corporation which ranked 55 on the 1983 *Fortune 500* list of the largest U.S. industrial corporations. A-B's subsidiary operations included the world's largest brewing organization, the second-largest U.S. producer of fresh baked goods (Campbell-Taggart, acquired in 1982, whose products were marketed under the brand names Colonial, Earth Grains, Rainbo, Manor, and Kilpatrick's), aluminum can manufacturing and recycling, malt and rice production, metalized label printing, baker's yeast, Eagle brand snack foods, Busch Gardens family entertainment parks, the St. Louis Cardinals major league baseball franchise, refrigerated rail car repair and transportation services, and cable TV sports programming. The aluminum can, malt and rice, and label printing operations represented vertical integration efforts aimed at supporting the corporation's beer products business. In 1983, beer and beer-related activities accounted for 75 percent of sales and 94 percent of operating profit; food products (including Campbell-Taggart, yeast, and snack foods) represented 22 percent of sales and 5 percent of operating profit; and the remaining diversification amounted to 3 percent of total sales and 1 percent of operating profit. The total company had expenses of $1.2 billion for marketing, administration, and research; advertising costs for all operations were $234 million in 1981, $322 million in 1982, and $404 million in 1983.

The company's flagship beer brand, Budweiser, had been the best-selling brand of beer in the United States since 1957 when its sales overtook those of Schlitz. A-B's Michelob brand was the dominant seller in the super-premium segment. However, A-B's first entry into the light beer segment, Natural Light, was generally conceded as a failure and its second entry, Bud Light, had been only a modest success so far. The company was said to be developing a low-alcohol beer for introduction in mid-1984.

MILLER BREWING/PHILIP MORRIS

Miller Brewing Company was the only brewer whose corporate parent did not have longstanding roots in the beer industry. In 1983, Philip Morris was a leading company in three major consumer goods businesses—cigarettes, beer, and soft drinks; the company ranked 35th on the 1983 *Fortune 500* list. Founded more than a century ago and incorporated in Virginia in 1919, the company had long been a major cigarette manufacturer; in 1982, it overtook R. J. Reynolds to become the largest U.S.-based international cigarette company. Philip Morris acquired full control of Miller Brewing in 1970 and proceeded to implement a long-term strategy that moved Miller from seventh to second place in the beer industry. In 1978, PM acquired The Seven-Up Company, the third-largest soft drink manufacturer in the world. Philip Morris had also diversified into the manufacture of specialty paper, tissues, packaging materials, and residential and community real estate.

PM had organized its businesses into six operating companies (Miller Brewing being one), each of which was managed on a decentralized basis. Cigarette sales accounted for 70 percent of corporate revenues and 86 percent of total operating profit; Miller Brewing generated 22 percent of revenues and 12 percent of operating profit; Seven-Up generated 5 percent of sales ($650 million) and had been marginally unprofitable since 1980.

During the past decade, PM's revenues had grown at an average annual rate of 17.4 percent and earnings had grown at a 19.8 percent rate; the firm's annual return on equity investment had consistently exceeded 20 percent. The company's cigarette business generated huge internal cash flows (in 1983, pre-tax operating profit was $1.7 billion on sales of just over $9 billion)—amounts substantially greater than dividend and capital needs. The company was cash rich and very strong financially. PM was the second-largest advertiser in the United States and was generally regarded as one of the finest marketing-oriented and marketing-astute companies in the world (despite its difficulties in trying to produce the same kind of market share growth at Seven-Up as it had at Miller Brewing).

During the 1980s, Miller's shipments of beer had declined, revenues had flattened, and market share had slipped, mostly due to a fall off in the sales of Miller High Life. However, Miller's operating profits rose 37 percent in 1982 (to $159 million) and another 43 percent in 1983 (to $227 million). The profit gains reflected selling price increases, lower material costs, and improved operating efficiencies; as a result of improved margins, Miller was able to increase its marketing expenditures and still boost profits substantially. Miller had revamped its "Miller Time" ads in an effort to reverse the decline in sales of its High Life brand. During the 1978–83 period, PM invested $1.3 billion in new plant facilities for Miller Brewing.

PM's management viewed competition in beer in 1983 as being at its fiercest level since its entry into the business in 1969. Price discounting was said to be particularly widespread. Miller introduced popular-priced Meister Brau nationwide in 1983—the company's first entry in the sizable popular-priced segment; Miller had also recently introduced a second popular-priced brand, Milwaukee's Best, on a regional basis. Miller's Lite beer commercials were voted by TV viewers as the outstanding television ads in 1982 and 1983. Most recently, Miller had begun to test market a new super-premium brand, Miller's Special Reserve, had arranged with a Canadian brewery to introduce Calgary Beer into U.S. test markets, and had licensed Miller High Life to be brewed and sold in Canada (market share had already reached 10 percent). Because of excess capacity, the company had yet to open up its new 10-million-barrel brewery in Ohio even though construction was complete.

THE STROH BREWERY COMPANY

Stroh Brewery was a family-owned, Detroit-based brewery which had acquired F&M Schaefer Corporation in 1981 and the Jos. Schlitz Brewing Company in 1982 to become the third-largest brewer in the United States. In 1980, Stroh was a single-plant operation; after its two acquisitions it was a 7-brewery (29-million-barrel capacity), 10-brand, six-container-plant operation and one of the 10 largest family-owned corporations in the United States. The Schaefer acquisition gave Stroh a presence in the northeastern U.S., and the Schlitz acquisition, given the national coverage of Schlitz brands, made Stroh a national contender.

Because it was privately held, financial data and operating statistics were not readily available. Sales were estimated at $1.3 billion in 1982, with earnings of only $1.2 million. Advertising expenditures for its operations were said to be $55.5 million in 1982 and $16.2 million in 1981; however, in 1983, Stroh reportedly budgeted $60 million for network TV advertising alone.

When Stroh assumed control of Schlitz in 1982, management moved quickly to install its own marketing approaches and to change the Schlitz corporate culture. New ad agencies were brought in and new ad campaigns were developed for Old Milwaukee, Schlitz, and Schlitz Malt Liquor. Special efforts were directed at reversing a 26 percent decline in the 1981 volume sales of the once-dominant Schlitz brand. Meanwhile, Stroh revamped the operations of the East Coast-based Schaefer, boosted marketing efforts to rebuild sales of the declining Schaefer brand, and launched new ad campaigns for its flagship Stroh's brand. Advertising for the Stroh's brands appeared in 65 percent of the United States in 1983. Plans called for full U.S. coverage in 1984. In a nationwide 1983 survey that asked 15,000 consumers to name the ad in any product category that came to mind first, Stroh's ads came out eighth. Stroh's beer shipments in 1983 were up 6 percent over 1982. Stroh's immediate objective was a 15 percent market share.

Stroh had the reputation of being a well-managed and conservative company. Peter W. Stroh was chairman and CEO. Because Stroh's own earnings had been volatile over the past five years in face of stiffening competition industrywide, and because Stroh was said to be taking on $320 million in debt to make the Schlitz purchase (making the combined companies' leverage figure 80 percent or more), there were doubts whether Stroh would have the financial wherewithal to turn Schlitz around, revive Schaefer, and make Stroh a national brand. While subsequent sale of some of Schlitz's assets reduced the debt burden, it was clear that the Schlitz brand was in deep trouble. Analysts who followed the company believed that the Schlitz brand was afflicted with tremendous brand disloyalty and that its image had been tarnished, perhaps irreversibly. The outlook for turning the sales of Schlitz around was said to be bleaker than it had ever been. In the mid-1950s Schlitz was the number-one-selling brand; as late as 1975, it was still number two; in 1982, it was ranked 10th among the top-ten best-selling brands.

Stroh was thought to be in a good cost competitive position. Completion in 1982 of a $35 million renovation of a Schaefer brewery in Pennsylvania allowed major cuts in shipping costs to the East and Southeast. Schlitz's plants in the South and West were cost efficient. In 1983, there were 1,230 distributors handling one or more of Stroh's 10 brands. In entering the Sunbelt states in 1983, Stroh used the theme "Stroh a Party" and ran specials on Schaefer beer at $2 a 6-pack.

G. HEILEMAN BREWING COMPANY

Heileman's competitive strategy was to corner regional markets with regional brands. Beginning in the 1970s, the company had made a practice of acquiring floundering regional brewers at bargain prices. Most of Heileman's brewing acquisitions had cost under $15 per barrel of capacity (some had come as low as $10 per barrel) compared to the $30 to $50 per barrel costs of building new plants. The company sold more brands (Exhibit 4) than any other company and gradually had acquired enough production capacity to achieve economies in material purchasing and general administration. The company had a debt to fixed asset ratio of about 28 percent, roughly equal to the industry norm. Eleven of the company's 50-plus labels accounted for over 80 percent of total beer sales—Old Style, Blatz, Rainier, Schmidt, Wiedemann, Black Label, Red White & Blue, Lone Star, Colt 45, Special Export, and Henry Weinhard's; most of Heileman's brands were popular-priced.

During the 1970s and early 1980s, G. Heileman's aggressive pricing was a key to its success in reviving the sales of a number of regional brands it acquired. The companies Heileman purchased all had excess capacity. Since the average cost of brewing beer at 85 percent of capacity was lower than at 60 percent, Heileman's strategy was to build volume by expanding into adjacent geographic markets, using sizable introductory price cuts to attract buyer attention. Market share thus achieved was sustained by continuing to offer consumers a regionally recognized premium brand at popular-brand prices. Heileman was in a position to use lower prices as a long-term promotional approach because of its low-cost production facilities, especially those acquired in its 1979 purchase of Carling National Breweries.

In 1983, G. Heileman, headquartered in LaCrosse, Wisconsin, was the fourth leading U.S. brewer. The company had 11 breweries, annual capacity of 26 million barrels, and approximately 2,400 distributors of its products (few of the distributors carried Heileman's brands exclusively and few carried all or even most of Heileman's brands). Sales had increased from $19 million in 1960 to $210 million in 1975 to $1.3 billion in 1983, making Heileman the fastest-growing company in the industry; the company had had 9 consecutive years of double-digit earnings increases and profits had risen in 21 of the last 22 years. Return on equity investment had averaged over 20 percent for the past five years, the highest in the industry and almost double the industry average.

G. Heileman was strongest in the midwestern states and had the leading market share in Illinois, Wisconsin, and Minnesota; its Rainier brand was number one in Washington and Montana. Chicago was a major market area and Heileman's Old Style brand was the best-selling brand with a 30 percent share. Heileman's Blatz brand (an original Milwaukee-brewed beer that had been one of Heileman's first two acquisitions) had recorded nine consecutive years of sales increases. The company had recently arranged to become a major U.S. distributor of Beck's beer, a German import which was one of the five best-selling import brands. Heileman's prolific array of brands (about 50), numerous packaging options (returnable and nonreturnable bottles, cans, 6-packs, 8-packs, 12-packs, 24-packs, and 7-oz., 12-oz., 16-oz., 32-oz., and 40-oz. sizes), and assorted beverage types (super-premium, premium, and popular-priced beers together with ales, malt liquors, light beers, imports, flavored malt liquors, near beers, and mineral waters) allowed the company to lay claim to the title of "America's Leading Full Line Brewer." Heileman had developed a number of clever and carefully designed regional marketing campaigns to undergird its approach to product, brand, and package segmentation.

Heileman's management was aggressive and had earned industry respect in the years following Russell Cleary's becoming president in 1971. One rival said of Cleary, "Cleary has always been the Lone Ranger, doing things his way." August A. Busch, CEO of Anheuser-Busch, observed, "That company, doomed by most analysts, has transformed the traditional don'ts into do's through innovative management, leadership, good products, and progressive marketing." Cleary believed Heileman's success was due to its strategy of staying on the offensive and building on the strengths of regionally popular beers:

> You can't win unless you stay on the attack. We made our acquisitions because if we hadn't, another company would have and used the brands and plants against us.
>
> This is a fiercely competitive business. We have to be aggressive. If we play by their rules, we are going to be killed.
>
> We have chosen not to force our brands into new markets but to build on the regionals we have acquired. They have been there for years and mean something to people. . . . Each brand sells well in a particular area.

In late 1983, it was clear that Cleary intended for Heileman to become more than a portfolio of regional brands, each with its own regional appeal and regional marketing strategy. Heileman had plans to expand the marketing of its popular-priced Carling Black Label and Blatz brands from 35 to all 50 states. Heileman's premium Old Style brand and super-premium Special Export brands, available in 17 midwestern and southern states, were slated for introduction throughout the Southeast. The company previously had stated that in the years ahead it would like to make Old Style a national premium flagship brand in the "House of Heileman" portfolio. In addition, the Rainier brand was scheduled for introduction in other states in the Pacific Northwest, while Henry Weinhard's Private Reserve, a super-premium beer that had been well received in Oregon and northern California was headed for test marketing in other parts of the United States. In years past, Heileman had used the strategy of low price backed with attention-catching ads to gain a foothold in areas where it was introducing new beers. With production capacity of 26 million barrels and sales of 17.5 million barrels (plus an agreement to provide another 3 million barrels annually to Pabst over the next five years), it was apparent that Heileman needed to seek additional sales. The location of Heileman's 11 breweries gave it access to reach all areas of the U.S. market without a freight disadvantage. Miller, A-B, Coors, and Stroh were all trying to carve out bigger shares for themselves in Heileman's midwestern stronghold, especially in the Chicago area.

ADOLPH COORS COMPANY

Coors was a single brewery company with extensive (in some cases completely self-sufficient) backward vertical integration into rice and malt, glass bottle and aluminum can manufacturing, can recycling, and paper converting, and forward integration into company-owned distributorships (five, as of 1983). At the company's main offices in Golden, Colorado, Coors operated the largest single brewery (15 million barrels annual capacity) and the largest aluminum can manufacturing plant in the United States. Most of the company's other facilities were in Colorado as well.

Until the late 1970s, Coors dominated the western U.S. beer market. A mystique surrounded its Coors brand, partly because of the favorable image generated by its slogan of "Made with Pure Rocky Mountain Spring Water." Customers in California, Texas, and 10 other western states where Coors was sold were convinced that Coors was the best beer money could buy—bar none. During most of the 1970s the company had a 50-plus percent market share in California, and in Colorado its market share was over 60 percent. Although Coors was marketed only in 12 states prior to 1975, its reputation was so strong elsewhere that it was bootlegged into other parts of the country (the bootlegging of Coors was fanned by the movie "Smoky and the Bandit" in which actor Burt Reynolds played a character who fought the law and the clock in order to sneak a cargo of Coors into Atlanta). Sales and earnings rose strongly year after year; between 1970 and 1974, Coors' shipments rose 70 percent to 12.3 million barrels, putting it in fourth place nationwide behind Anheuser-Busch, Miller, and Schlitz. Because of its strong reputation and image with beer drinkers, other brewers chose to focus elsewhere. However, in 1973, Anheuser-Busch launched a drive to expand into the West, opening a new brewery in northern California in 1976. For the first time, Coors had to defend its market position against a powerful rival.

In 1975, the Coors family decided to take the company public (partly to help pay inheritance taxes of $50 million), selling about $127 million in stock at $31 per share but retaining majority control. Coors' earnings declined in five of the seven years following 1976, and the company lost market share in its 12-state western stronghold. In 1983, Anheuser-Busch was nearing a 48 percent market share in California, compared to Coors estimated 18 percent share. Meanwhile, Miller successfully attacked Coors in Texas, gaining a 28 percent share to Coors' 20 percent share, as of 1983. Coors tried to counterattack by moving eastward, expanding sales into eight states by 1981 and into six more states east of the Mississippi in 1983, plus Alaska and Hawaii. A new advertising "The Best of the Rockies Is Here" was developed exclusively for the expansion areas.

Coors introduced Coors Light in 1978, Herman Joseph's (a full-bodied super-premium brand) in 1980, and Golden Lager (its second premium brand) in 1983; of these, only Coors Light had so far achieved much sales volume. The company had no plans to introduce a brand in the popular-priced segment. Coors sold 13.7 million barrels of beer in 1983 and had over 360 independent distributors of its brands. Coors brands were marketed in 31 states. Approximately 75 percent of Coors beer was shipped in insulated railcars (at distances up to 2,000 miles); the remainder was distributed in refrigerated trucks. The company had established beer distribution centers in California, Maryland, Tennessee, and South Carolina. One analyst estimated, in 1983, that the cost of shipping from Colorado into the southeast was $7 to $8 per barrel, compared to the normal $3 per barrel costs for deliveries from regionally located breweries. Coors required distributors to store and deliver Coors under refrigerated conditions and to adhere to a 60-day rotation policy to preserve product freshness. Coors' brewing process was the longest and most sophisticated of any major brewer, and refrigeration of the final product was required at all times to preserve quality and taste.

In addition to its beer business, Coors derived about 17 percent of sales and 14 percent of earnings from diversification efforts in snack foods, rice, porcelain products, and oil and gas. Coors was viewed by analysts as in strong financial condition.

A Coors executive predicted that in 1993 Coors would be the only remaining independent, family-owned brewery in the United States, would have national market coverage, and would be the third or fourth largest firm in the industry. Anheuser-Busch reportedly had an option on land to construct a brewery in Fort Collins,

Colorado. Recently, Coors had brought in new sales and marketing personnel to boost its capabilities, but observers doubted whether Coors had the marketing muscle and talent to go head-to-head with the two industry leaders.

PABST BREWING COMPANY

Pabst Brewing, formed in 1844, sold 18 brands of beer, operated four breweries (annual capacity of 14 million barrels), and had a nationwide network of 1,300 distributors. The company's best selling brands were Pabst Blue Ribbon, Hamm's, Olympia, and Olde English "800." Except for a can manufacturing plant at its Florida brewery, Pabst purchased all of its packaging materials and most of its ingredient supplies from outside suppliers. Sales volume had declined from 16.9 million barrels in 1976 to 12.2 million barrels in 1982; volume increased to 12.6 million barrels in 1983.

Between late 1980 and early 1983, Pabst was the object of a number of takeover attempts and efforts by dissident stockholders to gain control. A "new" Pabst emerged in 1983, with Justice Department approval. William Smith, after a three-year successful stint in turning Pittsburgh Brewing Company around, was appointed president of Pabst in September 1981.

Pabst's biggest problem was continuing decline in the sales of its Blue Ribbon brand, which accounted for 60 percent of the company's sales. Sales of Blue Ribbon were 7.7 million barrels in 1983 versus 9.8 million barrels in 1981. Pabst spent a company-record $60 million on advertising and point-of-sale material in 1983 (versus $42 million in 1982 and $47 million in 1981). Observers said younger beer drinkers looked upon Blue Ribbon "as the beer my father drank." Pabst had lagged behind other brewers in introducing light beers and was said to be weak in Sunbelt areas.

Pabst was not in strong financial condition. Long-term debt rose to $77 million in 1983, up from $13 million in 1981; earnings in 1983 were $5 million on sales of $800 million; and the stock price had recently fallen 50 percent. August U. Pabst, great grandson of the co-founder, resigned in 1983 as executive vice president and was quoted in *Forbes* as saying, "Unless Pabst merges with or acquires another brewer that gives them almost instant volume, I just don't see how they can turn it around."

William Smith, Pabst's new president, had made several comments about the industry and the company's prospects:

> The battle of the "Big Two" has introduced the era of the two "Ms"—megabucks and market share—which affect all brewers in determining their individual advertising appeals and executing effective marketing strategies.
>
> Increasing costs in all areas of operations, from production to shipping and transportation, continue to tax our ingenuity and resources.
>
> We need some success stories to survive. . . . Sure, we're slipping bad. But [Vince] Lombardi said, "If the game lasts long enough, we can win." I hope the game lasts long enough.
>
> There's no question Pabst is a target. If we go bankrupt, there are 13 million barrels of beer that will have to go somewhere. . . .
>
> When it's over, if it is, I hope people will say, "Bill Smith gave it a hell of a shot. But it was a little late when he got there."

CASE 14   THE ELECTRIC UTILITY INDUSTRY IN 1982*

There isn't a more difficult job in all of industry than the CEO of a power company.
        —Don D. Jordan, President and CEO Houston Lighting & Power Co.

In 1982 the electric utility industry in the United States had struggled through 12 years of unprecedented and turbulent change. More changes, perhaps equally dramatic, seemed to loom ahead. Prior to 1970, the industry was widely viewed as a stable, financially solid, minimum-risk business with a secure monopoly grip on supplying the steadily growing needs of customers for more electricity. But the utilities' long-run attractiveness began to change when the industry was transformed by the events of the 1970s from a decreasing unit cost business into an increasing unit cost business.

Even after allowing for the impact of recession, the industry in 1982 was still faced with subpar profitability and a historically weak financial condition, staggering capital requirements to construct new facilities, volatile interest rates and financial market conditions, stringent and costly regulatory requirements, significant downward shifts in the growth rates of electricity usage at the same time that new capacity was coming on line, mounting customer sensitivity to sharply higher electric rates, and potentially major technological developments in finding alternate ways to generate electricity economically and in reducing the amount of electricity needed to operate appliances and equipment. The combination of all these factors made the industry's outlook uncertain and complex to predict.

THE ELECTRIC UTILITY INDUSTRY: SIZE AND STRUCTURE

As of 1982 the electric utility industry in the United States had sales revenues approaching $120 billion and assets of over $300 billion. Some 240 investor-owned companies supplied about 75 percent of the retail market for electricity in the United States, with roughly 3,000 municipal electric systems, rural electric cooperatives, and publicly owned government corporations supplying the remainder. Even though the industry was comprised of many different enterprises, economies of scale in both the generation and distribution of electricity were so big as to make the business a "natural monopoly" from a geographical standpoint. Traditionally, each retail electric supplier had a monopoly franchise to serve a given geographic area.

Virtually all of the 240 investor-owned firms operated a fully integrated electric system that included large central-station generating plants, high-voltage transmission networks from the generating facilities to major distribution points, and local distribu-

---

* Prepared by Professor Arthur A. Thompson, Jr., The University of Alabama. Copyright © 1983 by Arthur A. Thompson, Jr.

Exhibit 1 Condensed Income Statement and Balance Sheet Data for

Income Statement Figures ($ millions)
Electric Operations only

Year	Total Operating Revenues	Fuel Costs	Main- tenance	Depreci- ation	Income Taxes	Other Taxes	Operating Income
1970	$18,830	$ 3,734	$1,373	$2,196	$1,322	$2,130	$ 4,483
1975	41,855	14,451	2,522	3,792	2,457	3,755	8,536
1976	47,080	16,239	2,918	4,217	3,038	4,183	9,444
1977	55,142	20,122	3,528	4,640	3,755	4,649	10,340
1978	61,299	22,225	4,153	5,120	4,055	4,985	11,123
1979	68,152	26,281	4,788	5,628	3,827	5,300	11,939
1980	80,636	31,622	5,616	6,079	4,402	5,866	13,718
1981	94,270	37,167	6,279	6,690	5,624	6,565	16,247

Balance Sheet Data ($ billions)

Year	Total Net Plant	Current Assets	Total Assets	Common Equity Capital	Preferred Stock
1970	$ 80.5	$ 5.3	$ 87.2	$26.6	$ 7.5
1975	138.3	13.0	155.3	45.8	16.9
1976	152.0	15.0	171.6	51.9	18.4
1977	167.6	17.6	190.7	58.3	20.0
1978	184.7	18.4	209.7	64.3	21.6
1979	205.6	21.6	235.8	70.8	23.9
1980	226.0	25.9	261.6	78.0	25.8
1981	247.3	28.1	287.7	86.8	26.8

Source: Edison Electric Institute.

tion facilities (substations, transformers, poles, and lines running to ultimate users). Sixty-nine of these investor-owned firms were part of 14 public utility holding companies; normally, the generation and transmission operations of firms that were part of a utility holding company were interconnected and integrated to function as one coordinated system for dispatching power to local distribution points. In 1981 investor-owned electric utilities controlled 78 percent of the total U.S. generating capacity, served 77 percent of all ultimate customers in the United States, and collected $93.8 billion in revenues from electricity sales. Exhibit 1 presents condensed income and balance sheet data for the investor-owned firms as a group.

Self-sufficient, fully integrated electric systems were much less common among municipalities, rural cooperatives, and government-owned corporations. The majority of the 1,900 municipal electric systems bought bulk power at wholesale and then resold it at retail through their own electric distribution network to customers within the municipality. Several hundred municipal utilities, however, were engaged in the generation of electricity, either on their own or in joint ventures, and supplied part or all of their requirements. In 1980 municipalities owned 5.6 percent of the total

Investor-Owned Electric Utility Industry

Allowance for Funds Used During Construction	Gross Income	Interest Costs	Preferred Stock Dividends	New Income	Common Stock Dividends
$ 594	$ 5,603	$ 2,270	$ 361	$ 2,972	$2,022
1,694	11,202	5,181	1,143	4,859	3,272
1,896	12,549	5,566	1,347	5,643	3,771
2,367	12,985	6,117	1,488	6,325	4,322
2,907	14,229	6,844	1,592	6,982	4,956
3,727	15,824	8,044	1,750	7,552	5,587
4,627	18,392	9,959	2,042	8,487	6,429
5,489	22,050	11,971	2,251	10,405	7,587

Long-Term Debt	Total Capital-ization	Current Liabilities
$ 42.2	$ 76.2	$ 7.4
69.9	132.6	15.3
75.8	146.1	15.4
82.0	160.3	17.0
87.5	173.4	20.5
96.3	190.9	26.0
105.6	209.3	29.6
114.6	228.1	32.4

U.S. generating capacity, generated 3.8 percent of the total electricity supplied, and served about 12 percent of the ultimate customers for electricity.

Rural electric cooperatives tended to be partly integrated, supplying some of their electricity requirements with internal generation and buying the remainder at wholesale from investor-owned firms or government-owned power projects; their ownership share of total U.S. generating capacity in 1980 was 2.5 percent, and they accounted for 2.8 percent of the total electricity generated. The role of the 925 rural co-ops in the industry was mainly one of operating transmission and distribution networks to service customers in less-populated geographic sections. Cooperatives served 10 percent of the ultimate customers for electricity.

The government-owned participants in the U.S. electric utility industry consisted of a variety of federal, state, and local power district corporations which operated generating and transmission facilities and sold their power output at wholesale to rural distribution cooperatives and municipal electric systems. A few government-owned systems were integrated forward into local retail distribution of electricity. Among the prominent government-owned electric utilities were the Tennessee Valley

Authority, Bonneville Power, and Salt River Project. In 1980 government-owned corporations (excluding municipalities) operated 14.1 percent of the total industry generating capacity, generated 15.5 percent of the total electricity, and provided direct service to less than 1 percent of the ultimate users.

ELECTRIC SYSTEM OPERATIONS

Historically, the technology and economics of supplying electricity to users favored building large-scale central station generating units, transmitting the electric output of these units in bulk over high-voltage wires to local substations that reduced the voltage levels, and extending local distribution systems to each customer location. While it was feasible for users of electricity to buy and install their own on-site generating unit (a combustion-powered generator or a windmill) sized to meet their load requirements, the electric energy from on-site units was more costly, less reliable (because of breakdowns), and inconvenient (because of attending to maintenance and operating requirements). The monopoly grip of electric utilities on their customers thus derived from the lower-cost economics, the reliability, and the convenience of central-station generation technology.

Types of Generating Plants   For most of the electric utility industry's existence, the dominant forms of central-station generation were hydroelectric dams and steam turbines powered by fossil fuels, such as fuel oil, natural gas, and coal. Smaller combustion turbines were also used by most companies to meet very high peak loads, but they were not as cost efficient as steam turbines and accounted for a small fraction of total electricity generation. Since 1970 a growing fraction of the electricity had been generated in nuclear-powered generating plants. Four major manufacturers supplied generating units to electric utilities: General Electric, Westinghouse, Babcock and Wilcox, and Combustion Engineering.

Because of sharply rising crude oil prices and concerns over the adequacy of natural gas reserves, those electric utilities which relied on fuel oil or natural gas to power their steam turbines had begun programs in the 1970s to shift their generation mix toward coal and nuclear fuel. The figures below show the changing generation mix of fuel sources, along with the 1990 forecasts:

Electricity Generation by Type of Fuel Source

	1960	1970	1980	1990
Coal	53.2%	45.9%	50.9%	52.7%
Fuel oil	6.1	11.9	10.7	8.0
Natural gas	20.8	24.3	15.2	4.8
Hydroelectric	19.2	16.1	12.1	8.2
Nuclear	0.1	1.4	11.0	25.0
Other	0.6	0.4	0.2	1.3
Total	100.0%	3.44%	100.0%	100.0%

Source: Edison Electric Institute and National Electric Reliability Council.

During the 1982–1986 period, utilities in the United States planned to spend $2.9 billion to convert fuel oil generating units to coal-fired units. Fuel oil consumption by electric utilities in 1981 was 351 million barrels, down from a peak of 636 million barrels in 1978. However, the shift to coal came under closer scrutiny in 1982 when the Canadian government complained of high and maybe rising levels of acidity in rainfall and in Canadian lakes and streams, said to be caused by sulfur emissions from power plants in the midwestern United States which burned high-sulfur coal. The construction of nuclear power plants, an alternative to fossil fuel generation, had been enveloped in a national controversy for many years.

The future of nuclear power became even more clouded following the accident at the Three Mile Island nuclear plant in March 1979, an event which shook confidence in nuclear power and strengthened the arguments of environmentalists and antinuclear groups with regard to the safety and desirability of nuclear plants. Other factors contributing to the uncertain role of nuclear energy in future years were:

1. The sharply rising construction costs and capital investment requirements associated with nuclear units [the projected costs per kilowatt (kw) of capacity as of 1982 were running in the $2,000–$4,000 range—well above coal-fired units at $1,000–$2,000 per kilowatt, and the total costs of an optimal-sized nuclear plant ran in the $3–$8 billion range].
2. Tedious procedures and long delays in the nuclear licensing process.
3. The absence of a national policy for the storage and disposal of spent nuclear fuels.
4. The probability that safety rules would be issued, requiring expensive retrofitting of safety equipment.
5. The probability of encountering additional construction costs and unexpected maintenance problems (maintenance problems and breakdowns could cause shutdowns lasting as long as three to six months).
6. The financial burden of constructing a $3–$8 billion project over a 10–13 year period.

No U.S. utility had placed an order for a new nuclear plant since 1978. A total of 70 previously announced nuclear plants had been canceled, some of which were already under construction. Pressures were building to halt construction on at least five others. Still, in 1982 there were 75 nuclear units with operating licenses, representing about 60,000,000 kw of capacity; construction permits had been issued for over 80 more units, about half of which were more than 50 percent complete. Some 52,000,000 kw of new nuclear generating capacity was expected to come on line during the 1982–1986 period. Industry sources did not expect any new orders for nuclear plants to occur unless and until the licensing processing could be streamlined, ways could be found to reduce capital costs and construction times, public confidence in nuclear power could be restored, and satisfactory answers to the safety and environmental issues were worked out.

Interconnections among the Separate Systems

It was normal for firms in the industry to share information on both technology and operating practices and, more important, to use the available generating capacity in the most economical fashion. To accomplish this, the transmission networks of adjacent firms were interconnected to form a supply grid that covered the entire United States. The interconnected grid facilitated the interchange and sale of power from company to company. It was common practice for a company to purchase power from a neighboring utility whenever the costs of purchased power were below its own internal generating costs; such a condition frequently arose at peak demand periods when older, less efficient generating equipment or units with high fuel costs (oil-fired combustion turbines) might otherwise have to be started up. Likewise, it was common for a company with spare capacity to supply power to neighboring companies to help them meet unusually high peak loads or to fill in for a generating unit which had unexpectedly broken down.

Customers and Their Use Characteristics   The demand side of the market for electricity was apportioned among five distinct customer groups: residential, commercial, industrial, government, and wholesale buyers (municipal electric systems, rural co-ops, neighboring power companies). The proportion of an electric company's sales to each customer group varied, depending on such factors as the amount of industry in the utility's service area, whether many or few of the industrial users used electricity-intensive production methods, how many residential customers had air conditioning and electric heat, and similar such economic and demographic considerations.

Moreover, there was wide variation in the usage patterns within and across customer groups. In the industrial sector, some firms operated energy-intensive process manufacturing plants on a 24-hours per day, 365 days-a-year schedule; their usage was thus both big and stable. Other firms operated their plants on a 40-hour, 5-day week schedule, which meant their usage was heavily concentrated within an 8-hour span on weekdays with much less electricity being demanded the remaining 16 hours of each weekday and all day long on weekends and holidays. Similarly, residential and commercial use patterns varied according to the time of the day, the day of the week, the season of the year, and the temperature and climatic conditions in the local area.

Residential and commercial usage was very weather and temperature sensitive. The use of air-conditioning was heavy in the hottest summer months and the use of electricity for heating peaked in the coldest winter months; the spring and fall months were generally low-use months because of reduced heating-cooling requirements. How much electricity a residential customer consumed was, in addition, a function of whether the customer used natural gas or electricity for water heating and cooking, the type of heating system in use (natural gas, fuel oil, electric heat pump, electric resistance heating, wood), whether the home was air-conditioned, the age and efficiency of any electric heating/cooling equipment in use, the thermostat setting which the customer preferred, the size of the home, the number of appliances in the house and their frequency of use, the degree to which the residence was well insulated, the number of household members, and the customer's income, habits, and lifestyle as concerns electricity-using devices. Depending on these variables, any one residential customer's electricity consumption could vary as much as from 500–1,000 kwh in a low-use month to 2,000–3,000 kwh in a high-use month.

By class of customer, residential customers tended to have the highest variation in usage and industrial customers the lowest, with commercial users in between. In 1981 the electric utility industry served 83.5 million residential customers, 9.9 million commercial customers, and 500,000 industrial customers. On a nationwide basis, industrial firms consumed the largest amount of electricity (37 percent of the total), followed in order by residential (34 percent), commercial (25 percent), and all others (4 percent). Exhibit 2 shows the historical and forecast consumption trends of these customer groups.

It was customary in the electric utility business to make a sharp distinction between a customer's electric energy *demand* and a customer's electric energy *usage*. Electric energy demand referred to the size of the "load" a customer placed on the utility's electric system—in other words, how many kilowatts of power it took to meet a customer's electricity requirements; an all-electric home might require as many as 15–20 kilowatts of generating capacity to meet load requirements, whereas a small apartment with neither electric heat nor air conditioning might impose a maximum power load of only 5–10 kilowatts. Energy usage was measured in kilowatt-hours (kwh) and took into account the length of time so many kilowatts of power were actually used (1 kw of power used for 1 hour equaled 1 kilowatt-hour). Residential electric rates were usually keyed to a customer's kilowatt-hour usage, whereas the pricing of electricity to commercial and industrial customers commonly included a capacity charge (a fee for the number of kilowatts of power required for service) and an energy charge (so many cents per kilowatt-hour used).

Electric utility customers could, of course, change the size of the energy load they placed upon the utility's electric system by simply pushing a button, pulling a switch, or otherwise exercising their freedom to turn electricity-using equipment on or off. They could also add new equipment and facilities powered by electric energy without prior notification to the utility. Most every electric utility, public- and investor-owned, firmly took the position that its electric system had to be of a size and capability to meet whatever energy loads and use patterns might be imposed by customers. This policy existed mainly out of a desire and legal responsibility to serve the full needs of customers and secondarily to protect against "brownouts" and "blackouts." A brownout resulted when total customer loads barely exceeded generating output, allowing the margin of difference to be managed by reducing voltage levels below desirable limits. Brownouts were damaging to both customers' equipment and the company's electric system. A blackout occurred when customer loads so overtaxed power delivery capacity that generating units ceased operating altogether. Once a blackout occurred, the system could be reactivated only when a balanced relationship was restored between customer demand and power delivery capability.

As a general rule of thumb, electric utilities sought to maintain a reserve generating capability (nameplate-rated capacity) at least 15–20 percent greater than the maximum peak demand load they expected to encounter. This 15–20 percent margin provided not only a measure of safety against an unusually large peak load but also allowed the firm to meet peak demands even if it should experience a breakdown in one of its generating units. In 1982 reserve margins on a nationwide basis had risen from the "normal" 15–20 percent range to the 30–35 percent range during the summer and to the 40–50 percent range during the winter (see Exhibits 3 and 4), reflecting

Exhibit 2 Actual and Projected Kilowatt-Hour Usage of Electricity in the United States, by Customer Group, 1971–2000   In Billions of kwh

| | | | | Customer Group | | | | | |
Year	Residential	Percent Change	Industrial	Percent Change	Commercial	Percent Change	Other	Percent Change	Total	Percent Change
1971	479.1	7.0%	592.7	3.5%	333.8	6.7%	60.9	4.5%	1,466.4	5.4%
1972	511.4	6.7	639.5	7.9	361.9	8.4	65.0	6.7	1,577.7	7.6
1973	554.2	8.4	687.2	7.5	396.9	9.7	64.9	-0.1	1,703.2	8.0
1974	555.0	0.1	689.4	0.3	392.7	-1.1	63.7	-1.9	1,700.8	-0.1
1975	586.1	5.6	661.6	-4.0	418.1	6.5	67.2	5.6	1,733.0	1.9
1976	613.1	4.6	725.2	9.6	440.6	5.4	70.8	5.2	1,849.6	6.7
1977	652.3	6.4	757.2	4.4	469.2	6.5	72.1	1.8	1,950.8	5.5
1978	679.2	4.1	782.1	3.3	480.7	2.5	75.8	5.2	2,017.8	3.4
1979	696.0	2.5	817.6	4.5	494.7	2.9r	76.1	0.4	2,084.4	3.3
1980	734.4	5.5	793.8	-2.9	524.1	5.9r	73.7	-3.0	2,126.1	2.0
1981	735.7	0.2	800.0	0.8	541.4	3.3	76.8	4.1	2,153.8	1.3
Forecast										
1982	747.7	1.6	743.4	-7.1	554.9	2.5	76.3	-0.6	2,122.3	-1.5
1983	761.8	1.9	769.6	3.5	568.2	2.4	77.6	1.6	2,177.3	2.6
1984	783.9	2.9	828.5	7.7	587.0	3.3	78.9	1.8	2,278.3	4.6
1985	813.5	3.8	862.8	4.1	610.5	4.0	80.4	1.9	2,367.2	3.9
1986	844.6	3.8	894.9	3.7	634.9	4.0	82.0	2.0	2,456.4	3.8
1987	875.4	3.6	933.8	4.3	659.0	3.8	83.6	2.0	2,551.8	3.9
1988	903.3	3.2	962.0	3.0	681.4	3.4	85.3	2.0	2,632.0	3.1
1989	930.6	3.0	990.9	3.0	703.2	3.2	86.9	2.0	2,711.7	3.0
1990	954.4	2.3	1,019.7	2.9	722.9	2.8	88.6	2.0	2,785.7	2.7
1995	1,076.8	2.2	1,164.0	2.4	817.9	2.5	97.7	2.0	3,156.4	2.4
2000	1,207.6	2.3	1,307.9	2.3	920.9	2.4	108.1	2.1	3,544.5	2.3

Source: *Electrical World,* September 1982, p. 79.

Exhibit 3   Summer Peak Capabilities, Peak Loads, and Reserve Margins   Total Electric
Utility Industry of the Contiguous United States

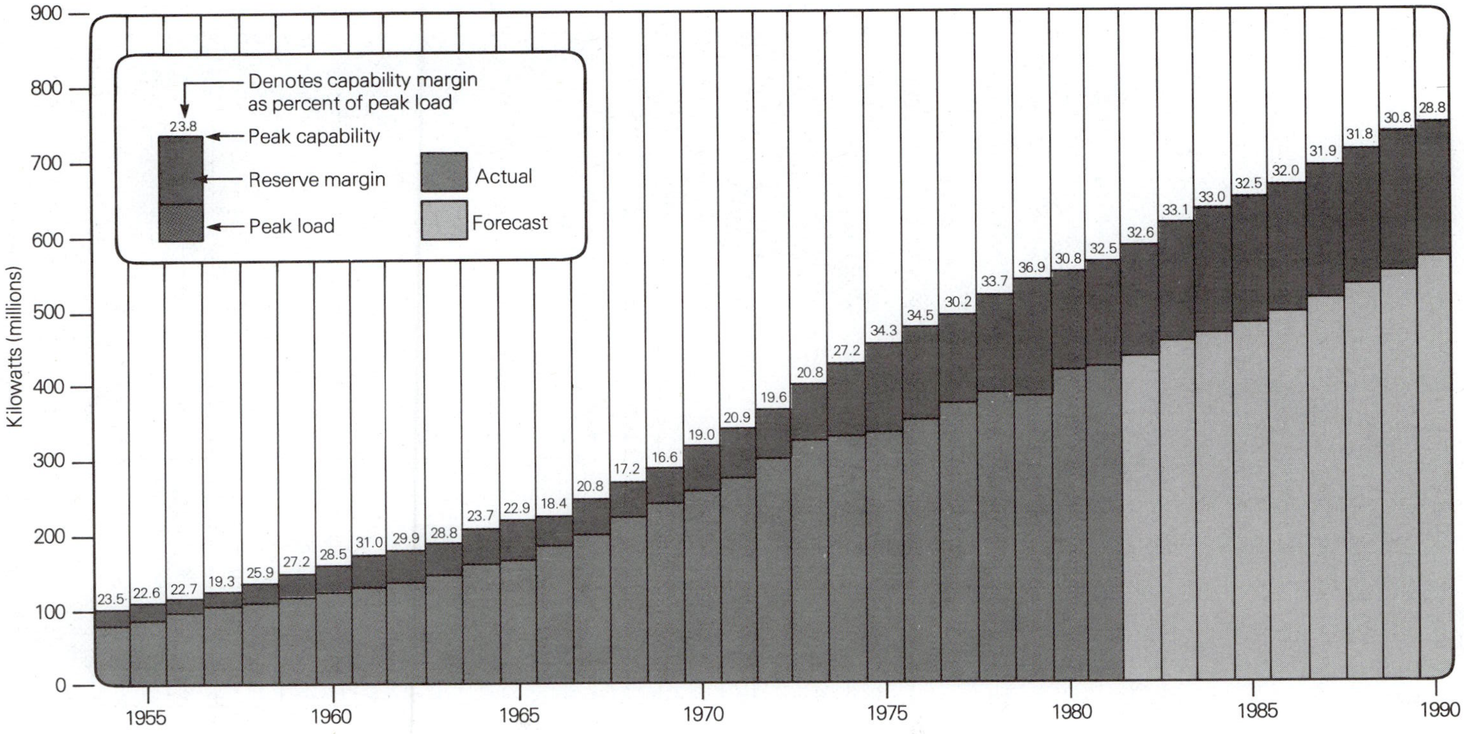

Source: Edison Electric Institute.

Exhibit 4   Winter Peak Capabilities, Peak Loads, and Reserve Margins   Total Electric Utility
Industry of the Contiguous United States

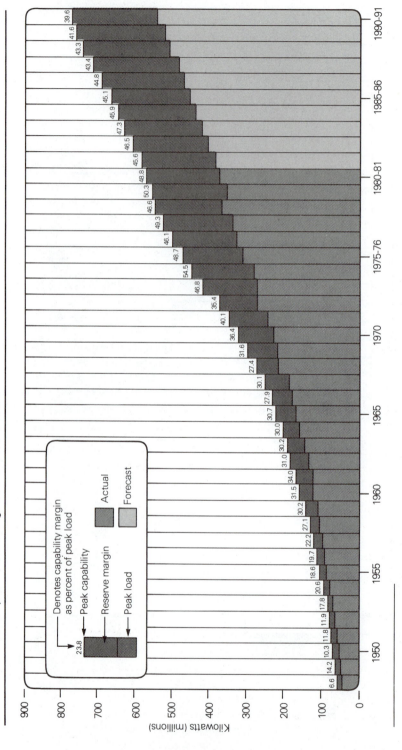

Source: Edison Electric Institute.

a general industry condition that new generating capacity additions were outrunning peak load growth. Above-average reserve margins were forecast to exist at least into the 1990s.

Regulation   Because electric utilities were monopoly providers of an essential public service, they were extensively regulated. State public utility commissions had jurisdiction over the retail rates which investor-owned utilities charged and, in the case of municipalities and cooperatives, rates were generally subject to review by political bodies or constrained by the organization's nonprofit status. Wholesale electric rates were generally subject to approval of the Federal Energy Regulatory Commission. The securities of utilities were subject to the rules and regulations of the Securities and Exchange Commission. The Nuclear Regulatory Commission closely regulated all aspects of nuclear plant operations. As concerns air and water pollution, utilities had to comply with the requirements of the Environmental Protection Agency, as well as state and local pollution control authorities. Moreover, the audit staffs of state regulatory commissions scrutinized virtually all aspects of electric utility operations under their jurisdiction, and the Federal Energy Regulatory Commission required extensive financial and operating reports on a regular basis. Extensive public hearings and regulatory approval were required before construction of new generating facilities could begin. State commissions and the Federal Energy Regulatory Commission could issue directives on a wide variery of utility company operations.

Throughout the 1970s and into the 1980s, regulatory rules and constraints greatly intensified in the areas of rates, air and water quality standards, all aspects of nuclear plant construction, and energy conservation requirements. Generally, the regulatory environment was hostile and unsympathetic to the operating and financial difficulties being encountered by power companies. Many utility executives attributed a great portion of the industry's problems to the tightening web of rules and regulations, to the added operating costs imposed by many of these rules and regulations, and to a failure to receive adequate rate increases.

THE "GOLDEN AGE" ERA OF DECREASING UNIT COSTS

Up until the late 1960s the electric utility industry was characterized by decreasing unit cost conditions. Technological advances in steam turbine manufacture led to the installation of bigger and bigger generating units which were more efficient and economical to operate. New technological applications and growing electricity demand also made high-voltage transmission lines an economical investment. The costs of fossil fuels (coal, fuel oil, and natural gas) to power steam turbines were low and stable, and the advent of nuclear-powered generating equipment offered promise of even cheaper generating costs. The construction of hydroelectric dams, with their virtually zero marginal generating costs (because water in the storage reservoirs was a "free" fuel), also contributed to a declining cost structure. The economics of the business were such that once the large fixed asset investment in generating and transmission facilities had been made and customers were hooked up to the system, then they could be supplied with additional kilowatt-hours (kwh) of electricity at a very low marginal cost (essentially fuel cost plus a small variable operating expense) per kwh. The high fixed costs of installing generating, transmission, and distribution equipment were recovered by encouraging greater kwh usage per customer and adding more customers, both of which served to increase the utilization of the existing investment in facilities and to spread total fixed expenses over more kilowatt-hours.

To capitalize upon the industry's decreasing unit-cost economics during the 1950s and 1960s, utilities pursued aggressive grow-and-build type strategies. Marketing strategies emphasized the simple theme of "promote and sell" more electricity to more customers for more uses, while in the other operating areas the strategy was to build new generating capacity, extend transmission and distribution networks, and improve the reliability of service (by lessening the frequency and duration of outages due to system failures). To help develop and broaden the market for electricity, companies gave away free light bulbs, ran ads to convince customers to "live better electrically" and pushed Reddy Kilowatt as the industry's cartoon mascot. Periodic sales promotion campaigns touted the advantages of electric cooking appliances, frost-free refrigerators, air conditioning, electric water heating and space heating, improved lighting, and other electric appliances. Some companies got into the appliance sales business. Sales forces were organized to develop and promote electric energy in commercial and industrial applications. Street lighting and security lights were heavily promoted as a desirable, economical, off-peak use of electricity.

Pricing strategy also played a prominent role. It was standard for all utilities to have rate incentives that benefited customers who increased their electricity consumption. "Declining-block" rates structures were designed such that as a customer used more electricity the price charged on the *extra* kilowatt-hours consumed was stepped down; these quantity discounts at successive intervals of consumption meant that a customer's monthly electric bill did not rise in proportion to the increased usage.

All of these strategies worked. Residential, commercial, and industrial customers understood the happy economics of declining block rates and they responded to the utilities' promotional campaigns to use more electricity for more purposes. Between 1950 and 1970, commercial usage of electricity in the United States rose 500 percent and industrial consumption rose 400 percent. Nationwide, the average annual usage per residential customer rose from 1,800 kwh in 1950 to 7,000 kwh in 1970, an increase of almost 300 percent. In geographic areas where summers were hot and air conditioning was prevalent, the average annual kwh usage of households was often in the 10,000 kwh to 12,000 kwh range. The monthly residential bill for 1,000 kwh (enough electricity to handle water heating, cooking, lighting, and power for the appliances of a well-equipped household— averaged about $25.00 in 1960 and was down to $18.50 in 1970; for a 2,000-square-foot, all-electric home with both air conditioning and electric heat, the monthly bill in 1970 averaged under $40 per month throughout most of the United States.

The electric utility industry thrived in this "golden age" era of decreasing unit-costs. The strategic performance that unfolded year after year up until 1970 was self-renewing: the more electricity that customers used, the lower were the average costs of producing it; the lower were the average costs per kwh, the lower the average price that companies could charge and still earn an attractive return on the fair value of their expanding investments in generating, transmission, and distribution facilities; the lower the price per kwh, the more that customer usage was stimulated; the greater the usage of electricity, the lower the average cost of producing it (due both to improved operating efficiencies and to spreading the high total fixed costs over more kwh of electricity). From 1950 through 1970 the sales revenues of investor-owned firms grew at a compound rate of 7.3 percent, total kwh usage grew at a 7.9 percent compound rate, profits rose at an 8.4 percentage rate, and the average revenue charged per kwh (all customers) dropped from 1.85 cents to 1.68 cents. The favorable technology and cost economics, combined with stable and predictable growth rates, made the business risk factor minimal; new investments in electric utility stocks and bonds were considered safe, and as shown in Exhibit 5 the profitability and price-earnings ratios of electric utility companies compared favorably with unregulated manufacturing companies and *Fortune 500* firms.

THE TRANSITION TO INCREASING UNIT COSTS

Beginning in the late 1960s, however, economic forces in the industry began to change dramatically. Four powerful economic conditions dominated the picture between 1968 and 1982:

1. Technology-based economies of scale were exhausted and companies could no longer count upon the installation of larger and larger generating units to produce lower operating costs. The most efficient size generating unit topped out at about 600,000 kw to 800,000 kw.
2. Inflation hit the industry especially hard. Between 1970 and 1980, fuel costs per kwh generated rose from 0.33¢ to 2.07¢ on an industrywide basis. The interest rates which companies had to pay on first mortgage bonds jumped from 4.5–5.0% in the mid-1960s to the 15–18% range in 1981–1982. Nonfuel operating and maintenance expenses per kwh doubled from 0.43¢ in 1970 to 0.86¢ in 1980.
3. Expenditures for the construction of new facilities mushroomed. Whereas companies were able to build and install new generating units at costs of $100–$200 per kw of capacity during the 1950–1970 period, the figure rose to the estimated $500–$1,000 per kw range for units coming on line in 1980–81; construction costs to complete units begun in the early 1980s were in the $1,500–$4,000 per kw range. One utility firm added a coal-fired plant in 1971 at a cost of $155 per kw, another plant of the same type in 1981 at a cost of $912 per kw, and estimated its costs for a 1990 coal-fired plant at $2,104 per kw. Another firm began plans for four nuclear plants in 1969. The first two were completed in 1978 and 1980 at a combined cost of $1.5 billion; the third one was halted in 1982 with construction 15 percent completed because the estimated costs to complete the project had escalated from $1.2 billion to $5.1 billion; plans for the fourth unit were scrapped. Industrywide, construction expenditures of investor-owned firms jumped from $10.1 billion in 1970 to $27.2 billion in 1981. Increased construction costs were a reflection of *(a)* inflation having driven up the costs of materials and labor; *(b)* added expenditures for pollution control equipment and safety regulations; *(c)* the building of nuclear-powered generating units (which entailed a higher fixed investment cost per kw of installed capacity than either hydro or fossil fuel units, but which had fuel and operating costs of about 50 percent or less that of fossil fuel plants); *(d)* the imposition of extensive and

time-consuming regulations and hearings regarding site selection, testing, safety, licensing, and environmental impact which pushed the start-to-finish construction interval from 3–5 years during the 1960s up to 10–13 years as of the early 1980s; and *(e)* the construction of larger increments of new generating capacity (about 1.5 times more new generating capacity was added during the 1970s as compared to the 1960s). During the 1980s it was estimated that the industry would increase generating capacity by 31 percent at a cost of about $250 billion.

4. Major expenditures to reduce the air pollution content of fossil-fuel plants and to comply with new environmental safety requirements for nuclear plants added to the burden of rising costs, and in some states higher sales and property taxes were also imposed on electric utility companies. Between 1970 and 1982, utilities spent over $20 billion to comply with pollution control requirements and legislation was pending in Congress regarding the "acid rain" issue and sulfur emissions from coal-fired plants that could result in additional environmental costs of $7–$15 billion annually.

During the decade of the 1970s, the costs incurred by investor-owned companies for fuel, operating and maintenance expenses, depreciation, interest, and taxes rose a combined $50 billion over and above the amounts attributable to greater kwh sales and larger-scale operations. This represented an annual upward shift in the industry's cost structure of $5 billion a year for each year of the decade, in an industry which had 1970 sales of $19 billion and after-tax profits of $3.0 billion.

Exhibit 5   Comparisons of Electric Utility P-E Ratios and Rates of Return on Equity Investment with Those of Other Firms, Selected Years, 1950–1981

Year	Price-Earning Ratios		Rates of Return on Stockholders' Equity		
	Moody's 24 Electric Utilities (annual average)	Dow Jones Industrials (end of year)	Fortune 500 Largest Industrial Corporations	All Manufacturing firms	Investor-Owned Electric Utilities
The Decreasing Cost Era					
1950	11.9x	7.7x	n.a.	15.4%	10.1%
1955	15.3	13.6	n.a.	12.6	10.4
1960	16.9	19.1	10.1%	9.2	10.7
1965	19.8	18.1	13.0	13.0	12.2
1969	13.7	14.0	11.5	11.5	11.8
The Increasing Cost Era					
1970	11.5x	16.4x	9.6	9.3	11.2
1975	6.6	11.3	11.4	11.6	10.5
1976	7.4	10.4	11.4	13.9	10.8
1977	7.8	9.3	13.5	14.2	10.8
1978	7.4	7.1	13.3	15.0	10.8
1979	6.8	6.7	14.2	16.4	10.6
1980	6.1	7.9	15.0	14.2	10.9
1981	5.5	7.7	14.3	13.6	12.0

n.a. = Not available.

Sources: Edison Electric Institute, *Statistical Yearbook;* Federal Trade Commission, *Quarterly Financial Report for Manufacturing, Mining, and Trade Corporations;* and *The Fortune Directory of the 500 Largest Industrial Corporations.*

As a consequence, electric utilities all across the country were forced to raise their rates on numerous occasions and by sizable amounts. Between 1969 and 1981 the retail electric rates of investor-owned utilities more than tripled:

Type of Customer	Average Revenue per Kwh (cents)				
	1969	1973	1977	1979	1981
Residential	2.21	2.54	4.06	4.63	6.19
Commercial	2.06	2.42	4.10	4.68	6.28
Industrial	0.99	1.26	2.52	3.06	4.29
All customers	1.63	1.97	3.44	3.99	5.45

Many companies by the mid-1970s found themselves caught in the position of either having a rate increase under review by their respective regulatory commission or else busy working on the elaborate documentation necessary to file on a new rate increase. Confronted with round after round of rate increase filings, regulatory commissions everywhere began to scrutinize rate requests more and more thoroughly. The hearing process became lengthy and protracted, involving weeks of testimony of expert witnesses, counterarguments from consumer groups protesting the need and validity of such increases, the processing of requests for additional data and documentation, all accompanied by extensive reviews of the proceedings and statistics by both the regulatory staffs and commission members. In 1982 the "regulatory lag" period was averaging 8.5 months.

More often than not regulatory commissions refused to grant all of the rate increase a company requested, thus prompting a company either to appeal the decision to the courts or else file another rate increase request asking for the amounts not previously granted plus additional amounts to cover the rising costs incurred since the last filing. Exhibit 6 shows the expanding volume of rate increase requests during

---

Exhibit 6 The Volume of Rate Increase Requests of Investor-Owned Electric Utilities

Year	Number of Rate Increases Filed	Amount Requested
1970	80	$ 796,784,000
1971	113	1,368,161,000
1972	110	1,204,935,000
1973	139	2,125,185,000
1974	212	4,555,061,000
1975	191	3,973,479,000
1976	169	3,747,294,000
1977	162	3,952,846,000
1978	154	4,494,132,000
1979	178	5,741,235,000
1980	254	10,871,485,000
1981	262	11,475,197,000
1982 (6 months)	188	11,776,826,000

Source: Edison Electric Institute.

the increasing unit-cost years. In 1982 state regulatory commissions were granting an average of 60 percent of the amounts requested, but the actual percentage in a given rate case filing varied greatly across both states and companies. By 1990, it was predicted that the price of electricity would average between 10¢ and 15¢ per kwh, depending on how inflation affected operating costs.

CONSTRUCTION EXPENDITURES AND THE "CASH-HOG" CHARACTER OF THE BUSINESS

The electric utility business was and is the most capital intensive of all businesses: As of 1980, it took about $2.80 of capital investment in fixed assets (generating plants, transmission lines, distribution equipment, office facilities, land) to produce $1 in sales revenue. In comparison, most businesses required less than 50¢ in fixed asset investment for each revenue dollar. Far and away the most expensive part of supplying electricity was the cost of the generating plant. Over 60 percent of the industry's fixed assets were invested in generating facilities.

The combined effects of capital intensity, rapidly rising construction costs, and lengthening times from beginning to completion of construction made it increasingly hard for electric utilities to finance their expansion programs. During the 1970s, total after-tax earnings averaged about 30–33 percent of gross construction expenditures as compared to 40–55 percent in the 1955–1965 period (see Exhibit 7). Moreover, the quality of the industry's reported net earnings was deteriorating in one important respect—a rising fraction of reported earnings was the result of an accounting treatment which, in effect, credited as net income an imputed return on funds tied up in construction work in progress. This imputed return, called allowance for funds used during construction or AFUDC, was calculated by multiplying a firm's weighted-average cost of capital by the value of the firm's dollar investment in construction work in progress; the resulting value was then divided into the "equity portion" and the "debt portion," based on the respective fractions of the company's capital structure which were equity financed and debt financed. The equity portion of AFUDC showed up on the income statement as "other income," thus adding to gross income (see Exhibit 1); the debt portion was shown on the income statement as a deduction from actual interest payments. The effect was to increase net income by the combined total of the equity and debt AFUDC amounts though, of course, no actual cash was involved. The full amount of the AFUDC calculation in a given year was then capitalized and included as part of the total cost of new construction.[1] Later, when

---

[1] Although there were other generally accepted accounting principles for handling the treatment of construction work, many regulatory commissions mandated the use of the AFUDC approach because it had the result of increasing a firm's reported net income without ratepayers having to pay the rates that would produce this income in cash dollars. However, while this caused rates to be lower during the construction phase, later, when the AFUDC amounts were rolled into total construction costs and the project was brought into service, rates had to be set higher to produce revenues to cover the added depreciation charges that the capitalization of AFUDC produced. The rate tradeoff was thus "lower now, higher later" because ratepayers paid the AFUDC "financing charges" as the facilities were used rather than as they were constructed (in accord with the accounting principle that revenues should be recognized at the same time the costs associated with those revenues are recognized). The size of a company's AFUDC charges reflected the size of its construction program.

Exhibit 7   The Electric Utility Industry's Inability to Finance Construction out of Earnings   Dollar Figures in Millions

Year	Gross Additions to Utility Plants	Size of AFUDC Components of Net Earnings			"Cash" Earnings (Net earnings − AFUDC)	Dividend Payments of Common Stock	Cash Surplus (Deficiency)
		After-tax Earnings	Dollars	Percent of Total			
The Decreasing Cost Era							
1950	$ 2,050	$ 711	n.a.	n.a.	—	$ 508	—
1955	2,719	1,093	n.a.	n.a.	—	792	—
1960	3,331	1,557	$ 100	6.4	$1,457	1,090	$ 367
1965	4,027	2,340	94	4.0	2,246	1,526	720
1969	8,294	2,823	405	14.3	2,418	1,880	538
The Increasing Cost Era							
1970	10,145	2,972	594	20.0	2,378	2,022	356
1975	15,130	4,859	1,694	34.9	3,165	3,272	(107)
1976	17,027	5,643	1,896	33.6	3,747	3,771	(24)
1977	19,806	6,325	2,367	37.4	3,958	4,322	(724)
1978	22,431	6,982	2,907	41.6	4,013	4,956	(943)
1979	24,445	7,552	3,727	49.4	3,825	5,587	(1,762)
1980	25,816	8,487	4,627	54.5	3,860	6,429	(2,569)
1981	27,255	10,405	5,489	52.8	4,916	7,587	(2,671)

Source: Edison Electric Institute, *Statistical Yearbook*, various issues.

the newly constructed facilities came into service, companies could, with commission approval, begin to charge rates which would, over the life of the facilities, produce revenues sufficient to recover the AFUDC income reported earlier (this was accomplished by including the capitalized AFUDC amounts in calculating depreciation charges on the new facilities).

Between 1970 and 1981, the AFUDC component of the industry's net earnings jumped from 20.0 percent to 52.8 percent (see column 5 of Exhibit 7)—a trend which caused Wall Street and the investment community to view the industry's earnings as becoming progressively of "lower quality." Because AFUDC was a noncash bookkeeping entry rather than real dollars, the cash component of the industry's earnings since 1975 was inadequate to cover dividend payments on common stock, much less help fund construction costs. And the cash flow deficiency was widening (see column 7 of Exhibit 7). Even when all other sources of internal funds were included, most companies came up far short of having the internal cash flow to pay construction costs. The industry's ratio of internal cash flow to actual construction outlays averaged 33 percent during the 1970s.

As a result, electric utilities depended heavily on external sources of capital. In the 1970s, investor-owned electric utilities raised a total of $113.1 billion externally; of this total, $28.0 billion came from new issues of common stock, $18.4 billion was raised through new issues of preferred stock, and $66.7 billion was in the form of new long-term bonds. Some companies were forced to depend on sales of commercial paper and short-term bank loans for interim construction financing, because lags in obtaining rate increases from state regulatory commissions temporarily depressed earnings and imperiled earnings coverage requirements on the issuance of new securities.

During the 1950s and 1960s, the times-interest-earned coverages throughout the industry were in the 4.0x to 6.0x range, solidly above the standard minimums of 2.0x on first mortgage bonds and 1.5x on preferred stock. Most companies enjoyed a desirable degree of financial flexibility in the sense that they could select from among the most timely and economical sources of external capital. But during the 1970s the once comfortable earnings coverage ratios were eroded to the 2.5x to 3.0x range by the combined effects of (1) higher interest rates on new security issues, (2) the large volume of new financing required to support a large, ongoing construction effort, and (3) a chronic squeeze on earnings brought on by the twin effects of "regulatory lag" in approving rate increases and sharply escalating, inflation-driven, cost increases. The sequence of events that power companies encountered was financially debilitating:

Scene 1:   Inflation-driven increases in construction costs for new generating plants pushed capital spending requirements well above the amount of internal cash flows available for investment purposes.

Scene 2:   To raise the monies to fund construction budgets, reliance had to be placed upon external sources of long-term capital—first mortgage bonds, preferred stock, and common stock.

Scene 3:   As more first mortgage bonds were issued and interest charges rose, new downward pressure was put on times-interest-earned coverages. Similarly, new issues of preferred stock created new preferred stock dividend requirements and these, along with higher interest rates on debt, acted to push the preferred stock coverages down toward the minimum 1.5x level. Once these coverages got down to the 2.0x and 1.5x minimums, respectively, further issues were blocked.

Scene 4:   Total dependence on the issuance of more shares of common stock for the rest of the funding was not practical for two reasons: first, more shares of stock diluted earnings per share, and second, more shares created additional dividend requirements—both of which put limitations on common stock as a source of capital.

Scene 5:   Hence, as new construction financing became necessary and with subpar coverages on security obligations, a company was pushed into filing for a rate increase sufficient to boost earnings coverages above the required minimum. The improved earnings coverages permitted more bonds and preferred stock to be issued. At the same time, higher net earnings renewed access to equity capital.

Scene 6:   But *the relief* provided by such a rate increase *was temporary*. When new bonds and preferred stock were sold, the added interest charges and dividend requirements prompted new downward pressure on coverage ratios and, also, cut into net profits after taxes. Meanwhile, relentless inflationary cost pressures added to the squeeze on earnings. Hence as the time came when another round of construction expenditures had to be financed, yet another rate increase was needed to continue to fund construction.

Exhibit 8   The Vicious Circle of Construction Financing

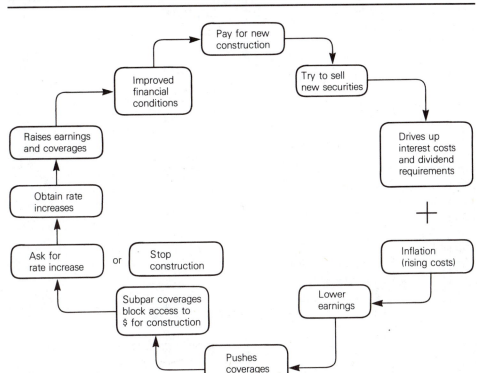

Much of the weakening financial condition of the industry was attributable to the combined impact of inflationary cost pressures and large, ongoing construction expenses. Since 1970 virtually every electric utility had cycled two or more times through the "vicious circle" shown in Exhibit 8. Despite round after round of rate increases, utility balance sheets and income statements were viewed by Wall Street and securities investors as looking worse, not better. During the 1971–1981 period Standard & Poor's issued 156 downgradings and only 41 upgradings on the bonds of electric utilities. Since 1973, the common stocks of most electric utility companies had traded on exchanges at 65 to 90 percent of book value and, as of March 1982, were selling at an average of 82 percent of book value versus an average of 150 percent of book for 399 S&P industrials.

The burden of construction financing was projected to be heavy throughout the 1980s. Exhibit 9 shows the scheduled additions of new generating capacity for the entire industry, both investor owned and publicly owned. The U.S. investor-owned companies had planned construction outlays for new facilities and equipment of $165 billion during the five-year period 1982–1986 (see Exhibit 10), an amount 38.5 percent above the previous five-year period. It was anticipated that at least $100 billion of the $165 billion total (60 percent) would have to be raised externally in the capital markets. In 1981, 68 percent of construction costs were financed externally.

Exhibit 9 Scheduled Additions to Electric Generating Capacity, U.S. Electric Utility Industry

	Thermal								Hydro				Total	
	Steam Turbine-Generators				Combustion Turbine Generators		Diesel Engine-Generators		Conventional		Pumped-Storage			
	Conventional		Nuclear											
	Number of Units	Kw	Number of Units	Kw	Number of Units	Kw	Number of Units	Kw	Number of Units	Kw	Number of Units	Kw	Number of Units	Kw
Total Scheduled	165	88,471,308	89	102,677,150	16	2,213,970	5	28,707	47	2,471,552	23	5,317,402	345	201,180,089
Scheduled Additions by Years as of April 1, 1981														
1981	27	9,751,643	4	4,426,631	8	739,570	4	22,707	10	542,220	4	107,868	57	15,590,639
1982	22	10,138,599	11	11,979,688	3	231,060	1	6,000	10	467,800	3	1,050,000	50	23,873,147
1983	14	6,977,157	11	12,066,312	1	96,440	—	—	15	570,682	1	31,000	42	19,741,591
1984	16	9,067,504	14	16,029,786	—	—	—	—	9	749,970	—	—	39	25,847,260
1985	23	12,347,827	6	6,800,805	1	72,900	—	—	3	140,880	5	1,103,934	37	20,393,446
1986	13	8,036,175	12	14,506,697	—	—	—	—	—	—	3	1,050,000	29	23,665,772
1987 and later	50	32,152,403	31	36,867,231	3	1,074,000	—	—	—	—	7	1,974,600	91	72,068,234
Scheduled Additions by Ownership														
Investor-owned	116	68,995,680	70	78,621,733	11	1,889,110	—	—	14	513,162	16	5,124,600	227	155,144,285
Federal	—	—	14	7,528,802	—	—	—	—	28	1,769,220	7	192,802	49	19,490,824
Municipal	16	3,596,142	—	—	4	266,360	5	28,707	1	40,000	—	—	26	3,931,209
Cooperatives	25	12,099,755	—	—	—	—	—	—	—	—	—	—	25	12,099,755
State and local	8	3,779,731	5	6,526,615	1	58,500	—	—	4	149,170	—	—	18	10,514,016

Source: Edison Electric Institute, *1981 Annual Electric Power Survey*, p. 23.

Exhibit 10   Estimated Construction Expenditures of Investor-Owned Electric Utility Industry, 1982–1986 In Millions of 1982 Dollars

Type of Facility	1982	1983	1984	1985	1986	Total 1982–1986
Electric generation:						
Nuclear plant	$13,720	$11,610	$ 8,590	$ 7,110	$ 5,550	$ 46,580
Nuclear fuel	1,390	1,590	2,110	2,560	2,310	9,960
Total nuclear	15,110	13,200	10,700	9,670	7,860	56,540
Coal	7,860	7,650	8,100	7,350	7,410	38,370
All other	1,810	1,700	1,870	2,100	2,230	9,710
Total generation	24,780	22,550	20,670	19,120	17,500	104,620
Transmission and distribution	7,860	9,380	9,860	9,830	10,190	47,120
All other (electric operations only)*	2,780	2,790	2,820	2,760	2,590	13,740
Total†	$35,420	$34,720	$33,350	$31,710	$30,280	$165,480

* Includes expenditures on programs designed for conservation, load management, and end-use efficiency.
† Includes AFUDC and expenditures for coal conversions and pollution control equipment at existing facilities.
Source: Edison Electric Institute.

THE STRATEGIC RESPONSES TO INCREASING
COST ECONOMICS

During the 1970s most electric utility managements responded to increasing unit-cost conditions with a three-pronged strategic approach:

1. Continue to invest heavily in new generating facilities, in anticipation of growing demand for electricity and a need to ensure adequate electric energy supplies for national economic growth.
2. Press hard for rate increases and convince regulators that timely rate increases were essential if the company's profits and overall financial condition are to be adequate to finance the amount of construction needed to serve customers.
3. Institute publicly visible programs to promote energy conservation and implement "load management" practices aimed at restricting peak load growth (the growth in peak loads was the driving force behind the need to construct new generating capacity).

By 1974 marketing strategies at most companies had shifted from aggressive promotion of more use to advocating wise use. Sales promotions campaigns ceased and advertising efforts were cut back. The remaining ads were directed wholly at conservation and educating customers to wise energy use practices. Sales force activities were redirected into providing energy audits, responding to customer complaints, and public relations. Many companies changed the name of their marketing departments to "energy services" or "customer services." As one observer expressed it, "marketing departments were dismantled." The industry's sales expenses fell from a peak of $307 million in 1970 to just $33 million in 1980.

As inflation-driven cost increases accelerated and fossil fuel prices skyrocketed, more and bigger rate increases became imperative. New and more sophisticated efforts had to be expended to convince regulators to grant rate increases. By 1982 it was apparent that even a modified grow-and-build strategy of trying to complete only those projects already under construction might not work to the advantage of either customers or investors. Round after round of rate increases had not prevented the financial condition of electric utilities from deteriorating, even though rate increases were large and frequent. The outcome of continuing a grow-and-build strategy seemed fairly predictable: sizable rate increases, above the inflation rate, would be needed to keep construction programs going. Customer resistance to higher rates could be expected to stiffen regulatory reluctance to grant rate relief and, also, to diminish consumer enthusiasm for using more electricity; peak loads and kwh usage could well become even more price elastic.

STRATEGY ALTERNATIVES FOR THE 1980s

As a consequence of the difficulties of continuing a grow-and-build strategy, there was much discussion throughout the electric utility industry of the various strategic options. A number of strategic alternatives had been identified and were either being studied or pursued:

1. Revamp functional area and internal operating strategies to generate new efficiencies and use the cost savings to help fund the basic "grow and build" strategy at the corporate level.
2. Diversify into other utility businesses, such as cable television and telephone interconnect services.
3. Diversify into alternate energy sources (coal mining, oil and gas exploration, solar energy).
4. Develop service businesses (data processing services, energy consulting, management and design of generation facilities, construction management).
5. Add complementary product lines (devices to promote energy conservation, sale of energy-efficient appliances and solar energy systems, repair and maintenance of electrical heating and cooling equipment).
6. Enter nonregulated, nonenergy-related businesses via either acquisition or internal start-up.
7. Divest part or all of the new generating facilities under construction.
8. Adopt a slow growth strategy with emphasis on increased utilization of existing generating capacity and selective marketing of available capacity at off-peak periods.

The degree to which companies were pursuing these options varied from company to company, but in all but a handful of companies diversification efforts accounted for less than 5 percent of revenues and profits as of 1982.

Four developments, however, were posing some new strategic issues for industry executives to contemplate: (1) the broadening effects of price-induced conservation efforts, (2) the introduction of new energy-saving equipment by manufacturers, (3) continued technological advances and cost-saving improvements in alternate ways of generating electricity, and (4) potential major technological developments in micro-processors and telecommunications which could throw electric utilities into the competitive arena with other firms to provide a whole new family of utility services.

THE BROADENING EFFECTS OF PRICE-INDUCED CONSERVATION

In 1982 there was no room to doubt the growing impact of customer efforts to conserve electricity. Peak load growth was in a state of decline:

Period	Average Annual Peak Load	Compound Growth Rate Kwh Usage
1960–1970	7.5%	7.4%
1970–1975	5.4	4.6
1975–1980	3.7	3.7
1978–1980	2.3	1.7
1980–1981	0.8	1.3

Projections of future peak load growth and energy usage had fallen steadily each year since 1974, as shown in Exhibit 11. The once stable and predictable growth rates in loads and usage became uncertain and unpredictable. Forecasts were being revised frequently and by significant amounts, and the views of the forecasters were diverging.

Since 1978 nationwide kwh usage had increased by an average of just 26 billion kwh per year, compared to average increases of 79 billion kwh annually between 1970 and 1978. The consensus industry forecast was for an average 83 billion kwh increase during the 1982–1990 period (see Exhibit 2). As shown in Exhibits 3 and 4, reserve generating capacity to meet summer and winter peaks was well in excess of the 15 to 20 percent rule-of-thumb. More and more companies were confronting overcapacity and since the early 1970s, the industry as a whole had experienced a steady decline in the number of kilowatt-hours of electricity generated per installed kw of capacity, a key index of capacity utilization (see Exhibit 12).

While some of the current slack in load growth was due to the deep economic recession that had shut down many industrial plants, stifled the construction of new homes and buildings, and created a national unemployment rate exceeding 10 percent, it was clear that conservation efforts were taking their toll on electricity energy sales. Efforts to eliminate wasteful practices and to conserve were taking many forms and involved all three major customer groups (residential, commercial, and industrial):

1. Daytime thermostat settings in homes and buildings were being raised to the 76 to 80 degree range during the summer and lowered to the 65 to 70 degree range in the winter, instead of being left at 72 degree settings year round.
2. Homeowners especially in warmer climates, were using their air conditioning systems less frequently, turning them on later in the spring, off earlier in the fall, and off on cooler summer nights and rainy summer days. In the place of air conditioning, they were substituting attic fans, ceiling fans, and open windows.

Exhibit 11   The Progressive Reduction in Forecast Electric Energy Growth Rates

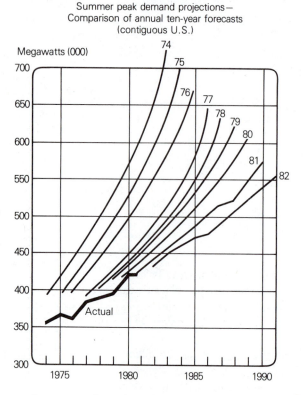

Summer peak demand projections—
Comparison of annual ten-year forecasts
(contiguous U.S.)

Megawatts (000)

Average annual growth rate (percent) projecting ten years

1974—7.6	1979—4.7
1975—6.9	1980—4.0
1976—6.4	1981—3.4
1977—5.7	1982—3.0
1978—5.2	

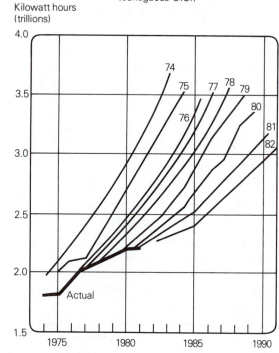

Net energy projections—
Comparison of annual ten-year forecasts
(contiguous U.S.)

Kilowatt hours
(trillions)

Average annual growth rate (percent) projecting ten years

1974—7.5	1979—4.8
1975—6.7	1980—4.1
1976—6.3	1981—3.7
1977—5.8	1982—3.3
1978—5.3	

Source: North American Electric Reliability Council.

3. In office buildings, programs were instituted to greatly reduce electricity usage at nights and on weekends.
4. More homeowners were retrofitting their residences with storm windows, storm doors, weatherstripping, and additional insulation.
5. A larger fraction of new homes and buildings were being constructed to energy-efficient specifications.
6. Manufacturing processes in industrial plants were being reexamined for energy-saving potentials and new investments in energy-saving technologies were being made when the payback in cost reductions was attractive. The search for energy-

---

Exhibit 12   Number of Kilowatt-Hours of Electricity Generated per
Kilowatt of Installed Generating Capacity, 1960–1981

Year	Total Electric Utility Industry	Investor-Owned	Cooperatives	Government-Owned
1960	4,638	4,677	3,929	4,536
1965	4,604	4,689	3,963	4,360
1970	4,681	4,707	4,949	4,570
1971	4,541	4,532	5,122	4,534
1972	4,557	4,510	5,210	4,693
1973	4,427	4,385	5,021	4,545
1974	4,075	3,991	4,585	4,371
1975	3,895	3,836	4,254	4,102
1976	3,920	3,884	4,320	4,024
1977	3,892	3,945	4,308	3,646
1978	3,872	3,859	4,326	3,877
1979	3,816	3,827	4,272	3,725
1980	3,773	3,789	4,344	3,641
1981	3,676	3,689	4,334	3,532

Source: Edison Electric Institute, *1981 Statistical Yearbook,* p. 22.

---

saving actions tended to be greatest in those industries where energy costs made up a big fraction of total costs.

The conservation efforts of customers were being further reinforced by the "load management" and demarketing programs which firms in the utility industry had instituted in response to the "energy crisis." Power companies were developing, studying, testing, and trying a number of techniques to curtail electricity usage:

1. Increased promotion of summer-winter price signals. In the case of summer-peak companies, residential rates were set higher in the summer to discourage greater use of air conditioning and lower in the winter months to stimulate greater penetration of the electric heating market.
2. The establishment of time-of-day or time-of-use rates whereby rates were set at a higher level during peak-use hours (usually 9 A.M. to 8 P.M.) and at a lower level at off-peak periods (nights, weekends, and holidays).
3. The use of so-called inverted rate designs where the rate per kwh increased once kwh usage passed a "basic necessity level of usage"; this was intended to discourage customers from "overusing" electricity and had the effect of increasing the cost to customers of using air conditioning and/or electric heating.
4. The use of advertising and "bill stuffers" to inform customers of ways to conserve on electric energy usage.
5. The establishment of voluntary "interruptible service contracts" with selected large commercial and industrial customers, whereby the utility could curtail service to such customers at peak periods; customers were offered a discount or rate incentive to enter into interruptible service contracts.
6. The use of remote-controlled devices which could be installed on water heaters,

air conditioners, and/or electric heating equipment thereby allowing the utility to transmit a signal that would cut such equipment off at peak periods; the idea was to install many such devices and then rotate them off-and-on at peak hours. (For example, if 30,000 homes had such devices, then 6,000 homes could be "rippled" off the system load for 12 minutes each hour, without greatly inconveniencing customers.) Detroit Edison, a leader in this approach to load management, gave an average discount of 27 percent to customers who agreed to allow their water heaters to be shut off as much as four hours per day and a 13 percent discount to customers who agreed to having their air conditioners rippled on and off.

7. Instituting programs to conduct "energy audits" of homes and buildings to recommend elimination of wasteful practices and to suggest cost-effective improvements in insulation, weather stripping, and the use of storm windows and doors.

8. Programs to educate architects and construction firms to the use of more energy-efficient construction practices.

Industry Responses to Growing Overcapacity Problems

Some power companies, however, were skeptical about the long-term wisdom of demarketing electricity at the same time they were building new plants to boost their generating capacity. In 1982 an increasing number of summer peak electric utilities were beginning to adopt a more aggressive marketing posture on electric heating. Whereas almost 100 percent of the air conditioners in use were powered by electricity, many homeowners switched to fuel oil and natural gas for heating. One midwestern utility discovered that 95 percent of its customers used electric air conditioning but only 5 percent used electric heating; to increase its winter loads, the company started offering $100 rebates to customers who installed energy-efficient electric heat pumps, and it established a winter rate for electricity that made electric heating cheaper than heating with fuel oil and natural gas. It also ran ads showing the cost savings to customers of electric heat pumps over fuel oil and natural gas. Most electric utilities that were promoting electric heat pumps had stopped short of offering rebates and establishing price competitive winter rates. Alabama Power Co., for instance, emphasized meetings with architects, engineers, and building contractors to sell them on the virtues of heat pumps and all-electric buildings. Indianapolis Power and Light set up a special telephone line for people with questions about heat pumps. Dozens of power companies had recently started to cosponsor advertising by heat pump manufacturers, work closely with local heat pump dealers, and promote heat pumps in bill stuffers and speeches to civic groups.

Aggressive selling of electric heating was seen by many utilities as an answer for their overcapacity problems and high generating reserve margins. Others were placing their emphasis on recruiting new industry as the best avenue for boosting load growth— Detroit Edison had a $500,000 budget for an international industry-recruiting ad campaign. However, some executives were skeptical of the benefits of such programs, arguing that they would produce little net gain in revenue and would antagonize the public. More than a few industry executives believed that electricity didn't have to be, or couldn't be, marketed; as one executive put it, "To go out and hawk electricity is just not going to cut it."

Another solution to the overcapacity problem was for capacity-long companies to enter into long-term contracts to supply bulk power to capacity-short companies. The Southern Company, the nation's largest electric utility holding company based in Atlanta, had recently entered into 10-year contracts to supply 3 million kw of power to several Florida and Texas utilities. Canadian utilities were negotiating to supply the New England Power Pool and the Power Authority of the State of New York with 150 billion kwh of electricity over the 1984–1997 period. It was estimated that Canadian firms had enough surplus power capacity to supply 90 percent of the estimated increased loads in New York State until the year 2000. TVA had at least 1 million kw of surplus capacity which it was anxious to contract to sell; so far it had not found any buyers. The bulk power market had in 1982 become so saturated by the efforts of capacity-long companies to find outlets for their excess generating capacity that the going prices on bulk power sales had already dropped by as much as 30 percent.

NEW ENERGY-SAVING EQUIPMENT AND SERVICES

While electric utilities were feeling the pinch of the "competitive" effects from such "substitute" products as insulation, higher/lower thermostat settings, attic and ceiling fans, wood-burning stoves, double-pane windows, and storm windows and doors, the potential for even more substitution was growing from the introduction of new energy efficient products and services:

1. General Electric was reportedly perfecting new-technology light bulbs that would use one third less electricity.
2. Appliance manufacturers were introducing dishwashers, refrigerators, freezers, and dryers that used less electricity and were publicizing the higher Energy Efficiency Ratios (EER) of their new models. In fact, federal regulations required retailers to post the EER ratings and average annual energy costs for operation on each appliance model to alert consumers to the potential of operating cost savings associated with higher EER-rated models. In many cases, the added cost of purchasing the highest EER-rated models was justified by the subsequent savings in operating costs and payback periods were steadily decreasing as electric utilities raised their residential rates.
3. Air conditioner manufacturers and makers of electric heating equipment were coming out with energy-efficient models that used 15–30 percent less electricity (fewer kwhs) to produce the same comfort levels; these new models also required as much as 50 percent less power (in terms of kw load) when in operation. Further energy-saving technological improvements were likely.
4. The thermal value of roofing, windows, doors, and insulation was being improved, with result that newly constructed or remodeled homes and buildings would have significantly lower energy-use requirements.
5. Manufacturers of electrical motors and electrical equipment for use in commercial and industrial applications were aggressively pushing the reduced energy requirements of their new models and further improvements were thought to be in the offing.
6. A number of consulting firms with expertise in energy conservation were being

formed in response to the growing interest among industrial and large commercial customers to implement conservation practices. Some of these consulting firms, in order to attract the interest of potential clients, were basing their fees on a percentage of the energy cost savings that they could generate.

It was arguable whether customers would wait until existing equipment wore out before undertaking replacement with new energy-efficient models or whether they would initiate replacement sooner because of the energy savings. Given the useful life of most appliances and heating/cooling equipment, it was virtually certain that all of the current installations would be replaced before the year 2000. It was also clear that all such changeovers would cut down on both peak loads and kilowatt-hour usage.

TECHNOLOGICAL DEVELOPMENTS IN ALTERNATE FORMS OF ELECTRICITY GENERATION

Since 1973, when the much-discussed "energy crisis" heightened national consciousness about the possibility of energy shortages and the beginnings of a high-cost energy era, active searches for new ways to produce energy economically had accelerated. By 1982 the payoffs from these searches were starting to emerge on a number of technological fronts. Three of the most important were solar thermal systems, photovoltaic cells, and cogeneration.

Solar Thermal Systems   Solar thermal systems based on air and liquid solar collectors were emerging as commercially viable, given tax credits and low-cost state and federal financing incentives. While problems remained, many of the technological problems had been solved and costs reduced. Further technological improvements and cost reductions were thought to be a matter of time. Proven active systems for hot water, space heating, and to a lesser extent space cooling were being marketed. Of these, solar water heating systems had already reached the point of being cost competitive with electric water heating.

There were about 300 manufacturers of solar thermal equipment, with another 3,000-plus firms involved in distributing, marketing, and servicing solar thermal equipment. While several major companies had withdrawn from the business (Exxon, PPG Industries, and Olin Corp.), others had recently entered (Corning Glass and the Harrison Radiator Division of General Motors). Other large companies with solar business interests included Standard Oil of California, Champion Homebuilders, City Investing, General Electric, Martin Marietta, Rockwell International, Westinghouse, and McDonnell-Douglas.

In 1980, 19.5 million square feet of solar collectors were produced, up 37 percent over 1979. About 60 percent of the collectors were used for heating swimming pools, about 21 percent were used for hot water heating, and 12 percent were used in space heating. An estimated total of 300,000 solar thermal systems had been installed by the end of 1980, up from 20,000 in 1974. Federal spending for further R&D on solar thermal systems totaled $844 million in 1980.

Electric utility involvement in solar energy projects was increasing. TVA was financing the installation of 12,000 solar water heaters in Tennessee. The California Public Utility Commission ordered 4 utilities in the state to offer cash rebates and 6 percent loans to consumers for a total of 175,000 solar water heater conversions over a three-year period, starting in September 1980. Long Island Lighting Co. offered a special incentive rate to customers who installed solar hot water systems. Similar solar incentive programs were under way in Florida, Washington, Montana, and Hawaii; 44 states offered tax-incentives to consumers who installed solar energy units. A 1980 survey showed that 236 utilities had over 700 ongoing experimental or demonstration projects involving solar thermal units.

Photovoltaic Cells   Photovoltaic cell technology was based on using crystal silicon solar arrays to capture and store energy and then convert it to electricity. In 1982 some 28 U.S. companies were active in technological developments relating to solar energy cells and photovoltaic production of electricity, including Westinghouse, General Electric, United Technologies, Motorola, National Semiconductor, Texas Instruments, Phillips Petroleum, Exxon, Mobil, Standard Oil of Indiana, and Arco. Westinghouse had publicly stated its belief in being able to provide photovoltaic electric energy for between 4 and 8 cents per kwh by 1986, using a single crystal silicon produced with its patented dendritic web process. Other firms were betting on amorphous silicon processes. The Japanese were testing a 1,000 kw generating system using amorphous silicon photovoltaic panels. Electric utilities involved in photovoltaic power project ventures to test state-of-the-art technology included Arizona Public Service, Southern California Edison, Southwestern Public Service, and West Texas Utilities.

The U.S. Department of Energy projected worldwide installations of photovoltaic power would reach 500,000 kw in 1986 and 50 million kw in the year 2000. DOE's goal was a 6 cents per kwh cost by 1986; toward this goal, it spent $157 million on R&D efforts for photovoltaics in 1980. A study on solar energy by a prominent energy consulting firm projected that the fledgling solar energy industry, only a $150 million a year business in 1980, would grow to a $20 billion industry by the year 2000 and that solar thermal systems and photovoltaic systems combined would supply as much as 15 percent of U.S. energy needs.

Cogeneration   Cogeneration involved harnessing the waste heat and process steam byproducts associated with certain manufacturing operations to generate electricity. Cogeneration thus allowed a manufacturing firm to generate all or part of its own electric energy requirements in the course of operating its industrial process. Energy savings from cogeneration averaged 15 to 20 percent. Small-scale diesel cogenerator units sold for $7,000 to $10,000, but the investment required for coal-fired steam turbine cogeneration facilities could run as high as $25 million. Cogeneration was thought to be most attractive in such energy-intensive operations as soybean processing, breweries, textile mills, pulp and paper plants, agricultural chemicals, and petroleum refining. Analysts estimated that if manufacturers took full advantage of the cogeneration potential, they would buy 275 billion fewer kilowatt-hours of electricity from power companies—an annual revenue loss of about $12.5 billion at 1982 prices.

Electric utilities were divided on the merits of cogeneration. Capacity-short utilities and utilities dependent on fuel oil generation tended to see cogeneration as helpful and were generally willing to assist customers in cogeneration efforts. Other utilities saw cogeneration as threatening the loss of an important market. Federal regulations made it possible for users of cogeneration to sell their surplus electricity to utilities.

Other Alternate Energy Technologies

Some proponents saw fuel cells, biomass, geothermal, and windpower technologies as becoming economical sources of electric energy. Fuel cells were viewed as a most promising energy technology; they represented an innovative way to use natural gas to generate electricity. Biomass generation involved converting plant life to energy, the use of synfuels, and using wastes as fuels (the Diamond Walnut Growers cooperative in California was completing a plant to burn walnut shells to produce steam and electricity; the co-op anticipated earning $1 million a year on electricity sales and natural gas savings). Geothermal generation focused on ways to use geysers, hot water springs, and superheated brine to drive turbine generators. Geothermal plants had been constructed on an experimental basis in California and Idaho.

Windpower was expected to provide as much as 2 percent of electric energy needs by the year 2000. In 1980, 1,500 windpower units were sold to homeowners and small businesses. The owner of a McDonald's restaurant in California installed two $17,000 windpower units in anticipation of realizing a three- to four-year payback from energy savings and tax credits. Windpower units for residential use were available at a cost of $7,000 and had the capability to supply 50 to 60 percent of a home's power needs. In 1980 over 90 utilities had a total of 152 windpower development projects under way.

The Implications of Alternate Energy Sources

Electric utility executives were aware that if solar thermal systems, photovoltaic cells, cogeneration systems, fuel cells, and other onsite electric generation technologies could be developed to the point of being reliable and less costly, then they would have high potential to undermine the electric utilities' monopoly position as a supplier of electricity. And even if such technologies were able to supply only part of a customer's electricity requirements, electric utilities could still find themselves in the unenviable position of becoming more and more of a secondary supplier, providing backup energy in case of breakdowns and serving only the peak load needs of customers.

As things stood in 1982, some technical experts were saying that while conventional central station generation and distribution represented *the* most economical technology presently available (accounting for why electric utilities had a solid monopoly grip), it was doubtful if its superiority would stand unchallenged in the future. They saw alternate forms of electricity generation as providing competition to conventional power companies. Since electric utilities were investing heavily in central station generation systems with a useful life of 30 to 40 years, the issue of when and to what extent new technologies might prove more economical was significant. Short-run technological breakthroughs in the cost competitiveness of alternate energy supplies were not probable but the situation in 5 to 10 years was another matter.

TECHNOLOGICAL DEVELOPMENTS IN
MICROPROCESSORS AND TELECOMMUNICATIONS

In 1982 technical experts were predicting that new product developments in electronics, microprocessors, and telecommunications systems would have a major, near-term impact on the electric power industry. Microprocessors and other two-way electronic communications devices were being marketed to permit centralized energy management systems to be installed in homes, buildings, and industries. According to some estimates, these automated energy management devices could produce enough savings in energy consumption to pay for themselves in three to five years. They could cut water heaters on and off at specified intervals, adjust thermostat settings up or down, cut lights on and off, manage the flow of electric energy to equipment, and in some cases allow remote meter reading and billing. A newly developed memory chip called EEPROM (short for electrically erasable, programmable, read-only memory) allowed the old program instructions in microprocessors to be instantaneously replaced with new instructions via radio or telephone signals. Houston Lighting and Power was testing an EEPROM system to read meters and print out customer bills. Over 100 companies were marketing a wide variety of load control and automatic energy management systems in 1982, including General Electric, Westinghouse, Rockwell International, Scientific Atlanta, Honeywell, IBM, Johnson Controls, Robertshaw, Climatron, Pacific Technology, Square-D, Tano, American Multiplex, Barber-Coleman, and Emerson Electric.

American Telephone and Telegraph had telecommunications products on the market capable of taking over day-to-day management of a customer's energy system. In a cooperative experiment with Duke Power, AT&T had tested a more elaborate two-way telecommunications system which had the capacity for meter reading and billing, energy management, cable TV service, electronic mail and banking services, security protection and security alarms, and customer access to a variety of information sources (sales catalogs, stock market quotations, shopping data).

AT&T was also a pioneer in fiberoptics cable that had the technological capability to handle both visual and data signal transmission and was being investigated as one of the ways to provide meter reading, energy management, television programming, teleconference hookups, security alarms, and electronic data transfer all in one package.

THE ELECTRIC UTILITY INDUSTRY'S OUTLOOK

Managers and technical analysts in the electric utility industry were aware of the numerous and diverse technological developments in energy-saving equipment, alternate energy sources, microprocessors, and telecommunications. These developments were not only widely reported and assessed in the business press and trade journals but from time to time the industry's trade associations (Edison Electric Institute and Electric Power Research Institute) commissioned special in-depth studies to appraise their implications. The estimated impacts of energy-saving equipment, price-induced conservation, and alternate energy sources had been factored into industry forecasts of peak load growth, total kilowatt-hour usage, and the need for additional capacity. However, there was a growing diversity of opinions among forecasters, as a September 1982 article in *Electrical World* noted:

> Forecasters seem to be slowly polarizing in their analyses of load growth—a common phenomenon in just about every issue concerning the industry today. There are those who see the growth in electricity consumption closely correlated with the growth in the Gross National Product. The second camp foresees a strongly declining or even negative trend, primarily the result of conservation induced by rising prices.

The thing that increasingly concerned many utility executives was not so much the uncertainty over the future forecasts as it was how to position their companies in the marketplace to deal with the potentially fundamental market and technological changes ahead. Recent statistics indicated a general public hostility toward investor-owned electric utilities. Only 28 percent of the customers surveyed felt that the industry was trying to serve the public well.

CASE 15 IOWA RESOURCES, INC.*

In January 1984 Iowa Resources reorganized its electric power and natural gas divisions into two separate operating subsidiaries, Iowa Power & Light and Iowa Gas, and then encouraged them to compete aggressively with each other. Virtually all of the residential, commercial, and industrial customers who bought their natural gas from Iowa Gas also bought their electricity from Iowa Power. By mid-1984 Iowa Power and Iowa Gas were embroiled in a hard-waged marketing fight, each running ads and special promotions to convince homeowners to go with its source of energy for home heating rather than the other's. The two companies were battling for revenues and market share with such vigor that some observers had trouble believing their profits were going to the same stockholders. A feature article in the *Des Moines Register* offered the following account of what was happening: [1]

> The focus of their sizzling advertising war is the heat pump, an energy machine the electricity industry is promoting heavily as a cost-saving supplement to a home's natural gas, fuel oil, or propane furnace. Power companies all over the country are trying to sell heat pumps to boost electricity sales in the winter months. . . .
>
> As Iowans gulped lemonade and dripped sweat in summer's worst heat last week, Iowa Power cast this bait: "Add a heat pump for cool comfort this summer and lower heating bills next winter."
>
> Iowa Power customers had heard this pitch before. What they hadn't heard before were Iowa Gas's sharp, retaliatory ads blasting the heat pump as a foolish investment that breaks down frequently and doesn't heat very well even when it works.
>
> Heat pumps, according to one of the caustic ads, "cost more to buy and install, to maintain, to repair, and to run than a gas furnace and central air conditioning combination. . . . Before you make a mistake, look into gas."
>
> This advertising war is the first public evidence of the lively intracorporate battle between Iowa Power and Iowa Gas, and utility observers are watching with fascination. "It's quite an experiment," said Horace Webb, spokesman for Iowa Electric Light and Power Co. of Cedar Rapids.
>
> Some say it will result in self-defeating marketing programs; some say it's evidence that Iowa Resources intends to sell the gas company, whose profits have been disappointing; others say such competition is just what the energy marketplace needs.
>
> The all-out attack on heat pumps by Iowa Gas, the underdog in this unorthodox corporate structure, is getting support from the corporate level, but it's hardly enthusiastic. Without directly criticizing the Iowa Gas campaign, Iowa Resources spokesman David Weiss said: "There are many ways you might choose to market your product. This certainly is one means. . . . But I think natural gas is a product that can stand on its own merits."

---

* Prepared by Professor Arthur A. Thompson, Jr., The University of Alabama. Copyright © 1986 by Arthur A. Thompson, Jr. The case researcher gratefully acknowledges the assistance and cooperation of Iowa Resources in preparing the case.

[1] David Westphal, "Iowa Power, Iowa Gas Clash in Sizzling Ad War on Worth of Heat Pumps," *Des Moines Register,* July 15, 1984.

At the same time, Weiss said this aggressive competition between Iowa Power and Iowa Gas is something their 230,000 customers should get used to. "This is the first head-to-head battle, the first spirited one, but there will be more, most certainly. We want competition between the two. It's a big reason why we decided to divide the companies."

Weiss and other utility experts in Iowa say, though, that the heat pump war reflects more than a corporate restructuring at Iowa Resources. By their account, it also points up the growing competition nationwide for the winter heating business.

Mark W. Putney, Iowa Resources' president and chief executive officer, gave management's account of what was behind the decision to foster competition between the two sister companies:

> Our utility operation is medium sized with total revenues of almost $500 million coming from 230,000 electric customers and 130,000 gas customers in central and southwest Iowa. About five years ago, in order to provide better opportunities for nonutility activities and growth, we formed a holding company called Iowa Resources, with our utility operation, Iowa Power & Light Company, the flagship subsidiary.
>
> As we continued to plan, the more we looked at the changing marketplace of the 80s . . . and the more we recognized the absolute need to purify a profit center approach, we moved toward separation of our major utility entities—natural gas, retail electric, and the generation portion of the business, which we might call wholesale electric. Finally about a year and a half ago, we set up three separate divisions within Iowa Power & Light Company . . . Iowa Power, the retail electric distribution entity; Iowa Generation, the wholesale electric generating and transmission unit; and Iowa Gas, our natural gas operation. Immediately, operational responsibilities were separated, as was marketing. Each of the divisions was and is headed by a vice president and general manager. It appeared obvious to us that if those people were to be held responsible for the financial success of their operations, it was essential that they have their own marketing staff and be able to develop their own strategic marketing plan.
>
> Our goal continued to be complete separation of the gas entity, and we methodically moved toward that goal when on January 1, 1984, Iowa Gas became a separate operating subsidiary of Iowa Resources, with its own board of directors, its own president, and its own customer service function along with operations and marketing. Certain administrative and staff services are provided to Iowa Gas on a fee basis by Iowa Power and Light . . . such responsibilities as finance, stockholder services, personnel, legal, and accounting.
>
> Our purpose is simple. Competition among the differing forms of energy has escalated rapidly during the past several years. If natural gas and electricity are to remain competitive, we must establish a climate in which each has the opportunity to develop to its full potential. Only then can their individual performances be measured.

IOWA RESOURCES' SITUATION IN 1984

Iowa Resources in 1984 was a holding company (formed in 1979) with two principal subsidiaries, Iowa Power & Light Company and Iowa Gas Company, that accounted for over 98 percent of the parent's revenues and profits. Other wholly owned subsidiary companies of Iowa Resources were:

- ENERCOR, Inc., an Iowa corporation which invested in energy-related ventures and owned 1,280 acres of land in the Powder River Basin in Wyoming for possible future coal mining development.
- Redlands, Inc., which owned approximately 3,800 acres of land near Des Moines, Iowa, for possible future use as a generating station site; in 1984 the land was being leased for farming operations.
- Middlewood, Inc., which owned and developed real estate for industrial, commercial, and residential uses; the principal project to date had been construction and operation of a three-block office complex in Des Moines called Capitol Center.
- Middlewood Mall, Inc., which had a one-third equity interest in a proposed $48 million retail and office mall in downtown Des Moines.
- UNITRAIN, Inc., which owned and leased unit coal trains, managed unit train operations and maintenance activities, and coordinated coal-hauling services for several electric utilities with coal-fired generating stations.
- Iowa Computer Resources, Inc., which was involved in the development and sale of computer software (much of this software had been developed for internal use but was also thought to be commercially marketable).
- ENSERCO, Inc.—a provider of financial and investment services for Iowa Resources and its other subsidiaries.
- Industries of Iowa, Inc., which held an investment in a grain alcohol venture.

These other subsidiaries had combined 1983 revenues of $2.1 million (0.5 percent of total corporate revenues), assets of $21.2 million, and an operating loss of $163,000. Exhibits 1 and 2 provide financial summaries.

Iowa Power & Light (IPL) provided electric service to some 232,000 customers in some 130 communities over a 5,560-square-mile region in central and southwestern Iowa; over 55 percent of IPL's customers were located in the Des Moines metropolitan area, the state capital and largest city in Iowa. Iowa Gas (IG) served mainly the Des Moines area and had some 134,000 customers in 1984. The population of IPL's total service area numbered about 560,000, while the population of Iowa Gas's service area totaled about 300,000. Iowa had experienced statewide population growth over the last 10 years of about 4 percent, compared to 11 percent nationally. Per capita income in Iowa was slightly less than the national average, and the economy of the company's service area was tied closely to agriculture and to a modest industrial base.

Southwestern and central Iowa had some of the most fertile and prosperous farm land in the United States; the primary agricultural products were corn, soybeans, grains, livestock, and dairy products. Des Moines was an insurance center, had a substantial printing and publishing industry, and was the major retail and jobbing point in Iowa. Some of the more important products produced in the Des Moines area were farm machinery, tires, livestock feeds, meats, food products, steel products, and building materials. Approximately 61 percent of Iowa Resources' 1983 operating revenues were derived from electric and gas service furnished by IPL and IG in the Des Moines metropolitan area. Council Bluffs, located across the Missouri River from Omaha, Nebraska, was the second largest city served by IPL; its 1980 population was 56,500. The unemployment rate in the state was 8.2 percent in January 1984 versus an 8.8 percent jobless rate nationwide.

Exhibit 1   Consolidated Income Statements, Iowa Resources, Inc., 1981–
1983   In Thousands, except per Share Amounts

| | Year Ended December 31 | | |
	1981	1982	1983
Revenues			
Electric	$220,120	$240,360	$284,856
Gas	106,215	142,245	170,902
Other	1,926	3,326	2,158
Total	328,261	385,931	457,916
Expenses			
Operation:			
Purchased power-nuclear	46,085	55,338	48,487
Interchange power, net	(10,566)	(21,177)	(5,993)
Fuel for electric generation	42,904	41,633	55,165
Gas purchased for resale	84,767	113,024	141,873
Other	42,079	50,506	49,641
Maintenance	19,638	19,448	18,010
Depreciation	26,066	28,506	30,433
Property and other taxes	19,376	19,471	20,053
Total	270,349	306,749	357,669
Operating income			
Electric	55,381	70,764	93,755
Gas	2,717	8,538	6,655
Other	(186)	(120)	(163)
Total	57,912	79,182	100,247
Other income			
Allowance for equity funds used during construction and carrying costs accrued on advances	6,417	9,564	10,175
Other, net	146	(899)	(27)
Total	6,563	8,665	10,148
Fixed charges			
Interest on debt	34,087	33,862	33,239
Allowance for borrowed funds used during construction and carrying costs accrued on advances	(13,321)	(9,353)	(6,763)
Preferred dividends of subsidiary	5,779	5,699	5,633
Total	26,545	30,208	32,109
Income before income taxes	37,930	57,639	78,286
Income taxes	6,804	22,218	32,682
Net income	$ 31,126	$ 35,421	$ 45,604

Source: 1983 Annual Report.

Exhibit 2 Selected Consolidated Financial Data, Iowa Resources, Inc., 1973–1983   Dollar Figures in Thousands, except per Share Amounts

	1973	1978	1979	1980	1981	1982	1983
Summary of operations							
Revenues	$111,634	$227,332	$269,341	$297,933	$328,261	$385,931	$457,916
Operating expenses	86,943	181,815	204,696	232,803	270,349	306,749	357,669
Operating income before income taxes	24,691	45,517	64,645	65,130	57,912	79,182	100,247
Other income, net	634	6,343	2,945	3,760	6,563	8,665	10,148
Fixed charges	7,549	14,877	20,643	23,694	26,545	30,208	32,109
Income before taxes	17,776	36,983	46,947	45,196	37,930	57,639	78,286
Income taxes	7,674	12,298	20,409	18,412	6,804	22,218	32,682
Net income	$ 10,102	$ 24,685	$ 26,538	$ 26,784	$ 31,126	$ 35,421	$ 45,604
Dividends on common stock declared	$ 6,687	$ 16,032	$ 18,710	$ 20,676	$ 24,795	$ 27,864	$ 30,235
Average number of common shares outstanding (000s)	3,942	6,814	7,430	7,835	8,792	9,673	10,221
Earnings per average share of common stock	$ 2.56	$ 3.62	$ 3.57	$ 3.42	$ 3.54	$ 3.66	$ 4.46
Dividends declared per share of common stock	$ 1.68	$ 2.34	$ 2.49	$ 2.62	$ 2.75	$ 2.86	$ 2.94
Average book value per share	$ 21.03	$ 25.59	$ 26.46	$ 27.48	$ 27.61	$ 27.53	$ 28.34
Return on average common equity	12.2%	14.2%	13.5%	12.4%	12.8%	13.3%	15.7%
Property, Plant, and Equipment							
Electric	$323,896	$612,672	$681,704	$751,031	$837,467	$878,830	$927,923
Gas	61,807	80,416	88,476	93,321	98,926	104,143	102,485
Other	1,425	6,876	8,661	16,199	17,984	22,845	21,986
Total gross plant	$387,128	$699,964	$778,841	$860,551	$954,377	$1,005,818	$1,052,394
Net after depreciation	$288,650	$546,886	$605,889	$665,470	$735,899	$775,147	$796,279
Accrued depreciation/property plant and equipment	25.4%	21.9%	22.2%	22.7%	22.9%	22.9%	24.3%
Annual depreciation/average plant in service	3.2%	3.7%	3.5%	3.8%	3.7%	3.6%	3.6%
Capital expenditures	$ 46,660	$ 86,632	$103,587	$ 91,806	$118,179	$ 74,809	$ 62,749
Total assets	$311,579	$834,813	$920,763	$980,632	$1,084,685	$1,102,475	$1,193,016
Capitalization							
Long-term debt	$110,417	$213,163	$250,471	$279,790	$293,810	$336,534	$339,381
Preferred stock equity	$ 30,000	$ 55,000	$ 54,500	$ 73,884	$ 73,453	$ 72,903	$ 70,374
Common stock equity	$ 90,858	$180,480	$205,347	$219,373	$252,856	$272,602	$301,546
Number of employees—year-end	1,394	1,518	1,548	1,577	1,559	1,504	1,456

Organization and Management   The top management of Iowa Resources, concerned about the traumatic decade of the 1970s in which energy costs had escalated and regulatory issues had become a dominant force, began in 1979 to rethink the risks and rewards of concentrating solely in the electric and gas utility businesses. To prepare for possible diversification, Iowa Power & Light shifted to a holding company structure and reorganized into four business units under the Iowa Resources umbrella:

- Iowa Generation—a unit responsible for electricity generation and transmission.
- Iowa Power & Light—a unit responsible for retail electric distribution.
- Iowa Gas—a unit responsible for gas operations.
- Industries Group—a unit to handle all diversification activities.

A fifth Corporate Group supplied such administrative services as accounting, communications, and legal services to the four business units. Following the reorganization, a Chicago-based consulting firm was called in to help institute a new strategic planning process supportive of the concept of free-standing business units. A major effort was made to educate and motivate managers in each business unit to act as separate entities—a change which went against the grain of the prevailing utility management culture. Dwight Swanson, Iowa Resources' chairman, explained the rationale for the change thusly:

> In the traditional combination (electric and gas) utility structure, responsibility for "bottom-line" profit performance rests at the top of the organization. Middle managers receive experience in functional, "cost center" management only. As a result, there is often strong emphasis on efficiency (cost minimization) and much less emphasis on overall effectiveness, as measured by profitability, in utility management. Changing the focus of all levels of management to profitability is essential to survival in the 1980s. The task is not a trivial undertaking, as management reporting and analysis capabilities are structured to analyze the business as a whole, masking the separate performance characteristics of the electric generation, electric distribution, and gas distribution businesses. Utility accounting systems have historically provided just data for regulatory commission reports—not performance information.

Iowa Resources management believed the establishment of individual business units would produce a number of important corporate benefits:

- Better financial performance in the face of adverse conditions.
- Improved planning and strategic thinking.
- A broader and more experienced management team.
- More opportunities for capable managers.
- Continued and increased focus on providing both effective and efficient utility operations.
- Better preparation for future environmental changes.

The consultants assisted in implementing ways to expand the role of line management in the annual strategic planning cycle. Business strategies and planning charters were developed for each business unit, with each containing

- Recommended mission statements and business definitions.
- Reassignment of responsibilities and associated manpower requirements.
- Assignment of assets.
- New performance and operating reports for corporate management.

In addition, management instituted an incentive compensation arrangement for the business unit managers designed to support and encourage a strong profit center orientation.

END-USE COMPETITION BETWEEN ELECTRICITY AND NATURAL GAS

Electricity and gas were long-standing energy competitors everywhere there were gas mains and power lines; this was true nationally as well as in Iowa. Natural gas utilities typically installed natural gas mains to serve areas which had a high enough concentration of customers to justify the investment in lines. Scattered residences in the countryside were almost never served by natural gas, and in many outlying suburbs and subdivisions gas mains had not been extended either for reasons of it being uneconomical or because of regulatory moratoriums on extending lines to new customers during the "energy crisis" years of 1975–81. Residential and commercial customers not served by natural gas did, however, have the option in most areas of the United States of using liquefied propane gas (distributed and sold by propane gas companies) for space heating, water heating, and cooking; LP gas was generally more expensive than natural gas but, depending on electric rates, could be cheaper to use than electricity. In Iowa, LP gas companies were a major factor in competing with electricity in geographic areas not served by natural gas. Residential customers who had a gas main running down their streets could rather easily choose between electricity and natural gas. Virtually all residential customers who used natural gas for space heating also used natural gas for water heating. Much smaller numbers of customers opted for gas ranges and gas clothes dryers. Nationally, about 67 percent of all residential gas consumption was for space heating; water heating accounted for 24 percent of total residential consumption; cooking, 5 percent; clothes drying, 2 percent; and miscellaneous end-uses, 2 percent. Exhibit 3 gives residential market share comparisons between electricity and natural gas for the United States as a whole.

Commercial customers served both by a gas company and a power company could choose to go with one or the other for cooking, water heating, space heating, clothes drying, and process steam applications. Nationally, about 68 percent of all commercial gas sales went to space heating. The biggest commercial users of natural gas were firms in real estate (including apartment buildings and commercial offices), hospitals, schools, restaurants, and retail trade establishments. Nearly half of the total commercial natural gas consumption in the United States took place in buildings in the north central states (which included Iowa).

Among industrial customers, electricity and gas were often in direct competition as the preferred energy source for firing boilers and furnaces, for a variety of process steam and process heating applications, for space heating, and for materials handling vehicles. Both gas and electricity competed against coal, no. 2 fuel oil, no. 6 fuel oil, and liquefied propane gas to serve the energy requirements of industrial customers in several heavy manufacturing and light industrial applications, particularly where steam, hot water, and cooling uses were involved. Usually, fuel cost was the primary criterion of industrial customers in choosing which energy source to use; in fact,

Exhibit 3   Residential Market Share Comparisons for Electricity and Natural Gas, United States, 1983

Types of Residential Uses	1983 Market Share Percentages		
	Natural Gas	Electricity	Other
Space heating, all existing			
residential housing	55%	19%	26%
Northeastern U.S.	42	n.a.	n.a.
Midwestern U.S.	71	n.a.	n.a.
Southeastern U.S.	46	n.a.	n.a.
Far western states	66	n.a.	n.a.
Space heating, newly constructed housing only			
Single-family units	43	45	12
Multifamily (more than four units)	28	70	2
New residential construction only in areas where gas mains were already installed	70	28	2
Ranges	39	61	0
Water heaters	54	45	1
Clothes dryers	22	78	0
Percentage share of all residential energy use	55%	40%	5%

n.a. = Not available.

Notes: In 1969, natural gas had market shares of 60 percent in new, single-family residential construction; 52 percent in cooking; 60 percent in water heating; and 25 percent in clothes drying.

The number of residences being converted over to natural gas house heating from alternative fuels was as follows:

1980	583,000
1981	452,000
1982	225,000
1983	132,000
1984 (projected)	125,000

Source: American Gas Association.

many industrial customers had by 1984 invested in energy conversion systems that gave them the capacity to use any of several fuel sources to meet their energy requirements. Industrial customers with fuel switching capability were nearly always extremely fuel price conscious; they monitored fuel prices constantly and were quick to switch over to whichever energy source was the cheapest for their end-use purposes. In 1984 over one half of the nationwide sales of industrial gas were to customers with installed multiple-fuel capability. Residential and commercial customers rarely had short-term capability to switch back and forth from one fuel to another, being temporarily locked in to whatever fuel their present appliances and heating equipment used. Residential and commercial customers, however, became candidates for long-term fuel switching (1) when the time came to replace worn-out equipment or (2) when early replacement of existing equipment could be justified with a quick investment payback from the savings generated by the use of a lower priced fuel or by greater energy-saving efficiency of new equipment.

THE ENERGY MARKET IN IOWA

Statewide, natural gas consumption in Iowa in 1984 was running about 40 percent below the pre-energy crisis levels of 10 years earlier. The decline in usage reflected sharply higher natural gas prices (most natural gas consumers in Iowa were paying four to six times as much for natural gas in 1984 than they had paid in 1973) and widespread attempts by users to conserve on natural gas usage in the wake of much higher rates, a continuing stream of information about wasteful energy use practices, and public concern about the depletion of irreplaceable oil and gas reserves. Many homeowners, especially those with older heating equipment, were investing in newly introduced high-efficiency gas furnaces and improved weatherization and insulation to curtail fuel usage and reduce heating bills. Surveys also indicated that a big majority of residential consumers had lowered their wintertime thermostat settings in an effort to reduce heating costs. Iowa had moderately severe winter weather and home heating costs were significant, running from $500 to $1,200 per heating season (depending on the homeowner's thermostat setting, home size, efficiency of the heating equipment, insulation characteristics of the house, and the severity of the winter weather). Gene Young, IPL's vice president for marketing, saw the top marketing opportunity for IPL as being the residential home heating market:

> With penetration of electric heating at only the 10–12 percent level, the availability of higher efficiency heat pumps, competent factory training for dealers, and Iowa Power's incentive heating rate of just under 5 cents per kwh, we are in an excellent position to compete effectively for the new home heating market. This is especially true in the multifamily apartment and condominium market where the installation of smaller electric furnaces and heat pumps result in lower first cost for the builder.

Residential gas sales in Iowa, as well as elsewhere, were heavily concentrated during the heating season months of November through March and were very weather sensitive; consumption could vary up or down as much as 20 percent depending on whether the winter was milder or colder than normal. The gas industry measured winter weather in terms of heating "degree days." A day in which the average outdoor temperature was 40 degrees Fahrenheit, as compared to a standard of 65 degrees when theoretically no heating (or cooling) is needed, was defined as a 25 degree day; the sum of the degree days over an entire heating season was a measure of overall winter weather severity and winter heating needs. In Iowa, a typical winter heating season totaled 6,500 degree days; the cooling season averaged about 1,000 degree days.

Commercial gas sales in Iowa, like residential gas sales, were strongly influenced by weather conditions. Industrial sales, however, were more a function of industrial development activity (new plant openings and plant expansions) and production ups and downs in the manufacturing segment of the economy.

At Iowa Gas 1983 unit sales of natural gas were only 20 percent below 1973 levels, a reflection of a comparatively prosperous Des Moines economy (relative to other parts of Iowa). IG's residential gas volume had declined at an average annual rate of 1 percent since 1973 and commercial-industrial usage had dropped about 3 percent annually (see Exhibit 4); the 1984–88 forecast for unit gas sales was for continued overall declines of about 2 percent annually (see Exhibit 5). Natural gas

Exhibit 4 Electric and Gas Statistics, Iowa Resources, 1973–1983

	1973	1978	1979	1980	1981	1982	1983
ELECTRIC							
Revenues ($000)							
Residential	$ 34,701	$ 68,278	$ 79,603	$ 92,671	$ 100,635	$ 109,395	$ 135,850
Small general service	19,791	39,800	48,110	53,516	61,135	65,906	77,466
Large general service	17,546	36,952	42,555	46,950	54,311	54,737	66,369
Other	3,545	5,458	9,896	8,982	4,039	10,322	5,171
Total revenues	$ 75,583	$ 150,488	$ 180,164	$ 202,119	$ 220,120	$ 240,360	$ 284,856
Sales (000s kwh)							
Residential	1,278,688	1,678,914	1,677,211	1,767,160	1,618,636	1,680,062	1,872,872
Small general service	738,864	1,012,729	1,052,509	1,059,840	1,034,899	1,063,833	1,116,924
Large general service	1,199,292	1,508,055	1,493,222	1,415,509	1,410,532	1,363,717	1,464,796
Other	107,492	107,413	106,002	108,072	105,666	108,051	110,861
Total sales	3,324,336	4,307,111	4,328,944	4,350,581	4,169,733	4,215,663	4,565,453
Customers (year-end)							
Residential	176,609	197,351	200,387	202,493	203,046	203,532	203,973
Small general service	24,280	25,447	25,708	26,021	26,138	26,195	26,932
Large general service	301	352	356	366	338	360	380
Other	849	935	954	965	985	987	995
Total customers	202,039	224,085	227,405	229,845	230,507	231,074	232,280
Other							
Peak demand—MW (summer–winter)	853–564	1,064–777	1,119–787	1,150–760	1,165–789	1,097–795	1,209–851
System load factor	48.4%	51.1%	48.8%	47.3%	44.7%	47.9%	46.8%
Average annual residential use—kwh	7,336	8,610	8,444	8,783	7,988	8,279	9,201
Average residential revenue per kwh	2.71¢	4.07¢	4.75¢	5.24¢	6.22¢	6.51¢	7.25¢
Utility plant investment per customer	$ 1,610	$ 2,734	$ 2,998	$ 3,268	$ 3,633	$ 3,803	$ 3,983

GAS

Revenues ($000)

Residential	$ 19,726	$ 40,847	$ 47,431	$ 48,059	$ 71,514	$ 87,617
Commercial and industrial—firm	9,822	21,279	25,200	25,791	40,628	51,813
Commercial and industrial—interruptible	6,227	13,670	16,303	18,172	27,224	29,642
Other	276	871	(209)	1,044	2,879	1,830
Total revenues	$ 36,051	$ 76,667	$ 88,725	$ 93,066	$ 142,245	$ 170,902

Sales (000s ccf)

Residential	168,766	178,962	173,898	153,374	150,770	151,930
Commercial and industrial—firm	103,582	104,534	102,223	91,215	93,407	96,768
Commercial and industrial—interruptible	123,940	88,041	85,928	81,781	72,589	70,175
Total sales	396,288	371,537	362,049	326,370	316,766	318,873

Customers (year-end)

Residential	112,023	116,771	117,523	118,984	119,190	119,373
Commercial and industrial—firm	13,104	13,385	13,685	13,781	13,976	14,015
Commercial and industrial—interruptible	356	294	246	240	128	129
Total customers	125,483	130,450	131,454	133,005	133,294	133,517

Other

Maximum daily sendout (000s ccf)	2,369	2,460	2,364	2,302	2,454	2,590
Heating degree days	5,788	7,217	7,173	6,334	5,560	6,599
Average annual residential use—ccf	1,520	1,543	1,490	1,301	1,145	1,276
Average residential revenue per ccf	11.69¢	22.82¢	27.28¢	31.33¢	39.31¢	57.67¢
Utility plant investment per customer	$ 494	$ 616	$ 673	$ 702	$ 742	$ 811

Source: 1983 Annual Report.

Exhibit 5 Iowa Resources, Inc., 1984–1988 Operating Forecast

	Actual 1983	Forecast 1984	1985	1986	1987	1988	Four-Year Growth Rate
IOWA POWER & LIGHT COMPANY							
Sales kwh (millions)	4,565	4,310	4,402	4,512	4,623	4,732	2.4%
Annual sales growth rate (percent)	8.3%	(5.6)%	2.1%	2.5%	2.5%	2.4%	
Customers	231,624	233,952	236,312	239,116	242,127	244,941	1.2%
Annual customer growth rate (percent)	.2%	1.0%	1.0%	1.2%	1.3%	1.2%	
Peak load (MW) (Note 1)	1,209	1,193	1,214	1,239	1,264	1,288	2.0%
Annual peak growth rate (percent)	10.2%	(1.3)%	1.8%	2.1%	2.0%	1.9%	
Generating capability (MW) (Notes 1, 3)							
Base load—Coal	547	745	745	745	745	745	
—Nuclear (Note 2)	380	380	380	380	380	380	
Intermediate—Coal	309	309	309	309	309	309	
Peak load—Oil/gas	275	275	275	275	275	275	
Net purchases (sales)	9	(288)	11	10	9	8	
Total net capability (MW)	1,520	1,421	1,720	1,719	1,718	1,717	

Fuel source for energy (percent based on MWH)	1983	1984	1985	1986	1987	1988	Five-Year Average
Coal	49%	57%	67%	51%	49%	50%	55%
Nuclear (Note 2)	31	36	26	44	46	45	39
Oil/gas	1	1	1	1	1	1	1
Other, net purchases	19	6	6	4	4	4	5
Total	100%	100%	100%	100%	100%	100%	100%

Fuel costs—Cents per kwh	1983	1984	1985	1986	1987	1988	
Coal	1.65¢	1.53¢	1.58¢	1.67¢	1.77¢	1.94¢	
Nuclear	1.08¢	0.64¢	0.85¢	0.91¢	0.97¢	0.85¢	
Construction expenditures ($ millions)	$45	$46	$55	$29	$28	$27	

	1983	1984	1985	1986	1987	1988	Four-Year Growth Rate, 1984–1988
IOWA GAS COMPANY							
Sales ccfs (millions)	319	294	285	280	276	272	(2.0%)
Annual sales growth rate (percent)	.7%	(7.8)%	(3.1)%	(1.8)%	(1.4)%	(1.4)%	
Customers	133,170	133,706	134,592	135,418	136,263	137,088	.6%
Annual customer growth rate (percent)	.2%	.4%	.7%	.6%	.6%	.6%	
Construction expenditures ($ millions)	$7	$7	$8	$8	$8	$9	

Notes to operating forecast:
(1) Net capability at time of peak.
(2) The company has a long-term power purchase agreement with the Nebraska Public Power District for one half of the capacity of the Cooper Nuclear Generating Station. The station went into service in 1974 and has generated significant amounts of energy for the company since that time.
(3) The Iowa State Commerce Commission, in its rate order of April 6, 1984, imposed an excess capacity penalty of $7.2 million for generating capability greater than 125 percent of peak load.

was sold in cubic feet, and the price was customarily stated as so much per hundred cubic feet (CCF) or per thousand cubic feet (MCF).

Sales of electricity at Iowa Power were up slightly however, growing at a 1.1 percent average annual rate from 1978 to 1983 (but down significantly from a 5.3 percent annual growth rate between 1973 and 1978)—see Exhibit 4. IPL had ample installed generating capacity. In 1984 the Iowa State Commerce Commission, imposed an excess capacity penalty reducing IPL's earnings by $7.2 million because IPL's generating capacity was greater than 125 percent of peak load. In 1984 IPL had generating capacity of 1,720 megawatts (mw).[2] IPL's summer peak load in 1984 was 1,209 mw; its winter peak load was only 851 mw. The 1988 load forecast for electricity called for a summer peak of 1,288 mw.

Because IPL was a summer peaking company and had generating reserves of almost 50 percent during the winter months, the company was anxious to find ways to boost sales during the winter. IPL's marketing officials believed that about 65 percent of the homes in the company's service territory were heated with natural gas; only about 10 percent were heated with electricity. The remaining 25 percent of the homes, many of which were in rural areas, were heated with fuel oil or propane gas. IPL's residential customers used an average of about 9,000 kwhs per year. However, all-electric customers (those who had homes equipped with electric space heating, electric water heaters, and all-electric appliances) had annual consumption levels in the range of 15,000 to 25,000 kwhs—the amount varied significantly depending on home size, home weatherization features, age and efficiency of appliances, number of people in the home, the preferred thermostat settings, each customer's living habits, the inventory of appliances, and so on.

ENERGY USE DECISIONS IN THE RESIDENTIAL MARKET

Residential customers in Iowa, because of sharp jumps in their monthly bills for natural gas and electricity over the past decade, had become cost and use sensitive. Company surveys of customers confirmed that efforts to conserve were common, with the most frequently used energy-saving actions being (1) lower thermostat settings during the winter (especially at night), (2) higher thermostat settings during the summer—about 75 percent of IPL's residential customers had air conditioning, (3) using heating and cooling equipment fewer hours (for example, waiting until later in June to even turn the air conditioning on at all and cutting the air conditioning off early in the fall as soon as hot daytime temperatures subsided), (4) being more conscious about turning lights off, (5) installing more energy-efficient heating-cooling equipment and appliances, and (6) investing in storm windows and doors, better insulation, and other weatherization efforts. Insofar as the installations of more energy-efficient heating-ventilation-air conditioning (HVAC) equipment and new appliances were concerned, there were two distinct market segments—the new construction market and the replacement/fuel conversion market.

---

[2] A megawatt was equal to 1,000 kilowatts; thus IPL's generating capacity of 1,720 mw was equal to 1,720,000 kw.

New Construction Market   The main participants in the decision to equip new homes were the utility companies and the builder. Architects, HVAC dealers, and appliance dealers also played significant roles. Decisions to extend gas distribution systems to serve new homes and subdivisions was usually made with the gas utility's own best financial and marketing interests in mind. In many cases, gas utilities imposed short-term payback requirements on investments in main extensions and, occasionally, builders were asked to share the costs of installing new gas lines. Iowa Gas was willing in 1984 to extend lines to all homes where the company could realize an adequate return on investment; lines were being extended to most new subdivisions in the greater Des Moines metropolitan area. Electric service was, of course, made available to every home, irrespective of the distance required to extend lines.

While prospective homebuyers often had a preference for gas or electric HVAC equipment and appliances, their preferences were rarely strong enough to outweigh such other home purchase factors as location, style, size, and price of a home. Homebuilders traditionally did not see their decision to install gas or electric equipment as one that would make or break a sale; the one exception to this in Iowa concerned space heating. Natural gas heating was generally perceived by the public as more economical than electric heating equipment; as a consequence, building contractors in Iowa had a distinct preference for installing gas furnaces and usually gas water heaters in new homes whenever natural gas service was available. Until recently, the majority of builders had opted to install "builder model" equipment and appliances in the new home they constructed; builder models were low-cost units, with low to moderate operating efficiency and comparatively high operating costs. However, more builders, in response to growing homebuyers' awareness about energy-efficient equipment and concern over monthly utility bills, were constructing energy-efficient homes and equipping them with high-efficiency HVAC units, water heaters, and kitchen appliances. In custom-built homes, the house owner played a big role in deciding what kind of HVAC equipment and appliances to install.

Gene Young believed IPL faced a number of hurdles in boosting electricity's share of the new home segment:

> We are dealing with perceptions that electric heat is somehow not quite as dependable and is more costly and with the long ingrained habits of people who have lived with gas most of their adult lives. The challenge is a two-pronged one—builders generally accept heat pumps and recognize their efficiency and good performance characteristics; yet they feel homebuyers prefer natural gas and are therefore hesitant to install electric heat in speculative building projects. On the other hand, when families are having a new home custom-built and have been comfortable with gas heat before, we find them reluctant to add the decision to switch to electric heat to the multitude of construction decisions already necessary. Nevertheless, we see the potential of developing a solid electric heat marketing effort and are beginning to try to overcome the attitude barriers we face. In some respects, though, we may be better off going after the replacement segment because for every new home built there are three or four homeowners in the market to replace their old furnaces.

The Replacement and Fuel Conversion Segment   The decision to replace heating/cooling equipment was usually made by the homeowner, nearly always after consulting with one or more heating/cooling dealers. Replacement decisions were influenced by the initial purchase cost, financing terms, the availability of natural gas service, equipment efficiency, and operating cost. In making a choice, homeowners tended to strike a balance between lower equipment cost and lower operating cost; increasing numbers of buyers were willing to invest in more expensive high-efficiency units if the payback from the operating cost savings was less than 5–8 years. On the other hand, owners of apartments, because they were not responsible for paying utility bills, were less likely to spend the extra dollars it cost to equip their rental units with high-efficiency equipment; a number of landlords opted for the cheapest, and usually the least efficient, heating/cooling equipment and appliances.

While many homeowners were still inclined to select heating/cooling units and appliances that used the same energy source as what was being replaced, more and more homeowners were willing to switch fuel sources if it was economical to do so or if they were concerned about future rate increases and fuel availability. Many Iowa homeowners with fuel oil heating equipment were switching over to gas furnaces. In addition, significant numbers of Iowa homeowners with old, low-efficiency heating equipment were investigating the economics of replacing their existing heating systems, irrespective of what fuel was used.

Decisions by homeowners to replace space heating equipment were made carefully. A national study showed that over half of the consumers surveyed took over three months to decide and often consulted with several dealers. Only a few contacted their local gas or electric company for advice. Over 25 percent were aware of the recent introduction of new generation high-efficiency gas furnaces with Annual Fuel Utilization Efficiencies (AFUEs) up to 96 percent; older model gas furnaces typically had AFUEs in the 55–65 percent range. The same survey showed that cooking and clothes dryer replacement decisions also took up to three months. In contrast, the decision for replacing a domestic water heater was usually immediate; 40 percent of the homeowners surveyed made the decision the day the need arose and almost 67 percent made the decision within one week (except for space heating and cooling, water heating was usually the most costly piece of domestic energy-using equipment to operate). The decisions to replace other major appliances tended either to coincide with home renovation plans or else came after a series of growing repair and maintenance calls. Other studies showed that when a home was sold, the new homeowners usually made changes in the appliances and heating/cooling equipment within the first 12 months.

Marketing Opportunities and Barriers in the Residential Segment   An assessment of the residential marketing opportunities and barriers from the perspective of natural gas was conducted in 1985 by the American Gas Association; the major conclusions were as follows:

Opportunities

1. There is widespread belief among residential customers that natural gas is the least expensive fuel, especially in comparison to electricity, for space heating and water heating.
2. A wide range of gas appliances and gas furnaces are available to consumers (the two biggest areas where natural gas is unable to serve as a residential energy source are refrigerators and air conditioning).

3. A gas heat pump is only a few years from commercialization (which could offer entry into space cooling).
4. The Gas Research Institute is actively engaged in developing new and better gas-using products and in finding companies to commercialize them.
5. There is substantial potential for improving existing gas-fueled equipment and for developing new appliance/equipment/process applications.
6. In many instances gas equipment either is cheaper to buy and install or is cheaper over the life-cycle (initial purchase and operating costs averaged over the life of the equipment).
7. A customer base of 46 million residential gas users provides a ready-made vehicle for information campaigns.
8. Natural gas prices are expected to stabilize, rising no faster than the general inflation rate (maybe less) for the remainder of the 1980s.

Problems and Barriers

1. Many consumers have the impression that the price of natural gas will continue to go substantially higher.
2. Some gas appliances are more expensive to buy and install than electric appliances (gas water heaters and clothes dryers, for example).
3. There is a lack of portable "quick-connect" gas appliances.
4. There are few "gas only" appliance and equipment manufacturers.
5. Competitors (especially power companies) outspend the gas industry by a factor of 10 for advertising and promotion.
6. Gas utility sales personnel are not consistently well-versed in new energy-efficient technological applications.
7. The costs of extending gas mains to prospective new residential customers are often prohibitive.

ENERGY USE DECISIONS IN THE COMMERCIAL MARKET

The great majority of commercial buildings were constructed for defined owners/tenants; a few were built for speculative sale. Owner-occupiers who built or remodeled buildings and occupied them in whole or in part were usually quite concerned about "life-cycle cost effectiveness" insofar as energy use was concerned since they paid for both the energy-using equipment and the monthly energy bills associated with operating this equipment. Speculative commercial builders and commercial landlords tended to be more concerned about initial installation costs than life-cycle costs because they wanted to minimize construction costs and because the new owners or tenants ended up paying the monthly utility bills. Other factors besides initial equipment costs and operating costs which affected the choice of energy-using equipment and fuel choices included:

*   Anticipated escalation in the costs of using alternative fuels.
*   Relative availability of alternative fuels.
*   Building design parameters and building use.
*   Building codes and construction standards.
*   Reliability and maintenance costs of the various types of energy-using equipment.

- Comfort and convenience.
- Utility hook-up costs.
- Utility company services and dependability.

Architects and mechanical design engineers often strongly influenced the energy choices made by building owners or building developers; others who could be influential in design and equipment selection included utility company representatives, HVAC manufacturers and distributors, contractors, real estate salespeople and property managers, and lenders. Almost all commercial buildings were developed in four phases: proposed purpose and use of the building, preliminary design, final design and preparation of working drawings, and construction. Owners, developers, and architects were typically receptive to ideas about alternative energy equipment and energy use design during the preliminary design stage. The choices of energy source and specific equipment were usually made during the preliminary design or working drawing phases when a financing package was being developed and when both construction costs and long-term operating costs were being scrutinized by lenders and the developer.

Energy-use decisions were made differently in the replacement or retrofit market segment. The choices of replacement equipment for existing commercial buildings usually were made by owners, property management firms, maintenance personnel, and sometimes energy consultants; local HVAC dealers might be called upon for advice and for bids on equipment and installation. It was the exception rather than the rule for decision makers to consult with utility company representatives because utility companies neither sold nor installed nor serviced energy equipment.

As of 1984, many commercial customers in Iowa were closely monitoring their energy use and were alert for ways to cut energy costs; this was particularly true among such large commercial users as hotels and motels, hospitals, schools, and office buildings where monthly bills could average $5,000 to $10,000 or more. Typical conservation measures applied in commercial buildings included (1) reduced lighting levels; (2) relamping lighting fixtures with bulbs which used less electricity; (3) the installation of computerized energy management systems, which automatically regulated energy use on a 24-hour, seven-day-a-week basis; (4) reduced wintertime thermostat settings to save on space heating costs; (5) higher summer thermostat settings to save on air-conditioning costs; and (6) shutting off HVAC equipment entirely during nonbusiness hours. Commercial customers, in increasing numbers, were willing to switch over to more economic fuels and equipment for space heating and cooling, for water heating, and for other needs, provided the return on investment and/or payback period justified conversion.

Opportunities and Barriers to Marketing Gas to Commercial Customers

In trying to compete with electricity (and to a much lesser extent LP gas, fuel oil, coal, and other commercial fuel sources), the American Gas Association noted the following opportunities and barriers:

Opportunities

1. There are life-cycle cost advantages to using natural gas in commercial water heating and space heating.
2. Gas prices are expected to stabilize in the next few years.
3. Leasing programs for gas equipment can be worked out.

4. High-efficiency space and water heating equipment is available.
5. Gas-fired fuel cells could be available for commercialization by late 1985.
6. Gas-fired cogeneration equipment could be economically installed by a number of commercial customers as a cheaper energy source alternative.
7. The American Gas Association has initiated attractive national co-op advertising programs with gas equipment manufacturers.
8. Programs whereby gas company employees are offered incentives for providing leads on new sales opportunities and new customer prospects are a major source for identifying prospective customers and drumming up more gas business.

Problems and Barriers

1. High first costs sometimes limit the attractiveness of installing natural gas equipment.
2. The perception among most commercial users is that gas prices will go higher.
3. Many energy purchase decision makers are not aware of the economic advantages of natural gas as an energy source.
4. The cost of extending gas mains to some commercial establishments (especially widely scattered ones in outlying surburban areas) is often prohibitive.
5. The gas industry has a "low-tech" image in comparison to electricity and some other emerging energy sources.
6. Rapid commercialization of new technologies is impeded by the "slow-to-change" character of natural gas utilities and by the low technical skills of commercial sales personnel.
7. Industrywide, natural gas utilities place a relatively low priority on marketing efforts to commercial customers.
8. The highly segmented nature of commercial end-uses for natural gas entails substantially higher marketing costs.
9. It is typical for gas company personnel to have only a very limited involvement in the energy use decision process of commercial customers.

ENERGY USE DECISIONS IN THE INDUSTRIAL MARKET

As of 1984 industrial users of energy nationwide had shifted their emphasis from one of being very concerned about ensuring they had access to adequate energy supplies both presently and later to one of how best to minimize energy costs. With electricity, natural gas, coal, and fuel oil in seemingly abundant supply for the forseeable future, availability played a weak second fiddle to economical energy use. Virtually all large industrial energy users were either actively exploring or had already installed fuel-switching equipment, and numerous energy-saving measures had been implemented. Industrial use of energy per unit of production volume fell over 20 percent nationwide between 1972 and 1984. Industrial customers were likely to invest in energy-saving equipment, provided payback and return on investment considerations could be met. A majority of industrial users of natural gas in the United States indicated that they expected either no change or a decrease in their natural gas usage over the next five years.

One of the most recent developments in the industrial gas segment was the growing interest of large industrial customers in contracting directly for their supplies with interstate pipeline suppliers and bypassing dealing with local retail gas companies except for the payment of a fee for use of the local pipeline in getting the pipeline supplier's gas to the industrial plant site. So-called "contract carriage" was seen as a step in the process of natural gas deregulation and, in effect, thrust both interstate pipeline companies and local gas companies into "common carrier" status insofar as big industrial customers were concerned.

Industrial energy decisions were made either by corporate-level managers or by plant management, depending on the company and the total dollar cost of the energy used. Big users typically had energy conservation engineers who monitored use, explored alternatives, and initiated energy-saving proposals. Major energy-saving investments nearly always required executive approval above the plant and division levels.

Both gas and electric utilities took more of a passive than an active posture in trying to stave off competition from alternative fuel sources such as no. 2 or no. 6 fuel oil, coal, and cogeneration equipment. From an industrywide standpoint, it was not common for either electric or gas companies to make regular, "drum up some more business" sales calls on industrial customers. When utility representatives did visit with industrial customers it was usually for such "goodwill" purposes as offering to help solve any outage or reliability problems, handling a service complaint, explaining a newly approved rate structure, and providing advice on how the customer could reduce monthly bills.

Opportunities and Barriers to Marketing Gas to Industrial Customers

The five-year gas industry marketing plan prepared by the American Gas Association for 1985 identified the following problems and opportunities regarding an improved competitive position for natural gas in industrial end-uses:

Opportunities
1. The recent ruling allowing direct retail sales by natural gas pipeline companies allows increased gas industry flexibility in pricing gas to large industrial users.
2. Increased research funding is becoming available for developing more economical industrial gas applications.
3. There is growing economic attractiveness of using natural gas in such industrial applications as steam recompressing systems, ceramic recuperators, scrap and ladle preheaters, and waste heat congregation.
4. Air quality restrictions make greater use of coal difficult despite worldwide declines in coal prices.
5. Natural gas has gotten increased exposure via a national advertising program sponsored by the American Gas Association and participation in a number of national trade shows.

Problem Areas and Barriers
1. Industrial customers are highly sensitive to the relative costs of alternative fuels and are willing to switch to whatever fuel source is cheapest.
2. Big industrial users of gas are very concerned about the upward trend in natural gas costs.

3. The diversity of energy use technologies among industrial customers makes technical understanding difficult for gas marketing personnel.

4. The gas industry has a low-tech image insofar as sophisticated industrial customers are concerned.

5. There has recently been a slight shift in customers' attitudes toward electricity as the ideal energy source.

6. A low priority is given to industrial advertising and sales promotion activities by most local gas utilities.

SPECIAL ASPECTS OF THE ENERGY MARKET IN IOWA

There were four primary differences between the energy marketplace nationwide and market conditions in the territory served by Iowa Resources:

• Natural gas was strongly perceived by residential customers in Iowa as more economical for space heating and water heating than was electricity. While it was, in fact, true in Iowa Resources' territory that natural gas was cheaper than electricity for water heating, the historical inability of IPL to compete effectively with IG for the space heating business of residential customers was due principally to the perception that electric heating was more expensive than gas heating and the long-standing familiarity of dealers and homeowners with gas furnaces. Recent technological improvements had made high-efficiency electric heat pumps capable of operating as economically as high-efficiency natural gas furnaces. To be fully competitive with natural gas, electric heat had to be priced at about 3.5 cents to 4.0 cents per kwh; IPL's average price for electricity for winter heating customers was about 4.5 cents per kwh.

• Because IPL, historically, had not aggressively gone after the market for residential space heating (letting its sister company dominate this end-use segment), IPL's residential electric rates had never really been downstepped in the winter months sufficiently to dispel the perception of customers that natural gas heating was cheaper than electric heating. In other parts of the United States, especially in Sunbelt states where heavy use of air conditioning caused electric utilities to hit much higher summer peak loads than winter peak loads, there had been a more aggressive posture on the part of electric utilities in capturing the residential space heating market and in getting builders to construct all-electric homes. A few Sunbelt power companies and many of the electric utilities in Oregon and Washington (where electric rates were the cheapest in the United States) had market shares in residential space heating of 40 to 80 percent—far above IPL's approximately 10 percent share. Several electric utilities utilized declining-block winter rate designs to make electric heat more price competitive with natural gas and alternate fuel sources (see Exhibit 6); and since their service area had also been among the national leaders in new residential construction, they had penetrated the home heating market with more all-electric homes than had power companies in low population growth states such as Iowa. Power companies which had been the most successful in promoting total electric homes generally had a smaller differential between summer and winter peak loads and their more even year-

Exhibit 6   Illustration of Use of a Declining-Block Rate Design to Make Electric Space-Heating Price Competitive with Natural Gas or Other Alternative Fuels

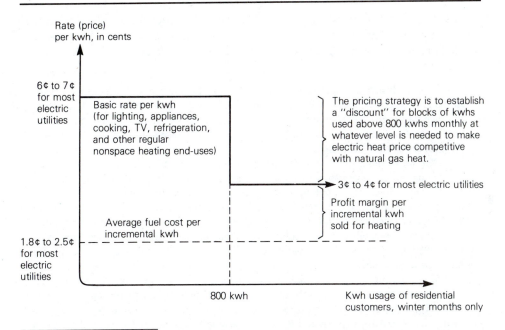

Note: A "typical" single-family residence used about 600 kwh per month for lighting, power for household appliances, cooking, TV, refrigerators, and so on; an electric water heater could add 200–300 kwh per month, depending on family size, hot-water-use habits, and setting of thermostat on hot water heater. Thus, the effective price for space-heating becomes 3–4 cents per kwh at usage levels past 800 kwh/month.

round capacity utilization allowed them to spread fixed overhead costs over greater kwh sales.

- The natural gas industry in Iowa had a strong tradition in serving the space heating and water heating needs of customers and had always seen electricity as its chief competition for these end-uses.
- The local HVAC dealers and distributors in Iowa were strongly aligned with the natural gas industry. A big majority of the dealers and distributors in Iowa Resources' territory were in 1984 aggressively pushing high-efficiency gas furnaces and gas water heaters. Many dealers, especially those in rural areas, did not stock or push electric heat pumps, selling them only when a prospect specifically asked for a heat pump. Moreover, many dealers believed heat pumps were inferior to the high-efficiency gas furnace and that they were not very suitable for the cold Iowa winters. Comparatively few dealers in Iowa handled as many as five electric heat pump installations annually, but virtually all were eager and equipped to sell, install, and service electric air-conditioning units. Virtually all Iowa dealers

and distributors recommended to both residential and commercial customers that they install gas heating equipment and electric air conditioning. (Gas air conditioners were notorious failures nationwide—a fact well known to dealers and consumers.)

IPL tried hard to work with local heating/cooling dealers, but there were both pros and cons of having to create a strong IPL-dealer alliance given the historically strong alliance between the dealers and the natural gas industry. Gene Young commented as follows:

> We have elected to attack the problem on two fronts. First, we've looked for ways to make it profitable and easier for dealers to sell heat pumps effectively. At the same time we have tried to create a demand, or at least a strong interest on the part of the public, for heat pumps so that dealers will recognize a new enthusiasm for the product on the part of their customers.
>
> What we've done in the last few years is rejuvenate and broaden our "registered heat pump dealer" program, something we started in 1975. All of the major Des Moines and Council Bluffs dealers are knowledgeable in heat pump installation and many carry heat pumps in stock. We're extending our efforts out into more rural areas now. We're working more closely with builders and architects, explaining the advances in heat pump efficiency and reliability. Our biggest success has come in the commercial market— since 1980 about 95 percent of major new construction over 25,000 square feet in size has been total electric.
>
> We are getting ready to launch a major add-on heat pump promotional program with area dealers in 1985. It will take time for all these efforts to pay off, of course. Natural gas appliances and furnaces have a good image with consumers, and dealers have a lot of experience with and trust in natural gas equipment. The natural gas folks aren't about to give in easily and they are well financed. It's going to be a struggle.

THE 1984 IPL—IG COMPETITIVE STRUGGLE

IPL's competitive strategy in 1984 centered around promoting the installation of "add-on" heat pumps in homes where residential customers were considering replacing their central air-conditioning units. The add-on heat pump had the capability to function both as an air conditioner and as an electric heating system; Exhibit 7 provides excerpts from an IPL brochure describing how the add-on heat pump worked. IPL spent $200,000 on a five-week TV, radio, and newspaper campaign urging customers who were purchasing an air conditioner to consider a heat pump instead and use it to complement their present heating system. IPL studies showed that 7,000 to 8,000 IPL customers replaced their worn out central air conditioners each year. The price of an add-on electric heat pump ran $600 to $800 more than a central electric air conditioner, but the extra costs could be justified by the fuel savings on heating. According to IPL estimates, an add-on electric heat pump could produce annual fuel savings of $374 for a 1,200-square-foot home heated with LP gas and annual fuel savings of $649 for a 1,300-square-foot home heated with fuel oil. Add-on heat pumps piggybacked with natural gas furnaces could generate fuel savings of up to $175 on large homes or as little as no savings in small homes. IPL's newspaper ads contained coupons in which customers could mail in certain heating data; an IPL computer program used this data to calculate the potential yearly savings, and the results were then mailed back to customers. Several hundred IPL customers mailed in the coupon, and about 200 subsequently installed add-on heat pumps, resulting in a net annual revenue gain to IPL of about $100,000 ($500 per customer). Gene Young, IPL's vice president for marketing, indicated that the campaign was aimed primarily at homeowners who heated with propane and fuel oil.

Iowa Gas fought back with a hard-hitting, six-week radio campaign of its own. Bill Davis, marketing manager for Iowa Gas, said:

> What they're trying to do is steal our market. If I seem adamant about this, I am. The heat pump is an attempt to take away our most profitable business, our gravy. So that's why our ads are hard-hitting. . . . The heat pump is not good for any customer—the existing customer or the new customer.

Iowa Gas's campaign was financed largely by Northern Natural Gas Co., IG's prime pipeline supplier, and by the Iowa Blue Flame Association, a consortium of gas suppliers and HVAC dealers. IG's ads were professionally produced by the American Gas Association and not only challenged the fuel savings of heat pumps but also gnawed at the most common criticisms of heat pumps: (1) that they produce a lukewarm air from the vents which many people complain of as having a "drafty feel," (2) that they are more costly to maintain and wear out quicker than gas furnaces,[3] and (3) that heat pumps were a negative factor when a home was up for sale. The dialogue in one IG ad ran as follows:

Wife:	Well, here we are in our new home . . . I mean igloo.
Husband:	Now, now give our heat pump a chance.
Wife:	Can't we turn it up?
Husband:	Oh, no resetting the thermostat upsets its operation, makes it less efficient.
Wife:	But feel. The air coming out of the vents isn't warm like our gas furnace's was. . . . Our heat pump is maladjusted and cold-hearted and we can't upset it. That's quite a machine we've got here. Oh, listen, let's go visit the kids. They've got gas heat.

In addition, Iowa Gas began a program whereby employees were paid $5 for each lead they gave the marketing department on homeowners who were not currently using gas for space heating and/or water heating.

COMPETITIVE MARKETING STRATEGY OF IOWA GAS

Iowa Gas's marketing objectives and marketing strategies were stated in its 1985 Marketing Plan as follows:

Residential Market

Marketing Objective   Maintain stable volume utilization of natural gas as a primary space and water heating fuel source. Approximately 93 percent of the natural gas utilized in the home is for these uses.

---

[3] The compressor units in heat pumps normally had an expected life of 8–10 years, whereas the main operating parts of gas furnaces were commonly guaranteed by the manufacturer for 20 years. However, the experience with the new style high-efficiency gas furnaces was too short for gas companies to claim a clear-cut advantage of high-efficiency gas furnaces over new-style heat pumps on overall maintenance costs.

Exhibit 7   Description of Add-On Heat Pump in Iowa Power and Light Advertising Brochure, 1984

It looks like a central air conditioner. It cools like a central air conditioner. It *is* a central air conditioner. And then some.

We're talking about the add-on heat pump, the air conditioner that heats, too.

The add-on heat pump operates like any other heat pump. The difference is it's added to and works with your home's furnace for superb energy efficiency and operating savings.

Cools All Summer

When it's hot outside, the add-on heat pump keeps you cool inside, just like an ordinary central air conditioner does. Today's heat pumps operate as efficiently as the new energy-efficient central air conditioner models, and must more efficiently than older central air units.

But while central air conditioners go into hibernation when summer's over, the heat pump's job is just beginning.

Warms All Winter

During the heating season, the add-on heat pump provides economical warmth on all but very cold days of winter. Then, the heat pump works with your furnace to keep your home comfortable at a lower cost than the furnace can working alone.

We hope you'll spend a few moments with this booklet to learn about the many advantages of adding a heat pump to your home. It'll be time well spent . . . and money well saved!

HOW IT WORKS

The name *heat pump* tells only part of what this energy-efficient machine can do. Actually, a heat pump is a central air conditioner that works in reverse, too.

In summer, the heat pump *absorbs* heat from the air inside your home and pumps it outside, just as any other central air conditioner does. So, you enjoy cool, dehumidified air throughout your home all summer long.

Then, in winter, the heat pump reverses this process. It absorbs heat from the outside air and pumps it into your home.

Heat from Outside Air? Yes.

The heat pump takes advantage of this surprising fact of nature: there is always solar heat in the air, even on cold winter days.

It requires less energy to *move* this heat from place to place—to pump it—than it does to *create* heat in the first place. And that's the key to the heat pump's energy-efficient operation.

Why an "Add-On"?

When outside temperatures drop to the 20° range or below, a heat pump that's sized to meet the cooling requirements of your home can't provide all the heating you need. That's when your furnace and heat pump work together to keep your home warm and comfortable. Result? Lower heating bills—lower than with either system working alone.

Summer cooling . . . winter heating. No other machine does both. And when you team the add-on heat pump with your furnace, you've got an unbeatable combination for year-round comfort and savings.

IS IT RIGHT FOR YOUR HOME?

Whatever the size, style, or age of your home, if it's ducted for forced-air heat, you can enjoy the advantages of an add-on heat pump.

The heat pump has been around for a long time. Its technology has been proved, and engineering refinements in recent years have increased the reliability and energy efficiency of new models to the highest levels ever.

Exhibit 7 *(concluded)*

In fact, today about one in four new homes is heated and cooled with a heat pump. Homeowners appreciate its clean, efficient operation and the fact that it provides comfort and economy all year long.

In northern climates like Iowa's, the heat pump requires supplementary heating during winter's coldest days. But you already have the supplementary heat source you need. It's your furnace!

Adding a heat pump gives you a "dual fuel" system that offers unmatched energy efficiency.

When to Add a Heat Pump

There are two situations where an add-on heat pump is likely to be the best choice you can make for your home.

If your old central air conditioner needs to be replaced, add a heat pump instead. An add-on heat pump does cost more to buy than a central air unit. But its economical operation will pay back this cost difference quickly and save you money season after season.

Or if you have forced air heating but no central air, you can add a heat pump and start enjoying cool comfort this summer . . . and lower heating bills next winter and for many winters to come.

Q: Who can use an add-on heat pump?

A: An add-on heat pump can be used with natural gas, oil, propane, or electric furnaces in both new and existing homes.

Q: How is the add-on heat pump different from a conventional, total electric heat pump system?

A: The conventional heat pump includes supplemental electric resistance heat to provide warmth on very cold days. The add-on heat pump uses the home's existing furnace for supplemental heating. Working together, the add-on heat pump and your furnace provide lower cost heating than either unit operating by itself.

Q: Isn't it true fossil fuel heating systems (furnaces) deliver heated air at warmer temperatures than those of a heat pump?

A: Fossil fuel systems do provide warmer air. However, hotter air moves upward far more quickly, collecting near the ceiling. By contrast, the air delivered by the heat pump tends to rise more slowly. So, more of it goes for warming people.

Q: I've heard that a heat pump runs longer than a furnace. Is this correct?

A: Yes, a heat pump usually does run longer. This is because the temperature of the heated air is closer to that being maintained in the room. By contrast, a fossil fuel furnace delivers large "bursts" of hot air, which quickly warm the room, then cool down. Heat pump heating is more comfortable because it doesn't cycle on and off as often, providing a more even heat.

Q: Does a heat pump require a larger duct system than a furnace?

A: No. In most cases, the ductwork required for an add-on heat pump is the same as that required by your current heating and cooling system.

Q: Are heat pumps less efficient in the cooling mode than central air conditioners?

A: No. Today's add-on heat pump operates in the cooling mode as efficiently as, or more efficiently than most electric central air conditioners.

Q: Are efficiencies (both heating and cooling) of heat pumps getting higher?

A: Yes. As energy costs increase, higher efficiency systems are becoming very cost-effective. The coefficient of performance (COP) of most heat pumps is now near 200 percent. This means that each BTU of electricity can deliver 2 BTUs of heat to the home. A furnace, on the other hand, can never reach even 100 percent efficiency. This is because combustion is never complete.

In fact, the typical furnace installed in many new homes today is only about 65 percent efficient. And as furnaces get older, they become less efficient. So, it makes good sense to team a low-efficiency machine like a furnace with a very high efficiency machine—the heat pump.

Marketing Strategies   Activities aimed at accomplishing the above objective will be directed toward:

- Supporting the continued use of natural gas by existing residential users. (IG research indicated that of homeowners now using natural gas for heating, only 67 percent, on the basis of factors other than cost, really preferred gas heat over other heating sources.)
- Increasing the amount of natural gas used by existing natural gas customers who can be identified as not using natural gas for space or water heating.
- Attracting new customers who are using alternate fuels for space or water heating.
- Maintaining a high level of natural gas space and water heating equipment installed in newly constructed single-family and multiple-family dwelling units within the confines and limitations of main and service extension policies.

Action Plans

- Use customers' billing history records to develop a prime prospect file of current customers showing the greatest potential for additional sales of natural gas. Launch a direct mail campaign targeted to these customers, promoting the benefits of natural gas space and water-heating conversions.
- Prepare bill stuffers to present the advantages of using gas for both space and water heating, and to reinforce current natural gas usage.
- Expand interest and participation in the Iowa Gas employee incentive campaign to generate leads for customer service representative follow-up among current customers not using natural gas for space and/or water heating.
- Prepare sales promotion materials for dealer use in conjunction with media campaigns and the use of co-op advertising programs.
- Develop a special *Iowa Gas Newsletter* directed to home builders. This communications vehicle will be published quarterly and contain timely information relevant to all applications of natural gas in the homebuilding business.
- Have trade show exhibits at:
  —Home & Garden Show (February).
  —Home Expo (June).
  —Parade of Homes (September).
  —Shopping Center Exhibit.
- Establish a personal working relationship and regular contact program with key lenders, real estate personnel, and members of the Iowa Energy Policy Council (an agency which distributed energy information to the general public).
- Develop energy usage cost comparisons for release to specific audiences on a regular and timely basis.

Commercial Market

Marketing Objective   Increase the use of natural gas as a primary fuel source for space and water heating *and* for use in the manufacturing or processing of products within the confines and limitations of main and service extension policies.

Marketing Strategies   Activities will be directed toward:

- Supporting continued use of natural gas by existing commercial customers.
- Increasing the percentage of natural gas space and water heating systems installed in low-rise offices and other commercial buildings.

- Increasing the use of natural gas systems installed for the purpose of manufacturing and/or processing of products within targeted light-industrial and commercial businesses. Give special emphasis to commercial and institutional food service category prospects.

Action Plans

- Execute a profile and attitude research study among all commercial market customers, prospects, and influencers. Use the findings to refine marketing directions and to develop communications messages appealing to specific needs within the market.
- Develop innovative rate structures designed to reflect actual cost of service among customer classes and to adequately compete against alternate energy sources.
- Develop specific informational material promoting the advantages and benefits of cogeneration energy utilization to those classes of customers generating high volumes of waste heat.
- Develop additional printed and audiovisual sales presentation materials for use by Iowa Gas personnel in presenting the advantages and benefits of natural gas energy to commercial market decision makers and influencers.
- Utilize the *Sales Prospector* and summary reports of the *F. W. Dodge Report* to establish prime contacts for ongoing communications and sales calling programs with decision makers and influencers of newly planned projects.
- Establish Iowa Gas *Commercial Markets Newsletter* to maintain regular contact with audience members.
- Continue the Iowa Gas employee incentive campaign to generate commercial leads for Customer Service Representative follow-up among potential customers.
- Attend and have displays at selected commercial market trade shows and conventions.

Industrial Market

Marketing Objective   Increase the volume of natural gas used in industrial manufacturing or processing operations.

Industrial Marketing Strategies   Activities will be directed toward:

- Supporting continued use of natural gas by existing large-volume category customers.
- Increasing the amount of natural gas used by existing large-volume customers who can be identified as having additional uses for our product in their manufacturing or processing operations.
- Attracting large-volume category industrial energy users who are prime prospects for conversion to natural gas processes within all or a portion of their operation.
- Establish personal working relationships and regular contact program among customers and prospects.
- Utilize the *Sales Prospector* and summary reports of the *F. W. Dodge Report* to establish prime contacts for ongoing communications and sales calling programs with decision makers and influencers of planned projects.
- Develop informational and sales material for use by Iowa Gas personnel in their contacts with industrial market decision makers and influencers, with particular emphasis on energy-use comparison data for the multitude of manufacturing and processing operations in use today.
- Develop specific information material promoting the advantages and benefits of cogen-

eration energy utilization to those classes of customers generating high volumes of waste heat.

- Establish sales incentive/bonus program for Iowa Gas personnel making regular sales calls on industrial customers and prospects.
- Establish an Iowa Gas *Industrial Information Bulletin* covering new developments for natural gas usage in manufacturing and processing.
- Attend and have displays at selected industrial market trade shows and conventions.
- Establish VIP tours for prospective new industrial customers showing the greatest potential of relocation in IG's service area.
- Establish an industrial incentive rate to enhance the attractiveness of locating within the Iowa Gas service area.
- Develop a direct mail and sales follow-up system targeted to businesses identified as having high natural gas requirements. Phase One will target firms with facilities already located in Iowa. Phase Two will target out-of-state firms.

COMPETITIVE MARKETING STRATEGY AT IPL

Gene Young, vice president for marketing at Iowa Power and Light, reflected on how the company's marketing approaches and marketing philosophy had changed over the years:

We've come almost full circle in the past 35 years . . . from direct promotion and merchandising of electric appliances in the 50s and 60s, to our conservation-centered marketing efforts in the 1970s, resulting from higher costs and the energy crisis . . . back to today's more selective marketing of specific kinds of energy usage, such as heat pumps.

During the 1950s, if you walked into an Iowa Power office you might have thought you were in an appliance store. Fact is . . . in some small towns, Iowa Power was the appliance store. Our role as marketers during this period was to expand the market for electric service. Showing consumers how appliances could improve their lives . . . how electric helpers could be used to cook, clean, cool, cut, bake, drill, polish, percolate, and entertain.

As the second half of the 1960s dawned, we were still experiencing impressive growth. We'd gotten out of the merchandising business and many of us in the utility industry were gradually becoming more *marketing* oriented instead of simply *sales* oriented. We had begun to focus on the profitability of selling and for the first time, the contribution of new load to the bottom line came to the forefront. At Iowa Power we began to build off-peak energy sales with the creation of a strong electric heating program. By promoting off-peak usage, the fixed cost of providing electric power can be spread over a greater number of kilowatt hours, making for more efficient operation of generating facilities.

Hardly had those efforts begun, however, when the oil embargo hit. Quickly many utilities stopped whatever marketing they were doing, got rid of their salespeople, pulled in their horns, and adopted the conservation ethic which permeated the industry for the next dozen years at least. At Iowa Power, we were one of the utilities leading the parade. We invented a cartoon character by the name of Dr. Wise Use, and we published an energy diet booklet and distributed almost 100,000 of them. We were one of the first utilities to recognize the value of insulation and the second in the country to develop an insulation financing program.

However, and this is important, we never stopped promoting the creation of off-peak energy use through electric heating. That sort of dual program (conservation and selling) did raise questions in the minds of some customers and we carefully attempted to explain why we were doing what we were doing . . . the idea that conservation was important, efficient energy use was important, but also that for a strongly summer peaking electric utility, wintertime electric sales were also essential.

Had we forgotten that concept during the 70s, I'm sure our electric heating market would not be nearly as developed as it is today, when electric heating customers contribute up to a third of our residential and small commercial revenues in a typical winter month. The Energy Diet, by the way, was an early effort to try to convince customers that they could indeed help control their energy budget, that indeed they were making a buying decision every time they pushed a button or flipped a switch.

By the late 70s, marketing research told us the conservation ethic had pretty well run its course. Most everybody who could afford to and wanted to add insulation and tighten up their homes had already done so. As we entered the 80s at Iowa Power, our fuel mix for generation was good and new plants were under construction and coming on-line on schedule. It seemed pertinent to implement a sophisticated marketing program that sold additional off-peak kilowatt hours at the same time that it voiced concerns for customer needs and continued to instruct on wise and efficient energy use.

Mr. Young went on to describe IPL's current efforts to market electricity to residential customers:

In the residential area our thrust is two-fold . . . an energy-efficient home program called Payback Plus, which identifies the heat pump as a major element in the construction of the most livable, energy efficient new homes, and a strong information program on the add-on heat pump for existing housing.

Our Add-on Heat Pump program is extremely vital for us. Only about 1,500 to 2,000 new homes are currently being built in our service area each year. Thus, in building wintertime usage, we must focus efforts on the 200,000 customers in homes already built who presently heat with something besides electricity. Our 1984 summer campaign was keyed to the theme "Sell the air conditioner that heats too!" That's the dealer message. To the customer we said, "Don't just replace your central air conditioner, buy a heat pump instead . . . it's the air conditioner that heats too!" Thus the add-on heat pump was positioned as a product that would provide highly efficient summer cooling, thereby reducing a customer's summer cooling bills . . . but since it is "the air conditioner that heats too," it also would reduce their wintertime heating bills. To prove that, we offer a computer savings estimate tailored to the customer's specific home and its energy usage. The media campaign is supported by a targeted mailing to prime add-on heat pump prospects, all designed to obtain customer response—a request that we provide a specific savings estimate for his home. That program is supplemented with telephone calls to people who phone dealers for information on the heat pump. There are dealer incentives for sales and for presentations and a co-op advertising program.

Our Payback Plus new home program is based on the premise that customers in the future are going to demand energy-efficient construction and that that's a beneficial idea that a utility should spearhead. We want to firmly implant in the customer's mind that a truly energy-efficient home includes a highly efficient heat pump. That's essential to our thinking. Payback Plus includes a strong builder marketing program with yard signs, pennants, and customer giveaways including balloons and key chains and special open house support. This year the centerpiece is a sophisticated consumer brochure which contains not only an explanation of Payback Plus building practices but four specific Payback Plus home plans created by four of Iowa's leading architects especially for Payback Plus.

We're also involved with builders in both Des Moines and Council Bluffs in a research and development program involving ground-loop, water-source heat pumps. We call it "The Super Home" because it includes not only state-of-the-art energy-efficient construction but also has heating and cooling featuring an earth-coupled, water-source heat pump—what we call "the solar system that keeps working even when the sun isn't shining."

Mr. Young described IPL's efforts among commercial and industrial customers thusly:

Our work in the commercial sector, I'm sure, is not much different than that conducted by other electric utilities. We hold seminars and we publish a series of memos detailing the features of new commercial buildings using total electric heating and cooling systems.

The emphasis however is on day-to-day contact with architects and consulting engineers and with appropriate personnel at our major industrial plants. Only by being out among them can you develop the intelligence that leads to success. Ninety-five percent of our new commercial construction is total electric, the majority using the very efficient closed-loop, water-source heat pump system.

The 1985 strategic plans for Iowa Power & Light included the following marketing objectives and marketing program activities:

Residential Objectives

1. Encourage installation of all-electric heat pumps in all new residential construction, add-on heat pumps as a replacement for central air units in existing structures, and focus on the efficiency of closed-loop, water-source heat pump systems as "the most economical heating system available."

   Supporting Program Activities   Consumer Heat Pump Campaign—April–June 1985.

   - Provide a major customer incentive for all installations during the campaign period, including both new and existing housing.
   - Work actively with dealers, identifying those who will concentrate on heat pump sales during the campaign period.
   - Develop a pilot program in which a temporary salesperson will be employed during the campaign period to directly follow leads, contact customers, and close sales for cooperating dealers.
   - Offer low-cost financing for all customers and no-cost financing for employees during the campaign period.
   - Produce ads, including testimonials, on the competitive operating cost of heat pumps in both new and existing structures.

2. Promote the cost-saving benefits of Payback Plus construction and recognize builders and home owners who construct Payback Plus homes.

Supporting Program Activities

- Develop print advertising campaign to run throughout the building season (April–September), featuring builders of Payback Plus homes and testimonials on the benefits of Payback Plus construction.
- Provide lighted house numbers and other Payback Plus identification for installation on all Payback Plus homes.
- Focus on Payback Plus with a major booth at the Home & Garden Show in Des Moines in February 1985.

3. Create levels of information and understanding that lead to a good feeling about electricity, its value, and customer control over its use.

Supporting Action Programs

- Prove in all the things we say and do that we are a group of people committed to consumer service and caring. We must empathize with their concern about their bill and offer energy-efficiency ideas and control options which will assist them in keeping their cost as low as possible.
- Show customers that we care by responding to all customer inquiries quickly and courteously and by insisting that all employees perform their jobs confidentially and with the customers' interest in mind.
- Demonstrate to the customers that we can work for our mutual interest by developing special programs that position Iowa Power as a caring organization.

Commercial/Industrial Objectives

1. To maintain close liaison with architects, consulting engineers, and major industrial customers in order to sell the benefits of electric heating and production applications.
2. Sell electric heating to 90 percent of all commercial structures over 25,000 square feet, and 50 percent of all commercial structures under 25,000 square feet.

Program Activities

- Sponsor and conduct an industrial heat pump school in spring of 1985 for representatives of major industrial customers.
- Hold an architect/engineer seminar in the fall of 1985.
- Arrange and carry out top-level executive visits with 30 of our largest industrial customers.

3. To create marketing strategies and undertake activities that will enable us to achieve greater kilowatt-hour growth through installation of efficient flood and security lighting in both residential and commercial sectors.

Program Activities

- Investigate creation of a subsidiary that would market private area lighting systems.
- Develop cheaper pricing for leased lighting systems.
- Develop a direct mail promotional campaign focusing on the benefits of flood lighting for large residential and commercial installations.

4. Improve economic prosperity throughout our service area by offering professional development services that will attract job-producing firms and help existing ones expand, in order to stimulate added sales of 2 million kwh and the creation of 1,000 new jobs.

Program Activities

- Coordinate efforts with the Economic Development Department.
- Sponsor national advertising in well-read trade magazines including *Site Selection Handbook, Area Development, Plant Sites and Parks,* and *Business Facilities.*
- Produce materials that would inform companies how we can assist them with their expansion plans.
- Produce a portable display unit that can be utilized at selected trade shows for prospect development.
- Participate and cooperate with other development groups including the Iowa Development Commission, the Iowa Professional Developers, the Bureau of Economic Development in Des Moines, and individual community development groups.
- Exert leadership to help produce a legislative economic development package that includes allowance for incentive rates for new and expanding industrial customers, eliminates the sales and use tax on equipment and machinery, and produces a more attractive climate for industry throughout Iowa.

Pricing Objective

1. Create optional rate design plans that customers can choose among and that also provide positive benefits for the company by improving capacity utilization, holding down summer peaks, and increasing off-peak and winter sales.

Program Activities

- Analyze time-of-use applications for electric heating customers.
- Design optional rate design plans that promote energy efficiency and reward customers for the installation of efficient equipment.
- Carefully evaluate optional pricing designs to minimize revenue disruption in the short term and maximize revenue gain in the long term.

Companywide Objective

1. Make all employees (particularly nonbargaining unit employees) an integral and vital part of the marketing organization through the creation of information and motivation programs that benefit participating employees and the company.

Program Activities

- Develop and promote a broad-based employee incentive plan, called "The I-Team," that will reward employee participation in a variety of marketing activities with point certificates redeemable for valuable merchandise.
- Provide data and information to participating employees on heat pumps, Payback Plus homes, and other specialized marketing programs.

- Develop testimonials from employees who have installed heat pumps in their own homes.
- Continue our 9 percent financing offer on heat pump equipment for employees throughout 1985, and offer no-cost financing on employee installation during the 1985 spring heat pump campaign.

Exhibit 8 shows comparative data for IPL and IG regarding the resource support for their marketing efforts. Exhibits 9, 10, and 11 present materials used by IPL in support of its 1985 heat pump campaign.

For IPL's marketing strategy to succeed, Gene Young believed a number of things would have to occur:

> In the existing home market we first have to position the heat pump successfully as "the air conditioner that heats too" and provide incentive financing packages that will reduce the first cost disadvantage (a heat pump generally retails for about $600 more than a replacement central air conditioner). At the same time the major dealers must become convinced that our sales tools will help them meet customer needs and desires effectively and close the sale expeditiously.

Midway through 1985, Young commented on the success that IPL's marketing strategy was having:

> Major strides toward our goals are in progress. Already in 1985 we've had a very successful add-on heat pump program in the preseason (April–June) air conditioning market. Over 400 add-on heat pumps were sold during this concentrated period, more than twice as many as in any previous heat pump campaign. We worked only with dealers who signed agreements to work actively with us, to use co-op advertising, and to send all their employees to an after-work seminar conducted by Iowa Power personnel. The sales tools that provided motivation for dealers and the consumer included 7 percent financing on purchase and installation (up to $3,000 over four years) and a $300 cash efficiency bonus paid directly to the customer by Iowa Power. In addition, we offered employees of the company zero-interest financing in an effort to improve heat pump saturation within the company. About 17 employees have taken advantage of the offer so far. In the new home market we've been successful in positioning the heat pump as an essential part of our Payback Plus energy efficient home program. Electric heating, preferably

Exhibit 8   Comparative Marketing Efforts of IPL and IG, 1984 and 1985

	IPL	IG
Overall marketing budget, 1984	$1,035,000	$457,000
Number of marketing personnel	19	8
"General office" staff	5	3
Customer reps/sales personnel	14	5
Residential	4	3
Commercial	5	1
Industrial	5	1
Advertising and promotion budget, 1984	$ 450,000	$250,000
Advertising and promotion budget, 1985	$ 514,000	$264,000
Number of *new* positions, 1985 over 1984	1	6

Source: Iowa Resources.

Exhibit 9   Sample Copy of Iowa Power's Dealer Agreement for Participating in 1985 Add-On Heat Pump Program

---

For _____ , I agree to participate in Iowa Power's 1985
(dealer name)

Add-On Heat Pump Program. I understand that Iowa Power will provide:

- A $300 cash rebate to customers buying an add-on heat pump (minimum SEER of eight) during the campaign period, April 1–June 15. Rebates will also be provided to the owner of a new home when they commit to an add-on or all-electric heat pump during the campaign period and have it installed by September 1, 1985. The rebate plan covers only installations made on single-family homes or in attached town house or condominium buildings of up to four units.
- Seven percent financing for qualified customers, up to a maximum of $3,000 for over four years. Financing available only for individual customers of Iowa Power and for existing structures only.
- Media support in my market area to include a statement stuffer to all Iowa Power customers, print, radio, and TV (where available).
- A listing of my dealership in print advertising placed by Iowa Power.
- Co-op advertising dollars to pay one half of my approved advertising schedule between April 1–June 1.
- Sales promotion materials for my personnel to use in sales presentations.
- An orientation meeting to explain the program and to solicit the support of my entire staff.
- FREE, computerized cost savings estimates for customers requesting additional information on savings with an add-on or all-electric heat pump.

As a participating dealer, I agree:

- To actively sell the add-on heat pump as a replacement for central air, particularly during the campaign period.
- To make this effort clear to my staff and encourage their emphasis on the add-on heat pump.
- To run print or radio co-op advertising featuring the add-on heat pump equipment during the campaign period. At a minimum, my radio schedule will include at least 10 spots per week for four weeks. Print advertising will consist of at least one 15-column-inch ad insertion each week for four weeks.
- To follow up on leads and referrals from Iowa Power within five working days.
- To allow Iowa Power to present the program to my staff at an orientation meeting prior to the media campaign.

I understand that only dealers who agree to these requirements will be included in the program. Their names will appear in Iowa Power's print ads and will be used on a rotating basis for referrals and leads. I understand that my commitment will be monitored in terms of timely follow-up on referrals and leads; actual add-on heat pump sales; and co-op advertising placed. I understand that Iowa Power reserves the right to withdraw my dealership from the program if any of the above requirements are not met.

Signed _____   Date _____

Exhibit 10   A Sample IPL Ad Promoting Add-On Electric Heat Pumps, 1985

Get $300 back on the air conditioner that's so advanced it even heats your home in the winter.

Imagine a high-efficiency central air conditioner...combined with a super-efficient heating system in one superior unit.

Imagine an add-on heating and cooling unit that works in *conjunction* with your present forced-air furnace...gas, electric, propane or oil! A unit that requires no special construction, no special duct systems.

Imagine a total heating and cooling system that could lower your *annual* energy bills by as much as $150 to $600!

Stop imagining...it's here today. It's called the add-on heat pump, the central air conditioner that heats, too!

$300 Efficiency Bonus*/ 7% APR Financing

If you're an Iowa Power customer, you can get a $300 Cash Efficiency Bonus *and* 7% APR financing — up to four years and $3,000 — when you buy this versatile add-on unit by June 15, 1985. Buy any brand from any participating dealer.

For a free brochure and computerized estimate that shows you *how much* an add-on heat pump could save you in your home, stop in or call your local Iowa Power office. Or telephone toll-free 1-800-553-4343/ Extension 11.

ip iowa power

*Efficiency Bonus offer valid on add-on heat pumps with an efficiency rating (SEER) of 9 or more. Efficiency bonus and financing available only for Iowa Power residential customers purchasing add-on heat pumps for existing single-family structures or for attached dwellings of up to four units. Contact any Iowa Power office for complete qualifying terms and details.

The cost of this ad will be paid for by the customers of Iowa Power.

Exhibit 11   Sample Materials Supporting IPL's Spring 1985 Heat Pump Promotion

Cost to Buy?

- Generally, an add-on heat pump costs about $800 more than a new central air conditioner of the same size and quality. A special $300 cash efficiency bonus eliminates part of that difference.
- The remaining extra investment is returned to you quickly in *energy savings*.
- Compare your return on this $500 investment:

Years	Savings with Add-On Heat Pump*	Return on Heat Pump Investment of $500†	5¼% Savings (compounded quarterly)	8½% C.D. (simple interest)
1	$ 140	$(360)	$526.77	$542.50
2	280	(220)	554.98	585.00
3	420	(80)	584.69	627.50
4	560	60	616.00	670.00
5	700	200	648.98	712.50
6	840	340	683.73	755.00
7	980	480	720.34	797.50
8	1,120	620	758.90	840.00
9	1,260	760	799.54	882.50
10	1,400	900	842.35	925.00

* Example based on an add-on heat pump added to an older, 55 percent efficient gas furnace. Savings would be greater with oil or propane.

† Example shows how $140 yearly savings pays back initial investment, then builds a cumulative cash flow. The savings figure assumes no increase in fuel costs. Actual savings could be greater if the cost for the furnace fuel (gas, oil, propane) increased faster than the cost of electricity.

$300 Cash Bonus!

- Buy and install an add-on heat pump by June 15, 1985, and receive a $300 cash efficiency bonus.

Save, Too, with 7% APR Financing!

- You can finance your purchase of an add-on heat pump—up to $3,000 for up to four years—on your Iowa Power service bill.

Finance $_____ for _____ Months = Monthly payment of $_____

Exhibit 11 *(concluded)*

Yearly Heating/Cooling Costs

Typical 1,500-Square-Foot Home*

	Heat-ing	Cool-ing	Heating/ Cooling	Heating/ Cooling with Add-On Heat Pump	Sav-ings	Heating/ Cooling with Add-On Heat Pump and Clock Thermostat	Sav-ings
Gas Furnace							
55% efficient	$585	$159	$744	$604	**$140**	$523	**$221**
65% efficient	495	159	654	581	**73**	503	**151**
85% efficient	379	159	538	552	**(14)**	478	**60**
Oil furnace							
55% efficient	706	159	865	634	**231**	548	**317**
65% efficient	597	159	756	607	**149**	525	**231**
85% efficient	456	159	615	572	**43**	495	**120**
Propane furnace							
55% efficient	717	159	876	637	**239**	551	**325**
65% efficient	607	159	766	609	**157**	527	**239**
85% efficient	464	159	623	574	**49**	497	**126**

* Examples based on typical 1,500-square-foot home with 60.4 million BTUs of heating requirement per season.

Note: Furnace efficiency decreases with age. While newer furnaces have high efficiency ratings, older units were likely 65 percent or less efficient when new. Furnaces more than 10 years old will generally have efficiencies of 55 percent or less.

Finance on Your Iowa Power Bill

Amount Financed at 7% APR	Monthly Payments			
	12 Months	24 Months	36 Months	48 Months
$ 800	$ 69.22	$ 35.82	$24.70	$19.16
1,000	86.53	44.77	30.88	23.95
1,200	103.83	53.73	37.05	28.74
1,400	121.14	62.68	43.23	33.52
1,600	138.44	71.64	49.40	38.31
1,800	155.75	80.59	55.58	43.10
2,000	173.06	89.54	61.76	47.89
2,200	190.36	98.50	67.93	52.68
2,400	207.67	107.45	74.11	57.47
2,600	224.97	116.40	80.28	62.26
2,800	242.28	125.36	86.46	67.05
3,000	259.58	134.32	92.63	71.84

heat pumps, are an integral part of the Payback Plus concept so that customers who desire energy efficiency think of electric heating as an important element in that concept. Five major builders in the Des Moines market are now building Payback Plus homes, apartments, and condominiums exclusively, and it's expected the program will expand to other builders in future years. Iowa Power has made a strong commitment to cost containment through closing of local offices, mothballing of certain generating plants and an early retirement program which reduced work force by about one-sixth. These measures, which will provide rate stability for a number of years, will help keep electric heating very competitive in all markets for some years to come.

CASE 16 THE U.S. ICE CREAM INDUSTRY*

Production of ice cream in the United States remained essentially flat throughout the 1970–85 period. As of 1985 sales in gallons were below the 1975 production peak. Underneath this calm surface of leveling sales volume, however, was a highly competitive, very lucrative superpremium ice cream segment averaging over 15 percent annual growth. Trying to capitalize on the trail blazed by Häagen-Dazs, many local and national ice cream companies had launched new superpremium brands, aggressively pursued ways to gain wider distribution, and tried to capture the interest of consumers with a stream of new ice cream-related products. A number of major developments highlighted the 1980–85 period:

1980: • Two superpremium ice cream brands with foreign names, Frusen Glädjé and Alpen Zauber, were introduced and positioned as direct competitors to Häagen-Dazs; distribution of these brands was mainly in the northeastern states.

• A superpremium brand, Rich and Creamy, was introduced by Flavorich in southeastern markets; consumers in the southeast had not taken to brands with foreign names as had consumers in the northeast.

• Ben and Jerry's Homemade Ice Cream began distributing pint cartons of its superpremium ice cream through supermarkets in Vermont.

1981: • The use of the "mix-in" at Steve's Ice Cream in Somerville, Massachusetts, became a widely recognized success. (A mix-in was crushed candy or cookies, nuts, fruit, or granola, blended with ice cream to create new flavor combinations.) Steve's already unique flavors developed a reputation that spread to New York.

• Alpen Zauber brought legal action against Häagen-Dazs for threatening to withhold its ice cream from distributors who also sold Alpen Zauber.

1982: • Gelare Ice Cream Italiano became available through dipping stores on the West Coast as did other brands and variations of gelato (an intensely flavored ice cream with Italian origins).

• Swensen's (a 290-store ice cream parlor chain) began testing an "ultra-premium" ice cream and announced plans to open 50 to 60 new stores in the following year.

• Häagen-Dazs opened 90 dipping stores in 18 months (late 1981 to early 1983) for a total of 210 franchises nationwide; 55 more were under construction.

1983: • Frusen Glädjé launched a national franchise effort and opened more than 50 stores.

• Häagen-Dazs was purchased by the Pillsbury Company for $75 million. The company introduced six ice cream liqueur desserts using Hiram Walker liqueurs such as cognac and amaretto.

• Integrated Resources purchased Steve's Ice Cream for $4.5 million and announced plans to expand from 25 outlets to 525 over the next four years.

• Borden Foods signed an agreement to produce and distribute Gelare Ice Cream Italiano on a nationwide basis.

* Prepared by graduate researcher Miriam Aiken and Professor Arthur A. Thompson, Jr., The University of Alabama. Copyright © 1986 by Arthur A. Thompson, Jr.

- Dreyer's Grand Ice Cream (Oakland, California), a long-time competitor in the premium ice cream market, launched a line of superpremium chocolate ice creams flavored after European candies.
- Campbell Soup began testing a superpremium line under its Pepperidge Farms brand name and introduced an even richer ice cream through its Godiva Chocolatier subsidiary.
- Baskin-Robbins (a chain of 2,700 dipping stores) began test marketing some reduced calorie frozen dessert items.
- Pet Inc.'s Dairy Division introduced three premium ice cream lines—Great Ice Creams of the South, Cellini (an Italian type of ice cream), and Creams of England.
- Popsicle Industries paired with Nabisco to introduce a line of Oreo ice cream products.
- Zack's Famous Frozen Yogurt (New Orleans) and I Can't Believe It's Yogurt (Dallas) initiated rapid regional franchising campaigns.

1984:
- Land O'Lakes began distributing its Country Creamery brand ice cream in Minnesota and Wisconsin.
- Häagen-Dazs began distribution of Le Sorbet, a low-calorie frozen fruit dessert similar to sherbet. Castle & Cooke's Dole Fruit Sorbet was test-marketed in several states.
- Pillsbury acquired Sedutto, a New York-based superpremium ice cream franchise chain.
- Frusen Glädjé set up a joint venture with fashion designer Gloria Vanderbilt to manufacture and market a frozen tofu dessert under the designer's name, while Häagen-Dazs began distributing Tofu Time's Tofutti through supermarkets.
- Larry's Ice Cream headquartered in Florida began interstate franchising with hopes of opening stores throughout the Southeast.
- Swensen's purchased two ice cream plants from Foremost Dairies in exchange for 2.4 million shares of Swensen's stock, which gave Foremost a controlling interest in Swensen's. Foremost was named the exclusive distributor of Swensen's new line of ice cream packaged for retail sale in supermarkets.

1985:
- Dart & Kraft acquired Frusen Glädjé and also started to introduce its Breyer's premium ice cream line in western and midwestern markets.
- Swensen's reversed its deal of 1984 with Foremost Dairies and reacquired the 2.4 million shares of stock, saying that it had decided to focus its resources on its parlor and package ice cream business. Foremost, however, continued in its role as the sole supplier of packaged ice cream for supermarket sales under the Swensen's brand.
- Baskin-Robbins announced a $20 million renovation program for its 3,000 franchised ice cream parlors and a $3 million advertising campaign to boost its image with consumers. B-R also filed a suit against Pillsbury and Häagen-Dazs, alleging trademark infringement of its "Pralines 'N Cream" flavor name.

HISTORY OF THE ICE CREAM INDUSTRY

Ice cream evolved from chilled wines and other iced beverages. The earliest known commercial venture was in 1660 in Paris where water ices and possibly cream ices were manufactured and sold. The date of ice cream's arrival in America is uncertain, but in 1700, guests of Maryland's governor were treated to an ice cream-like delicacy. George Washington and Thomas Jefferson both enjoyed ice cream; Dolley Madison greatly increased the popularity of ice cream, serving it as a dessert at her husband's second inauguration in 1812. An American, Nancy Johnson, invented the hand-cranked rock salt-and-ice freezer in 1846. The first commercial ice cream plant in this country was established in 1851, and Bassett's Ice Cream, introduced in 1861 in Philadelphia, ranked as the oldest brand still on the U.S. market in 1985. The first ice cream sodas were created by a Philadelphia businessman who added carbonated beverages to ice cream. When these concoctions were banned from sale on Sunday, a syrup was substituted for the carbonation, and the "sundae" came into being. The ice cream cone was first made and sold at the St. Louis World's Fair in 1904 when rolled waffles were used as "dishes" for ice cream.

The commercial production of ice cream was facilitated by a number of mechanical and technical advances: the homogenizer (which gave ice cream its smooth texture), freezers, mechanical refrigeration, electric motors, sophisticated test equipment, packaging machines, insulation methods, and the motorized delivery van. Dramatic boosts in production resulted—from 5 million gallons in 1899 to 30 million gallons in 1909 to 150 million gallons in 1919.

Other products such as ice cream on sticks, bars, and other forms of ice cream, ice milk, and sherbet (known as novelties) originated in the 1920s. By 1922, a million Eskimo Pie ice cream bars were being sold each day. The Good Humor bar on a stick followed, and in 1924, the Individual Drinking Cup Company began manufacturing its Dixie Cup containers for individual servings of ice cream. The banana split also came into popularity. By the 1920s, ice cream was a "typical American food," sold everywhere from corner drugstores to the best restaurants. Ice cream gained in popularity during the Prohibition era as people joked that the "cold stuff" was a substitute for the "hard stuff."

Rationing of milk and sugar during World War II greatly curtailed ice cream production, but production snapped back quickly in 1946, and sales of all kinds of ice cream products averaged over 16 quarts per capita by 1950. Consumption of ice cream alone remained around the 15-quart per capita level from 1955 to 1985 (see Exhibit 1), with total production tracking population growth. When drugstores began replacing their soda fountains with more profitable drug and cosmetic products in the 1950s, the bulk of ice cream sales shifted to custard stands, mom-and-pop stores, fast-food outlets, and supermarkets. By 1960 half of all ice cream sales were through supermarkets. Most supermarket chains wasted little time in introducing their own private label brands of ice cream, most of which were lower in butterfat, artificially flavored, higher in air content, and cheaper in price.

MARKET SIZE AND GROWTH

The retail value of ice cream and related products in 1984 was about $6 billion. Production of ice cream alone in 1984 was estimated at 884 million gallons. Increases in ice cream production had slowed significantly over the past four decades:

Period	Average Annual Growth Rate
1940–49	7.4%
1950–59	2.6
1960–69	.9
1970–80	.9
1981	.3
1982	2.4
1983	3.5
1984	.2

The slowdown was attributed mainly to the fact that consumers were already eating as much ice cream as often as they wanted. Total consumption was not expected to fluctuate greatly for the remainder of the decade.

INDUSTRY STRUCTURE

The ice cream industry in the United States had historically been comprised of a multitude of regional and local producers. For a century commercial ice cream was made in local dairies, neighborhood stores, or restaurants for limited distribution in the immediate area. As improvements in refrigeration techniques made it possible to transport the product long distances, larger dairy corporations and bigger ice

Exhibit 1   Total U.S. Production of Ice Cream and Related Products Selected years 1909–1984

	All Types of Ice Cream and Ice Cream-Related Products		Ice Cream Only	
	Total Gallons (in 000s)	Per Capita Production (in quarts)	Total Gallons (in 000s)	Per Capita Production (in quarts)
1909	29,637	1.31	29,637	1.31
1919	152,982	5.86	152,982	5.86
1920	171,248	6.43	171,248	6.43
1930	255,439	8.30	255,439	8.30
1940	339,544	10.29	318,088	9.64
1950	634,768	16.79	554,351	14.66
1955	819,934	19.96	628,525	15.30
1960	969,004	21.54	699,605	15.55
1965	1,130,215	23.36	757,000	15.65
1970	1,193,144	23.42	761,732	14.95
1975	1,263,213	23.45	836,552	15.53
1980	1,225,223	21.58	829,798	14.61
1981	1,238,712	21.61	832,450	14.52
1982	1,248,552	21.54	852,072	14.70
1983	1,295,294	22.14	881,543	15.07
1984	1,303,031	22.07	883,525	14.96

Source: *The Latest Scoop,* 1985, p. 9.

Exhibit 2   Number of Employees, Number of Plants, and Capital
Expenditures in the Frozen Desserts Industry, 1972–1982

Year	Number of Employees	Number of Plants Producing Ice Cream and Related Products	Capital Expenditures for New Plant and Equipment ($000)
1972	21,100	1,451	$35,800
1973	21,300	1,330	29,200
1974	21,300	1,239	27,800
1975	20,200	1,167	37,200
1976	20,300	1,124	43,200
1977	19,100	1,095	56,800
1978	18,500	1,062	56,400
1979	19,900	990	46,300
1980	19,600	949	46,800
1981	20,100	895	41,800
1982	17,800	884	79,900

Source: *The Latest Scoop,* 1985 edition, International Association of Ice Cream Manufacturers, pp. 6, 7.

cream producers began squeezing out or absorbing the smaller companies; about 1,700 ice cream plants closed between 1957 and 1970. Most dairy producers viewed ice cream as a sideline of selling milk.

In 1970 there were 1,628 plants producing ice cream in the United States; by 1985 this number had declined to 853 (see Exhibit 2). Many of these were small local operations, but major producers operated large fully equipped plants. In early 1983 Dreyer's Grand Ice Cream installed $2.5 million worth of new equipment in its Los Angeles plant, making this facility capable of producing more than 5 million gallons of ice cream per year. Ben & Jerry's had a 23,000 square-foot facility which could process up to 820 gallons of ice cream an hour. Some manufacturers preferred to operate relatively small, geographically scattered plants, feeling that it allowed stricter quality control and delivery of a fresher product to surrounding localities. It was not uncommon for a major ice cream marketer to contract with local dairy producers to make and distribute its brand locally so as to cut down on steep transportation charges from its own more distant plants.

Häagen-Dazs and the Superpremium Phenomenon

Reuben Mattus of the Senator Ice Cream Company in the Bronx, New York, viewed the increasing market share of the best-selling brands with alarm as he watched his company's products being edged out in the supermarkets. In response, he developed a rich, high butterfat ice cream with all natural ingredients and began to market it in 1961 under the brand name Häagen-Dazs. Although Mattus was soon able to sell all the ice cream he could make, the initial success of the Häagen-Dazs brand produced no overnight move to superpremium quality on the part of either consumer or producers. However, the 1960s did bring a proliferation of ice cream shops featuring

Exhibit 3   Major Ice Cream Producers, Brands Produced and Geographic Areas of Sales Strength

Company	Brand(s) of Ice Cream	Area(s) of Sales Strength
Kraft	Frusen Glädjé,	New York, New England, California
	Breyers	Eastern United States
	Sealtest	Eastern United States
Borden	Lady Borden	Southeast, Southwest
	Borden	Southeast, Southwest
(distributor for)	Gelare	West Coast, New York
Ben & Jerry's Homemade, Inc.	Ben & Jerry's Homemade	New England
Integrated Resources	Steve's	Massachusetts, New England, Mid-Atlantic
Pillsbury	Häagen-Dazs	New England, Mid-Atlantic, California
Friendly Restaurants	Friendly's	New England, Mid-Atlantic, Midwest
Bluebell Dairies	Bluebell	Texas
Dreyer's Grand Ice Cream	Dreyer's/Edy's	Midwest, Western United States
Schrafft's Ice Cream Company	Schrafft's	New York
Larry's Ice Cream	Larry's	Florida, Georgia, South Carolina, California
Swensen's	Swensen's	South Florida, Texas, Arizona, California, New England
Baskin-Robbins	Baskin-Robbins	Nationwide
Pet, Inc.	Great Ice Creams of the South	Florida, Georgia, North Carolina, South Carolina, Tennessee, Virginia, West Virginia
Mayfield Dairies	Mayfield's	Georgia, Tennessee
Bassett's Ice Cream Company	Bassett's	Pennsylvania, New York

high-quality products. Many were local businesses, while others, such as Baskin-Robbins, expanded across the nation.

Consumer enthusiasm for superpremium ice cream products spurted dramatically in the 1980s. By 1985 superpremium brands accounted for about 20 percent of the $6 billion in annual retail sales of ice cream. Despite the market penetration efforts of such major manufacturers as Kraft and Borden, no brand of ice cream commanded more than 14 percent of the market in 1984. Regional manufacturers were still a prominent factor, and many had established very respectable niches in local and regional markets (see Exhibit 3).

THE MANUFACTURING PROCESS

Ice cream consisted largely of cream and milk combined with sweeteners and flavoring. Depending on the variety and brand, ice cream ingredients could include fresh or frozen cream, whole milk, skim milk, buttermilk, butter, powdered milk products, sugar, honey, corn sweetners, sucrose, dextrose, fructose, fresh eggs, frozen or powdered eggs, salt, colorings, and flavorings; fruit and nuts were added to some varieties. Many manufacturers included additives such as stabilizers and emulsifiers. Stabilizers were used to prevent the formation of ice crystals in the product; emulsifiers produced a smooth, creamy texture. Many types and brands of ice cream were made with "all natural" ingredients, however.

The ingredients were blended in proper proportions in a mixing tank. The mix then went to a pasteurizer where it was heated and held at a predetermined temperature for a specified period of time. Homogenization was the next step in the process; under pressure of 2,000 to 2,500 pounds per square inch, the milk fat globules were broken into still smaller particles to make the ice cream smooth. The mix was then quickly cooled to a temperature of about 40° F.

The actual freezing of the mix could be done in a continuous freezer, which used a steady flow of mix, or in a batch freezer, which made a single quantity of ice cream at a time. While it was being frozen, the ice cream was whipped and aerated by blades (called dashers) in the freezers. The aeration, known as overrun, was controlled in all states by requirements regarding the weight and content of total food solids of all products labeled as ice cream. Overrun, stated as a percentage of two times the actual air content, could be as great as 100 percent, meaning that the product would actually be 50 percent air. Too little overrun resulted in a rock-hard frozen mass, while too much made ice cream thin and foamy.

Federal standards required that ice cream contain a minimum of 10 percent milk fat and weigh not less than 4.5 pounds per gallon. Ice cream that contained at least 1.4 percent egg yolks could be labeled as french ice cream or frozen custard.

If a continuous freezer were used, ingredients such as fruit and nuts could be added after the freezing stage by a mechanical flavor feeder. Otherwise they were added along with the liquid flavors to the mix before freezing. In the filling operation the ice cream was packaged in gallon, half-gallon, quart, or pint containers or was used to fill molds to make ice cream bars or other novelties. Ice cream was stored in subzero temperatures to further harden the product. From the hardening room it was loaded into refrigerated trucks for distribution. Production levels varied throughout the year with May, June, July, and August being peak production months.

The costs of manufacturing ice cream varied greatly according to the quality of ingredients, the amount of air incorporated, and the size and efficiency of facilities. On the average, ingredients cost the ice cream processor 52.5 percent of revenues; processing and packaging, 30.9 percent; distribution expense, 9.5 percent; and administrative expense, 2.8 percent; pretax profit margins averaged 4.3 percent of revenue.

TYPES OF ICE CREAM

The difference between ice creams was directly related to the quality, richness, and freshness of the ingredients and the way they were blended and treated. The "economy" brands used a higher proportion of dried products, air, stabilizers, and emulsifiers and had a lower milk fat content. High-quality ice creams contained fresh whole products, less air, as much as 20 percent milk fat, and a minimum of additives.

Butterfat and overrun were commonly used as criteria to classify ice creams as ordinary, premium, or superpremium. Typical supermarket brands contained the minimum 10 to 12 percent of butterfat and 80 to 100 percent overrun. Premium brands had 12 to 16 percent butterfat and 40 to 60 percent overrun, while the superpremium varieties included 16 to 20 percent butterfat and less than 40 percent overrun. Many premium and superpremium brands used no additives or artificial flavors or colors. A four-ounce scoop of superpremium vanilla contained about 260 calories; the same scoop of premium had only 180 while an economy brand had 150 or fewer calories. However, as of 1985, there was little industry standardization in the classification and labeling of various types of ice cream; producers who wanted to promote their brands as "premium" or "superpremium" could ignore the butterfat and overrun criteria observed by most sellers.

Ice milk was similar to ice cream except that it contained 2 to 7 percent milkfat. Sherbet had to include 1 to 2 percent milkfat and weigh not less than six pounds per gallon. The best known sherbets were those flavored with fruit, but other flavors of sherbet appeared in the 1970s. Frozen yogurt and tofu desserts were similar to ice milk, but the milkfat was replaced, in part or in whole, with vegetable fat. The minimum fat content for these products was 6 percent. Gelato had less butterfat and overrun than ice cream and carried a much stronger flavor impact. Exhibit 4 shows total and per capita production figures for ice cream and related products for 1984.

About 4 percent of ice cream was produced in a soft-serve form; in 1984 this amounted to 38,586,000 gallons. The vast majority of soft serve desserts were actually ice milk; Dairy Queen and Tastee Freeze were the leading dispensers of soft-serve products.

Exhibit 4   Total and Per Capita Production of Ice Cream Products, 1984

	1984	Percent Change from 1983
Total—ice cream and related products	1,303,031,000 gallons	+0.60
Per capita production	22.07 quarts	−0.32
Ice cream (hard and soft)	883,525,000 gallons	+0.22
Per capita production	14.96 quarts	−0.73
Ice milk (hard and soft)	299,624,000 gallons	+1.60
Per capita production	5.08 quarts	+0.79
Sherbet (hard and soft)	47,292,000 gallons	−0.92
Per capita production	0.80 quarts	−1.84
Water ices (hard)	41,613,000 gallons	+5.55
Per capita production	0.70 quarts	+4.60
Frozen yogurt and tofu desserts (hard and soft)	8,236,000 gallons	−18.34
Per capita production	0.14 quarts	−19.03

Source: *The Latest Scoop*, 1985, p. 4.

From a pricing perspective, the ice creams available in the United States in 1985 could be characterized as luxury-priced, superpremium, premium, standard-priced, and economy-priced. The luxury priced ice creams included such specialty brands as Godiva ($3.75 per pint) and Borden's Gelare ($2.49 per pint). In the superpremium group (the leaders being Häagen-Dazs, Frusen Glädjé, Ben & Jerry's Homemade) prices ranged from $1.69 per pint to $2.19. Most of the best selling ice creams (Breyers, Dreyer's/Edy's, Sealtest) fit into the premium category and retailed from $2.59 up to $3.49 per half-gallon in 1985. Where the luxury and superpremium priced ice creams were almost always sold in round pint cartons, premium and lower priced types were usually sold by half-gallons; 65 percent of all packaged ice cream sold was in half-gallon containers. Standard-priced ice creams (usually produced by local dairies) carried prices of $1.99 to $2.59 and included some premium-quality products at the lower price. The economy-priced category consisted of store brands and inexpensive local ice creams and were priced from $.99 to $1.99. It was not uncommon though for some premium-quality products (based on butterfat and overrun criteria) to be sold at superpremium prices; a few premium ice creams were marketed at popular prices.

DISTRIBUTION

While the majority of ice cream was sold in supermarkets, consumer desires for elaborate ice cream desserts and a variety of unusual flavors spawned numerous parlor franchise outlets, and dipping stores that featured cones, sundaes, sodas, milk shakes, ice cream dessert specialties, and hand-packed ice cream. As of 1985 there were 31 different franchisors operating almost 6,200 retail ice cream outlets. The number of stores, as well as store sales, had increased steadily since 1980:

Year	Number of Retail Outlets	Total Sales	Average Sales per Retail Outlet
1981	5,427	$793,518,000	$146,217
1982	5,547	856,466,000	154,402
1983	5,847	917,326,000	156,888
1984	6,193	998,714,000	161,265

Source: *Restaurant Business.*

Most ice cream companies who contracted out the manufacture of their brands to local dairies also relied on them to deliver their products to supermarkets and keep the freezer cases stocked with the most popular flavors. Other companies who produced their own ice cream, such as Ben & Jerry's and Häagen-Dazs, maintained a network of regional distributors to deliver their products to supermarkets. However, Dreyer's Grand Ice Cream operated its own plant-to-store delivery system in an effort to attain better control over product freshness and to secure better space in supermarket freezer displays.

Exhibit 5   Estimated Cost Structure for the Ice Cream Industry, 1985

	Estimated Cost Composition for Half-Gallon of Private Label	Estimated Cost Composition for Half-Gallon of Premium Ice Cream
1. Manufacturing costs:		
Raw materials	$0.71	$0.86
Processing and packing	.42	.51
Distribution expense	.13	.15
Administrative expense	.03	.05
Total manufacturing costs	1.29	1.58
2. Manufacturer's operating profit	.06	.07
3. Manufacturer's price to distributor	1.35	1.65
4. Average distributor mark-up over manufacturer's price	.35	1.17
5. Average distributor price to retailer	1.70	2.82
6. Average retail markup over cost	.49	.77
7. Average price to consumer at retail	$2.19	$3.59

Source: Compiled by the researcher from a variety of documents and field interviews.

INDUSTRY COST STRUCTURE

Raw materials comprised over half of the ice cream processor's costs. Cartons and labels were generally purchased from outside suppliers. The manufacturing cost of goods sold ran about 80 percent of the processor's selling price, although this varied according to product category (superpremium, premium, and so on). Producers tried to achieve about a 10 percent operating profit margin overall. Exhibit 5 shows the chain of costs from the manufacturer through to the price paid by shoppers in supermarkets.

For private-label ice cream the markups at the distributor levels were between 25 and 30 percent; distributors received much higher margins (up to 70 percent) on premium and superpremium brands. Margins at retail were similar for all types of ice cream, usually about 28 percent.

ICE CREAM CONSUMERS

Nine out of 10 households purchased ice cream, and 83 percent of the country's households bought it for home consumption. New Englanders consumed 23.1 quarts of ice cream and related products per person in 1984, while the rest of the nation averaged about 15 quarts per capita.

The maturation of the baby boom generation resulted in a large adult population for whom ice cream seemed to be the perfect snack or dessert. Adults ate three times as much ice cream as children, and men consumed more than women. Adults were more prone to purchase premium and superpremium brands, frequently equating price with quality and taking the superiority of higher-priced items for granted. The pint and single-serving containers were very popular with one- and two-person households.

Despite the apparent contradiction, many health-conscious people did not exclude rich ice cream from their diets. People might exercise more and eat more nutritiously, but they also tended to splurge more. With desserts instant gratification was often the goal; calories and cholesterol didn't count. Also, because of ice cream's "wholesome" image, some people viewed it as an appropriate reward for exercise or dieting. This was especially true for frozen yogurt and tofu desserts (which might contain little or no sugar, butterfat, or cholesterol) and for ice cream brands which contained no artificial ingredients.

It was also hypothesized that an ailing economy made people turn to small luxuries like ice cream. Purchases of premium and superpremium ice cream crossed economic and cultural lines, and there was little data on the makeup of these buyers or on brand loyalty. Foreign mystique was readily available by purchasing Frusen Glädjé (Swedish for "frozen delight"), Alpen Zauber (German for "alpine magic") or Häagen-Dazs (meaningless words in English or Danish), all of which were headquartered in New York.

Consumer willingness to try new flavors and ice cream creations often seemed unlimited. However, vanilla was still the preferred flavor of more than 30 percent of consumers. The most popular flavors are shown in Exhibit 6. Pralines 'N Cream (vanilla laced with praline-covered pecans and caramel) was voted the all-time favorite

---

Exhibit 6   Most Popular Ice Cream Flavors in the United States

	Flavors	Percent of Total Sales
1.	Vanilla	31.02%
2.	Chocolate	8.81
3.	Neopolitan	6.19
4.	Vanilla Fudge	4.16
5.	Cookies 'n Cream	3.89
6.	Butter Pecan	3.83
7.	Chocolate Chip	3.60
8.	Strawberry	3.53
9.	Rocky Road	1.31
10.	Tin Roof Sundae	1.26
11.	Cherry	1.26
12.	French Vanilla	1.21
13.	Praline Pecan	0.91
14.	Heavenly Hash	0.91
15.	Chocolate Almond	0.85

Source: *The Latest Scoop*, 1985, p. 28.

among Baskin-Robbins's more than 500 flavors. Variations of chocolate were in the 2nd through 10th positions. Several companies, including Dreyer's and Baskin-Robbins, had developed new lines of chocolate and chocolate-combination flavors.

Food critics proclaimed various brands of ice cream as best. Howard Johnson's ice cream, Swensen's, Häagen-Dazs, and Baskin-Robbins all had won assorted taste tests. In 1981, a test of 28 brands of vanilla was conducted by nine food experts. Häagen-Dazs received a second-place rating, while Alpen Zauber, Baskin-Robbins, Louis Sherry, and Dreyer's were far down the list. First place went to the Giant Food chain's economy vanilla "Kiss," which sold for $1.29 a half-gallon and contained preservatives, stabilizers, fillers, artificial color, and the legal minimum of 10 percent butterfat. Several guides for ice cream gourmets had appeared on the market; one was titled *The Very Best Ice Cream And Where To Find It.*

Consumer Reports rated Schrafft's, a superpremium ice cream made in Pelham, New York, "number one" out of about 30 brands tested. Expert tasters judged the ice cream against standards of excellence used by the American Dairy Science Association. Various brands of chocolate and vanilla ice cream were evaluated for firm body and a smooth velvety texture free from graininess or perceptible ice crystals. Appearance and flavor balance were other criteria. The vanilla ice creams produced by Schrafft's, Friendly, and Howard Johnson's were all rated "excellent." Judged "very good" were Baskin-Robbins, Louis Sherry, Sealtest, Dreyer's, and Breyers. Häagen-Dazs, Borden, and the house brand products of Safeway, A&P, and Kroger supermarkets received "good" ratings. None of the chocolate ice creams were rated excellent by *Consumer Reports;* Schrafft's, Friendly, Baskin-Robbins, Howard Johnson's, Dreyer's, Häagen-Dazs, and several others received a very good ranking. Lack of flavor, lack of flavor balance, and icy texture were among the defects noted. The panel of tasters asserted that the "all-natural" compositions of Breyers and Häagen-Dazs could account for many of the defects of these products; the lack of additives contributed to a deterioration of flavor and texture.

SUBSTITUTES

Ice milk and sherbet were relatively well-established substitutes for ice cream and had stable consumption patterns. Frozen yogurt and tofu-based desserts products gained more recognition in the early 1980s. Several regional chains emerged to sell the low-calorie, low-fat, frozen yogurt creations: I Can't Believe It's Yogurt of Dallas, Zack's Famous Frozen Yogurt of New Orleans, and The Country's Best Yogurt (TCBY) of Little Rock. The products were usually produced as soft-serve and in a wide range of flavors. Frozen yogurt outlets were usually patterned after ice cream parlors and dipping stores and often sold a tofu-based dessert as well. Zack's had 40 stores while The Country's Best Yogurt sold 224 franchises in less than two years after the company's formation. Independent yogurt stores appeared in many areas of the country, and many restaurants and delicatessens installed frozen yogurt machines.

Of the large yogurt producers, only TCBY was publicly owned. Many of the other producers did not report their sales volumes, so the total market for frozen yogurt could not be exactly determined. 1985 sales in California alone were 3.5 million gallons. Total sales for 1984 were estimated at 8 million gallons, worth about $125 million at retail. There were 57 plants producing mix for frozen yogurt and tofu products.

Development of the market for frozen yogurt varied according to geographic regions. Frozen yogurt was a familiar treat in California, Texas, and New York. Annual growth rates in these states ranged from 20 to 30 percent. More dramatic growth was witnessed in the rapidly developing markets in the southeastern states. One industry source estimated annual growth in the region at more than 30 percent. In other areas of the United States, frozen yogurt was not popular at all. The markets in the midwest and plains states were essentially undeveloped.

The best known of the tofu mixtures was Tofutti, a nondairy, bean curd–based dessert made by the Brooklyn-based company Tofu Time. Tofu Time experienced more than 600 percent growth in sales from 1983 to 1984; its 1985 sales were expected to top $4 million, an increase of 68 percent over the previous year. Tofutti had no butterfat or cholesterol, contained no dairy products, (which made it suitable for the 30 million lactose-intolerant Americans), and had only half the calories of ice cream. To gain acceptance in supermarkets for Tofutti, Tofu Time had entered into an agreement for Häagen-Dazs to act as distributor for its hard-serve product in the grocery segment. Tofutti retailed for about $2.50 per pint, and its packaging cultivated the same superpremium image as Häagen-Dazs. Tofu Time had opened its own dipping stores in New York, and Tofutti was also sold soft-serve through more than 300 Häagen-Dazs franchise stores. Reduced calorie tofu-based frozen desserts had appeared, and in late 1984 Frusen Glädjè teamed with fashion designer Gloria Vanderbilt to manufacture and market Gloria Vanderbilt's Glace Tofu Frozen Dessert.

A relative newcomer to the ice cream market was sorbet, a low-calorie frozen dessert with an intense fruit flavor and a creamier texture than regular sherbet. Castle & Cooke's Dole Fruit Sorbet and Häagen-Dazs's Le Sorbet were both introduced in 1984. Both companies emphasized the French origins of sorbet and the "all natural" compositions of their products. The round pint containers were similar to those for superpremium ice cream, and each pint sold for about $1.99. Sorbet contained no dairy products; Le Sorbet contained only fruit, water, and sugar and was available in such flavors as raspberry, mango, lemon, strawberry, cantelope, cassis, and passion fruit.

A multitude of new pudding and juice bars from companies such as General Foods, Castle & Cooke, and Welch's had appeared in the 1980s to compete with Eskimo Pies, Good Humor bars, and Popsicles. Many of the new products bore labels proclaiming "all natural" and describing the nutrients contained in the bars. Popsicle, Good Humor, and other companies known for ice cream novelties responded with new shapes and flavors of their own. The pudding bars and juice bars typically carried a higher price than traditional ice-cream-on-a-stick products.

Ice Cream Novelties

The ice cream novelty category included bars, sticks, cones, sandwiches, and parfaits made from ice cream, ice milk, and sherbet. Novelties typically accounted for between 20 and 25 percent of total ice cream sales.

In trying to capture more of the adult market, many manufacturers had begun to make high-quality, richer novelties. Often targeted at one- or two-person households, the premium or superpremium novelties were made larger and were sold in packages of fewer units. Typical of this trend was the Chipwich (ice cream sandwiched between two chocolate chip cookies and rimmed in chocolate morsels), which sold for about $1. Dove Bar International had a single product: a six-ounce ice cream bar with four ounces of superpremium ice cream hand-dipped in dark bittersweet chocolate; a single bar sold for $1.75 to $2, and a grocery store two-pack retailed for $2.99. Created by a candy maker, the Dove Bar was described by one ice cream expert as two ounces of "very fine candy—the ice cream is really the chaser."

COMPETITIVE RIVALRY

Rivalry among the ice cream processors revolved mainly around price, quality (or at least the image of quality), and variety. There was no clear price leader in any of the categories, although prices on the premium-priced, standard-priced, and econ-omy-priced brands were usually fairly close within their respective categories. Regional brands in these categories tended to be priced slightly below national brands. Price was seldom featured in the marketing of superpremium and luxury-priced ice creams, but supermarkets did run shopper discount specials on ice cream.

Most manufacturers chose to emphasize the natural, fine quality ingredients used and the superiority of the product that resulted. Quality claims based on low overrun and high butterfat seemed to reach an ultimate with Borden's Gelare; the product had no air and 18 percent butterfat, making it so hard that it had to sit out of the freezer for 15 minutes before it could be spooned from the carton. Foreign names or names that already carried prestige, such as Godiva, were used to further enhance the image of superpremium and luxury ice cream. New exotic flavors appeared frequently, and many dipping stores featured a variety of "mix-ins" or "add-ons" to differentiate their frozen creations.

With the proliferation of brands and flavors, the distribution battle became more heated. Competition for limited shelf space in the supermarket meant that advertising played an increasingly important role in attracting distributors as well as consumers. Traditionally ice cream marketers shunned advertising. Reuben Mattus was very proud of the fact that Häagen-Dazs's early success was due to word-of-mouth advertising. In 1981 the ice cream industry spent a total of $5 million on national advertising. This had risen to $14 million by 1983, but on the average, ice cream manufacturers spent less than 1 percent of sales on advertising.

In 1984, Häagen-Dazs's ads appeared in *Essence* and *Ebony* to reach the black market, while Spanish language advertising was used in New York and Miami. A 1984 Frusen Glädjé campaign challenged: "You'll like Frusen Glädjé ice cream better than Häagen-Dazs or we'll refund your money." Borden's Gelare targeted Häagen-Dazs with print ads that showed Gelare outweighing its competitor on a scale. Schrafft's offered incentives to retailers on a regular basis and also helped supermarkets with their product displays. Some sellers used newspaper ads and couponing to attract consumers.

Fancier cartons appeared as manufacturer's sought to catch the consumer's eye.

Kraft chose a round black carton for its introduction of Breyers ice cream into new western and midwestern markets.

Profiles of seven large ice cream manufacturers and of TCBY Yogurt follow. Exhibit 7 contains comparative financial data for these companies.

FRIENDLY ICE CREAM/HERSHEY FOODS CORP.

In 1985 Hershey Foods was a major producer of chocolate and confectionery products and pasta products. The company was best known for its Hershey candy bars. The company's management sometimes used a quote by founder Milton S. Hershey to summarize the approach to consumers: "Give them quality and value—that's the best kind of advertising there is."

Hershey purchased the Friendly Ice Cream Corporation in 1979. Friendly's was founded in 1935 in Springfield, Massachusetts, as one small store with a single ice cream freezer. At the end of 1984 there were 707 Friendly Restaurants in 16 states, primarily in the northeast and midwest. Friendly's sales in 1984 were $427 million; the Friendly division accounted for 23 percent of Hershey Foods' total revenues and for 17 percent of consolidated operating profits. Friendly's had both a strong mealtime menu and a strong ice cream specialty and was one of the largest nonfranchised chains. Most of the units were freestanding, but since about 1980, the company had begun opening units in shopping malls. During this time many of the older units were refurbished, and menu offerings were standardized.

Friendly increased advertising and promotional activities significantly in 1983 in response to greater competition in the fast-food industry. New ice cream desserts, such as pies and rolls, had recently been introduced, and Hershey candy had been incorporated into sundaes and parfait selections. Modest price increases were instituted in 1984. Ice cream represented about 40 percent of Friendly's business; 8 to 10 percent of ice cream was sold on a take-home basis.

Friendly did not discuss its ice cream's content of butterfat or other ingredients, stating only that the company made an ice cream that appealed to a broad range of tastes and that was affordable by the average family.

Friendly's expansion had taken it as far west as Illinois and as far south as Virginia. By the end of 1986, however, Friendly hoped to have 15 to 20 sites in the Orlando, Florida, area. Plans called for continued development of stores in the mid-Atlantic area and in the midwest, but management viewed the southeast region as a prime area for consideration. Friendly had recently acquired more than 30 properties from Sambo's, Howard Johnson Restaurants, and Roy Rogers Family Restaurants and converted them to Friendly restaurants; company plans included more such acquisitions. Friendly's also operated a small number of franchised ice cream shops called O'goodies, where customers created their own ice cream desserts.

DART & KRAFT, INC.

Dart & Kraft, Inc., in 1984 had consolidated net sales of $9.8 billion and net income of $456 million. The company was structured into four main divisions: (1) Kraft,

Exhibit 7 Comparative Financial Performances of Selected Producers of Ice Cream and Yogurt, 1979–1984 All Dollar Figures in Thousands

Company	1979	1980	1981	1982	1983	1984
Swensen's Inc.						
Franchising revenues and royalties	$ 4,963	$ 4,587	$ 8,313	$ 12,377	$ 14,929	$ 11,415
Net loss	(226)	(2,788)	(3,013)	(1,680)	(285)	(1,790)
Total assets	2,229	4,969	6,816	11,282	11,529	18,932
Shareholders' equity	11	404	149	1,585	5,481	7,491
Total sales at retail	51,904	64,615	79,615	88,575	92,050	99,600
Number of stores open	255	292	316	340	357	387
Hershey Foods Corp.						
Net sales	$1,161,295	$1,335,289	$ 4,451,151	$1,565,736	$1,706,105	$1,892,506
Operating profit	125,177	143,154	173,012	186,566	207,069	229,804
Net after-tax income	53,504	62,055	80,362	94,168	100,166	108,682
Total assets	607,199	684,472	829,447	904,754	983,944	1,122,567
Shareholders' equity	320,730	361,550	469,664	532,495	596,037	660,928
Friendly Restaurants division only						
Net sales		$ 272,297	$ 302,908	$ 335,836	$ 383,543	$ 427,122
Income from operations		25,567	29,309	34,279	39,428	41,770
Assets		219,196	223,265	234,860	251,781	273,356
Baskin–Robbins Ice Cream Co.*						
Revenues					$ 125,173	$ 145,978
Operating profit					19,589	25,046
Net after-tax income					10,446	13,396
Total assets					58,607	69,362
Shareholders' equity					36,502	43,164
Borden, Inc.						
Net sales	$4,312,533	$4,595,795	$ 4,415,174	$4,111,277	$4,264,771	$4,568,018
Operating profit	274,924	300,043	305,043	319,860	403,620	416,662
Net after-tax income	134,015	147,485	159,939	165,855	189,069	191,407
Total assets	2,468,860	2,649,644	2,508,816	2,589,702	2,720,471	2,884,127
Shareholders' equity	1,177,940	1,227,284	1,318,755	134,333	1,391,039	1,367,944

Dart & Kraft, Inc.

Net sales	$9,411,000	$10,211,000	$9,974,000	$9,714,000	$9,759,000
Operating profit	694,000	752,000	748,000	817,000	848,000
Net after-tax income	383,000	348,000	350,000	435,000	456,000
Total assets	4,650,000	5,054,000	5,134,000	5,418,000	5,285,000
Shareholders' equity	2,621,000	2,718,000	2,774,000	2,923,000	2,598,000

Food products division (Kraft) only

Net sales			$7,041,100	$6,660,400	$6,837,000
Operating profit			488,500	553,500	615,400
Assets			2,364,800	2,131,800	2,316,500

Pillsbury Company†

Net sales	$2,166,000	$3,032,000	$3,301,700	$3,685,900	$4,172,300
Operating profit	186,800	250,000	267,500	269,600	347,900
Net after-tax income	104,700	104,700	119,600	138,900	169,800
Total assets	1,804,500	1,983,700	2,174,500	2,366,600	2,608,300
Shareholders' equity	577,700	664,500	747,200	956,400	1,046,200

TCBY Enterprises

Franchising revenue			$ 406	$ 622	$ 1,989
Sales revenue			1,122	1,711	5,419
Operating profit			N/A	265	2,124
Net after-tax income			226	161	1,011
Total assets			845	4,594	8,136
Shareholders' equity			N/A	469	5,635
Systemwide sales			1,775	5,219	11,462
Number of stores open			18	41	102

Ben and Jerry's Homemade Inc.

Net sales	$ 374	$ 615	$ 968	$ 1,815	$ 4,010
Operating profit	40	33	16	97	297
Net after-tax income (loss)	33	29	(56)	57	213
Total assets	92	193	295	509	3,894
Shareholders' equity	48	77	21	154	1,068

* Privately held company; financial data from 1984, 1979–82 not available.
† Pillsbury's fiscal year ends May 31.
Source: Annual reports and 10-K reports.

Inc., the sole component of the Food Products Division; (2) Direct Selling—Tupperware; (3) Consumer Products—Duracell (batteries), West Bend (appliances), Health Care, and Kitchenaid; and (4) Commercial Products—Hobart Commercial equipment and Wilsonart brand decorative laminates. Food products accounted for 70 percent of 1984 corporate sales; the division's operating profit was $615.4 million, an 11 percent increase from 1983.

Kraft's mission was to become the world's leading food company. It marketed more than 3,300 food products under some 850 trademarks to consumers in about 130 nations. Most of the products fit into five broad categories:

1. Natural and process cheese.
2. Ice cream and other frozen desserts.
3. Cultured dairy products including cottage cheese, sour cream, and yogurt.
4. Vegetable oil–based products including salad dressings, mayonnaise, margarine, edible oils, and shortening.
5. Other grocery products including frozen foods, confections, condiments, juices, and other foods.

Ice cream accounted for less than 5 percent of the sales of Kraft's Food Products Division. Kraft's ice cream products were marketed under the brand names Sealtest, Breyers, and the newly acquired (1985) Frusen Glädjé brand. Sealtest and Breyers were widely available in states east of the Mississippi River. Although sales of Sealtest ice cream were down somewhat in 1984, Breyers continued to perform well, and Kraft held its position as the market share leader of ice cream in supermarkets. Breyers was one of the best selling premium ice creams in the country, and Kraft continued to extend the market coverage for this brand by initiating distribution in some western and midwestern areas. New packaging and extensive ad campaigns were developed for Breyers market expansion. Breyers was promoted as "all natural" and was positioned as a top-of-the-line brand in the premium ice cream segment. In the 1980s Breyers began to replace the Sealtest brand in many supermarket freezers.

Frusen Glädjé was the number-two-selling superpremium ice cream brand in the United States behind Häagen-Dazs at the time of its acquisition. Kraft management anticipated that the addition of Frusen Glädjé would help the dairy group achieve nationwide distribution of its ice cream and provide Kraft the means to gain a solid position in the superpremium segment. Kraft acquired the company's trademark, product formula, and pint retail business (90 percent of Frusen Glädjé's sales).

In its 1984 advertising, Frusen Glädjé did direct comparisons with Häagen-Dazs, urging consumers to compare the two brands. Kraft continued this approach with an advertising blitz including TV spots. Taste samples of Frusen Glädjé were offered in supermarkets as Kraft continued to expand distribution of the brand. Frusen Glädjé subsequently joined forces with Sunshine Biscuits to produce a line of cookies-and-cream products featuring Hydrox cookies. Frusen Glädjé also manufactured and marketed Gloria Vanderbilt's Glace Tofu frozen dessert. This product was sold through Frusen Glädjé's 50 or so dipping stores as well as through supermarkets. Frusen Glädjé also introduced a sorbet dessert in 1985.

PILLSBURY/HÄAGEN-DAZS ICE CREAM

The Pillsbury Company was a diversified international food and restaurant organization with 1984 sales of $4.6 billion. The company's first flour mill was built in 1869, and since then Pillsbury had grown through internal development and acquisitions to be a leading manufacturer of consumer packaged goods including dessert mixes, canned and frozen vegetables, refrigerated bread products, frozen pizza, frozen fish, and superpremium ice cream. The company was the largest diversified restaurant operator in the world in 1984, owning the Burger King Corporation, Steak & Ale Restaurants, and Bennigan's. Over the past 10 years its major acquisitions included Totino's Fine Foods, Green Giant Company, Häagen-Dazs, Van de Kamp's, and Diversifoods, Inc.

Pillsbury's Restaurants Group had sales of $2.05 billion (up 16 percent) and operating profit equal to $220 million (up 17 percent) in 1985. Included in the Restaurants Group were the more than 300 Häagen-Dazs Shoppes. Some of these shops were dipping stores, while others were larger dessert shop operations. Pillsbury purchased Häagen-Dazs in mid-1983 for $75 million. A family-held company for 23 years, Häagen-Dazs had annual sales of $115 million (excluding revenues from its franchised shops) at the time of the purchase. The annual growth rate for Häagen-Dazs then was between 25 and 35 percent, and the company held a 25 percent share of the superpremium ice cream market. During its first year with Pillsbury, physical volume for Häagen-Dazs increased 22 percent. Volume rose another 20 percent in fiscal 1985, despite a slight decline in total U.S. ice cream consumption. Häagen-Dazs sales were $130 million in 1985, up 34 percent over 1984. The opening of a second plant in 1985 increased capacity by 50 percent, allowing greater penetration of the markets in the western United States.

In 1984 Häagen-Dazs became the national distributor of Tofutti and Le Sorbet, as well as launching a line of Sorbet and Cream products. Sorbet and Cream combined fruit ices with Häagen-Dazs vanilla ice cream. Through a joint venture with Suntory of Japan, Häagen-Dazs ice cream became available through some Tokyo supermarkets, and Häagen-Dazs had dipping stores in Japan, Singapore, Hong Kong, and Korea. Häagen-Dazs planned to continue with rapid geographic and product expansion.

BORDEN, INC.

Borden, Inc., operated in two major industry segments: foods and chemicals. Net sales in 1984 were $4.6 billion; its Consumer Products Division accounted for 64 percent of sales and 53 percent of operating income in 1984.

Borden's food segment included a wide variety of dairy products, instant beverages, snack foods, confections jams and jellies, pasta, and seafood. Lady Borden was the company's premium brand of ice cream. Lady Borden had been a market leader in the premium category for many years and showed strong sales gains in 1982 due to richer formulas, new flavors, and new packaging. Pudding bars and fruit bars were first introduced in 1982 under the Borden label.

In 1983 Borden expanded its ice cream line by signing an agreement to produce and distribute Gelare, a superpremium all natural ice cream with 18 percent butterfat content and no overrun. The product had Italian origins and had become popular on the West Coast two and a half years before the licensing agreement. Borden hoped to capitalize on the "ice cream awareness" created by other superpremium brands and to entice some customers away from Häagen-Dazs and Frusen Glädjé.

BASKIN-ROBBINS ICE CREAM COMPANY

The Baskin-Robbins ice cream business was founded in 1946 by Burton Baskin and Irvine Robbins and was engaged in the development and manufacture of ice cream products, operation of retail ice cream stores, and granting of franchises for such stores. Allied-Lyons North America Corporation owned 100 percent of the shares of stock of Baskin-Robbins.

Retail sales for all 3,300 Baskin-Robbins stores were $470 million in 1984, $455 million in 1983, and $423 million in 1982. About one third of Baskin-Robbins 3,300 stores were company-owned, and two thirds were franchised. Baskin-Robbins's revenue from product sales to its 3,300 retail stores in 1984 were $152 million; 1983 sales were $146 million, up from $125.1 million in 1982. The parent derived revenue from product sales to its retail franchises and by charging each of its franchised factories a license fee. Baskin-Robbins charged its franchisees a royalty on ice cream rather than on gross sales. For many years Baskin-Robbins had viewed the interest in super-rich ice cream as a passing fad; their own product was classified as premium because of its butterfat content and 50 percent overrun. In 1982 the company chose to market a low-fat frozen dessert in hopes of appealing to health-conscious consumers. Management also decided against expanding its take-out stores into the higher-cost, sit-down parlors as some competitors had done.

A 1984 Tastes of America survey voted Baskin-Robbins the favorite fast-food chain for the second consecutive year. In 1985 the company implemented a multiphase program to update its image with consumers. The program included a $20 million renovation of its more than 3,000 franchised ice cream parlors, a $3 million advertising program that included network TV, and increased investment in new products. Baskin-Robbins president Robert Marley explained, "There is so much excitement in the ice cream industry today, and we are not getting our fair share. We've been silent too long. We have excellent product awareness and product preference. We just have to capitalize on it."

To entice more adults and professionals into its stores, Baskin-Robbins replaced its pink, white, and brown decor with new store graphics, new furniture, increased seating capacity, and softer color tones. For the first time Baskin-Robbins stores differed in appearance as the company allowed franchise owners to tailor their store decors to fit in with shopping centers or malls.

Advertising, sales promotions, and local publicity efforts reminded consumers that Baskin-Robbins offered more flavors and styles of ice cream to "families of all ages." Baskin-Robbins had a rotating lineup of 31 flavors with a repertoire of more than 500 flavors. Its ice cream products included American style, French-style with a higher butterfat content, sherbets, sorbets, ices, French-style mousse, and Special Diet frozen desserts.

In 1985 Baskin-Robbins filed suit against Pillsbury and Häagen-Dazs for trademark infringement of its "Pralines 'N Cream" flavor name. Häagen-Dazs ads had stated that "Pralines & Cream" was exclusively available at its shops. In keeping with its new aggressive stance, Baskin-Robbins had plans to file suit against other companies for similar infringements. The company also planned capacity expansions and additional efforts in new product development.

SWENSEN'S, INC.

Swensen's, Inc., through its wholly owned subsidiaries Swensen's Manufacturing Company, Swensen's Distributing Company, and Swensen's Ice Cream Company (Australia) Pty. Ltd., operated and franchised more than 380 ice cream parlors and dip shoppes through the United States and 14 foreign countries. In 1984 the company had entered into the packaged ice cream business and marketed its Swensen's Old Fashioned label ice cream products to supermarkets and convenience stores in Arizona. Plans for national distribution through supermarkets were contingent on consumer response.

Unlike many of its competitors, Swensen's ice cream was made in 20- or 40-quart batches by the operator of each store, either on the premises or in a nearby location. This method allowed each store to make small quantities of a wide variety of flavors, thus ensuring freshness. The company had recipes for 175 flavors with each store offering between 16 and 45 flavors at any one time. A new menu format was developed in 1983, and in the following year Swensen's Supreme, a superpremium ice cream, was offered. Swensen's stores ranged from ice-cream-only shops with no seats, to ice-cream-only stores with 25 to 30 seats, to limited-menu restaurants with 80 to 100 seats. These restaurants served sandwiches, soups, salads, and a full complement of ice cream and fountain items. Swensen's planned to have 390 stores in operation by the end of 1984. Sixteen new stores were to be located in other countries. Total sales for all Swensen's stores in 1984 were $99.6 million, up from $92 million in 1983 and $88.6 million in 1982. Management estimated that about 60 percent of Swensen's system sales were from the retail sales of its superpremium ice cream.

In August 1984 Swensen's acquired two ice cream manufacturing facilities from Foremost Dairies, Inc. Swensen's planned to maintain close control over its pints and half-gallons of ice cream for supermarket sale by owning and staffing these dairies. The "theme song" for introducing the packaged ice cream was "You Made Me Love You."

In late 1984 Swensen's president, E. C. Schoenleb, resigned following a dispute with the company's directors who viewed his plans to revamp Swensen's menus and decor as overaggressive. Schoenleb had joined the company in 1981 and was credited with helping to reverse the company's loss record. Losses in 1980 were $2.8 million and $3 million the following year. By February of 1985 Swensen's had reached an agreement to transfer ownership of the manufacturing facilities back to Foremost Dairies. The company stated that it decided to focus its resources on its parlor and packaged ice cream business. Foremost would continue to manufacture the pints and half-gallons of ice cream sold under Swensen's name in the supermarkets.

Over the past several years Swensen's new ice cream and food items had included the richer ice cream called Swensen's Supreme (16–18 percent butterfat), a "walkaway" sundae in a freshly baked, waffle batter cone, croissant sandwiches, new soups, and gourmet salads.

TCBY ENTERPRISES (THE COUNTRY'S BEST YOGURT)

TCBY franchised and owned soft serve frozen yogurt stores. A majority of the company-owned and franchised stores operated under the name "This Can't Be Yogurt!!" until December 1985, when the settlement of a trademark infringement lawsuit with "I Can't Believe It's Yogurt" of Dallas required TCBY to change its name. Afterward known as "TCBY" Yogurt!! and "The Country's Best Yogurt," the stores sold more than 20 flavors of yogurt in various ways as a dessert, snack, or light meal item. As of March 1985 there were 142 franchise stores and 19 company stores open or under construction with 72 more planned. TCBY intended to open 200 more shops each year in 1986 and 1987. TCBY was the only publicly owned franchisor of yogurt shops. Average annual net income per store was $22,500, about 15 percent of the average annual store sales of $150,000.

The yogurt was served in cones, sundaes, shakes, and cups and sometimes included cookies, crepes, or waffles, as well as a variety of toppings. The stores were patterned after ice cream shops, and TCBY operated under the slogan "All of the pleasure and none of the guilt." TCBY owned its yogurt supplier, Arthur's Food. The company began offering frozen tofu desserts in its shops in mid-1985, hoping to capitalize further on the public's concern with health and weight maintenance. Marketing programs were aimed at increasing the acceptance of the product and creating loyalty to the TCBY name.

BEN AND JERRY'S HOMEMADE, INC.

Ben and Jerry's Homemade, Inc., manufactured and marketed Ben and Jerry's super-premium ice cream to supermarkets, convenience stores, and restaurants, as well as franchising ice cream parlors in New England and upstate New York. Thirty flavors were available in bulk and 10 flavors in pints at retail food outlets. In 1984 about two thirds of company revenues resulted from the sale of the packaged pints. Bulk sales to restaurants and franchises accounted for one fourth of the revenues, while the remaining 8 percent came from sales at a company-owned ice cream parlors.

In 1978 Ben Cohen and Jerry Greenfield opened a retail store featuring homemade ice cream in a renovated gas station in Burlington, Vermont. They learned to make the ice cream from a $5 correspondence course and experimentation with a rock-salt freezer. In the beginning their ingredients were mostly free samples from suppliers, resulting in flavors like lemon-peppermint carob chip. Demand was such that by 1979 Ben and Jerry's began a wholesale operation selling ice cream to local restaurants.

Cohen drove around the state delivering ice cream from a cooler in the back of his Volkswagen.

More than 300 restaurants and supermarkets in New England, in addition to eight franchised stores, carried the product by the end of 1984. *Dairy Record* named the company its "Ice Cream Retailer of the Year" in 1984, and *Time* magazine called Ben and Jerry's "the best ice cream in the world." To meet the growing demand, in early 1985 the company built a plant capable of processing 820 gallons an hour. The factory was financed by a Vermont-only public stock offering of which hundreds of people purchased one or two shares.

Ben and Jerry's marketing emphasized the ice cream's high quality and natural ingredients and projected a "down home" Vermont image. Packaging and advertising carried pictures of Cohen and Greenfield, paintings of cows, and hand lettering. The company relied heavily on promotional events, free sampling, and word-of-mouth advertising to market its product. Four percent of total sales were put into radio, print, and TV advertising. Ben and Jerry's also sponsored community celebrations and contributed cash and merchandise equal to about 4 percent of its income before taxes to charitable events and enterprises.

The ice cream was primarily distributed through independent regional ice cream distributors. When Ben and Jerry's learned in 1984 that Häagen-Dazs had told some distributors that they would lose access to Häagen-Dazs products if they carried any other superpremium ice cream brands, Ben and Jerry's initiated an antitrust suit against Häagen-Dazs and Pillsbury. In fear of being shut out of new markets, Ben and Jerry's also instituted a "What's the Pillsbury Doughboy Afraid of?" campaign including bumper stickers, t-shirts and a toll-free information number. The litigation was settled in March 1985 when Ben and Jerry's agreed to discontinue this campaign and Häagen-Dazs agreed not to interfere with the distribution of Ben and Jerry's ice cream. The company planned to begin distribution in Washington, D.C., Virginia, and Florida during 1985. Management projected that at least 23 franchised dipping stores would be operating by the end of 1985.

CASE 17 NUCOR CORPORATION*

"It's the closest thing to a perfect company in the steel industry."

—*Daniel Roling, analyst for Merrill Lynch*

With earnings growth over the past decade averaging better than 23 percent per year, Nucor prospered in the steel industry while giant companies barely survived. Few "high-tech" companies could match Nucor's record (see Exhibit 1). But in 1986, Nucor was moving into an era where the easy pickings were over. One securities analyst believed that Nucor would not be able to find alluring new opportunities, stating: "Their rapid growth of the last 10 years is simply not repeatable."

BACKGROUND

Nuclear Corporation   Nuclear Corporation of America was formed by a merger of Nuclear Consultants, Inc., and parts of REO Motors in 1955. Between 1955 and 1964 various managements tried (unsuccessfully) by way of acquisitions and divestitures to make a profit. One of the acquisitions was Vulcraft, a steel joist manufacturer. By 1965 Nuclear Corporation was losing $2 million on sales of $22 million. A new group got control of the company in 1965 and installed Vulcraft general manager Ken Iverson (who headed the only profitable division) as president. "I got the job by default," Iverson said.

Entry into Steel Industry   Iverson decided that Vulcraft—a manufacturer of steel joists for buildings—ought to make its own steel. His goal was to match the prices of imported steel: "We had some vision that if we were successful, we could expand and create another business by selling steel in the general marketplace." In 1968 Nucor built its first steel mill in Darlington, South Carolina. By 1985 Nucor operated four steel mills, six joist plants, two cold finishing plants, three steel deck plants, and a grinding ball plant throughout the south, southwest, and west. About 65 percent of Nucor's steel was sold in open markets, while 35 percent went to Vulcraft and other Nucor products. Until the recession of 1982–83 sales and earnings grew at an astonishing clip. Even during the recession Nucor managed to eke out a profit while other integrated steel companies lost billions.

STEEL INDUSTRY CONDITIONS, 1985

Industry Participants   Companies competing in the U.S. steel industry in 1985 were of several distinct types: integrated U.S. companies, foreign manufacturers, mini-mills, and specialty steel producers. The large integrated domestic companies (see

---

* Prepared by Professors Charles I. Stubbart and Dean Schroeder, the University of Massachusetts.

Exhibit 1 Six-Year Financial Review, Nucor Corporation, 1980–1985

	1980	1981	1982	1983	1984	1985
Net sales	$482,420,363	$544,820,621	$486,018,162	$542,531,431	$660,259,922	$758,495,374
Costs and expenses:						
Cost of products sold	369,415,571	456,210,289	408,606,641	461,727,688	539,731,252	600,797,865
Marketing and administrative expenses	38,164,559	33,524,820	31,720,315	33,988,054	45,939,311	59,079,802
Interest expense (income)	(1,219,965)	10,256,546	7,899,110	(748,619)	(3,959,092)	(7,560,645)
	406,360,165	499,991,655	448,226,128	494,967,123	581,711,471	652,317,022
Earnings before taxes	76,060,198	44,828,966	37,792,034	47,564,308	78,548,451	106,178,352
Federal income taxes	31,000,000	10,100,000	15,600,000	19,700,000	34,000,000	47,700,000
Net earnings	$ 45,060,198	$ 34,728,966	$ 22,192,034	$ 27,864,308	$ 44,548,451	$ 58,478,352
Net earnings per share	$3.31	$2.51	$1.59	$1.98	$3.16	$4.11
Dividends declared per share	$.22	$.24	$.26	$.30	$.36	$.40
Percentage of earnings to sales	9.3%	6.4%	4.6%	5.1%	6.7%	7.7%
Return on average equity	29.0%	17.8%	10.0%	11.4%	16.0%	17.8%
Return on average assets	16.9%	10.3%	5.9%	7.0%	9.8%	11.2%
Capital expenditures	$ 62,440,354	$101,519,282	$ 14,788,707	$ 19,617,147	$ 26,074,653	$ 29,066,398
Depreciation	13,296,218	21,599,951	26,286,671	27,109,582	28,899,421	31,105,788
Sales per employee	150,756	155,663	133,156	148,639	176,069	197,011
Current assets	$115,365,727	$131,382,292	$132,542,648	$193,889,162	$253,453,373	$334,769,147
Current liabilities	66,493,445	73,032,313	66,102,706	88,486,795	100,533,684	121,255,828
Working capital	$ 48,872,282	$ 58,349,979	$ 66,439,942	$105,402,367	$152,919,689	$213,513,319
Property, plant and equipment	$173,074,273	$252,616,074	$239,071,390	$231,304,817	$228,102,790	$225,274,674
Total assets	$291,221,867	$384,782,127	$371,632,941	$425,567,052	$482,188,465	$560,311,188
Long-term debt	$ 39,605,169	$ 83,754,231	$ 48,229,615	$ 45,731,000	$ 43,232,384	$ 40,233,769
Percentage of debt to capital	18.2%	28.3%	17.2%	15.0%	12.6%	10.1%
Stockholders' equity	$177,603,690	$212,376,020	$232,281,057	$258,129,694	$299,602,834	$357,502,028
Per share	$12.96	$15.25	$16.60	$18.32	$21.16	$24.97
Shares outstanding	13,699,994	13,927,014	13,991,882	14,090,181	14,161,079	14,315,005
Stockholders	22,000	22,000	22,000	21,000	22,000	22,000
Employees	3,300	3,700	3,600	3,700	3,800	3,900

Exhibit 2   Production Capacity of Largest U.S. Integrated Steel Companies, 1984

Firm	Raw Steel Capacity (millions of tons per year)
1. U.S. Steel	26.2
2. LTV	19.1
3. Bethlehem	18.0
4. Inland	9.4
5. Armco	6.8
6. National	5.6
7. Wheeling–Pittsburgh	4.5
8. Weirton	4.0
9. Ford Motor Co. (Rouge Steel)	3.6
10. McLouth	2.0
11. CF&I	2.0 (partially closed)
12. Interlake	1.4
13. Sharon	1.0
14. California	2.1 (closed)
Total	105.7

Source: Company reports; Oppenheimer & Co., Metal Bulletin, *Iron and Steel Works of the World,* 8th edition.

Exhibit 2) got their start at the turn of the century. Integrated companies held about 45 to 55 percent of the market. Specialty steel producers manufactured relatively low volumes of steel with varying degrees of hardness, purity, and strength. Imports of steel into the United States accounted for about 20 to 25 percent of domestic sales. (Imports probably held a larger share, taking into account the steel in imported automobiles and other products.) Minimills, which transformed scrap metal into steel using electric furnaces, had a market share of about 20 to 25 percent of the domestic market.

Recent History   Since the early 1960s the integrated steel industry had suffered a painful decline. The stagnation of the early 1960s gave way to faster growth (and rising imports) in the late 1960s. During 1965–74 steel demand was strong, and industry officials expected major growth after 1974. But they were wrong. Steel production in the United States had fallen from its 1974 level, and many analysts believed that the 1974 levels would never be reached again (Exhibit 3). Much of this decline was traceable to the long-term trends toward smaller lighter cars, the inroads of competing materials (such as aluminum and plastics), a shift in emphasis away from smokestack industries to service industries, and greater use of imported steel in U.S. products.

Between 1960 and 1985 foreign competitors and domestic minimills invested heavily in building all-new facilities with the latest technology. Major integrated companies invested in older, more familiar technologies to try to spruce up existing plants and correct gross inefficiencies. Facing weak demand, having less efficient facilities, and with the U.S. dollar appreciating in value, the biggest domestic integrated companies suffered huge losses in the late 1970s and early 1980s (Exhibit 4).

Exhibit 3   U.S. Raw Steel Production, Finished Steel Shipments, and Steel Imports, 1956–1984

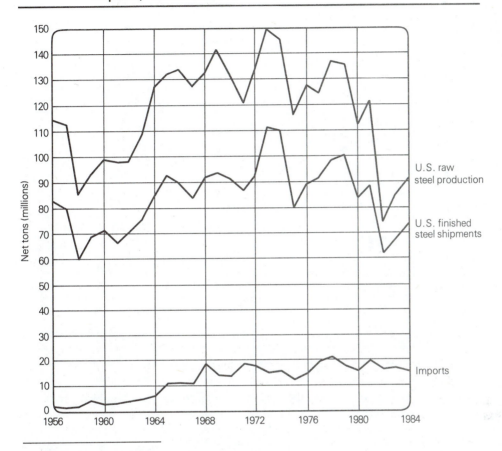

Source: American Iron and Steel Institute, *Annual Statistical Reports.*

Other problems also contributed to the rapid slide. The steelworkers union was able to negotiate large wage increases in 1968 and 1971, and union work rules hampered steel company efforts to increase productivity in their plants. Only in 1983 did the steelworkers union reluctantly agree to wage concessions and work rule modifications under the pressure of plant closings.

Poor Investments   Expecting major increases in demand for 1975–85, integrated companies made large investments in ore mines and iron pelletizing facilities. An important share of their investment dollars went into meeting environmental regulations. Integrated companies' financial calculations persuaded them to stick with modifications of existing plants instead of building new "greenfield" plants. As a result, not one all-new integrated steel plant had been built for over 20 years in the United States. Given the high cost of capital, the complex environmental constraints,

Exhibit 4   Profitability of U.S. Domestic Steel Industry Relative to All Other Manufacturing Industries, 1972–1984

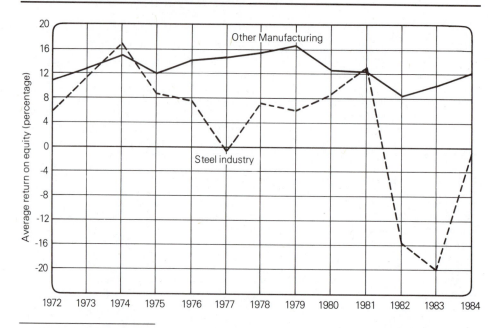

Source: *Forbes,* May 1986.

weak demand, and intense foreign/domestic competition, it was unlikely that any new integrated plants would be built in the United States in the foreseeable future.

Imports and Protection   The steel strike of 1959 provided the first opportunity for foreign steel firms to make inroads into the U.S. market. By the 1980s—despite several attempts to limit imports via voluntary restraints and trigger pricing (a minimum pricing rule)—the integrated companies found themselves with 140 million of tons of excess capacity, much of it in old inefficient plants. They had no choice but to face the music and close many plants and sell unproductive assets—a protracted and painful process for the companies, the steelworkers, and many local communities. Within one four-year period steelmakers wrote off $4.4 billion in assets and took $7 billion in losses. Steel companies, steelworkers, and endangered communities struggled mightily to persuade the Reagan administration and the Congress to limit steel imports. A reluctant Reagan administration agreed to negotiate "voluntary" restraints in 1985. Even so, to the integrated companies, the "rust bowl" communities, and to over 200,000 permanently laid off steelworkers, it seemed that too little had been done too late.

Foreign steel imports in 1985 accounted for about 25 percent of the U.S. market in spite of the Reagan administration's negotiating bilateral voluntary restraints with foreign governments. These restraint agreements aimed at limiting imports to about

21 percent of the market. Sentiment was growing in Congress to stem the tidal wave of foreign imports in the face of a $130 billion trade deficit during 1985. Ken Iverson, Nucor's CEO, steadfastly argued against protecting the domestic steel industry:

> We've had this "temporary" relief for a long time. We had a voluntary quota system in the early 1970s. We had trigger prices in the late 1970s. And what happened during these periods? As soon as prices began to rise so that steel companies would begin to be profitable, they stopped modernizing. It's only under intense competitive pressure—both internally from minimills and externally from the Japanese and the Koreans—that the big steel companies have been forced to modernize. . . . In 1980 the industry still had rolling mills dating from the Civil War. . . . Out of all this turmoil will come a lot of things which are beneficial: more of an orientation toward technology, greater productivity, certainly a lot of changes in management structure.

Future Prospects   Speculating about 1986, steel producers expected another year like 1985: declining tonnage, stable prices, slightly declining import shares, and overall profitability near zero for the industry. Their forecasts hinged on a GNP growth of approximately 3 percent. Industry analysts foresaw that a reduction in imports (traced to the falling value of the U.S. dollar) would offset an expected decline in steel consumption. Demand for steel in machinery, railroad equipment, farm equipment, and other capital items was falling. Analysts were also uncertain about the 1986 demand for autos. Some estimates placed 1986 domestic steel shipments in the range of 70 to 75 million tons (not counting imports). The prospect of labor negotiations beginning in the second half of 1986 represented a major uncertainty for steel producers and customers.

But there was a bright side too. Steel companies entered the year determined to extract concessions from the United Steelworkers Union. Companies had eliminated most of their grossly inefficient facilities. Prices were edging up. Capacity utilization approached 70 percent, compared to a low of 48 percent in 1982 (Exhibit 5). A weakening dollar made imports less attractive.

Analysts estimated that worldwide demand had stabilized. From 1979 to 1985 steel output in the industrial nations dropped precipitously from 442 million tons to 331 million tons. Capacity had been cut back 28 million tons in Europe, 23 million tons in the United States, and 17 million tons in Japan. One U.S. steel producer predicted that an additional 20 million tons in U.S. capacity would have to go. Exhibit 6 offers some industry projections for steel.

STEEL MINIMILLS: AN INDUSTRY WITHIN AN INDUSTRY

The United States had about 50 minimills. As U.S. Steel, Bethlehem, Republic, National, and LTV surrendered market share and lost billions, new entrants into the domestic market such as North Star, Nucor, Co-Steel, Florida Steel, and others prospered—and even displaced imports. Contrary to typical relationships between scale and efficiency, minimills manufactured high-quality steel inexpensively, with plants of 200,000 to 1 million tons of annual electric-furnace capacity; integrated plants

Exhibit 5   Utilization Rates of U.S. Steelmaking Capacity, 1975–1985

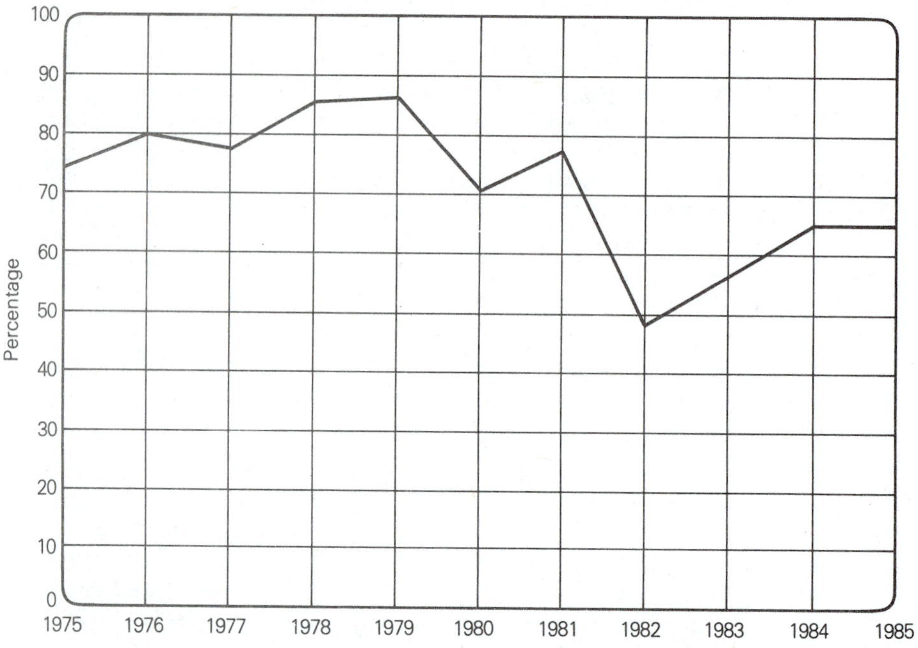

Source: AISI statistics.

producing 2 million to 10 million tons using open-hearth and basic oxygen furnace equipment were the high-cost producers.

Technology   The electric-furnace technology of minimills was first developed by Northwestern Steel and Wire in the 1930s. Exhibit 7 shows a comparison of the two processes, integrated versus minimill; the comparative simplicity of minimills is apparent. First, minimills use electric arc furnaces compared to integrated plants that use open-hearth (about 10 percent) or basic oxygen furnaces (about 90 percent), as shown in Exhibit 8. They simply charge scrap into an electric arc furnace to produce molten steel, then continuously cast the molten metal into semifinished shapes. Continuous casters eliminated reheating and increased the yield from molten metal to finished product. Unlike integrated mills, minimills were expressly designed for rebuilding and technical updating. Many integrated plants used obsolete ingot-casting technologies.

Product Specialization   Early on, minimills fashioned small specialized steel products like reinforcing rods for use in concrete work, rather than making huge beams, slabs, or sheets. Product specialization increased their efficiency. Steel slabs

Exhibit 6 Steel Industry Projections for 1985, 1990, and 2000

| | 1980 Actual | 1985 (Projected) | Projected Ranges | | | |
| | | | 1990 | | 2000 | |
			Low	High	Low	High
Import share of U.S. market (percent)	17.0	24.0	28.0	28.0	32.0	32.0
Domestic shipments (millions of tons)	83.9	76.0	73.1	75.6	71.4	78.2
Imports (millions of tons)	17.2	24.0	28.4	29.4	33.6	36.8
Total shipments (millions of tons)	86.7	77.0	74.1	76.6	72.4	79.2
Minimill shipments (millions of tons)	12.0	14.4	20.5	20.5	29.0	29.0
Minimill capacity (millions of tons)	16.0	22.0	27.0	27.0	35.0	35.0
Minimill productivity (work hours per ton)	4.0	2.8	2.2	2.2	1.5	1.5
Integrated shipments (millions of ton)	74.7	62.6	53.6	56.1	43.4	50.2
Integrated raw steel production (millions of tons)	102.3	82.3	67.8	71.0	49.9	57.7
Integrated capacity (millions of tons)	138.4	108.3	80.0	81.6	55.4	64.1
Integrated productivity (work hours per ton)	9.5	7.2	6.0	6.0	4.5	4.5
Capacity utilization rate (percent)	75.3	76.0	85.0	87.0	90.0	90.0
Total employment (in thousands)	401.6	247.9	195.0	201.6	129.6	141.7

Source: Barnett, *Minimills.*

were still predominantly the private preserve of the integrated companies. But, as time passed, minimill companies expanded their product lines. Exhibit 9 compares minimill product lines to integrated mill product lines. Nucor in 1985 produced cold-finished bars and was devoting a major innovative effort to the challenge of adapting minimill technology to sheet steel production. If Nucor could perfect this new technology, the company would be able to challenge integrated companies on their "home ground," the flat-rolled steel used in automobiles, appliances, and roofing.

Location   Only by the 1960s did minimills become a force within the industry. Their strategy was to utilize only electric furnaces and to locate their plants in regions near customer markets and scrap supplies but more distant from integrated plants (steel was expensive to ship). During the 1970s minimills grew explosively, capturing significant market shares (Exhibit 8).

Input Costs   Scrap steel was the principal raw material input for minimill production. While the cost of iron ore had constantly risen (as rich high-quality sources in the United States ran out), scrap remained plentiful. Over the last 10 years scrap prices had declined relative to iron ore prices.

Exhibit 7 Comparative Steelmaking Methods

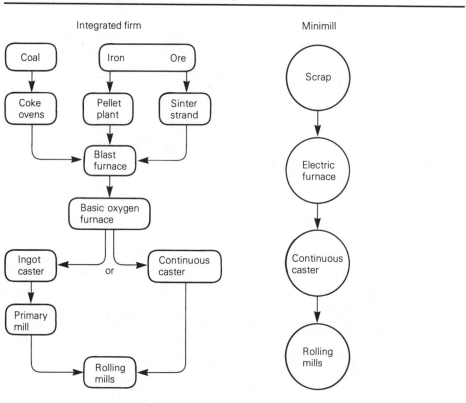

Workforce Flexibility Another important advantage of minimills was their workforce flexibility. Most minimills employed nonunion workers. Union attempts to organize minimills had met with little success. Although nonunion minimill wages were not always lower than union wages, their worker productivity was always much higher, primarily because of the flexibility and latitude management had in organizing work. Without union work rule restrictions, management could introduce labor-saving technology and link earnings to productivity.

Productivity Electric furnace technology, workforce flexibility, and constant efforts to operate facilities more efficiently added up to a significant cost advantage (that translated into a price advantage) for minimills. The advantage in 1985 was about $100 per ton ($375 for integrated firms versus $275 for minimills.) Much of the advantage stemmed from the fact that output per worker at minimills ran about double the 350 tons per employee at integrated companies. Because minimill wages were comparable (some lower but not much) to workers' earnings in the unionized plants of bigger, integrated producers, minimills had about half the labor costs per ton of integrated companies.

Exhibit 8 U.S. Steel Production Production by Process, 1975–1985

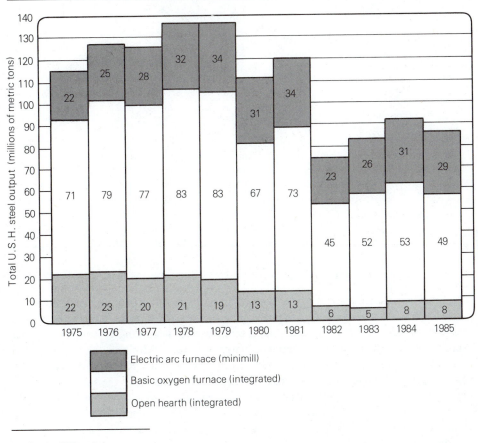

Source: AISI statistics.

Developmental Sequence Minimills did not win their market niche overnight. Some minimills failed. While minimills had advantages in low-cost labor and low-cost scrap, they faced scale disadvantages and began with an untested technology and no customer base. The initial market penetration successes came in low-grade steel products. Then, as they learned and made operating improvements, they moved gradually and selectively to challenge integrated mills and imports in an ever-broadening array of products but always where their relative cost position was strongest. The largest, and generally most successful, minimill companies in 1985 are shown in Exhibit 10.

Intensified Competition Contrary to popular impressions about imported steel, minimills' production accounted for more of the displacement of integrated companies' share than had imports. The relationship between the minimills and the

Exhibit 9 Product Categories of Integrated Mills and Minimills

Products of Integrated Mills	Capable of Being Made with Present Minimill Production Technology?
Slabs:	
Hot rolled sheets	No
Cold rolled sheets	No
Coated sheets	No
Plates	Yes
Welded pipe and tube	Limited
Blooms and Billets:	
Wire rods	Yes
Bars	Yes
Reinforcing bars	Yes
Small structural shapes	Yes
Large structural shapes	Limited
Rails	No
Seamless tube	Yes
Axles	No

integrated companies resembled a successful guerilla war. In 1985, however, the competitive scene was changing. Having used their lower costs to force integrated companies and imports out of many markets, minimills were beginning to compete against each other. An official at an integrated company noted: "Minimills have passed the stage of taking tonnage from integrated producers. We are concentrating on more sophisticated products where they can't compete. Let them have the inefficient products." Iverson observed: "We are now head to head against much tougher competition. It was no contest when we were up against the integrated companies. Now we are facing minimills who have the same scrap prices, the same electrical costs, and who use the same technologies."

Exhibit 10 Leading Minimill Companies in United States, 1985

Firm	Number of Plants	Capacity	Products
Nucor	4	2,100,000	Bars, small structurals
North Star	4	2,050,000	Bars, rods, small structural
Northwestern	1	1,800,000	Bars, rods, small and large structural
Co-Steel	2	1,750,000	Bars, rods, small and large structural
Florida Steel	5	1,560,000	Bars, small structurals

Note: The minimill segment consisted of 50 firms and 65 plants. Of total minimill production, 55 percent came from plants with less than 600,000 tons of annual capacity.

Minimills coveted the bigger market for flat-rolled steel where profit margins were higher. But they were shut out of this segment by technological limitations. In terms of technological capabilities, productivity, workforce practices, and expanding products, Nucor was viewed as the leader among minimill producers. Nucor operated four steel minimills located in South Carolina, Nebraska, Texas, and Utah with a total capacity of about 2 million tons; this made Nucor about the 10th largest steel company in the United States.

VULCRAFT: THE OTHER HALF OF NUCOR

Ken Iverson said:

> "Most people think of us as a steel company, but we are a lot more than a steel company. The business is really composed of two different factors. One is manufacturing steel and the other is steel products. We like it if in an average year each factor contributes about 50 percent of our sales and 50 percent of our earnings. It is important for the company in the long run that we keep this balance. If one of them began to dominate the company it would cause problems we wouldn't like to see."

Products   Vulcraft was the nation's largest producer of steel joists and joist girders. Steel joists and girders served as support systems in industrial buildings, shopping centers, warehouses, high rise buildings, and to a lesser extent in small office buildings, apartments, and single-family dwellings. Vulcraft had six joist plants and four deck plants. Steel deck was used for floor and roof systems. In 1985 Vulcraft produced 471,000 tons of joists and girders and 169,000 tons of steel deck (Exhibits 11 and 12).

Manufacturing Process   Joists were manufactured on assembly lines. The steel moved on rolling conveyors from station to station. Teams of workers at each station cut and bent the steel to shape, welded joists together and drilled holes in them, and painted the completed product.

Competition   Many competitors participated in the joist segment, and a large number and variety of customers bought joists. Competition centered around timely delivery and price. Joist manufacturing was not capital intensive like basic steel-making, but was more of an engineering business. Vulcraft bid on a very high percentage of all new buildings which needed joists. Sophisticated computer software was used to design the joists needed on a job and to develop bid estimates. Success also depended on marketing and advertising. Vulcraft had a 40 percent national market share in joists in 1985, making it the largest joist manufacturer in the United States. In 1985 Vulcraft manufactured joists for about 15,000 buildings. Vulcraft management pursued a strategy of being the low-cost supplier of joists.

Organization   Each Vulcraft plant was managed by a general manager who reported directly to Dave Aycock, president of Nucor. Each Vulcraft general manager had spent many years in the joist business. In general, the Vulcraft division's relationships with corporate headquarters paralleled those of the steel division.

Exhibit 11   Nucor's Steel Joist and Steel Production, 1975 to 1985

OTHER NUCOR BUSINESSES

In addition to steel and joists, Nucor operated three cold finish plants which produced steel bars used in shafting and machining precision parts; a plant which produced grinding balls used by the mining industry; and a research chemicals unit which produced rare earth oxides, metals, and salts.

KEN IVERSON AND THE NUCOR CULTURE

Iverson had consciously modeled Nucor on certain bedrock values: productivity, simplicity, thrift, and innovation.

Productivity   Iverson liked to contrast Nucor to integrated companies. He recounted a field trip he took to an integrated steel plant when he was a student at Purdue: "This was the late afternoon. We were touring through the plant, and we

Exhibit 12   Nucor's Steel Deck and Cold Finished Steel Sales,
             1977–1985

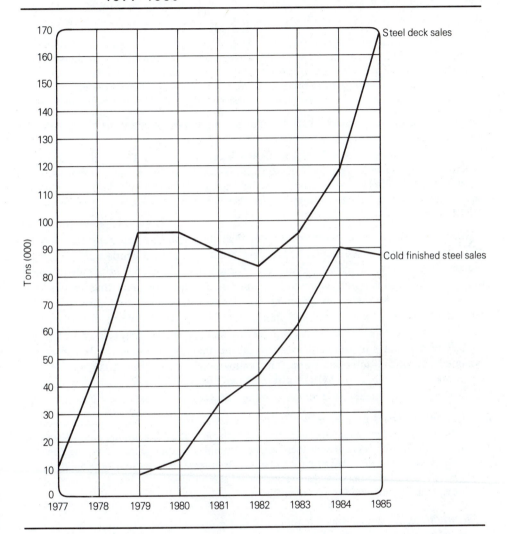

actually had to step over workers who were sleeping there. I decided right then that I didn't ever want to work for a big steel plant." The average Nucor worker produced 700 to 800 tons of steel per year versus 350 tons per employee at integrated companies; total labor costs at Nucor averaged less than half that at integrated producers. At the production level people were arranged into groups of 25 to 35 people. Each group had a production standard to meet and a steep bonus schedule for exceeding its standard. Nucor production workers could earn $30,000 or more in a good year. Producing steel and joists entailed hard, hot, dirty, and occasionally dangerous jobs. Performance at all levels of the company was rigidly tied to efficiency and profitability criteria.

Simplicity and Thrift   Iverson and other managers at Nucor had developed practices and symbols which conveyed simplicity. One of their notable achievements was a streamlined organizational structure. Only four levels separated the official hierarchy: workers, department managers, division managers, corporate. Iverson said:

> You can tell a lot about a company by looking at its organization charts. . . . If you see a lot of staff, you can bet that it is not a very efficient organization. . . . Secondly, don't have assistants. We do not have that title and prohibit it in our company. . . . And one of the most important things is to restrict as much as possible the number of management layers. . . . It is probably the most important single factor in business.

Iverson's pioneering approach in steel was beginning to be copied by the bigger companies:

> I spent two days as a lecturer at a business school not long ago. One of the students heard me talk about getting rid of management layers. He spoke up and said that when he visited U.S. Steel's new pipe mill near Birmingham, Alabama, the thing they were most proud of wasn't the technology but that they had only 4 management layers instead of the usual 10.

Nucor's spartan values were most evident at its corporate headquarters. Instead of having a handsome, expensive showcase building sited on landscaped grounds, Nucor rented a few thousand square feet of the fourth floor of a nondescript office building with an insurance company's name on it. The only clue that Nucor was there was its name (listed in ordinary size letters) in the building directory. The office decor was spartan, simple and functional. Only 16 people worked in the headquarters—no financial analysts, no engineering staff, no marketing staff, no research staff. The company assiduously avoided the normal paraphenalia of bureaucracy. No one had a formal job description. The company had no written mission statement, no strategic plan, and no MBO system. There was little paperwork, few regular reports, and fewer meetings. Iverson commented on his staff and how it functioned:

> They are all very sharp people. We don't centralize anything. We have a financial vice president, a president, a manager of personnel, a planner, internal auditing, and accounting. . . . With such a small staff there are opportunities you miss and things you don't do well because you don't have time . . . but the advantages so far outweigh the disadvantages. . . . We focus on what can really benefit the business. . . . We don't have job descriptions, we just kind of divide up the work.

Innovation   Nucor was a leading innovator among steel minimills and the joist business as well. Plant designs, organizational structure, incentives, and workforce allocations synchronized with cultural pressure for constant innovative advancements. Iverson projected that minimills could eventually capture as much as 35 to 40 percent of the steel business if they succeeded in developing technological advances which enabled them to produce a wider variety of steel products very economically. The breakthroughs hinged on revamping continuous casting technology. Currently, a minimill couldn't produce certain shapes. Iverson thought the key to unlock the door was the "thin-slab caster":

> We are trying to develop a thin slab. Then we could produce plate and other flatrolled products. Right now the thinnest slab that can be produced is 6 inches thick. If we

can get down to 1½ inches with the thin slab caster, then we can map out the growth for another 10 years. We could build those all over the country. We're trying to develop this new technology in our Darlington mill. The investment will probably run $10 to $20 million. Now, if we could do it, the new mills would probably cost about $150 million.

Many analysts doubted that such a breakthrough was really in the offing, but Iverson believed it would come within three years and was monitoring seven experimental programs.

Ken Iverson: Public Figure

Nucor's success had made Iverson a public figure. He had been interviewed by newspapers, magazines, radio, and TV; he spoke to industry groups and business schools; and he had been called to testify before Congress. He explained why he was willing to devote his time to these extracurricular activities:

Generally, our policy is to stay as far away as we can from government . . . except that I felt so strongly about protectionism that I thought I should make my views known—especially because our view is so different from the other steel mills. . . . Talking to investors is an important part of the company's relationship with the marketplace . . . the company gets a direct benefit and it makes good sense. . . . I do some talks at business schools just from the standpoint that I get pleasure out of that. . . . We do occasionally hire MBAs, but we haven't had much success with them.

Iverson had a casual, informal, and unaffected style. His office was neither large nor furnished with expensive decorations. For lunch he took visitors across the street to a delicatessen—their "executive dining room"—for a quick sandwich. Nucor had no executive parking spaces, no executive restrooms, no company cars. Everyone, including Iverson, flew coach class. When Iverson went to New York he rode the subway instead of taking a limosine or taxi. Other Nucor managers followed Iverson's example, shunning ostentation, luxury, and status symbols common among other successful companies.

Managers at Nucor described Iverson's management style:

Ken is straightforward. If he says something you can pretty well count on it. He sets the tone and the direction and everybody pitches in. That's the way he acts and approaches things—directly.

Ken is one of the greatest leaders the steel industry has ever had.

Ken is liberal with people and conservative with money.

ORGANIZATION

Organization Structure

Following Iverson's "lean management" philosophy, only four levels of management separated Iverson from the hourly employees. At corporate headquarters they joked that with four promotions, a janitor could become CEO! Exhibit 13 depicts Nucor's organization chart. Below the corporate level the company was organized into divisions. These divisions roughly corresponded to plant locations.

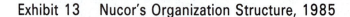

Exhibit 13   Nucor's Organization Structure, 1985

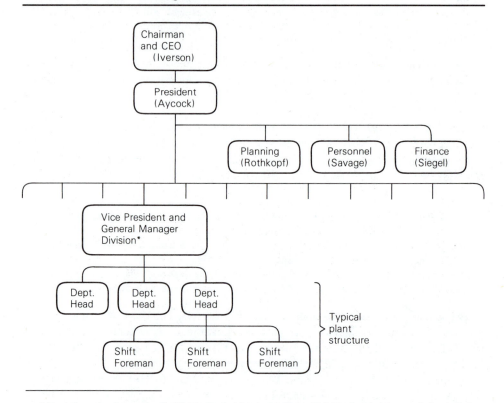

* Note: Nucor has four steel mills (divisions), six joist plants, three cold finished steel plants, a grinding ball plant, and a research chemicals division—each is headed by a vice president and general manager.

Recently, under the pressure of the growing size of the company and Iverson's busy public role, the jobs of president and CEO were separated. By trying to be "everything to everyone," Iverson was spreading himself a little thin. Dave Aycock was promoted from a plant manager's job to president, responsible for day-to-day operations of Nucor; Aycock talked about his new role:

> I worked at Vulcraft when it was acquired by Nucor in 1955. . . . I've been in this new job for about a year. . . . It's very exciting. . . . If I had actually known roughly half of what I thought I knew, I would probably have been more valuable. . . . Most of my time has been spent learning the personalities, the reactions, and philosophies of the operating personnel. . . . Many of them were glad to see the change because they thought Ken was overworked.

Division Management   Because Nucor had no headquarters staff and because of top management's great confidence in operating personnel, division managers played a key role in decision making. Iverson said of the division managers: "They are all vice presidents, and they are behind our success. He's at that division. He's responsible for that division. They make the policies of this company. Most of them have been with Nucor at least 10 years. But his pay is based on how this company does—not on how well his division does—it's the group concept again."

Corporate-Division Interaction   Contact between divisions and corporate headquarters was limited to a report of production volume, costs, sales, and margin— the "Monthly Operations Analysis." Each month every division received the "smiling face" report, comparing all the divisions across about a dozen categories of efficiency and performance. One division manager described how Iverson delegated and supervised:

> Mr. Iverson's style of management is to allow the manager all the latitude in the world. His involvement with managers is quite limited. As we have grown, he no longer has the time to visit with division managers more than once or twice a year. . . . In a way I feel like I run my own company because I don't get marching orders from Mr. Iverson. He lets you run the division the way you see fit, and the only way he will step in is if he sees something he doesn't like, particularly bad profits, high costs, or whatever. But in the four years I've worked with him I don't recall a single instance where he issued an instruction to me to do something differently.

The casewriters asked a division manager how the corporate officers would handle a division which wasn't performing as it should:

> I imagine he (Aycock) would call first and come out later, but it would be appropriate to the situation. Ken and Dave are great psychologists. Right now, for instance, the steel business is showing very poor return on assets, but I don't feel any pressure on me because the market is not there. I do feel pressure to keep my costs down, and that is appropriate. If something went wrong Dave would know.

How does Nucor respond to problems in management performance?

> We had a situation where we were concerned about the performance of a particular employee . . . a department manager. Ken, Dave, and I sat down with the general manager to let him know where we were coming from. So now the ball is in his court. We will offer support and help that the general manager wants. Later I spent a long evening with the general manager and the department manager. Now the department manager understands the corporate concern. Ken will allow the general manager to resolve this issue. To do otherwise would take the trust out of the system. . . . We are not going to just call someone in and say "We're not satisfied. You're gone.". . . But, eventually, the string may run out. Ken will terminate people. He takes a long time to do it. I respect that. Ken would rather give people too much time than too little.

Important issues merited a phone call or perhaps a visit from a corporate officer. A division manager told the casewriters that he talked to headquarters about once a week. Divisions made their own decisions about hiring, purchasing, processes, and equipment. There was no formal limit on a division manager's spending authority. Sales policy and personnel policy were set at corporate level. Divisions didn't produce a plan, but: "People in this company have real firm ideas about what is going on and what will be happening . . . mostly by word of mouth."

Relationships between the divisions were close. They shared ideas and information, and sold each other significant amounts of product.

Decision Making   Division managers met formally in a group with corporate management three times a year at the "Roundtable." Sessions began at 7 A.M. and ended at 8 P.M. At these meetings, budgets, capital expenditures, and changes in wages or benefits were agreed on, and department managers were reviewed. Iverson waited for a consensus to emerge about an alternative before going ahead with a decision. He did not impose decisions. Corporate officers described Nucor's decision making processes:

> Over a long period of time, decisions in this company have been made at the lowest level that they can—subject to staying within the philosophy of the company. We get a lot of work done without too many managers. Ken has the business courage to stay out of the small things. It takes a lot of courage for general managers to resist the temptation to control every event.

> I can walk into Ken's office anytime and talk about anything I want to talk about. Agree or disagree with anything he has done. I don't agree with every decision that is made. I have the right to disagree. Sometimes I disagree strongly. Ken hears me out. Ken listens to other people. He does not feel that he is always right. Sometimes he will change his mind.

> I remember when I first started to work for Nucor and I was sitting down with Ken Iverson. He told me, "John, you are going to make at least three mistakes with this company in the first few years that you are with us. Each one of these mistakes will cost us $50,000. I want you to be aggressive, and I want you to make decisions. One word of caution. We don't mind you making the mistakes, but please don't make them all in one year."

> Ken defers a decision when the executives are strongly divided to give people a chance to consider it more. Ken is a superb negotiator. He might look at the various positions and say "I have a compromise," and lay that out. Many times he can see a compromise that everyone is comfortable with.

FINANCIAL POSITION

The theme of simplicity also extended to financial matters. Sam Siegel, Nucor's vice president of finance, did not use a computer. He told the casewriters: "When you make too many calculations they get in the way of business. Each of the divisions uses computers for many purposes, including financial analysis. You could make an economic case for centralizing some of that here at corporate headquarters. We could save money and create all kinds of information, but then we would have to hire more people to study that information."

Investments   No financial analysts worked at corporate headquarters. Nucor did not use sophisticated models of discounted cash flow or complicated formulas to govern capital expenditures, preferring an eclectic capital investment policy. Iverson commented: "Priority? No. We don't even do that with capital expenditures. Sometimes we'll say . . . we won't put up any buildings this year. . . . But in recent years we've been able to fund anything we felt we needed. We don't do it by priorities." Responding to a query about whether the company used an internal hurdle rate of return, Iverson said:

We look at it from the standpoint of whether it's replacement and if it's modernization, what the payback period is, or if it is a new facility. In many cases the payback on a new steel mill is longer than you would like, but you can't afford not to do it. I think maybe that is where other manufacturing companies go wrong—where they have these rigid ideas about investments. If you don't put some of these investments in, after four or five years you are behind. . . . You can't afford to fall behind, even if you don't get the payback. That's why the integrated steel companies didn't put in continuous casters, because they couldn't get the payback they wanted. . . . Now they have got to do it. . . . From an economics point of view they didn't do anything wrong, they didn't make a mistake.

Financial Reporting   Each division had a controller who reported directly to the division manager and indirectly to Siegel. Siegel saw the role of his controllers as being broad: "Controllers who merely do financial work are not doing a good job. A controller should become involved with key plant operations . . . should learn the whole operation." Siegel spent only about one half of his own time on strictly financial matters, contributing the other half toward "problems, issues, and projects" of importance to the company.

Financial Condition   According to Siegel, the company was in good financial condition except for having too much invested in short-term assets (Exhibits 14 and 15). Wall Street analysts had speculated about what Nucor might decide to do with its excess short-term assets.

HUMAN RESOURCES

Besides being known for its stunning success in joists and steel, Nucor was also known for its remarkable human resources practices. The casewriters visited a Vulcraft plant and talked with a department manager who had worked at Vulcraft for 16 years about what made Nucor different:

> Our plants are located strategically. The company puts them in rural areas, where we can find a good supply of quality labor—people who believe in hard work. We have beaten back three unionizing campaigns in the last 10 years. These employees are very loyal. In fact, we had to hire a guard to protect the union organizers from some of our workers. We see about 3 percent turnover and very little absenteeism. They are proud of working with us. It's fun when they come to you and ask for work.

Why did Nucor do so well with employees?

> Most companies want to take their profits out of their employees. We treat employees right. They are the ones who make the profits. Other companies aren't willing to offer what is needed to allow people to work. They can't see the dollar down the road for the nickel in their hand. Nucor's people make it strong.

Nucor's incentive systems had been a subject of much discussion and comment. *Fortune* estimated in 1981 that Nucor's workers earned an average of $5,000 more than union steelworkers. Moreover, Nucor workers were the highest paid manufacturing, blue-collar workforce in the United States.

Exhibit 14 Balance Sheets, Nucor Corp., 1984 and 1985

	1984	1985
Assets		
Current assets:		
Cash	$ 2,863,680	$ 8,028,519
Short-term investments	109,846,810	177,115,954
Accounts receivable	58,408,244	60,390,448
Contracts in process	8,462,815	10,478,296
Inventories	73,797,302	78,641,805
Other current assets	74,522	114,125
Total current assets	253,453,373	334,769,147
Property, plant and equipment	228,102,790	225,274,674
Other assets	632,302	267,367
Total assets	$482,188,465	$560,311,188
Liabilities and Stockholders' Equity		
Current liabilities:		
Long-term debt due within one year	$ 2,402,462	$ 2,402,462
Accounts payable	32,691,249	35,473,011
Federal income taxes	23,705,195	27,597,464
Accrued expenses and other current liabilities	41,734,778	55,782,891
Total current liabilities	100,533,684	121,255,828
Other liabilities:		
Long-term debt due after one year	43,232,384	40,233,769
Deferred federal income taxes	38,819,563	41,319,563
	82,051,947	81,553,332
Stockholders' equity:		
Common stock	5,669,757	5,732,382
Additional paid-in capital	18,991,334	24,299,195
Retained earnings	275,035,788	327,816,850
	299,696,879	357,848,427
Treasury stock	(94,045)	(346,399)
Total stockholders' equity	299,602,834	357,502,028
Total liabilities and stockholders' equity	$482,188,465	$560,311,188

Casewriter: But doesn't that prove the point—that American steelworkers earning $30,000 per year have priced the industry out of business?

Iverson: They earn every bit of it! Sure, it's generous. . . . There's a reason for it. It's hot, hard, dirty, dangerous, skilled work. We have melters who earn more than $40,000, and I'm glad they earn it. It's not what a person earns in an absolute sense, it's what he earns in relation to what he produces that matters.

The incentive system at Nucor had several key elements. John Savage, manager of personnel services, explained the company's personnel philosophy:

Our employee relations philosophy has four primary components. . . . Management's first and foremost obligation to employees is to provide them the opportunity to earn according to their productivity. . . . Next, we are obligated to manage the company in such a way that employees can feel that if they are doing their job properly, they will have a job tomorrow. . . . Third, employees must believe that they are treated

Exhibit 15   Statement of Changes in Financial Position, Nucor Corp., 1983–1985

	1983	1984	1985
Funds provided:			
Operations:			
Net earnings	$27,864,308	$44,548,451	$58,478,352
Depreciation of plant and equipment	27,109,582	28,899,421	31,105,788
Deferred federal income taxes	8,200,000	5,600,000	2,500,000
Total funds provided by operations	63,173,890	79,047,872	92,084,140
Disposition of plant and equipment	274,138	377,259	788,726
Decrease in other assets	—	—	364,935
Issuance of common stock	2,201,183	2,006,460	5,387,182
Total funds provided	$65,649,211	$81,431,591	$98,624,983
Funds applied:			
Purchase of property, plant and equipment	$19,617,147	$26,074,653	$29,066,398
Increase in other assets	354,170	259,229	—
Reduction in long-term debt	2,498,615	2,498,616	2,998,615
Cash dividends	4,216,854	5,081,771	5,697,290
Acquisition of treasury stock	—	—	269,050
Increase in working capital	38,962,425	47,517,322	60,593,630
Total funds applied	$65,649,211	$81,431,591	$98,624,983
Analysis of change in working capital:			
Increase (decrease) in current assets:			
Cash	$ (4,283,370)	$ (3,521,115)	$ 5,164,839
Short-term investments	38,445,234	37,177,195	67,269,144
Accounts receivable	16,424,874	7,297,872	1,982,204
Contracts in process	8,402,160	1,404,012	2,015,481
Inventories	7,723,168	17,242,200	4,844,503
Other current assets	(366,052)	(35,953)	39,603
Net increase (decrease)	61,346,514	59,564,211	81,315,774
Increase (decrease) in current liabilities:			
Long-term debt due within one year	799,000	—	—
Accounts payable	14,186,217	(4,443,835)	2,781,762
Federal income taxes	2,278,813	8,891,286	3,892,269
Accrued expenses and other current liabilities	5,120,059	7,599,438	14,048,113
Net increase (decrease)	22,384,089	12,046,889	20,722,144
Increase in working capital	$38,962,425	$47,517,322	$60,593,630

fairly. . . . Lastly, employees must have an avenue of appeal if they believe they are being treated unfairly, to Mr. Iverson himself if necessary.

Everyone at Nucor participated in incentive plans. These incentives took several different forms depending on the type of work involved.

Production Incentives   Production groups of 25 to 30 employees were grouped around clearly measurable production tasks. About 3,000 Nucor employees made joists and steel under production incentives based on historical time standards. If, for example, a group produced a joist in 50 percent less than standard time, they got a 50 percent bonus. Bonuses were paid at the end of the following week. When equipment sat idle, no bonus accrued. If an employee was absent for a day, he or she lost a week's bonus—a difference amounting to as much as $7 per hour. Although workers often earned wages far above averages for manufacturing, the system was very tough:

> If you work real hard and you get performance, the payment is there next week. . . . You worked like a dog and here is the money. . . . There are lots of people who don't like to work that hard, and they don't last for long. We have had groups get so mad at a guy who wasn't carrying his weight that they chased him around a joist plant with a piece of angle iron and were gonna kill him. . . . Don't get the idea that we're paternalistic. If you are late even five minutes you lose your bonus for the day. If you are late by more than 30 minutes because of sickness or anything else, you lose your bonus for the week. We do grant four "forgiveness" days a year. We have a melter, Phil Johnson, down in Darlington. One day a worker arrived at the plant and said that Phil had been in an auto accident and was sitting by his car on Route 52 holding his head. The foreman asked, "Why didn't you stop to help him?" The guy said, "And lose my bonus?"

Many Nucor workers earned between $30,000 and $40,000 per year. Nucor's monetary incentives made the company attractive to jobseekers (see Exhibit 14). Iverson told a story about hiring new workers:

> We needed a couple new employees for Darlington, so we put out a sign and put a small ad in the local paper. The ads told people to show up Saturday morning at the employment office at the plant. When Saturday rolled around, the first person to arrive at the personnel office was greeted by 1,200 anxious jobseekers. There were so many of them that the size of the crowd began to interfere with access into and out of the plant. So the plant manager called the state police to send some officers over to control the crowd. But, the sergeant at the state police barracks told the plant manager that he couldn't spare any officers. You see, he was short-handed himself because three of his officers were at the plant applying for jobs!

Managerial Compensation

Department managers received a bonus based on a percentage of their division's contribution to corporate earnings. In an operating division such bonuses could run as high as 50 percent of a person's base pay. In the corporate office the bonus could reach 30 percent of base pay. Employees such as accountants, secretaries, clerks, and others who didn't work in production got a bonus based on either their division's profit contribution or corporate return on assets.

Senior officers had no employment contracts or pension plan. More than half of their compensation was based on company earnings. Their base salaries were set at about 70 percent of market rates for similar jobs. Ten percent of pretax earnings were set aside and allocated to senior officers according to their base salary. The base level was tied to a 12 percent return on shareholder's equity. Half the bonus was paid in cash, and half was deferred in the form of Nucor stock. In a profitable year officers could earn as much as 190 percent of their base salary as bonus and 115 percent on top of that in stock.

Other Compensation Incentives

Nucor also operated a profit sharing trust. The plan called for 10 percent of pretax earnings to be assigned to profit sharing each year. Of that amount, 20 percent was paid to employees in the following year, and the remainder was held to fund the worker retirement program. Vesting in the trust was 20 percent after one year and 10 percent each following year. The arrangement had the effect of making the retirement income of Nucor employees depend on the company's success. Additionally, Nucor paid 10 percent of whatever amount an employee was willing to invest in Nucor stock, gave employees five shares of stock for each five years of employment, and occasionally paid extraordinary bonuses.

Lastly, Nucor ran a scholarship program for children of full-time employees. In 1985 over 300 children were enrolled in universities, colleges, and vocational schools. Since the program's inception over 900 students had participated. One family had educated eight children on Nucor's plan.

No Layoffs   Nucor had never laid off or fired an employee for lack of work. Iverson explained how the company handled the need to make production cutbacks:

> When we have a difficult period, we don't lay anybody off. . . . We operate the plants four days a week or even three days. We call it our "share the pain program.". . . The bonus system remains in place, but it's based on four days' production instead of five. The production workers' compensation drops about 25 percent, the department managers' drops 35 to 40 percent, and the division managers' can drop as much as 60 to 80 percent. Nobody complains. They understand. And they still push to get that bonus on the days they work.

The Downside   Nucor's flat structure and steep incentives also had certain negative side effects. First, the incentive system was strictly oriented toward the short term. If a general manager was thinking about a major capital investment project, he was also thinking about reducing his short-term income. Iverson described how the ups and downs of the incentive plans affected officers: "If the company can hit about 24 percent return on equity, the officers salary can reach 300 percent of the base amount. It maxed out in 1979 and 1980. In 1980 and 1981 total officers' compensation dropped way off. In 1980 I earned about $400,000, but in 1981 I earned $108,000. So officers have to watch their lifestyle!" Iverson's 1981 pay made him, according to *Fortune,* the lowest paid CEO in the *Fortune 500* industrial ranking. Iverson commented that it was "Something I was really a little proud of."

Second, promotions came very slowly. Many managers had occupied their current jobs for a very long time. Additionally, Nucor experienced problems in developing the skills of its first-line supervisors.

Many other companies studied Nucor's compensation plans. The casewriters asked John Savage about the visits other companies made to study Nucor's system:

> Many companies visit us. We had managers and union people from General Motors' Saturn project come in and spend a couple of days. They were oriented toward a bureaucratic style. . . . You could tell it from their questions. I was more impressed with the union people than with the management people. The union people wanted to talk dirty, nitty-gritty issues. But the management people thought it was too simple, they didn't think it would work. Maybe their business is too complex for our system. . . . We never hear from these visitors after they leave. . . . I believe it would take five to seven years of working at this system before you could detect a measurable change.

High wages and employment stability got Nucor listed in the book *The 100 Best Companies to Work for in America.* A division manager summed up the Nucor human relations philosophy this way: "It's amazing what people can do if you let them.

Exhibit 16   Excerpts of Interviews with Hourly Employees at Nucor

---

Jim

Jim is 32 years old, did not finish school, and has worked at Vulcraft for 10 years. He works at a job that requires heavy lifting. Last year he earned about $38,500.

> This is hard physical work. Getting used to it is tough, too. After I started working as a spliceman my upper body was sore for about a month. . . . Before I came to work here I worked as a farmer and cut timber. . . . I got this job through a friend who was already working here. . . . I reckon I was very nervous when I started here, but people showed me how to work. . . . The bonuses and the benefits are mighty good here . . . and I have never been laid off. . . . I enjoy this work. . . . This company is good to you. They might let employees go if they had problems, but first they'd give him a chance to straighten out. . . . In 1981 things were slow and we only worked three or four days a week. Sometimes we would spend a day doing maintenance, painting, sweeping. . . . and there wasn't no incentive. I was glad I was working . . . I was against the union.

Kerry

Kerry is 31 years old, married, and expecting a child. He has worked on the production line for about three years.

> I was laid off from my last job after working there five years. I went without work for three months. I got this job through a friend. My brother works as a supervisor for Nucor in Texas. . . . This is good, hard work. You get dirty, too hot in the summer and too cold in the winter. They should air-condition the entire plant (laughs). On this joist line we have to work fast. Right now I'm working 8½ hours a day, six days a week. . . . I get good pay and benefits. Vulcraft is one of the better companies in Florence (South Carolina). . . . Everyone does not always get along, but we work as a team. Our supervisor has his off days. . . . I want to get ahead in life, but I don't see openings for promotion here. Most of the foremen have had their jobs for a long time, and most people are senior to me in line. . . . This place is very efficient. If I see a way to improve the work, I tell somebody. They will listen to you.

Other comments from hourly workers

> I am running all day long. It gets hot and you get tired. My wife doesn't like it because sometimes I come home and fall asleep right away.

> When something goes down, people ask how they can help. Nobody sits around. Every minute you are down it's like dollars out of your pocket. So everybody really hustles.

Nucor gives people responsibility and then stands behind them." Exhibit 16 presents selected excerpts from interviews with hourly employees about their jobs at Nucor.

STRATEGIC PLANNING

Nucor followed no written strategic plan, had no written objectives (except those stated in the incentive programs), and had no mission statement. Divisions promulgated no strategic plans. We asked Sam Siegel about long range strategic planning. He confided: "You can't predict the future. . . . No matter how great you may think your decisions are, the future is unknown. You don't know what will happen. . . . Nucor concentrates on the here-and-now. We do make five year projections, and they are good for about three months. Five to 10 years out is philosophy." We also asked Bob Rothkopf (planning director) about planning at Nucor:

I work on the strategic plan with Ken twice a year. It's formulated out of the projects we are looking at. He and I talk about the direction we feel the company is going. . . . The elements of the most recent plan are that we take the basic level of the company today and project it out for five years. We look at net sales, net income, under different likely scenarios. In this last plan I looked at the potential effects of a mild recession in 1986. . . . We add new products or projects to that baseline.

Rothkopf had responsibility for generating most of the information he used in his forecasts. He often used consultants or other companies to get the information he needed. None of the other senior executives or division managers got deeply involved in this planning process.

Nucor didn't rely on its strategic planning system to make strategic decisions. Rothkopf described how strategic decisions were reached:

Projects come from all over. Some come from our general managers, or from our suppliers, our customers . . . or come walking in the door here. Iverson is like a magnet for ideas, because of who he is and what Nucor is. . . . We evaluate each project on its own, as it comes up. As each opportunity arises, we go in and investigate it. Some investigations are short; we throw out quite a few of them. We don't make any systematic search for these ideas.

Rothkopf compared Nucor's planning to formal strategic planning done by other companies:

I think there might be some advantages for us to do that sort of thing. However, our business has been pretty simple. Our businesses are all related and easy to keep track of. When a big decision comes up we discuss it. That's easy because of the simple structure of the company. . . . Planning has disadvantages . . . time-consuming . . . expensive . . . hard to get the information for it . . . tends to get bureaucratic.

Although Nucor had no formal planning system, important strategic decisions loomed on the company horizon. Exhibit 17 provides information on Nucor's strategic options.

NUCOR'S FUTURE: WHAT NEXT?

In spite of Nucor's remarkable successes, Iverson stated a modest, cautious view of the company's capabilities:

We are not great marketers or financial manipulators. . . . We do two things well. We build plants economically and we run them efficiently. We stick to those two things. . . . Basically, that's all we do. We are getting better at marketing, but I wouldn't say we are strong marketers . . . that is not the base of the company. . . . We're certainly not financial manipulators. We recognized a long time ago how important it was for us to hold down overhead and management layers.

Iverson talked about the future of Nucor:

The company's position is much different than it was in past years. In the 60s we nearly went bankrupt. It was a miniconglomerate, so I got rid of half the company. We started all over again. We built steel mills. From the late 60s to the 80s our constraints were financial. We decided that we wanted debt to be less than 30 percent of capital.

Exhibit 17   A Summary Review of Nucor's Strategic Options

Strategic Considerations	Option 1 Build a Seamless Tube Mill	Option 2 Get into Preengineered Buildings
Market	About $2.5 billion Oilfield equipment companies Commodity Mature, competitive, low growth Integrated companies sell here	$350 million Small growth Numerous competitors, all sizes Regional, fragmented Not a commodity
Investment	$150–180 million	$5–7 million plant generates $15–20 million sales in four years. Want about 20 percent market share in five to six years
Time period needed	About two years	8–12 months
Fit to present activities	Could sell some product to joist division Increase efficiency	Already manufacturing parts for such buildings
Revenues/profits	Sales $240–270 million 20–25 percent profit before taxes	About same as present earning power
Support among executives	Some active support Analyses in process	Joist division favors it Corporate execs divided
Skills and resources	Know market Have most skills, others not too hard to learn	Selling to whole new market Manufacturing skills help
Downside risk	Risky, uncertain market	New market to understand Can do gradually Not very risky

Strategic Considerations	Option 3 Build Bar Minimill	Option 4 Acquire Bar Minimills
Market	Same as current	Same as current
Investment	$50–75 million for a 250,000 ton mill	A six to seven year old, 175,000 ton mill costs $50 million to build Earns $10–15/ton before tax ±1989, 1987 earliest
Time period needed	18 months	
Fit to present activities	Perfect fit	Obvious, yes
Revenues/profits	$65–75 million sales. Lose money years one and two. Over long term make $5–10 million before taxes.	$45 million sales, earns ±$1 million Under Nucor, such a mill can see sales of $60 million, earn ±$5 million
Support among executives	Quite a bit	Unknown
Skills and resources	In place, no problems	OK, in place
Downside risk	No growth in market. Must take business from entrenched competitors	Anti-trust? Company culture might not fit; exposure to union problems

Strategic Considerations	Option 5 Innovative Flat-Rolled Minimill	Option 6 Build Bolt Plant
Market	25–30 million tons Stable, a commodity Integrated mills dominant	$800 million Mature, stable Commodity dominated by four companies
Investment	$125–$175 million for 400,000, to 600,000 ton mill	$25 million/plant
Time period needed	Could build four plants in 5–10 years	

Exhibit 17 *(concluded)*

Strategic Considerations	Option 5 (cont.) Innovative Flat-Rolled Minimill	Option 6 (cont.) Build Bolt Plant
Fit to present activities	Extends product range Sales to joist division Keeps steel/joist "balance"	Steel currently produced goes into product
Revenues/profits	Must project 25 percent profit before tax to justify Lower cost $100/ton?	$28–32 million sales per plant
Support among executives	High company support; spending $10 million to develop process at Darlington	Agreed to build one plant
Skills and resources	Don't know marketing of flat-rolled products Must learn flat-rolling of steel	Need marketing skills
Downside risk	Must invest $10–15 million in any case Hard to invest new technology Competitors leap-frog with new processes Estimate 50–75 percent chance it will work	If foreign steel is barred in United States, bolts get "dumped" here. International prices of bolts unstable.

Strategic Considerations	Option 7 Increase Dividends ($.10/Share Now)	Option 8 Purchase Nucor Stock for Treasury
Market	Stockholder reaction uncertain Number of shares × increase	14,000,000 shares at $45 currently Number of shares × price
Time period needed	Anytime	One to two years
Fit to present activities	Change in philosophy	Underlines management confidence
Revenues/profits	N/A	Sell shares for profit? Enrich remaining stockholders? At the right price/earnings ratio
Support among executives	Iverson thinking about it	
Skills and resources	N/A	N/A
Downside risk	If earnings slip, could pressure ability to invest	Price of stock could decline

Strategic Considerations	Option 9 Diversification Outside Steel Products or Joists
Market	Faster growing markets open
Investment	Nucor has $100–150 million Could borrow more
Time period needed	One to two years
Fit to present activities	Depends on business
Revenues/profits	Greater profitability?
Support among executives	Very little
Skills and resources	Nucor understands heavy manufacturing Nucor has skills in streamlined management Employee-relations philosophy
Downside risk	Company has to learn new things? Might require different organizational set-up.

That restricted the number of mills we could finance. But then in the 1980s things changed. Our restraints are not financial now. We no longer see the opportunities in minimills which we saw in the 60s and 70s. So, what direction should the company go? We have about $120 million in cash and short-term securities.

Since we don't see much opportunity for building additional minimills, we have been looking at various alternatives . . . merger or acquisition, internal growth . . . buying back our own stock . . . and other things. It goes forward by project. We looked at buying another steel company that had problems. Dave visited their plant. Bob (the planner) did some projections on what it would cost us to put that mill in shape. We also have an outside consultant working on it. That is what we have done so far (Iverson points to a report). . . . We are looking at the bolt business too. About 95 percent of bolts used in the United States are made outside of the United States. We are studying whether we should spend $25 million to build a plant. . . . Maybe we ought to buy our own stock. It reduces the number of shares and increases the per share earnings. I feel comfortable with that with the price/earnings ratio we are at.

We are thinking about a seamless tube mill. That business seems to meet many of our requirements. Also, the Vulcraft people believe that we could easily enter the business of preengineered buildings. Although that is a new market for us, it's not very risky, and it is a logical extension of the joist business.

We are also talking to the Japanese about a joint venture to produce large and medium structural steel shapes. That's a six million ton market worth about $2 billion per year. It's cyclical because it's tied to the construction industry. Imports have about 32 percent of that. We might invest $200 million. We know this market, but we lack some technology which the Japanese can supply. We would be 51 percent partners and run the plant.

Was he worried about a takeover?

I really don't expect someone to try to take us over. We have a staggered board. So if someone tries to do it they will have to wait for quite a while to control enough directors. We have other provisions in the bylaws which would make a takeover difficult. Besides, we're in a lousy business—steel.

What about an acquisition by Nucor?

We have some problems with going that route. We don't have any experience with acquisitions, all our growth has been internally generated. The second thing, we would never acquire outside our business, which is the manufacture of steel and steel products. We might be able to go into some nonferrous metals. But if we went into, say, textiles or something else like that . . . it's not . . . If stockholders want to invest in those businesses, let them do it themselves. Conglomeration is a lot of nonsense.

CASE 18 DICKENSON MINES LIMITED*

In October 1981, Peter Munro, the new president of Dickenson Mines (Dickenson), sat in the Toronto offices of the gold-mining company and wondered what he could do to save Dickenson from bankruptcy. In 1979, Dickenson's former management had undertaken a major expansion of the company's mining and milling operations. Subsequently, interest rates on the debt financing of the project climbed and gold prices dropped. These problems were compounded by cost overruns on the expansion program and higher operating costs at the mine. These factors combined to produce a cash drain on the company, and Dickenson was no longer able to service its growing debt. Munro's first priority was to take the necessary steps to ward off bankruptcy and then to restore profitability. Exhibits 1, 2, and 3 show Dickenson's financial position as of October 1981.

COMPANY HISTORY

In 1981 Dickenson Mines conducted gold-mining operations in Ontario and silver-mining operations in British Columbia. Dickenson also held a number of investments in oil and gas ventures throughout Canada and the United States. Most of the company's revenues were generated at the Red Lake Gold Mine in northwestern Ontario.

The Dickenson property was first staked during the Red Lake gold rush of 1926. In 1945 Dickenson Red Lake Mines was incorporated and by 1947 the first shaft was sunk to a depth of 550 feet. The following year enough reserves were discovered to justify the construction of a 150 ton per day mill to treat ore. By 1959 the mill was expanded to 450 tons per day, again in response to the discovery of new reserves. In 1961 the first shaft was deepened to 3,300 feet and in 1968 a second internal shaft was sunk from the 3,300 foot level to 4,400 feet. By 1968 Dickenson was conducting mining operations on 30 different levels off the main shafts.

The period 1945–71 was difficult for the Canadian gold industry. The selling price of gold was fixed at U.S. $35.00 ounce and production costs were rising. Other metal producers were enjoying increasing prices for their products and therefore were able to lure away skilled miners with the promise of higher wages. These problems led to the introduction of the Emergency Gold Mining Act (EGMA) in 1947 to aid the faltering industry. This act made new gold mines tax exempt for the first three years of operation and allowed them to accumulate the depletion and depreciation allowances earned during those years for write-offs in the following years. Over this period government subsidies of this sort worked out to roughly $5 an ounce and allowed many companies to stay in operation. In 1971, when gold prices were allowed

---

* Prepared by Peter Nerby under the supervision of Professor David C. Shaw, School of Business Administration, University of Western Ontario.

Exhibit 1   Consolidated Balance Sheets, Dickenson Mines Ltd., 1979–1981   In Thousands of Dollars

	December 31, 1979	December 31, 1980	September 30, 1981 (Unaudited)
Assets			
Current assets			
Bullion and concentrates on hand and in transit, at net realizable value	$ 2,943	$ 1,561	$ 1,646
Accounts receivable	343	580	422
Income taxes recoverable	—	314	314
Marketable securities, at cost (quoted market value 1981–$213; 1980–$383; 1979–$965)	731	347	365
Prepaid expenses	53	110	133
Total current assets	4,070	2,912	2,880
Long-term investments (note 4)	15,826	22,881	15,245
Fixed, at cost			
Buildings, machinery, and equipment	12,041	16,383	24,349
Less: Accumulated depreciation	(8,404)	(9,293)	(9,749)
Net, after depreciation	3,637	7,090	14,600
Mining claims	1,179	1,089	929
Townsite lots	142	282	287
Total, fixed assets	4,958	8,461	15,816
Other, at cost			
Shaft deepening and renovation expenditure unamortized	2,922	6,722	11,838
Interest in and expenditure on outside mining properties	1,129	1,110	530
Interest in and expenditure on oil and gas properties	1,905	3,086	3,961
Stores and supplies	1,709	2,317	2,712
Deferred charges	186	348	136
Total, other assets	7,851	13,583	19,177
Total assets	$32,705	$47,837	$56,118
Liabilities and Shareholders' Equity			
Current liabilities			
Bank indebtedness (note 3)	$ 315	$ 4,043	$ 7,436
Accounts payable	2,239	4,604	4,378
Income and mining taxes payable	981	142	142
Current portion of long-term debt (notes 2 and 3)	1,200	1,043	6,250
Total current liabilities	4,735	9,832	18,206
Long-term debt (notes 2 and 3)	3,500	7,746	6,669
Deferred income taxes	3,223	4,916	5,435
Total liabilities	11,458	22,494	30,310
Capital stock (note 1)			
Authorized			
30,000,000 Class A shares without par value			
6,000,000 Class B shares without par value			
Issued			
Class A shares	4,489	4,879	4,901
Class B shares	4,489	4,879	4,898
Contributed surplus	1,466	1,466	1,466
Retained earnings	12,108	16,688	17,002
Deduct Company's shares of Kam Kotia Mines Limited's holdings of shares of Dickenson Mines Limited	(1,305)	(2,569)	(2,459)
Total shareholders' equity	21,247	25,343	25,808
Total liabilities and shareholders' equity	$32,705	$47,837	$56,118

Exhibit 1 *(continued)*

Notes to Financial Statements

1. **Amalgamation**

The consolidated financial statements give effect to the statutory amalgamation (under the Business Corporations Act of Ontario) of Dickenson Mines Limited (Dickenson) and Silvana Mines Inc. (Silvana), both under common control, into the continuing corporation, Dickenson Mines Limited, pursuant to an amalgamation agreement dated October 7, 1980, and the issue of a certificate of amalgamation on October 31, 1980.

(a) The amalgamation was accounted for on the basis of combining the assets and liabilities of the amalgamating corporations at their carrying value in each corporation's records. The income of the combined corporation includes income of the combining corporations for the year ended December 31, 1980. Income figures for the years 1979, 1978, 1977, and 1976 have been restated on the same basis.

(b) The amalgamation agreement provided that the authorized capital of the amalgamated corporation shall consist of 30,000,000 Class A common shares without par value and 6,000,000 Class B special shares without par value; each Class A share is entitled to one vote and each Class B share is entitled to ten votes at meetings of shareholders. The Class B shares rank equally with the Class A shares in all other respects.

2. **Long-term debt**

	In Thousands of Dollars		
	December 31, 1979	December 31, 1980	September 30, 1981 (Unaudited)
Term bank loan—U.S. $10,000,000, interest at prime plus 1¼%	$ —	$ —	$11,919
Term bank loan—interest at prime rate plus 1%	4,700	6,600	—
Notes payable—Carl O. Nickle—7% repayable $1,000,000 in September 1981 and $1,000,000 in September 1982	—	2,000	1,000
Finance contract payable—14% repayable U.S. $3,036 monthly up to and including May 1, 1985. Fixed assets have been pledged as security	—	189	—
	4,700	8,789	12,919
Less: Amounts due within one year	(1,200)	(1,043)	(6,250)
	$3,500	$7,746	$ 6,669

3. **Bank loan security**

The Company has pledged as security for the bank indebtedness and the term bank loan the following:

(a) A $25,000,000 demand debenture creating a fixed charge over the Red Lake Mine, a fixed charge over the major machinery and equipment of the Company, and a floating charge over all other assets of the Company.

(b) Security under Section 177 of the Bank Act (Canada) on mineral reserves, inventory, and equipment located at the Red Lake Mine site.

(c) Security under Section 178 of the Bank Act (Canada) with respect to the Red Lake and Silvana Mines.

(d) An hypothecation of the Company's portfolio of junior stocks, including oil and gas stocks and Kam-Kotia stock.

(e) An assignment of the promissory note from Oakwood Petroleum Limited.

Exhibit 1 *(concluded)*

4. Investments in companies accounted for by the equity method:

			In Thousands of Dollars		
			December 31,1979	December 31,1980	September 30,1981 (Unaudited)
Shares and convertible notes Kam Kotia Mines Limited					
	Shares	*Quoted Market Value*			
at September 30, 1981	2,119,108	$ 4,026,000			
at December 31, 1980	2,119,108	$19,602,000			
at December 31, 1979	2,112,108	$13,465,000	$ 2,992	$ 2,346	$ 1,041
Conventures Limited [Note 1(b)]					
1,453,686 shares and $4,700,000—5% convertible notes (quoted market value at December 31, 1980 $31,128,000)			—	16,826	—
Other (quoted market value)					
at September 30, 1981	$ 2,592,000				
at December 31, 1980	$10,365,000				
at December 31, 1979	$ 7,228,000		2,826	2,701	2,855
			5,818	21,873	3,896
Loans and advances, at cost			315	72	112
Subtotal			6,133	21,945	4,008
Investment in Conventures Limited [Note 1 (b)] At December 31, 1979,1,084,396 shares and $4,700,000—5% convertible notes (quoted market value at December 31, 1979, $23,406,000)			9,938	—	—
Portfolio investments, at cost					
Listed shares					
Shares and warrants of New Cinch Uranium Ltd. (quoted market value)					
at September 30, 1981	$ 274,000				
at December 31, 1980	$12,216,000				
at December 31, 1979	$ 1,388,000		198	345	275
Other listed shares (quoted market value)					
at September 30, 1981	$117,000				
at December 31, 1980	$385,000				
at December 31, 1979	$365,000		320	262	278
			518	607	553
Other shares, bonds, advances and participations			1,256	2,188	1,878
Subtotal			1,774	2,795	2,431
Note receivable from Oakwood Petroleum Limited, due September 5, 1983, bearing interest at the prime rate, not to exceed 23.5% and not less than 17.5%			—	—	13,535
Total			17,845	24,740	19,974
Less: Allowance for decline in value			(2,019)	(1,859)	(1,729)
			$15,826	$22,881	$18,245

The quoted market values referred to above do not necessarily represent the realizable value of these holdings that may be more or less than that indicated by market quotations.

The investment in Conventures Limited comprising 1,453,686 shares and $4,700,000 convertible notes was sold to Oakwood Petroleum Limited on September 29, 1981 (with effect from September 4, 1981) for the following considerations:

Cash*	$13,000,000
Note receivable, due September 5, 1983	13,535,000
	$26,535,000

* The cash portion of the proceeds were applied to reduce the Company's bank indebtedness.

to float on the open market, profitability returned to the Canadian industry, and the EGMA was no longer needed.

After the deregulation of the price of gold, Dickenson's fortunes improved considerably. By 1974, revenues had risen to $11 million, and profits were $3 million compared to 1971 when revenues were $3 million and profits were $264,000. The company's major activity was still gold mining, but diversification had begun. Dickenson owned a 36 percent share in Kam Kotia Mines, which had investments in several mining and oil and gas companies and was developing a silver–lead–zinc mine in British Columbia.

In 1975 Dickenson management made the strategic decision to diversify into oil and gas exploration and development. Dickenson entered into a joint venture agreement with Conventures Ltd. of Calgary to develop a gas field in Alberta. Conventures acted as the operating partner and Dickenson supplied a portion of the capital. From June 1975 to December 1978, Dickenson purchased 700,000 Conventures shares for a total of $2.1 million. In 1979 Dickenson invested an additional $1 million and supplied Conventures with some oil and gas leases in Alberta in exchange for 225,000 shares at a share purchase price valued at $8 per share by the two companies. Also in 1979, Dickenson loaned the company money on the basis of a $4.7 million note from Conventures that was convertible into another 681,000 common shares at $6.90 per share until December 31, 1981. If Dickenson decided to exercise the conversion option, they would own roughly 25 percent of the oil and gas company.

By early 1980 the Dickenson group of companies operated the Red Lake Gold Mine in Ontario and the Silvana silver mine in British Columbia. Besides Conventures, Dickenson held nonoperating interests in several oil and gas plays throughout Alberta, other parts of Canada, and the United States. In addition, Kam Kotia Mines Ltd. held similar oil and gas interests. Dickenson also held a portfolio of investments in Canadian junior mining companies.

THE MINE AND MILL EXPANSION

By 1979, after 31 years of production at the Red Lake Gold Mine, new high-grade ore reserves were no longer being discovered in sufficient quantities to maintain gold production at historical levels. However, Dickenson management believed that large quantities of low-grade ore reserves still existed and that these could best be mined by changing Dickenson from a medium-tonnage, high-grade ore producer to a high-tonnage, low-grade ore producer. The management believed that this shift in mining strategy could best be accomplished by changing the mining method from labor-intensive cut-and-fill mining to mechanized blast-hole mining. Consultants were hired to quantify these low-grade ore reserves and give an opinion on the application of blast-hole mining.

After several months of study, a four-part capital expenditure program was approved. This program would increase mill capacity, deepen the number-two internal shaft of the mine, increase ore hoisting capacity, and utilize newer more mechanized methods of mining. It was estimated that the two-year program would cost between $10 and $11 million and would increase the mine's capacity to 1,000 tons per day.

Exhibit 2 Consolidated Income Statements, Dickenson Mines, Ltd., 1976–1981 In Thousands of Dollars except Earnings per Share

	Year Ended December 31,					Nine Months Ended September 30, (Unaudited)	
	1976	1977	1978	1979	1980	1980	1981
Revenue:							
Gold bullion production	$6,857	$9,650	$13,594	$15,973	$19,857	$16,018	$ 9,439
Lead and zinc concentrates production	164	1,216	2,793	5,207	7,394	5,560	4,584
	7,021	10,866	16,387	21,180	27,251	21,578	14,023
Expense:							
Mining	4,212	5,227	6,256	6,979	9,299	6,548	8,972
Milling	1,051	1,343	1,757	2,257	3,073	2,014	2,484
Mine management, office and general	1,160	1,357	1,930	2,485	3,511	2,326	2,768
Transportation and treatment costs	407	498	597	1,627	1,666	1,251	1,314
Head office administration, general and short-term interest expense	28	340	897	796	1,015	629	2,703
Marketing	45	53	65	66	73	62	37
	6,903	8,818	11,502	14,210	18,637	12,830	18,278
Operating income (loss) before undernoted items	118	2,048	4,885	6,970	8,614	8,748	(4,255)
Amortization of shaft deepening and renovations	—	—	121	393	1,388	960	866
Depreciation and depletion	329	583	731	826	1,206	676	671
Outside exploration written off	87	28	9	436	757	516	695
Amortization of oil and gas properties	—	—	—	—	343	257	349
	416	611	861	1,655	3,694	2,409	2,581
Income (loss) from mining operations	(298)	1,437	4,024	5,315	4,920	6,339	(6,836)

Investment and other income and expense							
Share of net income (loss) of companies accounted for by the equity method	(62)	75	38	(94)	742	104	(106)
Dividends, interest, and net results of security transactions	221	258	267	844	1,093	910	736
Oil and gas revenue	—	—	—	16	70	53	52
Interest expense, long-term	—	—	—	(674)	(762)	(465)	(985)
Fire loss recovery (net)	—	—	—	—	464	—	32
Amalgamation expense	—	—	—	—	(332)	(50)	—
	159	333	305	92	1,275	552	(271)
Income (loss) before income taxes and extraordinary items	(139)	1,770	4,329	5,407	6,195	6,891	(7,107)
Income and mining taxes	(346)	541	1,648	2,691	1,750	2,200	—
Income (loss) before extraordinary items	207	1,229	2,681	2,716	4,445	4,691	(7,107)
Increase in the carrying value of the Company's interest in Kam Kotia Mines Limited arising from share issues by Kam Kotia	—	—	—	1,200	503	503	—
Provisions for decline in investment in New Cinch Uranium Ltd.	—	—	—	—	—	—	(477)
Share of extraordinary gains (loss) of companies accounted for by the equity method	(40)	(75)	(124)	367	93	93	(1,285)
Gain on sale of investment in Conventures Limited (net of deferred tax of $520)	—	—	—	—	—	—	9,183
Net income for the period	$ 167	$ 1,154	$ 2,557	$ 4,283	$ 5,041	$ 5,287	$ 314
Earnings per share:							
Before extraordinary items							
Class A	$ 0.03	$ 0.16	$ 0.32	$ 0.31	$ 0.48	$ 0.49	$ (0.76)
Class B	0.03	0.16	0.32	0.31	0.48	0.49	(0.76)
After extraordinary items							
Class A	0.02	0.15	0.31	0.48	0.55	0.55	0.03
Class B	0.02	0.15	0.31	0.48	0.55	0.55	0.03

Exhibit 3   Consolidated Statement of Changes in Financial Position, Dickenson Mines, Ltd., 1976–1981   In Thousands of Dollars

			Year Ended December 31,			Nine Months Ended September 30, (unaudited)	
	1976	**1977**	**1978**	**1979**	**1980**	**1980**	**1981**
Source of funds:							
Income (loss) before extra-ordinary items	$ 207	$1,229	$2,681	$ 2,716	$ 4,445	$ 4,691	$ (7,107)
Charges (credits) not affecting funds							
Amortization of shaft deepening and renovations	—	—	121	393	1,388	960	866
Depreciation and depletion	329	583	731	826	1,206	676	671
Outside exploration written off	87	28	9	436	757	516	695
Amortization of oil and gas properties	—	—	—	—	343	257	349
Share of loss (net income) of companies accounted for by the equity method	62	(75)	(38)	94	(742)	(104)	106
Deferred income taxes	2	123	710	1,705	1,692	2,200	—
Gain on sale of investment in Jameland Mines Ltd.	—	—	—	—	—	—	(118)
Funds provided from (applied to) operations	687	1,888	4,214	6,170	9,089	9,196	(4,538)
Long-term debt, noncurrent portion	—	—	—	3,500	4,246	4,100	1,077
Issue of capital stock	264	1,186	852	2,535	986	984	39
Decrease in stores and supplies	—	93	—	—	—	—	—
Decrease in deferred charges	—	—	147	14	—	—	219
Proceeds from sale of long-term investments	—	—	—	—	—	—	26,650
Increase in contributed surplus		—	6	—	—	—	—
	951	3,167	5,219	12,219	14,321	14,280	21,293
Application of funds:							
Purchase of fixed assets	1,686	1,519	869	874	4,482	3,130	8,196
Shaft deepening and renovation expenditure	—	35	650	2,185	5,100	3,332	5,982
Increase in stores and supplies	141	41	349	275	608	706	395
Investment in and advances to other companies	342	770	1,600	8,076	7,501	7,631	13,788
Exploration expenditure on outside mining, oil, and gas properties	115	591	796	2,238	2,262	1,388	1,338
Increase in deferred charges	173	8	—	—	162	9	—
Dividends paid	259	163	353	190	461	—	—
	2,716	3,127	4,617	13,838	20,576	16,196	29,699
Increase (Decrease) in funds during the period	(1,765)	40	602	(1,619)	(6,255)	(1,916)	(8,406)
Funds (deficiency) at beginning of period	2,076	311	352	954	(665)	(665)	(6,920)
Funds (deficiency) at end of period	$ 311	$ 351	$ (954)	$ (665)	$ (6,920)	$ (2,581)	$(15,326)

Deepening the number two internal shaft from a depth of 4,400 feet to 5,700 feet would open up eight more levels for mining (levels 31–38) and allow access to new ore that was believed to be promising. The cost of the project was estimated to be $2.5 million.

In order to remove 1,000 tons per day from the mine, additional hoisting capacity had to be built. After considerable study, it was decided to modify the number one shaft to permit utilization of the two hoisting compartments solely for hoisting ore and waste instead of combining this use with the lifting of men and materials. These services then were placed in a third compartment that required the installation of considerable auxiliary equipment. This was expected to cost $4 million.

Finally, milling capacity had to be increased to accommodate the increased ore volumes from the mine. To accomplish this, the consultants proposed that the ore-crushing process be speeded up by reducing the crushing time for a batch of ore and therefore increasing the crusher product size. The size of the crusher product would be doubled, which would increase crusher capacity to 1,400 tons per day. In addition, the fine ore storage bin would be increased in size from 600 to 2,000 tons. The cost of the mill expansion was estimated to be $4 million.

The consultants and Dickenson management believed that these operating changes would allow the company to mine lower ore grades at lower cost per ton. Combined with higher gold prices, these changes would ensure the profitability of the mine in years to come. Dickenson therefore negotiated a $10 million project term loan at a rate of bank prime plus 1 percent and an additional $5 million line of credit to finance the expansion program.

By the end of 1980 approximately $8 million had been spent on the expansion program, yet none of the four components was complete. Dickenson had run the term loan up to $6.6 million and the operating line of credit was up to $3.7 million. Gold production for the year had dropped from 44,000 ounces in 1979 to 29,000 ounces in 1980 primarily because of the mining of lower ore grades. The recovery rate at the mill also fell, as an enhanced recovery process involving the roasting of gold sulfide wastes produced by cyanide leaching had to be suspended because of environmental and employee health reasons. This lowered gold recovery from 93.7 percent to 83.3 percent. Lower ore grades and lower mill recovery rates meant that Dickenson had to treat 4.4 tons of ore in 1980 to produce 1 ounce of gold compared to 2.7 tons in 1979. Fortunately, the average price received per ounce of gold had risen from $356 to $675. The company had revised its estimates of the cost to complete the four-part expansion to an additional $9 million in 1981, because of severe cost overruns during 1980—see Exhibit 4. Exhibit 5 presents a diagram of the Red Lake Gold Mine operations; Exhibit 6 shows the mine's 1976–1981 operating results; and Exhibit 7 presents statistics on the mine's proven ore reserves.

PROBLEMS IN 1981

As the expansion program moved nto 1981, several new developments occurred that all started to work against Dickenson. For 1981, anticipating the commencement of the new mechanized mining operations, the company had set out a production budget to mine 210,000 tons of ore at a grade of 0.19 ounce of gold per ton, resulting in

Exhibit 4   Forecast of Expenditures to Complete Mine and Mill Expansion   In Thousands

Expenditure Category	*Actual 1980*	*Actual January 1– September 30, 1981*	*Estimate 1982*
(1) Working Capital and New Machinery for Mechanized Cut-and-Fill Mining	$1,042	$ 2,411	$ 35
(2) Mill Expansion	1,163	5,202	2,882
(3) Deepening of #2 Shaft	3,152	531	0
(4) New Hauling System	2,591	5,776	310
Totals	$7,948	$13,920	$3,227

Exhibit 5   Mill Operations

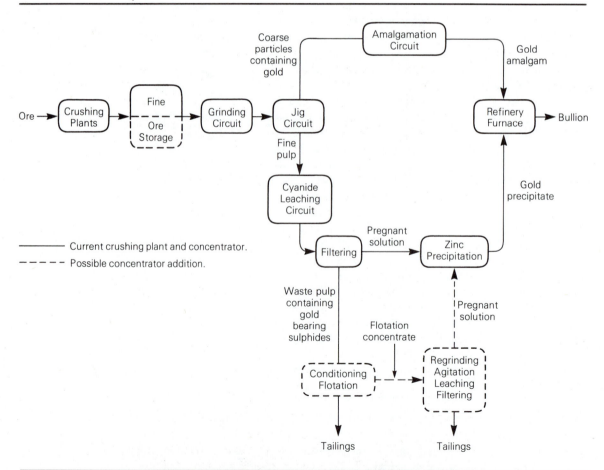

————— Current crushing plant and concentrator.

– – – – Possible concentrator addition.

Exhibit 6   Operating Results for the Red Lake Gold Mine, 1976–September 30, 1981

	Years Ended December 31,					1981		
	1976	1977	1978	1979	1980	First Quarter	Second Quarter	Third Quarter
Ore milled (tons)	117,000	129,000	110,000	118,000	128,000	36,549	46,467	49,360
Average grade of ore milled (ounces of gold per ton)	0.509	0.499	0.576	0.405	0.270	0.15	0.13	0.17
Production of gold (ounces)	55,488	60,019	59,957	44,367	29,281	4,282	5,047	7,142
Operating expenses								
Per ton milled	$ 58.36	$ 60.89	$ 80.94	$ 86.27	$ 91.79	$ 97.21	$ 83.22	$ 85.21
Per troy ounce recovered	$ 123.02	$ 130.89	$ 149.48	$ 229.45	$ 401.25	$798.77	$765.44	$588.33
Average price of gold per ounce received during the period	123.30	160.34	226.00	356.33	675.49	$687.43	$554.04	$501.19
Revenue received during the period (thousands of dollars)	$ —	$ —	$ 13,560	$ 15,807	$ 19,779	$ —	$ —	$ —

Exhibit 7   Proven Ore Reserves, Red Lake Gold Mine, 1975–1981

Year	Tons of Ore	Ounce/ Ton	Ounces of Gold
1975	393,057	0.538	211,464
1976	357,382	0.536	191,556·
1977	335,622	0.539	180,190
1978	350,909	0.571	200,369
1979	389,000	0.529	205,781
1980	425,000	0.450	191,250
1981[a]	653,700	0.289	189,300

[a] As estimated by consultants.

the production of 34,700 ounces of gold, assuming a mill recovery rate of about 87 percent. Costs of production were expected to be $63.10 per ton or $381.90 per ounce.

As the year progressed, it became clear that Dickenson could not meet this budget. The expansion work in the mine hindered the efficiency of the mining process and the control of ore-grade quality declined as the new mechanized mining methods were put into use. This resulted in lower tonnages mined at reduced ore grades. The operating and financial statements for the first three quarters clearly indicated the severity of the operating problems at the mine. For the nine months ending September 30, 1981, 133,000 tons of ore had been mined at an average grade of 0.15 ounce of gold per ton, resulting in production of only 16,471 ounces of gold. Once again the expansion program was experiencing major cost overruns, as total estimated expenditures for 1981 alone were now expected to be roughly $14 million (Exhibit 4).

Increased financing costs and lower gold prices added to these operating problems. The prime rate hit a high of 22 percent in 1981 and, by October 1981, the price of gold had fallen to U.S. $400 ounce. At that point, Dickenson's operating costs were estimated to be Cdn $631/ounce and interest expense was estimated at Cdn $91/ounce for a total cost of $722 an ounce. These problems were compounded by the complete lack of capital budgetary controls to the extent that the company relied solely on the external auditors to develop capital cost and cash flow projections. At this time the company's major banker was exerting considerable pressure to reduce bank debt and infuse new management.

Dickenson's problems were not limited to the gold-mining operations, as the silver division also was operating at a loss. This division was composed of Silvana Mines of British Columbia and it had been adversely affected by sharply reduced silver prices. For the nine months ending September 30, 1981, Silvana lost almost $1 million as opposed to a profit of $493,000 for the same period in 1980—see Exhibit 8.

Dickenson was also involved in a $21 million lawsuit with Willroy Mines Ltd. concerning the results of an exploration program conducted by New Cinch Uranium Mines of New Mexico, a company in which Dickenson held a 12 percent interest. Willroy was accusing Dickenson and 15 other firms of misrepresentation regarding the presentation of the New Cinch assay results. The original assays of New Cinch's reserves were found to be inaccurate, but not before Willroy had purchased a large

Exhibit 8   Results of Silvana Division[a]

	Years Ended December 31,			Nine Months Ended September 30,	
	1978	1979	1980	1980	1981
Revenue	$1,896,000	$3,580,000	$5,545,193	$4,214,497	$3,288,164
Operating income (Loss)[b]	246,000	1,255,000	413,140	560,190	(352,687)
Income (Loss) before income taxes[c]	123,000	1,006,000	369,488	493,126	(954,898)
Average price received:					
Silver (per ounce)	6.25	14.82	22.56	23.56	12.49
Lead (per pound)	0.37	0.63	0.48	0.48	0.44
Zinc (per pound)	0.33	0.41	0.42	0.42	0.50

[a] In 1976 and 1977 to August 1, Silvana Mines Inc. leased its property to Kam Kotia. Financial information for years prior to 1978 is not comparable to subsequent years.

[b] Before depreciation and depletion, deferred development expenses, oil and gas interests written off, and head office, administration, and general expenses and interest income.

[c] Results were adversely affected in 1981 by a change in the method of accounting for depreciation from the straight line method to the unit of production method.

	Years Ended December 31,			
	1977	1978	1979	1980
Ore milled (tons)	17,499	17,600	21,632	31,110
Average tons per month	1,459	1,467	1,803	2,593
Average grade				
Silver (ounces per ton)	19.34	14.84	13.96	8.63
Lead (%)	7.41	5.81	4.87	3.21
Zinc (%)	6.13	4.34	4.51	3.03
Lead concentrate produced (tons)	2,086	1,609	1,654	1,556
Metal content				
Silver (ounces)	224,311	174,799	185,744	183,684
Lead (pounds)	2,449,345	1,948,464	2,011,863	1,805,561
Zinc (pounds)	427,384	299,608	301,586	258,200
Zinc concentrate produced (tons)	1,582	1,071	1,458	1,359
Metal content				
Silver (ounces)	101,515	68,876	104,301	71,698
Zinc (pounds)	1,578,866	1,108,890	491,599	372,240
Cadmium (pounds)	12,055	8,209	10,937	9,542

portion of New Cinch shares. When the drilling cores were reassayed and found to be worthless, New Cinch stock dropped dramatically and Willroy Mines incurred a substantial loss. Dickenson contended that it had no knowledge of the inaccuracies in the original assays and indeed that it also suffered a loss on its holdings of New Cinch as a result of the new information.

THE SALE OF CONVENTURES LTD.

By September 1981 Dickenson owed $4.5 million in accounts payable and $33.4 million in bank debt, all of which was technically due and payable because the company was in default on servicing this debt. In light of these obligations, Dickenson management decided to sell the company's interest in Conventures Ltd. of Calgary, which now consisted of 1.4 million common shares and the $4.7 million convertible debenture.

Exhibit 9   Dickenson Mines' Common Stock Performance for 1980 and 1981

1981	Dickenson A Shares	Dickenson B Shares	TSE Gold Index	Gold Price (in U.S. $ per ounce)
September	$ 4.15	$3.60	3423	$431.75
August	5.00	5.00	4101	414.00
July	4.85	4.70	3819	401.50
June	5.37	5.12	3573	428.75
May	7.00	5.87	4449	479.25
April	8.50	7.50	4311	477.25
March	10.50	9.25	4288	539.50
February	8.25	8.00	3796	489.00
January	10.50	9.25	4056	506.50

Note: 1980 Range: $11.25–16.75; $9.75–$17.00.

On September 29, 1981, Dickenson was able to arrange to sell its interest in Conventures to Oakwood Petroleum of Calgary for $26.5 million. Dickenson received a note from Oakwood for $13.5 million bearing interest equal to the prime rate within a range of 17.5 percent to 23.5 percent. Dickenson also received $13 million in cash which was used to reduce the bank debt. In return, Dickenson gave up 1,453,686 shares of Conventures and the 5 percent–$4.7 million note from Conventures that could be converted into another 680,000 shares by December 31, 1981. On September 24, 1981, Conventure's common stock had closed at $9.

THE SITUATION IN OCTOBER 1981

When Peter Munro joined Dickenson from Falconbridge in October 1981, he called in his new vice president of finance, John Kachmar, also from Falconbridge, to review the situation. The cash proceeds from the Conventures investment had reduced Dickenson's floating rate bank debt to roughly $20.4 million. Interest payments amounted to $325,000 a month. Two creditors in particular had become adamant about receiving payment. One bank wanted $1 million by January and the company's cyanide supplier was threatening to cut off deliveries, which would shut down the mill, if outstanding bills were not settled.

With regard to the expansion program, which had been expected to cost between $9 and $10 million originally, the deepening of the number two shaft was now complete and enough equipment had been purchased to begin the mechanized mining processes, but mill capacity had only reached 700 tons per day and the ore haulage system was not finished. The consultants estimated that the cost to complete the program, in addition to the $22 million already spent in 1980 and 1981, was $3.2 million in 1982.

Munro and Kachmar knew that they had to raise cash to pay off their debts or face bankruptcy. They drew up a list of possible options:

1. A public financing issue to institutional investors.
2. A rights offering to existing shareholders and corporate management.
3. Sell assets.
4. Increase gold production with possible use of forward sales to ensure stable gold prices.
5. Reduce costs and cut capital expenditures.

Munro and Kachmar had had some discussions with the company's underwriters regarding the first two financing options. They had come up with a plan to issue a type of "debt unit." This unit would consist of seven $1,000 (U.S.) bonds and 40 gold purchase warrants. Each warrant would allow the holder to purchase one ounce of gold. The warrants would be exercisable in groups of 10 in the years 1986, 1987, 1988, and 1989. Dickenson wanted to sell each unit for U.S. $14,000, the purchase price representing seven U.S. $1,000 bonds and a prepayment of U.S. $175 towards the exercise price of each warrant. The coupon rate on the bonds, the exercise price of the warrants, and the overall size of the issue had yet to be decided.

A rights offering to existing shareholders and management would allow the present shareholders to maintain their proportionate share of ownership and give the new management an opportunity to participate in the ownership of the company at a low cost, given the current price level of Dickenson stock. It was, however, a risky proposition because Dickenson's future was by no means certain. Exhibit 9 shows the recent performance of the company's stock; Exhibit 10 shows recent prime lending rates at a major Canadian bank.

Exhibit 10   Prime Lending Rate of a Major Canadian Bank, January 1980–September 1981   At Month End

		Average Monthly Prime Rate (percent)
1980	January	15
	February	15
	March	16.12
	April	17.16
	May	15.18
	June	13.25
	July	12.63
	August	12.25
	September	12.25
	October	12.87
	November	13.83
	December	16.91
1981	January	17
	February	17.11
	March	17.75
	April	18
	May	19.25
	June	20
	July	21
	August	22.50
	September	22.00

Exhibit 11   *Pro Forma* Production Budget, Red Lake Gold Mine, 1982–1986

| | *Year Ending December 31,* | | | | |
	1982	*1983*	*1984*	*1985*	*1986*
Ore milled (tons)	240,000	350,000	350,000	350,000	350,000
Average grade of ore milled (ounces of gold per ton)	0.181	0.176	0.176	0.176	0.176
Recovery	83%	85%	85%	85%	85%
Production of gold (ounces)	36,000	52,500	52,500	52,500	52,500
Operating expenses (1982 dollars)					
Per ton milled	$ 56.25	$ 51.65	$ 51.65	$ 51.65	$ 51.65
Per troy ounce recovered	$375.05	$344.38	$344.38	$344.38	$344.38
Capital costs (thousands of 1982 dollars)					
Concentrator	$ 1,443				
Other	$ 1,265	$ 2,853	$ 1,372	$ 1,244	$ 1,244

Selling more company assets was not a pleasant proposition, but had to be considered. First, there was the note from Oakwood Petroleum with a par value of $13,535,000 and interest rates that varied with the prime rate between 17.5 percent to 23.5 percent. Munro and Kachmar also had to consider the possibility of selling a portion of Dickenson's oldest asset, the Red Lake Gold Mine. Munro wondered how much cash he might be able to raise by selling a 50 percent interest in the mine.

Both men clearly recognized the need to cut operating costs and increase gold production. They felt it might be possible to return to more traditional mining methods for a while and work the remaining higher grade stopes and pillars that were still left in the mine. They were also considering the use of the gold futures or options markets in order to gain security against further price drops. Munro was also considering delaying the rest of the capital expenditure program.

Both Munro and Kachmar realized that the initial goal of the mine and mill expansion was a good one in principle. However, it was also clear to them that bankruptcy was imminent if they could not develop a short-run survival plan to raise cash and retire debt. In light of the current problems, the company's five-year plan for the Red Lake Mine looked increasingly unrealistic (see Exhibit 11).

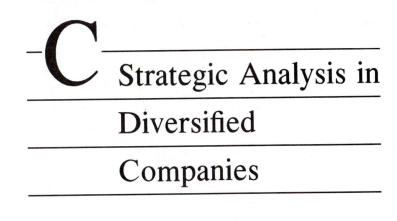

C Strategic Analysis in Diversified Companies

CASE 19   MOBIL CORPORATION (A) (revised)*

Mobil Corporation began the 1980s as a company with revenues of $49 billion, assets of $28 billion, earnings of $2 billion, and capital outlays of nearly $4 billion. The firm ranked as the third largest industrial corporation in the United States and the fifth largest in the world. The dominant portion of Mobil's business was concentrated in petroleum; its Mobil Oil division was one of the seven largest integrated petroleum companies in the world and accounted for 85 percent of Mobil's corporate revenues. In 1980 the Mobil Oil division owned or operated oil- and gas-producing properties in 16 nations, had interests in 38,000 miles of pipelines in the United States and abroad, operated some 35 refineries in various worldwide locations, operated a worldwide fleet of nearly 100 oceangoing vessels, and marketed its refined petroleum products in over 100 countries. In addition to its oil business, Mobil Corporation's business portfolio included Mobil Chemical Company, a manufacturer of disposable plastic packaging, phosphate rock, chemical coatings, and petrochemicals; Container Corporation of America, the nation's leading manufacturer of paperboard packaging; Montgomery Ward, one of the largest retail department store chains in the United States; and a number of developmental activities relating to coal, uranium, shale oil, and solar energy. Exhibit 1 provides financial highlights of Mobil's consolidated operations. Exhibit 2 shows a breakout by line of business.

---

* Prepared by Professor Arthur A. Thompson, Jr., The University of Alabama, and Victor Gray, The University of Otago. Copyright © 1986 by Arthur A. Thompson, Jr.

Exhibit 1   Mobil Corporation's Financial Summary, 1975–1979   Dollar Amounts Are in Millions except per Share Figures

	1975*	1976*	1977*	1978*	1979
Year ended December 31:					
Revenues	$22,355	$28,046	$34,443	$37,331	$48,241
Operating and other expenses	18,934	23,865	29,592	32,805	40,927
Interest and debt discount expense	224	315	397	420	459
Income taxes	2,374	2,893	3,428	2,975	4,848
Total costs and expenses	21,532	27,073	33,417	36,200	46,234
Net income	823	973	1,026	1,131	2,007
Net income per share, based on average shares outstanding ($)	4.04	4.69	4.85	5.34	9.46
Cash dividends	346	364	413	456	541
per share ($)	1.70	1.75	1.95	2.15	2.55
Return on average shareholders' equity	12.3%	13.3%	12.8%	13.0%	20.5%
Return on average capital employed†	10.0%	10.5%	9.9%	10.4%	16.0%
Net income per dollar of revenue	3.7¢	3.5¢	3.0¢	3.0¢	4.2¢
Energy earnings per gallon sold	1.6¢	2.0¢	2.1¢	2.4¢	4.4¢
Capital expenditures, exploration, and other outlays‡	1,469	2,485	1,786	2,175	3,812
At December 31:					
Current assets	6,160	8,157	9,174	9,800	11,889
Current liabilities	5,226	6,844	7,632	8,686	11,170
Working capital	934	1,313	1,542	1,114	719
Investments and long-term receivables	1,998	1,504	1,657	1,844	2,030
Net properties, plants, and equipment	6,885	9,366	9,973	10,816	13,103
Total assets	15,257	19,323	21,182	22,880	27,506
Long term debt	2,172	3,214	3,310	3,047	2,962
Shareholders' equity	6,897	7,739	8,358	9,037	10,513
Shareholders' equity per share, based on shares outstanding at end of year ($)	33.86	36.56	39.45	42.63	49.54
Number of shares outstanding (000)	203,729	211,663	211,852	211,978	212,229
Number of shareholders	229,000	265,200	268,100	268,000	274,200
Number of employees	73,200	199,500	200,700	207,700	213,500

* Restated to reflect adoption of *FASB 19*, "Financial Accounting and Reporting by Oil and Gas Producing Companies." Per share amounts and shares outstanding have been adjusted for the two-for-one stock split.

† Net income plus income applicable to minority interests plus interest expense net of tax divided by the sum of average shareholders equity, debt, capital lease obligations, and minority interests.

‡ Includes capital expenditures of majority owned unconsolidated companies and acquisitions.

Note: Mobil's 54 percent voting interest in the Marcor companies was accounted for on the equity method through July 1, 1976, when Mobil became the 100 percent owner of these companies.

Source: Mobil Corporation, *1979 Annual Report.*

HISTORY AND BACKGROUND

In 1866, Matthew Ewing, a carpenter, persuaded Hiram Bond Everest, a grocer, to invest in a venture to produce kerosene by distilling crude oil in a vacuum. Ewing believed his method would produce higher kerosene yields than the conventional distillation at atmospheric pressure. The increased yields did not transpire, but an important difference did result; because of the lower temperatures used in the vacuum

Exhibit 2   Mobil Corporation's Financial Performance by Line of Business, 1976–1979   Millions of Dollars

	1976	1977	1978	1979
Total revenues:				
Energy: United States	$ 6,994	$ 7,751	$ 8,225	$10,831
Foreign	19,301	21,530	22,953	31,814
Chemical	1,107	1,203	1,361	1,718
Retail merchandising	2,514	5,047	5,474	5,652
Paperboard packaging	540	1,145	1,284	1,487
Other	—	—	—	162
Adjustments and eliminations	(1,978)	(2,126)	(1,874)	(3,372)
Total	$28,478	$34,550	$37,423	$48,292
Segment earnings:				
Energy: United States	$ 456	$ 503	$ 474	$ 680
Foreign	392	435	586	1,341
Chemical	81	85	86	113
Retail merchandising	86	94	105	54
Paperboard packaging	38	45	5*	35
Other	(13)	(60)	(35)	(65)
Corporate expenses	(67)	(76)	(90)	(151)
Income before extraordinary item	$ 973	$ 1,026	$ 1,131	$ 2,007
Capital expenditures†:				
Energy: United States	$ 672	$ 643	$ 712	$ 1,187
Foreign	536	540	668	825
Chemical	113	90	104	146
Retail merchandising	63	127	179	250
Paperboard packaging	55	108	129	117
Corporate and other	2	6	70	117
Total	$ 1,441	$ 1,514	$ 1,862	$ 2,642
Depreciation, depletion, and amortization:				
Energy: United States	$ 281	$ 340	$ 468	$ 542
Foreign	245	272	283	334
Chemical	33	38	46	58
Retail merchandising	32	67	68	74
Paperboard packaging	26	56	59	65
Corporate and other	4	4	6	13
Total	$ 621	$ 777	$ 930	$ 1,086
Total segment assets at year-end:				
Energy: United States	$ 5,425	$ 5,766	$ 6,046	$ 7,830
Foreign	9,540	10,697	11,263	13,681
Chemical	739	835	955	1,160
Retail merchandising	3,021	3,343	3,569	3,746
Paperboard packaging	1,119	1,205	1,279	1,382
Other	10	(8)	45	229
Corporate assets	108	121	158	115
Adjustments and eliminations	(639)	(777)	(435)	(637)
Total	$19,323	$21,182	$22,880	$27,506

* Includes a $42 million after-tax provision for settlements of class action antitrust litigation.
† Excludes exploration expenses, major acquisitions, and the capital expenditures of majority-owned unconsolidated companies.
Source: Mobil Corporation, *1979 Annual Report*.

process, the residual undistilled oil proved to be of better lubricating quality than other oils on the market produced by the normal process. Ewing's method was patented in October 1866 and the Vacuum Oil Company was formed to capitalize upon it. Within a number of years, Vacuum Oil became a recognized leader in the industrial lubricant field.

The activities of the company attracted the interest of John D. Rockefeller who purchased a controlling interest in 1879. In 1882 the Standard Oil Company of New York (Socony) was formed and became part of Rockefeller's Standard Oil Trust. When Rockefeller's Standard Oil empire was broken up in 1911, Socony emerged as one of the 33 individual companies, with Vacuum as another. From 1911 until 1931 Socony and Vacuum separately set about building, acquiring, and expanding their operations. Vacuum's interests were toward additional refining capacity, while Socony sought production interests—since the breakup left it devoid of production facilities. Vacuum was recognized worldwide for its industrial lubricants. Socony had marketing operations throughout the United States and the Far East but mainly in the field of fuels. The interests, operation, and facilities of the two companies complemented each other and a court-approved merger was consummated in July 1931, with a new name being chosen: Socony–Vacuum Corporation. In 1934, the company's name was changed to Socony–Vacuum Oil Company, Inc. By 1955, the brand name for Socony–Vacuum's gasoline and lubricants—Mobil—had become so well recognized that the company decided to include it in its corporate name. The firm's name was thus changed to Socony–Mobil Oil Company, Inc.

In 1959, Socony–Mobil's four U.S. subsidiaries were merged into two major divisions: Mobil Oil Company, which operated in the United States and Canada, and Mobil International Oil Company, which had responsibility for operations throughout the rest of the world. In 1960 a new division was added: the Mobil Chemical Company. During 1966, the company's centennial year, the firm changed its name again, this time to Mobil Oil Corporation.

In 1969 the company withdrew from the domestic retail fertilizer business, selling a major portion of its retail fertilizer assets and business to Swift and Company at a loss of $22 million. Corporate management's explanation for the divestiture was: "We didn't do the proper analysis we should have. We didn't buy competent management and when they left, we were oil men running a business we didn't know much about."

In 1976, when Mobil Oil Corporation acquired Montgomery Ward and Container Corporation of America, it was deemed desirable to form the Mobil Corporation as the holding company for all the various Mobil interests. As of 1980, Mobil Corporation consisted of three major operating divisions: Mobil Oil Corporation (which included all of Mobil's worldwide energy operations and Mobil Chemical Company); Montgomery Ward and its subsidiaries; and Container Corporation of America and its subsidiaries.

MOBIL'S TOP MANAGEMENT TEAM

In 1969, Mobil got a new top management team: Rawleigh Warner, Jr., chairman (Exhibit 3) and William P. Tavoulareas, president (Exhibit 4). Warner had been described as a man who appeared to be more a diplomat than a businessman. He

---

Exhibit 3   Biographical Sketch of Rawleigh Warner, Jr.

1921   Born, Chicago. Father, chairman of Pure Oil Company.
1943   B.A. (cum laude), Princeton University.
1946   Secretary-treasurer: Warner–Bard Company.
1948   Continenial Oil Company, various positions; left as assistant treasurer.
1953   Joined Mobil as assistant to the financial director of Socony–Vacuum overseas supply company.
1958   Manager of economics department.
1959   Regional vice president for Middle East.
1960   Executive vice president of Mobil International.
1963   President of Mobil International.
1964   Director, executive vice president, and member of executive committee, responsible for Mobil International and Mobil Petroleum Company, Inc.
1965   President of Mobil.
1969   Chairman of the board of directors and chief executive officer.

Director of Time, Inc., American Telephone and Telegraph Company, American Petroleum Institute, Caterpillar Tractor Company, Chemical New York Corporation, and Chemical Bank, American Express Company. Republican.

Exhibit 4   Biographical Sketch of William P. Tavoulareas

1919   Born, Brooklyn. Father a butcher.
1941   B.B.A., St. John's University.
1947   Joined Mobil as an accountant.
1948   J.D., St. John's University.
1957   Manager of Middle East accounting department of Middle East Affairs.
1959   Manager of corporate planning and analysis department.
1961   Vice president of plans and programs of Mobil's international petroleum division.
1963   Vice president of supply and distribution and international sales.
1965   Director, member of the executive committee and a senior vice president of Mobil.
1967   President of North American Division.
1969   President and vice chairman of executive committee of Mobil.

Director of Bankers Trust Company, General Foods Corporation. Democrat.

---

was an urbane, trim, dapper executive who got intricately involved in the day-to-day operations of the company. Warner maintained an active role in Mobil's financial and legal affairs and took a special interest in the public relations of Mobil, particularly those dealing with government. Warner appointed William P. Tavoulareas as president of the company. Unlike Warner, whose father was an oil man, Tavoulareas was the first in his family to enter the oil industry. One observer described Tavoulareas as "an irreverent, fast talking numbers man who has the crucial Rockefeller talent for lightning arithmetic." Another described him thusly:

> Tavoulareas is now widely regarded as the ablest of the major oilmen. He sits in shirt-sleeves, talking at top speed, blinking, twitching, and staring, running to the telephone like an imp let loose: saying gimme and lemme, whadda ya want.[1]

Tavoulareas was well known in the industry for his negotiating skills.

---

[1] Anthony D. Sampson, *The Seven Sisters* (New York: Viking Press), p. 193.

Mobil's management was well regarded in business circles, mainly because of the reputations enjoyed by Warner and Tavoulareas. The company had been described as a financier-lawyer-businessman type company rather than an oilman-geologist company. The people Warner chose to work with him talked in terms of *managing assets* and *portfolios*. A term used by Mobil to describe its 1976 acquisition of Montgomery Ward and Container Corporation was *risk aversion investment.* Some suggested these terms were not the typical jargon of the oil industry. Warner developed within the company a strong commitment to planning and many analysts saw planning as Mobil's strongest management characteristic. Tavoulareas said of planning:

> The real virtue of centralized planning is that it provides a person whose main responsibility is to question what the operator is doing. By his very nature the person charged with day-to-day operations doesn't have time to worry about tomorrow's problems. The planner, on the other hand, can look over his shoulder and try to anticipate what kind of environment we will be operating in the future and how we can take advantage of it. In the end his decisions will help the operator do his job better.[2]

MOBIL'S PETROLEUM AND EXPLORATION OPERATIONS

Under Warner and Tavoulareas, Mobil accelerated efforts to find additional crude oil reserves to try to bring internal crude oil production into better balance with the firm's refinery capacity. Historically, Mobil had the lowest internal crude oil production capability relative to refining capacity among the major oil companies. Mobil had always been very cautious in its spending for exploration. Mobil's long-standing reputation in the oil industry as concerns exploration and crude oil production was one of "arriving in the oil patch too late with too little." Warner and Tavoulareas moved to correct Mobil's crude oil production and reserves deficiency; exploration and production outlays rose from 19 percent of Mobil's capital expenditures in 1969 to 67 percent in 1979. Even so, Mobil's crude reserves declined in 1977, 1978, and 1979—an outcome which perpetuated the company's long-standing short position in crude oil. And, like other transnational oil companies, Mobil had to scramble to maintain its sources of crude oil supply in foreign countries, particularly in the volatile OPEC nations where nationalization was very much in evidence. The following statement in Mobil's *1979 Annual Report* detailed Mobil's loss of control over its foreign investments in petroleum:

> Since the early 1970s many producing country governments have assumed an increasing control of the oil industry within their jurisdictions. In several countries terms of ownership and operation are not settled as yet.
>
> In Saudi Arabia negotiations contemplate government acquisition of substantially all of Mobil's assets and the establishment of future arrangements. Under these proposed arrangements Mobil will provide management and technical services, will conduct an exploration program for the government, and will receive certain payments. Also, Mobil will have access to substantial volumes of crude oil at a competitive price under a long-term contract.

---

[2] As quoted in *Dun's Review,* December 1972, p. 38.

In Iran the government has taken over all producing and refining operations and in effect has announced that it considers the prior arrangements to be no longer operative.

In Nigeria the government's participation in Mobil's exploration and producing operations was increased from 55 percent to 60 percent, effective July 1, 1979. The amount of compensation remains to be settled.

In addition, producing country governments have nationalized or negotiated a participation in Mobil's producing, refining, and pipeline assets and operations in Venezuela (100 percent), Qatar (100 percent), Abu Dhabi (60 percent), Libya (51 percent), and Iraq (100 percent). Compensation has generally been based on net asset values used for local tax purposes.

In all of these countries, except Iran and Iraq, Mobil or its affiliate has continued as the concession operator or is providing management and technical services for stated payments and, except in Iran and Venezuela, has access to quantities of crude oil under equity agreements and/or at competitive prices under long-term contracts. . . .

Mobil is hopeful that the ultimate compensation received will be at least equal to the carrying value of the assets that have been, or will be, given up. It is clear the ultimate compensation will be substantially less than the economic value of the reserves that have been, or will be, given up.

Tavoulareas cited two major strategic objectives for Mobil's oil business: (1) to increase crude supplies all around the world so as to bring the company closer to self-sufficiency in supplying its refineries with crude oil and (2) to maximize the efficiency with which the supplies of crude were carried to refineries and refined products to their marketing areas. To assist in achieving these objectives, Tavoulareas indicated that Mobil's "exploration program around the world is proceeding above historical levels." Nonetheless, between 1965 and 1979, 60 percent of Mobil's capital expenditures were in the United States and the bulk of its foreign exploration and production efforts remained concentrated in the Middle East, especially Saudi Arabia. According to one of Mobil's directors:

> It makes sense to put your investment where the oil is and Saudi Arabia's reserves are far larger than any other country's. The money we invest in Saudi ventures should help assure our access to this crude in the years ahead when oil supplies are tighter. Mobil has had more than 30 years of mutually beneficial relationships with the Saudis.

Examples of key Mobil projects in Saudi Arabia as of 1980 included:

1. A one-million-barrel-a-year lube oil refinery, a 30–70 Mobil/Saudi venture.
2. A 700,000-barrel-a-year petrolube plant, a 29–71 Mobil/Saudi project.
3. A 250,000-barrel-a-day export refinery, a 50–50 Mobil/Saudi deal.
4. A 750-mile, 48-inch crude pipeline, designed and constructed by Mobil but 100 percent Saudi-owned.
5. A petrochemical complex, a 50–50 Mobil/Saudi investment.
6. A dry cargo shipping company, a 60–40 Mobil/Saudi project.

Among the biggest oil companies, only Royal Dutch/Shell was more active than Mobil in the Middle East. Outside the Middle East, Mobil's foreign exploration efforts were focused in the North Sea (where in 1980 Britain and Norway raised their oil production tax rates to 70 percent and 82 percent respectively), in the Canadian

Atlantic (where Mobil was rumored to be on the verge of important new discoveries), off Cameroun in West Africa, and in Indonesia. Mobil's exploration expenditures in the United States were concentrated in Alaska (wells in Prudhoe Bay yielded an increase of some 200 million barrels of crude reserves to Mobil—the company had a 5 percent ownership in the Trans-Alaska Pipeline System) and in the Gulf of Mexico. In 1979 a promising gas discovery was made offshore Alabama in Mobile Bay.

To help boost its oil and gas reserves, Mobil in 1979 acquired the operations of General Crude Oil Company from International Paper Co. for $792 million; Trans-Ocean Oil Co. was acquired in 1980 from Esmark Inc. for $715 million. General Crude had daily net production of 26,700 barrels of oil and 103 million cubic feet of natural gas; in the transaction Mobil also obtained rights to drill on some 2,000,000 acres of International Paper's landholdings. In the TransOcean acquisition, Mobil reportedly obtained proved reserves totalling 20 million barrels of crude oil and 240 billion cubic feet of natural gas, as well as undeveloped acreage thought to have oil and gas potential. These acquisitions were in line with Mobil's avowed strategy of increasing its U.S. exploration program and boosting its U.S. reserves of crude oil.

However, industry analysts regarded Mobil's approach to exploration and development as one of the less adventurous in the industry. For several years Mobil had pushed efforts to maximize recovery of oil from fields already in production through expanded use of technology, such as waterflooding and thermal recovery. About 70 percent of Mobil's U.S. production of crude oil in 1976 came from fields where improved recovery processes were used. Mobil's lack of bold effort was illustrated by the number of exploratory wells it drilled in the United States in 1976 relative to other majors: Texaco 647, Gulf 629, Exxon 613, Mobil 377. On the list of companies drilling the "very risky" wildcat wells in 1976, Mobil was not among the top 10 drillers.

Joint ventures were frequently favored by Mobil in its exploratory programs and in bidding for leases on undeveloped properties:

> Mobil prefers to bid jointly with other companies both large and small because it believes it is prudent to hedge against the risk of failure by seeking a smaller interest in many tracts rather than a larger interest in a few and limited capital is available for investment in exploration and producing because of the high risk nature of offshore investment.
>
> In selecting partners with whom to bid, primary consideration is given to the financial capabilities of the company as well as to the potential partners' technical expertise. With the initiation of leasing high cost frontier areas, it is increasingly important that a company be financially capable of providing its share not only of the lease bonus, but also of the subsequent expense for wildcat drilling and development if hydrocarbons are found. The ability of a company to add data and expertise to the joint venture is very important given the risky nature of offshore exploration. The interpretation of data available at the surface as a means of predicting the state of nature many miles below the surface is not an exact science and interpretation by other qualified geologists and geophysicists is important.[3]

---

[3] From a statement by Mobil to the House Subcommittee on Monopolies and Commercial Law, 1976. (Serial No. 48, Part 1, Joint Ventures, p. 235.)

Upstream Activities from Crude Production

Tankers   To transport crude oil and refined products, Mobil in 1980 operated a worldwide fleet of 100 vessels with capacity of 12.6 million deadweight tons; Mobil's investment in marine activities was about $1.1 billion. Recently Mobil had upgraded the efficiency of its tankers by using 18 very large crude carriers (VLCCs) and making greater use of low-cost charter vessels. Plans were underway to convert the company's larger VLCCs from steam turbine to more cost-efficient diesel propulsion. Mobil's tanker fleet operations were profitable in 1979.

Pipelines   Mobil's involvement in pipelines was the fifth largest in the industry in 1980, equivalent to a 6.8 percent share of the market. Mobil ranked fourth in 1951 with 8.4 percent of the total U.S. market in interstate oil pipeline movements. In 1980 the company had ownership interests in almost 27,000 miles of crude oil, natural gas liquids, and product pipelines in the United States and 10,800 miles in foreign countries; Mobil's investment in pipeline facilities totaled about $700 million.

Refining   In 1980 Mobil had 7 U.S. refineries along with 10 wholly owned and 21 partly owned foreign refineries located in 21 different countries; total capacity was 2.6 million barrels daily and total capital investment in refinery operations was $3.9 billion. During the late 1970s Mobil ranked as the industry leader, in both the United States and worldwide, in upgrading refining facilities to increase yields of gasoline and distillate fuels, including home heating oil. In 1978 and 1979 Mobil operated its refineries at an average of about 79 percent of capacity.

Marketing   After the 1911 split-up of Standard Oil, many of the "new companies" had concentrated marketing operations in clearly defined areas of the United States. Mobil's home ground and strong area for 20 years following the split was Connecticut, Maine, Massachusetts, New Hampshire, Rhode Island, Vermont, and New York. Mobil's "claim" to these areas was through its Standard of New York (Socony) subsidiary. Texas and Oklahoma were also major areas, through its wholly owned subsidiary Magnolia Petroleum Company. By and large these areas were still the company's retail marketing stronghold in the United States. Marketing activities outside the United States were concentrated in Europe, Australia, Southeast Asia, and the Far East.

Mobil had always been an industry leader in lubricants and this was a continuing strategic goal. Worldwide about 33 percent of Mobil's unit volume sales of refined products were accounted for by automotive gasoline; distillate and jet fuels accounted for another 32 percent and residual fuels for about 17 percent. Lubricants amounted to less than 15 percent of unit volume.

In recent years Mobil's overall marketing strategy had been to restrict marketing investment in new outlets to areas where significant growth would be likely; older, less-efficient outlets were closed; and self-serve stations grew in number. At year-end 1979 there were 17,749 Mobil retail outlets in the United States; abroad the total was 20,088. Both totals reflected a continuing downward trend. However, the average annual gasoline sales in Mobil's U.S. stations increased 33 percent during the 1975-78 period—a reflection of Mobil's success in upgrading throughputs and profits in its retail outlets. All told, Mobil in 1980 had invested $2.8 billion in its marketing facilities and annual capital expenditures for marketing averaged about $150 million during the 1976-80 period.

A comparison of Mobil's earnings from various facets of its petroleum operations is summarized below:

	Operating Earnings (in millions of dollars)			
	1976	1977	1978	1979
Exploration and production:				
United States	$364	$379	$ 353	$ 491
Foreign	249	263	364	523
Refining, transportation (marine and pipelines), and marketing:				
United States	92	124	121	189
Foreign	143	172	222	818
	$848	$938	$1,060	$2,021

DIVERSIFICATION

Following an internal reorganization during the late 1950s and early 1960s, Mobil's management determined that one long-term corporate objective should be "some kind of meaningful diversification." Mobil's performance had been questioned and criticized by some petroleum analysts for the small proportion of its earnings derived from domestic operations; for instance, from 1973 through 1975, domestic earnings averaged only 35 percent of total earnings. Moreover, Mobil, like many companies in the industry, fully realized that at some point the opportunity to productively spend dollars on petroleum exploration would diminish. Mobil decided to pursue diversification outside of energy for reasons stated by Mobil's chairman, Rawleigh Warner:

> The oil industry in the past few years has been undergoing major changes in its relations with government in practically every country where it operates. Governments are interfering. The U.S. government certainly is. The Federal Energy Administration tells us to whom we must sell our crude and what we can charge. They threaten us with a federal oil company that will be a yardstick to how effective we are. There are 3,000 bills before Congress, each of which will do something to the oil industry. . . . We concluded that there was a lot of wisdom in diversifying into a large business completely apart from the energy industry because we could see the government becoming more and more involved in energy activities.[4]

In accord with Warner's dictum, Mobil directed its acquisition efforts toward companies which (1) were not subject to the same business cycles and risks as the petroleum industry and (2) were not likely to attract as much government intervention. Mobil's executive vice president for planning and economics, Lawrence M. Woods,

---

[4] As quoted by H. Lee Silberman, "Appear to Reason," *Finance Magazine,* November 1975, pp. 9–13.

headed the team that searched for a company which would fit Mobil's diversification strategy. During a five-year search, Mobil considered over 100 different firms in 25 industries. Eventually Woods reported that Marcor, Inc. (the merged parent of Montgomery Ward and Container Corporation of America), appeared to satisfy the major criteria that Mobil had set: a low price/earnings multiple, a large share of earnings from U.S. operations, a large enough firm to impact Mobil's earnings, a management team whose track record (in this case turning the sagging business of Montgomery Ward around) was satisfactory.

In 1973 Warner obtained approval from Mobil's board to purchase 4.5 percent of Marcor's common stock. The purchase was to be made in a brokerage house's name in an effort to take a closer look at the company as a potential investment without revealing Mobil's interest. After having secretly bought 1,235,000 shares at an average price of $20 per share, Mobil approached the management of Marcor about increasing the investment to 51 percent. On June 14, 1974, Warner and Tavoulareas flew to Chicago to meet with the management of Marcor. Leo H. Schoenhofen, Marcor's chairman, had a previous engagement, but the company's president, Edward S. Donnell, and Gordon R. Worley, the vice president, met with the two Mobil executives. Commenting on the meeting, Warner said:

> We told them we had one thing we wanted to tell them and one thing we wanted to propose to them. They were very surprised, just as I would be if someone walked into my office and told me they owned 10 million shares of Mobil. But it was all very cordial and businesslike . . . we told them we had financial resources that may be helpful to them, that we don't want to run their business, but we would be very interested as investors.[5]

Marcor's management was receptive and formal negotiations were initiated.

In an effort to get to know the company from the inside, four Mobil executives were appointed to the Marcor board. They reported no surprises and in fact reported some strengths that had not previously been identified. An acquisition agreement was reached whereby 3,577,970 shares of Mobil Corporation's common stock and $673 million principal amount of Mobil Corporation's 8½ percent debentures due 2001 were issued to Marcor shareholders. The total cost of Mobil of acquiring Marcor was $1.7 billion, approximately 13 times Marcor's 1975 earnings. The merger became effective on July 1, 1976.

The merger had an appeal to both companies. Short-term loans for working capital at that time were costing Marcor up to 16 percent and since part of Mobil's tender included $200 million for a new series of Marcor's voted preferred stock, this gave Marcor a cash inflow of $200 million at 7 percent. From Mobil's point of view, for the equivalent of one year's cash flow, Mobil had obtained two companies which in 1976 would add roughly $150 million to its net income from domestic operations.

Mobil made it plain from the beginning of new operations that it did not plan to pump further working capital into Marcor. Mobil intended for the two major companies which comprised Marcor (Montgomery Ward and the Container Corporation of America) to stand on their own feet. Addressing the question of autonomy, Warner said:

---

[5] As quoted by *Business Week*, June 29, 1974, p. 29.

I don't see an operating role for Mobil in Ward for one fundamental reason. We are not retailers; we learned that a long time ago, that you can't anoint someone and expect him to do an effective job in a business that he doesn't know. You can question a commitment to autonomy if we took over another oil company, but retailing is a unique exercise. We have not been involved in it except for gas, which is totally different. . . . When our diversification quest finally led us to Ward, we told our board and management committee that we weren't deep enough to divert our energies to another business. We weren't broadbased in our management skills, so any acquisition had to have good management.[6]

Edward S. Donnell, the president of Marcor, said:

[We] will check our management style against theirs. We will have financial counsel and advice and a lot of good, hard pragmatic questions in planning areas. But there will be full freedom in operating areas. Mobil people aren't retailers and they don't have the people to run the business; we're people intensive and they are capital intensive.[7]

After the merger, Fredrick H. Veach, Ward's vice president for corporate planning, expressed it in a different way:

We wondered if we would get the mushroom treatment. First, they (new owners) put you in the dark. Then they cover you with manure. Then they cultivate you. Then they let you steam for a while. Finally, they can you. We have been looking for evidence but haven't found any of these steps. Maybe it's too early, but we can depend on everything they have said. I have faith and confidence, naive as this may be.[8]

Formalized planning had been a strong feature at Mobil and Mobil's management quickly pressed Marcor's management to formalize its planning. "We want them to format what they have already been doing and what we have institutionalized since 1959. This will make things more understandable to us," said Woods. On the subject of long-range planning, Veach said,

There's always resistance to formal planning. First, line managers see it as a threat to their authority. Second, they feel their business instincts will take care of problems better. Third, they don't really want to be as open as they think they have to be. Fourth, most incentive compensation plans are based on short-term results, so they couldn't care less about the future. And finally, managers aren't interested in long range because they get promoted or otherwise judged on the basis of what happens this year. These are generic obstacles.[9]

MARCOR, INC.

On October 31, 1968 when the stockholders of Montgomery Ward and Container Corporation of America voted to combine the assets and managements of the two companies, they created Marcor, Inc., a diversified, marketing-oriented, multibillion dollar company that brought together two leaders of the merchandising and packaging

---

[6] As quoted by *Chain Store Age Executive,* September 1976.

[7] Ibid.

[8] Ibid.

[9] Ibid.

industries. Montgomery Ward was one of the nation's better known retailers of consumer goods and services with sales of almost $2 billion and profits of $33 million in 1968. Container Corporation provided a variety of packaging materials for consumer and industrial products; it had 1968 sales of $469 million and profits of $31.6 million.

After the merger, Marcor implemented no basic changes in the names, administration, or operation of its two subsidiaries. Montgomery Ward and Container continued to have their own boards of directors, officers, administrative staffs, and service functions. And each continued its own programs of growth and expansion in merchandising, marketing, and manufacturing.

The role of Marcor executives in the operation of Ward and Container was a blend of outside counselor and parent. While they tried to preserve what was best in each of the companies, they sought to introduce a new degree of objectivity and independent scrutiny, permitting a fresh look at both operations. Marcor's management remained small and "free-form" so that it could respond quickly and effectively to new problems. It drew freely on the management capabilities of both Ward and Container, from time to time assembling task forces to tackle particular projects and disbanding or reshaping them as each problem was solved or redefined. For the most part, Marcor's officers concentrated their effort and attention on developing and implementing broad corporate objectives.

One of the most direct and immediate benefits Marcor sought to produce was the infusion of many of the specialized management skills and techniques of each company into the other's management force. Marcor executives would direct and channel the available management talent into critical areas first, while evaluating additional opportunities in all parts of both operations. Marcor also served as a focal point for determining what management resources of one company were available for the other.

Part of Marcor's task was to combine the development programs of each of the subsidiaries to provide "cross-training" of the management. Exhibit 5 shows financial highlights of Marcor for three years prior to Mobil's acquisition.

MONTGOMERY WARD

Montgomery Ward was founded in 1872 by Aaron Montgomery Ward and his brother-in-law, George R. Thorne; the company pioneered the mail order merchandise business. The company was exclusively a mail order sales firm until 1926 when it opened the first of the chain of retail stores in Marysville, Kansas. Following World War II, when competitors undertook giant building and modernization programs, Wards—under the direction of Sewell Avery—refrained from store expansion for fear of impending return to the depressionary era of the 1930s. For 16 years no new stores were opened—a strategic decision which has become one of the legendary mistakes in all of business history. In 1957 new management began the tremendous task of rebuilding what had become an outdated and outmoded chain and trying to regain the lost ground that Sears had easily captured.

From 1958 to 1969 Ward invested $500 million in modernizing and moving the thrust of its retail operations from the small town to the metropolitan suburb, while developing and installing computerized systems for reducing costs and improving

Exhibit 5 Summary of Marcor Operations, 1973–1975 Prior to Acquisition by Mobil

	1973	1974	1975
Summary of Earnings (millions)			
Net sales	$4,077.4	$4,667.5	$4,822.3
Costs and expenses:			
Cost of goods sold	2,951.5	3,379.9	3,517.8
Operating, selling, administrative, and research expenses	818.3	886.6	902.6
Interest expense	127.5	174.9	145.6
Provisions for taxes on income†	83.4	105.7	121.1
Net earnings before change in accounting policy*†	96.7	120.4	135.2
Effect of change in accounting policy related to store preoperating expense	—	4.7	—
Net earnings*†	$ 96.7	$ 115.7	$ 135.2
Financial Data (millions except per share amounts)			
Accounts receivable—parent and consolidated subsidiaries	$ 369.6	$ 339.2	$ 440.6
Accounts receivable—owned by credit subsidiary	1,512.7	1,880.1	2,075.7
Inventories	850.1	958.4	942.6
Net investment in properties and equipment	984.3	1,087.1	1,146.2
Additions to properties and equipment	202.6	214.8	179.9
Depreciation and amortization	75.9	80.0	87.7
Long-term debt	741.1	742.4	827.3
Stockholders' equity*†	1,028.9	1,309.4	1,392.9
Book value per share	26.60	28.77	31.12
Primary earnings per share*†	3.01	3.40	3.60
Full diluted earnings per share*†	2.32	2.63	2.85
Cash dividends per common share§	0.87½	0.97½	1.00
Market price range of common shares (high-low)	29⅝–17¾	28⅛–13¼	29⅛–13⅞
Closing price year-end	20	13⅞	28⅞
Year-end price-earnings ratio (fully diluted earnings)	9	5	10

* Net earnings for 1974 includes a net loss of $4.5 from the sale of Pioneer Trust & Savings Bank. As of the beginning of 1974, the company adopted the LIFO method of determining inventory cost for a substantial portion of its domestic manufacturing inventories. This change in accounting had the effect of reducing net earnings for 1974 by $9.1.

† Amounts prior to November 1, 1968, have been reduced by the portions applicable to Container Corporation shares exchanged for debentures at that date.

§ Dividends prior to November 1, 1968, are those paid on common shares of Montgomery Ward & Co., incorporated.
Source: Marcor, *Annual Reports, 1973–1975.*

efficiencies in handling catalog sales. The company's diversification program added new markets to its operations.

At the time of its acquisition by Mobil, Ward was the third largest catalog and nonfood retail merchandiser in the United States (trailing Sears and J. C. Penney) and was the nation's fifth largest general merchandising chain; it also had the third largest automobile club (1.1 million members). In 1976 the company sold through 2,300 retail and catalog outlets and employed approximately 100,000 employees. The company operated 439 retail stores having more than 58 million square feet of gross space, over half of which was in retail selling areas.

M-W semiannually published two large general-merchandise catalogs, together with a number of small seasonal catalogs. Catalog sales were made through direct mail, catalog order decks in retail stores, 550 catalog stores, and some 1,300 independently owned sale agencies. A support network of nine catalog distribution centers shipped some 100,000 items of merchandise to consumers throughout the country. Credit sales were a major portion of Ward's business, accounting for more than half of its sales in 1975. At many of its urban and suburban store locations, M-W offered such services as auto and appliance repairs; driver education, interior design systems; kitchen planning; home cleaning and painting; pest control; key making; utility bill payment; postal services; tax return preparation; notary public service; ticket reservations for theatrical and sporting events; photocopying; and beauty, optical, and hearing aid shops. Exhibits 6 and 7 show details of Montgomery Ward's performance and how it compared with its two strongest competitors, Sears and J. C. Penney. Montgomery Ward's reputation as a consumer merchandiser and retailer was well below that enjoyed by Sears and Penney. Many industry observers were skeptical of Ward's ability

Exhibit 6   Comparative Statistics of Montgomery Ward, 1946–1976

Year	Sales (millions)	Net Earnings (millions)	Retail Stores	Catalog Stores	Catalog Sales Agencies
1946	$ 974.2	$52.3	628	215	—
1950	1,170.4	74.2	614	250	—
1955	969.9	35.2	566	301	—
1960	1,248.9	15.0	529	627	—
1965	1,748.4	23.9	502	864	287
1966	1,894.1	16.5	493	793	569
1967	1,879.0	17.4	475	719	632
1968	1,985.6	33.3	468	695	804
1969	2,155.2	39.6	464	669	894
1970	2,226.9	34.6	462	660	961
1971	2,376.9	36.8	465	644	1,014
1972	2,640.0	42.3	458	590	1,184
1973	3,231.0	54.9	449	419	1,239
1974	3,623.0	44.3	446	460	1,253
1975	3,779.3	67.7	443	555	1,288
1976	4,020.0	85.0	439	550	1,314

Source: Montgomery Ward, *Annual Reports*, various years.

Exhibit 7   Sales-Profit Comparisons of Top Three Leading Catalog Retailers, 1970–1979   Millions of Dollars

Year	Sears Roebuck		J. C. Penney		Montgomery Ward	
	Sales	Net Income	Sales	Net Income	Sales	Net Income
1970	$ 9,262	$464.2	$ 4,150	$114.1	$2,227	$ 34.6
1971	10,006	550.9	4,812	135.7	2,376	36.8
1972	10,991	614.3	5,529	162.7	2,640	42.3
1973	12,306	679.9	6,243	185.8	3,231	54.9
1974	13,101	511.4	6,935	125.1	3,623	44.3
1975	13,639	522.6	7,678	189.6	3,779	67.7
1976	14,950	695.0	8,354	228.1	4,020	85.0
1977	17,224	838.0	9,369	294.8	4,548	108.0
1978	17,946	921.5	10,845	276.2	5,014	119.0
1979	17,514	810.1	11,274	244.0	5,251	73.0

Source: Annual reports of the companies.

to strengthen its competitive market position either against Sears and Penney or against other retailers, given the highly competitive, fast-paced nature of the department store business.

Montgomery Ward—Since the Acquisition

In the three years following its acquisition by Mobil, M-W's performance was mediocre:

Year	Millions of Dollars		
	Revenues	Earnings	Assets
1977	$4,548	$108	$3,207
1978	5,014	119	3,477
1979	5,251	73	3,679

Credit sales continued to account for more than half of M-W's total sales. In 1980 M-W had 8.8 million active customers using its Charg-all credit card. The most rapidly growing part of M-W was the recently created Jefferson Ward division, a chain of 40 discount retail department stores featuring centralized check-out and both private label and national brand merchandise. Exhibits 8, 9, and 10 provide additional operating statistics for these three years against 1976, the year the acquisition became final.

Montgomery Ward's 1979 profit decline was attributed to a falloff in durable goods sales in the last nine months of 1979 and to higher financing and operating costs. Nonetheless, Mobil publicly noted several areas where Montgomery Ward was making progress:

> Retail store selling space was increased by 1.9 million square feet to a total of 31.1 million, with the opening of 11 large Ward stores and 10 in the Jefferson/Ward operations.

Exhibit 8 Montgomery Ward & Co., Inc., Selected Financial and Operating Highlights, 1976–1979

	1976	1977	1978	1979
Condensed Income Statement Items *(millions of dollars)*				
Net sales:				
Retail sales	$3,075	$3,514	$3,886	$4,077
Catalog operations	893	988	1,093	1,159
Other	52	46	35	15
Total net sales	4,020	4,548	5,014	5,251
Costs and Expenses:				
Cost of goods sold, including net occupancy and buying expense	2,862	3,274	3,637	3,863
Operating, selling, general, and administrative expenses	836	886	938	948
Provision for closing certain unprofitable stores	—	—	—	—
Interest and discount expense	150	169	231	331
Total cost and expenses	3,848	4,329	4,806	5,142
Income (loss) before income taxes and parent company interest charges	172	219	208	109
Income taxes	80	104	89	36
Income (loss) before parent company interest charges	92	115	119	73
Parent company interest charges, net of income taxes	7	7	—	—
Net income (loss)	$ 85	$ 108	$ 119	$ 73
Selected Balance Sheet Items *(millions of dollars)*				
Current assets	$1,613	$1,742	$1,846	$1,780
Current liabilities	1,187	1,310	1,482	1,647
Inventories	868	968	1,104	1,078
Properties, plant, equipment, net	896	947	1,026	1,192
Total assets	2,998	3,207	3,477	3,679
Long-term debt	267	268	286	279
Capital lease obligations	313	322	312	311
Shareholders' equity	1,179	1,247	1,323	1,345
Total liabilities and shareholders' equity	2,998	3,207	3,477	3,679
Other Items				
Capital expenditures ($ millions)	$ 114	$ 127	$ 179	$ 250
Number of employees—full-time equivalent (thousands)	102.0	103.1	107.7	106.3
Financing charges on accounts receivable— to support credit sales ($ millions)	$ 30	$ 59	$ 61	$ 80

Source: Mobil Corporation.

Exhibit 9   Operating Highlights for Montgomery Ward's Retail Store Operations, 1976–1979

	For the 52- or 53-Week Period Ended			
	Dec. 29, 1976	Dec. 28, 1977	Dec. 27, 1978	Dec. 26, 1979
Financial ratios:				
Income as percent of sales	2.3%	2.5%	2.4%	1.4%
Credit sales as percent of total revenues	48.5%	49.4%	51.2%	51.5%
Number of retail stores—year-end:				
Sales over $15 million	38	61	81	89
Sales $10–15 million	83	93	103	109
Sales $5–10 million	136	123	112	108
Sales under $5 million	157	140	106	92
Opened during this year, net	14	11	9	21
Total	428	428	411	419
Percent of retail store sales by size of store:*				
Sales over $15 million	24%	33%	40%	42%
Sales $10–15 million	31	31	31	32
Sales $5–10 million	32	26	21	19
Sales under $5 million	13	10	8	7
Total	100%	100%	100%	100%
Retail stores opened during year	14	11	9	23
Retail stores closed during year	18	11	26	15
Retail store selling space— year-end (million square feet):				
Major Metro markets†	15.8	16.7	16.7	18.3
Secondary and non-Metro markets	12.4	12.4	12.5	12.8
Total	28.2	29.1	29.2	31.1
Retail sales productivity per square foot of selling space:‡				
Major Metro markets†	$130	$142	$153	$153
Secondary and non-Metro markets	108	122	132	135
Average	120	133	144	145
Average equivalent full-time employees (thousands):				
Retail	75.3	76.9	80.0	77.2
Catalog	9.5	9.3	9.8	10.4
Administrative and other	17.2	16.9	17.9	18.7
Total	102.0	103.1	107.7	106.3
Sales per Ward employee ($000)	$39.4	$44.1	$46.6	$49.4

* Excludes stores open only a partial year.
† Major Metro markets are those large metropolitan areas in which Wards has two or more full-line retail stores.
‡ Calculations are based on only those sales units in operation for the full year.
Source: Mobil Corporation.

Exhibit 10   Operating Highlights for Montgomery Ward's Catalog and Other Operations, 1976–1979

	For the 52- or 53-Week Period Ended			
	Dec. 29, 1976	*Dec. 28, 1977*	*Dec. 27, 1978*	*Dec. 26, 1979*
Catalog desks in retail and neighborhood stores	31.5	30.3	27.2	25.6
Catalog sales agencies	34.2	35.3	36.1	36.8
Catalog budget centers, including catalog desks	.9	1.6	4.1	4.9
Catalog sales agencies	1,315	1,353		1,394
			1,367	
Catalog budget centers	7	7	10	10
Total	2,272	2,293	2,292	2,311
Percent of catalog sales by medium:				
Conventional catalog sales	12.2%	11.2%	10.6%	9.7%
Limited line catalog-retail outlets	14.6	15.4	16.1	17.4
Catalog desks in retail and neighborhood stores	31.5	30.3	27.2	25.6
Catalog sales agencies	34.2	35.3	36.1	
				36.8
Catalog budget centers, including catalog desks	.9	1.6	4.1	4.9
Direct mail	6.6	6.2	5.9	5.6
Total	100.0%	100.0%	100.0%	100.0%
Automotive service centers:*				
Number	634	644	655	654
Service bays	5,383	5,439	5,533	5,752
Montgomery Ward Insurance Group:				
Value of life insurance policies (millions)	$3,426	$3,853	$4,723	$5,354
Premium and investment income (millions)	$61	$81	$108	$131
Net income (millions)	$7	$10	$14	$17
Montgomery Ward Auto Club:*				
Members (thousands)	840	925	1,151	1,109
Customer service contracts:				
Number in force (thousands)*	2,200	2,800	2,950	3,200
Sales (millions)	$60	$70	$82	$91
Customer credit:				
Gross credit sales (millions)	$2,400	$2,800	$3,100	$3,400
Percent of total gross sales	53.5%	55.4%	56.4%	56.8%
Active credit customers (thousands)* ..	7,000	7,700	8,300	8,800
Accounts receivable outstanding (millions)	$2,638	$3,088	$3,559	$3,996
Average account balance*	$375	$400	$426	$452
Average account maturity (months) ...	16.2	16.6	16.5	16.9
Account balances delinquent (percent)	3.8	3.4	3.7	4.1
Net write-offs (millions)	$44	$53	$55	$73
Percent of credit sales	1.7%	1.6%	1.5%	1.9%
Percent of average receivables balances	2.0%	1.9%	1.8%	2.0%
Average monthly collection percentage	8.0%†	8.0%	8.0%	7.7%

* Year-end.
† 48-week period.
Source: Mobil Corporation.

Retail stores, including newly constructed and renovated stores acquired from others, totaled 419 at year-end, a net increase of 8. During the year 13 retail stores were closed.

Expansion of Jefferson/Ward operations will facilitate economical entry into some of those major metropolitan markets in the East where Ward's has never had retail representation. The concept of Jefferson stores is to maintain lower operating costs, yet provide customers with both private-label and national-brand merchandise that equals Ward's quality standards. The interiors and exteriors of these self-service stores acquired in 1979 are being redesigned to make them attractive as well as convenient. The Jefferson/Ward operations increased the number of stores from 11 to 21 and others are scheduled to be added during 1980.

Substantial progress was made by Montgomery Ward's merchandising group during 1979 to upgrade product quality and supplier services, as long-term buying agreements were signed with many of the nation's top-ranked manufacturers. An increasing proportion of Ward's private-label merchandise is not coming from industry leaders.

Continuing the practice of making the widest selection of goods and services available to its customers, Ward's during 1979 became the first U.S. department store chain to offer legal and family health care services. The first legal services clinics were opened at four stores and the first family health care center was opened at one. There are now six dental clinics in Ward stores.

To serve urban consumers more effectively, Ward's is accelerating its program for new retail stores within the city limits of many of its major urban markets.[10]

CONTAINER CORPORATION OF AMERICA

The other company Mobil obtained in the Marcor acquisition, the Container Corporation of America, was founded in 1926 and grew through internal expansion and acquisition to become a major factor in the packaging industry. A corollary to its development of packaging products was Container Corporation's innovation in the application of marketing and packaging design services, where the company's influence extended far beyond its own industry. Its design and market research laboratories, established in the mid-1940s, were the industry's first to use programmed application of market research, design, and scientific testing in the development of more effective consumer packaging.

By 1976, Container Corporation, with a total work force of more than 21,000, was the nation's largest producer of paperboard packaging and the second largest manufacturer of paperboard. In 1975 it operated 90 facilities throughout the United States. Its overseas affiliations employed 8,000 employees in the 56 different operations in Columbia, Mexico, Venezuela, Italy, Spain, and the Netherlands. The company's best year was in 1974 when it earned $74.6 million on sales of $965 million; earnings fell to $64 million in 1975 and to $59 million in 1976.

Finished packaging products, which represented over 80 percent of container sales, included corrugated shipping containers, folding paper cartons, composite cans, fiberboard and drums, and industrial plastic containers. Production of paperboard in 1975 totaled almost 2 million tons, of which 1.5 million tons were produced by domestic mills. Allied to its paperboard packaging, the company offered packaging services

---

[10] Mobil Corporation, 1979.

including graphic design, structural design, market research, packaging testing, packaging machinery development, and manufacturing. To supply its operation in 1976, the corporation owned or controlled over 744,000 acres of timberlands and had a 49 percent interest in the T. R. Miller Lumber Company, Inc. This company owned almost 200,000 acres close to the company's Alabama paperboard mill. Container also had short-term cutting rights to timber on some 103,000 acres. The company had a continuing policy of increasing its holdings in timberlands.

Container Corporation had an operating characteristic similar to that of Mobil. It was timber shy, just as Mobil was crude shy. Warner observed, "There is a kind of affinity between Container Corporation and ourselves. . . . I suppose we were attracted to someone who had to live by their wits like we have had to do."

Container Corporation in 1975 collected more than a million tons of waste paper for recycling. Approximately half of this collected material was used by its own domestic recycling mills and the balance was sold to other countries. Exhibit 11 presents sales and earnings for Container Corporation during the time it was a part of Marcor.

Container Corporation's Progress Since The Mobil Acquisition

In the 1977-79 period Container Corporation reported higher sales revenues every year, but earnings were lower and operating volume was relatively flat. Several new products were successfully introduced in each of the first three years following acquisition and Container increased its timberland holdings in the southeastern United States by 122,000 acres. The company's product line in 1980 included corrugated and solid fiber shipping containers, folding cartons, composite cans, fiber drums, paper bags, plastic packaging, containerboard, and boxboard. It operated 89 paperboard mills, fabricating plants, and other facilities in the United States and had 59 facilities in other countries. The company ranked as the nation's largest producer of paperboard

Exhibit 11   Highlights of Container Corporation's Performance under Marcor   Millions of Dollars

Year	Sales	Earnings
1968	$ 469	$31.6
1969	510	27.7
1970	527	30.1
1971	559	24.1
1972	624	33.7
1973	755	50.0
1974	965	74.6
1975	953	64.0
1976	1,099	59.0

Source: Container Corporation, *Annual Reports, 1968–1976.*

packaging, the third largest manufacturer of paperboard, and the leading recycler of paper. Nevertheless, Container Corporation's profits were lackluster, partly due to charges against earnings to settle alleged antitrust violations in folding cartons and shipping containers and partly due to competitive pressures which prevented prices from being raised fast enough to cover rising costs.

Exhibits 12 and 13 present Container Corporation's operating performance since its acquisition by Mobil.

Exhibit 12   Financial Highlights of Container Corporation of America, 1976–1979   Millions of Dollars

	1976	1977	1978	1979
Condensed Income Statement				
Net sales:				
Shipping containers	$ 496	$ 520	$ 564	$ 654
Paperboard cartons	256	274	314	350
Other packages	129	138	162	179
Paperboard and miscellaneous	198	212	232	279
Total net sales	1,079	1,144	1,272	1,462
Costs and expenses:				
Cost of products sold	859	974	1,068	1,228
Operating, selling, administrative, and research expenses	80	84	92	114
Interest expense, net	8	8	15	22
Provision for civil antitrust lawsuits	—	—	60*	8*
Income taxes	63	45	23	44
Total costs and expenses	1,010	1,084	1,258	1,416
Net income before effect of changes in accounting policies and Marcor interest charges	69	60	14	46
Cumulative effect, less applicable taxes, on prior years of changes in accounting policies	6	—	—	—
Net income before parent company interest charges	63	60	14	46
Marcor interest charges less applicable taxes	4	4	—	—
Net income	$ 59	$ 56	$ 14	$ 46
Selected Balance Sheet Items				
Current assets	$ 359	$ 425	$ 382	$ 415
Net receivables	199	209	165	203
Inventories	121	125	143	167
Properties, plant, and equipment, net	584	636	704	755
Total assets	1,041	1,101	1,127	1,213
Current liabilities	205	239	288	349
Short-term loans	31	38	46	86
Long-term debt	180	158	162	150
Shareholders' equity	557	592	548	568
Total liabilities and shareholders' equity	1,041	1,101	1,127	1,213

* Provisions for litigation related to the company's operations in years prior to Mobil's acquisition.
Source: Mobil Corporation.

Exhibit 13   Operating Highlights of Container Corporation of America, 1976–1979

	1976	1977	1978	1979
Percent of sales by area:				
United States	74.2%	74.3%	73.1%	69.9%
Foreign	25.8	25.7	26.9	30.1
Worldwide	100.0%	100.0%	100.0%	100.0%
Percent of sales by product category:				
Shipping containers	46.0%	45.2%	45.3%	45.3%
Paperboard cartons	23.7	24.1	24.4	23.7
Other packages	12.0	12.1	12.2	12.5
Finished packaging products	81.7	81.4	81.9	81.5
Paperboard and miscellaneous	18.3	18.6	18.1	18.5
Total	100.0%	100.0%	100.0%	100.0%
Paperboard produced (thousands of tons):				
United States	1,700	1,632	1,824	1,846
Foreign	524	551	558	632
Worldwide	2,224	2,183	2,382	2,478
Folding cartons shipped (thousands of tons)	334	345	378	389
Corrugated containers shipped billions of square feet)	17.9	18.7	20.4	20.7
Recycled paperboard produced as percent of total paperboard produced	49%	51%	49%	49%
U.S. timberland owned or under long-term lease (thousands of acres)	744	781	839	860
Net investment in properties and equipment (millions):				
United States	$440	$487	$550	$579
Foreign	136	141	154	179
Worldwide	$576	$628	$704	$758
Capital expenditures ($ millions)	$ 90	$108	$129	$117
Number of employees (thousands)	21.4	22.0	22.6	22.6

Source: Mobil Corporation.

MOBIL'S CHEMICAL DIVISION

Mobil's diversification into the chemical industry in 1960 was a move that many other large petroleum companies also pursued. Also, like the chemical divisions of other petroleum companies, Mobil Chemical Company was profitable. In 1979 Mobil Chemical contributed 5.6 percent of Mobil's total net income on only 3.4 percent of the total revenues. In 1980 the Mobil Chemical Company had 65 plants in operation in nine countries. It was the largest U.S. manufacturer of disposable plastic products, including (1) polyethylene, one use of which was the material for Mobil's Hefty Bags, (2) polystyrene, the base for foam containers, and (3) polypropylene, a transparent packaging film used in many industries and a low-cost substitute for cellophane.

The company in 1980 had a capacity to produce almost three billion pounds of petrochemicals per year. In addition, it ranked as the fourth largest producer in the United States of phosphate rock, sources of phosphorous chemicals, and fertilizer (however, Mobil had ranked as the third largest producer in 1977).

Mobil Chemical's profits for the years 1973 to 1979 were $36, $106, $89, $81, $85, $86, and $113 million, respectively; more detailed operating statistics are shown in Exhibit 14.

The primary strategic thrust of Mobil Chemical was to integrate its petrochemicals operation with the expanding needs of its plastics business. The basic idea was to

Exhibit 14   Selected Financial and Operating Highlights for Mobil Chemical Company, 1976–1979 Millions of Dollars

	1976	1977	1978	1979
Condensed Income Statement Items				
Revenues:				
Sales: Plastics	$ 464	$ 515	$ 574	$ 708
Petrochemicals	230	218	252	396
Chemical coatings	196	210	230	237
Phosphorus	137	163	174	221
Net sales to trade	1,027	1,106	1,230	1,562
Other revenues	80	97	131	156
Total revenues	1,107	1,203	1,361	1,718
Costs and expenses:				
Depreciation, depletion, and amortization	(33)	(38)	(46)	(58)
Other costs and expenses	(938)	(1,032)	(1,161)	(1,495)
Pretax operating profit	136	133	154	165
Income taxes	(48)	(44)	(65)	(51)
Earnings before finance charges	88	89	89	114
Finance charges	(7)	(4)	(3)	(1)
Segment earnings	$ 81	$ 85	$ 86	$ 113
Chemical Operations Highlights				
Total assets	$739	$835	$955	$1,160
Properties, plants, and equipment, at cost	$642	$724	$823	$961
Capital expenditures	$113	$90	$104	$146
Number of employees (thousands) . . .	10.8	11.1	12.3	13.6
Number of facilities worldwide	51	53	56	60
Percent of sales by product category:				
Plastics	45%	46%	47%	46%
Petrochemicals	23	20	20	25
Chemical coatings	19	19	19	15
Phosphorus	13	15	14	14
Net sales to trade	100%	100%	100%	100%

Source: Mobil Corporation.

devote a larger percentage of petrochemical feedstocks to supplying materials for Mobil's growing lineup of plastics product. The profit margins on Mobil's line of plastic products were higher than for other types of petrochemical products. In 1980, Mobil Chemical had several expansionary efforts underway:

- A stronger version of two-ply Hefty-brand trash bags was being introduced, as was a new 20-gallon size bag.
- Hefty-brand disposable foam plates were introduced.
- Greater distribution for a new Marketote-brand grocery sack with handles, which had wet strength and was reusable, was being sought in grocery stores (almost 500 grocery stores were already using the bags).
- Capacity to produce a new polypropylene film was being expanded by 25 percent and a new division was being established to consolidate worldwide production and sales under a single general manager.
- Capacity to produce Mobilrap brand stretch film products was also being expanded. This product was a strong, thin plastic film which could be used to wrap large loads of products stacked on pallets (it was a substitute for strapping, shrink film, and other unitization packaging methods).

MOBIL: THE LAND DEVELOPER

Another diversification move concerned land development. One venture was a 13,000-unit condominium apartment complex in Hong Kong which housed 70,000 people. In 1970, Mobil created a real estate company, named Mobil Oil Estates, Limited, which was involved in real estate development in California and Texas. Another major venture was a San Francisco Bay project at Redwood Shores, a residential community covering 1,300 acres. In October 1974 Mobil reached an understanding with majority owners on a bid to purchase the Irvine Company, owner of 77,700 acres of land in Orange County, California, approximately 73,000 acres of which were undeveloped. However, after two years of litigation and the entry of two other firms into a bidding war for Irvine, Mobil disengaged from its attempts at acquisition. The real estate and land development operations were not as of 1980 a significant factor in Mobil's overall business portfolio; statistics for the division are included under "Other" in Exhibit 2. Exhibit 15 shows the comparative credit ratings assigned to Mobil's various units by Moody's and Standard & Poor's.

FUTURE DIRECTIONS AT MOBIL CORPORATION

Between 1975 and 1980 Mobil made no further acquisitions aimed at diversifying its business portfolio. According to Lawrence Woods, a Mobil director (as well as an executive vice president and project leader for the Marcor acquisition), Mobil's strategy in investing in Montgomery Ward, Container Corporation, and land development was not an attempt to become a conglomerate:

> When we acquired Montgomery Ward and Container Corporation of America we merely implemented a diversification policy established a decade ago. Our goal with this policy

---

Exhibit 15   Comparative Credit Ratings Assigned to Various Mobil Operating Subsidiaries, 1980

| | Bond Rating Agency | |
	Moody's	Standard & Poor's
Mobil Oil Corporation:		
Debt	Aaa	AAA
Mobil Oil Credit Corp:		
Commercial paper	P-1	A-1
Montgomery Ward & Co., Inc.:		
Debt	Baa	BBB
Montgomery Ward Credit Corp:		
Senior debt	Baa	BBB
Subordinated debt	Ba	BBB-
Commercial paper	P-2	A-2
Container Corporation of America:		
Debt	A	A
Commercial paper	P-1	A-1
Mobil Corporation	Aa	AA

Source: Mobil Corporation.

---

was to increase Mobil's domestic revenue and earnings base and to engage in activities subject to different business cycles and regulatory climates than the energy companies. We believe these objectives have been met and we are not actively seeking other major diversifications. We see ourselves essentially as a diversified energy company.

Whether Mobil could seriously be considered as a diversified *energy* company as of 1980 was debatable, however. Mobil did own an estimated 4.1 billion tons of coal reserves, but it had no operating mines; construction on Mobil's first coal mine was tentatively scheduled to start in 1981, with initial deliveries in 1983. The company's first uranium plant (with only a 325 ton annual capacity) went into production in mid-1979; Mobil had only 18,000 tons of uranium reserves. Mobil was engaged in a joint venture with Tyco Laboratories to develop high-efficiency solar cells, but commercial sales were not expected until "the more distant future." The company had "extensive" oil shale lands in Colorado and tar sands reserves in Canada. These activities, as of 1980, constituted all of Mobil's noteworthy energy investments outside of petroleum and natural gas.

In December 1976, Rawleigh Warner summed up Mobil's strategic position as follows:

> Mobil is one of the world's largest companies. Energy is and will remain, our primary business, but a carefully balanced program begun in 1968 has broadened and strengthened our earnings base. . . .
>
> For 16 consecutive years, Mobil has increased the size of its dividends. It is a record of which we are proud—one we are determined to improve. . . .
>
> In the past Mobil has been known primarily as an international oil company. Today diversification has created an earnings mix which retains our ability to grow in the

petroleum industry while offering attractive new earnings sources in fields that are subject to different economic cycles and less stringent government regulations. . . .

A result of this strategy has been to strengthen our U.S. earnings base. In 1976 more than half of Mobil's earnings are coming from domestic sources. And our diversification has been accomplished without weakening our position in energy. . . .

Mobil is beginning to benefit from the results of strategic petroleum exploration and production investments that were made overseas during the earlier years of the decade, improving the company's already strong position internationally with as diversified a base of oil and gas supply as possible. . . .

Nothing is more basic to Mobil's business than the search for energy.

Wherever energy is to be found—as oil, gas, coal, shale, shale oil, uranium, the sun—Mobil is prepared to lead in its development. . . .

Mobil Oil's exploration and production division was recently reorganized on a world-wide basis to provide effective response to energy opportunities so investment can be channeled to those that are most promising. . . .

Montgomery Ward and Container Corporation bring to Mobil similar, sophisticated management processes adapted to their special needs. . . .

However, three years later in Mobil's *1979 Annual Report,* Warner's message to the shareholders suggested a strong strategic emphasis on petroleum rather than on either energy or on future diversification:

For the years immediately ahead, when industry supplies of oil and gas will become less abundant and higher priced, we expect to follow a multipronged strategy. We will continue heavy investments in exploration and producing, seeking in particular to expand and develop promising discoveries made in the 70s and investigating new prospective areas identified by our advanced exploration technology. Priority will continue to be given to finding new U.S. reserves. At the same time we will build on our industry leadership in the United States and abroad in upgrading refinery yields to obtain greater proportions of high-value fuels and we will continue our expansion into high-value chemicals. We intend also to seek attractive opportunities to build synthetic-fuel plants, looking toward the day when significant volumes of synthetic fuels can be produced on a commercial basis.

Although Mobil has achieved some diversification into businesses subject to different economic cycles and less government regulation, our main thrust will continue to be as an energy company. Evidencing this was the $792 million purchase of General Crude Oil Company's exploration and producing operations in 1979.

In the years immediately ahead we should be able to realize significant earnings improvement from the capital projects started in the 1970s, especially our large producing ventures and the new manufacturing facilities of Mobil Chemical Company.

In the section of the *1979 Annual Report* on "Prospects in the 80s," Mobil made no mention of any of its diversification investments or any of its energy activities other than petroleum, natural gas, and petrochemicals. The company had capital resources of at least $3 billion which could be deployed to strengthen its business portfolio.

CASE 20 EXXON CORPORATION, 1986*

Throughout the 20th century Exxon Corporation ranked as the largest company in the international petroleum industry and as one of the largest corporations in the world. In 1985 Exxon reported revenues of $92.9 billion, net income of $4.9 billion, and total assets of $69.1 billion. These results gave Exxon a worldwide ranking among corporations of all types of number two in sales, number two in after-tax profits, and number one in assets.

Exxon Corporation and its affiliated companies operated in the United States and more than 80 other countries. The company's business interests included exploring for and producing crude oil and natural gas, operating marine and pipeline facilities for transporting both crude and refined products, refining and marketing petroleum-based products, manufacturing petrochemicals, fabricating nuclear fuel, mining coal and other minerals, producing electric motors and electrical equipment, and the generation of electric power in Hong Kong. Over 70 percent of invested capital and over 85 percent of revenues were tied to Exxon's oil and natural gas activities. Exhibits 1 and 2 provide a financial overview.

COMPANY HISTORY AND BACKGROUND

Exxon Corporation is the surviving parent company from the legendary breakup of the Standard Oil Company of New Jersey in 1911, then headed by John D. Rockefeller—the man who dominated the oil industry in its early years and who became a symbol for both the sins and the virtues of capitalism. When the Supreme Court ruled in 1911 that the Rockefeller-controlled Standard Oil of New Jersey constituted a monopoly in restraint of trade, the court-ordered remedy was a breakup; Standard Oil (New Jersey) continued on as the largest of 34 new downsized companies.

In 1960 Standard Oil (New Jersey) consolidated a number of divisions into one U.S. subsidiary, Humble Oil and Refining Company. Humble's trademark, Esso, was one of the best known in the world and was widely used by Standard Oil (New Jersey) in many foreign countries. However, since the nationwide use of Esso as a trade mark had been ruled by the courts as inappropriate owing to conflicts with other trademarks established during the Rockefeller era, Humble marketed its products under the Esso brand in some areas, under the Enco (from Energy Company) brand in others, and under Humble in Ohio; retail operations were conducted in 35 states. In 1960 Humble announced its intention to market in all 50 states and to adopt a uniform design for its service stations. In 1972, frustrated by an inability to use any one of the existing trademarks under which to market and advertise nationwide, Standard Oil (New Jersey) and its domestic operating subsidiary, Humble Oil and

* Prepared by Professor Arthur A. Thompson, Jr., The University of Alabama, with the research assistance of Victor Gray and Miriam Aiken. Copyright © 1986 by Arthur A. Thompson, Jr.

Exhibit 1 Financial Summary, Exxon Corporation, 1981–1985 Dollar Figures in Millions, except per Share Amounts

	1981	1982	1983	1984	1985
Sales and other operating revenue					
Petroleum and natural gas	$102,418	$ 92,570	$ 83,622	$ 85,415	$ 81,399
Chemicals	7,116	6,049	6,392	6,870	6,670
Coal	204	288	272	327	357
Minerals	83	80	115	97	108
Reliance Electric	1,673	1,561	1,397	1,538	1,667
Hong Kong power generation	604	584	566	608	586
Other and eliminations	1,122	927	1,083	1,018	833
Total sales and other operating revenue	113,220	102,059	93,447	95,873	91,620
Earnings from equity interests and other revenue	1,702	1,500	1,287	1,415	1,249
Revenue	$114,922	$103,559	$ 94,734	$ 97,288	$ 92,869
Earnings:					
Petroleum and natural gas					
Exploration and production	$ 4,117	$ 3,431	$ 4,079	$ 4,789	$ 4,937
Refining and marketing	1,132	1,141	1,156	408	872
International marine	29	(76)	(101)	(63)	(65)
Total petroleum and natural gas	5,278	4,496	5,134	5,134	5,744
Chemicals	238	93	270	430	249
Coal	13	23	37	43	39
Minerals	(97)	(95)	(57)	(52)	21)
Reliance Electric	29	(32)	(33)	11	30
Hong Kong power generation	36	51	71	88	90
Other operations	(78)	14	44	47	(19)
Corporate and financing	(507)	(323)	(497)	(298)	(508)
Earnings before special items	4,912	4,227	4,969	5,403	5,604
Foreign exchange on debt	(32)	166	85	267	(2)
Facilities restructuring	(54)	(207)	(76)	(142)	(187)
Hawkins provision	—	—	—	—	(545)
Net income	$ 4,826	$ 4,186	$ 4,978	$ 5,528	$ 4,870
Net income per share	$ 5.58	$ 4.82	$ 5.78	$ 6.77	$ 6.46
Cash dividends per share	$ 3.00	$ 3.00	$ 3.10	$ 3.35	$ 3.45
Net income to average shareholders' equity *(percent)*	17.8	14.9	17.2	19.0	16.8
Net income to total revenue *(percent)*	4.2	4.0	5.3	5.7	5.2
Working capital	$ 5,500	$ 3,328	$ 3,556	$ 1,974	$ (1,734)
Total additions to property, plant and equipment	$ 9,003	$ 9,040	$ 7,124	$ 7,842	$ 8,844
Exploration expenses, including dry holes	$ 1,650	$ 1,773	$ 1,408	$ 1,365	$ 1,495
Research and development costs	$ 630	$ 707	$ 692	$ 736	$ 681
Total assets	$ 61,575	$ 62,289	$ 62,963	$ 63,278	$ 69,160
Long-term debt	$ 5,153	$ 4,556	$ 4,669	$ 5,105	$ 4,820
Total debt	$ 8,186	$ 7,303	$ 5,536	$ 6,382	$ 7,909
Shareholders' equity	$ 27,743	$ 28,440	$ 29,443	$ 28,851	$ 29,096
Average number of shares outstanding *(thousands)*	864,926	867,959	861,399	816,169	754,093
Number of shareholders at year end *(thousands)*	776	865	889	839	785
Wages, salaries, and employee benefits	$ 5,832	$ 5,993	$ 5,849	$ 5,550	$ 5,381
Average number of employees *(thousands)*	180	173	156	150	146

Source: *1985 Annual Report.*

Exhibit 2   Consolidated Balance Sheets, Exxon Corporation, 1983–1985
In Millions of Dollars

	December 31, 1983	December 31, 1984	December 31, 1985
Assets			
Current assets:			
Cash	$ 2,512	$ 1,384	$ 1,078
Marketable securities	1,584	1,906	1,396
Notes and accounts receivable, less estimated doubtful amounts	7,900	7,366	7,527
Inventories			
Crude oil, products and merchandise	3,598	3,600	3,803
Materials and supplies	1,373	1,102	993
Prepaid taxes and expenses	1,628	1,881	2,558
Total current assets	18,595	17,239	17,355
Investments and advances	1,747	1,743	2,311
Property, plant and equipment, at cost, less accumulated depreciation and depletion	40,868	42,776	48,262
Other assets, including intangibles	1,753	1,520	1,232
Total assets	$62,963	$63,278	$69,160
Liabilities and Shareholders' Equity			
Current liabilities:			
Notes and loans payable	$ 867	$ 1,277	$ 3,089
Accounts payable and accrued liabilities	11,001	10,845	13,359
Income taxes payable	3,171	3,143	2,641
Total current liabilities	15,039	15,265	19,089
Long-term debt	4,669	5,105	4,820
Annuity reserves and accrued liabilities	3,272	3,478	3,319
Deferred income tax credits	9,012	8,948	11,042
Deferred income	315	369	412
Equity of minority shareholders in affiliated companies	1,213	1,262	1,382
Total liabilities	33,520	34,427	40,064
Shareholders' equity	29,443	28,851	29,096
Total liabilities and shareholders' equity	$62,963	$63,278	$69,160

Source: *Annual Reports,* 1984 and 1985.

Refining Company, announced that they would, henceforth, use Exxon as their single primary trademark on a nationwide basis. Subsequently, Standard Oil (New Jersey) became known as Exxon Corporation, and Humble Oil and Refining became known as Exxon Company, U.S.A.

One of the most important strategic decisions in the company's history also unfolded in 1960 when Monroe J. Rathbone started a five-year stint as Exxon's CEO. Rathbone believed that the demand for oil, rising faster than new discoveries, would one day convert the presently abundant oil supplies into a scarcity and that the Middle East oil-producing countries would be able to charge much higher prices for their crude. Thus, even though Exxon then had more crude than its refined-products markets could absorb, Rathbone persuaded the company's board to approve major outlays for a search for oil outside the Middle East. Rathbone set up a new subsidiary called Esso Exploration and sent geologists and drilling crews into new areas of the world; Exxon's existing subsidiaries were ordered to begin combing their territories for more oil. In the period 1964-67 Exxon spent nearly $700 million on exploration, mostly in non-OPEC areas. Other major oil companies indicated their amusement at Exxon's move by declining to follow suit on any large scale. Mobil, for instance, with the greatest lack of crude oil reserves of any major U.S. company, spent just $267 million for exploration during the same period. Exxon's decision paid off; as of 1977 Exxon had more proven oil reserves outside the Middle East than any other major company. For his role and foresight in engineering Exxon's move, *Fortune* in 1975 named Monroe J. Rathbone to its Business Hall of Fame—he was one of four living executives so chosen (together with 15 other deceased laureates among whom was John D. Rockefeller).

ORGANIZATION AND MANAGEMENT

Exxon first adopted the principle of decentralized management of its operations in the late 1920s. Decentralized approaches were much in evidence in 1986. Generally speaking, strategy formulation, planning, and coordination were functions of Exxon Corporation's senior management and staff. Activities such as drilling wells, running refineries, and marketing products were delegated to local and division managements close to the scene of these activities. Management positions in Exxon's foreign affiliates and subsidiaries were, with few exceptions, staffed by personnel native to the countries where Exxon operated.

Prior to 1966 some 40 subsidiary companies were reporting directly to corporate headquarters in New York. Feeling that this system was becoming unwieldy and inefficient, Exxon reorganized into a smaller number of regional and operating units. The top official in each subunit was given broad responsibility and a sizable staff in an effort to permit quicker response to changing conditions and, further, to reduce the number of people reporting to corporate headquarters. Some subunits had geographic responsibilities for designated parts of the world—the United States, Europe and Africa, Latin America, and the Far East; others had worldwide responsibilities for particular segments of Exxon's business, such as chemicals or research. As of 1986 there were 14 such subunits, each headed by a senior executive: Exxon Company, U.S.A., Esso Middle East, Exxon Chemical Company, Exxon International Company, Esso Eastern, Inc., Esso Europe Inc., Esso Exploration Inc., Esso Inter-American, Inc., Exxon Enterprises, Inc., Exxon Research and Engineering Company, Imperial Oil Limited (70 percent owned by Exxon), Exxon Production Research Company, Reliance Electric Company, and Exxon Minerals Company.

In 1986 the principal link between Exxon and each regional or operating subunit was provided by one of seven senior management officials (either a senior vice president or the corporation president) who were on Exxon's board of directors. The officer-director was designated as the "contact executive" for at least one of the regional or operating subunits. The concept of "contact" responsibilities was, according to Exxon, a significant innovation when introduced in 1943. A contact executive's responsibilities were implicit rather than precisely defined, but the chief role was to provide strategic guidance over the assigned subunits. The contact executive endeavored to stay well informed about the plans of the regional or operating subunits and the problems they faced. On many matters the contact executive had final review authority; on big issues recommendations had to go before Exxon's management committee (composed of all seven officer-directors) or the compensation and executive development (COED) committee. From time to time the contact assignments of the officer-directors were rotated so as to provide new viewpoints and broaden their own experience.

In 1986 Exxon's board chairman was Clifton C. Garvin; he had been board chairman since August 1975 and director since 1968. Garvin began his career with Exxon in 1947. A graduate of Virginia Polytechnic Institute, he joined Exxon as a process engineer at Exxon's Baton Rouge refinery and became operating superintendent in 10 years. Later he moved through a series of positions in Exxon Company, U.S.A., gaining experience in other major functions of the oil business. In 1964 he went to New York as executive assistant to Exxon's president. During the three years prior to his election as a director he headed Exxon Chemical, U.S.A., and Exxon's worldwide chemical organization. Garvin regularly consulted with the corporation's management committee composed of all eight employee directors; he was chairman of this committee and was also chairman of the COED committee which was primarily concerned with the continuity and quality of Exxon's management. The COED committee directly concerned itself with about 200 senior management positions around the world and indirectly kept an eye on another 400 top management jobs in affiliated companies and subsidiary operations. The COED committee met weekly. Garvin had announced that he planned to retire at the end of 1986.

Exxon's president was Lawrence G. Rawl; he served as vice chairman of both the management committee and the COED committee. Rawl started with Exxon as an engineer in Texas in 1952, holding a variety of supervisory jobs in the Southwest United States. Rawl eventually took on U.S. marketing operations and was the number two executive of Exxon's Esso Europe unit. In 1980 Rawl was appointed to the Exxon board; he played a critical role in boosting Exxon's oil production and profits during the 1980s. Rawl was named president in early 1985 and was expected to take over the chairman's position when Garvin retired.

Anthony Sampson, in a book largely critical of the seven biggest international oil companies, said the following about Exxon and its management:

> In the middle of Manhattan, in the line of cliffs adjoining the Rockefeller Center, is the headquarters of the most famous and long-lived of them all: the company known in America as Exxon, and elsewhere as Esso, and for most of its hundred years' existence as Standard Oil of New Jersey or simply Standard Oil. It is a company which perhaps more than any other transformed the world in which we live. For much of its life it was automatically associated with the name of Rockefeller and some links still remain. The family still own two percent of the stock; Nelson Rockefeller once worked for it in Venezuela; and the desk of the founder, John D. Rockefeller I, is still preserved as a showpiece at the top of the building. But Exxon has long ago outgrown the control of a single family.
>
> The tranquil style of Exxon's international headquarters seems to have little in common with the passionate rhetoric of Arab politicians in Algiers. Beside a bubbling fountain and pool on Sixth Avenue, the fluted stone ribs soar up sheer for 53 storeys, and inside

the high entrance hall is hung with moons and stars. On the 24th floor is the mechanical brain of the company, where the movements of its vast cargoes are recorded. A row of TV screens are linked with two giant computers and with other terminals in Houston, London, and Tokyo, in a system proudly named LOGICS (Logistics Information and Communications Systems). They record the movement of 500 Exxon ships from 115 loading ports to 270 destinations, carrying 160 different kinds of Exxon oil between 65 countries. It is an uncanny process to watch: a girl taps out a question on the keyboard and the answer comes back in little green letters on the screen with the names of ships, dates, and destinations across the world. From the peace of the 24th floor, it seems like playing God—a perfectly rational and omniscient god, surveying the world as a single market.

Up on the 51st floor, where the directors are found, the atmosphere is still more rarefied. The visitor enters a high two-story lobby with a balcony looking down on high tapestries; the wide corridors are decorated with Middle East artifacts, Persian carpets, palms, or a Coptic engraving. It is padded and silent except for a faint hum of air-conditioning, and the directors' offices are like fastidious drawing rooms, looking down on the vulgar bustle of Sixth Avenue. It all seems appropriate to Exxon's reputation as a "United Nations of Oil."

But in this elegant setting, the directors themselves are something of an anticlimax. They are clearly not diplomats or strategists or statesmen; they are chemical engineers from Texas, preoccupied with what they call "the Exxon incentive." Their route to the top has been through the "Texas pipeline"—up through the technical universities, the refineries, and tank farms. The Exxon Academy, as they call it, is not a university or a business school, but the giant refinery at Baton Rouge, Louisiana. Watching the Exxon board at their annual meeting, I found it hard to imagine them as representatives of a world assembly. It was true that there were, in 1974, two foreign directors—Prince Colonna, the former commissioner of the Common Market, and Otto Wolff, the German industrialist; and there was also one director, Emilio Collado, with experience of government. But the core of the board was made up of the engineers, enclosed in their own specialized discipline.

Within their own citadel these men seem confident enough with some reason: they are directors of a company that has survived for a century, they have acquired great expertise, and they each earn over $200,000 a year. They move in a world enclosed by the rules of Exxon, which belongs to them. "I think of it as a proprietary relationship," said Garvin in 1973, "Like running a company of which I am the owner. It is not just my duty, but my deep personal desire, to keep it in the best shape possible for the men who will come after me." But once outside their own territory, their confidence easily evaporates. Confronting their shareholders they seem thoroughly nervous, sitting in a row, their fingers fidgeting and their cheekbones working, as they listen to questions about Exxon's African policy, Exxon's salary policy, Exxon's kidnap policy, Exxon's Middle East policy. They know well enough that their company, while one of the oldest, has also been the most hated.

It is in Texas, not New York, that the Exxon men feel more thoroughly at home: and it is the Exxon skyscraper in Houston, the headquarters of Exxon U.S.A., which seems to house the soul of the company. At the top is the Houston Petroleum Club with two entire storeys making up a single room where the oilmen can lunch off steaks and strawberries every day of the year. They like to show visitors the view of which they are justly proud. The flatlands stretch in every direction, broken only by the jagged man-made objects: the domes and tower-blocks in place of cliffs and hills; the curving freeways instead of rivers; the giant roadsigns instead of trees. The glaring gasoline signs stick up from the desolate landscapes like symbols leading to some distant shrine:

Exxon, Texaco, Shell, Gulf, Exxon. The fluid which has wrought all these changes is concealed from the view: around Houston there are only a few little pumps nodding in the fields, a few piles of pipelines to indicate the underground riches. But no one needs reminding: it was all done by oil.[2]

SIZE AND STRUCTURE OF THE PETROLEUM INDUSTRY

The business of supplying crude oil and petroleum products in 1985 was not only economically crucial but it was also the largest industry in the world. Worldwide sales of crude oil and petroleum products in 1985 approached $1 trillion, and worldwide petroleum consumption averaged over 50 million barrels per day. Billion-dollar oil companies were commonplace, and no nation was without at least one truly large-scale oil company. In 1985 11 of the 20 largest U.S. industrial corporations were primarily petroleum companies—Exxon Corporation, Mobil Corporation, Texaco, Inc., Chevron Corporation, Phillips Petroleum Company, Amoco Corporation, Atlantic Richfield Co., Shell Oil Company, (the U.S. subsidiary of Royal Dutch Petroleum), Tenneco Inc., Sun Company, Inc., and Occidental Petroleum Corporation. Exhibit 3 presents selected statistics for the leading oil companies.

The petroleum industry spanned a wide range of geographically separate and technically distant activities relating to getting oil from the ground to the final user. The main stages in the process were (1) finding and producing the crude oil, (2) transporting it to the point of processing, (3) refining it into marketable products, (4) transporting the products to regions of use, and (5) distributing them at retail. However, in the search for oil, producing companies were commonly involved in the production, use, and sales of natural gas; many of the major oil companies were suppliers of natural gas.

In the United States roughly 10,000 companies were involved in oil and gas exploration and production. No one firm accounted for more than 11 percent of oil and gas production. Over 80 percent of total U.S. crude oil output came from Texas, Louisiana, California, Alaska, and Oklahoma. It moved mainly through about 70,000 miles of gathering lines and 85,000 miles of trunk pipelines, as well as on oceangoing tankers, river barges, railroad tank cars, and trucks to some 200 operating refineries, with total 1984 capacity of about 15 million barrels/day. In 1984 the U.S. refining industry operated at about 80 percent of capacity. These refineries were operated by approximately 140 companies; in 1984 the top four companies accounted for under 35 percent of refining capacity. In 1985 over 75 pipeline companies were engaged in transporting crude oil and refined products on an interstate basis; additional companies operated intrastate. The top four pipeline companies accounted for less than 30 percent of total volume moved.

Most petroleum products moved from the refinery to the final customer via one or more intermediate storage facilities. Although residual fuel oil, for example, was delivered to large utility and industrial customers directly from the refinery, most products first went to large terminals, located generally at the outlet of a pipeline

---

[2] Anthony Sampson, *The Seven Sisters* (New York: The Viking Press, 1975), pp. 8–10. Quoted with permission.

Exhibit 3 Exxon's Performance in Comparison with Other Petroleum Companies, 1984

Primary Scope of Operation/Company	Revenues (in millions)	Net Income (in millions)	Five-Year Growth Rate in Earnings	Return on Equity	Return on Assets	Net Return on Sales	Debt as a Percent of Invested Capital	Debt as a Percent of Net Working Capital
Integrated companies—international:								
British Petroleum	$43,926.0	$1,624.0	-14.7%	11.9%	4.1%	3.7%	22.8%	165.7%
Chevron Corp.	26,798.0	1,534.0	-3.0	10.6	5.1	5.7	43.4	14,910.3
Exxon Corp.	90,854.0	5,528.0	5.2	19.0	8.8	6.1	11.6	258.6
Mobil Corp.	56,047.0	1,268.0	-8.8	9.2	3.3	2.3	40.9	2,723.2
Royal Dutch Petroleum	44,225.0	2,539.0	-9.4	14.6	6.0	5.7	17.3	110.8
Texaco Inc.	47,334.0	306.0	-29.5	1.8	0.9	0.6	41.0	761.9
Integrated companies—domestic:								
Amerada Hess Corp.	8,277.0	170.5	-19.6	6.7	2.7	2.1	40.1	287.1
American Petrofina	2,155.1	45.1	-11.5	7.2	2.9	2.1	39.1	580.6
Amoco Corp.	26,949.0	2,183.0	7.7	17.5	8.5	8.1	17.3	1,053.8
Atlantic Richfield Co.	23,768.0	1,129.0	-0.6	10.9	5.0	4.8	26.9	NM
Kerr McGee Corp.	3,537.0	65.0	-16.5	3.7	1.7	1.8	23.5	286.6
Phillips Petroleum Co.	15,537.0	810.0	-1.9	12.7	5.4	5.2	26.0	NM
Standard Oil Co. (Ohio)	11,692.0	1,488.0	4.6	18.1	8.8	12.7	26.4	NM
Sun Co. Inc.	14,466.0	538.0	-5.1	10.2	4.3	3.7	25.3	3,816.1
Unocal Corp.	10,838.4	700.4	6.9	12.9	7.2	6.5	15.3	417.3

NM = Not meaningful.
Source: Standard and Poor's, *Industry Surveys*.

or on a river, lake, or coastal port, where they could take barge or tanker delivery. By far most of these terminals were owned by refiners, although independent wholesaler-owned terminals took a substantial portion of the distillate and residual oils. Most gasoline and home heating oils were shipped next to local bulk storage facilities. From area bulk plants, the gasoline was transported to service stations and the heating oil to the storage tanks of homes and commercial establishments. However, in the case of gasoline it was not uncommon for the marketing departments of the refinery companies to bypass local bulk plants and ship gasoline directly to their own service stations from large area terminals. This development was made possible by the construction of large-volume retail outlets and the use of increasingly efficient truck carriers.

In 1985 there were over 12,000 wholesale distributors and about 150,000 service stations retailers (down from a peak of 226,000 in 1972). Another 100,000 outlets (convenience food stores, motels, and car washes) retailed gasoline as a secondary activity. The large oil companies owned less than 10 percent of the retail outlets which they supplied; most were owned (or leased) by wholesalers and retail resellers who established their own prices and operating practices.

EXXON'S PETROLEUM AND NATURAL GAS BUSINESS

Prior to the 1960s the strategic emphasis at Exxon had always been focused on strengthening the company's position as a major, transnational, fully integrated petroleum enterprise. Its operating scope was worldwide. Even though diversification efforts were begun in the 1960s, in 1986 Exxon was predominantly still an oil company (see the revenue and earnings breakdowns in Exhibit 1). The company was a major factor in all phases of the oil business.

Exploration and Production   Exxon's worldwide production of crude oil and natural gas liquids from internally generated sources declined in 1985 to about 1.7 million barrels a day (one barrel = 42 gallons)—down from the 1976 record high of 5.6 million barrels per day and from 4.0 million barrels per day in 1980. This was due to three factors: (1) weak economic conditions in many of the large industrial nations, (2) stagnating demand for petroleum products stemming from the meteoric climb of prices for petroleum products of the past seven years and growing conservation efforts by users, and (3) the expiration of long-term and special agreements with foreign governments for fixed supply amounts. Exxon in 1985 filled much of its needs for crude oil with purchases on the open market. Exxon was struggling to keep its discoveries of new oil and gas deposits abreast of current production rates from its own wells so as to stabilize its net proved reserves position. Exxon's crude oil reserves totaled nearly 7.5 billion barrels worldwide, and its natural gas reserves were about 45 trillion cubic feet; further statistics are presented in Exhibit 4.

Exxon drilled more than 2,400 wells in 1985, versus about 2,100 in 1984, 1,500 in 1983, 1,725 in 1978, and 1,550 in 1970. At year-end 1981 Exxon had drilling and exploration rights to some 596 million acres, up from 443 million acres in 1970. In 1985 additional exploration acreage was acquired in 15 countries. The company had increased its worldwide oil and natural gas reserves for four consecutive years—

Exhibit 4 Selected Petroleum and Natural Gas Operating Statistics, Exxon Corporation, 1980–1985

	1980	1981	1982	1983	1984	1985
	thousands of barrels daily					
Net production of crude oil and natural gas liquids and petroleum supplies available under special agreements:						
Net production, Exxon-owned wells						
United States	787	752	740	781	778	768
Canada	116	94	95	90	93	116
Other Western Hemisphere	11	11	10	14	16	18
Europe	155	194	289	370	412	417
Middle East and Africa	56	39	5	5	4	3
Australia and Far East	225	230	228	267	310	330
Total consolidated affiliates	1,350	1,320	1,367	1,527	1,613	1,652
Proportional interest in production of equity companies	351	32	33	32	21	20
Oil sands production—Canada	24	26	18	23	21	29
	1,725	1,378	1,418	1,582	1,655	1,701
Supplies available under long-term agreements with foreign governments	1,802	2,020	1,340	706	489	0
Other supplies available under special agreements	481	398	341	294	226	0
Worldwide	4,008	3,796	3,099	2,582	2,370	1,701
Petroleum product sales:						
Aviation fuels	336	323	330	316	312	326
Gasoline, naphthas	1,453	1,369	1,346	1,344	1,392	1,397
Home heating oils, kerosene, diesel oils	1,428	1,324	1,299	1,280	1,349	1,343
Heavy fuels	1,179	1,051	849	681	685	539
Specialty products	557	534	486	464	466	477
Total	4953	4,601	4,310	4,085	4,204	4,082
	millions of cubic feet daily					
Natural gas production available for sale:						
Net production, Exxon-owned wells						
United States	3,373	3,065	2,594	2,345	2,485	2,085
Canada	191	186	186	181	168	141
Other Western Hemisphere	78	82	72	70	70	69
Europe	719	799	773	851	1,069	1,086
Middle East and Africa	87	46	—	—	—	1
Australia and Far East	189	251	264	225	215	231
Total consolidated affiliates	4,637	4,429	3,889	3,672	4,007	3,613
Proportional interest in production of·equity companies	2,396	2,191	1,860	1,956	1,911	2,048
Supplies available under long-term agreements with foreign governments	104	107	—	—	—	—
Worldwide	7,137	6,727	5,749	5,628	5,918	5,661
	thousands of barrels daily					
Pipeline throughput	3,297	2,740	2,624	2,600	2,694	2,933

Source: *Annual Reports,* 1984 and 1985.

Exhibit 5   Summary of Exxon's Exploration and Production Operations   Millions of Dollars

	1970	*1978*	*1980*	*1983*	*1984*	*1985*
Earnings from operations:						
United States	$ 517	$ 1,202	$ 2,131	$ 1,866	$ 2,012	$ 2,111
Foreign	579	1,282	1,869	2,213	2,777	2,826
Total	1,096	2,484	4,000	4,079	4,789	4,937
Average capital employed:						
United States	2,418	5,871	7,306	11,625	11,907	12,312
Foreign	2,374	4,987	5,095	4,724	4,428	4,812
Total	4,792	10,858	12,401	16,349	16,335	17,124
Capital and exploration expenditures:						
United States	368	1,523	2,395	3,564	4,224	4,638
Foreign	370	1,884	2,818	2,521	2,715	2,923
Total	$ 738	$ 3,407	$ 5,213	$ 6,085	$ 6,939	$ 7,561
Research and development costs	$ 18	$ 61	$ 78	$ 151	$ 174	$ 159

Source: *Annual Reports*, 1979, 1981, 1984, 1985.

only a select group of oil companies were accumulating new reserves at a rate that more than replaced volumes currently produced.

Exxon's exploration teams were considered superior in selecting sites to drill for oil; in recent years Exxon had compiled a 20 percent success rate in finding oil and/or gas on new tracts where it has obtained drilling leases—compared to an industry average of 10 percent. Exxon U.S.A.'s senior vice president of exploration indicated that there was no real alternative to anteing up and accepting the drilling risks of dry holes: "You have nightmares going into these things, but an exploration man has to learn early that it's better to try and fail than not to try and have nothing.[3] To try to reduce the risk of choosing drill sites, Exxon, like other oil companies, sent out seismographic teams to assess the probability to discovery.

Operating and financial results for Exxon's exploration and production activities are highlighted in Exhibit 5.

Refining and Marketing
Exxon was the world's largest refiner with a capacity of roughly 5 million barrels a day. About 30 percent of Exxon's refining capacity was in the United States, and its domestic capacity advantage over other U.S. companies was much less than its size advantage elsewhere.

Total U.S. refining capacity in 1984 was 15.1 million barrels daily (down from 15.9 million barrels in 1983). Worldwide refining capacity was 74.5 million barrels in 1982, down from 76.4 million barrels in 1983. The declines reflected shutdowns of old inefficient refineries.

At Exxon, as well as at other integrated oil companies, the role of refining and marketing had shifted dramatically during the past decade. Prior to the 1973 Arab

---

[3] Ibid., p. 120.

oil embargo refining and marketing assets were considered a support conduit for transforming crude oil into profit-making capability. Most of the profit in the oil business was made at the wellhead, and refining and distribution operations were only marginally profitable. Beginning with the 1973 embargo, however, major oil companies lost their influence over world crude oil prices and supplies; effective control shifted to the OPEC nations. This reduced the need to protect the profitability of crude oil production via forward integration into refining and distribution. At the same time in the United States the oil and gas depletion allowance was phased out, and a windfall profit tax was imposed on the revenues from crude oil production, both of which limited profitability at the wellhead. In those foreign countries where oil companies were able to retain some ownership position in crude oil reserves, taxes imposed by government amounted to 80 percent or more of profits. The upshot was that the major integrated companies like Exxon came to regard refining and marketing investments as "stand alone" assets which were expected to generate returns on capital employed commensurate with alternative investment opportunities.

This "decoupling" of the investment/profitability links between production operations and refining/marketing operations came at a time when refining/marketing activities faced increased worldwide profit pressures. Chief among these were (1) the prospect of no long-range growth in demand for refined petroleum products in industrialized nations, (2) a need to alter refining capabilities to accommodate shifts in the demand mix for refined products and in the patterns of "light" and "heavy" (high-sulfur content) crude oil availability, (3) the possibilities that OPEC countries would acquire existing refinery capacity and integrate forward, and (4) a growing refinery overcapacity.

In the United States the demand for refined products topped out in 1978 at about 19.2 million barrels per day; declines were recorded each of the next six years—down to 16.0 million barrels in 1984; forecasts of U.S. demand to the year 2000 indicated very small amounts of demand growth (see Exhibit 6). The worldwide peak in refined product sales occurred in 1979 with declines registered the following five years. Over the longer term, prospects were for little if any growth in demand in the industrialized free-world nations, but small demand gains were projected to

Exhibit 6   U.S. Demand for Refined Petroleum Products   Millions of Barrels per Day

	Actual		Projected	
	1980	1984	1990	2000
Total demand	17.0	16.0	16.5	17.0
Gasoline	6.9	6.5	6.2	5.9
Kerosene	1.2	1.0	1.1	1.4
Distillate	3.0	3.0	3.2	3.4
Residual	2.5	1.5	1.7	1.9
Other	3.4	4.0	4.3	4.4

Source: *World Oil.*

occur in lesser-developed countries. The stagnant demand prospects reflected the sharp run-up in the prices of all petroleum products and the conservation effect of more fuel-efficient automobiles, altered driving habits, greater industrial energy efficiency, shifts of electric utilities from fuel oil to coal and nuclear powered generation, and growing efforts of homeowners to use less fuel oil for space heating. Long-term demand was proving to be much more price elastic than short-term demand.

These trends had greatly affected Exxon's refinery capacity utilization. In 1981 Exxon's refinery utilization averaged about 74 percent in the United States, about 61 percent in foreign countries, and about 65 percent overall—well below the 85–93 percent rates typical of previous decades and the levels needed for maximum efficiency. Exxon reacted by closing down its least efficient U.S. refining capacity, and eight refineries in Europe were sold or shut down between 1980 and 1986. In 1985 Exxon's U.S. refineries ran at 80 percent of capacity.

To improve the profitability of its refining and marketing operations, Exxon had undertaken several major cost reduction efforts. The energy efficiency of Exxon refiner-

Exhibit 7   Summary of Exxon's Refining and Marketing Operations Millions of Dollars

	1970	1978	1980	1983	1984	1985
Earnings from operations:						
United States	$ 103	$ 294	$ 202	$ 456	$ 161	$ 229
Foreign	187	563	1,702	674	196	643
Total	290	857	1,904	1,130	357	872
Average capital employed:						
United States	2,372	2,741	2,546	2,535	2,380	2,547
Foreign	7,058	5,349	7,541	6,151	5,730	6,297
Total	7,430	8,090	10,087	8,686	8,110	8,844
Capital expenditures:						
United States	315	271	250	363	380	624
Foreign	577	606	947	818	1,003	1,309
Total	892	877	1,197	1,181	1,383	1,933
Research and development costs	33	56	93	113	111	104
thousands of barrels a day						
Petroleum product sales:						
United States	1,753	1,736	1,503	1,146	1,149	1,123
Foreign	3,931	3,654	3,450	2,939	3,055	2,959
Total	5,684	5,390	4,953	4,085	4,204	4,082
Refinery crude oil runs:						
United States	989	1,426	1,246	958	1,021	1,054
Foreign	4,281	3,001	2,903	2,308	2,199	1,849
Total	5,270	4,427	4,149	3,266	3,220	2,903

Source: *Annual Reports,* 1979, 1981, 1984, 1985.

ies had been improved over 25 percent since 1974. Computer automation and job content studies in plants and distribution terminals had been completed. Marginal service station outlets had been eliminated (over 66,000 were closed between 1969 and 1981). Self-service pumps had been installed in most stations. In 1985 the company introduced 120 Exxon Shops to the U.S. motoring public; the shops carried convenience goods, beverages, and automotive items and were entirely self-service outlets staffed only by a cashier. Credit card operations had been tightened and 4 cents per gallon discounts for customers who paid cash at self-service pumps had been instituted to discourage credit card sales and thereby reduce working capital tied up in financing accounts receivable. Exhibit 7 presents selected statistics for Exxon's refining and marketing operations.

International Marine Transportation   In recent years a world tanker surplus combined with slumping crude oil production had made a money loser of Exxon's international tanker operations:

	1970	1978	1980	1983	1984	1985
	millions of dollars					
Earnings (losses) from operations	$112	$ (31)	$ 34	$ (126)	$(117)	$(65)
Average capital employed	581	1,676	1,438	1,031	828	640
Average expenditures	162	48	65	14	5	1
Research and development costs	3	4	5	3	2	2
	millions of deadweight tons					
Average capacity, owned and chartered						
Owned vessels	8.1	17.3	16.8	13.3	12.0	11.2
Chartered vessels	10.6	8.9	8.6	2.2	1.5	1.5
Total	18.7	26.2	25.4	15.5	13.5	12.7

Responding to the marine division losses during 1985, Exxon sold or scrapped six large crude oil carriers and three smaller vessels, reducing the capacity of fleet tonnage almost 25 percent to 9.7 million tons; these efforts followed on the heels of major fleet reductions between 1981 and 1984.

CHEMICAL OPERATIONS

Exxon's chemical plants were primarily in the United States, Canada, and Europe. Products included plastics and polyethylene, solvents and specialty chemicals, petroleum resins, lubricant additives, agricultural fertilizers, and primary petrochemicals. Revenues totaled $6.7 billion in 1985, and earnings from operations amounted to $249 million. Although its petrochemical business was inherently cyclical, Exxon's management felt bullish on the long-term prospects for its petrochemical operations because of Exxon's strong feedstock position and the company's long-standing experience in managing the technologies involved. Several chemical plants in Europe were sold or closed in 1985 to enhance long-term profit prospects.

Exhibit 8   Summary of Exxon's Chemical Operations   Millions of Dollars

	1970	1978	1980	1983	1984	1985
Earnings from operations:						
United States	$ 22	$ 154	$ 129	$ 118	$ 204	$ 123
Foreign	23	114	273	152	226	126
Total	45	268	402	270	430	249
Average capital employed:						
United States	410	1,052	1,480	1,890	1,858	1,767
Foreign	865	1,160	1,331	1,889	1,875	1,862
Total	1,275	2,212	2,811	3,779	3,733	3,627
Capital expenditures:						
United States	47	359	260	207	109	146
Foreign	54	111	155	338	194	187
Total	101	470	415	545	303	333
Research and development costs	31	40	72	105	124	133

Source: *Annual Reports,* 1979, 1980, 1984, 1985.

A profile of the performance of Exxon's chemical operations is shown in Exhibit 8.

EXXON'S STRATEGIC SHIFT TO BECOME AN ENERGY COMPANY

As far back as the 1960s Exxon management began to sense that oil and gas reserves would be inadequate to meet the world's need for energy. It was with this in mind that Exxon started laying the groundwork for a major strategic shift from being just a petroleum company to becoming an energy company.

Exxon's strategic move into nonpetroleum energy sources was motivated by two factors: (1) projections that all types of new and existing energy sources would be needed to meet a growing U.S. and world demand for energy and (2) the conviction that Exxon could meaningfully contribute to meeting these needs in a fashion that served both consumers and shareholders. Top management was convinced that the skills needed to develop these energy sources were similar to those Exxon had acquired in its existing business. A senior executive of Exxon described the desirability of diversifying thusly:

> Over many years Exxon has regularly prepared energy supply/demand outlooks for both the United States and the world. In the early 1960s we were projecting that oil and gas demand would continue to grow at about the same rate as the total demand for energy; however, it was not clear just where in the long term these supplies would come from. It appeared to us at that time that domestic production of both oil and gas could peak during the 1970s. We were also aware that there were very substantial reserves of oil and gas located overseas; however, like others, we were becoming increas-

ingly concerned over the national security aspects of increased imports. Thus, we concluded at this early date that there could be substantial future needs for synthetic oil and gas. It also appeared that since coal reserves are so plentiful in this country, a high percentage of the synthetic fuels would be made from coal. . . .

Another important conclusion reached by our appraisals during this period was that use of electricity was going to grow about twice as fast as the demand for total energy. The high projected growth rate for electricity led to our interest in uranium. Looking ahead it appeared to us that nuclear power would play a significant and increasingly important role in meeting the electric utility demand growth. . . .

Another important question which had to be answered before we made a decision to enter either the coal or uranium business was the availability of resources. . . . Our studies indicated that of this amount of potential reserves, approximately 65 percent were not owned or under lease by any company then producing coal. . . .

In the case of uranium, the reserves situation was quite different. Because uranium is difficult to find, it has a very high discovery value. This resource had been much more actively sought after than coal, and all known reserves were controlled by companies which were already active in the business. We believed, however, that the company's accumulated oil and gas exploration skills would offer a good start toward discovering new reserves . . . most of the known uranium deposits in the United States occur in sedimentary rocks. . . . Since oil and gas occur in a similar environment, we had a great deal of geological expertise which could be applied to uranium exploration. Also, Exxon U.S.A. had an extensive library of geological and geophysical information that had not yet been examined with the objective of locating uranium deposits. Many of the areas of the United States containing known or potential uranium deposits had been explored in the course of our oil and gas exploration efforts. It seemed possible that rock samples and detailed geological information could be reexamined for guides to locating uranium deposits. In addition, the company held mineral leases which covered not only oil and gas but also other minerals, including uranium. For all these reasons, we believed we could contribute to uranium discovery.

In addition to our exploration capabilities, we had other strengths which could be effectively used in establishing a position in the nuclear fuel and coal businesses. For example, we had developed over the years considerable expertise in processing hydrocarbons in our refineries. We believed that much of the research and development work we had done in refining would prove useful in developing processes for converting coal to gas or liquids.

It was determined at an early date that, to be successful, the coal and nuclear fuel businesses would require sizable amounts of front-end capital. Another important factor was that our company had considerable experience in the area of high-risk, capital-intensive, long-lead-time ventures. In short, we concluded that the needs to be met in these energy fuel areas were compatible with the capabilities of our company.[4]

Exxon's corporate strategy became one of using a sizable and growing fraction of the company's cash flow from oil and gas operations to diversify into other energy endeavors and gradually lessen the firm's total dependence on its petroleum-related operations. The strategy was to be implemented over a 10- to 20-year period with heavy investments in other energy sources coming during the 1980s; the strategic objective was to transform Exxon into a well-diversified, full-line energy supplier by sometime in the 1990s. Generally speaking the strategy called (1) for starting up

---

[4] Testimony before Senate Committee on Interior and Insular Affairs, December 6, 1973.

the new energy activities internally rather than via acquisition so as to avoid any antitrust problems or adverse public reaction associated with acquiring existing companies and (2) for energy diversification to be financed by investing an increasing percentage of Exxon's $8–$10 billion cash flows in developing new energy businesses. Meanwhile, in the near term, the bulk of Exxon's capital expenditures would be concentrated in protecting the company's long-term position as a leader in the worldwide petroleum industry.

EXXON'S ENTRY INTO COAL

Exxon's studies revealed that the economically recoverable domestic coal reserves in the United States were in the range of 200 billion tons. When compared to current annual coal production of about half a billion tons, these reserves represented more than a 400-year supply. Since coal was plentiful, it was expected to be a raw material for production of synthetic fuels. Synthetics were believed to be a likely future raw material for Exxon's refineries and chemical plants or to be substitutable as retail products.

Exxon's coal activities became the responsibility of a subsidiary, The Carter Oil Company. The purchase of undeveloped coal reserves began in 1965; bituminous coal reserves were purchased in Illinois, West Virginia, and Wyoming, and lignite reserves were obtained in Arkansas, Montana, North Dakota, and Texas. Coal marketing activities began in 1967. Initially coal from the Illinois reserves offered the best sales prospects because of its proximity to midwestern electric utilities—power companies with coal-fired generating plants used 75 percent of all the coal consumed in the United States (an average-sized coal-fired plant used 1 to 2 million tons of coal per year). In 1968 a sales contract was negotiated with Commonwealth Edison, a large electric utility based in Chicago, and Monterey Coal Company, a Carter subsidiary, was formed and began development of its first mine in southern Illinois; production commenced in mid-1970. The mine employed about 500 people, had a maximum capacity of about 3 million tons of coal per year, and was one of the largest and most modern underground mines in the country. A second mine was opened in 1977 to supply coal to Public Service Company of Indiana; its capacity was 3.6 million tons per year.

The Carter Mining Company, another subsidiary of the Carter Oil Company, developed Exxon's coal reserves in the West. By 1982 two surface mines were in operation near Gillette, Wyoming. Outside the United States Exxon had coal mining properties in operation or under development in Columbia, Canada, and Australia; in Columbia Exxon was one of the partners in a $3 billion project to construct and operate a coal mine, railroad, and port for coal exporting.

Management was proud of the company's coal mining efficiency. Exxon's underground coal mine productivity in 1975 was 23 tons/man-day; this compared with 17 tons/man-day for all underground mines in Illinois (1974) and less than 10 tons/man-day for all U.S. underground mines (1975). Even so, Exxon's coal business did not become profitable until 1980, 10 years after the first mine was opened in Illinois. Exhibit 9 shows operating statistics for Exxon's coal mining and development business.

Exhibit 9   Summary of Exxon's Coal Mining and Development Operations   Millions of Dollars

	1970	1978	1980	1983	1984	1985
Earnings from operations, after tax:						
Operating mines	$ —	$ 2	$ 22	$ 60	$ 65	$ 59
New business and mine development costs	(1)	(22)	(19)	(23)	(22)	(20)
	$ (1)	$ (20)	$ 3	$ 37	$ 43	$ 39
Research and development costs	$ —	$ 4	$ 2	$ 7	$ 8	$ 3
Average capital employed	$ 24	$ 271	$ 358	$ 792	$ 1,057	$ 1,333
Capital and exploration expenditures	$ 13	$ 87	$ 52	$ 336	$ 397	$ 367
			millions of short tons			
Recoverable reserves	7,000	9,500	10,500	10,566	11,070	11,040
Production	.3	5.2	11.4	20.5	25.1	28.9
Design capacity						
Existing operations	3.0	26.6	36.0	37.9	37.9	37.9
Under construction	—	1.0	9.3	8.3	8.3	9.1
Mines						
In operation	1	4	4	5	5	5
Under construction	—	1	2	1	1	1

Sources: *Annual Reports*, 1978, 1980, 1984, 1985.

EXXON'S ENTRY INTO NUCLEAR ENERGY

As far back as the mid-1960s, Exxon's analysis of the energy situation indicated that use of electricity was to grow about twice as fast as the demand for total energy; Exxon believed that nuclear power would supply as much as 30 percent of the U.S. electric energy supply by the 1990s—an outcome which would greatly increase uranium demand and make diversification into uranium mining and nuclear fuels a profitable business opportunity.

As Exxon saw it, the nuclear fuel business consisted of several distinct activities—uranium exploration, mining, and milling; uranium enrichment; fabrication of enriched uranium into nuclear fuel assemblies; chemical reprocessing of the spent fuel assemblies; chemical reprocessing of the spent fuel assemblies to recover uranium and plutonium for recycling into the fuel cycle, thus reducing requirements for new uranium supply and enrichment services; and ultimate safe storage and disposal of nuclear wastes. Exxon elected to enter only the first three of these segments.

Exploration, Mining, and Milling.   Exxon initiated its uranium exploration program in the United States in 1966. By 1977 the company had made two uranium discoveries that had been brought into production and two others that were in varying stages of evaluation. Exxon's petroleum activities played a key role in two of the four discoveries: one discovery was located on a lease which was originally obtained as a petroleum prospect and another resulted, in part, from information gained during geophysical exploration for hydrocarbons. Exxon estimated that in 1977 it had about 5 percent of the uranium reserves in the United States. The reserves that had been assessed as commercially viable were already committed under contract to the utility industry.

Nuclear Fuel Fabrication   During the 1970s Exxon entered into uranium marketing and into the design, fabrication, and sale of nuclear fuel assemblies to electric utilities with nuclear-generating plants. The company also began to provide a range of fuel management and engineering services to electric utility firms. Responsibility for these activities was assigned to a newly created subsidiary, Exxon Nuclear, Inc. Exxon Nuclear competed only in the market segment for refueling nuclear reactors. Nuclear reactors were refueled every 12 to 18 months during their 30 to 40 year life. Exxon Nuclear's primary rivals in the replacement fuel market were Westinghouse, General Electric, Combustion Engineering, Inc., and Babcock & Wilcox Co. Exxon Nuclear was the only fuel fabricator not engaged in selling nuclear reactors and supplied about 6 percent of the domestic fuel fabrication market.

Even though Exxon's nuclear operation lost money every year during the 1970s, Exxon continued to be optimistic about the outlook for its budding nuclear fuels business because of continued construction of nuclear plants all over the world. Over

Exhibit 10   Summary of Exxon's Uranium Mining and Nuclear Fuel Fabrication Activities   Millions of Dollars

	1970	*1978*	*1980*	*1981*	*1982*	*1983*	*1984*	*1985*
(Losses) from operations, after tax:								
Operating results	$ (3)	$ (33)	$ (18)	$ (41)	NA	NA	NA	NA
Exploration costs	(1)	(18)	(14)	(9)	NA	NA	NA	NA
Total	$ (4)	$ (51)	$ (32)	$ (50)	$(14)	$23	$20	$(19)
Research and development costs	$ 1	$ 25	$ 17	$ 14	NA	NA	NA	NA
Average capital employed	$ 7	$201	$229	$203	NA	NA	NA	NA
Capital and exploration expenditures	$10	$ 74	$ 72	$ 42	NA	NA	NA	NA
Revenue	$ 1	$142	$183	$273	NA	NA	NA	NA
				millions of pounds				
Production of uranium concentrates	—	3.3	3.6	3.1	.8	1.4	.4	0
Mines:								
In operation	—	3	3	3	1	1	—	—
Under development	1	—	—	—	—	—	—	—

NA = not available.
Source: *Annual Reports,* 1979, 1980, 1983, 1984, 1985.

270 nuclear plants were either in operation or under construction at various sites worldwide. However, by early 1982, the outlook for nuclear fuel was reversed. Although Exxon Nuclear had signed contracts with seven utilities for the fabrication of nuclear fuel through 1990, reduced demand projections for nuclear fuel (owing to numerous cancellations in nuclear plant construction and stretchouts in the construction of others) had caused management to begin planning in 1983 for shutdowns of Exxon Nuclear's U.S. mining operations. Moreover, Exxon's uranium exploration had been stopped, developmental engineering work at one mineable deposit was deferred, and a joint venture to develop techniques for separating uranium isotopes with laser beams was ended. The company halted its research activities in nuclear enrichment and reprocessing because of uncertainties in the outlook for profitable investment opportunities.

In mid-1984 the Wyoming uranium mine was closed due to low demand and depressed prices, terminating Exxon's uranium mining operations. In the meantime, both General Electric and Westinghouse had moved to divest their nuclear fuel businesses. So far Exxon had decided to remain in the nuclear fuel fabrication business; since 1969 Exxon Nuclear had provided fuel for more than 40 reactors in the United States, Europe, and the Far East. In the United States in 1985 there were 99 nuclear reactors in operation, and 32 more were under construction; outside the United States there were an additional 244 nuclear units in operation and another 137 under construction. In 1985 Exxon's shipments of nuclear fuel assemblies were up 22 percent.

Exhibit 10 summarizes the recent operating results of Exxon's ventures into uranium mining and nuclear fuel fabrication.

EXXON'S OTHER DIVERSIFICATION EFFORTS IN ENERGY

Exxon's diversification into other energy areas was motivated by some of the same factors that motivated its diversification into coal and nuclear fuel. As late as 1977 Exxon's total expenditures on these other diversification efforts were small relative to coal and nuclear fuel expenditures. The company's efforts were designed to learn about emerging technologies, to contribute to their development, and to position the company so that a competitive commercial contribution could be initiated when and if market demand led to profit opportunities that appeared to be commensurate with the risks involved.

Oil Shale   Oil shale from deposits in Colorado, Utah, and Wyoming represented a potential source of supplemental liquid and gaseous fuels many times that of the proved domestic reserves of crude petroleum. While considerable shale lands were held by oil companies, the vast majority—about 80 percent—of potential reserves were federally controlled.

Exxon's oil shale activities were relatively limited because of the high-cost economics and because of federal control of most oil shale lands. During the early 1960s Exxon acquired a number of small tracts of patented land and mining claims in the oil shale area of Colorado. These holdings, however, were widely scattered and would have to be consolidated to form mineable blocks. Exxon's expenditures in oil shale totaled more than $16 million as of 1977. Of this $8.8 million went to acquire oil shale reserves in the early 1960s, $4.9 million was spent on research and $2.8 million on core drilling, administrative expenses, and the like.

During the late 1970s Exxon became a 60 percent partner in the Colony oil shale project in northwestern Colorado. The project (scheduled to begin producing in 1986 with an ultimate production target of 47,000 barrels a day of upgraded synthetic oil) was halted in 1983 when a growing worldwide surplus of crude oil and declines in crude oil prices combined to make the production of synthetic fuel uneconomic; in 1983 Exxon wrote off losses of $106 million on the Colony project. An Australian oil shale project, in which Exxon was a joint venture partner, was halted for reappraisal in 1982.

Solar   Exxon started investigating commercial uses of solar energy in 1970 when a research program was initiated to develop advanced low-cost photovoltaic devices. Throughout the 1970s Exxon and other companies worked at developing applications for photovoltaic devices for use in microwave transmitters and ocean buoys. In 1979 Exxon's Solar Power Corp. recorded a 33 percent increase in unit sales of its solar photovoltaic products. It also obtained government contracts for several major demonstration projects in amounts sufficient to assure that 1980 sales would more than double the 1979 total. In the mid-1980s Exxon's efforts in solar energy were terminated, partly because the paths of solar technology that Exxon was pursuing were found to be less promising than those under development elsewhere; the solar activities were never profitable.

Batteries and Fuel Cells   Recognizing the increasing electrification of energy and the need for efficiently storing solar-generated electricity, Exxon funded research in electrochemistry during the 1970s. Fuel cells (devices that convert special fuels such as hydrogen to electricity) had been under study in Exxon Research and Engineering since 1960. In 1970 Exxon Enterprises entered a joint development effort with a French electrical equipment manufacturer to develop a more efficient power supply for electric vehicles and to replace generators driven by engines or gas turbines. Program costs through 1975 exceeded $15 million, but technical progress as of 1985 had not met expectations. Fuel cell technology had progressed to the point in 1986 where many electric utilities were engaged in constructing and operating small-scale pilot projects utilizing fuel cell technology.

A battery development program was initiated at Exxon in 1972 based on concepts developed by Exxon Research and Engineering Company. Batteries with increased energy densities were viewed as being useful as storage devices to help utilities meet peak electricity demands and as potential power sources for electric vehicles. Company experts felt the technological challenge was to develop new batteries that would store from two to five times more energy per unit weight than conventional batteries and be rechargeable hundreds of times without deterioration. In 1978 Exxon's Advanced Battery Division began selling a titanium disulfide button battery for uses in watches, calculators, and similar products. As of 1986, however, Exxon had not become a major factor in pioneering significant breakthroughs in either batteries or fuel cells.

Laser Fusion   Exxon Research and Engineering Company was one of the sponsors of a program at the University of Rochester begun in 1972 to study the feasibility of laser-ignited fusion of light atoms for the economical generation of power. Out of an estimated program cost of $5.8 million through August 1975, Exxon Research and Engineering Company had contributed about $917,000. This included the cost of Exxon scientists on direct loan to the university. In 1986 Exxon's laser fusion efforts were still in the long-range research and product development stage; the bulk of Exxon's activities were in monitoring results elsewhere.

HONG KONG POWER GENERATION

Exxon's biggest and most profitable nonoil energy venture was launched during the late 1970s and 1980s when Exxon became a 60 percent partner in a $3 billion joint venture with China Light and Power Co. to build and operate two large multiunit coal-fired electric power generation plants in Hong Kong. In 1986 five out of the eight generating units were operational, and construction was continuing on three 677-megawatt units. All of the facilities were managed and operated by China Light and Power. Eight percent of China Light and Power's total sales of electricity were to the People's Republic of China. Operating statistics for Exxon's Hong Kong venture are summarized below:

| | Millions of Dollars | | | | |
	1981	1982	1983	1984	1985
Revenues	$604	$584	$566	$608	$586
Operating earnings	36	51	71	88	90
Average capital employed				839	1,002
Capital expenditures				328	346

MINERALS MINING AND DEVELOPMENT

For about 10 years Exxon had been a participant in ventures to develop and operate several minerals projects. In 1986 these projects involved two copper mines in Chile, a gold mine in Australia, and a zinc/copper mine. The copper mines in Chile made their first profit from operations in 1985 after incurring losses of $500 million during the past decade. The gold mine in Australia also had a small profit for the year on production of about 35,000 ounces; mining began at midyear. Exxon was a 50 percent owner and was the operator of the gold mine. A profile of recent operating results for the Exxon Minerals division is shown in Exhibit 11.

EXXON'S ACQUISITION OF RELIANCE ELECTRIC COMPANY

During 1979 Exxon acquired 100 percent ownership of the Reliance Electric Company of Cleveland, Ohio, at a cost of $1.2 billion. With 31,000 employees and principal operations or subsidiaries in 16 states and 14 foreign countries, Reliance's primary domestic operating organizations were a rotating machinery group that made electric motors; a drives and systems group that made motor controls; a mechanical group that made mechanical power products and components; a weighing and controls

Exhibit 11   Operating Results—Exxon Minerals Division, 1982–1985   Millions of Dollars

	1982	1983	1984	1985
Revenues	$ 80	$ 115	$ 97	$ 108
Earnings (Losses):				
Operating results	(67)	(24)	(16)	1
Mine pre-development &				
development costs	(23)	(10)	(17)	(9)
Exploration costs	(24)	(23)	(19)	(13)
Total Earnings (losses)	$(114)	$(57)	$(52)	$(21)
Average capital employed	$325	$338	$352	$359
Capital and exploration				
expenditures	93	59	71	82
Research & development costs	7	5	4	2
		thousands of metric tons		
Recoverable reserves with				
contained metal:				
Copper	12,716	12,530	12,819	12,752
Zinc	4,454	4,212	4,212	4,088
Lead	366	353	353	388
Molybdenum	231	212	214	213
Gold (thousands of troy ounces)			354	330
Production:				
Copper			67	77
Gold (thousands of troy ounces)			—	18

group that was composed primarily of the Toledo Scale subsidiary; a telecommunications group, primarily a supplier to the telephone industry; and Federal Pacific Electric, a subsidiary which manufactured and marketed electric power distribution equipment.

Exxon's principal purpose in making the acquisition was to obtain the means for rapid development and marketing of a new energy-saving technology called alternating current synthesis (ACS). The technology held promise for a low-cost, efficient, and reliable means of converting standard utility alternating current electricity into variable voltage and variable frequency electricity with resulting savings in power consumption. The new technology, which grew out of Exxon's research efforts on an electric car, was thought to have the potential for cutting the energy required by a standard industrial electric motor as much as 50 percent (the equivalent of 1 million barrels of crude oil a day)—there were an estimated 20 million electric motors in industrial use. Exxon felt it needed to acquire a well-established electrical equipment manufacturer to manufacture and market the ACS device with a high probability of success. Reliance Electric in 1978 had sales of $966 million and profits of $65 million; about 12 percent of its sales were in electric motors.

Exxon was also interested in Reliance Electric because of Exxon's high-priority research into a new power system for automobiles. In 1979 Exxon had reached the prototype stage in its efforts and had come up with a hybrid car powered by both a battery-driven motor and a small gasoline engine. The electric motor, equipped with the new ACS device, provided the power for acceleration and steep grades;

the gasoline engine took over on level stretches and served to recharge the batteries. Exxon felt the new system would be very fuel efficient even on larger cars.

The Reliance Electric acquisition did not produce spectacular results for Exxon. Shortly after Exxon made the acquisition, antitrust violations surfaced in Reliance Electric's Federal Pacific Division and settlement damages ran into the millions. More importantly, development work on the ACS project hit major snags and it was determined that the concept would not be cost effective. An alternative concept was explored, but did not offer a significant competitive advantage over existing products. In August 1981 the whole ACS project was canceled. In 1985 the Federal Pacific unit of Reliance was sold. Reliance's revenues in 1985 were $1.67 billion, up from $1.54 billion in 1984; several new products were introduced. A profile of Reliance's performance since its acquisition is shown below:

	Millions of Dollars					
	1980	*1981*	*1982*	*1983*	*1984*	*1985*
Revenues	$1,595	$1,673	$1,561	$1,397	$1,538	$1,667
Operating results	1	39	(41)	(51)	15	NA
Business development costs	(7)	(8)	(9)	(7)	(4)	NA
Total operating earnings (loss)	(6)	31	(50)	(58)	11	30
Research and development costs	29	34	36	30	25	40
Average capital employed	1,586	1,566	1,451	1,307	1,230	1,085
Capital expenditures	83	102	98	56	51	49

NA = not available.
Reliance took $60 million of write-offs in 1984.

EXXON ENTERPRISES

A subsidiary, Exxon Enterprises, was started in the early 1970s to become the "new business development arm" of Exxon. By 1981 Exxon Enterprises had invested over $800 million in some two dozen new ventures, either by joining other investors in additional venture-capital deals or by funding new businesses created and run by its own employees. Most of these were fledgling firms far removed from Exxon's traditional business. Only two involved the energy industry—Solar Power and Daystar, both of which made equipment for collecting solar energy and both of which were divested in 1981–82 because they were no longer felt to be attractive investments. Scan-Tron sold scholastic tests that were automatically graded by its own machine; Environmental Data produced instruments for measuring air pollution; Qyx marketed computer-controlled office typewriters; Graftek made graphite shafts for golf clubs and fishing rods; Delphi had developed a way to store voice messages in a computer; Zilog manufactured microprocessors to transmit and process data; Qume made high-speed printers; Vydec produced wordprocessing display terminals and text-editing systems; and Periphonics made switching computers. Other companies that were a part of Exxon Enterprises included Amtek, Xentex, Qwip, Micro-Bit Corporation, Magnex Corp., Intecom, and Optical Information Systems.

The corporate role of the Exxon Enterprises division was to develop nonenergy options for Exxon's future, mainly in case Exxon's diversification into other energy sources did not prove to be as successful as anticipated, and also to take up slack from the eventual decline of the oil business. Unlike other oil companies such as Mobil and Atlantic Richfield which chose to diversify by acquiring well-established companies, Exxon opted for buying ownership interests in small entrepreneurial companies which were just getting started and which appeared to have products capable of achieving $100 million in sales. The idea was to grow up with a new industry as opposed to entering an established industry. In addition Exxon had a longer time horizon, less aversion to risk, more money, and a greater determination to "stick with the winners" than many other venture capital firms.

In 1980 Exxon Enterprises consolidated its several ventures in the office equipment and office systems field. Fifteen of the small "startup" companies were molded into a new unit called Exxon Information Systems; the combined sales of these companies totaled $200 million in 1979 and nearly all were experiencing rapid growth (though none were profitable). A drive was also launched to recruit senior executives away from other information processing companies—IBM and Xerox in particular. A senior vice president of Exxon Enterprises said, "We intend to be *the* systems supplier to the office market." The strategy was to become a major factor in advanced office systems equipment within three to five years using a "supermarket approach"—offering customers a wide variety of products (typewriters, word processors, fast printers, electronic files, voice-input devices, message units, and so on) with the potential of computer-controlled coordination. Most industry observers predicted that Exxon would try to challenge IBM and Xerox head-on in the office automation market which, by the end of the 1980s, was projected to be a $150–$200 billion industry.

Exxon indicated that revenues would probably have to reach $1 billion before the Exxon Information Systems unit became profitable. Management stated that Exxon was prepared to be patient in integrating the 15 companies into a single systems company and in "growing" the unit into a profitable and high competitive market position. However, the prospects for making EIS profitable got gloomier between 1980 and 1984. By 1984 Exxon had invested more than $600 million in the office systems units, but losses continued to mount—the cumulative total exceeded $250 million. In early 1985 the foreign operations of the Office Systems Division were sold to Italy's Olivetti and the U.S. operations were sold to Harris Corporation's Lanier Business Products unit; the sales price was undisclosed but Exxon did not come close to recovering its $600 million investment. The only company of significance from the original group of Exxon Enterprises companies still owned by Exxon in 1985 was Zilog. Several new companies had recently been added to Exxon Enterprise's business portfolio; the biggest of these was Gilbarco.

MAJOR NEW DEVELOPMENTS: 1981–1986

Between 1981 and 1986 conditions in the worldwide oil and gas market swung sharply from shortage to surplus. Worldwide crude oil supplies were plentiful as end-use demand fell well short of earlier projections. Crude oil prices softened slowly during 1982–84, began a slide from the $34–$38 range to the $25–$30 range in 1985, and crashed temporarily to the $10–$14 per barrel range in early 1986. In 1980–81 it had been widely predicted that crude oil prices would reach at least $50 per barrel by 1985 and perhaps $70–$100 per barrel by 1990.

Efforts to conserve all types of petroleum products, brought on by the sharp run-up of prices in the 1974–80 period and by expectations of further sharp increases to come, were the driving forces in the shift from shortages to surplus conditions. Energy-saving technology of all types was increasingly available and in 1986 automobiles were delivering about double the miles per gallon of the early 1970s. Conditional upon developments in energy-saving technology, on energy prices, and on economic growth rates, it seemed probable that worldwide demand for crude oil in 1990 would not be substantially higher than the 1979 peak of 63 million barrels per day. Supplies of natural gas had also shifted from short to abundant; prices were declining and a surplus of natural gas was expected at least through 1986.

The jolt to enterprises tied to the oil and gas business as the sellers' market turned into a buyers' market was far reaching. The belief that oil and gas prices were destined to rise indefinitely and that investing in drilling and exploration for oil and natural gas were certain payoff propositions had prompted a rush in the late 1970s and early 1980s to invest in oil and gas exploration by all kinds of small companies as well as the major oil companies like Exxon. Banks were willing to finance speculative drilling projects and many independent operators borrowed heavily. Multimillion dollar limited partnerships were formed to drill for new supplies. Du Pont acquired Conoco Oil and U.S. Steel bought Marathon Oil (both multibillion-dollar transactions) because of the lucrative long-term profit prospects in oil. But in 1982 when the glut became highly visible and several OPEC countries turned to price cuts to help them maintain production volumes, the near-term outlook for companies dependent on rising oil prices became desperate. Many oil companies began major restructuring to avoid possible takeover attempts and there were several buy-outs among the oil giants: Occidental Petroleum acquired Cities Service; Texaco bought Getty Oil; Chevron acquired the Gulf Oil Corporation; and Mobil acquired Superior Oil. Capital investments in drilling, coal-based synthetic fuels, and oil shale were cut back drastically. Drilling activity fell off sharply. Financing dried up for the programs of many small independent operators. Long-term contracts to supply oil and natural gas, which buyers had rushed to sign in the shortage era, became unattractive. The budding synthetic fuel business virtually collapsed. Many coal-based synthetic fuels projects, always looked upon as marginally viable and longer range than oil shale, were canceled or downsized. The bulk of the major oil shale projects in the United States were slowed, reduced in size, or halted; two multibillion-dollar Canadian projects were canceled. A $40 billion pipeline to transport Alaskan North Slope gas to the lower 48 states was put on hold. Most oil company exploration and production programs were tailored to maximize cash generation rather than to find reserves which might be recoverable at a profit later if prices rose enough.

Long-term, oil's share of total energy use was still expected to drop from 53 percent in 1980 to 40 percent by the year 2000; natural gas was expected to hold onto its roughly 18 percent share of the energy market. Coal, synthetic fuels, nuclear energy, and solar energy were expected to fill the gap. However, the potential for coal, oil shale, tar sands, coal liquefaction, and coal gasification really depended on (1) how much new oil and natural gas was discovered, (2) the extent to which energy-saving technologies were developed to permit conventional oil and gas to stretch further, (3) how much of the total energy demand would be supplied by nuclear power plants (the accident at Three Mile Island in the United States and the disaster at Chernobyl in Russia raised major safety questions), and (4) the speed with which developments in solar energy technology made solar power a cost effective and almost infinite energy source. Coal was coming under closer environmental scrutiny and there was now a consensus that the use of high-sulfur coal contributed to "acid rain." Tougher, more costly pollution regulations concerning coal use were a virtual certainty before 1990.

Exxon's chairman, Clifton Garvin, reflected on both the successes of 1985 and uncertainty about the future:[5]

> That we were able to do as well as we did in 1985 is attributable to strategies set in motion some time ago. A major emphasis in our planning over the past several years has been to prepare for a more competitive future. We have done this in a variety of ways, all directed toward making Exxon a more productive organization. In refining and marketing, for instance, we have systematically phased out less efficient capacity when it became apparent that it could no longer compete. Current refining capacity, as a result, is down about a quarter from its 1981 level. At the same time, we have upgraded to higher levels of efficiency and productivity those facilities that we have retained. Average sales volume in Exxon service stations is an example. Over the same four-year period this has increased some 30 percent. Emphasis on higher-value products and greater selectivity in geographical market participation have been other elements in our downstream strategy.
>
> In exploration and production our goal has been twofold: to develop and maximize recovery from existing oil and gas fields (about two thirds of our producing investments have gone for this purpose) and to strengthen our resource based through cost-effective additions to reserves. In 1985 we drilled a record number of development wells and the largest number of exploration wells in the last quarter of a century. The new discoveries and extensions to existing fields that resulted, along with purchases and revised recovery estimates, more than replaced volumes produced. For the fourth year running we increased our reserve base.
>
> All in all, then, it was a good year for Exxon. But as we all know much has happened since the year ended. Early in 1986 spot crude oil prices experienced their most drastic drop in the modern history of the oil industry. How far this may go, how permanent it may be, and all that it implies for the future remains to be seen. But that there will be far reaching consequences for our industry seems certain. As a result, we are having to rethink our entire strategy. Exploration ventures, capital investments, the lines of business that we are in—all must be reexamined to make sure that they continue to make sense in a radically new environment.

In April 1986 Exxon offered 40,000 employees the option to retire early or resign with compensation, citing the poor outlook for the oil industry due to recent drastic declines in oil prices. The company planned a major reorganization with staff reductions extending to all levels of the corporations. Some divisions faced a 30 to 50 percent reduction in staff, as the company sought a method of coping with $15 per barrel oil.

---

[5] Management's letter to the shareholder, *1985 Annual Report*.

The company was using portions of its $11 billion annual cash flow to (1) repurchase shares of its stock (a 125 million-share stock buyback campaign had helped boost earnings per share and keep Exxon's stock price in the $50–$65 dollar range), (2) make small acquisitions of distressed U.S. oil properties (about $600 million had been spent since early 1984 to acquire at least 100 million barrels of oil reserves and an undisclosed amount of natural gas), (3) search for new oil reserves in altogether new fields (30 percent of exploration expenditures) and in fields where oil had already been discovered (70 percent of exploration expenditures), and (4) fund the expansion efforts of existing operations. Analysts estimated that Exxon could take on an additional $4 to $5 billion in long-term debt without jeopardizing its AAA bond ratings.

CASE 21 THE THERMOMETER CORPORATION OF AMERICA: DIVISION OF FIGGIE INTERNATIONAL, INC.*

It was late November of 1982, when Harry Figgie, Jr., Chairman of Figgie International, and Joe Skadra, group vice president and treasurer, were meeting in the company's new headquarters complex in Richmond, Virginia. Figgie International (FI) was a diversified company which had 40 different business ranging from fire engines to clothing. Included in these businesses was the manufacture of thermometers which was conducted under the name of Thermometer Corporation of America (TCA). The TCA plant was located in Springfield, Ohio, a city of 86,000 in the west-central part of the state.

FI had recently received a proposal from Ohio Thermometer Co. (OTC) dated November 17, 1982, and entitled "An Analysis of a Merger and Future Between TCA and OTC" (Exhibit 1). The proposal was presented by Charles L. Wappner and Jerome P. Bennett, president and vice president, respectively (and co-owners), of OTC. OTC was a competitor in the thermometer business and was also located in Springfield, Ohio. Figgie and Skadra arranged this meeting to discuss the November 17 proposal. Their conversation began as follows:

Figgie: As you know, I met with Charlie [Wappner] and Jerry [Bennett] on November 17th at their request. At that meeting they presented their proposal, which calls for Figgie [International] to purchase OTC.

Skadra: As I recall, they [OTC] tried to acquire TCA from us back in 1978.

Figgie: Yes, but at that time we felt that the growth potential for TCA was too good to consider divesting. I have kept in touch with Charlie and Jerry since then, so their proposal wasn't a complete surprise.

Skadra: How did the meeting go?

Figgie: The atmosphere was very friendly. I pointed out, as best I could, that while we regard ourselves as a good parent company to work with, a number of changes would have to be made if we assimilated OTC. I'm sure from the comments they made that they understand this and would be willing to work with us.

Skadra: Living and working in the same community, they must know Bill Kieffer [TCA president].

Figgie: They know him and apparently have considerable respect for him and for his abilities as a manager, as do we. In the proposal they specifically refer to his [Kieffer's] "running a lean operation." This tells me that if a merger of TCA and OTC were to take place, they would be willing to accept Kieffer as their leader.

This case was prepared as a basis for class discussion rather than to illustrate either effective or ineffective handling of an administrative situation.

* Prepared by Per Jenster, Henry Odell, and Ken Burger, all of the University of Virginia. This case was used in the fourth McIntire Case Competition (MCI IV) held at the University of Virginia on February 9–11, 1985. We gratefully acknowledge the General Electric Foundation for support of the MCI and the writing of this case. © 1985. Distributed by the Case Research Association. All rights reserved to the authors and the Case Research Association. Reprinted with permission.

Skadra: In terms of return on investment, TCA has been one of our top businesses—until recently.

Figgie: True enough, but we haven't been able to get the sales growth we had hoped for. Bill [Kieffer] has, on several occasions, asked me for help in acquiring businesses that would help us expand the thermometer business and help him in getting that growth.

Skadra: I remember looking at a couple that just couldn't be justified.

Figgie: Despite the recent decline in sales at TCA I still think it has potential, and I don't want to consider selling it. We have a proven manager in Bill and a good operation. But we're not fully utilizing the managerial capabilities of Bill and his team.

Skadra: The proposal indicates a number of possible synergies that might be realized by combining the two operations. We'll certainly have to identify those before negotiating.

Figgie: Yes, and I also keep thinking about that idle manufacturing plant we have in Springfield, which is now being used for storage.

Skadra: As I recall, that plant has 65,000 square feet on one floor.

Figgie: Charlie said that their present plant has 100,000 square feet on one floor. Apparently it's not being fully used now. Charlie and Jerry own it personally.

Skadra: From a quick look at the figures, their asking price of $1,500,000 (Exhibit 2) seems very high. I'd like to take a closer look at the whole situation, especially the financial aspect.

Figgie: I agree. Let's analyze the offer from a strategic and financial standpoint, looking at all the angles.

Skadra: Since both TCA and OTC have had declining sales and profits in the last couple of years, I think we should pay special attention to costs.

BACKGROUND

In late 1963, Harry E. Figgie, Jr., acquired the controlling interest in "Automatic" Sprinkler Corporation of America, a family-owned firm with sales of $22 million. Figgie recalled:

> On January 2, 1964, I drove 90 miles to Youngstown, Ohio, to take over a company I'd never seen. Their top officer said to me, 'You've got to be the dumbest man alive.' I said, 'I'm the second dumbest. You sold it!'

Since then Figgie and his executive team had expanded the corporation to a multidivisional firm with sales of $770 million in 1981. This growth came about through an aggressive acquisition phase to obtain what Figgie referred to as a "critical mass" of $300 million in annual sales. To do this he applied a management concept of a lean organization with a small, highly mobile corporate staff. According to Harry Figgie: "In those days, it was not uncommon for the team to look over as many as 50 companies a month. In one rush of buying (in 1967), they closed five deals in just 25 days."

This phase ended in 1970 after Figgie had acquired more than 50 new divisions. Among these acquisitions was Mid-Con, Inc., a minor conglomerate consisting of a number of smaller companies in the Ohio Valley, one of which was the Thermometer Corporation of America. Most of the other small firms obtained in this particular acquisition had been divested since then.

Exhibit 1   An Analysis of a Merger and Future between TCA and OTC, Presented to Harry E. Figgie, Jr., by Jerome P. Bennett and Charles L. Wappner, November 17, 1982

We at Ohio Thermometer are of the opinion that our company's growth is tied to the economy. When times are good, sales are good and when times are bad, sales drop. The reason is our product base. Ohio Thermometer is very weak in the inexpensive category, kitchen or cooking category and almost nonexistent in the gift and decorator field. Without these three areas it is impossible for us to replace another thermometer company. We don't have the necessary capital to tool for all of these areas, hence our need for TCA's products. We feel, as competitors to TCA, that they have the same problems in the housewares field, only more severe. They have been unable to come up with a dial that is competitive with Ohio's, consequently they have no ammunition to replace any other company. Companies such as TCA are being replaced by Springfield or Taylor. Ohio Thermometer is, however, not being replaced mainly because everybody has to have our dials. We can't see TCA making much movement in the housewares industry because of the above problems. We feel TCA is also tied to the economy in this particular area.

In other areas of thermometry Ohio Thermometer has the advertising thermometer business locked up. This is an area that's up and expanding and profitable. TCA is in the auto field and scientific area, which are areas that we don't get into, so we really don't know how they are doing in those areas. They also have a gourmet thermometer line that we feel has tremendous potential, but they lack the customer base that we have. If they had our customer base, those items could perform miracles. In addition to the mentioned areas, Ohio has the Detroit automobile business under control, in our pocket, and we are the dominant people in the poultry industry.

Put the two companies together and you wind up with the most balanced thermometer company in the country. Together the companies would be the answer to many of our customers' problems. Most purchasing agents at this time want to cut down the list of vendors. In the thermometer field, if you talk to them, they say they must carry Taylor because of their name, and they must have Ohio because of their dials. Most have Springfield and they usually have a fourth vendor, which is either Chaney, Cooper or TCA, but very, very seldom do they ever have a fifth vendor, so they take their pick between one of the three, either Chaney, Cooper or TCA. With a combined company, TCA and Ohio, we certainly would be in a position to eliminate the fourth vendor and very possibly eliminate the third vendor. I am not too sure that, in certain areas, that you couldn't really take a good shot at Taylor. We know Chaney's and Cooper's customers and we know their weaknesses and we know their strengths. I think a combined company would have a field day or a Marianna's turkey shoot in the foreseeable future.

Looking at both sides, if Ohio could buy TCA, and I might add we have tried to do this in 1978, at this point it would probably stretch our finances. We feel that our borrowing would be somewhere close to $1,000,000. This would cover our current borrowing, allow $500,000 to be paid to Figgie International, with the rest going toward working capital. We would have to have some other type of financing for the remainder of the purchase price of TCA, and pay these off over a number of years. Could we get this financing? Questionable.

If Figgie International takes over Ohio these problems are eliminated and with Kiefer running a lean operation, we see immediate profits and probably large profits.

I, personally, feel that by taking the best sales reps from Ohio and the best sales reps from TCA and combining them, figures don't lie; we would have one of the strongest sales operations in the thermometer field. I feel that because of our contacts and our personal relationships with all of our customers, that we would keep all of them and be able to expand the entire base thermometer business. In addition, we sell to almost all of TCA's housewares accounts, so I can't see where we would lose any of that business. Quite frankly, with the two companies, the housewares end of the business would be a bonanza to the customers, at the same time solving their problems of too many vendors.

Our four or five year sales forecast would be in the $10 million-plus range. Even if the economy didn't bounce back, we could still project many inroads in the thermometer business and even if the economy stays as it is today, we would project a 10 percent to 15 percent to 20 percent sales increase per year. Again, with these sales and with the idea of running a lean company, there would be enough profit to go into the thermometer business with new items in depth. We look at weather stations that Taylor sells in the $300 to $400 range and it makes our mouths water. We sell to the same accounts that they sell to, only we can't compete with them, as we don't have the product.

Exhibit 1 *(concluded)*

Lastly, whether together or separately, both TCA and Ohio are going to have to get into the electronics area. Obviously TCA would have the jump on us, because they could use other Figgie operations. However, individually, we doubt that they would have the necessary profits to make the expenditures to do this.

A HAPPY MARRIAGE!!

Intangibles That Ohio Has to Sell

1. *Dial thermometer business.* Making TCA the major factor in the dial thermometer business with $2,750,000 in existing business; this is the heart of the thermometer business today.
2. *Advertising thermometer business.* This would make TCA the major and dominant supplier in the advertising and point of sale thermometer business with $550,000 of existing business. Ohio now supplies almost all of the major corporations with their advertising thermometer needs, controlling an estimated 95 percent of this business.
3. *Industrial and special products.* This would make TCA the dominant company in the automobile thermometer business and the major supplier of thermometers and instruments to the poultry industry, both in the United States and Canada.
4. *Customer base.* Ohio now has a very broad base of customers because all major accounts carry Ohio dials. The list of Ohio's customers is attached. This would automatically expose all TCA products to the major discounters, distributors, department and variety stores, hardware chains, drug chains, food chains and catalog and catalog showrooms.
5. *Ohio expertise in thermometer business.* Ohio Thermometer is about to start its 50th year in the thermometer business. Over the years we have consistently ranked number one or two with Taylor Instrument in accuracy and quality, according to past published consumer reports.
6. *Sales operation.* In looking over our customer base, it should be obvious that Ohio has the dominant sales rep organization between the two companies. In addition, Bennett and Reeder know the buyers on a first name basis at the major accounts such as K mart, Sears, Penney's, etc. We feel this will automatically prevent the loss of customers and would actually increase the thermometer base. Almost all accounts that Ohio now sells are TCA's accounts, which would add to protecting our business.

During the next 10 years the company grew from $356 million in sales to $770 million through internal growth. Harry Figgie recalled: "Such growth was not without problems as we chewed up working capital and sent our debt-to-equity ratio up to 1.36 to 1 [1979]."

In 1981 the company changed its name to Figgie International, Inc. and prepared itself for a new period of aggressive growth. As the recession hit the company in 1982 and overall sales dropped about 8 percent, cost reduction became Harry Figgie's number one priority in 1982 (see Exhibit 3 for balance sheet and income statement data).

FIGGIE INTERNATIONAL, INC.

In a recent interview in *The Craftsman,* an internal publication of FI, Harry Figgie discussed his ambitious plan of growth for the future. The plan entailed a new phase of acquisitions that would build on the company's present business groups. Figgie's goals for the future were to:

- Further reduce the company's debt-to-equity ratio.
- Top $1 billion in sales and start building towards $2 billion through an aggressive acquisition program.
- Continue to emphasize internal consolidation, bringing the minimum divisional size up to $25 million in sales.
- Pursue high technology and bring robotics and CAE/CAD/CAM into the workplace by adapting new techniques and strategies.
- Remain faithful to the company's commitment of producing quality products at competitive prices.

Harry E. Figgie, Jr., and his Management Philosophy   Most people would probably say that Harry Figgie was well prepared when he took over the small troubled Automatic Sprinkler Corp. in 1964. After earning his B.S. in metallurgical engineering at Case Institute of Technology, Harry Figgie earned an M.B.A. at Harvard Business School, a J.D. at Cleveland Marshall Law School, and an M.S. in industrial engineering at Case Western Reserve University. Later as a partner with Booz, Allen & Hamilton, a management consulting firm, Harry Figgie was exposed to a wide range of business situations in smaller and medium-size firms. The experience he gained in management consulting, as well as in his capacity as chairman and chief operating officer of Figgie

---

Exhibit 2   Proposed Terms of Sale of Assets of Ohio Thermometer to Figgie International

	Net Sound Value
Lloyd-Thomas Appraised Values May 31, 1982:	
Machinery	$ 555,985
Furniture and fixtures	135,361
Office furniture and fixtures	39,921
Office machines	19,808
Industrial power trucks	10,758
Dies*	213,473
Tools and trucks*	4,000
	979,306
Inventories complete at cost (September 30, 1982 values)	513,740
Total value	$1,493,046

Acceptable Terms: $1,493,000 cash at closing or at your option: $500,000 cash at closing and balance in acceptable securities or notes.

(a) Jerry Bennett and Charles Wappner would agree to stay for at least two years.

(b) We would agree to lease our 100,000 sq. ft. factory and office building to Figgie International for two years at $5,000 per month on a net net basis.

(c) Our NCR 8271 computer system is leased from U.S. Leasing. There are 30 months remaining at a rental of $1,672 per month. We would agree to transfer this lease to Figgie International if desired.

---

* Owners' valuation.

Exhibit 3   Income Statement and Balance Sheet Data, Figgie International, Inc., 1974–1982   Dollar Figures in Millions

Year Ended Dec. 31	Reve- nues	Opera- ting Income	Operating Income as % of Revenues	Capital Expen- ses	Depre- ciation	Interest Expen- ses	Income before Taxes	Effec- tive Tax Rate	Net Income	Net Profit Margin
1974	$476	$41.4	8.6%	$14.8	$ 6.6	$13.3	22.9	48.6%	11.2	2.4%
1975	480	40.2	8.4	13.5	7.7	9.9	23.7	48.2	12.2	2.5
1976	518	41.4	8.0	12.7	8.1	9.5	25.7	48.7	13.1	2.5
1977	568	40.5	7.1	34.4	9.7	12.5	21.8	47.1	11.5	2.0
1978	628	52.4	8.3	29.1	12.9	16.8	30.4	49.0	15.5	2.5
1979	691	62.0	9.0	24.0	16.1	21.3	33.8	48.0	17.6	2.5
1980[2]	760	65.2	8.6	22.4	13.8	23.6	40.3	48.8	20.6	2.7
1981[2,3]	770	72.3	9.4	28.1	14.5	22.2	48.1	46.6	25.7	3.3
1982[1]	708	51.0	7.2	31.9	14.9	21.4	38.6	32.4	26.1	3.7

Dec. 31	Cash	Current Assets	Current Liabilities	Current Ratio	Total Assets	Return on Assets	Long Term Debt	Com- mon Equity	Total Capital	% Long Term Debt to Total Capital	Return on Equity
1974	$14.8	$228	$ 80	2.9	$309	3.8%	$113	$ 72	$224	50.6%	14.1%
1975	15.2	213	63	3.4	300	4.0	112	79	232	48.2	13.9
1976	8.8	217	63	3.4	312	4.3	110	88	244	45.0	13.8
1977	9.2	256	108	2.4	376	3.5	117	90	260	45.0	11.5
1978	9.8	285	111	2.6	436	3.8	154	98	315	48.7	14.7
1979	7.0	316	143	2.2	478	3.8	145	111	326	44.5	15.2
1980	10.6	318	141	2.3	485	4.3	140	128	335	41.7	15.7
1981	6.8	298	131	2.3	475	5.4	127	146	335	37.8	17.6
1982[1]	15.6	268	111	2.4	465	5.5	122	164	343	35.7	15.9

[1] Estimated.
[2] Reflects acquisitions.
[3] Reflects accounting change.

International, had made him known as one of the foremost cost-reduction authorities in the world. In his book, *The Cost Reduction and Profit Improvement Handbook,* he stressed the importance of a lean organization:

> The first point to remember about the concept of cost reduction is that it can be used interchangeably with the term "profit improvement." If profit improvement is the glass of water half full, then cost reduction is the glass half empty. . . . [p. 1]
>
> As will be demonstrated, a 10 percent reduction in costs can increase profits by 25 percent to 50 percent, or more if the savings can be preserved. . . . [p. 3]

Harry Figgie's management concept also placed responsibility for profit-making decisions at the basic profit-center level—on the division president. Accordingly, each division president had "entrepreneurial" control of his division's profit and growth performance. He reported to a group vice president, who in turn, reported directly to Figgie. One subdivision president commented:

I have full responsibility for my division, but will receive help from corporate headquarters if I ask. And you'd better ask before the trouble arrives; they [corporate headquarters] don't like surprises. . . . Figgie International is our banker and advisor.

Organization   Figgie International was divided into five groups: Consumer, Fire Protection/Safety, Machinery, Technical, and Service. The contribution by group is shown in Table 1.

The Consumer Group included Rawlings sporting goods (baseballs, baseball gloves, basketballs, footballs, golf clubs, and related equipment), Adirondack baseball bats, Fred Perry sportswear (tennis clothing and other sportswear), home fire alarms, vacuum cleaners, and thermometers (TCA).

The Fire Protection/Safety Group consisted of custom-made fire engines, sprinkler systems, chemical fire extinguishers, aerial-type water delivery systems for fire-fighting apparatus, protective breathing equipment, and security systems and equipment.

The Machinery and Products Group encompassed capping, sorting and sealing machinery, high-speed automatic bottling equipment, road-building and maintenance equipment, hydraulic pumps, vibrating road rollers, material-handling systems, battery-powered vehicles, and mortar and concrete mixers.

The Technical Products Group consisted primarily of aircraft and missile components, aircraft display instruments and armament control systems, telemetry and electronic instrumentation systems, and electronic access control and monitoring systems.

The Service Group included sales financing, computer software, real estate, and natural resources investments.

Management Systems   Cash was managed centrally at Figgie International and divisions submitted all receivable collections to headquarters. Conversely, cash for payables was sent to divisions upon request. Corporate capital and headquarters expenses were paid for in two ways: "payment for debt services" (assets less current liabilities at FI's cost of capital rate) and "incremental costs of working capital" which were charged at slightly over prime for changes in working capital calculated on a monthly basis.

The capital budgeting procedure ran parallel to the allocation of working capital. Here a division manager could make discretionary decisions up to $1,000 and a

Table 1

Business Group (1982)*	Sales	Profits
Consumer	18%	8%
Fire protection/safety	43	41
Machinery and products	19	−6
Technical	19	21
Services	1	36

* Sales to the U.S. Government accounted for an estimated 21% of the total in 1982.

group vice president up to $5,000. All other capital investments had to be encompassed in the budget or submitted for Harry Figgie's approval.

Planning was also an integral part of the management process. In line with the management philosophy of keeping things simple, divisional presidents presented with their group officer the annual business plan between October 1 and November 30 to Harry Figgie and the corporate staff. The plan included a detailed budget for the coming year and a summary for the following four years. Operating performance (actual) and a rolling five-month forecast were reported by divisions on a monthly basis.

The reward system was a central part of the management system at Figgie International and was highly integrated with the planning and budgeting process. The division presidents received bonuses based on their achievement of pretax return on sales (50 percent) and pretax return on assets (50 percent).

THERMOMETER CORPORATION OF AMERICA (TCA)

The operations of TCA were in a 35,000 square-foot, two-story plant in the southern part of the city of Springfield. The office consisted of 2,500 square feet on the second floor. A wide variety of thermometer products was manufactured, including scientific and houseware products. The main manufacturing processes included:

1. The blowing of glass tubes to modify them by adding bulbs or joining tubes of different diameters. Standard lathes had been customized so that the glass tubes could be heated and rotated as the blowing took place.
2. Etching of glass tubes was needed to provide the degree markings for the scientific and other special-use thermometers. The tubes were coated with wax and a special machine formed slits through which acid could reach the glass surface.
3. Calibration of the thermometer required the right combination of tube bore and bulb size, amount of liquid enclosed (mercury or alcohol-based), and degree marking (etched on the glass or printed on an enclosure in the tube or on a mounting). The operators worked with controlled temperature baths and made the adjustments.

Since the operations did not lend themselves to automation, the machines required full-time operators to load each piece and perform the operations. Considerable manual skills were required, especially in the glass-blowing. Most operations required the glass to be in a heated, semimolten state so that the machines could process it. Heating attachments, some of which have been designed by TCA, maintained the processing temperature.

Many of the machines were "dedicated" for a particular operation and were not changed. As a result such machines, remaining idle for much of the time, were typically older machines, but were deemed to be as effective as newer models. The plant was operating at 40 percent of capacity. About 50 percent of the total cost of sales was raw materials and purchased parts.

There were 31 hourly paid employees in the plant, most of whom were women. They belonged to the United Auto Workers union. The average hourly wage rate was $4.39 plus $1.48 in fringe benefits. There had been one brief strike in recent

Exhibit 4   Thermometer Corporation of America Organization Chart, November 1982

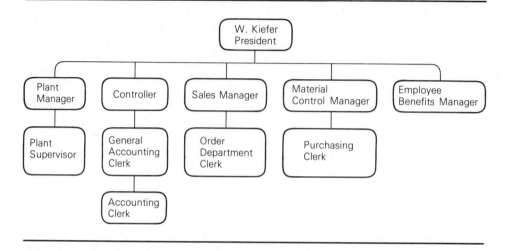

years. The relationship between management and workers seemed good; many of the employees had been with TCA for many years and turnover was low.

Salaried workers were shown in the organization chart (Exhibit 4). A manual accounting system was used, which Bill Kieffer considered adequate for generating needed information for his operating purposes and for the required reports to FI headquarters. He indicated that he would want to study the situation very carefully and find just the right hardware before shifting to computerization.

Financial information is shown in Exhibits 5, 6, 7, and 8.

OHIO THERMOMETER COMPANY (OTC)

OTC was located in a one-story, 100,000 square-foot building in Springfield. The plant was about five miles from the TCA plant. The current operations (equipment and storage) used 60 percent of the floor space. The primary product was dial thermometers of 12 inch and 18 inch diameters. The primary parts were the coated steel dial face (which was printed with the thermometer readings and other desired backgrounds), the aluminum outer band, brass bushings and shaft, temperature indicator, clear acrylic plastic dial cover (lens), and the bimetallic coil (which moved the indicator as the temperature varied). OTC used more durable materials than competitors. The total material purchases including raw materials and purchased parts, such as coils and indicators, were about 50 percent of the total cost of sales.

The plant operations were divided into three areas. One area contained the punch presses, which cut out the dial faces and the outer bands from sheet metal. A second area held the printing line with various printing presses and a drying oven connected by a circular conveyor belt. The third area was where the assembly took place. The punch presses were the only metalworking equipment used and were standard models.

Exhibit 5   Comparative Balance Sheet, Thermometer Corporation
of America, 1979–1981   Year Ended December 31

	1979	1980	1981
Assets			
Current assets:			
Cash	$ —	$ —	$ (27,000)
Accounts receivable (net)	193,000	211,000	162,000
Inventory	638,000	642,000	869,000
Prepaid expenses	1,000	2,000	1,000
Total current assets	$ 832,000	855,000	1,010,000
Property and equipment:			
Land	9,000	9,000	9,000
Machinery and equipment	1,164,000	1,176,000	1,192,000
Total	1,173,000	1,185,000	1,201,000
Less: accumulated depreciation	1,046,000	1,072,000	1,088,000
Total property and equipment	127,000	113,000	113,000
Other assets:			
Patents	47,000	42,000	36,000
Other assets	1,000	1,000	1,000
Total other assets	48,000	43,000	37,000
Total assets	$1,007,000	$1,011,000	$1,160,000
Liabilities and Stockholders' Equity			
Current liabilities:			
Accounts payable	$ 23,000	$ 78,000	$ 100,000
Unpaid withheld taxes	25,000	30,000	33,000
Accrued expenses	165,000	186,000	225,000
Total current liabilities	213,000	294,000	358,000
Long-term debt	0	0	0
Total liabilities	213,000	294,000	358,000
Stockholders' equity:			
Original investment	151,000	151,000	151,000
Retained earnings	93,000	1,015,000	1,121,000
Intracompany current	550,000	(449,000)	(470,000)
Total stockholders' equity	794,000	717,000	802,000
Total liabilities and stockholders' equity	$1,007,000	$1,011,000	$1,160,000

There were 70 hourly paid shop employees who belonged to the International Association of Machinists union. The average wage rate was $4.92 per hour. Fringe benefits were $1.60 per hour. The work in the plant was not highly skilled. As shown in Exhibit 5, the plant had five supervisors.

OTC had an art department, which generated a wide variety of advertising for printing on the dial face. The equipment provided photographic and silk-screening capabilities.

Exhibit 9 shows 23 salaried employees, including the three officers, Charlie Wappner

Exhibit 6   Thermometer Corporation of America, Comparative Income Statements 1979–1981

	1979	1980	1981
Net sales	$1,762,000	$1,730,000	$1,677,000
Cost of sales	1,220,000	1,193,000	1,096,000
Gross profit	542,000	537,000	581,000
Operating expenses:			
Selling	124,000	123,000	134,000
Administrative	160,000	153,000	172,000
Debt service	78,000	80,000	72,000
Other	8,000	(3,000)	7,000
Total operating expenses	370,000	353,000	385,000
Income (loss) from operations	172,000	184,000	196,000
Provision for income taxes	79,000	85,000	90,000
Net income (loss)	$ 93,000	$ 99,000	$ 106,000

Exhibit 7   Schedule of Cost of Goods Sold, Thermometer Corporation of America, 1981

	1981
Materials	$ 467,992
Direct labor	211,066
Manufacturing expenses:	
Indirect labor	$ 60,497
Supervision	59,760
Vacation and holiday	39,996
Payroll taxes	42,439
Industrial welfare	550
Employees insurance	43,534
Supplies	32,110
Maintenance and repairs	10,269
Truck	5,896
Freight	41,816
Utilities	49,161
Depreciation	12,352
Insurance	39,450
Taxes	—
Scrap	17,584
Travel	221
Rentals	17,018
Miscellaneous	—
	$ 472,653
Burden (absorbed)	(363,601)
Burden from inventory	307,593
Total manufacturing expenses	$ 416,645
Decrease in finished goods inventory	—
Cost of goods sold	$1,095,703

Exhibit 8   Schedule of Selling and Administrative Expenses, Thermometer Corporation of America, 1981

Selling expenses:	1981	Administrative expenses:	1981
	$ 9,586		$110,433
Salaries	61,295	Salaries	9,301
Commissions	715	Payroll taxes	11,000
Travel	31,172	Pension	4,278
Advertising	2,917	Travel	3,892
Samples	4,037	Office supplies	2,422
Telephone	20,460	Telephone	2,800
Show expense	899	Legal and professional	1,595
Payroll taxes	2,439	Depreciation	3,572
Depreciation	131	Dues and subscriptions	1,274
Supplies	—	Insurance	4,106
Miscellaneous	$133,651	Bank charges	914
		Contributions	4,238
		Data processing	3,643
		Rent—Autos	5,700
		Amortization patents	3,000
		Bad debt expense	386
		Miscellaneous	$172,554

Exhibit 9   Ohio Thermometer Organization Chart, November 1982

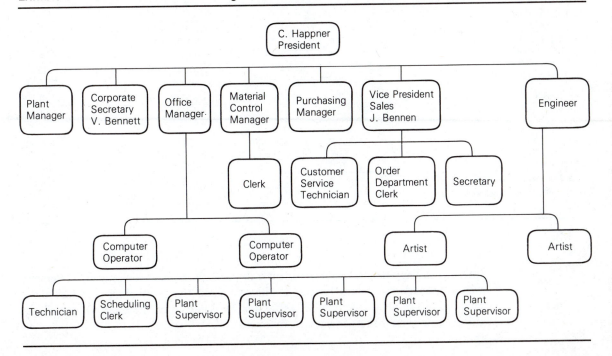

Exhibit 10   Comparative Balance Sheets, Ohio Thermometer Company, 1978–1982   Years Ended June 30

	1978	1979	1980	1981	1982
Assets					
Current assets:					
Cash	$ —	$ —	$ 4,330	$ 4,934	$ 7,939
Federal income tax refundable	—	—	90,546	55,216	—
Accounts receivable (net)	481,374	559,238	339,342	282,055	247,057
Inventory	795,181	903,762	853,579	708,409	626,796
Prepaid expenses	23,552	45,392	19,737	20,808	24,513
Total current assets	1,300,607	1,508,892	1,307,534	1,071,422	906,305
Property and equipment:					
Land	51,851	51,851	51,851	51,851	51,851
Building	308,418	308,418	308,418	308,418	308,418
Machinery and equipment	281,792	320,180	353,300	356,235	380,362
Trucks	9,518	9,518	9,518	9,518	9,518
Furniture	83,790	85,320	86,480	87,570	97,717
Total	735,369	775,287	809,567	813,592	847,866
Less: accumulated depreciation	577,634	610,816	635,337	663,478	691,896
Total property and equipment	157,735	164,471	174,230	150,114	155,970
Other assets:					
Cash value life insurance	135,833	135,833	109,958	21,679	21,860
Advances to employees	—	—	10,635	12,912	1,544
Deposits on leased equipment	5,410	5,256	2,220	2,220	1,202
Total other assets	141,243	141,089	122,813	36,811	24,406
Total assets	$1,599,585	$1,814,452	$1,604,577	$1,258,347	$1,086,881
Liabilities and Stockholders' Equity					
Current liabilities:					
Notes payable	$ 85,000	$ 175,000	$ 185,000	$ 175,000	$ 300,000
Current maturities on long-term debt	5,255	5,753	8,728	10,290	9,993
Accounts payable	450,094	506,937	418,566	519,981	418,671
Accrued expenses	132,510	106,679	83,414	67,136	73,390
Total current liabilities	672,859	794,369	695,708	772,407	802,054
Long-term debt	196,197	187,464	159,173	53,374	20,473
Total liabilities	869,056	981,833	854,881	825,781	822,527
Stockholders' equity:					
Common stock	250,000	250,000	250,000	250,000	250,000
Retained earnings	577,809	679,399	596,976	279,846	111,634
Less: treasury stock	97,280	97,280	97,280	97,280	97,280
Total stockholders' equity	730,529	832,619	749,696	432,566	264,354
Total liabilities and stockholders' equity	$1,599,585	$1,814,452	$1,604,577	$1,258,347	$1,086,881

(president), Jerry Bennett (vice president–sales), and V. Bennett (secretary). V. Bennett was Wappner's sister and Bennett's wife and filled the position of secretary on a part-time basis at a salary of $3,000 annually. Aside from these corporate officers the average annual salaries were as follows:

1. Managers and engineers.	$25,000
2. Supervisors, technicians, and artists.	$18,000
3. Clerks, computer operators, and secretaries.	$14,000

Fringe benefits were about 35 percent of salaries.

The NCR 8271 computer (leased) was used for accounting, inventory, and production control. It had far larger capabilities than were needed for the operation.

Financial information is shown in Exhibits 10, 11, 12, and 13.

Wappner stated that since July 1, 1982, several steps had been taken to increase profits. A 6 percent price increase was in effect. Improvements had been made in plant operations. Some overhead items, such as retirement benefits, had been reduced. As a result of these changes, Wappner was projecting income from operations for the fiscal year ending June 30, 1983 at $130,000.

THE THERMOMETER INDUSTRY

Market Structure   In the early 80s, the thermometer industry was composed of two major segments: the consumer market and the industrial market. The ratio of industrial to consumer sales for the total thermometer market was approximately 20 percent to 80 percent. TCA maintained an interest in both segments with about

Exhibit 11   Comparative Income Statements, Ohio Thermometer Company, 1978–82,   Years Ended June 30

	1978	*1979*	*1980*	*1981*	*1982*
Net sales	$4,367,128	$4,735,234	$4,286,345	$3,649,931	$3,654,311
Cost of sales	3,248,270	3,538,663	3,337,012	2,882,232	2,788,718
Gross profit	1,118,858	1,196,571	949,333	767,699	865,593
Operating expenses:					
Selling	525,870	615,489	654,647	593,627	513,136
Administrative	334,121	442,065	435,530	472,730	441,451
Interest	18,461	30,706	40,668	56,546	63,317
Bad debts	—	—	—	15,241	15,206
Other	41,950	(4,474)	(4,976)	—	—
Total operating expenses	920,402	1,063,786	1,125,869	1,138,144	1,033,110
Income (loss) from operations . .	198,456	132,785	(176,536)	(370,445)	(167,517)
Provision for income taxes	78,000	30,000	—	—	—
Tax benefit of net oper. loss carrybacks	—	—	70,546	54,010	—
Net income (loss) before special items	120,456	102,785	(105,990)	(316,435)	(167,517)
Insurance proceeds on deceased officer	—	—	23,762	—	—
Net income (loss)	$ 120,456	$ 102,785	$ (82,228)	$ (316,435)	$ (167,517)

Exhibit 12   Schedules of Cost of Goods Sold, Ohio Thermometer Company, 1981–1982

	1981	1982
Materials	$1,462,728	$1,423,055
Direct labor	$ 555,098	$ 513,231
Manufacturing expenses:		
Indirect labor	$ 59,041	$ 63,303
Production office	4,034	3,157
Engineers	41,984	41,780
Supervision	112,258	120,874
Vacation and holiday	91,659	88,482
Retirement	33,198	29,372
Payroll taxes	87,391	81,298
Industrial welfare	2,527	210
Employees insurance	94,604	109,956
Supplies	106,549	104,784
Maintenance and repairs	69,584	66,883
Truck	2,780	2,645
Freight	17,090	16,465
Utilities	50,676	58,373
Depreciation–Building	9,850	9,850
Depreciation–Other	11,312	14,918
Insurance	7,234	5,125
Taxes	5,788	5,616
Dues and subscriptions	1,148	420
Travel	267	222
Rent	442	490
Miscellaneous	2,187	2,236
	$ 811,877	$ 826,459
Total manufacturing expenses	$2,829,703	$2,762,745
Decrease in finished goods inventory	52,529	25,973
Cost of goods sold	$2,882,232	$2,788,718

the same split as the total industry. OTC, however, was predominantly focused in the consumer segment, especially the weather components of that market which comprised over 80 percent of its total thermometer sales.

Marketing information for the industrial sector was generally not available on a per-company basis or by type of thermometer instrument. This situation was due to the fact that the production of thermometers in most companies was but a small part of a huge product line of all types of recorders, gauges, and instruments. As a result it was virtually impossible to isolate meaningful information on the industrial market.

Therefore, the majority of information was on competitive activities within the consumer market. The product lines in this market included weather, houseware/decorator, cooking, and a miscellaneous line for medical, automobile, and other small uses of thermometers, as shown in Exhibit 14. The total market for thermometers (consumer and industrial) was estimated at $100 million in 1982.

Exhibit 13 Schedules of Selling and Administrative Expenses, Ohio Thermometer Company, 1981–1982

	1981	1982
Selling expenses:		
Salaries	$157,883	$135,936
Commissions	202,616	159,211
Travel	23,873	18,088
Advertising	15,219	20,662
Prospect	32	10
Samples	6,392	3,657
Freight	179,743	167,595
Telephone	4,780	5,818
Dues and subscriptions	3,089	2,159
	$593,627	$513,136
Administrative expenses:		
Executive salaries	$ 88,299	$ 99,611
Office salaries	126,898	124,401
Payroll taxes	24,862	36,584
Executive pension	60,638	28,293
Director fees	2,400	3,300
Travel	4,625	9,139
Postage	6,132	5,872
Office supplies	50,332	30,610
Telephone	7,194	8,109
Legal and professional	19,133	19,077
Depreciation	6,980	3,649
Dues and subscriptions	2,354	2,056
Insurance	14,468	17,007
Life insurance on officers	8,564	10,398
Contributions	753	3,520
Taxes	21,961	15,458
Rent–Computer	20,064	20,064
Rent–Autos	7,073	4,303
	$472,730	$441,451

Exhibit 14 Examples of Products Included in Each of the Product Lines

Weather:
12″ and 18″ dials—plain and decorated
Window units
Remote reading units
Wall weather units
Patio units

Houseware/decorator:
Gift lines
Clock component
Oven-refrigerator units

Cooking:
Meat units
Candy units
Thermo spoon/fork units
Cheese/yogurt units

Miscellaneous:
Mercury units
Car units
Dairy and poultry units
Laboratory/hobby units

Market Conditions   The sale of consumer thermometer lines generally fluctuated with the economy. A number of items within the decorator line, for example, were positioned as gift items and sales corresponded to the general consumer buying mood, especially during holidays.

Products within all categories ranged from low-price, mainly discount items to high-quality, high-price specialty items. Most of the seven major competitors within the consumer market had at least one strong product which acted as the anchor for the rest of their lines.

Distribution of consumer thermometer products was generally accomplished through retailers of all types, including department/variety, hardware, discount, drug, grocery, and showroom and catalog stores. Retail outlets that commonly carry thermometer products are shown in Exhibit 15. Because of shelf-space limitations and high costs of dealing with multiple vendors, most retail outlets preferred to do business with vendors who represented manufacturers that produced a wide variety of thermometers. Historically most retailers limited the number to three or, at most, four separate vendors. Most would welcome the opportunity to reduce that number if a manufacturer offered a full lineup of thermometers for all end-uses and price ranges.

Competitive Situation   The largest share of the thermometer market was held by Taylor with 30 percent. Not only did this company have a balanced array of products which spanned all of the consumer lines, it was also strongly positioned in the industrial market. Their industrial line included all types of sensing, recording, and control devices. Taylor had used its expertise in the industrial sector to develop specialized, high-quality products which competed at the high end of the consumer market. Decorator units included "top-of-the-line" thermometers and hydrometers as well as recording devices for amateur meteorologists. Taylor had positioned most of its products as specialty items or heterogenous shopping-good items.

Springfield held the second largest share of the market with 15 percent. This company concentrated on the price-sensitive consumer. It emphasized high volume, limited product lines, low raw material costs, and large production runs to hold down production costs. Springfield had strong positions in the weather, cooking, and decorator components of the consumer market.

Airguide had a narrow product line with 6 percent market share. Its initial entry into the consumer market was through its compass line. Since then the company had diversified into consumer weather thermometers. Airguide actively pursued international markets and currently imported many of its products.

Cooper maintained fourth position in the consumer market with 5 percent. This company had products in the weather segment; however, its main strength was its line of bimetal cooking thermometers. Patents on manufacturing processes provide a competitive edge in terms of best quality combined with the lowest production costs in the industry for these types of thermometers.

OTC occupied fifth position by virtue of its strength in round-dial thermometers with 3.5 percent. Springfield had captured the low end of this segment. OTC produced higher quality products and had an established reputation as the most reliable name in this segment of the market. In addition, OTC had captured the market dealing in promotional and scenic display thermometers (12 inch and 18 inch round-dial types). Its Achilles heel was the lack of competitive products across all parts of the

Exhibit 15　Examples of Retail Outlets by Type

Discounters

K mart	Fedco	Hill's
Woolworth	Service Merchandise	Western Auto
Target	Frank's Nursery	Meijer-Thrifty Acres
G. C. Murphy		

Department and Variety

Sears	Alden's	Allied
Montgomery Ward	Hammacher-Schlemmer	Ben Franklin
J. C. Penney's	Hoffritz	Neiman-Marcus
	Mercantile	T.G. & Y.

Hardware

American	Bostwick-Braun—Pro	Our Own Hardware
Ace	Clark-Siviter	Coast to Coast
Cotter-True Value	Stratton-Baldwin	United
Geo. Worthington—Sentry	Farwell, Ozmun, Kirk	Central
S & T		

Drug Stores

Walgreen	Rexall	McKesson
Super X	Skillern	Thrifty
Skaggs	Long's	Payless
Eckerds	Kerr	

Catalog and Show Rooms

E. F. MacDonald	Joan Cook	Eastern Mountain Sports
Top Value	Sportsman's Guide	Orvis Stitchery
Premium Corporation	Johnny Appleseed	Edmund Scientific
L. L. Bean	Brookstone	Gander Mountain
Century	Bolinds	Gokey's
Southern States	Miles Kimball	Taylor Gifts

Foods

Kroger's	Safeway	National Grocers
Lucky (Ch.)	National Tea	Lucky (L.A.)
Publix	Albertson's	Super Valu

Distributors

Dutch Peddler	Edwin Jay	Ideal School Supply
Peyton's	Comer-Hanby	Orchard Supply
Manor Sales	Superior Merchandise	Mid States Distributing

Advertising and Premium

General Motors	Coors	Cargill
Coca Cola	Anderson Anco	Goodrich
Pepsi	Plough	Fram
Seagrams	Jack Daniels	Homelite
Seven Up	Firestone	Briggs Stratton
Dr. Pepper	Calverts	Stihl
Monroe	Dupont	

consumer market. Over 80 percent of OTC's total thermometer sales were concentrated in dial thermometers. OTC did manufacture thermometers for miscellaneous uses such as automobiles, but these areas were considered to be rather limited in terms of growth potential. OTC had, however, compensated for its lack of a wide product selection by developing one of the best vendor representative groups in the consumer thermometer industry. This network of vendor representatives provided excellent breadth and depth of reach into all retail markets.

TCA struggled in sixth place in the total consumer market with 1.5 percent. Most of its revenues (80 percent) originated from weather and cooking thermometers. In addition, TCA maintained a small presence in the industrial market (15 percent of revenues) as well as the housewares and miscellaneous markets. Although TCA had managed to maintain product lines which crossed all consumer markets, it had failed to dominate in any of these markets. Consequently, it was experiencing low market share across the board and had no flagship product that could ultimately provide a dominant level of consumer awareness and interest in its products. TCA also appeared to have somewhat weak representation in the marketplace due to its inability to develop a strong, comprehensive vendor network.

Chaney was seventh among the top competitors with one percent and was really focused in only two areas. Its major strength was based on strong candy and meat thermometer products. The company did offer weather instruments, but none of its weather products were well known.

Exhibit 16 summarizes the relative positions of each of the seven top competitors in the consumer market and indicates which segments each one served.

Distribution Channels   Most of the companies had comparable channel configurations. For example, all of the seven competing manufacturers used vendor systems in which manufacturers' reps contacted all types of retail outlets.

Taylor, Springfield, and OTC had the strongest network of reps. Since most retail outlets preferred to do business with only those companies that carried broad, well-established product lines, it was difficult for the other companies to break into the retail marketplace. Thus, TCA used a combination of manufacturers reps and its own sales reps to maintain a stronger presence in the marketplace. Normally its sales force reps concentrated on key accounts based on geographical location and size.

Exhibit 16   Market Shares and Breadth of Product Lines

Company	Percent of Total Thermometer Market	Segments of Consumer Sector			
		Weather	Houseware and Decorator	Cooking	Miscellaneous
Taylor	30.0	Y	Y	Y	Y
Springfield	15.0	Y	Y	Y	N
Airguide	6.0	Y	N	N	Y
Cooper	5.0	Y	Y	Y	N
OTC	3.5	Y	N	Y	Y
TCA	1.5	Y	Y	Y	Y
Chaney	1.0	Y	N	Y	N

CONCLUDING DIALOGUE

The conversation between Figgie and Skadra continued:

Figgie: Jerry Bennett told me that he thought the addition of TCA products for his present OTC manufacturers' reps would immediately increase the rate of sales by $500,000 annually. He also thinks that within five years the combined companies would have a sales potential of $10,000,000.

Skadra: Very optimistic! He sounds like a salesman.

Figgie: I had a chance later to talk with Bill Kieffer. He has concerns about working with the OTC plant personnel. He thinks they are used to doing things in their own way and may be difficult to change. And he thinks that their processes can be made more efficient.

Skadra: Do you think we can assimilate Charlie and Jerry into TCA without losing their interest and effort?

Figgie: We'll have to do some thinking about that.

Skadra: By agreeing to cut their salaries by a combined total of $72,000 per year and by agreeing to work for two years they are demonstrating support for the continuing operation.

Figgie: Charlie and Jerry have apparently taken title to the building in their own names and would like to rent the building to us as part of a merger.

Skadra: With FI's vacant plant, we may have an alternative to renting from them.

Figgie: Springfield is a small town; we have little chance of leasing the idle plant. How much do you estimate we would have to spend for improvements to make the plant usable for manufacturing?

Skadra: About $100,000.

Figgie: The possible loss carry-forward does not justify assuming the risk of potential liabilities that would accompany the purchase of the stock of OTC Corporation.

There are a number of factors to consider here, Joe. Will you and your staff take a good look at the November 17th offer and prepare a complete counterproposal with supporting justification? Also I'd like to have a strategy for conducting the negotiations.

CASE 22 ALLIED CORPORATION—SULFURIC ACID OPERATIONS*

In 1984 Allied Corporation had just come through five years of unprecedented change. The company's whole management approach had been overhauled from top to bottom and its business portfolio had been massively restructured by a series of acquisitions and divestitures. Within 10 days of being appointed Allied's chief executive officer in May 1979, Edward L. Hennessy, Jr., had formed an Acquisition Task Force. By the end of his second month Hennessy had made a $598 million acquisition and had decided to divest several unprofitable businesses that he felt were in mature or unattractive industries. By the end of his fifth month he had eliminated 700 corporate staff jobs, cut annual corporate overhead by $30 million, and decentralized authority for division operations, delegating far more autonomy to Allied's business-level managers than had his predecessors. After six months Hennessy had negotiated settlements to three major lawsuits that had preoccupied Allied's top executives and was well into a program of corporate revitalization that included development of long-range strategies and comprehensive review of the company's internal policies and management practices. Two of Hennessy's long-run priorities were to build a strategically balanced business portfolio and to institute a new corporate culture at Allied. Exhibit 1 presents highlights of Allied's financial performance during the Hennessy years.

CORPORATE BACKGROUND

The company was first formed in 1920 as a merger of three complementary chemical and dye operations and a coal and coke producer; it operated under the name of Allied Chemical Corporation. By 1950, despite a long and tangled history of internal power struggles and management dissension, Allied had become an acknowledged leader in the U.S. chemical industry and was one of 30 "blue-chip" companies whose performance went into calculating the widely followed Dow Jones Industrial Average.

Between 1958 and 1968 Allied lost ground in the chemical industry principally because of (1) a weak research and development effort (Allied's "conservative" management never allocated more than a token percentage of revenues to research and development), (2) late entry into new specialty chemical markets (where profit margins were higher and proprietary technology and patents yielded a measure of protection from vigorous price competition), and (3) a top management leadership that spent more time on internal jockeying for power than on external jockeying for long-term position in the steadily changing markets for commodity and specialty chemicals. One business publication, commenting on this period, said:[1]

---

* This case was prepared by Professor Arthur A. Thompson, with the assistance of graduate researchers Sharon Henson and Kem King, The University of Alabama. Copyright © 1985 by Allied Corporation and Arthur A. Thompson, Jr.

[1] "Allied Chemical: A Long Rough Road Back," *Forbes*, May 15, 1969, p. 205.

Allied was a real blue chip. It was old . . . it was well established in chemicals that were basic to the entire economy. Spectacular, no. Solid, yes.

Then it turned out that Allied wasn't solid at all. In fact, its basic structure was rotten. What looked to the outside like conservative management turned out, in fact, to be no management at all.

For a time Allied's management was able to obscure the company's weakening market position from clear view by changing depreciation and tax accounting methods, capitalizing expenditures which had formerly been expensed currently, riding the crest of general chemical industry prosperity, and selling off unused land at a handsome profit. Between 1959 and 1965 Allied's revenues jumped almost 40 percent, yet its pretax operating income rose only 5 percent, a reflection of sharply lower margins on sales of basic commodity chemicals.

In January 1967 Allied's board of directors decided to act. John T. Connor, then secretary of commerce in Lyndon Johnson's administration, was hired as president and CEO. As Connor gradually saw through the mirage of his predecessors' creative accounting procedures and came to understand the deteriorating profit economics associated with Allied's chemical businesses, he realized that the company was in deeper difficulty than had appeared when he took the job to see if he "could breathe some life into the wheezing corporate giant." Connor's probing ended with three important conclusions: (1) Allied's plants were in bad repair, were inefficient, and were scattered haphazardly across the United States and overseas; (2) the company's chemical products mix consisted mainly of standard low-margin products such as soda ash, sulfuric acid, dyestuffs, and biodegradable detergents—all subject to strong price competition, cyclical ups and downs, and slow rates of growth; and (3) Allied no longer enjoyed the market clout and respected status that came from being an acknowledged industry leader.

Connor tried to shore up Allied's position by selling several unprofitable businesses, diversifying into polyester, and investing heavily in oil and gas exploration and production. Connor's biggest strategic decision was to pump over $1 billion into Allied's Union Texas Petroleum subsidiary to prospect for and develop oil and gas reserves—a move which Connor helped finance by redeploying the $400 million Allied obtained from the sale of the marginal businesses Connor singled out for divestiture. Even so, Allied's performance under Connor was lackluster, partly because of only spotty profit improvements in Allied's chemical businesses and because large losses in the coal and coke division offset gains elsewhere. By 1979 oil and gas was Allied's top performing business, generating about 30 percent of sales and 76 percent of income.

Three major incidents during the 1970s compounded Connor's and Allied's problems. In 1975 Allied was sued for over $1 billion when employees of a subcontractor firm developed Kepone poisoning while producing the chemical pesticide for Allied. It was discovered that the subcontractor firm was owned by former Allied employees and that Allied had discharged Kepone into the James River during the eight years it had produced the toxic chemical. The ordeal cost Allied $20 million in fines, settlements, and legal fees and also resulted in a qualified auditor's opinion for 1976 and 1977, diminished employee morale, and increased scrutiny of Allied's operations by government regulatory agencies such as EPA and OSHA.

The second incident took place in mid-1976 when Allied, responding to government

Exhibit 1   Allied Corporation, Selected Financial Performance, 1979–1983
Dollars in Millions except per Share Amounts

Years Ended December 31	1979[a]	1980	1981[a]	1982[a]	1983[a]
For the Year[b]					
Net sales	$ 4,160	$ 5,300	$ 6,142	$ 6,013	$10,022
Cost of goods sold	3,167	3,902	4,547	4,566	7,730
Income from operations	706	975	1,071	815	1,105
Nonrecurring items	(50)	(28)	84	(11)	—
Interest and other financial charges	(102)	(81)	(88)	(84)	(197)
Income from continuing operations before taxes on income	570	910	1,087	808	1,042
Taxes on income	391	630	711	524	592
Income from continuing operations	179	280	376	284	450
Discontinued operations:					
Operating income (losses), net of income taxes	(22)[c]	9	(28)	(12)	(55)
Estimated loss on disposals, net of income taxes	(146)[c]	—	—	—	(336)
Cumulative effect of change in accounting principle	—	—	—	—	39
Net income	11	289	348	272	98
Preferred stock dividend requirement	(5)	(23)	(38)	(68)	(91)
Earnings applicable to common stock	$ 6	$ 266	$ 310	$ 204	$ 7
Earnings per share of common stock:					
Income from continuing operations	$ 6.05	$ 7.85	$ 10.01	$ 6.59	$ 6.91
Income (losses) from discontinued operations	(5.85)[c]	.30	(.84)	(.37)	(7.52)
Cumulative effect of change in accounting principle	—	—	—	—	.74
Net earnings	$ .20	$ 8.15	$ 9.17	$ 6.22	$ .13
Weighted average number of common shares outstanding (in millions)	28.7	32.6	33.8	32.8	52.0
Dividends per share of common stock	$ 2.00	$ 2.15	$ 2.35	$ 2.40	$ 2.40
Salaries and wages	660	804	992	1,121	2,400
Oil and gas exploration costs expensed	91	120	189	245	223
Property, plant and equipment additions:					
Environmental improvement facilities	65	54	56	34	37
Capitalized oil and gas exploration and development	162	226	251	202	164
Plant improvements and additions	183	253	302	288	406
Total additions	409	533	609	524	607
At Year-End					
Net working capital	$ 279	$ 467	$ 638	$ 416	$ 458
Property, plant and equipment–net	2,169	2,384	2,866	2,858	3,553
Total assets	4,210	4,538	5,344	6,272	7,647
Long-term debt	866	814	804	669	1,080
Limited recourse financing	86	71	53	31	263
Preferred redeemable stock	199	260	591	586	434
Capital stock and other shareholders' equity	1,229	1,664	1,900	2,013	2,747
Book value per share of common stock	42.65	49.69	56.30	57.11	45.92
Number of common shares outstanding (in millions)	28.8	33.5	33.7	35.2	53.5
Common shareholders	60,304	58,022	56,648	58,046	68,187
Employees	49,014	46,269	58,224	44,337	117,750

Exhibit 1 *(concluded)*

Years Ended December 31	1979[a]	1980	1981[a]	1982[a]	1983[a]
Financial Statistics[b]					
Return on sales (pre-tax adjusted)	9.4	11.2	12.0	8.9	7.6
Return on average assets:					
Pre-tax (adjusted)	12.4	15.5	16.9	11.1	11.1
After-tax	5.4	7.3	8.6	5.9	6.5
Return on shareholders' equity	14.2	15.4	17.8	10.7	14.0
Long-term debt as a percent of total capital	35.6	28.4	23.3	19.5	28.4
Interest coverage ratio	7.1	9.9	9.4	7.3	5.1

[a] Includes the effect of acquisitions in the respective periods. The Company acquired Eltra Corporation effective July 1, 1979, which transaction was valued at approximately $598 million and was accounted for as a purchase.

[b] Restated to reflect discontinued operations. Sales applicable to discontinued operations prior to December 31, 1983, were as follows: 1983, $329 million; 1982, $154 million; 1981, $265 million; 1980, $219 million; and 1979, $172 million. Income taxes included in the caption "Discontinued operations: Operating income (losses), net of income taxes" for each period were: 1983, $(52) million; 1982, $(17) million; 1981, $(26) million; 1980, $7 million; and 1979, $(7) million.

[c] Substantially all of the amounts shown relate to businesses discontinued in 1979.

pressure, closed down a coke-producing facility in Kentucky to remedy environmental and safety problems. The plant's sole customer, Armco Steel, sued Allied for $217 million in damages for failure to meet its obligations to supply 95,000 tons of coke a month under a 10-year contract. Allied under Hennessy's guidance settled the suit out of court by giving Armco a coal mine with a $14 million book value and paying Armco $20 million in cash.

In 1979 Allied was indicted for allegedly conspiring to defraud the IRS. The company was charged with paying a General Tire and Rubber Company purchasing manager $220,000 for his assurance that General Tire would buy polyester cord yarn from Allied.

HENNESSY'S REVITALIZATION EFFORTS

Ed Hennessy began his business career as a junior accountant at Price Waterhouse—the worst job he ever had ("We had to wear straw hats and suits, and we spent days in warehouses" doing audits).[2] He held financial staff positions at Textron (five years), Lear Siegler (four years), ITT (four years under Harold Geneen, with exposure to Geneen's theories about making acquisitions and managing broad diversification), Colgate–Palmolive (one year), and Heublein (seven years, where he played a key role in Heublein's acquisition of Kentucky Fried Chicken). He then spent seven years at United Technologies, a large *Fortune 500* company noted for the aggressive way it pursued diversified growth via acquisition. At United Technologies, Hennessy rose through the ranks to occupy the number two post of executive vice president. At the time of his selection as Allied's CEO, he was perceived by some people as a

[2] As quoted in Colin Leinster, "Allied-Signal's Tough Skipper," *Fortune,* June 24, 1985, p. 92.

strong-willed financial manager whose chief accomplishments had been engineering active acquisition campaigns on behalf of Heublein, Inc., and United Technologies. He was attracted to Allied by the opportunity to run his own show at a "blue-chip" company. Unlike Connor, when Hennessy came on board he was well aware that Allied was what one industry analyst described as "a doggy commodity chemical company . . . that was not growing or building stockholder value or even providing its employees with a very interesting place to work."[3]

Hennessy hit the ground running at Allied, not only because Allied's position was deteriorating, but also because there were signs that Allied might be the target of an acquisition takeover and because he learned that Standard & Poor's, a major bond rating agency, was considering lowering Allied's bond rating from A to BBB. Having just moved over to Allied, Hennessy had no interest in Allied's being acquired (having been on the other end many times during his days at United Technologies) and he feared a downgrading of Allied's bond rating would lessen the financial flexibility and maneuvering ability he would need to launch Allied on a new course. As it turned out a takeover attempt never materialized and Hennessy convinced S&P to hold back on its bond downgrading until he had had a few months to turn Allied around.

In mid-June 1979, six weeks after taking command, Hennessy formed a policy and management committee consisting of Allied's 11 top managers. Over the next six months the committee discussed what changes to institute in Allied's operations. Through the committee Hennessy got widespread support for a revitalization plan consisting of four parts: (1) diversification by acquisition, (2) divestiture of businesses that were losing money or only marginally profitable, (3) decentralization of operating responsibilities to the business and division levels, and (4) upgrading internal administrative systems, incentive compensation, and the company's public image.

In early 1980 Hennessy started to concentrate on Allied's corporate strategy and strategic planning process. Quarterly strategic review sessions were initiated. While Allied's operating divisions had business strategies, some of which Hennessy felt were good, he still felt that the aggregate of the business strategies did not yield a coordinated or meaningful whole. Hennessy's probing into Allied's strategic management practices led him to several other conclusions:

- Allied's corporate management did not have a good overview of all the businesses the company was in and how attractive their future prospects were.
- Allied needed to have a strategic planning cycle whereby the managers of Allied's divisions and businesses would be motivated to make realistic assessments of the potential and attractiveness of the businesses they managed—a cycle and a discipline which would then lead to the development of sound business strategies and division-level (or business-level) accountability for successful strategy execution. Hennessy believed, based on his own personal experiences, that the managers of unattractive, poorly-performing business units could not be expected on their own initiative to document clearly the dim outlook for their divisions and to recommend it be divested; as Hennessy put it, "How many managers are going to say, 'This business will never get an 18 percent return so I think you better

---

[3] "Allied After Bendix: R&D is the Key," *Business Week*, December 12, 1983, p. 76.

sell it and me.' It won't happen." Hence, Hennessy believed he had to push for the establishment of a strategic planning process that could be counted upon to expose the future prospects of each of Allied's businesses.

- The task of managing the formulation of a sound corporate strategy and the simultaneous formulation of sound business strategies in each business area was so big that consultants were needed to help.

Consultants were hired to come up with a new strategic planning process for Allied. The consultants trained Allied managers to "profile a business" and then spent three days with each of Allied's business areas helping them go through the profiling task. A standard profiling form was developed to facilitate comparing all of Allied's businesses. Using data from the business profiles, each Allied business was positioned on a corporatewide business portfolio matrix that used competitive standing and industry maturity as the variables on the two axes.

The profiling and business portfolio matrix analysis documented that 75 percent of Allied's businesses were in mature and aging industries. Hennessy and the rest of Allied's top management reached a consensus that Allied needed to be in more growth businesses. A financial objective of an 18 percent pretax return on assets was established for the corporation (at the time only Allied's fiber business and oil and gas business earned more than the 18 percent target).

The corporate strategy that emerged centered around two themes. First, the company's business portfolio would consist of four or five groups of related core businesses. Hennessy often described the successful modern corporation as needing to be structured like a wheel with strong spokes. In his view the three spokes that Allied had in 1980—chemicals, oil and gas, and polyester fibers—were not enough "to keep the wheel round and true and the company rolling along." Hence the need for Allied to diversify further, primarily through acquisition. The second strategic theme was that Allied's existing businesses in mature and aging industries were to be managed for long-term profit and cash flow. Resources were to be allocated to these units primarily for cost reductions, productivity improvements, and protection of assets. For any of these businesses to receive capital appropriations from corporate headquarters, Allied's senior management had to be convinced that the business had a good strategic plan with which they agreed, that the business plan was consistent with the corporate-level financial strategy, that the business had adequate long-run attractiveness, and that the business had realistic prospects for meeting the corporate objective of an 18 percent pretax return on assets. Insofar as Allied's chemical businesses were concerned, the strong preference of corporate management was to try over the long-run to diversify out of bulk chemicals into specialty chemicals and out of both into other faster-growing, more attractive industries. Hennessy stated:[4]

> Our goal is to become a leader—not necessarily number one but no worse than a close number two or three—in every business we're in. If we can't build a business to a leadership position—by becoming the low-cost producer or perhaps by extending our product line through acquisitions—then we should divest it.

By 1985 over 30 business units had been divested.

---

[4] As quoted in Allied Corporation (B), Harvard Case Services 0-383-078, p. 13.

NEW ACQUISITIONS

Between 1979 and 1984, Hennessy spearheaded a series of important acquisitions that gave Allied's business portfolio a new look:

1979   Acquired Eltra Corporation, a diversified manufacturer of consumer and industrial goods, including batteries, motors, cables, and athletic footwear. Eltra, with a net worth of almost $392 million, sales of $1 billion, and net income of $48 million, was acquired at a total cost to Allied of approximately $598 million. (Since the acquisition, some of Eltra's business divisions had been sold off and several others were up for sale in 1985.)

1981   Acquired Bunker Ramo Corporation, a producer of electrical and electronic connectors, information systems, and specialty textiles, with a net worth of $176.8 million, sales of $468 million, and net income of $27 million. Allied's total cost was approximately $347 million in cash, notes, and preferred stock.

Acquired Fisher Scientific Company, a manufacturer of scientific laboratory equipment and supplies, with a net worth of nearly $112 million, sales of $425 million, and net profit of $16 million. Allied's cost was approximately $311 million in preferred stock and cash.

1982   Acquired 50 percent of the Supron Energy Corporation, an oil and gas company with sales of $78 million and net profit of nearly $18 million. Allied's cost was $357 million.

1983   Acquired The Bendix Corporation, a diversified company whose operations consisted primarily of automotive components and aerospace-electronics and industrial tools, with a net worth of nearly $1.5 billion, sales over $4 billion, and net profit of $204.5 million. The merger (expected to reduce Allied's dependence upon oil and gas, diversify its operations into higher tech, higher value-added products, and make the company much less capital intensive) cost Allied approximately $1.8 billion.

Acquired Semi-Alloys, Inc., manufacturer of components for high-reliability semiconductor packages, to expand Allied's position as a leading supplier of chemicals and components to the semiconductor industry. Semi-Alloys' 1982 sales were $70 million. Allied paid approximately $97 million in cash and common stock.

Acquired Instrumentation Laboratory, Inc., producer of biomedical and analytical instruments, to add more high-technology products to the health and scientific products line acquired with Fisher Scientific. IL had 1982 revenues of $137.6 million and net income of $4.6 million. Allied paid approximately $115 million in cash and common stock.

These acquisitions led Allied in 1983 to organize into five core business groups (see Exhibit 2). To reflect the broader scope and corporate strategy that Hennessy was pursuing, the company's name was changed in 1981 from Allied Chemical Corporation to Allied Corporation.

ALLIED'S SULFURIC ACID BUSINESS

Spurred by Hennessy's drive to assess the long-term attractiveness of each of Allied's business units, in 1980 the managers in charge of Allied's sulfuric acid business area formed an internal task force, under the direction of the Chemical Company Planning

Group, to reevaluate Allied's entire sulfuric acid operations and to make recommendations for improving the area's return on assets. The sulfuric acid area's pretax return on assets of 7.6 percent in 1980 was judged to be unacceptable. An in-depth study of the overall U.S. sulfuric acid industry was conducted as a basis for the evaluation.

THE U.S. SULFURIC ACID INDUSTRY IN 1980

Sulfuric acid (H_2SO_4) was classified as a standard industrial commodity chemical and was commercially marketed in bulk railcar or tank truck lots. Three production methods existed; it could be (1) manufactured from Frasch mined sulfur (referred to as virgin or sulfur-burned sulfuric acid), (2) reconstituted from spent or waste acid, or (3) gathered as a by-product of metallic ore smelting (referred to as smelter or by-product acid). All three methods were in use in 1980. About 70 percent of total sulfuric acid production in the United States was consumed directly by the producer for intracompany use in making other products (referred to as the captive market). The remaining 30 percent was sold commercially to a wide variety of users (in what was known as the merchant market).

During the past two decades dramatic shifts in the end-use patterns for sulfuric acid had occurred. The use of sulfuric acid for manufacturing phosphoric acid (a basic fertilizer material) had mushroomed to over 60 percent of total demand. At the same time demand for sulfuric acid had declined in many of the traditional end-use segments (such as steel pickling and manufacturing titanium dioxide—a paint pigment). The major end-use changes are shown in Exhibit 3.

A number of reasons accounted for the end-use declines in sulfuric acid demand:

Other Fertilizers—The use of sulfuric acid in other fertilizers was on the decline due to their being replaced by newer, more concentrated fertilizers that used phosphoric acid as an ingredient.

Petroleum Refining—The use of sulfuric acid was declining moderately because of refiners' preferences for using another chemical process to serve the same purpose.

Alcohols—Users were shifting to another process for making ethyl alcohol that did not use sulfuric acid.

Titanium Dioxide—The sulfate process for making titanium dioxide (which required sulfuric acid) was being slowly replaced by the cloride process (which did not use sulfuric acid).

Hydrofluoric Acid—The manufacture of hydrofluoric acid was being shifted to new plants in Mexico and Canada, plus the use of hydrofluoric acid was waning because of sharp cutbacks in the use of fluorocarbons in aerosol packaging.

Rayon—Rayon demand had been declining because of competition from nylon and polyesters.

The only two industrial end-uses of sulfuric acid showing significant gains in demand from 1960–78 were for copper leaching and uranium ore processing.

From 1968 through 1978 overall use of sulfuric acid increased by about 30 percent—an average annual growth rate of 2.7 percent. The phosphoric acid end-use grew at an 8.1 percent annual rate; however, over 90 percent of the sulfuric acid used in making phosphoric acid was captively supplied. As a group the other end-uses, mainly industrial, experienced a 23 percent decline over the ten-year period (see Exhibit 4).

Exhibit 2   Allied Corporation's Core Business Groups, 1983

Business Groups	*Principal Products*
Chemical Sector Allied's chemical businesses produce a wide variety of commodity and specialty chemicals, synthetic fibers and plastics for most of the key basic industries. The company is the largest producer of soda ash in North America and the world's largest producer of hydrofluoric acid, type 6 nylon and fluorine-derived chemicals, one of which, fluorinated carbon, is shown being packaged for use in lithium batteries.	Nylon filaments/staple fibers • nylon and polyester industrial fibers • nylon apparel fibers • fibers intermediates • ammonium sulfate • soda ash • fluorocarbons • fluorine, electronic, chrome, water treatment, and fine chemicals • tar products • hydrofluoric acid • sulfuric acid • uranium hexafluoride • engineered plastics • fluoropolymers • high-density polyethylene • low-molecular-weight polyethylene
Oil and Gas Sector Allied's oil and gas businesses are managed by its Union Texas Petroleum subsidiary, one of the largest independent oil and gas companies in the United States. UTP engages in worldwide oil and gas exploration and production such as in West Texas where this pipeline is part of a project to recover additional oil reserves at the Wellman Field. UTP also processes and distributes natural gas liquids, manufactures petrochemicals, and markets petroleum products.	Crude oil and condensate • natural gas • liquefied natural gas • liquefied petroleum gases • natural gasoline • residue gas • ethylene
Automotive Sector Allied's automotive businesses, which include Bendix, Fram, Autolite, and Prestolite products, manufacture components and systems for passenger cars and trucks. Products are used in original equipment and as replacement parts. Bendix is the world's leading independent manufacturer of car and truck brake components and friction materials.	Disc/drum brakes • air/hydraulic disc and drum brakes • brake components • friction materials • air/oil/fuel filters • spark plugs • steering systems • engine controls • engine cooling fans • air cleaner assemblies • electric motors • wire products • ignition components • safety restraints • die castings and metal stampings
Aerospace Sector Allied's aerospace businesses, primarily Bendix operations, manufacture products used in military and civil aircraft, spaceflight vehicles, missiles, and other national defense projects and space exploration, including the altitude pointing and control systems incorporated in the space telescope. Other aerospace units manage government-owned facilities and provide technical services for the Department of Energy and NASA.	Integrated avionic systems • weather radar systems • communications/navigation/identification systems • electronic cockpit displays • flight control systems • fuel control/ignition systems • electric generating systems • wheels/brakes • dynamic control systems • transmission shafts • test systems • gyroscopic guidance systems • tactical missile systems • antisubmarine systems • communications systems • technical services
Industrial and Technology Sector Allied's industrial and technology businesses were added to the Corporation's portfolio largely through acquisitions since 1979. Among them are businesses in electronics and health care, whose markets have good growth potential.	Electrical/electronic connectors/components • flat ribbon cable/assemblies • seal lids/die attach preforms • analytical and measuring instruments/apparatus/appliances • biomedical instruments/supplies • reagent chemicals and diagnostics • glassware and plasticware • laboratory furniture • electronic information systems • phototypesetting equipment • batteries • refractory materials

Markets/Industries	Year	1981–1983 Results of Operations by Sector (in millions of dollars)			
		Net Sales	Percent of Total Sales	Income from Operations	Percent of Total Profits
Carpet • automotive • cordage • lingerie, loungewear • fertilizer • glass • paper • nuclear • refrig- eration • water treatment • semiconductor devices • elec- tronics • plastics • packaging • metal finishing • aluminum and steel • wood treatment • addi- tives • coatings	1983	$2,337	23%	$227	24%
	1982	2,143	36	136	22
	1981	2,387	39	199	24
Oil refining • gas pipelines • chemical feedstocks • home, farm, utility, and industrial fuels	1983	$1,989	20%	$413	43%
	1982	1,992	33	486	77
	1981	2,068	35	570	69
Passenger cars • light/medium/ heavy trucks • industrial/off- road/recreational vehicles • air- craft • railway • powered equip- ment	1983	$2,370	24%	$203	21%
	1982	298	5	6	1
	1981	371	7	17	2
Military aricraft • civil aircraft • commercial aircraft • air traffic control • missiles and spacecraft • ships • oceanics • military land vehicles • refinery/industrial process control • industrial tur- bines	1983	$1,603	16%	$152	16%
	1982	48	2	—	0
	1981	42	2	(5)	(1)
Military/aerospace • telecom- munications • computers • elec- tronics • industrial/medical/ government/educational institu- tion laboratories • brokerage and banking • publishing • auto- motive • iron and steel	1983	$1,708	17%	$(43)	(4)%
	1982	1,392	24	1	0
	1981	963	17	49	6

Exhibit 3   Percent of Total Use of Sulfuric Acid

End-Uses	1960	1970	1978
Phosphoric acid	19.0%	41.0%	63.0%
Other fertilizers	14.0	3.8	2.5
Petroleum refining	9.0	7.0	5.1
Copper leaching	negl.	2.6	2.7
Ammonium sulfate	6.0	5.2	4.0
Alcohols	9.0	6.2	2.7
Titanium dioxide	9.0	5.5	2.2
Hydrofluoric acid	2.7	3.2	2.1
Uranium and vanadium	1.8	1.1	1.8
Aluminum	2.5	2.1	1.7
Rayon	3.6	2.2	1.3
Steel pickling	5.6	1.6	0.9
Surfectants	1.5	1.2	0.8
Batteries	0.5	0.4	0.5
Other	15.7	16.9	7.3
Total	100.0%	100.0%	100.0%

Demand projections for the next five years indicated that phosphoric acid end-use would continue to expand and that industrial end-use demand for sulfuric acid would be essentially flat.

Although smelter acid was acceptable for some end-uses, it could not be used in many applications because of differences in quality, variations in concentration, and the presence of impurities. In 1979 smelter acid accounted for about 10 percent of the total end-use market; virgin and reconstituted acid producers supplied the remaining 90 percent. Smelter acid producers netted about $5 to $15 per ton for their acid—a price which, after adding freight and handling charges, allowed smelter acid to compete favorably with the delivered prices of virgin acid at $50 to $75 per ton

Exhibit 4   U.S. Sulfuric Acid Demand, 1968–1978
Thousands of Metric Tons

	Total	Phosphoric Acid	All Other Uses
1968	27,514	10,358	17,156
1969	28,455	10,797	17,658
1970	28,462	11,581	16,881
1971	27,718	12,514	15,204
1972	29,708	14,410	15,298
1973	30,282	14,766	15,516
1974	32,375	15,433	16,942
1975	30,541	17,267	13,274
1976	31,733	18,028	13,705
1977	33,911	20,567	13,344
1978	35,766	22,540	13,266
10-year change	8,252	12,182	(3,930)

f.o.b. manufacturing plant, with the price being largely influenced by proximity to sulfur sourcing. Mining companies, the main source of smelter acid, were willing to unload their acid at very low prices because of the low-cost, by-product nature of smelter acid (any revenue they got for a largely unwanted by-product was considered as "gravy"); buyers of smelter acid bore the expensive freight charges (as much as $40 to $50 per ton depending on distance and freight rates) in transporting the substance.

Smelter acid had only recently become generally available in the merchant market, but low prices and growing availability had stimulated demand. Smelter acid production had grown from 1.6 million tons in 1955 to almost 4 million tons in 1979. A number of virgin acid producers bought smelter acid from mining companies for resale through their own marketing organization. Allied, in fact, was the dominant U.S. marketer of smelter acid with sales concentrated in the Northeast and the Midwest; this resale acid was marketed through Allied's distribution channels and was sold at a price just under the going market prices for virgin acid. Allied also purchased smelter acid for internal company use. The growing demand for smelter acid by price conscious end-users who were not concerned with its variable quality (because the nature of their use did not require pure acid) was having an adverse competitive effect on virgin sulfuric acid prices in 1980.

Industry Structure   In 1980 the U.S. sulfuric acid industry consisted of about 5,000 customers served by over 50 producers. Domestic producers operated about 140 plants having a combined capacity of about 45 million tons. Industry revenues totaled about $2 billion. No producer supplied more than 8 percent of the total market and a number of producers had less than a 1 percent market share. Ten companies accounted for about 55 percent of the industry's production capacity as shown in Exhibit 5.

Exhibit 5   Major U.S. Producers of Sulfuric Acid, 1979

Company	Annual Capacity in Tons (1979)	Percent of Total U.S. Capacity
Stauffer Chemical	3,800,000	8.4%
CF Industries*	3,430,000	7.6
Allied	2,532,000	5.6
DuPont	2,445,000	5.4
Agrico Chemical*	2,400,000	5.3
Freeport Minerals*	2,296,000	5.1
Occidental Chemical*	2,184,000	4.9
Texasgulf*	2,072,000	4.6
IMC*	2,010,000	4.5
Beker Industries*	1,575,000	3.5

* Production capacity was almost exclusively dedicated to captive fertilizer requirements.

For the past 10 years the industry had suffered from substantial overcapacity. Excess supply conditions had resulted in industrywide capacity utilization rates in the 69 to 79 percent range—the 1968 through 1978 average was 73 percent.

In 1980 approximately 90 percent of all sulfuric acid shipments were made by truck; the remaining 10 percent of the shipments were carried by rail to final destinations. Truck shipments were favored over rail shipments because most acid was shipped only a short distance and because trucking could be arranged on shorter notice than could rail shipments.

COMPETITION AND PRICING

Because shipping costs were high relative to the actual production cost of acid, the output of most plants was marketed regionally. Historically producers had located their plants close to end-use destinations. The supply network was more fully developed in the northeast which for many years had had the strongest concentration of end-use demand. Plants had gradually been built in other regions as end-use demand sprung up in more and more geographic areas of the United States. By 1980 each major geographic region had developed its own unique characteristics of competition and pricing, largely based on supply-demand conditions in the region.

Regional demand patterns were in a state of flux. In recent years some regions had experienced declines in demand (for example the northeast and midwest regions where much of Allied's capacity was located); two regions, the west and the southwest, had experienced growth in end-use demand. Meanwhile, continuing excess capacity conditions had caused shutdowns of older, higher cost plants and a number of producers had sold their sulfuric acid plants, either getting out of the business entirely or ridding themselves of unprofitable plants. Industrywide, however, companies had added nearly 5 million annual tons of new capacity since 1975—almost 2.5 million annual tons in the southwest region (1975–77), about 400,000 annual tons in the eastern region (1976–79), and about 2 million annual tons in eastern Canada (1977–79). Much of the new capacity, however, was being installed by end-users to put their own acid supply capability right next to their consuming operations; the rest of the expansion had been undertaken by smelters to collect sulfur dioxide gas that was causing an environmental problem.

Although reliable regional supply-demand figures were not available, regional production and merchant market sales figures were typically relied upon as reasonable proxies of regional market conditions. Examples of the regional production-merchant sales shifts during 1968–78 are shown in Exhibit 6.

The decline in production in the Northeast and North Central regions reflected declining end-use demand in these regions and growing availability of lower cost smelter acid entering the country from Canada. In 1955 Canadian imports of sulfuric acid were a fairly insignificant 28,000 tons, but during the 1973–80 period Canadian imports were in the 180,000–450,000 metric ton range. The major Canadian supplier to the U.S. market was CIL (Canadian Industries, Ltd.), an expansion-minded firm which manufactured and marketed Canadian smelter acid. Projections indicated that Canadian production capacity would be more than ample to meet Canadian demand

---

Exhibit 6   Sales Shifts between the Merchant and Captive Segments

---

Regional Trends

Northeast:	Production—34 percent decline
	Merchant Market Shipments—35 percent decline
North Central:	Production—25 percent decline
	Merchant Market Shipments—8 percent decline

Trends in Selected States (where data was available)

States	Production	Approximate Merchant Market Sales
Pennsylvania	37% decline	38% decline
Illinois	43% decline	11% decline
Virginia	10% increase	28% decline
Louisiana	203% increase	83% increase
California	27% decline	21% increase

---

over the next five years and that the excess of about 325,000 net tons would likely be exported to the United States at least through 1984 and 1985.

In addition to the entry of Canadian imports, new sulfuric acid supplies were expected to come onto the market from electric utilities by 1985. Some coal-burning electric power plants, in response to new sulfur emission regulations, were projected to be equipped with sulfuric acid recovery systems. A minimum of 200,000 tons of acid was expected from these sources by 1985 and additional supplies were likely to be forthcoming after 1985. The collection of sulfuric acid by electric utilities was the result of desulfurizing flue gases, as opposed to turning the waste material into sludge to be disposed. Indications in 1980 were that the Environmental Protection Agency would institute regulations that would make sludge disposal so costly that the collection of sulfuric acid could become a more cost efficient alternative for dealing with sulfur emissions. Even collection of a small fraction of the estimated potential of 49.4 million tons of sulfuric acid could have a dramatic effect on the competitive positions of traditional suppliers.

Sulfuric acid prices were historically determined largely by the cost of Frasch-mined sulfur, the major ingredient in producing virgin acid. As Frasch prices rose, sulfuric acid producers traditionally passed the higher costs through to end-users, explaining to customers that the price increases were a direct cause of the higher costs of Frasch-mined sulfur. 1980 projections showed a tightening of Frasch sulfur supply for several years and conditions were not expected to improve until 1983–85. The tight supply could be expected to push Frasch sulfur prices up again. According to the findings of Allied's Sulfuric Task Force:

> Sulfur is expected to remain in tight supply for the next few years with any substantial relief not expected to occur prior to the 1983–85 period. During this period, sulfur recovery projects from the Middle East, especially Saudi Arabia, could narrow the supply-demand gap sufficiently to begin some rebuilding of inventories. Recent curtailments in Iranian sulfur recovery illustrates, however, the vulnerability of supply from this area of the world. Tight supplies should continue to put upward pressure on price although

some moderation is expected from recent sharp levels of escalation. Allied is continuing to try to minimize adverse cost effects by switching from costly Frasch sulfur to sulfur recovered from oil refineries or natural gas processing plants.

The regional nature of competition created variations in virgin sulfuric acid prices from region to region:

Region	Average Annual Price per Ton of Sulfuric Acid	
	1979	*1980*
Northeast	$62.30	$81.92
Midwest	57.15	71.21
Gulf Coast	55.75	74.81
Southwest	59.30	71.85

Because of the commodity nature of the product, if one major company changed its price to buyers in a region, other sellers in the region could be expected to follow the change.

ALLIED'S POSITION IN THE U.S. SULFURIC ACID INDUSTRY

Over 75 percent of Allied's sulfuric acid capacity was located in the northeast and midwest, where the industrial market for sulfuric acid had steadily declined in the last 10 years. In 1980, Allied operated ten sulfuric acid producing plants in the United States, as shown in Exhibit 7. Seven of the ten plants operated at a profit in 1979; their combined 1979 return on assets was 8 percent. In addition, between 1968 and 1978 Allied was the dominant domestic marketer of by-product acid, handling an average of 650,000 net tons annually; of this, 40 percent was consumed by other Allied businesses (captive use) and the balance was sold in the merchant market.

Exhibit 7   Allied's Sulfuric Acid Plant Operations, 1979

Plant Location	Capacity (Tons/Year)	1979 Production Volume (Tons)	1979 Sales (in 000s)
Harrisburg, Pa.	145,000	122,550	$ 5,641
Philadelphia, Pa.	360,000	356,059	14,845
Pittsburgh, Pa.	160,000	112,166	5,319
Syracuse, N.Y.	114,000	93,823	4,443
Cumberland, Md.	130,000	85,654	3,057
Baltimore, Md.	153,000	133,404	4,953
Little Rock, Ark.	100,000	86,981	3,532
Toledo, Ohio	160,000	142,011	7,511
Sacramento, Calif.	150,000	92,728	3,749
Bakersfield, Calif.	90,000	80,677	2,788
Total	1,562,000	1,306,053	$55,838

As of 1980, Allied had contracts with seven smelter acid producers to resell 772,000 tons per year:

Smelter Acid Producer	Location	Tons per Year
Bunker Hill	Idaho	90,000
Phelps Dodge	New Mexico	157,000
Amax	Iowa	50,000
NJ Zinc	Pennsylvania	115,000
Getty Oil	Delaware	130,000
Amax	Pennsylvania	90,000
Noranda	Canada	140,000
Total		772,000

Allied estimated that in 1978–79 its pretax return on assets employed in resale operations was 29 percent.

The third segment of Allied's sulfuric operations involved spent acid conversion. Spent sulfuric acid was generated as a residual product when virgin acid was not totally consumed during its use in a manufacturing process. The waste acid was typically contaminated with water, organics, or other impurities making it unsuitable for reuse directly in the same process. Spent acid regenerators, such as Allied, refortified, reprocessed, or resold these waste products for their customers. The charge for converting these spent acids coupled with the raw material and, in certain cases, fuel values contained in the waste acids made this business segment, in Allied's opinion, particularly attractive. Allied's Sulfuric Task Force concluded that recent sharp increases in the price of Frasch sulfur, together with tougher environmental and toxic regulations, would enhance future profitability of this segment. The Task Force reported:

> This is a service oriented, value added business. It is well protected from byproduct incursions, has raw material supply protection, and is partially insulated from business cycles. Almost 90 percent of the business is done with oil companies which are strong financially and see sulfuric acid as a relatively small element of refinery costs. The seasonality of the business does require additional investment in storage in excess of that which normally supports the sulfuric businesses.

Allied operated seven plants to handle spent acid conversion; five were in the declining industrial areas of the northeast and north central regions.

A summary of the overall performance of Allied's sulfuric acid operations is contained in Exhibit 8.

Competition   In the virgin acid manufacturing and spent acid conversion segments, the number of Allied's competitors varied from plant to plant. At one plant Allied had to confront eight competitors; at another there were no nearby competitors. Most plants, however, had three to five competitors. Among Allied's biggest rivals were Du Pont, CIL, Essex, Stauffer, and American Cyanamid, lesser competitors included Coulton Chemical, National Distillers, Mobil, Esmark, Beker, and Monsanto. In the resale segment Allied's primary competitor was Canadian Industries Limited (CIL). Allied considered it was the leading U.S. marketer of by-product or smelter acid. CIL was the only other major acid producer with a significant by-product

Exhibit 8   Profitability of Allied's Sulfuric Acid Operations, 1970–1978

| Year | Volume (in thousands of tons) | | | Combined Revenues ($ millions) | Pretax Income ($ millions) | Pretax Income as a Percent of Sales Revenues |
	Virgin Acid Production	Spent Acid Conversion	Resale of By-Product Acid	Total			
1970	1,590	498	568	2,656	$56.3	$ 8.1	14.4%
1971	1,542	486	563	2,591	51.7	5.6	10.8
1972	1,474	489	623	2,586	52.8	4.2	7.9
1973	1,359	429	707	2,495	54.9	5.4	9.9
1974	1,320	357	742	2,419	63.9	7.5	11.7
1975	1,025	284	510	1,819	68.8	12.3	17.9
1976	1,080	318	628	2,026	81.7	15.4	18.9
1977	1,123	328	714	2,165	86.3	8.9	10.3
1978	1,052	319	755	2,126	86.4	6.8	7.9

Source: Allied Corporation, Sulfuric Task Force Report.

acid strategy; CIL handled about 1.6 million tons of by-product acid annually, about double Allied's 1980 volume, but much of CIL's volume was marketed to Canadian end-users. Allied expected CIL to challenge Allied's leadership in the resale segment in the United States. Other producers who competed with Allied in reselling byproduct acid included Stauffer Chemical, Du Pont, Olin, and Esmark—all of which handled substantially smaller volumes than Allied.

The Sulfuric Task Force evaluated Allied's business characteristics and competitive strength in both virgin acid manufacture and the resale of by-product acid. The findings are summarized in Exhibits 9 and 10.

Allied's 1980 pretax return on assets for sulfuric acid operations was 7.6 percent. The Task Force came up with the capital requirements projections through 1984 as follows:

Allied's Plants	Capital Needs Estimates (in thousands of dollars)					
	1980	1981	1982	1983	1984	Total
Syracuse, New York	$ 440	$ 440	$ 440	$ 440	$ 440	$ 2,200
Pittsburgh, Pennsylvania	765	825	795	1,545	1,320	5,250
Cumberland, Maryland	117	350	277	455	450	1,649
Toledo, Ohio	1,167	1,768	929	459	506	4,829
Philadelphia, Pennsylvania	1,800	2,695	1,450	1,795	4,755	12,495
Harrisburg, Pennsylvania	695	615	600	330	330	2,570
Little Rock, Arkansas	332	550	725	650	470	2,727
Bakersfield, California	570	489	335	457	300	2,151
Sacramento, California	950	1,000	700	200	375	3,225
Baltimore, Maryland	400	1,085	340	175	325	2,325
Total	$8,216	$12,557	$7,811	$6,811	$10,506	$45,901

SULFURIC TASK FORCE RECOMMENDATIONS

The Task Force concluded that the sulfuric acid industry, despite the problems of overcapacity and declining industrial end-use demand, was attractive—at least from Allied's standpoint. However, the Task Force recommended that Allied close several plants and consolidate operations to improve profitability in line with the corporate target of an 18 percent pretax return on assets. The specific plant-related recommendations were as follows:

1. *Harrisburg*—Shut the plant down and serve customers on contract from Allied's Philadelphia plant. (The plant was incurring substantial financial losses.)

2. *Syracuse*—Continue to operate and maintain for the time being. (The economics for this location were integrated with Allied's production of nitric, ammonium thiosulfate, oxalic and metallic nitrates, all of which were attractively profitable. The Task Force noted that this plant's profitability could also be enhanced by shifting some production over from the Harrisburg and Pittsburgh plants.)

3. *Pittsburgh*—Shut the plant down. (This plant had had an unacceptable ROA in the past and was projected to stay well below 18 percent in the future. The plant was at a competitive disadvantage and opportunities existed to shift a large part of the plant's output to other Allied plants where excess capacity existed.)

Exhibit 9 Allied's Business Characteristics and Competitive Strength, Sulfuric Acid Manufacturing Operations and Spent Acid Conversion Operations

Plant Evaluations

Business Characteristics	Philadelphia	Harris-burg	Syracuse	Pitts-burgh	Cumber-land	Toledo	Little Rock	Bakers-field	Sacra-mento	Balti-more
Number of Competitors	5	4	3	3	2	8	5	0	3	2
Cyclicality	High	Moderate	High	High	High	High	High	Low	Low	High
Growth	Low	Low	Low	Low	Low	Low	Moderate	Low	Low	Low
Environmental problems	Moderate	High	High	Moderate	High	Moderate	High	Low	Moderate	High
Customer price concerns	Moderate	Moderate	Moderate	Moderate	Moderate	Moderate	Moderate	Low	Low	Moderate
Seasonality	Yes	Yes	Yes	No	No	Yes	No	Yes	Yes	No
Barriers to entry	High	High	High	High	High	High	High	High	High	High
Importance of capacity util.	High	High	High	High	High	High	High	High	High	High
Asset intensity	High	High	High	High	High	High	High	High	High	High
Raw material security	Concerns	No	Concerns	Concerns	Concerns	Concerns	Concerns	No	No	Concerns
Energy/labor intensity	Low	Low	Low	Low	Low	Low	Low	Low	Low	Low
Number—customer base	Moderate	Low	High	High	High	High	Moderate	Low	Moderate	Low
Product differentiation	Low	Low	Low	Low	Low	Low	Low	Low	Low	Low
Service content	High (Spent Acid)	High	High (Spent Acid)	High (Spent Acid)	Low	High (Spent Acid)	Low	High	High	High
Marketing content	Low	Low	Low	Low	Low	Low (Spent Acid)	Low	Low	Low	Low

Competitive Strengths

Market share	Strong	Strong	Strong	Strong	Strong	Tenable	Weak	Strong	Equal	Strong
Cost	Equal	Weak	Tenable	Tenable	Tenable	Equal	Tenable	Strong	Strong	Equal
Raw material position	Strong (Spent Acid)	Strong	Strong (Spent Acid)	Equal	Weak	Strong (Spent Acid)	Equal	Strong	Strong	Equal
Base load	Strong	Strong	Equal	Strong	Strong	Strong	Strong	Strong	Strong	Strong
Facilities	Strong	Tenable	Tenable	Tenable	Equal	Equal	Tenable	Strong	Equal	Equal
Service	Equal	Equal	Equal	Equal	Equal	Equal	Equal	Strong	Strong	Strong
Environmental/ leg. impact	Strong	Weak	Weak	Strong	Tenable	Strong	Strong	Strong	Strong	Tenable
Labor	Equal	Tenable	Equal	Equal	Equal	Equal	Equal	Equal	Equal	Equal
Organization	Equal	Tenable	Equal	Equal	Equal	Equal	Equal	Equal	Equal	Equal
Financial	Tenable	Weak	Tenable	Weak	Equal	Equal	Tenable	Strong	Strong	Strong
Technology	Equal	Equal	Tenable	Tenable	Tenable	Equal	Tenable	Strong	Strong	Tenable

Source: Allied Corporation, Sulfuric Task Force Report.

Exhibit 10   Allied's Business Characteristics and Competitive Strength, Resale of By-product Acid Segment

Business Characteristics	Evaluation
Number of competitors	8
Cyclicality	High
Growth	Moderate
Environmental impact/concerns/problems	High
Application critical	Yes
Customer price concern	Moderate
Seasonality	No
Barriers to entry	Low
Capacity utilization importance	Low
Asset intensity	Moderate
Raw material security	Moderate concern
Energy/labor intensity	Low
Product differentiation	Low
Service content	Low
Material content	Low

Competitive Strengths	Evaluation
Market share	Strong
Cost	Equal
Base load	Strong
Service	Strong
Environmental impact/concerns/problems	Equal
Labor	Equal
Organization	Equal
Financial	Strong
Market position/market niche	Strong
Product	Equal
Price	Equal
Selling	Equal
Distribution	Strong
Image	Strong
Product mix	Equal
Customer mix	Equal

Source: Allied Corporation, Sulfuric Task Force Report.

4. *Cumberland*—Continue to operate for the time being with cheaper sulfur sources currently used at Newell. To improve this plant's economics, the high cost sulfur contract with Allied's Frasch sulfur supplier should be bought out at a $12 per ton penalty. Periodic make-buy analyses should be made to determine longer term viability.

5. *Little Rock*—Shut the plant down and purchase Allied's captive acid requirements in the open market. (As an option, the Task Force indicated that one of Allied's sister divisions, a major customer of this plant's output, could be approached to fund the operation at Little Rock at an adequate transfer price.)

6. *Toledo*—Operate for three years with restricted capital outlays (until mid-1983) while attempting to build a clientele and sales base for the plant with spent

acid and other chemical products. If this is not successful, then take an orderly phase-out of operations.

7. *Philadelphia*—Attack the current low ROA by aggressively seeking out more customers and by filling out capacity through Harrisburg shutdown. Improved plant economics can be expected from absorbing activities formerly performed at Harrisburg and Pittsburgh plants.

8. *Other Locations*—Continue to operate Baltimore, Bakersfield, and Sacramento plants, as all are operating at acceptable profit levels.

Because of weakening demand and forecasts of growing Canadian imports of by-product acid in the northeast and north central regions, the Task Force concluded that insofar as expansion of Allied's resale business was concerned it would be best to pursue a "southwest strategy." The supporting reasons offered were:

1. Additional growth in the demand for smelter-produced by-product acid was anticipated in the southwest and west regions.

2. Mining operations in the southwest were expected to grow, thus offering good sources of smelter acid for resale.

3. Allied was recognized as a major marketer of sulfuric acid.

4. Allied's other divisions had a continuing need for sulfuric acid as a raw material.

5. A continuing position in the marketplace would insure Allied of a reliable and economic supply of acid.

The initial recommended action for the southwest strategy was the negotiation of a contract with an Arizona mining operation to handle the resale of 500,000 tons of by-product acid. The Task Force developed a marketing plan and financial analysis for the proposed 500,000 ton arrangement which projected a 24 percent pretax return on assets based on prevailing market conditions.

The Task Force identified three opportunity areas where Allied could expand profits in reprocessing spent acid, stating its findings as follows:

1. *Expansion into new spent acid opportunity areas.* Basically this area includes those waste acids previously disposed of by neutralizing disposal facilities or reused directly. Nitration spent acids containing nitrates and possibly halogen products, as well as those spents deemed unsuitable for the direct manufacture of fertilizers or other related products, will be forced into treatment and reprocessing over the next five years as tougher environmental standards are implemented. The company's technical and research efforts in this area will give us the expertise to initiate reprocessing of these acids in increasing quantities.

2. *The use of available excess capacity* at Allied's remaining plants (assuming the shutdown recommendation are followed) to achieve economies of scale and greater plant utilization economics. Opportunities exist to shift the spent acid operations at Harrisburg over to the Philadelphia plant, to debottleneck spent acid conversion at Pittsburgh once the Syracuse plant is closed, and to use the excess capacity at Toledo to handle spent acids currently serviced by Stauffer in Hammond, Indiana and by U.S.I. in Kansas.

3. *The expansion of Allied into the Southwest market* by investing in spent acid facilities to serve an Arizona operation. This would enable Allied to share a

Exhibit 11   Financial Effects of Sulfuric Task Force Recommendations, Allied Corporation, 1980

Recommended Plant Changes	Projected Financial Effects (in millions of dollars)		Suggested Timing
	Increase or (Decrease) in Pretax Income	Increase (Decrease) in Assets	
Shut down Harrisburg	2.0	(3.7)	1983
Shut down Pittsburgh	(0.8)	(3.5)	1984
Pittsburgh spent acid to Philadelphia	1.3	2.0	1983
Product mix change-Syracuse	0.2	—	1983
Spent acid increase-Syracuse	0.7	0.1	1984
Product mix change-Syracuse	0.5	0.2	1984
Product mix change-Toledo	0.3	0.1	1982
Spent acid increase-Toledo	1.5	0.2	1982
Total-plant changes	5.7	(4.6)	
Additional 500,000 ton resale	2.6	10.9	1982
Total changes	8.3	6.3	

Summary Comparisons	Increase or (Decrease) in Pretax Income	Increase (Decrease) in Assets	ROA (Percent)
Current operations (1980 second half)	7.4	73.5	10.1
Current planned improvements	6.2	12.7	
Recommended plant changes	5.7	(4.6)	
Additional 500,000 ton resale	2.6	10.9	
Total impact, Sulfuric operations	21.9	92.5	23.7

Source: Allied Corporation, Sulfuric Task Force Report.

portion of this growing market to counteract expected declines or lack of growth in Allied's existing Northern U.S. market areas.

The Task Force saw spent acid reprocessing as "an important area for future profit growth."

The projected financial effects of the combined task force recommendations are outlined in Exhibit 11.

ALLIED'S RESPONSE TO THE TASK FORCE REPORT

Shortly after Allied's Sulfuric Task Force presented its recommendations, senior management took action. A $28 million pretax nonrecurring charge was made in the last quarter of 1980 to cover the write-off of sulfuric acid facilities which it was decided would be sold or shut-down in 1981. In October 1981 the Toledo and Syracuse plants were sold and the Harrisburg plant was shut down. In January 1982 the

Pittsburgh plant was shut down. In response to the Task Force's southwest strategy recommendation, by mid-1982 Allied had implemented a major expansion of its West Coast sulfuric acid facility located at Bakersfield, California. Allied's strategy for the sulfuric acid area was revised and profiled in June 1982 (Exhibit 12). The Little Rock plant was shut down in December 1982.

Frank Biermann, marketing manager for Allied's sulfuric acid business, reflected on the changes that were implemented:

> As a result of our actions in 1981, our sulfuric acid business is far healthier now and has the strong support of corporate management. Our current production locations, our captive demand, and our distribution systems have us well positioned to take advantage of further directional changes in both supply and demand for sulfuric acid in the years ahead.
>
> I arrived on the scene in Spring 1981 to implement much of the plant rationalization strategy that had been formulated. Certainly the business is far healthier today because people made the tough decisions back in 1980 to shed assets that were marginal at best in markets that were to be increasingly dominated by smelter acid.
>
> Our company's management has attained some notoriety in recent years for its aggressive acquisition program, but product or plant rationalization deserves even more credit because that is often a more difficult task. When Hennessy was brought aboard in 1979, he put renewed emphasis on ROA. The response by the Sulfuric Acid business group was right on target. Profit has been increased and assets have been reduced.
>
> One of the ways that we have improved ROA is to put increased emphasis on individual asset bases. In the old days the Allied sulfuric business was viewed more as a nationwide "system" where profits were measured as a percentage of total business investment because of the number of plant locations and their intersecting shipping circles. This type of management approach can make a rationalization strategy difficult to conceive or implement because good locations can cover up poor ones when they are averaged. Nowadays, each location must stand on its own, either as a manufacturing plant or as a resale (smelter acid) location. Every location is expected to produce an acceptable ROA.
>
> The real credit for Allied's strength today, from a marketing sense, probably belongs to my predecessors in the 1960s and early 1970s. They had the foresight to recognize that Allied should be in the business of marketing sulfuric acid, rather than merely manufacturing it. They recognized that copper smelters, electric utilities, and other environmentally related acid producers were going to need some help in marketing by-product acid. We now have in place the distribution systems (barges, rail fleet, tank trucks, order entry, sales force) to do the job . . . to provide a service where select opportunities allow us to earn an acceptable return on assets involved in selling by-product acid.

Exhibit 13 shows the 1981–83 operating results for Allied's sulfuric operations.

DEVELOPMENTS IN THE SULFURIC ACID INDUSTRY, 1982

In addition to the actions taken by Allied, several other sulfuric acid production facilities in the United States changed ownership during 1982 as shown in Exhibit 14.

Exhibit 12   Allied's 1982 Strategic Profile for its Sulfuric Acid Unit

A. Situation analysis

1. *Statement of Scope:*
   - Sulfuric acid manufactured or purchased for resale is sold to domestic petroleum, fibers, steel, paint, paper, chemical, and agricultural industries.
   - Reprocessing sulfur-containing products for specialty markets.
   - Provide sulfur products for upgrading into other Allied products.

2. *Industry Description*
   1982: $2.3 billion: 34 metric tons (MM): 60 percent capacity.

   Approximately ⅔ of total industry volume is consumed captively for fertilizer manufacture.

   Major merchant market producers include:

	Capacity—MM Tons
Stauffer	3.7
Du Pont	2.5
Allied	1.9
Olin	1.1
American Cyanamid	1.1
Canadian Industries, Ltd.	0.6

   Sulfuric acid, the largest volume commodity chemical in the United States, is produced both by burning sulfur and as a recovered by-product. Historically, sulfuric acid has been manufactured from Frasch mined sulfur, while selected locations have used spent acid regeneration and other sulfur bearing sources (e.g., H_2S: Hydrogen Sulfide) to augment raw material requirements. Frasch sulfur pricing has generally set acid pricing, but now environmentally-dictated acid tends to sell at a lower price. The U.S. industry comprises 170 producing locations and about 5,000 customers. Markets are primarily regional in nature with minor exceptions involving movement of by-product acid.
   - Cyclicality: Linked to GNP
   - Timing: Coincident
   - Amplitude: Medium

3. *Industry Maturity*
   Current: *Aging*   Future: *Aging*

4. *Market Statistics (nonfertilizer segment)*

Nonfertilizer End Uses	*U.S. MM*	*Allied MM*	*Allied Growth Rate*	
			Past 5 Years	*Next 5 Years*
Chemicals	3.2	.5	−6.0	2.0
Petroleum	2.5	.2	−9.6	—
Other	7.6	.4	−4.4	2.0
Total	13.3	1.1	−5.8	1.7

5. *Market Description*
   Sulfuric acid is used to digest phosrock in the production of phosphate fertilizer. Most of the required sulfuric acid is produced captively. Chemical end uses are numerous; usually requiring high quality acid. Distribution systems and reliability of supply are important. In the petroleum industry it is used as a catalyst for alkylate and in other uses resulting in spent acids and sludges from which the acid must be recovered by decomposition techniques. Coke production by the steel industry requires large quantities of sulfuric acid for ammonium sulfate. Use for processing uranium ore in the West has grown; however, current demand for this use has slowed. Sulfuric acid supply has increased due to by-product acid recoveries in Canada and the Southwest. This by-product acid is sold throughout the United States.

6. *Strategic Unit Description*
   Allied's plants are managed to support captive requirements of about 316 million tons/ year ($23 million) for upgraded Chemical group products, profitable service related reprocessing of sulfur containing materials, and stand-alone profitable locations which have defendable competitive positions.

   Manufacturing plants include:

Exhibit 12 *(continued)*

	Capacity	*Millions of Net Tons*	
		1984 Volume Estimate	*Utilization*
Bakersfield	90	77	86%
Sacramento	150	100	67
Philadelphia	370	337	91
Baltimore	152	113	74
Total	762	667	82%

Additionally, approximately 450M tons/year of by-product acid is either resold or captively consumed.

8 customers = 50% of Allied's total trade tons
24 customers = 80% of Allied's total trade tons

7. *Competitive Analysis*

	Du Pont	*Stauffer*	*CIL*	*AmCy*	*Essex*
Protected Market Position	+	=	+	+	+
Total Cost	=	+	=	=	=
Profitability	=	=	+	=	−
Net Cash Throw-Off	=	=	+	=	=
Location & Size of Facility	=	+	=	+	=

Summary: Equal/Favorable

8. *Past Strategies*
   - Maintenance
   - Market Rationalization
   - Product Rationalization

B. Plan Analysis

1. *Key Assumptions*
   - Economic recovery in 1983.
   - Decomposition volume remains stable.
   - Contracts with big customers will continue.
   - Increased competition—East Coast.
   - No change in government regulations.
   - By-product acid resale arrangements continue.

STRATEGIES/PROGRAMS		1982	1983	1984	1985	1986	1987
Same Products/Same Markets Negotiate Major contracts							
Methods and Functions Efficiency Inventory Reduction Cost Reduction Program at Delaware (Indirects) Energy Conservation at Richmond							
MEASURES							
Inputs (Investments) Marketing effort-contracts	Work Years	.5	.5	.5	.5	.5	.5
Inventory Reduction from 1982 Plan	$MM	3.0					
Sacramento Capital Projects:							
Heat Reclaim (cum)	$MM	0.15	.15	.15	.15	.15	.15
Smaller Blower Motor (cum)	$MM	0.15	.15	.15	.15	.15	.15
OUTPUTS (PERFORMANCE) Maintenance of System Loadings	M NT	1129	1162	1195	1194	1212	1229
Inventory Levels	$MM	3.0	3.3	3.6	3.9	4.2	4.5
Philadelphia Cost Reductions	$MM	2.0	3.0				
Sacramento—Natural Gas Savings	$MM	0.1	0.3	0.3	0.3	0.3	0.3

Exhibit 12 *(concluded)*

2. *Strategic Thrust and Positioning*
   • Hold niche.
   Stand alone manufacturing locations (product/market segments) will be managed to maximize return and cash flow. Resale arrangements will be continued wherever profitable.

3. *Acquisition Activities*
   None

4. *Current/Future Strategic Situation*

	Embryo	Growth	Mature	Aging
LEADING				
STRONG				
FAVORABLE				X
TENABLE				
WEAK				

5. *Major Threats/Concerns*
   East Cost competition will result in lower market share and margins.
   Major customer plant closings could be announced.
   By-product acid availability is growing.

Industry analysts attributed many of the plant sales to the growing strength of lower priced smelter acid, as well as to the aggressive efforts of CIL to gain a bigger share of the U.S. market for both virgin and smelter acids. Also, virgin sulfuric acid profits were squeezed hard by depressed virgin acid prices, increased Frasch sulfur costs, and a significant economywide recession. Many companies began looking to dispose of unprofitable or out-of-date facilities.

There were a number of other developments in 1982:

July: Smelter acid producers began running low on inventories brought about by depressed copper, lead, and zinc markets. (Producers of these metals generated smelter acid as a by-product of their ore processing operations.) Many mining companies began to shut down for indefinite lengths of time in an effort to work off excess inventories and adjust production to reduced demand. However, the curtailment of smelter acid availability gave smelter acid producers an opening to boost prices, though not so much as to get above the posted prices on virgin sulfuric acid.

October: Frasch sulfur producers reduced prices by $12.50 per ton which meant a cost savings for virgin sulfuric acid producers of around $3.80 per ton.

November: CIL Chemicals announced it would spend $1 million at its newly acquired Sayreville, New Jersey operations to upgrade its acid storage capacity, sulfur delivery, and railway car loading facilities. This announcement was preceded by the U.S. Department of Transportation's decision to extend the amount of allowable loaded train movement between the United States and Canada.

November: Du Pont announced that it would drastically cut its sulfuric acid prices in an effort to reaffirm its market position, a move widely interpreted as signal-

Exhibit 13   Financial Performance of Allied Corporation's Sulfur Products Operations, 1981–1983   Dollar Figures in Millions

	Baltimore			Sacramento		
	1981	*1982*	*1983*	*1981*	*1982*	*1983*
Sales and Operating Revenue	$ 8.9	$ 7.7	$ 7.3	$ 7.8	$ 6.8	$ 8.9
Pretax Income	$ 1.4	$ 0.7	$ 1.0	$ 2.9	$ 2.4	$ 2.4
Average Assets	$ 4.6	$ 4.0	$ 4.1	$ 4.9	$ 5.3	$ 5.6
ROA	30.5%	17.5%	24.3%	59.2%	45.3%	42.8%

	Bakersfield			Philadelphia		
	1981	*1982*	*1983*	*1981*	*1982*	*1983*
Sales and Operating Revenue	$ 5.6	$ 5.5	$ 7.0	$ 33.1	$35.0	$33.6
Pretax Income	$ 2.2	$ 2.4	$ 3.5	$ 3.5	$ 4.0	$ 3.7
Average Assets	$ 6.1	$ 5.8	$ 5.7	$ 29.6	$26.4	$26.6
ROA	36.1%	41.4%	61.4%	11.8%	15.2%	13.9%

	Resale/Other			Discontinued		
	1981	*1982*	*1983*	*1981*	*1982*	*1983*
Sales and Operating Revenue	$24.8	$21.2	$ 19.8	$19.7		
Pretax Income	$ 2.6	$ 0.9	$ 2.0	$ (4.4)		
Average Assets	$ 2.7	$ 2.9	$ 2.0	$ 20.9		
ROA	96.3%	31.0%	100.0%	−21.1%		

	Total		
	1981	*1982*	*1983*
Sales and Operating Revenue	$99.9	$76.2	$ 76.6
Pretax Income	$ 7.7	$10.3	$ 12.5
Average Assets	$68.8	$44.7	$ 44.0
ROA	11.2%	23.1%	28.4%

Source: Allied Corporation.

Exhibit 14   Sales/Purchases of U.S. Sulfuric Acid Plants, 1982

Buyer	*Seller*	*Location*	*Annual Capacity In Tons*
PVS Chemicals	Ozark-Mahoning	Tulsa, Okla.	90,000
PVS Chemicals	3M	Copley, Ohio	98,000
Koch Industries	N-Ren	Pine Bend, Minn.	98,000
Koch Industries	Northeast Chemical	Wilmington, N.C.	120,000
Smith-Douglas	Bordon, Inc.	Streator, Ill.	30,000
Amax Phosphate	Bordon, Inc.	Piney Point, Pa.	550,000
Mobil	Olin Corp.	Pasadena, Texas	500,000
J. R. Simplot Co.	Valley Nitrogen	Helm, Calif.	2,000,000
Tennessee Chemical	Cities Service Co.	Copperhill, Tenn.	1,260,000

ling strong retaliation to CIL's aggressive attempts to grab market share. Du Pont's announced price cuts were as follows:

Market	Old Price per Ton	New Price per Ton
New Jersey	$95.90	$61.00
West Pennsylvania	80.25	55.80
Chicago	77.00	55.80
Gulf Coast	88.50	83.50
Virginia	95.90	90.90
Ohio Valley	80.25	75.25

November: CIL matched Du Pont's price cuts, despite having some operating problems in meeting its supply commitments from its Sayreville plant.

December: Other companies were slow to follow the deep price cuts announced by Du Pont and CIL. Industry observers speculated that this was because profit margins were already squeezed by a 10 to 20 percent falloff in demand in the Northeast.

SULFURIC ACID INDUSTRY DEVELOPMENTS, 1983

New competitive developments and capacity changes continued to keep the industry in a state of flux during 1983:

January: Sulfuric acid prices in the northeastern one third of the United States began to stabilize around the Du Pont levels.

February: A slight increase in sulfuric acid demand occurred in the highly competitive Midwest and Northeast markets. The Southeast experienced some increase in demand, although not as much as was seen elsewhere; industry analysts suggested this might have been because the southeast had not experienced the sharp price cuts which had hit the industrial northeast and midwest.

February: Chemical Marketing Services announced it would acquire two facilities which would have a combined production capacity of 75,000 tons of virgin sulfuric acid. (However, the acquisition never materialized.)

May: Frasch sulfur producers in Florida cut prices as much as $12.50 per long ton (2,240 pounds). Industry analysts familiar with the southeast region believed the price cuts were an effort to stave off the entry of Canadian-produced Frasch sulfur into the Gulf Coast market. Canadian producers had begun shipping their sulfur to customers in the region just a few months earlier.

May: Japanese suppliers began exporting sulfuric acid to the Gulf Coast, adding to oversupply conditions in that area. The Japanese prices were said to be in the $35–39 per ton range; the posted prices of domestic producers selling in the Gulf Coast region were $48 to $52 per ton.

July: Phelps Dodge Corporation's copper mine workers went on strike and similar actions were being threatened at other major U.S. mines; the potential reduction in smelter acid supplies brought "a ray of hope" to producers plagued with general oversupply conditions. Without a steady stream of new smelter

	acid to handle, smelter acid suppliers were expected to be able to work off inventories to meet demand; inventories were said to be big enough to handle two months of sales.
August:	Demand for sulfuric acid remained low, particularly in fertilizer end-uses where demand was not expected to recover until fall 1984. End-use demand in mining from 1981 to 1982 had fallen 800,000 tons.
August:	Asarco, Incorporated announced plans to increase daily capacity of smelter acid in the near future at its Hayden, Arizona facility from its present 750 tons a day to 2,800 tons a day. Kennecott Corporation also announced plans to increase its daily smelter acid capacity approximately 65 percent to 600 tons a day.
September:	Announcements indicated phosphate fertilizer exports were increasing and that by the spring of 1984 domestic sulfuric acid demand might in turn be boosted (sulfuric acid was needed to make phosphoric acid which was a prime ingredient in producing phosphate fertilizers). The rise in phosphoric fertilizer production was also expected to assist in undergirding Frasch sulfur prices. Meanwhile, continued discounting of sulfuric acid on the Gulf Coast prompted Stauffer Chemical, the area's biggest producer, to drop its prices from $83.50 to $65 per ton. Prices in Houston remained between $95 and $100 per ton and Louisiana prices were about $5 higher. On the West Coast, increasing supply and limited demand prompted producers of sulfuric acid to turn to exporting their products. Exports had recently risen 65 percent and carried prices of $82 per ton.
October:	Du Pont signed an agreement with Asarco, Inc. to purchase 300,000 tons of smelter acid per year from Asarco's Hayden, Arizona plant. Speculations about the purchase were that Du Pont (1) might use the new supplies to cut back on its own sulfuric acid production, (2) might use the new supplies in place of other ways to meet its sulfuric requirements along the Gulf Coast, or (3) might have made the purchase to prevent another supplier from making that same purchase and using it to compete with Du Pont. Du Pont maintained the purchase was made in an effort to supply the midwest market that it presently could not serve.
October:	Cutbacks in virgin sulfuric acid production, coupled with a growing optimism in the fertilizer industry, improved the outlook for bringing sulfuric acid demand and supply conditions into better balance in 1984. However, excess capacity and a dormant uranium end-use market continued to depress prices, particularly in the Gulf Coast area. Acid prices elsewhere were showing signs of firming up.

ALLIED'S STRATEGY IN SULFURIC ACID, 1984

Going into 1984 about 30 percent of Allied's surfuric acid supplies were shipped to other Allied divisions and about 70 percent was sold in the merchant market. Allied had a base of approximately 600 customers for its various sulfur products. Overall U.S. consumption of sulfuric acid was projected to grow at an average annual rate of 2.5 percent from a 1984 base. Allied's strategy for the sulfuric acid business was reviewed and profiled in 1984 (Exhibit 15).

Exhibit 15   Allied's 1984 Strategic Plan for Its Sulfuric Acid Business

---

A. Situation analysis

1. *Statement of Scope*

   Sulfuric acid manufactured or purchased for resale is sold to domestic petroleum, fibers, steel, paint, paper, chemical, and agricultural industries. Related activities also include specialty reprocessing of sulfur-containing products.

   About 30 percent of Allied's sulfur products produced in this business unit are captively consumed in upgraded products (used by other Allied businesses), with the remaining 70 percent moving to the merchant market. Specifically excluded from the scope of this unit are sulfuric manufacturing facilities where product is totally consumed in captive on-site upgrading for fibers, agriculture and Hydrofluric Acid (HF) products.

2. *Industry Description*

   Sulfuric acid, the largest volume commodity chemical in the United States, is produced both by burning sulfur and as a recovered by-product. Total sulfuric acid production in the United States is valued at about $2.0 billion, typically representing 40 million net tons of product annually. Most sulfuric acid is consumed captively in production of other industrial chemicals, primarily fertilizers. Only about 30 percent of U.S. production moves to the merchant market. However, included in this percentage is acid used for alkylation and other sludge-producing operations that must be purchased from specific plants capable of recycling sludges. Historically, sulfuric acid has been manufactured from Frasch mined sulfur, while selected locations have used spent acid regeneration and other sulfur bearing sources to augment raw material requirements. Frasch sulfur pricing has generally set acid pricing, but now environmentally-dictated acid tends to sell at a lower price. The U.S. industry comprises 140 producing locations with capacity of about 55 million net tons, and about 5,000 customers. Markets are primarily regional in nature with minor exceptions involving movement of by-product acid.

   Cyclicality: Linked to GNP; Strong agricultural influences because of big fertilizer end-use.
   Timing: Coincident
   Amplitude: Medium

   There are 70 companies producing sulfuric acid in the United States at 140 producing locations.

   Major merchant market producers include:

	Capacity—MM Tons
Stauffer	3.8
Du Pont	2.5
Allied	1.2
Tennessee Chemical	1.4
American Cyanamid	1.1
Canadian Industries, Ltd.	0.6
Essex Chemical	0.6

3. *Industry Maturity*

   Current: *Aging*   Future: *Aging*

4. *Market Statistics*

   Total consumption of sulfuric acid in the United States grew at an average annual rate of 3.0 percent from 1972 to 1981. Consumption declined significantly in 1982 and 1983 due to the general economic slowdown. This has been particularly true in the hard-hit fertilizer sector, which (excluding ammonium sulfate) accounts for some 60 percent of sulfuric acid consumption. Overall, U.S. consumption of sulfuric acid is projected to grow at an average annual rate of 2.5 percent from a 1984 base for the next several years, reflecting in part a recovery from the economic downturn. Growth in fertilizer use will exceed this rate, while other uses will be static or exhibit slower growth.

Nonfertilizer End Uses	U.S. MM	Allied MM	Allied Growth Rate Past 5 Years
Chemicals	4.9	.6	−6.0
Petroleum	2.0	.2	−9.6
Other	7.5	.4	−4.4
Total	14.2	1.2	−5.8

Exhibit 15 (continued)

5. *Market Description*
   Sulfuric acid is used to digest phosrock in the production of phosphate fertilizer. Most of the required sulfuric acid is produced captively. Chemical end uses are numerous, usually requiring high quality acid. Distribution systems and reliability of supply are important. In the petroleum industry it is used as a catalyst for alkylate and in other uses resulting in spent acids and sludges from which the acid must be recovered by decomposition techniques. Coke production by the steel industry requires large quantities of sulfuric acid for ammonium sulfate. Use for processing uranium ore in the West has grown; however, current demand for this use has slowed. Sulfuric acid supply has increased due to by-product acid recoveries in Canada and the Southwest. This by-product acid is sold throughout the United States.

6. *Strategic Unit Description*
   Regional business units, that is, producing location and/or resale arrangements, are managed to support captive requirements of about 300M tons/year for upgraded products, profitable service related reprocessing of sulfur containing materials, and stand-alone profitable locations which have defendable competitive positions.

   Manufacturing plants include:

	Capacity	Millions of Net Tons	
		1984 Volume Estimate	Utilization
Bakersfield	100	89	89%
Sacramento	150	141	94
Philadelphia	370	275	74
Baltimore	152	126	83
Total	772	631	82%

   Additionally, approximately 340M tons/year of by-product acid is either resold or captively consumed by Allied.

   8 customers = 50% of Allied's total trade tons
   24 customers = 80% of Allied's total trade tons

   Current Operating Rate: 82%

7. *Competitive Analysis*

	Du Pont	Stauffer	CIL	AmCy	Essex
Protected Market Position	=	=	+	+	=
Total Cost	=	=	+	=	=
Profitability	=	=	+	+	+
Net Cash Throw-Off	=/+	=	+	+	=
Location and Size of Facility	=	+	+	+	=
Overall	=	=	+	+	=

   Summary: Equal/Favorable

8. *Past Strategies*
   - Maintenance
   - Market Rationalization
   - Product Rationalization

B. Plan analysis
1. *Key Assumptions*
   - Economic Recovery in 1984; fertilizer demand improves.
   - Captive demand remains stable at 1984 levels.
   - Decomposition volume remains constant on East Coast; customer mix changes.
   - Avtex business continues viable.
   - Continuation of long term contractual arrangements.
   - Continued supply/demand imbalance on East Coast limits margin improvement near term.
   - Du Pont shutdown at Rapunto, New Jersey facility 1984; Allied to supply.

Exhibit 15 *(concluded)*

- Additional production rationalization occurs within three to five years.
- By-product acid resale arrangements continue, but greater competitive pressure for participation.
- Acid rain issue resolution will not impact in plan period.

2. *Strategic Thrust and Positioning*
   Hold Niche/Defend Position

   Stand alone manufacturing locations (product/market segments) will be managed to maximize return and cash flow. Resale arrangements will be continued wherever profitable. Bakersville and Sacramento will focus on maintaining existing niche, while Baltimore, Cumberland, and Philadelphia locations will orient to defending position based upon geographical advantage.

3. *Acquisition Activities*
   None

4. *Current/Future Strategic Situation*

	Embryo	Growth	Mature	Aging
LEADING				
STRONG				
FAVORABLE				X
TENABLE				
WEAK				

5. *Major Threats/Concerns*
   - East Coast competition will result in lower market share and margins as new producers establish position and excess capacity continues.
   - Major customer plant closings. Viability of Allied's chrome chemical business.
   - Acceleration of resolution of acid rain issue could impact on sulfuric acid.
   - Additional imported acid on East Coast (Canada, Europe).

6. *Major Action Programs*
   - Maintenance of long-term contractual positions to defend positions.
   - Continuation of cost reduction program at Philadelphia.
   - Continue to explore potential change in Philadelphia customer/product mix to isolate from Northeast merchant market.
   - Improve efficiencies on inventory and distribution management.

7. *Expected Competitive Response*
   Expect continued price and margin pressures in East Coast market due to:
   - CIL operation of Sayreville, New Jersey Plant (600 M tons) at one train rate to provide backup for smelter acid resale position.
   - Essex operation of Baltimore, Maryland plant (350 M tons) continues tenable near term.
   - American Cyanamid will operate Warners, New Jersey for energy value.
   - Du Pont will consolidate capacity on East Coast.
   - By-product acid (longer-term).
   - Increased competition for Allied resale arrangements.

8. *Strategic Manufacturing Focus*
   Objective is to be a dependable supplier with a competitive cost structure, including a secure sulfur raw material supply, while controlling investment in investories and facilities.

9. *Strategic Technological Development Focus*
   Research and development spending is focused on process improvement (spent decomposition efficiencies) and energy savings projects.

Frank Biermann, Allied's marketing manager for sulfuric acid products, indicated his thoughts about what future market conditions in the industry would be like:

The industry scene today is marked by the dominance of agricultural demand (largely captive supply) in certain geographical areas, continued retrenchment of producers who use Frasch sulfur to make virgin acid, and ambiguities in the supply of by-product acid.

Open market prices for sulfuric acid continue to be threatened by excess capacity among the fertilizer producers; the demand for agricultural fertilizers is down and some fertilizer producers are said to be considering selling sulfuric acid in the industrial market given that they temporarily do not need all of their acid-producing capacity in-house. However, their high concentration in Florida and the Gulf States, coupled with customer skepticism over just how long the fertilizer companies will be willing to commit their acid-making term commitment of capacity to outside merchant sales, has certainly minimized the impact of the current weak agricultural demand on industrial marketers such as Allied. Where it does hurt, though, is where large quantities of smelter acid are suddenly freed up because some of the fertilizer producers are no longer buying smelter acid on the open market to supplement their own inhouse acid-producing capacity.

I expect to see some further shutdowns of sulfur based plants because of the impact of smelter acid. Generally, they are smaller plants that either have no specialty niche (upgrading to Oleum, regeneration of spent acids) or are facing large capital investments. Some of these plants are sold to smaller firms with presumably lower overhead who seem to hang in there longer than the larger companies. Sometimes they make very little sense from a marketing viewpoint. Large quantities of new sulfuric acid were predicted to arrive by the mid-80s as the acid rain issue received attention. This has just not happened anywhere near on-schedule. Electric utilities have just not moved to collect sulfur gases from their stacks via the sulfuric acid route to any degree at all. A number of copper smelters have improved their operations, resulting in more efficient collection of sulfur gases. While this has resulted in increased acid production at certain locations, in general the copper industry has been hurt badly by producers in South America and Africa who have higher grade ore deposits and often are accused of producing only to generate foreign exchange.

CASE 23 CAMPBELL SOUP COMPANY*

In mid-1985, five years after he had been appointed president and chief executive officer of Campbell Soup Company, Gordon McGovern decided it was time to review the key strategic theme he had initiated—new product development. Shortly after he became Campbell's CEO, McGovern reorganized the company into autonomous business units to foster entrepreneurial attitudes; his ultimate objective was to transform Campbell from a conservative manufacturing company into a consumer-driven, new product-oriented company. As a result of McGovern's push, Campbell had introduced 334 new products in the past five years—more than any other company in the food processing industry.

During the 1970s Campbell's earnings had increased at an annual rate just under 9 percent—a dull performance compared to the 12 percent average growth for the food industry as a whole. With prior management's eyes fixed mainly on production aspects, gradual shifts in consumer buying habits caused Campbell's unit volume growth to flatten. McGovern's five-year campaign for renewed growth via new product introduction had produced good results so far. By year-end 1984 sales were up 31 percent—to $3.7 billion—and earnings had risen by 47 percent—to $191 million. But now it appeared that Campbell's brand managers may have become so involved in new product development that they had neglected the old stand-by products, as well as not meeting cost control and profit margin targets. Campbell's growth in operating earnings for fiscal year 1985 fell far short of McGovern's 15 percent target rate. Failure to control costs and meet earnings targets threatened to leave Campbell without the internal cash flows to fund its new-product strategy. Exhibit 1 offers a summary of Campbell Soup's recent financial performance.

THE FOOD PROCESSING INDUSTRY

In the early 19th century small incomes and low urban population greatly limited the demand for packaged food. In 1859 one industry—grain mills—accounted for over three fifths of the total U.S. food processing. Several industries were in their infancy: evaporated milk, canning, candy, natural extracts, and coffee roasting. From 1860 to 1900 the industry entered a period of development and growth that made food processing the leading manufacturing industry in the United States. The driving forces behind this growth were increased urbanization, cheaper rail transport, and the advent of refrigeration and tin can manufacturing.

At the beginning of the 20th century the food processing industry was highly fragmented; the thousands of local and regional firms were too small to capture scale economies in mass production and distribution as was occurring in other indus-

---

* Prepared by graduate researcher, Sharon Henson, under the supervision of Professor Arthur A. Thompson, The University of Alabama. Copyright © 1986 by Sharon Henson and Arthur A. Thompson.

Exhibit 1 Financial Summary, Campbell Soup Company, 1979–1985 In Thousands of Dollars

	1979	1980	1981	1982	1983	1984	1985
Total sales (includes interdivisional)	n.a.	$2,566,100	$2,865,600	$2,995,800	$3,359,300	$3,744,600	$4,060,800
Net sales (excludes interdivisional)	$2,248,692	2,560,569	2,797,663	2,955,649	3,292,433	3,657,440	3,988,705
Cost of products sold	1,719,134	1,976,754	2,172,806	2,214,214	2,444,213	2,700,751	2,950,204
Marketing and sales expenses	181,229	213,703	256,726	305,700	367,053	428,062	478,341
Administrative and research expenses	94,716	102,445	93,462	136,933	135,855	169,614	194,319
Operating earnings	253,613	276,869	280,355	309,283	349,116	378,316	389,488
Interest—net	1,169	10,135	30,302	21,939	39,307	26,611	32,117
Earnings before taxes	252,444	257,532	244,367	276,863	306,005	332,402	333,724
Taxes on earnings	119,700	122,950	114,650	127,250	141,000	141,200	135,800
Net earnings, after taxes	119,817	134,582	129,717	149,613	165,005	191,202	197,824
Percent of sales	5.3%	5.3%	4.6%	5.1%	5.0%	5.2%	5.0%
Percent of stockholders' equity	13.8%	14.6%	13.2%	14.6%	15.0%	15.9%	15.0%
Per share of common stock	1.80	2.04	2.00	2.32	2.56	2.96	3.06
Dividends declared per share	.86	.93	1.02	1.05	1.09	1.14	1.22
Average shares outstanding	66,720	65,946	64,824	64,495	64,467	64,514	64,572
Salaries, wages, pensions, etc.	$ 543,984	$ 609,979	$ 680,946	$ 700,940	$ 755,073	$ 889,450	$ 950,143
Current assets	680,955	861,845	845,343	921,501	932,099	1,063,330	1,152,761
Working capital	362,187	405,628	368,246	434,627	478,899	541,515	579,490
Plant assets—gross	1,134,571	1,248,735	1,368,663	1,472,693	1,607,634	1,744,866	1,856,122
Accumulated depreciation	520,603	560,730	613,643	657,315	718,478	774,004	828,662
Plant assets purchased and acquired	159,603	155,796	155,275	175,928	178,773	201,864	222,321
Total assets	1,325,823	1,627,565	1,722,876	1,865,519	1,991,526	2,210,115	2,437,525
Long-term debt	36,298	137,879	150,587	236,160	267,465	283,034	297,146
Stockholders' equity	900,017	958,443	1,000,510	1,055,762	1,149,404	1,259,908	1,382,487
Depreciation	60,360	67,958	75,118	83,813	93,189	101,417	119,044

Source: Annual reports of Campbell Soup Company.

Exhibit 2 The Top 15 Companies in the Food Processing Industry, 1985 Millions of Dollars

Company		Sales	Profits	Assets	Return on Common Equity	Example Brands
1. RJR Nabisco	1985	$ 16,595	$2,163	$16,930	20.3%	Nabisco, Del Monte
	1984	12,974	1,619	9,272	22.1	
2. Dart & Kraft	1985	9,942	466	5,502	17.0	Velveeta, Parkay,
	1984	9,759	456	5,285	16.5	Miracle Whip
3. Beatrice	1985	12,595	479	10,379	21.8	Swiss Miss, Wesson,
	1984	9,327	433	4,464	20.4	Tropicana
4. Kellogg	1985	2,930.1	281.1	1,726.1	48.0	Mrs. Smith's, Eggo,
	1984	2,602.4	250.5	1,667.1	27.0	Rice Krispies
5. H. J. Heinz	1985	4,047.9	266	2,473.8	22.6	Star-Kist Tuna,
	1984	3,953.8	237.5	2,343	21.0	Heinz Ketchup
6. Ralston Purina	1985	5,863.9	256.4	2,637.3	26.7	Hostess Twinkies,
	1984	4,980.1	242.7	2,004.2	23.1	Meow Mix
7. Campbell Soup	1985	3,988.7	197.8	2,437.5	15.0	Prego, Le Menu,
	1984	3,657.4	191.2	2,210.1	15.9	Vlasic pickles
8. General Mills	1985	4,285.2	(72.9)	2,662.6	(6.5)	Cheerios, Betty
	1984	5,600.8	233.4	2,858.1	19.0	Crocker
9. Sara Lee	1985	8,117	206	3,216	20.5	Popsicle, Bryan,
	1984	7,000	188	2,822	19.4	Rudy's Farm
10. CPC International	1985	4,209.9	142.0	3,016.6	10.5	Mazola, Skippy,
	1984	4,373.3	193.4	2,683.4	14.7	Hellmann's
11. Borden	1985	4,716.2	193.8	2,932.2	14.3	Wyler's, Bama,
	1984	4,568	182.1	2,767.1	13.7	Cracker Jack
12. Pillsbury	1985	4,670.6	191.8	2,778.5	17.3	Green Giant,
	1984	4,172.3	169.8	2,608.3	17.0	Häagen-Dazs
13. Archer Daniels	1985	4,738.8	163.9	2,967.1	10.8	LaRosa,
	1984	4,907	117.7	2,592.7	NA	Fleischmann's
14. Quaker Oats	1985	3,520.1	156.6	2,662.6	20.3	Gatorade, Van-
	1984	3,334.1	138.7	1,806.8	19.8	Camp's
15. Hershey Foods	1985	1,996.2	112.2	1,197.4	16.6	Delmonico, Hershey's
	1984	1,848.5	108.7	1,122.6	17.3	Chocolate
Industry composite	1985	$101,669	$4,004	$58,294	16.5%	

Ranking by market value of common stock according to *Business Week*, April 18, 1986.
Financial data from annual reports.
NA = Not available.

tries. During the 1920s industry consolidation via acquisition and merger began; the process was evolutionary not revolutionary and continued on into the 1960s and 1970s. Companies such as Del Monte and Kraft, whose names have since become household words, were established, as were the first two multiline food companies— General Foods and Standard Brands (later part of Nabisco Brands). With consolidation came greater production cost efficiency and national market coverages. Following World War II the bigger food companies made moves toward more product differentiation and increased emphasis on advertising. Some became multinational in scope, establishing subsidiaries in many other countries. Starting in the 1960s and continuing into the 1980s the industry went through more consolidation; this time the emphasis was on brand diversification and product line expansion. Acquisition-minded companies shopped for smaller companies with products having strong brand recognition and brand loyalty.

Then in the 1980s giants began acquiring other giants. In 1984 Nestle acquired Carnation for $3 billion. In 1985 R. J. Reynolds purchased Nabisco Brands for $4.9 billion (and then changed its corporate name to RJR Nabisco), and Philip Morris acquired General Foods Corporation for $5.7 billion—the biggest nonoil deal in U.S. industry. In 1985 the U.S. food processing industry had sales over $100 billion and combined net profits of over $4 billion. Exhibit 2 shows data for leading companies in the industry in 1985.

COMPANY BACKGROUND

Campbell Soup Company was one of the world's leading manufacturers and marketers of branded consumer food products. In 1985 the company had approximately 44,000 employees and 80 manufacturing plants in 12 nations, with over 1,000 products on the market. Its major products were Prego spaghetti sauces, Le Menu frozen dinners, Pepperidge Farm baked goods, Mrs. Paul's frozen foods, Franco-American canned spaghettis, Vlasic pickles, and its flagship red-and-white-label canned soups.

Founded in 1869 by Joseph Campbell, a fruit merchant, and Abram Anderson, an ice box maker, the company was originally known for its jams and jellies. In 1891 it was incorporated as the Joseph Campbell Co. in Camden, New Jersey. In 1899 John T. Dorrance, a brilliant 24-year-old with a Ph.D. from MIT, developed a process for canning soup in condensed form. He was also a master salesman who came up with the idea of attaching snappy placards to the sides of New York City streetcars as a way of promoting the company's products.

From 1900 to 1954 the company was owned entirely by the Dorrance family. It was incorporated as the Campbell Soup Company in 1922. When Dorrance died in 1930 after running the company for 16 years, he left an estate of over $115 million, the third-largest up to that time. He also left a company devoted to engineering, committed to supplying value (in recessions it would rather shave margins than lower quality or raise prices), and obsessed with secrecy. John T. Dorrance, Jr., ran the company for the next 24 years (1930-54) and few, if any, important decisions were made at Campbell without his approval. In 1954 the company went public, with the Dorrance family retaining majority control. In 1985 the Dorrance family still held about 60 percent of Campbell's stock and picked the top executives of the company. In 1984 John Dorrance III became a member of the board. The more than eight decades of family dominance contributed to what some insiders described as a conservative and paternalistic company culture at Campbell.

Over the years Campbell had diversified into a number of food and food-related businesses—Swanson frozen dinners, Pepperidge Farm bakery products, Franco-American spaghetti products, Recipe pet food, fast-food restaurant chains, Godiva chocolates, and even retail garden centers. Still, about half of the company's revenues came from the sale of its original stock-in-trade: canned soup. Throughout most of its history, the company picked its top executives from among those with a production background in the soup division—most had engineering training and good track records in furthering better manufacturing efficiency. One such person, Harold A. Shaub, a 30-year veteran of the company, was named president in 1972. An industrial engineer, Shaub placed a premium on controlling production cost while maintaining acceptable product quality. There were occasions when Shaub, during unannounced inspection tours, had shut down a complete plant that didn't measure up to the strict standards he demanded.

During his tenure Shaub began to set the stage for change at Campbell, acknowledging that "The company needed changes for the changing times."[2]* He restructured the company into divisions built around major product lines. Then in 1978, realizing that Campbell's marketing skills were too weak, he hired aggressive outsiders to revitalize the company's marketing efforts. That same year Campbell purchased Vlasic Foods, Inc., the largest producer of pickles in the United States.

Also in 1978 Campbell launched Prego spaghetti sauce products, the first major new food items introduced by Campbell in 10 years. The former Campbell policy required that a new product had to show a profit within a year and the pay-out on Prego was expected to be three years. But because the policy held back new product development, Shaub changed it and set a goal of introducing two additional products each year.

In 1980 Campbell broke a 111-year-old debt-free tradition, issuing $100 million in 10-year notes. Until then the company had relied primarily on internally generated funds to meet long-term capital requirements.

Because of company tradition, everyone expected Shaub's successor to come from production. Thus it came as a surprise to Gordon McGovern, president of Connecticut-based Pepperidge Farm and a marketing man, when Shaub called him into his office and said, "I'd like you to come down here and take my place."[1] When McGovern became Campbell's president and CEO on December 1, 1980, Shaub remained on the board of directors.

McGovern was at Pepperidge Farm when the company was bought by Campbell in 1961. He was in business school when Margaret Rudkin, founder of Pepperidge Farm, spoke to his class. She told how she had built her bread company from scratch in an industry dominated by giants. McGovern was impressed. He wrote to Rudkin for a job, received it in 1956, and began his climb through the ranks. When Campbell acquired Pepperidge Farm in 1961 it had sales of $40 million. When McGovern became its president in 1968 sales had reached $60 million. When he left to become president of Campbell in 1980, Pepperidge Farms' sales had climbed to $300 million. McGovern brought some of what he considered Pepperidge's success strategy with him to Campbell: experimentation, new product development, marketing savvy, and creativity.

MANAGEMENT UNDER McGOVERN

Every Saturday morning McGovern did his family's grocery shopping, stopping to straighten Campbell's displays and inspect those of competitors, studying packaging and reading labels, and trying to learn all he could about how and what people were eating. He encouraged his managers to do the same. Several board meetings

---

* Numbers in brackets refer to references listed at the end of this case.

were held in the backrooms of supermarkets so that afterward directors could roam the store aisles interviewing customers about Campbell products.

McGovern's style of management was innovative to a company known as much for its stodginess as for its red and white soup can. For decades Campbell Soup operated under strict rules of decorum. Eating, smoking, or drinking coffee was not permitted in the office. Managers had to share their offices with their secretaries, and an unwritten rule required executives to keep their suitcoats on in the office. When McGovern joined Campbell he drove to work in a yellow Volkswagen that stuck out in his parking space so much that the garagemen quietly arranged to have it painted. Finding the atmosphere at headquarters stifling, he promised a change.

He began wandering through the corridors every day, mingling easily among the employees. McGovern's voluble personality and memory for names made him popular with many employees. But not everyone was impressed by McGovern's style. Some production people were suspicious of his marketing background. Others believed that his grocery trips and hobnobbing with employees were ploys calculated to win him support and a reputation. But McGovern pressed forward with several internal changes: (1) a day care center for the children of employees (complete with Campbell Kids posters on the wall), (2) a health program including workouts in a gymnasium, and (3) an unusual new benefit program which covered adoption expenses up to $1,000 and gave time off to employees who adopted children—in the same way that women were given maternity leave. He appointed the first two women vice presidents in the company's history; one of these, a former director of the Good Housekeeping Institute, was hired to identify consumers' food preferences and needs.

McGovern decentralized Campbell management to facilitate entrepreneurial risk-taking and new product development, devising a new compensation program to reward these traits. He restructured the company into some 50 autonomous units and divided the U.S. division into eight strategic profit centers: soups, beverages, pet foods, frozen foods, fresh produce, main meals, grocery, and food service. Units were encouraged to develop new products even if another unit would actually produce the products. Thus, the Prego spaghetti sauce unit—not the frozen food group—initiated frozen Mexican dinners. And although it wasn't his job, the director of market research created "Today's Taste," a line of refrigerated entrees and side dishes. "It's like things are in constant motion," the director said. "We are overloaded, but it's fun."[3]

The new structure encouraged managers, who had to compete for corporate funding, to be more aggressive in developing promising products. According to McGovern:

> These integral units allow the company to really get its arms around chunks of the business. The managers are answerable to the bottom line—to their investments, their hiring, their products—and it's a great motivation for performance.[4]

As part of this motivation, Campbell began annually allotting around $30 million to $40 million to support new ventures, each requiring a minimum of $10 million. This strategy was intended to encourage star performers while enabling management to weed out laggards. McGovern felt that this was much easier to determine when everyone knew where the responsibilities lay—but that it was no disgrace to fail if the effort was a good one. An employee noted that McGovern was endorsing "the right to fail," adding that "it makes the atmosphere so much more positive."[4]

Every Friday McGovern held meetings to discuss new products. The fact-finding sessions were attended by financial, marketing, engineering, and sales personnel. Typical McGovern questions included: "Would you eat something like that?" "Why not?" "Have you tried the competition's product?" "Is there a consumer niche?" The marketing research director noted that in Shaub's meetings the question was "Can we make such a product cost-effectively?"[3]

Under Shaub the chain of command was inviolable, but McGovern was not hesitant about circumventing the chain when he felt it was warranted. He criticized one manager's product to another manager, expecting word to get back to the one with the problem. Although this often motivated some to prove McGovern wrong, others were unnerved by such tactics. When he became aware of this, McGovern eased up a bit.

In the past under prior CEOs, cost-cutters got promoted; now in McGovern's more creative atmosphere, the rules weren't so well defined. As one insider put it, "There's a great deal of uncertainty. No one really knows what it takes to get ahead. But that makes us all work harder."[3]

When hiring managers McGovern, himself a college baseball player, tended to favor people with a competitive sports background. "There's teamwork and determination, but also the idea that you know how to lose and get back up again. 'Try, try, try' is what I say. I can't stress how important that is."[4]

STRATEGY

The strategic focus was on the consumer—considered to be the key to Campbell's growth and success in the 1980s. The consumer's "hot buttons" were identified as nutrition, convenience, low sodium, price, quality, and uniqueness—and managers were urged to "press those buttons." General managers were advised to take into account the consumer's perceptions, needs, and demands regarding nutrition, safety, flavor, and convenience. Key strategies were: (1) improving operating efficiency, (2) developing new products for the modern consumer, (3) updating advertising for new and established products, and (4) high quality.

When he took over, McGovern developed a five-year plan that included four financial performance objectives: a 15 percent annual increase in earnings, a 5 percent increase in volume, a 5 percent increase in sales (plus inflation), and an 18 percent return on equity by 1986. His long-range strategy included making acquisitions every two years that would bring in $200 million in annual sales. Campbell's acquisition strategy was to look for small, fast-growing food companies strong in product areas where Campbell was not and companies on the fast track that were in rapidly growing parts of their industries. Under McGovern Campbell made a number of acquisitions:

1982 • Mrs. Paul's Kitchens, Inc., a processor and marketer of frozen prepared seafood and vegetable products, with annual sales of approximately $125 million (acquired at a cost of $55 million).

• Snow King Frozen Foods, Inc., engaged in the production and marketing of a line of uncooked frozen specialty meat products, with annual sales of $32 million.

• Juice Bowl Products, Inc., a Florida producer of fruit juices.

• Win Schuler Foods, Inc., a Michigan-based producer and distributor of specialty cheese spreads, flavored melba rounds, food service salad dressings, party dips and sauces, with annual sales of $6.5 million.

Exhibit 3   Examples of Major Acquisitions in the Food Processing Industry, 1982–1985

Buyer	Acquired Company	Year	Price (millions of dollars)	Products/Brands Acquired
Beatrice	Esmark	1984	$2,800	Swift, Hunt-Wesson brands
CPC	C. F. Mueller	1983	122	Makes CPC biggest U.S. pasta maker
ConAgra	Peavey	1982	NA	Jams & syrups
	ACLI Seafood	1983	NA	
	Armour Food	1983	166	Processed meats
	Imperial Foods' Country Poultry	1984	18	
Dart & Kraft	Celestial Seasonings	1984	25	Herbal teas
Esmark	Norton Simon	1983	1,100	Hunt-Wesson
General Foods	Entenmann's	1982	315	Baked goods
	Otto Roth	1983	NA	Specialty cheeses
	Monterey	1983	NA	
	Peacock Foods	1983	NA	
	Ronzoni	1984	NA	Pasta
	Oroweat	1984	60	Bread
McCormick	Patterson Jenks	1984	53	Major British spice and food distributor
Nestle	Carnation	1984	3,000	Evaporated milk, Friskies pet food
Philip Morris	General Foods	1985	5,750	Jell-O, Maxwell House
Pillsbury	Häagen-Dazs	1983	75	Ice cream
	Sedutto	1984	5	
Quaker Oats	Stokely-Van Camp	1983	238	Baked beans, canned goods
Ralston Purina	Continental Baking	1984	475	Hostess Twinkies, Wonder Bread
R. J. Reynolds	Nabisco Foods	1984	4,900	Oreo cookies, Ritz crackers,
	Canada Dry	1984	175	ginger ale, soda, tonic

NA = Not available.
Data compiled from various sources.

- Costa Apple Products, Inc., a producer of apple juice retailed primarily in the Eastern United States, with annual sales of $6 million.

1983
- Acquired several small domestic operations at a cost of $26 million, including:
- Annabelle's restaurant chain of 12 units in the southeastern United States.
- Triangle Manufacturing Corp., a manufacturer of physical fitness and sports medicine products.

1984
- Mendelson-Zeller Co., Inc., a California distributor of fresh produce.

1985
- Continental Foods Company S.A. and affiliated companies which produced sauces, confectioneries, and other food products in Beligum and France; the cost of the acquisition was $17 million.

Campbell was by no means alone in adding companies to its portfolio; many major mergers in the food industry were taking place (see Exhibit 3). Several factors were at work:

- Many food companies had been stung by ill-fated diversification forays outside food. In the 1960s when industry growth had slowed, it was fashionable to diversify into nonfoods. Many of the acquired companies turned out to be duds, draining earnings and soaking up too much top management attention. Now food companies were refocusing their efforts on food—the business they knew best.
- Even though the food industry was regarded as a slow-growth/low-margin business, the fact remained that stable demand, moderate capital costs, and high cash flows had boosted returns on equity to almost 20 percent for some companies. Food processors discovered that they were earning better returns on their food products than they were earning in the nonfood businesses they had earlier diversified into.

While companies such as Beatrice, the nation's largest food company, and Nestle, the world's largest, paid substantial sums to buy out large established companies with extensive brand stables, others—such as Campbell—followed the route of concentrating on internal product development and smaller, selective acquisitions to complement their existing product lines. In fact Campbell was considered the leader among the food processors who were striving to limit acquisitions in favor of heavy, in-house product development. Campbell's emphasis on new product development was not without risk. It took $10 to $15 million in advertising and couponing to launch a brand. Because of the hit-or-miss nature of new products, only about one out of eight products reaching the test market stage were successful. Moreover, industry analysts predicted that the continuing introduction of new products would lead to increased competition for shelf space and for the consumer's food dollar.

MARKETING

The outsiders Shaub had hired to revitalize Campbell's marketing included a vice president for marketing who was an eight-year veteran of a New York advertising firm and a soup general manager who was a former Wharton business school professor. In addition to those hired by Shaub, the rest of McGovern's marketing-oriented executive team included: a frozen foods manager (a former marketing manager with General Foods), the head of the Pepperidge Farm division, and the head of the Vlasic Foods division (both marketing men from Borden). This team boosted Campbell's marketing budget to $428 million by 1984 (up 57 percent from 1982). Advertising spending grew from $67 million in 1980 to $179 million in 1985. Prior to McGovern, Campbell used to cut ad spending at the end of a quarter to boost earnings. Besides hurting the brands, it gave the company an unfavorable reputation among the media. In 1985 the marketing expenditures (including advertising and promotion) of some of the leading food companies were: Campbell—approximately $488 million, Quaker—$619 million, Heinz—$303 million, Pillsbury—$365 million, and Sara Lee—$594 million.

In 1982 McGovern was named *Advertising Age's* Adman of the Year for his efforts in transforming Campbell into "one of the most aggressive market-driven companies in the food industry today."[4] *Advertising Age* noted that McGovern had almost doubled the advertising budget and had replaced the company's longtime ad agency for its soups, leading to a new ad campaign that helped reverse eight years of flat or lower sales. The new campaign emphasized nutrition and fitness, as opposed to the former "mmm,mmm,good" emphasis on taste. Print ads included long copy that referred to major government research studies citing soup's nutritional values. The new slogan was: "Soup is good food." New products and advertising were aimed at shoppers who were dieting, health conscious, and usually in a hurry. In keeping with the new fitness image, the 80-year-old Campbell Kids, although still cerubic, acquired a leaner look. Campbell's marketing strategy under McGovern was based on several important market research findings and projections:

- Women now comprised 43 percent of the workforce and a level of 50 percent was projected by 1990.
- Two-income marriages represented 60 percent of all U.S. families. These would take in three out of every five dollars earned.
- Upper-income households would grow 3.5 times faster than total household formations.
- More than half of all households consisted of only one or two members.
- There were 18 million singles, and 23 percent of all households contained only one person.
- The average age of the population was advancing with the number of senior citizens totaling 25 million-plus and increasing.
- The percentage of meals eaten at home was declining.
- Nearly half of the adult meal-planners in the United States were watching their weight.
- Poultry consumption had increased 26 percent since 1973.
- Ethnic food preparation at home was increasing, with 40 percent, 21 percent, and 14 percent of households preparing Italian, Mexican, and Oriental foods, respectively, at home from scratch.
- There was growing consumer concern with food avoidance: sugar, salt, calories, chemicals, cholesterol, and additives.
- The "I am what I eat" philosophy had tied food in to lifestyles along with Nautilus machines, hot tubs, jogging, racquet ball, backpacking, cross-country skiing, and aerobic dancing.

In response to growing ethnic food demand, Campbell began marketing ethnic selections in regions where interests were highest for particular food types. For instance, it marketed spicy Ranchero Beans only in the south and southwest and planned to market newly acquired Puerto Rican foods in New York City.

The product development priorities were aimed at the themes of convenience, taste, flavor, and texture. The guidelines were:

- Prepare and market products that represent superior value to consumers and constantly strive to improve those values.
- Develop products that help build markets.
- Develop products that return a fair profit to Campbell and to customers.

In support of these guidelines, Campbell adopted several tactics:

- Use ongoing consumer research to determine eating habits by checking home menus, recipe preparation, and foods that are served together. Study meal and snack eating occasions to determine which household members participate so that volume potential can be determined for possible new products and product improvement ideas.

- Develop new products and produce them in small quantities that simulate actual plant production capabilities.
- Test new or improved products in a large enough number of households which are so distributed throughout the United States that results can be projected nationally. Once the product meets pretest standards, recommend it for market testing.
- Once packaging and labels have been considered, design and pretest introductory promotion and advertising.
- Introduce a new product into selected test markets to determine actual store sales which can be projected nationally.
- If test marketing proves successful, roll out the new product on a regional or national plan using test market data as a rationale for expansion.

A key part of the strategy was the "Campbell in the Kitchen" project, consisting of some 75 homemakers across the country. Three to five times a year Campbell asked this "focus group" to try different products and give opinions. McGovern regularly dispatched company executives to the kitchens of these homemakers to observe eating patterns and see how meals were prepared. He sent Campbell's home economists into some of the households to work with the cooks on a one-to-one basis.

All this was in sharp contrast to the preMcGovern era. Campbell averaged about 18 new product entries a year through the late 1970s. Many of these were really line extensions rather than new products. Substantial numbers flopped, partly because they had often been subjected to only the most rudimentary and inexpensive tests. Sometimes the testing had consisted only of a panel of the company's advertising and business executives sipping from teaspoons.

In 1983 Campbell was the biggest new products generator in the combined food and health and beauty aids categories with a total of 42 new products. Second was Esmark, 36; followed by Lever/Lipton, 33; Nabisco Brands, 25; Beatrice and General Foods, 24 each; American Home Products, 23; Quaker Oats, 21; Borden, 19, and General Mills and Noxell, 17 each. Exhibit 4 shows Campbell's leading new products from 1982 to 1985.

Exhibit 4   Campbell's Leading New Products   Total $600 Million in Sales for Fiscal 1985

1985 Ranking	Year Introduced
Le Menu Frozen Dinner	1982
Prego Spaghetti Sauce	1982
Chunky New England Clam Chowder	1984
Great Starts Breakfasts	1984
Prego Plus	1985

Source: *The Wall Street Journal*, August 14, 1985.

PRODUCTION

McGovern summarized Campbell's philosophy on quality: "I want zero defects. If we can't produce quality, we'll get out of the business." [5] In 1984 Campbell held its first Worldwide Corporate Conference dedicated to quality. Hundreds of Campbell managers from all levels and most company locations spent three days at this conference. Campbell believed that the ultimate test of quality was consumer satisfaction and its goal was to maintain a quality-conscious organization at every employee level in every single operation.

Before McGovern took over, Campbell used to emphasize new products compatible with existing production facilities. For example, a square omelet was designed for Swanson's frozen breakfasts because it was what the machine would make. After McGovern's appointment, although low-cost production was still a strategic factor, consumer trends—and not existing machinery—were the deciding factors for new product development. Other important factors considered in the production process included:

- The growing move toward consumption of refrigerated and fresh produce in contrast to canned or frozen products.
- The emerging perception that private label and/or generic label merchandise would drive out weak national and secondary brands unless there was a clear product superiority and excellent price/value on the part of the brands supported by consumer advertising.
- The polarization of food preparation time with long preparation on weekends and special occasions, but fast preparation in between via microwaves, quick foods, and instant breakfasts.
- The cost of the package—especially metal packaging—which was outrunning the cost of the product it contained.
- Energy and distribution costs—these were big targets for efficiency with regional production, aseptic packaging, and packages designed for automatic warehouse handling and lightweight containers becoming standard.

The bulk of $154 million in capital expenditures in 1983 went into improvement of production equipment, expenditures for additional production capacity, the completion of the $100 million canned foods plant in North Carolina, and the start of a mushroom-producing facility at Dublin, Georgia. In 1984 construction began on a $9 million Le Menu production line in Sumter, South Carolina. Capital expenditures in 1985 totaled $213 million. Most of this went into improvements of production equipment, packaging technology, and expenditures for additional production capacity.

Campbell was considered a model of manufacturing efficiency. Production was fully integrated from the tomato patch to the canmaking factory. Campbell was the nation's third largest can manufacturer behind American Can Company and Continental Group. Yet Campbell, which made the red and white soup can with the gold medallion an American institution, had recently concluded that food packaging was headed in the direction of snazzier and more convenient containers. McGovern compared sticking with the can to the refusal of U.S. automobile makers to change their ways in the face of the Japanese challenge:

There's a tremendous feeling of urgency because an overseas company could come in here with innovative packaging and technology and just take us to the cleaners on basic lines we've taken for granted for years. [6]

Other soup companies—including Libby, McNeill & Libby, a Nestlé Enterprises, Inc., unit that made Crosse & Blackwell gourmet soup—had already started experimenting with can alternatives. Campbell's testing was considered the most advanced, but a mistake could mean revamping production facilities at a cost of $100 million or more.

Researchers at the Campbell Soup Company's DNA Plant Technology Corporation were working toward the development of the "perfect tomato." They were seeking ways to grow tasty, high solids tomatoes under high-temperature conditions that would cause normal plants to droop and wither. They also hoped to crossbreed high quality domestic tomatoes with tough, hardy, wild tomatoes that could withstand cold weather. A breakthrough in this area could result in two harvests a year. Conceding that they were latecomers (Heinz began similar research several years after Campbell), Campbell researchers estimated that they were four to five years ahead of Heinz.

Campbell believed its key strengths were: (1) a worldwide system for obtaining ingredients, (2) a broad range of food products that could be used as a launching pad for further innovation, and (3) an emphasis on low-cost production.

Exhibit 5   Sales and Earnings of Campbell Soup, by Division, 1980–1985   Millions of Dollars

	1980	*1981*	*1982*	*1983*	*1984*	*1985*
Campbell U.S.:						
Sales	$1,608	$1,678	$1,773	$1,987	$2,282	$2,500
Operating earnings	205	190	211	250	278	292
Pepperidge Farm:						
Sales	283	329	392	433	435	426
Operating earnings	29	35	41	43	35	39
Vlasic Foods:						
Sales	130	137	149	168	193	199
Operating earnings	8	10	12	13	14	16
Mrs. Paul's Kitchens:						
Sales				108	126	138
Operating earnings				10	14	11
Other United States:						
Sales	35	27	56	64	84	81
Operating earnings	1	(1)	(1)	(1)	(2)	(3)
International:						
Sales	512	694	643	599	624	716
Operating earnings	33	46	46	33	34	35

Source: Campbell's annual reports.

CAMPBELL'S OPERATING DIVISIONS

Campbell Soup Company was divided into six operating units—Campbell U.S., Pepperidge Farm, Vlasic Foods, Mrs. Paul's Kitchens, Other United States, and International. Sales and profit performance by division are shown in Exhibit 5.

CAMPBELL U.S.

In 1985 the Campbell U.S. Division was Campbell's largest operating unit, accounting for almost 62 percent of the company's total consolidated sales. Operating earnings increased 5 percent over 1984. Unit volume rose 7 percent in 1983, 9 percent in 1984, and 4 percent in 1985. The Campbell U.S. division was divided into eight profit centers: Soup, Frozen Foods, Grocery Business, Beverage Business, Food Service Business, Poultry Business, Fresh Produce Business, and Pet Foods Business. Exhibit 6 shows the brands Campbell had in this division and the major competitors each brand faced.

The soup business group alone accounted for more than 25 percent of the company's consolidated sales (as compared to around 50 percent in the 1970s). Campbell's flagship brands of soups accounted for 80 percent of the $1 billion-plus annual canned soup market; in 1985 Campbell offered grocery shoppers over 50 varieties of canned soups. Heinz was second with 10 percent of the market. Heinz had earlier withdrawn from producing Heinz-label soup and shifted its production over to making soups for sale under the private labels of grocery chains; Heinz was the leading private-label producer of canned soup, holding almost an 80 percent share of the private-label segment. See Exhibit 6 for information on competitors and their brands.

Although the soup business was relatively mature (McGovern preferred to call it underworked), Campbell's most ambitious consumer research took place in this unit. McGovern planned to speed up soup sales by turning out a steady flow of new varieties in convenient packages: "Ethnic, dried, refrigerated, frozen, microwave—you name it, we're going to try it." (7)

In 1985 Campbell began an assault on the $290 million dry-soup mix market dominated by Thomas J. Lipton Inc., a unit of the Anglo-Dutch Unilever Group. This move was made because dry-soup sales in the United States were growing faster than sales of canned soup. Lipton's aggressive response to test marketing of an early Campbell dry-soup product resulted in Campbell's rushing a six-flavor line into national distribution ahead of schedule.

In 1982 McGovern caused a stir when he announced publicly that Campbell's Swanson TV-dinner line was "junk food": "It was great in 1950, but in today's world it didn't go into the microwave; it didn't represent variety or a good eating experience to my palate." [7] He maintained that consumers had discovered high-quality options to the TV-dinner concept. The market niche for more exotic, better quality entrees was being exploited by Nestle's Stouffer subsidiary and Pillsbury's Green Giant division (Exhibit 6).

Campbell's Frozen Foods group answered the challenge by producing its own frozen gourmet line, Le Menu. Campbell committed about $50 million in manufactur-

Exhibit 6   The Campbell U.S. Division; Products, Rival Brands, Competitors

Division   Product/brand   Rival brands (competing company or brand owner)

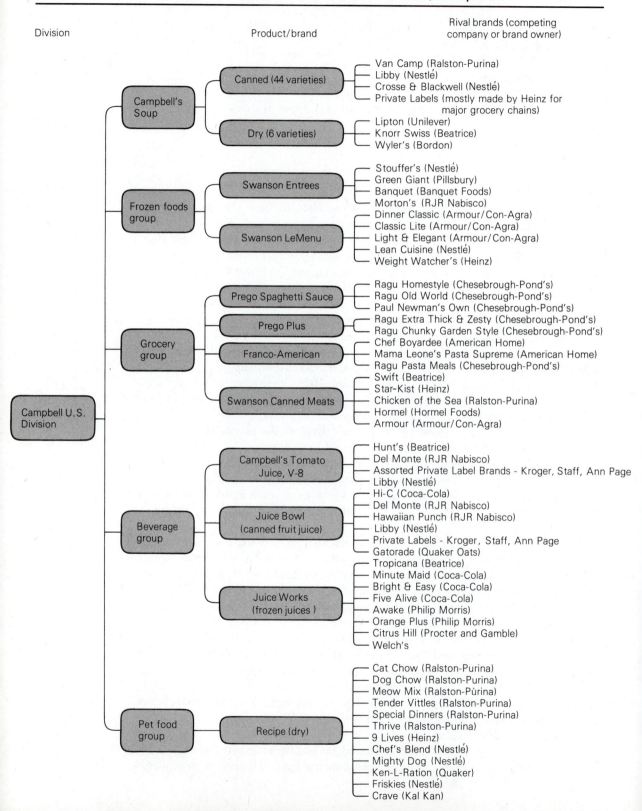

Campbell U.S. Division

Campbell's Soup

- Canned (44 varieties)
  - Van Camp (Ralston-Purina)
  - Libby (Nestlé)
  - Crosse & Blackwell (Nestlé)
  - Private Labels (mostly made by Heinz for major grocery chains)
- Dry (6 varieties)
  - Lipton (Unilever)
  - Knorr Swiss (Beatrice)
  - Wyler's (Bordon)

Frozen foods group

- Swanson Entrees
  - Stouffer's (Nestlé)
  - Green Giant (Pillsbury)
  - Banquet (Banquet Foods)
  - Morton's (RJR Nabisco)
- Swanson LeMenu
  - Dinner Classic (Armour/Con-Agra)
  - Classic Lite (Armour/Con-Agra)
  - Light & Elegant (Armour/Con-Agra)
  - Lean Cuisine (Nestlé)
  - Weight Watcher's (Heinz)

Grocery group

- Prego Spaghetti Sauce
  - Ragu Homestyle (Chesebrough-Pond's)
  - Ragu Old World (Chesebrough-Pond's)
  - Paul Newman's Own (Chesebrough-Pond's)
- Prego Plus
  - Ragu Extra Thick & Zesty (Chesebrough-Pond's)
  - Ragu Chunky Garden Style (Chesebrough-Pond's)
- Franco-American
  - Chef Boyardee (American Home)
  - Mama Leone's Pasta Supreme (American Home)
  - Ragu Pasta Meals (Chesebrough-Pond's)
- Swanson Canned Meats
  - Swift (Beatrice)
  - Star-Kist (Heinz)
  - Chicken of the Sea (Ralston-Purina)
  - Hormel (Hormel Foods)
  - Armour (Armour/Con-Agra)

Beverage group

- Campbell's Tomato Juice, V-8
  - Hunt's (Beatrice)
  - Del Monte (RJR Nabisco)
  - Assorted Private Label Brands - Kroger, Staff, Ann Page
  - Libby (Nestlé)
- Juice Bowl (canned fruit juice)
  - Hi-C (Coca-Cola)
  - Del Monte (RJR Nabisco)
  - Hawaiian Punch (RJR Nabisco)
  - Libby (Nestlé)
  - Private Labels - Kroger, Staff, Ann Page
  - Gatorade (Quaker Oats)
- Juice Works (frozen juices)
  - Tropicana (Beatrice)
  - Minute Maid (Coca-Cola)
  - Bright & Easy (Coca-Cola)
  - Five Alive (Coca-Cola)
  - Awake (Philip Morris)
  - Orange Plus (Philip Morris)
  - Citrus Hill (Procter and Gamble)
  - Welch's

Pet food group

- Recipe (dry)
  - Cat Chow (Ralston-Purina)
  - Dog Chow (Ralston-Purina)
  - Meow Mix (Ralston-Pùrina)
  - Tender Vittles (Ralston-Purina)
  - Special Dinners (Ralston-Purina)
  - Thrive (Ralston-Purina)
  - 9 Lives (Heinz)
  - Chef's Blend (Nestlé)
  - Mighty Dog (Nestlé)
  - Ken-L-Ration (Quaker)
  - Friskies (Nestlé)
  - Crave (Kal Kan)

ing, marketing, and trade promotion costs on the basis of encouraging marketing tests. In the five years prior to Le Menu, Swanson's sales volume had slipped 16 percent, its biggest volume decline (23 percent) was in the area that had been its stronghold: sales of dinners and entrees. Overall industry sales in dinners and entrees grew to $2 billion during 1982. The single dish entree market had increased 58 percent since 1978 with sales being dominated by Stouffer's Lean Cuisine selections.

Le Menu—served on round heatable plates and consisting of such delicacies as chicken cordon bleu, al dente vegetables, and sophisticated wine sauces—produced 20 percent growth in the frozen meal unit with sales of $150 million during its first year of national distribution (1984). This was double Campbell's earlier projection of sales.

Under Project Fix Swanson dinners were overhauled, putting in less salt and more meat stock in gravies and adding new desserts and sauces. The revamped line had new packaging and a redesigned logo. The Frozen Foods Business Unit reported an overall volume increase of 3 percent in 1983, 27 percent in 1984, and 2 percent in 1985. In 1985 the unit had a 52 percent increase in operating earnings as sales rose 10 percent.

Meanwhile, Pillsbury had targeted the $4 billion-a-year frozen main meal market and the rapidly expanding market in light meals and snacks as vital to its future. In 1984 Pillsbury purchased Van de Kamp's, a market leader in frozen seafood and ethnic entrees for $102 million. During 1985 Van de Kamp's became the number one seller of frozen Mexican meals. Pillsbury also sold more than one third of the 550 million frozen pizzas consumed in the United States in 1985 and made substantial investments in quality improvements and marketing support to maintain the number one position in frozen pizza.

The Grocery Business Unit's star was Prego Spaghetti Sauce that in 1984 had obtained 25 percent of the still growing spaghetti sauce market and was the number two sauce, behind Chesebrough-Pond's Ragu. (Exhibit 6 lists competing brands.) Chesebrough had recently introduced Ragu Chunky Gardenstyle sauce to try to convert cooks who still made their own sauce (about 45 percent of all spaghetti sauce users still cooked their own from scratch). The new Ragu product came in three varieties: mushrooms and onions, green peppers and mushrooms, and extra tomatoes with garlic and onions. Campbell had no plans for a similar entry because copying Ragu wouldn't be innovative. However, a Prego Plus Spaghetti Sauce line completed its first year of national distribution in 1985. To show "old-fashioned concern," all three sizes of Prego sauce came in jars with tamper-evident caps; Campbell would buy back from grocery shelves all jars that had been opened.

The Beverage Group's 1985 operating earnings were affected by a slower-than-anticipated introduction of Juice Works—a line of 100 percent natural, no-sugar-added, pure, blended fruit juices for children. This was attributed to intense competitive pressure and major technological problems. Campbell's Tomato Juice and V-8 Cocktail Vegetable Juice also reported disappointing earnings. Juice Bowl, however, showed improved earnings in 1985. Campbell's competition in this area came from Hunt's, Del Monte, and private label brands (Exhibit 6).

The Poultry Business Unit sales were up 13 percent in 1985. Operating earnings for the year were positive, compared to a loss in 1984. These results stemmed from the national rollout of frozen "finger foods"—Plump & Juicy Dipsters, Drumlets, and Cutlets—and sales of Premium Chunk White Chicken. Some of the competitors were Banquet's Chicken Drum-Snackers and Tyson's Chick'n Dippers.

PEPPERIDGE FARM

Pepperidge Farm, Campbell's second-largest division with 12 percent of the company's consolidated sales, reported a decline in operating income and a sales gain of less than 1 percent between 1983 and 1984. In 1980 it was one of the fastest growing units; sales had risen 14 percent annually, compounded.

1984's disappointing results were largely blamed on losses incurred in the apple juice (Costa Apple Products, Inc., purchased in 1982) and "Star Wars" cookies businesses. When Pepperidge Farm introduced Star Wars cookies, McGovern called them a "travesty" because they were faddish and did not fit the brand's high-quality, upscale adult image. Plus, at $1.39 a bag, he maintained that it was a "lousy value." But he didn't veto them because, "I could be wrong." [6] As the popularity of the movie series waned, so did sales.

The frozen biscuit and bakery business unit volume was also down. New products such as Vegetables in Pastry and Deli's reportedly did not receive enough marketing support.

To remedy the division's growth decline, a number of steps were taken:

- Apple juice operations were transferred to the Campbell U.S. Division Beverage Unit.
- During the year Pepperidge divested itself of operations that no longer fit into its strategic plan, including Lexington Gardens, Inc., a garden center chain.
- Deli's went back into research and development to improve quality.
- By the start of the 1985 fiscal year a new management team was in place and a comprehensive review of each product was being conducted in a effort to return emphasis to traditional product lines and quality standards which accounted for its success and growth in the past.

At the end of 1985 Pepperidge Farm showed an 11 percent increase in operating earnings over the previous year in spite of a 2 percent drop in sales. This was considered a result of the transfer of Pepperidge Farm beverage operations to the Campbell U.S. Beverage Group and the sale of the Lexington Gardens nursery chain. During 1985 sales in the Confectionery Business Unit increased 22 percent and seven Godiva boutiques were added. Goldfish Crackers and Puff Pastry contributed to a volume increase in the Food Service Business Unit, while some varieties of Deli's and the Snack Bar products were discontinued.

One of Pepperidge Farm's major competitors in frozen bakery products was Sara Lee, which had 40 percent of the frozen sweet goods market and an ever-increasing 33 percent share of the specialty breads category. Pepperidge Farm's fresh breads and specialty items competed against a host of local, regional, and national brands. Exhibit 7 presents more details.

Exhibit 7   The Pepperidge Farm Division: Products, Rival Brands, Competitors

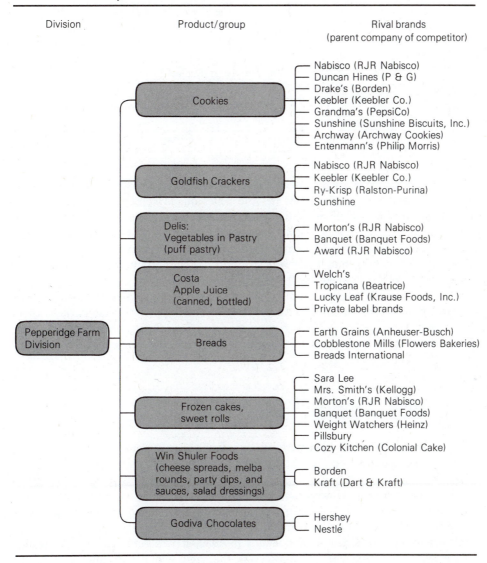

Division	Product/group	Rival brands (parent company of competitor)
Pepperidge Farm Division	Cookies	Nabisco (RJR Nabisco) Duncan Hines (P & G) Drake's (Borden) Keebler (Keebler Co.) Grandma's (PepsiCo) Sunshine (Sunshine Biscuits, Inc.) Archway (Archway Cookies) Entenmann's (Philip Morris)
	Goldfish Crackers	Nabisco (RJR Nabisco) Keebler (Keebler Co.) Ry-Krisp (Ralston-Purina) Sunshine
	Delis: Vegetables in Pastry (puff pastry)	Morton's (RJR Nabisco) Banquet (Banquet Foods) Award (RJR Nabisco)
	Costa Apple Juice (canned, bottled)	Welch's Tropicana (Beatrice) Lucky Leaf (Krause Foods, Inc.) Private label brands
	Breads	Earth Grains (Anheuser-Busch) Cobblestone Mills (Flowers Bakeries) Breads International
	Frozen cakes, sweet rolls	Sara Lee Mrs. Smith's (Kellogg) Morton's (RJR Nabisco) Banquet (Banquet Foods) Weight Watchers (Heinz) Pillsbury Cozy Kitchen (Colonial Cake)
	Win Shuler Foods (cheese spreads, melba rounds, party dips, and sauces, salad dressings)	Borden Kraft (Dart & Kraft)
	Godiva Chocolates	Hershey Nestlé

VLASIC FOODS

Campbell's third largest domestic division enjoyed an 11 percent increase in operating earnings in 1985. Vlasic maintained its number one position with a 31 percent share of the pickles market. Seventeen percent of Vlasic's sales were in the food service category.

Exhibit 8   Vlasic Division: Products, Rival Brands, and Competitors

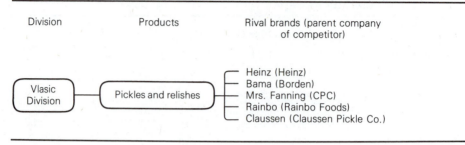

In 1985 Vlasic implemented new labels which used color bands and a flavor rating scale to help consumers find their favorite tastes quickly on the supermarket shelf. Taking advantage of their marketing research, which indicated consumer desires for new and interesting flavors, Vlasic introduced "Zesty Dills" and "Bread & Butter Whole Pickle" lines in 1985. Heinz was Campbell's leading national competitor in this area (Exhibit 8), but there were a number of important regional and private label brands which competed with Heinz and Vlasic for shelf space.

Win Schuler, the Vlasic subsidiary purchased in 1982, reported flat sales in 1984 due to a general economic decline in the Michigan and upper midwest markets where its products were sold. In 1985 it was moved to Campbell's Refrigerated Foods Business Unit where there were plans to begin producing a wider range of food products under the Win Schuler brand name.

MRS. PAUL'S KITCHENS

Sales of this division for 1984 were up 16 percent over the previous year, operating earnings increased 36 percent, and unit volume increased 9 percent. Mrs. Paul's sales represented just over 3 percent of Campbell's total business; all results exceeded goals set for the year. However, strong competitive pressure on its traditional lines was blamed for the unit's drop in operating earnings for 1985. Competing brands included Hormel and Gorton's (Exhibit 9).

When Campbell acquired Mrs. Paul's in 1982, it was rumored that Heinz and Pillsbury, among others, were considering the same acquisition. Shortly after the acquisition, Campbell responded to consumer preferences for convenience seafood products that were nutritious, low in calories, microwavable, and coated more lightly, by introducing Light & Natural Fish Fillets in 1983. Quality improvements were made to existing products, and a promising new product, Light Seafood Entrees, was introduced in 1984. Market share increased about 25 percent over 1983, and Light Seafood Entrees went national in 1985. This line, which featured seven varieties of low-calorie, microwavable, seafood dishes, accounted for 11 percent of 1985's volume. However, sales of the company's established product lines of breaded frozen seafood items dipped below the 1984 level.

Exhibit 9   The Mrs. Paul's Kitchen Division: Products, Rival Brands, National Competitors

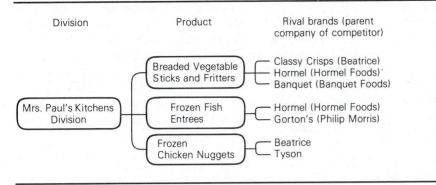

Division	Product	Rival brands (parent company of competitor)
Mrs. Paul's Kitchens Division	Breaded Vegetable Sticks and Fritters	Classy Crisps (Beatrice) / Hormel (Hormel Foods) / Banquet (Banquet Foods)
	Frozen Fish Entrees	Hormel (Hormel Foods) / Gorton's (Philip Morris)
	Frozen Chicken Nuggets	Beatrice / Tyson

CAMPBELL'S OTHER U.S. BUSINESSES

Beyond the base of Campbell's main operating groups there were several additional small businesses: Triangle Manufacturing Corp., a health and fitness products manufacturer; Campbell Hospitality, the restaurant division; and Snow King Frozen Foods, Inc., a manufacturer of frozen meat specialty products.

In 1984 the Hospitality Division, encompassing 59 Pietro's restaurants, 15 Annabelle's, and 6 H. T. McDoogal's, reported an operating loss slightly less than 1983. During the year the division added one H. T. McDoogal's, two Annabelle's, and nine Pietro's units.

In 1985 Annabelle's experienced a 14 percent increase in sales and a 43 percent rise in operating earnings. During the year Campbell announced its intention to sell four H. T. McDoogal's restaurants. Snow King reported a sales decline of 19 percent and an operating loss of almost $1 million.

Competing food companies in the restaurant business included General Mills and Pillsbury. General Mills' Red Lobster unit was the nation's largest full-service dinnerhouse chain. Red Lobster had 1985 sales of $827 million—an all-time high—and its operating profits also set a record. Pillsbury's Restaurants Group was comprised of Burger King and Steak & Ale Restaurants; both achieved record sales and earnings in 1985. Pillsbury opened 477 new restaurants in 1985—the most ever in a single year—bringing the total to 4,601.

Triangle, Campbell's physical fitness subsidiary, in its second full year of operation in 1985, reported that sales had more than tripled, but that increased marketing costs aimed at securing brand recognition resulted in an operating loss. Sales growth was a result of doubling the size of Triangle's distribution system. It's best known product line, "The Band" wrist and ankle weights, maintained the number two position in its category with a 14 percent market share. Triangle planned to build on its strengths by entering the exercise equipment category and by marketing its products internationally.

CAMPBELL'S INTERNATIONAL DIVISION

Campbell's International Division provided 18 percent of the company's consolidated sales in 1984. Campbell had subsidiaries in 11 foreign countries and was planning to expand further. Total restructuring of the International Division was in progress with goals of increasing sales and earnings and building a solid base for growth.

In 1985 steps were taken toward the division's goal of contributing 25 percent of Campbell's corporate sales and earnings. A number of operations were consolidated, and new businesses were added. Other international objectives were to improve Campbell's presence in all international markets and to make Campbell into a premier international company.

RECENT EVENTS

During 1985 the market price of Campbell's stock reached a new high of $80.50 a share. In July the stock was split two for one. At year-end 1985 the market price was $51.50 and the stock price was up $4 during one December week. Analysts were puzzled by this sudden rise in market price, and there were rumors of a takeover.

Analysts observed that the company had been hurt by fierce competition in 1985, an increasing softness in many of its markets, and mistakes on new product introduction. In its *1985 Annual Report* Campbell acknowledged increased competition in the marketplace:

> The supermarket has become an arena of intense competitive activity as food companies introduce a steady stream of new consumer-oriented products and support them with massive marketing dollars in an attempt to carve out a first or second place position in the respective categories. That competitive activity is keeping the pressure on Campbell's operating results.

REFERENCES

1. *Forbes,* December 7, 1981, p. 44.
2. *The Wall Street Journal,* September 17, 1984, p. 1.
3. *The Wall Street Journal,* September 17, 1984, p. 10.
4. *Advertising Age,* January 3, 1983, p. 38.
5. *Savvy,* June 1984, p. 39.
6. *Business Week,* November 21, 1983, p. 102.
7. *Business Week,* December 24, 1984, p. 67.

CASE 24 THE CHARTER COMPANY*

In 1982 Raymond K. Mason could look back over his years as chairman and chief executive officer of The Charter Company and see a dramatic shift in the firm's portfolio of business interests. When Mason took over Charter's reins in 1963 the company consisted only of his father's old lumberyard business and a variety of small real estate and mortgage interests, all located in Florida. Total sales were under $15 million. In barely more than a decade, Mason built Charter into a major multi-faceted U.S. corporation whose chief businesses were oil refining and gasoline retailing. Charter had 1974 sales of $1.1 billion and an up-and-coming ranking among the *Fortune 500*. But Mason was just getting started. In 1975 he launched The Charter Company on a course of unusually aggressive acquisition and deal-making that by 1982 made Charter a $5 billion-plus conglomerate with a portfolio of interests in oil, insurance, publishing, and radio and TV broadcasting. Charter ranked 75th in sales on the 1981 *Fortune 500* list. The manner in which Ray Mason engineered Charter's growth gained him an international reputation as a high-powered wheeler-dealer.

CHARTER'S EARLY YEARS

The company was first incorporated in Florida in 1959 under the name of Pearce-Uible Co. as a consolidation of 14 small Florida real estate-related businesses. Company offices were headquartered in Jacksonville. In 1962 the company's name was changed to Charter Mortgage and Investment Co., and in 1963 this was shortened to The Charter Company following a merger with the lumberyard business of the W. K. Mason Company. Later that same year Ray Mason became president, and in 1964 he assumed the additional title of chairman. The acorn was adopted as Charter's corporate symbol.

Because of early Mason family connections with Charter, Ray Mason was one of Charter's major stockholders; in 1982 he and members of his immediate family were owners of the second largest block of Charter's common stock. The largest block of shares came to be effectively controlled by Edward Ball who, until his death in 1981, was senior trustee for the Alfred I. Du Pont Testamentary Trust and also chairman of the board of St. Joe Paper Company. The Du Pont Trust owned about 75 percent of the voting stock of St. Joe and in a 1972–73 exchange of stock between Charter and St. Joe the latter ended up with control of 23 percent of Charter's stock and a seat on Charter's board. The interlocking directorate relationship continued; St. Joe's president had been a member of Charter's board since 1972, and in 1982 two other St. Joe directors were also members of Charter's board.

---

* Prepared by Professor Arthur A. Thompson, Jr., The University of Alabama. Copyright © 1983 by Arthur A. Thompson, Jr.

Ray Mason and Ed Ball were longtime close friends as well as business associates and in the 1970s Mason wrote a biography of Ed Ball named *Confusion to the Enemy,* the title being Ball's favorite sundown toast. Together Mason and Ball (until his death) exercised near-total control of Charter, with Mason playing the lead role in his capacity as CEO and Ball staying in the background but serving as Mason's mentor, advisor, confidant, and key supporter. Ball was more than just interested in Charter's development though; he owned over 375,000 shares of Charter common stock at the time of his death in 1981.

From the outset Charter thrived on new acquisitions. Among the first acquirees were Jacksonville National Bank, a title insurance company, and a convenience item/ gasoline retail operation; a mortgage company in Puerto Rico was cofounded. While the company's size restricted early acquisitions to small companies, Mason and Ball began to involve Charter in big transactions in the late 1960s when Mason worked out a tentative agreement to merge Charter with Armand Hammer's Occidental Petroleum Corp. and, later, when Mason discussed with billionaire J. Paul Getty the possibilities of a joint venture to set up gasoline stations along the eastern coast of the United States. Neither deal went through. Mason also met several times with then much-publicized Robert Vesco about buying the assets of Vesco's high-flying Investors Overseas Services Corp. (later Vesco was accused of draining funds illegally from the Switzerland-based financial complex and fled to exile in the Caribbean; the collapse of IOS grew into one of the biggest scandals in business history).

Charter's breakout from its mostly Florida-area business interests came in 1970 in the form of a major acquisition. Mason, on a trip to examine some property that he was planning to buy from the Irvine Ranch in California, by chance learned that Signal Oil and Gas Co. wanted to make a quick sale of some of its less attractive petroleum operations. Mason felt the 500 Billups and Super-Test gas stations which were part of the asset package that Signal wished to dispose of would fit neatly with Charter's recently acquired small chain of Dixie Vim gasoline stations and tire stores. Charter's offer of $71 million in cash and notes were readily agreed to by Signal. At the time Charter had annual sales revenues of $20 million and a net worth of $19 million, so the $71 million deal constituted a big financial hurdle.

The acquisition boosted Charter's revenues tenfold to almost $350 million, but along with the leap in revenues came some serious problems. The Billups and Super-Test stations, scattered across 12 states, were in run-down condition and had to be consolidated and revitalized. The Venezuelan oil exploration and production operation, also part of the Signal package, was nationalized. A third piece of the package, a shipping division, began incurring substantial losses ($7 million in 1972, leaving Charter with net earnings of $6.5 million on sales of $451 million). And a fourth piece, a World War II vintage Houston refinery with a rust-coated catalytic cracker, required over $100 million to refurbish. About this same time, Charter encountered some significant losses on a few of its Florida real estate investments.

Charter was so hard pressed to cope with all of these problems that several Charter managers believed the company was "about to bite the dust."[1] St. Joe Paper and Gulf Oil Co. stepped in to help Charter financially—Gulf purchased $7.5 million in

---

[1] A quote attributed to a former Charter executive in a *Wall Street Journal* article on August 20, 1979, pp. 1, 6.

preferred stock from Charter, and Charter and St. Joe arranged an exchange of stock in 1972–73. Then the 1973 oil embargo appeared, and the combination of oil shortages and sharply higher retail gasoline prices turned Charter's petroleum business into a highly profitable operation with sizable cash flows. The crisis dissolved into a bonanza.

The Arab oil embargo gave Mason another idea—sell Gulf Oil Corp. to Saudi Arabia. Mason, who saw the chance to earn a handsome agent's commission if he could engineer the sale, reasoned that Arab ownership of Gulf Oil would assure the United States a supply of Arab oil because the Saudis would likely not cut off oil supplied to their own U.S. outlet. Feeling that his idea was sound, Mason flew to Saudi Arabia to present his proposal to King Faisal. The king, so the rumors say, was interested enough to pursue the plan and later came to Jacksonville to visit at Mason's estate. Mason's ambitious plan collapsed when Gulf Oil rejected the proposal.

Mason was viewed by others and by himself as an irrepressible optimist with an affinity for pushing a good thing to its limit. One close friend was said to have described Mason as a "hayseed tycoon." Observers saw him as using the risky acquisition strategy of buying troubled companies at bargain prices and betting that Charter, via management's hard work, could pull off a profitable turnaround. As of 1974, while some of Charter's acquisitions proved harder to turnaround than originally supposed and threatened to make the strategy backfire, the company had still been able, as one Mason associate put it, "to hold on long enough for the game to turn."

THE CHARTER COMPANY IN 1974

When The Charter Company closed out 1974, management could look back upon a truly successful year: Sales revenues totaled $1.2 billion; after-tax earnings were a record $40.2 million, equal to $10.71 per share (up from $4.61 in 1973) and representing a 31.4 percent return on equity investment (versus a *Fortune 500* median of 13.6 percent and an all-manufacturing average of 14.9 percent). The company ranked 173 in sales in the 1974 *Fortune 500* listing (up from 317 in 1973); it ranked number 8 among the 500 on return on equity investment; and its 32.3 percent average annual return to investors (dividends plus capital gains) during the 1964–74 period was second best among all the 500 firms. The company's 1974 net worth was $128 million as compared to $12 million in 1963 a few years after the company was formed.

Exhibit 1 shows the structure of Charter's businesses as of 1974. The company's activities were heavily concentrated in petroleum refining and marketing (46.6 percent of revenues) and foreign oil production and trading (50.5 percent of revenues). Other business interests included (1) a financial services group (Jacksonville National Bank, mortgage servicing activities) which accounted for 2.3 percent of revenues and (2) real estate (sales of lots to builders, land, and income-producing properties) which generated 0.6 percent of revenues. Neither the financial services group nor real estate were profitable in 1974 although both groups were profitable each of the preceding four years. In addition Charter had major investments in Downe Communications, St. Joe Paper Company, Charter Bankshares (a bank holding company), and International Charter Mortgage Company (which originated and serviced mortgage loans in Puerto Rico and the Virgin Islands).

Exhibit 1   The Charter Company, Organization and Subsidiaries, 1974

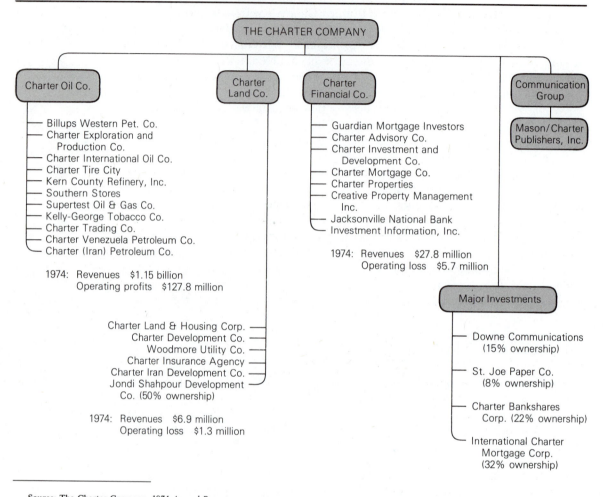

Source: The Charter Company, *1974 Annual Report.*

A CHRONOLOGY OF KEY STRATEGIC ACTIONS AND EVENTS, 1975–1982

The events of the next seven and a half years brought major change. A month-by-month chronology of the key actions and events from January 1975 through June 1982 conveys the corporate strategy course that Charter took:

1975

January: Increased its ownership percentage of Downe Communications, Inc. from 15.5 percent to 43 percent through the purchase of an additional

1,470,220 shares of Downe's common stock for $8.7 million. Downe's operations included publishing *Ladies' Home Journal* (circulation: 7 million copies monthly), *Family Weekly* (distributed weekly through 300 newspapers having combined circulation of 10 million), *Sport* (circulation: 1.4 million copies monthly), and several special-interest publications, as well as five radio stations, a subscription fulfillment service, and two mail order marketing businesses (Joy's Ltd. and The Hamilton Mint). The radio stations included WOKY-AM, Milwaukee; KCBQ-AM, San Diego; KSLQ-FM, St. Louis; WDRQ-FM, Detroit; and WMJX-FM, Miami.

April:
Announced revisions in a letter of agreement under which the Charter Land unit would acquire 51 percent of Louisiana and Southern Insurance Co.'s stock in exchange for certain assets. Louisiana and Southern was a Louisiana-based insurance company which offered ordinary life, limited life, term, endowment, and annuity policies; the company discontinued its line of individual health and disability insurance in March 1974. Louisiana and Southern was licensed to do business in 28 states, but 70 percent of its premium income came from sales in California, Texas, and Louisiana. The company had about 250 agents, of which 60 produced over half of the company's premiums. In 1974 Louisiana and Southern had premium income and revenues of $25.6 million, a net loss of $755,000, assets of $33.0 million, and a shareholders' equity of $1.4 million.

April:
Began preliminary discussion to acquire Commonwealth Oil and Refining Co. Commonwealth Oil's principal business asset was a 161,000-barrel-per-day oil refinery in Puerto Rico; it also engaged in producing aromatics and other petrochemicals. Most of Commonwealth's crude oil came from Venezuela, with lesser amounts from Africa and the Persian Gulf. In 1974 Commonwealth reported sales of $1.1 billion, net earnings of $8.7 million, total assets of $531 million, and total shareholders' equity of $215 million.

June:
Agreed to purchase the common stock of Redbook Publishing Co. and most of the assets of the Dayton Printing Division of McCall Corporation from Norton Simon, Inc. in a transaction valued at about $25 million. Redbook Publishing published *Redbook* magazine, a nationally distributed women's service magazine directed toward the 18–34 age group. The magazine had a circulation of about 4.5 million and ranked 16th in average monthly circulation among 989 general magazines and 7th out of 8 women's service magazines. The Dayton Printing Division of McCall had a 1,360,000 + square-foot plant and printed all or portions of *McCall's, Reader's Digest, Esquire, Scholastic, Redbook, American Home, Newsweek,* and *Sport.* Charter merged the facilities of Dayton Printing into a new subsidiary called Dayton Press, Inc.

August:
Completed the acquisition of approximately 51 percent of common stock of Louisiana and Southern Life Insurance Co. in exchange for $5.3 million in cash and certain other assets.

September: Agreed in principle that its Charter Publishing Co. unit would acquire *womenSports* magazine from Billie Jean King; *womenSports* had an average monthly circulation of 200,000 copies.

October: Reached an agreement with American Financial Corp. to buy three subsidiaries for cash and securities.

November: Signed a letter of intent to sell its Kern County Refinery, Inc. to Russell B. Newton, Jr. in a transaction valued at about $16 million.

December: Terminated its agreement with American Financial Corp. to purchase three subsidiaries.

December: Acquired over 90 percent of the common stock of American Home Publishing Co., which published *American Home* magazine. *American Home,* first published in 1904, was a monthly women's shelter magazine containing articles about food, decorating, home building, and gardening; it had an average monthly circulation of 2.5 million copies.

1976

January: Revealed that the Securities and Exchange Commission was investigating trades in company's stock in late 1973 and early 1974 that were linked to inside data.

May: Revealed that the company's independent auditors had qualified their opinion of Charter's 1975 financial statements.

June: Announced a letter of agreement to sell oil and gas assets of Charter Exploration and Production Co. to Crystal Oil Co. for $16 million.

1977

January: Sold two Jacksonville-based subsidiaries to Jack Uible for $14.3 million. Uible resigned as president of Charter Financial Co. to head the newly purchased units.

January: Negotiated a $100 million credit line with eight banks.

March: Negotiated a $20 million loan from certain units of American Financial Corp.

August: Bought an additional 710,000 common shares of Downe Communications for about $2.8 million, increasing Charter's ownership percentage in Downe from 43 percent to about 56 percent.

September: Proposed a merger between Downe Communications and a Charter subsidiary in an effort to expand and consolidate Charter's publishing industry businesses.

November: Agreed to acquire the remaining 44 percent of Downe Communications by purchasing some 2.2 million shares for $4.50 per share ($10.6 million total) and announced plans to seek stockholder approval of merger of Downe's operations into Chartcom, Inc., a Charter subsidiary.

December: Announced that *Redbook* and *American Home* magazines would be combined in an effort to improve the profitability of Charter's publishing holdings. The publishing of *American Home* ceased with the February 1978 issue.

1978

January: Sold a book publishing subsidiary.

February: Terminated publication of *womenSports* magazine.

March: Completed arrangements for new financing totaling $150 million.

March: Acquired the 44 percent minority interest in Downe Communications through a cash merger and, subsequently, changed the name of Downe to Chartcom, Inc.

March: Announced the initiation of consolidated strategic planning on a formalized basis. Charter's management said there would be major changes in strategy including (1) organizing operations into three major groups—petroleum, communications, and insurance; (2) revising the freewheeling acquisition strategy to focus only on acquisitions within the bounds of its three groups; (3) eliminating unprofitable operations; and (4) instituting accounting controls and budgetary plans so as to improve profitability and reduce wide swings in earnings.

It was announced that, whereas much of the petroleum division's growth had previously been internal (owing to a recently completed $100 million expansion of the company's Houston oil refinery and a resulting ability to use the 70,000 barrel per day capacity to produce a wider and more profitable mix of products), the future growth in this division would come from new acquisitions. Charter indicated it planned to expand its chain of about 500 Billups and Supertest gas stations by acquiring other small chains and that it was in the process of equipping its stations with self-service pumps as well as adding facilities for the sale of nongasoline items—"everything from beer to gun racks." In addition, Charter said its retail gasoline business would integrate backward to acquire distributors of nongasoline items "to cut out middlemen who wholesale products we could sell in our stations." Raymond Mason, Charter's chairman and president, said the petroleum group would eventually expand into other energy fields, probably beginning with coal on "a limited basis, so we can first learn the business."

The head of Charter's insurance group indicated that the group was "seriously searching" for acquisitions that would triple the group's assets to about $150 million; it was acknowledged, however, that the acquisitions might not take place in 1978 unless Charter could "find companies that suit our needs." Charter's insurance operations were unprofitable in 1977, but expectations were for a $2 million profit in 1978 and growth of about 15 percent.

The head of Charter's communications group, also unprofitable in 1977, said, "we'll be on a shakedown cruise this year," and forecast group profits of $4 million in 1978. He indicated that the group had eliminated operations in a book publishing unit and in two magazines that in 1977 had a combined loss of $7 million. Plans for the communications group were to "very aggressively pursue acquisitions in publishing and broadcasting. We are right on the threshold of significant expansion."

Management stated five objectives for the company: (1) become a high-performance company in growth and earnings, (2) enhance the confidence and respect of investors and the business/financial community, (3) increase overall financial strength, (4) move toward a balanced mix of investments in Charter's three operating groups, and (5) manage the company as a decentralized, closely coordinated enterprise.

April: Announced a proposal to acquire Commonwealth Oil Refining Co., which had filed for Chapter XI reorganization in March 1978; the value of Charter's offer was pegged at $180 million and included some cash and securities of a subsidiary of Charter.

May: Was reported to be contending with Tenneco and Coastal States Gas in efforts to acquire ownership of Commonwealth Oil Refining Co.; Commonwealth's board of directors authorized its management to explore the feasibility of a merger proposal from Charter Oil Co., a Charter subsidiary.

September: Filed with the Securities and Exchange Commission (SEC) a proposed public offering of $40 million of 20-year debentures with warrants to purchase shares of Charter's common stock.

September: Agreed to pay $27 million to acquire Riffe Petroleum Co. which was operating under Chapter XI of the Federal Bankruptcy Act. (The acquisition was completed on November 22, 1978). Riffe had two asphalt processing subsidiaries, one on the east coast of the United States and one which had 12 asphalt emulsion plants in the southwestern United States; it also marketed paving asphalt and roofing asphalts in the midwest.

September: Completed sale of $50 million (up from the originally filed $40 million) in 20-year debentures that carried warrants to purchase shares of Charter's common stock.

October: Considered increasing its takeover offer for Commonwealth Oil Refining Co. in order to outbid a group of Arab investors.

October: Announced that it had agreed to acquire Pacific Fidelity Life Insurance Co. from its parent owner Piedmont Management Co. for about $15 million.

October: Received an offer from Roger Tamsez, a Lebanese-born, Harvard-trained entrepreneur, to buy two refineries jointly owned by Charter and another firm, on behalf of Arab investors.

October: Sold its New York City radio station which had revenues of $2.2 million and operating profit of $500,000 for the 10 months ended October 31, 1978.

December: Announced that its proposed purchase of Pacific Fidelity Life Insurance Co. from Piedmont Management Co. had been terminated.

1979

February: Announced plans to spin off its Riverside Group, Inc., unit into an independent company by paying out all of the common stock of Riverside Group as a "special dividend" to Charter shareholders. Riverside was formerly Charter Land & Housing Corp. and conducted the majority of Charter's real estate operations. As a result of the spinoff Charter's real estate and related assets were reduced by $24.5 million, and Charter's retained earnings were reduced by $7.6 million. Riverside's had negatively impacted Charter's consolidated earnings with losses of $1,088,000 in 1978, $2,553,000 in 1977, $3,811,000 in 1976, and $5,451,000 in 1975.

March: Paid $4 million to acquire a 20 percent interest in Carey Energy Corporation. Carey was the largest independent marketer of fuel oil on the east coast of the United States but was in severe financial straits. In 1978 Carey Energy reported consolidated revenues of $1.04 billion and losses of $91.1 million.

May: Signed a $477 million merger agreement with Carey Energy Corp. and acquired the remaining 80 percent interest in Carey Energy for convertible preferred stock having a value of $26 million. Subsequently, Charter negotiated plans to settle the claims of creditors against Carey Energy for $447 million. The funds relied upon by Charter to settle these claims included borrowings under a new $200 million revolving bank credit arrangement, a $100 million public offering of convertible preferred stock, and cash payments from operating capital generated through a processing agreement between a Charter subsidiary and Carey Energy's creditors. Charter's planned settlements with two of the creditors, National Oil Corporation of Libya and National Iranian Oil Company, included agreements to supply crude oil to Charter. (Charter's arrangements with the National Iranian Oil Co. were later disrupted by the hostage crisis.) The third major creditor was Standard Oil of California and Charter negotiated with SoCal to pay $63 million in cash and to transfer 25 percent ownership interest in Carey Energy's share of the Bahamas Refinery in Freeport (capacity of 500,000 barrels per day— fifth largest in world) to SoCal; this left Charter with a 50 percent ownership share.

June: Following a sharp decline in Charter's stock price on the NYSE (which had earlier shot up from $6 to $40 after the news of the bid for Carey), Charter assured investors that its proposed acquisition of Carey Energy was sound and could increase 1979 second-quarter earnings by as much as 1,400 percent, to between $2 and $3 per share. There were indications that Carey's large debt could be paid back in tax-free dollars, that foreign-flag ships could be used to transport the refinery's output at substantial savings over U.S.-registered ships, and that the refinery's product mix would command very attractive prices in Europe.

June: Hideca Trading Corp., a Venezuelan firm, entered a competing bid to acquire Carey Energy. Charter's stock price dropped to below $30 but stock analysts speculated that if Charter succeeded in its acquisition bid for Carey, Charter's added profits could push the stock price up to as much as $70. (The earlier run-up in Charter's stock price from $6 to $44 made it the leading gainer on the NYSE during the first six months of 1979. During this run-up in Charter's stock, Norton Simon, Inc., in the seventh largest trade in NYSE history, sold its 2 million shares of Charter stock for over $40 per share. Norton had obtained these shares as partial payment for Redbook Publishing and Dayton Printing which Charter purchased in 1975.)

July: Was officially placed by the Council on Wage and Price Stability on its list of violators of antiinflation price guidelines.

July: Announced plans to build a $50 million office building in Jacksonville, Florida to be leased to Southern Bell Telephone and Telegraph Co.

August: *The Wall Street Journal* carried a front-page story outlining Charter's attempts to acquire Carey Energy and, in reference to the Mason-led attempt by Charter to win the bidding for Carey, quoted Edward Ball as saying, "Ray's got himself a gusher. He's on his way to making a million dollars a day." The same article quoted another associate, "There ain't no stoppin' Ray now. He's got a potful of cash and a headful of dreams."[2]

September: Obtained a favorable ruling from a Bahamian court agreeing to halt liquidation proceedings of Carey Energy Corp., thereby paving the way for Charter to complete its acquisition of Carey Energy.

September: Raised additional capital in an offering of $35 million in Eurodollar convertible subordinated debentures.

October: Was reported to be near an agreement to acquire City Gas Co. of Florida.

October: Announced an agreement to form a joint venture with E. F. Hutton Group and Alaska Petrochemical Co. to build a 150,000 barrel-per-day refinery in Valdez, Alaska. The project had an estimated cost of $1 billion.

October: Announced that the acquisition of Carey Energy and its Freeport refinery was a "bonanza" for Charter. Charter spokesman said that the newly acquired refinery was earning about $40 million per month due to the exceptional strength of the oil market and forecast that continuation of such earnings would permit Charter to pay off its Carey-related debt by the end of 1980.

December: Was blocked by the Securities and Exchange Commission from acquiring City Gas Co. of Florida.

December: Awarded a $1.7 billion contract to Foster Wheeler Energy Corp. and Thyssen AG to design and build the Valdez refinery.

December: Announced plans to acquire ERC Corp. for a combination of debentures and preferred stock valued at about $547.8 million. ERC was one of the largest reinsurance companies in the United States and had been resisting a takeover attempt from Connecticut General Insurance Co.

December: Became engaged in a bidding war with Connecticut General for control of ERC. Charter offered debentures and preferred stock worth about $90 per share and Connecticut General offered $80 per share in cash (about $480 million total).

---

[2] *The Wall Street Journal,* August 20, 1979, p. 6.

December: Completed purchase of two Crum & Forster life insurance companies from Crum and Forster for $19 million in cash and changed their names to Charter Security. The executive and administrative functions of one of the companies were transferred to Jacksonville and integrated with those of Charter Security (Louisiana) which formerly was Louisiana and Southern Insurance Co.; the operations of the other Crum & Forster insurance company became known as Charter Security (New York) with headquarters in New York City. Charter became attracted to the Crum & Forster insurance businesses when they introduced single premium deferred annuity policies and gave Dean Witter Reynolds distribution rights for 18 months. Sales were excellent and business boomed to such an extent that the parent Crum and Forster had to make a decision whether to exploit the business potential and become a diversified financial company or else stay primarily in the property-casualty segment of the insurance business. C&F opted for the latter and put its life insurance operations up for sale.

1980

January: Ceased efforts to acquire ERC Corp. when ERC's board of directors failed to support Charter's increased offer of securities worth $100 per share.

February: Agreed in principle to acquire assets of Permian Corp., a domestic crude oil marketing subsidiary of Occidental Petroleum Corp., for $500 million. Occidental also agreed to sell Charter, at prices to be negotiated, a minimum of 100,000 barrels of foreign crude oil a day for five years. The transaction was intended by Charter to help give it access to 500,000 barrels of oil per day for its Freeport, Bahamas, refinery.

February: Gained approval of the Federal Communications Commission to acquire WMIL-FM in Milwaukee for $1,540,000.

March: Moved to acquire 35 percent of the shares of Republic National Life Insurance for $100 million in cash and notes and tentatively agreed to offer to purchase the remaining shares of Republic National within a year of completing the first transaction. The acquisition of Republic would more than triple the size of Charter's insurance business. Republic National operated exclusively in the life insurance industry, marketing life insurance policies, accident and health policies, and annuities; the company also engaged in the business of reinsuring a portion of the risks of other life insurance companies. Republic's business was concentrated in group life and health insurance, and sales activities were concentrated in Texas (30 percent). California (21 percent), Tennessee (6 percent), Illinois (5 percent), and 16 other states (38 percent). At year-end 1979 Republic National had total life insurance in force at $14.3 billion, total assets of $694 million, premium revenues of $330.7 million, investment income of $32.2 million, a net worth of $111.4 million, and net profits of $20.2 million.

March:	Terminated negotiations with Occidental Petroleum to acquire Permian Corp. and 150,000 barrels of oil per day.
March:	Agreed to form a new media firm called Charter Media Co. with Karl Eller, former head of Combined Communications. Plans called for Charter to contribute to Charter Media its magazine publishing operations, its subscription fulfillment services, and its radio broadcasting interests. Charter Media also proposed to acquire radio station KIOI-FM in San Francisco for $12 million cash.
April:	Agreed to sell the stock of two subsidiaries, Charter Insurance, Inc., and Woodmere Jacksonville, Inc., to a corporation owned by J. Steven Wilson, Charter's senior vice president and chief financial officer.
April:	Announced that discussions were under way for Charter to acquire *The Philadelphia Bulletin,* an evening newspaper in Philadelphia, which was experiencing financial difficulties and losing circulation.
April:	Announced that it was revising its earlier agreement with Republic National Life Insurance Co. and that an accord had been signed with certain shareholders which provided for Charter to make an exchange offer for all of Republic's common stock in a transaction valued at approximately $282 million.
April:	Was removed from the list of violators of the Carter Administration's antiinflation program.
May:	Renewed its bid to acquire financially troubled $1.2 billion Commonwealth Oil Refining Co. which operated a 161,000 barrel-a-day refinery in Puerto Rico.
May:	Learned that one of the joint venture partners in the Valdez, Alaska, refinery project was withdrawing from participation.
May:	Presented a plan to the Federal Bankruptcy Court in San Antonio to take over Commonwealth Oil. Commonwealth had been in bankruptcy proceedings for 2½ years. The plan called for an exchange of four shares of Commonwealth for one share of Charter, giving the exchange a value of about $100 million (this was well below Charter's $180 million offer in April 1978).
June:	Announced that plans for the Valdez, Alaska, oil refinery were being scaled down.
June:	Announced plans to drill for oil at two promising sites in the United States by the end of 1980.
June:	Gained shareholder approval for the proposed $282 million acquisition of Republic National Life Insurance Co.
June:	Completed the acquisition of The Bulletin Co., owner of *The Philadelphia Bulletin,* for $2 million in cash and about $29 million in promissory notes. The acquisition was by Charter Media Co., a venture headed by Karl Eller and 50 percent owned by Eller and by Charter.
July:	Reached definitive agreements with Commonwealth Oil's creditors and with Tesoro Petroleum (which owned 37 percent of Commonwealth's stock), moving a step closer to acquisition of Commonwealth.

July: Announced that high crude oil prices and a soft market for refined products would likely lead to consolidated losses of as much as $5 million during the second quarter of 1980; filed with SEC to issue $50 million of subordinated debentures due in 2000 and warrants to purchase shares of Charter's common stock.

July: Confirmed that Billy Carter [the brother of Jimmy Carter, then President of the United States] was assisting Charter in obtaining oil from Libya. Reports in the media said Charter had agreed to pay Billy Carter up to a 50-cents-per-barrel commission; there were rumors that this payment would have actually been, in part, an indirect payment to fugitive financier Robert Vesco. Several days later, it came to light that Charter had a contract with Libya for 100,000 barrels of crude oil per day and was trying to have this amount doubled with Billy Carter's assistance. In testimony before the U.S. Senate Committee investigating Billy Carter's dealings with Libya, it was revealed that Charter representatives had met with Vesco five times during 1978 and 1979.

July: Reported a second-quarter loss of almost $8.7 million on sales of $1.11 billion and announced that the company's attempts to acquire Republic National and Commonwealth Oil might be too expensive. There was considerable speculation that Charter could not afford the extra debt on its already leveraged balance sheet.

August: A *Fortune* article on Charter and Ray Mason observed, "Raymond Mason is contemplating his biggest acquisitions yet. If he can get them, they're a beautiful fit." According to the article, if Charter was able to bring off its pending deals to (1) acquire Republic National and Commonwealth Oil, (2) build a refinery in Valdez, Alaska, and (3) form a successful joint venture with Karl Eller to store up and expand Charter's publishing and radio broadcasting interests (1979 sales: $197 million), then Charter would gain "the kind of breadth and solidity" that Mason dreamed of. The article pointed out that while pursuing all these efforts would saddle Charter with a heavy load of debt and stretch Charter's thin management ranks even thinner there were still some pluses: (1) Charter had always bounced back from its troubles, and each time it had come back bigger than before; (2) some earlier acquisitions had been divested, leaving Charter in a stronger and more cohesive condition; and (3) the company's balance sheet was stronger than in years past when it had been heavily loaded with debt securities. Should all the deals go through, Mason indicated to the *Fortune* reporter that the company would slow down on its acquisitions and assimilate the businesses it had, even though there would probably always be "something cooking" in the way of new deals.

August: Confirmed that it would go ahead with the Republic National and Commonwealth Oil acquisitions and would issue enough debt and convertible preferred stock to come up with the necessary $850 million to make the two acquisitions. However, the next day Charter announced that it was terminating its agreement to buy Commonwealth Oil and canceling its proposal to buy Republic National. Later Commonwealth Oil officials acknowledged that the acquisition fell through because of Charter's financial difficulties in raising the needed funds.

August: Announced that Charter Media would acquire New York Subways Advertising Co. and KITT-FM in San Diego.

August: Announced that E. F. Hutton Group had agreed to sell its 8 percent interest in the Valdez, Alaska, refinery project to Charter.

August: Learned that a U.S. Senate panel would investigate dealings of Charter and Billy Carter with Libya.

August: Reported that workers at Dayton Press had voted to buy the money-losing facility under an employee stock ownership plan devised by Kelso & Co., a banking and consulting firm. Acknowledged that *McCall's* and *Reader's Digest* had decided not to renew their printing contracts with Dayton Press.

August: Announced that Robert Vesco was seeking a $5 million fee in connection with Charter's acquisition of Carey Energy.

September: Reported that Alpetco Co., a joint venture of Charter Co., Seatrain Lines, and six Alaska corporations, would be allowed to build a scaled-down refinery at Valdez, Alaska, and would purchase reduced amounts of Alaska's royalty oil.

September: Had no comment on reports that Karl Eller, Charter's partner in Charter Media, was becoming dissatisfied with the way his relationship with Charter was turning out. According to rumors, Raymond Mason and Karl Eller had a personality clash.

October: Ended its media venture with Karl Eller by acquiring Eller's ownership interest and taking back the properties it had contributed to Charter Media.

October: Arranged for a $115 million working capital revolving loan and a letter of credit to finance Alpetco Co., the Charter subsidiary building the Valdez, Alaska, refinery to process Alaska's royalty oil.

October: Reported a third-quarter 1980 loss of $22.4 million.

November: Agreed in principle to sell *Sport* magazine to CBS, Inc.

December: Suspended discussions to sell *Sport* to CBS, Inc.

December: Announced that it was restructuring its Charter Security Life Insurance Cos. into an operation with a different distribution system and a different set of products. Termination notices were sent out to the 5,000 agents along with a notice that Charter Security would not be accepting any more life insurance business as of January 1, 1982. In place of the conglomeration of agents and life policies of the former Louisiana and Southern and Crum & Forster companies, Charter Security elected to narrow its operations to focus on the annuity market segments with policies distributed through brokerage offices. When the earlier negotiated 18-month exclusive sales arrangement with Dean Witter expired, Charter Security promptly expanded its outlets to include other brokerage firms, including Shearson Loeb Rhoades, E. F. Hutton, and Merrill Lynch. The top management of Charter Security believed that distribution through stock brokerage offices was more efficient than the agent system and, further, that the new system would give better market access to the buyers of annuities and new-type life policies (still being developed) with features offering tax benefits and/or higher rates of return on cash values.

1981

January: Settled charges of overpricing its refined petroleum products, bringing an end to federal price-control violations. The consent order signed by the company and the U.S. Department of Energy required Charter to make payments totaling $15 million and to grant discounts totaling $10 million to former and current customers; in addition, DOE allowed $67 million in increased costs claimed by Charter as justification for charging increased prices under the regulatory program.

February: Renegotiated its terms for purchasing *The Philadelphia Bulletin* from an initial $31 million price down to about $21 million.

February: Agreed, as part of the purchase of Karl Eller's ownership interest in Charter Media, to sell New York Subways Advertising to Eller for cash.

February: Announced that former president Gerald R. Ford had been hired as a consultant.

March: Decided to terminate the active business operations of several foreign subsidiaries engaged in marine transportation.

March: Revealed that Bass Equity Enterprises had purchased about 7.4 percent of the convertible preferred stock of Charter for $4.4 million.

March: In Charter's *1980 Annual Report,* the traditional message to the stockholders, signed jointly by Raymond Mason, chairman and CEO, and Jack T. Donnell, president and chief operating officer, had this to say:

In terms of crystallizing our direction for the long-term . . . 1980 was our most significant year yet. It was a year when several achievements and policy changes meshed to put a sharper focus on where The Charter Company is going in this decade and beyond. . . .

Our posture toward future acquisitions was placed under a more stringent discipline. We have been an acquisition-oriented enterprise and expect to maintain this philosophy as a way to growth. But in mid-1980 the Board of Directors and senior management strengthened our strategic policy. Within months, as the business environment became less favorable, two major projects became casualties of our more demanding position: proposed acquisitions of Commonwealth Oil Refining Company and Republic National Life Insurance Company. We had hoped to add these operations for sound strategic reasons and there will be other proposals to come before us in the 80s. However, they must meet tougher hurdle levels for profitability, compatibility, and durability.

A major revision to our long-range plan was begun as part of a whole new approach to asset management. Growth of existing businesses is a parallel objective to growth by acquisition, and we initiated a fresh process to reexamine present assets for their return on investment potential. Marginal or nonproductive operations were examined and during 1980 we eliminated the following: retail home heating oil business in the northeast; automobile and truck tire distributing in the southeast; marketing of oil well drilling equipment; manufacturing and marketing of materials handling equipment; real estate in California; wholesale food operations in the southwest; and in early 1981, retail petroleum operations in Canada and seafood processing and marketing in the northwest.

Executive management was substantially restructured. We are moving aggressively to capitalize on the outstanding capabilities of our people . . . to improve our productivity . . . to increase our responsiveness to business trends and opportunities . . . to promote unity and teamwork across all organizational lines. . . .

Looking back over time, it is satisfying to us as business managers to observe the return we have achieved on stockholders' equity. Our compounded return on equity for the past 10 years is 32 percent—among the top 5 percent of all major U.S. companies.

But now it is time to look ahead. Never in our history has it been so important to view The Charter Company for its long-term growth potential. Like some of America's most dynamic companies, we are entrepreneurial by nature. We have grown in several directions. We became very big very quickly. We have a high-spirited management team that is not afraid to take risks, learns from mistakes, profits from successes, and searches for more.

That's the Charter way. And it will continue to characterize our future. But our size and events of the world have now imposed a new discipline on us. Not a tempering of our spirit . . . more a sobering of our approach. Led by a management team that is deeper and more experienced than ever, we are preserving the best of our past . . . seizing on the strengths of our present . . . focusing on the priorities of the future. . . .

March:	Announced that employees of the financially ailing Dayton Press facility had, to date, been unable to get private loans to buy the plant.
April:	Sold *Sport* magazine to Ray Hunt, president of Hunt Oil Corporation. Through the date of sale Charter reported that *Sport* had revenues of $3.5 million and an operating loss of $1.8 million.
May:	Agreed to sell its 11.4 percent stake in Century Banks to investor Marvin Warner in exchange for promissory notes; in addition, members of Ray Mason's family agreed to sell another 2 percent of Century Bank's common stock to Warner for promissory notes equal to $12.19 per share.
May:	Agreed to sell Charter Distributing Co. to American Agronomics Corp. for cash and the assumption of certain lease obligations.
May:	Said it would consider selling its 50 percent interest in its Freeport, Bahamas, refinery (acquired in the Carey Energy transaction).
May:	Announced that it was calling off its plans to build a refinery in Valdez, Alaska, because of an inability to secure financing and was initiating action to terminate its royalty crude oil contract with the State of Alaska under which it had been purchasing 75,000 barrels per day of crude oil since July 1980. Charter's investment in this project, as of September 30, 1981, was $37.2 million.
June:	Announced plans to close Dayton Press by mid-1982 due to heavy losses; took a pretax write-off of $40.7 million against second-quarter earnings to provide for expected losses and termination costs. The company at-

tributed the closedown decision to labor disputes, unfavorable labor agreements, paper shortages, bad weather, start-up problems with new equipment, and the unattractiveness of making further capital investments to replace obsolete equipment.

June: Reported that it was seeking partnerships with other oil companies to run its Bahamas refinery.

June: Was sued by an employee of *The Philadelphia Bulletin* over plans to withdraw $5 million in assets from the *Bulletin's* employee pension fund.

June: Indicated that it planned to sell two radio stations and, also, that it was seeking more oil drilling concessions in the Middle East.

July: Revealed that it had purchased 5 percent of the common stock of E. H. Crump Cos. for investment purposes. E. H. Crump conducted a nationwide insurance agency and insurance brokerage business, operated a property and casualty company, owned an electronic data processing service company, and engaged in real estate sales and development. The company had offices in 51 cities. In 1980 Crump had consolidated revenues of $27.9 million, net income of $2.8 million, total assets of $48.5 million, and net worth of $16.7 million.

July: Revealed that it had purchased 158,920 shares in W. R. Berkley Corp., about 5.1 percent of the company's outstanding stock. W. R. Berkley was a Delaware insurance holding company whose operating subsidiaries participated in regional property casualty insurance, reinsurance, and excess and surplus lines insurance. In 1980 the company had revenues of $117.5 million, net income of $3.7 million, total assets of $213.1 million, and net worth of $42.3 million.

August: Announced that all unions at *The Philadelphia Bulletin* had agreed to a variety of cost-cutting concessions which, coupled with actions taken in nonunion departments, would result in payroll savings of approximately $6.6 million. Charter let it be known that unless its comprehensive plan to revitalize the newspaper achieved certain targeted financial goals it would reevaluate its investment and possibly terminate publication of the *Bulletin*. In the event of shutdown, the pretax charge against earnings was estimated at between $16 and $22 million.

September: Confirmed that the Bahamas refinery was still experiencing operating losses because of an excess of supply over demand in the world markets for refined petroleum products and increased costs of crude oil to supply the Bahamas refinery. The company said its plans were to utilize "only a small portion of its capacity at the Bahamas refinery" until conditions improved. (Previously Charter had acknowledged that the Bahamas refinery was at a "conversion disadvantage" because the high sulfur crude oil stocks processed at this refinery yielded a high percentage of relatively low-priced fuel oils and intermediate feedstocks. In early 1981 Charter was operating the Bahamas refinery at only 7 percent of capacity and was considering whether to undertake capital expenditures to reduce its conversion disadvantage.)

November: Was said, according to published reports, to be abandoning efforts to put together a major publishing "empire." The report noted that Charter was still losing money on its publishing operations despite having closed Dayton Press and sold *Sport* magazine. Efforts were said to be underway to dispose of several radio stations and to find a buyer for *The Philadelphia Bulletin.*

November: Filed a statement with the Securities and Exchange Commission that Charter Security Life Insurance Co., a subsidiary, had purchased 5.3 percent of the common stock (204,800 shares) of Centran Corporation, a diversified bank holding company whose principal operations included six banks in Ohio and Colonial Financial Service in Birmingham, Alabama. In 1981 Centran reported assets of $3.0 billion, a net worth of $163.4 million, and a net loss of $22 million.

December: Filed a statement with the SEC that Charter Security had purchased 962,000 shares (5.1 percent) of the common stock of Liberty National Insurance Holding Co. of Birmingham, Alabama, at a cost to Charter of $25 million. Liberty National Insurance Holding Company was the parent of Liberty National Insurance Company (which marketed life insurance, accident and health insurance, group insurance, and annuities) and Globe Life and Accident Insurance Co. of Oklahoma (which sold life, accident, and health insurance through 54 sales offices in 37 states, as well as through a national direct mail program). LNIH Co. had 1981 assets of $2.7 billion, revenues of $585.2 million, earnings of $69.6 million, and total life insurance in force of $25.5 billion. A *Wall Street Journal* story quoted a Charter official as saying that Charter's purchase of Liberty National stock was "part of the normal investment portfolio of our insurance group." Charter's SEC filing statement declared that it "may consider seeking control" of Liberty National later.

1982

January: Closed down the operations of *The Philadelphia Bulletin* after efforts to find a buyer were unsuccessful. Earlier, Charter had announced that it would not put more money into its efforts to turn around the newspaper's operations (pretax losses were $7 million for the last four months of 1981, about double what Charter expected) and that Charter would try to find a buyer to take over the *Bulletin's* operations. *The Wall Street Journal* quoted a securities analyst who followed the newspaper industry closely as saying, "Anyone trying to sell a newspaper in that condition would need a mask and a gun." The same analyst said Charter was "foolish" to buy the *Bulletin* if the purpose was to earn a return on its investment.

January: Increased its holdings of Liberty National stock by open market purchases of an additional 255,000 shares, giving Charter Security ownership of 6.5 percent of the 18.9 million Liberty National shares.

February: Liberty National filed suit in Federal District Court seeking to stop Charter from buying additional Liberty National stock and alleging that

Charter had (1) violated securities laws by making misleading and inaccurate disclosures to the SEC regarding its December purchases of Liberty National stock and (2) used illegal means to manipulate the market price of Liberty National stock (traded on the NYSE). The suit asked for damages of $100 million.

February: Announced that additional shares of Liberty National stock had been bought, increasing Charter's ownership from 6.5 percent to 6.9 percent.

March: Signed a definitive agreement for the sale of its six radio stations to Surrey Broadcasting Co. for $32 million in cash and notes.

March: Boosted its stakeholding of Liberty National stock to 7.9 percent.

April: Declared that it had purchased 456,000 shares, or 5.2 percent, of the stock of Monarch Capital Corporation. Monarch Capital was a Delaware holding company with three life insurance company subsidiaries: Monarch Life Insurance Co., Springfield Life Insurance Co., and Fidelity Bankers Life Insurance Co.; the three companies marketed life insurance, health and accident insurance, and annuities. In 1981 Monarch Capital reported life insurance in force of $7.7 billion, assets of $975 million, revenues of $226.6 million, and net income of $26.7 million.

April: Increased its ownership share of Liberty National common stock to 8.2 percent and indicated it did not plan immediately to buy more.

April: The Federal District Court dismissed on technical grounds the suit filed by Liberty National charging that Charter had violated securities laws and tried to manipulate the price of Liberty National's stock.

May: Agreed in principle to sell two communications operations, including *Redbook* magazine, to Hearst Corp. for $23 million in cash and notes, plus a contingent payment based on *Redbook's* future performance.

May: Acquired 9.8 percent of Naples Federal Savings and Loan Association's common stock and said it would keep its holdings below 10 percent temporarily.

May: Paid $31.5 million for Gulf United Corp. convertible debentures, equivalent to 5.4 percent or 1.5 million shares of Gulf's outstanding common stock. Gulf United was a holding company with six life insurance companies (8,400 agents selling a full line of life, group, accident and health, and annuity policies in Florida, Georgia, Alabama, Texas, Utah, California, and Tennessee) and had lesser interests in broadcasting (2 TV stations and 11 radio stations) and in the wholesale distribution of health care products. Gulf United reported 1981 revenues of $1 billion, total assets of $3 billion, operating income of $89 million, a net worth of $548 million, and a return on equity of 16.1 percent.

June: Announced that it had increased its stock ownership in Gulf United to the equivalent of 9.9 percent of the common stock outstanding.

June: Announced that it had purchased enough additional shares of Monarch Capital Corp. stock to give Charter a 9.9 percent ownership.

In addition to the above developments, Charter had over the years made limited investments in oil shale research, coal mining, and aquaculture. Its primary oil shale operation in 1982 involved testing a method of processing oil shale containing the minerals nahcolite and dawsonite. Raw nahcolite had been demonstrated to be an effective dry desulfurization agent for coal-fired electrical power plants and could potentially be marketed to electric utilities as an aid in meeting pollution control standards. Charter controlled 8,300 acres of nahcolite leases on oil shale lands and was working to acquire more oil shale rights from the U.S. government. Charter's management believed that commercial development of its "Multi Mineral venture" would require new financing and a joint venture with an equity partner.

In 1981 the Company sold its Oregon-based seafood processing and aquaculture operations but retained and was expanding its aquaculture research and consulting and its hatchery and fish-rearing operations. Some of these activities were joint ventures and were located in both the United States and Ireland.

CHARTER'S INSURANCE GROUP

Between 1979 and 1982 Charter's activities in the insurance field mushroomed. In 1982 Charter's insurance businesses consisted of a holding company, Charter Insurance Group, Inc., with three life insurance subsidiaries, a financial services subsidiary, and a data products subsidiary. The three life insurance subsidiaries companies were all formed as stock life insurance companies. In 1981 the three wrote a combined $1.37 billion of new life insurance and $1.23 billion of new annuities and at year-end had $3.4 billion of life insurance in force and $1.66 billion of annuities in force. Some of the key operating statistics of the insurance group are summarized below (very little of which is reflected in The Charter Company's consolidated financial statements—see Exhibits 5 to 7, because of the different accounting treatments given to insurance company operations):

	Year ended December 31 ($000)				
	1977	1978	1979	1980	1981
Premium income*	$ 9,069	$11,576	$ 19,633	$372,165	$1,259,411
Investment income*	2,193	2,762	3,924	46,911	124,171
Operating profit*	655	910	2,295	7,380	12,625
Net income*†	817	2,453	1,490	6,201	14,847
Total assets‡	45,221	53,354	247,178	653,478	1,922,327
Stockholders' equity‡§	6,851	9,267	24,934	50,851	69,698

* Includes only Charter Security (Louisiana) for years prior to 1980.
† Includes realized gains on investments of $8.1 million in 1981, $2.2 million in 1980, and $1.2 million in 1978.
‡ 1981, 1980, and 1979 data represent the three life insurance subsidiaries on a consolidated basis. Prior years include only Charter Security (Louisiana).
§ Includes capital contributions of $5.4 million in 1981, $17.7 million in 1980, and $14.1 million in 1979.

Substantial amounts of Charter's purchases of stock in Liberty National, Gulf United, Monarch Capital, and others were financed with the cash flows being generated by the Group's premium income.

THE CHARTER COMPANY IN 1982

The flurry of activity in building and rebuilding Charter's business portfolio made The Charter Company of 1982 different from The Charter Company of 1974, as can been seen by comparing Exhibit 2 with Exhibit 1. Not surprisingly, Charter's many deals were a factor in the movements of its stock price (Exhibit 3). Exhibits 4 and 5 contain information on Charter's board of directors and executive officers. The financial performance of Charter is summarized in Exhibits 6 through 9.

Exhibit 2   The Charter Company, Organization and Subsidiaries, 1982

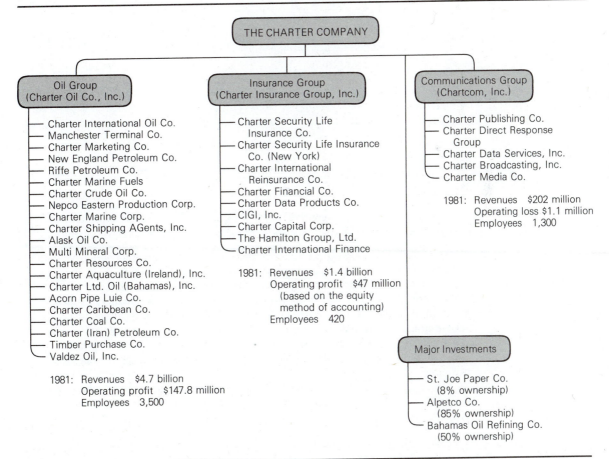

Exhibit 3 Quarterly Trading Range of Charter's Common Stock on the NYSE

	Market Price			*Market Price*	
Year/Quarter	*Low*	*High*	*Year/Quarter*	*Low*	*High*
1981:			1977:		
4	7½	11⅛	4	3⅞	4⅜
3	6½	11⅞	3	3⅞	4¾
2	9¾	11⅛	2	3¾	3¾
1	11⅞	20⅜	1	3¾	5
1980:			1976:		
4	17⅝	25¾	4	2⅝	3¾
3	15¾	24⅜	3	3⅜	3⅞
2	20⅝	27⅜	2	3⅜	4½
1	17	44¼	1	3⅞	5⅜
1979:			1975:		
4	31¾	38⅜	4	3⅛	5⅞
3	28¼	49¾	3	4⅜	6⅜
2	17⅝	44½	2	5⅜	6⅞
1	5	10	1	3½	7
1978:					
4	4	6½			
3	5½	7½			
2	6	8			
1	3⅞	6½			

Source: The Charter Company, *Annual Reports, 1975–1981.*

THE VIEW FROM THE TOP

In March 1982 the two top executive officers of Charter, Ray Mason and Jack Donnell, provided their public assessment of the company's strategy and restructuring:[3]

> We are proud to report a great deal of accomplishment in our program of restructuring our company and building a new foundation for growth in the future.
>
> The results of all our efforts—good in 1980—were even more significant in 1981. Within just the past 12 months an agreement to sell six of our seven radio stations was reached, the Philadelphia *Bulletin* ceased publication, the thrust of our highly successful life insurance business was redirected, discussions began with possible partners in our Multi Mineral venture, plans to build a refinery in Alaska were suspended, the phaseout of printing operations at Dayton Press began, *Sport* magazine was sold—and more.
>
> A year ago we had $486 million in long-term debt and a long-term debt to total capitalization ratio of .42 to 1. Today we have $333 million in long-term debt, a ratio of .34 to 1.

[3] The Charter Company, *1981 Annual Report.*

Exhibit 4   Board of Directors of The Charter Company, 1982

Name/Occupation/Affiliation	Age	Year First Elected	Number of Shares Held
Raymond K. Mason, chairman and chief executive officer, The Charter Company	55	1963	2,670,608 shares of common
Jack T. Donnell, president and chief operating officer, The Charter Company	52	1980	59,676 shares of common
J. C. Belin, president, St. Joe Paper Company, Port St. Joe, Florida	67	1972	386,200 shares of common
Joseph M. Cline, investment banker, Nashville, Tennessee	71	1965	5,100 shares of common; 80 shares of preferred
Newton C. Ebaugh, consulting engineer, retired, Gainesville, Florida	74	1977	22,000 shares of common
Philip C. Jackson, chairman and chief executive officer, Central Bank of Birmingham, and vice chairman, Central Bank Shares of the South, Birmingham, Alabama	53	1979	5,000 shares of common
W. Guy McKenzie, chairman, McKenzie Tank Lines, Tallahassee, Florida	71	1977	None
B. K. Roberts, partner in law firm of Roberts, Miller, Baggett, La Face, Richard & Wiser, Tallahassee, Florida	75	1977	None
William C. Ruffin, Jr., M.D., chief of staff of Shands Teaching Hospital and Clinic; professor and assistant dean of College of Medicine, University of Florida; Gainesville, Florida	56	1965	279,010 shares of common
Lloyd Smith, partner of Smith, Hulsey, Schwalbe & Nichols, general counsel for The Charter Co., Jacksonville, Florida*	67	1963	174,100 shares of common
W. L. Thornton, president, Florida East Coast Railway (a subsidiary of St. Joe Paper Company), St. Augustine, Florida*	54	1972	375,300 shares of common†
Edward M. Carey, chairman, Carey Energy Corp. (an energy and shipping company separate from companies acquired by Charter)	65	1981	480,500 shares of common; 126,000 shares of preferred

Note: As a group, all officers and directors held 20.4 percent of the voting shares of common stock outstanding and 0.5 percent of the outstanding preferred stock.

* Also a director of St. Joe Paper Company. St. Joe owned 4,115,000 shares of Charter's common stock.

† This total includes 375,200 shares held by the estate of Edward Ball of which Belin and Thornton were representatives.

Source: The Charter Company, *1981 10-K Report.*

Exhibit 5   Executive Officers of The Charter Company, 1982

Name	Age	Present Position	Appointed to Present Position	Year First Employed by Charter	Previous Position/Background Experience
Raymond K. Mason	55	Chairman of the Board of Directors; Member of Executive Committee; and Chief Executive Officer	1964	1959	President, The Charter Company
Jack T. Donnell	52	President, and Chief Operating Officer	1981	1971	President, Charter Oil Company
J. Dix Druce, Jr.	34	President, Charter Insurance Group, Inc.	1977	1972	Various management positions, The Charter Company
Dudley K. Parker	48	President, Charter Oil Company	1981	1971	Various management positions, The Charter Company
James P. Smith, Jr.	38	President, Chartcom, Inc.	1981	1975	Various management positions, The Charter Company
Carl A. Steighner	35	Chief Financial Officer	1981	1971	Various management positions, The Charter Company
Thomas E. Burke	51	Senior Vice President, Corporate Relations	1981	1981	Vice President, Pittsbury Co.; various management positions, Marriott Corp.
T. Malcolm Graham	32	Senior Vice President, Secretary and Corporate Counsel	1980	1976	Secretary, The Charter Company; Corporate Counsel, The Charter Company
Norman K. Green	57	Senior Vice President, International	1980	1980	Rear Admiral, U.S. Navy
Curtis W. Loftin	35	Seniro Vice President, Corporate Planning and Development	1981	1978	Vice President, Jacksonville National Bank
Ray M. VanLandingham	39	Senior Vice President, Administration Chief Accounting Officer	1972	1971	Chief Accounting Officer, The Charter Company
Kimball R. Bobbitt	39	Vice President, Finance	1981	1979	Accountant, Touche Ross & Co.
K. C. Caldabaugh	35	Vice President, Corporate Development	1981	1979	Vice President, Jacksonville National Bank
Paul A. Grant	36	Vice President, Corporate Taxes	1981	1977	Tax Manager, Peat, Marwick, Mitchell & Co.
Richard S. Holtz	34	Vice President, Internal Audit	1982	1977	Accountant, Peat, Marwick, Mitchell & Co.
Wallace A. Patzke, Jr.	34	Vice President and Controller	1979	1972	Various management positions, The Charter Company
Gilbert O. Rogers	55	Vice President and Treasurer	1956	1964	Treasurer, The Charter Company
James R. Whitley	33	Vice President Finance	1981	1979	Senior Vice President, Century First National Bank, St. Petersburg, Florida

Source: The Charter Company, *1981 10-K Report.*

Exhibit 6 Financial Highlights, The Charter Company, 1975-1981   In Thousands, except per Share Amounts

	1975	1976	1977	1978	1979	1980	1981
Revenues	$1,046,159	$1,190,908	$1,481,645	$2,046,330	$4,211,806	$4,421,142	$4,966,171
Earnings from continuing operations	9,785	17,562	18,612	25,777	369,539	59,359	55,946
Gain (loss) on discontinued operations	(302)	(2,794)	1,049	(2,489)	(1,813)	(9,122)	(48,229)
Earnings before extraordinary items	9,483	14,768	19,661	23,288	367,726	50,237	7,717
Extraordinary items	(4,089)	2,094	300	—	2,388	—	—
Net earnings	5,394	16,862	19,961	23,288	365,338	50,237	7,717
Earnings per share, fully diluted	.43	.80	.89	1.09	13.02	1.56	.06
Cash dividends per common share . .	.08	.06	.13	.24	.52	.95	1.00
Working capital	38,675	27,769	51,919	98,369	292,539	238,205	149,882
Total assets	544,404	522,854	669,740	689,803	1,728,694	1,726,260	1,541,326
Long-term debt and redeemable preferred stock	191,526	198,430	211,133	246,361	501,938	486,964	333,808
Stockholder's equity	140,941	126,291	142,976	165,869	646,885	676,669	653,871
Book value per common share . . .	5.74	6.56	7.52	8.89	26.04	26.02	24.97
Common shares outstanding . . .	17,566	17,566	17,566	17,463	20,166	21,592	21,592

Source: The Charter Company, annual reports.

Exhibit 7   Consolidated Income Statements, The Charter Company, 1979-1981
In Thousands except per Share Amounts

	1979	1980	1981
Revenues	$4,211,806	$4,421,142	$4,966,171
Expenses:			
Cost of sales and operating	3,551,337	4,057,921	4,512,215
Selling, general, and administrative	145,912	102,185	190,656
Depreciation, depletion, and amortization	24,190	29,527	32,511
Interest	42,140	75,995	89,196
Total expenses	3,763,579	4,265,628	4,824,578
Earnings before equity in affiliates, etc.	448,227	155,514	141,593
Equity in net earnings of affiliates	2,357	3,321	14,080
Earnings before income taxes, etc.	450,584	158,835	155,673
Income taxes	81,045	99,476	99,727
Earnings from continuing operations	369,539	59,359	55,946
Discontinued operations, net:			
Loss from operations	(1,813)	(9,122)	(13,150)
Provision for loss on disposal			(35,079)
Total discontinued operations	(1,813)	(9,122)	(48,229)
Earnings before extraordinary items	367,726	50,237	7,717
Extraordinary items, net	(388)		
Net earnings	$ 367,338	$ 50,237	$ 7,717
Earnings (loss) per share of common stock:			
Primary:			
Continuing operations	$ 15.00	$ 1.92	$ 1.77
Discontinued operations	(.07)	(.33)	(1.71)
Before extraordinary items	14.93	1.59	1.71
Extraordinary items	(.10)		
Net earnings	14.93	1.59	.06
Fully diluted:			
Continuing operations	13.08	1.88	1.77
Discontinued operations	(.06)	(.32)	(1.71)
Before extraordinary items	13.02	1.56	.06
Extraordinary items	(.08)	—	—)
Net earnings per share	$ 12.94	$ 1.56	$ .06

Source: The Charter Company, *1981 Annual Report.*

Exhibit 8 Consolidated Balance Sheets, The Charter Company, 1980-1981 In Thousands

	1980	1981
Assets		
Current assets:		
Cash	$ 94,112	$ 69,283
Receivables:		
Trade accounts	322,237	343,862
Other	32,142	25,967
Affiliates	16,312	11,479
Short-term notes and current portion of long-term receivables	3,133	8,815
	373,824	390,123
Less: Allowance for doubtful receivables	6,062	14,464
Net receivables	367,762	375,659
Inventories:		
Petroleum	270,094	111,313
Other	25,477	25,374
	295,571	136,687
Prepaid expenses	16,217	27,316
Total current assets	773,662	608,945
Investments:		
Bahamas refinery affiliates	407,402·	389,060
Charter Security (La.) and other affiliates	83,190	76,751
Other	39,990	41,160
Total investments	530,582	506,971
Property, plant, and equipment:		
Cost	468,851	403,187
Less: Accumulated depreciation, depletion, and amortization	122,225	124,409
Net property, plant, and equipment	346,626	278,778
Net assets of discontinued operations	—	2,717
Intangibles resulting from acquisitions, net	44,293	74,115
Other assets	51,097	69,800
Total assets	$1,746,260	$1,541,326
Liabilities and Stockholders' Equity		
Current liabilities:		
Notes payable	$ 76,563	$ 50,500
Current installments of long-term debt	21,402	17,192
Accounts payable	348,312	309,285
Accrued expenses	71,747	54,939
Income taxes	17,433	27,207
Total current liabilities	535,457	459,123
Long-term debt, excluding current installments	404,631	251,425
Subordinated debentures, net of discount	81,316	81,673
Deferred income taxes	27,377	43,820
Deferred subscription income, net		23,053
Deferred credits and other	19,793	27,651
Redeemable preferred stock (aggregate liquidation preference $826,000 in 1981 and $1,249,000 in 1980)	1,017	710
Nonredeemable preferred stock, common stock, and other stockholders' equity:		
Nonredeemable preferred stock (aggregate liquidation preference $114,684,000 in 1981 and $114,686,000 in 1980)	116,900	116,898
Common stock, shares outstanding: 21,592,230 in 1981 and 21,591,785 in 1980	21,592	21,592
Additional paid-in capital on common stock	67,202	67,233
Retained earnings	470,476	447,555
Net unrealized gain in investment securities of an unconsolidated subsidiary, net of income taxes	499	593
	676,669	653,871
Total liabilities and stockholders' equity	$1,746,260	$1,541,326

Source: The Charter Company, *1981 Annual Report.*

Exhibit 9   Consolidated Statements of Changes in Financial Position, The Charter Company, 1979-1981   In Thousands

	1979	1980	1981
Funds provided:			
Operations:			
Earnings from continuing operations	$ 369,539	$ 59,359	$ 55,946
Charges (credits) to earnings not affecting working capital:			
Depreciation, depletion, and amortization	24,190	29,527	32,511
Deferred income taxes and other	3,474	1,350	4,254
Equity in net earnings of affiliates	(2,357)	(3,321)	(14,080)
Equity in net loss of Bahamas refinery, included in cost of sales	10,376	16,775	27,548
Funds provided by continuing operations	405,179	103,690	106,179
Funds provided (used) by discontinued operations	(4,217)	(326)	7,138
Funds provided by extraordinary items	6,100	—	—
Total funds provided by operations	415,539	103,364	99,041
Additional long-term debt	253,741	16,020	19,849
Proceeds from sales of property, plant, and equipment	5,255	26,353	35,025
Issuance of common and preferred stock	144,104	11,360	6
Decrease in investments and other, net	—	—	8,132
Decrease in working capital	—	54,334	88,383
	818,639	211,431	250,436
Funds applied:			
Cash dividends	14,625	29,390	30,522
Noncash dividend	7,593	—	—
Expenditures for property, plant, and equipment	51,650	106,611	58,472
Acquisition of subsidiaries	439,411	—	—
Redemption and conversion of preferred and common stock	24,126	7,455	425
Reduction of long-term debt	65,742	25,385	161,017
Increase in investment and other net	21,312	42,590	—
Increase in working capital	194,170	—	—
	818,639	211,431	250,438
Increase (decrease) in working capital:			
Cash	61,471)	(1,520)	(24,829)
Receivables	132,861	34,691	7,807
Inventories and prepaid expenses	287,066	(53,363)	(147,785
Current debt	(14,199	(73,744)	30,273
Accounts payable and accrued expenses	(251,575)	28,827	55,845
Income taxes	(21,454)	(10,775)	(9,784)
Increase (decrease) in working capital	$ 194,170	$ (54,334)	$ (88,383)

Clearly, as we enter 1982, we are a much different company. Leaner. Stronger. More mature.

We also have a sound sense of direction for the long run. In 1981 we continued to broaden our management team and, augmented by international management consulting expertise, we are operating with the following basic strategy.

We are a company primarily of oil industry professionals operating petroleum assets—and of insurance, financial, and investment specialists and magazine publishers. We will concentrate our people and our capital resources on doing what we do best.

We are an independent refiner with the flexibility to process a wide range of crude oil into various petroleum products. Our Houston refinery operates at a much higher percentage of capacity than the industry average, converting cheaper and more available sour crudes into a flexible state of products, heavily weighted toward the more valuable unleaded gasolines and petrochemicals. The Bahamas refinery, while capable of producing only lower-grade petroleum products, is a modern off-shore facility with deep-water port advantages.

We are a balanced, versatile marketer of petroleum products—those we refine and those purchased from domestic and international oil sources. Residual fuels, petrochemicals, and asphalts go to a wide range of industrial and utility customers. Gasoline and convenience items are marketed through 430 retail outlets in the southeastern United States—a system with considerable promise for further development. Gasoline is also sold through wholesale and interrefinery markets.

We have a concession interest in Abu Dhabi and domestic gathering operations which provide us good sources of crude oil. We still obtain a significant portion of our crude oil from the spot market but will continue to seek favorable long-term contractual supplies, as appropriate.

We will give higher priority to the company's fastest growing operations today—insurance. Our Insurance Group is one of the nation's largest sellers of single premium deferred annuities and net income has jumped almost tenfold in two years. Assets are up eightfold to $1.9 billion, ranking Charter Security Life now as one of the country's 50 largest life insurance companies. A whole new system for marketing annuities through national securities firms went into effect in 1981. New ways to develop and sell insurance products, to capitalize on our investment expertise, and to provide new financial services are being explored.

We publish two of America's most respected magazines, *Ladies' Home Journal* and *Redbook,* but have significantly pruned our third business segment, communications.

We will maintain our financial focus on the return our stockholders receive for their investment. We are dedicated to building a steady stream of earnings and to maintaining a healthy balance sheet. With less complexity of operations and more consistency in performance, we hope to achieve the kind of confidence and predictability for which the financial community pays a high premium.

We will continue to hone our growing management skills. Charter reached $1 billion in sales just a few years ago and already we are five times larger. The core of management that brought us through this rapid transition to a major company has reached a new level of experience and seasoning. We will use this experience and advanced management techniques to prepare us for an exciting future.

Charter has come a long way to become a major American corporation in a relatively few years—evolving rapidly into one of America's 100 largest industrial companies. Our revenues have increased more than fourfold in the past five years, our assets have tripled. If we added the insurance revenues and assets, which must be accounted for separately, the increase would be about sixfold in each case.

In many ways we came even further in just the last year—disposing of various operations . . . earning $56 million from continuing operations that will do even better in a healthier economy . . . refinancing debt . . . shaping a new strategic plan to fit the changing environment.

We believe that the progress achieved in 1981 and the strategic direction which we have mapped out have brightened the future for Charter and its stockholders, employees, and others interested in the company.

D
Strategy
Implementation and
Administration

CASE 25   CLUB MÉDITERRANÉE (A)*

Sipping a cognac and smoking one of his favorite cigars on his way back to Paris from New York on the Concorde, Serge Trigano was reviewing the new organization structure that was to be effective November 1981. In the process he was listing the operational problems and issues that were yet to be resolved. Son of the chief executive of "Club Med," Serge Trigano was one of the joint managing directors and he had just been promoted from director of operations to general manager of the American zone, responsible for operations and marketing for the whole American market. Having experienced a regional organization structure that was abandoned some four years ago, he wanted to make sure that this time the new structure would better fit the objectives of Club Med and allow its further development in a harmonious way.

COMPANY BACKGROUND AND HISTORY

Club Med was founded in 1950 by a group of friends led by Gérard Blitz. Initially it was a nonprofit organization set up for the purpose of going on vacation together in some odd place. The initial members were essentially young people who liked sports and especially the sea. The first "village," a tent

---

* Prepared by Professor Jacques Horovitz as a basis for class discussion rather than to illuminate either effective or ineffective handling of an administrative situation. Copyright 1981 by IMEDE (International Management Development Institute), Lausanne, Switzerland. Reprinted with permission.

Exhibit 1   Financial Performance   Thousands of French Francs

Years	Sales	Net Income	Cash Flow	EPS
1969–70	313,000	NA	NA	5.31
1970–71	363,000	NA	NA	5.73
1971–72	427,000	13,400	25,100	7.41
1972–73	502,000	22,500	37,000	10.88
1973–74	600,000	27,300	42,800	12.78
1974–75	791,000	40,000	56,790	16.08
1975–76	1,060,000	51,800	70,900	20.78
1976–77	1,350,000	67,870	103,645	20.98
1977–78	1,616,000	72,135	114,578	23.78
1978–79	1,979,000	85,900	138,300	28.42
1979–80	2,462,000	111,600	173,100	36.91

village, was a camping site in the Balearic Isles. After four years of activities, Gilbert Trigano was appointed the new managing director. Gilbert Trigano came to Club Med from a family business involved in the manufacture of tents in France, a major supplier to Club Med. With this move, and in the same year, the holiday village concept was expanded beyond tent villages to straw hut villages, the first of which was opened in 1954. Further expanding its activities, in 1956 Club Med opened its first ski resort at Leysin, Switzerland. In 1965 its first bungalow village was opened, and in 1968 the first village started its operation in the American zone. Club Med's main activity was, and still is today, to operate a vacation site for tourists who would pay a fixed sum (package) to go on vacation for a week, two weeks, or a month and for whom all the facilities were provided in the village. Club Med has always had the reputation of finding beautiful sites which were fairly new to tourists (for instance, Moroccan tourism was "discovered" by Club Med) which offered many activities, especially sports activities, to its members.[1] In 1981 Club Med operated 90 villages in 40 different countries on five continents. In addition to its main activity it had extended to other sectors of tourism in order to be able to offer a wider range of services. In 1976 Club Med acquired a 45 percent interest in an Italian company (Valtur) which had holiday villages in Italy, Greece, and Tunisia, mainly for the Italian market. In 1977 Club Med took over Club Hotel, which had built up a reputation over the last 12 years as a leader in the seasonal ownership time-sharing market. The result of this expansion had been such that in 1980 more than 770,000 people had stayed in the villages of Club Med or its Italian subsidiary, whereas there were 2,300 in 1950. Most members were French in 1950, and in 1980 only 45 percent were French. In addition, 110,000 people had stayed in the apartments or hotels managed by its time-sharing activity. Actually, in 1980, Club Med sales were about 2.5 billion French francs (FF) and its cash flow around FF170 million. (See Exhibit 1 for the last 10 years' financial performance.) Exhibits 2–4 show the

---

[1] When going on vacation to any of Club Med's villages, one becomes a "member" of Club Med.

number of people who had stayed at the holiday centers of Club Med, the number of beds it had as of 1980, and the nationality of its members. The present case focuses exclusively on the organization structure of the holiday village operations and not on the time-sharing activities of the company.

Exhibit 2   Growth in Number of Club Members

Year	Number of Members
1950	2,300
1955	10,000
1960	45,000
1965	90,000
1970	293,000
1975	432,000
1980	770,000*

* Includes Valtur.

Exhibit 3   Number of Facilities, 1981

	Number of Holiday Centers	Number of Beds
Club Med and Valtur	102	60,500
Hotels	7	1,000
Apartment buildings	24	11,000
Total	133	72,500

Exhibit 4   Members of Club Med According to Country of Origin, 1979*

France	301,000	43.1%
United States/Canada	124,000	17.8
Belgium	41,600	6.0
Italy	34,400	4.9
West Germany	34,100	4.9
Switzerland	18,500	2.6
Austria	6,800	1.0
Australia	18,400	26.0
Others	84,900	12.1
Conferences and seminars	34,700	5.0†
	698,500	100.0%

* Excluding Valtur.
† Most seminars are in France for French customers.

Exhibit 5   Countries of Operations   Before New Structure

Country	Separate Commercial Office	Country Manager	Country Manager Supervising Commercial Operations	Villages
Germany	x			
Switzerland	x	x		x
Turkey			x	x
Italy	x	x		x
Venezuela	x			
Belgium	x			x
Mexico			x	x
United States	x	x		
Bahamas		x ⎫ Same as United States		x
Haiti		x ⎭		x
Brazil			x	x
Japan	x			
Great Britain	x			
Tunisia			x	x
Morocco		x		x
Holland	x			
Greece	x	x		x
Israel			x	x
Malaysia	x	x		x
France	x	x		
New Zealand	x			
Australia	x			x
Egypt		x		x
Singapore	x			
Canada	x			
Tahiti		x		x
South Africa	x			
Spain	x	x		x
Senegal		x Same		x
Ivory Coast		x		
Mauritius		x Same as Reunion		x
Sri Lanka		x Same as Mauritius		x
Guadeloupe		x ⎫ Same as United States		x
Martinique		x ⎭		x
Reunion Island		x		x
Dominican Republic		x Same as United States		x
United Arab Emirates				x

SALES AND MARKETING

In 1981 Club Med was international, with vacation sites all over the world, and so were its customers. They came from different continents, backgrounds, market segments, and did not look for the same thing in a vacation package. Club Med offered different types of villages and a wide range of activities to accommodate all the people who chose to go on a package deal.[2] The club offered ski villages in ski

---

[2] Most villages offered by Club Med are rented by the company or run under a management contract.

resorts for those who liked to ski; straw hut villages with a very Spartan comfort on the Mediterranean, mainly for young bachelors; and hotel and bungalow resort villages with all comforts open throughout the year, some with special facilities for families and young children. An average client who went to a straw hut village on the Mediterranean usually did not go to a plush village at Cap Skirring in Senegal (and the price was different too), although the same type of person might go to both.

A family with two or three children who could afford the time and money needed to travel to a relatively nearby village was, however, less likely to go to a village in Malaysia due to the long journey and the cost of transportation. Broadly speaking, diverse kinds of holiday seekers were represented among the Club's customers. However, there was a larger proportion of office workers, executives, and professional people and a small proportion of workers and top management. The sales and marketing of the Club, which began in Europe, had expanded to include two other important markets: the American zone, including the United States, Canada, and South America, and the Far Eastern Zone, including Japan and Australia. The Club's sales network covered 29 countries; sales were either direct through the Club-owned offices, 23 of which existed at the moment (see Exhibit 5 for countries where the Club owns commercial offices as well as villages and operations) or indirect through travel agencies (in France Havas was the main retailer). Originally all the villages were aimed at the European market; in 1968 with the opening of its first village in America, the Club broke into the American market and opened an office in New York. Since then the American market had grown more or less independently. Eighty percent of the beds in the villages located in the American geographical area were sold to Club members in the United States and Canada. Sixty-five percent of French sales, which represent 47 percent of the Club's turnover, were direct by personal visits to the office, by telephone or letter. However, in the United States, direct sales accounted for only 5 percent of the total, the remaining 95 percent being sold through travel agencies. These differences were partly explained by national preferences but also by a deliberate choice on the part of the Club. Until the appointment of Serge Trigano to lead the U.S. zone, all sales and marketing officers reported to a single worldwide marketing director. (The capital structure of Club Med is shown in Exhibit 6.)

Exhibit 6   Providers of Capital to Club Med, 1981

Compagnie Financière Group (Rothschild)	7.0%
Banque de Paris et des Pays Bas	6.0
REDEC Group	5.0
Credit Lyonnais	7.5
Union des Assurances de Paris	7.5
The IFI International Group	7.0
The Company Personnel's Common Investment Fund	5.0
	45.0
Public	55.0
	100%

THE VILLAGE

Club Med had around 90 villages, and it was growing fast. In the next three years (1981–84) about 20 new villages were scheduled to open. At Club Med a village was typically either a hotel, bungalows, or huts in usually a very nice area offering vacationers a series of several activities, among which were swimming, tennis, sailing, waterskiing, windsurfing, archery, gymnastics, snorkling, deep sea diving, horseback riding, applied arts, yoga, golf, boating, soccer, circuits, excursions, bike riding, and skiing. There were also usually on site a shop, a hairdresser, even some cash changing, car renting, and so on, and a baby or mini club in many places. Club Med was well known for having chosen sites which were the best in any country where they were, not only from a geographical point of view but also from an architectural point of view and the facilities provided. Exhibit 7 shows the number of villages which were open during the winter or summer season by type.

Essentially there were three types of villages. Hut villages were the cheapest, open only during the summer season. All the hut villages had been built early in Club Med's history and were on the Mediterranean. They did not offer all the comfort that the wealthy traveler was used to (common showers). Then there were bungalows or hotels or "hard type" villages which were more comfortable with private bathrooms. Most were still double-bedded which meant that two single men or women would have to share the same bedroom. In a village there were two types of people: the GMs or "gentils membres," who were the customers and came usually for one, two, three, or four weeks on a package deal to enjoy all the facilities and activities of any village and the GOs, or "gentils organisateurs," who helped people make this vacation the best. There were GOs for sports, for applied arts, for excursions, for food, for the bar, as disk jockeys, as dancing instructors, for the children or babies in the miniclubs, for maintenance, for traffic, for accounting, for receptions, and so forth.[3] On average there were 80 to 100 GOs per village.

There was a third category of people who were behind the scenes: the service people, usually local people hired to maintain the facilities and the garden, to clean up, and so on (about 150 service people per village). They could also be promoted to GOs.

Every season (either after the summer season from May to September or the winter season in April, or every six months) all the GOs would be moved from one village to another; that was one of the principles of the Club since its inception so that nobody would stay for more than six months in any particular site. The village chief of maintenance was an exception. He stayed one full year; if a village was closed in the winter, he remained for the painting, the repair, and so forth. The service people (local people) were there all the year around or for six months, if the village was only open in the summer (or winter for ski resorts). Exhibit 8 shows a typical organization structure of a village from the GO's point of view.

Under the chief of the village there were several coordinators: one for entertainment, responsible for all of the day and night activities (shows, music, night club, plays,

---

[3] Although the GOs were specialized by "function," they had also to be simply "gentils organisateurs," i.e., making the GM's life easy and participating in common activities, such as arrival cocktails, shows, and games.

Exhibit 7   Number of Villages by Type and Season

| | Sea | | | | |
	Huts	Bungalows	Hotels	Mountain	Total
Summer season	14	31	26	10	81
Winter season	0	19	11	23	53

Source: Club Méditerranée Trident N123/124, Winter 1980–81, Summer 1981.

games, and so on); the sports chief who coordinated all the sports activities in any particular village; the maintenance chief who would see to the maintenance of the village, either when there was a breakdown or just to repaint the village or keep the garden clean, grow new flowers, etc., and who was assisted by the local service people; the food and beverage chief who coordinated the cooking in the different restaurants as well as the bar. Usually there was a bazaar for miscellaneous, a garment boutique and a hairdresser under a boutique's coordinator. There was a coordinator for the baby club (if existent) within the village to provide the children with some special activities; this coordinator was also responsible for the medical part of the village (nurses and doctor). Many times there was a doctor on site, especially when a village was far from a big town. A coordinator of excursions and applied arts was on duty to help the GM to go somewhere or propose accompanied excursions (one, two, three days) for those who wanted it, or to assist a GO in making a silk scarf or pottery. There was a coordinator of administration, accounting, and control who dealt with cash, telephone, traffic, planning and reception, basic accounting, salaries for GOs and service personnel, taxes, and so forth. The food and beverage service and maintenance operations were heavy users of local service personnel.

Exhibit 8   Organization Chart of a Typical Village

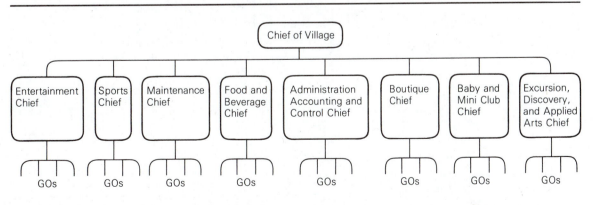

COMPANY ORGANIZATION STRUCTURE

Exhibit 9 shows the organization structure of Club Med's holiday village activity just before Serge Trigano's appointment as director of the U.S. zone. (The rest—time-sharing activities—are additional product-market subsidiaries).

There were several joint managing directors who participated in the management committee. Essentially the structure was a functional one with a joint managing director for marketing and sales, another one for operations, and several other function heads like accounting, finance, and tax. Exhibit 10 shows how the operations part of the organization was structured.

Essentially the structure was composed of three parts. As there was an entertainment chief in the village, there was a director of entertainment at the head office and the same for sports. There were several product directors who mirrored the structure of the village. There were country managers in certain countries where the club had several villages in operation, and then there were the 90 villages. All reported to Serge Trigano.

Exhibit 9   Organization Chart before November 1981, Holiday Villages Activity Only

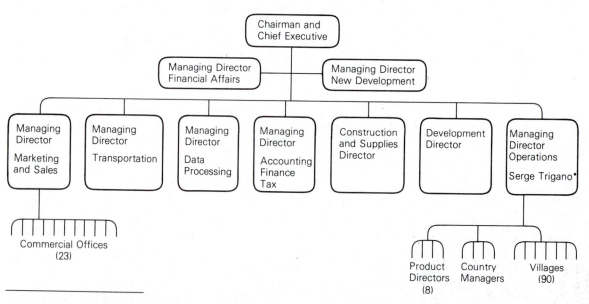

* Until his recent appointment as managing director, American zone.

Exhibit 10   Organization Chart—Operations Just before the New Move in November 1981

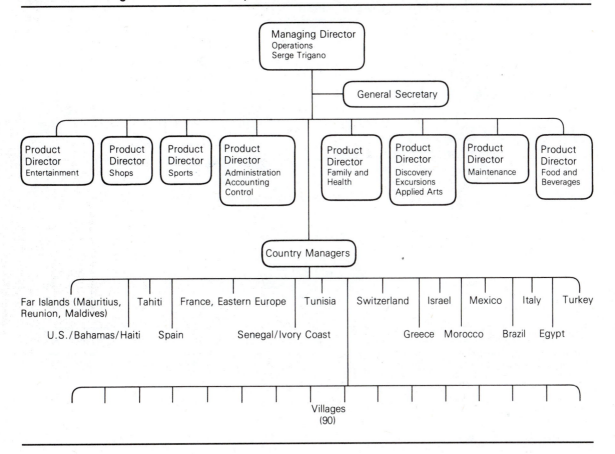

THE ROLE OF THE PRODUCT DIRECTORS

Product directors were responsible for the product policy. They made decisions with respect to the policy of Club Med in all the villages, such as the type of activities that should be in each village and the maintenance that should be done. They recruited and trained the various GOs needed for their domain (e.g., sports GOs, entertainment GOs, administration GOs, cooks). They staffed the villages by deciding with the director of operations which chief of village would go where and how many people would go with him. They made investment proposals for each village either for maintenance, new activities, extension, or renovation purposes. They also assumed the task of preparing the budgets and controlling application of policies in the villages by traveling extensively as "ambassadors" of the head office to the villages. Each one

Exhibit 11   Examples of Product Management

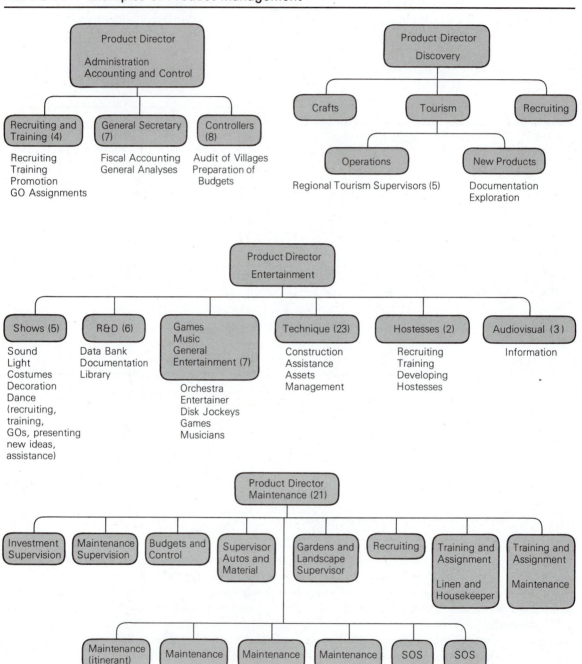

of them was assigned a certain number of villages. When visiting the village, he would go there representing not his particular product but Club Med's product as a whole. Also, each of them, including the director of operations, was assigned, on a rotating basis, the task of answering emergency phone calls from any village and making emergency decisions or taking action if necessary. Exhibit 11 presents examples of product organization. In the new regional structure their role and place were questioned.

THE ROLE OF THE COUNTRY MANAGER

Country managers were mainly the ambassadors of Club Med in the countries where Club Med had village(s). Usually they were located in countries with more than one village. They would handle political relations themselves, maintaining lasting relationships with elected bodies, mayors, civil servants, regional offices, and so forth. They would introduce to the new team coming every six months what the country had to offer, its constraints, local mores, the local people to be invited, local artists to be invited, the traps to be avoided, the types of suppliers, the type of local events that might be of interest for the village (so that the village would not forget, for instance, national holidays). They would try to get Club Med more integrated politically and socially in the host country, in particular in less developed countries where there was a gap between the abundance and richness of the club as compared to its immediate environment. They also had an assistance role, such as getting work permits for GOs and also finding suppliers; sometimes, in fact, the country manager had a buyer attached to his staff who would purchase locally for the different villages to get economies of scale. In addition, the country managers personally recruited and maintained lists of the service personnel available to Club Med. They would go and negotiate the salaries, wages, and working conditions of the service personnel with the unions so that the village was free of being involved every six months in a renegotiation. Also, they might have an economic role by helping develop local production or culture as the Club was a heavy buyer of local food and products. They could also act as a development antenna looking for new sites or receiving proposals from local investors and submit them to head office. They would also handle legal and tax problems when Club Med had a local legal entity as well as maintain relationships with the owners of the land, hotels, or bungalows when Club Med—as was often the case—was only renting the premises.

PROBLEMS WITH THE CURRENT STRUCTURE

The current structure had been set up about four years ago. It had also been Club Med's structure before 1971, but in between (1971–76) there had been a change in the operations side only which had involved setting up area managers; instead of having one director of operations, there had been five directors who had under their control several countries and villages. From 1971 to 1976 there had been no country managers and each of the area managers had had about 10 or 15 villages under his supervision. This structure was changed in 1976 because it seemed to have created several Club Meds in one. The area managers had started to try to get the best chiefs of village and people for their area. As a result GOs were not moving around every six months from one area of the world to another as was the policy, and also area managers started giving different types of services to their customers so that, for instance, a Frenchman going to one of the zones one year and to another the next year would find a different Club Med. These reasons had led to the structure presented in Exhibit 4 for the operations. But until now marketing had always been worldwide.

Of course the structure in operation until now had created the reverse problem: it seemed to Serge Trigano and others that it was too centralized. In fact Serge Trigano had a span of control (which is rarely achieved in industry) of 90 chiefs of villages plus 8 product directors and 14 country managers, all reporting to him from all over the world. There was an overload of information, too much detail, and too many issues being entrusted to him which would be worse as time would go by since Club Med was growing and doubling its capacity every five years. Beside the problem of centralization and information overload, another problem seemed to appear because Club Med's operations had not adapted enough to the international character of its customers. Most of the GOs were still recruited in France whereas now 15–20 percent of the customers came from the American zone. France was not even the best location to find GOs, who often needed to speak at least one other language. They had to be unmarried, under 30; they had to change countries every six months, with no roots; and they had to work long hours and be accessible 24 hours a day, seven days a week for a relatively low salary. The feeling was that maybe one could find happier and more enthusiastic people in Australia or Brazil than in France. Too much centralization, information overload, and lack of internationalization in operations were among the big problems in the current structure.

Also, there was a feeling that a closer local coordination between marketing and operations could give better results since customers seemed to concentrate on one zone (American in the United States, European in Europe) because of transportation costs, and a coordination might lead to a better grasp of customer needs, price, product, offices, and so on. For example, when Club Med was smaller and only in Europe, departure from its villages was done only once a week. As a result, reception at the village was also once a week. Lack of local coordination between operations and marketing had created arrivals and departures almost every day in certain villages, overburdening the GO's staff and disrupting the organization of activities. As another illustration, the American customer was used to standard hotel services (bathroom, towels, etc.), which may be different than in Europe. Closer local ties might help respond better to local needs.

Centralization had also created bottlenecks in assignments and supervision of people. Every six months everybody—all GOs—were coming back to Paris from all over the world to be assigned to another village. Five or 10 years ago this was in fact a great happening that allowed everybody to discuss with the product people, see headquarters, and find friends who had been in other villages, but now with 5,000 GOs coming almost at the same time—and wanting to speak to the product directors—reassigning them was becoming somewhat hectic. It was likely to be even worse in the future because of the growth of the company.

PLANNING AND CONTROL

The planning cycle could be divided into two main parts: first, there was a three-year plan started two years ago, which involved the product directors and the country managers. Each product director would define his objectives for the next three years and the action programs that would go with it and propose investments that he would like to make for his product in each of the 90 villages. All the product directors would meet to look at the villages one by one and see how the investment fit together as well as consider the staffing number of GOs and service personnel in broad terms for the next three years. Of course the big chunk of the investment program was the maintenance of the facilities since 55 percent of the investment program concerned such maintenance programs. The rest was concerned with additions or modifications of the villages, such as new tennis courts, theater, or restaurant, revamping a boutique, and so on. The country managers were involved in that same three-year plan. First of all they would give the product directors their feelings and suggestions for investments as well as for staffing the villages. In addition, they would provide some objectives and action programs in how they would handle personnel problems, political problems, economic problems, cultural and social integration, sales of Club Med in their country, and development.

Besides this three-year operational plan, there was the one-year plan whch was divided into two six-month plans. For each season a budget was prepared for each of the villages. This budget was mostly prepared by the product director for administration accounting, and it concerned the different costs, such as goods consumed, personnel charges, and rents. This budget was given to the chief of the village when he left with his team. In addition to this operational budget, there was an investment budget every six months in more detail than the three-year plan. This investment budget was prepared by the maintenance director under the guidance and proposal from the different product directors. It was submitted to the operations director and then went directly to the chief executive of the company. It had not been unusual (before the three-year plan) for the investment budget proposals of product directors to the maintenance director to run three times as high as what would in fact be given and allowed by the chief executive.

On the control side, there was a controller in each of the villages (administrator chief of accounting and control) as well as central controllers who would be assigned a region and would travel from one village to the other. But the local controller and his team in fact were GOs like any other ones and they were changing from one village to another every six months. There was a kind of "fact and rule book" that was left in the village so that the next team would understand the particular ways and procedures of the village. But mostly speaking, each new team would start all over again each time it was coming with a new budget and standard, rules, and procedures from the central head office as well as with the help of the fact and

Exhibit 12   The Club Growth in Numbers

	1969–70	*1970–71*	*1971–72*	*1972–73*	*1973–74*
Membership objective	255,000	293,000	299,000	318,000	339,000
Villages	25	55	55	60	61
Beds		33,900	34,300	36,400	37,000
Number of hotel nights—winter		881,000	948,000	1,018,000	1,044,000
Number of hotel nights—summer		2,651,000	2,801,000	2,850,000	2,920,000
Occupancy rate (percent)		68.07%	69.52%	66.81%	66.76%
Number of permanent employees	793	938	950	978	977
Number of GOs in villages (summer season)*					
Number of service personnel in villages (summer season)*					
Number of employees in Paris (operations only)					
Number of employees, country management					

* Number is approximate.

rule book. These two tools—the three-year plan and the six-month (season) budgets—were the main planning and control tools used.

OBJECTIVES AND POLICIES

Five objectives seemed to be important to Serge Trigano when reviewing the structure. One was that the club wanted to continue to grow and double its capacity every five years, either by adding new villages or increasing the size of the current ones (see Exhibit 12).

The second objective, which had always guided Club Med, was that it would have to continue to innovate, not to be a hotel chain but to be something different as it had always been and to continue to respond to the changing needs of the customers.

A third objective stemmed from the fact that Club Med was no longer essentially French. The majority of its customers (GMs) in fact did not come from France; as a result, it would have to continue to internationalize its employees, its structure, its way of thinking, training, and so on (see Exhibit 13).

The fourth objective was economic. Costs were increasing, but not all of these costs could be passed on to the gentils membres unless the club wanted to stop its growth. One way of not raising prices to the customer was to increase productivity by standardization, better methods, and procedures.

The fifth objective was to keep the basic philosophy of Club Med: to keep the village concept an entity protected as much as possible from the outside world but integrated in the country in which it was; to keep the package concept for GMs; and, finally, continue social mixing. Whatever your job or your social position, at Club Med, you were only recognized by two things: the color of your bathing suit

1974–75	1975–76	1976–77	1977–78	1978–79	1979–80
408,000	475,000	540,000	578,000	615,000	698,500
69	70	74	74	78	83
49,300	50,400	53,800	55,600	58,600	64,600
1,240,000	1,628,000	1,790,000	1,940,000	2,011,000	2,250,000
3,210,000	3,400,000	3,550,000	3,710,000	3,970,000	4,265,000
69.63%	70.70%	71.19%	71.65%	72.87%	72.88%
1,035	1,157	1,132	1,192	1,286	1,297
					6,000
					10,000
					250
					100

and the beads you wore around your neck which allowed you to pay for your scotch, orange juice, and so on, at the bar. Part of the philosophy, in addition, was to make sure that the GO's nomadism would continue: change every season.

THE PROPOSED NEW STRUCTURE

With these objectives in mind, the new structure to be effective November 1981 had just been sketched as shown in Exhibit 14. The idea would be to move the operations and marketing closer together in three zones. One would be America (North and South); another Europe and Africa; and the third (in the long run when this market would be more developed), the Far East. In each area a director would manage the operations side, that is, the villages and the marketing side—promotion,

Exhibit 13   Evolution of General Managers by Nationality

	1972–73	1978–79
France	60.0%	47.2%
United States	7.7	17.8
Belgium	8.7	6.0
Italy	7.5	5.6
West Germany	7.4	4.9
Switzerland	2.4	1.0
Others	5.7	12.2
	100%	100%

Exhibit 14   The Proposed Structure

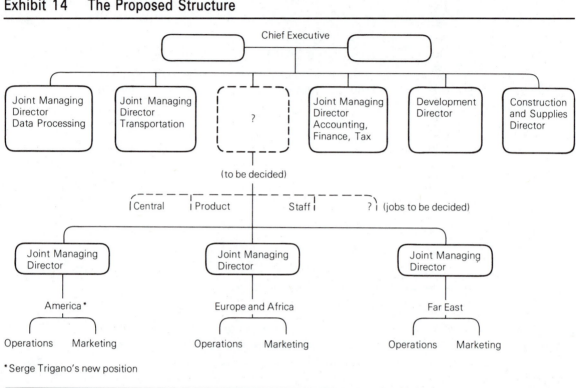

*Serge Trigano's new position

selling, pricing, distributing Club Med's concept. In fact, most of the American GMs were going to the American zone villages; most of the European GMs to the European zone; and most of the Asian GMs to the Asian zone—mainly because the cost of transportation from one zone to another was prohibitive.

This was the general idea, and now it had to be pushed further. Among the main interesting and troublesome aspects of the new structure were the following: how to avoid with this structure separating Club Med into three different entities with three different types of products? Should such occurrence be avoided? It seemed that this should not be allowed; that's why the structure which had been there four years ago with five regions failed. It had transformed Club Med into five mini Club Meds, although even at that time the five area managers did not have marketing and sales responsibility. In addition to this major issue of how to preserve the unity and uniqueness of Club Med with a geographic structure, several other questions were of great importance:

- Who would decide what activities would take place in a village?
- Who would decide the investments to be made in a village?

- Who would staff a village?
- Would there be a central hiring and training of all GOs or only some of them?
- How would the geographic managers be evaluated in terms of performance?
- If they wanted to continue with the GOs and give them the right and possibility to move every six months from one part of the world to another, how would the transfer of GOs be done?
- How should the transfer of GOs be coordinated?
- Should there be some common basic procedures, like accounting and reporting, and in that case, who would design and enforce those procedures?
- How could there be some coordination and allocation of resources among the three regions; who would do it; and how would it be done?

Also of importance was the problem of transition.

- What would happen to the country managers?
- What would happen to the product directors?
- What would happen to central marketing and sales?

These were some of the questions that bothered Serge Trigano on the flight to Paris from New York.

CASE 26 THE SPECIALTY PRODUCTS UNIT OF BMF INTERNATIONAL*

CONTINENTAL PACKAGING COMPANY'S PRODUCT LINE AND CUSTOMERS

Continental Packaging Company (CPC) was founded almost 150 years ago. After a long and successful history, Continental was acquired by BMF International in 1967. CPC's products included a wide variety of paper packaging materials and office products. CPC was organized into three businesses based on types of customers. Of the three business units, the Distributor Division concentrated its efforts on several thousand distributors of office and stationery products; the Retail Division sold directly to several hundred large retail outlets; and the Specialty Products unit handled a few very large accounts which required slightly customized products in large batches. Specialty Products was considerably smaller in sales dollars than its sister units, and its managers took care not to intrude on the territory and customers of the Distributor Division or the Retail Division.

In recent years CPC had experienced performance problems, and its leadership position had eroded in some geographic markets. Exhibit 1 shows a strategic capability profile for CPC. Some of CPC's strengths included its superior distribution channels, ability to manage financial affairs, availability of financial resources (being a division of BMF International), and its market share in college and commercial markets. On the other hand, CPC's executives had three big concerns: the company was relatively weak in product development, costs were too high, and CPC's profitability lagged behind that of competitors.

THE 1984 STRATEGIC PLANNING EFFORT

When Neil Greene was appointed president of CPC in 1982, the division faced serious difficulties. Because CPC's business depended on a derived demand and because CPC customers were very sensitive to general economic conditions, CPC suffered during the 1981–82 recession. Some executives felt that, prior to Greene's arrival, the division had been (perhaps unconsciously) "milked." Greene concluded that many long-standing problems had progressed to a dangerous stage, that the business was "unfocused," and that some type of genuine strategic planning was long overdue. Strategic planning attempts during earlier years produced plans that were never adequately implemented.

---

* Prepared by Professor Chuck Stubbart, University of Massachusetts at Amherst. The names of the company and key managers have been disguised to preserve the company's desire for anonymity.

Executives' sentiments generally converged with Greene's thinking—something "big" was needed—a turnaround.

During the summer of 1984, using the guidance of a consultant, 15 top executives of CPC met frequently to get a strategic planning effort on track. Six entire working days were spent off-site, and several series of three half-day, on-site sessions were held. Hundreds of executive working-hours were spent preparing and going over strategic capability profiles, environmental analysis, customer profiles, competitor profiles, product analysis, critical success factors, scenario generation, setting objectives, and alternative action plans. Initially some executives felt skeptical about the value of this planning exercise; other participants were reluctant to share freely and fully everything they knew and felt.

Comments by Executives about the 1984 Strategic Planning Effort

During the fall of 1984 (after that first year's planning sessions had concluded) CPC executives characterized the planning done that summer:

"The first thing I wondered was, 'How honest do they really want us to get?' "

"I knew it would be successful because I've seen strategic planning done elsewhere."

"Greene initiated it, but he stayed in the background. He wanted to know what we thought. Greene makes me nervous when he does this."

"I learned an incredible amount about our business."

"When Greene came in he realized we needed some direction. This was his way of getting it."

"We did planning before, but that planning never really amounted to much. Distractions were pouring over the walls. The plans never got implemented. Those plans didn't have actions specified. These do. For example, the old plan said 'deemphasize a certain business,' but nothing happened. The new plan says 'stop doing a certain business by Tuesday' and it gets stopped."

"It was a good idea to go off-site."

"The plan gives us a common language."

"The plan suits Greene's style perfectly. He is a man who wants thorough preparations and no loose ends. Greene says, 'Do it right, do it once, do it now.' "

"Given the history of the company and the style of Greene's predecessor this is a hard religion for us to practice. But we are making strides."

"Greene inherited some good programs."

"When we did planning before Greene arrived, the same problems and issues came up. But the management situation couldn't resolve conflicts so nothing much was done. Fortunately Greene doesn't have to face that."

"Jesus, I'm not sure we can do the things the plan calls for."

"I'm not sure we understand what we're doing."

"Implementing the plans is forcing some painful issues."

"Planning is worthwhile; it changed our direction."

"The good recent results we've had don't really come from the plan."

"The plan identified goals. But that was the easy part. Now we're down to the level of people, systems, dollars, information. It's getting harder."

Exhibit 1   Consolidated Packaging Company's Strategic Capability Profile

	Strength Rating (+3 to −3)[a]	Importance Rating (0 to +3)[b]
Marketing:		
Market share		
Retail Division	+1	+2
Distributor Division	+3	+2
Specialty Products Division	0	+1
Product line	+1	+2
Recognition by market	+1	+2
Market research	+2	+1
Awareness customer needs	−1	+3
Advertising	−1	+2
Sales force	−1	+3
Distribution	+2	+3
Product management	−1	+3
Product design	0	+2
Product Development:		
New products design	0	+2
Rate of new products introduction	−2	+1
Product development Facilities and personnel	+1	+1
Manufacturing:		
Costs	−2	+3
Manufacturing costs	−2	+3
Production control	+3	+2
Flexibility	0	+1
Adequate facilities	−1	+2
Cost of materials	−1	+1
Reliability of supplies	+1	+1
Capacity	0	+2
Financial		
Financial abilities	+1	+2
Management information systems	+2	+1
Financial resources	0	+2
Human Resources:		
Personnel policies	0	+1
Union relations	+2	+2
Turnover	+2	+1
Skill and commitment of work force	+1	+2
Corporate Management:		
Profitability	−1	+3
Senior management	−1	+3
Planning	−2	+2
Control	+1	+1
Coordination and communications	+1	+2
Organizational structure	−1	+1
Climate	−1	+2

[a] +3 to −3, where +3 is very strong, −3 very weak in comparison to competitors.
[b] 0 to 3, where 3 is very important.

Exhibit 1 *(concluded)*

Principal Opportunities and Threats—1984

Opportunities:
Expand market share in fast-growing wholesale segment
Expand market share in fast-growing info-processing market
Cost reduction
Develop human resources
Expand Specialty Products segment

Threats:
Not positioned for new products
Changing wholesaler strategies
Undermotivatd, uninspired work force
Specialty Products diverts resources better used elsewhere
Unresponsive to customer needs
Change in competitor's strategies
Commodity orientation of customers

"Greene was quite a shock to the CPC system. He's very different from his predecessor, MacDonald. . . . Greene is aloof and reserved, MacDonald was gregarious. Greene is circumspect, while MacDonald was a 'straight-ahead' fellow. Greene understands marketing and strategy; MacDonald was an operations man. . . . Strategic planning served as a way for us to get to know Greene, and vice versa."

The strategic plan stated several ambitious financial and product objectives for CPC:

- Earn $20 million after-tax profit by 1987.
- Increase sales 12–15 percent per year.
- Increase productivity 15 percent by 1987.
- Boost the after-tax return on sales to 8 percent.

Actions plans included:

- Pruning the product line.
- Reorganization.
- Improving service to customers.
- Installing an MBO system.

A renewed emphasis was placed on concentrating CPC efforts on critical challenges to the firm.

PAUL GOODMAN

Paul Goodman worked as the operations manager for CPC. He was in his mid-30s with a wife and two children and was a jogger and an ex-smoker. Paul graduated from Lowell Tech with a bachelor of science degree in industrial management in 1971. His first job was with American Optical Company where he held positions in distribution, warehousing, engineering, and production control. Paul came to CPC in 1977. He moved from production control manager to bindery plant manager. In

1981 corrugated products were added to his responsibilities. In July 1984 he was appointed operations manager for CPC.

His office was located in a hundred-year-old manufacturing facility beside a canal, astride several sets of railroad tracks. The plant site was in an old, somewhat run-down, New England manufacturing center of intermediate size; CPC headquarters was located in a modern glass building about 10 minutes away.

A consistent management style and philosophy shaped Paul's interactions with co-workers; he always noticed and dealt with the interpersonal elements of situations—the intentional and unintentional impacts of words and events. He demonstrated particularly good skills for giving feedback or direction in "sticky" situations, such as performance appraisals, or when failures occurred. But his style also accommodated open expressions of anger or enthusiasm. Paul constantly tried to find the positive elements in a situation and work with them—what he called "problem-tunities." Paul liked numbers. On the other hand, he didn't have extraordinary faith in "bean-counting," although he usually seemed to know exactly how many beans there were.

Paul was strongly committed to his marriage and his family. He sometimes put aside work demands in favor of pressing family concerns. He worried that the work demands placed on a company executive might erode the quality of his family life. Paul left the plant at quitting time, usually taking work home in his briefcase.

In the late summer and early fall of 1984 Paul Goodman was a very busy man. He had just received a promotion and was enrolled in an executive MBA program at a well-known nearby university. Besides all that, he was a member of the strategic planning group which met regularly to chart the future strategy of CPC.

Exhibit 2   Consolidated Packaging Company's Organization Structure, Fall 1984

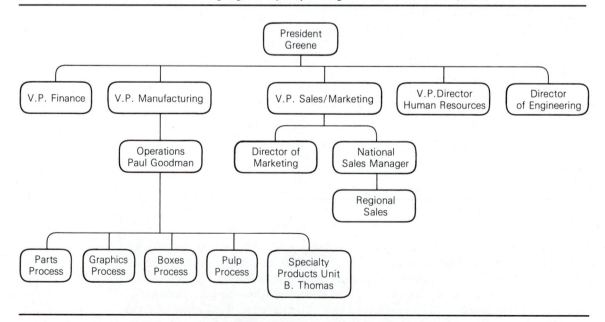

Among Paul's numerous new responsibilities in fall 1984 was serving as general manager of Specialty Products. Paul remarked that he found his assignment as head of Specialty Products ironic because, as a factory executive, "I used to be against this business!" He explained that the special requirements and operations of Specialty Products diverted plant personnel from more important operations supporting the Distributor Division and Retail Division. Actually Paul welcomed the chance to take responsibility for a profit center, realizing that his upward mobility would be limited if he didn't broaden his experience beyond manufacturing operations.

Exhibit 2 depicts CPC organization in fall 1984. Under this organization, Specialty Products reported to the manufacturing vice president. CPC executives explained that they couldn't afford a traditional product-line divisional setup because of the extra "costs" required.

In the past Specialty Products had never been considered an important part of CPC. In fact, during the 1984 strategic planning sessions, executives among the planning group seriously considered whether Specialty Products ought to be divested or, more likely, simply disbanded. Many executives argued that Specialty Products was a distraction, that margins would never reach satisfactory levels. CPC nearly abandoned Specialty Products. At times, however, Specialty Products "looked good." When Retail Division and Distributor Division (the other two business units of CPC) lagged, causing excess capacity in the plant to hurt profits, Specialty Products was the mechanism for soaking up that excess capacity. However, when business was good for Retail Division and Distributor Division—Specialty Products faded into a distinctly secondary role. Paul called this phenomenon "the light switch business." Ultimately, Specialty Products survived this scrutiny—but only as a means for soaking up unused capacity—not as a genuine opportunity area. In fact, Specialty Products' mission expressly ruled out additional investment for Specialty Products except under extraordinary circumstances.

Exhibits 3 and 4 show financial data for the BMF International Company and the CPC. Although Specialty Products was expected to lose money in 1984, certain ambiguities remained. First, executives at Specialty Products argued that they received allocations for too much division overhead. Second, analysts could not calculate precisely how much assets were committed to Specialty Products. The reason for this confusion was that all three business units shared the same products (to a degree) and the same intermingled manufacturing equipment and processes in the plant.

Exhibit 3   BMF International's Recent Performance

	1980	1981	1982	1983	Projected 1984
Net sales ($000)	$899,188	$910,965	$968,491	$990,122	$1,130,000
Earnings as a percent of sales	5.6	4.7	5.3	3.6	4.5
Return on equity	17.9%	14.7%	16.5%	10.8%	15.1%

Exhibit 4 Operating Performance and Projections for Consolidated Packaging Company, a Division of BMF International   Thousands of Dollars

	1980	1981	1982	1983	1984	Projected 1985	1986	1987
Sales	$131,682	$152,524	$151,846	$175,883	$185,477	$190,816	$220,245	$237,861
Gross profit from sales	43,191	51,400	47,831	59,624	61,763	66,976	80,389	87,532
General and administrative expenses	29,628	35,843	37,354	46,608	47,111	49,039	53,960	55,897
Selling expenses	29,628	35,843	37,354	46,608	47,111	49,039	53,960	55,897
Depreciation	3,400	3,400	2,500	5,300	3,820	4,120	4,400	4,400
Capital expenditures	8,200	9,600	5,000	2,500	2,800	6,000	6,000	6,000
Net earnings	8,296	9,304	7,896	7,563	8,160	9,350	12,554	15,461

THE SITUATION AT SPECIALTY PRODUCTS: FALL 1984

Bob Thomas managed the Specialty Products unit. He'd been working for CPC about 20 years. Prior to managing Specialty Products, Bob held positions in manufacturing, customer service, and sales. Bob was a friendly, open person, with a smile always ready. People at CPC commented that Bob knew the products particularly well and that he loved new ideas. Occasionally Bob had been criticized for what some people called his tendency to "charge off in too many directions at once." Bob countered, "You've got to take advantage of your opportunities when you get them, not necessarily when you are ready for them."

Specialty Products concentrated its efforts in New England. The customer base included mainly very large divisions of *Fortune 500* companies with a need for customized, packaging products. Special, decorated boxes constituted the principal product. Specialty Products' mission was stated in the 1984 strategic plan:

> Specialty Products is specifically authorized to pursue any customer who offers the potential for large orders of custom merchandise for resale. Specialty Products will be addressed as a growth business with the particular intent to use excess capacity. New business will be at 20 percent margin or better. Major capital investment to support this market will not be made except in unusual circumstances and after very careful examination and justification.

Recently Specialty Products had suffered several serious reverses:

- Customers, shocked by the economic contraction and high interest rates, began managing their inventories more tightly to help their cash flow.
- Although Specialty Products produced custom products, customers remained sensitive to prices. Specialty Products' standard costs rose 13 percent in the most recent year in spite of continued efforts (such as installing a class "A" MRP system) to drive down labor and materials costs.
- Several serious quality problems upset sales efforts.
- Salesforce morale hit an all-time low. Without clear objectives, having little training, and believing themselves "second-class citizens" compared to salespeople in other divisions, the Specialty Products' sales effort floundered.

On the other hand, Thomas believed that Specialty Products could produce the best-made products on the market, that his in-house customer service constituted an important advantage, and that CPC's vertical integration and skillful inventory planning formed an advantage. The key problem was, according to Thomas, "How can I increase sales, increase market share, increase margins . . . in the face of high costs and no investment?"

Specialty Products had a large number and variety of competitors. Many of its rivals made only a very narrow product line from a single type of material, in just a few types of construction, and chose to compete in local or regional markets. Typically Specialty Products faced a different set of competitors for nearly every account. Customers ordinarily divided their purchases among two, three, or four suppliers, preferring not to rely on a single supplier. Most supply relationships in the industry lasted a long time, and there was not much shuffling by customers from supplier to supplier. Although this type of packaging didn't constitute a significant cost for most customers, mistakes and shortages in supply could severely disrupt a customer's operations—imposing large costs.

Specialty Products' affiliation with CPC provided an advantage insofar as customers believed that they could rely on CPC's distribution efficiency and financial health. But the image of "bigness" also carried a cost. Customers regarded Specialty Products (and CPC) as "stodgy," not dynamic. Worse, some customers (with justification) doubted CPC's long-term commitment to their particular market.

In fall 1984, Paul Goodman and Bob Thomas tried to define Specialty Products' competitive situation. They called in a consultant to help them with strategic planning—an exchange between Paul and Bob laid out some of the issues:

Bob: As you know, Paul, Specialty Products is only a small part of the CPC pie. First, you've got Distributor Division serving the wholesalers, the contract stationers, and dealers. That's $140 million. Then there's Retail Division which takes care of another large market. Another $50 million there. Also, there's Chain, which was about $15 million—but CPC decided as a result of the 1984 planning to get out of that business. Finally, here we are at Specialty Products. We take our business from large corporate accounts. We only take very large orders, at least $500,000 each, and we provide semicustomized products.

Paul: We get the low margin business.

Bob: That's it.

Paul: What do we have going for us?

Bob: Well, CPC is one of the biggest, oldest, and most respected firms in the industry. The customers say that CPC can provide fast service, a broad line of products, and we have distribution everywhere. Also, in the past anyway, our quality has been superior in areas such as packaging, shipping, and products themselves.

Paul: But, we've got high costs, right?

Bob: Yes, and that's a constant problem. Our customers will sometimes pay a little extra for quality, service, and so forth, but not much more.

Paul: That's why we've always been forced into price-cutting and that's why margins are never good for Specialty Products.

Bob: Exactly. The salesforce, whose compensation is tied to sales volume, can't resist the temptation to cut price and promise the world. The salesforce is coming off a very bad year. No bonuses. They are very demoralized.

Paul: So the problem is, how do you differentiate and innovate in a traditional, high-cost, business?

Bob: Right.

Paul: According to the objectives for Specialty Products contained in the 1984 strategic plan, we need 20 percent margins and 4 percent return after taxes while increasing business from $8.2 million to $10.9 million.

Bob: A mighty tall order. Plus, you've got to consider that CPC won't make any capital expenditures for Specialty Products.

Paul: How do we define this market, where do we start?

Bob: Well, one problem is that nobody keeps organized data about our business. All we have to go on is rumors and our experience. We presently serve a number of very large accounts. These people always use multiple sources. For most of these accounts we are number one or number two.

Paul: We've been losing ground with some of these accounts, right?

Bob: That's right. We've lost our relative share with some accounts, such as Western. . . . Others, like Macintosh, have even displaced us to a lower slot. Most of these defeats have been caused by quality problems. There was that "green gunk" on some binders that we shipped to Phillips. . . . There was that mistaken color for Becker. . . . Altogether we've got 12 big accounts. Our competitors for this business are basically small, poorly financed outfits who serve very limited geographic areas or who go for a product niche.

Paul: We're going for customized business on basically standard products.

Bob: Yes. But I've got an idea for a four-color printing process that we could work on. For this, we would go to all kinds of corporations who publish boxes holding product information, for example. We can provide a colorful, splashy product that other suppliers can't touch. CPC even has the printing capability for this. I've already talked to advertisers about this idea. . . .

THE COURSE OF EVENTS

This section contains a brief synopsis of important events involving implementation of CPC's plans for Specialty Products during the time between summer 1984 and fall 1985.

Late Summer 1984

In July CPC presented its strategic plan to BMF International. Executives at the parent company examined financial relationships, how much profit CPC would contribute, and how much investment would be needed. They seemed to view Greene's planning efforts as slightly eccentric—"Greene's thing." Nevertheless, there was enough in Greene's plan to justify his requests, and the parent company went along with the overall CPC plan as submitted.

Serious quality problems continued to plague Specialty Products. For example, there was the infamous case of the "green gunk" on a product. Extensive investigation revealed that the "green gunk" originated in a chemical reaction brought about by exposing plated metals to moisture. Another emergency rocked the unit when a large customer received a shipment of boxes with discolored covers.

October 1984

Goodman and Thomas remained uncertain about what to submit for their upcoming Planning Review meeting within the CPC division. They suspected that Greene harbored ideas about what Specialty Products' strategy ought to entail, but Greene would not reveal his ideas. What did Greene want? Goodman took advantage of occasions when Greene was present to initiate informal discussions with Greene. The closest Greene came to evaluating Goodman's "trial balloons" during these asides was to remark cryptically: "You are teetering on the edge of the acceptable."

Goodman and Thomas were having trouble answering basic strategy questions about Specialty Products: What was their market position? How did customers view

Specialty Products/CPC? How could Goodman and Thomas discern whether a particular approach would be acceptable to Greene before having to recommend and present it to him? The most troublesome question was, "How can Specialty Products differentiate itself?" Goodman jokingly referred to one possible strategy, "We can ship you high-cost products better than anyone." Goodman made informal contacts with quality control, accounting, marketing, and finance to check out other departments' reactions to the preliminary plans and ideas that Specialty Products was thinking about proposing.

Thomas approached advertising agencies with his idea about a four-color lithographed cover for boxes. He claimed that nobody else had anything like it. He felt sure that CPC could manufacture this technically difficult product.

Specialty Products was experiencing paperwork snafus in October. Other departments found it hard and/or annoying to deal with the special routines needed for Specialty Products shipments, customer service, and accounting.

Goodman and Thomas tried to outline a strategy for Specialty Products. Some of the major uncertainties they wondered about were: What should they include? What sequence should they follow for presenting topics? How much quantitative data? What promises were they willing to make? What did Greene want? Goodman and Thomas met to discuss their efforts:

Bob: Well, I've got an idea of what the plan should contain. Here it is (shows Goodman some notes). I'd say we have 20 percent of the publisher's business. High costs hurt us. The market size is probably $400 million. Maybe the market is called "Custom Decorated Products."

Paul: We need more information about competitors in there.

Bob: OK. I'll put in Benson, Coral, and Great Lakes.

Paul: You're kidding, Benson is in there?

Bob: Sure, they're in there, they do Washington Products.

Paul: Well, suppose the segment is $60 million, and we should say we have 10–20 percent.

Bob: I'd say $75 million.

Paul (who is figuring on a pad): Let's call it 15 percent. Do we have 80 percent of our business in publishers? What do you call Honeywell? Western is different?

Bob: Call it the corporate segment.

Paul: Who else is a big competitor for the corporate business?

Bob: Nickelstone.

Paul: I never heard of Nickelstone.

Paul: Can we classify these competitors? Who is the toughest?

Bob: Probably Denton, then Creighton.

Paul: How do these competitors see us?

Bob: We're General Motors. We're an ocean liner, and they are rowboats. Our size worries them. When we sneeze they catch cold.

Paul: Let's hope we are not the Titanic!

Paul (reaching into his filing cabinet): I think we should take another look at the CPC plan to get more ideas.

Bob: You know, what worries me most is that our excess capacity is in the traditional boxes. That area is not growing. That is not the best place to look for new business. I've got ideas for new materials, special printing, exciting new constructions. . . . there are your growth areas. I personally feel we should go more for the growth areas.

Paul: We don't have the capacity. That's not our mission.

Bob: What does Greene want to see in this plan? He's a marketing man.

Paul: I'm not sure. He plays it pretty close to the vest. He'll make changes. If there are problems he'll see them.

Bob: I feel as if we're in a defensive position.

Paul: Yeah, the squeaky wheel at CPC.

Bob: I hope the plan isn't set in concrete. Costs are the major issue.

Goodman began attacking Specialty Products' quality problems. Goodman revamped procedures for shipping Specialty Products items, adding a final, extra quality control inspection. He conducted meetings with manufacturing and shipping personnel in the plant to impress on them that Specialty Products couldn't afford any more quality slip-ups.

The Executive Committee (CPC's senior executives) met on October 15 to examine budgets—based on functional and business unit plans derived from CPC's strategic plan. After hearing the Specialty Products plan (see Exhibit 5), Greene announced,

---

Exhibit 5   Outline of Specialty Products Strategic Plan October 15, 1983

1. *Charter/Mission*
    Growth business . . . unused production capacity . . . large corporate customers . . . custom products . . . no investment except unusual circumstances
2. *Situation*
    Concentrate in Northeast
    Few customers, mostly large divisions of *Fortune 500* firms
    Binder products
    "Good" market share
3. *Problems*
    Economy hurt customers
    High costs, heavy overhead allocations
    Quality problems
    Demoralized salesforce
    Long lead-time on new product
    Regional approach limits sales
    Paperwork confusion
4. *Strengths*
    Good service due to MRP and specialized customer service
    Part of a *Fortune 500* company.
    Excess capacity?
    Broad line in collateral products
    Excellent distribution system
    Good product engineering
5. *Product Strategy*
    Use excess capacity
    New products
6. *Projections*

	1984	1985	1986	1987
Sales (millions)	10.0	11.3	13.5	16.5
Percent increase	0	13	20	22
Margin percent	20	23	22	21.5

"Sounds like the same old stuff to me. You wanted support. I'm giving it (in reference to an approval for a new job position for Specialty Products). Now . . . go out and get some growth."

The executive committee raised the 1985 Specialty Products sales target to $14 million from Goodman's proposal of $13 million. After the meeting, in an aside, marketing vice president McCracken confided to Goodman "what you have is OK . . . but it needs a spark." Goodman considered that meeting "a base hit, not a home run."

Comments about Specialty Products from Top Executives after Hearing Goodman's Presentation

Joe Parker, vice president of manufacturing:

> In the past CPC has never taken Specialty Products seriously. Now that is changed. . . . The plan Goodman and Thomas are proposing is good. . . . Our competitors are vulnerable. . . . Perhaps the plan is even too modest. . . . Goodman and Thomas are too conservative. . . . They do have organizational problems at Specialty Products, especially in the area of salesforce training. . . . Unit needs strong direction. . . . You can achieve more sales and higher margins with better sales effort. . . . Sure, it's unusual for a business unit to report to manufacturing, but we can't afford high-priced organizational structures. . . . I'm thrilled about the prospects for Specialty Products. . . . I like a challenge. . . . In six or eight months we'll know.

Frank Holden, vice president for finance:

> Specialty Products is only 5 percent of CPC's business. Some people think it could be more. I'm not sure. . . . You could call me a borderline believer. . . . In 1984 we missed all our targets for Specialty Products. . . . Specialty Products has a low margin and it's declining . . . quality problems. . . . Specialty Products isn't even as good as it looks because allocations of costs are dubious. . . . It reminds me of a business we had at another company where I worked; people kept asking "When will we crack this big market?" We never did. . . . Getting more business and more margin will be tough. . . . We need to see good progress in 1985. A critical year.

Dick McCracken, vice president of marketing:

> The Goodman-Thomas plan needs more work. . . . Right now there is a widening gap between the plans and slipping results. Maybe they are now bottoming out. . . . Specialty Products has to grow like Hell . . . bigger steps . . . run fast. . . . New organizational setup is real good. They need the sales manager position. . . . Problems with the customer service department. . . . The four color idea is interesting. . . . Thomas knows the factory and he knows the products. . . . Unless we come up with something new, we can't get the margins. . . . Nasty quality problems must be solved. . . . I think Specialty Products can meet the objectives, we just don't know all the steps yet . . . plans aren't finished. We need to pin our hopes to attainable things . . . solid steps, no panaceas. . . . Thomas shouldn't conclude that everything is OK now that they have a sales manager. . . . My role is to help them with their marketing.

Phil Townsend, vice president of human resources:

I don't really know much about the Specialty Products plan, except in those respects which involve personnel. . . . My experience has been that you can't consider national accounts a real market. Customers want a broad-based supplier for these products. I don't think you can be a specialty supplier of particular products over the long run. . . . I would only intervene in their planning if they were screwing up.

Neil Greene, president:

I'm supporting Specialty Products because I think they have a market there.

November 1984

At Goodman's initiative Specialty Products reorganized as shown in Exhibit 6. Thomas returned to an inside office (next to Goodman) from working in the field. Discussion began concerning prospects for a sales manager position. New positions were at that time very hard to get approved. Greene promised Goodman that the position would receive approval.

Goodman and Thomas met with their Specialty Products salesforce to explain the thrust of strategic planning and the recent changes in Specialty Products' organization. Thomas was particularly enthusiastic during the sessions. A salesman remarked, "For the first time, we have a direction." Goodman and Thomas concluded that morale had improved.

Goodman intervened to smooth ruffled feathers in disputes between Thomas and Callahan. Customer Service found Specialty Products' demands increasingly difficult to satisfy. Callahan didn't like working for Thomas. Emotions ran high as Goodman

Exhibit 6   Specialty Products Unit Reorganization

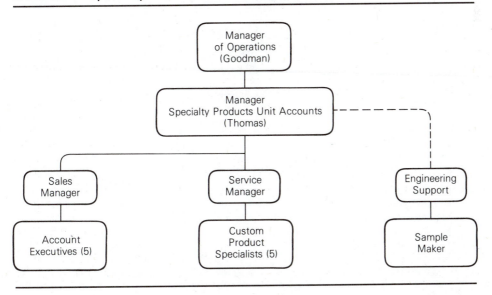

spent hours with the two of them, seeking resolutions for their problems. After an extended meeting of Goodman, Thomas, and Callahan, the issue seemed ironed out.

"The Spirit is here," commented Goodman. "It was a big move to get Thomas inside instead of on the road."

Improved quality control procedures were now firmly in place.

Goodman began working with flow charts, trying to translate the strategy he had presented to the executive committee into specifics. He said "We need to know who is going to do what." He began to draft a written plan, which he said he would give to Greene. The consultant helped Goodman write the plan. Greene hadn't asked for a written plan.

December 1984

Goodman confided to the consultant, "I wish we were moving faster." Sales and profit figures revealed that Specialty Products fell far short of its 1984 budget requirements (see Exhibit 7). Goodman and Thomas could feel the psychological pressure—

Exhibit 7   1984 Actual Performance versus Budget, Specialty Products   In Thousands

	1984 Budget	1984 Actual
Revenues:		
Net sales	$12,309	$ 9,600
Direct costs	9,594	7,815
Gross margin	2,715	1,785
As percent of net sales	22.1%	18.6%
Variances (see Note)	374	794
Gross profit	2,341	991
As percent of net sales	19.0%	10.3%
Operating expenses:		
Selling	663	666
Warehousing	1,047	850
Transportation	85	68
Total operating expense	1,795	1,584
As percent of net sales	14.6%	16.5%
Contribution	546	(593)
As percent of net sales	4.4%	(6.1)%
Overhead expenses:		
Research and engineering	215	204
General and administrative	511	345
Corporate overhead	129	126
Total overhead	855	675
As percent of net sales	7.0%	7.0%
Earnings before tax	$ (309)	$(1,268)

Note: Consolidated Packaging Company computed "direct costs" at a standard, then figured in any variance from standard costs as an expense.

level rising. Specialty Products' shortcomings became a topic of frequent, sometimes biting comment. At the December profit and loss meeting Greene commented, "Either we are going to grow this business (Specialty Products) or we are going to shut it down." Goodman and Thomas worried. Goodman remarked that the excitement had left him sleepless at night "once or twice."

Discussions and feedback between Thomas and a higher-up outside the official chain-of-command confused Thomas and annoyed Goodman. Angry words were exchanged between Goodman and one of his superiors.

The marketing vice president, McCracken, continued to make supportive asides to Goodman. McCracken commented that he was pleased by changes in Specialty Products.

The Thomas/Callahan dispute continued to simmer.

January 1985

The Specialty Products plan, revamped to reflect changes mandated by November's budget meeting, was formally presented to Greene. At that meeting, Goodman used transparencies to convey their plans (see Exhibit 8). Basically the revised plan entailed pushing three new product variations, continuing to investigate the new four-color process, solving quality problems, increasing penetration into existing accounts, and reorganization. Sales volume growth targets were upped from the original 12 to 22 percent yearly, to 25 percent yearly. The executive committee agreed that more work on the Specialty Products plan was needed. Some executives remained skeptical. Greene decided that the latest month for Specialty Products was "semi-solid."

End-of-the-year work overwhelmed planning. Planning projects were all put on a back burner. Goodman's other operating responsibilities dominated his time.

CPC executives and salesmen attended their annual sales meeting in Florida. At an awards banquet (where Specialty Products received no awards) Goodman commented to Greene, "Next year we are going to win all the prizes." Greene responded, "I'd love to worry about that."

Exhibit 8   Notes from Goodman's Presentation to Executive Committee, January 1985, Specialty Products's Strategic Plan

---

Tasks Needing Attention

I. Organization
   Improved sales training
   Clear up problems with Customer Service
II. Quality
   Enhance work-in-process audits
   Continue workshops on quality
III. Market
   Document market strategy
   Review pricing policy, increase prices? (Paul Goodman said no)
   Introduce four-color process
IV. Issues
   Problems with capacity allocations

February 1985

Goodman and Thomas met with their salesforce for three days. They discovered that the salesforce was "loaded with useful competitive information." The salesforce evidently appreciated the attention.

Greene remarked to Goodman (after two months of improving sales volume), "It's no longer a question of whether Specialty Products will succeed, it is a question of when." Goodman was pleased with the recent sales-volume increases, but he still worried that the key to a successful strategy was somehow missing. He also worried that his gross margins weren't high enough (Exhibit 9).

According to Goodman, Thomas was beginning to lose sight of their strategic trajectory. Goodman constantly coaxed Thomas away from tempting new products and out from under operating details. Goodman told Thomas to concentrate on the strategic aspects of the situation.

March 1985

Thomas now had his sights set on the VHS/video market, an exciting, rapidly growing business. According to Thomas, Specialty Products could manufacture and print the product-packaging for video tapes. "The computer revolution will replace paper. It's so exciting! But not if you sell traditional products. If you sell traditional products, it stinks," he explained.

Specialty Products' gross margins hovered around 16 percent. Goodman complained, "This is not good enough." A senior consultant observed that CPC remained wedded to sales performance rather than profitability. Improving sales volume for Specialty Products seemed to relieve some pressure from top management.

Goodman was now convinced that what Specialty Products needed was more business from its present customers, rather than new customers: "We need to make them addicts." Until then he had been uncertain whether the strategy should concentrate on getting more business from old customers or finding new customers. Thomas

---

Exhibit 9   1984 Monthly Gross Margins for Specialty Products

Month	Actual Margin	Budgeted Margin
January	17.7	25.1
February	21.2	24.7
March	22.5	26.3
April	17.9	26.0
May	21.9	25.3
June	21.0	27.1
July	22.0	25.6
August	18.0	24.4
September	20.4	26.6
October	20.4	25.9
November	21.0	24.7
December	26.1	25.1

was not happy with Goodman's conclusion. Thomas favored finding new products and new customers.

Goodman mentioned a recent visit of two important customers of Specialty Products who confided that, with the improvement in Specialty Products' quality they had experienced and the resulting increased reliability of Specialty Products, they would give Specialty Products a greater proportion of their business.

Goodman learned about a letter from Greene to another unit, advising that unit "you ought to copy the activities of Specialty Products." Goodman felt this proved that Specialty Products was "gaining credibility."

Goodman reflected: "Greene has given us everything we've asked for so far. He's letting us do it our way. If we don't produce, we have no rock to hide behind."

Specialty Products' new quality control system detected a big quality problem, saving an important shipment. Goodman and Thomas were ecstatic.

Problems between the Customer Service department and Specialty Products reached another boiling point. Thomas and Callahan argued vehemently. Goodman intervened.

Goodman was now working on competitive analyses. He still wasn't quite sure whether Specialty Products had a competitive advantage—or could develop one. "What is CPC? What is Specialty Products? What the hell are we? How can we make them (customers) want us?", Paul wondered.

Martha Appleton (administrative assistant to Goodman) was busy learning to use a newly installed microcomputer. Martha's analysis of the margin shortfall helped Goodman and Thomas to stave off pressure from their superiors (and a consultant) advocating price hikes. The microcomputer provided forecasts of margins based on different pricing structures, various mixtures of accounts, and various volumes of sales. Everyone was quite impressed with the new technology.

Goodman wondered if he could find a way to use an inventory management system called MRP to achieve a competitive advantage. MRP strived to limit work-in-process and other inventories to levels adequate to maximum efficiency. About 5,000 firms used MRP in some form. CPC claimed that it was among the 5 percent "best" users of MRP. Goodman had been a major force behind the installation of MRP at CPC.

April 1985

Goodman concluded that Specialty Products could double its business through its existing accounts. "Do what you've got right. Get more of what you've got," he reasoned.

At a meeting of CPC's Executive Committee, Goodman presented Specialty Products' latest financial results (Exhibit 10) and ideas. Specialty Products' continuing failure to meet margin requirements was noted by finance vice president, Frank Holden. However, Greene encouraged Goodman saying, "If you can do what you say you can do, you'll be doing fine." Some Executive Committee members expressed concern about Thomas's performance. Goodman's reaction to meeting: "We're in better shape than we were, we've bought some time."

Specialty Products' tight quality control procedures were now creating a more than desired amount of scrap and waste, raising costs. Goodman was concerned.

Exhibit 10   Specialty Products' Actual Performance versus Budget, 1985 In Thousands

	1985 Budget	Projected 1985 Actual*
Revenues:		
Net sales	$10,000	$12,000
Direct costs	8,581	10,189
Gross margin	2,401	2,185
As percent of net sales	21.9%	17.7%
Variances	204	85
Gross profit	2,197	2,100
As percent of net sales	20.0%	17.0%
Operating expenses:		
Selling	635	639
Warehousing	992	1,115
Transportation	88	136
Total operating expense	1,715	1,890
As percent of net sales	15.6%	15.3%
Contribution	482	210
As percent of net sales	4.4%	1.7%
Overhead expenses:		
Research and engineering	210	272
General and administrative	489	516
Corporate overhead	112	113
Total overhead	811	901
As percent of net sales	7.4%	7.3%
Earnings before tax	$ (329)	$ (482)

* Based on 9 months of 1985.

May 1985

Goodman received his personal performance appraisal covering the prior year. Goodman said of his appraisal: "There is nothing specifically relating to Specialty Products."

"What if" scenarios regarding prices and gross margins produced a consensus forecast of a 19.5 percent margin for 1985.

Strategic planning sessions for 1985 began. CPC executives spent one day at a pleasant mountain resort. Topics included a review of the 1984 plan, critiques of the 1984 planning process, stating expectations for 1985's planning process, and compiling competitor profiles. Goodman was uncertain about what should go into his 1985 plan. He observed, "No new issues seem to be coming up at the sessions. People seem to have the attitude, 'We've agreed upon what should be done, let's get on with it.'" Sessions seemed too heavily focused on marketing issues. Greene admonished executives about "backsliding, not thinking strategically."

The surge in CPC sales during the prior four months now threatened maximum capacity for some types of products—especially products of Specialty Products (Exhibit 11). Thomas and Goodman were increasingly worried that they would get the "short

---

Exhibit 11   Work Center Capacity Analysis, 1984

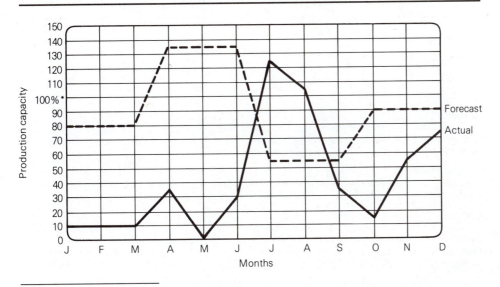

* 100 percent capacity means two shifts and average downtime for maintenance and breakdowns.

---

end of the stick." The situation reminded Goodman of the "light switch" history of Specialty Products. Goodman complained, "They're taking my capacity while asking me to grow."

An important Specialty Products customer visited the plant. According to Goodman, "They say we are outstanding. They love us." He believed that this feedback was a sign that the new strategy was working.

Goodman and a consultant worked on a written plan to encapsulate Specialty Products' strategy. While Greene had never asked for a formal, written plan, Goodman thought the plan should be written down (see Exhibit 12).

Goodman invited several customers to send some of their operations personnel to Specialty Products. He offered seminars on MRP systems for them. He reasoned that Specialty Products customers struggled under heavy pressure from their parent companies to reduce costs. If Specialty Products could persuade them to use MRP, not only would the customers feel grateful, but more importantly, the resulting tight connection between Specialty Products' systems and customer systems would constitute a switching cost for these customers.

Although Specialty Products' mission only specified, "to use excess capacity," Goodman began to consider making a capital expenditures request of $1 million for 1985. "I think we can get it," he concluded.

CPC's engineering department responded slowly to requests about product design for Specialty Products items. "They don't think we're a high priority business. Almost all their attention is given to the Retail Division and Distributor Division," observed Goodman.

Exhibit 12   Selected Parts of Specialty Products' Written Plan, April 1985   Draft

---

MEMO TO: Neil Greene

FROM: Bob Thomas

SUBJECT: Strategy

Introduction
For years Specialty Products has drifted. The aim of the present management of Specialty Products is to give purpose and direction to this business. This plan outlines the way we think this can be done.

Critical Issue
How can we transform a business with relatively high costs, a history of quality problems, and a near-commodity product into a strong leadership position in satisfying customer needs?

Specialty Products' Mission
Specialty Products focuses on customers having a potential for large orders of custom products using standard construction. Principal market segments presently include accountants and we plan to extend this market to high-tech industries and advertising agencies (as a conduit to new customers). While Specialty Products is seen as a growth business, the growth is limited by available capacity.

Objectives
Penetration of existing accounts (specifics)
Margin (specifics)
Sales (specifics)
New products (specifics)
Reputation (specifics)
Quality (specifics)
Personnel (specifics)

Target Markets
Present main markets
  Others
New markets
  High tech/computer
  Advertising agencies
  Others

Competitive Advantage
In order to achieve the ambitious objectives outlined above, Specialty Products must create a competitive advantage. We believe that this competitive advantage can be secured by combining some advantages Specialty Products has with some of our "hidden assets."
The advantages we plan on using are ones which create added value for customers of Specialty Products. The overall logic is to be better and different in ways that are not traditional in this business and which cannot be easily copied by our rivals.

Quality
We expect to achieve a level of quality that cannot be matched by smaller competitors. This is attainable through manufacturing, engineering.

Service
Because of our size, sophistication, and experience we can be a leader in service.

MRP
We will use the MRP system to lower our costs, to help our customers lower their inventories, and as a promotional technique.

Innovation
(Several new products mentioned)

Exhibit 12 *(concluded)*

Action Plans

We have already made a number of strides in the right direction, but much remains to be done. Here is our report of progress and our work-in-progress. (This part of the plan gave details of actions accomplished and actions remaining.)

Forecasts

The steps we have taken and those we plan to take should result in financial performance as follows:

Forecast for Specialty Products

	1984 Actual	*1985*	*1986*
Sales	9,600,000	14,200,000	18,000,000
Margin percent	18.0	20.2	21.0

Conclusion

Being a high-cost competitor places a constraint on strategy. Because of our position, we need to find ways to add value to our offerings that steer us away from price competition. It is our judgment that the combinations of quality, service, reliability . . . can support the higher prices *and* higher volume we need in order to attain the objectives which have been set.

June 1985

CPC executives gathered at a nearby resort for three more days of strategic planning. For the first time (according to Goodman), Greene discussed his objectives and expectations. Some executives said that Greene should have made his expectations clear in the beginning. Other issues were discussed:

- Goodman wanted to change Specialty Products mission to remove the "no investment criterion," but his proposal was rejected.
- Some executives complained about "staff infection."
- Numerous human resources difficulties had cropped up in connection with efforts to implement plans.
- Goodman stated, "We have done a good job of planning; the planning is important, but enough is enough. It's time to make it all happen."

Thomas and Goodman found themselves under heavy workload pressure. "I can't afford a hiccup," commented Bob Thomas.

Specialty Products' growing sales, combined with good growth in sister divisions' sales, maintained heavy pressure on capacity. "We have diesel acceleration and disc brakes at CPC," joked Goodman.

Goodman met with Thomas to discuss Thomas's performance appraisal. Among the comments which various senior executives had written:

- "The next 12 months are crucial to Specialty Products and Bob Thomas."
- "It's evident that BT's efforts should be directed toward general management and marketing."
- "Does Specialty Products really require the additional staffing that Thomas has requested?"

Preliminary work on CPC's 1986 budget began.

July 1985

Goodman attributed the sales-volume resurgence of Specialty Products partly to MRP and partly to the conquest of quality problems; he went on to say:

> Our customers are doing good business, so we do good business. Where would Specialty Products be without the economic recovery? Even without the recovery we would have done OK, maybe not as good. If the economy took another nosedive, our growth would suffer, but our base would stick. No declines . . . from here on.

Thomas continued to talk about getting into the computer software packaging business in a bigger way. At the time, Specialty Products had a few software accounts to whom only binders were sold. Bob noted that several expanded avenues seemed open:

- Specialty Products could manufacture and print materials for manuals and discs. BMF International's software development division could even provide the program-product.
- Specialty Products could manufacture and sell to printers.
- Specialty Products could sell directly to computer firms.
- Specialty Products could manufacture cases for software systems (Specialty Products already had some accounts of this type).

Goodman observed that this printing/packaging proposal did not fit within the Specialty Products mission. He told Thomas that it's a "distraction." Thomas, unmoved by Goodman's objections, promoted the idea to Greene.

More strategic planning meetings. Goodman ordered t-shirts for the participants which read "S.O.B." (strategically operated businesses). Goodman, reflecting on latest conference, mused, "I think the fun overshadowed the planning." Goodman noticed quite a bit of "plugging one's own turf." At one point Goodman came under some group pressure about Specialty Products during an open session, but Greene himself choked off the debate, saying "Sure, we've got problems, but they are not strategic." Goodman said with a hint of disappointment in his voice, "Most people here still don't understand Specialty Products, and Specialty Products doesn't get much attention at these meetings. It's 99 percent everything else."

The formal Specialty Products plan remained in Goodman's desk drawer.

FALL 1985 PROBLEMS AND PROSPECTS

In the early fall of 1985 Thomas was preparing to meet with Greene to discuss the Specialty Products 1986 plan. At the same meeting Thomas hoped to present his idea for software packaging to Greene. He believed that Specialty Products could double its 1985 business in three or four years, but only if new product opportunities such as software publishing were aggressively pursued. (On the other hand, Goodman felt that the same goals could be reached without the "publishing software" move.) In arguing for the software publishing alternative, Thomas made the following main points:

- A market is there.
- Many competitors for this business, but none who can do it all.
- CPC can make the product, including printing, decorating.
- Price is important.
- On-time delivery is important.
- Specialty Products can sell "CPC" image.

As Neil Greene sat in his office at the Executive Office Building awaiting Bob Thomas' arrival, he reflected on the year's events and the future of the Specialty Products unit. Noting the difficulties Specialty Products experienced in reaching its margins, he wondered if their strategic plans were "enough" to reach those ambitious goals. His attention fell upon the latest monthly reports on Specialty Products' 1985 performance (Exhibit 13). He knew that others serving on the Executive Committee

Exhibit 13   Sales Performance versus Budget of Consolidated Packaging Company's Three Principal Business Segments, 1985   Nine Months

1985	Sales (in 000s)	Percent Sales Above (+)/Below (−) Budget	Actual Margin	Budgeted Margin
		Distributor Division		
January	$ 8,387	+3	42.6	42.3
February	10,805	−8	42.4	42.1
March	13,003	−18	41.5	41.4
April	14,227	+1	35.9	39.1
May	9,652	−12	40.3	41.4
June	12,032*	−11	39.5	41.8
July	8,753	+14	41.2	42.6
August	10,082	−5	40.9	41.8
September	12,199	+9	39.8	42.2
		Retail Division		
January	$ 1,696	+0	28.9	34.5
February	1,628	+5	31.3	36.9
March	1,616	−2	25.7	36.4
April	1,694	−15	36.4	36.4
May	2,159	−4	31.6	35.3
June	4,000	+21	30.2	32.7
July	8,210	+3	32.5	32.5
August	4,968	−27	27.3	32.3
September	3,189	−4	31.8	34.3
		Specialty Products		
January	$ 600	+20	18.1	24.6
February	703	+23	16.4	23.5
March	1,018	+4	15.5	23.7
April	873	+52	16.1	24.3
May	1,005	−34	22.3	24.0
June	1,208	−27	18.0	18.1
July	1,050	+22	16.0	17.5
August	750	+25	12.8	17.4
September	1,566	+18	17.4	18.6

Exhibit 14   Selected Details of Thomas's Software Packaging Proposal

This proposal involves a complete packaging operation. Specialty Products would provide printed materials, vinyl jackets, disks (from sister division of BMF International), indexing, color printing decoration, warehousing, and distribution.

Why Software Packaging?
  Fast-growing segment
  Market potential $150–$200 by 1986
  Large volume customers
  Quality image important
  Distribution important
  Fits Specialty Products plans

Strengths of Specialty Products:
  Have full-line of products
  Warehousing
  National distribution network
  Class "A" MRP system
  Brand recognition high
  Excess capacity
  Competitors can't do *packaging*
  (Low vertical integration)

Threats:
  More competition
  Volatile market
  Credit problems of customers?

Market strategy:
  A one-step shopping center for software
    publishers with sales ≥ $5 million.

Market requires:
  Quality product
  Dependable service
  Creativity
  Competitive prices
  Prompt service

Weaknesses:
  Lack of product engineering support
  Sales and service depts. lack product
    knowledge
  High costs
  Some elements strain capacity

Forecast ($000)

| | Total Sales (with no new marketing personnel) | Proposals | |
| | | Add Software Specialists | Add New Sales Person |
		Additional Sales	Additional Sales
1986	$ 500	$1,000	$ 800
1987	700	2,250	950
1988	1,200	3,800	1,750

		1985	1986	1987
	Total Software	2,300	4,900	8,560

still doubted Specialty Products long-term potential. Was Specialty Products really worth the trouble? He wondered whether he should approve Thomas's software-packaging idea (Exhibit 14). Looking ahead to the annual capital budgeting process, he wondered whether a request for $1 million in investment for Specialty Products ought to be granted. Was strategic planning taking hold at CPC? Greene had a lot on his mind as his secretary announced Bob Thomas' arrival. Bob Thomas walked in, carrying details of his plans and projections (Exhibit 15).

**Exhibit 15   Selected Information from Thomas's Presentation of Specialty
Products' Strategic Plan to Greene, October 11, 1985**

Strengths
- Outstanding service
- Commitment to market
- Financial strength
- Vertical integration
- Specialized sales force
- High-level of quality assurance
- Using MRP system to "tie" customers

Threats:
- Price cutting by competitors
- Increasing industry capacity
- High interest rates
- Don't know competitors in software

Weaknesses:
- Poor engineering support/product development
- High prices
- "Red tape" of Company systems
- Limited capacity
- Shortage of skilled production personnel for some key areas
- Seasonal capacity problem brought on by sharing facilities with other company units
- Outdated equipment

1985 Market Strategy:
- Increase market share with
- Establish position in software publishing
- Develop auditing, consulting, professional education markets
- MRP, service, quality as main competitive weapons

	Projections		
	1986	*1987*	*1988*
Sales (millions)	18.5	22.5	26.6
Margin (dollar)	3.3	4.2	5.3
Margin (percent)	18	19	20

CASE 27   THE LINCOLN ELECTRIC COMPANY, 1985*

The Lincoln Electric Company is the world's largest manufacturer of welding machines and electrodes. Lincoln employs 2,400 workers in two U.S. factories near Cleveland and approximately 600 in three factories located in other countries. This does not include the field sales force of more than 200 persons. It has been estimated that Lincoln's market share (for arc-welding equipment and supplies) is more than 40 percent.

The Lincoln incentive management plan has been well known for many years. Many college management texts make reference to the Lincoln plan as a model for achieving high worker productivity. Certainly Lincoln has been a successful company according to the usual measures of success.

James F. Lincoln died in 1965, and there was some concern, even among employees, that the Lincoln system would fall into disarray, that profits would decline, and that year-end bonuses might be discontinued. Quite the contrary, 20 years after Lincoln's death, the company appears as strong as ever. Each year, except the recession years 1982 and 1983, has seen higher profits and bonuses. Employee morale and productivity remain high. Employee turnover is almost nonexistent except for retirements. Lincoln's market share is stable. Consistently high dividends continue on Lincoln's stock.

A HISTORICAL SKETCH

In 1895, after being "frozen out" of the depression-ravaged Elliott–Lincoln Company, a maker of Lincoln-designed electric motors, John C. Lincoln, took out his second patent and began to manufacture his improved motor. He opened his new business, unincorporated, with $200 he had earned redesigning a motor for young Herbert Henry Dow, who later founded the Dow Chemical Company.

Started during an economic depression and cursed by a major fire after only one year in business, Lincoln's company grew, but hardly prospered, through its first quarter century. In 1906 John C. Lincoln incorporated his company and moved from his one-room, fourth-floor factory to a new three-story building he erected in east Cleveland. In his new factory he expanded his work force to 30 and sales grew to over $50,000 a year. John Lincoln preferred being an engineer and inventor rather than a manager, though, and it was to be left to another Lincoln to manage the company through its years of success.

In 1907, after a bout with typhoid fever forced him from Ohio State University in his senior year, James F. Lincoln, John's younger brother, joined the fledgling

---

* Prepared by Arthur D. Sharplin, Northeast Louisiana University. Copyright © 1985 by Arthur D. Sharplin. Reproduced with permission.

company. In 1914 he became the active head of the firm, with the titles of general manager and vice president. John Lincoln, while he remained president of the company for some years, became more involved in other business ventures and in his work as an inventor.

One of James Lincoln's early actions as head of the firm was to ask the employees to elect representatives to a committee which would advise him on company operations. The advisory board has met with the chief executive officer twice monthly since that time. This was only the first of a series of innovative personnel policies which have, over the years, distinguished Lincoln Electric from its contemporaries.

The first year the advisory board was in existence, working hours were reduced from 55 per week, then standard, to 50 hours a week. In 1915 the company gave each employee a paid-up life insurance policy. A welding school, which continues today, was begun in 1917. In 1918 an employee bonus plan was attempted. It was not continued, but the idea was to resurface and become the backbone of the Lincoln Management System.

The Lincoln Electric Employees' Association was formed in 1919 to provide health benefits and social activities. This organization continues today and has assumed several additional functions over the years. In 1923 a piecework pay system was in effect, employees got two-week paid vacations each year, and wages were adjusted for changes in the consumer price index. Approximately 30 percent of Lincoln's stock was set aside for key employees in 1914 when James F. Lincoln became general manager, and a stock purchase plan for all employees was begun in 1925.

The board of directors voted to start a suggestion system in 1929. The program is still in effect, but cash awards, a part of the early program, were discontinued several years ago. Now suggestions are rewarded by additional "points," which affect year-end bonuses.

The legendary Lincoln bonus plan was proposed by the advisory board and accepted on a trial basis by James Lincoln in 1934. The first annual bonus amounted to about 25 percent of wages. There has been a bonus every year since then. The bonus plan has been a cornerstone of the Lincoln management system, and recent bonuses have approximated annual wages.

By 1944 Lincoln employees enjoyed a pension plan, a policy of promotion from within, and continuous employment. Base pay rates were determined by formal job evaluation, and a merit rating system was in effect.

In the prologue of James F. Lincoln's last book, Charles G. Herbruck writes regarding the foregoing personnel innovations:

> They were not to buy good behavior. They were not efforts to increase profits. They were not antidotes to labor difficulties. They did not constitute a "do-gooder" program. They were expressions of mutual respect for each person's importance to the job to be done. All of them reflect the leadership of James Lincoln, under whom they were nurtured and propagated.

By the start of World War II, Lincoln Electric was the world's largest manufacturer of arc-welding products. Sales of about $4 million in 1934 had grown to $24 million by 1941. Productivity per employee more than doubled during the same period.

During the war Lincoln Electric prospered as never before. Despite challenges to Lincoln's profitability by the Navy's Price Review Board and to the tax deductibility of employee bonuses by the Internal Revenue Service, the company increased its profits and paid huge bonuses.

Certainly since 1935 and probably for several years before that, Lincoln productivity has been well above the average for similar companies. Lincoln claims levels of productivity more than twice those for other manufacturers from 1945 onward. Information available from outside sources tends to support these claims.

COMPANY PHILOSOPHY

James F. Lincoln was the son of a Congregational minister and Christian principles were at the center of his business philosophy. The confidence that he had in the efficacy of Christ's teachings is illustrated by the following remark taken from one of his books:

> The Christian ethic should control our acts. If it did control our acts, the savings in cost of distribution would be tremendous. Advertising would be a contact of the expert consultant with the customer, in order to give the customer the best product available when all of the customer's needs are considered. Competition then would be in improving the quality of products and increasing efficiency in producing and distributing them; not in deception, as is now too customary. Pricing would reflect efficiency of production; it would not be a selling dodge that the customer may well be sorry he accepted. It would be proper for all concerned and rewarding for the ability used in producing the product.

There is no indication that Lincoln attempted to evangelize his employees or customers—or the general public for that matter. The current board chairman, William Irrgang, and the president, George Willis, do not even mention the Christian gospel in their recent speeches and interviews. The company motto, "The actual is limited, the possible is immense," is prominently displayed, but there is no display of religious slogans and there is no company chapel.

Attitude toward the Customer

James Lincoln saw the customer's needs as the *raison d'être* for every company. "When any company has achieved success so that it is attractive as an investment," he wrote, "all money usually needed for expansion is supplied by the customer in retained earnings. It is obvious that the customer's interests, not the stockholder's, should come first." In 1947 he said, "Care should be taken . . . not to rivet attention on profit. Between 'How much do I get?' and 'How do I make this better, cheaper, more useful?' the difference is fundamental and decisive." George Willis still ranks the customer as Lincoln's most important constituency. This is reflected in Lincoln's policy to "at all times price on the basis of cost and at all times keep pressure on our cost." Lincoln's goal, often stated, is "to build a better and better product at a lower and lower price." "It is obvious," James Lincoln said, "that the customer's interests should be the first goal of industry."

Attitude toward Stockholders

Stockholders are given last priority at Lincoln Electric. This is a continuation of James Lincoln's philosophy: "The last group to be considered is the stockholders who own stock because they think it will be more profitable than investing money in any other way." Concerning division of the largess produced by incentive management, Lincoln wrote, "The absentee stockholder also will get his share, even if undeserved, out of the greatly increased profit that the efficiency produces."

Attitude toward Unionism

There has never been a serious effort to organize Lincoln employees. While James Lincoln criticized the labor movement for "selfishly attempting to better its position at the expense of the people it must serve," he still had kind words for union members. He excused abuses of union power as "the natural reactions of human beings to the abuses to which management has subjected them." Lincoln's idea of the correct relationship between workers and managers is shown by this comment: "Labor and management are properly not warring camps; they are parts of one organization in which they must and should cooperate fully and happily."

Beliefs and Assumptions about Employees

If fulfilling customer needs is the desired goal of business, then employee performance and productivity are the means by which this goal can best be achieved. It is the Lincoln attitude toward employees, reflected in the following comments by James Lincoln, which is credited by many with creating the record of success the company has experienced:

> The greatest fear of the worker, which is the same as the greatest fear of the industrialist in operating a company, is the lack of income. . . . The industrial manager is very conscious of his company's need of uninterrupted income. He is completely oblivious, evidently, of the fact that the worker has the same need.

> He is just as eager as any manager is to be part of a team that is properly organized and working for the advancement of our economy. . . . He has no desire to make profits for those who do not hold up their end in production, as is true of absentee stockholders and inactive people in the company.

> If money is to be used as an incentive, the program must provide that what is paid to the worker is what he has earned. The earnings of each must be in accordance with accomplishment.

> Status is of great importance in all human relationships. The greatest incentive that money has, usually, is that it is a symbol of success. . . . The resulting status is the real incentive. . . . Money alone can be an incentive to the miser only.

> There must be complete honesty and understanding between the hourly worker and management if high efficiency is to be obtained.

LINCOLN'S BUSINESS

Arc-welding has been the standard joining method in the shipbuilding industry for decades. It is the predominant way of joining steel in the construction industry. Most industrial plants have their own welding shops for maintenance and construction. Manufacturers of tractors and all kinds of heavy equipment use arc-welding extensively in the manufacturing process. Many hobbyists have their own welding machines and use them for making metal items such as patio furniture and barbeque pits. The popularity of welded sculpture as an art form is growing.

While advances in welding technology have been frequent, arc-welding products, in the main, have hardly changed except for Lincoln's Innershield process. This process, utilizing a self-shielded, flux-cored electrode, has established new cost-saving opportunities for construction and equipment fabrication. The most popular Lincoln electrode, the Fleetweld 5P, has been virtually the same since the 1930s. The most popular engine-driven welder in the world, the Lincoln SA-200, has been a gray-colored assembly including a four-cylinder continental "Red Seal" engine and a 200 ampere direct-current generator with two current control knobs for at least three decades. A 1980 model SA-200 even weighs almost the same as the 1950 model, and it certainly is little changed in appearance.

Lincoln and its competitors now market a wide range of general purpose and specialty electrodes for welding mild steel, aluminum, cast iron, and stainless and special steels. Most of these electrodes are designed to meet the standards of the American Welding Society, a trade association. They are thus essentially the same as to size and composition from one manufacturer to another. Every electrode manufacturer has a limited number of unique products, but these typically constitute only a small percentage of total sales.

Lincoln's research and development expenditures have recently been less than one and one-half percent of sales. There is evidence that Lincoln's competitors spend several times as much as a percentage of sales.

Lincoln's share of the arc-welding products market appears to have been about 40 percent for many years, and the welding products market has grown somewhat faster than the level of industry in general. The market is highly price-competitive, with variations in prices of standard products normally amounting to only a percent or two. Lincoln's products are sold directly by its engineering-oriented sales force and indirectly through its distributor organization. Advertising expenditures amount to less than one fourth of 1 percent of sales, one third as much as a major Lincoln competitor with whom the casewriter checked.

The other major welding process, flame-welding, has not been competitive with arc-welding since the 1930s. However, plasma-arc-welding, a relatively new process whch uses a conducting stream of super-heated gas (plasma) to confine the welding current to a small area, has made some inroads, especially in metal tubing manufacturing, in recent years. Major advances in technology which will produce an alternative superior to arc-welding within the next decade or so appear unlikely. Also, it seems likely that changes in the machines and techniques used in arc-welding will be evolutionary rather than revolutionary.

Products

The company is primarily engaged in the manufacture and sale of arc-welding products—electric welding machines and metal electrodes. Lincoln also produces electric motors ranging from ½ horsepower to 200 horsepower. Motors constitute about 8 to 10 percent of total sales.

The electric welding machines, some consisting of a transformer or motor and generator arrangement powered by commercial electricity, and others consisting of an internal combustion engine and generator, are designed to produce from 30 to 1,000 amperes of electrical power. This electrical current is used to melt a consumable metal electrode with the molten metal being transferred in a super hot spray to the metal joint being welded. Very high temperatures and hot sparks are produced, and operators usually must wear special eye and face protection and leather gloves, often along with leather aprons and sleeves.

Welding electrodes are of two basic types: (1) coated "stick" electrodes, usually 14 inches long and smaller than a pencil in diameter, which are held in a special insulated holder by the operator who must manipulate the electrode in order to maintain a proper arc-width and pattern of deposition of the metal being transferred. Stick electrodes are packaged in 6- to 50-pound boxes; (2) coiled wire, ranging in diameter from 0.035 inch to 0.219 inch, which is designed to be fed continuously to the welding arc through a "gun" held by the operator or positioned by automatic positioning equipment. The wire is packaged in coils, reels, and drums weighing from 14 to 1,000 pounds.

MANUFACTURING OPERATIONS

The main plant is in Euclid, Ohio, a suburb on Cleveland's east side. The layout of this plant is shown in Exhibit 1. There are no warehouses. Materials flow from the half-mile long dock on the north side of the plant through the production lines to a very limited storage and loading area on the south side. Materials used on each workstation are stored as close as possible to the workstation. The administrative offices, near the center of the factory, are entirely functional. Not even the president's office is carpeted. A corridor below the main level provides access to the factory floor from the main entrance near the center of the plant. A new plant, just opened in Mentor, Ohio, houses some of the electrode production operations that were moved from the main plant.

Manufacturing Processes

Electrode manufacturing is highly capital intensive. Metal rods purchased from steel producers are drawn or extruded down to smaller diameters, cut to length, and coated with pressed-powder "flux" for stick electrodes or plated with copper (for conductivity) and spun into coils or spools for wire. Some of Lincoln's wire, called "Inner-shield," is hollow and filled with a material similar to that used to coat stick electrodes.

Exhibit 1   Main Factory Layout

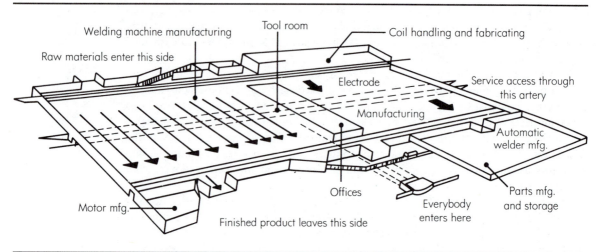

Welding machine manufacturing

Tool room

Coil handling and fabricating

Raw materials enter this side

Electrode

Service access through this artery

Manufacturing

Automatic welder mfg.

Motor mfg.

Offices

Everybody enters here

Parts mfg. and storage

Finished product leaves this side

Lincoln is highly secretive about its electrode production processes, and the casewriter was not given access to the details of those processes.

Welding machines and electric motors are made on a series of assembly lines. Gasoline and diesel engines are purchased partially assembled, but practically all other components are made from basic industrial products (e.g., steel bars and sheets and bar copper conductor wire) in the Lincoln factory.

Individual components, such as gasoline tanks for engine-driven welders and steel shafts for motors and generators, are made by numerous small "factories within a factory." The shaft for a certain generator, for example, is made from a raw steel bar by one operator who uses five large machines, all running continuously. A saw cuts the bar to length, a digital lathe machines different sections to varying diameters, a special milling machine cuts a slot for a keyway, and so forth, until a finished shaft is produced. The operator moves the shafts from machine to machine and makes necessary adjustments.

Another operator punches, shapes, and paints sheetmetal cowling parts. One assembles steel limitations onto a rotor shaft, then winds, insulates, and tests the rotors. Finished components are moved by crane operators to the nearby assembly lines.

Worker Performance and Attitudes

Exceptional worker performance at Lincoln is a matter of record. The typical Lincoln employee earns about twice as much as other factory workers in the Cleveland area. Yet the labor cost per sales dollar at Lincoln, currently (1985) 23.5 cents, is well below industry averages.

Sales per Lincoln factory employee currently exceed $157,000. An observer at the factory quickly sees why this figure is so high. Each worker is proceeding busily and thoughtfully about the task at hand. This is no idle chatter. Most workers take no coffee breaks. Many operate several machines and make a substantial component unaided. The supervisors, some with as many as 100 subordinates, are busy with planning and recordkeeping duties and hardly glance at the people they supervise. The manufacturing procedures appear efficient—no unnecessary steps, no wasted motions, no wasted materials. Finished components move smoothly to subsequent workstations.

Worker turnover at Lincoln is practically nonexistent except for retirements and departures by new employees. The Appendix includes summaries of interviews with Lincoln employees.

ORGANIZATION STRUCTURE

Lincoln has never had a formal organization chart. The objective of this policy is to ensure maximum flexibility. An open door policy is practiced throughout the company, and personnel are encouraged to take problems to the persons most capable of resolving them. Once Harvard Business School researchers prepared an organization chart reflecting the below-mentioned implied relationships. The chart became available within the Lincoln organization, and present Lincoln management feels that it had a disruptive effect. Therefore, the casewriter was asked not to include any kind of organizational chart in this report.

Perhaps because of the quality and enthusiasm of the Lincoln work force, routine supervision is almost nonexistent. A typical production foreman, for example, supervises as many as 100 workers, a span of control which does not allow more than infrequent worker-supervisor interaction. Position titles and traditional flows of authority do imply something of an organizational structure, however. For example, the vice president, sales and the vice president, electrode division, report to the president, as do various staff assistants such as the personnel director and the director of purchasing. Using such implied relationships it has been determined that production workers have two or, at most, three levels of supervision between themselves and the president.

PERSONNEL POLICIES

Recruitment and Selection

Every job opening at Lincoln is advertised internally on company bulletin boards and any employee can apply for any job so advertised. External hiring is done only for entry level positions. Selection for these jobs is done on the basis of personal interviews—there is no aptitude or psychological testing. Not even a high school diploma is required except for engineering and sales positions, which are filled by graduate engineers. A committee consisting of vice presidents and superintendents interviews candidates initially cleared by the personnel department. Final selection is made by the supervisor who has a job opening. Out of over 3,500 applicants interviewed by the personnel department during a recent period fewer than 300 were hired.

Job Security

In 1958 Lincoln formalized its lifetime employment policy, which had already been in effect for many years. There have been no layoffs at Lincoln since World War II. Since 1958 every Lincoln worker with over one year's longevity has been guaranteed at least 30 hours per week, 49 weeks per year.

The policy has never been so severely tested as during the 1981–83 recession. As a manufacturer of capital goods, Lincoln's business is highly cyclical. In previous recessions Lincoln has been able to avoid major sales declines. However, sales plummeted 32 percent in 1982 and another 16 percent the next year. Few companies could withstand such a sales decline and remain profitable. Yet, Lincoln not only earned profits, but no employee was laid off and year-end incentive bonuses were paid. To weather the storm, Lincoln cut most of the nonsalaried workers back to 30 hours a week for varying periods of time. Many employees were reassigned, and the total work force was slightly reduced through normal attrition and restricted hiring. Many employees grumbled at their unexpected misfortune, probably to the surprise and dismay of some Lincoln managers. However, a modest sales resurgence in 1984 and 1985 seemed to portend brighter days.

Performance Evaluations

Each supervisor formally evaluates subordinates twice a year using the cards shown in Exhibit 2. The employee performance criteria, "quality, dependability, ideas and cooperation," and "output," are considered to be independent of each other. Marks on the cards are converted to numerical scores which are forced to average 100 for each evaluating supervisor. Individual merit rating scores normally range from 80 to 110. Any score over 110 requires a special letter to top management. These scores (over 110) are not considered in computing the required 100-point average for each evaluating supervisor. Suggestions for improvements often result in recommendations for exceptionally high performance scores. Supervisors discuss individual performance marks with the employees concerned. Each warranty claim on a Lincoln product is traced to the individual employee whose work caused the defect. The employee's performance score may be reduced by one point, or the worker may be required to repay the cost of servicing the warranty claim by working without pay.

Compensation

Basic wage levels for jobs at Lincoln are determined by a wage survey of similar jobs in the Cleveland area. These rates are adjusted quarterly in accordance with changes in the Cleveland Area Consumer Price Index. Insofar as possible, base wage rates are translated into piece rates. Practically all production workers and many others—for example, some forklift operators—are paid by piece rate. Once established, piece rates are never changed unless a substantive change in the way a job is done results from a source other than the worker doing the job. In December of each year, a portion of annual profits is distributed to employees as bonuses. Incentive bonuses since 1934 have averaged about the same as annual wages and somewhat more than after-tax profits. The average bonus for 1981 was $20,759. Bonuses averaged

Exhibit 2   Merit Rating Cards

QUALITY

⊃⇢   Increasing Quality   ⊃⇢

This card rates the QUALITY of work you do.

It also reflects your success in eliminating errors and in reducing scrap and waste.

This rating has been done jointly by your department head and the Inspection Department in the shop and with other department heads in the office and engineering.

DEPENDABILITY

⊃⇢ Increasing Dependability ⊃⇢

This card rates how well your supervisors have been able to depend upon you to do those thing that have been expected of you without supervision.

It also reflects your ability to supervise yourself including your work safety performance, your orderliness, care of equipment, and the effective use you make of your skills.

This rating has been done by your department head.

IDEAS & COOPERATION

⊃⇢   Increasing Ideas & Cooperation   ⊃⇢

This card rates your Cooperation, Ideas and Initiative.

OUTPUT

⊃⇢   Increasing Output   ⊃⇢   Days Absent

This card rates HOW MUCH PRODUCTIVE WORK you actually turn out.

It also reflects your willingness not to hold back and recognizes your attendance record.

New ideas and new methods are important to your company in our continuing effect to reduce costs, increase output, improve quality, work safety and improve our relationship with our customers. This card credits you for your ideas and initiative used to help in this direction.

It also rates your cooperation—how you work with others as a team. Such factors as your attitude towards supervision, co-workers and the company, your efforts to share knowledge with others, and your cooperation in installing new methods smoothly, are considered here.

This rating has been done jointly by your department head and the Production Control Department in the shop and with other department heads in the office and engineering.

$13,998 and $8,557, respectively, for the recession years 1982 to 1983. Individual bonuses are proportional to merit-rating scores. For example, assume the amount set aside for bonuses is 80 percent of total wages paid to eligible employees. A person whose performance score is 95 will receive a bonus of 76 percent (0.80×0.95) of annual wages.

Vacations

The company is shut down for two weeks in August and two weeks during the Christmas season. Vacations are taken during these periods. For employees with over 25 years of service, a fifth week of vacation may be taken at a time acceptable to superiors.

Work Assignment

Management has authority to transfer workers and to switch between overtime and short time as required. Supervisors have undisputed authority to assign specific parts to individual workers, who may have their own preferences due to variations in piece rates. During the 1982–83 recession, 50 factory workers volunteered to join sales teams and fanned out across the country to sell a new Lincoln welder designed for automobile body shops and small machine shops. The result—$10 million in sales and a hot new product.

Employee Participation in Decision Making

When a manager speaks of participative management, he usually thinks of a relaxed, nonauthoritarian atmosphere. This is not the case at Lincoln. Formal authority is quite strong. "We're very authoritarian around here," says Willis. James F. Lincoln placed a good deal of stress on protecting management's authority. "Management in all successful departments of industry must have complete power," he said, "Management is the coach who must be obeyed. The men, however, are the players who alone can win the game." Despite this attitude, there are several ways in which employees participate in management at Lincoln.

Richard Sabo, manager of public relations, relates job enlargement/enrichment to participation. He said, "The most important participative technique that we use is giving more responsibility to employees. We give a high school graduate more responsibility than other companies give their foremen." Lincoln puts limits on the degree of participation which is allowed, however. In Sabo's words,

> When you use "participation," put quotes around it. Because we believe that each person should participate only in those decisions he is most knowledgeable about. I don't think production employees should control the decisions of Bill Irrgang. They don't know as much as he does about the decisions he is involved in.

The advisory board, elected by the workers, meets with the chairman and the president every two weeks to discuss ways of improving operations. This board has been in existence since 1914 and has contributed to many innovations. The incentive bonuses, for example, were first recommended by this committee. Every Lincoln employee has access to advisory board members, and answers to all advisory board suggestions are promised by the following meeting. Both Irrgang and Willis are quick to point out, though, that the advisory board only recommends actions. "They do not have direct authority," Irrgang says. "And when they bring up something that management thinks is not to the benefit of the company, it will be rejected."

A suggestion program was instituted in 1929. At first employees were awarded one half of the first year's savings attributable to their suggestions. Now, however, the value of suggestions is reflected in performance evaluation scores, which determine individual incentive bonus amounts.

Training and Education

Production workers are given a short period of on-the-job training and then placed on a piecework pay system. Lincoln does not pay for off-site education. The idea behind this latter policy is that everyone cannot take advantage of such a program, and it is unfair to expend company funds for an advantage to which there is unequal access. Recruits for sales jobs, already college graduates, are given on-the-job training in the plant followed by a period of work and training at one of the regional sales offices.

Fringe Benefits and Executive Perquisites

A medical plan and a company-paid retirement program have been in effect for many years. A plant cafeteria, operated on a break-even basis, serves meals at about 60 percent of usual costs. An employee association, to which the company does not contribute, provides disability insurance and social and athletic activities. An employee stock ownership program, instituted in about 1925, has resulted in employee ownership of about 50 percent of Lincoln's stock. Under this program, each employee with more than one year of service may purchase stock in the corporation. The price of these shares is established at book value. Stock purchased through this plan may be held by employees only and must be offered back to the company upon termination of employment. Dividends and voting rights are the same as for stock which is owned outside the plan. Approximately 75 percent of the employees own Lincoln stock.

As to executive perquisites, there are none—crowded, austere offices, no executive washrooms or lunchrooms, and no reserved parking spaces. Even the company president pays for his own meals and eats in the cafeteria.

FINANCIAL POLICIES

James P. Lincoln felt strongly that financing for company growth should come from within the company—through initial cash investment by the founders, through retention of earnings, and through stock purchases by those who work in the business. He saw the following advantages of this approach:

1. Ownership of stock by employees strengthens team spirit. "If they are mutually anxious to make it succeed, the future of the company is bright."
2. Ownership of stock provides individual incentive because employees feel that they will benefit from company profitability.
3. "Ownership is educational." Owners-employees "will know how profits are made and lost; how success is won and lost. . . . There are few socialists in the list of stockholders of the nation's industries."
4. "Capital available from within controls expansion." Unwarranted expansion will not occur, Lincoln believed, under his financing plan.
5. "The greatest advantage would be the development of the individual worker. Under the incentive of ownership, he would become a greater man."
6. "Stock ownership is one of the steps that can be taken that will make the worker feel that there is less of a gulf between him and the boss. . . . Stock ownership

---

Exhibit 3 Balance Sheets, The Lincoln Electric Company, 1980–1984 In Thousands of Dollars

	1980	1981	1982	1983	1984
Assets					
Cash	$ 1,307	$ 3,603	$ 1,318	$ 1,774	$ 3,580
Bonds and CDs	46,503	62,671	72,485	77,872	57,212
Notes and accounts receivable	42,424	41,521	26,239	31,114	34,469
Inventories (LIFO basis)	35,533	45,541	38,157	30,773	37,433
Deferred taxes and prepaid expenses	2,749	3,658	4,635	4,704	5,095
Total current assets	$128,516	$156,994	$142,834	$146,237	$137,789
Other assets	$ 19,723	$ 21,424	$ 22,116	$ 21,421	$ 20,216
Investment in foreign divisions	4,695	4,695	7,696	8,696	8,696
	$ 24,418	$ 26,119	$ 29,812	$ 30,117	$ 28,912
Property, plant, equipment					
Land	$ 913	$ 928	$ 925	$ 925	$ 926
Buildings (net)	22,982	24,696	23,330	22,378	20,860
Machinery and equipment (net)	25,339	27,104	26,949	27,146	28,106
	$ 49,234	$ 52,728	$ 51,204	$ 50,449	$ 49,892
Total Assets	$202,168	$235,841	$223,850	$226,803	$216,593
Liabilities and Shareholders' Equity					
Accounts payable	$ 15,608	$ 14,868	$ 11,936	$ 16,228	$ 15,233
Accrued wages	1,504	4,940	3,633	3,224	4,358
Taxes payable	5,622	14,755	5,233	6,675	4,203
Dividends payable	5,800	7,070	6,957	6,675	6,207
Total current liabilities	$ 28,534	$ 41,633	$ 27,759	$ 32,802	$ 30,001
Other long-term debt	$ 3,807	$ 4,557	$ 5,870	$ 7,805	$ 10,313
Shareholders' equity					
Common stock	$ 276	$ 272	$ 268	$ 257	$ 239
Additional paid-in capital	2,641	501	1,862	0	0
Retained earnings	166,910	188,878	188,392	186,318	176,569
Foreign currency adjustment			(301)	(379)	(529)
	$169,827	$189,651	$190,221	$186,196	$176,279
Total Liabilities and Shareholders' Equity	$202,168	$235,841	$223,850	$226,803	$216,593

will help the worker to recognize his responsibility in the game and the importance of victory."

Lincoln Electric Company uses a minimum of debt in its capital structure. There is no borrowing at all, with the debt being limited to current payables. Even the new $20 million plant in Mentor, Ohio, was financed totally from earnings.

The unusual pricing policy at Lincoln is succinctly stated by President Willis: "At all times price on the basis of cost and at all times keep pressure on our cost." This policy resulted in Lincoln's price for the most popular welding electrode then in use going from 16 cents a pound in 1929 to 4.7 cents in 1938. More recently, the SA-200 Welder, Lincoln's largest selling portable machine, decreased in price from 1958 through 1965. According to Dr. C. Jackson Grayson of the American Productivity Center in Houston, Texas, Lincoln's prices in general have increased only one fifth as fast as the consumer price index from 1934 to about 1970. This has resulted in a welding products market in which Lincoln is the undisputed price leader for the products it manufactures. Not even the major Japanese manufacturers, such as Nippon Steel for welding electrodes and Asaka Transformer for welding machines, have been able to penetrate this market.

Huge cash balances are accumulated each year preparatory to paying the year-end bonuses. The bonuses totaled $32,718,000 for 1984. This money is invested in short-term U.S. government securities and bank certificates of deposit until needed. Financial statements are shown in Exhibits 3 and 4. Exhibit 5 shows how Lincoln's revenue has been distributed.

Exhibit 4   Income Statements, The Lincoln Electric Company, 1980–1984   Dollar Amounts in Thousands

	1980	1981	1982	1983	1984
Revenue					
Net sales	$387,374	$450,387	$310,862	$263,129	$321,759
Other income	13,817	18,454	18,049	13,387	11,814
	401,191	468,841	328,911	276,516	333,573
Costs and expenses					
Cost of products sold	260,671	293,332	212,674	179,851	222,985
Selling, general, and administrative expenses	37,753	42,656	37,128	36,348	40,164
Year-end incentive bonus	43,249	55,718	36,870	21,914	32,718
Payroll taxes related to bonus	1,251	1,544	1,847	1,186	1,874
Pension expense	6,810	6,874	5,888	5,151	5,139
Interest on tax assessments	0	0	0	1,946	99
	349,734	400,124	294,407	246,396	302,979
Income					
Income before income taxes	51,457	68,717	34,504	30,120	30,594
Federal income tax	20,300	27,400	13,227	14,246	12,429
State and local income taxes	3,072	3,885	2,497	(989)	1,423
	23,372	31,285	15,724	13,257	13,852
Net income	$ 28,085	$ 37,432	$ 18,780	$ 16,863	$ 16,742
Employees eligible for bonus	2,637	2,684	2,634	2,561	2,469

Exhibit 5   How Lincoln's Revenue Dollar Was Disbursed, 1974–1983

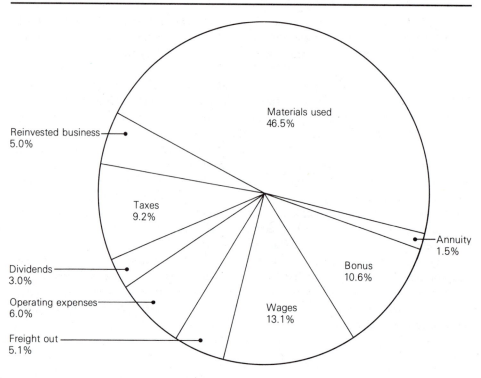

HOW WELL DOES LINCOLN SERVE ITS PUBLIC?

Lincoln Electric differs from most other companies in the importance it assigns to each of the groups it serves. Willis identifies these groups, in the order of priority Lincoln ascribes to them, as (1) customers, (2) employees, and (3) stockholders.

Certainly Lincoln customers have fared well over the years. Lincoln prices for welding machines and welding electrodes are acknowledged to be the lowest in the marketplace. Lincoln quality has consistently been so high that Lincoln "Fleetweld" electrodes and Lincoln SA-200 welders have been the standard in the pipeline and refinery construction industry, where price is hardly a criterion, for decades. The cost of field failures for Lincoln products was an amazing four one hundredths of 1 percent in 1979. A Lincoln distributor in Monroe, Louisiana, says that he has sold several hundred of the popular AC-225 welders and, though the machine is warranted for one year, he has never handled a warranty claim.

Perhaps best-served of all Lincoln constituencies have been the employees. Not the least of their benefits, of course, are the year-end bonuses, which effectively double an already average compensation level. The foregoing description of the personnel program and the comments in the Appendix further illustrate the desirability of a Lincoln job.

While stockholders were relegated to an inferior status by James F. Lincoln, they have done very well indeed. Recent dividends have exceeded $7 a share and earnings per share have exceeded $20. In January 1980 the price of restricted stock committed by Lincoln to employees was $117 a share. By February 4, 1983, the stated value, at which Lincoln will repurchase the stock if tendered, was $166. A check with the New York office of Merrill Lynch, Pierce, Fenner, & Smith on February 4, 1983, revealed an estimated price on Lincoln stock of $240 a share, with none being offered for sale. Technically, this price applies only to the unrestricted stock owned by the Lincoln family, a few other major holders, and employees who have purchased it on the open market, but it gives some idea of the value of Lincoln stock in general. The risk associated with Lincoln stock, a major determinant of stock value, is minimal because of the absence of debt in Lincoln's capital structure, because of an extremely stable earnings record, and because of Lincoln's practice of purchasing the restricted stock whenever employees offer it for sale.

A CONCLUDING COMMENT

It is easy to believe that the reason for Lincoln's success is the excellent attitude of Lincoln employees and their willingness to work harder, faster, and more intelligently than other industrial workers. However, Richard Sabo, manager of publicity and educational services at Lincoln, suggests that appropriate credit be given to Lincoln executives, whom he credits with carrying out the following policies:

1. Management has limited research, development, and manufacturing to a standard product line designed to meet the major needs of the welding industry.
2. New products must be reviewed by manufacturing and all production costs verified before being approved by management.
3. Purchasing is challenged to not only procure materials at the lowest cost, but also to work closely with engineering and manufacturing to assure that the latest innovations are implemented.
4. Manufacturing supervision and all personnel are held accountable for reduction of scrap, energy conservation, and maintenance of product quality.
5. Production control, material handling, and methods engineering are closely supervised by top management.
6. Material and finished goods inventory control, accurate cost accounting, and attention to sales cost, credit, and other financial areas have constantly reduced overhead and led to excellent profitability.
7. Management has made cost reduction a way of life at Lincoln, and definite programs are established in many areas, including traffic and shipping, where tremendous savings can result.
8. Management has established a sales department that is technically trained to reduce customer welding costs. This sales technique and other real customer services have eliminated nonessential frills and resulted in long-term benefits to all concerned.

9. Management has encouraged education, technical publishing, and long-range programs that have resulted in industry growth, thereby assuring market potential for the Lincoln Electric Company.

Sabo writes, "It is in a very real sense a personal and group experience in faith—a belief that together we can achieve results which alone would not be possible. It is not a perfect system and it is not 'easy.' It requires tremendous dedication and hard work. However, it does work and the results are worth the effort."

APPENDIX: INTERVIEWS WITH LINCOLN ELECTRIC
EMPLOYEES

Typical questions and answers from employee interviews are presented below. In order to maintain each employee's personal privacy, fictitious names are given to the interviewees.

I

Interview with Betty Stewart, a 52-year-old high school graduate who had been with Lincoln 13 years and who was working as a cost accounting clerk at the time of the interview.

Q: What jobs have you held here besides the one you have now?

A: I worked in payroll for a while, and then this job came open and I took it.

Q: How much money did you make last year, including your bonus?

A: I would say roughly around $20,000, but I was off for back surgery for a while.

Q: You weren't paid while you were off for back surgery?

A: No.

Q: Did the Employees Association help you out?

A: Yes. The company doesn't furnish that, though. We pay $6 a month into the Employee Association. I think my check from them was $105 a week.

Q: How was your performance rating last year?

A: It was around 100 points, but I lost some points for attendance with my back problem.

Q: How did you get your job at Lincoln?

A: I was bored silly where I was working, and I had heard that Lincoln kept their people busy. So I applied and got the job the next day.

Q: Do you think you make more money than similar workers in Cleveland?

A: I know I do.

Q: What have you done with your money?

A: We have purchased a better home. Also my son is going to the University of Chicago, which costs $10,000 a year. I buy the Lincoln stock which is offered each year, and I have a little bit of gold.

Q: Have you ever visited with any of the senior executives, like Mr. Willis or Mr. Irrgang?

A: I have known Mr. Willis for a long time.

Q: Does he call you by name?

A: Yes. In fact he was very instrumental in my going to the doctor that I am going to with my back. He knows the director of the clinic.

Q: Do you know Mr. Irrgang?

A: I know him to speak to him, and he always speaks, always. But I have known Mr. Willis for a good many years. When I did Plant Two accounting I did not understand how the plant operated. Of course you are not allowed in Plant Two, because that's the Electrode Division. I told my boss about the problem one day and the next thing I knew Mr. Willis came by and said, "Come on, Betty, we're going to Plant Two." He spent an hour and a half showing me the plant.

Q: Do you think Lincoln employees produce more than those in other companies?

A: I think with the incentive program the way that it is, if you want to work and achieve, then you will do it. If you don't want to work and achieve, you will not do it no matter where you are. Just because you are merit rated and have a bonus, if you really don't want to work hard, then you're not going to. You will accept your 90 points or 92 or 85 because, even with that, you make more money than people on the outside.

Q: Do you think Lincoln employees will ever join a union?

A: I don't know why they would.

Q: What is the most important advantage of working for Lincoln Electric?

Q: You have an incentive, and you can push and get something for pushing. That's not true in a lot of companies.

Q: So you say that money is a very major advantage?

A: Money is a major advantage, but it's not just the money. It's the fact that having the incentive, you do wish to work a little harder. I'm sure that there are a lot of men here who, if they worked some other place, would not work as hard as they do here. Not that they are overworked—I don't mean that—but I'm sure they wouldn't push.

Q: Is there anything that you would like to add?

A: I do like working here. I am better off being pushed mentally. In another company if you pushed too hard you would feel a little bit of pressure and someone might say, "Hey, slow down; don't try so hard." But here you are encouraged, not discouraged.

II

Interview with Ed Sanderson, 23-year-old high school graduate who had been with Lincoln four years and who was a machine operator in the Electrode Division at the time of the interview.

Q: How did you happen to get this job?

A: My wife was pregnant, and I was making three bucks an hour and one day I came here and applied. That was it. I kept calling to let them know I was still interested.

Q: Roughly what were your earnings last year including your bonus?

A: $37,000.

Q: What have you done with your money since you have been here?

A: Well, we've lived pretty well and we bought a condominium.

Q: Have you paid for the condominium?

A: No, but I could.

Q: Have you bought your Lincoln stock this year?

A: No, I haven't bought any Lincoln stock yet.

Q: Do you get the feeling that the executives here are pretty well thought of?

A: I think they are. To get where they are today, they had to really work.

Q: Wouldn't that be true anywhere?

A: I think more so here because seniority really doesn't mean anything. If you work with a guy who has 20 years here, and you have two months and you're doing a better job, you will get advanced before he will.

Q: Are you paid on a piece rate basis?

A: My gang does. There are nine of us who make the bare electrode, and the whole group gets paid based on how much electrode we make.

Q: Do you think you work harder than workers in other factories in the Cleveland area?

A: Yes, I would say I probably work harder.

Q: Do you think it hurts anybody?

A: No, a little hard work never hurts anybody.

Q: If you could choose, do you think you would be as happy earning a little less money and being able to slow down a little?

A: No, it doesn't bother me. If it bothered me, I wouldn't do it.

Q: What would you say is the biggest disadvantage of working at Lincoln, as opposed to working somewhere else?

A: Probably having to work shift work.

Q: Why do you think Lincoln employees produce more than workers in other plants?

A: That's the way the company is set up. The more you put out, the more you're going to make.

Q: Do you think it's the piece rate and bonus together?

A: I don't think people would work here if they didn't know that they would be rewarded at the end of the year.

Q: Do you think Lincoln employees will ever join a union?

A: No.

Q: What are the major advantages of working for Lincoln?

A: Money.

Q: Are there any other advantages?

A: Yes, we don't have a union shop. I don't think I could work in a union shop.

Q: Do you think you are a career man with Lincoln at this time?

A: Yes.

III

Interview with Roger Lewis, 23-year-old Purdue graduate in mechanical engineering who had been in the Lincoln sales program for 15 months and who was working in the Cleveland sales office at the time of the interview.

Q: How did you get your job at Lincoln?

A: I saw that Lincoln was interviewing on campus at Purdue and I went by. I later came to Cleveland for a plant tour and was offered a job.

Q: Do you know any of the senior executives? Would they know you by name?

A: Yes, I know all of them—Mr. Irrgang, Mr. Willis, Mr. Manross.

Q: Do you think Lincoln salesmen work harder than those in other companies?

A: Yes. I don't think there are many salesmen for other companies who are putting in 50 to 60-hour weeks. Everybody here works harder. You can go out in the plant or you can go upstairs and there's nobody sitting around.

Q: Do you see any real disadvantage of working at Lincoln?

A: I don't know if it's a disadvantage but Lincoln is a spartan company, a very thrifty company. I like that. The sales offices are functional, not fancy.

Q: Why do you think Lincoln employees have such high productivity?

A: Piecework has a lot to do with it. Lincoln is smaller than many plants, too; you can stand in one place and see the materials come in one side and the product go out the other. You feel a part of the company. The chance to get ahead is important, too. They have a strict policy of promoting from within, so you know you have a chance. I think in a lot of other places you may not get as fair a shake as you do here. The sales offices are on a smaller scale, too. I like that. I tell someone that we have two people in the Baltimore office, and they say "You've got to be kidding." It's smaller and more personal. Pay is the most important thing. I have heard that this is the highest paying factory in the world.

IV

Interview with Jimmy Roberts, a 47-year-old high school graduate who had been with Lincoln 17 years and who was working as a multiple-drill press operator at the time of the interview.

Q: What jobs have you had at Lincoln?

A: I started out cleaning the men's locker room in 1963. After about a year I got a job in the flux department where we make the coating for welding rods. I worked there for seven or eight years and then got my present job.

Q: Do you make one particular part?

A: No, there are a variety of parts I make—at least 25.

Q: Each one has a different piece rate attached to it?

A: Yes.

Q: Are some piece rates better than others?

A: Yes.

Q: How do you determine which ones you are going to do?

A: You don't. Your supervisor assigns them.

Q: How much money did you make last year?

A: $47,000.

Q: Have you ever received any kind of award or citation?

A: No.

Q: Was your rating ever over 110?

A: Yes. For the past five years, probably, I made over 110 points.

Q: Is there any attempt to let others know. . . ?

A: The kind of points I get? No.

Q: Do you know what they are making?

A: No. There are some who might not be too happy with their points and they might make it known. The majority, though, do not make it a point of telling other employees.

Q: Would you be just as happy earning a little less money and working a little slower?

A: I don't think I would—not at this point. I have done piecework all these years and the fast pace doesn't really bother me.

Q: Why do you think Lincoln productivity is so high?

A: The incentive thing—the bonus distribution. I think that would be the main reason. The paycheck you get every two weeks is important too.

Q: Do you think Lincoln employees would ever join a union?

A: I don't think so. I have never heard anyone mention it.

Q: What is the most important advantage of working here?

A: Amount of money you make. I don't think I could make this type of money anywhere else, especially with only a high school education.

Q: As a black person, do you feel that Lincoln discriminates in any way against blacks?

A: No. I don't think any more so than any other job. Naturally, there is a certain amount of discrimination, regardless of where you are.

V

Interview with Joe Trahan, 58-year-old high school graduate who had been with Lincoln 39 years and who was employed as a working supervisor in the tool room at the time of the interview.

Q: Roughly what was your pay last year?

A: Over $50,000; salary, bonus, stock dividends.

Q: How much was your bonus?

A: About $23,000.

Q: Have you ever gotten a special award of any kind?

A: Not really.

Q: What have you done with your money?

A: My house is paid for—and my two cars. I also have some bonds and the Lincoln stock.

Q: What do you think of the executives at Lincoln?

A: They're really top notch.

Q: What is the major disadvantage of working at Lincoln Electric?

A: I don't know of any disadvantage at all.

Q: Do you think you produce more than most people in similar jobs with other companies?

A: I do believe that.

Q: Why is that? Why do you believe that?

Q: We are on the incentive system. Everything we do, we try to improve to make a better product with a minimum of outlay. We try to improve the bonus.

Q: Would you be just as happy making a little less money and not working quite so hard?

A: I don't think so.

Q: You know that Lincoln productivity is higher than that at most other plants. Why is that?

A: Money.

Q: Do you think Lincoln employees would ever join a union?

A: I don't think they would ever consider it.

Q: What is the most important advantage of working at Lincoln?

A: Compensation.

Q: Tell me something about Mr. James Lincoln, who died in 1965.

A: You are talking about Jimmy, Sr. He always strolled through the shop in his shirt sleeves. Big fellow. Always looked distinguished. Gray hair. Friendly sort of guy. I was a member of the advisory board one year. He was there each time.

Q: Did he strike you as really caring?

A: I think he always cared for people.

Q: Did you get any sensation of a religious nature from him?

A: No, not really.

Q: And religion is not part of the program now?

A: No.

Q: Do you think Mr. Lincoln was a very intelligent man, or was he just a nice guy?

A: I would say he was pretty well educated. A great talker—always right off the top of his head. He knew what he was talking about all the time.

Q: When were bonuses for beneficial suggestions done away with?

A: About 15 years ago.

Q: Did that hurt very much?

A: I don't think so, because suggestions are still rewarded through the merit rating system.

Q: Is there anything you would like to add?

A: It's a good place to work. The union kind of ties other places down. At other places, electricians only do electrical work, carpenters only do carpenter work. At Lincoln Electric we all pitch in and do whatever needs to be done.

Q: So a major advantage is not having a union?

A: That's right.

CASE 28 MARY KAY COSMETICS, INC.*

In spring 1983 Mary Kay Cosmetics Inc. (MKC), the second largest direct sales distributor of skin care products in the United States, encountered its first big slowdown in recruiting women to function as Mary Kay beauty consultants and market the Mary Kay cosmetic lines. As of April, MKC's sales force of about 195,000 beauty consultants was increasing at only a 13 percent annual rate, down from a 65 percent rate of increase in 1980. The dropoff in the percentage of new recruits jeopardized MKC's ability to sustain its reputation as a fast-growing company. MKC's strategy was predicated on getting ever larger numbers of beauty consultants to arrange "skin care classes" at the home of a hostess and her three to five guests; at the classes consultants demonstrated the Mary Kay approach to skin care, gave makeup instruction with samples from the Mary Kay Cosmetics line, and usually sold anywhere from $50 to $200 worth of Mary Kay products. MKC's historically successful efforts to build up the size of its force of beauty consultants had given the company reliable access to a growing number of "showings" annually.

Even though MKC's annual turnover rate for salespeople was lower than that of several major competitors (including Avon Products), some 120,000 Mary Kay beauty consultants had quit or been terminated in 1982, making the task of recruiting a growing sales force of consultants a major, ongoing effort at MKC. Recruiting success was seen by management as strategically important. New recruits were encouraged to spend between $500 and $3,000 for sales kits and startup inventories; the initial orders of new recruits accounted for over one third of MKC's annual sales. The newest recruits were also instrumental in helping identify and attract others to become Mary Kay beauty consultants.

Richard Rogers, MKC's cofounder and president, promptly reacted to the recruiting slowdown by announcing five changes in the company's sales force program:

- The financial incentives offered to active beauty consultants for bringing new recruits into the Mary Kay fold were increased by as much as 50 percent.
- A new program was instituted whereby beauty consultants who (1) placed $600 a month in wholesale orders with the company for three consecutive months and (2) recruited five new consultants who together placed $3,000 in wholesale orders a month for three straight months would win the free use of a cream-colored Oldsmobile Firenza for a year (this program supplemented the existing programs whereby top-performing beauty consultants could win the use of a pink Cadillac or pink Buick Regal).
- The minimum order size required of beauty consultants was increased from $400 to $600.

* Prepared by graduate researcher Robin Romblad and Professor Arthur A. Thompson, Jr., The University of Alabama. The assistance and cooperation provided by many people in the Mary Kay organization is gratefully acknowledged. Copyright © 1986 by Arthur A. Thompson, Jr.

- The prices at which MKC wholesaled its products to consultants were raised by 4 percent.
- The requirements for attaining sales director status and heading up a sales unit were raised 25 percent; a sales director had to recruit 15 new consultants (instead of 12), and her sales unit was expected to maintain a monthly minimum of $4,000 in wholesale orders (up from $3,200).

In addition, MKC's 1984 corporate budget for recruiting was more than quadrupled and, as a special recruiting effort, the company staged a National Guest Night in September 1984 that consisted of a live closed-circuit telecast to 78 cities aired from Dallas, Texas, where MKC's corporate headquarters was located. Mary Kay sales people all over the United States were urged to invite prospective recruits and go to one of the 78 simulcast sites.

NATIONAL GUEST NIGHT IN BIRMINGHAM

Jan Currier, senior sales director for MKC in the Tuscaloosa, Alabama, area, invited two other ladies and the casewriter to drive to Birmingham in her pink Buick Regal to attend what was billed as "The Salute to the Stars." On the way, Jan explained that as well as being entertaining, the evening's event would give everyone a chance to see firsthand just how exciting and rewarding the career opportunities were with MKC; she noted with pride that Mary Kay Cosmetics was one of the companies featured in the recent book *The 100 Best Companies to Work For in America*. As the Tuscaloosa entourage neared the auditorium in Birmingham, the casewriter observed numerous pink Cadillacs and pink Buick Regals in the flow of traffic and in the parking lot. Mary Kay sales directors were stationed at each door to the lobby enthusiastically greeting each person and presenting a gift of Mary Kay cosmetics. Guests were directed to a table to register for prizes to be awarded later in the evening.

Inside the auditorium over 1,500 people awaited the beginning of the evening's program. A large theater screen was located at center stage. The lights dimmed promptly at 7 P.M. and the show began. The casewriter used her tape recorder and took extensive notes to capture what went on:

Mark Dixon: [*National Sales Administrator for the South Central Division, appears on stage in Birmingham*]: Welcome, ladies and gentlemen, to National Guest Night, Mary Kay's Salute to the Stars. Tonight, you're going to be a part of the largest teleconference ever held by a U.S. corporation.

Now please help me welcome someone all of us at Mary Kay love very dearly, National Sales Director from Houston, Texas, Lovie Quinn.

[*The crowd stands and greets Lovie with cheers and applause.*]

Lovie Quinn: [*comes out on stage in Birmingham to join Mark Dixon. Lovie is wearing this year's Mary Kay national sales director suit of red suede with black mink trim.*]: Good evening ladies and gentlemen and welcome to one of the most exciting events in the history of Mary Kay. An evening with Mary Kay as she Salutes the Stars. . . . During the evening you'll learn about career opportunities. There will be recognition of our stars. We'll see the salute to them with gifts and prizes you hear about at Mary Kay. You'll hear about . . . pink Cadillacs . . . pink Buick Regals, and Firenza Oldsmobiles.

You're going to hear about and see diamond rings and beautiful full-length mink coats. And of course we'll talk about MONEY.

If you've never attended a Mary Kay function you might very easily get the impression that we brag a lot. We like to think of it as recognition . . . But we would not be able to give this recognition of success if you, the hostesses, our special guests, did not open up your homes so we may share with you and some of your selected friends the Mary Kay skin care program. For that reason we would like to show our appreciation at this time. Will all the special guests please stand up.

[*About 40 percent of the audience stands and the remainder applaud the guests.*]

Lovie Quinn: Now I need to have all our directors line up on stage. [*Each one is dressed in a navy blue suit with either a red, green, or white blouse—the color of the blouse signifies director, senior director, or future director status.*] Enthusiasm and excitement are at the root of the Mary Kay philosophy. This is why we always start a meeting like this with a song. We invite all of you to join with the directors and sing the theme song, "That Mary Kay Enthusiasm."

[*Lovie motions for the audience to stand; the choir of directors begins to clap and leads out in singing. The audience joins in quickly.*]

> I've got that Mary Kay enthusiasm up in my
> head, up in my head, up in my head.
> I've got that Mary Kay enthusiasm up in my
> head, up in my head to stay.
> I've got that Mary Kay enthusiasm down in my
> heart, down in my heart, down in my heart.
> I've got that Mary Kay enthusiasm down in my
> heart, down in my heart to stay.
>
> I've got that Mary Kay enthsiasm down in my
> feet, down in my feet, down in my feet.
> I've got that Mary Kay enthusiasm down in my
> feet, down in my feet to stay.
>
> all over me, all over me.
> all over me to stay.
> I've got that Mary Kay enthusiasm up in my
> head, down in my heart, down in my feet.
> I've got that Mary Kay enthusiasm all over me,
> all over me to stay.

[*The song concludes to a round of applause. The crowd is spirited.*]

Lovie Quinn: Now we'd like to recognize a group of very special consultants. These ladies have accepted a challenge from Mary Kay and have held 10 beauty shows in one week. This is something really terrific. It demonstrates the successful achievement of a goal. We have found when you want to do something for our Chairman of the Board, Mary Kay Ash . . . you don't have to give furs. The most special gift you can give to Mary Kay is your own success. . . .

[*All of those recognized are seated in the first 10 rows with their guests; seating in the front rows is a special reward for meeting the challenge. The crowd applauds.*]

Lovie Quinn: It is almost time for the countdown to begin, but before it does one more special group must be recognized. These ladies are Mary Kay's Gold Medal winners. In one month they recruited *five* new consultants. [*A number of ladies stand; they beam* *with pride and each has been awarded a medal resembling an Olympic Gold. The audience gives them a nice round of applause.*]

Lovie Quinn [*Lovie continues to fill the crowd with excitement and anticipation.*]: The countdown is going to be in just a few moments. It will be a treat for those of you that have not met Mary Kay before. Please help me count down the final 10 seconds before the broadcast.

[*But the crowd is so excited it starts the countdown when one minute appears on the screen. As the seconds wind down, the crowd gets louder with anticipation and then gets in sync chanting: 10, 9, 8, 7, 6, 5, 4, 3, 2 1. More screams and applause.*

On the screen a Gold Mary Kay medallion appears, then the production lines at the plant are shown, and then trucks shipping the products. The audience claps as they see these on the screen. Headquarters is shown. Now a number of the Mary Kay sales directors are shown framed in stars on the screen. People clap when they recognize someone from their district. Loud applause fills the auditorium when Mary Kay Ash, MKC's chairman of the board and company cofounder, is shown in a star.

The Dallas-based part of the simulcast opens with female dancers dressed in pink and male dancers dressed in gray tuxedos. They perform the "Mary Kay Star Song" which includes a salute to various regions in the United States. The Birmingham crowd cheers when the South is highlighted.

A woman is chosen out of the audience in Dallas. Her name is Susan; the audience is told that at various intervals in the broadcast we will see her evolution into a successful Mary Kay Beauty consultant. Initially we see her get a feeling that maybe she can be a Mary Kay star. The message is that personal dreams of success can come true. Will she be successful? The answer comes back, "Yes, She Can Do It."

Mary Kay Ash is escorted on stage by her son Richard Rogers. She is elegantly dressed with accents of diamonds and feathers. The applause, the loudest so far, is genuinely enthusiastic and many in both the Dallas and Birmingham audiences are cheering loudly.]

Mary Kay Ash: Welcome everyone to our very first Salute to the Stars, National Guest Night. How exciting it is to think that right now over 100,000 people are watching this broadcast all over the United States. . . . Even though I can't see all of you, I can feel your warmth all the way to Dallas.

During the program this evening one expression you're going to hear over and over again is YOU CAN DO IT. . . . This is something we really believe in. What we have discovered is the seeds of greatness are planted in every human being. . . . Tonight we hope to inspire you, to get you to reach within yourself, to bring out some of those star qualities that I know you have. And no matter who you are and no matter where you live, I believe you can take those talents and go farther than you ever thought possible and we have a special place waiting just for you.

Now I would like to introduce someone who has a special place in my heart. Someone who has been beside me from the very beginning. Without him Mary Kay Cosmetics would not be what it is today. Please welcome your president and cofounder of our company, my son, Richard Rogers.

Richard Rogers [*Steps to the microphone, accompanied by respectful applause.*]: When we started this company over 20 years ago my mother and I never dreamed we would be standing here talking live to over 100,000 of you all across the country. . . . Tonight we've planned a memorable evening just for you. A program that conveys the spirit of Mary Kay. Going back 21 years ago, Mary Kay saw a void in the cosmetics industry. The observation she made was that others were just selling products. No one was teaching women about their skin and how to care for it. . . . This is the concept on which she based her company. So on September 13, 1963, Mary Kay Cosmetics opened its doors in Dallas, Texas.

Throughout the decade Mary Kay's concept continued to flourish. . . . By the end of the 60s Mary Kay Cosmetics had become a fully integrated manufacturer and distributor of skin care products. In 1970 the sales force had grown to 7,000 consultants in Texas and four surrounding states.

California was the first state MKC designated for expansion. When we first went there no one had ever heard of Mary Kay Cosmetics. Within three years California had more consultants selling Mary Kay Cosmetics than the state of Texas. . . . With this success, expansion continued throughout the United States. . . . By 1975 MKC had grown to 700 sales directors, 34,000 consultants, and $35 million in sales.

International expansion was initiated in 1978 by selling skin care products in Canada. In just 36 months MKC became the fourth largest Canadian cosmetic company. . . . Since that time Mary Kay has expanded to South America, Australia, and in September we opened for business in the United Kingdom.

At the end of 1983 MKC had over 195,000 consultants. Sales had reached over $600 million around the world. . . . With total commitment to excellence setting the pace, MKC is still working towards achieving the goal of being the finest teaching-oriented skin care organization in the world. . . . Mary Kay is proud to have the human resources necessary to meet this goal. At Mary Kay P&L means more than profit and loss. It also stands for People and Love. People have helped MKC reach where it is today, and they will play a big part in where it will be tomorrow.

Tonight we're proud to announce the arrival of a book that expresses the Mary Kay philosophy of Golden Rule management, a book that outlines the management style that has contributed to the success of Mary Kay Cosmetics. The new book is *Mary Kay on People Management.*

[*The crowd applauds at this announcement.*]

Mary Kay Ash [*Reappears on stage.*]:We're so excited about the new book. I am pleased to have the opportunity to talk with you about it tonight. Actually, I started to write that book over 20 years ago. I had just retired from 25 years of direct sales. I wanted to share my experiences, so I wrote down my thoughts about the companies I had worked for. What had worked and what had not. . . . After expressing my ideas I thought how wonderful it would be to put these ideas of a company designed to meet women's needs into action. That is when Mary Kay Cosmetics was born. . . . The company helps women meet the goals they set for themselves. . . . I feel this is what has contributed to the success of the organization. Everyone at MKC starts at the same place, as a consultant, and everyone has the same opportunities for success.

[*The broadcast returns to the scenario of Susan as she becomes a new Mary Kay consultant. Susan sings about the doubts people have about her joining Mary Kay. She disregards this and decides to climb to success. At the end of the scene, she projects a positive, successful image that her friends and family recognize. The audience responds favorably.*]

Dale Alexander [*National Sales Administrator for Mary Kay Cosmetics appears on stage in Dallas.*]: It is a great honor to be with you tonight and I want to add my most sincere welcome. . . . Recognition is one of the original principles on which our company is based. It's an essential ingredient in the Mary Kay formula for success. . . . I want to start out by recognizing the largest group. The group of independent businesswomen who are out there every day holding beauty shows, teaching skin care, selling our products, and sharing the Mary Kay opportunity. At this time will all of the Mary Kay beauty consultants across the nation stand to be recognized? [*In Birmingham the lights go up and the crowd applauds the consultants in the audience.*] Next we want to recognize the Star Consultants. . . . Will these ladies stand?

Many of our people are wearing small golden ladders. This is our Ladder of Success.

Each ladder has a number of different jewels awarded for specific accomplishments during a calendar quarter. Star consultants earn rubies, sapphires, and diamonds to go on their ladders. The higher they climb the more dazzling their ladders become. A consultant with all diamonds is known at Mary Kay as a top Star Performer. It is like wearing a straight A report card on your lapel.

In addition to Ladders, consultants have an opportunity to earn great prizes each quarter. . . . This quarter's theme is Salute to the Stars . . . and these prizes are out of this world.

[The scene shifts to a description of the fall 1984 sales program; it utilizes a "Star Trek" theme, and across the screen is emblazoned "Starship Mary Kay in Search of the Prize Zone." Captain Kay appears with members of her crew on Starship Mary Kay. She remarks their mission is to seek out prizes to honor those that reach for the sky. They are approaching the prize zone. The awards and prizes are flashed onto the screen.]

The Prize Zone
Bonus Prizes Available
Based on Fourth Quarter Sales

$1,800 Wholesale sales	Cubic zirconia necklace and earrings or travel set with hair dryer
$2,400 Wholesale sales	Leather briefcase with matching umbrella
$3,000 Wholesale sales	Diamond earrings with 14K gold teardrops
$3,600 Wholesale sales	Telephone answering machine
$4,200 Wholesale sales	Sapphire ring
$4,800 Wholesale sales	Electronic printer by Brother—fits in a briefcase
$6,000 Wholesale sales	Diamond pendant—nine diamonds—.5 karat on a 18K gold chain

[Even though this "space" presentation of prizes is humorous, the ladies know that the rewards are real; they respond as the scene ends with a round of applause and a buzz of excitement. The scene concludes with the message, "When you reach for the sky you bring home a star."]

Mary Kay [*Returns to the stage.*]: You can climb that ladder of success at Mary Kay. It is up to you to take that very first step. . . . There are so many rewards for being a Mary Kay consultant. There are top earnings, prizes, and lots of recognition. But there is even more to a Mary Kay career and that is the fulfillment of bringing beauty into the lives of others. . . . .

When a woman joins our company she knows she can do it. But not alone. She'll receive support from many people. A big sister relationship will form between a new consultant and her recruiter. . . . Whoever invited you tonight thought you were a special person. She wanted to share this evening and introduce you to our company and let you see for yourself the excitement and enthusiasm Mary Kay people have when they are together. . . . The enthusiasm of our consultants and directors is responsible for our success.

[The vignette about Susan returns to the screen. This time she is thinking about concentrating her efforts on recruiting. After five recruits she will become a team leader. A good goal to strive for, she thinks. A woman that had doubted Susan's career earlier is the first one recruited. Then four more ladies are recruited: a waitress, a teacher, a stewardess, and a nurse. All kinds of people can be Mary Kay consultants. Susan has reached her goal—she is a team leader. The crowd applauds her success.]

Dale Alexander [*Returns to the microphone in Dallas.*]: There is the perfect goal of a Mary Kay career. And now it is time to recognize a very special group of individuals who are proof of this point. Will all the team leaders please stand and remain standing for a few moments? [*The lights go up and team leaders stand. All are wearing red jackets.*]

To qualify for a team leader each consultant must recruit five new consultants. . . . And now will you please recognize these ladies' achievements with a round of applause? [*The audience applauds.*] Now it is time to draw for the prizes. In each of the 75 locations two names will be drawn. These lucky people will both win this exquisite 14K diamond earring and pendant set. [*The crowd oohs and aahs when the jewelry is shown on the screen.*] These two winners will also be eligible for the prize to be given by Mary Kay when the broadcast resumes.

[*The lights go up in the Birmingham auditorium. Lovie draws two tickets from a big box. When she calls out the names, the winners scream and run on stage to accept their gifts. The crowd applauds the winners.*]

Lovie Quinn [*On the stage in Birmingham*]: Please join me in counting down the final seconds left before we rejoin the broadcast.

[*Everyone stands and enthusiastically counts off 11, 10, 9, 8, 7, 6, 5, 4, 3, 2, 1." The crowd applauds and cheers.*]

Mary Kay [*Appears on the screen as the broadcast from Dallas is rejoined.*]: I wish I could be there to congratulate each winner. . . . The two lucky winners in each of the 75 cities are eligible to win the grand prize. . . . It used to be you just drew a number out of a hat. Now that is considered old-fashioned. Tonight, we'll use a computer. All I have to do is push a button and a city will be randomly selected. The local winners in that city will also win this .75 karat diamond ring. [*The crowd buzzes as a close-up of the ring is shown on the giant screen.*] Are you ready? OK Here goes. [*Mary Kay presses a button.*] The lucky city is Philadelphia. [*The crowd applauds.*] Congratulations Philadelphia, and we will be sending each of you a ring real soon.

By the way, while we are talking about prizes. Would you happen to have a spare finger for a diamond ring? [*The crowd cheers.*] Or could you squeeze into your closet room for a full-length mink coat? [*The crowd is really excited.*] Or is there by any chance, a space in your driveway for a car? [*The crowd cheers and applauds. One member of the audience remarks how she would be glad to get rid of that old blue thing she is driving.*] Well, all you have to do is set your Mary Kay career goals high enough to achieve the recognition and rewards available just for you. . . .

I remember the first sales competition I set my goals to win. I worked so hard and all I won was a flounder light. [*The audience laughs.*] Does anyone know what you do with it? It is something you use when you put on waders and gig fish. [*The audience laughs again.*] I thought the prize was awful . . . but my manager was a fisherman and he thought it was great.

Winning that flounder light taught me a lesson. I decided if I was ever in a position to give awards they would be things women appreciate, *not* flounder lights. . . . Prizes would be things women would love to have. Absolutely no washing machines and certainly no ironing boards. [*The audience shows their approval by cheers and applause.*] At MKC you are rewarded for consistent sales and recruiting performance. . . . This past spring a new program was added. . . . We call it our VIP program. It stands for Very Important Performer. . . . This program allows a person to win a cream-colored Oldsmobile Firenza with rich brown interior. . . . A consultant is eligible for this prize only three months after joining MKC. . . .

Mary Kay Cosmetics can offer several unique career opportunities:

A 50 percent commission on everything you sell.

Earnings of a 12 percent commission on your recruit's sales.

You work your own hours.

After three months you can be eligible for a car. The car is free. MKC pays the insurance.

When you do well you get a lot of recognition. Not dumb old things like turkeys and hams. We're talking diamonds and furs.

You work up to management because of your own efforts and merit.

Other companies would think these things are part of a dream world. At Mary Kay we do live in a dream world and our dreams do come true.

[*The audience applauds loudly. The broadcast then returns to the scenario about Susan. She sets a goal to be a VIP. Through song and dance her group illustrates setting goals and receiving recognition. Step by step they climb the ladder of recognition. The audience applauds this short scene on success.*]

Dale Alexander [*Comes back to the Dallas stage.*]: We have some VIPs among us tonight. . . . Mary Kay's Very Important Performers. Will all the VIPs now stand? [*The lights go up in Birmingham; the VIPs stand and the audience applauds.*] Through her enthusiasm and hard work each VIP has worked hard to achieve this status. And to recognize her accomplishments she was awarded an Oldsmobile Firenza to show off her achievement of success. Now let's give all our VIPs a round of applause. [*The Birmingham and Dallas audiences respond with more applause.*]

Mary Kay Ash [*Comes onto the stage in Dallas and the crowd in Birmingham turns its attention to the screen.*]: With Mary Kay you can achieve success. . . . All you have to do is break down your goals into small manageable steps. . . . You are able to move on to bigger accomplishments as you gain confidence in yourself.

Let's look at some of the provisions of the Mary Kay career plan and see how it works:

Your products are purchased directly from the company.

Generous discounts are offered on large orders.

There are no territories. You can sell and recruit wherever you want.

We provide our customers the best possible way to buy cosmetics. They can try the products in their own home before they buy.

All Mary Kay products are backed by a full 100 percent money back guarantee.

Mary Kay is a good opportunity to go into business for yourself. . . . There are many benefits of running your own business. . . . You meet new people and at the same time you enjoy the support of the Mary Kay sisterhood. . . . Plus you earn financial rewards as well as prizes. . . .

Now we need to talk about the position of Mary Kay Sales Director. Directors receive income not only from shows, facials, and reorders but also from recruit commissions. . . . In addition they earn unit and recruiting bonuses from Mary Kay. . . . Some earn the privilege to drive pink Regals and Cadillacs. . . . Each year hundreds of Sales Directors earn over $30,000 a year. And today in our company we have more women earning over $50,000 a year than any other company in America. [*The audience applauds.*] At the very top are our National Sales Directors. . . . Their average is about $150,000 a year in commissions. How about that? [*The audience applauds.*] Everyone at Mary Kay starts at the same place with the same beauty showcase. I've always said you can have anything in this world if you want it badly enough and are willing to pay the price. With that kind of attitude anyone can succeed at Mary Kay.

[*The vignette about Susan comes back onto the screen. Susan sets a goal to achieve Sales Director. She sings about how invigorating her new career is and how she now wants to be a coach, a teacher, a counselor, and a friend to others. Everyone around her recognizes how her success has positively affected her whole life. The scene ends and the audience applauds.*]

Dale Alexander [*Comes onto the screen from Dallas.*]: Those individuals that advance on to directorship lead our organization. They set the pace for their units. Will all our Sales Directors please stand? [*The sales directors stand as the lights go up in Birmingham and the audience applauds.*] Among all our directors there are some that have reached a very special level. They have earned the privilege of driving one of Mary Kay's famous pink cars. . . . One thing is guaranteed. Whenever you see one of those pink cars on the road you know there is a top achiever behind the wheel. At this time we want to honor all these ladies. [*First the Regal drivers stand and then the Cadillac drivers. The audience recognizes each group with applause.*] Finally, there is one last group we want to recognize. A group whose members have already committed to a future with Mary Kay. . . . They are our DIQs or Directors in Qualification. They are working towards meeting the goals to qualify for Directorship. . . . Will all the DIQs stand for a round of applause?

[*The lights go up and the DIQs stand. They are recognized with applause from the audience. The lights fade and the scene shifts back to Dallas.*]

Mary Kay: I want to congratulate these ladies. Next week I'll have the pleasure of hostessing our traditional tea for the DIQs at my home. [*The audience applauds.*] Our DIQs are a perfect example of one of the points we have tried to make this evening. . . . You can set your goals and achieve them if you want them badly enough.

    I've always felt our most valuable asset is not our product but our people. . . . I wish I could tell you all the success stories of consultants at MKC. . . . We have chosen a few stories we think best represent Mary Kay consultants. The first person you'll meet is Rena.

[*The audience applauds; Rena is recognized by the Mary Kay people present. The narrator of the film clip tells us that Rena has been with MKC for 17 years. She has been Queen of Unit Sales four consecutive years, an honor which was earned when the sales unit she managed exceeded $1 million in sales in one year. Her reward was four $5,000 shopping sprees at Neiman-Marcus Co. in Dallas. When she started she was living on $300 a month in government housing with her husband and three small children. One day a friend offered to buy her dinner and pay for a babysitter if she would attend a meeting. She couldn't pass up this offer so she went to the Mary Kay meeting. The meeting inspired her and she joined MKC. At the end we learn that Rena has had cancer for the last eight years, a fact that is not well known; the point is made that it has never affected her ability to succeed with Mary Kay Cosmetics. The crowd applauds her success story.*

Next comes a film clip about Ruel; the audience is told that Ruel was raised in Arkansas, a daughter of a sharecropper. She joined Mary Kay in 1971. By 1976 she was a National Sales Director. A career with Mary Kay has given her confidence. She has two children in medical school and one of her sons just won a national honor, the Medal of Valor. All of this she attributes to Mary Kay. Her children saw her achieve and they knew they could too. Her career with Mary Kay has allowed her to climb up the scale from a poor sharecropper's daughter to become financially independent. Along the way she has the opportunity to meet many wonderful people. As her success story ends, the audience applauds.

The third story is about Arlene. Arlene has been a National Sales Director since 1976. She achieved this just five short years after joining MKC. She had been at home for 13 years and wanted to have her own business, set her own hours, and write her own checks. She found she could achieve these goals in a career with Mary Kay. Arlene, we are told, has been able to reach inside herself and achieve great success. Arlene testifies that one of her biggest rewards at Mary Kay has been helping other women achieve the goals they set. The audience loudly applauds the last of the success stories.]

Mary Kay: I am so proud of all these ladies. . . . It makes me feel good to be able to offer all these wonderful opportunities to so many women.

Every journey begins with just a single step. All you have to do is make up your mind that YOU can do it! Isn't it exciting. You CAN do it.

All you need to start a Mary Kay career is a beauty case. It carries everything: vanity trays, mirrors, products, and product literature.

Tonight it becomes easier. . . . If you join us as a beauty consultant tonight, we will give you your beauty showcase. [*The audience interrupts with a round of applause.*] When you submit your Beauty Consultant agreement along with your first wholesale order, you will receive the beauty case free, an $85 value.

At Mary Kay you'll make lasting friends and you'll achieve a feeling of growth. . . . Tonight we wanted to give you a feel for Mary Kay Cosmetics. We have a place for you to shine. . . . Believe in yourself and you can do anything.

[*The broadcast from Dallas concludes; the audience stands and applauds the program.*]

Lovie Quinn [*Comes onto stage in Birmingham.*]: I started at Mary Kay just to earn money for Christmas. I told Mary Kay I could only work four hours a week. Believe it or not Mary Kay welcomed me into the organization.

Things were different then. There were no manuals or guides. I was given my first cosmetics in a shoe box. Mary Kay Cosmetics has come a long way. Each consultant has her own beauty case and is trained in skin care.

Last year I earned over $112,000. This does not include my personal sales. . . . I am now driving my 13th pink Cadillac. . . . For three years I have been in the half million dollar club. The prizes for this honor include either a black mink, a white mink, or a diamond ring, all worth $10,000 each. I have all three.

Mary Kay Cosmetics offers many opportunites to women. . . . Tonight, if you join MKC, I would be honored to sign your agreement. This will let Mary Kay know you made your commitment tonight.

[*Lovie invites the new consultants to meet her up front. The audience applauds her. Many of the women eagerly go up to meet Lovie and have their agreements signed.*]

THE DIRECT SALES INDUSTRY

In 1984 Avon was the acknowledged leader among the handful of companies that chose to market cosmetics to U.S. consumers using direct sales techniques; Avon, with its door-to-door sales force of 400,000 representatives, had worldwide sales of about $2 billion. Mary Kay Cosmetics was the second leading firm (see Exhibit 1). Other well-known companies whose salespeople went either door-to-door with their products or else held "parties" in the homes of prospective customers included Amway Corp. (home cleaning products), Shaklee Corp. (vitamins and health foods), Encyclopaedia Britannica, Tupperware (plastic dishes and food containers), Consolidated Foods' Electrolux division (vacuum cleaners), and StanHome (parent of Fuller Brush). The direct sales industry also included scores of lesser known firms selling about every product imaginable—clothing, houseplants, toys, and financial services. Although Stanley Home Products invented the idea, Mary Kay and Tupperware were the best-known national companies using the "party plan" approach to direct selling.

Exhibit 1   Estimated Sales Of Leading Direct Selling Cosmetic Companies, 1983

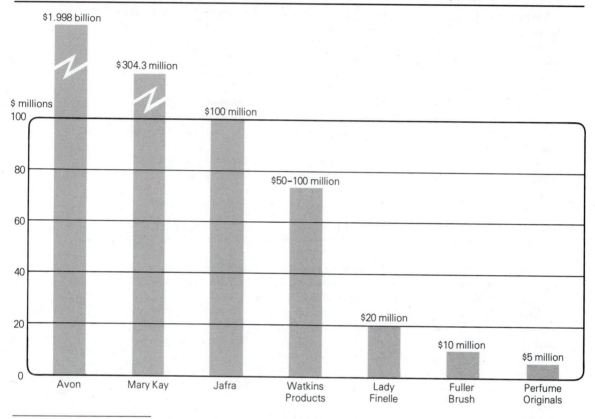

Source: "Reopening the Door to Door-to-Door Selling," *Chemical Business,* February 1984.

The success enjoyed by Avon and Mary Kay was heavily dependent upon constantly replenishing and expanding their sales forces. New salespeople not only placed large initial orders for products but they also recruited new people into the organization. Revenues and revenue growth thus were a function of the number of representatives as well as the sales productivity of each salesperson. Market size was not seen as a limiting factor for growth because direct sales companies typically reached fewer than half the potential customer base.

Direct selling was grounded in capitalizing on networking relationships. Salespeople usually got their starts by selling first to relatives, friends, and neighbors, all the while looking for leads to new prospects. Direct sales specialists often believed that party plan selling was most successful among working class, ethnic, and small-town population groups where relationships were closer knit and where the social lives of women had a high carryover effect with work and high school. However, industry analysts saw several trends working against the networking approach and party plan type of direct-selling—rising divorce rates, the scattering of relatives and families across wider geographic areas, weakening ties to ethnic neighborhoods, declines in the number and strength of "the old girls" networks in many towns and neighborhoods, increased social mobility, the growing popularity of apartment and condominium living where acquaintances and relationships were more transient, and the springing up of bedroom communities and subdivisions populated by commuters and/or by families that stayed only a few years.

In the 1980s direct selling companies began to have problems recruiting and retaining salespeople, partly because of these trends but even more because of shifting employment patterns and preferences. During the two most recent recessionary periods in the United States, it was thought that the pool of potential saleswomen available for recruitment into direct sales careers would expand owing to above-normal unemployment rates. It didn't happen. As it turned out, many women became the sole family support and even greater numbers sought steady, better paying jobs in other fields. Part-time job opportunities mushroomed outside the direct-sales field as many service and retailing firms started hiring part-time permanent workers rather than full-time permanent staffs because part-time workers did not have to be paid the same extensive fringe benefits that full-time employees normally got. When the economy experienced upturns, the pool of direct sales recruits shrank even more as people sought security in jobs offering regular hours and a salary; in 1983 all direct sales companies reported increased difficulty in getting people to accept their part-time, sales-oriented, commission-only offers of employment.

Avon and Mary Kay were both caught offguard by these unpredicted events. Staffing plans at Avon had originally called for expansion in the number of sales force representatives from 400,000 in 1983 to 650,000 by 1987; in 1984 the company revised the 1987 goal down to 500,000 representatives. Four straight years of declining earnings convinced Avon that the traditional approach of depending on increasing the number of representatives for growth was not feasible any longer.

Sarah Coventry, a home party jewelry firm, decided in 1984 that relying solely upon direct selling approaches would not only be a continuing problem but a growing problem. The company began to look for ways to supplement its direct sales methods and shortly announced a plan to begin to sell Sarah Coventry products in retail stores. Fuller Brush, a long-standing door-to-door seller, began to distribute mail-order catalogs displaying a wider line of "househelper" products.

As of 1984 virtually every company in the direct sales industry was critically evaluating the extent to which changes in the economy and in employment demographics would affect the success of direct selling. Many firms, including Avon and Mary Kay, were reviewing their incentive programs and sales organization methods. A number of industry observers as well as company officials believed some major changes would have to be made in the way the direct sales industry did business.

MARY KAY ASH

Before she reached the age of 10, Mary Kay had the responsibility of cleaning, cooking, and caring for her invalid father, while her mother worked to support the family. During these years, Mary Kay's mother encouraged her daughter to excel. Whether at school or home, Mary Kay was urged to put forth her best efforts. By the time she was a teenager, Mary Kay had become a classic overachiever, intent on getting good grades and winning school contests. Over and over again she heard her mother say "you can do it." Years later Mary Kay noted on many occasions, "The confidence my mother instilled in me has been a tremendous help."[1]

Deserted by her husband of 11 years during the Great Depression, Mary Kay found herself with the responsibility of raising and supporting three children under the age of eight. Needing a job with flexible hours, she opted to try a career in direct sales with Stanley Home Products, a home party housewares firm. One of the first goals Mary Kay set at Stanley was to win Stanley's Miss Dallas Award, a ribbon honoring the employee who recruited the most new people in one week; she won the award during her first year with Stanley. After 13 years with Stanley Mary Kay joined World Gift, a direct sales company involved in decorative accessories; a few years later she was promoted to national training director. Her career and life were threatened in 1962 by a rare paralysis of one side of the face.

After recovery from surgery she decided to retire from World Gift; by then she had remarried and lived in a comfortable Dallas neighborhood. She got so bored with retirement she decided to write a book on her direct sales experiences. The more she wrote, the more she came to realize just how many problems women faced in the business world. Writing on a yellow legal pad at her kitchen table, Mary Kay listed everything she thought was wrong with male-run companies; on a second sheet she detailed how these wrongs could be righted, how a company could operate in ways that were responsive to the problems of working women and especially working mothers, and how women could reach their top potential in the business world. Being restless with retirement, she decided to do something about what she had written on the yellow pad and began immediately to plan how she might form a direct sales company that had no sales quotas, few rules, flexible work hours, and plenty of autonomy for salespeople.

Finding a product to market was not a problem. In 1953 when she was conducting a Stanley home party at a house "on the wrong side of Dallas" she had noticed that all the ladies present had terrific-looking skin. It turned out that the hostess was a cosmetologist who was experimenting with a skin care product and all the guests were her guinea pigs. After the party everyone gathered in the hostess's kitchen to get samples of her latest batch. The product was based on a formula that the woman's father, a hide tanner, developed when he accidentally discovered that some tanning lotions he made and used regularly had caused his hands to look much younger than his face. The tanner decided to apply these solutions to his face regularly, and after a short time his facial skin began looking more youthful too. The woman had since worked with her father's discovery for 17 years, making up batches which had the chemical smell of tanning solutions, putting portions in empty jars and bottles, and selling them as a sideline; she gave out instructions for use written in longhand on notebook paper. Mary Kay offered to try some of the hostess's latest batch and, despite the fact that it was smelly and messy, soon concluded that it was so good she wouldn't use anything else. Later, she became convinced that the only reason the woman hadn't made the product a commercial success was because she lacked marketing skills.

---

[1] Mary Kay Ash, *Mary Kay* (New York: Harper & Row, 1981), p. 3.

In 1963, using $5,000 in savings as working capital, she bought the formulas and proceeded to organize a beauty products company that integrated skin care instruction into its direct sales approach. The company was named Beauty by Mary Kay; the plan was for Mary Kay to take responsibility for the sales part of the company and for her second husband to serve as chief administrator. One month before operations were to start, he dropped dead of a heart attack. Her children persuaded her to go ahead with her plans, and Mary Kay's 20-year-old son, Richard Rogers, agreed to take on the job of administration of the new company. In September 1963 they opened a small store in Dallas with one shelf of inventory and nine of Mary Kay's friends as saleswomen. Mary Kay herself had limited expectations for the company and never dreamed that its sphere of operations would extend beyond Dallas.

All of Mary Kay's life-long philosophies and experiences were incorporated into how the company operated. The importance of encouragement became deeply ingrained in what was said and done. "You Can Do It" was expanded from a technique used by her mother to a daily theme at MKC. Mary Kay's style was to "praise people to success." She put into practice again the motivating role which positive encouragement had played in her own career; recognition and awards were made a highlight of the sales incentive programs that emerged. By 1984, recognition at MKC ranged from a simple ribbon awarded for a consultant's first $100 show to a $5,000 shopping spree given to million-dollar producers.

The second important philosophy which Mary Kay stressed concerned personal priorities: "Over the years I have found that if you have your life in the proper perspective, with God first, your family second, and your career third, everything seems to work out."[2] She reiterated this belief again and again, regularly urging employees to take stock of their personal priorities and citing her own experience and belief as a positive example. She insisted on an all-out, firmwide effort to accommodate the plight of working mothers. Mary Kay particularly stressed giving beauty consultants enough control over how their selling efforts were scheduled so that problems with family matters and sick children were not incompatible with a Mary Kay career. A structure based on no sales quotas, few rules, and flexible hours was essential, Mary Kay believed, because working mothers from time to time needed the freedom to let work demands take a backseat to pressing problems at home.

Fairness and personal ethics were put in the forefront, too. The Golden Rule (treating others as you would have them treat you) was high on Mary Kay's list of management guidelines:

> I believe in the Golden Rule and try to run the company on those principles. I believe that all you send into the lives of others will come back into your own. I like to see women reaching into themselves and coming out of their shells as the beautiful person that God intended them to be. In my company women do not have to claw their way to the top. They can get ahead based on the virtue of their own ethics because there's enough for everyone.[3]

To discourage interpersonal rivalry and jealousy, all rewards and incentives were pegged to reaching plateaus of achievement; everybody who reached the target level

---

[2] Ibid., p. 56.

[3] As quoted in "The Beauty of Being Mary Kay," *Marketing and Media Decisions,* December 1982, pp. 150 and 152.

of performance became a winner. Sales contests based on declaring first place, second place, and third place winners were avoided.

MKC INC.

The company succeeded from the start. First-year wholesale sales were $198,000; in the second year sales reached $800,000. At year-end 1983 wholesale revenues exceeded $320 million and MKC's staff of consultants numbered over 195,000. Major geographical expansion was initiated during the 1970s. Distribution centers were opened in California, Georgia, New Jersey, and Illinois, and the company expanded its selling efforts internationally to Canada, Argentina, Australia, and the United Kingdom.

Early on, Mary Kay and Richard decided to consult a psychologist to learn more about their personalities. Testing revealed that Mary Kay was the type who, when encountering a person bleeding all over a fine carpet, would think of the person's plight first while Richard would think first of the carpet. This solidified their decision for Mary Kay to be the company's inspirational leader and for Richard to concentrate on overseeing all the business details.

In 1968 the company name was changed to Mary Kay Cosmetics, Inc. Also, during 1968 the company went public and its stock was traded in the over-the-counter market; in 1976 MKC's stock was listed on the New York Stock Exchange. Income per common share jumped from $0.16 in 1976 to $1.22 in 1983. A 10-year financial summary is presented in Exhibit 2; Exhibits 3 and 4 provide additional company data.

Richard Rogers, president, gave two basic reasons for the success of MKC:

> We were filling a void in the industry when we began to teach skin care and makeup artistry and we're still doing that today. And second, our marketing system, through which proficient consultants achieve success by recruiting and building their own sales organization, was a stroke of genius because the by-product has been management. In other words, we didn't buy a full management team, they've been trained one by one.[4]

One of the biggest challenges MKC had to tackle during the 1970s was how to adapt its strategy and operating style in response to the influx of women into the labor force. Full- and part-time jobs interfered with attending beauty shows during normal working hours, and many working women with children at home had a hard time fitting beauty shows on weeknights and weekends into their schedules. To make the beauty show sales approach more appealing to working women, the company began to supplement its standard "try before you buy" and "on-the-spot-delivery" sales pitch themes. Consultants were trained to tout the ease with which MKC's scientifically formulated skin care system could be followed, the value of investing in good makeup and attractive appearance, the up-to-date glamor and wide selection associated with MKC's product line, the flexibility of deciding what and when to buy, and the time-saving convenience of having refills and "specials" delivered to their door instead of having to go out shopping. Mary Kay consultants quickly

---

[4] Mary Kay Cosmetics, Inc., "A Company and a Way of Life," Company Literature.

Exhibit 2 Selected Financial Data, Mary Kay Cosmetics, Inc., 1973–1983 In Thousands Except per Share Data

	1973	1974	1975	1976	1977	1978	1979	1980	1981	1982	1983
Net sales	$22,199	$30,215	$34,947	$44,871	$47,856	$53,746	$91,400	$166,938	$235,296	$304,275	$323,758
Cost of sales	6,414	9,054	10,509	14,139	14,562	17,517	27,584	52,484	71,100	87,807	88,960
Selling, general, and administrative expenses	9,674	13,128	15,050	19,192	21,394	27,402	45,522	86,998	120,880	154,104	168,757
Operating income	6,111	8,033	9,388	11,540	11,900	8,827	18,304	27,456	43,316	62,364	66,041
Interest and other income, net	377	443	202	501	175	660	493	712	1,485	2,763	3,734
Interest expense	58	54	60	43	212	504	958	635	1,014	1,284	2,886
Income before income taxes	6,430	8,422	9,530	11,998	11,863	8,983	17,839	27,533	43,787	63,843	66,889
Provision for income taxes	3,035	3,973	4,480	5,854	5,711	4,110	8,207	12,398	19,632	28,471	30,235
Net income	$ 3,395	$ 4,449	$ 5,050	$ 6,144	$ 6,152	$ 4,873	$ 9,632	$ 15,135	$ 24,155	$ 35,372	$ 36,654
Net income per common share	$ .09	$ .11	$ .13	$ .16	$ .17	$ .15	$ .33	$ .52	$ .82	$ 1.18	$ 1.22
Cash dividends per share	$ .01	$ .03	$ .03	$ .05	$ .05	$ .06	$ .06	$ .09	$ .10	$ .11	$ .12
Average common shares	38,800	38,864	38,928	39,120	35,480	33,408	29,440	28,884	29,324	29,894	30,138
Total assets	$19,600	$24,743	$27,996	$34,331	$35,144	$36,305	$50,916	$ 74,431	$100,976	$152,457	$180,683
Long-term debt	$ 756	$ 87	$ 42	—	$ 5,592	$ 3,558	$ 4,000	$ 3,000	$ 2,366	$ 4,669	$ 3,915
Return on average stockholders' equity			21%	23%	24%	20%	38%	48%	48%	45%	32%
Stock prices											
Year high			2¾	2⅞	2⅝	1⅞	3⅞	8¾	18¾	28½	47⅞
Year low			1⅞	1¾	1½	1¼	1¼	3	6⅛	8⅜	13⅛

Source: Mary Kay Cosmetics, Inc., *1983 Annual Report.*

Exhibit 3   Growth in the Number of MKC Sales Directors and Beauty Consultants, 1973–1983

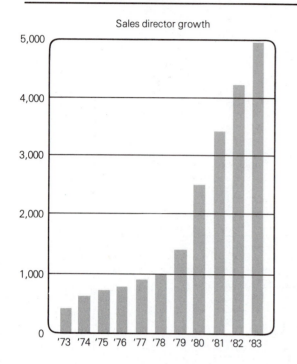

Sales director growth

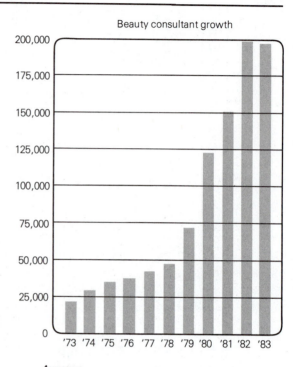

Beauty consultant growth

	Average Number of Consultants	Net Sales ($000)	Average Annual Sales Productivity per Consultant
1983	195,671	$323,758	$1,655
1982	173,137	304,275	1,757
1981	134,831	235,296	1,745
1980	94,983	166,938	1,758
1979	57,989	91,400	1,576

Source: *1983 Annual Report.*

picked up on the growing popularity of having beauty shows on Tuesday, Wednesday, and Thursday nights; a lesser proportion of weekday hours were used for morning and afternoon showings, and a greater proportion came to be used for seeking and delivering reorders from ongoing users.

MKC's corporate sales goal for the 80s was to reach $500 million in revenues by 1990. As of 1984 about 65 percent of total sales were made to customers at beauty shows. However, it was expected that as the size of the company's customer base grew, the percentage of orders from repeat buyers would rise well above the present 35 percent level. MKC estimated that the average client spent over $200 a year on cosmetics. The company saw its target clientele as middle-class women in

---

Exhibit 4   Percentage Breakdown of Product Sales at Mary Kay Cosmetics, 1979–1983

	1979	1980	1981	1982	1983
Skin care products for women	49%	52%	49%	46%	44%
Skin care products for men	1	2	1	1	1
Makeup items	26	22	26	26	30
Toiletry items for women	10	10	10	12	11
Toiletry items for men	2	2	2	2	2
Hair care	2	2	2	2	2
Accessories	10	10	10	11	10
TOTAL	100%	100%	100%	100%	100%

Source: *1983 Annual Report.*

---

the 18–34 age group primarily and in the 35–44 age group secondarily, and believed that a big percentage of its customers consisted of suburban housewives and white-collar clerical workers. The company's literature always pictured upscale women, dressed in a classy and elegant yet understated way, in either the role of a Mary Kay beauty consultant or the role of a user of Mary Kay cosmetics. As company figurehead, Mary Kay Ash personally made a point of being fashionably and expensively dressed, with perfect makeup and hairdo—a walking showcase for the company's products and a symbol of the professionally successful businesswoman (Exhibit 5).

MANUFACTURING

When Mary Kay Cosmetics commenced operations in 1963, the task of making the products was contracted out to a private Dallas-based manufacturing company. Mary Kay explained why:

> In 1963 I had no previous experience in the cosmetics industry; my forte was recruiting and training salespeople. After I acquired the formulas for the skin-care products, the first thing I did was seek out the most reputable cosmetics manufacturer I could find. Specifically I wanted a firm that not only made quality products, but observed the Food and Drug Administration's regulatory requirements to the letter. I knew it would be a fatal mistake to attempt to cut corners. With the right people in charge, we would never have to concern ourselves with that aspect of the business.[5]

In 1969 MKC built a 300,000-square-foot manufacturing and packaging facility adjacent to corporate headquarters. Packaging, warehousing, purchasing, and research labs were all housed in this location. Also included was a printing set-up which

---

[5] Mary Kay Ash, *Mary Kay on People Management* (New York: Warner Books, 1984), p. 13.

Exhibit 5   Mary Kay Ash in 1983

Source: *1983 Annual Report* (picture on front cover).

created Mary Kay labels in English, Spanish, and French. Many of the operations were automated.

The company's scientific approach to skin care was supported by a staff of laboratory technicians skilled in cosmetic chemistry, dermatology, physiology, microbiology, and package engineering. Ongoing tests were conducted to refine existing items and to develop new products. Laboratory staffs were provided with the comments and reactions about the products that came in from beauty consultants and their customers; consultants were strongly encouraged to report on their experiences with items and to relay any problems that consultants had directly to the laboratory staff. About 80 percent of the R&D budget was earmarked for improving existing products.

MKC believed that it was an industry leader in researching, one, the biophysical properties of the skin (as concerning skin elasticity and moisture) and, two, skin structure and anatomical quality. Much of the research at MKC was performed in cooperation with academic institutions, particularly the University of Pennsylvania and the University of Texas Health Science Center.

PRODUCT LINE AND DISTRIBUTION POLICIES

As of 1984 the Mary Kay product line consisted of the Basic Skin Care Program for various skin types, the glamour collection, the body care products line, and a line of men's products called Mr. K. Most of the women's products were packaged in pink boxes and jars. When the company first began operations, Mary Kay personally put a lot of thought into packaging and appearance:

> Since people do leave their toiletries out, I wanted to package our cosmetics so beautifully that women would *want* to leave them out. So I was looking for a color that would make a beautiful display in all those white bathrooms. There were some shades of blue that were attractive, but the prettiest complementary color seemed to be a delicate pink. It also occurred to me that pink is considered a more feminine color. But my main reason for choosing it was that delicate pink seemed to look prettier than anything else in those white tile bathrooms. And from that I gained a *pink* reputation![6]

Mr. K, the men's line, was introduced in the 1960s in response to a number of confessions from men who used their wives' Mary Kay products. A rich chocolate brown package accented with silver was chosen for Mr. K. The men's line included a Basic Skin Care Program as well as lotions and colognes. The majority of Mr. K purchases were made by women for their husbands and boyfriends.

Consultants bought their supplies of products directly from MKC at wholesale prices and sold them at a 100 percent markup over wholesale. To make it more feasible for consultants to keep an adequate inventory on hand, the product line at MKC was kept streamlined, about 50 products. Mary Kay consultants were encouraged to carry enough products in their personal inventories that orders could be filled on the spot at the beauty shows. As an incentive to support this practice, MKC offered special awards and prizes when consultants placed orders of $1,500 or more.

A consultant could order as many or as few of the company's products as she chose to inventory. Most consultants stockpiled those items that sold especially well with their own individual clientele, and consultants also had the freedom to offer special promotions or discounts to customers. Nearly 50 percent of sales were for the skin care products which had evolved from the hide tanner's discovery. Consultants were required to pay for all orders with cashier's checks or money orders prior to delivery. MKC dealt only on a cash basis to minimize accounts receivables problems; according to Mary Kay, "Bad debts are a major reason for failure in other direct sales companies." In 1984 the average initial order of new consultants for inventory was about $1,000 ($2,000 in retail value). Consultants who decided to get out of the business could resell their inventories to MKC at 90 percent of cost.

During the company's early years, consultants were supplied only with an inventory of items to sell; shipments arrived in plain boxes. There were no sales kits and no instruction manuals to assist in sales presentations. However, by the 1970s each new recruit received training in skin care techniques and was furnished with a number of sales aids. Later new consultants were required to buy a beauty showcase containing everything needed to conduct a beauty show (samples, pink mirrors, pink trays used

---

[6] Ash, *Mary Kay*, pp. 150–51.

to distribute the samples, and a step-by-step sales manual that included suggested dialogue. In 1984 the showcase was sold to new consultants for $85. Along with the showcase came a supply of beauty profile forms to use at showings; guests filled out the form at the beginning of the show, and from the information supplied a consultant could readily prescribe which of several product formulas was best suited for the individual's skin type.

In addition to the income earned from product sales, consultants earned bonuses or commissions on the sales made by all of the recruits they brought in. MKC paid consultants with one to four recruits a bonus commission equal to 4 percent of the wholesale orders of the recruits. A consultant with five or more recruits earned an 8 percent commission on the orders placed by recruits, or 12 percent if she also placed $600 a month in wholesale orders herself. MKC consultants who were entitled to a 12 percent commission and who had as many as 24 recruits were averaging about $950 monthly in bonuses and recruitment commissions as of 1984.

MKC'S SALES ORGANIZATION

The basic field organization unit for MKC's 195,000-person force of beauty consultants was the sales unit. Each sales unit was headed by a sales director who provided leadership and training for her group of beauty consultants. The top-performing sales directors were designated as national sales directors, a title that signified the ultimate achievement in the Mary Kay career sales ladder. A corporate staff of seven national sales administrators oversaw the activities of the sales directors in the field and their units of beauty consultants.

The sales units were not organized along strict geographical lines, and sales directors were free to recruit consultants anywhere:

> One of the first things I wanted my dream company to eliminate was assigned territories. I had worked for several direct-sales organizations in the past, and I knew how unfairly I had been treated when I had to move from Houston to St. Louis because of my husband's new job. I had been making $1,000 a month in commissions from the Houston sales unit that I had built over a period of eight years and I lost it all when I moved. I felt that it wasn't fair for someone else to inherit those Houston salespeople whom I had worked so hard to recruit and train.
>
> Because we don't have territories at Mary Kay Cosmetics, a director who lives in Chicago can be vacationing in Florida or visiting a friend in Pittsburgh and recruit someone while there. It doesn't matter where she lives in the United States; she will always draw a commission from the company on the wholesale purchases made by that recruit as long as they both remain with the company. The director in Pittsburgh will take the visiting director's new recruit under her wing and train her; the recruit will attend the Pittsburgh sales meetings and participate in the local sales contests. Although the Pittsburgh director will devote a lot of time and effort to the new recruit, the Chicago director will be paid the commissions. We call this our "adoptee" program.
>
> The Pittsburgh recruit may go on to recruit new people on her own. No matter where she lives, she becomes the nucleus for bringing in additional people for the director who brought her into the business. As long as they're both active in the company, she will receive commissions from the company on her recruit's sales activity.
>
> Today we have more than 5,000 sales directors, and most of them train and motivate

people in their units who live outside their home states. Some have beauty consultants in a dozen or more states. Outsiders look at our company and say "Your adoptee program can't possibly work!" But it does work. Each director reaps the benefits from her recruits in other cities and helps other recruits in return.[7]

THE BEAUTY CONSULTANT

Nearly all of MKC's beauty consultants had their first contact with the company as a guest at a beauty show. A discussion of career opportunities with Mary Kay was a standard part of the presentation at each beauty show. As many as 10 percent of the attendees at beauty shows were serious prospects as new recruits.

All beauty consultants were self-employed and worked on a commission basis. Everyone in the entire MKC sales organization started at the consultant level. The progression of each consultant up the "ladder of success" within the MKC sales organization was tightly linked to (1) the amount of wholesale orders the consultant placed with MKC, (2) her abilities to bring in new sales recruits, and (3) the size of the wholesale orders placed by these recruits. There were five rungs on the ladder of success for consultants, with qualifications and rewards as follows:

1. *New Beauty Consultant* (member of "Perfect Start Club").
   "Perfect Start Club" qualifications:

   Study and complete Perfect Start workbook.

   Observe three beauty shows.

   Book a minimum of eight shows within two weeks of receiving beauty showcase.

   Awards and recognition:

   Receives "Perfect Start" pin.

   Earns 50 percent commission on retail sales (less any discounts given to customers on "special promotions").

   Becomes eligible for a 4 percent recruiting commission on wholesale orders placed by active personal recruits (to be considered active a consultant had to place at least a $600 minimum wholesale order during the current quarter).

   Is eligible for special prizes and bonuses given for current quarter's sales and recruiting contest.

2. *Star Consultant.*
   Qualifications:

   Must have three active recruits.

   Be an active beauty consultant (place a minimum wholesale order of $600 within the current calendar quarter.

   Awards and recognition:

   Earns a red blazer.

   Earns a star pin.

---

[7] Ash, *People Management*, pp. 2–3.

Earns "Ladder of Success" status by placing $1,800 in wholesale orders in a three-month period.

Earns 50 percent commission on personal sales at beauty shows.

Earns 4 percent personal recruiting commissions on wholesale orders placed by active personal recruits.

Is eligible for special prizes and awards offered during quarterly contest.

Receives a Star of Excellence ladder pin by qualifying as a star consultant for 8 quarters (or a Double Star of Excellence pin for 16 quarters).

3. Team Leader.
   Qualifications:

   Must have five or more active recruits.

   Be an active beauty consultant.

   Awards and recognitions:

   Earns 50 percent commission on sales at own beauty shows.

   Earns a "Tender Loving Care" emblem for red blazer.

   Earns an 8 percent personal recruiting commission on wholesale orders of active personal recruits.

   Earns a 12 percent personal recruiting commission if *(a)* five or more active personal recruits place minimum $600 wholesale orders during the current month and *(b)* the team leader herself places a $600 wholesale order during the current month.

   Receives Team Leader pin in ladder of success program.

   Is eligible for quarterly contest prizes and bonuses.

4. *VIP (Very Important Performer).*
   Qualifications:

   Must have obtained Team Leader status.

   Must place wholesale orders of at least $600 for three consecutive months.

   Team must place wholesale orders of at least $3,000 each month for three consecutive months.

   Awards and recognition:

   Earns the use of an Oldsmobile Firenza.

   Earns 50 percent commission on sales at own beauty shows.

   Earns a 12 percent personal recruiting commission.

   Receives VIP pin in ladder of success program.

   Is eligible for quarterly contest prizes and bonuses.

5. Future Director.
   Qualifications:

   Must have qualified for Team Leader status.

   Must have 12 active recruits at time of application.

   Must make a commitment to Mary Kay to become a Sales Director by actually giving her letter of intent date.

Awards and recognition:

Earns a Future Director crest for red jacket.

Plus all the benefits accorded Team Leaders and VIPs, as appropriate, for monthly and quarterly sales and recruiting performance.

New recruits were required to submit a signed Beauty Consultant Agreement, observe three beauty shows conducted by an experienced consultant, book a minimum of eight beauty shows, and hold at least five beauty shows within their first two weeks. Each consultant was asked to appear in attractive dress and makeup when in public and to project an image of knowledge and confidence about herself and the MKC product line. Mary Kay felt the stress on personal appearance was justified: "What we are selling is beauty. A woman is not going to buy from someone who is wearing jeans and has her hair up in curlers. We want our consultants to be the type of woman others will want to emulate."[8]

Consultants spent most of their work hours scheduling and giving beauty shows. A showing took about two hours (plus about an hour for travel time), and many times the hostess and one or more of the guests turned out to be prospective recruits. New consultants were coached to start off by booking showings with friends, neighbors, and relatives and then network these into showings for friends of friends and relatives of relatives.

Consultants were instructed to follow up each beauty show by scheduling a second facial for each guest at the showing. Many times a customer would invite friends to her second facial and the result would be another beauty show. After the follow-up facial, consultants would call customers periodically to check on whether the customer was satisfied, to see if refills were needed, and to let the customer know about new products and special promotions. Under MKC's "dovetailing" plan, a consultant with an unexpected emergency at home could sell her prearranged beauty show to another consultant and the two would split the commissions generated by the show.

THE SALES DIRECTOR

Consultants who had climbed to the fifth rung of the consultants' ladder of success were eligible to become sales directors and head up a sales unit. In addition to conducting her own beauty shows, a sales director's responsibilities included training new recruits, leading weekly sales meetings, and providing assistance and advice to the members of her unit. Sales directors, besides receiving the commissions on sales made at their own showings, were paid a commission on the total sales of the unit they headed and a commission on the number of new sales recruits. In June 1984 the top 100 recruiting commissions paid to sales directors ranged from approximately $660 to $1,900. It was not uncommon for sales directors to have total annual earnings in the $50,000 to $100,000 range; in 1983 the average income of the 4,500 sales directors was between $25,000 and $30,000.

[8] Rebecca Fannin, "The Beauty of Being Mary Kay," *Marketing & Media Decisions* 17 (December 1982), pp. 59–61.

There were six achievement categories for sales directors, with qualifications and awards as shown below:

1. *Director in Qualification (DIQ).*
   Qualifications:

   Must have 15 active personal recruits.

   Submits a Letter of Intent to obtain Directorship.

   Gets the Director of her sales unit to submit a letter of recommendation.

   Within three consecutive months:

   Must recruit an additional 15 consultants for a total of 30 personal active recruits.

   The unit of 30 personal active recruits must place combined wholesale orders of $4,000, $4,500, and $5,000 for months one, two, and three respectively.

   Awards and recognition:

   Earns personal sales and personal recruiting commissions (as per schedules for at least Team Leader status).

   Eligible for prizes and bonuses in quarterly contests.

2. *Sales Director.*
   Qualifications:

   Sales unit must maintain a minimum of $4,000 in wholesale orders each month for the sales director to remain as head of her unit.

   Awards and recognition:

   Receives commissions of 9 percent to 13 percent on unit's wholesale orders.

   Receives monthly sales production bonuses:
   - a $300 monthly bonus if unit places monthly wholesale orders of $3,000–$4,999.
   - a $500 monthly bonus if unit places monthly wholesale orders of $5,000 and up.

   Receives a monthly recruiting bonus (for personal recruits or for recruits of other consultants in the sales unit):
   - $100 bonus if three to four new recruits come into unit.
   - $200 bonus if five to seven new recruits come into unit.
   - $300 bonus if 8 to 11 new recruits come into unit.
   - $400 bonus for 12 or more recruits.

   Is given a designer Director suit.

   Is entitled to all commission schedules and incentives of Future Sales Directors.

3. *Regal Director.*
   Qualifications:

   Members of sales unit must place wholesale orders of at least $24,000 for two consecutive quarters.

   Must qualify every two years.

Awards and recognition:

>Earns the use of a pink Buick Regal.

>Is entitled to all the commission percentages, bonuses, and other incentives of a Sales Director.

4. *Cadillac Director.*
   Qualifications:

   >Sales unit members must place at least $36,000 in wholesale orders for two consecutive quarters.

   >Must qualify every two years.

   Awards and recognition:

   >Earns the use of pink Cadillac.

   >Is entitled to all the commission percentages, bonuses, and other incentives of a Sales Director.

5. *Senior Sales Director.*
   Qualifications:

   >One to four Sales Directors emerge from her unit.

   Awards and recognition:

   >Earns a 4 percent commission on offspring Director's consultants.

   >Is entitled to all the commission percentages, bonuses, and other incentives of at least a Sales Director.

6. *Future National Director.*
   Qualifications:

   >Five or more active Directors emerge from her unit.

   Awards and recognition:

   >Is entitled to all the commission percentages, bonuses, and other incentives of a Senior Sales Director.

As of late 1983 the company had about 700 Regal Directors and about 700 Cadillac Directors; in one recent quarter 81 sales directors had met the qualifications for driving a new pink Cadillac.

THE NATIONAL SALES DIRECTOR

Top-performing sales directors became eligible for designation as a National Sales Director, the highest recognition bestowed on field sales personnel. NSDs were inspirational leaders and managers of a group of sales directors and received commissions on the total dollar sales of the group of sales units they headed. In 1984 MKC's 50 national sales directors had total sales incomes averaging over $150,000 per year. A 1985 *Fortune* article featured Helen McVoy, a MKC National Sales Director since 1971, as one of the most successful salespeople in the United States; in 1984 she earned $375,000. McVoy began her career with Mary Kay in 1965 at the age of 45. Her family was on a tight budget, having lost all of their savings in a bad mining investment. To support her plant collecting hobby, Helen started selling Mary Kay products on a part-time basis—two hours a week. Her original investment was for a beauty case; by the end of her first year she had made $17,000. From 1970 through 1984 she was the company's top volume producer.

TRAINING

Before holding a beauty show a new consultant had to observe three beauty shows, attend orientation classes conducted by a Sales Director, and complete a self-study set of MKC training materials. This training covered the fundamentals of conducting skin care shows, booking future beauty shows, recruiting new Mary Kay consultants, personal appearance, and managing a small business. Active consultants were strongly encouraged to continue to improve their sales skills and product knowledge. In addition to weekly sales meetings and frequent one-on-one contact with other consultants and sales directors, each salesperson had access to a variety of company-prepared support materials—videotapes, films, slide shows, and brochures.

In 1983 a new educational curriculum was introduced to support each phase of a Mary Kay career. A back-to-basics orientation package provided a foundation for the first stage of career development. A recruitment notebook provided dialogue of mock recruiting conversations, and sales directors were provided with an organizational kit to help them make a smooth transition from being purely a consultant to being a sales manager as well as a consultant.

Additional learning opportunities were provided in the form of special product knowledge classes, regional workshops, and annual corporate-sponsored seminars.

MOTIVATION AND INCENTIVES

New sales contests were introduced every three months. Prizes and recognition awards were always tied to achievement plateaus rather than declaring first, second, and third place winners. Top performers were spotlighted in the company's full-color monthly magazine, *Applause* (which had a circulation of several hundred thousand).

Mary Kay Ash described why MKC paid so much attention to recognition and praise:

> I believe praise is the best way for a manager to motivate people. At Mary Kay Cosmetics we think praise is so important that our entire marketing plan is based upon it.[9]

> Praise is an incredibly effective motivator; unfortunately, many managers are reluctant to employ it. Yet I can't help feeling that they know how much praise means, not only to others, but to themselves. . . . I believe that you should praise people whenever you can; it causes them to respond as a thirsty plant responds to water.[10]

[9] Ash, *People Management.* p. 21.
[10] Ibid., p. 23.

The power of positive motivation in a goal-oriented structure such as ours cannot be overstated. This is what inspires our consultants to maximize their true potentials.[11]

As a manager you must recognize that everyone needs praise. But it must be given sincerely. You'll find numerous occasions for genuine praise if you'll only look for them.[12]

Because we recognize the need for people to be praised, we make a concentrated effort to give as much recognition as possible. Of course with an organization as large as ours not everyone can make a speech at our Seminars, but we do attempt to have many people appear on stage, if only for a few moments. During the Directors' March, for example, hundreds of directors parade on stage before thousands of their peers. In order to appear in the Director's March a director must purchase a special designer suit. Likewise we have a Red Jacket March, in which only star recruiters, team leaders, and future directors participate. Again, a special uniform is required for participation.[13]

How important are these brief stage appearances? Frankly I think it means more for a woman to be recognized by her peers on stage than to receive an expensive present in the mail that nobody knows about! And once she gets a taste of this recognition, she wants to come back next year for more![14]

SEMINAR

MKC staged an annual "Seminar" as a salute to the company and to the salespeople who contributed to its success. The first Seminar was held on September 13, 1964 (the company's first anniversary); the banquet menu consisted of chicken, jello salad, and an anniversary cake while a three-piece band provided entertainment. By 1984 Seminar had grown into a three-day spectacular repeated four consecutive times with a budget of $4 million and attended by 24,000 beauty consultants and sales directors who paid their own way to attend the event. The setting, the Convention Center in Dallas (see Exhibit 6), was decorated in red, white, and blue in order to emphasize the theme, "Share the Spirit." The climactic highlight of Seminar was Awards Night, when the biggest prizes were awarded to the people with the biggest sales. The company went to elaborate efforts to ensure the Awards Night was charged with excitement and emotion; as one observer of the 1984 Awards Night in Dallas described it, "The atmosphere there is electric, a cross between a Las Vegas revue and a revival meeting. Hands reach up to touch Mary Kay; a pink Cadillac revolves on a mist-shrouded pedestal; a 50-piece band plays; and women sob."

Mary Kay Ash customarily made personal appearances throughout the Seminar period. In addition to Awards Night, Seminar featured sessions consisting of informational and training workshops, motivational presentations by leading sales directors, and star entertainment (Paul Anka performed in 1984, and in previous years there had been performances by Tennessee Ernie Ford, John Davidson, and Johnny Mathis). Over the three days Cadillacs, diamonds, mink coats, a $5,000 shopping spree at Neiman-Marcus for any director whose team sold $1 million worth of Mary Kay

---

[11] Ibid., p. 26.

[12] Ibid., p. 27.

[13] Ibid., p. 25.

[14] Ibid., p. 26.

Exhibit 6   "Share the Spirit," 1984 Annual Seminar, Mary Kay Cosmetics

Source: Mary Kay Cosmetics, Inc., Interim Report, 1984.

products, and lesser assorted prizes were awarded to the outstanding achievers of the past year. Gold-and-diamond bumblebee pins, each containing 21 diamonds and retailing for over $3,600, were presented to the Queens of Sales on Pageant Night; these pins were not only the company's ultimate badge of success, but Mary Kay felt they also had special symbolism:

> It's a beautiful pin, but that isn't the whole story. We think the bumblebee is a marvelous symbol of woman. Because, as aerodynamic engineers found a long time ago, the bumblebee cannot fly! Its wings are too weak and its body is too heavy to fly, but fortunately, the bumblebee doesn't know that, and it goes right on flying. The bee has become a symbol of women who didn't know they could fly but they DID! I think the women who own these diamond bumblebees think of them in their own personal ways. For most of us, it's true that we refused to believe we couldn't do it. Maybe somebody said, "It's really impossible to get this thing off the ground." But somebody else told us, "You can do it!" So we did.[15]

---

[15] Ash, *Mary Kay*, p. 9.

On the final day of seminar the Sue Z. Vickers Memorial Award—Miss Go Give—was presented. This honor was given to the individual who best demonstrated the Mary Kay spirit—a spirit described as loving, giving, and inspirational.

CORPORATE ENVIRONMENT

The company's eight-story, gold-glass corporate headquarters building in Dallas was occupied solely by Mary Kay executives. An open-door philosophy was present at MKC. Everyone from the mailroom clerk to the chairman of the board was treated with respect. The door to Mary Kay Ash's office was rarely closed. Often people touring the building peeked in her office to get a glimpse of the pink and white decor. Mary Kay and all other corporate managers took the time to talk with any employee.

First names were always used at MKC. Mary Kay herself insisted on being addressed as Mary Kay; she felt people who called her Mrs. Ash were either angry at her or didn't know her. In keeping with this informal atmosphere, offices didn't have titles on the doors, executive restrooms didn't exist, and the company cafeteria was used by the executives (there was no executive dining room).

To further enhance the informal atmosphere and enthusiasm at MKC, all sales functions were started with a group sing-along. Mary Kay offered several reasons for this policy:

> Nothing great is ever achieved without enthusiasm. . . . We have many of our own songs, and they're sung at all Mary Kay get-togethers, ranging from small weekly meetings to our annual Seminars. Our salespeople enjoy this activity, and I believe the singing creates a wonderful esprit de corps. Yet outsiders, especially men, often criticize our singing as being "strictly for women." I disagree. Singing unites people. It's like those "rah-rah-rah for our team" cheers. If someone is depressed, singing will often bring her out of it.[16]

The company sent Christmas cards, birthday cards, and anniversary cards to every single employee each year. Mary Kay personally designed the birthday cards for consultants. In addition, all the sales directors received Christmas and birthday presents from the company.

THE PEOPLE MANAGEMENT PHILOSOPHY AT MKC

Mary Kay Ash had some very definite ideas about how people ought to be managed, and she willingly shared them with employees and, through her books, with the public at large. Some excerpts from her book on *People Management* reveal the approach taken at Mary Kay Cosmetics:

> People come first at Mary Kay Cosmetics—our beauty consultants, sales directors, and employees, our customers, and our suppliers. We pride ourselves as a "company known for the people it keeps." Our belief in caring for people, however, does not

---

[16] Ash, *People Management*, p. 59.

conflict with our need as a corporation to generate a profit. Yes, we keep our eye on the bottom line, but it's not an overriding obsession.[17]

Ours is an organization with few middle management positions. In order to grow and progress, you don't move upward; you expand outward. This gives our independent sales organization a deep sense of personal worth. They know that they are not competing with one another for a spot in the company's managerial "pecking order." Therefore the contributions of each individual are of equal value. No one is fearful that his or her idea will be "stolen" by someone with more ability on the corporate ladder. And when someone—anyone—proposes a new thought, we all analyze it, improve upon it, and ultimately support it with the enthusiasm of a team.[18]

Every person is special! I sincerely believe this. Each of us wants to feel good about himself or herself, but to me it is just as important to make others feel the same way. Whenever I meet someone, I try to imagine him wearing an invisible sign that says: MAKE ME FEEL IMPORTANT! I respond to this sign immediately and it works wonders.[19]

At Mary Kay Cosmetics we believe in putting our beauty consultants and sales directors on a pedestal. Of all people I most identify with them because I spent many years as a salesperson. My attitude of appreciation for them permeates the company. When our salespeople visit the home office, for example, we go out of our way to give them the red-carpet treatment. Every person in the company treats them royally.[20]

We go first class across the board, and although it's expensive, it's worth it because our people are made to feel important. For example, each year we take our top sales directors and their spouses on deluxe trips to Hong Kong, Bangkok, London, Paris, Geneva, and Athens to mention a few. We spare no expense, and although it costs a lot extra per person to fly the Concorde, cruise on the Love Boat, or book suites at the elegant Georges V in Paris, it is our way of telling them how important they are to our company.[21]

My experience with people is that they generally do what you expect them to do! If you expect them to perform well, they will; conversely, if you expect them to perform poorly, they'll probably oblige. I believe that average employees who try their hardest to live up to your high expectations of them will do better than above-average people with low self-esteem. Motivate your people to draw on that untapped 90 percent of their ability and their level of performance will soar!"[22]

A good people manager will never put someone down; not only is it nonproductive—it's counterproductive. You must remember that your job is to play the role of problem solver and that by taking this approach instead of criticizing people you'll accomplish considerably more.

While some managers try to forget problems they encountered early in their careers, I make a conscious effort to remember the difficulties I've had along the way. I think

---

[17] Ibid., p. xix.

[18] Ibid., p. 11–12.

[19] Ibid., p. 15.

[20] Ibid., p. 19.

[21] Ibid., p. 20.

[22] Ibid., p. 17.

it's vital for a manager to empathize with the other person's problem, and the best way to have a clear understanding is to have been there yourself![23]

Interviews with Mary Kay consultants gave credibility to the company's approach and methods. One consultant described her experience thusly:

I had a lot of ragged edges when I started. The first time I went to a Mary Kay seminar, I signed up for classes in diction and deportment, believe me, I needed them. I didn't even have the right clothes. You can only wear dresses and skirts to beauty shows, so I sank everything I had into one nice dress. I washed it out every night in Woolite and let it drip dry in the shower.

But I was determined to follow all the rules, even the ones I didn't understand—*especially* the ones I didn't understand. At times, it all seemed foolish, especially when you consider that all my clients were mill workers and didn't exactly appreciate my new grammar. But I kept telling myself to hang in there, that Mary Kay knew what was good for me.

When I first started, I won a pearl and ruby ring. A man or a man's company may say I'd have been better off with the cash, but I'm not so convinced. Mary Kay is on to something there. From the moment I won that ring, I began thinking of myself as a person who deserved a better standard of living. I built a new life to go with the ring.[24]

Another consultant observed:

The essential thing about Mary Kay is the quality of the company. When you go to Dallas, the food, the hotel, and the entertainment are all top notch. Nothing gaudy is allowed in Mary Kay.[25]

When asked if she didn't think pink Cadillacs were a tad gaudy, she responded in a low, level tone: "When people say that, I just ask them what color car their company gave them last year."

On the morning following Awards Night 1984, a group of Florida consultants were in the hotel lobby getting ready to go to the airport for the flight home.[26] One member had by chance met Mary Kay Ash in the ladies room a bit earlier and had managed to get a maid to snap a Polaroid photograph of them together. She proudly was showing her friends the snapshot and was the only one of the group who had actually met Mary Kay. The consultant said to her friends, "She told me she was sure I'd be up there on stage with her next year. She said she'd see me there." Her sales director, in noting the scene, observed, "She's got the vision now. She really did meet her. And you've got to understand that in Mary Kaydom that's a very big deal."

THE BEAUTY SHOW

It was a few minutes past 7 P.M. on a weeknight in Tuscaloosa, Alabama. Debbie Sessoms and three of her friends (including the casewriter) were seated around the

---

[23] Ibid., p. 6.

[24] As quoted in Kim Wright Wiley, "Cold Cream and Hard Cash," *Savvy,* June 1985, p. 39.

[25] Ibid., p. 41.

[26] Ibid.

dining room table in Debbie's house. In front of each lady was a pink tray, a mirror, a pencil, and a blank personal Beauty Profile form. Jan Currier stood at the head of the table. She welcomed each of the ladies and asked them to fill out the personal Beauty Profile form in front of them.

When they were finished, Jan started her formal presentation, leading off with how MKC's products were developed by a tanner. She used a large display board to illustrate the topics she discussed. Next Jan told the group about the company and the founder, Mary Kay Ash. She showed a picture of Mary Kay and explained she was believed to be in her 70s—though no one knew for sure because Mary Kay maintained that "A woman who will tell her age will tell anything." Jerri, one of the guests, remarked that she couldn't believe how good Mary Kay looked for her age. Jan told her that Mary Kay had been using her basic skin care formulas since the 1950s.

Jan went on to talk about the growth of the sales force from nine consultants to over 195,000 in 1984. She explained how the career opportunities at MKC could be adapted to each consultant's ambitions. A consultant, she said, determined her own work hours and could choose either a full-time or part-time career. Advancement was based on sales and recruiting abilities. The possible rewards included diamonds, minks, and pink Cadillacs.

Before explaining the basic skin care program, Jan told the ladies that with the Mary Kay money-back guarantee products could be returned for any reason for a full refund. Jan distributed samples to each of the guests based on the information provided in the personal Beauty Profiles. Under Jan's guidance the ladies proceeded through the complete facial process, learning each of the five basic skin care steps advocated by Mary Kay. There was a lot of discussion about the products and how they felt on everyone's skin.

When the presentation reached the glamour segment, each guest was asked her preference of makeup colors. Jan encouraged everyone to try as many of the products and colors as they wanted. Jan helped the guests experiment with different combinations and worked with each one personally, trying to make sure that everyone would end up satisfied with her own finished appearance.

After admiring each other's new looks, three of the ladies placed orders. Jan collected their payments and filled the orders on the spot. No one had to wait for delivery.

When she finished with the orders, Jan talked with Debbie's three guests about hostessing their own shows and receiving hostess gifts. Chris agreed to book a show the next week. Debbie was then given her choice of gifts based on the evening's sales and bookings. To close the show, Jan again highlighted the benefits of a Mary Kay career—being your own boss, setting your own hours—and invited anyone interested to talk with her about these opportunities. Debbie then served some refreshments. Shortly after 9 P.M., Jan and Debbie's three guests departed.

Walking to Jan's car, the casewriter asked Jan if the evening was a success. Jan replied that it had been "a pretty good night. Sales totaled $150, I got a booking for next Wednesday, I made $75 in commissions in a little over two hours, the guests learned about skin care and have some products they are going to like, and Debbie got a nice hostess gift."

Exhibit 7   Excerpt from Sales Director's Mimeographed Weekly Newsletter Distributed to Members of Sales Unit

---

You Are Special

Once upon a time a very competent woman went into a beautiful designer furniture store and said to the owner, "Sir, I would like to work for you. I will work hard. I will do a *Great* job for you, but I ask for the following:

1. For everything I sell I want to make a 50 percent profit.
2. I know others that I will get to sell for you too, and I want to be paid a commission on all they do, say 4 percent to 12 percent.
3. I want to work my own hours. No Sundays—just a few nights. . . . God and my family will *always* come first.
4. I will also need a car after I bring in five successful people to work for you, at no cost to me—not even insurance.
5. When I do really well, I want to receive bonuses, not little meaningless things, but things like *mink coats* and *diamonds!*

"Can you give these things to me?"

The store owner was in shock with her requests. He roared with condescending laughter. Then came his reply, "No, not one! No one could."

Only your own beautiful *Mary Kay!* You have it all right at your fingertips! Go after it! You and your family deserve it! This is your year, 1984!

Consider this story and think seriously about what you have in this wonderful opportunity!!!

You are indeed *special!* You are appreciated and loved. I'm so very proud of you. Share what you have. . . .

Jan

THE WEEKLY SALES MEETING

Jan Currier, senior sales director, welcomed the consultants to the weekly Monday night meeting of the members of her sales unit.[27] After calling everyone's attention to the mimeographed handout on everybody's chair (Exhibit 7), she introduced the casewriter to the group and then invited everyone to stand and join in singing the Mary Kay enthusiasm song. As soon as the song was over Jan started "the Crow Period" by asking Barbara, team leader, to stand and tell about her achievement of VIP (Very Important Performer) status. Barbara told of setting and achieving the goals necessary to win the use of an Oldsmobile Firenza. Her new goal was to assist and motivate everyone on her team to do the same. Jan recognized Barbara again for being both the Queen of Sales and the Queen of Recruiting for the previous month.

---

[27] Most sales directors had their sales meetings on Monday night, a practice urged upon them by Mary Kay Ash. Mary Kay saw the Monday night meeting as a good way to start the week: "If you had a bad week—you need the sales meeting. If you had a good week, the sales meeting needs you! When a consultant leaves a Monday meeting excited, she has an entire week to let excitement work for her." Ash, *Mary Kay,* p. 40.

Jan began the educational segment by instructing the consultants on color analysis and how it related to glamour. She continued the instruction by explaining the proper techniques of a man's facial.

Next everyone who had at least a $100 week in sales was asked to stand. Jan began the countdown "110, 120, 130 . . . 190." Barbara sat down to a round of applause for her $190 week in sales. "200, 220 . . . 270." Melissa sat down. The ladies applauded her efforts. Mary was the only one left standing. There was anticipation of how high her sales reached as the countdown resumed. "280, 290, 300 . . . 335." Mary sat down. Everyone applauded this accomplishment of a consultant who had only been with MKC for four months and who held a 40-hour-week full-time job in addition to her Mary Kay sales efforts.

At this time Jan asked Linda and Susan to join her up front. She pinned each lady and congratulated them on joining her team. The Mary Kay pin was placed upside down on the new consultant's lapels. Jan explained this was so people would notice and ask about it. When they did, a consultant was to respond by saying; "My pin is upside down to remind me to ask you if you've had a Mary Kay facial. The pin would be turned right side up when the consultant got her first recruit. Each of the new consultants also received a pink ribbon. This marked their membership in the Jan's Beautiful People sales unit. Both Linda and Susan were given some material Jan had prepared (Exhibits 8, 9, and 10); Jan said she would go over it with them after the meeting.

Next a new competition was announced. This contest focused on recruiting. For each new recruit a consultant would receive one stem of Romanian crystal. So everyone could see how beautiful the rewards were, Jan showed a sample of the crystal.

A final reminder was made for attendance at the upcoming workshop on motivation. Jan sweetened the pot by providing a prize to the first one in her unit to register and pay for the seminar. Next week she would announce the winner.

The meeting was adjourned until next Monday evening.

AN INTERVIEW WITH JAN CURRIER

One night shortly after attending the meeting of Jan's Beautiful People sales unit, the casewriter met with Jan to ask some questions:

Casewriter: How many are in your unit?

Jan: We're down right now. I had a small unit to start with. I only had 56. . . . A decent unit has got a hundred, 75 to 100 at least.

Casewriter: Is it the size of the town that hampers you?

Jan: No, no it's me who hampers me. The speed of the leader is the speed of the unit. If I'm not out there doing it, then they're not going to be doing it. If I'm recruiting, they're recruiting.

Casewriter: What about your leader, is your leader not fast?

Jan: No it's me, see when you point a finger, three come back.

Casewriter: How do you handle a situation where a consultant would like to do well but she doesn't put in the time necessary to do well?

Jan: You have to go back to that premise, that whole philosophy that you're in

Exhibit 8 Example of a Sales Director's Mimeographed Handout to New Mary Kay Recruits

GETTING STARTED

Jan Currier,
Senior Sales Director

HELLO . . . AND WELCOME TO. . . .
THE BEAUTIFUL PEOPLE UNIT!!

1. You will need:
   A. Cotton balls.
   B. Swabs.
   C. Large and small zip-lock bags.
   D. Five subject spiral notebook for note-taking.
2. This is the time to decide which merchandise order you will need. Just fill in your name and address on one of the sample orders. It's ready to go. Or change one to suit you, using the blank order. Beginning with at least $1,500 section one only. . . . makes you a ladder or success winner.
3. Be a professional consultant by ordering the "consultants kit." (1,000 gold labels, rubber stamp, name badge, 500 facial cards—style B—"Rip-off type"—for $21.95.) Send check or money order to Labeling Inc., P.O. Box 476, Lakewood, CA 90714.
4. "Buff brushes" may be ordered from Silverset Brush Co., P.O. Box 53 Greenvale, New York 11548 . . . 20 cents each ($2.00 shipping charge) style 2900 *pink* handle . . . *minimum* order $25. Suggest sharing an order with other Beauty Consultants where possible.
5. Write your mileage in your datebook today . . . for income tax purposes.
6. Memorize:
   A. Hide tanners story. (It *is* a true story.)
   B. Correct booking approach.
   C. Four Point Recruiting plan.
7. Read and read again your beauty consultants guide. *Everything* you really need to know is in this book!! Listen to your training tape over and over again. If yours hasn't arrived yet, ask to borrow your recruiter's.
8. Obtain list of Beauty Consultants and their telephone numbers in your area from your Recruiter or local Director. Call and ask to observe shows. *If you are out of town* . . . call the local Director, ask to attend her training classes and meetings, be helpful, and let her know that you support her. Always keep a positive attitude . . . especially at the sales meetings.
9. Begin booking your shows for two weeks from now. You will want to get off to a *"Perfect Start"* by *Holding* at least five shows during your beginning two weeks. Realizing that some of these may *postpone* (never "cancel") you will want to book *twice as many.* These are only *practice* shows. (You will have products with you should they decide to buy, of course!)

   Submit names, dates, times, and telephone numbers to your recruiter. She will call or write them, thanking them for helping you get started.

   Again, these are just "practice" shows. Simply ask your friends to "help you" get started by letting you "practice" on them. (Part of your training is to get their *honest opinions.*)

Rebook each and every basic customer for a *second* facial. . . . preferably within a week to 10 days. Then . . . "Oh, by the way, you are *entitled* to invite a few friends over to *share* your second facial. It's so much more fun and *you* win some *free!* In other words, you receive a *discount* on whatever *they* buy. In other words, THE MORE THEY BUY . . . THE *MORE YOU* RECEIVE *FREE!!"* "BUT WE CAN'T DO MORE THAN SIX. . . . IT'S NOT A PARTY. . . . IT'S A CLASS. SO WE ARE LIMITED. YOU CAN DECIDE WHAT YOU PREFER TO DO. . . . I'LL JUST GIVE YOU THIS *SUGGESTIONS FOR THE HOSTESS* (comes with your Beauty Case) AND I WILL BE CALLING YOU IN A DAY OR SO." Give her: *Beauty Book, Suggestions for the Hostess,* and *Saturday Evening Post* reprint if she looks like she would be a good recruit. *BE SURE YOUR NAME IS ON EVERYTHING!!* Send a reminder card within two days.

Vow never to miss a sales meeting. This is your continuous training . . . and it is for you. And . . . always try to bring prospective recruits as your guests. And a very very positive attitude.

AND . . . YOU ARE OFF TO A BEAUTIFUL START!!!!

Exhibit 9   Example of Material Provided to New Beauty Consultants at Weekly Sales Meeting

---

Goal Setting is the most powerful force for human motivation
    Goal + Plans + Action = Success!!!

My Goal Is: _____

Circle Number of Classes You Will Put On Each Week	Class Time Plus Travel Time	Sales Based on each $150 Class (minutes)	Approximate Gross Profit per Week (before expenses)
1	3 hours	$ 150	$ 75
2	6	300	150
3	9	450	225
4	12	600	300
5	15	750	375
6	18	900	450
7	21	1,059	525
8	24	1,200	600
9	27	1,350	675
10	30	1,500	750
11	33	1,650	825
12	36	1,800	900
13	39	1,950	975
14	42	2,100	1,050
15	45	2,250	1,125
16	48	2,400	1,200
17	51	2,550	1,275
18	54	2,700	1,350
19	57	2,850	1,425
20	60	3,000	1,500

Note: Hostess credit and hostess gifts will be deducted from your gross profit. However, everything you give away is tax deductible.

Your *Attitude* and Your *Consistency* Will Determine . . .
Your Goals . . . Your Success!

Jan Currier
Senior Sales Director

---

business for yourself but not by yourself. So if a girl comes in and says I want to make X number of dollars, then I will work with her and we will do it. I try to get them to set goals and really look at them every week and work for it. One gal comes in and wants to make $25 a week and another says "I have to support my family." There's a big difference.

Casewriter: How do you handle those that only want to make $25 a week?

Jan: If you get rid of the piddlers you wouldn't have a company. It's the piddlers that make up the company. There are only going to be one or two superstars.

Casewriter: How do you motivate the girls in your unit?

Jan: The only way you can really motivate is to call, encourage, write notes, and encourage recognition at the sales meetings and recognition in the newsletter. If they're not doing anything they usually won't come to the sales meeting, but once in a while maybe, they'll find excuses.

Exhibit 10　Example of Material Provided to New Beauty Consultants at Weekly Sales Meeting

---

The Mary Kay Opportunity

Yearly Total

3	Shows per week with $150.00 sales per show Less 15 percent hostess credit = $191.25 profit (per week) Three persons buying per show, three shows per week	$ 9,945
	468 prospective customers per year Average selling to 7 out of 10 327 new customers per year Call customers at least six times per week Average $15.00 in sales per call Yearly reorder profits will be	14,715
1	Facial per week—52 prospective customers per year Average selling to 7 of 10, 36 new customers If each buys a basic, your facial profits will be	702
36	New customers from facials Call each customer six times per year Average $15.00 in sales per call Your yearly *reorder* profit will be	1,620
	Recruit one person per month Each with at least a $1,500 initial order (wholesale) Ordering only $500.00 every month thereafter Your 4 percent—8 percent commission checks from these 12 recruits	3,490
	Your yearly profits will be approximately	$30,472

This is a simple guideline designed to show you, in figures, approximately how much you can benefit from your Mary Kay career. These figures may vary a little, due to price changes. These totals are based on orders placed at our maximum discount level and do not include referrals, dovetail fees, and prizes.

Working hours per week for the above should not exceed 20 hours, if your work is well planned. Attitude and consistency are the keys to your success.

Jan Currier
Senior Sales Director

Casewriter: What do you do when a girl hits that stage?

Jan: Everybody has to go through that phase . . . If you're smart, you'll go to your director, read your book and go back to start where you were before—with what was working to begin with and you'll pull out of it. There are a lot of them who never pull out of it. They came in to have fun.

Casewriter: And the fun wears out.

Jan: Let's face it. This is a job. It's work, it's the best-paying hard work around, but it's work. I just finished with one gal last week who ended up saying "Well, I just thought it would be fun. I thought it was just supposed to be fun." And I said "Yes, but it's a job."

Casewriter: Can you tell before a girl starts if she'll be successful?

Jan: There's no way to predict who's going to make it, the one you think is going to be absolutely a superstar isn't. You give everybody a chance. I measure my time with their interest and I tell them that. I'll encourage them, but they are going to pretty much do what they want to do. I learned that the hard way. There is no point to laying guilt trips, no point pestering them to death, and pressure doesn't work.

Casewriter: Do you feel recognition is the best motivator?

Jan: Absolutely, recognition and appreciation. I think appreciation more than anything else. Little notes, I'm finally learning that too. Some of us are slow learners. . . . So I'll write little notes telling someone, I really appreciate your doing this, or I'm really proud of you for being a star consultant this quarter, or I'm so glad you went with us to Birmingham to the workshop.

Casewriter: Does it upset you when people don't come to the sales meetings?

Jan: I use to grieve when they wouldn't come to sales meetings. I'd ask what am I doing wrong. . . . Finally I realized that no matter how many people aren't there, the people who are there care and they are worth doing anything for. It's strange we seem to get a different batch every meeting.

Casewriter: I get the impression that you are always looking for new recruits.

Jan: Yes, I've gotten more picky. I'm looking more for directors. I'm looking for people who really want to work. I look for someone who is older, not just the 18-year-olds because they don't want to work. They want to make money but they don't want to work. . . . I'd like to build more offspring directors.

Casewriter: What kind of people do you look for?

Jan: Not everybody's right for Mary Kay. It takes somebody who genuinely cares about other people.

Casewriter: Is there a common scenario that fits most new recruits?

Jan: Mary Kay attracts a lot of insecure women who are often married to insecure men. And that woman is told over and over by Mary Kay how wonderful she is and how terrific she is and how she can do anything with God's help. She can achieve anything. And like me she is dumb enough to believe it and go along with it.

Casewriter: What do you feel is the reason for the slowdown in recruiting at Mary Kay?

Jan: The key to this drop has been partly the economy but partly a lot of people are weeding out. That's OK because the cream is going to rise to the top. I really believe that. We're going to have a stronger, much better company. I could see it at leadership (conference). The quality of people was much higher. It gets higher every year.

MKC'S FUTURE

MKC's sales in 1984 fell 14 percent to $278 million (down from $324 million in fiscal year 1983). The company's stock price, after a two for one split at about $44, tumbled from $22 in late 1983 to the $9–$12 range in 1984. Profits were down 8 percent to $33.8 million. The declines were blamed on a dropoff in recruiting and retention (owing to reduced attractiveness of part-time employment) and to the expense of starting up the European division. As of December 31, 1984, the company had about 152,000 beauty consultants and 4,500 sales directors as compared to 195,000 beauty consultants and 5,000 sales directors at year-end 1983. Average sales per consultant in 1984 was $1,603, versus $1,655 in 1983 and a 1980-82 average of $1,753; only 60,000 of the 152,000 consultants was thought to be significantly productive. A cosmetic analyst for one Wall Street securities firm, in talking about the company's prospects, said, "Brokers loved this stock because it had such a great story. But the glory days, for the time being, are certainly over."[28]

The company's mystique was upbeat, however. Mary Kay Ash was on the UPI list of the most interviewed women in America. And when the Republicans chose Dallas for its 1984 convention, the Chamber of Commerce had to persuade Mary Kay to change the date of the 1984 Seminar which was slated for the same week in the same convention center. Positive anecdotes about Mary Kay Ash and how MKC was operated were cited in numerous books and articles.

Mary Kay Ash indicated that the company had no plans for changing the main thrust of company's sales and recruiting strategies:

> This is an excellent primary career for women, not just a way to get pin money. We see no need to alter our basic approach. It's taken us this far.[29]

> We have only 4 percent of the total retail cosmetics market. The way I see it 96 percent of the people in the United States are using the wrong product. There's no reason why we can't become the number one cosmetics company in the United States.[30]

---

[28] As quoted in Wiley, "Cold Cream and Hard Cash," p. 40.

[29] Ibid.

[30] As quoted in *Business Week,* March 28, 1983, p. 130.

CASE 29 WAL-MART STORES, INC.*

"Give me a W!" shouts Sam Walton, the founder and CEO of Wal-Mart Stores, Inc., to associates at the weekly Saturday morning headquarters meeting in Bentonville, Arkansas (population approximately 9,000). "W!" the crowd of some several hundred roars back. "Give me an A!" says Walton. And so it goes down to the last T. Then everyone joins in a final ringing chorus: "Wal-Mart, we're Number 1!" This rah-rah style keynoted the tone for each meeting, and the upbeat spirit carried over to the rest of the company's operations. Enthusiasm and dedication were factors in Wal-Mart's ranking as the second largest national discount department store chain (Exhibit 1).

Sam Walton's goal for Wal-Mart was continued, controlled, profitable growth. During the 1976–85 period the company recorded average annual compound rates of growth of 38.5 percent in sales and 42.6 percent in profitability (see Exhibit 2 for a 10-year financial summary). This was good enough to firmly establish Wal-Mart as one of the fastest-developing major retailers in the nation and to cause its NYSE-listed common stock to command a price-earnings ratio that was far and away the highest among the leading discount chains. One Wall Street securities analyst noted, "Wal-Mart leads all other companies of its type in every quantitative measure I know."

The company opened 103 new discount stores, 8 Sam's Wholesale Clubs (a wholesale outlet which sold in bulk on a membership-only basis), and 1 Helen's Arts & Crafts store during 1984. On January 31, 1985, Wal-Mart had 745 Discount Cities and 11 Sam's Wholesale Clubs in operation in 20 states in the Southeast and Midwest (see Exhibit 3); plans called for entering Colorado and Wisconsin next. The company's aggressive store opening program reflected a strategy of saturating target rural market areas first and then entering that area's major population center, a process Sam Walton dubbed "backwards expansion." About 80 percent of all Wal-Mart stores were located in towns with a resident population of 15,000 or less and a "shopping area" draw of about 25,000 people. Wal-Mart's small town focus was Sam Walton's brainchild; his idea was that if Wal-Mart offered prices as good or better than stores in cities that were several hours away by car, people would shop at home.

Walton's backwards expansion strategy called first for building a cluster of 30 or 40 Discount City stores in a targeted rural area within a 600-mile radius of a distribution center. Once stores were opened in most of the selected towns around a more populous city, Wal-Mart would locate one or more stores in the metropolitan area and begin major market advertising. When a geographic area approached its store saturation target, the expansion effort shifted to penetrating adjoining market areas.

Complementing the store location strategy were a number of management practices concerning people, planning, discipline, and challenge. From its inception Wal-Mart

---

* Prepared by graduate researcher Kem A. King under the supervision of Professor Arthur A. Thompson, Jr., the University of Alabama.

Exhibit 1   Discount Department Store Rankings, 1984

Chain	General Merchandise Volume 1984*	Net Earnings 1984*	Number of Stores	Net Selling Space†
1. K mart Corp.	$21,040	$492.9	2,196	125,500
2. Wal-Mart Stores, Inc.	6,268	270.8	860	43,115
3. Target Stores	3,550	235.6	230	22,481
4. Best Products Co., Inc.	2,253	13.6	214	6,420
5. Zayre Corp.	2,195	122.2	325	17,907
6. T.G.&Y.	2,020	n/a	733	21,650
7. Toys "R" Us, Inc.	1,701	111.4	233	5,825
8. Service Merchandise	1,607	44.6	290	5,800
9. Bradlees	1,404	82.5	150	10,538
10. Gemco National, Inc.	1,247	12.7	80	6,400

* In millions of dollars.
† In thousands of square feet.

had followed participatory management practices, extending from decision-making to profit-sharing plans involving each of the 81,000 Wal-Mart employees (called "associates"). At the Saturday morning associates meetings in Bentonville, new action thrusts were regularly announced and mapped out for all aspects of the business, ranging from what areas to expand in next, to what product lines to add, to how to better motivate associates. Wal-Mart believed it had to become a very cost effective organization to reach its profit objectives via selling mostly name brand merchandise at discount prices.

Driven by the need to be a low-cost operator, Wal-Mart modeled its warehouse-type, open-air store offices with two factors in mind: (1) to avoid the added cost of building and furnishing store offices and (2) to create a close feeling between store management and customers while promoting a better working bond between co-workers. Wal-Mart officers were so cost-control conscious that the company's total travel cost did not expand from 1983 to 1984 despite the opening of 95 new stores. Keeping costs low was also set up as a challenge for Wal-Mart associates to achieve, and Wal-Mart effectively used this challenge as a motivational technique. All stores were given the objective of achieving a 10 percent increase over the previous year's sales, and individual departments were pitted against one another to improve productivity in terms of sales per square foot. Sam Walton strongly advocated trying new ideas and suggestions, all the while recognizing that not all of what was tried would be successful.

SAM WALTON

"Sam Walton is the warmest, most genuine human being who's ever walked the face of the earth."

—Bill Avery
Wal-Mart management recruiter

Exhibit 2   Ten-Year Financial Summary, Wal-Mart Stores, Inc. and Subsidiaries
Dollar Amounts in Thousands except Per Share Data

	1976	1977	1978	1979
Earnings				
Net sales	$340,331	$478,807	$678,456	$900,298
Licensed department rentals and other income—net	3,803	5,393	7,767	9,615
Cost of sales	251,473	352,669	503,825	661,062
Operating, selling, and general administrative expenses	66,427	95,488	134,718	182,365
Interest costs:				
Debt	1,758	1,680	2,068	3,119
Capital leases	2,419	3,506	4,765	6,595
Taxes on income	10,925	14,818	19,656	27,325
Net income	11,132	16,039	21,191	29,447
Per share of common stock:				
Net income				
Primary	.10	.15	.19	.24
Full diluted	.10	.14	.18	.24
Dividends	.008	.011	.02	.028
Stores in operation at the end of the period				
Wal-Mart Stores	125	153	195	229
Sam's Wholesale Clubs	—	—	—	—
Financial position				
Current assets	$ 76,070	$ 99,493	$150,986	$191,860
Net property, plant, equipment, and capital leases	48,744	68,134	100,550	131,403
Total assets	125,347	168,201	251,865	324,666
Current liabilities	33,953	43,289	74,891	98,868
Long-term debt	17,531	19,158	21,489	25,965
Long-term obligations under capital leases	26,534	41,190	59,003	72,357
Preferred stock with mandatory redemption provisions	—	—	—	—
Common stockholders' equity	47,195	4,417	96,482	127,476
Financial ratios				
Current ratio	2.2	2.3	2.0	1.9
Inventories/working capital	1.5	1.6	1.8	1.9
Return on assets*	11.2	12.8	12.6	11.7
Return on stockholders' equity*	30.9	34.0	32.9	30.6

* On beginning of year balances.
Source: 1985 Annual Report.

Walton graduated from the University of Missouri with a degree in business and began his retail career as a management trainee with the J. C. Penney Co., an experience which began to shape his thinking about department store retailing. His career with Penney's was interrupted, however, by a stint in the military during World War II. When the war was over, Walton decided to open a Ben Franklin retail variety store in Newport, Arkansas, rather than return to Penney's. Five years later when the lease on the Newport building was lost, Walton relocated his Ben Franklin in Bentonville, Arkansas, where he bought a building and opened Walton's 5 & 10 as a Ben

1980	1981	1982	1983	1984	1985
$1,248,176	$1,643,199	$2,444,997	$3,376,252	$4,666,909	$6,400,861
10,092	12,063	17,650	22,435	36,031	52,167
919,305	1,207,802	1,787,496	2,458,235	3,418,025	4,722,440
251,616	331,524	495,010	677,029	892,887	1,181,455
4,438	5,808	16,053	20,297	4,935	5,207
8,621	10,849	15,351	18,570	29,946	42,506
33,137	43,597	65,943	100,416	160,903	230,653
41,151	55,682	82,794	124,140	196,244	270,767
.33	.43	.63	.91	1.40	1.91
.33	.43	.63	.91	1.40	1.91
.038	.05	.065	.09	.14	.21
276	330	491	551	642	745
—	—	—	—	3	11
$ 266,617	$ 345,204	$ 589,161	$ 720,537	$1,005,567	$1,303,254
190,562	245,942	333,026	457,509	628,151	870,309
457,879	592,345	937,513	1,187,448	1,652,254	2,205,229
170,221	177,601	339,961	347,318	502,763	688,968
24,862	30,184	104,581	106,465	40,866	41,237
97,212	134,896	154,196	222,610	339,930	449,886
—	—	7,438	6,861	6,411	5,874
164,844	248,309	323,942	488,109	737,503	984,672
1.6	1.9	1.7	2.1	2.0	1.9
2.4	1.7	2.0	1.5	1.5	1.8
12.7	12.2	14.0	13.2	16.5	16.4
32.3	33.8	33.3	38.3	40.2	36.7

Franklin–affiliated store. During the next nine years, eight more Walton-owned Ben Franklin stores were opened in four states.

In 1961 Walton became very concerned about the long-term competitive threat to variety stores posed by the emerging popularity of giant supermarkets and discounters. Walton, an avid pilot, took off in his plane on a cross-country tour studying the changes in stores and retailing trends, then put together a plan for a discount store of his own. The first Wal-Mart Discount City was opened July 2, 1962, in Rogers, Arkansas. Twenty-three years later Wal-Mart was a $6.4 billion dollar com-

Exhibit 3   Locations of Wal-Mart Facilities

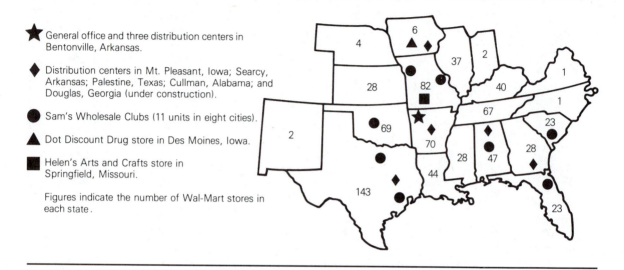

★ General office and three distribution centers in Bentonville, Arkansas.

◆ Distribution centers in Mt. Pleasant, Iowa; Searcy, Arkansas; Palestine, Texas; Cullman, Alabama; and Douglas, Georgia (under construction).

● Sam's Wholesale Clubs (11 units in eight cities).

▲ Dot Discount Drug store in Des Moines, Iowa.

■ Helen's Arts and Crafts store in Springfield, Missouri.

Figures indicate the number of Wal-Mart stores in each state.

pany. In a 1985 *Forbes* magazine article Sam Walton, at 67, was designated as the richest man in America based on his 39 percent ownership of Wal-Mart's common stock, worth about $2.8 billion at Wal-Mart's then current stock price of $51.

Despite his wealth and the demands placed upon his time as a result of the phenomenal growth of the Wal-Mart chain, Walton's outgoing personality and personal demeanor toward the Wal-Mart associates who worked for him were a source of admiration and inspiration. The comments of several associates indicated the regard and esteem he commanded:

He's a beautiful man. I met him when this store opened. He came back two and one half years later and still remembered me. He walked over to this department and said, "Grace, you and I have been around a long time, I'm gonna hug your neck." That's just the type of guy he is. He's just a wonderful person.

I was just . . . I was thrilled (to meet him). He's a very special person. He is a very outgoing person, and it kind of motivates you just to sit and listen to him talk. He listens—that's another thing.

I think he's a fine person. He's just an everyday person like one of us. When you meet him he's just like one of us. You can talk to him. Anything you want to ask him—you can just go right up and ask.

He's really down-to-earth. He'll put his arm around you, hug you, and tell you you're doing a good job.

Mr. Walton cares about his employees. You get the feeling that you're working for him instead of Wal-Mart. And although he may not need the money, he's good to us and we try to be good to him.

WAL-MART'S NEAR-TERM GROWTH STRATEGY

Using Walton's backwards expansion strategy and aided by some acquisitions, Wal-Mart's 1-store operation in 1962 had become a 745-store operation in 1985, and the growth era seemed far from over. Wal-Mart's 1985 plans called for expanding in a number of directions simultaneously:

- Adding 20 percent more floor space in the form of 115 new store openings and the expansion of 60 existing stores (another 30 stores were scheduled for remodeling).
- Opening 10 to 12 new Sam's Wholesale Clubs and doubling the sales of this division.
- Adding several more units of Helen's Arts & Crafts.
- Opening one new DOT Discount Drug Store.
- Trying out 25,000- to 35,000-square-foot store prototypes in small communities (the regular Discount City store had 60,000 to 90,000 square feet of sales space).
- Installing electronic scanning devices at checkout counters in more than 200 stores so that Uniform Product Codes (UPC) could be used instead of price tags.
- Instituting a "Buy American" plan to give preference to stocking merchandise manufactured in the United States.

In mid-1985 Wal-Mart announced plans for capital expenditures of $250 million to construct 9 million square feet of additional retail space (a 22 percent increase over 1984). In terms of in-store sales growth the company had a goal of $200 in sales per square foot (in 1985 Wal-Mart was realizing sales of $166 per square foot versus an industry average of around $100 per square foot). The company also began an "aggressive hospitality" program that featured a customer greeter at the front door of each store and enhanced efforts on the part of associates to "aggressively" make more contacts with shoppers, offering a cheerful word, a smile, help in finding items, and information about products.

NEW STORE INNOVATION

Wal-Mart's future was not dependent solely upon opening more Wal-Mart Discount Cities—Sam Walton was a strong advocate of continuously experimenting with new types of stores. Four new store prototypes were being explored. Wal-Mart intended to open several 25,000- to 30,000-square-foot Discount Cities in communities smaller than typical Wal-Mart towns. One Wal-Mart associate told the casewriter that since the smaller Discount City was only in the concept-testing phase it was too early to know how it would mesh with other Wal-Mart growth options, but "it ought to be an interesting way to gain increased penetration of Wal-Mart's present geographic markets." The smaller stores were scheduled to carry a narrower selection of merchandise specially targeted to the tastes, incomes, and lifestyles of rural area residents.

Another store prototype, Sam's Wholesale Club, a membership only, cash-and-carry warehouse, appeared in the Wal-Mart family in 1983. These stores were approximately 100,000 square feet in size and carried mostly best-selling brands of a particular item; a Sam's storefront is pictured in Exhibit 4. The concept of membership wholesale clubs represented a new retailing trend, and Wal-Mart was in the vanguard of companies trying to develop this segment (see Exhibit 5). Cash-and-carry warehouses were located in population centers and targeted the small business owner who was not able to buy directly from manufacturers or wholesalers in large enough quantities to receive bulk discounts. The merchandise mix stocked in Sam's was a variable because many products were bought whenever Wal-Mart ran across a special deal from suppliers. Expected operating margins were 8 to 9 percent of total sales. Three Sam's Wholesale Clubs were opened in 1983, and within two years 8 more were in operation, with plans to build another 10 to 12 by 1986. Small business proprietors paid a $25 membership fee to join Sam's Wholesale Club; membership entitled them to buy materials at 10 percent above wholesale, prices that were cheaper than in the Wal-Mart Discount City stores. The idea of opening a Sam's Wholesale Club adjacent to a Wal-Mart Discount City was being considered as an experiment for 1986 or 1987.

In 1984 Wal-Mart opened its first Helen's Arts & Crafts store in Springfield, Missouri. The store carried a broader range of arts and crafts supplies than was generally found in a Wal-Mart store, plus assorted hobby equipment. Three more Helen's stores were opened in 1985, all with a full line of hobby equipment. The store sites selected were in free-standing or strip-store locations, not in connection with Wal-Mart Discount Cities, and were targeted to very selective markets. Although the mark-up in these stores was such that an excellent profit was made, plans for further expanding this prototype were not definite in 1986.

Wal-Mart also opened two Dot Discount Drug Stores in Des Moines and Kansas City. These were deep discount pharmacies that primarily carried a full line of drugs and personal care goods. As with the Helen's stores the Dot stores were either free-standing or strip-stores and had no publicly visible Wal-Mart connection.

MARKETING POLICIES AND PROGRAMS

Leased Departments   Wal-Mart both owned and leased space for pharmacies and shoe departments in its Discount City stores. When Wal-Mart decided to add pharmacy departments to the Discount Cities, the strategy of leasing space to outside interests was a way of spreading the risk of adding previously untried lines of merchandise. But as one Wal-Marter put it, "We began leasing (pharmacies) and found we knew better than anyone else how to conduct our business—how to better enforce the Wal-Mart way, so we will continue to lease a few (pharmacies), but primarily will open our own." Plans called for deep discount pharmacies to be added to most existing stores. For similar reasons, all the leased shoe departments in the Discount Cities were scheduled to be acquired from Morse Shoe in three phases: 25 percent in February 1986; 25 percent in July 1986; and 50 percent in February 1987. Sales in leased-out departments totaled $117.2 million in 1985, $76.8 million in 1984, and $71.5 million in 1983; Wal-Mart's rental income from the leased space was $13.1 million in 1985, $10.2 million in 1984, and $7.3 million in 1983.

Exhibit 4   Sample Layouts and Scenes at Wal-Mart

Exhibit 5 Membership Warehouse Clubs

Chain (headquarters)	Volume in Millions		Number of Stores	
	Sales Last Fiscal Year	Sales Previous Fiscal Year	January 1985	January 1986
Price Club (Califorinia)	$1,164	$643	19	25
Sam's Wholesale (Arkansas)	220	34	11	23
Makro (Ohio)	170	162	4	4
Warehouse Club (Illinois)	150	15	5	10
Value Club (Texas)	125	120	5	6
Costco (Washington)	102	0	12	21
Price Savers (Utah)	80	0	4	4
The Wholesale Club (Indiana)	46	11	3	5
BJ's Wholesale (Maryland)	40	0	3	6

Products   When customers walked into a Wal-Mart Discount City, it was very clear that Wal-Mart had a lot of merchandise to sell. Stock was stacked high along the walls and filled free-standing displays along narrow aisles. Wal-Mart tried to fully utilize the floor space in a Discount City without having a cluttered look. In comparison to other well-known national chain stores, such as Sears Roebuck & Co. and J.C. Penney, Wal-Mart was positioned as a deeper discounter and carried a narrower product line. In comparison to K mart, Wal-Mart stores had very much the same appearance, were somewhat smaller in square footage, packed more merchandise in a cleaner fashion into its sales spaces, and priced its merchandise at fractionally lower levels. The merchandise in Wal-Mart departments was a mixture of deeply discounted name brands and even lower priced off-brands. The front of every Wal-Mart store was emblazoned with the declaration "We Sell for Less" (see Exhibit 3).

In selecting which new items to carry and in experimenting with different merchandising techniques, Wal-Mart conducted tests in a selected market area to see if the new line or new merchandising technique was successful. If the item had successful sales figures in test stores, then it was "rolled out" or expanded to other stores.

Since the early 80s, Wal-Mart had increased the percentage of soft goods in its stores because of their higher gross margins. Wal-Mart also shifted toward more name brands. The women's clothing department began carrying more famous maker labels which appeared at lower-than-retail prices; plus-size and maternity wear lines were also added.

A number of changes had recently been made to upgrade product offerings in the electronics department. The space given to LP records was cut back to make room for the addition of telephones. In larger stores big-ticket items such as "boomboxes" and home-and-go stereo units, with price tags ranging to $290 and $360, as well as videocassette recorders priced up to $1,000 were added. Some stores began to carry satellite dish TV receivers at prices exceeding $2,000. A film-processing plant was purchased in 1981 to support the camera department's activities and services. Name brand cameras, color video cameras, and videodisk players were added to lend credibility to the department and to help build customer traffic in the department.

These and other similar changes were all part of a "merchandise intensification" program which focused on adding more big-ticket items to the product mix. New lines added included paint, microwave ovens, jewelry, and an elementary education reading center. These complemented the merchandising of tried-and-true volume-producers such as housewares, garden supplies, auto supplies, health and beauty aids, and hardware. The newer "soft" items were added in expectation of producing both new store traffic and greater dollar sales per customer.

Customer Relations and Customer Service

One store manager expressed to the casewriter that making the customer number one was what put Wal-Mart on top. He explained that Wal-Mart believed in standing behind the products it sold and said that it was much better for the company to replace a dissatisfied customer's merchandise and maintain a loyal patron than to chance incurring the wrath of the individual and the possibility of loss of future sales through negative publicity. Displayed above the door of every Wal-Mart store and even on the shopping bags was Wal-Mart's promise to its customers, "Satisfaction Guaranteed." Wal-Mart's newly instituted aggressive hospitality program represented an attempt by associates to provide "the warmest, most friendly, most helpful, and most appreciative environment in which to shop"—from the time the customers entered the store until they left.

When Wal-Mart associates were asked about their own customer relations activities, the following comments were made:

> The thing they teach us first is that the customer comes first and they pay our salaries, so always be nice to your customers, no matter what. That's the main thing, just always be nice to your customer. Always try to help your customer. Always go up to someone in your department and ask them if you can be of help—never be rude.

> That's one of our most important things—our customers. . . . We do our best to go out of our way for our customers.

> You're always supposed to drop what you're doing, the customer always comes first. Customer satisfaction—that's the Wal-Mart way. They start talking about that from day one.

> We're never supposed to point out where something is. We're supposed to take the customer to the item they're looking for.

> We try to please the customer. If they have any complaints we try to do something about it immediately. You know, the customers always come first at Wal-Mart.

PURCHASING AND WAREHOUSE DISTRIBUTION

Wal-Mart's buyers purchased merchandise in large quantities directly from the vendor and inventoried them in Wal-Mart distribution centers for shipment via Wal-Mart's own trucking fleet to Wal-Mart stores. Being able to receive bulk discount rates and to use its own distribution network gave Wal-Mart cost savings, which were in turn reflected in prices and profits. Approximately 70 to 80 percent of the merchandise was blanket ordered for all stores, although each store was allowed some latitude in stocking to meet differences in buying patterns. As one company official noted, "If you're in Cajun country in Louisiana and you don't stock a crayfish pot, you're out of it."

Store managers telephoned their orders weekly into a central computer. Merchandise was then sorted by automated equipment onto the trucks and delivered to the stores, usually within a 24–48 hour period. Managers could swap stock between stores to assure that merchandise was sold and was in the best store location to meet customer demand.

The Buy American Plan   One of Wal-Mart's newer purchasing programs was announced in 1985, the "Buy American" plan. In a letter sent to about 3,000 domestic vendors, dated March 14, 1985, Sam Walton discussed the "serious threat" of the nation's balance-of-trade deficit and conveyed his plans for carrying more U.S.-made goods in Wal-Mart's stores; yet, he assured the Buy American plan was not an anti-import effort:

> Our Wal-Mart company is firmly committed to the philosophy of buying everything possible from suppliers who manufacture their products in the United States. We are convinced that with proper planning and cooperation between retailers and manufacturers many products can be supplied to us that are comparable, or better, in value and quality to those we have been buying offshore.

In upholding his commitment to buying U.S.-manufactured goods, Walton offered longer lead times for placing orders and a willingness to take a lesser markup or to pay a slightly higher price for American made goods. Walton added his own belief, "Wal-Mart believes our American workers can make the difference if management provides the leadership." Along with the Buy American program, Wal-Mart instituted a new promotional slogan: "Wal-Mart—Keeping America Working and Strong."

Projections by one store manager indicated that approximately 2,000 U.S. jobs had been saved as a result of the Buy American plan. In their search for American-made goods, Wal-Mart buyers located a flannel shirt maker in Arkansas who could supply shirts of an as good or better quality than those produced by the previous Hong Kong supplier; the Arkansas-made shirts were also obtained at a cost below what Wal-Mart was paying the Hong Kong supplier.

HUMAN RESOURCES

"The customer is Number 1; the sales associate is Number 2. You take care of those and the rest will just come along."

—*Bill Avery*
Wal-Mart management recruiter

Wal-Mart's 81,000 employees were referred to as associates—a practice Walton insisted on from the outset. Walton preferred this term because it implied ownership, and Wal-Mart associates did have a stockholder interest through a profit-sharing plan which was transmitted to the associate through company stock. Walton believed when he first started Wal-Mart that if a partnership could be developed rather than an employer-employee relationship, the work would go a lot smoother. Associates were eligible to participate in the profit-sharing/stock ownership plan the month following one year of continuous full-time service in which the individual had worked 1,000 hours or more. At the end of an associate's second year of service, the company began contributing to the plan, in the associate's name, a certain percentage of its profits. The money, contributed solely by the company, became vested at the rate of 20 percent per year beginning the third year of participation in the plan. After seven years of continuous employment the associate became fully vested; however, if the associate left the company prior to that time, the unvested portions were redirected into a company fund and redistributed to all remaining employees. As of January 1985 almost 2.2 million shares of stock had been issued under the profit-sharing/stock option plan.

Although only full-time associates were allowed to participate in Wal-Mart's benefits programs, one associate related that Wal-Mart did not try to hire a large ratio of part-time employees to avoid having to pay benefits. The associate indicated that in her store there was approximately a five-to-one full-time to part-time associate ratio.

Associates at Wal-Mart were hired at higher than minimum wage and could expect to receive a raise within the first year at one or both of two annual job evaluations. An associate told the casewriter that at least one raise was guaranteed in the first year if Wal-Mart planned to keep the individual on the staff. The other raise depended on how well the associate worked and improved during the year. At Wal-Mart only the store managers were salaried. All other associates, including the department managers, were considered hourly employees.

Wal-Mart stressed participatory management from the top to the bottom, and listening was a very important part of each manager's job. It was not unusual to find Walton showing up on the loading docks at midnight with a bag of donuts to talk to the guys. One manager told the casewriter that up to 90 percent of his day was spent walking around the store communicating with the associates—praising them for a job well done, discussing how improvements could be made, listening to their comments, and soliciting suggestions. A steady stream of ideas from associates on how to improve performance was the rule rather than the exception. Moreover, Wal-Mart associates were encouraged to put their ideas into action, whether it was an associate contributing an idea for a volume-producing item (VPI) contest or a corporate officer suggesting a new type of department or specialty store. According to Walton:

> Our philosophy is that management's role is simply to get the right people in the right places to do a job and then to encourage them to use their own inventiveness to accomplish the task at hand.

Task forces to evaluate ideas and to plan for future actions on those ideas were common; and it was not unusual for the person who developed the idea to be appointed the leader of the group. This encouraged a commitment to follow through on new ideas. Rewards for successful ideas took the form of company-wide recognition such as mention in Saturday morning headquarters meetings and sometimes personal praise from Walton himself.

The planning process at Wal-Mart began with store management asking each associate what they could do individually or what could be changed to improve store operations. If anyone believed a policy or procedure detracted from operations, associates at all levels were encouraged to challenge and change it. "LTC" (meaning low threshold for change) was a highly valued concept at Wal-Mart.

The Friday Morning Store Meetings   On Friday morning general store meetings were held in each Discount City store; associates at every level could ask questions and expect to get straightforward answers from management concerning departmental and store sales and cost figures, along with other pertinent store figures or information. The meeting might also include information on new company initiatives, policy change announcements, and perhaps video training films (the use of video films was a popular Wal-Mart training technique.)

As David Glass, Wal-Mart's president and chief operating officer, said, "Most of us wear a button that says, 'Our People Make the Difference'—that is not a slogan at Wal-Mart, it is a way of life. Our people really do make a difference." Believing in this and encouraging superior performance was ingrained in all Wal-Mart staffers. Each week department and store figures were posted on the back wall of the store. That way asssociates could see how their departments ranked against other depart-

---

Exhibit 6   A Scene from a Wal-Mart Saturday Morning Meeting at Headquarters in Bentonville

ments and how the store was doing overall. If the figures were better than average, associates were praised verbally and given pats on the back; associates in departments that regularly outperformed the averages could expect annual bonuses and raises. When departmental performances came out lower than average, then the store manager would talk with department associates to see what was wrong and how it could be corrected.

The Saturday Morning Headquarters Meetings   At 7:30 A.M. every Saturday morning since 1961, the top officers, the merchandising staff, the regional managers who oversaw the store districts, and the Bentonville headquarters' staff—over 100 people in all—gathered to discuss Wal-Mart issues (see Exhibit 6). Topics covered might include the week's sales, store payroll percentages, special promotion items, and any unusual problems. Reports on store construction, distribution centers, transportation, loss prevention, information systems, and so on were also given to keep everyone up-to-date.

The meetings were deliberately very informal and relaxed. Those attending might show up in tennis or hunting clothes so that when the meeting was over they could go on to their Saturday activities. The meetings, normally attended by Walton, were always up-beat and were sometimes begun by Walton "calling the hogs," a practice common in Arkansas razorback country. Walton used his cheerleading and hog-calling tactics to loosen everyone up, create some fun and excitement, and get things started on a stimulating note.

MANAGEMENT AND ASSOCIATE TRAINING

"At Wal-Mart we guarantee two things: Opportunity and hard work."
—*Bill Avery*
Wal-Mart management recruiter

Management Training   Wal-Mart managers were hired in one of three ways. Hourly associates could move up through the ranks from sales to department manager to manager of the check lanes into store management training. Second, people from other retail companies with outstanding merchandising skills were recruited to join the ranks of Wal-Mart managers. And third, Wal-Mart recruited college graduates to enter the company's management training program.
According to Wal-Mart's president:

We create more opportunity for people in this company than most companies I know. If you want to advance, you can in Wal-Mart. If you want to do better, you can in Wal-Mart. If you don't like the area you are in and you want to try something else, the process we call crosspollinization, you can do that. If you have the desire and want to apply yourself, then we will work to help you do it. We involve our people in all of our areas.

Casewriter interviews with Wal-Mart associates revealed a positive attitude concerning advancement opportunities and the company's work climate:

You have the option to go as far as you want to go if you do a good job.

It's up to you; if you do the work, you'll get the raises.

I think it's a good place to work. There's a lot here (as far as advancement) if you want to work for it. It's a good open relationship with management. The benefits are good and the pay is above average for most discount stores.

The management training program involved two phases. In the first phase the trainee completed a 16-week on-the-job training program:

Week 1	Checkouts/Service desk
Week 2	Cash office
Weeks 3 and 4	Receiving
Week 5	Invoicing
Weeks 6, 7, and 8	Hardlines merchandising
Weeks 9, and 10	Merchandise office
Weeks 11, 12, and 13	Home and seasonal merchandising
Weeks 14, 15, and 16	Apparel merchandising

At designated times during Phase I trainees were tested and evaluated by the store manager. During this time the individual was encouraged to complete a "self-critique" of his/her own progress and the caliber of guidance being received from the training effort. At the end of Phase I the trainee moved at once into Phase II.

The initial three weeks of Phase II were structured to cover such management topics as internal/external theft, scheduling, store staffing, retail math, merchandise replenishment, and the Wal-Mart "Keys to Supervision" series which dealt with interpersonal skills and personnel responsibilities. After completion of the first three weeks of Phase II the trainee was given responsibility for an area of the store. The length of time during the remainder of Phase II varied according to the rate at which each trainee progressed. After showing good job performance, demonstrated leadership, and job knowledge, the trainee was promoted to an assistant manager. As an assistant manager training continued with the Retail Management Training Seminar which was designed to complement the in-store training with other vital management fundamentals. With the quickly paced growth rate of Wal-Mart stores, the above-average trainee could progress to store manager within five years. Through bonuses for sales increases above projected amounts and company stock options, the highest performing store managers earned salaries of around $70,000 to $80,000 annually.

To further promote management training, in November 1985 the Walton Institute of Retailing was opened in affiliation with the University of Arkansas. Within a year of its inception every Wal-Mart manager from the stores, the distribution facilities, and the general office were expected to take part in special programs at the Walton Institute to strengthen and develop the company's managerial capabilities.

Associate Training   Wal-Mart did not provide a specialized training course for its hourly associates. Upon hiring, an associate was immediately placed in a position for on-the-job-training. From time to time training films were shown in the Friday morning associates' meetings, but no other formalized training aids were provided by Wal-Mart headquarters. Store managers and department managers were expected to train and supervise the associates under them in whatever ways were needed.

A number of associates commented on the Wal-Mart training programs:

Mostly you learn by doing. They tell you a lot; but you learn your job every day.

They show you how to do your books. They show you how to order and help you get adjusted to your department.

We have tapes we watch that give us pointers on different things. They give you some training to start off—what you are and are not supposed to do.

The training program is not up to par. They bring new people in so fast—They try to show films, but it's just so hard in this kind of business. In my opinion you learn better just by experience. The training program itself is just not adequate. There's just not enough time.

We have all kinds of films and guidelines to go by, department managers' meetings every Monday, and sometimes we have quizzes to make sure we're learning what we need to know.

The most training you get is on the job—especially if you work with someone who has been around awhile.

MOTIVATION AND INCENTIVES

Developing new programs to encourage sales was one way Wal-Mart motivated its associates. One of Wal-Mart's most successful incentive programs was its VPI (Volume Producing Item) contests. In this contest, departments within the store were able to do special promotion and pricing on items they themselves wanted to feature. Management believed the VPI contests boosted sales, breathed new life into an otherwise slow-selling item, and helped keep associates thinking about how to help bolster sales; two sales associates commented on the VPI incentive scheme:

We have contests. You feature an item in your department and see how well it sells each week. If your feature wins, you get a half day off.

They have a lot of contests. If you're the top seller in the store you can win money. For four weeks in a row I've won money. That gives you a little incentive to do the very best you can. You kind of compete with other departments even though we're a big family in the long run. You like a little competition, but not too much.

Wal-Mart also had an incentive plan whereby associates received bonuses for "good ideas," such as how to reduce shoplifting or how to improve merchandising. As a result of the shoplifting reduction bonus plan, between 1977 and 1982 shrinkage dropped from 2.2 percent to 1.3 percent of total sales (as compared to an industrywide average of over 2 percent; in 1985 shrinkage dropped to a Wal-Mart record low of 1.06 percent). Fifty percent of the savings Wal-Mart realized from this shoplifting reduction plan was given to the associates as bonuses.

Another motivational tactic that Wal-Mart employed involved dress-up days in which associates dressed according to a theme (for instance, Western days or Halloween); these added fun and excitement for associates and the upbeat mood was transferred to the customer.

The Work Atmosphere at Wal-Mart

Throughout company literature, comments could be found referring to Wal-Mart's "concern for the individual"; such slogans as "Our people make the difference," "We care about people," and "People helping People" were often repeated by Wal-Mart executives. "It's a lot of hard work, but it's so much fun," one Wal-Mart executive told this casewriter concerning his job with Wal-Mart. He indicated he enjoyed working for a company that promoted a concerned feeling toward its associates. He also stated that work at Wal-Mart was never dull. New challenges were always cropping up in the form of new products to be marketed or new merchandising techniques to be tested or implemented. In interviewing a number of Wal-Mart management associates, the casewriter was told several times that Wal-Mart was a wonderful place to work because of all the human resource practices carried out by the company.

> It's a special feeling you get when you walk in a Wal-Mart store. And when you're working there is when you really notice it because the people care about each other. It's like being with a successful football team, that feeling of togetherness, and everyone is willing to sacrifice in order to stay together.
>
> *Bill Avery*
> *Wal-Mart management recruiter*

In questioning Wal-Mart associates about how they liked working at Wal-Mart, a number of comments were made to the casewriter about the family-oriented atmosphere that was fostered at the store:

> There is no comparison between Wal-Mart and other places I've worked. Wal-Mart is far above. They just treat customers and associates really nice.

> It's more of a family-oriented place than anywhere I've ever worked. They seem to really care about their employees. It's not just the money they're making, but a true concern for the people working here.

> We're just like a family. Everybody cares for each other. The management is fantastic. You can go to them for anything and feel free to contradict them if you want to.

> They select such nice people to work with. We get along well.

> I care about my responsibilities. You're just more proud of it. You're more apt to care about it. You'll want people to come in and see what you've done. I guess the pats on the back let you know that what you've done is appreciated. And when they show their appreciation you're going to care more and do better.

> We're a united group. We may be from different walks of life, but once we get here we're a group. You may leave them at the door, but when you're in here you're part of a family. You help each other; you try to be everybody's friend. It's a united feeling.

To fire the managers up, Walton sent them and their spouses to a resort each year for strategy sessions and merchandising seminars. A highlight of the event was the spouses only gripe-session. The program agenda was designed to reinforce Wal-Mart's down-home "concern for the individual" atmosphere.

Wal-Mart was founded and ingrained with old-fashioned beliefs which in 1985 still permeated the corporation. Restrictions on hiring persons over 65 were not formally lifted until Sam Walton himself approached the mandatory retirement age of 65. Other holdover practices that might seem out of step remained intact. For example, associates were not allowed to date one another without authorization from the executive committee. Women were rarely hired for executive positions. In 1985 only 12 (17 percent) of the merchandise buyers were women; and in 1984 Walton resisted naming a woman to the board of directors despite the urgings of Ferold G. Arend, a past president of Wal-Mart.

These old-line values did not seem to disturb any of the female associates at Wal-Mart. At the close of a number of interviews with the Wal-Mart associates, the casewriter asked the associate to relate what made Wal-Mart associates special and what made Wal-Mart so successful:

They tell us that we are the best.

I like working at Wal-Mart better than any other place. I'm freer to handle the work better. . . . I can go at my own speed and do the work the way I want to do it.

I enjoy Wal-Mart; I've been here eight years. Of course, we work, but that's what we're here for. You've got potential with Wal-Mart.

I think Wal-Mart is one of the best companies there is. I wouldn't want to work for anyone else.

I think Wal-Mart is successful because it's geared to the needs of the average family from low-income families on up. And they have good merchandise. Since Wal-Mart has been here I've made very few trips to the city (30 miles away).

Our low prices!!!

MANAGEMENT CHANGES AT WAL-MART HEADQUARTERS

Until 1984 Jack Shewmaker, 47, was president and chief operating officer. However, in late 1984 Shewmaker shifted to vice chairman and chief financial officer with responsibilities that included overseeing Sam's Wholesale Club, special divisions, data processing, real estate and construction, and finance and accounting. David Glass, 49, stepped in as president and chief operating officer at that time. The flip-flop in positions was explained as a means of giving both men an equal opportunity and the broad organizational experience for stepping into Walton's shoes when the time came. Robson Walton, 40, Sam Walton's eldest son, was also being prepared to assume the lead position.

FUTURE PROSPECTS AT WAL-MART

With a mind to the future, Wal-Mart planned to continue its established aggressive growth plans in terms of number of stores and sales increases. Two new southeastern distribution centers were to be completed in 1985, and a search was undertaken to locate a site for another distribution center in the western Wal-Mart territory. The western region distribution center would act as a springboard into greater western expansion. Top management indicated that people development would remain its number one priority. Wal-Mart executives believed that in a growing company the decision-making process would have to be pushed to lower levels and that management at all levels would need to be broadened in preparation for that responsibility. Wal-Mart projected that sales would top $8 billion in fiscal 1986, up from $6.4 billion in 1985. During the bull market of early 1986 Wal-Mart's stock price set record highs and was selling at a price-earnings ratio of 34 to 1.

CASE 30 McDONALD/FRAZER (A)*

In early 1985 John Crump was appointed president and chief operating officer of McDonald/Frazer, a $2.8 million advertising agency (see Exhibit 1) located in New York City. Prior to accepting the position he had discussed the situation at McDonald/Frazer only with the CEO of the parent company, Marlowe Advertising. From this discussion he knew that the agency was in danger of losing its biggest client, Serrally Distillery. He also began to suspect that most of his account executives were unable to perform as their major client wanted.

Adding to Crump's concerns was the realization that his CEO and board chairman, who had been pushed aside by Marlowe Advertising to accommodate Crump, was a long-time friend and former protegé of Serrally's president. For all these reasons, as Crump prepared to move to New York, he knew that his first days at McDonald/Frazer would be critical to his future success there.

COMPANY BACKGROUND

McDonald/Frazer was an old-line advertising agency founded in Detroit in 1930 that had specialized in handling industrial business clients. In 1947 the agency won its first and only major consumer product account—Serrally Distillers, a producer and importer of vodka and rum spirits. Serrally's production was primarily offshore and was imported to a distribution subsidiary in the United States. Since Serrally had offices in New York and since New York was the acknowledged capitol of consumer products advertising, McDonald/Frazer decided to open an office there in order to service the account.

During the next decade, largely because of McDonald/Frazer's reputation for industrial advertising in Detroit, the New York office expanded its base to include such clients as Union Carbide Corporation, ITT Corporation and General Electric Company. Nevertheless, Serrally remained the dominant client (see Exhibit 2).

In 1966 Joe Stillwell, who had been creative director on the Serrally account and head of the New York office since 1961, was hired by Serrally to become marketing director, which left 42-year-old Mike Hedstrom, who had been the creative director on the industrial accounts and the number two man in the New York office, in charge. When he left, Stillwell, a minor shareholder in the McDonald/Frazer operation, sold his shares to Mike Hedstrom.

Although Hedstrom had dealt mainly with industrial accounts, he had done some work on Serrally's international advertising and was known and liked by the executives in Serrally's International Division. Because of his good relationship with Stillwell

---

* Prepared by Frank DeVotie under the supervision of Professor William E. Fulmer. Copyright © 1986 by the Colgate Darden Graduate Business School Sponsors, Charlottesville, VA. Reproduced with permission. The names of the company, some of its clients, and some individuals have been disguised to preserve anonymity.

Exhibit 1   Income Statement, McDonald/Frazer, 1984   In Thousands

Total commissions and fees	$2,799.1
Operating expenses	
Compensation	1,312.2
Direct charges	116.0
Overhead expenses	820.7
Total operating expenses	2,248.9
Interest expense	141.9
Executive incentive payments	
(to Mike Hedstrom)	105.0
Profit before taxes	303.3
Corporate income taxes	164.0
Net income	$ 139.3

---

and Serrally, he followed Stillwell's precedent and took over most of the creative work on the Serrally account.

Throughout the 1960s and early 1970s Serrally profited immensely from two changes in consumer preferences: (1) a switch from dark liquors, such as Scotch and bourbon, to lighter liquors such as rum and vodka; and (2) a growing taste for mixing spirits with a variety of soft drinks and juices rather than drinking them straight or with water. Because Serrally's products were both light and mixable, Serrally's case sales tripled in slightly over a decade. During most of this growth era, Serrally was a sales-dominated organization in which little thought was given to long-term positioning of brands. Nevertheless, the advertising budget grew as sales did, and the account became extremely important and profitable to McDonald/Frazer.

Exhibit 2   McDonald/Frazer, 1984 Revenue by Client   In Thousands

FBM Distillers (Serrally Canada)	$ 246.0
Serrally	1,851.6
General Electric	108.4
ITT USTS*	0
ITT Rayonier	138.4
ITT Blue Marble*	0
Copper Development	95.3
A. Sahadi	62.7
Arco Polymers	73.7
Pro Hardware	66.9
Coco Lopez	80.0
Union Carbide	28.9
Sandvik	43.3
Silicones*	0
Miscellaneous	3.9
Totals	$2,799.1

* McDonald/Frazer was the agency of record for these clients, but they were inactive during 1984.

Stillwell became president of Serrally in 1974. Because the organization was still small, he was able to continue working directly with Hedstrom at McDonald/Frazer in producing Serrally's advertising.

MARLOWE ADVERTISING

By 1984 Marlowe Advertising was one of the 20 largest agencies in the United States and, if ranked on the basis of international billings, probably one of the 10 largest in the world. Since its founding in 1907, its largest and oldest client had been Procter & Gamble. In addition to handling some of P&G's largest and best-known products, the agency also handled some of Johnson & Johnson's consumer products and part of the American Motors account. The agency was best known for its marketing and account management expertise; its creative output was known for being "solid" but unspectacular.

Robert Drysdale, Marlowe's CEO, typified the agency's normal career pattern. He had been with Marlowe since very early in his career and had been assigned mainly to P&G brands. Although originally a copywriter, he had spent the last 10 years as a manager and had a good understanding of marketing. A majority of the parent agency's other top executives also had spent most of their careers with Marlowe and had a great deal of experience working on P&G brands.

Marlowe was a privately held agency. Employees were allowed to buy stock in amounts commensurate with their rank but had to sell their stock back upon leaving or retiring. A controlling interest was held by the group of 10 men who made up the executive committee. This group included such people as the CEO, the president, the CFO, the head of International, and the vice presidents in charge of subsidiaries, the creative department, and account management.

Like many of the large agencies, Marlowe began acquiring smaller agencies during the 1970s. The major motivation was growth; in recent years Marlowe had not been particularly successful in gaining new accounts and felt that buying smaller agencies would be an effective way to grow. In fact, most of the agency's recent U.S. growth had come as a result of acquisitions and increased billings from existing clients.

Marlowe became interested in buying McDonald/Frazer's New York office in the late 1970s. Serrally was the type of client that Marlowe wanted: the account was large (in excess of $10 million) and required the kind of creative "image" advertising that current Marlowe clients did not. Marlowe felt that by having Serrally on their client list they would gain entry into other such "image" accounts.

After Marlowe had convinced Hedstrom of the merits of selling McDonald/Frazer, Hedstrom in turn urged the other partners to accept the proposal. A deal was finally struck in 1982 in which Marlowe bought 49 percent ownership in McDonald/Frazer and agreed to buy an additional 10 percent each year for the next five years. The agreement required that the subsequent payments would include a specified minimum plus an incentive payment, made to the principals, that would depend on McDonald/Frazer's reported earnings. Serrally was consulted prior to the final agreement and did not voice any objections. They did, however, state a preference for Hedstrom continuing as CEO for the immediate future.

PROBLEMS WITH SERRALLY

In the early 1980s Joe Stillwell at Serrally had begun to realize that, despite an annual growth rate of 7 percent for the company's case sales, the U.S. consumption of spirits was flat and probably would soon begin to decline. Consequently, he began looking to new-product introductions as a means for diversification and began hiring professional package-goods marketers to look after the company's long-term positioning.

By 1984 Stillwell had hired several young brand managers from such package-goods giants as P&G, The Clorox Company, and R. J. Reynolds Industries, Inc. In addition, he met with Hedstrom and told him that McDonald/Frazer should become more concerned with strategic positioning of Serrally's products rather than simply coming up with new campaigns.

For new products, Serrally began to act as distributor for Almondette, an imported almond liqueur, and Undarraga, a fine South American wine. Both introductions were unsuccessful, however, The wine was too delicate to travel and frequently turned sour by the time it got to the shelves. The new marketing people that Stillwell had brought in loudly complained that McDonald/Frazer was not doing a good job and was merely acting as an order taker rather than contributing any ideas.

Stillwell met with Marlowe's CEO Drysdale late in 1980 and expressed his opinion that McDonald/Frazer was not providing the strategic thought that he felt was necessary and that Serrally's main brands had been neglected in the agency's rush to write ads for the new products. Although he acknowledged that sales were still climbing, he felt that Serrally had not established an image that would provide for loyal consumers and long-term growth. He cited research which showed that consumers perceived Serrally products to be sweet and fattening. Although no specific names were mentioned, Drysdale left the meeting feeling that perhaps Hedstrom had "lost his handle on the situation" and should be replaced.

After considerable thought and discussion within Marlowe, Drysdale asked John Crump to become the chief operating officer at McDonald/Frazer and to "save the Serrally account." Hedstrom would remain as CEO and as chairman of the board for the time being. Hedstrom, who had had a brief meeting with Crump during his interview trip, agreed to the new arrangement, feeling that it would allow him to spend more of his time giving strategic direction to Serrally's problems.

JOHN CRUMP

John Crump was a large, quiet-spoken man with a shock of dark hair and a face that could best be described as outdoorsy. He had spent all of his career in advertising, starting two days after he graduated from the University of Illinois in 1966. Most of his career had been at Marlowe and had included several overseas assignments.

The shelves occupying one wall of his office were lined with native bric-a-brac from Mexico, the Philippines, and Puerto Rico. The most striking adornment was an 18-inch clay figurine with the likeness of John Wayne, Crump's favorite actor. Crump described his background:

I grew up in suburban Chicago; my father ran Marlowe's Chicago office, and for me there was never any doubt that I would go into advertising. I was a good golfer as a kid and played on the team at Illinois. I even played against Jack Nicklaus while he was at Ohio State; he beat me, though. I majored in the liberal arts at Illinois because that was supposedly the best degree for advertising. I also took several advertising courses from a guy named Sandage, one of the best-known professors of advertising. I learned a lot, but I still think that advertising is better learned by doing than in a classroom.

I interviewed only with Chicago agencies as I was getting ready to graduate. I guess, since I'm from Chicago, it never even occurred to me to look at the New York agencies. I couldn't work for Marlowe since my father was there, but I had offers from both Leo Burnett and from Tatham, Laird, Kudner. I chose TLK because they had a very good training program and because they offered me the opportunity to work on the Procter & Gamble account. I spent four years there and was account executive on the Mr. Clean and Head & Shoulders accounts. I've always admired the way P&G does business and most of what I know about marketing has been learned from them. Since I was still in Chicago I saw a lot of my parents, and through my father I was able to meet both Bart Cummings, Marlowe's CEO at the time, and Bob Drysdale, the current CEO. I used to go over for dinner when they were in town and got to know and like them.

Finally in 1970 Marlowe offered me a job to go down to Mexico as an account supervisor. They had recently purchased a minority ownership in a local agency and felt that with me down there they might attract some P&G business. I accepted the offer, partly because I had always wanted to work at Marlowe and partly because I was excited about going international and felt that it offered me a chance to become a manager more quickly. I spent two and a half years in Mexico and enjoyed the experience, though we never did get any of P&G's business. Their local agency had an in with Mexico's media baron, which gave them almost a complete monopoly on local network air time, and it was tough for other agencies to get time for their clients. I did work on some Nestlé business as well as some Richardson-Vicks business. I also picked up a love of bullfighting. I bought a small share in a ranch that raised fighting bulls and used to go on weekends to get in the ring myself. I sort of like to test my courage in that way. I read a lot of Hemingway's stories on bulls and am a big fan of his.

After two and a half years, though, it appeared that the local agency wasn't going to do much, and Marlowe had bought a share in a Puerto Rican agency that did look as if it would prosper. They offered me the chance to go as a management supervisor with an opportunity to run it in a few years. I spent another three and a half years there handling the P&G account as well as Nabisco and some Richardson-Vicks business.

The man running the agency there died of cancer about a year after I got there, and I expected to get the job as general manager. Marlowe decided that I was still too young and gave the job to Jim Adler instead. I was quite bitter at the time, but in retrospect I definitely think that it was for the better. Jim Adler was very good about giving me responsibility for my accounts and letting me negotiate agency contracts with media and suppliers. He eventually recommended that Marlowe find a place for me to run my own agency.

In 1976 Marlowe offered me the chance to go to the Philippines to run their agency there. They had originally bought into a small agency there as a means to service P&G's account, and things had not gone very well. In some ways the situation there reminded me a little of the situation at McDonald/Frazer. P&G was providing 80 percent of the agency's income (the agency was losing money), and they were upset that the local management was not servicing their account properly. They had criticized the agency very heavily, and the morale was very low as a result. To make matters worse, the first month and a half that we were there the monsoons caused such heavy rain that almost half of the agency personnel were flooded into their homes and couldn't work. Finally, to top it all off, the Marcos government declared martial law three months after I got there and imposed a news blackout for over a month. Since there was no news, there was no advertising, hence no income.

During that time I started working with the people at P&G and discovered that the problem was that the agency had not been working with strategies, but rather, wrote ads simply to be creative. Once I began working on strategies and teaching our creative people how to write to them and our account people how to implement them, the problems began to straighten out and I discovered that I actually had a pretty talented group of people there. The problem had been that the man who was running the agency before me (one of the original partners and still a part owner of the local equity) had no concept of how to use strategy to drive advertising. Once I got the problems with P&G straightened out, I gained the respect of all of the local owners and got complete control of the agency. I have to give part of the credit to P&G for all of this. They had originally agreed to pay part of my salary to come out, and this gave me more credibility with their local managers than they would have given someone else.

Things went well in the Philippines almost from the beginning. We turned a profit even the first year, and I never had to fire anyone. We took the Pepsi-Cola account from J. Walter Thompson, and we convinced Johnson & Johnson, an account that we already had but who hadn't advertised much, to start advertising as soon as the media blackout was lifted. The results were that we were able to increase billings enough to start hiring new creative talent and ended up with a strong grip on the creative talent pool on the islands. By the end of three years, we had also gotten the Warner Lambert and Pfizer accounts, had become the largest agency on the island, and were the sixth largest contributor in the Marlowe system. The local owners (who by now owned less than 50 percent) had asked me to stay, but I felt that it was time to move on, and Marlowe wanted me to go back to Mexico to run an agency that they were thinking of purchasing.

The deal in Mexico fell through, but I was still sent back to the United States as a management supervisor on the Procter & Gamble account while I waited for another international job to open up. I stayed in New York for a year and then was sent back to Puerto Rico to take over as general manager of our agency there. My old boss, Jim Adler, was being promoted to director of international, and I was to be director of Latin America as well as general manager.

I arrived in San Juan in the summer of 1980 to find an agency that was already in pretty good health. Marlowe had already bought out the local managers, so there was no problem to worry about on that score, and the agency itself already had a good base of clients, none of whom were unhappy with the agency. I did institute the purchase of in-house typesetting capabilities, which allowed us to handle a couple of large retail accounts with a much greater profit margin. Rather than contracting the business out and taking a 15 percent commission, we were able to use our own people and get a better margin for ourselves while providing them with cheaper, faster service, and it allowed us to provide faster service in helping our package-goods clients in preparing their print material.

We had several local managers who were quite capable, so I was able to groom them to become managers by letting them handle day-to-day operations while I worked on strengthening the Latin American network.

Unfortunately, the exchange rate fluctuations in the late 70s made any investment a risky one and we were not able to purchase the larger agencies that we had originally wanted.

By late 1984 the Puerto Rican agency had become the largest one on the island (it had been one of the top two before I got there), and I felt that I was ready to move on to new challenges. About that time Robert Drysdale called and asked me if I was willing to come up and run the McDonald/Frazer operation. Although McDonald/Frazer was a smaller agency than Badillo/Marlowe (the Puerto Rican agency) and was an agency in trouble, I decided to accept the job for a number of reasons. To begin with, I have always been loyal to the company and I felt that there was a genuine need for me here. By this time I had a wife and two kids and felt that they would be better off growing up in the United States. I had been out of the United States for most of 14 years, and I felt that I had to come back if I really wanted to go far in advertising. Finally, I wanted the challenge. If I hadn't accepted I would either have finished my career in Puerto Rico or come back to the United States as a management supervisor at Marlowe. I felt that I would go stale in Puerto Rico, and I knew that I could never settle for being a management supervisor after having run my own agency for eight years.

McDONALD/FRAZER PERSONNEL

During Crump's interview with Drysdale at Marlowe, he learned that McDonald/Frazer's account handling department was the only one that was completely divided by account (Exhibit 3). The Serrally account supervisors were Tom East, established brands; Larry Walling, liqueur; and Moe Drabowski, imported wines.

Tom East was an old hand in the advertising business, having spent 22 years as an account executive at Foote, Cone, Belding. Prior to joining McDonald/Frazer in 1978, East had supervised a large pharmaceutical account and had several contacts

Exhibit 3   McDonald/Frazer, Organization Chart

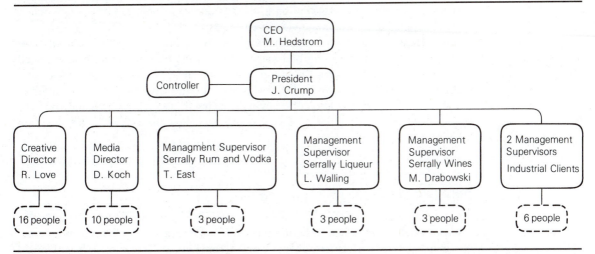

in that industry. He was 55 and probably would be retiring soon. He was currently earning $50,000.

Larry Walling, 42, had been at McDonald/Frazer for three years and also earned $50,000. He had spent the most recent part of his career as a sales manager for Buitoni Foods. Walling originally had been hired by Hedstrom when Stillwell began pushing the agency to become more knowledgeable in new products and in strategic positioning. Hedstrom had felt that Walling's knowledge of distribution systems would be crucial in introducing new products; Walling was known to be very ambitious.

Moe Drabowski originally had worked at a small New York agency but later spent several years as a marketing manager in a supermarket chain where his duties included both buying and advertising. Originally from the Midwest, Drabowski was 33 years old and was making $34,000.

Two other account supervisors worked exclusively on the industrial accounts and knew very little about consumer marketing.

Although the agency had no research department, it did have a creative department consisting of Ron Love, the creative director, and eight creative teams who reported to him. Ron had worked at McDonald/Frazer since 1966 and had done much of the creative work on Serrally. He was essentially an art director because the copywriting had been supervised by Hedstrom. He had previously worked at a video production agency in which he had been a partner. Love was currently making $55,000.

Each creative team consisted of an art director and a copywriter. They varied in ages from mid-50s to early 20s. The teams were not assigned to any one particular account, but worked on a project basis as needed. All had worked on Serrally as well as the industrial accounts. Working primarily with magazines and some newspaper advertising, none had any experience in nonprint media. Neither had any experience working with tightly defined and enforced strategic parameters.

The media department was similar to the creative department in that no one had any experience in buying broadcast media, but the media planners and media buyers had a great deal of experience in buying print media. The media director was Doug Koch, an expert chess player with six years of work experience at McDonald/Frazer. He was working on a masters degree in philosophy at night school. Koch was making approximately $34,000.

Mike Hedstrom, the 60-year-old CEO, was essentially a copywriter who had been converted into a manager. He had spent much of his time working on the Serrally account. He seemed to enjoy working with the creative director and his creative teams to ensure that the copy flowed nicely. From his days as a copywriter on industrial accounts, he had the reputation of enjoying working in the creative area and appreciating a clever turn of a phrase. Mike's salary was close to $100,000, not including his incentive bonuses.

CRUMP'S MANAGEMENT APPROACH

"It is clear that much has to be done if McDonald/Frazer and John Crump are to continue to be star performers for Marlowe," Crump noted. "My goal with McDonald/ Frazer is to make it into a strong midsize package goods agency with a more diversified client base. I think that if I do well I can convince Bob Drysdale to let me merge with one of the other subsidiaries and turn it into a large midsized agency."

As Crump reflected on the future, he was asked by the casewriter about his management style and philosophy:

Well, it's not something I think about very much, but I suppose I do have a method that I usually follow. To begin with, I always think that people are essentially good and that with proper motivation they can manage themselves and do a lot better than even they think that they can.

I've heard of this concept of "Management by Walking Around," and I guess it describes me pretty much. I always take a tour of the office in the morning and, if possible, another one during the afternoon. I want my people to know that I know them personally and that I'm interested in what they are doing. I generally believe in giving positive feedback, but if somebody screws up more than a couple of times on the same thing, I have been known to "kick some ass."

I like to think of myself as a delegator, but I never delegate the tough things like firing people or telling someone that they don't get a bonus or a raise. Sometimes I wish that I could delegate more, because I realize that I have a high need for control; I hate to fly, and I don't like to be in a car when other people are driving because I lose that sense of control.

One of the things that I definitely believe in is management by objectives. I always set my own personal objectives to reach, and I always meet with my top people in each department and set goals with them to aim for. Sometimes they are quantifiable goals, such as maintaining personnel costs at a certain level, and sometimes they are less quantifiable, such as improving morale in their department, but there is always some goal.

I also believe strongly in keeping an open-door policy and letting people tell me their views on the agency. I believe that it serves two purposes: one, it allows me to keep my fingers on the agency's pulse, and two, it provides my people with a place to blow off steam. Many of the complaints are actually pretty trivial and will take care of themselves if given time. I am pretty jealous of my personal time, though, and I like to be out of the office by 5:30 to make the 6:00 train. I am willing to stay late if there is a problem that has come up with little warning, but if it is simple procrastination or poor planning, then somebody is going to be in trouble if I have to stay late.

I strongly believe that the two most important things in running an ad agency are keeping the creative people happy and keeping the clients happy. I think that my own strengths are marketing and keeping clients happy, but I am definitely not creative so I really work at keeping them happy.

Keeping the creatives happy requires that you know something about the nature of their work. By nature it requires a certain amount of ego and a certain spark that is often hard to find. I don't expect them to be brilliant every time, and in fact I am happy if they are only brilliant half the time, and maybe even 20 percent is enough sometimes. The rest of the time they only have to be solid. I also do a great deal to gratify their egos. If a creative person doesn't have a big ego, then they probably aren't any good. The way to take care of their egos is best done by letting them enter as many creative contests as they want. There are many of them, and I have made it a policy to pay whatever the entrance fee if the creatives think that they have a decent chance to win. If they do win I also make it a policy to let them go to the awards ceremony and pick up their own prize. Surprisingly, many agencies have the management supervisor or a member of top management pick up the awards.

I will also take on a small account if I think that it can become a creative showcase.

We currently handle the account for The Church of the Nazarene as creative consultants. The account bills almost nothing, but it lets the creatives take flights of fancy without having to worry about getting product demos or fitting a constricting strategy.

One last thing that I do is delegate some of the decisions to them. For instance, I always let the creative director make out his own personnel budget and will always approve it, within reason. It makes him feel as though he does more than just pump out ads, and it also commits him to his budget. If somebody wants more than they are allotted, he can take care of it without coming to me. Anything having to do with office decor (and in this business you have to have nice office space) is automatically deferred to a decision of the creative director.

Since I came up through the account side, I tend to be a little tougher on account executives, but that is because I expect them to provide the leadership. This is definitely a strategy-driven business, and the majority of the strategic input is always going to come from the account people, not from the creatives. And if the strategy is bad, even the greatest creative person in the world isn't going to save the account.

Most of what I know about writing copy strategies comes from working on P&G, and they have a little presentation on the nuts and bolts of it that I often give to my people if I see that they are going off course. When I judge account people I always look for an ability to think in terms of long-term positioning. When I judge a creative person I always look for their ability to understand strategic thinking and to execute it concisely and originally.

Dealing with clients requires listening to them and knowing what they mean instead of what they say. We had a client recently that did not complain about the advertising, but kept wondering when the creative would be as good as the first ads that were produced. This was a campaign that had been running for quite some time. After looking at a reel of the advertising that we had done for them, I realized that it had become a little flat and decided to rotate the creative team that was working on this particular account. The creative team was relieved to be able to get to a fresh account without being asked to leave by the client, and the client felt as though they had exercised some influence with the agency.

Treating people with dignity in this business is essential. In the example that I just mentioned I used an account rotation, which is fairly common, as a means for protecting the dignity of both the client and the creative people. In my career I have had to retire several people and have always done it with dignity. The guy that I replaced in the Philippines was one of the founders of the agency and well liked by many of the employees, as well as in the business community. I arranged to make him a very good offer to retire and let him stay on as president for a little while until he had found another job. The same thing in San Juan. The founder of the agency was enormously well respected by the employees and by the business community and, in fact, had contributed a great deal to the agency's success before his age started catching up with him. I ensured that he was able to retire in comfortable circumstances. He was allowed to keep his own office, although we needed the space, and he remained as chairman of the board of the local company even after he had been completely bought out. I realize that I will probably outlive my usefulness someday, and I only hope that I am allowed to go with some dignity.

CASE 31 SIGNETICS CORPORATION: IMPLEMENTING A QUALITY IMPROVEMENT PROGRAM (A)*

In 1979, as part of a four-year planning process at Signetics, D. C. McKenzie, director of corporate quality control, was asked to forecast his department's growth through 1984. McKenzie believed that "quality" would become the battleground of the future. However, his management and budget forecasts—showing exponential increases in inspectors and QC activities—convinced him that if Signetics were to compete successfully against other U.S. and Japanese manufacturers, it would require the complete reorganization of the quality control function. A new philosophy would have to be implemented—one that would hold every employee accountable for quality and that would have zero defects as its goal.

During the fall of 1979 McKenzie held several meetings with his staff to define a major program for implementing this new philosophy. That program also incorporated quality as a measure in all Signetics' managers' semiannual performance reviews.

By the spring of 1980 substantial progress had been made in defining a redirected quality improvement program at Signetics, getting top management support, and taking initial steps toward its implementation. However, in April McKenzie decided there was a need to assess just what had and had not been accomplished and to evaluate several possible next steps. In particular, McKenzie and his quality managers had come up with three different types of projects, each of which would require a significant commitment on the part of his organization. One option emphasized working with vendors, another working with customers, while a third focused on internal operations. McKenzie felt that this next step would be an important one; it had to keep the momentum growing while guarding against a major setback in the overall program or a dilution of effort from trying to do too much at once.

The remainder of this case describes the company background, the circumstances that led to the redirecting of its quality philosophy in late 1979, and a review of some of the specific actions taken as part of that redirection program. In addition, the three types of projects under consideration in April 1980 are described, and data on their resource requirements and other issues in their evaluation are provided.

COMPANY BACKGROUND

Signetics Corporation was founded in Sunnyvale, California, in 1961. It was the first company in the world established for the sole purpose of designing, manufacturing, and selling integrated circuits (ICs). By 1980 Signetics had become the sixth largest U.S. semiconductor company, and it offered one of the broadest lines of integrated

---

* Reprinted with permission of Stanford University Graduate School of Business, ©1982 by the Board of Trustees of the Leland Stanford Junior University. Selected data have been disguised to protect the proprietary interests of the company.

circuits in the industry. Since 1972 the company had experienced a compound annual growth rate of 26 percent. In 1980 gross sales were expected to exceed $360 million.

From 1962 to 1975 Signetics was owned by Corning Glass Works. In 1975 Signetics was purchased by the U.S. Philips Corporation, a subsidiary of N. V. Philips of the Netherlands. With worldwide sales in 1979 in excess of 33 billion guilders (approximately $16 billion 1979 U.S. dollars), N. V. Philips was a diversified manufacturing firm participating in industries ranging from lighting products to consumer electronics to scientific instruments and semiconductors.

Although operated independently of N. V. Philips, by 1980 Signetics' relationship with the Netherlands firm had become very important. Philips bought and sold products under the Signetics name and provided its subsidiary access to its worldwide research and development capability, advanced manufacturing process know-how, and technology.

Company Products and Markets

Signetics had developed several thousand different circuits for such diverse markets as data processing, industrial controls, instrumentation, consumer products, telecommunications, automotive, and defense. Product lines included PROMs (Programmable Read Only Memory), Fuse Programmable Logic Arrays, LSI (Large Scale Integration), logic, and analog circuits. (Exhibit 1 provides a glossary of semiconductor terminology, and Exhibit 2 summarizes generic product categories offered by Signetics.)

Signetics' major U.S. competitors were: Texas Instruments Incorporated, National Semiconductor Corporation, Motorola, Inc., Intel Corporation, and Fairchild Camera & Instrument Corp. Exhibit 3 provides comparative sales data for 1979.

Memory components accounted for at least 40 percent of the semiconductor industry's global sales, which were projected to reach some $13 billion in 1980 and had been rising at the impressive rate of 18 percent annually. By 1979 U.S. manufacturers were doing about two thirds of that volume. By 1988 semiconductor output in the United States was expected to increase to $30 billion, about 55 percent of the world total.

Semiconductors had been dubbed "the crude oil of the 1980s," partly because of the size and growth anticipated in the semiconductor industry and partly because of the pervasiveness of the applications of ICs. Many other manufacturers were expanding their commitment and capabilities in the field, most notably the Japanese who, owing in part to their product quality record, were making significant inroads in world markets (see Exhibit 4).

In early 1980, to take advantage of the fast growth anticipated for MOS (metal-oxide-silicon) technology, Signetics began a four-year program to invest in new manufacturing facilities and equipment. A new 250,000-square-foot plant was built in Albuquerque, New Mexico, primarily for MOS manufacturing. It was the company's objective to become a major supplier in the mainstream of MOS technology by 1984.

In addition to an extensive program to develop its own new products, Signetics had joined with Motorola, Inc. to manufacture that company's family of 16-bit microprocessors. Through this agreement, Signetics was able to offer one of the most sophisticated 16-bit microprocessors available. In keeping with the company's family-of-prod-

Exhibit 1 Glossary of Technical Terms

Semiconductor: A solid material (e.g., silicon or germanium) with properties of both a conductor and an insulator.

Transistor: A small chip of semiconductor material that amplifies or switches electrical current. Known as discrete (single-function) semiconductors, transistors replaced vacuum tubes and started the solid-state revolution.

Integrated circuit (ICs): Many transistors and other circuit elements "integrated" on a single silicon chip.

LSI: Large Scale Integration, where more transistors are put on a chip than on an IC, enabling the chip to perform several functions rather than one. LSIs are then interconnected on a circuit board to make up entire computers.

Microprocessor: Called the "computer-on-a-chip" because the arithmetic and logic functions of a computer are placed on a single silicon chip.

Microcomputer: A microprocessor with memory chips for storing software (e.g., operating instructions) and communication chips for "talking" to the outside world.

MOS: Metal-oxide-silicon, one of two basic IC designs, is the fastest growing because it is cheaper and easier to use.

Bipolar: The second fundamental design for ICs. Bipolar chips are faster but more costly to manufacture.

Wafer: A 3- or 4-inch thin disc of silicon on which up to 500 separate chips can be printed and then cut into individual ICs.

Logic: The part of the computer that does the arithmetic or makes decisions.

Memory: Stores needed facts along with instructions on what to do with them and when. Each memory component stores a number of bits of binary data normally denoted in multiples of kilobits where one kilobit equals 1,024 bits.

RAM: Random Access Memory, which stores digital information temporarily and can be changed by the user. It constitutes the basic storage element in computer terminals and is replacing magnetic core memories in mainframe computers.

ROM: Read Only Memory, which stores information used repeatedly such as tables of data, characters for electronic displays, and so on. Unlike RAM, ROM cannot be altered.

E/PROM: Erasable Programmable Read Only Memories are similar to ROMs but enable the user to erase stored information and replace it with new information at the end of a normal operation.

Source: "How to Talk High Tech," *Forbes,* November 26, 1979, p. 54.

ucts philosophy, Signetics had begun to offer a line of high-performance peripheral input/output and communication chips as well.

On the research side, Signetics and Philips had organized a team of scientists and engineers to explore complex IC technologies and processes of the future and to advance Signetics' capabilities in both Bipolar and MOS technology. Planning was underway for a 120,000-square-foot Signetics Advanced Technology Center to be located in Sunnyvale. When completed, the Center was expected to be one of the most sophisticated research and development facilities in the industry, providing space for more than 100 scientists and engineers.

Internal Organization and Operations

Signetics was organized into eight divisions, as shown in Exhibit 5. Six designed, manufactured, and marketed ICs. The remaining two finished and tested these products for conformance to the rigid specifications demanded by the military and automotive/

Exhibit 2　Generic Product Categories Offered by Signetics

Logic
  Arithmetic units/microprocessor CPUs
  Decoder/drivers
  Parity generators
  Encoders
  Latches
  Comparators
  Counters
  Data selector/multiplexer
  Decoders/multiplexers
  Flip-flops
  Registers
  Seven segment decoder/drivers with
    zero suppression and lamp test
  Line receivers
  Line drivers
  Buffers/inverters
  Special functions
  Bus transceiver
  Semicustom LSI design (T^2L compatible)
    gate arrays
  Composite cell logic (CCL)

MOS microprocessor
  Microprocessors and microcomputers
  I/O peripheral interface
  Training
  Development hardware
  LSI support devices
  Development systems

Bipolar memory
  CAMs
  RAMs
  FPLAs
  FPGAs
  FPLSs
  PROMs

Analog
  TV circuits
  Audio circuits
  Radio circuits
  Interface
  Video amplifiers
  MOSFET-analog/digital switches (D-MOS)
  Microminiature packages
  MOSFET-RF (D-MOS)
  Op amps
  Data acquisition
  Timers
  Phase locked loops
  Transistor arrays
  Display drivers
  Power control circuits
  Comparators

MOS memory
  ROMs

Bipolar LSI
  Microprocessors
  Sequencers
  I/O interface
  Special-purpose circuits
  Memories (PROMs and ROMs)
  Memories (RAMs)
  Support circuits
  Field programmable logic arrays
  Development hardware and kits
  Development software
  8 × 300 software training materials

Source: Company brochure.

---

telecommunication markets. The eight divisions reported to one of two major technology groups: Bipolar Digital and MOS/Analog.

Divisions in the MOS/Analog Group designed and manufactured MOS microprocessors (the so-called "computers on a chip") and their peripheral circuits. Applications included those that transmitted computer data over telephone lines, MOS memory circuits, and Analog ICs used in computer products, industrial products, and consumer products such as radios, TVs, and electronic games.

The divisions in the Bipolar Digital Group made high-speed memory circuits and families of complex logic microprocessors and control ICs for computers and their peripheral equipment, as well as a variety of industrial, telecommunications, and consumer control systems.

Exhibit 3   1979 Integrated Circuit Sales by U.S. Manufacturers

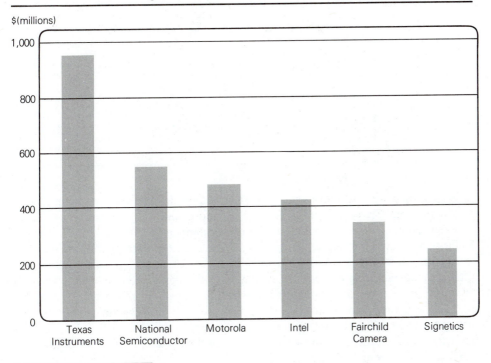

$(millions)

Source: *Business Week,* April 14, 1980, p. 94.

Exhibit 4   World IC Production   Millions of Dollars

Producing Region	1978	1979
United States		
IC merchant	$3,238	$4,071
IC captive	1,344	2,010
IC total United States	4,582	6,081
Western Europe		
IC total	453	600
Japan		
IC total	1,195	1,750
Rest of world		
IC total	782	675
Total ICs	$7,012	$9,106

Source: Company estimates.

Exhibit 5   Signetics Organization—1980

Groups	Divisions
MOS/Analog Products Group	{ Analog MOS microprocessor MOS memory
Bipolar Digital Products Group	{ Logic Bipolar LSI Bipolar Memory Military } Market segment divisions Auto/Telecom }

Most of Signetics' facilities were located in Sunnyvale. The corporate offices were nearby in Santa Clara, California; Wafer Fabrication and Test Operations were split between Orem, Utah, and Sunnyvale; and the company's three assembly and test facilities were in Seoul, Korea, Bangkok, Thailand, and Manila, the Philippines.

Making semiconductor devices involved more than 150 steps and required extremely intricate manufacturing processes. A silicon ingot was sliced into thin wafers. Through miniaturization involving photographic reduction and photo lithography, some 200 to 3,000 elaborate chips were created on each wafer. Following the proper buildup of layers of metals and chemicals, each wafer was cut into individual dice (or chips), gold leads were attached, and each die was packaged on a frame with electrical connectors to become a final unit.

DEVELOPMENT OF THE QUALITY IMPROVEMENT PROGRAM

Before the fall of 1979 the quality and reliability (Q&R) philosophy at Signetics had functioned as though Q&R staff had full responsibility for quality, while production was responsible only for output (see Exhibit 6). D. C. McKenzie expressed a firm conviction as to why the quality control concept within the company had to be revamped:

> My feelings about the inappropriateness of our philosophy came to a head in the fall of 79 when I began to prepare my part of a long-range corporate growth plan. I concluded that the number of Q&R personnel operating as "police people" would have to expand exponentially to keep pace with Signetics' forecasted growth in volume. Q&R had been concentrating on establishing test procedures and setting specifications (commonly thought of as appraisal and gating/screening activities) and then trying to make sure that everyone adhered to our specs. It was just hopeless to continue down that path. The requirements of the future clearly called for quality performance levels possible only through more sophisticated prevention programs.

McKenzie's Q&R staff had met to examine two options—continue past practices or initiate change. During the spring of 1979 alternatives to past practices were dis-

Exhibit 6   Signetics Corporation, 1980 Organization Chart

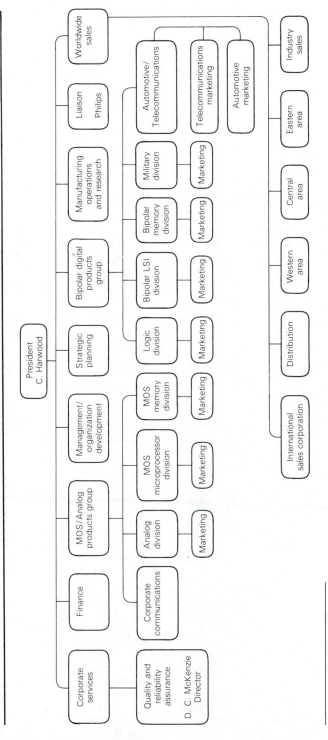

Source: Company document.

Exhibit 7   Before and After Contrast of Quality—Fall 1979

Before	*After*
Screen for quality	Plan for quality
Quality is Q&R's responsibility	Quality is everybody's responsibility
Some mistakes are inevitable	Zero defects is possible
Quality means inspection	Quality means conformance to requirements
Scrap and rework are the major costs of poor quality	Scrap and rework are only a small part of the costs of nonconformance
Quality is a tactical issue	Quality is a strategic imperative
Production units are where quality should be measured	Individual accountability is where quality should be measured

cussed. Determined to explore those further, McKenzie organized an off-site three-day planning meeting in September 1979 for all the corporate Q&R managers. He enlisted the help of one of Signetics' Organization Development staff, who opened the meeting with an introduction to a problem-solving technique called ABC. As McKenzie explained it:

> ABC stands for Assumptions, Behavior, and Consequences. The idea is that by looking at the current state for each of those three areas and then looking at what is desired, it's possible to concentrate on problem solving without having to point blame.

McKenzie then presented the problem he wanted his staff to focus on—that the philosophy that Q&R should act as a police force in Signetics operations needed to be changed radically.

> I was nervous when I got through writing it on the board and turned back to get my staff's response; but right off the bat four of the six agreed with me 100 percent, and the other two agreed as soon as they understood more about it. The two who weren't right with me at first don't work directly in the police force role.
>
> We spent the rest of the meeting outlining the before and after contrast of a quality philosophy and the details of the transition plan. (See Exhibits 7 and 8.)

Exhibit 8   Rough Outline of a Four-Year Quality Improvement Program

1980–1981
  Raise the quality consciousness level of all personnel
  Division and plant managers begin active leadership roles
  Quality tied to everyone's performance review

1981–1982
  Utilization of the cost of nonconformance as an improvement planning tool
  Zero defects a part of the culture—ppm is standard notation
  Greater emphasis on technical planning
  Major quality improvements made through the quality improvement teams

1983–1984
  Logistics and technical data systems working
  Cooperating routinely with key customers on special programs

Initial Q&R Program Actions

As a skeletal framework for the new Q&R philosophy, McKenzie introduced a 14-point program based on the book, *Quality Is Free,* by Philip B. Crosby.

While the group viewed Crosby's program, originally developed for ITT, as not totally complete, it felt the need to have an anchor and a method of instruction—one that had been articulated and would be recognized by other companies and in some published works. In addition, the initial success was based on the humanistic aspects of the program and not its technical content.

Throughout the fall of 1979 the Q&R managers held a series of meetings to develop the methods required to implement the program. A division was chosen for a pilot program, the training that would be required was defined, the people who could do the training were identified, and the changes in responsibilities that would result from the new philosophy were examined.

In early 1980 the Q&R staff met with Signetics president Chuck Harwood to ask his approval and support for the detailed pilot program. It proposed that all the basic elements be in place by late 1980. Throughout the company the Q&R police role would be replaced by individual accountability with a goal of zero defects. In describing their program to Harwood the Q&R staff even made rough comparisons of how each manager's Responsibility, Measures, and Objectives (RMO) goals (a management by objectives type of system in place throughout Signetics) would change after the pilot program. Harwood was asked to communicate his personal support by presenting the program to employees and key customers and by chairing a corporate quality committee that would meet monthly to review the program's progress.

Harwood agreed to the program, but one of the group vice presidents had serious concerns, typical of the conventional wisdom, about the quality department abdicating its role of keeping the people honest with regard to quality. Since the manager of the division chosen to serve as the pilot site was anxious to get going on the program, approval to begin was given with the understanding that such questions would be answered to corporate satisfaction before the program was adopted companywide.

Reorganization of the Quality Department

The first of two organizational steps was taken in early 1980. This step included a series of organization changes that decentralized the quality functions into the operating groups. Starting in the Analog Division, the plan was to proceed throughout the other product divisions and manufacturing operations so that by the end of 1980 the transition would be completed. As McKenzie explained:

> The essence of the reorganization consisted of consolidating the various quality activities—wafer fabrication quality control (QC), product assurance, electrical sort quality control, quality engineering, and reliability engineering—under the Divisional Quality/Reliability Assurance (QRA) managers. The QRA managers became direct members of the division vice presidents' staffs; the previous structure had them reporting to Corporate Q&R. In the manufacturing/operations groups a similar transition was accomplished with Assembly and Incoming QC. The Assembly QC functions became part of the

Exhibit 9   Q&R Organization Evolution

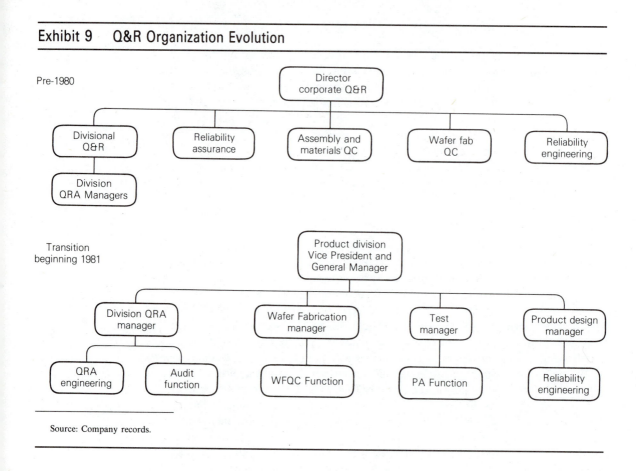

Source: Company records.

Sunnyvale Manufacturing operation, and Incoming QC was transferred to Material Control (Purchasing). (See Exhibit 9).

The fundamental reason behind this organizational change was to put the control tools into the hands of the responsible parties. We hoped this would generate a team atmosphere and a sense of ownership. By eliminating the check-and-balance system which had existed, it was hoped that there would be an intensification in the involvement with quality at the earliest possible time and lowest possible level. The greatest benefit was expected to come from stressing prevention instead of inspection and corrective action after the fact.

By the end of 1980 Corporate Q&R would consist of the five functional activities it had prior to the transition but with different objectives. Elimination of the inspection function would make it possible for Corporate Q&R to improve planning and overview activities. In addition to previous activities—such as qualification programs, corrective action, and monitors/audits—anticipated new corporate responsibilities included data compilation/trend analysis, corporate quality systems standards/procedures, training, quality improvement, and prevention programs.

STATUS OF THE QUALITY IMPROVEMENT PROGRAM
(April 1980)

While the pilot program had been set up to run from early 1980 through November of 1980, by April McKenzie and his Q&R management people felt a need to reassess their progress to date and decide just which avenues should be pursued, and how fast, over the next several months. While external (competitor and customer) pressures were adding support to the types of ideas incorporated in the quality improvement program, McKenzie and his people were concerned that they not confuse their own enthusiasm for and agreement on the program with that in the rest of the organization. Thus, in late March, McKenzie asked his group to provide him with information on the progress they thought Signetics had made over the preceding several months and to identify some of the major options that might be pursued as further steps in Signetics' quality improvement efforts.

As McKenzie reviewed these reports, he concluded that significant progress had been made among his own quality and reliability management people with regard to terminology and definitions. Some things that seemed to be clearly in place included:

1. The Q&R managers generally understood the philosophy change represented by the decentralization of the Q&R function (illustrated in Exhibit 5). While that decentralization was still in progress, at least those managers whose reporting relationships would be directly affected seemed to have a good understanding of what those organizational changes hoped to accomplish.
2. "Quality" had been redefined as "conformance to specification." Q&R people seemed to be in general agreement that everyone should "perform exactly like the stated requirements or cause those requirements to be officially changed to what the process could produce and what the customers really wanted."
3. The Q&R group agreed that the major thrust of the improvement program was to stress prevention rather than correction. The notions that "it is better to plan for quality than to screen for it" and that "mistakes are not a way of life" seemed to be tying in nicely with the belief that a zero defects philosophy could be developed.

While McKenzie felt confident that a strong consensus had formed within his own Q&R group, it was clear that others within the company still had a long way to go. One aspect of this was that of measurement and reporting. As part of the quality improvement program, McKenzie and his group had decided that the cost of nonconformance should be used as the performance measure for quality. Working with the financial controller, they proposed measurement procedures aimed at identifying the cost of "not doing things right the first time." As shown in Exhibit 10, this approach required data gathering and reporting on a variety of dimensions. While those procedures were not yet functioning, it was clear that there was already some growing opposition to this whole notion of the cost of poor quality. For some in accounting this looked like a lot of work, and they were already under pressure as an "overhead group" to keep the costs of accounting under control. A number of

---

Exhibit 10   Cost of Nonconformance

Internal
Rework
Scrap
Yield loss—standard is 100 percent
Screens
Corrective actions

External
Customer returns
Failure analysis (field failures)

Appraisal
Quality costs (QA/QC)—inspections
Production—test/inspection
Reliability engineering monitors (SURE)

Prevention
Training
Reliability (testing/qualifications)
Quality activities—quality circles/qualification engineering
Preventative maintenance/calibrations
Design reviews and process release interviews

---

line managers had voiced considerable doubt both as to the likelihood of ever getting and maintaining accurate data on the factors in Exhibit 10 and the negative motivational impact of telling manufacturing that their poor quality was the source of 15–20 percent (the preliminary number cited by Q&R) of total costs.

A second aspect of measurement and reporting that was still in the early stages of implementation was the inclusion of quality, both in each manager's job specifications and in his or her responsibility, measures, and objectives statement. While those involved in the pilot program seemed to be making good progress on this, it had been hoped that the entire organization would adopt it in 1980. However, the results seemed to be mixed, depending on the division and the level of support coming from division senior management. For many managers it looked like another "procedure" that kept them from their real task of producing product to meet customer needs at a profit (that is, emphasis on volume, delivery, and profit).

McKenzie and his people also had been able to gather some information about the attitudes of managers throughout the company. As McKenzie had anticipated, the behavior and response varied from extremely negative to extremely positive. At the former end of the spectrum was the whole notion of the quality improvement program of keeping people honest and quality having to compete with productivity, which was already lower than it should have been. Clearly, they hadn't made much progress in areas where such a view prevailed.

At the other end were the results achieved to date in the Orem, Utah, plant, which was part of the pilot program. The plant manager, Dennis Peasenell, was extremely enthusiastic about the program, and performance statistics already indicated that:

- Wafer lines were running at rates consistently higher than both the U.S. industry average and the plant's own 1979 performance.

- The number of defective circuits uncovered in destructive physical analysis performed in Sunnyvale on Orem-made products had plummeted from 12 percent to something down in the 1 to 2 percent range.
- One fab line seemed well on its way to doubling the number of good dies per wafer and expected to reach that goal in another three months.
- Reworks had declined from 20 percent in 1979 to what the plant manager projected would be 2 percent by the end of 1980 if the current trend continued.

McKenzie and his people were extremely pleased with the results at the Orem plant. The plant manager was highly committed, as was his boss; several other people were also playing key roles, including the work force, which seemed to be particularly receptive to the whole idea. The results had come not from simply following a 14-step program, but from broad-based support and commitment to the entire philosophy.

MAJOR OPTIONS FOR FUTURE QUALITY
IMPROVEMENT ACTIONS

McKenzie had also asked his managers to think about what additional projects might support Signetics' quality improvement activities. Based on his discussions with several of his managers, as well as many of the other managers throughout Signetics, he saw three major areas that might be pursued at various activity levels or in various sequences during coming months. These grouped roughly into internal activities (aimed at Signetics' own employees and managers), external activities involving materials suppliers and vendors, and activities involving customers. The commitment to each of these three areas could range from very low to that required for a significant change in direction.

Possible Vendor-Related Activities

One type of purchasing and supplier-related activity that had already received some discussion within Signetics was what McKenzie viewed as an educational program for suppliers. While not yet completely defined, it would include discussing specifications with suppliers, giving them exposure to the terminology and framework being used within Signetics, and gradually trying to improve their adherence to specifications. Given the range of suppliers, their sizes, current levels of quality, and various orientations, even such an educational program could take a significant amount of time and resources (on the order of three or four work years) on Signetics' part.

Another option that McKenzie was considering amounted to a shock treatment for Signetics' suppliers. The Signetics purchasing manager, who had been with the firm 18 years, prided himself on never shutting down a production line because of a lack of components. Although that was an admirable record, Q&R had found that many incoming materials did not meet Signetics' stated specifications (specs). Incoming materials were being put into one of three categories when they arrived at the plant: acceptable because they met specs; returned to the vendor because they were totally unacceptable; or set aside because even though they did not fully meet specs they probably could be used with some modification to keep production lines running. As Q&R had examined Signetics' behavior with regard to these three categories, they found that those items traditionally set aside (about 15 percent of all incoming materials) eventually got "waived" into production because they were needed immediately. It was then production's job to make them usable.

A radical approach to dealing with vendor quality would require convincing the purchasing and production managers to eliminate the "waived" category so that there would be only two categories in which materials could be placed upon receipt—either they would meet specs and move into production or they would not meet specs and would be returned immediately. McKenzie knew that purchasing would view an immediate shift to such a policy as disastrous to the company's reputation among its vendors. Production, too, would view such a policy as disastrous to its productivity and shipment schedules. Thus, if such a program were to be undertaken, Q&R would have to convince Signetics' own purchasing department that it made sense and also to convince vendors of the need to change their behavior. Moreover, they would need the cooperation of the plant so that materials would be rejected when they didn't meet specifications, no matter how badly they were needed.

Although there were several drawbacks to such an approach (and considerable risks if it was adopted and failed), McKenzie also thought it had many attractions. One of these was that if it could be done and adhered to, he felt certain that most vendors would get very involved in figuring out either how to meet Signetics' specs or convincing the company as to why a different and more appropriate set of specs should be adopted. This source of ideas for quality improvements might be very helpful throughout the Signetics organization and lead to higher quality products going to customers. He also felt that such a radical change in policy would provide a clear signal, not only to vendors but to everybody within Signetics, that the company was serious about quality and was making a major reorientation in its position.

Internal Signetics Projects

When the pilot program was adopted in 1980 the plan had been to work with a single part of the Signetics organization to get it to assimilate the Crosby 14-point framework for quality, to incorporate a quality objective in each person's RMO, and to establish procedures for timely data collection and feedback to management on the cost of nonconformance. It was hoped, in addition, that some significant improvements in the quality performance in that pilot organization would take place, but the pilot program was viewed primarily as establishing the groundwork for a subsequent significant improvement in Signetics' quality efforts. Debugging the measurement of the cost of nonconformance, making sure that the other management procedures required to support the RMO program and the new philosophy were in place, and beginning the decentralization of the Q&R organization were the pilot program's primary goals.

One option available to McKenzie with regard to Signetics' internal quality improvement efforts was to continue the pilot program and simply to extend it to the rest of the organization by the end of 1980. That had been the original plan; this option was simply to stick with that for the next several months, at least as far as the internal quality improvement efforts were concerned.

A very different kind of option had been triggered by the significant progress that had already been made in the wafer fabrication and test operations in Orem, Utah. It now appeared feasible to think about taking something like the Orem operation and using it not only as a pilot program for procedural and groundwork-type changes, but also to demonstrate what might be possible in other parts of the organization. This would involve going well beyond the pilot program stage for Orem and setting some very significant targets for the remainder of 1980. As those targets were met, Orem might well become the "model" within the company. If this were done, the types of activities that might be adopted included quality circles, increased commitment to process changes that produced more reliable products, and revising product designs to improve quality. (In a sense, this would amount to giving the Orem operation first priority on resources that were generally shared across multiple facilities.)

While McKenzie was sure that Dennis Peasenell, the plant manager in Orem, would be pleased to take on this challenge (and in fact was already taking a lot of initiative in this direction), he also saw potential problems in taking resources from other operations—which might be able to show a better payback and greater need—and giving them to Orem. In addition, if the Orem operation set its goals too high and didn't make them, it might be a major setback for the overall program.

Customer-Linked Quality Improvement Activities

As part of the original proposal for the quality improvement program, McKenzie and his Q&R group had anticipated the development of an atmosphere of open communication with customers. At a minimum this included presentations to each of the company's major customers explaining Signetics' commitment to quality. From preliminary discussions with selected customers it was anticipated that those like the military, who had always emphasized high reliability, would simply respond by congratulating Signetics on finally "getting with it." Other industrial customers who viewed quality as a particularly important aspect of their business were also likely to have high praise for Signetics' efforts. However, those firms who viewed quality in their own organization as a "police function" would probably be unimpressed by such a presentation. Even among those customers who would applaud Signetics' efforts, it was unclear whether such presentations would have any significant impact on Signetics' ability to attract new business. Thus, the results were likely to be a gradual change in Signetics' image as a supplier. This would become a factor in customer decisions only as Signetics' actual performance improved relative to that of competitors.

An alternative project linking Signetics' efforts directly with customer efforts had recently surfaced in the Automotive Division and was referred to as the parts-per-million program. This program represented a radical departure from what had been Signetics' traditional relationship with its customers. In fact, it was a type of approach that Signetics had rejected, at least implicitly, a few years earlier.

During the last half of the 70s, Signetics, like many other American semiconductor manufacturers, had been approached by Japanese firms looking for additional suppliers. However, Japanese quality requirements appeared formidable and unfamiliar to most potential American suppliers, including Signetics. Since World War II American manufacturers had largely utilized the AQL (acceptable quality level) criterion. AQLs that allowed more than 1 percent defects were common in U.S. industry.

In the late 1970s potential Japanese semiconductor customers required much lower levels, stating quality requirements in terms of PPM (parts-per-million). These firms were perceived as asking for legal guarantees on the level of commitment that a firm like Signetics would make to improve quality and specifying targets of performance that would change over time. Under such a PPM program defect levels less than 0.1 percent were not uncommon goals. Because of the liability issue and the difficulty of working with an entirely new type of customer under such stringent specifications, Signetics had chosen not to negotiate contracts with Japanese firms.

In late 1979 Signetics was approached by a U.S. automotive parts manufacturer which required extremely high IC quality levels to assure reliability through a five-year, 50,000-mile auto warranty period. In a presentation to Signetics management the manufacturer spelled out its quality requirements for the coming years, which included a failure rate of no more than 200 parts-per-million, a level significantly lower than that achieved by most U.S. IC manufacturers.

Military contracts had required similar low defect rates for years, but the semiconductor industry had traditionally filled those contracts through 100 percent testing. While this tended to weed out any defective parts before delivery to the customer, such testing was applied to normal production runs, significantly increasing the cost per unit shipped. Generally, military contracts for high reliability (hi-rel) products had been priced at levels that covered the additional testing and screening costs incurred by the semiconductor manufacturers and still made the business very attractive.

With a major prospective automotive customer wanting a parts-per-million program, there was a sudden interest on the part of Signetics in considering such an agreement. In addition, with increasing pressure for improved quality coming from international competitors, it was clear that this particular proposal might be a good learning experience for the company. This prospect made Signetics somewhat nervous, however, since it required not just higher testing levels but a commitment to eliminate the causes of poor quality, that is, potential problems in engineering/design, manufacturing processes, work force procedures, material defects, and so on.

Tom Endicott, PPM program manager in the Automotive Division, felt that this appeared to be a business where Signetics could achieve a substantial market share if it moved quickly. However, accepting the contract meant making a significant—and relatively open-ended—commitment. Not only would Signetics have to commit resources to set up a new manufacturing line (at a cost of more than $15 million) but, since the automotive division was basically a marketing operation, pursuing this particular program would require bringing together people from wafer fabrication, assembly production, and design into a much closer working arrangement than currently existed. Endicott felt that they couldn't really separate those functions if a true PPM program were to be successful, because what one function did might well put others beyond the limits of their own technical capabilities.

Signetics management recognized that the proposed PPM automotive relationship would be unique. As part of the contract the customer was prepared to supply capital for development and testing, to negotiate lead times acceptable to both parties, and to specify minimum order values with penalty payments in the event of future contract cancellations. While this was fairly standard for large supply contracts, the arrangement would also involve both the customer and Signetics in identifying types of defects and their sources. This represented an unusual relationship between customer and supplier and required a high level of teamwork: "our product problems" would be solved jointly. In the PPM program were to be truly successful, the automotive parts manufacturer would have to participate in Signetics' decision-making process, systems would have to be agreed to, and a technical interchange would have to be established. (Q&R's preliminary estimates of the internal feedback activities required to support the PPM effort are summarized in Exhibit 11.)

McKenzie felt that this option had perhaps the greatest leverage of any being considered, but also held some of the greatest risks. On the positive side, the parts-per-million concept complemented the zero defects philosophy that Signetics was already introducing internally. Both approaches defined quality as "performance to specification." PPM, however, was both a concept and a precise measurement of defects arrived at through statistical analysis, testing, materials, and assemblies. If pursued, it was intended to reduce the level of unacceptable product being produced by at least an order of magnitude. Zero defects, on the other hand, offered an overall philosophy but did not necessarily include such precise and significant targets.

Exhibit 11   PPM Assembly/Test Operations—Feedback Requirements

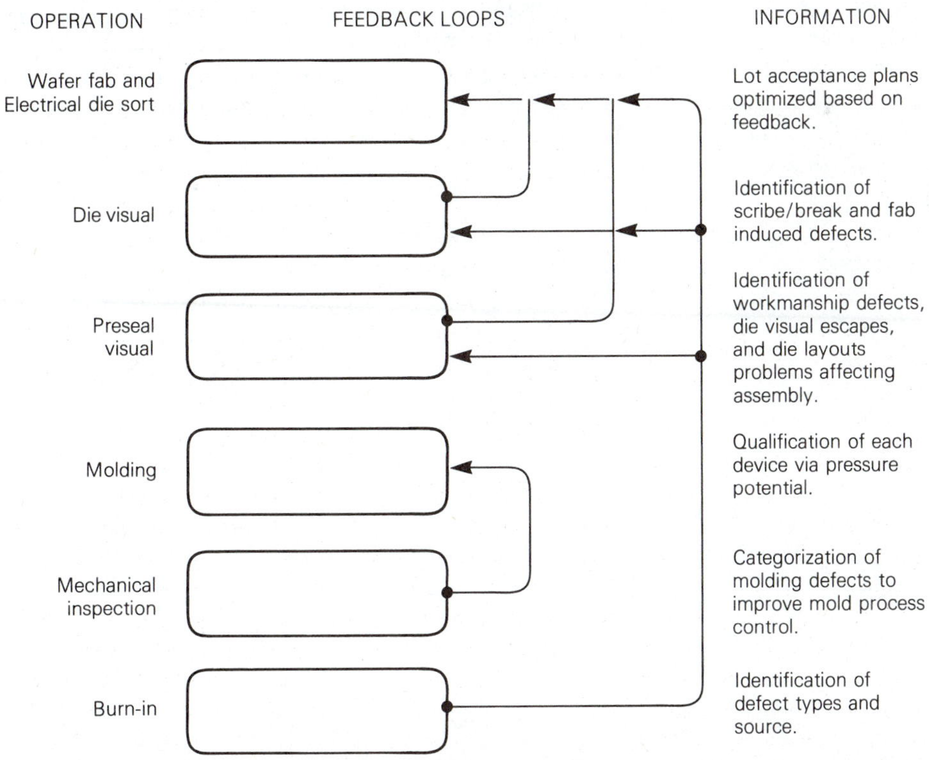

OPERATION	FEEDBACK LOOPS	INFORMATION
Wafer fab and Electrical die sort		Lot acceptance plans optimized based on feedback.
Die visual		Identification of scribe/break and fab induced defects.
Preseal visual		Identification of workmanship defects, die visual escapes, and die layouts problems affecting assembly.
Molding		Qualification of each device via pressure potential.
Mechanical inspection		Categorization of molding defects to improve mold process control.
Burn-in		Identification of defect types and source.

Such a PPM program would clearly demonstrate commitment to those within Signetics' own organization, as well as to customers. There was the possibility, however, that in order to solve some problems within the PPM framework, Signetics would have to commit significantly more resources than was currently envisioned. That is, until the contract was undertaken and the feedback loops started to operate, Signetics would not know just what kinds of resources and what level of resource commitments would be required. Thus, it could find itself having to choose between not living up to its part of the contract and committing resources that would cause the contract to be unprofitable.

Worse, this might prevent Signetics from committing resources to other potentially more profitable projects and products. Thus, if this approach were to have any hope of being successful, Signetics would have to commit itself philosophically and then follow through, even if, operationally, it became uncomfortable to do so. McKenzie wasn't sure the company was far enough along in its own internal quality improvement efforts to make such an ironclad commitment.

A TIME FOR DECISION

As McKenzie reviewed these alternatives and thought about comments he'd received from his colleagues in the past few weeks, he knew that the PPM proposal required an immediate decision. While Signetics might currently have the leading edge in getting that contract, there were certain to be other suppliers who would take over if Signetics chose not to accept the offer within the next week or two. The other alternatives did not present any pressing need for decision—they could simply continue with the pilot program and gradually educate vendors as originally planned. However, McKenzie felt he should consider the full set of options as he made this PPM decision.

CASE 32   VILLAGE INN*

The Village Inn, located on Bermuda Boulevard in San Diego, was only a few blocks away from San Diego State University and was within several miles of some of California's largest tourist attractions. Visiting lecturers, speakers, professors interviewing for jobs, and people attending conferences at the university resulted in a considerable amount of business for Village Inn.

The Inn was also near a concentrated area of light and heavy industry. The largest shopping mall in San Diego was under construction across the street from the Inn. A relatively new VA hospital and the University Community Hospital were both located within one mile. The Inn's very favorable locational features, together with the fact that it was a franchise of a major national noted chain, had made it a profitable investment. During the past 12 months the Inn had an average occupancy rate of between 65 and 70 percent, some 15 or more percentage points above the break-even occupancy rate of 50 percent.

Although the Village Inn had only modest competition from other hotel or motel facilities in the immediate vicinity, a new Travelodge Inn was under construction next door. The other closest competitors were nearly three miles away at the intersection of Bermuda Boulevard and Interstate 8. Village Inn offered a full range of services to its guests, including a restaurant and bar. The new Travelodge next door was going to have just a coffee shop. Insofar as its restaurant/bar business was concerned, the Village Inn's strongest competitor was the popular priced University Restaurant, two blocks away. Village Inn did not consider its own food service operations to be in close competition with the area's fast-food franchises or with higher priced restaurants.

OWNERSHIP OF VILLAGE INN

Mr. Johnson, a native of Oregon, opened the first Village Inn in San Diego in 1958. Since that time he had shared ownership in 15 other Village Inns, several which were in the San Diego area. He opened the Bermuda Boulevard Inn in October 1966. Prior to his focusing on the motel and restaurant business, Johnson had owned and operated a furniture store and a casket manufacturing plant. A suggestion from a business associate in Oregon influenced his decision to seek out Village Inn franchises and get into the motel business. In some of his Village Inn locations Johnson leased out the restaurant operations; however, the restaurant and bar at the Bermuda Boulevard Village Inn was not leased out. Johnson felt that because the occupancy rate at this location was so favorable it was more profitable to own and operate these facilities himself.

---

* Prepared by Diana Johnston, Russ King, and Professor Jay T. Knippen, the University of South Florida.

MANAGEMENT OF THE INN

Johnson had employed Mrs. Deeks as the innkeeper and manager of the entire operation. She had worked in Village Inns for the past seven and one half years. Previously Deeks had done administrative work for San Diego General Hospital and before that had been employed as a photo lab technician for two years. Her experience in the motel/restaurant business included working for several restaurants and lounges for five years as a cocktail waitress just prior to joining Village Inns.

Deeks stated that her main reason for going to work for Village Inns was because she felt there was more money to be made as a waitress than anything else she had tried. Her formal education for her present position of innkeeper consisted of a three-week training course at the Home Office Training Center in Louisville, Kentucky, and one-week refresher courses each year at the Training Center.

Recently the assistant innkeeper had been promoted and transferred to another location. Both Johnson and Deeks agreed that there was a pressing need to fill the vacancy quickly. It was the assistant innkeeper's function to supervise the restaurant/bar area and this was the area which always presented the toughest problems to management. Unless the food was well prepared and the service was prompt, guests were quick to complain. Poor food service caused many of the frequent visitors to the area to prefer to stay at other motels. Moreover, it was hard to attract and maintain a sizable lunchtime clientele without having well-run restaurant facilities. With so many restaurant employees to supervise, menus to prepare, and food supplies to order, it was a constant day-to-day struggle to keep the restaurant operating smoothly and, equally important, to see that it made a profit. Deeks, with all of her other duties and responsibilities, simply did not have adequate time to give the restaurant/bar enough close supervision by herself.

While searching for a replacement, Johnson by chance happened to see a feature article in the *Village Inn Magazine,* a monthly publication of the Village Inns of America chain—copies of which were placed in all of the guest rooms of the Inns, describing the operation of a successful Village Inn in nearby San Bernardino. The article caught Johnson's attention because it described how the Inn at San Bernardino had gained popularity and acclaim from guests because of the good food and fast service provided by the head chef of the restaurant operations. After showing the article to Deeks, Johnson wasted no time in getting in touch with the head chef of that Inn, Mr. Bernie, and persuading him to assume the new role of restaurant/bar manager for the Bermuda Boulevard Village Inn in San Diego.

FOOD SERVICE FACILITIES AND LAYOUT

Exhibit 1 depicts the arrangement of the lobby area and food service facilities at the Inn. A brief description of the restaurant/bar area follows.

Restaurant   The restaurant itself consisted of a dining room which seated 74 people, a coffee shop which seated 62 persons, and a bar which seated 35 people. The Inn's banquet facilities were just behind the main dining room and could seat 125 people.

Exhibit 1

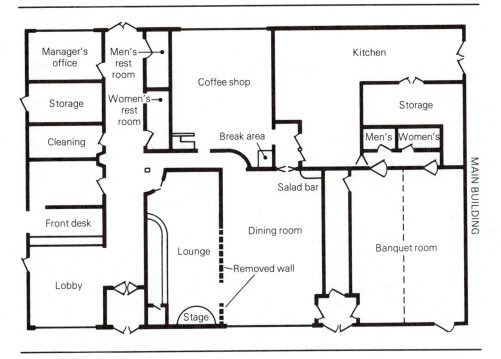

The essential role of the restaurant and bar area was to provide pleasant and convenient facilities for the Inn's guests. The contractual franchise agreements with the national chain required all owners to provide these services in conjunction with the overnight accommodations. There were periodic inspections of the facilities by a representative from Village Inn's corporate officer. Village Inn required each franchisee to comply with minimum standards for its food service facilities in an effort to promote comparability and ensure attractiveness. Restaurant services were to be available to guests from 6:30 A.M. until 11 P.M.

Coffee Shop   The coffee shop was open from 6:30 A.M. to 11 A.M. to serve breakfast to motel guests. At 11 A.M. these facilities were closed and the main dining area was opened. The coffee shop was occasionally used beyond scheduled hours to serve customers for lunch and dinner when there was an overflow from the dining area. Tables in both the coffee shop and the dining room were decorated and set uniformly.

Dining Room   The dining area was open from 11 A.M. until 11 P.M. It was located next to the lounge and was physically separated from the coffee shop by a wall. The lunch and dinner offerings featured a salad bar along with menu items which were somewhat uniform with other Village Inns and which were prescribed by the franchise agreement. However, menu deviations were allowed if approved by corporate representatives from Village Inn's central office.

Bar   The bar, separated from the dining room by a partition, was open for business from 10 A.M. until 1 A.M. It had tables and booths and customers who preferred to do so could have their food served to them in the bar area. A small dance floor was located in front of the entertainer stage near the front window; a juke box furnished music when there was no live entertainment. A small bar stockroom was located at one end of the bar counter. The cash register area was centrally located to receive payments from customers in all three areas—dining room, coffee shop, and bar.

Kitchen   The kitchen facilities, located beside the coffee shop and dining room, had a stainless steel counter at the entrance door from the restaurant area. It was here that waitresses turned orders in to the cooks and that the cooks served the orders up to the waitresses. The cooking area was located in the center of the room and sinks were located along the sides of the kitchen.

RESTAURANT OPERATIONS

As was to be expected, customers' activity in the restaurant area fluctuated widely. Busy periods were generally at the traditional meal hours, but the peak load at any given mealtime period often varied by as much as an hour from one day to the next. At lunchtime, for example, customers sometimes seemed to come all at once, while on other days the arrival times were more evenly distributed throughout the 11:30 A.M. to 1:30 P.M. interval. Experience had shown that these peaks were hard to anticipate and that the staff had to be prepared for whatever occurred. Moreover, on Monday, Tuesday, Wednesday, and Thursday evenings, the customers were mostly business people, sales representatives, and university visitors, whereas on weekends there were more family travelers. Because of the Inn's location, its clientele consisted somewhat more of the former than the latter.

The Inn's restaurant business was also subject to some seasonal fluctuations. There were always a certain number of people who spent the winter in Southern California to escape the harsh northern and Canadian winters; these included not only winter tourists but also the "Canadian Snow Birds" who came to Southern California to work in the late fall and returned to Canada in March or April. In addition, the Inn's business picked up noticeably during the June graduation exercises at San Diego State University and during the week when the fall term opened. By and large the daily fluctuations were harder to predict than the seasonal fluctuations.

RESTAURANT STAFFING

Because of the alternating between peak periods and slack periods, the employees in the food service area tended to work together, take breaks together, and eat their meals together. In commenting on the kind of people who tended to work in hotel-motel operations, Deeks indicated that employees were typically gregarious and were there because they wanted to be. They had to contend with an uneven work pace, a low-wage scale (often no more than the minimum wage), and irregular working hours. Since waitresses often earned only a token wage ($0.75 to $1 per hour) and relied mainly on tips for their income, they could not afford many "slow days" or "bad days" at work. Their livelihood and degree of service was dependent upon how well they greeted customers, a friendly smile, prompt service, and, in general, an ability to make customers feel satisfied with the attention they received. When the food was cold or ill-prepared or the service less than expected, customers left smaller tips and the waitresses' disgruntlement carried over to the kitchen staff, the hostess, and the busboys. But even more disruptive than the loss of tips were the customers who complained directly to the Inn's management; if this occurred frequently then the pressure and anxiety felt by the restaurant staff increased noticeably. Deeks noted that people who could not adjust to the tempo and temperament of the restaurant business usually did not stay in it long. She noted further that it was extremely difficult to "standardize" the human service aspects of the restaurant business and that trying to attract and keep a good, experienced food service staff was a challenging task.

Deeks supplied the following job descriptions of the restaurant staff. These descriptions, however, came from her thoughts and perceptions and had never been formally set forth in writing to the Inn's employees:

Bartender   Cut up fruit for drinks, wash glasses, serve counter drinks, clean behind bar, stock liquor and mixes, stock beer, fill room service orders, ring up checks, balance register, and help with inventory.

Hostess/Cashier   Take room service orders, seat guests, deliver menu, direct seating, supervise waitresses and busboys, perform any functions within their prescribed area that speeds service, check out customers from dining area, check out register, file cash register receipts, and assign stations.

Waitresses   Take food orders, deliver orders to kitchen, pick up and serve orders, serve food and beverages, and perform any function that speeds service as directed by the hostess.

Busboys   Bus tables, put clean place settings on tables, clean dining rooms, stock supplies, take ice to all areas, get supplies for cooks, help set up banquets, deliver room service orders, help with maintenance, and perform any function that will speed service as directed by the hostess and manager.

Dishwasher   Wash dishes, pots, and pans, sweep and mop floors.

Cook   Prepare meals, schedule meals for prep cook, assist management in stock orders, receive food supplies, supervise and direct kitchen help, and assist management in menu changes. Report to management any changes or problems that occur.

Prep Cook   Prepare all food that the cook needs for the dinner and evening meals. Assist cook in any meal preparation that is necessary to expedite service to guests. Inform cook of any problems that need attention and help cook see that facilities are clean at all times.

Breakfast Cook   Open the kitchen in the morning. Prepare breakfast food for motel guests. Provide information necessary to maintain in-stock supplies.

MR. BERNIE

When Mr. Bernie arrived to assumed his new duties as restaurant/bar manager, he wasted no time in demanding and receiving total obedience from the personnel under his direction. He made it clear that he would not tolerate insubordination and that the consequence would be immediate discharge. Although Bernie stayed in his new job less than three months (from January to March), he nonetheless created an almost instantaneous climate of ill will and hatred with his subordinates. The intense dislike for Bernie was voiced by nearly every employee. One example of this was a statement by Elaine, the day hostess/cashier who had been employed in this capacity for the past two and one half years: "I enjoy my job because I like people. But Mr. Bernie was something else! I generally do not use this term in my vocabulary, but Mr. Bernie was a bastard from the day he arrived until the day he left."

Bernie's unpopularity was further brought out by a busboy's impromptu comment. Elaine was trying to possibly justify Bernie's temperament by pointing out that he was not of American nationality. Unable to recall his nationality she inquired of a nearby busboy if he could remember. The busboy immediately and sincerely replied, "He crawled out from under a rock."

Bernie spent considerable time trying to impress upon his staff the "right way" (his way) of accomplishing tasks (see Exhibits 2 and 3). Most of the employees resented Bernie's close supervision. Ann, a veteran employee and waitress, describing her resentment, said, "No one really needs to supervise us, especially the way Mr. Bernie stood over us. Usually the hostess is the supervisor, but all the old girls know what they are doing and everyone does their job."

Although an intense dislike for Bernie was foremost in the minds of the employees, he did manage to make a number of improvements and innovations. Physical changes became obvious within all departments under his authority. In the kitchen a general

---

Exhibit 2   Memo Number One from Mr. Bernie to Food Service Staff

People,

   Please help keep the floor clean.
   If you drop something, pick it up.
   Wipe table off in a trash can.
   If you spill something the mops and brooms are outside.
   It's no fun scrubbing the floor Saturday, and if you don't believe it, be here Saturday night at 11:00 P.M.

                                                                Mr. "B"

Exhibit 3   Memo Number Two from Mr. Bernie to Food Service Staff

---

March 11

TO ALL FOOD AND BEVERAGE EMPLOYEES:

I wish to thank each and every one of you for the very good job you have done in the past two weeks. The service has greatly improved on both shifts. There has been a better customer/employee relationship, but there is a long way to go yet. We are nearing the end of our winter season so it is most important to all of us that we concentrate on more service in order to obtain a local year-round business. Appearance, neatness, and good conduct on the floor will obtain this, along with good food.

A waitress and busboy are like salesmen. The hostess/cashier can determine the quality of service in this organization.

I expect my waitresses while on duty to be on the dining room cafe floor at all times. I should find waitresses and busboys at the cashier stand only when getting a ticket or paying a check.

I smoke myself—probably more than the rest of you put together. Your service area is beginning to look like a cigarette factory. I do not expect people to give up their smoking habit, but I do expect them to curtail to the rules and regulations of Village Inn, Inc., and those of the health department, "No Smoking on Premises." I would not like to enforce the law.

In the last two weeks I have walked into the operation after a busy breakfast or dinner and found everyone sitting around the first three booths of the cafe. I do not say it cannot be used, but when I find no waitresses on either floor day or night and customers have to call for service because waitresses are off the floor, I believe each waitress and busboy on all shifts should ask themselves one thing; what kind of service would I like if I were a guest? There is only one thing I know, in this part of California when the tourist is gone, half of the employees are worked on a part-time basis, which is not good on anyone's pocketbook. Therefore, I say let's not be second best but let's be first.

With regard to employees taking their meal breaks, I do not wish to schedule them but I cannot have everyone eating at once. Busboys will eat one at a time.

Thank you once again for your good performance.

                                                                Mr. "B"

---

cleanup campaign was instituted, an order spindle was added, and new oven equipment installed. In the coffee shop and restaurant new silverware, china, and glasses were purchased, and the menu was improved and complemented by the use of a salad bar. *Explicit* work duties were written and verbally defined to all employees under Bernie.

Bernie separated the cashier/hostess function into two distinct jobs. The cashier was confined to the cash register station and given instructions as to the duties she was to perform in that area. The hostess was given instructions to greet people, seat them, and supply menus. When Bernie was absent, he instructed the hostess to see that the waitresses and busboys carried out their jobs efficiently and effectively. According to Gay, one of the two day hostesses:

When Mr. Bernie was here I never had any employee problems. Waitresses and busboys did what I asked. But now if we have a busboy absent or we are crowded, some of the waitresses inform me they will not bus tables. Today there's no one in charge of anything. We need more employees here. It is always better to have more help than not enough. That's one thing Mr. Bernie did, he doubled the help the day he came.

The changes that Bernie instituted regarding the waitresses were significant in several aspects. All waitresses were required to wear fitted uniforms. This necessitated them driving across town for a uniform fitting. Bernie's detailed scrutinizing consisted of specific instructions on how to serve customers and which station locations each waitress would serve. He even went as far as to show them how to wrap the silverware and the napkins and gave explicit instructions to veteran waitresses on how to fill out the order tickets.

Bernie had the wall between the dining room and bar taken down. He then brought in an entertainer who supplied dinner music for both the restaurant and bar guests. Today the waitresses are getting some dysfunctional effects from this innovation; according to one:

> Mr. Bernie brought in an organ player. While this was conducive to a more pleasant dining atmosphere, the organist was not good enough to keep the people beyond their meal. But now that Mr. Bernie is gone our new entertainer is causing some serious problems. For example, last night I had a family of five sit at a table in my station for two and a half hours after their dinner. If people won't leave and they won't buy drinks, I can't make tips.

Bernie instilled an atmosphere of insecurity and day-to-day doubt in the minds of the employees as to how long they could weather the barrage of innovation and directives. To some, just remaining on the job became a challenge in itself. Elaine (the day hostess) phrased it in this manner:

> I have been employed with the Village Inn for almost two and one half years. I have worked most of my life and have never felt insecure in any of my jobs. The last job I held was a swimming instructor for 10 years with the Academy of Holy Names in San Diego. The reason I had to leave there was because of the change in the educational background requirement which called for a college degree.
>
> My children are all college graduates with highly responsible positions. They achieved this by hard work. I instilled this in their minds because I am a hard worker. But when Mr. Bernie was here, I experienced for the first time in my life the feeling of not knowing from one day to the next if my job would be there when I came to work. What few personnel he failed to drive away, he fired.

Linda, who was a bartender in the lounge area, commented further on Bernie's supervisory tactics:

> Bernie was a rover. When he walked into an area, including my area, the bar, he could not stand to see someone not involved with busy work. He even made me clean under the bar on the customer's side. I'm not a maid and I often wanted to tell him so. But the way he was hiring and firing employees, I just kept my mouth closed and did as he told me. My experiences with Mr. Bernie were nothing compared to the relationship he had with the busboys. From the bar he would sneak around and watch them in the dining area. If they did anything the least bit out of line, he would call them aside and give them lectures that could last for half an hour. He really treated the busboys like the scum of the earth. When the boys did get a break, they would come over to the bar and get a coke and ice. You know, he even started charging them 25 cents for that!

Sam, a cook hired by Bernie, offered a slightly different perspective view of Bernie:

> My wife was working here as a hostess and I used to bring her to work everyday. One day I came in with her and for some reason they were short of help in the kitchen. They needed a dishwasher. I was sitting in the coffee shop and Mr. Bernie walked over and asked me if I could use a job. I had been interested in cooking ever since I was in the Navy. There are two things you can do in your spare time in the Navy . . . drink and chase women or find a hobby. I found a hobby, which was cooking. On my two days off I used to go down to the galley and help the cooks. There I learned everything I know today. When I got out of the service I worked as a prep cook in a restaurant in Pennsylvania for a year or so. My real specialty is soups, though. Anyway, I had been a dishwasher here for about two days when the cook walked off the job after three years of service here. Mr. Bernie came in and asked how I'd like to be the new cook and here I am today. Mr. Bernie really taught me a lot. He taught me that a restaurant has three things it must give a customer: service, good food, and a pleasing environment to dine. If you have these three, customers will return.
>
> I've spent most of my working career in the automotive business doing such things as driving trucks. But I'm really into this cooking thing. Mr. Bernie taught me that about 50 percent of the customers who come in and order from the menu have no idea what they are ordering. The menu is too complicated. The customer doesn't know what he thinks he ordered and what you think he ordered. Another thing that fascinates me is trying to think like the customer. His definition of rare, medium, and well done is altogether different from my idea of how it should be. One addition by Mr. Bernie was the salad bar. This is a tremendous help to my job. If the waitress can get to the customer before they go to the salad bar and take their order, this gives me plenty of lead time to be sure the meal will be cooked right and served in the attractive manner that Mr. Bernie was so particular about. This lead time is especially important on those days that we are unusually busy. For example, I have prepared as many as 250 meals on some days and as few as 40 on others.

The employees who left or were dismissed by Bernie included two hostesses, two waitresses (one had an employment record at the Inn that dated back five years), and two busboys. Two of the personnel that Bernie fired have since returned to their old jobs. One of the waitresses that subsequently was rehired described her reason for leaving as follows:

> I really enjoy being a waitress and have been here for about five years. The work isn't really too hard and the pay is good. I took all the "directives" I could take from Mr. Bernie! A week before he left, I gave my resignation and took a vacation. When I returned, I learned of his departure and here I am again. I'm really glad things have worked out as they did.

Deeks' opinion of Bernie's performance was one of general dissatisfaction with the way he handled his dealings with employees:

> Mr. Bernie was highly trained, but he was an introvert who stood over his subordinates and supervised everything they did. Cooks are a rare breed of people all to themselves. The help situation has changed greatly in the past few years. It used to be that you could give orders and tell people what they were supposed to do. Now, you have to treat them with "kid gloves" or they'll just quit and get a job down the street. This problem is particularly true with cooks. They are very tempermental and introverted and they expect to be treated like "prima donnas."

> Mr. Johnson and I really tried to work with Mr. Bernie during his 90-day trial period. We knew that terminating him without a replacement would be hard on us, but we had no choice. We are now without a restaurant/bar manager or assistant innkeeper. We have been looking for a replacement, but finding a person that is knowledgeable in both the hotel and restaurant management is something of a chore.

CONDITIONS AFTER MR. BERNIE'S DEPARTURE

Since Mr. Bernie had departed, the restaurant personnel were in general agreement that their operation was understaffed. Often guests were seated in both the dining area and coffee shop waiting to be served; even though the waitresses were apparently busy, many customers experienced waits of 20 to 30 minutes. Elaine, one of the two hostesses, explained the lack of prompt service as follows:

> The coffee shop is supposed to take care of the guests until 11 A.M. and then the restaurant part is to be opened. Mr. Bernie handled the situation differently than we do now. When he was here he would not open the dining hall in the morning no matter how crowded the coffee shop was. I can remember mornings when people were lined into the hallway and all the way outside the front door. I guess he knew two girls and two busboys could not handle two rooms.
>
> But today we handle the situations differently. If the coffee shop gets crowded or we have many dirty tables we open up both rooms. This really makes it hard on the girls trying to serve both rooms. What we generally have when this happens is poor service to all concerned and consequently some guests leave unhappy and without tipping the waitresses.

Ralph, a busboy, indicated the problem was not exclusively felt in the restaurant only. He seemed to feel the lack or absence of a manager was the primary problem:

> Mrs. Deeks just can't run this operation by herself. It is physically impossible for her to be here seven days a week from 6:30 A.M. until 11 P.M. and manage the kitchen, restaurant, bar, coffee shop, front desk, maid service, and maintenance crew all at the same time.

Some of the employees perceived their duties and functions differently. For instance, the restaurant's two day hostesses alternated work shifts. Elaine would seat customers, give them their menu, take beverages to customers to help out the waitresses, help out busing tables when it was very busy, and had very little to say in supervising the waitresses and busboys. On the other hand, the other day hostess, Gay, would seat customers and give them menus but would not do what she perceived to be the duties of waitresses and busboys. Instead, she exercised supervisory authority over these personnel and when they were not able to get everything done, she would try to find out why not, rather than doing them herself.

There were similar discrepancies in the ways the waitresses and busboys performed their duties. In some cases, waitresses would help busboys clear tables during overcrowded periods and busboys would also help out the waitresses by bringing water and coffee to the people who were waiting to be served. The other side of the coin occurred also. Some of the waitresses, particularly those who had been employed for some time, felt that it was the busboys' responsibility to clear tables and would not life a finger to help them. In these instances the busboys did not go out of their way to help the waitresses.

Gene, the other bartender, offered yet another view of the Inn's problems:

> You know, I could tell management a few things about the restaurant business if they asked me. I knew from the first day Mr. Bernie arrived that he wouldn't work out. But Mr. Bernie is not the only problem they had. One of the biggest problems they have with this restaurant is in the banquets they have. We have a luncheon here every week with such clubs as the Sertoma, Kiwanis, and the like. Their luncheons start at noon and last until 1:30 or so. Have you ever noticed how they park outside? Well, I'll tell you they park all over the front parking lot and when local people drive by they assume our restaurant is full and go on down the street. These businessmen tie up most of our help and yet the dining room may be empty. These banquet people don't buy drinks with lunch like the local businessmen do who take clients out to lunch and often have a bigger bar bill than their restaurant checks. There's only one successful way to have a banquet business and that's not next to your dining room. If the banquet room was on the opposite side of the restaurant, then it would be okay.

EMPLOYEE TRAINING

The Village Inn provided a minimal amount of job training for employees with the exception of the management staff. The contractual agreement between franchise owners and Village Inns of America required all innkeepers, assistant innkeepers, and restaurant managers to attend the Home Office Training Center within a year of being hired. They also had to attend refresher courses on a yearly basis.

The restaurant personnel, in contrast, were given little job training. Instead, efforts were made to hire cooks, waitresses, and bartenders who had previous experience in the field. But in practice this policy was not always adhered to—as was exemplified by the way Linda became a bartender:

> My training on the job was really short and sweet. Mr. Bernie came in one day and inquired, "How would you like to be a bartender?" At the same time he handed me a book on mixing drinks. I went home and studied it and "poof" I was a bartender.
>
> Within a short time on the job I began getting a lot of help and advice from the waitresses who came over to the bar for drink orders. Sometimes when we do get a drink mixup they are very nice about it. I've even had people from other departments in the Inn to help me when the situation called for it. One night I had two ladies in here, one from the "crazy house" and the other her bodyguard. After a few "shooters" as they referred to the drinks, they asked for their check. They wanted to use a credit card instead of paying cash. This was not a problem but so I would get my tip I offered to carry the check and credit card to the front desk. Then they said I would cheat them on their bill once I was out of their sight. The front desk man heard the hassle and came in and escorted the ladies to the desk. This type of working together happens here all the time. Mrs. Deeks, my boss, is really a nice person to work for. She doesn't come around very much, except if she needs information or to advise me about something.

PAY SCALES

Management indicated that there was a shortage of good employees and that a low pay scale was characteristic of the restaurant business. Some of the employees expressed their awareness of this also.

(Bartender) Linda: The pay scale is really low compared to other areas. My first job as a cocktail waitress in San Diego was in a dive downtown. They paid us $2 an hour plus tips, but the tips were lousy. Here they're paying $3 an hour plus tips which is somewhat better, but it's still way below the wages elsewhere. I really don't feel like I'm suited for this work, but I make more money at the bar than I did as a cocktail waitress.

(Hostess) Gay: I make $4 an hour here. With all the responsibility and experience I've had, the pay scale here compared to other parts of the country is deplorable. The busboys make almost as much as I do. They make $3.50 an hour plus 15 percent of the waitress's tips. Even though the pay scale is low, there is always overtime available to most of all of the employees who want it. My husband who is a cook here has worked 145 hours so far in this two-week pay period and he still has five more days to go.

Barb, one of the waitresses, further substantiated the availability of overtime by saying she got at least one hour overtime each day. She attributed the extra hours of overtime to the fact that the Inn's restaurant staff always seemed to have at least one person unexpectedly absent each day.

The problem in the restaurant was apparently compounded by the fact that it was operating with a minimum number of employees. Timmy, a busboy, indicated the wide range of activities that were expected of him and the other busboys:

> We do everything; I clean and bus tables, sweep floors, and do janitorial work. I don't mean in just my area either. If the front desk needs a porter or runner or if some type of room service is needed. I do that too. Mr. Bernie was really hard to work under but he always confined us to restaurant duties. When he was here we didn't do all those jobs outside our area. Those duties were handled by a front desk porter. But, I'd still rather have to do things all over the place than have to put up with Mr. Bernie.

SEARCHING FOR MR. BERNIE'S REPLACEMENT

In outlining her thoughts on trying to replace Bernie, Deeks stated:

> I really had a good track record with personnel before Mr. Bernie came along. I strongly objected to his dictatorial supervision. In my experience I have learned employees perform their jobs better when left alone most of the time. I once tried to set up off-job activities for my employees. I reserved a room at the hotel for employees to meet together after working hours to play cards and drink coffee. Unfortunately the room was not used enough to merit keeping it on reserve. However, I still support functions that the employees suggest. We are presently sponsoring a bowling team that two of my waitresses belong to.
>
> Most of the waitresses would rather work night shifts if they have their choice. Some of the girls have children and husbands that require them to be home at night. This balances the shifts real well. One reason I prefer to schedule the waitresses is because of peculiar problems which occur. For example, I have two extremely good

waitresses that will not work on Saturdays and Sundays. The other waitresses do not know this and I feel if I were to allow the hostess to do the scheduling I would have some immediate personnel problems. To further complicate any benefits that might be derived by allowing the hostesses to make out schedules, it would be necessary to reveal my awareness of the slower waitresses we have which I schedule on Saturday and Sunday—our slower business days.

I am really more active in management and day-to-day problems than most of the employees realize. Any significant changes in rules or policies are usually passed in the form of a written memo. I prefer to handle communication in this way for two reasons: first, there is no room for distortion, and second, it does not give the employees a feeling that they are being closely supervised. However, I do need an assistant to help me manage this place. I have verbally put the word out to other Inns and motels. I'm really not concerned whether I get a restaurant manager or an assistant innkeeper so long as he has a knowledge of the food and beverage service. I'm really going to be cautious in the selection of this person as I don't want to jump out of the frying pan into the fire.

The absence of Bernie is now a well-known fact by all of the Inn's personnel. However, it was not known to everyone. One day, Mr. Trainor, a well-liked sales representative walked into the restaurant and inquired, "Where is Mr. Bernie today?" There was a hush of silence and then in answer to his own question he replied, "Why is everyone smiling?"

CASE 33 DAVIS GENERAL HOSPITAL*

As Fred White drove to work on Monday morning, he reflected on his past three years as administrator of Davis General Hospital. Twelve years ago, after receiving a BS in public health and an MBA/MPH from a well-known southern university, Fred began his career in health administration with the Mobile County, Alabama, Department of Public Health. As an idealistic college graduate, Fred felt he could better serve society in the public sector. He was, therefore, willing to forgo the larger salaries his classmates earned in order to help his community.

Fred's idealism was, over time, replaced with reality. As an associate administrator and later administrator of a large public hospital, he saw funds cut and the quality of care decline due to financial constraints. With no end in sight to soaring inflation and increasing competition for state funds, budgets would certainly be slashed, followed by personnel and health care reductions. Therefore, in 1973 Fred moved his family to Charleston, South Carolina, and accepted the position of administrator of Davis General Hospital, a small, private, for-profit institution.

Transition from public to private administration went smoothly for Fred. In his opinion, a hospital needed to cover its costs—just like any other institution—in order to survive. The only difference between profit and nonprofit hospitals was that nonprofit hospitals called the surplus "excess revenue" while proprietary hospitals referred to the surplus as "profit." To Fred it did not matter if the excess revenue was put in the bank to build an endowment or paid to stockholders as dividends. Davis had been quite successful in following the latter procedure; it was able to raise the necessary funds for expansion in the capital markets. To preserve its independence as a private institution, the hospital had not relied on federal or state funding for construction. Therefore, Davis was not required to accept a federally mandated quota of indigent patients on a charity basis.

Fred was specifically attracted to Davis General because of its reputation in the community. Davis was originally built by a partnership of doctors to provide the kind of high-quality care the doctors felt was not available in the area. Patients appreciated the additional amenities available at Davis General, including wine with dinner, newspapers every morning, and special-run movies. Davis maintained one of the highest nurses per patient ratio in the state. Small and relatively specialized, Davis was licensed for 175 beds and maintained no facilities to treat infectious diseases or psychiatric or maternity patients.

During Fred's three years at Davis, staff morale had been high. Davis had a relatively low turnover of nurses, which Fred felt was due to good working conditions and competitive salary policies. Recently, however, a local labor group had tried to unionize Davis's nonprofessional employees. Fred had also noticed some tension within

* Prepared by Lynne Atwood, Kerry Krisher, Lisa Lauricella, and Lynda Levy under the direction of Associate Professor Jeffery A. Barach, School of Business, Tulane University, as a basis for class discussion and not to illustrate either effective or ineffective administration practices. Copyright © 1983 by the School of Business, Tulane University. Reproduced with permission.

the administrative staff, but he attributed this to the potential that the hospital would be sold to a large national medical chain.

Pulling into the parking lot of Davis General, Fred knew he had a tough day and an even more difficult week ahead of him. This morning, he was meeting with officers of the hospital management company which had shown an interest in purchasing Davis. In addition, the final budget proposal had to go to the board of directors by Thursday. Finally, Fred had to complete annual performance reviews of hospital personnel and discuss the results with each member of the staff.

On his way to his office, Fred was stopped by Karl Smith, his associate administrator. Karl was concerned about a resignation letter from a disgruntled staff member (see Exhibit 1). The letter was circulating around the hospital, and Karl was worried about its effect on employee morale. Fred took the letter and sat down at his desk to read it.

Fred was astounded. He knew that "Health Care Is a Human Right" was the slogan for the Medical Committee on Human Rights, a radical left-wing student organization dedicated to socialized medicine and welfare-state nurses. Were Jessica Armstrong's attitudes shared by other employees as she maintained in the letter, or was this letter written in the hopes of starting a controversy, perhaps to jeopardize the sale of the hospital or to interest employees in unionizing? To answer these questions and to determine if a problem really existed in the Admissions Department, Fred decided to discuss the letter first with Mary Johnson, the Admissions Department supervisor, and then with Russell Adams, the director of Personnel. Fred wanted to find out *who* Jessica Armstrong was and if she was any threat to the continued success of the hospital before investigating the specific grievances stated in her letter.

Before meeting with the hospital management company representatives, Fred called Mary and Russell to set up afternoon meetings. They confirmed that the letter was being circulated throughout the hospital. Discretion was necessary in handling this matter. Any obvious show of concern on his part might turn a minor employee dissatisfaction into a major hospital problem.

When Fred returned from his morning meeting, he was enthusiastic about the hospital management company's plans and the role he might play in the broader scope of events. However, Fred had to attend to several immediate concerns before he could speculate about the future.

Fred met with Mary Johnson right after lunch to discuss Jessica Armstrong's job performance as an admit staff member, as well as Mary's personal feelings about her. According to Mary, Jessica was competent in her job and caught on quickly to departmental procedures. She kept to herself a lot, but Mary attributed this to her being new to the job. Mary felt Jessica was sensitive to the needs of patients and was very surprised by her resignation and reasons for it.

Fred's discussion with Russell Adams in personnel did not uncover anything unusual about Jessica either. Fred was furnished with a copy of her resume, shown in Exhibit 2. Russell's only hesitation about hiring Jessica had been that she might be overqualified for the admit clerk position. In addition, Russell feared that the lack of upward mobility in this department might frustrate Jessica in the long run. Russell agreed with Mary that admissions was a very sensitive department and that the ability to effectively handle situations that arose and to deal with the professional staff was not developed overnight.

Exhibit 1

Fred R. White
Administrator
Davis General Hospital
Charleston, S.C.

March 14, 1984

Dear Mr. White:

When I first came to work at Davis General it was made clear to me by you that the admitting office was the focal point of the hospital. During my three weeks of working here my position as an admitting officer has indeed provided me with a vantage point to see the policies, attitudes, and practices of the hospital and professional staff. It has left me horrified and disgusted. I am therefore submitting my resignation for the following reasons:

1) Doctors' attitudes toward and treatment of non-professional staff, in my experience, the admitting office.
2) The position of women and minority groups, primarily blacks, in the hospital structure.
3) Preferential treatment of wealthy patients.
4) The lack of involvement of everyone except doctors and higher professionals in decision-making.

So far, the hospital administration has successfully managed to convince the admitting office personnel that in essence their job is to take whatever abuse may come from all directions, the doctors, and other professionals and patients. It has also instilled in them a commitment toward the hospital and the patients which places working conditions and personal integrity far below this "commitment." The admitting clerk is there to serve at all costs, despite the fact that Davis General is in no way a service institution, but to the contrary, a private corporation dedicated to making a profit for its shareholders and the doctors who participate in it. It has no commitment toward adequate health care for all segments of the community, and in fact, perpetuates the inequities of good health care for the rich, and poor-to-no health care for lower-income families and the poor. Yet, despite this, the admitting staff are expected to sacrifice their integrity by not offending a patient who claims she will not be admitted if a private room is not available. Why? Because that patient will not receive adequate medical attention? Hardly. The patient who can afford to make that demand is not in dire need of medical attention. Because that patient may be offended, she will not add to the profit figure of the hospital.

I was also told that I would have to deal with doctors' temperaments, and as though temperament were their exclusive right. A doctor has no right to temperament. He is outrageously overpaid for his services by the community with both money and status. When Dr. Curtis calls and tells me to find any scrap of paper I can find to write down a reservation and asks no questions that's not a matter of temperament. Dr. Curtis as an example, is a pig, a pig living off people's illnesses. He has been coddled by the American private health care system, and that system, this hospital, continues to perpetuate pigs like him maintaining their overrated, awesome status in society.

Certainly the fact that the admitting staff are all women facilitates doctors' condescending treatment of them. Women are there to serve a male-dominated corporation. The typical liberal line was also presented to me upon hiring. Many women and blacks not only worked at the hospital, but also held positions of status. Housekeeping, admitting, dietary, patient representative and PBX's are all primarily staffed with women. In essence, all the typically women-dominated jobs are held by women, the lesser-status jobs primarily by black women.

Not only does this hospital exclude a large section of the community, those unable to afford health care insurance and those covered by the Department of Public Welfare, it also bends its policies to accomodate its wealthier patients. The waiting list for a private room is overlooked when a doctor demands one for his daughter. In fact, in one instance,

Exhibit 1 *(concluded)*

I was told to offer a certain doctor the VIP room for $75. The very doctors who fight viciously against socialized medicine have their own system of socialized medicine benefiting only themselves—professional courtesy. Another patient, because of her wealthy position in the community was moved from the bottom of the waiting list to the top because she screamed the loudest and the longest. This move was ordered by Dr. Hawley. Meanwhile, someone in the emergency room waiting for a room, is transferred to another hospital because he does not have insurance or cannot afford the $500 deposit.

With regard to the involvement of paraprofessionals (read to mean anyone other than doctors and hospital executives and minimally department heads) in the cooperative delivery of care to patients in this hospital—it is blatantly non-existent. It appears these other hospital staff are here primarily for the purpose of serving (servitude) the erratic, emotional, and authoritarian dictates and whims of the medical staff and hospital executives, and only secondarily the needs of the patients, privileged as they may be. The concept of the team approach to delivery of health care to the patient, although bandied around much today, is nonexistent in this hospital. Indicative of how unimportant the rank and file staff is regarded by the administration, a meeting was called this past Saturday by the directors, which all admitting staff were required to attend, had to be cancelled after an hour's wait because neither of the directors showed up or had the decency to notify those waiting of their not coming. While the admitting staff gave up their Saturday to attend this mandatory meeting, we were never informed of its purpose.

It is for these reasons that I can only come to one conclusion. Institutions such as Davis General are not only immoral and inhumane, but they are counterproductive to the delivery of adequate health care to all our community's people. In these three weeks of my employment here, I have spoken with many others who share these frustrations and grievances, but their financial responsibility to their families and the insecurities of their jobs deny them the mobility that I have to make this decision to leave.

I am therefore submitting my resignation, for I can no longer be part of this institution which feels no responsibility toward the total community or its workers, a bureaucratic parasite that only profits itself and other elitist segments of this society.

HEALTH IS A HUMAN RIGHT

Jessica Armstrong

cc: All Departments

Note: Casewriters were unable to reproduce the letter in its original form. Fred White had received a typed copy on onionskin paper. Department heads received poorly reproduced copies of the original. No corrections have been made to the original.

Exhibit 2   Resume of Jessica Armstrong

Permanent Address:
12 Highland Drive
Shaker Heights, Ohio

Current Address:
1221 34th Street, N.E.
Apartment 20B
Charleston, S.C.

Education

1977–83: The University of Wisconsin, Madison. BA, American History, magna cum laude. MA, American History. Graduate thesis: The Impact of Middle-Aged Women Re-Entering the American Work Force after Divorce or Death of a Spouse. Peer counselor, History Department; Chairman, Michelson for Senate Campaign.

1973–77: The Hathaway School. Received diploma with honors. Member: Journalism Club, Debate Club. Editor, Yearbook. Vice president, senior class. Treasurer, junior class.

Work Experience

1982–84: The University of Wisconsin, Madison. Research Associate for Professor David Cavanaugh. Lecturer, American History. Duties included coordinating research efforts among affiliated campuses, updating publication libraries, editing journals for publication.

Summer 1981: Wisconsin State Senate, Madison, Wisconsin. Senate aide to Robert Michelson. Responsibilities included legislative research and legislative correspondence with constituents.

References: Available upon request.

Fred's discussions with Jessica's supervisors made it clear to him that she was a capable, intelligent woman, but he still did not have a clear picture of her motives for writing the letter. Davis General administrative staff did not recognize any problems, but perhaps they were too close to the situation. If a new employee could point out serious trouble spots after only three weeks on the job, then these same areas might catch the eyes of the hospital management company while examining the hospital.

At this stage, Fred concluded that if there were problems at Davis General, they were probably not unique to his hospital. Fred needed data to compare Davis to other hospitals in the area, and he knew just where to get it. Two months before, a former classmate of Fred's, and now a public health professor at their alma mater, asked Fred and Davis General to participate in a survey of local hospital standards, policies, and procedures. The survey consisted of interviews with staff from all levels of the hospitals to assess employee attitudes toward standards of health care, job expectations and responsibilities, and hospital admissions and treatment policies. Fred called his friend, Dr. Jim Rutledge, to inquire about the survey's conclusions. Jim said that he would send the final report, completed just last week, to Fred the following morning. Meanwhile Fred decided to put this issue aside and tackle a budget problem he had put off all day.

Tuesday morning on the way up to his office Fred encountered Dr. Curtis, a staff doctor mentioned by name in the Armstrong letter. Fred chose this moment to casually ask Dr. Curtis if he had any recent problems with the Admissions Department. The doctor replied that there were no unusual problems aside from the difficulty of securing a private room for his city councilman's wife when she had surgery last week. Dr. Curtis joked with Fred about adding another floor to the hospital to expand the VIP rooms.

The hospital survey report was on Fred's desk when he arrived. The survey results indicated that admit staff below the supervisory level at many hospitals wanted to have some input in the formulation of hospital policy. The report affirmed that many policies at Davis General were shared by other hospitals. Preferential treatment existed everywhere, only the degree of such treatment differed. Davis General allowed its doctors to request preferential treatment at their discretion, while other hospitals had more formalized policies regarding preferential treatment based on illness and association with the hospital.

Another area that Fred noted was the attitude of hospital employees regarding the treatment of uninsured indigent patients. Davis's policy had always been to accept these patients into the emergency room, to stablize the patient, and then to transfer the patient to a county or charity hospital when stable enough to be moved. This policy was designed to reduce the likelihood of unpaid hospital bills. However, many employees surveyed disagreed with this policy. The report also highlighted negative feelings about hospitals as profit-making institutions, particularly when staff doctors were major shareholders. How could a doctor be objective about admitting borderline patients to his hospital when he was concerned about the hospital's profit picture? (For sample report data, see Exhibit 3.)

One area the survey did not explore was the position of minorities and women as hospital employees. If Jessica's letter created a controversy, Davis could be the target of affirmative action suits. Five other hospitals in the community had recently been charged with violating the equal opportunity laws. Fred asked Karl Smith to bring him the hospital's most recent EEOC compliance report and to get the population breakdown by race and sex for the surrounding standard metropolitan statistical area (see Exhibits 4, 5, and 6).

In Fred's opinion the hospital had no discriminatory hiring practices. Minorities certainly held positions of lower responsibility, however, Davis had very few job applications from minority nurses and doctors. Most minorities applied for service or clerical duties. The only thing that worried Fred was whether Davis was doing everything it could through training programs and community involvement to improve the skill level of minority groups.

Should Davis General hire inexperienced minorities and train them to fill management positions, or would this be viewed by the stockholders as an inefficient use of resources? Davis currently maintained an excellent reputation in the community as a provider of excellent patient care. Fred did not know if such a liberalized hiring policy would improve this image; in fact it might harm the quality of care by moving resources away from the hospital's patient care functions. But if employees were dissatisfied with advancement opportunities or working conditions, unionization might be just around the corner.

Fred also examined the hospital's admissions policies. A patient without insurance was only admitted if he could put down a $500 deposit. Every time the patient's bill went over $500 an additional deposit was required. David also accepted Medicare and Medicaid patients even though these patients were not as financially attractive as patients with private insurance. (Davis's patient mix was approximately 35 percent Medicare, 10 percent Medicaid, 30 percent Blue Cross, and 25 percent private insur-

Exhibit 3   Davis General Hospital, Hospital Survey Report

1. Did your preemployment interview contain a realistic preview of what you would encounter at work?

   Fair. But you really have to work in an admit office for a year or more to really understand the service *you perform.*

   My interviews tried to make me understand what was expected of me as an admit clerk.

   Not really. No mention of hassles by doctors or pressure by doctors and supervisors was mentioned. Also, anyone coming into this area should be made aware of favoritism for "VIP" patients.

2. How do you as an employee feel that you are treated by the professional staff?

   Very well. The patients and the professional staff are what keep me interested in my job. Each is so different. I find the professional staff most interesting.

   I feel the professional staff has treated me with respect at all times. Our hospital's very fortunate to have such a fine staff.

   The doctors treat the admitting staff as servants to their every whim. We're never asked to do anything, we're told to get it done by yesterday.

3. What input does the admit staff have on hospital policy?

   On a supervisory level administration is interested in any suggestions to improve hospital routine. Just have to make sure you send things through proper channels.

   Since we are not in supervisory positions we only perform the duties set by our department. We have no input in setting hospital policy. The only time we hear from the top is when a doctor complains.

4. What criteria do you use to admit an individual?

   Have a hospital policy and procedure that must be followed. Doctors admit patients not hospitals. All we can do is go along with the physician's diagnosis and classification of patient.

   We usually use information obtained from the emergency room or pre-admitting. I feel that patients are treated with the utmost compassion, consideration, etc.

   I follow the policies of the hospital. My personal opinion about a patient means nothing to the doctors or my supervisor.

5. On what basis and frequency is preferential treatment given?

   According to illness first. Then, we, as the hospital, like to extend courtesy to physicians and their families and hospital employees.

   I always treat every patient with kindness and try to make them feel as comfortable as possible. I don't care which doctor admits the patient, they're all the same to me. Preferential treatment is given much too often, and for too many people.

6. On what grounds are individuals denied admission?

Exhibit 3 *(concluded)*

Depends on medical classification. No emergency is denied. Elective can be put off or denied because patient is unable to handle financial responsibility.

If a patient isn't an emergency, sometimes an admission must be rescheduled if rooms aren't available.

We don't admit patients if we think they won't be able to pay their bills. Sometimes I've had to humiliate people into admitting they couldn't pay.

7. What are the general procedures in the Emergency Room?

Am not directly involved but I do know they also follow the degree of medical illness or classification.

We aren't involved in the emergency room, but I would assume they're a little more lenient than us.

I've known times when the emergency room has turned away people seriously hurt if they couldn't pay. I couldn't work in the emergency room; I'd have to be too callous.

8. What kind of image does the hospital want?

That we care for our patients and their families. Also, that we have an excellent medical staff and give the best medical treatment available.

The hospital tries for a good image. We stress the special care we give our patients. When you're sick you want to feel at home; that's the image we want.

We serve the rich. The hospital wants the image of being a place where the rich can be with their own kind. Who else gets served wine for dinner and a complimentary morning newspaper?

9. To what extent does financial status facilitate admittance? Quality of care?

Financial status has nothing to do with quality of care. Financial status should not facilitate an admission—unless one thinks that taking time to verify an insurance program delays an admission. This is done for both the patient and the hospital's benefit.

Financial arrangements are made to assist such individuals if necessary. The policy of this hospital, however, involves deposits or guarantees at admitting time. It is also expected that the bill be paid in full at checkout time. The quality of care is equal once you're admitted.

Financial status determines where a patient is put (what type of room). Welfare patients get ward beds. Medicare and most private insurance patients are assigned semiprivate rooms, and people with money get privates.

10. Should a hospital be profit-oriented, and at what expense?

I have never worked in a profit making hospital—so I really cannot answer this question. Except to say that I am very conscious of the fact that every thing we spend—or use— is paid for by the patient in our hospital (which is a nonprofit).

A hospital should be mostly concerned with offering quality care at a reasonable cost. Of course, income has to cover expenses, but if income drastically overcompensates, something is wrong.

A hospital should not be concerned with profits.

Exhibit 4   Population Breakdown of Charleston Standard Metropolitan Statistical Area

---

	1984	
Total males:	569,979	48.02%
Total females:	617,094	51.98

	Total	*Charleston SMSA*	*Davis General Primary Area of Service*
White males:	377,406	31.79%	20.32%
Black males:	179,662	15.14	25.38
Other males:	12,911	1.09	1.14
Total males:	569,979	48.02%	46.84%
White females:	397,015	33.44%	22.18%
Black females:	207,720	17.50	29.89
Other females:	12,359	1.04	1.09
Total females:	617,094	51.98%	53.16%

Note: Office of Economic Analysis did not consider Hispanic or Spanish origin as a race. Although there was a blank on the bottom of the survey to allow one to indicate that he (she) was of Spanish origin, the OEA did not consider the statistics compiled as reliable, presuming that most of those people of Spanish origin probably check cff "white."

The State's courts had determined the guidelines for EEOC compliance in hospitals. The employee mix had to reflect the racial and ethnic makeup of the hospital's primary area of service.

Source: Office of Economic Analysis.

---

ance and private pay patients.) Was the bottom line so important, Fred asked himself, that the hospital should be selective in who was admitted? Should ability to pay really determine the quality of health care a person was to receive?

Preferential treatment and patient transfer policies also concerned Fred, in light of the Armstrong letter and Dr. Rutledge's survey. At Davis General, doctors demanded preferential treatment for their patients for all sorts of reasons. While Fred agreed that seriously ill patients should have private rooms, it was hard for him to justify a doctor's request to move a patient because of racial prejudice, for example. Yet this had been done on more than one occasion in the past.

Fred examined his feelings toward the hospital's procedures for transferring patients who had no health insurance. Did this policy give Davis General a reputation as an elitist institution which catered to the wealthy? Was this the reputation the hospital wanted? And when Medicare and Medicaid patients were treated was it right that government reimbursements included, in addition to costs for the hospital services, a fixed percentage pre-tax return on equity to a for-profit hospital such as Davis General? Did this payment discriminate against nonprofit hospitals? After all, government reimbursement before this return on equity covered approximately 75 percent of the cost of services rendered; that is, Medicare and Medicaid basically covered variable costs, but not fixed costs, for nonprofit hospitals. Fred wondered if the assurance of profit should be the sole reason for a hospital to provide service.

Fred found himself sympathizing with some of Jessica Armstrong's concerns. He

Exhibit 5   Davis General Hospital, EEOC Statistics as of March 21, 1984

Section D—EMPLOYMENT DATA

Employment at this establishment—Report all permanent, temporary, or part-time employees including apprentices and on-the-job trainees unless specifically excluded as set forth in the instructions. Enter the appropriate figures on all lines and in all columns. Blank spaces will be considered as zeros.

JOB CATEGORIES	Overall Totals (Sum of Cols. B thru K) A	MALE					FEMALE				
		White (Not of Hispanic Origin) B	Black (Not of Hispanic Origin) C	Hispanic D	Asian or Pacific Islander E	American Indian or Alaskan Native F	White (Not of Hispanic Origin) G	Black (Not of Hispanic Origin) H	Hispanic I	Asian or Pacific Islander J	American Indian or Alaskan Native K
Officials and managers	34	15					18	1			
Professionals	72	4					60	5	1	1	1
Technicians	98	12	2				58	25	1		
Sales workers											
Office and clerical	81	2	4				24	51			
Craft workers (skilled)	4	3	1								
Operatives (semi-skilled)	6	5	1								
Laborers (unskilled)	1	1									
Service workers	179	7	35				4	133			
TOTAL	475	49	43				164	215	2	1	1
Total employment reported in previous EEO-1 report	472	50	49	1			166	203	1	2	

(The trainees below should also be included in the figures for the appropriate occupational categories above)

Former on-the-job trainees	White collar										
	Production										

1. NOTE: On consolidated report, skip questions 2-5 and Section E.
2. How was information as to race or ethnic group in Section D obtained?
   1 ☐ Visual survey   3 ☐ Other—Specify . . . .
   2 ☒ Employment record   . . . .
3. Dates of payroll period used: March 8-21, 1984

4. Pay period of last report submitted for this establishment:

5. Does this establishment employ apprentices?
   This year? 1 ☐ Yes   2 ☒ No
   Last year? 1 ☐ Yes   2 ☒ No

Section E—ESTABLISHMENT INFORMATION

1. Is the location of the establishment the same as that reported last year?
   1 ☐ Yes   2 ☐ No   3 ☐ Did not report last year.   4 ☐ Reported on combined basis.

2. Is the major business activity at this establishment the same as that reported last year?
   1 ☒ Yes   2 ☐ No   3 ☐ No report last year.   4 ☐ Reported on combined basis.

OFFICE USE ONLY

3. What is the major activity of this establishment? (Be specific, i.e., manufacturing steel castings, retail grocer, wholesale plumbing supplies, title insurance, etc. Include the specific type of product or type of service provided, as well as the principal business or industrial activity.
   General Hospital

Section F—REMARKS

Use this item to give any identification data appearing on last report which differs from that given above, explain major changes in composition or reporting units and other pertinent information.

Exhibit 6 Davis General Hospital, EEOC Statistical Breakdown by Job Skill Level and Ethnic Background

MONTHLY/QUARTERLY MINORITY & FEMALE REPORT

Division/Subsidiary: Davis General Hospital
Location: Charleston, S.C.
Month/Quarter: First Quarter/March   Year/1984

NUMBER OF EMPLOYEES

108 CATEGORIES	Overall Totals (Sum of Cols. B thru K) A	MALE White (Not of Hispanic Origin) B	MALE Black (Not of Hispanic Origin) C	MALE Hispanic D	MALE Asian or Pacific Islander E	MALE American Indian or Alaskan Native F	FEMALE White (Not of Hispanic Origin) G	FEMALE Black (Not of Hispanic Origin) H	FEMALE Hispanic I	FEMALE Asian or Pacific Islander J	FEMALE American Indian or Alaskan Native K	Percentages % MALE	Percentages % FEMALE
Total Employment	475	49	43	0	0	0	164	215	2	1	1	19.4%	80.6%
Officials and Managers													
Professionals	106 / 100%	19 / 18%	0	0	0	0	78 / 74%	6 / 6%	1 / 1%	1 / 1%	1 / 1%	18%	82%
Technicians	98(100%)	12(12%)	2(2%)	0	0	0	58(59%)	25(26%)	1(1%)	0	0	14%	86%
Salesworkers													
Office and Clerical	85 / 100%	5 / 6%	5 / 6%	0	0	0	24 / 28%	51 / 60%	0	0	0	12%	88%
Craft Workers (skilled)													
Operatives (semi-skilled)	6(100%)	5(83%)	1(17%)	0	0	0	0	0	0	0	0	100%	0
Laborers (unskilled)	180 / 100%	8 / 4%	35 / 19%	0	0	0	4 / 2%	133 / 75%	0	0	0	23%	77%
Service workers													
Percentage TOTAL	100%	10.3%	9.1%	0	0	0	34.5%	45.3%	0.4%	0.2%	0.2%	19.4%	80.6%

remembered his idealism when he was her age. But he also liked his job as administrator of Davis General. Fred was torn: Should he recommend an investigation into any or all of the complaints raised in the Armstrong letter and risk a controversy? If so, which complaints should he take seriously? Or should he keep quiet? Fred had to decide that afternoon, since the letter was already making its way through the hospital grapevine, and urgent action was needed to keep it out of the wrong hands.

CASE 34 PIK-NIK FOODS, INC. (E)*

As he was coming off the golf course in early July 1983, Joe Grimes, president of Pik-nik Foods, Inc., began to contemplate the future of the company and his involvement with it.

He was reflecting, too, on his own objectives and the extent to which the situation at Pik-nik was meeting those objectives. His goals were clear. First of all, he wanted to run his own business. Secondly, he had two types of financial criteria to satisfy. One was to increase his current income because, as Joe said, "While I think I am being adequately compensated for running a company this size, the fact of the matter is that I have a family with four high school- and college-age children to support." Joe's other major financial objective was to be able to sell his equity in Pik-nik in 5 to 10 years at a substantial capital gain.

At this time only one of Joe's major goals was being met—he was running a company and truly enjoying it. His financial objectives, however, were not being satisfied. Joe reasoned that there were two main causes for this. First, he was still grappling with the dilemma of how to grow Pik-nik. Growth had been a key issue ever since Joe and the investor partners had purchased Pik-nik in 1978 from Beatrice Foods. Growth was an objective all the partners shared and to which they were all dedicated. The second obstacle to Joe's meeting his financial objectives stemmed from Pik-nik's small size and Joe's limited ownership in the business—"less than half the action," as he said. In fact Joe held 42.5 percent of the equity while the investor partners owned 57.5 percent.

As Joe walked toward the clubhouse thinking of his current income and the probability of low payoff in 5 to 10 years, his mind turned again to a set of well-considered alternatives that he had shared with his partners at the February 1983 board of directors meeting. He had predicted that during the coming year one of the following events would occur:

1. Pik-nik Foods would make an acquisition.
2. Joe would leave Pik-nik and find another, presumably larger, company to run.
3. The current investors would sell the company.
4. Joe would buy out the other partners.

Several other important issues also needed to be reckoned with in the near future: (1) Joe wanted to transfer Pik-nik's long-term debt and working-capital financing to another lender; (2) a recession was in full force, and not only had Pik-nik's fiscal year 1983 sales not met the projections, but additional uncertainty surrounded the future; (3) the increased strength of the U.S. dollar was making the export market a more difficult selling environment.

* Prepared by Clare C. Swanger, Research Associate, under the supervision of John R. Berthold, Lecturer in Management, Stanford University Graduate School of Business. Selected names and data have been disguised to protect the proprietary interests of Pik-nik Foods, Inc. Reprinted with permission of Stanford University Graduate School of Business, © 1984 by the Board of Trustees of the Leland Stanford Junior University.

As he reached the clubhouse, Joe decided that immediately after his return to Chicago he would review the events of fiscal year 1983 and then evaluate each of the possible alternatives more closely so that he could proceed with a chosen course of action and try to have these issues resolved by the end of year.

BACKGROUND OF PIK-NIK FOODS, INC.

Pik-nik Foods, Inc. was one of the country's leading producers of shoestring potatoes. These snack food items were sold under the "Kobey's" brand name and enjoyed national distribution through major retail grocery chains. Net sales during fiscal year 1982 (ended June 30) were $8.3 million with net income of $178,000. The company had been consistently profitable and had a net worth of $900,000.

PIK-NIK IN FISCAL YEAR 1983

During 1983 Pik-nik had sales of $7 million and net income of $71,000 after a $30,000 write-off for development costs of its new Nachupas chip product. Exhibits 1, 2, and 3 present Pik-nik's financial statements; the notes to the financial statements are in Exhibit 4.

Pik-nik sold 667,804 cases of shoestrings, a decrease from the 1982 level which management attributed to the effects of the recession and a tougher export market environment (see Exhibit 5).

Exhibit 1　Pik-nik Foods, Income Statement 1979–1983　Years Ended June 30

	1979	1980	1981	1982	1983
Number of cases shipped	76 ,000	881,000	872,000	849,000	668,000
Net sales	$6,154,988	$7,545,164	$8,133,182	$8,304,251	$6,959,447
Cost of sales	4,163,216	5,236,723	5,526,611	5,758,337	4,921,485
Gross profit	1,991,772	2,308,441	2,606,571	2,545,914	2,037,962
Operating expenses:					
Selling, general and administrative	1,540,308	1,756,203	1,977,994	1,919,239	1,747,900
New product expense	—	—	—	94,683	30,642
Interest	238,277	260,424	228,457	210,094	142,615
Total expenses	1,778,585	2,016,627	2,206,451	2,224,016	1,921,157
Income before taxes	213,187	291,814	400,120	321,898	116,805
Taxes on income	90,000	127,000	176,000	143,000	45,000
Net income	$ 123,187	$ 164,814	$ 224,120	$ 178,898	$ 71,805

* Totals may not add exactly due to rounding.
See accompanying notes, which refer to 1983 and 1982.

Exhibit 2 Pik-nik Foods, Balance Sheets, 1980–1983 Fiscal Years Ended June 30

	1980	1981	1982	1983
Assets				
Current assets:				
Cash	$ 11,171	$ 28,082	$ 16,247	$ 14,536
Accounts receivable, net of allowance for doubtful accounts of $6,000 in both years (Notes 2 and 4)	629,340	577,661	441,722	484,629
Inventories (Notes 1, 2, and 4):				
Raw materials	48,919	65,710	48,311	39,015
Finished goods	1,122,862	892,976	1,272,934	993,211
	1,171,781	958,686	1,321,245	1,032,226
Prepaid expenses	128,765	103,715	117,968	110,158
Total current assets	1,941,057	1,668,144	1,897,182	1,641,549
Property and equipment, at cost (Notes 1, 2, and 4):				
Machinery and equipment	561,557	590,576	626,286	621,520
Leasehold improvements	51,522	51,522	74,491	75,341
	613,079	642,098	700,777	698,861
Less: Accumulated depreciation and amortization	(121,622)	(188,407)	(268,875)	(347,085)
Net property and equipment	491,457	453,691	431,902	349,776
Trademarks (Notes 1, 2 and 4)	67,263	63,276	58,689	55,302
Other assets	8,045	1,200	1,200	—
Total assets	$2,507,822	$2,186,311	$2,388,973	$2,046,627
Liabilities and Shareholders' Equity				
Current liabilities:				
Note payable to bank (Note 2)	$ 455,000	$ 1,000	$ 125,000	$ 350,000
Accounts payable	633,626	645,027	604,114	419,346
Income taxes payable (Notes 1 and 3)	67,053	80,240	83,334	—
Accrued liabilities	137,658	141,540	101,087	95,035
Long-term debt due within one year (Note 4)	23,434	101,000	160,000	110,000
Total current liabilities	1,316,771	968,807	1,073,535	974,381
Long-term debt, including subordinated notes payable, due July 24, 1981, to be refined (Note 4)	—	632,080	—	—
Long-term debt due after one year (Note 4)	335,522	—	339,164	229,167
Deferred taxes on income (Note 3)	17,128	22,903	34,855	29,855
Subordinated notes payable (Note 4)	500,000	—	200,000	—
Commitments (Note 5)				
Shareholders' equity (Notes 2, 4 and 6):				
Common stock, Class A, $1 par value; 500 shares authorized, 100 shares issued and outstanding	400	400	100	100
Common stock, Class B, $1 par value; 400 shares authorized, issued and outstanding	400	400	400	400
Common stock, Class C, $1 par value; 300 shares authorized, issued and outstanding	—	—	300	300
Capital in excess of par value	49,600	49,600	49,600	49,600
Retained earnings	288,001	512,121	691,019	762,824
Total shareholders' equity	338,401	562,521	741,419	813,224
Total liabilities and shareholders' equity	$2,507,822	$2,186,311	$2,388,973	$2,046,627

* Totals may not add exactly due to rounding.
See accompanying notes, which refer to 1983 and 1982.

Exhibit 3   Pik-nik Foods, Inc., Statement of Changes in Financial Position; 1980–1983   In Thousands

	Fiscal Years Ended June 30			
	1980	1981	1982	1983
Sources:				
Working capital provided from operations:				
Net income	$ 164	$ 224	$ 178	$ 71
Charges to operations not requiring the current use of working capital:				
Depreciation and amortization	79	87	86	91
Deferred taxes on income	2	5	11	(5)
Total working capital provided from operations	246	317	277	158
Long-term debt, due July 24, 1981, to be refinanced	—	632	—	—
Net book value of machinery and equipment sold	2	—	1	11
Total sources of working capital	248	949	278	169
Applications:				
Additions to machinery and equipment	88	39	61	15
Reduction of long-term debt due after one year	22	335	92	109
Reduction of subordinated note payable		500	—	200
Total applications of working capital	111	874	154	325
Increase in working capital	$ 137	$ 75	$ 124	$(156)
Changes in components of working capital:				
Increases (decreases) in current assets:				
Cash	$ 1	$ 16	$ (11)	$ (1)
Accounts receivable	(7)	(51)	(135)	42
Inventories	(64)	(213)	362	(289)
Prepaid expenses	7	(25)	14	(7)
	(62)	(272)	(229)	(255)
Increases (decreases) in current liabilities:				
Note payable to bank	(45)	(454)	124	255
Accounts payable	(145)	11	(40)	(184)
Income taxes payable	3	13	3	83
Other accrued liabilities	(5)	3	(40)	(6)
Long-term debt due within one year		77	59	(50)
	(199)	(347)	(104)	99
Increase in working capital	$ 137	$ 75	$ 124	$(156)

* Totals may not add exactly due to rounding.
See accompanying notes, which refer to 1983 and 1982.

Products and Brands

In 1983 the company's management replaced the Pik-nik brand in all remaining markets with a redesigned Kobey's label, identical to the Pik-nik label except for the name. During fiscal year 1983 (year ending June) 83 percent of Pik-nik's product was sold under the Kobey name, while 17 percent was in private label such as Lady Lee (Lucky Stores), Planters, and Monarch. Both Planters and Monarch were export lines (Exhibit 2).

Exhibit 4　Notes to Pik-nik's Financial Statements

---

1. *Principal accounting policies.*

Inventories.　Inventories are stated at the lower of cost (first-in, first-out) or market.

Depreciation and amortization.　Depreciation on machinery and equipment is being provided using the straight-line method for financial reporting purposes and an accelerated method for income tax purposes. Estimated useful lives are 3–10 years. Leasehold improvements are being amortized over the lesser of the life of the lease or the estimated useful lives of the improvements. Trademarks are amortized over 20 years.

Investment tax credit.　The company accounts for investment tax credits using the flowthrough method. The 1983 and 1982 taxes on income are net of investment tax credits of $1,500 and $2,600, respectively.

Net income per share.　Net income per share is calculated using the weighted average number of Class A, Class B, and Class C common shares outstanding during each period.

2. *Note payable to bank.*　The Company has a $1,100,000 revolving line of credit with St. Joseph Bank and Trust Company bearing interest at the bank's prime lending rate (11.25 percent at June 30, 1983). The note balance under the line of credit at June 30, 1983, is $350,000 and is secured by accounts receivable, inventory, property, equipment, and trademarks. The note is due on demand or September 30, 1983, if not previously paid.

Provisions of the revolving line of credit and term loan agreement (Note 4) restrict the company from entering into certain transactions and require the company to maintain minimum levels of working capital, net worth, and certain financial ratios. In addition, the company is required to maintain with the bank average daily demand deposit balances equal to $99,000. The compensating balance arrangement does not legally restrict the use of cash.

As of June 30, 1983, the company was in compliance with the provisions of the loan agreement or had obtained a waiver from the bank.

3. *Taxes on income.*　The provisions for taxes on income consists of the following:

		1983	*1982*
Federal:			
	Current	$36,000	$110,000
	Deferred	(3,000)	11,000
		33,000	121,000
State:			
	Current	14,000	21,000
	Deferred	(2,000)	1,000
		12,000	22,000
		$45,000	$143,000

Deferred income taxes result primarily from timing differences in reporting depreciation expense for financial statement and tax purposes.

4. *Long-term debt.*　At June 30, 1982 the company owed $250,000 on subordinated notes payable to four shareholders and a related party pursuant to subscription agreements executed July 7, 1978. Each note was for $50,000 and was subordinated to all debts, liabilities, and creditors of the company. The company was to make payments of $50,000 per year for five years with an interest rate of 20 percent per year with the first payment in July 1982. The company prepaid these notes in June 1983.

At June 30, 1983, the company owed $339,167 on a term loan payable to St. Joseph Bank and Trust Company with interest at the bank's prime lending rate. The loan is being repaid with principal payments of $9,167 plus interest each month. The term loan payable has the same provisions and is secured by the same assets as the note payable to the bank (Note 2).

5. *Commitments.*

Lease commitments.　Total annual rental expense for the manufacturing and office facility for the periods ended June 30, 1983, and 1982 was approximately $21,000. Annual minimum rentals under an operating lease agreement expiring in 1986 are as follows:

1984	$21,000
1985	21,000
1986	15,750
	$57,750

Exhibit 4 *(concluded)*

The company has an option to extend the lease for an additional five-year term commencing April 1, 1986, at an annual rental of $23,100.

    Purchase commitments.   The company has entered into commitments for the purchase of certain raw materials over the next year, amounting to approximately $1,028,000.

    6. *Capitalization.*   The relative powers, preferences, and rights and the qualifications, limitations, or restrictions of the Class A, Class B, and Class C common shares are in all respects identical except as to the following:

a. The holders of more than 75 percent of Class B shares may at any time elect to convert to Class A shares on a one for one basis at which time the Class B shares will be canceled and not eligible for reissuance. Four hundred shares of Class A common stock have been reserved for the sole purpose of Class B conversions.

b. Commencing with the fiscal year ending June 30, 1984, Class B common shareholders shall have the right to receive a dividend equal to 20 percent of net income for the year then ended. The right to this dividend shall continue as long as the Class B shares are outstanding.

c. In any fiscal year during which a dividend is declared on the Class A common stock, a like dividend shall be payable on each share of the Class C common stock. Similarly, when a dividend is declared on the Class C common stock, except for the first $5 per share of a cash dividend, a like dividend shall be payable on each share of Class A common stock. Dividends to Class A and Class C shareholders must be approved by a majority of Class B shares except for the first $5 of a cash dividend to Class C common stock.

d. Holders of more than 50 percent of the initial Class A and Class C issuances reserve the right to direct the Company to redeem all (but not less than all) of the Class B common shares and all (but not less than all) of the Class A shares converted from Class B for $1,-450,000 at June 30, 1983, increasing annually to a maximum of $2,000,000 through July 24, 1986.

e. All of the outstanding shares of Class C common stock at June 30, 1983, are owned by the president of the company. In the event that the president should die before July 1, 1987, all outstanding shares of Class C common stock issued to him shall be redeemed by the company based at a price equal to the book value of such shares as of the fiscal year ended immediately prior to such redemption.

    The company has obtained an insurance policy on the life of the president, the proceeds of which would be used to fund the purchase of the stock.

    7. *New product expense.*   In fiscal year 1982, the company abandoned the distribution of a new product. Cost and expenses related to the abandonment amounted to $30,642 and $94,683 for the years ended June 30, 1983, and 1982, respectively.

The private label business was very price competitive, and Pik-nik decided not to bid against Allen Canning for the Winn-Dixie account. Pik-nik estimated that it had supplied most of Winn Dixie's needs since 1980.

Pik-nik added a four-ounce "no salt added" shoestring product for sale to the growing salt-free consumer market. Reports indicated that the product was successful and should produce additional sales, possibly as much as 10 percent of current revenues.

Seasonality

Sales continued to exhibit seasonal variations in 1983 and even larger monthly fluctuations than in the previous year. (See Exhibit 6 for quarterly sales history from 1978 through 1983 and Exhibit 7 for monthly sales during 1982 and 1983.)

Exhibit 5   Pik-nik Foods, Inc., Selected Sales and Price Data, 1982–1983

Case Sales by Location, Type, and Size (Fiscal Year 1983)

| | United States | | Export | | |
	Brand*	Private	Brand	Private	Total
1¾ ounces	189,545	41,382	9,976	39,464	280,368
4 ounces	107,103	—	5,637	19,514	132,254
7 ounces	16,348	2,350	860	14,163	33,722
9 ounces	157,730	—	8,301	—	166,032
14 ounces	50,438	—	2,654	—	53,093
20 pounds	870	—	—	—	870
5½ pounds	1,465	—	—	—	1,465
Total	523,499	43,732	27,428	73,141	667,800

Shoestrings Average price, Fiscal Year 1983
United States Delivered $12/case (includes approximately $1.50/case freight)

Export, FOB $10.50/case

Case Sales by Location, Type, and Size (Fiscal Year 1982)

| | United States | | Export | | |
	Brand*	Private	Brand*	Private	Total†
1¾ ounces	228,085	52,422	12,004	85,635	378,147
4 ounces	128,036	—	6,738	13,795	148,570
7 ounces	46,142	—	2,428	21,673	70,244
9 ounces	163,307	—	8,595	—	171,903
14 ounces	74,502	—	3,921	—	78,424
20 pounds	8	—	—	—	8
5½ pounds	1,694	—	—	—	1,694
Total	641,774	52,422	33,686	121,103	848,990

* These figures are calculated assuming that brand name sales are 95 percent United States and 5 percent export.
† Totals may not add exactly due to rounding.

Distribution

Domestic sales were virtually nationwide, with the Midwest remaining the predominant area and Texas the largest single state for Pik-nik's shoestrings. (See Exhibit 8 for 1983 sales by state.) Joe worked on reestablishing brokers and distribution in several states.

Export sales declined from approximately $1.2 million during 1982 to $650,000 in 1983. Management attributed the decrease to unfavorable foreign exchange rates and to stiffer competition from Allen Canning, which supplied a large Middle Eastern customer. Pik-nik made shoestrings for Nabisco under the Planters label, and these products were sold mainly in South America and the Orient, with a small amount going to the Middle East.

Exhibit 6   Pik-Nik Foods, Inc., Sales History for Fiscal Years 1978—First Half 1984
Thousands of Cases

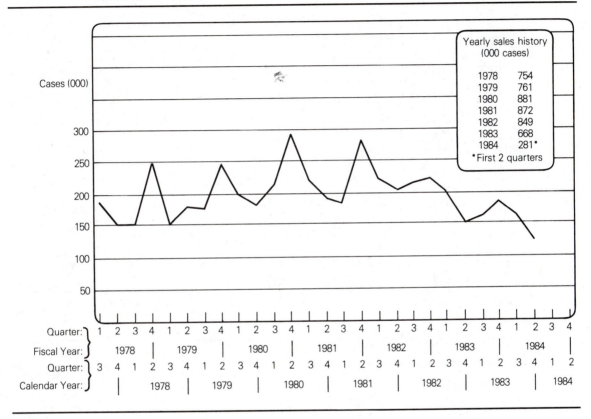

Yearly sales history (000 cases)	
1978	754
1979	761
1980	881
1981	872
1982	849
1983	668
1984	281*

*First 2 quarters

Growth Opportunities

Product Development   Pik-nik focused its internal product line expansion on improving existing products which had already been successfully marketed by others. The company worked with a major food company to develop an onion-piece product for snacking and spicing. The product was cashew-size and would be eaten as is for a snack or in salads. Pik-nik would package and distribute the product after it had passed through a period of test-marketing, expected to begin in mid-1984. Estimates of start-up costs for the test market had not been made. Durkee was the only company which had marketed a similar product. Best estimates of total market size for onion pieces were between $50 million and $60 million (2.5 million cases) retail annually, of which roughly 25 percent was estimated to be West Coast sales. In the long run, Pik-nik was targeting a 30–50 percent share of these West Coast sales or as much as $6 million annually.

Exhibit 7   Pik-Nik Foods, Inc., Sales by Month for Fiscal Years 1982, 1983, and First Half 1984   Thousands of Cases

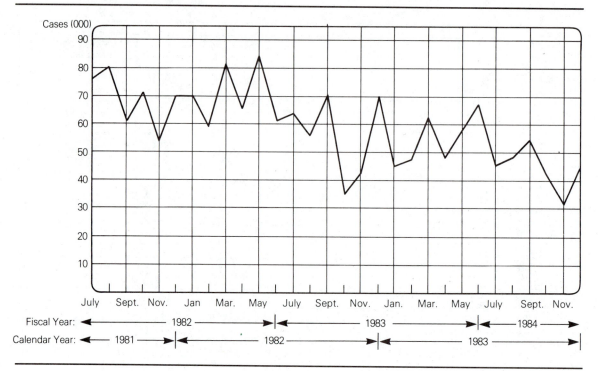

Pik-nik also expended some effort during 1983 developing their potato stick product, which was a thicker version of the existing shoestring potato. Potato sticks were considered a line extension very closely related to the shoestrings. Consequently, no decision had been made whether to proceed with this item.

Acquisition Possibilities   During fiscal 1982 Pik-nik management and Doug Adams had expended considerable effort negotiating to acquire Diane's Foods (a corn and tortilla chip manufacturer based in McMinnville, Oregon). Ultimately Diane's was purchased by Gruma/Mission Foods, Inc. Everyone at Pik-nik believed that a good acquisition opportunity had been lost and, as a result, they were even more eager to find a suitable replacement. Beginning in the spring of 1983 several acquisition candidates came to Joe's attention, and Doug Adams also actively looked for companies.

Joe first heard of a West Coast beef snacks company. The company made 110 products, 15 of which were profitable. Meat snacks required processing techniques different from shoestrings. However, there were several potential advantages to the company: it was in the snack food market, participated in a unique though small segment of that market, and had an established West Coast distribution network as well as administration and marketing synergies with Pik-nik. Joe quickly realized, however, that the manufacturing facility had been overbuilt for the company's volume.

Exhibit 8   Pik-Nik Foods, Inc. 1983 Sales by State   In Thousands

MN	$488.5
IA	129.0
MO	81.6
WS	174.3
IL	564.6
MI	298.0
IN	12.1
OH	186.2
	$1,934.3

AK $0.0

WA	$230.4
OR	133.1
CA	758.5
ID	0.0
NV	6.0
MT	0.0
WY	0.0
UT	0.0
AZ	210.9
CO	205.1
NM	0.0
ND	72.9
SD	23.5
NE	52.7
KS	183.3
OK	266.6
TX	1,245.2
	$3,388.2

HI $62.9

ME	$ 0.0
NH	0.0
VT	0.0
MA	0.0
CN	0.0
RI	0.0
NY	80.2
PA	456.3
NJ	20.7
MD	0.0
DE	0.0
DC	477.7
	$1,034.9

AR	$45.3
MS	5.3
AL	0.0
LA	171.0
	$221.6

VA	$ 47.3
NC	386.0
SC	184.8
GA	17.7
FL	659.0
WV	33.4
KY	2.3
TN	37.7
	$1,368.2

Note: Revenues by state are reported as *gross* sales. Therefore, the total of all sales shown adds to more than the comparable *net* sales figure.

Joe's initial thrust with the company would have been to cut the volume in half in order to increase profits but, given the large plant, there was too much capital and debt burden. Hence, Pik-nik never made an offer to acquire the company.

Two popcorn companies were for sale also. Both manufactured popcorn and one marketed popcorn for microwaves. Joe considered these briefly, but his conclusion was the same as the previous year—that four to five small merged popcorn companies such as this one would be necessary to create a viable market position.

The final and most significant acquisition candidate was Laura Scudder's, owned by PET, Inc. (St. Louis) which in turn was a subsidiary of IC Industries, Inc. Laura

Scudder's produced a full line of snack foods, including peanut butter, potato chips, corn and tortilla chips, carmel corn, popcorn, and a variety of bagged and canned nut snacks. Eighty percent of the products was delivered directly to the stores. The company had sales of about $100 million, profit before tax of $2 million, and book value of $20 million plus. It was the leading snack food company in Los Angeles. One of Joe's partners had talked with the Laura Scudder management in Chicago and then notified Joe of the opportunity. Joe contacted a major food company that was interested in the peanut butter part of the business with the idea that Pik-nik would acquire the other product lines. Joe had been familiar with the company for years, and he believed the purchase price would be about $30 million. Laura Scudder's decided to hold a closed bid for the company and to sell to the highest bidder. Since Joe's information about Laura Scudder's was superficial at this time and due diligence had not been performed, he submitted a conservative bid which PET did not accept. The company ultimately was acquired by a leveraged buyout group.

Management

In early 1983 Pik-nik's plant manager, Jerry Duggan, retired, and Joseph F. Dubreil was hired to replace him. (See Exhibit 9 for information in Dubreil's background.)

Pik-nik's new national broker accounts manager, Wilbert F. Dobbins, and Joe Grimes expected to focus considerable attention on adding or changing brokers, improving broker support, and adding new geographic markets as needed, as well as

---

Exhibit 9   Managers and Investors, Pik-nik Foods, 1983

Existing Managers and Investors, Pik-nik Foods, 1983

Joseph F. Grimes, President and Chief Executive Officer, 42.5 percent
Douglas L. Adams, Financial Adviser, 20.0 percent
Dorothy S. Johnson, Legal Counsel, 12.5 percent
Arthur W. Lawrence, Investor, 12.5 percent
Herman C. Lawrence, Investor, 12.5 percent
Michael A. Teeter, Vice President and General Manager of Operations

New Managers as of Fiscal Year 1983

Joseph S. Dubreuil, 48, came to Pik-nik as plant manager in October 1982. His previous experience covered all aspects of production, including managing a work force of 150 union employees and 6 salaried supervisors; inventory control, scheduling, budget preparation, purchasing, and so on. He spent seven years as production superintendent for the Paul Masson Vineyards in Saratoga, California (1975–82). He was also Champagne Department supervisor (1973–75) and production planner (1972–73) for the same firm and· has held other line management and accounting positions with Lucky Breweries and Bethlehem Steel Corp. Joe, who was married, with three children, served in the U.S. Navy and had studied accounting and business at Golden Gate College, City College of San Francisco, and LaSalle Extension University.

Wilbert F. Dobbins, 45, joined Pik-nik as national broker accounts manager in August 1983. Will was with American Home Foods for the past 16 years, most recently as major account sales manager. Prior to American Home Foods, he was with Sun Oil Co. of Philadelphia. Will was married and had two children. He worked out of the Chicago area, covering accounts east of the Rockies.

Exhibit 10   Pik-Nik Foods' Organization Chart

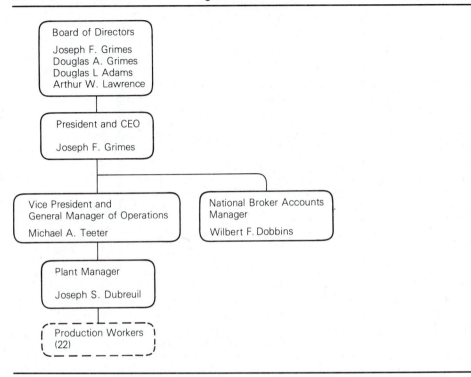

developing new private label, large client, and military business. (See Exhibit 6 for background information on Dobbins.)

Organization

Mike Teeter, Pik-nik's controller, was promoted to vice president and general manager of operations during 1983. Exhibit 10 presents Pik-nik's revised organization chart.

THE SNACK FOOD AND SHOESTRING MARKETS

Snack Food Industry

The snack food industry as a whole grew from $5.2 billion in 1981 to $5.7 billion in 1982 (see Exhibit 11). This growth rate of 8.8 percent was well below the 16.3 percent rate of the previous year, due primarily to the recession that was underway. The potato chip and corn/tortilla chip segments were least affected, while all the other categories suffered substantial slowdowns and, in several cases, absolute declines.

Exhibit 11 Snack Foods Market Data, 1980–1983

| | Total Sales (millions) | | | Growth Rates Percent | | | | | | | |
| | | | | Total Sales* | | | | Units | | | |
	1980	1981	1982	1979–1980	1980–1981	1981–1982	1982–1983 (estimated)	1979–1980	1980–1981	1981–1982	1982–1983 (estimated)
Potato chips	$1,900	$2,200	$2,540	17.7%	16.3%	14.7%	10.2%	6.4%	6.5%	7.1%	26.8%
Corn/Tortilla chips	1,000	1,190	1,330	24.0	19.1	11.6	22.1	10.0	10.0	8.0	19.0
Salted meat snacks (pork rinds and meat sticks)	200	277	297	N/A	38.5	7.2	N/A	N/A	N/A	N/A	N/A
Extruded snacks (cheese curls primarily)	200	259	262	N/A	17.6	1.4	24.8	N/A	6.5	1.5	14.6
Popped popcorn	100	126	131	N/A	26.3	3.7	20.0	N/A	16.8	(1.3)	9.3
Salted nuts	900	927	884	N/A	3.0	(4.6)	(6.5)	(4.5)	1.0	2.7	3.8
Pretzels	210	265	260	16.5	26.0	(1.8)	23.8	9.5	7.8	(4.5)	13.0
TOTAL	$4,510	$5,244	$5,704	N/A	16.3%	8.8%	N/A	N/A	N/A	N/A	N/A

* Total sales growth rates may not match exactly the rates calculated from the Total Sales ($ millions) data in this table due to rounding of the total Sales ($ millions) data.

Projections for 1983 were considerably higher because (1) many people believed that the recession was ending and (2) the snack food market was not nearly saturated.

Shoestring Industry

The shoestring potato industry followed the same pattern as the broader snack food industry during 1982. The extruded snacks category, of which shoestrings were a part, grew only 1.4 percent in sales and 1.5 percent in units.

The recession hit Pik-nik during the fourth quarter of fiscal 1982 (second quarter calendar 1982) and continued all through fiscal 1983. However, due to improving general economic trends, Pik-nik's management predicted a rebound in demand to 1981 levels and significantly improved performance for fiscal 1984.

COMPETITION

The competitive situation in shoestrings remained generally unchanged in 1983. Durkee led the industry with a 38 percent share, followed by Allen Canning with 29 percent, Pik-nik 23 percent, and Butterfield 3 percent. All of Allen Canning's business was private label, and Durkee and Pik-nik each had about 3.5 percent share in private label in addition to their brand name business mentioned above. Generally private label product quality was well below that of the brand name products.

In the broader snack food market, Planters was gaining share with its line of cannister-filled snacks.

AUGUST 1983

By August 1983 Joe Grimes had evaluated all four of the alternatives (listed at the beginning of this case) that he had been considering the previous few months.

The acquisition idea, while it still appealed to Joe in theory, hadn't materialized in the past two years, although Joe and the other investors and managers had spent considerable time and effort searching for and evaluating acquisition candidates. Consequently, Joe wanted to try another approach.

A second idea had been to leave Pik-nik and work for another firm. Joe hadn't fully tested this idea, partly because he liked Pik-nik and preferred to remain there. He had had preliminary discussions with another snack food manufacturer in the Midwest, however, and that firm had indicated that it considered Joe's investment in Pik-nik to be a major problem due to potential conflict of interest issues.

The third idea, to sell the firm, had also been just moderately evaluated. One of the partners had spent some time exploring potential interest in Pik-nik Foods within the investment community; the reactions were not particularly encouraging.

Finally, the compensation issue continued to be a significant one for Joe. Much as Joe enjoyed Pik-nik, the combination of his current income, the outlook for Pik-nik's growth, and his having only 42.5 percent of the equity was not sufficient. Therefore, Joe decided to try to buy out his partners.

PROPOSED FINANCING

As a first step Joe contacted an investment banker, Jack Laband of First San Francisco Corporation. Jack had represented the sellers in the Diane's Food transaction and even though Pik-nik was unsuccessful in acquiring Diane's, the two men had kept in contact. Jack offered to assist Joe with his plans to buy out the other investors and concurrently to change Pik-nik's lending institution, which Joe had wanted to do for quite some time.

Joe wanted to change the lending institution because the primary relationship between the current bank and Pik-nik was with Doug Adams (one of the investors who served as chief financial officer on a part-time basis). Joe wanted to have the primary relationship with the bank himself and also felt it would be more appropriate and convenient to deal with a West Coast financial institution since Pik-nik was based in San Jose, California.

Next, following initial discussions with Jack Laband, Joe suggested to his partners at the August directors meeting that he buy them out. He offered to pay $488,000 (57.5 percent of Pik-nik's $850,000 book value).

A repurchase agreement existed whereby Joe, as the leader of the investor group, had an option to purchase the stock held by his investor partners at a price linked to the net worth of the company. The prices were calculated as multiples of the company's net worth and were specified to increase each year. Accordingly, the buy-back agreement would have called for a repurchase price of $1.7 million in mid-1983, placing Pik-nik's total value at approximately $2.9 million. In view of the condition of the business, the agreement among the partners to permit Joe to purchase their holdings, and the partners' greater interest in terms (i.e., cash) than price, the rights of the other partners under the original repurchase agreement was waived in favor of the revised agreement (shown as Exhibit 12). All the partners and Joe agreed on a total valuation of $1,150,000 and a final purchase price of $660,000.

With the purchase price agreed on, Joe had to determine the financial structure for the deal. He and Jack Leband worked closely together on this. As one input to the financial structuring, Jack suggested that Joe get an appraisal on Pik-nik's fixed assets. The summary of the appraisal is shown in Exhibit 13. The details of the proposed financing are shown in Exhibit 14 (excerpted from the Pik-nik Prospectus that First San Francisco Corporation prepared). First San Francisco Corporation contacted five banks and sent them copies of the proposal. Joe waited for their reply and wondered how they would react to the proposed financing. He knew one of the first things they would do would be to calculate cash flows and debt service levels for the deal.

Exhibit 12

Pik-nik Foods, Inc.
214 Dupont Street
P.O. Box 1609
San Jose, California 95109

Phone (408) 286-2680
TWX 910-338-0287

November 10, 1983

<u>Revised Agreement among Pik-nik Partners</u>

To: Belard Company, c/o Douglas L. Adams
    Arthur W. Lawrence
    Herman C. Lawrence
    Dorothy S. Johnson

Gentlemen and Ladies:

This letter is being written to confirm our recent discussions concerning my desire to buy and your desire to sell your interest in Pik-nik Foods, Inc., a Delaware corporation ("Pik-nik") upon the following terms and conditions.

I have the right and option to purchase for cash after January 1, 1984, but no later than January 16, 1984, on behalf of myself or on behalf of a group to be formed in which I will participate, all of your respective shares of Pik-nik for your proportionate share of $1,150,000 (hereinafter referred to as "Total Value"). Therefore, based on 800 shares of Pik-nik outstanding, if a stockholder owns 100 shares of Pik-nik the stockholder's proportionate share of the Total Value will be 12½ percent of $1,150,000 or the sum of $143,750.

In the event I do not purchase your shares as set forth above, I have the right and option to cause the redemption by Pik-nik after January 1, 1984, but no later than January 16, 1984, of all of your shares so long as you would receive the same cash payment as you would have received if your shares had been purchased, as described above. If I choose a plan of redemption to accomplish the intention expressed herein, you will each vote your shares in favor of the redemption and will not incur any liability of any kind, including any personal guaranties, in order to effectuate this redemption.

In the event that I do not purchase your shares or cause a redemption of your shares, under the terms and time limitations as set forth above, I will sell or vote my shares of Pik-nik in order to effect a sale of the shares or assets of Pik-nik to a third party on terms of purchase agreeable to you. My agreement will stay in effect through December 31, 1984. I will further agree, if a sale is consummated, to remain with Pik-nik or its successor for a period of up to one year, or for a shorter term as the buyer may desire, so long, however, as my present base salary is maintained.

It is further understood that I will not enter into or prepay any contractual obligations involving consultants or market research analysts without the prior unanimous written approval of the Board of Directors, unless I first exercise an option set forth in paragraphs two or three above.

If you are in agreement with the terms of this letter, please acknowledge your concurrence on the copy attached hereto and return it to Scott Hodes for safekeeping.

Very truly yours,

Joseph F. Grimes
President

JFG/j
encl.

ACKNOWLEDGED AND AGREED

Exhibit 13

Appraisals by
MARSHALL
AND STEVENS
INCORPORATED

Fixed Assets Appraisal

File Reference: 14-3040

December 16, 1983

Michael Teeter
Vice President and General Manager
PIK-NIK FOODS, INC.
214 Dupont Street
San Jose, California 94126

Dear Mr. Teeter:

We have prepared an appraisal of the value in use and orderly liquidation value of the assets belonging to Pik-nik Foods, Inc., located at 214 Dupont Street in San Jose, California.

Based on the data and conclusions presented in the attached report, it is our opinion that the value in use and orderly liquidation value of the subject assets, as of December 2, 1983, are:

	Value in Use	Orderly Liquidation
Machinery and equipment	$ 960,400	$446,175
Office furniture and equipment	41,030	20,735
Leasehold improvements*	74,600	*
Totals	$1,076,030	$466,910

   * As per our contract, only value in use is given for leasehold improvements.

The opinions of value expressed in this appraisal are contingent on the analyses, facts, and limiting conditions presented in the accompanying report.

The field data from which this report was prepared are retained in our files and are available for inspection on request.

Very truly yours,

MARSHALL AND STEVENS INCORPORATED
John A. Thomson
Area Vice President

JAT/mjl

381 Bush Street, Suite 200,
San Francisco, California 94104
(415) 788-4970
Offices Around the World

Exhibit 14   Details of Proposed Financing

This section explains the details of the proposed financing including amounts and proposed terms. It provides information regarding projected cash flow over the next three years and discusses the quality of security assets.

Line of Credit and Term Financing

Line of Credit

Until July of this year, the company has had a $1.1 million revolving line of credit with St. Joseph Bank and Trust Company of South Bend, Indiana, bearing interest at the Bank's prime lending rate. As a result of careful inventory and cash management, and because the line's limit was never needed, Pik-nik initiated a reduction in that line to $900,000. The amount drawn down under this line of credit at September 30 was $185,000. The average month's end drawdown during fiscal year 1983 was $417,000. Borrowing exceeded $500,000 only during April and May when it was needed to support a brief, seasonal buildup in inventories. The line of credit is secured by accounts receivable, inventory, property, equipment, and trademarks.

Pik-nik is seeking to replace its $900,000 line of credit with a $640,000 line with its new lender. Additional borrowing may be requested during the next two years to support expanded business in new product lines.

Term Loan

A term loan, with a 1983–84 current portion of $110,000, is payable to St. Joseph Bank and Trust Company with interest at the Bank's prime lending rate. At the beginning of fiscal year 1984, the loan's balance was $320,000; by November it had been reduced to $300,000. The loan is being repaid with principal payments of $9,167 plus interest each month and is secured by the same assets as the line of credit. Pik-nik intends to refinance this debt with a new term loan in the same amount for a period of five years, with monthly principal payments of approximately $5,000 plus interest at prime.

Buyout Financing

The current five owners, consisting of the president and four passive investor partners, purchased the Company in 1978. The president holds 42.5 percent of the equity, and the remaining 57.5 percent is divided among the other partners. There are 800 shares outstanding of two classes (Class A and Class C) of common stock, all at $1 par value. The Company is seeking a loan for $660,000 to finance redemption of the stock belonging to the passive investors. Pik-nik is seeking a secured, long-term loan with interest payments only during the first one to two years or a combination of a term loan and line of credit financing.

Valuation and Terms of Equity Purchase

The shareholders have reached agreement for the structure of the sale and have set mid-December as the transaction date. The president has the right to cause the Company to redeem the shares of the other shareholders for their proportionate share of the defined total value of the firm. Total value has been set at $1,150,000; this is based on estimated book value as of November 30 of $900,000, plus a premium of $250,000. Total value of the stock to be redeemed therefore will be 57.5 percent of $1,150,000, or $661,250.

Cash Flow and Working Capital Requirements

Management projections and historical performance demonstrate that Pik-nik will have adequate cash flow in excess of debt service and repayment requirements.

Pik-nik does not expect it will require additional capital assets in order to meet these sales projections, so that changes in working capital, namely receivables and inventory, plus modest increases in new product development and certain other expenses are the only anticipated use of additional funds beyond current loan amounts. Furthermore, virtually all payables are current; no additional cash will be needed to satisfy bank loan requirements related to payables. Table 1 shows expected average and annual high and low levels for receivables and inventories for fiscal year 1984. Table 2 summarizes estimated annual cash available to pay interest and taxes, and to repay loan principal for the next three years.

Exhibit 14 *(continued)*

Table 1
Projected Receivables and Inventories, Fiscal Year 1984

	High Month ($000)	Low Month ($000)	Average Month ($000)
Accounts receivable	$ 477 (December, March, May)	$324 (October)	$ 388
Finished goods inventory	1,171 (March)	967 (April–June)	1,076

Table 2
Cash Flow Available for
Interest, Taxes, and Repayment of Loan Principal,
Fiscal Year Ended June 30

	1984	1985	1986
Cash receipts	$6,788	$7,329	$7,952
Cash disbursements	5,942	6,638	7,223
Net cash flow	$ 846	$ 691	$ 729

Securing Assets

Pik-nik will secure all debt with its accounts receivable, inventory, property, equipment, and trademarks. Receivables and inventory are exceptionally high in quality, and we believe warrant advances against them of 90 percent and 70 percent of book value, respectively (see Table 3).

Table 3
Summary of Securing Assets
In Thousands of Dollars

Asset	Valued at	Value	Percent Advance	Amount Advanced on Assets
Receivables	Annual	$ 407.5 (fiscal year 1983)	90%	$ 367
Inventory	Annual average	1,313.0 (fiscal year 1983)	70	919
Fixed assets	Book*	330.0 (quarter one fiscal year 1984)	80	264
Total		$2,050.5 (fiscal year 1983)		$1,550
		$1,758.3 (quarter one fiscal year 1984)		

Total financial request
($640,000 line of credit,
$300,000 term loan,
$660,000 buyout financing) $1,600

* Probably underestimates market value.

High-Quality Receivables

Pik-nik's customers are large, creditworthy, retail food store operators with excellent payment records, such as Safeway, Associated Grocers, Super Value, and so on.

Pik-nik's receivables are exceptionally high quality. Receivables as of September 30 this year were *91percent current.* On August 30, they were more than *93 percent current,* and only one half of 1 percent were 120 days or older (see Table 4 for an aging). Furthermore, Pik-nik offers its customers 2/10 net 30 terms, and most take the discount, so that current receivables are collected quickly. Finally, Pik-nik had only $9,000 bad debt expense on gross sales of $7.9 million in 1983—only one tenth of 1 percent of sales. The figure for prior years has been comparably low.

Exhibit 14 *(concluded)*

Table 4
Receivables—Percent of Balance Due

	August 30	September 30
Current	93.3%	91.0%
30 days	1.6	2.1
60 days	2.1	0.8
90 days	2.3	2.5
120 days	0.6	3.6
	100.0%	100.0%

High Velocity Inventory

Virtually all of Pik-nik's inventories are in finished goods, with a small amount of packaging materials and raw materials constituting the remainder. Finished goods inventory turns more than six times a year. Since 1978, when Pik-nik was acquired by present management, there has been only one write-off for obsolete inventories, $40,000 in 1983. Pik-nik's finished goods inventories are all readily salable, high-velocity product with shelf life of 12 months, well beyond any conceivable holding periods.

The company has no work-in-process inventory, and raw inventory turns more than once each day. This is a result of careful production scheduling and materials ordering practices, so that all potatoes are processed the day they arrive at the plant.

Finished goods inventory reports allow management to track all inventories at Pik-nik's 18 public warehouses and the on-site warehouse in San Jose. Management knows exactly what that inventory is at any given time, by product and by warehouse, as well as product in transit by destination. Physical inventory is taken at each warehouse every six months. Production schedules are set and monitored weekly to allow for shortened work weeks, and so on, as needed to keep sales, inventories, and production in balance. As a result, unintentional buildup of inventory is avoided. All product in transit in public warehouses is insured.

Fixed Assets

An appraisal of liquidation values for fixed assets is underway and will be completed in early December; until that time, we will assume book values for the liquidation values in estimating acceptable advances against fixed assets. However, we believe that the appraisal will demonstrate liquidation values in excess of current book value of $330,000. We anticipate a loan advance against fixed assets of at least 80 percent. Almost all of the fixed assets are equipment which has been depreciated more rapidly than its true useful life and virtually all of which is still in excellent operating condition. The Company also has trademarks valued at $54,000.

Total book value of fixed assets at September 30 was $330,000; original cost was $698,000. Nearly $250,000 of remaining book value is for cooking and packing equipment; some $14,000 is in computer equipment for billing and reporting; $13,000 in rolling stock; and almost $40,000 in leasehold improvements.

Pik-nik holds an operating lease for its manufacturing plant and warehouses, expiring in 1991. At $21,000 per year, this lease is considerably below market rental rates, and can be considered an off-balance sheet asset.

CASE 35 DAFOE AND DAFOE, INC. (A)*

On September 12, 1984, Ken Dafoe, president of Dafoe and Dafoe, Inc., a Canadian-owned manufacturer of various consumer products, was visiting his California plant when he received the following message from Henkel Corporation, a large German chemical corporation:

> We need a decision from you in one week. We will sell our factory in France for one franc plus the existing stocks of raw materials and finished goods for cash. There are now only 25 people in the factory. Contact Mr. Jacobi by the 19th.

Ken Dafoe's initial reaction to the message was that the offer from Henkel to sell Cypris (pronounced "Sepree"), a manufacturing company in France, sounded like a marvelous deal, but he wondered about the sudden change in the terms of the proposal. Earlier in the year Henkel wanted $1.5 million (U.S.) for Cypris, and after thinking about it for a couple of months, Ken decided he was not interested. Now, however, one franc seemed tempting.

KEN DAFOE'S BACKGROUND

Ken Dafoe was born and raised in Hamilton, Ontario. He attended Michigan State University on a track scholarship. As he put it: "The scholarship was my only chance at a formal education. My parents couldn't afford to send me and I couldn't afford to send myself."

In his second year at Michigan State he married his high school sweetheart, Heather. He graduated with a Bachelor of Arts degree in Business Administration in 1958.

After graduation he sold insurance for a few months. He then worked as a salesman for Procter & Gamble in London, Ontario for about a year. Ken recalled moving his sales territory from 21st to 2nd place in sales volume. He left the company when they wouldn't give him the promotion he requested.

His next job proved to have a particularly significant impact on Ken as a manager. In 1960 he accepted a sales manager position with Johnson & Johnson of New Brunswick, New Jersey, and was sent to the Caribbean. He traveled the islands for several years and was then put in charge of a new plant in Trinidad that manufactured sanitary napkins. He had heard stories about how lazy the people there were, how they would not work for a "white man," and all the trouble he would encounter running the Trinidadian plant. Ken encountered no difficulties. He attributed this to treating his workers with respect. He said:

> I don't care what colour people are. As long as you treat them with respect and show them why something has to be done, they will respond. I worked right along side them.

* Prepared by Mark C. Baetz with the assistance of Paul W. Beamish, Wilfrid Laurier University. Copyright © 1986 by Wilfrid Laurier University. Reprinted with permission.

When they saw me climbing over bales of paper, they figured if I was willing to work and J was the boss, they certainly could work hard as well.

Ken was determined to make the plant a success. He wanted his workers to show the head office in New Jersey that they could be profitable right from the start. The workers volunteered to work Saturdays for free during the initial start-up to make the plant profitable. In the first year the plant showed a minimal $1,000 deficit.

Trinidad was where Ken acquired certain philosophies about how to manage and motivate people. It was also where he learned about putting a sanitary napkin plant together from scratch. Ken attributed some of his success in Trinidad to his boss. He explained as follows:

My boss at Johnson & Johnson only saw me twice a year. This gave me the independence to use my common sense in starting up and managing the new plant. I like to use the same philosophy with the start-up and ongoing management of various plants. I like to give my plant managers the same sort of independence I had at Johnson & Johnson.

In 1966 Ken was transferred to Jamaica. He spent four years there. When civil strife broke out in 1970, Ken asked to be transferred. He was sent to Mexico, which was another place where Ken was supposed to find himself a social outcast. Apparently no Johnson & Johnson manager had ever been able to break into the Mexican social scene, but Ken claimed he had no difficulties with the Mexican people. The Dafoes were always invited to parties. At these parties the Dafoes were the only ones who could not speak Spanish. Their effort to communicate was appreciated and they were able to transcend the language barrier.

By this time Ken had two children and Heather wanted them educated in Canada. Ken could not get Johnson & Johnson to transfer him, so he resigned. He found a job as a general manager of the Texpack plant in Brantford, Ontario. Texpack, later called McGaw Manufacturing, was a division of American Hospital Supply Corp. of Chicago. Six weeks after Ken joined Texpack the employees went on strike. The strike turned out to be one of the most bitter in Brantford's history, and Ken Dafoe was in the center of it.

Ken loathed the way the union "used" its people, and as a result he was determined to break the strike. After 96 days, the head office gave in. Ken commented on the situation:

It broke my heart. We were winning. I have nothing against unions and fair negotiations, but when the union turns a bunch of people into an angry mob then uses them for its own purpose, I'll fight back. I'm a fighter! If I think you're playing unfair or trying to use me, I'll fight you 'til the end.

Ken left Texpack in 1973 to become vice president and general manager of Stearns & Foster Canada Limited, a Cincinnati-based company with plants in Brantford, Toronto, and Montreal. The company manufactured material used in sanitary napkins and disposable diapers.

COMPANY ORIGINS AND HISTORY

At Stearns & Foster Ken sensed that an opportunity existed in the Canadian sanitary napkin market. At the time private label and generic products were becoming more and more prevalent in the consumer goods industry, but no one in Canada was manufacturing sanitary napkins for that market. In 1975 Ken Dafoe decided to exploit the market opportunity and he set up a company called Safex Ltd., to be run by his wife. He located the company in 10,000 square feet of leased space in Brantford and soon began manufacturing sanitary napkins. The original financing of $250,000 for Safex came partly from the bank, a mortgage on the Dafoe house, a $138,000 loan from the Federal Business Development Bank (FBDB), and $2,000 in equity financing from FBDB. (On December 23, 1977, FBDB sold its equity interest back to the company for $40,000). Later financing came from the Ontario Development Corporation ($1 million: half in the form of a five-year interest-free loan and half as a bank guarantee) and venture capital of $300,000 from International Nickel Company (Inco) whch became major shareholders. Ken described the episode with Inco as follows:

> Inco hired Venture Founders of Boston for a handsome fee to find entrepreneurs with sound ideas. After Venture Founders located what they considered to be suitable entrepreneurs, they would recommend them to Inco who in turn would put up seed money to get these entrepreneurs off the ground in return for a minority interest.
>
> After we had been rejected by five more traditional venture capital firms, I wrote to Venture Founders in Boston and they did not reply to my letter. When I called them they said that they were not interested in sanitary napkins. I kept talking on the phone long enough to get a personal interview the next day in Toronto. In this interview they told me they had received 600 applications and were picking 25 for their weekend seminars. They said that I would probably not get into the seminar but that they would try to see if it was possible. Before I arrived back home in Brantford, they phoned to say I had been accepted. After attending these weekend seminars Heather and I traveled to Boston and put on a four-and-a-half hour presentation to seven members of the Venture Founders firm. At this presentation I was told that while I might be successful in Canada, I would have a tougher time convincing U.S. chains to jump into private label sanitary napkins. I got mad with them and told them they were crazy; the day before I'd signed up K mart Corp. in the United States to sell our products! They were convinced and agreed to recommend that Inco provide us with some capital. After that Venture Founders used us as an example of the kind of firm they can find for those with venture capital!

The original two employees in Safex were Heather Dafoe and Don Brennan. Ken Dafoe worked in the company part-time, planning to join full-time once business reached a certain level. Before this level was reached, Stearns & Foster fired him in 1976 for conflict of interest. Ken commented: "I got caught six months early."

In May 1978 Safex was renamed Dafoe and Dafoe Inc. (hereafter D&D), and the plant space was increased to 20,000 square feet at the same location. By this time the company was manufacturing sanitary napkins, tampons, and diapers. In September 1979 the company purchased and moved to a modern 87,000-square-foot plant on the outskirts of Brantford. Several acres of land were purchased with the plant which allowed for possible future expansion.

In December 1979 in a joint venture with one of its suppliers, the company opened a plant in Milton Keynes, England, in 11,000 square feet of leased space. The plant employed 24 people.

Within two years D&D opened three new plants in the United States as wholly owned subsidiaries. In April 1980 a 40,000-square-foot plant of leased space was opened in Atlanta, Georgia, with 56 people. In September 1981 a 42,000-square-foot plant of leased space with 31 employees was opened in San Diego, California. In July 1982 a 71,000-square-foot plant of leased space with 56 employees was opened in Philadelphia, Pennsylvania.

Once the Pennsylvania plant was fully operational, the company had enough productive capacity to support approximately $80 million in sales. The company had a total of 19 sanitary napkin machines, 11 cotton swab machines, 5 diaper machines, and 1 tampon machine in a total of five plants in three countries.

In mid-1984 D&D signed a lease to expand its plant in the U.K. to 40,000 square feet, effective November 1, 1984.

CORPORATE OBJECTIVES

Ken Dafoe described the objectives for D&D as follows:

> One of our objectives is to be the best company in Brantford for people to work for. Johnson Wax (S.C. Johnson & Son Ltd.) has the best name now, and I told them I'm after them.
>
> Another objective is to have a $100 million company by 1985. If all goes as planned 1990 sales should be $248 million. In fact, I see no reason why we can't be a billion-dollar company!

In terms of his personal objectives, Ken Dafoe commented:

> Even though I have been approached a number of times to sell the business, I'm not interested in selling now. I want to keep my options open. I may go public, if all goes well, but Heather and I will still keep 51 percent of the business (see Exhibit 1 for current share ownership). If I sold the company, I'd have a lot of money in the bank and I'd go nuts! You don't just work for the money, it's working for the sake of accomplishment. At the same time, I aim to hire people who want to work hard to get rich.

Exhibit 1   Percentage Ownership of Dafoe and Dafoe, Inc., 1984

Kenneth F. Dafoe	34.001%
Heather M. Dafoe	32.999
Inco Ltd.*	24.300
Ventures Founders†	2.700
Don Brennan	2.000
Stock Options	4.000
	100.000 %

* Inco had one seat on the company's six-person board of directors.

† Venture Founders Corp. of Boston was a consulting firm which recommended that Inco invest in D&D. The consulting firm investigated several hundred businesses before recommending D&D. As a finder's fee Venture Founders received 2.7 percent equity interest in D&D.

Another of my objectives is to run this company as though my employees are family. I want to know all their birthdays, anniversaries, etc. I want to make them feel proud to work here. I already have 11 people with a company car. Also, I make sure my employees know what things cost and I talk in percentages, otherwise they'll think I'm rich and take things for granted. I have acquired an airplane and a limousine. Not wanting to hide these acquisitions from my employees, I showed them off at a company party.

MARKETING STRATEGY

D&D had to initially overcome four major problems in successfully marketing a private label sanitary napkin: (1) customer loyalty to two brands—Modess (made by Johnson & Johnson) and Kotex (made by Kimberly-Clark Corporation); (2) store buyer bias—the buyers felt women would not change their brand loyalty; (3) lack of advertising—D&D did not advertise since this would compete with the private labeled products; this lack of advertising meant the woman customer was unaware of D&D's product; (4) large company discount buying—Johnson & Johnson and Kimberly-Clark offered greater "package" discounts the larger the total purchase, and therefore, any purchase from D&D would reduce the size of the "package" discounts received from these other firms.

Ken Dafoe and Jason Taggart, vice president of marketing, developed a strategy to overcome the above barriers. This strategy had the following components:

1. Forty percent lower price for similar quality product. (According to Ken Dafoe, D&D was able to offer the lower price because of more effective overhead utilization through increased volume, virtually no advertising, selling only to major chains, and taking lower profit margins from the name brand manufacturers).
2. Unique packaging—a resealable flip-top box and four- and five-color artwork.
3. Emphasis on the greater profit potential for the retailer of a private label program (the retailer could expect to receive a margin of 30 percent versus the 10 percent margin offered in comparable national brands).
4. Fast service, (one week turnaround) so that one week after the order is placed, it is on its way to the customer.

With this strategy, D&D captured several major accounts, including Shoppers Drug Mart, Woolco, The Bay, and Sears Roebuck & Co. In the United States some of the firm's major accounts were Revco (1,560 drugstores), K mart (2,400 stores), and Krogers (1,750 stores). By 1984 no one customer accounted for more than 5 percent of total company sales. The company manufactured its products under 100 brand names, including its own controlled brands.

Most of the company's dollar volume of sales came from sanitary napkins, which were sold to the consumer/retail segment of the market in Canada, the United States, and U.K. from the plants in those countries, as well as being exported to Australia, the Caribbean, and Africa. D&D also competed in the Canadian industrial/institutional and hospital segments but on a much smaller scale. The second largest component of company sales was diapers. Tampons and cotton swabs accounted for a very small percentage of company sales.

D&D CORPORATE ENVIRONMENT

It was estimated that the total North American market (including generics) for product categories in which D&D competed in 1980 was as follows:

Sanitary napkins and tampons	$ 770 million
Disposable baby diapers	1,000 million
Adult diapers	250 million
Cotton swabs	15 million

As noted earlier, sanitary napkins represented, by far, the greatest single component of D&D sales, and furthermore, Ken Dafoe expected this to remain the case in the future. For these reasons, the description of D&D's corporate environment will focus on the sanitary napkin industry.

The North American sanitary napkin market was dominated by Johnson & Johnson (J&J) and Kimberly-Clark (K-C). These two companies captured respectively about 50 percent and 30 percent of the market in 1984. Other competitors were Scott Paper and Playtex. The market had grown about 113 percent from 1970 to 1980, partly because of product improvements. In addition, a ban on television and radio advertising was lifted in 1972. As a result, most companies began major TV advertising campaigns, which increased consumer awareness and encouraged greater use of the product. Both product innovation and advertising established brand loyalty.

None of the major companies were selling to generic or private label markets in 1984. Ken Dafoe explained why: "The multinational name brand companies can't sell generics or private label of the same quality or they will kill their own brand, and they can't compete on price." Before 1975 some private labeling had been done by K-C and J&J, which supplied such Canadian customers as Zellers and The Bay. However, these companies only put private labels on the irregular products, which at the time were beginning to lose market share to the newer versions. Furthermore, these private label products were eventually phased out—they were merely cheaper versions of K-C's and J&J's name brands, they were no real bargain for the consumer, and they were resented by the store because they were inferior.

In 1981 Ken Dafoe described the competitive threat in the sanitary napkin market as follows: "Kimberly-Clark has said specifically that they are coming after us. They recently copied our packaging. This is the first time I've ever heard of a major manufacturer stealing a packaging design from the little guy."

One of the most recent trends in the menstrual care industry was a shift away from tampons (internal protection) to feminine napkins (external protection). This shift occurred partly because of the popularity of the minipad, partly because increased absorbency permitted the need for fewer tampons, and partly because of a suspected link between tampon use and toxic shock syndrome, a rare but sometimes fatal illness primarily affecting young women during their menstrual period. A number of companies producing tampons removed their products from the market in 1980 because of the suspected link to toxic shock syndrome. Up to 1977 tampons had been capturing an ever-increasing percentage of the menstrual care market. In 1980 napkins had about 53 percent of this market, while tampons had 47 percent, up from 35 percent

10 years earlier. Not all companies competed in both the tampon and napkin markets. For example, Tampax and Procter & Gamble (P&G) produced only tampon products. After P&G had to remove its tampon product from the market because of a suspected link with toxic shock syndrome, the company indicated it would attempt to break into the napkin market with a new type of napkin.

Ken Dafoe summarized his company's approach to the sanitary napkin market as follows:

> I am not interested in being a leader in research and development in sanitary napkins. Let someone else spend the money. Besides, the feminine protection business is a growth business. Although it has changed dramatically over the past decade to more convenient and smaller products, our market will remain fairly steady. Our product is a needed product and could not be "outdated" overnight. Furthermore, from our travels around the world, we are sufficiently aware of market trends and developments to change with the market.

PRODUCTION STRATEGY

D&D had a number of operating policies which embodied its production strategy as follows:

- D&D plants employed no more than 200 employees. In 1981 Ken Dafoe noted: "A company of 1,000 employees cannot run as efficiently as a company of 100 or 200. We are not running as efficiently now as we were when we only had 60 employees because people start taking the telephone and photocopying machine for granted . . . the bigger we get, the more the waste."
- All products in the D&D line were manufactured at world headquarters in Brantford (about 65 percent of Brantford production was shipped to the United States).
- All new products and their corresponding machines were first tested in Brantford before ordering new machines for other plants.
- D&D aimed to make plants as attractive as possible; Ken Dafoe noted: "The competition has schlocky plants. A clean plant impresses our customers. After all, we are in a sanitary business."
- D&D employed mainly females in the plants.
- All plants operated 24 hours per day, five days a week; preventive maintenance was supposed to be one shift per month per machine, but did not occur this often.
- D&D paid higher than average wages and provided better than average fringe benefits.
- D&D used two suppliers for every raw material.

Despite its well-defined production policies, D&D had experienced some problems in the production area. From 1979 to 1981 Ken fired three plant managers in two different plants. There seemed to be many reasons for the firings—inability to get machines operating at capacity, not paying enough attention to quality control resulting in customer dissatisfaction, not getting to know the employees, little interest in learning about accounting. Ken seemed to sense a slight weakness in the production function of D&D when he commented as follows:

I am not really a manufacturing person. One of the few people in the company who *has* manufacturing and engineering expertise is Don Brennan. When some of our equipment arrived eight months late from Sweden, Don completely assembled it and got it running in about one month. He also contributed immensely to the success of the company, and we could not have grown so quickly without him. However, I think we need to supplement his expertise by hiring some engineering graduates.

Instead of hiring engineering graduates Ken and Heather decided to hire a number of young, inexperienced business graduates, and within a short period of time these recent graduates were given various key assignments including the plant manager positions for the company's newly opened plants (see Exhibit 2 for a profile of the D&D management group in 1984). In general Ken was quite pleased with the performance of these new managers, and in turn these new managers were excited and enthusiastic about their jobs.

STRATEGY-MAKING PROCESS AND CORPORATE ORGANIZATION

Ken was clearly the key figure in the strategy-making process of D&D. For example, Ken described how Atlanta was chosen as the location of the first U.S. plant for the company:

For several reasons we had decided to manufacture in the United States. The market potential for generic and private label products seemed to be greater in the United States than in Canada. I knew we could not service many of the large and rapidly growing U.S. markets from our Brantford plant because of transportation costs and because we needed to give good service to build up our customer base. Inco carried out a study of population density and growth for us and told us that after the eastern seaboard, the U.S. Southeast was projected to be the fastest-growing U.S. market. The next issue was to choose a specific location. I had a lead on a site in Kentucky. The local government was going to give us some assistance. However, it took several plane connections and a long car ride to reach the potential plant site. I decided that Atlanta seemed far more suitable since it was easy to reach by plane and was clearly the hub of the U.S. Southeast.

While Heather admitted that Ken typically made the final decisions on strategy for the company, she usually played the role of devil's advocate "to question the assumptions in Ken's dreams for the company." Ken commented on the management relationship with his wife in the following way:

We have our problems at times. I've made decisions and she has changed them. She has made decisions and I've changed them. But in general we work together. Nevertheless, our people know who to go to for whatever they want. Some of them will come to me for certain things, and some will go to Heather for things. Basically, Heather is the tough one. I'm the easy guy. If you want something, come to me.

The D&D corporate structure was quite informal. For example, Jason Taggart, the vice president of marketing, often called the shipper directly to see if an order had been shipped. Ken Dafoe sometimes spoke to one of the shift supervisors directly

Exhibit 2   Profile of Dafoe & Dafoe Management Group, 1984

Name	Age	Present Position	Previous Position	Education/Full-Time Experience with other Companies
Ken Dafoe	49	Chairman/CEO	President	BA, Michigan State University; salesman, Procter & Gamble; sales manager, Johnson & Johnson; managing director, Johnson & Johnson; director, marketing, J & J Mexico; general manager, Texpack; vice president and general manager, Stearns & Foster.
Heather Dafoe	48	President	Vice President/ General Manager	High school: Delta Secondary. Worked in one-woman office doing everything. Unable to work in West Indies or Mexico. Started own company when children started school.
Jason Taggart	39	Senior Vice President	Vice President/ Marketing	BA from Mount Allison University. Worked for Uniroyal in Private Label Tires. Director of marketing at Victor Comptometer in Cambridge, Ontario. Part owner of Hamilton-Taggart, making truck cabs for camping. Joined D&D when sales were below $1 million annually.
Jim Harrison	39	Corporate Quality Control Manager	General Manager Canada	Joined Dafoe & Dafoe, Inc. in 1983 as general manager of Canada. Harding Carpets: 14 years holding various positions in the plant and quality control areas. Prior to joining Dafoe was plant manager of the Brantford Harding plant.
Blair McEwen*	24	Plant Manager, Pennsylvania	Product Manager Canada	Joined Dafoe immediately following graduation from University of Western Ontario (UWO) undergraduate business program in 1981. No full-time work experience, only various summer jobs during school.
Kevin McGraw*	24	General Manager, California	Summer Employment, Dafoe	Joined Dafoe immediately following graduation from undergrad business program at UWO in 1981. Worked for Dafoe during summers and various school breaks. Immediately upon joining Dafoe full-time was sent to start the company in California.
Eric Johnson*	24	General Manager, Pennsylvania	Personnel Manager, Dafoe Canada	Joined Dafoe following graduation from undergrad business program at UWO in 1981. Worked in various positions such as product manager, personnel manager, and sales coordinator in Canada prior to going to Pennsylvania.

* While at UWO, all three of these managers had worked together on a business policy field project to study Dafoe and Dafoe.

Note: In addition to those above, there were also plant managers in each plant under the general managers. There were also salespeople both as representatives and sales managers.

rather than going through the vice president of manufacturing. Further, Ken and Heather maintained an "open door" policy. They urged any employee to come directly to them for any problem they felt was not being resolved. Ken handled the "external" side of the business—marketing, arranging financing, finding suppliers, and so on— and Heather handled the "internal" side of the business—production, accounting, and so forth.

When new plants were established, Ken Dafoe and Jason Taggart usually did the initial selling themselves rather than give that job to the local vice president and general manager. All selling for D&D was done out of Brantford, but it was the responsibility of each plant manager to become acquainted with their local customers.

In terms of information and control systems, all plant managers prepared monthly production budgets and sent monthly cost and production output reports to headquarters in Brantford. Standard costs were established for each product group. These standard costs were used in pricing decisions. D&D monitored costs by comparing current and previous months' material costs as a percentage of sales. To facilitate financing with the banks, Ken Dafoe prepared monthly production budgets for each plant, based on projected sales levels.

D&D's inventory control system consisted of perpetual inventory records which kept track of incoming and outgoing stock, whether it was new materials or finished goods. D&D had been experiencing out-of-stock situations in its Brantford plant which resulted in shutting down the line. These problems seemed to be a result of the fact that minimum-maximum stock levels and order quantities for new materials had not yet been adjusted for the increased production capacity at Brantford.

As part of its reward and punishment system, D&D rewarded various managers with company cars, bonuses, and stock options (e.g. Don Brennan, vice president of engineering, had 2 percent ownership). Both factory and office workers were eligible for a share of D&D profits. In 1979 the profit-sharing plan paid each employee $1,000, and in 1980 the plan paid $1,500 for each employee. The company also added fringe benefits as they could afford them. Many of these benefits were given without the workers knowing about it until they were in effect. The company had no unions in any of its plants. When a union did try to organize the firm early in 1980, the employees voted against it.

In April 1981, 130 D&D employees gathered for a champagne luncheon at the Brantford Golf and Country Club. Ken promised the party to his employees when D&D reached $1 million in sales in one month, a milestone passed in March 1981. In addition to drinks and meals, the employees received an interim profit-sharing check for $740. Several also received gold pins under D&D's service award program.

In general the D&D president, Ken Dafoe, was highly motivated, enthusiastic, energetic, and seemed to have captured both the loyalty and energy of other company managers. For example, his vice president of marketing, who once managed his own company, commented as follows:

> I didn't think I could work for someone else again, but Ken is different. He offers you the avenue to rise to your own potential. He is the keenest businessman I have ever worked for and does not hesitate to share his knowledge. He'll tell you anything you want to know if he is able.

CORPORATE PERFORMANCE

At the end of October 1981, D&D received an Industrial Achievement Award from the Ontario government. This award was given to 10 Ontario businesses every year for superlative performance over a three-year period. More specifically, the award publicly recognized companies which created new jobs, increased production, improved sales, broke into new markets, increased exports, replaced imported goods, and showed technological or product innovation. A release from the Ministry of Industry and Tourism stated that from 1978 to 1980, D&D met all of these criteria.

For competitive reasons, Ken Dafoe did not want to be too specific about his sales and profit levels. He was willing to say the following in mid-1984:

> After a loss in the first year of our operations, we have had our ups and downs; one of our plants which had been experiencing losses is now showing a profit. There has been quite a variation in the profits among the plants. Generally the profits have been reasonable. In 1983 we turned the company around in terms of profits and expect a much larger profit in 1984. We have capacity now for just over $100 million in sales, and our actual sales this year will likely be about $50 million.

CYPRIS

Ken Dafoe was first told about the Cypris company in the fall of 1983. Ken was having lunch one day in Dusseldorf, West Germany, with Arno Jacobi, vice president—marketing of Henkel Corp., a large chemical company manufacturing and retailing such products as soaps, hair dyes, and perfumes. Henkel had been supplying Dafoe and Dafoe with tampons for the U.K. market. Ken described the conversation with Jacobi that day:

> Jacobi told me that Henkel had bought a large cosmetics company in France. This company, given the name Henkel Bonetti, owned a small cotton manufacturer in France known as Cypris. According to Jacobi, the Cypris products did not fit into the strategy of Henkel, so they wanted to get rid of Cypris and wondered if I was interested. I said I am interested so send me more information on the company.

In March 1984 Jacobi sent a package of details about Cypris with the message that Henkel intended to close the Cypris deal as soon as possible. Ken reviewed the materials and summarized the pertinent details (Exhibit 3).

Soon after receiving the information on Cypris, Ken went to France to tour the plant and was impressed on a number of counts. The plant was quite modern and well situated, given that 85 percent of the European market was located within 500 kilometers and excellent transportation was nearby. Because the plant was located near the German border, many of the employees were of the work-oriented German background. Although the machinery in the plant was old, there had not been much technological change in the kinds of machines involved in the production process.

Arno Jacobi indicated to Ken Dafoe that the asking price for Cypris was $1.5 million (U.S.). After two months of thinking about it, Ken decided to write back

Exhibit 3   Summary of Cypris Operations

	Sales and Profitability 1983	
	*Millions of French Francs**	*Number of Machines*
Cotton swabs	10.5	5
Zigzag cotton†	10.0	2
Cosmetic pads/discs	6.3	4
Cotton balls	6.0	5
Gross sales	32.8	16
Volume rebates	4.6	
Bonuses (e.g., salesmen)	3.5	
Net sales	24.7	
Freight/warehousing	2.5	
Production cost (full costing)	17.2	
Contribution to overhead and profit	5.0	
Overhead	3.5	
Profit before tax	1.5	
Profit after tax	.8 × 10 Price/earning ratio = 8.0 Profitability value	

Book Value of Cypris
(as of December 31, 1983)

	Millions of French Francs
Down payments and interest fees on leasing/purchase of land and buildings	1.6
Capital investments as installations (air filter, and so on)	3.1
Book value of production machines	3.1
Total	FF 7.8

Other Key Facts

1. As of March 14, 1984, there was FF4.1 (million) of finished goods and packaging materials in stock.
2. The leasing/purchasing contract will be fulfilled in 1993; remaining payments total FF5.8 (million).
3. Fifty-nine people are involved directly in the production process (49 workers, mostly young women).
4. Three clients represented one half of Cypris' business in the Cypris brand sales.
5. One third of Cypris sales were private label products and the remaining two thirds were the Cypris brand; about one third of the Cypris brand sales were contracted centrally, without the intervention of the salemen.
6. Cypris had a capacity of 1,200 tons and produced 678 tons in 1983. According to the Cotton Association, French production capacity in 1983 was 20,000 tons, actual production was 14,000 tons, and French consumption was 13,000 tons. This market included foods, pharmacies, and hospitals.
7. The largest single competitor to Cypris was Tempo Sanys with 4,200 tons of capacity and actual production of 3,500 tons.
8. The volumes (in million tons) and trends in the food market in 1983 were as follows:

Cotton swabs	132 (strong increase)
Zigzag cotton	281 (slow decline)
Cosmetic pads/discs	68 (strong increase)
Cotton balls	60 (slow increase)
	560 (increased 11.5 percent)

---

* 7 French francs = $1 Canadian.

† Zigzag cotton was either 100 or 200 grams of cotton folded in a zigzag or accordian style and either perforated or not. When perforated, a definite amount could be removed. Zigzag cotton was similar to 1-pound cotton sold in pharmacies in Canada and was used for medical reasons and for a variety of other uses including removing makeup, removing nail polish, and so on.

to say he was not interested. He explained why as follows: "I did not want to put $1.5 million into France, and I did not really have anyone in our management group who was fluent in French. Only two of our people had any experience with French: Eric Johnson, who grew up in Ottawa and spoke very little French, and Jason Taggart who grew up in Montreal and could converse but was not actually fluent."

After receiving the negative response from Dafoe, Henkel continued to keep the issue of the Cypris plant on the agenda in all meetings with D&D. This was because there were two major problems facing Henkel if it could find no buyer and it simply shut down Cypris. First, Henkel Bonetti had been the recipient of extensive government assistance in France, and Henkel was concerned about a backlash if the plant was shut down. Secondly, French labour laws were quite restrictive, and Henkel would face significant severance costs to employees in the event of a plant shutdown. These concerns led Henkel to make the offer to Ken Dafoe to sell Cypris for one French franc.

A DECISION

When Ken received the message that Henkel would sell Cypris for one French franc, he was delighted. He felt Cypris could give D&D a big boost to sales and profit. He expected he would export all the production from France to the United States for the first 6 to 12 months while rebuilding the business in Europe, and he felt additional machines could be ordered to increase the productive capacity. In general he felt the Cypris product line could fit in well with the D&D product line.

On the plane back from California Ken thought about the response he might give to Jacobi. He drafted the following telex:

We are pleased to purchase Cypris for one French franc. We will purchase subject to the following conditions:

1. We are given 30 days to arrange financing with a French bank.

2. Inventory amounts and costs will be approved by outside auditors.

3. You will give us three months to pay for the inventory following closing.

Ken wondered if he should add any further conditions. He suspected that Cypris was in receivership and wondered how that might affect things.

CASE 36 JEROLD W. "BILL" BROWN (A)*

Bill Brown sat at his desk pondering his uncertain future. In front of him lay the weekly sales report dated December 12, 1975. There remained only two weeks in the fiscal year and from Bill's vantage point it looked as if the affiliate would not even surpass last year's sales. The year had started out so successfully, and the home office had been very impressed by the affiliate's performance. He thought, "Why did I boast to Mr. Arnold (vice president, region) that I would be able to better last year's sales?"

BACKGROUND—BILL BROWN

Bill was happily married, with three children. The family lived comfortably on his salary with the help of company scholarships for his two sons in college. Bill's career ambitions were motivated by his desire to better his family's style of living, as well as personal ambitions.

Bill Brown had moved up the corporate ranks through various marketing positions, establishing a good record. He had worked for a number of firms in an attempt to find the fastest track to an upper-management position. At 40 his dreams had failed to materialize. At that point in time he was offered a position with a large multinational firm, which he believed would provide the fast track he had so eagerly searched for. In taking this job, he had to enter at one level lower than his previous position. In his new position he was marketing manager for the company's largest affiliate in Latin America. Within two years, a problem arose in a smaller but more promising affiliate. John Arnold decided that Bill Brown was the man to turn the troubled affiliate around because of his success in increasing sales and market share in his present position. The troubled affiliate was located in Puerto Rico.

Until 1968 Puerto Rico had been handled by a distributor. However, at that time the company eliminated the distributor and established an affiliate to assume direct control over the marketing of its products. Unfortunately sales had declined since then. This state of affairs had been embarrassing as well as unprofitable for the parent company. Nonetheless, the Puerto Rican market had great sales potential and impact on cash flow for the parent company because Puerto Rico did not limit the amount of profits that a U.S.-based company could repatriate, while most Latin American countries limited such amounts.

Bill Brown was promoted in October 1974 to marketing manager–Caribbean and

* Prepared by August E. Doskey, Abel A. Lopez, and Paul Vander Heyden, under the supervision of Associate Professor Jeffrey A. Barach, Graduate School of Business Administration, Tulane University. Copyright © 1977 by the Graduate School of Business Administration, Tulane University. Reproduced with permission.

The events described herein do not apply in their entirety to a specific company but came to the attention of the case researchers from various sources. Some of the events depicted are fictional, but the writers believe them adequately close to reality to be useful for class discussion.

managing director–Puerto Rico. He believed this would be a stepping-stone to area manager, as the current area manager was near retirement (see Exhibit 1).

When Brown arrived in Puerto Rico he found a very unprofessional marketing department plagued by older, unaggressive employees. There were other frictions within the department stemming from the different ethnic backgrounds of Puerto Ricans and Cuban refugees who made up the marketing department. After observing the department's performance, Brown dismissed the Cuban employees and replaced them with young, aggressive Puerto Ricans. This action relieved some of the tensions; however, Brown also brought in an aggressive and proven headquarters man, Jim Caldwell, as sales manager, whose hard-driving manner aggravated the present salesmen. The salesmen, wanting to stay with the old ways, formed a union. The union in effect diminished the sales manager's effectiveness in establishing a well-organized sales department. In July 1975, after searching for several months, Brown hired Juan Gomez as general manager. This was the first time a Puerto Rican had occupied this position.

Exhibit 1   Partial Organization Chart, December 1975

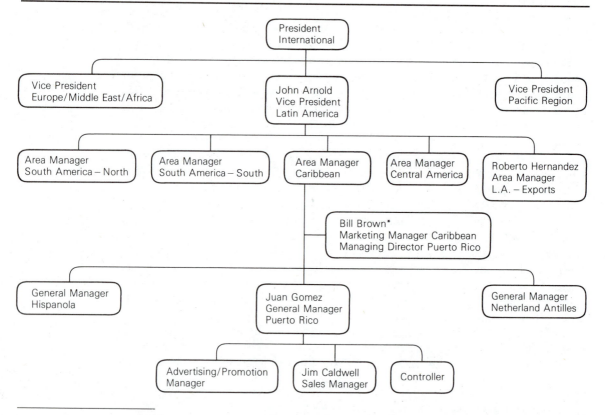

---

* This ad hoc position was created to spearhead the turning around of the Puerto Rico market. It is also a potential stepping-stone to the position of area manager.

Brown faced several other problems in turning around Puerto Rican sales. One of these was the company's advertising strategy. Headquarters demanded that all affiliates use the standard advertising campaign. The campaign was not culturally geared to Puerto Rico and, in effect, proved detrimental to its marketing strategy.

Faced with these problems which were contributing to declining sales, Brown took three basic steps in attempting to turn around the situation. First, he initiated a wholesale pricing strategy which called for a 2 percent discount to all wholesalers over and above the existing industry discount. Furthermore, Brown gave free merchandise to selected large wholesalers who could instantly increase sales. The effect of this free merchandise was to give large wholesalers an additional discount of 4 percent.

Second, Brown initiated a shelf-space strategy in major chain supermarkets which called for more eye-level shelf space. Sales had been found to be positively correlated with the use of eye-level shelf space. He was able to implement this strategy by signing favorable contracts with the major chains. However, one of the largest chains failed to adhere to the contract. Brown's quandary was that he wanted the extra shelf space immediately. In his mind the quickest way to obtain the extra shelf space was through a questionable payment to the general manager of the chain. This payment proved ineffective because in the course of the year Brown did not receive all of the shelf space agreed upon.

Brown's third step was to open another channel for distribution of his products by convincing a local distributor to set up a ship-chandling operation. This distributor represented 20 percent of the total sales of the affiliate. Ship chandlers sold duty-free merchandise to oceangoing vessels, both passenger and cargo. The only drawback to this type of operation was, according to the distributor, that in order to get the business a ship chandler would have to comply with many ship stewards' demands for kickbacks.

BACKGROUND—JOHN ARNOLD

John Arnold, the vice president of the region, climbed the corporate ladder through dealings in the export markets. These dealings included bona fide transactions as well as dubious operations with reputed smugglers. However, he had a reputation within the company as a discreet manager who accomplished results. The corporation felt that he was the right man for this region. Furthermore, it was Arnold's job to decide who would be promoted to area manager.

DECISION

Considering the adverse conditions he had faced throughout the year, sales were better than could have been expected. However, Brown felt that he must better last year's sales in order to get his promotion. His conviction was based upon sales reports from two other affiliates whose general managers he believed were also in the running for the promotion. These two affiliates had already surpassed their sales goals for that year and had been on an increasing trend of sales and market share for several years. However, he believed that substantially turning around a declining market would enhance his chances of promotion in the eyes of Arnold. With two weeks remaining in the year, Brown realized he would fall short of last year's sales and therefore felt that he would not get promoted.

Caldwell, the sales manager, knew of Brown's predicament. He felt that he had to protect Brown in order to protect himself. Caldwell knew that the ship chandler, a friend of his, could be induced to purchase enough merchandise to put the affiliate's sales figures over last year's. The catch was that the ship chandler would not sell the product to oceangoing vessels. Instead, the merchandise would be sold in another Latin American country outside of Brown's designated territory. This action would infringe upon the territory of another area manager within the region. Caldwell knew that the company could even be hurt by the "extra-curricular" ship-chandler deal because Francisco Diaz, the licensed distributor for the area where the excess product would be pushed, had a larger contribution to overall company sales than Brown's whole area. If Diaz found out that somebody else was muscling in on his area from within the parent firm, it would lead to friction and could possibly hurt the relationship between the distributor and the company. Further, this relationship was built through the distributor's close friendship with Arnold.

Brown told Caldwell that he would have to think it over and would let him know in half an hour. Bill was telling himself that at his age he needed the promotion immediately. He felt there was a low probability of being caught. In fact, he had heard through the grapevine that such maneuvers were being practiced elsewhere in the company. However, he thought upper management could not condone this action if the facts became publicly known. He based his belief on headquarters' newly released form to be signed by all management personnel regarding knowledge of questionable dealings by company employees. Brown reasoned that there were several options before him and he had to make a decision quickly.

Index

This book has been set VideoComp in 10 and 9 point Times Roman, leaded 2 points. Part numbers are 16 point Univers Medium Condensed and 72 point Time Bold Condensed; part titles are 27 point Times Bold. Chapter numbers are 72 point Times Bold Condensed and chapter titles are 24 point Times Bold. The size of the type area is 30 by 48 picas.